OXFORD PAPER

The Concise Ox

Quotati

Oxford Paperback Reference

The most authoritative and up-to-date reference books for both students and the general reader.

Abbreviations
ABC of Music
Accounting
Archaeology*
Architecture
Art and Artists
Art Terms
Astronomy
Better Wordpower
Bible
Biology
British History*
Buddhism*
Business
Card Games
Celtic Mythology
Chemistry
Christian Church
Classical Literature
Classical Mythology*
Colour Medical
Computing
Concise Quotations*
Dance*
Dates
Earth Sciences
Ecology
Economics
Engineering*
English Etymology
English Folklore*
English Grammar
English Language
English Literature
English Place-Names
Euphemisms
Film*
Finance and Banking
First Names
Food and Nutrition
Foreign Words and Phrases
Fowler's Modern English
  Usage
Geography
Handbook of the World
Humorous Quotations*
Idioms
Irish Literature
Jewish Religion
Kings and Queens of Britain
King's English
Law
Linguistics
Literary Quotations
Literary Terms

Local and Family History
London Place Names
Mathematics
Medical
Medicines
Modern Design*
Modern Quotations
Modern Slang
Music
Nursing
Opera
Paperback Encyclopedia
Philosophy
Physics
Plant-Lore
Plant Sciences
Political Biography
Political Quotations
Politics
Popes
Proverbs
Psychology*
Quotations
Sailing Terms
Saints
Science
Scientists
Shakespeare
Ships and the Sea
Slang
Sociology
Spelling
Statistics*
Superstitions
Synonyms and Antonyms
Theatre
Twentieth-Century Art
Twentieth-Century Poetry
Twentieth-Century World
  History
Weather
Weather Facts
Who's Who in Opera
Who's Who in the Classical
  World
Who's Who in the Twentieth
  Century
World History
World Mythology
World Religions
Writers' Dictionary
Zoology

*forthcoming

The Concise
Oxford Dictionary of

Quotations

FOURTH EDITION

Edited by

ELIZABETH KNOWLES

OXFORD
UNIVERSITY PRESS

OXFORD
UNIVERSITY PRESS

Great Clarendon Street, Oxford OX2 6DP

Oxford University Press is a department of the University of Oxford.
It furthers the University's objective of excellence in research, scholarship,
and education by publishing worldwide in

Oxford New York

Athens Auckland Bangkok Bogotá Buenos Aires Calcutta
Cape Town Chennai Dar es Salaam Delhi Florence Hong Kong Istanbul
Karachi Kuala Lumpur Madrid Melbourne Mexico City Mumbai
Nairobi Paris São Paulo Shanghai Singapore Taipei Tokyo Toronto Warsaw

with associated companies in Berlin Ibadan

Oxford is a registered trade mark of Oxford University Press
in the UK and in certain other countries

Published in the United States
by Oxford University Press Inc., New York

British Library Cataloguing in Publication Data
Data available

Library of Congress Cataloging in Publication Data
Data available

ISBN 0-19-866268-8

1 3 5 7 9 10 8 6 4 2

Typeset in Swift
by Interactive Sciences Ltd, Gloucester
Printed in Great Britain by
Cox & Wyman Ltd, Reading, Berkshire

CONTENTS

Introduction   vii

Quotations   1

Index   346

Sayings and Slogans   532

Advertising slogans   532

Catchphrases   533

Film lines   535

Modern sayings and slogans   536

Newspaper headlines and leaders   537

Official advice   538

Political slogans   538

INTRODUCTION

The fourth edition of the *Concise Oxford Dictionary of Quotations* is drawn from the latest (fifth) edition of the *Oxford Dictionary of Quotations*, published in 1999. This is the most comprehensive, as well as the most extensive, version of the *Dictionary* to have appeared, and in making our selection we have given priority to reflecting the richness and diversity of the parent text.

This new edition, therefore, gives proper place to the sacred texts of world religions. We now have the verse from the *Bhagavadgita*, 'I [Krishna] am all-powerful Time which destroys all things', as well as the related comment by the American physicist Robert Oppenheimer on witnessing the explosion of the first atomic bomb in New Mexico in 1945, 'I remembered the line from the Hindu scripture, the *Bhagavad Gita*, "I am become Death, the destroyer of worlds." '

New quotations from the classics of earlier centuries are found here, as comments and criticism on contemporary concerns. 'Everyone's quick to blame the alien' says Aeschylus, and Plutarch comments on Cicero's ability 'to see beneath the surface of Caesar's public policy and fear it, as one might the shining surface of the sea.' Tacitus tells us that 'Rumour is not always wrong.' The 16th-century merchant Robert Thorne gives his view on exploration, 'There is no land unhabitable, nor sea innavigable,' but Francis Bacon looks nearer home, to his garden: 'Nothing is more pleasing to the eye than green grass kept finely shorn.' The eighth amendment (1791) to the Constitution of the United States is revealed as the source of the now familiar phrase 'cruel and unusual punishment.'

Nearer our own time, Barbara Castle gives her recipe for longevity, 'I will fight for what I believe in until I drop dead. And that's what keeps you alive.' Jermey Paxman takes a firm line on conformity: 'Speaking for myself, if there is a message I want to be off it.' Sometimes the most recent quotations echo earlier sayings: listening to Bob Hope's comment 'Well, I'm still here' after erroneous reports of his death in 1998 led to tributes being paid to him in Congress, we are reminded of the famous summary of Mark Twain's protest of one hundred years before, 'Reports of my death have been greatly exaggerated.' There are many views of fame and its effects throughout the *Dictionary*: Walt Disney in his last illness comments, 'Fancy being remembered around the world for the invention of a mouse!'

The text has been further enhanced by a supplement of 'Sayings and Slogans', covering an extensive range of advertising and political slogans, catchphrases, film lines, newspaper headlines, and modern sayings.

HOW TO USE THE DICTIONARY

The sequence of entries is by alphabetical order of author, usually by surname but with occasional exceptions such as members of royal families (e.g. **Diana, Princess of Wales** and **Elizabeth II**, or authors known by a pseudonym ('**Saki**') or nickname (**Caligula**). Authors' names are given in their most familiar form, so that we have **Harold Macmillan** (not Lord Stockton), **George Eliot** (not Mary Ann Evans), and **H. G. Wells** (not Herbert George Wells). Collections such as **Anonymous** and the **Bible** are included in the alphabetical author sequence.

Author names are followed by dates of birth and death (where known). Cross-references are made to other entries in which the author appears, e.g. '*see also* **Lennon and McCartney**. Within each author entry, quotations are separated by literary form: novels, plays, poems, with the form for which the author is best known taking precedence. Quotations from diaries, letters, and speeches are given in chronological order, and usually follow the literary or published works quoted. Quotations from secondary sources which can be dated within the author's lifetime are arranged in sequence with diary entries and letters; undated and attributed quotations are arranged in alphabetical order of quotation text at the end of the entry.

Contextual information regarded as essential to a full appreciation of the quotation precedes the text in an italicized note; information providing amplification follows the text. Each quotation is accompanied by a bibliographical note of the source from which it is taken.

Spellings have been Anglicized and modernized except in those cases, such as **Burns** or **Chaucer**, where this would have been inappropriate. Capitalization has been retained only for personifications, and (with rare exceptions) verse has been aligned with the left-hand margin. Italic type has been used for all foreign-language originals.

Index

The most significant words from each quotation appear in the keyword index, allowing individual quotations to be traced. Both the keywords, and the context lines following each keyword, are in strict alphabetical order. Singular and plural nouns (with their possessive forms) are grouped separately: for 'some old lover's ghost) see **lover**; for 'at lovers' perjuries' see **lovers**. Variant forms of common words (fresshe/fresh, luve/love) are grouped under a single heading: **fresh**, **love**. References are to the author's name, usually in abbreviated form (as AUST for Jane Austen), followed by the page number and the number of the unique quotation on the page.

Acknowledgements

The book of course builds on the efforts of editors of earlier editions of the *Oxford Dictionary of Quotations* and the *Concise Oxford Dictionary of Quotations*, and due tribute must be paid to them. Particular thanks are due to Susan Ratcliffe, Associate Editor for Oxford Quotations Dictionaries, and members of the *Oxford Dictionary of Quotations* Project Team. Proof-reading has been expertly carried out by Kim Allen, Fabia Claris, Carolyn Garwes, and Penny Trumble.

ELIZABETH KNOWLES
Oxford 2000

Diane Abbott 1953-

1 Being an MP is the sort of job all working-class parents want for their children—clean, indoors and no heavy lifting.

in *Independent* 18 January 1994

Peter Abelard 1079-1142

2 *O quanta qualia sunt illa sabbata,*
Quae semper celebrat superna curia.
O what their joy and glory must be,
Those endless sabbaths the blessèd ones see!

Hymnarius Paraclitensis bk. 1 (tr J. M. Neale, 1854)

Dannie Abse 1923-

3 I know the colour rose, and it is lovely,
But not when it ripens in a tumour;
And healing greens, leaves and grass, so springlike,
In limbs that fester are not springlike.

'Pathology of Colours' (1968)

Accius 170-*c*.86 BC

4 *Oderint, dum metuant.*
Let them hate, so long as they fear.

from *Atreus*, in Seneca *Dialogues* bks. 3-5

Goodman Ace 1899-1982

5 TV—a clever contraction derived from the words Terrible Vaudeville . . . we call it a medium because nothing's well done.

letter to Groucho Marx, in *The Groucho Letters* (1967)

Dean Acheson 1893-1971

6 Great Britain has lost an empire and has not yet found a role.

speech at the Military Academy, West Point, 5 December 1962

7 A memorandum is written not to inform the reader but to protect the writer.

in *Wall Street Journal* 8 September 1977

Lord Acton 1834-1902

8 Power tends to corrupt and absolute power corrupts absolutely.

letter to Bishop Mandell Creighton, 3 April 1887; cf. **Pitt** 245:10

Abigail Adams 1744-1818

9 In the new code of laws which I suppose it will be necessary for you to make I desire you would remember the ladies . . . Do not put such unlimited power into the hands of the husbands. Remember all men would be tyrants if they could.

letter to John Adams, 31 March 1776; cf. **Defoe** 107:18

Charles Francis Adams 1807-86

10 It would be superfluous in me to point out to your lordship that this is war.

of the situation in the United States during the American Civil War

dispatch to Earl Russell, 5 September 1863

Douglas Adams 1952-

11 The Answer to the Great Question Of . . . Life, the Universe and Everything . . . [is] Forty-two.

The Hitch Hiker's Guide to the Galaxy (1979) ch. 27

Frank Adams
and Will M. Hough

12 I wonder who's kissing her now.

title of song (1909)

Franklin P. Adams 1881-1960

13 Years ago we discovered the exact point, the dead centre of middle age. It occurs when you are too young to take up golf and too old to rush up to the net.

Nods and Becks (1944)

14 Elections are won by men and women chiefly because most people vote against somebody rather than for somebody.

Nods and Becks (1944); cf. **Fields** 127:22

Henry Brooks Adams 1838-1918

15 A friend in power is a friend lost.

The Education of Henry Adams (1907) ch. 7

16 Practical politics consists in ignoring facts.

The Education of Henry Adams (1907) ch. 22

17 Nothing in education is so astonishing as the amount of ignorance it accumulates in the form of inert facts.

The Education of Henry Adams (1907) ch. 25

John Adams 1735-1826

18 The law, in all vicissitudes of government . . . will preserve a steady undeviating course . . . On the one hand it is inexorable to the cries of the prisoners; on the other it is deaf, deaf as an adder to the clamours of the populace.

argument in defence of the British soldiers in the Boston Massacre Trials, 4 December 1770; cf. **Sidney** 295:6

19 A government of laws, and not of men.

in *Boston Gazette* (1774) no. 7; later incorporated in the Massachusetts Constitution (1780); cf. **Ford** 131:4

20 In politics the middle way is none at all.

letter to Horatio Gates, 23 March 1776

21 The jaws of power are always opened to devour.

A Dissertation on the Canon and the Feudal Law (1765)

John Quincy Adams 1767-1848

22 Think of your forefathers! Think of your posterity!

Oration at Plymouth 22 December 1802

1 *Fiat justitia, pereat coelum* [Let justice be done, though heaven fall]. My toast would be, may our country be always successful, but whether successful or otherwise, always right.

> letter to John Adams, 1 August 1816; cf. **Decatur** 107:11, **Schurz** 265:21, **Watson** 329:2

Samuel Adams 1722–1803

2 What a glorious morning is this.

> *on hearing gunfire at Lexington, 19 April 1775; traditionally quoted as, 'What a glorious morning for America'*
> J. K. Hosmer *Samuel Adams* (1886) ch. 19

3 A nation of shopkeepers are very seldom so disinterested.

> *Oration in Philadelphia* 1 August 1776 (the authenticity of this publication is doubtful); cf. **Napoleon** 231:10, **Smith** 297:9

Sarah Flower Adams 1805–48

4 Nearer, my God, to thee,
Nearer to thee!

> 'Nearer My God to Thee' in W. G. Fox *Hymns and Anthems* (1841)

Harold Adamson 1906–80

5 Comin' in on a wing and a pray'r.

> *words derived from the contemporary comment of a war pilot, speaking from a disabled plane to ground control*
> title of song (1943)

Joseph Addison 1672–1719

6 And, pleased th' Almighty's orders to perform,
Rides in the whirlwind, and directs the storm.

> *The Campaign* (1705) l. 291

7 'Tis not in mortals to command success,
But we'll do more, Sempronius; we'll deserve it.

> *Cato* (1713) act 1, sc. 2, l. 43

8 The woman that deliberates is lost.

> *Cato* (1713) act 4, sc. 1, l. 31

9 What pity is it
That we can die but once to serve our country!

> *Cato* (1713) act 4, sc. 1, l. 258

10 When vice prevails, and impious men bear sway,
The post of honour is a private station.

> *Cato* (1713) act 4, sc. 1, l. 320

11 From hence, let fierce contending nations know
What dire effects from civil discord flow.

> *Cato* (1713) act 5, sc. 1, closing lines

12 Sir Roger told them, with the air of a man who would not give his judgement rashly, that much might be said on both sides.

> *The Spectator* no. 122 (20 July 1711)

13 I have often thought, says Sir Roger, it happens very well that Christmas should fall out in the Middle of Winter.

> *The Spectator* no. 269 (8 January 1712)

14 If we may believe our logicians, man is distinguished from all other creatures by the faculty of laughter.

> *The Spectator* no. 494 (26 September 1712)

15 'We are always doing', says he, 'something for Posterity, but I would fain see Posterity do something for us.'

> *The Spectator* no. 583 (20 August 1714)

16 See in what peace a Christian can die.

> *dying words to his stepson Lord Warwick*
> Edward Young *Conjectures on Original Composition* (1759)

George Ade 1866–1944

17 After being turned down by numerous publishers, he had decided to write for posterity.

> *Fables in Slang* (1900)

18 It is no time for mirth and laughter,
The cold, grey dawn of the morning after.

> *The Sultan of Sulu* (1903) act 2

Adi Granth *see* Sikh Scriptures

Alfred Adler 1870–1937

19 The truth is often a terrible weapon of aggression. It is possible to lie, and even to murder, for the truth.

> *The Problems of Neurosis* (1929) ch. 2

Polly Adler 1900–62

20 A house is not a home.

> title of book (1954)

Theodor Adorno 1903–69

21 It is barbarous to write a poem after Auschwitz.

> I. Buruma *Wages of Guilt* (1994)

Æ (George William Russell) 1867–1935

22 In ancient shadows and twilights
Where childhood had strayed,
The world's great sorrows were born
And its heroes were made.
In the lost boyhood of Judas
Christ was betrayed.

> 'Germinal' (1931)

Aeschylus *c.*525–456 BC

23 Hell to ships, hell to men, hell to cities.

> *of Helen (literally 'Ship-destroyer, man-destroyer, city-destroyer')*
> Agamemnon

24 Everyone's quick to blame the alien.

> *The Suppliant Maidens*

Herbert Agar 1897–1980

25 The truth which makes men free is for the most part the truth which men prefer not to hear.

> *A Time for Greatness* (1942) ch. 7; cf. **Bible** 47:36

James Agate 1877–1947

1 My mind is not a bed to be made and re-made.
diary, 9 June 1943

2 A professional is a man who can do his job when he doesn't feel like it. An amateur is a man who can't do his job when he does feel like it.
diary, 19 July 1945

Agathon b. c.445 BC

3 Even a god cannot change the past.
literally, 'The one thing which even God cannot do is to make undone what has been done'
Aristotle *Nicomachaean Ethics* bk. 6

Bertie Ahern 1951–

4 It is a day we should treasure. Today is about the promise of a bright future, a day when we hope a line will be drawn under the bloody past.
in Guardian 11 April 1998

Alfred Ainger 1837–1904

5 No flowers, by request.
summarizing the principle of conciseness for contributors to the Dictionary of National Biography
Supplement to the Dictionary of National Biography 1901–1911 (1912)

Arthur Campbell Ainger 1841–1919

6 God is working his purpose out as year succeeds to year;
God is working his purpose out and the time is drawing near;
Nearer and nearer draws the time, the time that shall surely be,
When the earth shall be filled with the glory of God as the waters cover the sea.
'God is working his purpose out' (1894 hymn)

Max Aitken *see* Lord Beaverbrook

Zoë Akins 1886–1958

7 The Greeks had a word for it.
title of play (1930)

Alain (Émile-Auguste Chartier) 1868–1951

8 *Rien n'est plus dangereux qu'une idée, quand on n'a qu'une idée.*
Nothing is more dangerous than an idea, when you have only one idea.
Propos sur la religion (1938) no. 74

Edward Albee 1928–

9 Who's Afraid of Virginia Woolf?
title of play (1962)

Alcuin c.735–804

10 *Nec audiendi qui solent dicere, Vox populi, vox Dei, quum tumultuositas vulgi semper insaniae proxima sit.*

And those people should not be listened to who keep saying the voice of the people is the voice of God, since the riotousness of the crowd is always very close to madness.
letter 164 in *Works* (1863) vol. 1; cf. **Pope** 248:26

Richard Aldington 1892–1962

11 Patriotism is a lively sense of collective responsibility. Nationalism is a silly cock crowing on its own dunghill.
The Colonel's Daughter (1931) pt. 1, ch. 6

'Buzz' Aldrin 1930–

12 Beautiful! Beautiful! Magnificent desolation.
of the lunar landscape
on the first moon walk, 20 July 1969

Alexander the Great 356–323 BC

see also **Diogenes** 112:1

13 If I were not Alexander, I would be Diogenes.
Plutarch *Parallel Lives* 'Alexander' ch. 14, sect. 3

14 Is it not worthy of tears that, when the number of worlds is infinite, we have not yet become lords of a single one?
when asked why he wept on hearing from Anaxarchus that there was an infinite number of worlds
Plutarch *Moralia* 'On Tranquillity of the Mind'

Alexander II ('the Liberator')1818–81

15 Better to abolish serfdom from above than to wait till it begins to abolish itself from below.
speech in Moscow, 30 March 1856

Cecil Frances Alexander 1818–95

16 All things bright and beautiful,
All creatures great and small,
All things wise and wonderful,
The Lord God made them all.
'All Things Bright and Beautiful' (1848)

17 Once in royal David's city
Stood a lowly cattle-shed,
Where a mother laid her baby
In a manger for his bed:
Mary was that mother mild,
Jesus Christ her little child.
'Once in royal David's city' (1848)

18 There is a green hill far away,
Without a city wall.
'There is a green hill far away' (1848)

William Alexander, Lord Stirling c.1567–1640

19 The weaker sex, to piety more prone.
'Doomsday' 5th Hour (1637)

Alfonso 'the Wise' 1221–84

20 Had I been present at the Creation, I would have given some useful hints for the better ordering of the universe.
on studying the Ptolemaic system
attributed

Nelson Algren 1909–

1 A walk on the wild side.
> title of novel (1956)

2 Never play cards with a man called Doc.
Never eat at a place called Mom's. Never
sleep with a woman whose troubles are
worse than your own.
> in *Newsweek* 2 July 1956

Ali ibn-Abi-Talib *c.*602–661

3 He who has a thousand friends has not a
friend to spare,
And he who has one enemy will meet him
everywhere.
> *A Hundred Sayings*

Muhammad Ali (Cassius Clay) 1942–

4 I'm the greatest.
> adopted as his catchphrase from 1962, in
> *Louisville Times* 16 November 1962

5 Float like a butterfly, sting like a bee.
> *summary of his boxing strategy (probably
> originated by his aide Drew 'Bundini' Brown)*
> G. Sullivan *Cassius Clay Story* (1964) ch. 8

Abbé d'Allainval 1700–53

6 *L'embarras des richesses.*
The embarrassment of riches.
> title of comedy (1726)

Fred Allen (John Florence Sullivan) 1894–1956

7 Committee—a group of men who
individually can do nothing but as a group
decide that nothing can be done.
> attributed

Woody Allen 1935–

8 It's not that I'm afraid to die. I just don't
want to be there when it happens.
> *Death* (1975)

9 On bisexuality: It immediately doubles your
chances for a date on Saturday night.
> in *New York Times* 1 December 1975

10 I don't want to achieve immortality through
my work . . . I want to achieve it through
not dying.
> Eric Lax *Woody Allen and his Comedy* (1975) ch. 12

11 I recently turned sixty. Practically a third of
my life is over.
> in *Observer* 10 March 1996 'Sayings of the Week'

William Allingham 1824–89

12 Up the airy mountain,
Down the rushy glen,
We daren't go a-hunting,
For fear of little men.
> 'The Fairies' (1850)

St Ambrose *c.*339–97

13 *Ubi Petrus, ibi ergo ecclesia.*
Where Peter is, there must be the Church.
> 'Explanatio psalmi 40' in *Corpus Scriptorum
> Ecclesiasticorum Latinorum* (1919) vol. 64

14 When I go to Rome, I fast on Saturday, but
here [Milan] I do not. Do you also follow the
custom of whatever church you attend, if
you do not want to give or receive scandal.
> *St Augustine: Letters* vol. 1 (tr Sister W. Parsons,
> 1951) 'Letter 54 to Januarius' (AD *c.*400)

Leo Amery 1873–1955

15 Speak for England.
> to Arthur Greenwood in the House of
> Commons, 2 September 1939; see **Boothby**
> 64:10

16 I will quote certain other words. I do it with
great reluctance, because I am speaking of
those who are old friends and associates of
mine, but they are words which, I think, are
applicable to the present situation. This is
what Cromwell said to the Long Parliament
when he thought it was no longer fit to
conduct the affairs of the nation: 'You have
sat too long here for any good you have
been doing. Depart, I say, and let us have
done with you. In the name of God, go.'
> speech, House of Commons, 7 May 1940; cf.
> **Cromwell** 103:20

Fisher Ames 1758–1808

17 A monarchy is a merchantman which sails
well, but will sometimes strike on a rock,
and go to the bottom; whilst a republic is a
raft which would never sink, but then your
feet are always in the water.
> attributed to Ames, speaking in the House of
> Representatives, 1795, but not traced in Ames's
> speeches

Hardy Amies 1909–

18 It is totally impossible to be well dressed in
cheap shoes.
> *The Englishman's Suit* (1994)

Kingsley Amis 1922–95

19 His mouth had been used as a latrine by
some small creature of the night, and then
as its mausoleum.
> *Lucky Jim* (1953) ch. 6

20 Outside every fat man there was an even
fatter man trying to close in.
> *One Fat Englishman* (1963) ch. 3; cf. **Connolly**
> 99:2, **Orwell** 237:8

21 Should poets bicycle-pump the human
heart
Or squash it flat?
Man's love is of man's life a thing apart;
Girls aren't like that.
> 'A Bookshop Idyll' (1956); cf. **Byron** 78:18

22 We men have got love well weighed up; our
stuff
Can get by without it.
Women don't seem to think that's good
enough;
They write about it.
> 'A Bookshop Idyll' (1956)

1 No pleasure is worth giving up for the sake of two more years in a geriatric home in Weston-super-Mare.

in *The Times* 21 June 1994; attributed

Martin Amis 1949-

2 To be more interested in the writer than the writing is just eternal human vulgarity.

on BBC2 *Bookmark*, 9 March 1996

Anacharsis

3 Written laws are like spiders' webs; they will catch, it is true, the weak and poor, but would be torn in pieces by the rich and powerful.

Plutarch *Parallel Lives* 'Solon' bk. 5, sect. 2; cf. **Swift** 306:17

Anatolius

4 Fierce was the wild billow,
Dark was the night;
Oars laboured heavily,
Foam glimmered white;
Trembled the mariners,
Peril was nigh:
Then said the God of God,
'Peace! it is I.'

'Fierce was the wild billow' (tr John Mason Neale, 1862)

Hans Christian Andersen 1805-75

5 The Emperor's new clothes.

title of story in *Danish Fairy Legends and Tales* (1846)

6 'But the Emperor has nothing on at all!' cried a little child.

Danish Fairy Legends and Tales (1846) 'The Emperor's New Clothes'

Maxwell Anderson 1888-1959

7 But it's a long, long while
From May to December;
And the days grow short
When you reach September.

'September Song' (1938 song)

Maxwell Anderson 1888-1959 and Lawrence Stallings 1894-1968

8 What price glory?

title of play (1924)

Robert Anderson 1917-

9 Tea and sympathy.

title of play (1957)

Lancelot Andrewes 1555-1626

10 It was no summer progress. A cold coming they had of it, at this time of the year; just, the worst time of the year, to take a journey, and specially a long journey, in.

The ways deep, the weather sharp, the days short, the sun farthest off *in solstitio brumali*, the very dead of Winter.

Of the Nativity (1622) Sermon 15; cf. **Eliot** 122:7

Norman Angell 1872-1967

11 The great illusion.

on the futility of war

title of book (1910), first published as 'Europe's optical illusion' (1909)

Anonymous

English

12 An abomination unto the Lord, but a very present help in time of trouble.

definition of a lie

an amalgamation of Proverbs 12.22 and Psalms 46.1, often attributed to Adlai **Stevenson**; Bill Adler *The Stevenson Wit* (1966); cf. **Bible** 37:28, **Book of Common Prayer** 61:25

13 Action this day.

annotation as used by Winston Churchill at the Admiralty in 1940

14 Adam
Had 'em.

on the antiquity of microbes

noted as an example of a short poem

15 All human beings are born free and equal in dignity and rights.

Universal Declaration of Human Rights (1948) article 1

16 All present and correct.

King's Regulations (Army) Report of the Orderly Sergeant to the Officer of the Day

17 Along the electric wire the message came:
He is not better—he is much the same.

parodic poem on the illness of the Prince of Wales, later King **Edward VII**

F. H. Gribble *Romance of the Cambridge Colleges* (1913); sometimes attributed to Alfred Austin (1835-1913), Poet Laureate

18 And they lived happily ever after.

traditional ending to a fairy story

recorded (with slight variations) from the 1850s

19 Any officer who shall behave in a scandalous manner, unbecoming the character of an officer and a gentleman shall . . . be CASHIERED.

Articles of War (1872) 'Disgraceful Conduct' Article 79; the Naval Discipline Act, 10 August 1860, Article 24, uses the words 'conduct unbecoming the character of an Officer'

20 Appeal from Philip drunk to Philip sober.

paraphrase of the words of an unidentified woman in Valerius Maximus *Facta ac Dicta Memorabilia* (AD c.32) bk. 6, ch. 2

21 Are we downhearted? No!

expression much taken up by British soldiers during the First World War

1 A beast, but a just beast.
a schoolboy's description of Dr Temple,
Headmaster of Rugby School
> F.E. Kitchener *Rugby Memoir of Archbishop Temple*
> *1857–1869* (1907) ch. 3

2 Be happy while y'er leevin,
For y'er a lang time deid.
Scottish motto for a house
> in *Notes and Queries* 9th series, vol. 8, 7
> December 1901

3 Betwixt the stirrup and the ground
Mercy I asked, mercy I found.
epitaph for 'A gentleman falling off his horse
[who] brake his neck'
> William Camden *Remains Concerning Britain*
> (1605) 'Epitaphs'

4 Bigamy is having one husband too many.
Monogamy is the same.
> Erica Jong *Fear of Flying* (1973) ch. 1 (epigraph)

5 The cloud of unknowing.
> title of mystical prose work (14th century)

6 Collapse of Stout Party.
supposed standard dénouement in Victorian
humour
> R. Pearsall *Collapse of Stout Party* (1975)
> introduction

7 A committee is a group of the unwilling,
chosen from the unfit, to do the
unnecessary.
> various attributions (origin unknown)

8 A community in which power, wealth and
opportunity are in the hands of the many
not the few, where the rights we enjoy
reflect the duties we owe . . . in which the
enterprise of the market and the rigour of
competition are joined with the forces of
partnership and cooperation.
> new Clause Four of the Labour Party
> constitution, passed at a special conference 29
> April 1995; cf. **Anonymous** 10:13

9 A Company for carrying on an undertaking
of Great Advantage, but no one to know
what it is.
> The South Sea Company Prospectus (1711), in
> Virginia Cowles *The Great Swindle* (1963) ch. 5

10 Conduct . . . to the prejudice of good order
and military discipline.
> *Army Discipline and Regulation Act* (1879) Section
> 40

11 [Death is] nature's way of telling you to slow
down.
> American life insurance proverb, in *Newsweek*
> 25 April 1960

12 The difficult we do immediately; the
impossible takes a little longer.
> US Armed Forces' slogan; cf. **Calonne** 80:12,
> **Nansen** 231:1

13 Do not fold, spindle or mutilate.
> instruction on punched cards (found in this
> form in the 1950s, and in differing forms from
> the 1930s)

14 Do not stand at my grave and weep:
I am not there. I do not sleep.
I am a thousand winds that blow.

I am the diamond glints on snow.
I am the sunlight on ripened grain.
I am the gentle autumn's rain.
When you awaken in the morning's hush,
I am the swift uplifting rush
Of quiet birds in circled flight.
I am the soft stars that shine at night.
Do not stand at my grave and cry;
I am not there, I did not die.
> *quoted in letter left by British soldier Stephen*
> *Cummins when killed by the IRA, March 1989*
> origin uncertain; attributed to various authors

15 Early one morning, just as the sun was
rising,
I heard a maid sing in the valley below:
'Oh, don't deceive me; Oh, never leave me!
How could you use a poor maiden so?'
> 'Early One Morning' (traditional song)

16 The eternal triangle.
> book review title, in *Daily Chronicle* 5 December
> 1907

17 Every country has its own constitution; ours
is absolutism moderated by assassination.
> Count Münster, quoting 'an intelligent Russian',
> in *Political Sketches of the State of Europe, 1814–1867*
> (1868)

18 Everyman, I will go with thee, and be thy
guide,
In thy most need to go by thy side.
spoken by Knowledge
> *Everyman* (c.1509–19) l. 522

19 Expletive deleted.
> in *Submission of Recorded Presidential Conversations*
> *to the Committee on the Judiciary of the House of*
> *Representatives by President Richard M. Nixon* 30
> April 1974, appendix 1

20 Exterminate . . . the treacherous English,
walk over General French's contemptible
little army.
allegedly a copy of Orders issued by the Kaiser
Wilhelm II *but most probably fabricated by the*
British
> annexe to BEF [British Expeditionary Force]
> Routine Orders of 24 September 1914, in
> Arthur Ponsonby *Falsehood in Wartime* (1928) ch.
> 10; cf. **Cromwell** 103:22

21 Faster than a speeding bullet! . . . Look! Up
in the sky! It's a bird! It's a plane! It's
Superman! Yes, it's Superman! Strange
visitor from another planet . . . Who can
change the course of mighty rivers, bend
steel with his bare hands, and
who—disguised as Clark Kent, mild-
mannered reporter for a great metropolitan
newspaper—fights a never ending battle for
truth, justice and the American way!
> *Superman* (US radio show, 1940 onwards)
> preamble

22 Fifty million Frenchmen can't be wrong.
> saying popular with American servicemen
> during the First World War; later associated
> with Mae **West** and Texas Guinan (1884–1933),
> it was also the title of a 1927 song by Billy Rose
> and Willie Raskin

1 From ghoulies and ghosties and long-leggetty
beasties
And things that go bump in the night,
Good Lord, deliver us!

> 'The Cornish or West Country Litany', in
> Francis T. Nettleinghame *Polperro Proverbs and
> Others* (1926) 'Pokerwork Panels'

2 From Moses to Moses there was none like
unto Moses.

> later inscription on the tomb of the Jewish
> scholar Moses **Maimonides** (1135–1204)

3 From the halls of Montezuma,
To the shores of Tripoli.

> 'The Marines' Hymn' (1847)

4 God be in my head,
And in my understanding . . .
God be in my mouth,
And in my speaking . . .
God be at my end,
And at my departing.

> *Sarum Missal* (11th century)

5 God save our gracious king!
Long live our noble king!
God save the king!
Send him victorious,
Happy, and glorious,
Long to reign over us:
God save the king!

> 'God save the King', attributed to various
> authors of the mid eighteenth century,
> including Henry **Carey**; Jacobite variants, such
> as James Hogg 'The King's Anthem' also exist

6 Go to jail. Go directly to jail. Do not pass go.
Do not collect £200.

> instructions on 'Community Chest' card in the
> game 'Monopoly'; invented by Charles Brace
> Darrow (1889–1967) in 1931

7 Greensleeves was all my joy,
Greensleeves was my delight,
Greensleeves was my heart of gold,
And who but Lady Greensleeves?

> 'A new Courtly Sonnet of the Lady
> Greensleeves, to the new tune of
> "Greensleeves" ', in *A Handful of Pleasant Delights*
> (1584)

8 Hereabouts died a very gallant gentleman,
Captain L. E. G. Oates of the Inniskilling
Dragoons. In March 1912, returning from
the Pole, he walked willingly to his death in
a blizzard to try and save his comrades,
beset by hardships.

> *epitaph on cairn erected in the Antarctic, 15
> November 1912, by E. L. Atkinson (1882–1929)
> and Apsley Cherry-Garrard (1882–1959)*
>
> Apsley Cherry-Garrard *The Worst Journey in the
> World* (1922)

9 Here lies Fred,
Who was alive and is dead:
Had it been his father,
I had much rather;
Had it been his brother,
Still better than another . . .
But since 'tis only Fred,
Who was alive and is dead,—

There's no more to be said.

> *of Frederick Louis, Prince of Wales (1707–1751),
> son of **George II** and **Caroline** of Ansbach*
>
> Horace Walpole *Memoirs of George II* (1847) vol. 1

10 Here's tae us; wha's like us?
Gey few, and they're a' deid.

> Scottish toast, probably of 19th-century origin;
> the first line appears in T. W. H. Crosland *The
> Unspeakable Scot* (1902), and various versions of
> the second line are current

11 He was her man, but he done her wrong.

> 'Frankie and Albert', in John Huston *Frankie and
> Johnny* (1930) (St Louis ballad later better known
> as 'Frankie and Johnny')

12 How different, how very different from the
home life of our own dear Queen!

> *comment overheard at a performance of
> Cleopatra by Sarah Bernhardt*
>
> Irvin S. Cobb *A Laugh a Day* (1924) (probably
> apocryphal)

13 Icham of Irlaunde
Ant of the holy londe of irlonde
Gode sir pray ich ye
for of saynte charite,
come ant daunce wyt me,
in irlaunde.

> fourteenth century

14 If it moves, salute it; if it doesn't move, pick
it up; and if you can't pick it up, paint it.

> 1940s saying, in Paul Dickson *The Official Rules*
> (1978)

15 If you really want to make a million . . . the
quickest way is to start your own religion.

> previously attributed to L. Ron Hubbard
> (1911–86) in B. Corydon and L. Ron Hubbard Jr.
> *L. Ron Hubbard* (1987), but attribution
> subsequently rejected by L. Ron Hubbard Jr.,
> who also dissociated himself from this book

16 I'll go no more a-roving
With you fair maid.

> 'A-roving' (traditional song)

17 I'll sing you twelve O.
Green grow the rushes O.
What is your twelve O?
Twelve for the twelve apostles,
Eleven for the eleven who went to heaven,
Ten for the ten commandments,
Nine for the nine bright shiners,
Eight for the eight bold rangers,
Seven for the seven stars in the sky,
Six for the six proud walkers,
Five for the symbol at your door,
Four for the Gospel makers,
Three for the rivals,
Two, two, the lily-white boys,
Clothed all in green O,
One is one and all alone
And ever more shall be so.

> 'The Dilly Song'; cf. **Burns** 75:11

18 I'm armed with more than complete
steel—The justice of my quarrel.

> *Lust's Dominion* (1657) act 4, sc. 3 (attributed to
> **Marlowe**, though of doubtful authorship)

1 I met wid Napper Tandy, and he took me by the hand,
And he said, 'How's poor ould Ireland, and how does she stand?'
She's the most disthressful country that iver yet was seen,
For they're hangin' men an' women for the wearin' o' the Green.

    'The Wearin' o' the Green' (c.1795 ballad)

2 It became necessary to destroy the town to save it.

    statement by unidentified US Army Major, referring to Ben Tre in Vietnam

    in Associated Press Report, *New York Times* 8 February 1968

3 Jacques Brel is alive and well and living in Paris.

    title of musical entertainment (1968–72) which triggered numerous imitations

4 John Brown's body lies a mould'ring in the grave,
His soul is marching on.

    inspired by the execution of the abolitionist John **Brown**, *after the raid on Harper's Ferry, on 2 December 1859*

    song (1861), variously attributed to Charles Sprague Hall, Henry Howard Brownell, and Thomas Brigham Bishop

5 The King over the Water.

    Jacobite toast (18th-century)

6 Liberty is always unfinished business.

    title of 36th Annual Report of the American Civil Liberties Union, 1 July 1955–30 June 1956

7 Licensed to kill.

    popular description of the status of Secret Service agent James Bond, 007, in the novels of Ian **Fleming**

8 Lions led by donkeys.

    associated with British soldiers during the First World War

    attributed to Max Hoffman (1869–1927) in Alan Clark *The Donkeys* (1961); this attribution has not been traced elsewhere, and the phrase is of much earlier origin

9 Little Englanders.

    term applied to anti-imperialists

    in *Westminster Gazette* 1 August 1895; in *Pall Mall Gazette* 16 September 1884 the phrase 'believe in a little England' occurs

10 Lizzie Borden took an axe
And gave her mother forty whacks;
When she saw what she had done
She gave her father forty-one!

    after the acquittal of Lizzie Borden, in June 1893, from the charge of murdering her father and stepmother at Fall River, Massachusetts on 4 August 1892

    popular rhyme

11 Lloyd George knew my father,
My father knew Lloyd George.

    two-line comic song, sung to the tune of 'Onward, Christian Soldiers' and possibly by Tommy Rhys Roberts (1910–75)

12 London, thou art the flower of cities all!
Gemme of all joy, jasper of jocunditie.

    'London' l. 16

13 Love me little, love me long,
Is the burden of my song.

    'Love me little, love me long' (1569–70)

14 Mademoiselle from Armenteers,
Hasn't been kissed for forty years,
Hinky, dinky, parley-voo.

    song of the First World War, variously attributed to Edward Rowland and to Harry Carlton

15 CHILD: Mamma, are Tories born wicked, or do they grow wicked afterwards?
MOTHER: They are born wicked, and grow worse.

    G. W. E. Russell *Collections and Recollections* (1898) ch. 10

16 The ministry of all the talents.

    name given ironically to William Grenville's coalition of 1806, and also applied to later coalitions

    G. W. Cooke *The History of Party* (1837) vol. 3

17 Matthew, Mark, Luke, and John,
The bed be blest that I lie on.
Four angels to my bed,
Four angels round my head,
One to watch, and one to pray,
And two to bear my soul away.

    traditional (the first two lines in Thomas Ady *A Candle in the Dark*, 1656)

18 Members [of civil service orders] rise from CMG (known sometimes in Whitehall as 'Call Me God') to the KCMG ('Kindly Call Me God') to—for a select few governors and super-ambassadors—the GCMG ('God Calls Me God').

    Anthony Sampson *Anatomy of Britain* (1962) ch. 18

19 Miss Buss and Miss Beale
Cupid's darts do not feel.
How different from us,
Miss Beale and Miss Buss.

    of the Headmistress of the North London Collegiate School and the Principal of the Ladies' College, Cheltenham

    rhyme, c.1884

20 My name is George Nathaniel Curzon,
I am a most superior person.

    of Lord **Curzon**

    The Masque of Balliol (c.1870), in W. G. Hiscock *The Balliol Rhymes* (1939); cf. **Beeching** 27:10

21 The nature of God is a circle of which the centre is everywhere and the circumference is nowhere.

    said to have been traced to a lost treatise of Empedocles; quoted in the *Roman de la Rose*, and by St Bonaventura in *Itinerarius Mentis in Deum* ch. 5, closing line

22 The noise, my dear! And the people!

    of the retreat from Dunkirk, May 1940; the saying has also been attributed to Ernest Thesiger of the First World War

    Anthony Rhodes *Sword of Bone* (1942) ch. 22

1 No more Latin, no more French,
No more sitting on a hard board bench.
children's rhyme for the end of term
> Iona and Peter Opie *Lore and Language of Schoolchildren* (1959) ch. 13

2 Not so much a programme, more a way of life!
title of BBC television series, 1964

3 Now I lay me down to sleep;
I pray the Lord my soul to keep.
If I should die before I wake,
I pray the Lord my soul to take.
> first printed in a late edition of the *New England Primer* (1781)

4 O Death, where is thy sting-a-ling-a-ling,
O grave, thy victory?
The bells of Hell go ting-a-ling-a-ling
For you but not for me.
> 'For You But Not For Me', in S. Louis Guiraud (ed.) *Songs That Won the War* (1930); cf. **Bible** 50:8

5 O God, if there be a God, save my soul, if I have a soul!
prayer of a common soldier before the battle of Blenheim, 1704
> in *Notes and Queries* vol. 173, no. 15 (9 October 1937); quoted in John Henry Newman *Apologia pro Vita Sua* (1864)

6 Once upon a time . . .
traditional opening to a story, especially a fairy story
> Anonymous, recorded from 1595

7 One Cartwright brought a Slave from Russia, and would scourge him, for which he was questioned: and it was resolved, That England was too pure an Air for Slaves to breathe in.
> 'In the 11th of Elizabeth' (17 November 1568–16 November 1569), in John Rushworth *Historical Collections* (1680–1722) vol. 2; cf. **Cowper** 101:29

8 O rare Ben Jonson.
> inscription on the tomb of Ben **Jonson** in Westminster Abbey

9 O ye'll tak' the high road, and I'll tak' the low road,
And I'll be in Scotland afore ye,
But me and my true love will never meet again,
On the bonnie, bonnie banks o' Loch Lomon'.
> 'The Bonnie Banks of Loch Lomon'' (traditional song)

10 A place within the meaning of the Act.
> usually taken to be a reference to the Betting Act 1853, sect. 2, which banned off-course betting on horse-races

11 Please do not shoot the pianist. He is doing his best.
printed notice in a dancing saloon
> Oscar Wilde *Impressions of America* 'Leadville' (c.1882–3)

12 Please to remember the Fifth of November, Gunpowder Treason and Plot.
We know no reason why gunpowder treason
Should ever be forgot.
> traditional rhyme on the Gunpowder Plot (1605)

13 The [*or* A] quick brown fox jumps over the lazy dog.
used by keyboarders to ensure that all letters of the alphabet are functioning
> R. Hunter Middleton's introduction to *The Quick Brown Fox* (1945) by Richard H. Templeton Jr.

14 The rabbit has a charming face:
Its private life is a disgrace.
I really dare not name to you
The awful things that rabbits do.
> 'The Rabbit', in *The Week-End Book* (1925)

15 Raise the stone, and there thou shalt find me, cleave the wood and there am I.
> Oxyrhynchus Papyri, in B. P. Grenfell and A. S. Hunt (eds.) *Sayings of Our Lord* (1897) Logion 5, l. 23

16 Rest in peace. The mistake shall not be repeated.
> inscription on the cenotaph at Hiroshima, Japan

17 Say it ain't so, Joe.
'Shoeless' Joe Jackson and seven other Chicago players were charged with being bribed to lose the 1919 World Baseball Series
> plea said to have been made by a boy as Jackson emerged from the hearing, September 1920

18 See the happy moron,
He doesn't give a damn,
I wish I were a moron,
My God! perhaps I am!
> in *Eugenics Review* July 1929

19 Seven wealthy towns contend for HOMER dead
Through which the living HOMER begged his bread.
> epilogue to *Aesop at Tunbridge; or, a Few Selected Fables in Verse* By No Person of Quality (1698); cf. **Heywood** 158:23

20 She was poor but she was honest
Victim of a rich man's game.
First he loved her, then he left her,
And she lost her maiden name . . .
It's the same the whole world over,
It's the poor wot gets the blame,
It's the rich wot gets the gravy.
Ain't it all a bleedin' shame?
> 'She was Poor but she was Honest' (sung by British soldiers in the First World War)

21 A soldier of the Great War known unto God.
standard epitaph for the unidentified dead of World War One
> adopted by the War Graves Commission

22 Some talk of Alexander, and some of Hercules;
Of Hector and Lysander, and such great names as these;
But of all the world's brave heroes, there's none that can compare

With a tow, row, row, row, row, row, for the
British Grenadier.
'The British Grenadiers' (traditional song)

1 So much chewing gum for the eyes.
*small boy's definition of certain television
programmes*
James Beasley Simpson *Best Quotes of '50, '55, '56*
(1957)

2 So on the Twelfth I proudly wear the sash
my father wore.
'The Sash My Father Wore', traditional Orange
song

3 Sumer is icumen in,
Lhude sing cuccu!
Groweth sed, and bloweth med,
And springth the wude nu.
'Cuckoo Song' (*c.*1250), sung annually at
Reading Abbey gateway and first recorded by
John Fornset, a monk of Reading Abbey; cf.
Pound 250:5

4 Swing low, sweet chariot—
Comin' for to carry me home.
Negro spiritual (*c.*1850)

5 Their name liveth for evermore.
*standard inscription on the Stone of Sacrifice in
each military cemetery of World War One,
proposed by Rudyard* **Kipling** *as a member of the
War Graves Commission*
Charles Carrington *Rudyard Kipling* (rev. ed.
1978); cf. **Bible** 41:30, **Sassoon** 265:4

6 There is a lady sweet and kind,
Was never face so pleased my mind;
I did but see her passing by,
And yet I love her till I die.
found on the reverse of leaf 53 of 'Popish
Kingdome or reigne of Antichrist', in Latin
verse by Thomas Naogeorgus, and Englished by
Barnabe Googe; printed in 1570; sometimes
attributed to Thomas Forde

7 There is one thing stronger than all the
armies in the world; and that is an idea
whose time has come.
in *Nation* 15 April 1943; cf. **Hugo** 166:16

8 There is so much good in the worst of us,
And so much bad in the best of us,
That it hardly becomes any of us
To talk about the rest of us.
attributed, among others, to Edward Wallis
Hoch (1849–1945) on the grounds of it having
appeared in his Kansas publication, the *Marion
Record*, though in fact disclaimed by him
('behooves' sometimes substituted for
'becomes')

9 They haif said: Quhat say they? Lat thame
say.
motto of the Earls Marischal of Scotland,
inscribed at Marischal College, Aberdeen, 1593;
a similarly defiant motto in Greek has been
found engraved in remains from classical
antiquity

10 Thirty days hath September,
April, June, and November;
All the rest have thirty-one,
Excepting February alone,
And that has twenty-eight days clear

And twenty-nine in each leap year.
Stevins MS (*c.*1555)

11 Though I yield to no one in my admiration
for Mr Coolidge, I do wish he did not look as
if he had been weaned on a pickle.
anonymous remark, in Alice Roosevelt
Longworth *Crowded Hours* (1933) ch. 21

12 'Tis bad enough in man or woman
To steal a goose from off a common;
But surely he's without excuse
Who steals the common from the goose.
'On Inclosures'; in *The Oxford Book of Light Verse*
(1938)

13 To secure for the workers by hand or by
brain the full fruits of their industry and the
most equitable distribution thereof that
may be possible upon the basis of the
common ownership of the means of
production, distribution, and exchange.
Clause Four of the Labour Party's Constitution
of 1918 (revised 1929); the commitment to
common ownership of services was largely
removed in 1995; cf. **Anonymous** 6:8

14 We hold these truths to be self-evident, that
all men are created equal, that they are
endowed by their Creator with certain
unalienable rights, that among these are
life, liberty and the pursuit of happiness.
The American Declaration of Independence, 4
July 1776; cf. **Jefferson** 171:12

15 We're here
Because
We're here.
sung to the tune of 'Auld Lang Syne', in John
Brophy and Eric Partridge *Songs and Slang of the
British Soldier 1914–18* (1930)

16 Were you there when they crucified my
Lord?
title of Negro spiritual (1865)

17 We want eight, and we won't wait.
on the construction of Dreadnoughts
George Wyndham, speech in *The Times* 29
March 1909

18 Western wind, when will thou blow,
The small rain down can rain?
Christ, if my love were in my arms
And I in my bed again!
'Western Wind' (published 1790) in *New Oxford
Book of Sixteenth-Century Verse* (1991)

19 What's the use of worrying?
It never was worth while,
So, pack up your troubles in your old kit-
bag,
And smile, smile, smile.
'Pack up your Troubles' (1915 song), written by
George Asaf (1880–1951)

20 When Israel was in Egypt land,
Let my people go,
Oppressed so hard they could not stand,
Let my people go.
*Go down, Moses,
Way-down in Egypt land,
Tell old Pharaoh
To let my people go.*
'Go Down, Moses' (Negro spiritual); cf. **Bible**
34:5

1 Who dares wins.

  motto of the British Special Air Service
  regiment, from 1942

2 When war is declared, Truth is the first
casualty.

  attributed to Hiram Johnson, speaking in the
  US Senate, 1918, but not recorded in his
  speech; the first recorded use is as epigraph to
  Arthur Ponsonby's *Falsehood in Wartime* (1928);
  see **Johnson** 173:17

3 A willing foe and sea room.

  naval toast in the time of **Nelson**

  W. N. T. Beckett *A Few Naval Customs, Expressions,
  Traditions, and Superstitions* (1931) 'Customs'

4 With a heart of furious fancies,
Whereof I am commander;
With a burning spear,
And a horse of air,
To the wilderness I wander.

  'Tom o' Bedlam'

5 Would you like to sin
With Elinor Glyn
On a tigerskin?
Or would you prefer
To err
With her
On some other fur?

  1907 rhyme, in A. Glyn *Elinor Glyn* (1955) bk. 2,
  sect. 30

6 Yankee Doodle came to town
Riding on a pony;
Stuck a feather in his cap
And called it Macaroni.

  'Yankee Doodle' (song, 1755 or earlier);
  Nicholas Smith *Stories of Great National Songs*
  (1899) ch. 2; cf. **Cohan** 95:14

7 Your King and Country need you.

  recruitment slogan for First World War, coined
  by Eric Field, July 1914; *Advertising* (1959); cf.
  Rubens 261:19

8 You should make a point of trying every
experience once, excepting incest and folk-
dancing.

  Arnold Bax (1883–1953), quoting 'a sympathetic
  Scot' in *Farewell My Youth* (1943)

French

9 *Ça ira.*

  Things will work out.

  refrain of 'Carillon national', popular song of
  the French Revolution (c.July 1790), tr William
  Doyle; the phrase is believed to originate with
  Benjamin **Franklin**, who may have uttered it
  in 1776 when asked for news of the American
  Revolution

10 *Cet animal est très méchant,
Quand on l'attaque il se défend.*

  This animal is very bad; when attacked it
  defends itself.

  'La Ménagerie' (1868 song) by 'Théodore P. K.'

11 *Chevalier sans peur et sans reproche.*

  Fearless, blameless knight.

  description in contemporary chronicles of
  Pierre Bayard (1476–1524)

12 *Honi soit qui mal y pense.*

  Evil be to him who evil thinks.

  motto of the Order of the Garter, originated by
  Edward III, probably on 23 April of 1348 or
  1349; cf. **Sellar and Yeatman** 267:17

13 *Il ne faut pas être plus royaliste que le roi.*

  You mustn't be more of a royalist than the
  king.

  saying from the time of Louis XVI; François
  René, Vicomte de Chateaubriand *De la monarchie
  selon la charte* (1816) ch. 81

14 *Ils ne passeront pas.*

  They shall not pass.

  slogan used by the French army at the defence
  of Verdun in 1916; variously attributed to
  Marshal **Pétain** and to General Robert Nivelle,
  and taken up by the Republicans in the Spanish
  Civil War in the form '*No pasarán!*'; cf. **Ibarruri**
  168:8

15 *Je suis Marxiste—tendance Groucho.*

  I am a Marxist—of the Groucho tendency.

  slogan used at Nanterre in Paris, 1968

16 *Laissez-nous-faire.*

  Allow us to do [it].

  remark dating from c.1664, in *Journal
  Oeconomique* Paris, April 1751: 'Monsieur Colbert
  assembled several deputies of commerce at his
  house to ask what could be done for commerce;
  the most rational and the least flattering
  among them answered him in one word:
  "Laissez-nous-faire"'; cf. **Argenson** 14:5

17 *L'ordre règne à Varsovie.*

  Order reigns in Warsaw.

  after the brutal suppression of an uprising, the
  newspaper *Moniteur* reported, 16 September
  1831, '*L'ordre et la tranquillité sont entièrement
  rétablis dans la capitale* [Order and calm are
  completely restored in the capital]'; on the
  same day Count Sebastiani, minister of foreign
  affairs, declared: '*La tranquillité règne à Varsovie*
  [Peace reigns in Warsaw]'

18 *Nous n'irons plus aux bois, les lauriers sont
coupés.*

  We'll to the woods no more,
  The laurels all are cut.

  old nursery rhyme, quoted by Théodore de
  Banville in *Les Cariatides, les stalactites* (1842–6); tr
  A. E. Housman in *Last Poems* (1922) introductory

19 *Revenons à ces moutons.*

  Let us get back to these sheep [i.e. 'Let us get
  back to the subject'].

  Maistre Pierre Pathelin l. 1191 (often quoted as
  '*Retournons à nos moutons* [Let us return to our
  sheep]')

20 *Tout passe, tout casse, tout lasse.*

  Everything passes, everything perishes,
  everything palls.

  Charles Cahier *Quelques six mille proverbes* (1856)
  no. 1718

German

21 *Arbeit macht frei.*

  Work liberates.

  words inscribed on the gates of Dachau
  concentration camp, 1933, and subsequently on
  those of Auschwitz

1 *Jedem das Seine.*

To each his own.

often quoted as 'Everyone gets what he deserves'

inscription on the gate of Buchenwald concentration camp, *c.*1937

2 *Kommt der Krieg ins Land*
Gibt's Lügen wie Sand.

When war enters a country
It produces lies like sand.

epigraph to Arthur Ponsonby *Falsehood in Wartime* (1928)

Greek

3 Nothing in excess.

inscribed on the temple of Apollo at Delphi

variously ascribed to the Seven Wise Men

4 Whenever God prepares evil for a man, He first damages his mind, with which he deliberates.

scholiastic annotation to Sophocles's *Antigone* l. 622

5 Let no one enter who does not know geometry [mathematics].

*inscription on **Plato**'s door, probably at the Academy at Athens*

Elias Philosophus *In Aristotelis Categorias Commentaria*; in A. Busse (ed.) *Commentaria in Aristotelem Graeca* (1900) vol. 18, pt. 1

Latin

6 *Adeste, fideles.*

O come, all ye faithful.

French or German hymn (*c.*1743) in *Murray's Hymnal* (1852); translation based on that of F. Oakeley (1841)

7 *Ad majorem Dei gloriam.*

To the greater glory of God.

motto of the Society of Jesus

8 *Ave Caesar, morituri te salutant.*

Hail Caesar, those who are about to die salute you.

gladiators saluting the Roman Emperor

Suetonius *Lives of the Caesars* 'Claudius' ch. 21

9 *Ave Maria, gratia plena, Dominus tecum: Benedicta tu in mulieribus, et benedictus fructus ventris tui, Jesus.*

Hail Mary, full of grace, the Lord is with thee: Blessed art thou among women, and blessed is the fruit of thy womb, Jesus.

'Ave Maria' or 'Hail Mary', also known as 'The Angelic Salutation', dating from the 11th century; cf. **Bible** 45:33

10 *Ave verum corpus,*
natum ex Maria Virgine.

Hail the true body, born of the Virgin Mary.

Eucharistic hymn, probably dating from the 14th century

11 *Dominus illuminatio mea.*

The Lord is my light.

motto of the University of Oxford; cf. **Bible** 52:29

12 *Et in Arcadia ego.*

And I too in Arcadia.

tomb inscription, of disputed meaning, often depicted in classical paintings, notably by Poussin in 1655; E. Panofsky 'Et in Arcadia ego' in R. K. Klibansky and H. J. Paton (eds.) *Philosophy and History: Essays Presented to E. Cassirer* (1936)

13 *Gaudeamus igitur,*
Juvenes dum sumus.

Let us then rejoice,
While we are young.

medieval students' song, traced to 1267, but revised in the 18th century

14 *Nemo me impune lacessit.*

No one provokes me with impunity.

motto of the Crown of Scotland and of all Scottish regiments

15 *Nisi Dominus frustra.*

In vain without the Lord.

motto of the city of Edinburgh; see **Bible** 53:2

16 *Nullius in verba.*

In the word of none.

emphasizing reliance on experiment rather than authority

motto of the Royal Society

17 *Per ardua ad astra.*

Through struggle to the stars.

motto of the Mulvany family, quoted and translated by Rider **Haggard** in *The People of the Mist* (1894) ch. 1; still in use as motto of the R.A.F., having been proposed by J. S. Yule in 1912 and approved by King **George V** in 1913

18 *Post coitum omne animal triste.*

After coition every animal is sad.

post-classical saying

19 *Quidquid agis, prudenter agas, et respice finem.*

Whatever you do, do cautiously, and look to the end.

Gesta Romanorum no. 103

20 *Semper eadem.*

Ever the same.

motto of **Elizabeth I**

21 *Sic semper tyrannis.*

Thus always to tyrants.

motto of the State of Virginia; cf. **Booth** 64:8

22 *Sic transit gloria mundi.*

Thus passes the glory of the world.

said during the coronation of a new Pope, while flax is burned to represent the transitoriness of earthly glory

used at the coronation of Alexander V in Pisa, 7 July 1409, but earlier in origin; cf. **Thomas à Kempis** 315:18

23 *Similia similibus curantur.*

Like cures like.

motto of homeopathic medicine, although not found in this form in the writings of C. F. S. Hahnemann (1755–1843); the Latin appears as an anonymous side-note in Paracelsus *Opera Omnia* (*c.*1490–1541, ed. 1658) vol. 1

1 *Si monumentum requiris, circumspice.*
If you seek a monument, gaze around.
  inscription in St Paul's Cathedral, London,
  attributed to the son of Sir Christopher Wren
  (1632–1723), its architect

2 *Vox et praeterea nihil.*
A voice and nothing more.
describing a nightingale
  Plutarch *Moralia* sect. 233a, no. 15

Italian

3 *Se non è vero, è molto ben trovato.*
If it is not true, it is a happy invention.
  common saying from the 16th century

Old English

4 Listen!
  The fame of Danish kings
in days gone by, the daring feats
worked by those heroes are well known to
us.
  Beowulf, translated by Kevin Crossley-Holland

5 Thought shall be the harder, heart the
keener, courage the greater, as our might
lessens.
  The Battle of Maldon (tr R. K. Gordon, 1926)

6 Men said openly that Christ slept and His
saints.
  *of England during the civil war between Stephen
  and Matilda*
  Anglo-Saxon Chronicle for 1137

Jean Anouilh 1910–87

7 God is on everyone's side . . . And, in the last
analysis, he is on the side of those with
plenty of money and large armies.
  L'Alouette (1953); cf. **Bussy-Rabutin** 77:1,
  Voltaire 326:9

8 There is love of course. And then there's
life, its enemy.
  Ardèle (1949)

Susan Brownell Anthony
1820–1906

9 Marriage, to women as to men, must be a
luxury, not a necessity; an incident of life,
not all of it.
  speech, 1875

Guillaume Apollinaire 1880–1918

10 *Les souvenirs sont cors de chasse
Dont meurt le bruit parmi le vent.*
Memories are hunting horns
Whose sound dies on the wind.
  'Cors de Chasse' (1912)

11 *Sous le pont Mirabeau coule la Seine.
Et nos amours, faut-il qu'il m'en souvienne?
La joie venait toujours après la peine.*
Under Mirabeau Bridge flows the Seine.
And our loves, must I remember them?
Joy always came after pain.
  'Le Pont Mirabeau' (1912)

12 When man wanted to make a machine that
would walk he created the wheel, which
does not resemble a leg.
  Les Mamelles de Tirésias (1918)

Thomas Gold Appleton 1812–84

13 Good Americans, when they die, go to Paris.
  Oliver Wendell Holmes *The Autocrat of the
  Breakfast Table* (1858) ch. 6; cf. **Wilde** 335:10

14 A Boston man is the east wind made flesh.
  attributed

Arabian Nights Entertainments, or the Thousand and one Nights

15 Who will change old lamps for new ones?
. . . new lamps for old ones?
  'The History of Aladdin'

16 Open Sesame!
  'The History of Ali Baba'

William Arabin 1773–1841

17 Prisoner, God has given you good abilities,
instead of which you go about the country
stealing ducks.
  also attributed to a Revd Mr Alderson, in
  Frederick Pollock *Essays in the Law* (1922)

18 They will steal the very teeth out of your
mouth as you walk through the streets. *I
know it from experience.*
  on the citizens of Uxbridge
  Sir W. Ballantine *Some Experiences of a Barrister's
  Life* (1882) vol. 1, ch. 6

Louis Aragon 1897–1982

19 *Ô mois des floraisons mois des métamorphoses
Mai qui fut sans nuage et Juin poignardé
Je n'oublierai jamais les lilas ni les roses
Ni ceux que le printemps dans ses plis a gardé.*
O month of flowerings, month of
metamorphoses,
May without cloud and June that was
stabbed,
I shall never forget the lilac and the roses
Nor those whom spring has kept in its folds.
  'Les lilas et les roses' (1940)

Diane Arbus 1923–71

20 A photograph is a secret about a secret. The
more it tells you the less you know.
  Patricia Bosworth *Diane Arbus: a Biography* (1985)

John Arbuthnot 1667–1735

21 Law is a bottomless pit.
  The History of John Bull (1712) title of first
  pamphlet

Archilochus

22 The fox knows many things—the hedgehog
one *big* one.
  E. Diehl (ed.) *Anthologia Lyrica Graeca* (3rd ed.,
  1949–52) vol. 1, no. 103; cf. **Berlin** 30:23

Archimedes *c.*287–212 BC

1 Eureka! [I've got it!]
Vitruvius Pollio *De Architectura* bk. 9, preface, sect. 10

2 Give me but one firm spot on which to stand, and I will move the earth.
on the action of a lever
Pappus *Synagoge* bk. 8, proposition 10, sect. 11

Robert Ardrey 1908–80

3 Not in innocence, and not in Asia, was mankind born.
African Genesis (1961)

Hannah Arendt 1906–75

4 It was as though in those last minutes he was summing up the lessons that this long course in human wickedness had taught us—the lesson of the fearsome, word-and-thought-defying *banality of evil*.
of Adolf Eichmann, responsible for the administration of the Nazi concentration camps
Eichmann in Jerusalem (1963) ch. 15

Marquis d'Argenson (René Louis de Voyer d'Argenson) 1694–1757

5 *Laisser-faire.*
No interference.
Mémoires et Journal Inédit du Marquis d'Argenson (1858 ed.) vol. 5; cf. **Anonymous** 11:16

Comte d'Argenson 1696–1764

6 DESFONTAINES: I must live.
D'ARGENSON: I do not see the necessity.
on Desfontaines having produced a pamphlet satirizing D'Argenson, his benefactor
Voltaire *Alzire* (1736) 'Discours Préliminaire' footnote, in *Oeuvres Complètes Théâtre* (1877) vol. 2

Ludovico Ariosto 1474–1533

7 *Natura il fece, e poi roppe la stampa.*
Nature made him, and then broke the mould.
Orlando Furioso (1532) canto 10, st. 84

Aristophanes *c.*450–*c.*385 BC

8 How about 'Cloudcuckooland'?
naming the capital city of the Birds
The Birds (414 BC) l. 819

9 This Second Logic then, I mean the Worse one,
They teach to talk unjustly, and—prevail.
The Clouds (423 BC) l. 113; cf. **Milton** 221:17

10 The old are in a second childhood.
The Clouds (423 BC) l. 1417

11 Brekekekex koax koax.
cry of the Frogs
The Frogs (405 BC) l. 209 and *passim*

12 Under every stone lurks a politician.
Thesmophoriazusae l. 530

Aristotle 384–322 BC

13 We make war that we may live in peace.
Nicomachean Ethics bk. 10, 1177b 5–6 (tr M. Ostwald); cf. **Vegetius** 323:8

14 Tragedy is thus a representation of an action that is worth serious attention, complete in itself and of some amplitude . . . by means of pity and fear bringing about the purgation of such emotions.
Poetics ch. 6, 1449b 24–8

15 A whole is that which has a beginning, a middle, and an end.
Poetics ch. 7

16 Probable impossibilities are to be preferred to improbable possibilities.
Poetics ch. 24, 1460a 26–7

17 Man is by nature a political animal.
Politics bk. 1, 1253a 2–3

18 He who is unable to live in society, or who has no need because he is sufficient for himself, must be either a beast or a god.
Politics bk. 1, 1253a 27–9

19 Nature does nothing without purpose or uselessly.
Politics bk. 1, 1256b 20–21

20 *Amicus Plato, sed magis amica veritas.*
Plato is dear to me, but dearer still is truth.
Latin translation of a Greek original ascribed to Aristotle

21 When he was asked 'What is a friend?' he said 'One soul inhabiting two bodies.'
Diogenes Laertius *Lives of Philosophers* bk. 5, sect. 20

Lewis Addison Armistead 1817–63

22 Give them the cold steel, boys!
during the American Civil War, 1863
attributed

Harry Armstrong 1879–1951

23 There's an old mill by the stream, Nellie Dean,
Where we used to sit and dream.
'Nellie Dean' (1905 song)

John Armstrong 1709–79

24 'Tis not for mortals always to be blest.
The Art of Preserving Health (1744) bk. 4, l. 260

25 'Tis not too late tomorrow to be brave.
The Art of Preserving Health (1744) bk. 4, l. 460

Louis Armstrong 1901–71

26 If you still have to ask . . . shame on you.
when asked what jazz is; sometimes quoted as, 'Man, if you gotta ask you'll never know'
Max Jones et al. *Salute to Satchmo* (1970)

Neil Armstrong 1930–

1 That's one small step for a man, one giant leap for mankind.
as the craft touched down, he had radioed 'Houston. Tranquillity Base here. The Eagle has landed'
in *New York Times* 21 July 1969; interference in the transmission obliterated 'a'

Robert Armstrong 1927–

2 It contains a misleading impression, not a lie. It was being economical with the truth.
during the 'Spycatcher' trial in New South Wales
in *Daily Telegraph* 19 November 1986; cf. **Burke** 74:16, **Clark** 93:16, **Twain** 321:5

Edwin Arnold 1832–1904

3 Nor ever once ashamed
So we be named
Press-men; Slaves of the Lamp; Servants of Light.
'The Tenth Muse' (1895) st. 18

Matthew Arnold 1822–88

4 The Sea of Faith
Was once, too, at the full, and round earth's shore
Lay like the folds of a bright girdle furled.
But now I only hear
Its melancholy, long, withdrawing roar.
Ah, love, let us be true
To one another!
'Dover Beach' (1867) l. 21

5 And we are here as on a darkling plain
Swept with confused alarms of struggle and flight,
Where ignorant armies clash by night.
'Dover Beach' (1867) l. 35

6 Come, dear children, let us away;
Down and away below!
'The Forsaken Merman' (1849) l. 1

7 Now the wild white horses play,
Champ and chafe and toss in the spray.
'The Forsaken Merman' (1849) l. 4

8 Where great whales come sailing by,
Sail and sail, with unshut eye,
Round the world for ever and aye.
'The Forsaken Merman' (1849) l. 43

9 Say, has some wet bird-haunted English lawn
Lent it the music of its trees at dawn?
'Parting' (1852) l. 19

10 Eternal Passion!
Eternal Pain!
of the nightingale
'Philomela' (1853) l. 31

11 Cruel, but composed and bland,
Dumb, inscrutable and grand,
So Tiberius might have sat,
Had Tiberius been a cat.
'Poor Matthias' (1885) l. 40

12 Not deep the Poet sees, but wide.
'Resignation' (1849) l. 214

13 Go, for they call you, Shepherd, from the hill.
'The Scholar-Gipsy' (1853) l. 1

14 All the live murmur of a summer's day.
'The Scholar-Gipsy' (1853) l. 20

15 Tired of knocking at Preferment's door.
'The Scholar-Gipsy' (1853) l. 35

16 Crossing the stripling Thames at Bab-lock-hithe.
'The Scholar-Gipsy' (1853) l. 74

17 The line of festal light in Christ-Church hall.
'The Scholar-Gipsy' (1853) l. 129

18 Thou waitest for the spark from heaven! and we,
Light half-believers in our casual creeds . . .
Who hesitate and falter life away,
And lose to-morrow the ground won to-day—
Ah, do not we, Wanderer, await it too?
'The Scholar-Gipsy' (1853) l. 171

19 Still nursing the unconquerable hope,
Still clutching the inviolable shade.
'The Scholar-Gipsy' (1853) l. 211

20 Others abide our question. Thou art free.
We ask and ask: Thou smilest and art still,
Out-topping knowledge.
'Shakespeare' (1849)

21 Truth sits upon the lips of dying men.
'Sohrab and Rustum' (1853) l. 656

22 And that sweet City with her dreaming spires.
of Oxford
'Thyrsis' (1866) l. 19

23 The bloom is gone, and with the bloom go I.
'Thyrsis' (1866) l. 57

24 Who saw life steadily, and saw it whole:
The mellow glory of the Attic stage;
Singer of sweet Colonus, and its child.
*of **Sophocles***
'To a Friend' (1849)

25 France, famed in all great arts, in none supreme.
'To a Republican Friend—Continued' (1849)

26 And bade betwixt their shores to be
The unplumbed, salt, estranging sea.
'To Marguerite—Continued' (1852) l. 24

27 The pursuit of perfection, then, is the pursuit of sweetness and light . . . He who works for sweetness and light united, works to make reason and the will of God prevail.
Culture and Anarchy (1869) ch. 1; cf. **Forster** 131:12, **Swift** 306:15

28 When I want to distinguish clearly the aristocratic class from the Philistines proper, or middle class, [I] name the former, in my own mind *the Barbarians.*
Culture and Anarchy (1869) ch. 3

29 Whispering from her towers the last enchantments of the Middle Age . . . Home

of lost causes, and forsaken beliefs, and
unpopular names, and impossible loyalties!
of Oxford
  Essays in Criticism First Series (1865) preface; cf.
  Beerbohm 27:12

1 In poetry, no less than in life, he is 'a
beautiful and ineffectual angel, beating in
the void his luminous wings in vain'.
  Essays in Criticism Second Series (1888) 'Shelley'
  (quoting from his own essay on Byron in the
  same work)

2 Poetry is at bottom a criticism of life.
  Essays in Criticism Second Series (1888)
  'Wordsworth'

3 I am past thirty, and three parts iced over.
  letter, 12 February 1853

4 The true meaning of religion is thus not
simply morality, but morality touched by
emotion.
  Literature and Dogma (1873) ch. 1

5 Have something to say, and say it as clearly
as you can. That is the only secret of style.
  G. W. E. Russell *Collections and Recollections* (1898)
  ch. 13

Samuel James Arnold

6 England, home and beauty.
  'The Death of Nelson' (1811 song)

Thomas Arnold 1795–1842

7 My object will be, if possible, to form
Christian men, for Christian boys I can
scarcely hope to make.
  *on appointment to the Headmastership of Rugby
  School*
  letter to Revd John Tucker, 2 March 1828

8 As for rioting, the old Roman way of dealing
with that is always the right one; flog the
rank and file, and fling the ringleaders from
the Tarpeian rock.
  from an unpublished letter written before 1828

L. A. Artsimovich 1909–73

9 The joke definition according to which
'Science is the best way of satisfying the
curiosity of individuals at government
expense' is more or less correct.
  in *Novy Mir* January 1967

Roger Ascham 1515–68

10 I said ... how, and why, young children,
were sooner allured by love, than driven by
beating, to attain good learning.
  The Schoolmaster (1570) preface

11 There is no such whetstone, to sharpen a
good wit and encourage a will to learning,
as is praise.
  The Schoolmaster (1570) bk. 1

Daisy Ashford 1881–1972

12 Mr Salteena was an elderly man of 42.
  The Young Visiters (1919) ch. 1

13 Bernard always had a few prayers in the hall
and some whiskey afterwards as he was

rarther pious but Mr Salteena was not very
addicted to prayers so he marched up to
bed.
  The Young Visiters (1919) ch. 3

14 Oh I see said the Earl but my own idear is
that these things are as piffle before the
wind.
  The Young Visiters (1919) ch. 5

Isaac Asimov 1920–92

15 The three fundamental Rules of Robotics ...
One, a robot may not injure a human being,
or, through inaction, allow a human being
to come to harm ... Two ... a robot must
obey the orders given it by human beings
except where such orders would conflict
with the First Law ... three, a robot must
protect its own existence as long as such
protection does not conflict with the First or
Second Laws.
  I, Robot (1950) 'Runaround'

Anne Askew 1521–46

16 Like as the armèd knight
    Appointed to the field,
  With this world will I fight,
    And faith shall be my shield ...
  I am not she that list
    My anchor to let fall,
  For every drizzling mist
    My ship substantial.
  'The Ballad which Anne Askew made and sang
  when she was in Newgate' (1546)

Cynthia Asquith 1887–1960

17 I am beginning to rub my eyes at the
prospect of peace ... One will at last fully
recognize that the dead are not only dead
for the duration of the war.
  diary, 7 October 1918

Herbert Asquith 1852–1928

18 We had better wait and see.
  *phrase used repeatedly in speeches in 1910,
  referring to the rumour that the House of Lords
  was to be flooded with new Liberal peers to ensure
  the passage of the Finance Bill*
  Roy Jenkins *Asquith* (1964)

19 It is fitting that we should have buried the
Unknown Prime Minister by the side of the
Unknown Soldier.
  *of Andrew **Bonar Law***
  Robert Blake *The Unknown Prime Minister* (1955)

20 [The War Office kept three sets of figures:]
one to mislead the public, another to
mislead the Cabinet, and the third to
mislead itself.
  Alistair Horne *Price of Glory* (1962) ch. 2

Margot Asquith 1864–1945

21 Kitchener is a great poster.
  More Memories (1933) ch. 6

1 The *t* is silent, as in *Harlow*.
to Jean Harlow, who had been mispronouncing 'Margot'
  T. S. Matthews *Great Tom* (1973) ch. 7

2 He can't see a belt without hitting below it.
of **Lloyd George**
  in *Listener* 11 June 1953 'Margot Oxford' by Lady Violet Bonham Carter

Violet Asquith 1887–1969

3 HOW DARE YOU BECOME PRIME MINISTER WHEN I'M AWAY GREAT LOVE CONSTANT THOUGHT VIOLET.
telegram to her father, H. H. **Asquith**, *7 April 1908*
  Mark Bonham Carter and Mark Pottle (eds.) *Lantern Slides* (1996)

Mary Astell 1668–1731

4 Fetters of gold are still fetters, and the softest lining can never make them so easy as liberty.
  An Essay in Defence of the Female Sex (1696)

Jacob Astley 1579–1652

5 O Lord! thou knowest how busy I must be this day: if I forget thee, do not thou forget me.
prayer before the Battle of Edgehill, 1642
  Philip Warwick *Memoires* (1701)

Nancy Astor 1879–1964
see also **Churchill** 92:15

6 I married beneath me, all women do.
  in *Dictionary of National Biography 1961–1970* (1981)

Brooks Atkinson 1894–1984

7 After each war there is a little less democracy to save.
  Once Around the Sun (1951) 7 January

David Attenborough 1926–

8 I'm not over-fond of animals. I am merely astounded by them.
  in *Independent* 14 January 1995

Clement Attlee 1883–1967

9 The voice we heard was that of Mr Churchill but the mind was that of Lord Beaverbrook.
  speech on radio, 5 June 1945

10 Few thought he was even a starter
There were many who thought themselves smarter
But he ended PM
CH and OM
An earl and a knight of the garter.
describing himself in a letter to Tom Attlee, 8 April 1956
  Kenneth Harris *Attlee* (1982)

11 [Russian Communism is] the illegitimate child of Karl Marx and Catherine the Great.
  speech at Aarhus University, 11 April 1956

12 Democracy means government by discussion, but it is only effective if you can stop people talking.
  speech at Oxford, 14 June 1957

John Aubrey 1626–97

13 And when he saw the cheese-cakes:—'What have we here, *crinkum crankum*?'
  Brief Lives 'Ralph Kettel'

14 Oval face. His eye a dark grey. He had auburn hair. His complexion exceeding fair—he was so fair that they called him *the lady of* Christ's College.
  Brief Lives 'John Milton'

15 He pronounced the letter R (*littera canina*) very hard—a certain sign of a satirical wit.
  Brief Lives 'John Milton'

16 Sciatica: he cured it, by boiling his buttock.
  Brief Lives 'Sir Jonas Moore'

17 Anno 1670, not far from Cirencester, was an apparition; being demanded whether a good spirit or a bad? returned no answer, but disappeared with a curious perfume and most melodious twang. Mr W. Lilly believes it was a fairy.
  Miscellanies (1696) 'Apparitions'

Auctoritates Aristotelis

18 Habit is second nature.

19 You cannot argue with someone who denies the first principles.

20 God and nature do nothing in vain.

21 All men naturally desire to know.

22 Parents love their children more than children love their parents.

23 Time is the measure of movement.

W. H. Auden 1907–73

24 I'll love you till the ocean
Is folded and hung up to dry
And the seven stars go squawking
Like geese about the sky.
  'As I Walked Out One Evening' (1940)

25 The glacier knocks in the cupboard,
The desert sighs in the bed,
And the crack in the teacup opens
A lane to the land of the dead.
  'As I Walked Out One Evening' (1940)

26   Make intercession
For the treason of all clerks.
  'At the Grave of Henry James' (1945); cf. **Benda** 29:9

27 August for the people and their favourite islands.
  title of poem (1936)

28 The desires of the heart are as crooked as corkscrews
Not to be born is the best for man.
  'Death's Echo' (1937); cf. **Sophocles** 299:10

29 To save your world you asked this man to die:
Would this man, could he see you now, ask why?
  'Epitaph for the Unknown Soldier' (1955)

1 When he laughed, respectable senators
   burst with laughter,
   And when he cried the little children died
   in the streets.
   'Epitaph on a Tyrant' (1940); cf. **Motley** 229:13

2 He was my North, my South, my East and
   West,
   My working week and my Sunday rest,
   My noon, my midnight, my talk, my song;
   I thought that love would last for ever: I was
   wrong.
   'Funeral Blues' (1936)

3 You were silly like us; your gift survived it
   all:
   The parish of rich women, physical decay,
   Yourself. Mad Ireland hurt you into poetry.
   'In Memory of W. B. Yeats' (1940) pt. 2

4 Earth, receive an honoured guest:
   William Yeats is laid to rest.
   Let the Irish vessel lie
   Emptied of its poetry.
   In the nightmare of the dark
   All the dogs of Europe bark,
   And the living nations wait,
   Each sequestered in its hate.
   'In Memory of W. B. Yeats' (1940) pt. 3

5 Time that with this strange excuse
   Pardoned Kipling and his views,
   And will pardon Paul Claudel,
   Pardons him for writing well.
   'In Memory of W. B. Yeats' (1940) pt. 3

6 Look, stranger, at this island now.
   title of poem (1936)

7 Lay your sleeping head, my love,
   Human on my faithless arm.
   'Lullaby' (1940)

8 About suffering they were never wrong,
   The Old Masters.
   'Musée des Beaux Arts' (1940)

9 Even the dreadful martyrdom must run its
   course
   Anyhow in a corner, some untidy spot
   Where the dogs go on with their doggy life
   and the torturer's horse
   Scratches its innocent behind on a tree.
   'Musée des Beaux Arts' (1940)

10 To the man-in-the-street, who, I'm sorry to
   say,
   Is a keen observer of life,
   The word 'Intellectual' suggests straight
   away
   A man who's untrue to his wife.
   New Year Letter (1941) l. 1277 n.

11 This is the Night Mail crossing the Border,
   Bringing the cheque and the postal order,
   Letters for the rich, letters for the poor,
   The shop at the corner, the girl next door.
   'Night Mail' (1936) pt. 1

12 Private faces in public places
   Are wiser and nicer
   Than public faces in private places.
   Orators (1932) dedication

13 Out on the lawn I lie in bed,
   Vega conspicuous overhead.
   'Out on the lawn I lie in bed' (1936)

14 O what is that sound which so thrills the ear
   Down in the valley drumming, drumming?
   Only the scarlet soldiers, dear,
   The soldiers coming.
   'O what is that sound' (1936)

15 Some thirty inches from my nose
   The frontier of my Person goes,
   And all the untilled air between
   Is private *pagus* or demesne.
   Stranger, unless with bedroom eyes
   I beckon you to fraternize,
   Beware of rudely crossing it:
   I have no gun, but I can spit.
   'Prologue: the Birth of Architecture' (1966)
   postscript

16 I and the public know
   What all schoolchildren learn,
   Those to whom evil is done
   Do evil in return.
   'September 1, 1939' (1940)

17 There is no such thing as the State
   And no one exists alone;
   Hunger allows no choice
   To the citizen or the police;
   We must love one another or die.
   'September 1, 1939' (1940)

18 A shilling life will give you all the facts.
   title of poem (1936)

19 At Twenty I tried to
   vex my elders, past Sixty it's the young
   whom
   I hope to bother.
   'Shorts I' (1969)

20 A poet's hope: to be,
   like some valley cheese,
   local, but prized elsewhere.
   'Shorts II' (1976)

21 History to the defeated
   May say Alas but cannot help or pardon.
   'Spain 1937' (1937) st. 23

22 Some books are undeservedly forgotten;
   none are undeservedly remembered.
   The Dyer's Hand (1963) 'Reading'

23 Art is born of humiliation.
   Stephen Spender World Within World (1951) ch.
   2

24 Nothing I wrote in the thirties saved one
   Jew from Auschwitz.
   attributed

Émile Augier 1820–89

25 *La nostalgie de la boue!*
   Longing to be back in the mud!
   Le Mariage d'Olympe (1855) act 1, sc. 1

St Augustine of Hippo AD 354–430

26 Give me chastity and continency—but not
   yet!
   Confessions (AD 397–8) bk. 8, ch. 7

27 When he was reading, he drew his eyes
   along over the leaves, and his heart

searched into the sense, but his voice and tongue were silent.

of St Ambrose
> Confessions (AD 397–8) bk. 6, ch. 3

1 *Tolle lege, tolle lege.*
Take up and read, take up and read.
> Confessions (AD 397–8) bk. 8, ch. 12

2 *Sero te amavi, pulchritudo tam antiqua et tam nova, sero te amavi! et ecce intus eras et ego foris, et ibi te quaerebam.*
Too late came I to love thee, O thou Beauty both so ancient and so fresh, yea too late came I to love thee. And behold, thou wert within me, and I out of myself, where I made search for thee.
> Confessions (AD 397–8) bk. 10, ch. 27

3 There is no salvation outside the church.
> De Baptismo contra Donatistas bk. 4, ch. 17, sect. 24; cf. **Cyprian** 105:10, 105:12

4 *Dilige et quod vis fac.*
Love and do what you will.
> *often quoted as* 'Ama et fac quod vis'
> In Epistolam Joannis ad Parthos (AD 413) tractatus 7, sect. 8

5 *Cum dilectione hominum et odio vitiorum.*
With love for mankind and hatred of sins.
> *often quoted as* 'Love the sinner but hate the sin'
> letter 211 in J.-P. Migne (ed.) Patrologiae Latinae (1845) vol. 33; cf. **Dryden** 116:29, **Pope** 247:2

6 *Roma locuta est; causa finita est.*
Rome has spoken; the case is concluded.
> traditional summary of words found in Sermons (Antwerp, 1702) no. 131, sect. 10

Augustus 63 BC–AD 14

7 Quintilius Varus, give me back my legions.
> *on Varus' loss of three legions in battle with Germanic tribes, AD 9*
> Suetonius Lives of the Caesars 'Divus Augustus' sect. 23

8 *Festina lente.*
Make haste slowly.
> Suetonius Lives of the Caesars 'Divus Augustus' sect. 25

9 He could boast that he inherited it brick and left it marble.
> *referring to the city of Rome*
> Suetonius Lives of the Caesars 'Divus Augustus' sect. 28

Aung San Suu Kyi 1945–

10 It's very different from living in academia in Oxford. We called someone vicious in the *Times Literary Supplement*. We didn't know what vicious was.
> *on returning to Burma (Myanmar)*
> in Observer 25 September 1988 'Sayings of the Week'

11 In societies where men are truly confident of their own worth, women are not merely tolerated but valued.
> videotape speech at NGO Forum on Women, China, early September 1995

Marcus Aurelius AD 121–80

12 Be like a headland of rock on which the waves break incessantly: but it stands fast and around it the seething of the waters sinks to rest.
> Meditations bk. 4, sect. 49

13 Nothing happens to anybody which he is not fitted by nature to bear.
> Meditations bk. 5, sect. 18

14 Mankind have been created for the sake of one another. Either instruct them, therefore, or endure them.
> Meditations bk. 8, sect. 59

Decius Magnus Ausonius
*c.*309–392 AD

15 *Nemo bonus Britto est.*
No good man is a Briton.
> Epigrams 119

Jane Austen 1775–1817

16 An egg boiled very soft is not unwholesome.
> Emma (1816) ch. 3

17 One has no great hopes from Birmingham. I always say there is something direful in the sound.
> Emma (1816) ch. 36

18 Let other pens dwell on guilt and misery. I quit such odious subjects as soon as I can.
> Mansfield Park (1814) ch. 48

19 'Oh! it is only a novel! . . . only Cecilia, or Camilla, or Belinda:' or, in short, only some work in which the most thorough knowledge of human nature, the happiest delineation of its varieties, the liveliest effusions of wit and humour are conveyed to the world in the best chosen language.
> Northanger Abbey (1818) ch. 5

20 From politics, it was an easy step to silence.
> Northanger Abbey (1818) ch. 14

21 Every man is surrounded by a neighbourhood of voluntary spies, and where roads and newspapers lay every thing open.
> Northanger Abbey (1818) ch. 34

22 'My idea of good company, Mr Elliot, is the company of clever, well-informed people, who have a great deal of conversation; that is what I call good company.' 'You are mistaken,' said he gently, 'that is not good company, that is the best.'
> Persuasion (1818) ch. 16

23 Men have had every advantage of us in telling their own story. Education has been theirs in so much higher a degree; the pen has been in their hands.
> Persuasion (1818) ch. 23

24 It is a truth universally acknowledged, that a single man in possession of a good fortune, must be in want of a wife.
> Pride and Prejudice (1813) ch. 1

25 In his library he had been always sure of leisure and tranquillity; and though

prepared . . . to meet with folly and conceit in every other room in the house, he was used to be free of them there.
Pride and Prejudice (1813) ch. 15

1 For what do we live, but to make sport for our neighbours, and laugh at them in our turn?
Pride and Prejudice (1813) ch. 57

2 3 or 4 families in a country village is the very thing to work on.
letter to Anna Austen, 9 September 1814

3 The little bit (two inches wide) of ivory on which I work with so fine a brush, as produces little effect after much labour?
letter to J. Edward Austen, 16 December 1816

4 Pictures of perfection as you know make me sick and wicked.
letter to Fanny Knight, 23 March 1817

5 I am going to take a heroine whom no-one but myself will much like.
on starting Emma
J. E. Austen-Leigh *A Memoir of Jane Austen* (1926 ed.)

J. L. Austin 1911–60

6 In such cases we should not know what to say. This is when we say 'words fail us' and mean this literally. We should need new words. The old ones just would not fit. They aren't meant to cover this kind of case.
on being asked how one might describe the predicament of the character in **Kafka**'s Metamorphosis *who wakes to find himself transformed into a giant cockroach; cf.* **Kafka** 180:7
Isaiah Berlin 'Austin and the Early Beginnings of Oxford Philosophy' in *Essays on J. L. Austin* (1973)

Earl of Avon *see* Anthony Eden

Revd Awdry 1911–97

7 You've a lot to learn about trucks, little Thomas. They are silly things and must be kept in their place. After pushing them about here for a few weeks you'll know almost as much about them as Edward. Then you'll be a Really Useful Engine.
Thomas the Tank Engine (1946)

8 I should like my epitaph to say, 'He helped people see God in the ordinary things of life, and he made children laugh.'
in *Independent* 22 March 1997, obituary

Alan Ayckbourn 1939–

9 This place, you tell them you're interested in the arts, you get messages of sympathy.
Chorus of Disapproval (1986) act 2

A. J. Ayer 1910–89

10 The criterion which we use to test the genuineness of apparent statements of fact is the criterion of verifiability. We say that a sentence is factually significant to any given person, if, and only if, he knows how to verify the proposition which it purports to express—that is, if he knows what observations would lead him, under certain conditions, to accept the proposition as being true, or reject it as being false.
Language, Truth, and Logic (1936) ch. 1

11 Why should you mind being wrong if someone can show you that you are?
attributed

Pam Ayres 1947–

12 Medicinal discovery,
It moves in mighty leaps,
It leapt straight past the common cold
And gave it us for keeps.
'Oh no, I got a cold' (1976)

W. E. Aytoun 1813–65

13 'He is coming! he is coming!'
Like a bridegroom from his room,
Came the hero from his prison
To the scaffold and the doom.
'The Execution of Montrose' (1849) st. 14

14 The earth is all the home I have,
The heavens my wide roof-tree.
'The Wandering Jew' (1867) l. 49

Charles Babbage 1792–1871

15 Every moment dies a man,
Every moment 1¹⁄₁₆ is born.
parody of **Tennyson**'s 'Vision of Sin', in an unpublished letter to the poet, in *New Scientist* 4 Dec 1958; cf. **Tennyson** 314:2

Isaac Babel 1894–1940

16 No iron can stab the heart with such force as a full stop put just at the right place.
Guy de Maupassant (1932)

Johann Sebastian Bach 1685–1750

17 There is nothing to it. You only have to hit the right notes at the right time and the instrument plays itself.
when complimented on his organ playing
K. Geiringer *The Bach Family* (1954)

Francis Bacon 1561–1626

18 If a man will begin with certainties, he shall end in doubts; but if he will be content to begin with doubts, he shall end in certainties.
The Advancement of Learning (1605) bk. 1, ch. 5, sect. 8

19 Words are the tokens current and accepted for conceits, as moneys are for values.
The Advancement of Learning (1605) bk. 2, ch. 16, sect. 3

20 A dance is a measured pace, as a verse is a measured speech.
The Advancement of Learning (1605) bk. 2, ch. 16, sect. 5

21 Ancient times were the youth of the world.
De Dignitate et Augmentis Scientiarum (1623) bk. 1 (tr. Gilbert Watts, 1640)

1 He is the fountain of honour.
An Essay of a King (1642); attribution doubtful; cf. **Bagehot** 22:11

2 A little philosophy inclineth man's mind to atheism, but depth in philosophy bringeth men's minds about to religion.
Essays (1625) 'Of Atheism'

3 Virtue is like a rich stone, best plain set.
Essays (1625) 'Of Beauty'

4 There is no excellent beauty that hath not some strangeness in the proportion.
Essays (1625) 'Of Beauty'

5 He said it that knew it best.
referring to **Demosthenes**
Essays (1625) 'Of Boldness'

6 In civil business; what first? boldness; what second and third? boldness: and yet boldness is a child of ignorance and baseness.
Essays (1625) 'Of Boldness'; cf. **Danton** 106:1, **Demosthenes** 108:12

7 Books will speak plain when counsellors blanch.
Essays (1625) 'Of Counsel'

8 I knew one that when he wrote a letter he would put that which was most material in the postscript, as if it had been a bymatter.
Essays (1625) 'Of Cunning'; cf. **Steele** 302:2

9 Men fear death as children fear to go in the dark; and as that natural fear in children is increased with tales, so is the other.
Essays (1625) 'Of Death'

10 Revenge triumphs over death; love slights it; honour aspireth to it; grief flieth to it.
Essays (1625) 'Of Death'

11 Cure the disease and kill the patient.
Essays (1625) 'Of Friendship'

12 God Almighty first planted a garden; and, indeed, it is the purest of human pleasures.
Essays (1625) 'Of Gardens'

13 Nothing is more pleasant to the eye than green grass kept finely shorn.
Essays (1625) 'Of Gardens'

14 If a man be gracious and courteous to strangers, it shows he is a citizen of the world.
Essays (1625) 'Of Goodness, and Goodness of Nature'

15 All rising to great place is by a winding stair.
Essays (1625) 'Of Great Place'

16 He that will not apply new remedies must expect new evils; for time is the greatest innovator.
Essays (1625) 'Of Innovations'

17 He that hath wife and children hath given hostages to fortune; for they are impediments to great enterprises, either of virtue or mischief.
Essays (1625) 'Of Marriage and the Single Life'; cf. **Lucan** 204:9

18 He was reputed one of the wise men that made answer to the question when a man should marry? 'A young man not yet, an elder man not at all.'
Essays (1625) 'Of Marriage and the Single Life'; cf. **Punch** 252:7

19 It is generally better to deal by speech than by letter.
Essays (1625) 'Of Negotiating'

20 Children sweeten labours, but they make misfortunes more bitter.
Essays (1625) 'Of Parents and Children'

21 Fame is like a river, that beareth up things light and swollen, and drowns things weighty and solid.
Essays (1625) 'Of Praise'

22 Age will not be defied.
Essays (1625) 'Of Regimen of Health'

23 Revenge is a kind of wild justice.
Essays (1625) 'Of Revenge'

24 Money is like muck, not good except it be spread.
Essays (1625) 'Of Seditions and Troubles'

25 The remedy is worse than the disease.
Essays (1625) 'Of Seditions and Troubles'

26 Some books are to be tasted, others to be swallowed, and some few to be chewed and digested.
Essays (1625) 'Of Studies'

27 Reading maketh a full man; conference a ready man; and writing an exact man.
Essays (1625) 'Of Studies'

28 Neither is money the sinews of war (as it is trivially said).
Essays (1625) 'Of the True Greatness of Kingdoms'; cf. **Cicero** 92:28

29 Travel, in the younger sort, is a part of education; in the elder, a part of experience. He that travelleth into a country before he hath some entrance into the language, goeth to school, and not to travel.
Essays (1625) 'Of Travel'

30 What is truth? said jesting Pilate; and would not stay for an answer.
Essays (1625) 'Of Truth'; cf. **Bible** 48:9

31 All colours will agree in the dark.
Essays (1625) 'Of Unity in Religion'

32 It was prettily devised of Aesop, 'The fly sat upon the axle-tree of the chariot-wheel and said, what a dust do I raise.'
Essays (1625) 'Of Vain-Glory'

33 Be so true to thyself as thou be not false to others.
Essays (1625) 'Of Wisdom for a Man's Self'; cf. **Shakespeare** 271:9

34 It is the nature of extreme self-lovers, as they will set a house on fire, and it were but to roast their eggs.
Essays (1625) 'Of Wisdom for a Man's Self'

35 It is the wisdom of the crocodiles, that shed tears when they would devour.
Essays (1625) 'Of Wisdom for a Man's Self'

1 I have taken all knowledge to be my province.

'To My Lord Treasurer Burghley' (1592) in J. Spedding (ed.) *The Letters and Life of Francis Bacon* vol. 1 (1861)

2 *Nam et ipsa scientia potestas est.*

For also knowledge itself is power.

Meditationes Sacrae (1597) 'Of Heresies'

3 God's first Creature, which was Light.

New Atlantis (1627)

4 *Magna ista scientiarum mater.*

That great mother of sciences.

of natural philosophy

Novum Organum (1620) bk. 1, Aphorism 80 (tr. J. Spedding)

5 Printing, gunpowder, and the mariner's needle [compass] . . . these three have changed the whole face and state of things throughout the world.

Novum Organum (1620) bk. 1, Aphorism 129 (tr. J. Spedding); cf. **Carlyle** 82:16

6 Anger makes dull men witty, but it keeps them poor.

often attributed to Queen **Elizabeth I** *from a misreading of the text*

J. Spedding (ed.) *The Works of Francis Bacon* vol. 7 (1859) 'Baconiana'

7 The world's a bubble; and the life of man Less than a span.

The World (1629)

8 What then remains, but that we still should cry,

Not to be born, or being born, to die?

The World (1629)

Lord Baden-Powell 1857–1941

9 The scouts' motto is founded on my initials, it is: BE PREPARED.

Scouting for Boys (1908)

Walter Bagehot 1826–77

10 In such constitutions [as England's] there are two parts . . . first, those which excite and preserve the reverence of the population—the *dignified* parts . . . and next, the *efficient* parts—those by which it, in fact, works and rules.

The English Constitution (1867) 'The Cabinet'

11 The Crown is, according to the saying, the 'fountain of honour'; but the Treasury is the spring of business.

The English Constitution (1867) 'The Cabinet'; cf. **Bacon** 21:1

12 It has been said that England invented the phrase, 'Her Majesty's Opposition'; that it was the first government which made a criticism of administration as much a part of the polity as administration itself. This critical opposition is the consequence of cabinet government.

The English Constitution (1867) 'The Cabinet'; cf. **Hobhouse** 160:7

13 *The Times* has made many ministries.

The English Constitution (1867) 'The Cabinet'

14 It has been said, not truly, but with a possible approximation to truth, that in 1802 every hereditary monarch was insane.

The English Constitution (1867) 'Checks and Balances'

15 Like Count Moltke, 'silent in seven languages'.

The English Constitution (1867) 'Checks and Balances'

16 It is nice to trace how the actions of a retired widow and an unemployed youth become of such importance.

of Queen **Victoria** *and the future* **Edward VII**

The English Constitution (1867) 'The Monarchy'

17 Throughout the greater part of his life George III was a kind of 'consecrated obstruction'.

The English Constitution (1867) 'The Monarchy'

18 There are arguments for not having a Court, and there are arguments for having a splendid Court; but there are no arguments for having a mean Court.

The English Constitution (1867) 'The Monarchy'

19 The Queen . . . must sign her own death-warrant if the two Houses unanimously send it up to her.

The English Constitution (1867) 'The Monarchy'

20 Our royalty is to be reverenced, and if you begin to poke about it you cannot reverence it . . . We must not let in daylight upon magic.

The English Constitution (1867) 'The Monarchy (continued)'

21 The Sovereign has, under a constitutional monarchy such as ours, three rights—the right to be consulted, the right to encourage, the right to warn.

The English Constitution (1867) 'The Monarchy (continued)'

22 Writers, like teeth, are divided into incisors and grinders.

Estimates of some Englishmen and Scotchmen (1858) 'The First Edinburgh Reviewers'

Abdul Baha 1844–1921

23 In this century, which is the century of light and the revelation of mysteries . . . it is well established that mankind and womankind as parts of composite humanity are coequal and that no difference in estimate is allowable, for all are human.

at a woman's suffrage meeting in New York, 1912

Bahya ibn Paquda fl. 1080

24 You should know, O man, that the greatest enemy you have in the world is your inclination.

The Duties of the Heart Gate 5, ch. 5

David Bailey 1938–

25 It takes a lot of imagination to be a good photographer. You need less imagination to be a painter, because you can invent things.

But in photography everything is so ordinary; it takes a lot of looking before you learn to see the ordinary.
interview in *The Face* December 1984

Philip James Bailey 1816–1902

1 America, thou half-brother of the world;
  With something good and bad of every land.
  Festus (1839) sc. 10

Beryl Bainbridge 1933–

2 Women are programmed to love completely, and men are programmed to spread it around.
  interview in *Daily Telegraph* 10 September 1996

Bruce Bairnsfather 1888–1959

3 Well, if you knows of a better 'ole, go to it.
  Fragments from France (1915)

Henry Williams Baker 1821–77

4 The King of love my shepherd is,
  Whose goodness faileth never;
  I nothing lack if I am his
  And he is mine for ever . . .
  'The King of love my shepherd is' (1868 hymn)

Michael Bakunin 1814–76

5 The urge for destruction is also a creative urge!
  Jahrbuch für Wissenschaft und Kunst (1842) 'Die Reaktion in Deutschland' (under the pseudonym 'Jules Elysard')

James Baldwin 1924–87

6 Money, it turned out, was exactly like sex, you thought of nothing else if you didn't have it and thought of other things if you did.
  in *Esquire* May 1961 'Black Boy looks at the White Boy'

7 If they take you in the morning, they will be coming for us that night.
  in *New York Review of Books* 7 January 1971 'Open Letter to my Sister, Angela Davis'

Stanley Baldwin 1867–1947

8 They [parliament] are a lot of hard-faced men who look as if they had done very well out of the war.
  J. M. Keynes *Economic Consequences of the Peace* (1919) ch. 5

9 There are three classes which need sanctuary more than others—birds, wild flowers, and Prime Ministers.
  in *Observer* 24 May 1925

10 The bomber will always get through. The only defence is in offence, which means that you have to kill more women and children more quickly than the enemy if you want to save yourselves.
  speech in the House of Commons, 10 November 1932

11 I shall be but a short time tonight. I have seldom spoken with greater regret, for my lips are not yet unsealed. Were these troubles over I would make a case, and I guarantee that not a man would go into the lobby against us.
  on the Abyssinian crisis; popularly quoted as, 'My lips are sealed'
  speech in the House of Commons, 10 December 1935

12 This House today is a theatre which is being watched by the whole world. Let us conduct ourselves with that dignity which His Majesty is showing in this hour of his trial.
  speech, House of Commons, 10 December 1936

13 Do not run up your nose dead against the Pope or the NUM!
  R. A. Butler *The Art of Memory* (1982) 'Iain Macleod'; cf. **Macmillan** 208:11

Arthur James Balfour 1848–1930

14 His Majesty's Government view with favour the establishment in Palestine of a national home for the Jewish people, and will use their best endeavours to facilitate the achievement of this object, it being clearly understood that nothing shall be done which may prejudice the civil and religious rights of existing non-Jewish communities in Palestine, or the rights and political status enjoyed by Jews in any other country.
  known as the 'Balfour Declaration'
  letter to Lord Rothschild 2 November 1917

15 I thought he was a young man of promise, but it appears he is a young man of promises.
  of Winston **Churchill**
  Winston Churchill *My Early Life* (1930) ch. 17

Ballads

16 All in the merry month of May,
  When green buds they were swellin',
  Young Jemmy Grove on his death-bed lay,
  For love of Barbara Allen.
  'Barbara Allen's Cruelty'

17 Ye Highlands and ye Lawlands,
  O where hae ye been?
  They hae slain the Earl of Murray,
  And hae laid him on the green.
  'The Bonny Earl of Murray'

18 I am a man upon the land,
  I am a selkie in the sea;
  When I am far and far from land,
  My home it is the Sule Skerry.
  'The Great Selkie of Sule Skerry'

19 Och, Johnny, I hardly knew ye!
  'Johnny, I hardly knew Ye'

20 'What gat ye to your dinner, Lord Randal, my Son?
  What gat ye to your dinner, my handsome young man?
  'I gat eels boil'd in broo'; mother, make my bed soon,
  For I'm weary wi' hunting, and fain wald lie down.'
  'Lord Randal'

1 This ae nighte, this ae nighte,
  —*Every nighte and alle*,
  Fire and fleet and candle-lighte,
  And Christe receive thy saule.
  'fleet' = corruption of 'flet', meaning house-room
  'Lyke-Wake Dirge'

2 When captains courageous whom death
    could not daunt,
  Did march to the siege of the city of Gaunt,
  They mustered their soldiers by two and by
    three,
  And the foremost in battle was Mary
    Ambree.
  'Mary Ambree'

3 For in my mind, of all mankind
  I love but you alone.
  'The Nut Brown Maid'

4 For I must to the greenwood go
  Alone, a banished man.
  'The Nut Brown Maid'

5 Yestreen the Queen had four Maries,
  The night she'll hae but three;
  There was Marie Seaton, and Marie Beaton,
  And Marie Carmichael, and me.
  'The Queen's Maries'

6 Ile lay mee downe and bleed a while
  And then Ile rise and fight againe.
  'Sir Andrew Bartton'

7 The king sits in Dunfermline town
  Drinking the blude-red wine.
  'Sir Patrick Spens'

8 To Noroway, to Noroway,
  To Noroway o'er the faem;
  The king's daughter o' Noroway,
  'Tis thou must bring her hame.
  'Sir Patrick Spens'

9 I saw the new moon late yestreen
  Wi' the auld moon in her arm.
  'Sir Patrick Spens'

10 Half-owre, half-owre to Aberdour,
   'Tis fifty fathoms deep;
   And there lies good Sir Patrick Spens,
   Wi' the Scots lords at his feet!
   'Sir Patrick Spens'

11 She's mounted on her milk-white steed,
   She's ta'en true Thomas up behind.
   'Thomas the Rhymer'

12 They waded thro' red blude to the knee;
   For a' the blude that's shed on the earth
   Rins through the springs o' that countrie.
   'Thomas the Rhymer'

13 As I was walking all alane,
   I heard twa corbies making a mane:
   The tane unto the tither did say,
   'Where sall we gang and dine the day?'
   '—In behint yon auld fail dyke
   I wot there lies a new-slain knight;
   And naebody kens that he lies there
   But his hawk, his hound, and his lady fair.
   'The Twa Corbies' (*corbies* ravens; *fail* turf)

14 The wind doth blow to-day, my love,
   And a few small drops of rain;
   I never had but one true love;
   In cold grave she was lain.

I'll do as much for my true-love
As any young man may;
I'll sit and mourn all at her grave
For a twelvemonth and a day.
'The Unquiet Grave'

15 O waly, waly, gin love be bonnie
   A little time while it is new!
   But when 'tis auld it waxeth cauld,
   And fades awa' like morning dew.
   'Waly, Waly'

16 Tom Pearse, Tom Pearse, lend me your grey
     mare,
   All along, down along, out along, lee.
   For I want for to go to Widdicombe Fair,
   Wi' Bill Brewer, Jan Stewer, Peter Gurney,
   Peter Davey, Dan'l Whiddon, Harry Hawk,
   Old Uncle Tom Cobbleigh and all.
   Old Uncle Tom Cobbleigh and all.
   'Widdicombe Fair'

J. G. Ballard 1930–

17 Some refer to it as a cultural Chernobyl. I
   think of it as a cultural Stalingrad.
   of Euro Disney
   in *Daily Telegraph* 2 July 1994; cf. **Mnouchkine**
   225:7

Whitney Balliett 1926–

18 A critic is a bundle of biases held loosely
   together by a sense of taste.
   Dinosaurs in the Morning (1962) introductory note

19 The sound of surprise.
   title of book on jazz (1959)

Pierre Balmain 1914–82

20 The trick of wearing mink is to look as
   though you were wearing a cloth coat. The
   trick of wearing a cloth coat is to look as
   though you are wearing mink.
   in *Observer* 25 December 1955

Honoré de Balzac 1799–1850

21 Man is neither good nor bad; he is born
   with instincts and abilities.
   La Comédie Humaine (1842) vol. 1, foreword

22 Hatred is a tonic, it makes one live, it
   inspires vengeance; but pity kills, it makes
   our weakness weaker.
   La Peau de Chagrin (1831) ch. 1

Tallulah Bankhead 1903–68

23 Cocaine habit-forming? Of course not. I
   ought to know. I've been using it for years.
   Tallulah (1952)

24 I'm as pure as the driven slush.
   in *Saturday Evening Post* 12 April 1947

John Barbour c.1320–95

25 Storys to rede ar delitabill,
   Suppos that thai be nocht bot fabill.
   The Bruce (1375) bk. 1, l. 1

26 A! fredome is a noble thing!
   Fredome mayse man to haiff liking.
   The Bruce (1375) bk. 1, l. 225

Alexander Barclay c.1475-1552

1 The lords will alway that people note and see
Between them and servants some diversity,
Though it to them turn to no profit at all;
If they have pleasure, the servant shall have small.
Eclogues (1514) no. 2, l. 790

R. H. Barham 1788-1845

2 The Jackdaw sat on the Cardinal's chair!
Bishop, and abbot, and prior were there.
The Ingoldsby Legends (First Series, 1840) 'The Jackdaw of Rheims'

3 Heedless of grammar, they all cried, 'That's him!'
The Ingoldsby Legends (First Series, 1840) 'The Jackdaw of Rheims'

4 Here's a corpse in the case with a sad swelled face,
And a 'Crowner's Quest' is a queer sort of thing!
in later editions: 'a Medical Crowner's a queer sort of thing!'
The Ingoldsby Legends (First Series, 1840) 'A Lay of St Gengulphus'

Sabine Baring-Gould 1834-1924

5 Onward, Christian soldiers,
Marching as to war,
With the cross of Jesus
Going on before.
'Onward, Christian Soldiers' (1864 hymn)

6 Through the night of doubt and sorrow
Onward goes the pilgrim band.
'Through the night of doubt and sorrow' (1867 hymn); translated from the Danish of B. S. Ingemann (1789-1862)

Frederick R. Barnard

7 One picture is worth ten thousand words.
in *Printers' Ink* 10 March 1927

Julian Barnes 1946-

8 Books say: she did this because. Life says: she did this. Books are where things are explained to you; life is where things aren't.
Flaubert's Parrot (1984) ch. 13

9 Does history repeat itself, the first time as tragedy, the second time as farce? No, that's too grand, too considered a process. History just burps, and we taste again that raw-onion sandwich it swallowed centuries ago.
A History of the World in 10½ Chapters (1989) 'Parenthesis'; cf. **Marx** 214:6

10 Love is just a system for getting someone to call you darling after sex.
Talking It Over (1991) ch. 16

Richard Barnfield 1574-1627

11 The waters were his winding sheet, the sea was made his tomb;

Yet for his fame the ocean sea, was not sufficient room.
on the death of Sir John Hawkins
The Encomion of Lady Pecunia (1598) 'To the Gentlemen Readers'

Phineas T. Barnum 1810-91
see also **Lincoln** 199:15

12 There's a sucker born every minute.
attributed

J. M. Barrie 1860-1937

13 His lordship may compel us to be equal upstairs, but there will never be equality in the servants' hall.
The Admirable Crichton (performed 1902, published 1914) act 1

14 Every time a child says 'I don't believe in fairies' there is a little fairy somewhere that falls down dead.
Peter Pan (1928) act 1

15 To die will be an awfully big adventure.
Peter Pan (1928) act 3; cf. **Frohman** 134:2

16 Do you believe in fairies? Say quick that you believe! If you believe, clap your hands!
Peter Pan (1928) act 4

17 There are few more impressive sights in the world than a Scotsman on the make.
What Every Woman Knows (performed 1908, published 1918) act 2

Sebastian Barry 1955-

18 Do you not feel that this island is moored only lightly to the sea-bed, and might be off for the Americas at any moment?
Prayers of Sherkin (1991)

Roland Barthes 1915-80

19 I think that cars today are almost the exact equivalent of the great Gothic cathedrals: I mean the supreme creation of an era, conceived with passion by unknown artists, and consumed in image if not in usage by a whole population which appropriates them as a purely magical object.
Mythologies (1957) 'La nouvelle Citroën'

Bernard Baruch 1870-1965

20 We are today in the midst of a cold war.
'cold war' was suggested to him by H. B. Swope, former editor of the New York World
speech to South Carolina Legislature, 16 April 1947

21 To me old age is always fifteen years older than I am.
in *Newsweek* 29 August 1955

Jacques Barzun 1907-

22 If it were possible to talk to the unborn, one could never explain to them how it feels to be alive, for life is washed in the speechless real.
The House of Intellect (1959) ch. 6

Matsuo Basho 1644–94

1 How pleasant—
just once *not* to see
Fuji through mist.
  tr. Lucien Stryk

2 Old pond,
leap-splash—
a frog.
  tr. Lucien Stryk

3 You, the butterfly—
I, Chuang Tzu's
dreaming heart.
  tr. Lucien Stryk; cf. **Chuang Tzu** 90:21

Edgar Bateman
and George Le Brunn

4 Wiv a ladder and some glasses,
You could see to 'Ackney Marshes,
If it wasn't for the 'ouses in between.
  'If it wasn't for the 'Ouses in between' (1894
  song)

Katherine Lee Bates 1859–1929

5 America! America!
God shed His grace on thee
And crown thy good with brotherhood
From sea to shining sea!
  'America the Beautiful' (1893)

Charles Baudelaire 1821–67

6 *Hypocrite lecteur,—mon semblable,—mon frère.*
Hypocrite reader—my likeness—my
  brother.
  Les fleurs du mal (1857) 'Au Lecteur'

7 *Là, tout n'est qu'ordre et beauté,
Luxe, calme et volupté.*
Everything there is simply order and
  beauty, luxury, peace and sensual
  indulgence.
  Les fleurs du mal (1857) 'L'Invitation au
  voyage'—'Spleen et idéal' no. 56

8 *Quelle est cette île triste et noire? C'est Cythère,
Nous dit-on, un pays fameux dans les chansons,
Eldorado banal de tous les vieux garçons.
Regardez, après tout, c'est un pauvre terre.*
What sad, black isle is that? It's Cythera, so
  they say, a land celebrated in song, the
  banal Eldorado of all the old fools. Look,
  after all, it's a land of poverty.
  Les fleurs du mal (1857) 'Un voyage à
  Cythère'—'Les fleurs du mal' no. 121

9 *Il faut épater le bourgeois.*
One must astonish the bourgeois.
  attributed; also attributed to Privat
  d'Anglemont (*c.*1820–59) in the form '*Je les ai
  épatés, les bourgeois* [I flabbergasted them, the
  bourgeois]'

L. Frank Baum 1856–1919

10 The road to the City of Emeralds is paved
with yellow brick.
  The Wonderful Wizard of Oz (1900) ch. 2; cf.
  Harburg 151:10

Beachcomber *see* J. B. Morton

David Beatty 1871–1936

11 There's something wrong with our bloody
ships today.
  at the Battle of Jutland, 1916
  Winston Churchill *The World Crisis 1916–1918*
  (1927) pt. 1

Pierre-Augustin Caron de
Beaumarchais 1732–99

12 Drinking when we are not thirsty and
making love all year round, madam; that is
all there is to distinguish us from other
animals.
  Le Mariage de Figaro (1785) act 2, sc. 21

13 Because you are a great lord, you believe
yourself to be a great genius! . . . You took
the trouble to be born, but no more.
  Le Mariage de Figaro (1785) act 5, sc. 3

Francis Beaumont 1584–1616
and John Fletcher 1579–1625
*see also **John Fletcher***

14 Those have most power to hurt us that we
love.
  The Maid's Tragedy (written 1610–11) act 5

15 There is no other purgatory but a woman.
  The Scornful Lady (1616) act 3

Lord Beaverbrook (Max Aitken,
Lord Beaverbrook) 1879–1964

16 Now who is responsible for this work of
development on which so much depends?
To whom must the praise be given? To the
boys in the back rooms. They do not sit in
the limelight. But they are the men who do
the work.
  in Listener 27 March 1941

17 With the publication of his Private Papers in
1952, he committed suicide 25 years after
his death.
  *of Earl **Haig***
  Men and Power (1956)

18 Our cock won't fight.
  *to Winston **Churchill** of **Edward VIII**, during
  the abdication crisis of 1936*
  Frances Donaldson *Edward VIII* (1974) ch. 22

Samuel Beckett 1906–89

19 One of the thieves was saved. (*Pause*) It's a
reasonable percentage.
  Waiting for Godot (1955) act 1

20 ESTRAGON: Charming spot. Inspiring
prospects. Let's go.
VLADIMIR: We can't.
ESTRAGON: Why not?
VLADIMIR: We're waiting for Godot.
  Waiting for Godot (1955) act 1

21 Nothing happens, nobody comes, nobody
goes, it's awful!
  Waiting for Godot (1955) act 1

1 They give birth astride of a grave, the light
gleams an instant, then it's night once
more.
Waiting for Godot (1955) act 2

2 Ever tried. Ever failed. No matter. Try again.
Fail again. Fail better.
Worstward Ho (1983)

3 I am what her savage loving has made me.
of his mother
James Knowlson *Damned to Fame* (1996)

Thomas Lovell Beddoes 1803–49

4 If there were dreams to sell,
What would you buy?
'Dream-Pedlary' (written 1830, published 1851)

The Venerable Bede AD 673–735

5 'Such,' he said, 'O King, seems to me the
present life of men on earth, in comparison
with that time which to us is uncertain, as if
when on a winter's night you sit feasting
with your ealdormen and thegns,—a single
sparrow should fly swiftly into the hall, and
coming in at one door, instantly fly out
through another. In that time in which it is
indoors it is indeed not touched by the fury
of the winter, but yet, this smallest space of
calmness being passed almost in a flash,
from winter going into winter again, it is
lost to your eyes. Somewhat like this
appears the life of man; but of what follows
or what went before, we are utterly
ignorant.'
Ecclesiastical History of the English People (tr. B.
Colgrave, 1969) bk. 2, ch. 13

Harry Bedford
and Terry Sullivan

6 I'm a bit of a ruin that Cromwell knocked
about a bit.
'It's a Bit of a Ruin that Cromwell Knocked
about a Bit' (1920 song; written for Marie Lloyd)

Barnard Elliott Bee 1823–61

7 There is Jackson with his Virginians,
standing like a stone wall. Let us determine
to die here, and we will conquer.
*referring to General T. J. ('Stonewall') Jackson at
the battle of Bull Run, 21 July, 1861 (in which Bee
himself was killed)*
B. Perley Poore *Perley's Reminiscences* (1886) vol. 2,
ch. 7

Thomas Beecham 1879–1961

8 There are two golden rules for an orchestra:
start together and finish together. The
public doesn't give a damn what goes on in
between.
Harold Atkins and Archie Newman *Beecham
Stories* (1978)

9 Too much counterpoint; what is worse,
Protestant counterpoint.
of J. S. Bach
in *Guardian* 8 March 1971

H. C. Beeching 1859–1919

10 First come I; my name is Jowett.
There's no knowledge but I know it.
I am Master of this college:
What I don't know isn't knowledge.
The Masque of Balliol (composed by and current
among members of Balliol College in the late
1870s) in W. G. Hiscock (ed.) *The Balliol Rhymes*
(1939); cf. **Anonymous** 8:20

Max Beerbohm 1872–1956

11 Enter Michael Angelo. Andrea del Sarto
appears for a moment at a window. Pippa
passes.
Seven Men (1919) 'Savonarola Brown' act 3

12 The fading signals and grey eternal walls of
that antique station, which, familiar to
them and insignificant, does yet whisper to
the tourist the last enchantments of the
Middle Age.
Zuleika Dobson (1911) ch. 1; cf. **Arnold** 15:29

13 Fate wrote her a most tremendous tragedy,
and she played it in tights.
of Caroline of Brunswick, wife of **George IV**
The Yellow Book (1894) vol. 3

Ethel Lynn Beers 1827–79

14 All quiet along the Potomac to-night,
No sound save the rush of the river,
While soft falls the dew on the face of the
dead—
The picket's off duty forever.
'The Picket Guard' (1861) st. 6; cf. **McClellan**
206:23

Ludwig van Beethoven 1770–1827

15 *Muss es sein? Es muss sein.*
Must it be? It must be.
String Quartet in F Major, Opus 135, epigraph

Brendan Behan 1923–64

16 PAT: He was an Anglo-Irishman.
MEG: In the blessed name of God what's
that?
PAT: A Protestant with a horse.
Hostage (1958) act 1

17 When I came back to Dublin, I was
courtmartialled in my absence and
sentenced to death in my absence, so I said
they could shoot me in my absence.
Hostage (1958) act 1

18 There's no such thing as bad publicity
except your own obituary.
Dominic Behan *My Brother Brendan* (1965)

Aphra Behn 1640–89

19 Oh, what a dear ravishing thing is the
beginning of an Amour!
The Emperor of the Moon (1687) act 1, sc. 1

20 Variety is the soul of pleasure.
The Rover pt. 2 (1681) act 1; cf. **Cowper** 102:1

21 Come away; poverty's catching.
The Rover pt. 2 (1681) act 1

1 The soft, unhappy sex.
   The Wandering Beauty (1698) para. 1

John Hay Beith *see* Ian Hay

Alexander Graham Bell 1847–1922

2 Mr Watson, come here, I want you!
   to his assistant, Thomas Watson, in the next room; the first words spoken on the telephone, 10 March 1876
   Thomas A. Watson *Exploring Life* (1926)

George Bell 1883–1958

3 The policy is obliteration, openly acknowledged. This is not a justifiable act of war.
   speech, House of Lords, 9 February 1944

Francis Bellamy 1856–1931

4 I pledge allegiance to the flag of the United States of America and to the republic for which it stands, one nation under God, indivisible, with liberty and justice for all.
   The Pledge of Allegiance to the Flag (1892)

St Robert Bellarmine 1542–1621

5 Nobody can remember more than seven of anything.
   reason for omitting the eight beatitudes from his catechism
   John Bossy *Christianity in the West 1400–1700* (1985)

Hilaire Belloc 1870–1953

6 Child! do not throw this book about;
   Refrain from the unholy pleasure
   Of cutting all the pictures out!
   Preserve it as your chiefest treasure.
   A Bad Child's Book of Beasts (1896) dedication

7 I shoot the Hippopotamus
   With bullets made of platinum,
   Because if I use leaden ones
   His hide is sure to flatten 'em.
   A Bad Child's Book of Beasts (1896) 'The Hippopotamus'

8 And mothers of large families (who claim to common sense)
   Will find a Tiger well repay the trouble and expense.
   A Bad Child's Book of Beasts (1896) 'The Tiger'

9 Believing Truth is staring at the sun.
   title of poem (1938)

10 Physicians of the Utmost Fame
   Were called at once; but when they came
   They answered, as they took their Fees,
   'There is no Cure for this Disease.'
   Cautionary Tales (1907) 'Henry King'

11 And always keep a-hold of Nurse
   For fear of finding something worse.
   Cautionary Tales (1907) 'Jim'

12 Sir! you have disappointed us!
   We had intended you to be
   The next Prime Minister but three:
   The stocks were sold; the Press was squared;

The Middle Class was quite prepared.
   But as it is! . . . My language fails!
   Go out and govern New South Wales!
   Cautionary Tales (1907) 'Lord Lundy'

13 For every time She shouted 'Fire!'
   They only answered 'Little Liar!'
   Cautionary Tales (1907) 'Matilda'

14 Here richly, with ridiculous display,
   The Politician's corpse was laid away.
   While all of his acquaintance sneered and slanged
   I wept: for I had longed to see him hanged.
   'Epitaph on the Politician Himself' (1923)

15 I said to Heart, 'How goes it?' Heart replied:
   'Right as a Ribstone Pippin!' But it lied.
   'The False Heart' (1910)

16 I'm tired of Love: I'm still more tired of Rhyme.
   But Money gives me pleasure all the time.
   'Fatigued' (1923)

17 Remote and ineffectual Don
   That dared attack my Chesterton.
   'Lines to a Don' (1910)

18 Whatever happens we have got
   The Maxim Gun, and they have not.
   The Modern Traveller (1898) pt. 6

19 The Llama is a woolly sort of fleecy hairy goat,
   With an indolent expression and an undulating throat
   Like an unsuccessful literary man.
   More Beasts for Worse Children (1897) 'The Llama'

20 Oh! let us never, never doubt
   What nobody is sure about!
   More Beasts for Worse Children (1897) 'The Microbe'

21 Lord Finchley tried to mend the Electric Light
   Himself. It struck him dead: And serve him right!
   It is the business of the wealthy man
   To give employment to the artisan.
   More Peers (1911) 'Lord Finchley'

22 Like many of the Upper Class
   He liked the Sound of Broken Glass.
   New Cautionary Tales (1930) 'About John'; cf.
   Waugh 329:17

23 I am a sundial, and I make a botch
   Of what is done much better by a watch.
   'On a Sundial' (1938)

24 When I am dead, I hope it may be said:
   'His sins were scarlet, but his books were read.'
   'On His Books' (1923)

25 Pale Ebenezer thought it wrong to fight,
   But Roaring Bill (who killed him) thought it right.
   'The Pacifist' (1938)

26 Do you remember an Inn,
   Miranda?
   Do you remember an Inn?
   'Tarantella' (1923)

1 There's nothing worth the wear of winning,
But laughter and the love of friends.
Verses (1910) 'Dedicatory Ode'

Saul Bellow 1915-

2 If I am out of my mind, it's all right with
me, thought Moses Herzog.
Herzog (1961)

3 It is sometimes necessary to repeat what we
all know. All mapmakers should place the
Mississippi in the same location, and avoid
originality.
Mr Sammler's Planet (1969)

4 Nobody likes being written about in their
lifetime, it's as though the FBI and the CIA
were suddenly to splash your files in the
paper.
in *Guardian* 10 September 1997

Du Belloy 1725-75

5 The more foreigners I saw, the more I loved
my homeland.
Le Siège de Calais (1765) act 2, sc. 3

Robert Benchley 1889-1945

6 The biggest obstacle to professional writing
is the necessity for changing a typewriter
ribbon.
Chips off the old Benchley (1949) 'Learn to Write'

7 In America there are two classes of
travel—first class, and with children.
Pluck and Luck (1925)

8 STREETS FLOODED. PLEASE ADVISE.
message sent on arriving in Venice
R. E. Drennan (ed.) *Wits End* (1973) 'Robert
Benchley'

Julien Benda 1867-1956

9 La trahison des clercs.
The treachery of the intellectuals.
title of book (1927)

Stephen Vincent Benét 1898-1943

10 I have fallen in love with American names,
The sharp, gaunt names that never get fat.
'American Names' (1927)

11 Bury my heart at Wounded Knee.
'American Names' (1927)

12 And kept his heart a secret to the end
From all the picklocks of biographers.
of Robert E. Lee
John Brown's Body (1928)

William Rose Benét 1886-1950

13 Blake saw a treefull of angels at Peckham
Rye,
And his hands could lay hold on the tiger's
terrible heart.
Blake knew how deep is Hell, and Heaven
how high,
And could build the universe from one tiny
part.
'Mad Blake' (1918)

Tony Benn 1925-

14 Not a reluctant peer but a persistent
commoner.
at a Press Conference, 23 November 1960

15 Some of the jam we thought was for
tomorrow, we've already eaten.
attributed, 1969; cf. **Carroll** 84:8

16 If you file your waste-paper basket for 50
years, you have a public library.
in *Daily Telegraph* 5 March 1994

17 A quotation is what a speaker wants to
say—unlike a soundbite which is all that an
interviewer allows you to say.
letter to Antony Jay, August 1996

18 When I think of Cool Britannia, I think of
old people dying of hypothermia.
at the Labour Party Conference, in *Daily Star* 30
September 1998

George Bennard 1873-1958

19 I will cling to the old rugged cross,
And exchange it some day for a crown.
'The Old Rugged Cross' (1913 hymn)

Alan Bennett 1934-

20 Standards are always out of date. That is
what makes them standards.
Forty Years On (1969) act 2

21 Sapper, Buchan, Dornford Yates,
practitioners in that school of Snobbery
with Violence that runs like a thread of
good-class tweed through twentieth-century
literature.
Forty Years On (1969) act 2

22 To be Prince of Wales is not a position. It is a
predicament.
The Madness of King George (1995 film); in the
1992 play *The Madness of George III* the line was
'To be heir to the throne . . . '

Arnold Bennett 1867-1931

23 'What great cause is he identified with?'
'He's identified . . . with the great cause of
cheering us all up.'
The Card (1911) ch. 12

24 A cause may be inconvenient, but it's
magnificent. It's like champagne or high
heels, and one must be prepared to suffer
for it.
The Title (1918) act 1

25 Literature's always a good card to play for
Honours.
The Title (1918) act 3

Jill Bennett 1931-90

26 Never marry a man who hates his mother,
because he'll end up hating you.
in *Observer* 12 September 1982 'Sayings of the
Week'

A. C. Benson 1862-1925

27 Land of Hope and Glory, Mother of the Free,
How shall we extol thee who are born of
thee?

Wider still and wider shall thy bounds be
set;
God who made thee mighty, make thee
mightier yet.
'Land of Hope and Glory' written to be sung as
the Finale to **Elgar**'s *Coronation Ode* (1902)

Stella Benson 1892–1933

1 Call no man foe, but never love a stranger.
This is the End (1917)

Jeremy Bentham 1748–1832

2 Natural rights is simple nonsense: natural
and imprescriptible rights, rhetorical
nonsense—nonsense upon stilts.
Anarchical Fallacies in J. Bowring (ed.) *Works* vol. 2
(1843)

3 The greatest happiness of the greatest
number is the foundation of morals and
legislation.
*Bentham claimed to have acquired the 'sacred
truth' either from Joseph* **Priestley** *or Cesare
Beccaria (1738–94)*
The Commonplace Book in J. Bowring (ed.) *Works*
vol. 10 (1843); cf. **Hutcheson** 167:13

4 All punishment is mischief: all punishment
in itself is evil.
Principles of Morals and Legislation (1789) ch. 13,
para. 2

5 Every law is contrary to liberty.
Principles of the Civil Code (1843)

6 Prose is when all the lines except the last go
on to the end. Poetry is when some of them
fall short of it.
M. St. J. Packe *The Life of John Stuart Mill* (1954)
bk. 1, ch. 2

Edmund Clerihew Bentley
1875–1956

7 The Art of Biography
Is different from Geography.
Geography is about Maps,
But Biography is about Chaps.
Biography for Beginners (1905) introduction

8 George the Third
Ought never to have occurred.
One can only wonder
At so grotesque a blunder.
More Biography (1929) 'George the Third'

Richard Bentley 1662–1742

9 It would be port if it could.
on claret
R. C. Jebb *Bentley* (1902) ch. 12

Lloyd Bentsen 1921–

responding to Dan **Quayle**'s *claim to have 'as
much experience in the Congress as Jack* **Kennedy**
had when he sought the presidency':
10 Senator, I served with Jack Kennedy. I knew
Jack Kennedy. Jack Kennedy was a friend of
mine. Senator, you're no Jack Kennedy.
in the vice-presidential debate, 5 October 1988

Pierre-Jean de Béranger
1780–1857

11 *Nos amis, les ennemis.*
Our friends, the enemy.
'L'Opinion de ces demoiselles' (written 1815) in
Chansons de De Béranger (1832)

Henri Bergson 1859–1941

12 *L'élan vital.*
The vital spirit.
L'Évolution créatrice (1907) ch. 2 (section title)

George Berkeley 1685–1753

13 They are neither finite quantities, or
quantities infinitely small, nor yet nothing.
May we not call them the ghosts of departed
quantities?
on **Newton**'s *infinitesimals*
The Analyst (1734) sect. 35

14 [Tar water] is of a nature so mild and benign
and proportioned to the human
constitution, as to warm without heating, to
cheer but not inebriate.
Siris (1744) para. 217; cf. **Cowper** 102:3

15 Westward the course of empire takes its
way;
The first four acts already past,
A fifth shall close the drama with the day:
Time's noblest offspring is the last.
'On the Prospect of Planting Arts and Learning
in America' (1752) st. 6.

Irving Berlin 1888–1989

16 I seem to find the happiness I seek
When we're out together dancing cheek-to-
cheek.
'Cheek-to-Cheek' (1935 song) in *Top Hat*

17 God bless America,
Land that I love.
'God Bless America' (1939 song)

18 There may be trouble ahead,
But while there's moonlight and music and
love and romance,
Let's face the music and dance.
'Let's Face the Music and Dance' (1936 song) in
Follow the Fleet

19 A pretty girl is like a melody
That haunts you night and day.
'A Pretty Girl is like a Melody' (1919 song)

20 There's no business like show business.
title of song in *Annie Get Your Gun* (1946)

21 I'm dreaming of a white Christmas,
Just like the ones I used to know.
'White Christmas' (1942 song) in *Holiday Inn*

22 Listen, kid, take my advice, never hate a
song that has sold half a million copies.
to Cole **Porter**, *of the song 'Rosalie'*
Philip Furia *Poets of Tin Pan Alley* (1990)

Isaiah Berlin 1909–97

23 There exists a great chasm between those,
on one side, who relate everything to a

single central vision . . . and, on the other side, those who pursue many ends, often unrelated and even contradictory . . . The first kind of intellectual and artistic personality belongs to the hedgehogs, the second to the foxes.

The Hedgehog and the Fox (1953) sect. 1; cf. **Archilochus** 13:22

1 Liberty is liberty, not equality or fairness or justice or human happiness or a quiet conscience.

Two Concepts of Liberty (1958)

Georges Bernanos 1888–1948

2 The wish for prayer is a prayer in itself.

Journal d'un curé de campagne (1936) ch. 2

3 Hell, madam, is to love no more.

Journal d'un curé de campagne (1936) ch. 2

Bernard of Chartres d. *c.*1130

4 We are like dwarfs on the shoulders of giants, so that we can see more than they, and things at a greater distance, not by virtue of any sharpness of sight on our part, or any physical distinction, but because we are carried high and raised up by their giant size.

John of Salisbury *The Metalogicon* (1159) bk. 3, ch. 4, quoted in R. K. Merton *On the Shoulders of Giants* (1965) ch. 9; cf. **Coleridge** 96:22, **Newton** 233:14

St Bernard of Clairvaux 1090–1153

5 You will find something more in woods than in books. Trees and stones will teach you that which you can never learn from masters.

Epistles no. 106; cf. **Shakespeare** 269:14

6 I am a kind of chimaera of my age, neither cleric nor layman.

Epistles no. 250

Eric Berne 1910–70

7 Games people play: the psychology of human relationships.

title of book (1964)

Yogi Berra 1925–

8 The future ain't what it used to be.

attributed

9 It ain't over till it's over.

comment on National League pennant race, 1973, quoted in many versions

10 It was déjà vu all over again.

attributed

John Berryman 1914–72

11 People will take balls,
Balls will be lost always, little boy,
And no one buys a ball back.

'The Ball Poem' (1948)

12 We must travel in the direction of our fear.

'A Point of Age' (1942)

13 I seldom go to films. They are too exciting, said the Honourable Possum.

77 Dream Songs (1964) no. 53

Theobald von Bethmann Hollweg 1856–1921

14 Just for a word 'neutrality'—a word which in wartime has so often been disregarded—just for a scrap of paper, Great Britain is going to make war on a kindred nation who desires nothing better than to be friends with her.

summary of a report by Sir Edward Goschen to Sir Edward **Grey**

British Documents on Origins of the War 1898–1914 (1926) vol. 11; *The Diary of Edward Goschen 1900–1914* (1980) Appendix B discusses the contentious origins of this statement

John Betjeman 1906–84

15 He sipped at a weak hock and seltzer
As he gazed at the London skies
Through the Nottingham lace of the
curtains
Or was it his bees-winged eyes?

'The Arrest of Oscar Wilde at the Cadogan Hotel' (1937)

16 And girls in slacks remember Dad,
And oafish louts remember Mum,
And sleepless children's hearts are glad,
And Christmas-morning bells say 'Come!'

'Christmas' (1954)

17 And is it true? And is it true,
This most tremendous tale of all,
Seen in a stained-glass window's hue,
A Baby in an ox's stall?
The Maker of the stars and sea
Become a Child on earth for me?

'Christmas' (1954)

18 Oh! Chintzy, Chintzy cheeriness,
Half dead and half alive!

'Death in Leamington' (1931)

19 Spirits of well-shot woodcock, partridge,
snipe
Flutter and bear him up the Norfolk sky.

'Death of King George V' (1937)

20 Old men who never cheated, never doubted,
Communicated monthly, sit and stare
At the new suburb stretched beyond the
run-way
Where a young man lands hatless from the
air.

'Death of King George V' (1937)

21 Phone for the fish-knives, Norman
As Cook is a little unnerved;
You kiddies have crumpled the serviettes
And I must have things daintily served.

'How to get on in Society' (1954)

22 Think of what our Nation stands for,
Books from Boots' and country lanes,
Free speech, free passes, class distinction,
Democracy and proper drains.
Lord, put beneath Thy special care
One-eighty-nine Cadogan Square.

'In Westminster Abbey' (1940)

1 Gaily into Ruislip Gardens
Runs the red electric train,
With a thousand Ta's and Pardon's
Daintily alights Elaine.
'Middlesex' (1954)

2 Come, friendly bombs, and fall on Slough!
It isn't fit for humans now.
'Slough' (1937)

3 Miss J. Hunter Dunn, Miss J. Hunter Dunn,
Furnish'd and burnish'd by Aldershot sun.
'A Subaltern's Love-Song' (1945)

4 Love-thirty, love-forty, oh! weakness of joy,
The speed of a swallow, the grace of a boy,
With carefullest carelessness, gaily you
won,
I am weak from your loveliness, Joan
Hunter Dunn.
'A Subaltern's Love-Song' (1945)

5 Ghastly good taste, or a depressing story of
the rise and fall of English architecture.
title of book (1933)

Bruno Bettelheim 1903–90

6 The most extreme agony is to feel that one
has been utterly forsaken.
Surviving and other essays (1979)

Aneurin Bevan 1897–1960

7 This island is made mainly of coal and
surrounded by fish. Only an organizing
genius could produce a shortage of coal and
fish at the same time.
speech at Blackpool, 24 May 1945

8 The Tory Party . . . So far as I am concerned
they are lower than vermin.
speech at Manchester, 4 July 1948

9 If you carry this resolution you will send
Britain's Foreign Secretary naked into the
conference chamber.
*speaking against a motion proposing unilateral
nuclear disarmament by the UK at Labour Party
Conference in Brighton, 3 October 1957*
in *Daily Herald* 4 October 1957

10 I read the newspapers avidly. It is my one
form of continuous fiction.
in *The Times* 29 March 1960

11 I stuffed their mouths with gold.
*of his handling of the consultants during the
establishment of the National Health Service*
Brian Abel-Smith *The Hospitals 1800–1948* (1964)
ch. 29

William Henry Beveridge
1879–1963

12 Want is one only of five giants on the road
of reconstruction . . . the others are Disease,
Ignorance, Squalor and Idleness.
Social Insurance and Allied Services (1942) pt. 7

Ernest Bevin 1881–1951

13 My [foreign] policy is to be able to take a
ticket at Victoria Station and go anywhere I
damn well please.
in *Spectator* 20 April 1951

14 If you open that Pandora's Box, you never
know what Trojan 'orses will jump out.
on the Council of Europe
Roderick Barclay *Ernest Bevin and the Foreign
Office* (1975) ch. 3

*on the observation that Aneurin **Bevan** was
sometimes his own worst enemy:*
15 Not while I'm alive 'e ain't!
*also attributed to Bevin of Herbert **Morrison***
Roderick Barclay *Ernest Bevin and Foreign Office*
(1975)

Bhagavadgita
textual translations are those of J. Mascaro, 1978

16 If any man thinks he slays, and if another
thinks he is slain, neither knows the ways
of truth. The Eternal in man cannot kill: the
Eternal in man cannot die.
He is never born, and he never dies. He is in
Eternity, he is for evermore. Never-born and
eternal, beyond times gone or to come, he
does not die when the body dies.
ch. 2, v. 19; cf. **Emerson** 124:8, **Upanishads**
321:24

17 I [Krishna] am all-powerful Time which
destroys all things, and I have come here to
slay these men. Even if thou does not fight,
all the warriors facing thee shall die.
ch. 11, v. 32; cf. **Oppenheimer** 236:16

18 Only by love can men see me, and know
me, and come unto me.
ch. 11, v. 54

Benazir Bhutto 1953–

19 Every dictator uses religion as a prop to
keep himself in power.
interview on *60 Minutes*, CBS-TV, 8 August 1986

The Bible (Authorized Version, 1611)
*see also **Book of Common Prayer** (Psalms)*

20 Upon the setting of that bright Occidental
Star, Queen Elizabeth of most happy
memory.
The Epistle Dedicatory

Old Testament: Genesis

21 In the beginning God created the heaven
and the earth. And the earth was without
form, and void; and darkness was upon the
face of the deep. And the Spirit of God
moved upon the face of the waters.
And God said, Let there be light: and there
was light.
Genesis ch. 1, v. 1

22 And the evening and the morning were the
first day.
Genesis ch. 1, v. 5

23 And God saw that it was good.
Genesis ch. 1, v. 10

24 And the Lord God planted a garden
eastward in Eden.
Genesis ch. 2, v. 8

25 And out of the ground made the Lord God
to grow every tree that is pleasant to the

sight, and good for food; the tree of life also in the midst of the garden, and the tree of knowledge of good and evil.
Genesis ch. 2, v. 9

1 But of the tree of the knowledge of good and evil, thou shalt not eat of it: for in the day that thou eatest thereof thou shalt surely die.
Genesis ch. 2, v. 17

2 It is not good that the man should be alone; I will make him an help meet for him.
Genesis ch. 2, v. 18

3 And the rib, which the Lord God had taken from man, made he a woman.
Genesis ch. 2, v. 22

4 Bone of my bones, and flesh of my flesh.
Genesis ch. 2, v. 23; cf. **Milton** 222:20

5 Therefore shall a man leave his father and his mother, and shall cleave unto his wife: and they shall be one flesh.
Genesis ch. 2, v. 24

6 Now the serpent was more subtil than any beast of the field.
Genesis ch. 3, v. 1

7 And they sewed fig leaves together, and made themselves aprons.
And they heard the voice of the Lord God walking in the garden in the cool of the day.
'and made themselves breeches' in the Geneva Bible, 1560, known for that reason as the 'Breeches Bible'
Genesis ch. 3, v. 7

8 The woman whom thou gavest to be with me, she gave me of the tree, and I did eat.
Genesis ch. 3, v. 12

9 The serpent beguiled me, and I did eat.
Genesis ch. 3, v. 13

10 It shall bruise thy head, and thou shalt bruise his heel.
Genesis ch. 3, v. 15

11 In sorrow thou shalt bring forth children.
Genesis ch. 3, v. 16

12 In the sweat of thy face shalt thou eat bread.
Genesis ch. 3, v. 19

13 For dust thou art, and unto dust shalt thou return.
Genesis ch. 3, v. 19; cf. **Longfellow** 201:25

14 Am I my brother's keeper?
Genesis ch. 4, v. 9

15 And the Lord set a mark upon Cain.
Genesis ch. 4, v. 15

16 And Cain went out from the presence of the Lord, and dwelt in the land of Nod, on the east of Eden.
Genesis ch. 4, v. 16

17 And Enoch walked with God: and he was not; for God took him.
Genesis ch. 5, v. 24

18 There were giants in the earth in those days.
Genesis ch. 6, v. 4

19 There went in two and two unto Noah into the Ark, the male and the female.
Genesis ch. 7, v. 9

20 But the dove found no rest for the sole of her foot.
Genesis ch. 8, v. 9

21 Whoso sheddeth man's blood, by man shall his blood be shed.
Genesis ch. 9, v. 6

22 I do set my bow in the cloud, and it shall be for a token of a covenant between me and the earth.
Genesis ch. 9, v. 13

23 Even as Nimrod the mighty hunter before the Lord.
Genesis ch. 10, v. 9

24 His [Ishmael's] hand will be against every man, and every man's hand against him.
Genesis ch. 16, v. 12

25 But his [Lot's] wife looked back from behind him, and she became a pillar of salt.
Genesis ch. 19, v. 26

26 A ram caught in a thicket.
Genesis ch. 22, v. 13

27 Esau selleth his birthright for a mess of pottage.
chapter heading in Geneva Bible, 1560
Genesis ch. 25

28 Behold, Esau my brother is a hairy man, and I am a smooth man.
Genesis ch. 27, v. 11

29 The voice is Jacob's voice, but the hands are the hands of Esau.
Genesis ch. 27, v. 22

30 And he dreamed, and behold a ladder set up on the earth, and the top of it reached to heaven: and behold the angels of God ascending and descending on it.
Genesis ch. 28, v. 12

31 And Jacob served seven years for Rachel.
Genesis ch. 29, v. 20

32 The Lord watch between me and thee, when we are absent one from another.
Genesis ch. 31, v. 49

33 He made him a coat of many colours.
Genesis ch. 37, v. 3

34 Jacob saw that there was corn in Egypt.
Genesis ch. 42, v. 1

35 Then shall ye bring down my grey hairs with sorrow to the grave.
Genesis ch. 42, v. 38

36 Ye shall eat the fat of the land.
Genesis ch. 45, v. 18

37 Unstable as water, thou shalt not excel.
Genesis ch. 49, v. 4

Exodus

38 I have been a stranger in a strange land.
Exodus ch. 2, v. 22

39 Behold, the bush burned with fire, and the bush was not consumed.
Exodus ch. 3, v. 2

1 Put off thy shoes from off thy feet, for the place whereon thou standest is holy ground.
Exodus ch. 3, v. 5

2 A land flowing with milk and honey.
Exodus ch. 3, v. 8

3 I AM THAT I AM.
Exodus ch. 3, v. 14

4 And I will harden Pharaoh's heart, and multiply my signs and my wonders in the land of Egypt.
Exodus ch. 7, v. 3

5 Let my people go.
Exodus ch. 7, v. 16

6 And they shall eat the flesh in that night, roast with fire, and unleavened bread; and with bitter herbs they shall eat it.
Exodus ch. 12, v. 8

7 Ye shall eat it in haste; it is the Lord's passover.
Exodus ch. 12, v. 11

8 For I will pass through the land of Egypt this night, and will smite all the firstborn in the land of Egypt, both man and beast.
Exodus ch. 12, v. 12

9 And they spoiled the Egyptians.
Exodus ch. 12, v. 36

10 And the Lord went before them by day in a pillar of a cloud, to lead them the way; and by night in a pillar of fire, to give them light.
Exodus ch. 13, v. 21

11 Would to God we had died by the hand of the Lord in the land of Egypt, when we sat by the flesh pots, and when we did eat bread to the full.
Exodus ch. 16, v. 3

12 Thou shalt have no other gods before me.
Exodus ch. 20, v. 3

13 I the Lord thy God am a jealous God, visiting the iniquity of the fathers upon the children unto the third and fourth generation of them that hate me.
Exodus ch. 20, v. 5; cf. **Book of Common Prayer** 59:19

14 Thou shalt not take the name of the Lord thy God in vain.
Exodus ch. 20, v. 7

15 Remember the sabbath day, to keep it holy.
Exodus ch. 20, v. 8

16 Honour thy father and thy mother: that thy days may be long upon the land which the Lord thy God giveth thee.
Thou shalt not kill.
Thou shalt not commit adultery.
Thou shalt not steal.
Thou shalt not bear false witness against thy neighbour.
Thou shalt not covet thy neighbour's house, thou shalt not covet thy neighbour's wife, nor his manservant, nor his maidservant, nor his ox, nor his ass, nor any thing that is thy neighbour's.
Exodus ch. 20, v. 12; cf. **Book of Common Prayer** 59:21

17 Life for life,
Eye for eye, tooth for tooth.
Exodus ch. 21, v. 23

18 These be thy gods, O Israel.
Exodus ch. 32, v. 4

19 Thou art a stiffnecked people.
Exodus ch. 33, v. 3

Leviticus

20 Let him go for a scapegoat into the wilderness.
Leviticus ch. 16, v. 10

21 Ye shall therefore keep my statutes and my judgments: which if a man do, he shall live in them: I am the Lord.
Leviticus ch. 18, v. 5; cf. **Talmud** 309:7

22 Thou shalt love thy neighbour as thyself.
Leviticus ch. 19, v. 18; cf. **Bible** 44:29

Numbers

23 The Lord bless thee, and keep thee:
The Lord make his face shine upon thee, and be gracious unto thee:
The Lord lift up his countenance upon thee, and give thee peace.
Numbers ch. 6, v. 24

24 These are the names of the men which Moses sent to spy out the land.
Numbers ch. 13, v. 16

25 What hath God wrought!
quoted by Samuel Morse in the first electric telegraph message, 24 May 1844
Numbers ch. 23, v. 23

26 Be sure your sin will find you out.
Numbers ch. 32, v. 23

Deuteronomy

27 Hear, O Israel: The Lord our God is one Lord.
Deuteronomy ch. 6, v. 4; cf. **Siddur** 295:4

28 If there arise among you a prophet, or a dreamer of dreams . . . Thou shalt not hearken.
Deuteronomy ch. 13, v. 1

29 He found him in a desert land, and in the waste howling wilderness; he led him about, he instructed him, he kept him as the apple of his eye.
Deuteronomy ch. 32, v. 10

30 The eternal God is thy refuge, and underneath are the everlasting arms.
Deuteronomy ch. 33, v. 27

Joshua

31 When the people heard the sound of the trumpet, and the people shouted with a great shout, that the wall fell down flat.
Joshua ch. 6, v. 20

32 Let them live; but let them be hewers of wood and drawers of water unto all the congregation.
Joshua ch. 9, v. 21

33 I am going the way of all the earth.
Joshua ch. 23, v. 14

Judges

1 I arose a mother in Israel.
Judges ch. 5, v. 7

2 The stars in their courses fought against Sisera.
Judges ch. 5, v. 20

3 She brought forth butter in a lordly dish.
Judges ch. 5, v. 25

4 Why tarry the wheels of his chariots?
Judges ch. 5, v. 28

5 Faint, yet pursuing.
Judges ch. 8, v. 4

6 Then said they unto him, Say now Shibboleth: and he said Sibboleth: for he could not frame to pronounce it right. Then they took him, and slew him.
Judges ch. 12, v. 6

7 Out of the eater came forth meat, and out of the strong came forth sweetness.
Judges ch. 14, v. 14

8 He smote them hip and thigh.
Judges ch. 15, v. 8

9 With the jawbone of an ass . . . have I slain a thousand men.
Judges ch. 15, v. 16

10 The Philistines be upon thee, Samson.
Judges ch. 16, v. 9

11 From Dan even to Beer-sheba.
Judges ch. 20, v. 1

12 The people arose as one man.
Judges ch. 20, v. 8

Ruth

13 Intreat me not to leave thee, or to return from following after thee: for whither thou goest, I will go; and where thou lodgest, I will lodge: thy people shall be my people, and thy God my God:
Where thou diest, will I die, and there will I be buried: the Lord do so to me, and more also, if ought but death part thee and me.
Ruth ch. 1, v. 16

I Samuel

14 Speak, Lord; for thy servant heareth.
I Samuel ch. 3, v. 9

15 And she named the child I-chabod, saying, The glory is departed from Israel.
I Samuel ch. 4, v. 21

16 And the asses of Kish Saul's father were lost. And Kish said to Saul his son, Take now one of the servants with thee, and arise, go seek the asses.
I Samuel ch. 9, v. 3; cf. **Milton** 222:27

17 Is Saul also among the prophets?
I Samuel ch. 10, v. 11

18 God save the king.
I Samuel ch. 10, v. 24

19 A man after his own heart.
I Samuel ch. 13, v. 14

20 For the Lord seeth not as man seeth: for man looketh on the outward appearance, but the Lord looketh on the heart.
I Samuel ch. 16, v. 7

21 Go, and the Lord be with thee.
I Samuel ch. 17, v. 37

22 And he . . . chose him five smooth stones out of the brook.
I Samuel ch. 17, v. 40

23 Saul hath slain his thousands, and David his ten thousands.
I Samuel ch. 18, v. 7; cf. **Porteus** 249:23

24 David therefore departed thence, and escaped to the cave Adullam: and when his brethren and all his father's house heard it, they went down thither to him.
And every one that was in distress, and every one that was in debt, and every one that was discontented, gathered themselves unto him.
I Samuel ch. 22, v. 1; cf. **Bright** 67:2

25 And Saul said, God hath delivered him into mine hand.
I Samuel ch. 23, v. 7

II Samuel

26 The beauty of Israel is slain upon thy high places: how are the mighty fallen!
II Samuel ch. 1, v. 19

27 Tell it not in Gath, publish it not in the streets of Askelon; lest the daughters of the Philistines rejoice.
II Samuel ch. 1, v. 20

28 Saul and Jonathan were lovely and pleasant in their lives, and in their death they were not divided.
II Samuel ch. 1, v. 23

29 I am distressed for thee, my brother Jonathan: very pleasant hast thou been unto me: thy love to me was wonderful, passing the love of women.
How are the mighty fallen.
II Samuel ch. 1, v. 26

30 The poor man had nothing, save one little ewe lamb.
II Samuel ch. 12, v. 3

31 Thou art the man.
II Samuel ch. 12, v. 7

32 For we needs must die, and are as water spilt on the ground, which cannot be gathered up again; neither doth God respect any person.
II Samuel ch. 14, v. 14

33 And the king was much moved, and went up to the chamber over the gate, and wept: and as he went, thus he said, O my son Absalom, my son, my son Absalom! would God I had died for thee, O Absalom, my son, my son!
II Samuel ch. 18, v. 33

34 By my God have I leaped over a wall.
II Samuel ch. 22, v. 30

35 David . . . the sweet psalmist of Israel.
II Samuel ch. 23, v. 1

I Kings

36 And Zadok the priest took an horn of oil out of the tabernacle, and anointed Solomon.

And they blew the trumpet; and all the people said, God save king Solomon.
I Kings ch. 1, v. 39

1 Then will I cut off Israel out of the land which I have given them; and this house, which I have hallowed for my name, will I cast out of my sight; and Israel shall be a proverb and a byword among all people.
I Kings ch. 9, v. 7

2 And when the queen of Sheba had seen all Solomon's wisdom . . . there was no more spirit in her.
I Kings ch. 10, v. 4

3 Behold, the half was not told me.
I Kings ch. 10, v. 7

4 Once in three years came the navy of Tharshish, bringing gold, and silver, ivory, and apes, and peacocks.
I Kings ch. 10, v. 22; cf. **Masefield** 214:16

5 But king Solomon loved many strange women.
I Kings ch. 11, v. 1

6 My little finger shall be thicker than my father's loins.
I Kings ch. 12, v. 10

7 My father hath chastised you with whips, but I will chastise you with scorpions.
I Kings ch. 12, v. 11

8 To your tents, O Israel.
I Kings ch. 12, v. 16

9 An handful of meal in a barrel, and a little oil in a cruse.
I Kings ch. 17, v. 12

10 How long halt ye between two opinions?
I Kings ch. 18, v. 21

11 There ariseth a little cloud out of the sea, like a man's hand.
I Kings ch. 18, v. 44

12 He girded up his loins.
I Kings ch. 18, v. 46

13 But the Lord was not in the wind: and after the wind an earthquake; but the Lord was not in the earthquake:
And after the earthquake a fire: but the Lord was not in the fire: and after the fire a still small voice.
I Kings ch. 19, v. 11

14 Elijah passed by him, and cast his mantle upon him.
I Kings ch. 19, v. 19

15 Hast thou found me, O mine enemy?
I Kings ch. 21, v. 20

16 I saw all Israel scattered upon the hills, as sheep that have not a shepherd.
I Kings ch. 22, v. 17

17 Feed him with bread of affliction and with water of affliction, until I come in peace.
I Kings ch. 22, v. 27

18 And a certain man drew a bow at a venture, and smote the king of Israel between the joints of the harness.
I Kings ch. 22, v. 34

II Kings

19 Elijah went up by a whirlwind into heaven.
II Kings ch. 2, v. 11

20 The spirit of Elijah doth rest on Elisha.
II Kings ch. 2, v. 15

21 Go up, thou bald head.
II Kings ch. 2, v. 23

22 Is it well with the child? And she answered, It is well.
II Kings ch. 4, v. 26

23 There is death in the pot.
II Kings ch. 4, v. 40

24 Are not Abana and Pharpar, rivers of Damascus, better than all the waters of Israel?
II Kings ch. 5, v. 12

25 I bow myself in the house of Rimmon.
II Kings ch. 5, v. 18

26 Whence comest thou, Gehazi?
II Kings ch. 5, v. 25

27 Is thy servant a dog, that he should do this great thing?
II Kings ch. 8, v. 13

28 The driving is like the driving of Jehu, the son of Nimshi; for he driveth furiously.
II Kings ch. 9, v. 20

29 She painted her face, and tired her head, and looked out at a window.
II Kings ch. 9, v. 30

30 Had Zimri peace, who slew his master?
II Kings ch. 9, v. 31

31 Who is on my side? who?
II Kings ch. 9, v. 32

32 They found no more of her than the skull, and the feet, and the palms of her hands.
II Kings ch. 9, v. 35

33 Thou trustest upon the staff of this bruised reed, even upon Egypt, on which if a man lean, it will go into his hand, and pierce it.
II Kings ch. 18, v. 21

I Chronicles

34 For we are strangers before thee, and sojourners, as were all our fathers: our days on the earth are as a shadow, and there is none abiding.
I Chronicles ch. 29, v. 15

Esther

35 And if I perish, I perish.
Esther ch. 4, v. 16

Job

36 And the Lord said unto Satan, Whence comest thou? Then Satan answered the Lord, and said, From going to and fro in the earth, and from walking up and down in it.
Job ch. 1, v. 7

37 The Lord gave, and the Lord hath taken away; blessed be the name of the Lord.
Job ch. 1, v. 21

38 All that a man hath will he give for his life.
Job ch. 2, v. 4

1 Curse God, and die.
   Job ch. 2, v. 9

2 Let the day perish wherein I was born.
   Job ch. 3, v. 3

3 There the wicked cease from troubling, and there the weary be at rest.
   Job ch. 3, v. 17

4 Then a spirit passed before my face; the hair of my flesh stood up.
   Job ch. 4, v. 15

5 Man is born unto trouble, as the sparks fly upward.
   Job ch. 5, v. 7

6 Man that is born of a woman is of few days, and full of trouble.
   He cometh forth like a flower, and is cut down: he fleeth also as a shadow, and continueth not.
   Job ch. 14, v. 1; cf. **Book of Common Prayer** 60:23

7 Miserable comforters are ye all.
   Job ch. 16, v. 2

8 I am escaped with the skin of my teeth.
   Job ch. 19, v. 20

9 I know that my redeemer liveth, and that he shall stand at the latter day upon the earth:
   And though after my skin worms destroy this body, yet in my flesh shall I see God.
   Job ch. 19, v. 25

10 The root of the matter is found in me.
   Job ch. 19, v. 28

11 The price of wisdom is above rubies.
   Job ch. 28, v. 18

12 I am a brother to dragons, and a companion to owls.
   Job ch. 30, v. 29

13 Canst thou bind the sweet influences of Pleiades, or loose the bands of Orion?
   Job ch. 38, v. 31

14 He saith among the trumpets, Ha, ha; and he smelleth the battle afar off, the thunder of the captains, and the shouting.
   Job ch. 39, v. 25

15 Behold now behemoth, which I made with thee; he eateth grass as an ox.
   Job ch. 40, v. 15

16 Canst thou draw out leviathan with an hook?
   Job ch. 41, v. 1

Proverbs

17 Surely in vain the net is spread in the sight of any bird.
   Proverbs ch. 1, v. 17

18 For whom the Lord loveth he correcteth.
   Proverbs ch. 3, v. 12

19 Her ways are ways of pleasantness, and all her paths are peace.
   Proverbs ch. 3, v. 17

20 Wisdom is the principal thing; therefore get wisdom: and with all thy getting get understanding.
   Proverbs ch. 4, v. 7

21 Go to the ant thou sluggard; consider her ways, and be wise.
   Proverbs ch. 6, v. 6

22 Yet a little sleep, a little slumber, a little folding of the hands to sleep.
   Proverbs ch. 6, v. 10

23 Wisdom hath builded her house, she hath hewn out her seven pillars.
   Proverbs ch. 9, v. 1

24 Stolen waters are sweet.
   Proverbs ch. 9, v. 17

25 A wise son maketh a glad father: but a foolish son is the heaviness of his mother.
   Proverbs ch. 10, v. 1

26 A virtuous woman is a crown to her husband.
   Proverbs ch. 12, v. 4

27 A righteous man regardeth the life of his beast: but the tender mercies of the wicked are cruel.
   Proverbs ch. 12, v. 10

28 Lying lips are abomination to the Lord.
   Proverbs ch. 12, v. 22; cf. **Anonymous** 5:12

29 Hope deferred maketh the heart sick.
   Proverbs ch. 13, v. 12

30 The way of transgressors is hard.
   Proverbs ch. 13, v. 15

31 He that spareth his rod hateth his son.
   Proverbs ch. 13, v. 24

32 A soft answer turneth away wrath.
   Proverbs ch. 15, v. 1

33 A merry heart maketh a cheerful countenance.
   Proverbs ch. 15, v. 13

34 Better is a dinner of herbs where love is, than a stalled ox and hatred therewith.
   'Better is a mess of pottage with love, than a fat ox with evil will' in Matthew's Bible (1535)
   Proverbs ch. 15, v. 17

35 A word spoken in due season, how good is it!
   Proverbs ch. 15, v. 23

36 Pride goeth before destruction, and an haughty spirit before a fall.
   Proverbs ch. 16, v. 18

37 There is a friend that sticketh closer than a brother.
   Proverbs ch. 18, v. 24

38 Wine is a mocker, strong drink is raging.
   Proverbs ch. 20, v. 1

39 Train up a child in the way he should go: and when he is old, he will not depart from it.
   Proverbs ch. 22, v. 6

40 Look not thou upon the wine when it is red.
   Proverbs ch. 23, v. 31

1 A word fitly spoken is like apples of gold in pictures of silver.
Proverbs ch. 25, v. 11

2 Withdraw thy foot from thy neighbour's house; lest he be weary of thee, and so hate thee.
Proverbs ch. 25, v. 17

3 If thine enemy be hungry, give him bread to eat; and if he be thirsty, give him water to drink.
For thou shalt heap coals of fire upon his head, and the Lord shall reward thee.
Proverbs ch. 25, v. 21

4 As cold waters to a thirsty soul, so is good news from a far country.
Proverbs ch. 25, v. 25

5 Answer not a fool according to his folly, lest thou also be like unto him.
Answer a fool according to his folly, lest he be wise in his own conceit.
Proverbs ch. 26, v. 4

6 As a dog returneth to his vomit, so a fool returneth to his folly.
Proverbs ch. 26, v. 11

7 The wicked flee when no man pursueth: but the righteous are bold as a lion.
Proverbs ch. 28, v. 1

8 He that maketh haste to be rich shall not be innocent.
Proverbs ch. 28, v. 20

9 Where there is no vision, the people perish.
Proverbs ch. 29, v. 18

10 There be three things which are too wonderful for me, yea, four which I know not:
The way of an eagle in the air; the way of a serpent upon a rock; the way of a ship in the midst of the sea; and the way of a man with a maid.
Proverbs ch. 30, v. 18

11 Who can find a virtuous woman? for her price is far above rubies.
Proverbs ch. 31, v. 10

Ecclesiastes

12 Vanity of vanities; all is vanity.
Ecclesiastes ch. 1, v. 2; cf. **Bible** 53:4

13 All the rivers run into the sea; yet the sea is not full.
Ecclesiastes ch. 1, v. 7

14 The thing that hath been, it is that which shall be; and that which is done is that which shall be done: and there is no new thing under the sun.
Ecclesiastes ch. 1, v. 9

15 He that increaseth knowledge increaseth sorrow.
Ecclesiastes ch. 1, v. 18

16 To every thing there is a season, and a time to every purpose under the heaven:
A time to be born, and a time to die; a time to plant, and a time to pluck up that which is planted.
Ecclesiastes ch. 3, v. 1

17 A time to weep, and a time to laugh; a time to mourn, and a time to dance.
Ecclesiastes ch. 3, v. 1

18 A time to love, and a time to hate; a time of war, and a time of peace.
Ecclesiastes ch. 3, v. 1

19 A threefold cord is not quickly broken.
Ecclesiastes ch. 4, v. 12; cf. **Burke** 73:20

20 The sleep of a labouring man is sweet.
Ecclesiastes ch. 5, v. 12

21 As the crackling of thorns under a pot, so is the laughter of a fool.
Ecclesiastes ch. 7, v. 6

22 God hath made man upright; but they have sought out many inventions.
Ecclesiastes ch. 7, v. 29

23 There is no discharge in that war.
Ecclesiastes ch. 8, v. 8

24 A man hath no better thing under the sun, than to eat, and to drink, and to be merry.
Ecclesiastes ch. 8, v. 15; cf. **Bible** 39:27, 46:22

25 A living dog is better than a dead lion.
Ecclesiastes ch. 9, v. 4

26 Whatsoever thy hand findeth to do, do it with thy might; for there is no work, nor device, nor knowledge, nor wisdom, in the grave, whither thou goest.
Ecclesiastes ch. 9, v. 10

27 The race is not to the swift, nor the battle to the strong.
Ecclesiastes ch. 9, v. 11; cf. **Davidson** 106:14

28 He that diggeth a pit shall fall into it.
Ecclesiastes ch. 10, v. 8

29 Woe to thee, O land, when thy king is a child.
Ecclesiastes ch. 10, v. 16; cf. **Shakespeare** 286:4

30 Wine maketh merry: but money answereth all things.
Ecclesiastes ch. 10, v. 19

31 Cast thy bread upon the waters: for thou shalt find it after many days.
Ecclesiastes ch. 11, v. 1

32 In the place where the tree falleth, there it shall be.
Ecclesiastes ch. 11, v. 3

33 Remember now thy Creator in the days of thy youth.
Ecclesiastes ch. 12, v. 1

34 And desire shall fail: because man goeth to his long home, and the mourners go about the streets:
Or ever the silver cord be loosed, or the golden bowl be broken, or the pitcher be broken at the fountain, or the wheel broken at the cistern.
Then shall the dust return to the earth as it was: and the spirit shall return unto God who gave it.
Ecclesiastes ch. 12, v. 5

35 Of making many books there is no end; and much study is a weariness of the flesh.
Ecclesiastes ch. 12, v. 12

1 Fear God, and keep his commandments: for this is the whole duty of man.
  Ecclesiastes ch. 12, v. 13

Song of Solomon

2 I am black, but comely.
  Song of Solomon ch. 1, v. 5

3 I am the rose of Sharon, and the lily of the valleys.
  Song of Solomon ch. 2, v. 1

4 The time of the singing of birds is come, and the voice of the turtle is heard in our land.
  Song of Solomon ch. 2, v. 10

5 My beloved is mine, and I am his: he feedeth among the lilies.
  Until the day break, and the shadows flee away.
  Song of Solomon ch. 2, v. 16

6 Behold, thou art fair, my love; behold, thou art fair.
  Song of Solomon ch. 4, v. 1

7 A garden inclosed is my sister, my spouse; a spring shut up, a fountain sealed.
  Song of Solomon ch. 4, v. 12

8 Love is strong as death; jealousy is cruel as the grave.
  Song of Solomon ch. 8, v. 6

9 Many waters cannot quench love, neither can the floods drown it.
  Song of Solomon ch. 8, v. 7

Isaiah

10 Though your sins be as scarlet, they shall be as white as snow.
  Isaiah ch. 1, v. 18

11 They shall beat their swords into plowshares, and their spears into pruninghooks: nation shall not lift up sword against nation, neither shall they learn war any more.
  Micah ch. 4, v. 3, Joel ch. 3, v. 10 have same image
  Isaiah ch. 2, v. 4; cf. **Rendall** 255:17

12 What mean ye that ye beat my people to pieces, and grind the faces of the poor?
  Isaiah ch. 3, v. 15

13 Woe unto them that join house to house, that lay field to field, till there be no place.
  Isaiah ch. 5, v. 8

14 I saw also the Lord sitting upon a throne, high and lifted up, and his train filled the temple.
  Above it stood the seraphims: each one had six wings; with twain he covered his face, and with twain he covered his feet, and with twain he did fly.
  And one cried unto another, and said, Holy, holy, holy, is the Lord of hosts: the whole earth is full of his glory.
  Isaiah ch. 6, v. 1

15 Whom shall I send, and who will go for us? Then said I, Here am I; send me.
  Isaiah ch. 6, v. 8

16 Then said I, Lord, how long?
  Isaiah ch. 6, v. 11

17 Behold, a virgin shall conceive, and bear a son, and shall call his name Immanuel. Butter and honey shall he eat, that he may know to refuse the evil, and choose the good.
  Isaiah ch. 7, v. 14

18 The people that walked in darkness have seen a great light: they that dwell in the land of the shadow of death, upon them hath the light shined.
  Isaiah ch. 9, v. 2

19 For unto us a child is born, unto us a son is given: and the government shall be upon his shoulder: and his name shall be called Wonderful, Counsellor, The mighty God, The everlasting Father, The Prince of Peace. Of the increase of his government and peace there shall be no end.
  Isaiah ch. 9, v. 6

20 The zeal of the Lord of hosts will perform this.
  Isaiah ch. 9, v. 7

21 And there shall come forth a rod out of the stem of Jesse, and a branch shall grow out of his roots.
  Isaiah ch. 11, v. 1

22 The wolf also shall dwell with the lamb, and the leopard shall lie down with the kid; and the calf and the young lion and the fatling together; and a little child shall lead them.
  Isaiah ch. 11, v. 6

23 And the sucking child shall play on the hole of the asp, and the weaned child shall put his hand on the cockatrice' den.
  They shall not hurt nor destroy in all my holy mountain: for the earth shall be full of the knowledge of the Lord, as the waters cover the sea.
  Isaiah ch. 11, v. 8

24 Dragons in their pleasant palaces.
  Isaiah ch. 13, v. 22

25 How art thou fallen from heaven, O Lucifer, son of the morning!
  Isaiah ch. 14, v. 12

26 Watchman, what of the night? Watchman, what of the night?
  The watchman said, The morning cometh, and also the night.
  Isaiah ch. 21, v. 11

27 Let us eat and drink; for to morrow we shall die.
  Isaiah ch. 22, v. 13; cf. **Bible** 38:24, 46:22

28 He will swallow up death in victory; and the Lord God will wipe away tears from off all faces.
  Isaiah ch. 25, v. 8

29 For precept must be upon precept, precept upon precept; line upon line, line upon line; here a little, and there a little.
  Isaiah ch. 28, v. 10

30 We have made a covenant with death, and with hell are we at agreement.
  Isaiah ch. 28, v. 15; cf. **Garrison** 136:12

1 The bread of adversity, and the waters of affliction.
Isaiah ch. 30, v. 20

2 This is the way, walk ye in it.
Isaiah ch. 30, v. 21

3 And thorns shall come up in her palaces, nettles and brambles in the fortresses thereof: and it shall be an habitation of dragons, and a court for owls.
Isaiah ch. 34, v. 13

4 The desert shall rejoice, and blossom as the rose.
Isaiah ch. 35, v. 1

5 Set thine house in order.
Isaiah ch. 38, v. 1

6 Comfort ye, comfort ye my people, saith your God.
Speak ye comfortably to Jerusalem, and cry unto her, that her warfare is accomplished.
Isaiah ch. 40, v. 1

7 The voice of him that crieth in the wilderness, Prepare ye the way of the Lord, make straight in the desert a highway for our God.
Every valley shall be exalted, and every mountain and hill shall be made low: and the crooked shall be made straight, and the rough places plain:
And the glory of the Lord shall be revealed, and all flesh shall see it together: for the mouth of the Lord hath spoken it.
Isaiah ch. 40, v. 3; cf. **Bible** 42:6

8 The voice said, Cry. And he said, What shall I cry? All flesh is grass, and all the goodliness thereof is as the flower of the field:
The grass withereth, the flower fadeth: because the spirit of the Lord bloweth upon it: surely the people is grass.
Isaiah ch. 40, v. 6; cf. **Bible** 51:25

9 He shall feed his flock like a shepherd: he shall gather the lambs with his arm, and carry them in his bosom, and shall gently lead those that are with young.
Isaiah ch. 40, v. 11

10 Have ye not known? have ye not heard? hath it not been told you from the beginning?
Isaiah ch. 40, v. 21

11 They shall mount up with wings as eagles; they shall run, and not be weary; and they shall walk, and not faint.
Isaiah ch. 40, v. 31

12 A bruised reed shall he not break, and the smoking flax shall he not quench.
Isaiah ch. 42, v. 3

13 There is no peace, saith the Lord, unto the wicked.
Isaiah ch. 48, v. 22

14 How beautiful upon the mountains are the feet of him that bringeth good tidings, that publisheth peace; that bringeth good tidings of good, that publisheth salvation.
Isaiah ch. 52, v. 7

15 For they shall see eye to eye, when the Lord shall bring again Zion.
Break forth into joy, sing together, ye waste places of Jerusalem: for the Lord hath comforted his people, he hath redeemed Jerusalem.
Isaiah ch. 52, v. 8

16 He is despised and rejected of men; a man of sorrows, and acquainted with grief.
Isaiah ch. 53, v. 3

17 But he was wounded for our transgressions, he was bruised for our iniquities: the chastisement of our peace was upon him; and with his stripes we are healed.
All we like sheep have gone astray; we have turned every one to his own way; and the Lord hath laid on him the iniquity of us all.
Isaiah ch. 53, v. 5

18 He is brought as a lamb to the slaughter, and as a sheep before her shearers is dumb, so he openeth not his mouth.
Isaiah ch. 53, v. 7

19 Mine house shall be called an house of prayer for all people.
Isaiah ch. 56, v. 7; cf. **Bible** 44:25

20 Arise, shine; for thy light is come, and the glory of the Lord is risen upon thee.
Isaiah ch. 60, v. 1

21 Stand by thyself, come not near to me; for I am holier than thou.
Isaiah ch. 65, v. 5

22 For, behold, I create new heavens and a new earth.
Isaiah ch. 65, v. 17

Jeremiah

23 The harvest is past, the summer is ended, and we are not saved.
Jeremiah ch. 8, v. 20

24 Is there no balm in Gilead?
Jeremiah ch. 8, v. 22

25 Can the Ethiopian change his skin, or the leopard his spots?
Jeremiah ch. 13, v. 23

26 The heart is deceitful above all things, and desperately wicked.
Jeremiah ch. 17, v. 9

Lamentations

27 Is it nothing to you, all ye that pass by? behold, and see if there be any sorrow like unto my sorrow.
Lamentations ch. 1, v. 12

28 Remembering mine affliction and my misery, the wormwood and the gall.
Lamentations ch. 3, v. 19

29 O Lord, thou hast seen my wrong: judge thou my cause.
Lamentations ch. 4, v. 59

Ezekiel

30 As is the mother, so is her daughter.
Ezekiel ch. 16, v. 44

1 The fathers have eaten sour grapes, and the children's teeth are set on edge.
Ezekiel ch. 18, v. 2

2 When the wicked man turneth away from his wickedness that he hath committed, and doeth that which is lawful and right, he shall save his soul alive.
Ezekiel ch. 18, v. 27

3 The king of Babylon stood at the parting of the ways.
Ezekiel ch. 21, v. 21

4 The valley which was full of bones.
Ezekiel ch. 37, v. 1

5 Can these bones live?
Ezekiel ch. 37, v. 3

6 O ye dry bones, hear the word of the Lord.
Ezekiel ch. 37, v. 4

Daniel

7 Cast into the midst of a burning fiery furnace.
Daniel ch. 3, v. 4

8 And this is the writing that was written, MENE, MENE, TEKEL, UPHARSIN.
This is the interpretation of the thing:
MENE; God hath numbered thy kingdom, and finished it.
TEKEL; Thou art weighed in the balances and art found wanting.
PERES; Thy kingdom is divided, and given to the Medes and Persians.
Daniel ch. 5, v. 25

9 Now, O king, establish the decree, and sign the writing, that it be not changed, according to the law of the Medes and Persians, which altereth not.
Daniel ch. 6, v. 8

10 The Ancient of days did sit, whose garment was white as snow, and the hair of his head like the pure wool: his throne was like the fiery flame, and his wheels as burning fire. A fiery stream issued and came forth from before him: thousand thousands ministered unto him, and ten thousand times ten thousand stood before him: the judgement was set, and the books were opened.
Daniel ch. 7, v. 9

11 O Daniel, a man greatly beloved.
Daniel ch. 10, v. 11

Hosea

12 They have sown the wind, and they shall reap the whirlwind.
Hosea ch. 8, v. 7

Joel

13 I will restore to you the years that the locust hath eaten.
Joel ch. 2, v. 25

14 Your sons and your daughters shall prophesy, your old men shall dream dreams, your young men shall see visions.
Joel ch. 2, v. 28

Amos

15 Ye were as a firebrand plucked out of the burning.
Amos ch. 4, v. 11

Micah

16 But thou, Bethlehem Ephratah, though thou be little among the thousands of Judah, yet out of thee shall he come forth unto me that is to be ruler in Israel.
Micah ch. 5, v. 2

17 What doth the Lord require of thee, but to do justly, and to love mercy, and to walk humbly with thy God?
Micah ch. 6, v. 8

Habakkuk

18 Write the vision, and make it plain upon tables, that he may run that readeth it.
Habakkuk ch. 2, v. 2

Malachi

19 But unto you that fear my name shall the Sun of righteousness arise with healing in his wings.
Malachi ch. 4, v. 2

Apocrypha

20 Great is Truth, and mighty above all things.
I Esdras ch. 4, v. 41; cf. **Bible** 53:14

21 But the souls of the righteous are in the hand of God.
Wisdom of Solomon ch. 3, v. 1

22 And in the time of their visitation they shall shine, and run to and fro like sparks among the stubble.
Wisdom of Solomon ch. 3, v. 7

23 We will fall into the hands of the Lord, and not into the hands of men: for as his majesty is, so is his mercy.
Ecclesiasticus ch. 2, v. 18

24 Laugh no man to scorn in the bitterness of his soul.
Ecclesiasticus ch. 7, v. 11

25 Judge none blessed before his death.
Ecclesiasticus ch. 11, v. 28; cf. **Solon** 298:26

26 He that toucheth pitch shall be defiled therewith.
Ecclesiasticus ch. 13, v. 1

27 A merchant shall hardly keep himself from doing wrong.
Ecclesiasticus ch. 26, v. 29

28 Honour a physician with the honour due unto him for the uses which ye may have of him: for the Lord hath created him.
Ecclesiasticus ch. 38, v. 1

29 Let us now praise famous men, and our fathers that begat us.
Ecclesiasticus ch. 44, v. 1

30 And some there be, which have no memorial . . . and are become as though they had never been born . . .
But these were merciful men, whose righteousness hath not been forgotten . . .
Their seed shall remain for ever, and their glory shall not be blotted out.

Their bodies are buried in peace; but their
name liveth for evermore.
  Ecclesiasticus ch. 44, v. 9

1 When he was at the last gasp.
  II Maccabees ch. 7, v. 9

New Testament: St Matthew

2 There came wise men from the east to
Jerusalem,
Saying, Where is he that is born King of the
Jews? for we have seen his star in the east,
and are come to worship him.
  St Matthew ch. 2, v. 1

3 They presented unto him gifts; gold, and
frankincense, and myrrh.
  St Matthew ch. 2, v. 11

4 In Rama was there a voice heard,
lamentation, and weeping, and great
mourning, Rachel weeping for her children,
and would not be comforted, because they
are not.
  referring to Jeremiah ch. 31, v. 15
  St Matthew ch. 2, v. 18

5 Repent ye: for the kingdom of heaven is at
hand.
  St Matthew ch. 3, v. 2

6 The voice of one crying in the wilderness,
Prepare ye the way of the Lord, make his
paths straight.
  St Matthew ch. 3, v. 3; cf. **Bible** 40:7

7 John had his raiment of camel's hair, and a
leathern girdle about his loins; and his meat
was locusts and wild honey.
  St Matthew ch. 3, v. 4

8 O generation of vipers, who hath warned
you to flee from the wrath to come?
  St Matthew ch. 3, v. 7

9 This is my beloved Son, in whom I am well
pleased.
  St Matthew ch. 3, v. 17

10 Man shall not live by bread alone, but by
every word that proceedeth out of the
mouth of God.
  echoing Deuteronomy ch. 8, v. 3
  St Matthew ch. 4, v. 4

11 Thou shalt not tempt the Lord thy God.
  echoing Deuteronomy ch. 6, v. 16
  St Matthew ch. 4, v. 7

12 The devil taketh him up into an exceeding
high mountain, and sheweth him all the
kingdoms of the world, and the glory of
them.
  St Matthew ch. 4, v. 8

13 Follow me, and I will make you fishers of
men.
  St Matthew ch. 4, v. 19

14 Blessed are the poor in spirit: for theirs is
the kingdom of heaven.
Blessed are they that mourn: for they shall
be comforted.
Blessed are the meek: for they shall inherit
the earth.
Blessed are they which do hunger and thirst
after righteousness: for they shall be filled.

Blessed are the merciful: for they shall
obtain mercy.
Blessed are the pure in heart: for they shall
see God.
Blessed are the peacemakers: for they shall
be called the children of God.
  St Matthew ch. 5, v. 3

15 Ye are the salt of the earth: but if the salt
have lost his savour, wherewith shall it be
salted?
  St Matthew ch. 5, v. 13

16 Ye are the light of the world. A city that is
set on an hill cannot be hid.
  St Matthew ch. 5, v. 14

17 Let your light so shine before men, that
they may see your good works.
  St Matthew ch. 5, v. 16

18 Resist not evil: but whosoever shall smite
thee on thy right cheek, turn to him the
other also.
  St Matthew ch. 5, v. 39

19 Whosoever shall compel thee to go a mile,
go with him twain.
  St Matthew ch. 5, v. 41

20 He maketh his sun to rise on the evil and on
the good, and sendeth rain on the just and
on the unjust.
  St Matthew ch. 5, v. 45; cf. **Bowen** 65:15

21 Be ye therefore perfect, even as your Father
which is in heaven is perfect.
  St Matthew ch. 5, v. 48

22 When thou doest alms, let not thy left hand
know what thy right hand doeth.
That thine alms may be in secret: and thy
Father which seeth in secret himself shall
reward you openly.
  St Matthew ch. 6, v. 3

23 After this manner therefore pray ye: Our
Father which art in heaven, Hallowed be
thy name.
Thy kingdom come. Thy will be done in
earth, as it is in heaven.
Give us this day our daily bread.
And forgive us our debts, as we forgive our
debtors.
And lead us not into temptation, but deliver
us from evil: For thine is the kingdom, and
the power, and the glory, for ever. Amen.
  St Matthew ch. 6, v. 9; cf. **Book of Common
  Prayer** 58:8, **Missal** 224:5

24 Lay not up for yourselves treasures upon
earth, where moth and rust doth corrupt,
and where thieves break through and steal:
But lay up for yourselves treasures in
heaven.
  St Matthew ch. 6, v. 19

25 Where your treasure is, there will your
heart be also.
  St Matthew ch. 6, v. 21

26 No man can serve two masters . . . Ye cannot
serve God and mammon.
  St Matthew ch. 6, v. 24

27 Consider the lilies of the field, how they
grow; they toil not, neither do they spin:

And yet I say unto you, That even Solomon in all his glory was not arrayed like one of these.
St Matthew ch. 6, v. 28

1 Take therefore no thought for the morrow: for the morrow shall take thought for the things of itself. Sufficient unto the day is the evil thereof.
St Matthew ch. 6, v. 34

2 Judge not, that ye be not judged.
St Matthew ch. 7, v. 1

3 Why beholdest thou the mote that is in thy brother's eye, but considerest not the beam that is in thine own eye?
St Matthew ch. 7, v. 3

4 Neither cast ye your pearls before swine.
St Matthew ch. 7, v. 6

5 Ask, and it shall be given you; seek, and ye shall find; knock, and it shall be opened unto you.
St Matthew ch. 7, v. 7

6 Or what man is there of you, whom if his son ask bread, will he give him a stone?
St Matthew ch. 7, v. 9

7 Therefore all things whatsoever ye would that men should do to you, do ye even so to them: for this is the law and the prophets.
St Matthew ch. 7, v. 12

8 Wide is the gate, and broad is the way, that leadeth to destruction, and many there be that go in thereat.
St Matthew ch. 7, v. 13

9 Strait is the gate, and narrow is the way, which leadeth unto life, and few there be that find it.
St Matthew ch. 7, v. 14

10 Beware of false prophets, which come to you in sheep's clothing, but inwardly they are ravening wolves.
St Matthew ch. 7, v. 15

11 By their fruits ye shall know them.
St Matthew ch. 7, v. 20

12 The winds blew, and beat upon that house; and it fell not: for it was founded upon a rock.
St Matthew ch. 7, v. 25

13 Lord I am not worthy that thou shouldest come under my roof.
St Matthew ch. 8, v. 8; cf. **Missal** 224:7

14 I am a man under authority, having soldiers under me: and I say to this man, Go, and he goeth; and to another, Come, and he cometh; and to my servant, Do this, and he doeth it.
St Matthew ch. 8, v. 9

15 But the children of the kingdom shall be cast out into outer darkness: there shall be weeping and gnashing of teeth.
St Matthew ch. 8, v. 12

16 The foxes have holes, and the birds of the air have nests; but the Son of man hath not where to lay his head.
St Matthew ch. 8, v. 20

17 Let the dead bury their dead.
St Matthew ch. 8, v. 22

18 Why eateth your Master with publicans and sinners?
St Matthew ch. 9, v. 11

19 They that be whole need not a physician, but they that are sick.
St Matthew ch. 9, v. 12

20 I am not come to call the righteous, but sinners to repentance.
St Matthew ch. 9, v. 13

21 Neither do men put new wine into old bottles.
St Matthew ch. 9, v. 17

22 Thy faith hath made thee whole.
St Matthew ch. 9, v. 22

23 The maid is not dead, but sleepeth.
St Matthew ch. 9, v. 24

24 When ye depart out of that house or city, shake off the dust of your feet.
St Matthew ch. 10, v. 14

25 Be ye therefore wise as serpents, and harmless as doves.
St Matthew ch. 10, v. 16

26 Are not two sparrows sold for a farthing? and one of them shall not fall on the ground without your Father.
The very hairs of your head are all numbered.
St Matthew ch. 10, v. 29; cf. **Bible** 46:21

27 I came not to send peace, but a sword.
St Matthew ch. 10, v. 34

28 He that findeth his life shall lose it: and he that loseth his life for my sake shall find it.
St Matthew ch. 10, v. 39

29 Art thou he that should come, or do we look for another?
St Matthew ch. 11, v. 3

30 What went ye out into the wilderness to see? A reed shaken with the wind?
St Matthew ch. 11, v. 7

31 Come unto me, all ye that labour and are heavy laden, and I will give you rest.
St Matthew ch. 11, v. 28

32 For my yoke is easy, and my burden is light.
St Matthew ch. 11, v. 28

33 He that is not with me is against me.
St Matthew ch. 12, v. 30 and St Luke ch. 11, v. 23

34 The blasphemy against the Holy Ghost shall not be forgiven unto men.
St Matthew ch. 12, v. 31

35 Behold, a greater than Solomon is here.
St Matthew ch. 12, v. 42

36 Then he saith, I will return into my house from whence I came out; and when he is come, he findeth it empty, swept, and garnished.
St Matthew ch. 12, v. 44

1 Behold, a sower went forth to sow;
And when he sowed, some seeds fell by the
wayside.
St Matthew ch. 13, v. 3

2 The kingdom of heaven is like to a grain of
mustard seed.
St Matthew ch. 13, v. 31

3 The kingdom of heaven is like unto a
merchant man, seeking goodly pearls:
Who, when he had found one pearl of great
price, went and sold all that he had, and
bought it.
St Matthew ch. 13, v. 45

4 A prophet is not without honour, save in his
own country, and in his own house.
St Matthew ch. 13, v. 57

5 Be of good cheer; it is I; be not afraid.
St Matthew ch. 14, v. 27

6 O thou of little faith, wherefore didst thou
doubt?
St Matthew ch. 14, v. 31

7 If the blind lead the blind, both shall fall
into the ditch.
St Matthew ch. 15, v. 14

8 The dogs eat of the crumbs which fall from
their masters' table.
St Matthew ch. 15, v. 27

9 Can ye not discern the signs of the times?
St Matthew ch. 16, v. 3

10 Thou art Peter, and upon this rock I will
build my church; and the gates of hell shall
not prevail against it.
St Matthew ch. 16, v. 18

11 Get thee behind me, Satan.
St Matthew ch. 16, v. 23

12 If ye have faith as a grain of mustard seed,
ye shall say unto this mountain, Remove
hence to yonder place; and it shall remove.
St Matthew ch. 17, v. 20

13 Except ye be converted, and become as little
children, ye shall not enter into the
kingdom of heaven.
St Matthew ch. 18, v. 3

14 Whoso shall receive one such little child in
my name receiveth me.
But whoso shall offend one of these little
ones which believe in me, it were better for
him that a millstone were hanged about his
neck, and that he were drowned in the
depth of the sea.
St Matthew ch. 18, v. 5

15 If thine eye offend thee, pluck it out, and
cast it from thee.
St Matthew ch. 18, v. 9

16 For where two or three are gathered
together in my name, there am I in the
midst of them.
St Matthew ch. 18, v. 20

17 Lord, how oft shall my brother sin against
me, and I forgive him? till seven times?
Jesus saith unto him I say not unto thee,
Until seven times: but Until seventy times
seven.
St Matthew ch. 18, v. 21

18 What therefore God hath joined together,
let not man put asunder.
St Matthew ch. 19, v. 6; cf. **Book of Common
Prayer** 60:20

19 If thou wilt be perfect, go and sell that thou
hast, and give to the poor, and thou shalt
have treasure in heaven.
St Matthew ch. 19, v. 21

20 It is easier for a camel to go through the eye
of a needle, than for a rich man to enter
into the kingdom of God.
St Matthew ch. 19, v. 24. See also St Luke ch. 18,
v. 24

21 With God all things are possible.
St Matthew ch. 19, v. 26

22 But many that are first shall be last; and the
last shall be first.
St Matthew ch. 19, v. 30

23 The burden and heat of the day.
St Matthew ch. 20, v. 12

24 I will give unto this last, even as unto thee.
St Matthew ch. 20, v. 14

25 It is written, My house shall be called the
house of prayer; but ye have made it a den
of thieves.
St Matthew ch. 21, v. 13; cf. **Bible** 40:19

26 For many are called, but few are chosen.
St Matthew ch. 22, v. 14

27 Render therefore unto Caesar the things
which are Caesar's; and unto God the things
that are God's.
St Matthew ch. 22, v. 21

28 For in the resurrection they neither marry,
nor are given in marriage.
St Matthew ch. 22, v. 30

29 Thou shalt love the Lord thy God with all
thy heart, and with all thy soul, and with all
thy mind.
This is the first and great commandment.
And the second is like unto it, Thou shalt
love thy neighbour as thyself.
St Matthew ch. 22, v. 38; cf. **Bible** 34:22

30 Woe unto you, scribes and Pharisees,
hypocrites!
St Matthew ch. 23, v. 23

31 Ye blind guides, which strain at a gnat, and
swallow a camel.
St Matthew ch. 23, v. 24

32 Ye are like unto whited sepulchres.
St Matthew ch. 23, v. 27

33 Ye shall hear of wars and rumours of wars.
St Matthew ch. 24, v. 6

34 For nation shall rise against nation, and
kingdom against kingdom.
St Matthew ch. 24, v. 7

35 The abomination of desolation, spoken of
by Daniel the prophet
referring to Daniel ch. 12, v. 11
St Matthew ch. 24, v. 15

1 Wheresoever the carcase is, there will the eagles be gathered together.
St Matthew ch. 24, v. 28

2 Heaven and earth shall pass away, but my words shall not pass away.
St Matthew ch. 24, v. 35

3 One shall be taken, and the other left.
St Matthew ch. 24, v. 40

4 Watch therefore: for ye know not what hour your Lord doth come.
St Matthew ch. 24, v. 42

5 Well done, thou good and faithful servant.
St Matthew ch. 25, v. 21

6 Lord, I knew thee that thou art an hard man, reaping where thou hast not sown, and gathering where thou hast not strawed.
St Matthew ch. 25, v. 24

7 Unto every one that hath shall be given, and he shall have abundance: but from him that hath not shall be taken away even that which he hath.
St Matthew ch. 25, v. 29

8 And he shall set the sheep on his right hand, but the goats on the left.
St Matthew ch. 25, v. 33

9 I was a stranger, and ye took me in:
St Matthew ch. 25, v. 35

10 Inasmuch as ye have done it unto one of the least of these my brethren, ye have done it unto me.
St Matthew ch. 25, v. 40

11 And they covenanted with him [Judas Iscariot] for thirty pieces of silver.
St Matthew ch. 26, v. 15

12 It had been good for that man if he had not been born.
St Matthew ch. 26, v. 24

13 Jesus took bread, and blessed it, and brake it, and gave it to the disciples, and said, Take, eat; this is my body.
St Matthew ch. 26, v. 26

14 This night, before the cock crow, thou shalt deny me thrice.
to St Peter
St Matthew ch. 26, v. 34

15 If it be possible, let this cup pass from me.
St Matthew ch. 26, v. 39

16 What, could ye not watch with me one hour?
St Matthew ch. 26, v. 40

17 Watch and pray, that ye enter not into temptation: the spirit indeed is willing but the flesh is weak.
St Matthew ch. 26, v. 41

18 All they that take the sword shall perish with the sword.
St Matthew ch. 26, v. 52

19 He [Pilate] took water, and washed his hands before the multitude, saying, I am innocent of the blood of this just person: see ye to it.
St Matthew ch. 27, v. 24

20 He saved others; himself he cannot save.
St Matthew ch. 27, v. 42

21 Eli, Eli, lama sabachthani? . . . My God, my God, why hast thou forsaken me?
St Matthew ch. 27, v. 46

22 And, lo, I am with you alway, even unto the end of the world.
St Matthew ch. 28, v. 20

St Mark

23 The sabbath was made for man, and not man for the sabbath.
St Mark ch. 2, v. 27

24 How can Satan cast out Satan?
St Mark ch. 3, v. 23

25 If a house be divided against itself, that house cannot stand.
St Mark ch. 3, v. 25; cf. **Lincoln** 199:6

26 He that hath ears to hear, let him hear.
St Mark ch. 4, v. 9

27 My name is Legion: for we are many.
St Mark ch. 5, v. 9

28 For what shall it profit a man, if he shall gain the whole world, and lose his own soul?
St Mark ch. 8, v. 36; cf. **Bolt** 57:17

29 Lord, I believe; help thou mine unbelief.
St Mark ch. 9, v. 24

30 Suffer the little children to come unto me, and forbid them not: for of such is the kingdom of God.
St Mark ch. 10, v. 14

31 Go ye into all the world, and preach the gospel to every creature.
St Mark ch. 16, v. 15

St Luke

32 Hail, thou that art highly favoured, the Lord is with thee: blessed art thou among women.
the angel to the Virgin Mary
St Luke ch. 1, v. 28

33 And Mary said,
My soul doth magnify the Lord,
And my spirit hath rejoiced in God my Saviour.
For he hath regarded the low estate of his handmaiden: for, behold, from henceforth all generations shall call me blessed.
known as the Magnificat; beginning 'Tell out my soul, the greatness of the Lord' in New English Bible
St Luke ch. 1, v. 46; cf. **Bible** 53:7

34 He hath shewed strength with his arm; he hath scattered the proud in the imagination of their hearts.
He hath put down the mighty from their seats, and exalted them of low degree.
He hath filled the hungry with good things; and the rich he hath sent empty away.
the Magnificat
St Luke ch. 1, v. 51

1 To give light to them that sit in darkness and in the shadow of death, to guide our feet into the way of peace.
St Luke ch. 1, v. 79

2 And it came to pass in those days, that there went out a decree from Caesar Augustus, that all the world should be taxed.
St Luke ch. 2, v. 1

3 She brought forth her firstborn son, and wrapped him in swaddling clothes, and laid him in a manger; because there was no room for them in the inn.
And there were in the same country shepherds abiding in the field, keeping watch over their flock by night.
And, lo, the angel of the Lord came upon them, and the glory of the Lord shone round about them: and they were sore afraid.
St Luke ch. 2, v. 7

4 Behold, I bring you good tidings of great joy.
the angel to the shepherds
St Luke ch. 2, v. 10

5 Glory to God in the highest, and on earth peace, good will toward men.
the angels to the shepherds
St Luke ch. 2, v. 14; cf. **Missal** 223:28

6 But Mary kept all these things, and pondered them in her heart.
St Luke ch. 2, v. 19

7 Lord, now lettest thou thy servant depart in peace, according to thy word.
said by Simeon
St Luke ch. 2, v. 29; cf. **Bible** 53:8

8 Wist ye not that I must be about my Father's business?
St Luke ch. 2, v. 49

9 Physician, heal thyself.
St Luke ch. 4, v. 23

10 Love your enemies, do good to them which hate you.
St Luke ch. 6, v. 27

11 Give, and it shall be given unto you; good measure, pressed down, and shaken together, and running over, shall men give into your bosom.
St Luke ch. 6, v. 38

12 Her sins, which are many, are forgiven; for she loved much.
St Luke ch. 7, v. 47

13 No man, having put his hand to the plough, and looking back, is fit for the kingdom of God.
St Luke ch. 9, v. 62

14 For the labourer is worthy of his hire.
St Luke ch. 10, v. 7

15 A certain man went down from Jerusalem to Jericho, and fell among thieves.
St Luke ch. 10, v. 30

16 He passed by on the other side.
St Luke ch. 10, v. 31

17 Go, and do thou likewise.
St Luke ch. 10, v. 37

18 But Martha was cumbered about much serving.
St Luke ch. 10, v. 40

19 Mary hath chosen that good part.
St Luke ch. 10, v. 42

20 No man, when he hath lighted a candle, putteth it in a secret place, neither under a bushel, but on a candlestick, that they which come in may see the light.
St Luke ch. 11, v. 33

21 Are not five sparrows sold for two farthings, and not one of them is forgotten before God?
St Luke ch. 12, v. 6; cf. **Bible** 43:26

22 Soul, thou hast much goods laid up for many years; take thine ease, eat, drink, and be merry.
St Luke ch. 12, v. 19; cf. **Bible** 38:24, 39:27

23 Thou fool, this night thy soul shall be required of thee.
St Luke ch. 12, v. 20

24 Friend, go up higher.
St Luke ch. 14, v. 10

25 For whosoever exalteth himself shall be abased; and he that humbleth himself shall be exalted.
St Matthew ch. 23, v. 12 is similar
St Luke ch. 14, v. 11

26 I have married a wife, and therefore I cannot come.
St Luke ch. 14, v. 20

27 Bring in hither the poor, and the maimed, and the halt, and the blind.
St Luke ch. 14, v. 21

28 Go out into the highways and hedges, and compel them to come in.
St Luke ch. 14, v. 23

29 Leave the ninety and nine in the wilderness.
St Luke ch. 15, v. 4

30 Rejoice with me; for I have found my sheep which was lost.
St Luke ch. 15, v. 6

31 Joy shall be in heaven over one sinner that repenteth, more than over ninety and nine just persons, which need no repentance.
St Luke ch. 15, v. 7

32 There wasted his substance with riotous living.
St Luke ch. 15, v. 13

33 I will arise and go to my father, and will say unto him, Father, I have sinned against heaven, and before thee,
And am no more worthy to be called thy son: make me as one of thy hired servants.
St Luke ch. 15, v. 18

34 Bring hither the fatted calf, and kill it.
St Luke ch. 15, v. 23

35 This my son was dead, and is alive again; he was lost, and is found.
St Luke ch. 15, v. 24

36 The children of this world are in their generation wiser than the children of light.
St Luke ch. 16, v. 8

1 Make to yourselves friends of the mammon of unrighteousness.
St Luke ch. 16, v. 9

2 He that is faithful in that which is least is faithful also in much.
St Luke ch. 16, v. 10

3 The crumbs which fell from the rich man's table.
St Luke ch. 16, v. 21

4 Between us and you there is a great gulf fixed.
St Luke ch. 16, v. 26

5 The kingdom of God is within you.
St Luke ch. 17, v. 21

6 Remember Lot's wife.
St Luke ch. 17, v. 32

7 God, I thank thee, that I am not as other men are.
St Luke ch. 18, v. 11

8 God be merciful to me a sinner.
St Luke ch. 18, v. 13

9 He shall show you a large upper room furnished.
St Luke ch. 22, v. 12

10 Not my will, but thine, be done.
St Luke ch. 22, v. 42

11 Father, forgive them: for they know not what they do.
St Luke ch. 23, v. 34

12 Lord, remember me when thou comest into thy kingdom.
said by the Penitent Thief
St Luke ch. 23, v. 42

13 To day shalt thou be with me in paradise.
to the Penitent Thief
St Luke ch. 23, v. 43

14 Father, into thy hands I commend my spirit.
St Luke ch. 23, v. 46; cf. **Book of Common Prayer** 61:12

St John
15 In the beginning was the Word, and the Word was with God, and the Word was God.
St John ch. 1, v. 1

16 All things were made by him; and without him was not any thing made that was made.
St John ch. 1, v. 3

17 And the light shineth in darkness; and the darkness comprehended it not.
St John ch. 1, v. 5

18 There was a man sent from God, whose name was John.
St John ch. 1, v. 6

19 He was not that Light, but was sent to bear witness of that Light.
That was the true Light, which lighteth every man that cometh into the world.
St John ch. 1, v. 8

20 He was in the world, and the world was made by him, and the world knew him not.
He came unto his own, and his own received him not.
St John ch. 1, v. 10

21 And the Word was made flesh, and dwelt among us, (and we beheld his glory, the glory as of the only begotten of the Father), full of grace and truth.
St John ch. 1, v. 14; cf. **Missal** 224:9

22 He it is, who coming after me is preferred before me, whose shoe's latchet I am not worthy to unloose.
said by St John the Baptist
St John ch. 1, v. 27

23 Behold the Lamb of God, which taketh away the sin of the world.
St John ch. 1, v. 29; cf. **Missal** 224:6

24 Can there any good thing come out of Nazareth?
St John ch. 1, v. 46

25 Behold an Israelite indeed, in whom is no guile!
St John ch. 1, v. 47

26 Woman, what have I to do with thee? mine hour is not yet come.
St John ch. 2, v. 4

27 The wind bloweth where it listeth, and thou hearest the sound thereof, but canst not tell whence it cometh, and whither it goeth.
St John ch. 3, v. 8

28 God so loved the world, that he gave his only begotten Son, that whosoever believeth in him should not perish, but have everlasting life.
St John ch. 3, v. 16

29 Except ye see signs and wonders, ye will not believe.
St John ch. 4, v. 48

30 Rise, take up thy bed, and walk.
St John ch. 5, v. 8

31 I am the bread of life: he that cometh to me shall never hunger; and he that believeth on me shall never thirst.
St John ch. 6, v. 35

32 Verily, verily, I say unto you, He that believeth on me hath everlasting life.
St John ch. 6, v. 47

33 And the scribes and the Pharisees brought unto him a woman taken in adultery.
St John ch. 8, v. 3

34 He that is without sin among you, let him first cast a stone at her.
St John ch. 8, v. 7

35 Neither do I condemn thee: go, and sin no more.
St John ch. 8, v. 11

36 And ye shall know the truth, and the truth shall make you free.
St John ch. 8, v. 32

37 I am the door.
St John ch. 10, v. 9

38 I am the good shepherd: the good shepherd giveth his life for the sheep.
St John ch. 10, v. 11

39 I am the resurrection, and the life.
St John ch. 11, v. 25

1 Jesus wept.
St John ch. 11, v. 35

2 It is expedient for us, that one man should die for the people.
said by Caiaphas
St John ch. 11, v. 50

3 The poor always ye have with you.
St John ch. 12, v. 8

4 Let not your heart be troubled.
St John ch. 14, v. 1

5 In my Father's house are many mansions . . . I go to prepare a place for you.
St John ch. 14, v. 2

6 I am the way, the truth, and the life: no man cometh unto the Father, but by me.
St John ch. 14, v. 6

7 Peace I leave with you, my peace I give unto you: not as the world giveth, give I unto you.
St John ch. 14, v. 27

8 Greater love hath no man than this, that a man lay down his life for his friends.
St John ch. 15, v. 13; cf. **Thorpe** 317:24

9 Pilate saith unto him, What is truth?
St John ch. 18, v. 38; cf. **Bacon** 21:30

10 Now Barabbas was a robber.
St John ch. 18, v. 40; cf. **Campbell** 81:4

11 A place called the place of a skull, which is called in the Hebrew Golgotha.
St John ch. 19, v. 17

12 What I have written I have written.
said by Pilate
St John ch. 19, v. 22

13 Woman, behold thy son! . . .
Behold thy mother!
to the Virgin Mary and, traditionally, St John
St John ch. 19, v. 26

14 I thirst.
St John ch. 19, v. 28

15 It is finished.
St John ch. 19, v. 30; cf. **Bible** 53:12

16 The first day of the week cometh Mary Magdalene early, when it was yet dark, unto the sepulchre, and seeth the stone taken away from the sepulchre.
St John ch. 20, v. 1

17 They have taken away my Lord, and I know not where they have laid him.
said by St Mary Magdalene
St John ch. 20, v. 13

18 Jesus saith unto her, Woman, why weepest thou? whom seekest thou? She supposing him to be the gardener saith unto him, Sir, if thou have borne him hence, tell me where thou hast laid him, and I will take him away.
St John ch. 20, v. 15

19 Touch me not.
to St Mary Magdalene
St John ch. 20, v. 17; cf. **Bible** 53:13

20 Except I shall see in his hands the print of the nails, and put my finger into the print

of the nails, and thrust my hand into his side, I will not believe.
said by St Thomas
St John ch. 20, v. 25

21 Blessed are they that have not seen, and yet have believed.
St John ch. 20, v. 29

22 Feed my sheep.
St John ch. 21, v. 16

Acts of the Apostles

23 Ye men of Galilee, why stand ye gazing up into heaven?
Acts of the Apostles ch. 1, v. 11

24 And suddenly there came a sound from heaven as of a rushing mighty wind, and it filled all the house where they were sitting. And there appeared unto them cloven tongues like as of fire.
Acts of the Apostles ch. 2, v. 2

25 Thy money perish with thee.
to Simon Magus
Acts of the Apostles ch. 8, v. 20

26 Saul, Saul, why persecutest thou me?
Acts of the Apostles ch. 9, v. 4

27 It is hard for thee to kick against the pricks.
Acts of the Apostles ch. 9, v. 5

28 The street which is called Straight.
Acts of the Apostles ch. 9, v. 11

29 Dorcas: this woman was full of good works.
Acts of the Apostles ch. 9, v. 36

30 God is no respecter of persons.
Acts of the Apostles ch. 10, v. 34

31 What must I do to be saved?
Acts of the Apostles ch. 16, v. 30

32 Certain lewd fellows of the baser sort.
Acts of the Apostles ch. 17, v. 5

33 Those that have turned the world upside down are come hither also.
Acts of the Apostles ch. 17, v. 6

34 I found an altar with this inscription, TO THE UNKNOWN GOD.
Acts of the Apostles ch. 17, v. 22

35 For in him we live, and move, and have our being.
Acts of the Apostles ch. 17, v. 28

36 We have not so much as heard whether there be any Holy Ghost.
Acts of the Apostles ch. 19, v. 2

37 Great is Diana of the Ephesians.
Acts of the Apostles ch. 19, v. 34

38 It is more blessed to give than to receive.
Acts of the Apostles ch. 20, v. 35

39 But Paul said, I am a man which am a Jew of Tarsus, a city in Cilicia, a citizen of no mean city.
Acts of the Apostles ch. 21, v. 39

40 And the chief captain answered, With a great sum obtained I this freedom. And Paul said, But I was free born.
Acts of the Apostles ch. 22, v. 28

1 I appeal unto Caesar.
  Acts of the Apostles ch. 25, v. 11

2 Hast thou appealed unto Caesar? unto Caesar shalt thou go.
  Acts of the Apostles ch. 25, v. 12

3 Paul, thou art beside thyself; much learning doth make thee mad.
  Acts of the Apostles ch. 26, v. 24

4 Almost thou persuadest me to be a Christian.
  Acts of the Apostles ch. 26, v. 28

Romans

5 Patient continuance in well doing.
  Romans ch. 2, v. 7

6 A law unto themselves.
  Romans ch. 2, v. 14

7 Let us do evil, that good may come.
  Romans ch. 3, v. 8

8 For where no law is, there is no transgression.
  Romans ch. 4, v. 15

9 Who against hope believed in hope, that he might become the father of many nations.
  of Abraham
  Romans ch. 4, v. 18

10 Shall we continue in sin, that grace may abound?
  Romans ch. 6, v. 1

11 We also should walk in newness of life.
  Romans ch. 6, v. 4

12 Christ being raised from the dead dieth no more; death hath no more dominion over him.
  Romans ch. 6, v. 9; cf. **Thomas** 316:2

13 The wages of sin is death.
  Romans ch. 6, v. 23

14 I had not known sin, but by the law.
  Romans ch. 7, v. 7

15 For the good that I would I do not: but the evil which I would not, that I do.
  Romans ch. 7, v. 19; cf. **Ovid** 238:15

16 All things work together for good to them that love God.
  Romans ch. 8, v. 28

17 If God be for us, who can be against us?
  Romans ch. 8, v. 31

18 For I am persuaded, that neither death, nor life, nor angels, nor principalities, nor powers, nor things present, nor things to come,
  Nor height, nor depth, nor any other creature, shall be able to separate us from the love of God, which is in Christ Jesus our Lord.
  Romans ch. 8, v. 38

19 Present your bodies a living sacrifice, holy, acceptable unto God.
  Romans ch. 12, v. 1

20 Vengeance is mine; I will repay, saith the Lord.
  Romans ch. 12, v. 19

21 The night is far spent, the day is at hand: let us therefore cast off the works of darkness, and let us put on the armour of light.
  Romans ch. 13, v. 12

I Corinthians

22 For the Jews require a sign, and the Greeks seek after wisdom.
  I Corinthians ch. 1, v. 22

23 We preach Christ crucified, unto the Jews a stumbling-block, and unto the Greeks foolishness.
  I Corinthians ch. 1, v. 23

24 Absent in body, but present in spirit.
  I Corinthians ch. 5, v. 3

25 Know ye not that a little leaven leaveneth the whole lump?
  I Corinthians ch. 5, v. 6

26 It is better to marry than to burn.
  I Corinthians ch. 7, v. 9

27 I am made all things to all men.
  I Corinthians ch. 9, v. 22

28 For the earth is the Lord's and the fulness thereof.
  I Corinthians ch. 10, v. 26; cf. **Book of Common Prayer** 61:8

29 Doth not even nature itself teach you, that if a man have long hair, it is a shame unto him?
  But if a woman have long hair, it is a glory to her.
  I Corinthians ch. 11, v. 14

30 Though I speak with the tongues of men and of angels, and have not charity, I am become as sounding brass, or a tinkling cymbal.
  And though I have the gift of prophecy, and understand all mysteries, and all knowledge; and though I have all faith; so that I could remove mountains; and have not charity, I am nothing.
  I Corinthians ch. 13, v. 1

31 Charity suffereth long, and is kind; charity envieth not; charity vaunteth not itself, is not puffed up . . .
  Beareth all things, believeth all things, hopeth all things, endureth all things.
  Charity never faileth
  I Corinthians ch. 13, v. 4

32 For we know in part, and we prophesy in part.
  I Corinthians ch. 13, v. 9

33 When I was a child, I spake as a child, I understood as a child, I thought as a child: but when I became a man, I put away childish things.
  For now we see through a glass, darkly; but then face to face: now I know in part; but then shall I know even as also I am known.
  And now abideth faith, hope, charity, these three; but the greatest of these is charity.
  I Corinthians ch. 13, v. 11

34 Let all things be done decently and in order.
  I Corinthians ch. 14, v. 40

1 Last of all he was seen of me also, as of one
born out of due time.
For I am the least of the apostles, that am
not meet to be called an apostle, because I
persecuted the church of God.
But by the grace of God I am what I am.

I Corinthians ch. 15, v. 8

2 But now is Christ risen from the dead, and
become the first fruits of them that slept.
For since by man came death, by man came
also the resurrection of the dead.
For as in Adam all die, even so in Christ
shall all be made alive.

I Corinthians ch. 15, v. 20

3 The last enemy that shall be destroyed is
death.

I Corinthians ch. 15, v. 26

4 If after the manner of men I have fought
with beasts at Ephesus, what advantageth it
me, if the dead rise not? let us eat and
drink; for to morrow we die.

I Corinthians ch. 15, v. 32; cf. **Bible** 38:24,
39:27, 46:22

5 Evil communications corrupt good
manners.

I Corinthians ch. 15, v. 33

6 The first man is of the earth, earthy.

I Corinthians ch. 15, v. 47

7 Behold, I shew you a mystery; We shall not
all sleep, but we shall all be changed,
In a moment, in the twinkling of an eye, at
the last trump; for the trumpet shall sound,
and the dead shall be raised incorruptible,
and we shall be changed.

I Corinthians ch. 15, v. 51

8 O death, where is thy sting? O grave, where
is thy victory?

I Corinthians ch. 15, v. 55

II Corinthians

9 The letter killeth, but the spirit giveth life.

II Corinthians ch. 3, v. 5

10 We have a building of God, an house not
made with hands, eternal in the heavens.

II Corinthians ch. 5, v. 1; cf. **Browning** 69:24

11 God loveth a cheerful giver.

II Corinthians ch. 9, v. 7

12 For ye suffer fools gladly, seeing ye
yourselves are wise.

II Corinthians ch. 11, v. 19

13 There was given to me a thorn in the flesh,
the messenger of Satan to buffet me.

II Corinthians ch. 12, v. 7

Galatians

14 Ye are fallen from grace.

Galatians ch. 5, v. 4

15 Be not deceived; God is not mocked: for
whatsoever a man soweth, that shall he also
reap.

Galatians ch. 6, v. 7

16 Let us not be weary in well doing: for in due
season we shall reap, if we faint not.

*'Be not weary in well doing' in II Thessalonians ch.
3, v. 13*

Galatians ch. 6, v. 9

Ephesians

17 The unsearchable riches of Christ.

Ephesians ch. 3, v. 8

18 We are members one of another.

Ephesians ch. 4, v. 25

19 Be ye angry and sin not: let not the sun go
down upon your wrath.

Ephesians ch. 4, v. 26

20 See then that ye walk circumspectly, not as
fools, but as wise,
Redeeming the time, because the days are
evil.

Ephesians ch. 5, v. 15

21 Ye fathers, provoke not your children to
wrath.

Ephesians ch. 6, v. 4

22 Put on the whole armour of God.

Ephesians ch. 6, v. 11

23 For we wrestle not against flesh and blood,
but against principalities, against powers,
against the rulers of the darkness of this
world, against spiritual wickedness in high
places.
Wherefore take unto you the whole armour
of God, that ye may be able to withstand in
the evil day, and having done all, to stand.
Stand therefore, having your loins girt
about with truth, and having on the
breastplate of righteousness.

Ephesians ch. 6, v. 12

Philippians

24 At the name of Jesus every knee should
bow, of things in heaven, and things in
earth, and things under the earth.

Philippians ch. 2, v. 10; cf. **Noel** 234:18

25 Work out your own salvation with fear and
trembling.

Philippians ch. 2, v. 12

26 Rejoice in the Lord alway: and again I say,
Rejoice.

Philippians ch. 4, v. 4

27 The peace of God, which passeth all
understanding, shall keep your hearts and
minds through Christ Jesus.

Philippians ch. 4, v. 7; cf. **James I** 170:11

28 Whatsoever things are true, whatsoever
things are honest, whatsoever things are
just, whatsoever things are pure,
whatsoever things are lovely, whatsoever
things are of good report; if there be any
virtue and if there be any praise, think on
these things.

Philippians ch. 4, v. 8

29 I can do all things through Christ which
strengtheneth me.

Philippians ch. 4, v. 13

Colossians

1 For by him were all things created, that are in heaven, and that are in earth, visible and invisible, whether they be thrones, or dominions, or principalities, or powers.
Colossians ch. 1, v. 16; cf. **Milton** 222:11

2 Husbands, love your wives, and be not bitter against them.
Colossians ch. 3, v. 19

3 Let your speech be alway with grace, seasoned with salt.
Colossians ch. 4, v. 6

I Thessalonians

4 Remembering without ceasing your work of faith and labour of love.
I Thessalonians ch. 1, v. 3

5 Prove all things; hold fast that which is good.
1 Thessalonians ch. 5, v. 21

II Thessalonians

6 If any would not work, neither should he eat.
II Thessalonians ch. 3, v. 10

I Timothy

7 Sinners; of whom I am chief.
I Timothy ch. 1, v. 15

8 Refuse profane and old wives' fables, and exercise thyself rather unto godliness.
I Timothy ch. 4, v. 7

9 Use a little wine for thy stomach's sake.
I Timothy ch. 5, v. 23

10 For we brought nothing into this world, and it is certain we can carry nothing out.
I Timothy ch. 6, v. 7

11 The love of money is the root of all evil.
I Timothy ch. 6, v. 10

12 Fight the good fight of faith, lay hold on eternal life.
I Timothy ch. 6, v. 12; cf. **Monsell** 225:22

II Timothy

13 I have fought a good fight, I have finished my course, I have kept the faith.
II Timothy ch. 4, v. 7

Titus

14 Unto the pure all things are pure.
Titus ch. 1, v. 15; cf. **Lawrence** 194:11

Hebrews

15 It is a fearful thing to fall into the hands of the living God.
Hebrews ch. 10, v. 31

16 Wherefore seeing we also are compassed about with so great a cloud of witnesses, let us lay aside every weight, and the sin which doth so easily beset us, and let us run with patience the race that is set before us,
Hebrews ch. 12, v. 1

17 Whom the Lord loveth he chasteneth.
Hebrews ch. 12, v. 6

18 Be not forgetful to entertain strangers: for thereby some have entertained angels unawares.
Hebrews ch. 13, v. 2

19 Jesus Christ the same yesterday, and to day, and for ever.
Hebrews ch. 13, v. 8

20 For here have we no continuing city, but we seek one to come.
Hebrews ch. 13, v. 14

James

21 Faith without works is dead.
James ch. 2, v. 20

22 The tongue can no man tame; it is an unruly evil.
James ch. 3, v. 8

23 Ye have heard of the patience of Job.
James ch. 5, v. 11

24 Let your yea be yea; and your nay, nay.
James ch. 5, v. 12

I Peter

25 All flesh is as grass, and all the glory of man as the flower of grass. The grass withereth, and the flower thereof falleth away.
I Peter ch. 1, v. 24; cf. **Bible** 40:8

26 But ye are a chosen generation, a royal priesthood, an holy nation, a peculiar people.
I Peter ch. 2, v. 9

27 Honour all men. Love the brotherhood. Fear God. Honour the king.
I Peter ch. 2, v. 17

28 Giving honour unto the wife, as unto the weaker vessel.
I Peter ch. 3, v. 7

29 Charity shall cover the multitude of sins.
I Peter ch. 4, v. 8

30 Be sober, be vigilant; because your adversary the devil, as a roaring lion, walketh about, seeking whom he may devour.
I Peter ch. 5, v. 8

II Peter

31 The dog is turned to his own vomit again.
II Peter ch. 2, v. 22

I John

32 If we say that we have no sin, we deceive ourselves, and the truth is not in us.
I John ch. 1, v. 8

33 He that loveth not knoweth not God; for God is love.
I John ch. 4, v. 8

34 There is no fear in love; but perfect love casteth out fear.
I John ch. 4, v. 18

35 If a man say, I love God, and hateth his brother, he is a liar: for he that loveth not his brother whom he hath seen, how can he love God whom he hath not seen?
I John ch. 4, v. 20

III John

1 He that doeth good is of God: but he that doeth evil hath not seen God.
III John v. 11

Revelation

2 The seven churches which are in Asia.
Revelation ch. 1, v. 4

3 I am Alpha and Omega, the beginning and the ending, saith the Lord.
Revelation ch. 1, v. 8

4 I have somewhat against thee, because thou hast left thy first love.
Revelation ch. 2, v. 4

5 Be thou faithful unto death, and I will give thee a crown of life.
Revelation ch. 2, v. 10

6 Because thou art lukewarm, and neither cold nor hot, I will spew thee out of my mouth.
Revelation ch. 3, v. 16

7 Behold, I stand at the door, and knock.
Revelation ch. 3, v. 20

8 Holy, holy, holy, Lord God Almighty, which was, and is, and is to come.
Revelation ch. 4, v. 8; cf. **Book of Common Prayer** 60:3, **Missal** 224:4

9 And I looked, and behold a pale horse: and his name that sat on him was Death.
Revelation ch. 6, v. 8

10 These are they which came out of great tribulation, and have washed their robes, and made them white in the blood of the Lamb.
Revelation ch. 7, v. 14; cf. **Lindsay** 199:16

11 God shall wipe away all tears from their eyes.
Revelation ch. 7, v. 17

12 And when he had opened the seventh seal, there was silence in heaven about the space of half an hour.
Revelation ch. 8, v. 1

13 And there appeared a great wonder in heaven; a woman clothed with the sun, and the moon under her feet, and upon her head a crown of twelve stars.
Revelation ch. 12, v. 1

14 And there was war in heaven: Michael and his angels fought against the dragon; and the dragon fought and his angels.
Revelation ch. 12, v. 7

15 And that no man might buy or sell, save he that had the mark, or the name of the beast, or the number of his name.
Revelation ch. 13, v. 17

16 Let him that hath understanding count the number of the beast: for it is the number of a man; and his number is Six hundred threescore and six.
Revelation ch. 13, v. 18

17 Babylon is fallen, is fallen, that great city.
Revelation ch. 14, v. 8

18 And the smoke of their torment ascendeth up for ever and ever: and they have no rest day or night, who worship the beast and his image.
Revelation ch. 14, v. 11

19 Behold, I come as a thief.
Revelation ch. 16, v. 15

20 And he gathered them together into a place called in the Hebrew tongue Armageddon.
Revelation ch. 16, v. 16

21 And upon her forehead was a name written, MYSTERY, BABYLON THE GREAT, THE MOTHER OF HARLOTS AND ABOMINATIONS OF THE EARTH.
Revelation ch. 17, v. 5

22 And I saw a great white throne.
Revelation ch. 20, v. 11

23 And the sea gave up the dead which were in it.
Revelation ch. 20, v. 13

24 And I saw a new heaven and a new earth: for the first heaven and the first earth were passed away; and there was no more sea. And I John saw the holy city, new Jerusalem, coming down from God out of heaven, prepared as a bride adorned for her husband.
Revelation ch. 21, v. 1

25 And God shall wipe away all tears from their eyes; and there shall be no more death, neither sorrow, nor crying, neither shall there be any more pain: for the former things are passed away.
And he that sat upon the throne said, Behold, I make all things new.
Revelation ch. 21, v. 4; cf. **Pound** 250:6

26 I will give unto him that is athirst of the fountain of the water of life freely.
Revelation ch. 21, v. 6

27 And the leaves of the tree were for the healing of the nations.
Revelation ch. 22, v. 2

28 Amen. Even so, come, Lord Jesus.
Revelation ch. 22, v. 20

Vulgate

29 *Dominus illuminatio mea, et salus mea, quem timebo?*
The Lord is the source of my light and my safety, so whom shall I fear?
Psalm 26, v. 1; cf. **Anonymous** 12:11

30 *Cantate Domino canticum novum, quia mirabilia fecit.*
Sing to the Lord a new song, because he has done marvellous things.
Psalm 97, v. 1 (Psalm 98, v. 1 in the Authorized Version); cf. **Book of Common Prayer** 62:21

31 *Jubilate Deo, omnis terra; servite Domino in laetitia.*
Sing joyfully to God, all the earth; serve the Lord with gladness.
Psalm 99, v. 2 (Psalm 100, v. 2 in the Authorized Version); cf. **Book of Common Prayer** 62:22

32 *Beatus vir qui timet Dominum, in mandatis ejus volet nimis!*

Happy is the man who fears the Lord, who is only too willing to follow his orders.

Psalm 111, v. 1 (Psalm 112, v. 1 in the Authorized Version)

1 *Non nobis, Domine, non nobis; sed nomini tuo da gloriam.*

Not unto us, Lord, not unto us; but to thy name give glory.

Psalm 113 (second part), v. 1 (Psalm 115, v. 1 in the Authorized Version); cf. **Book of Common Prayer** 63:6

2 *Nisi Dominus aedificaverit domum, in vanum laboraverunt qui aedificant eam. Nisi Dominus custodierit civitatem, frustra vigilat qui custodit eam.*

Unless the Lord has built the house, its builders have laboured in vain. Unless the Lord guards the city, the watchman watches in vain.

Psalm 126, v. 1 (Psalm 127, v. 1 in the Authorized Version); cf. **Anonymous** 12:15, **Book of Common Prayer** 63:18

3 *De profundis clamavi ad te, Domine; Domine, exaudi vocem meam.*

Up from the depths I have cried to thee, Lord; Lord, hear my voice.

Psalm 129, v. 1 (Psalm 130, v. 1 in the Authorized Version); cf. **Book of Common Prayer** 63:21

4 *Vanitas vanitatum, dixit Ecclesiastes; vanitas vanitatum, et omnia vanitas.*

Vanity of vanities, said the preacher; vanity of vanities, and everything is vanity.

Ecclesiastes ch. 1, v. 2; cf. **Bible** 38:12

5 *Rorate, coeli, desuper, et nubes pluant Justum; aperiatur terra, et germinet Salvatorem.*

Drop down dew, heavens, from above, and let the clouds rain down righteousness; let the earth be opened, and a saviour spring to life.

Isaiah ch. 45, v. 8

6 *Benedicite, omnia opera Domini, Domino; laudate et superexaltate eum in secula.*

Bless the Lord, all the works of the Lord; praise him and exalt him above all things for ever.

Daniel ch. 3, v. 57; cf. **Book of Common Prayer** 58:15

7 *Magnificat anima mea Dominum; Et exsultavit spiritus meus in Deo salutari meo.*

My soul doth magnify the Lord: and my spirit hath rejoiced in God my Saviour.

St Luke ch. 1, v. 46; cf. **Bible** 45:33

8 *Nunc dimittis servum tuum, Domine, secundum verbum tuum in pace.*

Lord, now lettest thou thy servant depart in peace: according to thy word.

St Luke ch. 2, v. 29; cf. **Bible** 46:7

9 *Pax Vobis.*

Peace be unto you.

St Luke ch. 24, v. 36

10 *Quo vadis?*

Where are you going?

St John ch. 16, v. 5

11 *Ecce homo.*

Behold the man.

St John ch. 19, v. 5

12 *Consummatum est.*

It is achieved.

St John ch. 19, v. 30; cf. **Bible** 48:15

13 *Noli me tangere.*

Do not touch me.

St John ch. 20, v. 17; cf. **Bible** 48:19

14 *Magna est veritas, et praevalet.*

Great is truth, and it prevails.

III Esdras ch. 4, v. 41; cf. **Bible** 41:20, **Brooks** 68:6

Isaac Bickerstaffe 1733–*c*.1808

15 Perhaps it was right to dissemble your love, But—why did you kick me downstairs?

'An Expostulation' (1789)

16 I care for nobody, not I, If no one cares for me.

Love in a Village (a comic opera with music by Thomas Arne, 1762) act 1, sc. 2

E. H. Bickersteth 1825–1906

17 Peace, perfect peace, in this dark world of sin? The Blood of Jesus whispers peace within.

Songs in the House of Pilgrimage (1875) 'Peace, perfect peace'

Ambrose Bierce 1842–*c*.1914

18 ALLIANCE, *n*. In international politics, the union of two thieves who have their hands so deeply inserted in each other's pocket that they cannot separately plunder a third.

The Cynic's Word Book (1906)

19 BATTLE, *n*. A method of untying with the teeth a political knot that would not yield to the tongue.

The Cynic's Word Book (1906)

20 HISTORY, *n*. An account, mostly false, of events, mostly unimportant, which are brought about by rulers, mostly knaves, and soldiers, mostly fools.

The Cynic's Word Book (1906)

21 PEACE, *n*. In international affairs, a period of cheating between two periods of fighting.

The Devil's Dictionary (1911)

Steve Biko 1946–77

22 The liberal must understand that the days of the Noble Savage are gone; that the blacks do not need a go-between in this struggle for their own emancipation. No true liberal should feel any resentment at the growth of black consciousness.

'Black Souls in White Skins?' (written 1970), in *Steve Biko—I Write What I Like* (1978); cf. **Dryden** 116:28

Josh Billings 1818–85

1 Love iz like the meazles; we kant have it bad but onst, and the latter in life we hav it the tuffer it goes with us.
Josh Billings' Wit and Humour (1874)

Maeve Binchy 1940–

2 Those lighting devils that go by the wrong name of innocent children.
The Copper Beech (1992)

3 It's not perfect, but to me on balance Right Now is a lot better than the Good Old Days.
in *Irish Times* 15 November 1997

Laurence Binyon 1869–1943

4 They shall grow not old, as we that are left grow old.
Age shall not weary them, nor the years condemn.
At the going down of the sun and in the morning
We will remember them.
regularly recited as part of the ritual for Remembrance Day parades
'For the Fallen' (1914)

5 Now is the time for the burning of the leaves.
'The Ruins' (1942)

Bion c.325–c.255 BC

6 Boys throw stones at frogs for fun, but the frogs don't die for 'fun', but in sober earnest.
Plutarch *Moralia*

Nigel Birch 1906–81

7 My God! They've shot our fox!
on hearing of the resignation of Hugh Dalton, Labour Chancellor of the Exchequer, after the leak of Budget secrets
comment, 13 November 1947

Lord Birkenhead *see* F. E. Smith

Augustine Birrell 1850–1933

8 That great dust-heap called 'history'.
Obiter Dicta (1884) 'Carlyle'; cf. **Trotsky** 320:3

Harrison Birtwistle 1934–

9 You can't stop. Composing's not voluntary, you know. There's no choice, you're not free. You're landed with an idea and you have responsibility to that idea.
in *Observer* 14 April 1996 'Sayings of the Week'

Elizabeth Bishop 1911–79

10 The armoured cars of dreams, contrived to let us do
so many a dangerous thing.
'Sleeping Standing Up' (1946)

11 I am sorry for people who can't write letters. But I suspect also that you and I . . . love to write them because it's kind of like working without really doing it.
letter to Kit and Ilse Barker, 5 September 1953

Otto von Bismarck 1815–98

12 If the Princess can leave the Englishwoman at home and become a Prussian, then she may be a blessing to the country.
on the marriage of Victoria, Princess Royal, to Prince Frederick William of Prussia
letter, c.1857

13 Politics is the art of the possible.
in conversation with Meyer von Waldeck, 11 August 1867; cf. **Butler** 77:4, **Galbraith** 135:11, **Medawar** 215:19

14 We will not go to Canossa.
during his quarrel with Pope Pius IX regarding papal authority over German subjects, in allusion to the Emperor Henry IV's submission to Pope Gregory VII at Canossa in Modena in 1077
speech to the Reichstag, 14 May 1872

15 Not worth the healthy bones of a single Pomeranian grenadier.
of possible German involvement in the Balkans; cf. **Harris** 152:14
speech to the Reichstag, 5 December 1876

16 Whoever speaks of Europe is wrong, [it is] a geographical concept.
marginal note on a letter from the Russian Chancellor Gorchakov, November 1876; cf. **Metternich** 217:14

17 I do not regard the procuring of peace as a matter in which we should play the role of arbiter between different opinions . . . more that of an honest broker who really wants to press the business forward.
speech to the Reichstag, 19 February 1878

18 This policy cannot succeed through speeches, and shooting-matches, and songs; it can only be carried out through blood and iron.
speech in the Prussian House of Deputies, 28 January 1886

19 If there is ever another war in Europe, it will come out of some damned silly thing in the Balkans.
attributed by Herr Ballen and quoted by Winston S. **Churchill** in the House of Commons, 16 August 1945

Björk 1965–

20 Icelandic peoples were the ones who memorized sagas . . . We were the first rappers of Europe.
attributed, January 1996

James Black 1924–

21 In the culture I grew up in you did your work and you did not put your arm around it to stop other people from looking—you took the earliest possible opportunity to make knowledge available.
on modern scientific research
in *Daily Telegraph* 11 December 1995

Valentine Blacker 1728–1823

1 Put your trust in God, my boys, and keep your powder dry.

*often attributed to Oliver **Cromwell** himself*
'Oliver's Advice' in E. Hayes *Ballads of Ireland* (1856) vol. 1

William Blackstone 1723–80

2 The king never dies.

Commentaries on the Laws of England (1765) bk. 1, ch. 7

3 The royal navy of England hath ever been its greatest defence and ornament; it is its ancient and natural strength; the floating bulwark of the island.

Commentaries on the Laws of England (1765) bk. 1, ch. 13; cf. **Coventry** 101:2

4 That the king can do no wrong, is a necessary and fundamental principle of the English constitution.

Commentaries on the Laws of England (1765) bk. 3, ch. 17

5 It is better that ten guilty persons escape than one innocent suffer.

Commentaries on the Laws of England (1765) bk. 4, ch. 27

Tony Blair 1953–

6 Labour is the party of law and order in Britain today. Tough on crime and tough on the causes of crime.

as Shadow Home Secretary
speech at the Labour Party Conference, 30 September 1993

7 Ask me my three main priorities for Government, and I tell you: education, education and education.

speech at the Labour Party Conference, 1 October 1996

8 We are not the masters. The people are the masters. We are the servants of the people ... What the electorate gives, the electorate can take away.

*addressing Labour MPs on the first day of the new Parliament, 7 May 1997; cf. **Burke** 74:18*
in *Guardian* 8 May 1997

9 She was the People's Princess, and that is how she will stay ... in our hearts and in our memories forever.

*on hearing of the death of **Diana**, Princess of Wales, 31 August 1997*
in *The Times* 1 September 1997

Eubie Blake 1883–1983

10 If I'd known I was gonna live this long, I'd have taken better care of myself.

on reaching the age of 100
in *Observer* 13 February 1983 'Sayings of the Week'

William Blake 1757–1827

11 To see a world in a grain of sand
And a heaven in a wild flower,
Hold infinity in the palm of your hand

And eternity in an hour.
'Auguries of Innocence' (*c*.1803) l. 1

12 A robin red breast in a cage
Puts all Heaven in a rage.
'Auguries of Innocence' (*c*.1803) l. 5

13 A truth that's told with bad intent
Beats all the lies you can invent.
'Auguries of Innocence' (*c*.1803) l. 53

14 The strongest poison ever known
Came from Caesar's laurel crown.
'Auguries of Innocence' (*c*.1803) l. 97

15 The whore and gambler, by the State
Licensed, build that nation's fate.
The harlot's cry from street to street
Shall weave old England's winding sheet.
'Auguries of Innocence' (*c*.1803) l. 113

16 Can wisdom be put in a silver rod?
Or love in a golden bowl?
The Book of Thel (1789) plate i 'Thel's Motto'

17 I am sure this Jesus will not do
Either for Englishman or Jew.
The Everlasting Gospel (*c*.1818) (f) l. 1

18   Near mournful
Ever weeping Paddington.
Jerusalem (1815) 'Chapter 1' (plate 12, l. 27)

19 I give you the end of a golden string;
Only wind it into a ball:
It will lead you in at Heaven's gate,
Built in Jerusalem's wall.
Jerusalem (1815) 'To the Christians' (plate 77) "I give you the end of a golden string"

20 Energy is Eternal Delight.
The Marriage of Heaven and Hell (1790–3) 'The voice of the Devil'

21 The reason Milton wrote in fetters when he wrote of Angels and God, and at liberty when of Devils and Hell, is because he was a true Poet, and of the Devil's party without knowing it.
The Marriage of Heaven and Hell (1790–3) 'The voice of the Devil' (note)

22 The road of excess leads to the palace of wisdom.
The Marriage of Heaven and Hell (1790–3) 'Proverbs of Hell'

23 If the fool would persist in his folly he would become wise.
The Marriage of Heaven and Hell (1790–3) 'Proverbs of Hell'

24 Prisons are built with stones of Law, brothels with bricks of Religion.
The Marriage of Heaven and Hell (1790–3) 'Proverbs of Hell'

25 The tygers of wrath are wiser than the horses of instruction.
The Marriage of Heaven and Hell (1790–3) 'Proverbs of Hell'

26 If the doors of perception were cleansed everything would appear to man as it is, infinite.
The Marriage of Heaven and Hell (1790–3) 'A Memorable Fancy' plate 14

27 And did those feet in ancient time
Walk upon England's mountains green?

And was the holy Lamb of God
On England's pleasant pastures seen?
And did the Countenance Divine
Shine forth upon our clouded hills?
And was Jerusalem builded here
Among these dark Satanic mills?
Bring me my bow of burning gold:
Bring me my arrows of desire:
Bring me my spear: O clouds, unfold!
Bring me my chariot of fire.
I will not cease from mental fight,
Nor shall my sword sleep in my hand,
Till we have built Jerusalem,
In England's green and pleasant land.
  Milton (1804–10) preface 'And did those feet in
  ancient time'

1 The atoms of Democritus
And Newton's particles of light
Are sands upon the Red sea shore,
Where Israel's tents do shine so bright.
  MS Note-Book

2 He who binds to himself a joy
Doth the winged life destroy;
But he who kisses the joy as it flies
Lives in Eternity's sunrise.
  MS Note-Book 'Several Questions
  Answered'—"He who binds to himself a joy"

3 What is it men in women do require?
The lineaments of gratified desire.
What is it women do in men require?
The lineaments of gratified desire.
  MS Note-Book 'Several Questions
  Answered'—"What is it men in women do
  require"

4 Piping down the valleys wild,
Piping songs of pleasant glee,
On a cloud I saw a child
  Songs of Innocence (1789) introduction

5 Your chimneys I sweep, and in soot I sleep.
  Songs of Innocence (1789) 'The Chimney Sweeper'

6 For Mercy has a human heart,
Pity a human face,
And Love, the human form divine,
And Peace, the human dress.
  Songs of Innocence (1789) 'The Divine Image'

7 Then cherish pity, lest you drive an angel
from your door.
  Songs of Innocence (1789) 'Holy Thursday'

8 Little Lamb who made thee?
Dost thou know who made thee?
  Songs of Innocence (1789) 'The Lamb'

9 My mother bore me in the southern wild,
And I am black, but O! my soul is white;
White as an angel is the English child:
But I am black as if bereaved of light.
  Songs of Innocence (1789) 'The Little Black Boy'

10 My mother groaned! my father wept.
Into the dangerous world I leapt:
Helpless, naked, piping loud;
Like a fiend hid in a cloud.
  Songs of Experience (1794) 'Infant Sorrow'

11 I was angry with my friend;
I told my wrath, my wrath did end.
I was angry with my foe:

I told it not, my wrath did grow.
  Songs of Experience (1794) 'A Poison Tree'

12 In the morning glad I see,
My foe outstretched beneath the tree
  Songs of Experience (1794) 'A Poison Tree'

13 O Rose, thou art sick!
The invisible worm
That flies in the night,
In the howling storm:
Has found out thy bed
Of crimson joy:
And his dark secret love
Does thy life destroy.
  Songs of Experience (1794) 'The Sick Rose'

14 Tyger Tyger, burning bright,
In the forests of the night;
What immortal hand or eye,
Could frame thy fearful symmetry?
  Songs of Experience (1794) 'The Tiger'

15 When the stars threw down their spears
And watered heaven with their tears:
Did he smile his work to see?
Did he who made the Lamb make thee?
  Songs of Experience (1794) 'The Tiger'

16 Cruelty has a human heart,
And Jealousy a human face;
Terror the human form divine,
And Secrecy the human dress.
  'A Divine Image'; etched but not included in
  Songs of Experience (1794); cf. **Blake** 56:6

Susanna Blamire 1747–94

17 I've gotten a rock, I've gotten a reel,
I've gotten a wee bit spinning-wheel;
An' by the whirling rim I've found
How the weary, weary warl goes round.
  'I've Gotten a Rock, I've Gotten a Reel' (*c.*1790) l.
  1

Jean Joseph Louis Blanc 1811–82

18 In the Saint-Simonian doctrine, the problem
of the distribution of benefits is resolved by
this famous saying: *To each according to his
ability; to each ability according to its fruits.*
  *Blanc cites Saint-Simon in order to disagree with
  his ideas*
    Organisation du travail (1841 ed.); cf. **Marx** 214:5

Lesley Blanch 1907–

19 She was an Amazon. Her whole life was
spent riding at breakneck speed towards the
wilder shores of love.
  of Jane Digby El Mezrab (1807–81)
    The Wilder Shores of Love (1954) pt. 2, ch. 1

Karen Blixen *see* Isak Dinesen

Philip Paul Bliss 1838–76

20 Hold the fort, for I am coming.
  suggested by a flag message from General
  Sherman*; see* **Sherman** 294:25
    Gospel Hymns and Sacred Songs (1875) no. 14

Gebhard Lebrecht Blücher
1742–1819

1 *Was für Plunder!*
What rubbish!
*of London, as seen from the Monument in June
1814; often misquoted as, 'Was für plündern!
[What a place to plunder!]'*
Evelyn Princess Blücher *Memoirs of Prince Blücher*
(1932)

Edmund Blunden 1896–1974

2 All things they have in common being so
poor,
And their one fear, Death's shadow at the
door.
'Almswomen' (1920)

3 I am for the woods against the world,
But are the woods for me?
'The Kiss' (1931)

John Ernest Bode 1816–74

4 O Jesus, I have promised
To serve thee to the end;
Be thou for ever near me,
My Master and my Friend.
'O Jesus, I have promised' (1869 hymn); written
for the confirmation of Bode's three children

Ivan F. Boesky 1937–

5 Greed is all right . . . Greed is healthy. You
can be greedy and still feel good about
yourself.
commencement address, Berkeley, California,
18 May 1986

Boethius AD *c.*476–524

6 For in every ill-turn of fortune the most
unhappy sort of unfortunate man is the one
who has been happy.
De Consolatione Philosophiae bk. 2, prose 4; cf.
Chaucer 88:26, **Dante** 105:20

Louise Bogan 1897–1970

7 Women have no wilderness in them,
They are provident instead,
Content in the tight hot cell of their hearts
To eat dusty bread.
'Women' (1923)

John B. Bogart 1848–1921

8 When a dog bites a man, that is not news,
because it happens so often. But if a man
bites a dog, that is news.
often attributed to Charles A. Dana
F. M. O'Brien *The Story of the* [New York] *Sun*
(1918) ch. 10

Niels Bohr 1885–1962

9 Anybody who is not shocked by this subject
has failed to understand it.
of quantum mechanics
attributed; in *Nature* 23 August 1990

10 Never express yourself more clearly than
you think.
Abraham Pais *Einstein Lived Here* (1994)

Alan Bold 1943–

11 This happened near the core
Of a world's culture.
'June 1967 at Buchenwald' (1969)

12 Scotland, land of the omnipotent No.
'A Memory of Death' (1969)

Henry St John, Lord Bolingbroke 1678–1751

13 They make truth serve as a stalking-horse to
error.
Letters on the Study and Use of History (1752) No. 4,
pt. 1

14 Truth lies within a little and certain
compass, but error is immense.
Reflections upon Exile (1716)

15 The greatest art of a politician is to render
vice serviceable to the cause of virtue.
comment (*c.*1728)

Robert Bolt 1924–95

16 This country's planted thick with laws from
coast to coast—Man's laws, not God's—and
if you cut them down—and you're just the
man to do it—d'you really think you could
stand upright in the winds that would blow
then?
A Man for All Seasons (1960) act 1

17 It profits a man nothing to give his soul for
the whole world . . . But for Wales—!
A Man for All Seasons (1960) act 2; cf. **Bible** 45:28

Elizabeth Patterson Bonaparte 1785–1879

18 Even quarrels with one's husband are
preferable to the ennui of a solitary
existence.
Eugene L. Didier *The Life and Letters of Madame
Bonaparte* (1879)

Andrew Bonar Law 1858–1923

19 I can imagine no length of resistance to
which Ulster will not go, in which I shall
not be ready to support them.
at a Unionist meeting at Blenheim in 1912
Robert Blake *The Unknown Prime Minister* (1955)

20 If I am a great man, then all great men are
frauds.
Lord Beaverbrook *Politicians and the War* (1932)

St Bonaventura 1221–74

21 Reason is the natural image of the Creator.
Itinerarium Mentis in Deum

Carrie Jacobs Bond 1862–1946

22 When you come to the end of a perfect day.
'A Perfect Day' (1910 song)

David Bone 1874–1959

1 It's 'Damn you, Jack — I'm all right!' with you chaps.
Brassbounder (1910) ch. 3

Dietrich Bonhoeffer 1906–45

2 In me there is darkness, but with you there is light.
prayer written for fellow-prisoners in a Nazi prison, 1943
Letters and Papers from Prison (1971)

3 It is the nature, and the advantage, of strong people that they can bring out the crucial questions and form a clear opinion about them. The weak always have to decide between alternatives that are not their own.
Widerstand und Ergebung (Resistance and Submission, 1951) 'Ein paar Gedanken über Verschiedenes'

The Book of Common Prayer
1662

4 Dearly beloved brethren, the Scripture moveth us in sundry places to acknowledge and confess our manifold sins and wickedness; and that we should not dissemble nor cloke them before the face of Almighty God our heavenly Father; but confess them with an humble, lowly, penitent, and obedient heart.
Morning Prayer Sentences of the Scriptures

5 We have erred, and strayed from thy ways like lost sheep. We have followed too much the devices and desires of our own hearts.
Morning Prayer General Confession

6 We have left undone those things which we ought to have done; And we have done those things which we ought not to have done; And there is no health in us.
Morning Prayer General Confession

7 And grant, O most merciful Father, for his sake; That we may hereafter live a godly, righteous, and sober life.
Morning Prayer General Confession

8 And forgive us our trespasses, As we forgive them that trespass against us.
Morning Prayer The Lord's Prayer; cf. **Bible** 42:23, **Missal** 224:5

9 Glory be to the Father, and to the Son: and to the Holy Ghost; As it was in the beginning, is now, and ever shall be: world without end. Amen.
Morning Prayer Gloria

10 We praise thee, O God: we acknowledge thee to be the Lord.
All the earth doth worship thee: the Father everlasting.
To thee all Angels cry aloud: the Heavens, and all the Powers therein.
Morning Prayer Te Deum

11 The glorious company of the Apostles: praise thee.
The goodly fellowship of the Prophets: praise thee.

The noble army of Martyrs: praise thee.
Morning Prayer Te Deum

12 When thou hadst overcome the sharpness of death: thou didst open the Kingdom of Heaven to all believers.
Morning Prayer Te Deum

13 Day by day: we magnify thee;
And we worship thy Name: ever world without end.
Morning Prayer Te Deum

14 O Lord, in thee have I trusted: let me never be confounded.
Morning Prayer Te Deum

15 O all ye Works of the Lord, bless ye the Lord.
Morning Prayer Benedicite

16 I believe in God the Father Almighty, Maker of heaven and earth:
And in Jesus Christ his only Son our Lord, Who was conceived by the Holy Ghost, Born of the Virgin Mary, Suffered under Pontius Pilate, Was crucified, dead, and buried, He descended into hell; The third day he rose again from the dead, He ascended into heaven, And sitteth on the right hand of God the Father Almighty; From thence he shall come to judge the quick and the dead. I believe in the Holy Ghost; The holy Catholic Church; The Communion of Saints; The Forgiveness of sins; The Resurrection of the body, And the life everlasting. Amen.
Morning Prayer The Apostles' Creed; cf. **Book of Common Prayer** 59:22, **Missal** 224:1

17 Give peace in our time, O Lord.
Morning Prayer Versicle

18 O God, who art the author of peace and lover of concord, in knowledge of whom standeth our eternal life, whose service is perfect freedom; Defend us thy humble servants in all assaults of our enemies.
Morning Prayer The Second Collect, for Peace

19 Grant that this day we fall into no sin, neither run into any kind of danger.
Morning Prayer The Third Collect, for Grace

20 In Quires and Places where they sing, here followeth the Anthem.
Morning Prayer rubric following Third Collect

21 Almighty God, the fountain of all goodness.
Morning Prayer Prayer for the Royal Family

22 Almighty God, who hast given us grace at this time with one accord to make our common supplications unto thee; and dost promise, that when two or three are gathered together in thy Name thou wilt grant their requests: Fulfil now, O Lord, the desires and petitions of thy servants, as may be most expedient for them.
Morning Prayer Prayer of St Chrysostom

23 O God, from whom all holy desires, all good counsels, and all just works do proceed; Give unto thy servants that peace which the world cannot give.
Evening Prayer Second Collect

1 Lighten our darkness, we beseech thee, O Lord; and by thy great mercy defend us from all perils and dangers of this night.
Evening Prayer Third Collect

2 Whosoever will be saved: before all things it is necessary that he hold the Catholic Faith.
At Morning Prayer Athanasian Creed 'Quicunque vult'

3 Have mercy upon us miserable sinners.
The Litany

4 From envy, hatred, and malice, and from all uncharitableness,
Good Lord, deliver us.
The Litany

5 From all the deceits of the world, the flesh, and the devil,
Good Lord, deliver us.
The Litany

6 From battle and murder, and from sudden death,
Good Lord, deliver us.
The Litany

7 In the hour of death, and in the day of judgement,
Good Lord, deliver us.
The Litany

8 That it may please thee to preserve all that travel by land or by water, all women labouring of child, all sick persons, and young children; and to shew thy pity upon all prisoners and captives;
We beseech thee to hear us, good Lord.
The Litany

9 O God, the Creator and Preserver of all mankind, we humbly beseech thee for all sorts and conditions of men.
Prayers . . . upon Several Occasions 'Collect or Prayer for all Conditions of Men'

10 We commend to thy fatherly goodness all those, who are any ways afflicted, or distressed, in mind, body, or estate; that it may please thee to comfort and relieve them, according to their several necessities, giving them patience under their sufferings, and a happy issue out of all their afflictions.
Prayers . . . upon Several Occasions 'Collect or Prayer for all Conditions of Men'

11 O God our heavenly Father, who by thy gracious providence dost cause the former and the latter rain to descend upon the earth.
Thanksgivings For Rain

12 Almighty God, give us grace that we may cast away the works of darkness, and put upon us the armour of light.
Collects The first Sunday in Advent

13 Blessed Lord, who hast caused all holy Scriptures to be written for our learning; Grant that we may in such wise hear them, read, mark, learn, and inwardly digest them, that by patience, and comfort of thy holy Word.
Collects The second Sunday in Advent

14 O God, forasmuch as without thee we are not able to please thee; Mercifully grant,

that thy Holy Spirit may in all things direct and rule our hearts.
Collects The nineteenth Sunday after Trinity

15 Stir up, we beseech thee, O Lord, the wills of thy faithful people.
Collects The five and twentieth Sunday after Trinity

16 An open and notorious evil liver.
Holy Communion introductory rubric

17 The Table, at the Communion-time having a fair white linen cloth upon it.
Holy Communion introductory rubric

18 Almighty God, unto whom all hearts be open, all desires known, and from whom no secrets are hid.
Holy Communion The Collect

19 I the Lord thy God am a jealous God, and visit the sins of the fathers upon the children unto the third and fourth generation of them that hate me.
the phrase 'sins of the fathers' is also used in the Douay/Rheims Bible (1609) in Numbers ch. 14, v. 18
Holy Communion The Ten Commandments; cf. **Bible** 34:13

20 Incline our hearts to keep this law.
Holy Communion The Ten Commandments (response)

21 Thou shalt do no murder.
Holy Communion The Ten Commandments; cf. **Bible** 34:16

22 I believe in one God the Father Almighty, Maker of heaven and earth, And of all things visible and invisible:
And in one Lord Jesus Christ, the only-begotten Son of God, Begotten of his Father before all worlds, God of God, Light of Light, Very God of very God, Begotten, not made, Being of one substance with the Father, By whom all things were made.
Holy Communion Nicene Creed; cf. **Book of Common Prayer** 58:16, **Missal** 224:1

23 And I believe one Catholick and Apostolick Church.
Holy Communion Nicene Creed; cf. **Missal** 224:1

24 Let us pray for the whole state of Christ's Church militant here in earth.
Holy Communion Prayer for the Church Militant

25 We humbly beseech thee most mercifully to accept our alms and oblations.
Holy Communion Prayer for the Church Militant

26 To inspire continually the universal Church with the spirit of truth, unity, and concord.
Holy Communion Prayer for the Church Militant

27 We do earnestly repent, And are heartily sorry for these our misdoings; The remembrance of them is grievous unto us; The burden of them is intolerable.
Holy Communion General Confession

28 Hear what comfortable words our Saviour Christ saith unto all that truly turn to him.
Holy Communion Comfortable Words (preamble)

1 Lift up your hearts.
Holy Communion versicles and responses; cf.
Missal 224:3

2 It is meet and right so to do.
Holy Communion versicles and responses

3 It is very meet, right, and our bounden duty,
that we should at all times, and in all places,
give thanks unto thee.
Holy Communion Hymn of Praise; cf. **Bible** 52:8,
Missal 224:4

4 Who made there (by his one oblation of
himself once offered) a full, perfect, and
sufficient sacrifice, oblation, and
satisfaction, for the sins of the whole world.
Holy Communion Prayer of Consecration

5 Who, in the same night that he was
betrayed, took Bread; and, when he had
given thanks, he brake it, and gave it to his
disciples, saying, Take, eat, this is my Body
which is given for you: Do this in
remembrance of me.
Holy Communion Prayer of Consecration

6 Among all the changes and chances of this
mortal life.
Holy Communion Collects after the Offertory

7 O merciful God, grant that the old Adam in
this Child may be so buried, that the new
man may be raised up in him.
Public Baptism of Infants Invocation of blessing on
the child

8 QUESTION: Who gave you this Name?
ANSWER: My Godfathers and Godmothers in
my Baptism.
Catechism

9 I should renounce the devil and all his
works, the pomps and vanity of this wicked
world, and all the sinful lusts of the flesh.
Catechism

10 To keep my hands from picking and
stealing.
Catechism

11 QUESTION: What meanest thou by this word
Sacrament?
ANSWER: I mean an outward and visible sign
of an inward and spiritual grace.
Catechism

12 Lord, hear our prayers.
And let our cry come unto thee.
Order of Confirmation

13 If any of you know cause, or just
impediment, why these two persons should
not be joined together in holy Matrimony,
ye are to declare it. This is the first [*second*,
or *third*] time of asking.
Solemnization of Matrimony The Banns

14 Dearly beloved, we are gathered together
here in the sight of God, and in the face of
this congregation, to join together this Man
and this Woman in holy Matrimony.
Solemnization of Matrimony Exhortation

15 Not by any to be enterprised, nor taken in
hand, unadvisedly, lightly, or wantonly, to
satisfy men's carnal lusts and appetites, like
brute beasts that have no understanding.
Solemnization of Matrimony Exhortation

16 If any man can shew any just cause, why
they may not lawfully be joined together,
let him now speak, or else hereafter for ever
hold his peace.
Solemnization of Matrimony Exhortation

17 Wilt thou love her, comfort her, honour,
and keep her in sickness and in health; and,
forsaking all other, keep thee only unto her,
so long as ye both shall live?
Solemnization of Matrimony Betrothal

18 To have and to hold from this day forward,
for better for worse, for richer for poorer, in
sickness and in health, to love, cherish, and
to obey, till death us do part, according to
God's holy ordinance; and thereto I give
thee my troth.
*the man having used the words 'I plight thee my
troth' and not having promised 'to obey'; the
woman may also omit the promise 'to obey'*
Solemnization of Matrimony Betrothal

19 With this Ring I thee wed, with my body I
thee worship, and with all my worldly
goods I thee endow.
Solemnization of Matrimony Wedding

20 Those whom God hath joined together let
no man put asunder.
Solemnization of Matrimony Wedding; cf. **Bible**
44:18

21 Unto God's gracious mercy and protection
we commit thee.
The Visitation of the Sick

22 The Office ensuing is not to be used for any
that die unbaptized, or excommunicate, or
have laid violent hands upon themselves.
The Burial of the Dead introductory rubric

23 Man that is born of a woman hath but a
short time to live, and is full of misery.
The Burial of the Dead First Anthem; cf. **Bible**
37:6

24 In the midst of life we are in death.
The Burial of the Dead First Anthem

25 Forasmuch as it hath pleased Almighty God
of his great mercy to take unto himself the
soul of our dear brother here departed, we
therefore commit his body to the ground;
earth to earth, ashes to ashes, dust to dust;
in sure and certain hope of the Resurrection
to eternal life.
The Burial of the Dead Interment

26 Why do the heathen so furiously rage
together: and why do the people imagine a
vain thing?
Psalm 2, v. 1

27 Out of the mouth of very babes and
sucklings hast thou ordained strength,
because of thine enemies.
Psalm 8, v. 2

28 Up, Lord, and let not man have the upper
hand.
Psalm 9, v. 19

1 The fool hath said in his heart: There is no God.

Psalm 14, v. 1

2 The lot is fallen unto me in a fair ground: yea, I have a goodly heritage.

Psalm 16, v. 7; 'The lines are fallen unto me in pleasant places' as Psalm 16, v. 6 in Authorized Version of the Bible

3 The heavens declare the glory of God: and the firmament sheweth his handy-work.

Psalm 19, v. 1

4 The judgements of the Lord are true, and righteous altogether.
More to be desired are they than gold, yea, than much fine gold: sweeter also than honey, and the honey-comb.

Psalm 19, v. 10

5 They part my garments among them: and cast lots upon my vesture.

Psalm 22, v. 18

6 The Lord is my shepherd: therefore can I lack nothing.
He shall feed me in a green pasture: and lead me forth beside the waters of comfort.

Psalm 23, v. 1; cf. **Herbert** 157:21, **Scottish Metrical Psalms** 266:28; see also Psalm 23, v. 1, Authorized Version of the Bible, 'The Lord is my shepherd; I shall not want. He maketh me to lie down in green pastures: he leadeth me beside the still waters'

7 Yea, though I walk through the valley of the shadow of death, I will fear no evil: for thou art with me; thy rod and thy staff comfort me.
Thou shalt prepare a table before me against them that trouble me: thou hast anointed my head with oil, and my cup shall be full.
But thy loving-kindness and mercy shall follow me all the days of my life: and I will dwell in the house of the Lord for ever.

Psalm 23, v. 4; cf. **Scottish Metrical Psalms** 266:29

8 The earth is the Lord's, and all that therein is: the compass of the world, and they that dwell therein.

Psalm 24, v. 1

9 Lift up your heads, O ye gates, and be ye lift up, ye everlasting doors: and the King of glory shall come in.

Psalm 24, v. 7

10 I should utterly have fainted: but that I believe verily to see the goodness of the Lord in the land of the living.

Psalm 27, v. 15

11 Heaviness may endure for a night, but joy cometh in the morning.

Psalm 30, v. 5

12 Into thy hands I commend my spirit.

Psalm 31, v. 6; cf. **Bible** 47:14

13 Great plagues remain for the ungodly: but whoso putteth his trust in the Lord, mercy embraceth him on every side.

Psalm 32, v. 11

14 Sing unto the Lord a new song: sing praises lustily unto him with a good courage.

Psalm 33, v. 3

15 O deliver my soul from the calamities which they bring on me, and my darling from the lions.

Psalm 35, v. 17

16 I have been young, and now am old: and yet saw I never the righteous forsaken, nor his seed begging their bread.

Psalm 37, v. 25

17 I myself have seen the ungodly in great power: and flourishing like a green bay-tree.

Psalm 37, v. 36

18 I held my tongue, and spake nothing: I kept silence, yea, even from good words; but it was pain and grief to me.

Psalm 39, v. 3

19 Lord, let me know mine end, and the number of my days: that I may be certified how long I have to live.

Psalm 39, v. 5

20 Yea, even mine own familiar friend, whom I trusted.

Psalm 41, v. 9

21 Like as the hart desireth the water-brooks: so longeth my soul after thee, O God.
My soul is a thirst for God, yea, even for the living God.

Psalm 42, v. 1; cf. **Tate** 309:11
As the hart panteth after the water brooks, so panteth my soul after thee, O God.
My soul thirsteth for God, the living God.
Psalm 42, v. 1 in the Authorized Version of the Bible

22 My heart is inditing of a good matter: I speak of the things which I have made unto the King.
My tongue is the pen: of a ready writer.

Psalm 45, v. 1

23 Thou hast loved righteousness, and hated iniquity: wherefore God, even thy God, hath anointed thee with the oil of gladness above thy fellows.

Psalm 45, v. 8

24 The King's daughter is all glorious within: her clothing is of wrought gold.

Psalm 45, v. 14

25 God is our hope and strength: a very present help in trouble.

Psalm 46, v. 1; cf. **Anonymous** 5:12

26 Be still then, and know that I am God.

Psalm 46, v. 10

27 Behold, I was shapen in wickedness: and in sin hath my mother conceived me.

Psalm 51, v. 5

28 Make me a clean heart, O God: and renew a right spirit within me.

Psalm 51, v. 10

29 Deliver me from blood-guiltiness, O God.

Psalm 51, v. 14

1 O that I had wings like a dove: for then would I flee away, and be at rest.
Psalm 55, v. 6

2 It was even thou, my companion: my guide, and mine own familiar friend.
We took sweet counsel together: and walked in the house of God as friends.
Psalm 55, v. 14

3 They have digged a pit before me, and are fallen into the midst of it themselves.
Psalm 57, v. 7

4 They are as venomous as the poison of a serpent: even like the deaf adder that stoppeth her ears;
Which refuseth to hear the voice of the charmer: charm he never so wisely.
Psalm 58, v. 4

5 Moab is my wash-pot; over Edom will I cast out my shoe.
Psalm 60, v. 8

6 Let God arise, and let his enemies be scattered: let them also that hate him flee before him.
Psalm 68, v. 1

7 The mountains also shall bring peace: and the little hills righteousness unto the people.
Psalm 72, v. 3

8 For promotion cometh neither from the east, nor from the west: nor yet from the south.
Psalm 75, v. 7

9 As one out of sleep: and like a giant refreshed with wine.
Psalm 78, v. 66

10 Yea, the sparrow hath found her an house, and the swallow a nest where she may lay her young: even thy altars, O Lord of hosts, my King and my God.
Psalm 84, v. 3

11 Blessed is the man whose strength is in thee: in whose heart are thy ways.
Who going through the vale of misery use it for a well: and the pools are filled with water.
They will go from strength to strength.
Psalm 84, v. 5

12 For one day in thy courts: is better than a thousand.
I had rather be a door-keeper in the house of my God: than to dwell in the tents of ungodliness.
Psalm 84, v. 10

13 Mercy and truth are met together: righteousness and peace have kissed each other.
Psalm 85, v. 10

14 For a thousand years in thy sight are but as yesterday: seeing that is past as a watch in the night.
Psalm 90, v. 4

15 The days of our age are threescore years and ten; and though men be so strong that they come to fourscore years: yet is their strength then but labour and sorrow; so soon passeth it away, and we are gone.
Psalm 90, v. 10

16 For he shall deliver thee from the snare of the hunter.
Psalm 91, v. 3

17 Thou shalt not be afraid for any terror by night: nor for the arrow that flieth by day;
For the pestilence that walketh in darkness: nor for the sickness that destroyeth in the noon-day.
Psalm 91, v. 5

18 O come, let us sing unto the Lord: let us heartily rejoice in the strength of our salvation.
Let us come before his presence with thanksgiving: and shew ourselves glad in him with psalms.
Psalm 95, v. 1

19 To-day if ye will hear his voice, harden not your hearts: as in the provocation, and as in the day of temptation in the wilderness.
Psalm 95, v. 8

20 O worship the Lord in the beauty of holiness: let the whole earth stand in awe of him.
Psalm 96, v. 9

21 O sing unto the Lord a new song: for he hath done marvellous things.
With his own right hand, and with his holy arm: hath he gotten himself the victory.
Psalm 98, v. 1; cf. **Bible** 52:30

22 O be joyful in the Lord, all ye lands: serve the Lord with gladness, and come before his presence with a song.
Be ye sure that the Lord he is God: it is he that hath made us, and not we ourselves; we are his people, and the sheep of his pasture.
Psalm 100, v. 1; cf. **Bible** 52:31

23 The days of man are but as grass: for he flourisheth as a flower of a field.
For as soon as the wind goeth over it, it is gone: and the place thereof shall know it no more.
Psalm 103, v. 15

24 Thou makest darkness that it may be night: wherein all the beasts of the forest do move.
The lions roaring after their prey: do seek their meat from God.
Psalm 104, v. 20

25 There go the ships, and there is that Leviathan: whom thou hast made to take his pastime therein.
Psalm 104, v. 26

26 The iron entered into his soul.
Psalm 105, v. 18

27 Thus were they stained with their own works: and went a whoring with their own inventions.
Psalm 106, v. 38

28 Such as sit in darkness, and in the shadow of death.
Psalm 107, v. 10

1 They that go down to the sea in ships: and occupy their business in great waters; These men see the works of the Lord: and his wonders in the deep.
    Psalm 107, v. 23

2 They reel to and fro, and stagger like a drunken man: and are at their wit's end.
    Psalm 107, v. 27

3 Thou art a Priest for ever after the order of Melchisedech.
    Psalm 110, v. 4

4 The fear of the Lord is the beginning of wisdom.
    Psalm 111, v. 10

5 The mountains skipped like rams: and the little hills like young sheep.
    Psalm 114, v. 4

6 Not unto us, O Lord, not unto us, but unto thy Name give the praise.
    Psalm 115, v. 1; cf. **Bible** 53:1

7 They have mouths, and speak not: eyes have they, and see not. They have ears, and hear not: noses have they, and smell not. They have hands, and handle not: feet have they, and walk not: neither speak they through their throat.
    Psalm 115, v. 5

8 The snares of death compassed me round about: and the pains of hell gat hold upon me.
    Psalm 116, v. 3

9 I said in my haste, All men are liars.
    Psalm 116, v. 10

10 The same stone which the builders refused: is become the head-stone in the corner. This is the Lord's doing: and it is marvellous in our eyes.
    Psalm 118, v. 22

11 Blessed be he that cometh in the Name of the Lord.
    Psalm 118, v. 26

12 I will lift up mine eyes unto the hills: from whence cometh my help.
    Psalm 121, v. 1; cf. **Scottish Metrical Psalms** 267:1

13 So that the sun shall not burn thee by day: neither the moon by night.
    Psalm 121, v. 6

14 The Lord shall preserve thy going out, and thy coming in: from this time forth for evermore.
    Psalm 121, v. 8

15 O pray for the peace of Jerusalem: they shall prosper that love thee.
    Psalm 122, v. 6

16 Our soul is escaped even as a bird out of the snare of the fowler: the snare is broken, and we are delivered.
    Psalm 124, v. 6

17 They that sow in tears: shall reap in joy. He that now goeth on his way weeping, and beareth forth good seed: shall doubtless come again with joy, and bring his sheaves with him.
    Psalm 126, v. 6

18 Except the Lord build the house: their labour is but lost that build it. Except the Lord keep the city: the watchman waketh but in vain.
    Psalm 127, v. 1; cf. **Bible** 53:2

19 Like as the arrows in the hand of the giant: even so are the young children. Happy is the man that hath his quiver full of them.
    Psalm 127, v. 5

20 Thy wife shall be as the fruitful vine: upon the walls of thine house. Thy children like the olive-branches: round about thy table.
    Psalm 128, v. 3

21 Out of the deep have I called unto thee, O Lord: Lord, hear my voice.
    Psalm 130, v. 1; cf. **Bible** 53:3

22 O give thanks unto the Lord, for he is gracious: and his mercy endureth for ever.
    Psalm 136, v. 1; cf. **Milton** 220:8

23 By the waters of Babylon we sat down and wept: when we remembered thee, O Sion.
    Psalm 137, v. 1

24 If I forget thee, O Jerusalem: let my right hand forget her cunning.
    Psalm 137, v. 5

25 If I take the wings of the morning: and remain in the uttermost parts of the sea; Even there also shall thy hand lead me: and thy right hand shall hold me.
    Psalm 139, v. 8

26 I will give thanks unto thee, for I am fearfully and wonderfully made.
    Psalm 139, v. 13

27 O put not your trust in princes, nor in any child of man.
    Psalm 146, v. 2

28 He hath no pleasure in the strength of an horse: neither delighteth he in any man's legs.
    Psalm 147, v. 10

29 To bind their kings in chains: and their nobles with links of iron.
    Psalm 149, v. 8

30 Praise him upon the well-tuned cymbals: praise him upon the loud cymbals. Let every thing that hath breath: praise the Lord.
    Psalm 150, v. 5

31 Be pleased to receive into thy Almighty and most gracious protection the persons of us thy servants, and the Fleet in which we serve.
    Forms of Prayer to be Used at Sea First Prayer

32 That we may be . . . a security for such as pass on the seas upon their lawful occasions.
    Forms of Prayer to be Used at Sea First Prayer

1 We therefore commit his body to the deep,
to be turned into corruption, looking for the
resurrection of the body (when the Sea shall
give up her dead).
Forms of Prayer to be Used at Sea At the Burial of
their Dead at Sea

2 Holy Scripture containeth all things
necessary to salvation.
Articles of Religion (1562) no. 6

3 Man is very far gone from original
righteousness.
Articles of Religion (1562) no. 9

4 It is a thing plainly repugnant to the Word
of God, and the custom of the Primitive
Church, to have publick Prayer in the
Church, or to minister the Sacraments in a
tongue not understanded of the people.
Articles of Religion (1562) no. 24

5 The Bishop of Rome hath no jurisdiction in
this Realm of England.
Articles of Religion (1562) no. 37

6 It is lawful for Christian men, at the
commandment of the Magistrate, to wear
weapons, and serve in the wars.
Articles of Religion (1562) no. 37

7 A Man may not marry his Mother.
A Table of Kindred and Affinity

John Wilkes Booth 1838–65

8 *Sic semper tyrannis!* The South is avenged.
*having shot President **Lincoln**, 14 April 1865*
in *New York Times* 15 April 1865; the second part
of the statement does not appear in any
contemporary source, and is possibly
apocryphal; cf. **Anonymous** 12:21

William Booth 1829–1912

9 The submerged tenth.
*defined by Booth as 'three million men, women,
and children, a vast despairing multitude in a
condition nominally free, but really enslaved'*
In Darkest England (1890) pt. 1, title of ch. 2

Robert Boothby 1900–86

10 *You* speak for Britain!
*to Arthur Greenwood, acting Leader of the Labour
Party, after Neville **Chamberlain** had failed to
announce an ultimatum to Germany; perhaps
taking up an appeal already voiced by Leo **Amery***
Harold Nicolson, diary, 2 September 1939; cf.
Amery 4:15

Betty Boothroyd 1929–

11 My desire to get here [Parliament] was like
miners' coal dust, it was under my fingers
and I couldn't scrub it out.
of Parliament
Glenys Kinnock and Fiona Millar (eds.) *By Faith
and Daring* (1993)

James H. Boren 1925–

12 Guidelines for bureaucrats: (1) When in
charge, ponder. (2) When in trouble,
delegate. (3) When in doubt, mumble.
in *New York Times* 8 November 1970

Jorge Luis Borges 1899–1986

13 The original is unfaithful to the translation.
*of Henley's translation of **Beckford**'s* Vathek
Sobre el 'Vathek' de William Beckford (1943)

14 The Falklands thing was a fight between
two bald men over a comb.
application of a proverbial phrase
in *Time* 14 February 1983

Cesare Borgia 1476–1507

15 *Aut Caesar, aut nihil.*
Caesar or nothing.
motto inscribed on the sword of Cesare Borgia
(1476–1507)

George Borrow 1803–81

16 Sun, moon, and stars, brother, all sweet
things: there's likewise a wind on the heath.
Life is very sweet, brother; who would wish
to die?
Lavengro (1851) ch. 25

Pierre Bosquet 1810–61

17 *C'est magnifique, mais ce n'est pas la guerre.*
It is magnificent, but it is not war.
*on the charge of the Light Brigade at Balaclava,
25 October 1854*
Cecil Woodham-Smith *The Reason Why* (1953) ch.
12

John Collins Bossidy 1860–1928

18 And this is good old Boston,
The home of the bean and the cod,
Where the Lowells talk to the Cabots
And the Cabots talk only to God.
verse spoken at Holy Cross College alumni
dinner in Boston, Massachusetts, 1910, in
Springfield Sunday Republican 14 December 1924

Jacques-Bénigne Bossuet
1627–1704

19 *L'Angleterre, ah, la perfide Angleterre, que le
rempart de ses mers rendait inaccessible aux
Romains, la foi du Sauveur y est abordée.*
England, ah, faithless England, which the
protection afforded by its seas rendered
inaccessible to the Romans, the faith of the
Saviour spread even there.
first sermon on the feast of the Circumcision,
in *Oeuvres de Bossuet* (1816) vol. 11; cf. **Ximénèz**
342:8

James Boswell 1740–95

20 I am, I flatter myself, completely a citizen of
the world. In my travels through Holland,
Germany, Switzerland, Italy, Corsica,
France, I never felt myself from home.
Journal of a Tour to the Hebrides (ed. F. A. Pottle,
1936) 14 August 1773

21 A page of my Journal is like a cake of
portable soup. A little may be diffused into a
considerable portion.
Journal of a Tour to the Hebrides (ed. F. A. Pottle,
1936) 13 September 1773

1 JOHNSON: Well, we had a good talk.
BOSWELL: Yes, Sir; you tossed and gored
several persons.

The Life of Samuel Johnson (1791) Summer 1768

Horatio Bottomley 1860–1933

*reply to a prison visitor who asked if he were
sewing:*

2 No, reaping.

S. T. Felstead *Horatio Bottomley* (1936) ch. 16

3 What poor education I have received has
been gained in the University of Life.

speech at the Oxford Union, 2 December 1920

Dion Boucicault 1820–90

4 Men talk of killing time, while time quietly
kills them.

London Assurance (1841) act 2, sc. 1; cf. **Sitwell**
296:14

Antoine Boulay de la Meurthe 1761–1840

5 It is worse than a crime, it is a blunder.

*on hearing of the execution of the Duc d'Enghien,
captured in Baden by Napoleon's forces, in 1804*
C.-A. Sainte-Beuve *Nouveaux Lundis* (1870) vol. 12

Harold Edwin Boulton 1859–1935

6 Speed, bonnie boat, like a bird on the wing,
'Onward,' the sailors cry;
Carry the lad that's born to be king,
Over the sea to Skye.

'Skye Boat Song' (1908)

Matthew Boulton 1728–1809

7 I sell here, Sir, what all the world desires to
have—POWER.

*speaking to **Boswell** of his engineering works*
James Boswell *Life of Samuel Johnson* (1791) 22
March 1776

F. W. Bourdillon 1852–1921

8 The night has a thousand eyes,
And the day but one.

Among the Flowers (1878) 'Light'; cf. **Lyly** 204:24

E. E. Bowen 1836–1901

9 Forty years on, when afar and asunder
Parted are those who are singing to-day.

'Forty Years On' (Harrow School Song,
published 1886)

Elizabeth Bowen 1899–1973

10 There is no end to the violations committed
by children on children, quietly talking
alone.

The House in Paris (1935) pt. 1, ch. 2

11 Fate is not an eagle, it creeps like a rat.

The House in Paris (1935) pt. 2, ch. 2

12 Jealousy is no more than feeling alone
against smiling enemies.

The House in Paris (1935) pt. 2, ch. 8

Lord Bowen 1835–94

13 The man on the Clapham omnibus.

the average man
in *Law Reports* (1903); attributed

14 When I hear of an 'equity' in a case like
this, I am reminded of a blind man in a dark
room—looking for a black hat—which isn't
there.

John Alderson Foote *Pie-Powder* (1911)

15 The rain, it raineth on the just
And also on the unjust fella:
But chiefly on the just, because
The unjust steals the just's umbrella.

Walter Sichel *Sands of Time* (1923) ch. 4: cf.
Bible 42:20

David Bowie (David Jones) 1947–

16 Ground control to Major Tom.

'Space Oddity' (1969 song)

Boy George 1961–

17 She's a gay man trapped in a woman's body.

*of **Madonna***
Take It Like a Man (1995)

18 Sex has never been an obsession with me.
It's just like eating a bag of crisps. Quite
nice, but nothing marvellous.

in *Sun* 21 October 1982

John Bradford c.1510–55

19 But for the grace of God there goes John
Bradford.

*on seeing a group of criminals being led to their
execution; usually quoted as, 'There but for the
grace of God go I'*
in *Dictionary of National Biography* (1917–)

F. H. Bradley 1846–1924

20 Metaphysics is the finding of bad reasons
for what we believe upon instinct; but to
find these reasons is no less an instinct.

Appearance and Reality (1893) preface

21 The world is the best of all possible worlds,
and everything in it is a necessary evil.

Appearance and Reality (1893) preface

Omar Bradley 1893–1981

22 The way to win an atomic war is to make
certain it never starts.

speech on Armistice Day, 1948

23 We have grasped the mystery of the atom
and rejected the Sermon on the Mount.

speech on Armistice Day, 1948
Collected Writings (1967) vol. 1

John Bradshaw 1602–59

24 Rebellion to tyrants is obedience to God.

suppositious epitaph

Anne Bradstreet c.1612–72

25 I am obnoxious to each carping tongue,
Who says my hand a needle better fits.

'The Prologue' (1650)

James Bramston *c.*1694–1744

1 What's not destroyed by Time's devouring hand?
Where's Troy, and where's the Maypole in the Strand?
The Art of Politics (1729) l. 71

Louis D. Brandeis 1856–1941

2 Fear of serious injury alone cannot justify suppression of free speech and assembly. Men feared witches and burned women. It is the function of speech to free men from the bondage of irrational fears.
in *Whitney v. California* (1927)

Richard Branson 1950–

3 We spend most of our lives working. So why do so few people have a good time doing it?
interview in *New York Times* 28 February 1993

Georges Braque 1882–1963

4 Art is meant to disturb, science reassures.
Le Jour et la nuit: Cahiers 1917–52

5 Truth exists; only lies are invented.
Le Jour et la nuit: Cahiers 1917–52

John W. Bratton
and James B. Kennedy

6 If you go down in the woods today
You're sure of a big surprise
If you go down in the woods today
You'd better go in disguise
For every Bear that ever there was
Will gather there for certain because,
Today's the day the Teddy Bears have their Picnic.
'The Teddy Bear's Picnic' (1932 song)

Werner von Braun 1912–77

7 Basic research is what I am doing when I don't know what I am doing.
R. L. Weber *A Random Walk in Science* (1973)

Bertolt Brecht 1898–1956

8 The aim of science is not to open the door to infinite wisdom, but to set a limit to infinite error.
The Life of Galileo (1939) sc. 9

9 Don't tell me peace has broken out, when I've just bought some new supplies.
Mother Courage (1939) sc. 8

10 The resistible rise of Arturo Ui.
title of play (1941)

11 Oh, the shark has pretty teeth, dear,
And he shows them pearly white.
Just a jackknife has Macheath, dear
And he keeps it out of sight.
The Threepenny Opera (1928) prologue

12 What is robbing a bank compared with founding a bank?
The Threepenny Opera (1928) act 3, sc. 3

Gerald Brenan 1894–1987

13 Those who have some means think that the most important thing in the world is love. The poor know that it is money.
Thoughts in a Dry Season (1978)

Sydney Brenner 1927–

14 A modern computer hovers between the obsolescent and the nonexistent.
attributed in *Science* 5 January 1990

Nicholas Breton *c.*1545–1626

15 I wish my deadly foe, no worse
Than want of friends, and empty purse.
'A Farewell to Town' (1577)

Aristide Briand 1862–1932

16 The high contracting powers solemnly declare . . . that they condemn recourse to war and renounce it . . . as an instrument of their national policy towards each other . . . The settlement or the solution of all disputes or conflicts of whatever nature or of whatever origin they may be which may arise . . . shall never be sought by either side except by pacific means.
draft, 20 June 1927, later incorporated into the Kellogg Pact, 1928

Edward Bridges 1892–1969

17 I confidently expect that we shall continue to be grouped with mothers-in-law and Wigan Pier as one of the recognized objects of ridicule.
of civil servants
Portrait of a Profession (1950)

Robert Bridges 1844–1930

18 All my hope on God is founded.
'All my hope on God is founded' (1899 hymn)

19 When men were all asleep the snow came flying,
In large white flakes falling on the city brown,
Stealthily and perpetually settling and loosely lying,
Hushing the latest traffic of the drowsy town.
'London Snow' (1890)

John Bright 1811–89

20 The angel of death has been abroad throughout the land; you may almost hear the beating of his wings.
on the effects of the war in the Crimea
speech in the House of Commons, 23 February 1855

21 A gigantic system of outdoor relief for the aristocracy of Great Britain.
of British foreign policy
speech at Birmingham, 29 October 1858

22 I am for 'Peace, retrenchment, and reform', the watchword of the great Liberal party 30 years ago.
speech at Birmingham, 28 April 1859

1 England is the mother of Parliaments.
  speech at Birmingham, 18 January 1865

2 The right hon Gentleman . . . has retired into what may be called his political Cave of Adullam—and he has called about him every one that was in distress and every one that was discontented.
  referring to Robert Lowe, leader of the dissident Whigs opposed to the Reform Bill of 1866
  speech in the House of Commons, 13 March 1866; cf. **Bible** 35:24

Anthelme Brillat-Savarin
1755–1826

3 Tell me what you eat and I will tell you what you are.
  Physiologie du Goût (1825) aphorism no. 4; cf. **Feuerbach** 127:5

4 The discovery of a new dish does more for human happiness than the discovery of a star.
  Physiologie du Goût (1825) aphorism no. 9

Russell Brockbank 1913-

5 Fog in Channel—Continent isolated.
  newspaper placard in cartoon, *Round the Bend with Brockbank* (1948); the phrase 'Continent isolated' was quoted as already current by John Gunther *Inside Europe* (1938)

Jacob Bronowski 1908–74

6 The essence of science: ask an impertinent question, and you are on the way to a pertinent answer.
  The Ascent of Man (1973) ch. 4

7 The wish to hurt, the momentary intoxication with pain, is the loophole through which the pervert climbs into the minds of ordinary men.
  The Face of Violence (1954) ch. 5

Charlotte Brontë 1816–55

8 There was no possibility of taking a walk that day.
  Jane Eyre (1847), opening words

9 Reader, I married him.
  Jane Eyre (1847) ch. 38

10 Be a governess! Better be a slave at once!
  Shirley (1849) ch. 13

11 I shall soon be 30—and I have done nothing yet . . . I feel as if we were all buried here.
  letter to Ellen Nussey, 24 March 1845

Emily Brontë 1818–48

12 No coward soul is mine,
  No trembler in the world's storm-troubled sphere;
  I see Heaven's glories shine,
  And faith shines equal, arming me from fear.
  'No coward soul is mine' (1846)

13 Cold in the earth—and fifteen wild Decembers,

From those brown hills, have melted into spring.
  'Remembrance' (1846)

14 My love for Heathcliff resembles the eternal rocks beneath:—a source of little visible delight, but necessary.
  Wuthering Heights (1847) ch. 9

15 I lingered round them, under that benign sky; watched the moths fluttering among the heath and hare-bells; listened to the soft wind breathing through the grass; and wondered how any one could ever imagine unquiet slumbers for the sleepers in that quiet earth.
  Wuthering Heights (1847), closing words

Patrick Brontë 1777–1861

16 Charlotte has been writing a book, and it is much better than likely.
  to his younger daughters, on first reading Jane Eyre
  Elizabeth Gaskell *The Life of Charlotte Brontë* (1857)

17 No quailing, Mrs Gaskell! no drawing back!
  apropos her undertaking to write the life of Charlotte **Brontë**
  letter from Mrs Gaskell to Ellen Nussey, 24 July 1855

Henry Brooke 1703–83

18 For righteous monarchs,
  Justly to judge, with their own eyes should see;
  To rule o'er freemen, should themselves be free.
  Earl of Essex (performed 1750, published 1761) act 1; cf. **Johnson** 176:18

Rupert Brooke 1887–1915

19 Blow out, you bugles, over the rich Dead!
  There's none of these so lonely and poor of old,
  But, dying, has made us rarer gifts than gold.
  These laid the world away; poured out the red
  Sweet wine of youth.
  'The Dead' (1914)

20 Unkempt about those hedges blows
  An English unofficial rose.
  'The Old Vicarage, Grantchester' (1915)

21 Stands the Church clock at ten to three?
  And is there honey still for tea?
  'The Old Vicarage, Grantchester' (1915)

22 Now, God be thanked Who has matched us with His hour.
  'Peace' (1914)

23 If I should die, think only this of me:
  That there's some corner of a foreign field
  That is for ever England.
  'The Soldier' (1914)

Anita Brookner 1938-

1 Good women always think it is their fault when someone else is being offensive. Bad women never take the blame for anything.
Hotel du Lac (1984) ch. 7

2 They were reasonable people, and no one was to be hurt, not even with words.
Hotel du Lac (1984) ch. 9

3 Dr Weiss, at forty, knew that her life had been ruined by literature.
A Start in Life (1981) ch. 1

J. Brooks

4 A four-legged friend, a four-legged friend, He'll never let you down.
sung by Roy Rogers about his horse Trigger
'A Four Legged Friend' (1952)

Phillips Brooks 1835-93

5 O little town of Bethlehem,
How still we see thee lie!
Above thy deep and dreamless sleep
The silent stars go by.
Yet in thy dark streets shineth
The everlasting light;
The hopes and fears of all the years
Are met in thee to-night.
'O Little Town of Bethlehem' (1868 hymn)

Thomas Brooks 1608-80

6 For (*magna est veritas et praevalebit*) great is truth, and shall prevail.
The Crown and Glory of Christianity (1662); cf.
Bible 53:14

Robert Barnabas Brough 1828-60

7 My Lord Tomnoddy is thirty-four;
The Earl can last but a few years more.
My Lord in the Peers will take his place:
Her Majesty's councils his words will grace.
Office he'll hold and patronage sway;
Fortunes and lives he will vote away;
And what are his qualifications?—ONE!
He's the Earl of Fitzdotterel's eldest son.
Songs of the Governing Classes (1855) 'My Lord Tomnoddy'

Lord Brougham 1778-1868

8 All we see about us, King, Lords, and Commons, the whole machinery of the State . . . end in simply bringing twelve good men into a box.
in the House of Commons, 7 February 1828

9 The schoolmaster is abroad! and I trust more to the schoolmaster, armed with his primer, than I do to the soldier in full military array, for upholding and extending the liberties of his country.
sometimes quoted as 'Look out, gentlemen, the schoolmaster is abroad!'
in the House of Commons, 29 January 1828

Heywood Broun 1888-1939

10 Everybody favours free speech in the slack moments when no axes are being ground.
in *New York World* 23 October 1926

11 A fanatic is a great leader who is just entering the room.
in *New York World* 6 February 1928

Christy Brown 1932-81

12 Painting became everything to me . . . Through it I made articulate all that I saw and felt, all that went on inside the mind that was housed within my useless body like a prisoner in a cell.
My Left Foot (1954)

H. Rap Brown 1943-

13 I say violence is necessary. It is as American as cherry pie.
speech at Washington, 27 July 1967

John Brown 1800-59

14 I, John Brown, am now quite certain that the crimes of this guilty land will never be purged away but with blood.
written on the day of his execution, 2 December 1859

Lew Brown 1893-1958

15 Life is just a bowl of cherries.
title of song (1931)

T. E. Brown 1830-97

16 A garden is a lovesome thing, God wot!
'My Garden' (1893)

Thomas Brown 1663-1704

17 A little before you made a leap into the dark.
Letters from the Dead to the Living (1702) 'Answer to Mr Joseph Haines'

18 I do not love thee, Dr Fell.
The reason why I cannot tell;
But this I know, and know full well,
I do not love thee, Dr Fell.
written while an undergraduate at Christ Church, Oxford, of which Dr Fell was Dean
A. L. Hayward (ed.) *Amusements Serious and Comical by Tom Brown* (1927); cf. **Martial** 213:7

Cecil Browne 1932-

19 But not so odd
As those who choose
A Jewish God,
But spurn the Jews.
reply to verse by William Norman **Ewer**; cf.
Ewer 125:14

Sir Thomas Browne 1605-82

20 Old mortality, the ruins of forgotten times.
Hydriotaphia (Urn Burial, 1658) Epistle Dedicatory

21 What song the Syrens sang, or what name Achilles assumed when he hid himself

among women, though puzzling questions, are not beyond all conjecture.
Hydriotaphia (Urn Burial, 1658) ch. 5

1 Generations pass while some trees stand, and old families last not three oaks.
Hydriotaphia (Urn Burial, 1658) ch. 5

2 Man is a noble animal, splendid in ashes, and pompous in the grave.
Hydriotaphia (Urn Burial, 1658) ch. 5

3 I have often admired the mystical way of Pythagoras, and the secret magic of numbers.
Religio Medici (1643) pt. 1, sect. 12

4 We carry within us the wonders we seek without us: there is all Africa and her prodigies in us.
Religio Medici (1643) pt. 1, sect. 15

5 All things are artificial, for nature is the art of God.
Religio Medici (1643) pt. 1, sect. 16

6 Persecution is a bad and indirect way to plant religion.
Religio Medici (1643) pt. 1, sect. 25

7 This trivial and vulgar way of coition; it is the foolishest act a wise man commits in all his life, nor is there any thing that will more deject his cooled imagination, when he shall consider what an odd and unworthy piece of folly he hath committed.
Religio Medici (1643) pt. 2, sect. 9

8 We all labour against our own cure, for death is the cure of all diseases.
Religio Medici (1643) pt. 2, sect. 9

9 For the world, I count it not an inn, but an hospital, and a place, not to live, but to die in.
Religio Medici (1643) pt. 2, sect. 11

10 That children dream not in the first half year, that men dream not in some countries, are to me sick men's dreams, dreams out of the ivory gate, and visions before midnight.
'On Dreams'

William Browne 1692–1774

11 The King to Oxford sent a troop of horse, For Tories own no argument but force: With equal skill to Cambridge books he sent,
For Whigs admit no force but argument.
reply to **Trapp**'s epigram on **George I**, in J. Nichols *Literary Anecdotes* vol. 3 (1812); cf. **Trapp** 319:5

Elizabeth Barrett Browning 1806–61

12 And lips say, 'God be pitiful,' Who ne'er said, 'God be praised.'
'The Cry of the Human' (1844) st. 1

13 What was he doing, the great god Pan, Down in the reeds by the river?
'A Musical Instrument' (1862)

14 How do I love thee? Let me count the ways. I love thee to the depth and breadth and height
My soul can reach.
Sonnets from the Portuguese (1850) no. 43

15 I love thee with the breath, Smiles, tears, of all my life!—and if God choose,
I shall but love thee better after death.
Sonnets from the Portuguese (1850) no. 43

Frederick 'Boy' Browning 1896–1965

16 I think we might be going a bridge too far.
expressing reservations about the Arnhem 'Market Garden' operation to Field Marshal **Montgomery**
on 10 September 1944; R. E. Urquhart *Arnhem* (1958)

Robert Browning 1812–89

17 Ah, but a man's reach should exceed his grasp,
Or what's a heaven for?
'Andrea del Sarto' (1855) l. 97

18 But all the play, the insight and the stretch—
Out of me, out of me!
'Andrea del Sarto' (1855) l. 115

19 We fall to rise, are baffled to fight better, Sleep to wake.
Asolando (1889) 'Epilogue'

20 The grand Perhaps!
'Bishop Blougram's Apology' (1855) l. 190

21 You, for example, clever to a fault.
'Bishop Blougram's Apology' (1855) l. 420

22 He said true things, but called them by wrong names.
'Bishop Blougram's Apology' (1855) l. 996

23 Boot, saddle, to horse, and away!
'Boot and Saddle' (1842)

24 When earth breaks up and heaven expands, How will the change strike me and you In the house not made with hands?
'By the Fireside' (1855) st. 27; cf. **Bible** 50:10

25 Oh, the little more, and how much it is! And the little less, and what worlds away!
'By the Fireside' (1855) st. 39

26 Setebos, Setebos, and Setebos! 'Thinketh, He dwelleth i' the cold o' the moon.
'Caliban upon Setebos' (1864) l. 24

27 Dauntless the slug-horn to my lips I set, And blew. '*Childe Roland to the Dark Tower came.*'
'Childe Roland to the Dark Tower Came' (1855) st. 34; cf. **Shakespeare** 277:28

28 How sad and bad and mad it was— But then, how it was sweet!
'Confessions' (1864) st. 9

29 Stung by the splendour of a sudden thought.
'A Death in the Desert' (1864) l. 59

1 . . . Progress, man's distinctive mark alone,
Not God's, and not the beasts': God is, they
  are,
Man partly is and wholly hopes to be.
  'A Death in the Desert' (1864) l. 586

2 Open my heart and you will see
Graved inside of it, 'Italy'.
  'De Gustibus' (1855) pt. 2, l. 43

3 'Tis well averred,
A scientific faith's absurd.
  'Easter-Day' (1850) l. 123

4 Beautiful Evelyn Hope is dead!
  'Evelyn Hope' (1855)

5 If you get simple beauty and naught else,
You get about the best thing God invents.
  'Fra Lippo Lippi' (1855) l. 217

6 This is our master, famous calm and dead,
Borne on our shoulders.
  'A Grammarian's Funeral' (1855) l. 27

7 That low man seeks a little thing to do,
Sees it and does it:
This high man, with a great thing to pursue,
Dies ere he knows it.
That low man goes on adding one to one,
His hundred's soon hit:
This high man, aiming at a million,
Misses an unit.
  'A Grammarian's Funeral' (1855) l. 113

8 Oh, to be in England
Now that April's there.
  'Home-Thoughts, from Abroad' (1845)

9 That's the wise thrush; he sings each song
twice over,
Lest you should think he never could
recapture
The first fine careless rapture!
  'Home-Thoughts, from Abroad' (1845)

10 Nobly, nobly Cape Saint Vincent to the
North-west died away;
Sunset ran, one glorious blood-red, reeking
into Cadiz Bay.
  'Home-Thoughts, from the Sea' (1845)

11 'Here and here did England help me: how
can I help England?'—say,
  'Home-Thoughts, from the Sea' (1845)

12 'With this same key
Shakespeare unlocked his heart,' once
more!
Did Shakespeare? If so, the less Shakespeare
he!
  'House' (1876); cf. **Wordsworth** 341:2

13 How they brought the good news from
Ghent to Aix.
  title of poem (1845)

14 I sprang to the stirrup, and Joris, and he;
I galloped, Dirck galloped, we galloped all
three.
  'How they brought the Good News from Ghent
  to Aix' (1845) l. 1

15 'You're wounded!' 'Nay,' the soldier's pride
Touched to the quick, he said:
'I'm killed, Sire!' And his chief beside,
Smiling the boy fell dead.
  'Incident of the French Camp' (1842) st. 5

16 Just for a handful of silver he left us,
Just for a riband to stick in his coat.
  of **Wordsworth**
  'The Lost Leader' (1845)

17 We that had loved him so, followed him,
honoured him,
Lived in his mild and magnificent eye,
Learned his great language, caught his clear
accents,
Made him our pattern to live and to die!
Shakespeare was of us, Milton was for us,
Burns, Shelley, were with us—they watch
from their graves!
  'The Lost Leader' (1845)

18 Never glad confident morning again!
  'The Lost Leader' (1845)

19 God for King Charles! Pym and such carles
To the Devil that prompts 'em their
treasonous parles!
  'Marching Along' (1842)

20 A tap at the pane, the quick sharp scratch
And blue spurt of a lighted match,
And a voice less loud, through its joys and
fears,
Than the two hearts beating each to each!
  'Meeting at Night' (1845)

21 Ah, did you once see Shelley plain.
  'Memorabilia' (1855)

22 That's my last Duchess painted on the wall,
Looking as if she were alive.
  'My Last Duchess' (1842) l. 1

23 She had
A heart—how shall I say?—too soon made
glad,
Too easily impressed; she liked whate'er
She looked on, and her looks went
everywhere.
  'My Last Duchess' (1842) l. 21

24 Never the time and the place
And the loved one all together!
  'Never the Time and the Place' (1883)

25 It was roses, roses, all the way.
  'The Patriot' (1855)

26 Rats!
They fought the dogs and killed the cats,
And bit the babies in the cradles,
And ate the cheeses out of the vats,
And licked the soup from the cooks' own
ladles.
  'The Pied Piper of Hamelin' (1842) st. 2

27 The year's at the spring
And day's at the morn;
Morning's at seven;
The hill-side's dew-pearled;
The lark's on the wing;
The snail's on the thorn:
God's in his heaven—
All's right with the world!
  Pippa Passes (1841) pt. 1, l. 221

28 That moment she was mine, mine, fair,
Perfectly pure and good.
  'Porphyria's Lover' (1842) l. 36

1 All her hair
In one long yellow string I wound
Three times her little throat around,
And strangled her. No pain felt she;
I am quite sure she felt no pain.
'Porphyria's Lover' (1842) l. 38

2 I was ever a fighter, so—one fight more,
The best and the last!
I would hate that death bandaged my eyes,
and forbore,
And bade me creep past.
No! let me taste the whole of it, fare like my
peers
The heroes of old,
Bear the brunt, in a minute pay glad life's
arrears
Of pain, darkness and cold.
'Prospice' (1864)

3 Grow old along with me!
The best is yet to be,
The last of life, for which the first was
made.
'Rabbi Ben Ezra' (1864) st. 1

4 O lyric Love, half-angel and half-bird.
The Ring and the Book (1868–9) bk. 1, l. 1391

5 Gr-r-r—there go, my heart's abhorrence!
Water your damned flowerpots, do!
If hate killed men, Brother Lawrence,
God's blood, would not mine kill you!
'Soliloquy of the Spanish Cloister' (1842) st. 1

6 There's a great text in Galatians,
Once you trip on it, entails
Twenty-nine distinct damnations,
One sure, if another fails.
'Soliloquy of the Spanish Cloister' (1842) st. 7

7 Any nose
May ravage with impunity a rose.
Sordello (1840) bk. 6, l. 881

8 And the sin I impute to each frustrate ghost
Is—the unlit lamp and the ungirt loin,
Though the end in sight was a vice, I say.
'The Statue and the Bust' (1863 revision) l. 246

9 Hark, the dominant's persistence till it must
be answered to!
'A Toccata of Galuppi's' (1855) st. 8

10 What of soul was left, I wonder, when the
kissing had to stop?
'A Toccata of Galuppi's' (1855) st. 14

11 Dear dead women, with such hair,
too—what's become of all the gold
Used to hang and brush their bosoms? I feel
chilly and grown old.
'A Toccata of Galuppi's' (1855) st. 15

12 I would that you were all to me,
You that are just so much, no more.
'Two in the Campagna' (1855) st. 8

13 When it was written, God and Robert
Browning knew what it meant; now only
God knows.
on Sordello
attributed; cf. **Klopstock** 189:10

Lenny Bruce 1925–66

14 I'll die young, but it's like kissing God.
on his drug addiction
attributed

Robert Bruce 1554–1631

15 Now, God be with you, my children: I have
breakfasted with you and shall sup with my
Lord Jesus Christ this night.
Robert Fleming *The Fulfilling of the Scripture* (3rd
ed., 1693)

Cathal Brugha 1874–1922

16 Don't you realize that, if you sign this thing,
you will split Ireland from top to bottom?
*to **de Valera**, December 1921, on the Treaty*
Jim Ring *Erskine Childers* (1996)

Beau Brummell 1778–1840

17 Who's your fat friend?
*referring to the Prince of Wales, later **George IV***
Capt. Jesse *Life of George Brummell* (1844) vol. 1

18 No perfumes, but very fine linen, plenty of
it, and country washing.
Memoirs of Harriette Wilson (1825) vol. 1

Gro Harlem Brundtland 1939–

19 I do not know of any environmental group
in any country that does not view its
government as an adversary.
in *Time* 25 September 1989

Frank Bruno 1961–

20 Boxing's just show business with blood.
in *Guardian* 20 November 1991

21 Know what I mean, Harry?
supposed to have been said in interview with
sports commentator Harry Carpenter, possibly
apocryphal

William Jennings Bryan
1860–1925

22 You shall not press down upon the brow of
labour this crown of thorns, you shall not
crucify mankind upon a cross of gold.
opposing the gold standard
speech at the Democratic National Convention,
Chicago, 1896

Zbigniew Brzezinski 1928–

23 Russia can be an empire or a democracy, but
it cannot be both.
in *Foreign Affairs* March/April 1994 'The
Premature Partnership'

John Buchan 1875–1940

24 It's a great life if you don't weaken.
Mr Standfast (1919) ch. 5

25 An atheist is a man who has no invisible
means of support.
H. E. Fosdick *On Being a Real Person* (1943) ch. 10

Frank Buchman 1878–1961

1 There is enough in the world for everyone's need, but not enough for everyone's greed.
   Remaking the World (1947)

Gene Buck 1885–1957
and Herman Ruby 1891–1959

2 That Shakespearian rag,—
   Most intelligent, very elegant.
   'That Shakespearian Rag' (1912 song); cf. **Eliot** 122:25

George Villiers, 2nd Duke of Buckingham 1628–87

3 Ay, now the plot thickens very much upon us.
   The Rehearsal (1672) act 3, sc. 2

H. J. Buckoll 1803–71

4 Lord, dismiss us with Thy blessing,
   Thanks for mercies past receive.
   Pardon all, their faults confessing;
   Time that's lost may all retrieve.
   Psalms and Hymns for the Use of Rugby School Chapel (1850) 'Lord, Dismiss us with Thy Blessing'

J. B. Buckstone 1802–79

5 And we won't go home till morning.
   Billy Taylor (performed 1829) act 1, sc. 2

Eustace Budgell 1686–1737

6 What Cato did, and Addison approved, Cannot be wrong.
   lines found on the desk of Eustace Budgell (1686–1737), after he, too, had taken his own life
   Colley Cibber *Lives of the Poets* (1753) vol. 5 'Life of Eustace Budgell'

Comte de Buffon 1707–88

7 Style is the man himself.
   Discours sur le style (address given to the Académie Française, 25 August 1753)

8 Genius is only a greater aptitude for patience.
   Hérault de Séchelles *Voyage à Montbar* (1803); **Carlyle** 82:17

Arthur Buller 1874–1944

9 There was a young lady named Bright,
   Whose speed was far faster than light;
   She set out one day
   In a relative way
   And returned on the previous night.
   'Relativity' in *Punch* 19 December 1923

Gerald Bullett 1894–1958

10 My Lord Archbishop, what a scold you are!
   And when your man is down how bold you are!
   Of charity how oddly scant you are!
   How Lang, O Lord, how full of Cantuar!
   on the role of Cosmo Gordon Lang, Archbishop of Canterbury, in the abdication of **Edward VIII**
   composed *c.*1936

Bernhard von Bülow 1849–1929

11 We desire to throw no one into the shade [in East Asia], but we also demand our own place in the sun.
   in the Reichstag, 6 December 1897; cf. **Wilhelm II** 335:27

Edward George Bulwer-Lytton 1803–73

12 It was a dark and stormy night.
   Paul Clifford (1830), opening words

13 Here Stanley meets,—how Stanley scorns, the glance!
   The brilliant chief, irregularly great,
   Frank, haughty, rash,—the Rupert of Debate!
   on Edward Stanley, 14th Earl of **Derby**
   The New Timon (1846) pt. 1, sect. 3, l. 202; cf. **Disraeli** 112:6

14 Out-babying Wordsworth and out-glittering Keats.
   on **Tennyson**
   The New Timon (1846) pt. 2, sect. 1, l. 62

15 Beneath the rule of men entirely great
   The pen is mightier than the sword.
   Richelieu (1839) act 2, sc. 2, l. 307; cf. **Burton** 76:14

16 In science, read, by preference, the newest works; in literature, the oldest.
   Caxtoniana (1863) 'Hints on Mental Culture'

Edward Robert Bulwer, Earl of Lytton *see* Owen Meredith

Alfred 'Poet' Bunn *c.*1796–1860

17 I dreamed that I dwelt in marble halls
   With vassals and serfs at my side.
   The Bohemian Girl (1843) act 2 'The Gipsy Girl's Dream'

Basil Bunting 1900–85

18 Praise the green earth. Chance has appointed her
   home, workshop, larder, middenpit.
   Her lousy skin scabbed here and there by
   cities provides us with name and nation.
   'Attis: or, Something Missing' (1931) pt. 1

19 Dance tiptoe, bull,
   black against may.
   'Briggflatts' (1965) pt. 1

Luis Buñuel 1900–83

20 Thanks to God, I am still an atheist.
   in *Le Monde* 16 December 1959

John Bunyan 1628–88

21 As I walked through the wilderness of this world.
   The Pilgrim's Progress (1678) pt. 1, opening words

22 The name of the slough was Despond.
   The Pilgrim's Progress (1678) pt. 1

23 Down into the valley of Humiliation.
   The Pilgrim's Progress (1678) pt. 1

1 A foul Fiend coming over the field to meet him; his name is Apollyon.
 The Pilgrim's Progress (1678) pt. 1

2 It beareth the name of Vanity-Fair, because the town where 'tis kept, is lighter than vanity.
 The Pilgrim's Progress (1678) pt. 1

3 Hanging is too good for him, said Mr Cruelty.
 The Pilgrim's Progress (1678) pt. 1

4 Yet my great-grandfather was but a water-man, looking one way, and rowing another.
 The Pilgrim's Progress (1678) pt. 1; cf. **Burton** 76:12

5 Then I saw that there was a way to Hell, even from the gates of heaven.
 The Pilgrim's Progress (1678) pt. 1

6 So I awoke, and behold it was a dream.
 The Pilgrim's Progress (1678) pt. 1

7 A man that could look no way but downwards, with a muckrake in his hand.
 The Pilgrim's Progress (1684) pt. 2; cf. **Roosevelt** 260:2

8 He that is down needs fear no fall,
He that is low no pride.
He that is humble ever shall
Have God to be his guide.
 The Pilgrim's Progress (1684) pt. 2 'Shepherd Boy's Song'

9 Who would true valour see,
Let him come hither;
One here will constant be,
Come wind, come weather.
There's no discouragement
Shall make him once relent
His first avowed intent
To be a pilgrim.
Who so beset him round
With dismal stories,
Do but themselves confound—
His strength the more is.
 The Pilgrim's Progress (1684) pt. 2

10 The last words of Mr Despondency were, Farewell night, welcome day. His daughter went through the river singing, but none could understand what she said.
 The Pilgrim's Progress (1684) pt. 2

11 I am going to my Fathers, and tho' with great difficulty I am got hither, yet now I do not repent me of all the trouble I have been at to arrive where I am. My sword, I give to him that shall succeed me in my pilgrimage, and my courage and skill to him that can get it. My marks and scars I carry with me, to be a witness for me, that I have fought his battles, who will now be my rewarder.
 Mr Valiant-for-Truth
 The Pilgrim's Progress (1684) pt. 2

12 So he passed over, and the trumpets sounded for him on the other side.
 Mr Valiant-for-Truth
 The Pilgrim's Progress (1684) pt. 2

Samuel Dickinson Burchard
1812–91

13 We are Republicans and don't propose to leave our party and identify ourselves with the party whose antecedents are rum, Romanism, and rebellion.
 speech at the Fifth Avenue Hotel, New York, 29 October 1884

Julie Burchill 1960–

14 Now, at last, this sad, glittering century has an image worthy of it: a wandering, wondering girl, a silly Sloane turned secular saint, coming home in her coffin to RAF Northolt like the good soldier she was.
 in *Guardian* 2 September 1997

Anthony Burgess 1917–93

15 A clockwork orange.
 title of novel (1962)

16 The US presidency is a Tudor monarchy plus telephones.
 George Plimpton (ed.) *Writers at Work* (4th Series, 1977)

Gelett Burgess 1866–1951

17 I never saw a Purple Cow,
I never hope to see one;
But I can tell you, anyhow,
I'd rather see than be one!
 The Burgess Nonsense Book (1914) 'The Purple Cow'

Lord Burghley *see* William Cecil

John William Burgon 1813–88

18 A rose-red city—half as old as Time!
 Petra (1845) l. 132

John Burgoyne 1722–92

19 You have only, when before your glass, to keep pronouncing to yourself nimini-pimini—the lips cannot fail of taking their plie.
 The Heiress (1786) act 3, sc. 2

Edmund Burke 1729–97

20 The king, and his faithful subjects, the lords and commons of this realm,—the triple cord, which no man can break.
 A Letter to a Noble Lord (1796); cf. **Bible** 38:19

21 Many have been taught to think that moderation, in a case like this, is a sort of treason.
 Letter to the Sheriffs of Bristol (1777)

22 It is the nature of all greatness not to be exact; and great trade will always be attended with considerable abuses.
 On American Taxation (1775)

23 Falsehood has a perennial spring.
 On American Taxation (1775)

24 To tax and to please, no more than to love and to be wise, is not given to men.
 On American Taxation (1775)

1 I do not know the method of drawing up an indictment against an whole people.
On Conciliation with America (1775)

2 Instead of a standing revenue, you will have therefore a perpetual quarrel.
On Conciliation with America (1775)

3 Slavery they can have anywhere. It is a weed that grows in every soil.
On Conciliation with America (1775)

4 Custom reconciles us to everything.
On the Sublime and Beautiful (1757) pt. 4, sect. 18

5 Whenever our neighbour's house is on fire, it cannot be amiss for the engines to play a little on our own.
Reflections on the Revolution in France (1790)

6 I thought ten thousand swords must have leapt from their scabbards to avenge even a look that threatened her with insult.
*of **Marie-Antoinette***
Reflections on the Revolution in France (1790)

7 The age of chivalry is gone.— That of sophisters, economists, and calculators, has succeeded; and the glory of Europe is extinguished for ever.
Reflections on the Revolution in France (1790)

8 In the groves of *their* academy, at the end of every vista, you see nothing but the gallows.
Reflections on the Revolution in France (1790)

9 Because half a dozen grasshoppers under a fern make the field ring with their importunate chink, whilst thousands of great cattle, reposed beneath the shadow of the British oak, chew the cud and are silent, pray do not imagine that those who make the noise are the only inhabitants of the field.
Reflections on the Revolution in France (1790)

10 We begin our public affections in our families. No cold relation is a zealous citizen.
Reflections on the Revolution in France (1790)

11 Ambition can creep as well as soar.
Third Letter . . . on the Proposals for Peace . . . (1797)

12 When . . . [people] imagine that their food is only a cover for poison, and when they neither love nor trust the hand that serves it, it is not the name of the roast beef of old England that will persuade them to sit down to the table that is spread for them.
Thoughts on the Cause of the Present Discontents (1770)

13 When bad men combine, the good must associate; else they will fall, one by one, an unpitied sacrifice in a contemptible struggle.
Thoughts on the Cause of the Present Discontents (1770); cf. **Burke** 74:22

14 Of this stamp is the cant of *Not men, but measures*; a sort of charm by which many people get loose from every honourable engagement.
Thoughts on the Cause of the Present Discontents (1770); cf. **Canning** 81:15, **Goldsmith** 143:25

15 Laws, like houses, lean on one another.
A Tract on the Popery Laws (planned *c.*1765) ch. 3

16 Falsehood and delusion are allowed in no case whatsoever: But, as in the exercise of all the virtues, there is an economy of truth.
Two Letters on the Proposals for Peace with the Regicide Directory (1796) pt. 1; cf. **Armstrong** 15:2

17 Your representative owes you, not his industry only, but his judgement; and he betrays, instead of serving you, if he sacrifices it to your opinion.
speech, 3 November 1774, in *Speeches at his Arrival at Bristol* (1774)

18 The people are the masters.
speech, House of Commons, 11 February 1780; cf. **Blair** 55:8

19 Not merely a chip of the old 'block', but the old block itself.
*on the younger **Pitt**'s maiden speech, February 1781*
N. W. Wraxall *Historical Memoirs of My Own Time* (1904 ed.) pt. 2

20 Old religious factions are volcanoes burnt out.
speech on the Petition of the Unitarians, 11 May 1792; cf. **Disraeli** 112:11

21 Dangers by being despised grow great.
speech on the Petition of the Unitarians, 11 May 1792

22 It is necessary only for the good man to do nothing for evil to triumph.
attributed (in a number of forms) to **Burke**, but not found in his writings; cf. **Burke** 74:13

Johnny Burke 1908–64

23 Every time it rains, it rains
Pennies from heaven.
Don't you know each cloud contains
Pennies from heaven?
'Pennies from Heaven' (1936 song)

24 Like Webster's Dictionary, we're Morocco bound.
The Road to Morocco (1942 film) title song

Fanny Burney 1752–1840

25 A little alarm now and then keeps life from stagnation.
Camilla (1796) bk. 3, ch. 11

26 'The whole of this unfortunate business,' said Dr Lyster, 'has been the result of PRIDE AND PREJUDICE.'
Cecilia (1782) bk. 10, ch. 10

27 O! how short a time does it take to put an end to a woman's liberty!
of a wedding
diary, 20 July 1768

John Burns 1858–1943

28 The Thames is liquid history.
to an American who had compared the Thames disparagingly with the Mississippi
in *Daily Mail* 25 January 1943

Robert Burns 1759–96

1 Address to the unco guid.
   title of poem, 1787

2 Ae fond kiss, and then we sever;
   Ae fareweel, and then for ever!
   'Ae fond Kiss' (1792)

3 Flow gently, sweet Afton, among thy green
   braes,
   Flow gently, I'll sing thee a song in thy
   praise.
   'Afton Water' (1792)

4 Should auld acquaintance be forgot
   And never brought to mind?
   'Auld Lang Syne' (1796)

5 We'll tak a cup o' kindness yet,
   For auld lang syne.
   'Auld Lang Syne' (1796)

6 Ye banks and braes o' bonny Doon,
   How can ye bloom sae fresh and fair;
   How can ye chant, ye little birds,
   And I sae weary fu' o' care!
   'The Banks o' Doon' (1792)

7 O saw ye bonnie Lesley,
   As she gaed o'er the border?
   She's gane, like Alexander,
   To spread her conquests farther.
   To see her is to love her,
   And love but her for ever.
   'Bonnie Lesley' (1798)

8 Gin a body meet a body
   Comin thro' the rye,
   Gin a body kiss a body
   Need a body cry?
   'Comin thro' the rye' (1796)

9 I wasna fou, but just had plenty.
   'Death and Dr Hornbook' (1787) st. 3

10 A man's a man for a' that.
   'For a' that and a' that' (1790)

11 Green grow the rashes, O,
   Green grow the rashes, O;
   The sweetest hours that e'er I spend,
   Are spent among the lasses, O.
   'Green Grow the Rashes' (1787)

12 There's death in the cup—so beware!
   'Inscription on a Goblet' (published 1834)

13 Corn rigs, an' barley rigs,
   An' corn rigs are bonnie.
   'It was upon a Lammas Night' (1796)

14 John Anderson my jo, John,
   When we were first acquent,
   Your locks were like the raven,
   Your bonny brow was brent.
   'John Anderson my Jo' (1790)

15 Some have meat and cannot eat,
   Some cannot eat that want it:
   But we have meat and we can eat,
   Sae let the Lord be thankit.
   'The Kirkudbright Grace' (1790), also known as
   'The Selkirk Grace'

16 Man's inhumanity to man
   Makes countless thousands mourn!
   'Man was made to Mourn' (1786) st. 7

17 Go fetch to me a pint o' wine,
   An' fill it in a silver tassie.
   'My Bonnie Mary' (1790)

18 My heart's in the Highlands, my heart is not
   here;
   My heart's in the Highlands a-chasing the
   deer;
   Chasing the wild deer, and following the
   roe,
   My heart's in the Highlands, wherever I go.
   'My Heart's in the Highlands' (1790)

19 My love she's but a lassie yet.
   title of poem, 1787

20 O whistle, an' I'll come to you, my lad.
   title of poem (1788); cf. **Fletcher** 130:9

21 O, my Luve's like a red, red rose
   That's newly sprung in June;
   O my Luve's like the melodie
   That's sweetly play'd in tune.
   'A Red Red Rose' (1796), derived from various
   folk-songs

22 Scots, wha hae wi' Wallace bled,
   Scots, wham Bruce has aften led,
   Welcome to your gory bed,—
   Or to victorie.
   'Robert Bruce's March to Bannockburn' (1799),
   also known as 'Scots, Wha Hae'

23 Liberty's in every blow!
   Let us do—or die!!!
   'Robert Bruce's March to Bannockburn' (1799)

24 Nae man can tether time or tide.
   'Tam o' Shanter' (1791) l. 67

25 Inspiring, bold John Barleycorn,
   What dangers thou canst make us scorn!
   Wi' tippenny, we fear nae evil;
   Wi' usquebae, we'll face the devil!
   'Tam o' Shanter' (1791) l. 105

26 The mirth and fun grew fast and furious.
   'Tam o' Shanter' (1791) l. 144

27 Tam tint his reason a' thegither,
   And roars out—'Weel done, Cutty-sark!'
   'Tam o' Shanter' (1791) l. 185

28 Fair fa' your honest, sonsie face,
   Great chieftain o' the puddin'-race!
   Aboon them a' ye tak your place,
   Painch, tripe, or thairm:
   Weel are ye wordy o' a grace
   As lang's my arm.
   'To a Haggis' (1787)

29 O wad some Pow'r the giftie gie us
   To see oursels as others see us!
   It wad frae mony a blunder free us,
   And foolish notion.
   'To a Louse' (1786)

30 Wee, sleekit, cow'rin', tim'rous beastie,
   O what a panic's in thy breastie!
   Thou need na start awa sae hasty,
   Wi' bickering brattle!
   I wad be laith to rin an' chase thee,
   Wi' murd'ring pattle!
   'To a Mouse' (1786)

31 The best laid schemes o' mice an' men
   Gang aft a-gley.
   'To a Mouse' (1786)

1 Don't let the awkward squad fire over me.
said shortly before his death
> A. Cunningham *The Works of Robert Burns; with his Life* vol. 1 (1834)

Burnum Burnum 1936–97

2 We wish no harm to England's native people. We are here to bring you good manners, refinement and an opportunity to make a *Koompartoo*, a fresh start.
in 1988, the year of Australia's bicentenary, on planting an Aboriginal flag on the white cliffs of Dover and claiming England for the Aboriginal people
> on 26 January 1988; in obituary, *Independent* 20 August 1997

Aaron Burr 1756–1836

3 Law is whatever is boldly asserted and plausibly maintained.
> attributed

William S. Burroughs 1914–97

4 The face of 'evil' is always the face of total need.
> *The Naked Lunch* (1959) introduction

Benjamin Hapgood Burt 1880–1950

5 'You can tell a man who "boozes" by the company he chooses'
And the pig got up and slowly walked away.
> 'The Pig Got Up and Slowly Walked Away' (1933 song)

6 When you're all dressed up and no place to go.
> title of song (1913)

Nat Burton

7 There'll be bluebirds over the white cliffs of Dover,
Tomorrow, just you wait and see.
> 'The White Cliffs of Dover' (1941 song)

Richard Burton 1821–90

8 Don't be frightened; I am recalled. Pay, pack, and follow at convenience.
note to his wife, 19 August 1871, on being replaced as British Consul to Damascus
> Isabel Burton *Life of Captain Sir Richard F. Burton* (1893) vol. 1, ch. 21

Robert Burton 1577–1640

9 All my joys to this are folly,
Naught so sweet as Melancholy.
> *The Anatomy of Melancholy* (1621–51) 'The Author's Abstract of Melancholy'

10 A loose, plain, rude writer . . . I call a spade a spade.
> *The Anatomy of Melancholy* (1621–51) 'Democritus to the Reader'

11 I had not time to lick it into form, as she [a bear] doth her young ones.
> *The Anatomy of Melancholy* (1621–51) 'Democritus to the Reader'

12 Like watermen, that row one way and look another.
> *The Anatomy of Melancholy* (1621–51) 'Democritus to the Reader'; cf. **Bunyan** 73:4

13 All poets are mad.
> *The Anatomy of Melancholy* (1621–51) 'Democritus to the Reader'

14 From this it is clear how much the pen is worse than the sword.
> *The Anatomy of Melancholy* (1621–51) pt. 1; cf. **Bulwer-Lytton** 72:15

15 See one promontory (said Socrates of old), one mountain, one sea, one river, and see all.
> *The Anatomy of Melancholy* (1621–51) pt. 1

16 What is a ship but a prison?
> *The Anatomy of Melancholy* (1621–51) pt. 2

17 To enlarge or illustrate this power and effect of love is to set a candle in the sun.
> *The Anatomy of Melancholy* (1621–51) pt. 3; cf. **Sidney** 295:5, **Young** 344:13

18 Be not solitary, be not idle.
> *The Anatomy of Melancholy* (1621–51), closing words

Hermann Busenbaum 1600–68

19 *Cum finis est licitus, etiam media sunt licita.*
The end justifies the means.
> *Medulla Theologiae Moralis* (1650); literally 'When the end is allowed, the means also are allowed'

Barbara Bush 1925–

20 Somewhere out in this audience may even be someone who will one day follow in my footsteps, and preside over the White House as the President's spouse. I wish him well!
> remarks at Wellesley College Commencement, 1 June 1990

George Bush 1924–

21 Oh, the vision thing.
responding to the suggestion that he turn his attention from short-term campaign objectives and look to the longer term.
> in *Time* 26 January 1987

22 Read my lips: no new taxes.
campaign pledge on taxation
> in *New York Times* 19 August 1988

23 And now, we can see a new world coming into view. A world in which there is the very real prospect of a new world order.
> speech, in *New York Times* 7 March 1991

Comte de Bussy-Rabutin 1618–93

24 Love comes from blindness,
Friendship from knowledge.
> *Histoire Amoureuse des Gaules: Maximes d'Amour* (1665) pt. 1

25 Absence is to love what wind is to fire;
It extinguishes the small, it kindles the great.
> *Histoire Amoureuse des Gaules: Maximes d'Amour* (1665) pt. 2; cf. **Francis** 132:20, **La Rochefoucauld** 193:21

1 As you know, God is usually on the side of the big squadrons against the small.
letter to the Comte de Limoges, 18 October 1677; cf. **Anouilh** 13:17, **Tacitus** 308:19, **Voltaire** 326:9

Joseph Butler 1692–1752

2 Sir, the pretending to extraordinary revelations and gifts of the Holy Ghost is a horrid thing—a very horrid thing.
to John **Wesley**, 16 August 1739

Nicholas Murray Butler 1862–1947

3 An expert is one who knows more and more about less and less.
Commencement address at Columbia University (attributed)

R. A. ('Rab') Butler 1902–82

4 Politics is the Art of the Possible. That is what these pages show I have tried to achieve—not more—and that is what I have called my book.
The Art of the Possible (1971); cf. **Bismarck** 54:13

5 In politics you must always keep running with the pack. The moment that you falter and they sense that you are injured, the rest will turn on you like wolves.
Dennis Walters *Not Always with the Pack* (1989)

Samuel Butler 1612–80

6 For rhyme the rudder is of verses,
With which like ships they steer their courses.
Hudibras pt. 1 (1663), canto 1, l. 457

7 Love is a boy, by poets styled,
Then spare the rod, and spoil the child.
Hudibras pt. 2 (1664), canto 1, l. 843

8 He that complies against his will,
Is of his own opinion still.
Hudibras pt. 3 (1680), canto 3, l. 547

9 For Justice, though she's painted blind,
Is to the weaker side inclined.
Hudibras pt. 3 (1680), canto 3, l. 709

Samuel Butler 1835–1902

10 The best liar is he who makes the smallest amount of lying go the longest way.
The Way of All Flesh (1903) ch. 39

11 It was very good of God to let Carlyle and Mrs Carlyle marry one another and so make only two people miserable instead of four.
letter, 21 November 1884

12 An apology for the Devil: It must be remembered that we have only heard one side of the case. God has written all the books.
Notebooks (1912) ch. 14

13 A definition is the enclosing a wilderness of idea within a wall of words.
Notebooks (1912) ch. 14

14 Jesus! with all thy faults I love thee still.
Further Extracts from Notebooks (1934)

15 Dusty, cobweb-covered, maimed, and set at naught,
Beauty crieth in an attic, and no man regardeth.
O God! O Montreal!
'Psalm of Montreal', in *Spectator* 18 May 1878

William Butler 1535–1618

16 Doubtless God could have made a better berry, but doubtless God never did.
of the strawberry
Izaak Walton *The Compleat Angler* (3rd ed., 1661) pt. 1, ch. 5

A. S. Byatt 1936–

17 What literature can and should do is change the people who teach the people who don't read the books.
interview in *Newsweek* 5 June 1995

William Byrd 1543–1623

18 The exercise of singing is delightful to Nature, and good to preserve the health of man. It doth strengthen all parts of the breast, and doth open the pipes.
Psalms, Sonnets and Songs (1588)

John Byrom 1692–1763

19 Christians, awake! Salute the happy morn,
Whereon the Saviour of the world was born.
Hymn (*c.*1750)

20 Strange! that such high dispute should be
'Twixt Tweedledum and Tweedledee.
'On the Feuds between Handel and Bononcini' (1727)

21 God bless the King, I mean the Faith's Defender;
God bless—no harm in blessing—the Pretender;
But who Pretender is, or who is King,
God bless us all—that's quite another thing.
'To an Officer in the Army, Extempore, Intended to allay the Violence of Party-Spirit' (1773)

Lord Byron 1788–1824

22 Year after year they voted cent per cent
Blood, sweat, and tear-wrung millions—why? for rent!
'The Age of Bronze' (1823) st. 14; cf. **Churchill** 91:14

23 Did'st ever see a gondola? . . .
It glides along the water looking blackly,
Just like a coffin clapt in a canoe.
Beppo (1818) st. 19

24 In short, he was a perfect cavaliero,
And to his very valet seemed a hero.
Beppo (1818) st. 33; cf. **Cornuel** 100:11

25 There was a sound of revelry by night.
Childe Harold's Pilgrimage (1812–18) canto 3, st. 21

26 On with the dance! let joy be unconfined;
No sleep till morn, when Youth and Pleasure meet

To chase the glowing Hours with flying feet.
Childe Harold's Pilgrimage (1812–18) canto 3, st. 22

1 Sapping a solemn creed with solemn sneer.
of Edward **Gibbon**
Childe Harold's Pilgrimage (1812–18) canto 3, st. 107

2 I stood in Venice, on the Bridge of Sighs:
A palace and a prison on each hand.
Childe Harold's Pilgrimage (1812–18) canto 4, st. 1

3 Oh Rome! my country! city of the soul!
Childe Harold's Pilgrimage (1812–18) canto 4, st. 78

4 Of its own beauty is the mind diseased.
Childe Harold's Pilgrimage (1812–18) canto 4, st. 122

5 Time, the avenger! unto thee I lift
My hands, and eyes, and heart, and crave of thee a gift.
Childe Harold's Pilgrimage (1812–18) canto 4, st. 130

6 *There* were his young barbarians all at play,
There was their Dacian mother— he, their sire,
Butchered to make a Roman holiday.
Childe Harold's Pilgrimage (1812–18) canto 4, st. 141

7 While stands the Coliseum, Rome shall stand;
When falls the Coliseum, Rome shall fall;
And when Rome falls—the World.
Childe Harold's Pilgrimage (1812–18) canto 4, st. 145

8 There is a pleasure in the pathless woods,
There is a rapture on the lonely shore,
There is society, where none intrudes,
By the deep sea, and music in its roar:
I love not man the less, but nature more.
Childe Harold's Pilgrimage (1812–18) canto 4, st. 178

9 Roll on, thou deep and dark blue Ocean—roll!
Ten thousand fleets sweep over thee in vain;
Man marks the earth with ruin—his control
Stops with the shore.
Childe Harold's Pilgrimage (1812–18) canto 4, st. 179

10 The glory and the nothing of a name.
'Churchill's Grave' (1816)

11 There was a laughing devil in his sneer.
The Corsair (1814) canto 1, st. 9

12 And she for him had given
Her all on earth, and more than all in heaven!
The Corsair (1814) canto 3, st. 17

13 The Assyrian came down like the wolf on the fold,
And his cohorts were gleaming in purple and gold;
And the sheen of their spears was like stars on the sea,
When the blue wave rolls nightly on deep Galilee.
'The Destruction of Sennacherib' (1815) st. 1

14 For the Angel of Death spread his wings on the blast,
And breathed in the face of the foe as he passed.
'The Destruction of Sennacherib' (1815) st. 3

15 And Coleridge, too, has lately taken wing,
But, like a hawk encumbered with his hood,
Explaining metaphysics to the nation—
I wish he would explain his explanation.
Don Juan (1819–24) canto 1, dedication st. 2

16 What men call gallantry, and gods adultery,
Is much more common where the climate's sultry.
Don Juan (1819–24) canto 1, st. 63

17 A little still she strove, and much repented,
And whispering 'I will ne'er consent'—consented.
Don Juan (1819–24) canto 1, st. 117

18 Man's love is of man's life a thing apart,
'Tis woman's whole existence.
Don Juan (1819–24) canto 1, st. 194; cf. **Amis** 4:21

19 There's nought, no doubt, so much the spirit calms
As rum and true religion.
Don Juan (1819–24) canto 2, st. 34

20 Let us have wine and women, mirth and laughter,
Sermons and soda-water the day after.
Don Juan (1819–24) canto 2, st. 178

21 And thus they form a group that's quite antique,
Half naked, loving, natural, and Greek.
Don Juan (1819–24) canto 2, st. 194

22 Think you, if Laura had been Petrarch's wife,
He would have written sonnets all his life?
Don Juan (1819–24) canto 3, st. 8

23 The isles of Greece, the isles of Greece!
Where burning Sappho loved and sung,
Where grew the arts of war and peace,
Where Delos rose, and Phoebus sprung!
Eternal summer gilds them yet,
But all, except their sun, is set!
Don Juan (1819–24) canto 3, st. 86 (1)

24 The mountains look on Marathon—
And Marathon looks on the sea;
And musing there an hour alone,
I dreamed that Greece might still be free.
Don Juan (1819–24) canto 3, st. 86 (3)

25 We learn from Horace, Homer sometimes sleeps;
We feel without him: Wordsworth sometimes wakes.
Don Juan (1819–24) canto 3, st. 98; cf. **Horace** 163:18

26 Now my sere fancy 'falls into the yellow Leaf,' and imagination droops her pinion.
Don Juan (1819–24) canto 4, st. 3; cf. **Shakespeare** 281:20

27 . . . That all-softening, overpowering knell,
The tocsin of the soul—the dinner bell.
Don Juan (1819–24) canto 5, st. 49

1 A lady of a 'certain age', which means
Certainly aged.
Don Juan (1819–24) canto 6, st. 69

2 Read your own hearts and Ireland's present
story,
Then feed her famine fat with Wellesley's
glory.
Don Juan (1819–24) canto 8, st. 125

3 When Bishop Berkeley said 'there was no
matter',
And proved it—'twas no matter what he
said.
Don Juan (1819–24) canto 11, st. 1

4 Merely innocent flirtation,
Not quite adultery, but adulteration.
Don Juan (1819–24) canto 12, st. 63

5 Now hatred is by far the longest pleasure;
Men love in haste, but they detest at leisure.
Don Juan (1819–24) canto 13, st. 4

6 The English winter—ending in July,
To recommence in August.
Don Juan (1819–24) canto 13, st. 42

7 'Tis strange—but true; for truth is always
strange;
Stranger than fiction.
Don Juan (1819–24) canto 14, st. 101

8 With just enough of learning to misquote.
English Bards and Scotch Reviewers (1809) l. 66

9 The petrifactions of a plodding brain.
English Bards and Scotch Reviewers (1809) l. 416

10 Friendship is Love without his wings!
'L'Amitié est l'amour sans ailes' (written 1806,
published 1831)

11 So he has cut his throat at last!—He! Who?
The man who cut his country's long ago.
on Castlereagh's suicide, c.1822
'Epigram on Lord Castlereagh'

12 The Cincinnatus of the West.
of George **Washington**
'Ode to Napoleon Bonaparte' (1814) st. 19

13 My hair is grey, but not with years,
Nor grew it white
In a single night,
As men's have grown from sudden fears.
The Prisoner of Chillon (1816) st. 1

14 She walks in beauty, like the night
Of cloudless climes and starry skies;
And all that's best of dark and bright
Meet in her aspect and her eyes:
Thus mellowed to that tender light
Which heaven to gaudy day denies.
'She Walks in Beauty' (1815) st. 1

15 Eternal spirit of the chainless mind!
Brightest in dungeons, Liberty! thou art.
'Sonnet on Chillon' (1816)

16 So, we'll go no more a-roving
So late into the night,
Though the heart be still as loving,
And the moon be still as bright.
'So we'll go no more a-roving' (written 1817)

17 I knew it was love, and I felt it was glory.
'Stanzas Written on the Road between Florence
and Pisa, November 1821'

18 Still I can't contradict, what so oft has been
said,
'Though women are angels, yet wedlock's
the devil.'
'To Eliza' (1806)

19 If I should meet thee
After long years,
How should I greet thee?—
With silence and tears.
'When we two parted' (1816)

20 Near this spot are deposited the remains of
one who possessed beauty without vanity,
strength without insolence, courage
without ferocity, and all the virtues of Man,
without his vices.
'Inscription on the Monument of a
Newfoundland Dog' (1808)

21 My Princess of Parallelograms.
*of his future wife Annabella Milbanke, a keen
amateur mathematician; Byron explains: 'Her
proceedings are quite rectangular, or rather we
are two parallel lines prolonged to infinity side by
side but never to meet'*
letter to Lady Melbourne, 18 October 1812

22 The place is very well and quiet and the
children only scream in a low voice.
letter to Lady Melbourne, 21 September 1813

23 Pure invention is but the talent of a liar.
letter to John Murray from Venice, 2 April 1817

24 I awoke one morning and found myself
famous.
on the instantaneous success of Childe Harold
Thomas Moore *Letters and Journals of Lord Byron*
(1830) vol. 1

25 You should have a softer pillow than my
heart.
to his wife, who had rested her head on his breast
E. C. Mayne (ed.) *The Life and Letters of Anne
Isabella, Lady Noel Byron* (1929) ch. 11

James Branch Cabell 1879–1958

26 The optimist proclaims that we live in the
best of all possible worlds; and the pessimist
fears this is true.
The Silver Stallion (1926) bk. 4, ch. 26

Augustus Caesar *see* Augustus

Irving Caesar 1895–

27 Picture you upon my knee,
Just tea for two and two for tea.
'Tea for Two' (1925 song)

Julius Caesar 100–44 BC

28 *Gallia est omnis divisa in partes tres.*
Gaul as a whole is divided into three parts.
De Bello Gallico bk. 1, sect. 1

29 Caesar's wife must be above suspicion.
*divorcing his wife Pompeia after unfounded
allegations were made against her*
oral tradition, based on Plutarch *Parallel Lives*
'Julius Caesar' ch. 10, sect. 9

1 Caesar had rather be first in a village than second at Rome.
> Francis Bacon *The Advancement of Learning* pt. 2, ch. 23, sect. 36; based on Plutarch

2 *Iacta alea est.*
The die is cast.
at the crossing of the Rubicon, the boundary beyond which he was forbidden to lead his army
> Suetonius *Lives of the Caesars* 'Divus Julius' sect. 32; originally spoken in Greek, Plutarch *Parallel Lives* 'Pompey' ch. 60, sect. 2

3 *Veni, vidi, vici.*
I came, I saw, I conquered.
> inscription displayed in Caesar's Pontic triumph, according to Suetonius *Lives of the Caesars* 'Divus Julius' sect. 37; or, according to Plutarch *Parallel Lives* 'Julius Caesar' ch. 50, sect. 2, written in a letter by Caesar, announcing the victory of Zela which concluded the Pontic campaign

4 *Et tu, Brute?*
You too, Brutus?
> traditional rendering of Suetonius

John Cage 1912–

5   I have nothing to say and I am saying it and that is poetry.
> 'Lecture on nothing' (1961)

James M. Cain 1892–1977

6 The postman always rings twice.
> title of novel (1934)

Caligula (Gaius Julius Caesar Germanicus) AD 12–41

7 Would that the Roman people had but one neck!
> Suetonius *Lives of the Caesars* 'Gaius Caligula' sect. 30

8 Strike him so that he can feel that he is dying.
> Suetonius *Lives of the Caesars* 'Gaius Caligula' sect. 30

James Callaghan 1912–

9 You never reach the promised land. You can march towards it.
> in a television interview, 20 July 1978

10 I had known it was going to be a 'winter of discontent'.
> television interview, 8 February 1979

Callimachus c.305–c.240 BC
see also **Cory** 100:14

11 A great book is like great evil.
> R. Pfeiffer (ed.) *Callimachus* (1949–53) Fragment 465

Charles Alexandre de Calonne 1734–1802

12 *Madame, si c'est possible, c'est fait; impossible? cela se fera.*
Madam, if a thing is possible, consider it done; the impossible? that will be done.
> in J. Michelet *Histoire de la Révolution Française* (1847) vol. 1; cf. **Nansen** 231:1

C. S. Calverley (born Blayds) 1831–84

13 The farmer's daughter hath soft brown hair;
(Butter and eggs and a pound of cheese)
And I met with a ballad, I can't say where,
Which wholly consisted of lines like these.
> 'Ballad' (1872)

14 How Eugene Aram, though a thief, a liar, and a murderer,
Yet, being intellectual, was amongst the noblest of mankind.
> 'Of Reading' (1861); cf. **Hood** 162:2

Helder Camara 1909–99

15 When I give food to the poor they call me a saint. When I ask why the poor have no food they call me a communist.
> attributed

Pierre, Baron de Cambronne 1770–1842

16 *La Garde meurt, mais ne se rend pas.*
The Guards die but do not surrender.
attributed to Cambronne when called upon to surrender at Waterloo, 1815, but later denied by him
> H. Houssaye *La Garde meurt et ne se rend pas* (1907); an alternative version is that he replied, '*Merde!* [Shit!]', known in French as the '*mot de Cambronne*'

Julia Margaret Cameron 1815–79

17 I longed to arrest all beauty that came before me.
> *Annals of my Glass House* 1874

Jane Montgomery Campbell 1817–78

18 We plough the fields, and scatter
The good seed on the land,
But it is fed and watered
By God's almighty hand.
> 'We plough the fields, and scatter' (1861 hymn); translated from the German of Matthias Claudius (1740–1815)

Mrs Patrick Campbell 1865–1940

19 The deep, deep peace of the double-bed after the hurly-burly of the chaise-longue.
on her recent marriage
> Alexander Woollcott *While Rome Burns* (1934) 'The First Mrs Tanqueray'

20 It doesn't matter what you do in the bedroom as long as you don't do it in the street and frighten the horses.
> Daphne Fielding *The Duchess of Jermyn Street* (1964) ch. 2

Roy Campbell 1901–57

21 You praise the firm restraint with which they write—

I'm with you there, of course:
They use the snaffle and the curb all right,
But where's the bloody horse?
'On Some South African Novelists' (1930)

Thomas Campbell 1777–1844

1 O leave this barren spot to me!
Spare, woodman, spare the beechen tree.
'The Beech-Tree's Petition' (1800); cf. **Morris** 228:15

2 On the green banks of Shannon, when Sheelah was nigh,
No blithe Irish lad was so happy as I;
No harp like my own could so cheerily play,
And wherever I went was my poor dog Tray.
'The Harper' (1799)

3 'Tis distance lends enchantment to the view,
And robes the mountain in its azure hue.
Pleasures of Hope (1799) pt. 1, l. 7

4 Now Barabbas was a publisher.
also attributed, wrongly, to **Byron**
attributed, in Samuel Smiles *A Publisher and his Friends: Memoir and Correspondence of the late John Murray* (1891) vol. 1, ch. 14; see **Bible** 48:10

Thomas Campion 1567–1620

5 There is a garden in her face
Where roses and white lilies grow;
A heavenly paradise is that place,
Wherein all pleasant fruits do flow.
There cherries grow, which none may buy
Till 'Cherry ripe' themselves do cry.
The Fourth Book of Airs (c.1617) no. 7; music by Richard Alison, who published the song in *An Hour's Recreation in Music* (1606)

Albert Camus 1913–60

6 You know what charm is: a way of getting the answer yes without having asked any clear question.
The Fall (1956)

7 What is a rebel? A man who says no.
The Rebel (1951)

8 All modern revolutions have ended in a reinforcement of the State.
The Rebel (1951)

9 What I know most surely about morality and the duty of man I owe to sport.
often quoted as '. . . I owe to football'
Herbert R. Lottman *Albert Camus* (1979)

Elias Canetti 1905–94

10 All the things one has forgotten scream for help in dreams.
Die Provinz der Menschen (1973)

George Canning 1770–1827

11 In matters of commerce the fault of the Dutch
Is offering too little and asking too much.
The French are with equal advantage content,

So we clap on Dutch bottoms just twenty per cent.
dispatch, in cipher, to the English ambassador at the Hague, 31 January 1826
Sir Harry Poland *Mr Canning's Rhyming 'Dispatch' to Sir Charles Bagot* (1905)

12 A steady patriot of the world alone,
The friend of every country but his own.
on the Jacobin
'New Morality' (1821) l. 113; cf. **Disraeli** 112:13

13 Give me the avowed, erect and manly foe;
Firm I can meet, perhaps return the blow;
But of all plagues, good Heaven, thy wrath can send,
Save me, oh, save me, from the candid friend.
'New Morality' (1821) l. 207

14 Pitt is to Addington
As London is to Paddington.
'The Oracle' (c.1803)

15 Away with the cant of 'Measures not men'!—the idle supposition that it is the harness and not the horses that draw the chariot along. If the comparison must be made, if the distinction must be taken, men are everything, measures comparatively nothing.
speech on the Army estimates, 8 December 1802, in *Speeches* (1828) vol. 2; the phrase 'measures not men' may be found as early as 1742 (in a letter from Chesterfield to Dr Chevenix, 6 March); cf. **Burke** 74:14, **Goldsmith** 143:25

16 I called the New World into existence, to redress the balance of the Old.
speech on the affairs of Portugal, in House of Commons 12 December 1826

17 [The Whip's duty is] to make a House, and keep a House, and cheer the minister.
J. E. Ritchie *Modern Statesmen* (1861) ch. 7; attributed

Hughie Cannon 1877–1912

18 Won't you come home Bill Bailey, won't you come home?
'Bill Bailey, Won't You Please Come Home' (1902 song)

Eric Cantona 1966–

19 When seagulls follow a trawler, it is because they think sardines will be thrown into the sea.
to the media at the end of a press conference, 31 March 1995

Robert Capa 1913–54

20 If your pictures aren't good enough, you aren't close enough.
Russell Miller *Magnum: Fifty years at the Front Line of History* (1997)

Truman Capote 1924–84

21 Other voices, other rooms.
title of novel (1948)

Al Capp 1907–79

1 A product of the untalented, sold by the unprincipled to the utterly bewildered.
of abstract art
  in *National Observer* 1 July 1963; cf. **Zappa** 345:2

Francesco Caracciolo 1752–99

2 In England there are sixty different religions, and only one sauce.
  attributed

Ethna Carbery 1866–1902

3 Young Rody MacCorley goes to die
On the Bridge of Toome today.
  'Rody MacCorley' (1902)

Neville Cardus 1889–1975

4 If everything else in this nation of ours were lost but cricket—her Constitution and the laws of England of Lord Halsbury—it would be possible to reconstruct from the theory and practice of cricket all the eternal Englishness which has gone to the establishment of that Constitution and the laws aforesaid.
  Cricket (1930)

Richard Carew 1555–1620

5 Will you have all in all for prose and verse?
Take the miracle of our age, Sir Philip Sidney.
  William Camden *Remains concerning Britain* (1614) 'The Excellency of the English Tongue'

Thomas Carew *c.*1595–1640

6 Here lies a king, that ruled as he thought fit
The universal monarchy of wit.
  'An Elegy upon the Death of Dr John Donne' (1640)

7 Ask me no more where Jove bestows,
When June is past, the fading rose;
For in your beauty's orient deep
These flowers, as in their causes, sleep.
  'A Song' (1640)

George Carey 1935–

8 We must recall that the Church is always 'one generation away from extinction.'
  Working Party Report *Youth A Part: Young People and the Church* (1996) foreword

Henry Carey *c.*1687–1743

9 Let the verse the subject fit,
Little subject, little wit.
  'Namby-Pamby: or, A Panegyric on the New Versification' (1725)

10 Of all the girls that are so smart
There's none like pretty Sally,
She is the darling of my heart,
And she lives in our alley.
  'Sally in our Alley' (1729)

Jane Carlyle 1801–66

11 I am not at all the sort of person you and I took me for.
  letter to Thomas Carlyle, 7 May 1822

Thomas Carlyle 1795–1881

12 In epochs when cash payment has become the sole nexus of man to man.
  Chartism (1839) ch. 6

13 The foul sluggard's comfort: 'It will last my time.'
  Critical and Miscellaneous Essays (1838) 'Count Cagliostro. Flight Last'

14 A well-written Life is almost as rare as a well-spent one.
  Critical and Miscellaneous Essays (1838) 'Jean Paul Friedrich Richter'

15 To the very last he [Napoleon] had a kind of idea; that, namely, of *La carrière ouverte aux talents*, The tools to him that can handle them.
  Critical and Miscellaneous Essays (1838) 'Sir Walter Scott' (*La carrière . . .* Career open to the talents)

16 The three great elements of modern civilization, Gunpowder, Printing, and the Protestant Religion.
  Critical and Miscellaneous Essays (1838) 'The State of German Literature'; cf. **Bacon** 22:5

17 'Genius' (which means transcendent capacity of taking trouble, first of all).
  History of Frederick the Great (1858–65) bk. 4, ch. 3; cf. **Buffon** 72:8

18 A whiff of grapeshot.
  History of the French Revolution (1837) vol. 1, bk. 5, ch. 3

19 The seagreen Incorruptible.
  describing **Robespierre**
  History of the French Revolution (1837) vol. 2, bk. 4, ch. 4

20 France was long a despotism tempered by epigrams.
  History of the French Revolution (1837) vol. 3, bk. 7, ch. 7

21 Aristocracy of the Moneybag.
  History of the French Revolution (1837) vol. 3, bk. 7, ch. 7

22 The true University of these days is a collection of books.
  On Heroes, Hero-Worship, and the Heroic (1841) 'The Hero as Man of Letters'

23 A Parliament speaking through reporters to Buncombe and the twenty-seven millions mostly fools.
  Latter-Day Pamphlets (1850) 'Parliaments'; cf. **Walker** 326:23

24 The Dismal Science.
  on political economy
  Latter-Day Pamphlets (1850) 'The Present Time'

25 Transcendental moonshine.
  on the influence of a romantic imagination in motivating Sterling to enter the priesthood
  The Life of John Sterling (1851) pt. 1, ch. 15

26 Captains of industry.
  Past and Present (1843) bk. 4, ch. 4 (title)

1 Man is a tool-using animal . . . Without tools
he is nothing, with tools he is all.
Sartor Resartus (1834) bk. 1, ch. 5

2 The everlasting No.
Sartor Resartus (1834) bk. 2, ch. 7 (title)

3 What a sad want I am in of libraries, of
books to gather facts from! Why is there not
a Majesty's library in every county town?
There is a Majesty's jail and gallows in every
one.
diary, 18 May 1832

4 Gad! she'd better!
*on hearing that Margaret Fuller 'accept[ed] the
universe'*
William James *Varieties of Religious Experience*
(1902) lecture 2

5 Macaulay is well for a while, but one
wouldn't *live* under Niagara.
R. M. Milnes *Notebook* (1838)

Stokely Carmichael 1941–98

6 The only position for women in SNCC is
prone.
*response to a question about the position of
women*
at a Student Nonviolent Coordinating
Committee conference, November 1964

Andrew Carnegie 1835–1919

7 The man who dies . . . rich dies disgraced.
North American Review June 1889 'Wealth'

Dale Carnegie 1888–1955

8 How to win friends and influence people.
title of book (1936)

Julia A. Carney 1823–1908

9 Little drops of water,
Little grains of sand,
Make the mighty ocean
And the beauteous land.
'Little Things' (1845)

Caroline of Ansbach 1683–1737
*see also **George II** 137:22*

10 My dear firstborn is the greatest ass, and the
greatest liar, and the greatest *canaille*, and
the greatest beast in the whole world, and I
heartily wish he was out of it.
*of her eldest son, Frederick, Prince of Wales, father
of **George III***
in *Dictionary of National Biography* (1917–)

Joseph Edwards Carpenter
1813–85

11 What are the wild waves saying
Sister, the whole day long,
'What are the Wild Waves Saying?' (1850 song)

J. L. Carr 1912–

12 *You* have not had thirty years' experience . . .
You have had one year's experience 30
times.
The Harpole Report (1972)

Lewis Carroll 1832–98

13 'What is the use of a book', thought Alice,
'without pictures or conversations?'
Alice's Adventures in Wonderland (1865) ch. 1

14 'Curiouser and curiouser!' cried Alice.
Alice's Adventures in Wonderland (1865) ch. 2

15 How doth the little crocodile
Improve his shining tail,
And pour the waters of the Nile
On every golden scale!
Alice's Adventures in Wonderland (1865) ch. 2; cf.
Watts 329:5

16 'You are old, Father William,' the young
man said,
'And your hair has become very white;
And yet you incessantly stand on your
head—
Do you think, at your age, it is right?'
Alice's Adventures in Wonderland (1865) ch. 5; cf.
Southey 299:16

17 He only does it to annoy,
Because he knows it teases.
Alice's Adventures in Wonderland (1865) ch. 6

18 This time it vanished quite slowly,
beginning with the end of the tail, and
ending with the grin, which remained some
time after the rest of it had gone.
the Cheshire Cat
Alice's Adventures in Wonderland (1865) ch. 6

19 'Then you should say what you mean,' the
March Hare went on. 'I do,' Alice hastily
replied; 'at least—at least I mean what I
say—that's the same thing, you know.' 'Not
the same thing a bit!' said the Hatter. 'Why,
you might just as well say that "I see what I
eat" is the same thing as "I eat what I see!" '
Alice's Adventures in Wonderland (1865) ch. 7

20 Twinkle, twinkle, little bat!
How I wonder what you're at!
Up above the world you fly!
Like a teatray in the sky.
Alice's Adventures in Wonderland (1865) ch. 7; cf.
Taylor 309:21

21 Off with her head!
the Queen of Hearts
Alice's Adventures in Wonderland (1865) ch. 8

22 Take care of the sense, and the sounds will
take care of themselves.
Alice's Adventures in Wonderland (1865) ch. 9

23 'Will you walk a little faster?' said a whiting
to a snail.
Alice's Adventures in Wonderland (1865) ch. 10

24 Will you, won't you, will you, won't you,
will you join the dance?
Alice's Adventures in Wonderland (1865) ch. 10

25 Soup of the evening, beautiful Soup!
Alice's Adventures in Wonderland (1865) ch. 10

26 Begin at the beginning,' the King said,
gravely, 'and go on till you come to the end:
then stop.
Alice's Adventures in Wonderland (1865) ch. 12

1 'It's the oldest rule in the book,' said the King.
  Alice's Adventures in Wonderland (1865) ch. 12

2 No! No! Sentence first—verdict afterwards.
  Alice's Adventures in Wonderland (1865) ch. 12

3 'Twas brillig, and the slithy toves
  Did gyre and gimble in the wabe;
  All mimsy were the borogoves,
  And the mome raths outgrabe.
  'Beware the Jabberwock, my son!
  The jaws that bite, the claws that catch!'
  Through the Looking-Glass (1872) ch. 1

4 'And hast thou slain the Jabberwock?
  Come to my arms, my beamish boy!
  O frabjous day! Callooh! Callay!'
  He chortled in his joy.
  Through the Looking-Glass (1872) ch. 1

5 Now, *here*, you see, it takes all the running *you* can do, to keep in the same place. If you want to get somewhere else, you must run at least twice as fast as that!
  Through the Looking-Glass (1872) ch. 2

6 'The time has come,' the Walrus said,
  'To talk of many things:
  Of shoes—and ships—and sealing wax—
  Of cabbages—and kings—
  And why the sea is boiling hot—
  And whether pigs have wings.'
  Through the Looking-Glass (1872) ch. 4

7 But answer came there none.
  Through the Looking-Glass (1872) ch. 4; cf. **Scott** 266:5

8 The rule is, jam to-morrow and jam yesterday—but never jam today.
  Through the Looking-Glass (1872) ch. 5; cf. **Benn** 29:15

9 Why, sometimes I've believed as many as six impossible things before breakfast.
  Through the Looking-Glass (1872) ch. 5

10 They gave it me,—for an un-birthday present.
  Through the Looking-Glass (1872) ch. 6

11 'The question is,' said Humpty Dumpty, 'which is to be master—that's all.'
  Through the Looking-Glass (1872) ch. 6; cf. **Shawcross** 292:7

12 You see it's like a portmanteau—there are two meanings packed up into one word.
  Through the Looking-Glass (1872) ch. 6

13 It's as large as life, and twice as natural!
  Through the Looking-Glass (1872) ch. 7

14 What I tell you three times is true.
  The Hunting of the Snark (1876) 'Fit the First: The Landing'

15 But oh, beamish nephew, beware of the day,
  If your Snark be a Boojum! For then
  You will softly and suddenly vanish away,
  And never be met with again!
  The Hunting of the Snark (1876) 'Fit the Third: The Baker's Tale'

16 For the Snark *was* a Boojum, you see.
  The Hunting of the Snark (1876) 'Fit the Eighth: The Vanishing'

William Herbert Carruth
1859–1924

17 Some call it evolution,
  And others call it God.
  'Each In His Own Tongue' (1908)

Edward Carson 1854–1935

18 We must be prepared . . . the morning Home Rule passes, ourselves to become responsible for the government of the Protestant Province of Ulster.
  speech at Craigavon, 23 September 1911

19 From the day I first entered parliament up to the present, devotion to the union has been the guiding star of my political life.
  in *Dictionary of National Biography* (1917–)

Rachel Carson 1907–64

20 Over increasingly large areas of the United States, spring now comes unheralded by the return of the birds, and the early mornings are strangely silent where once they were filled with the beauty of bird song.
  The Silent Spring (1962)

Henry Carter d. 1806

21 True patriots we; for be it understood,
  We left our country for our country's good.
  prologue, written for, but not recited at, the opening of the Playhouse, Sydney, New South Wales, 16 January 1796, when the actors were principally convicts
  previously attributed to George Barrington (b. 1755)

Howard Carter 1874–1939

22 Yes, wonderful things.
  when asked what he could see on first looking into the tomb of Tutankhamun, 26 November 1922; his notebook records the words as 'Yes, it is wonderful'
  The Tomb of Tut-ankh-amen (1933)

James Earl 'Jimmy' Carter 1924–

23 I've looked on a lot of women with lust. I've committed adultery in my heart many times. This is something that God recognizes I will do—and I have done it—and God forgives me for it.
  in *Playboy* November 1976

Sydney Carter 1915–

24 Dance then wherever you may be,
  I am the Lord of the Dance, said he,
  And I'll lead you all, wherever you may be
  And I'll lead you all in the dance, said he.
  'Lord of the Dance' (1967)

25 One more step along the world I go.
  'One More Step'

Jacques Cartier 1491–1557

1 I am rather inclined to believe that this is the land God gave to Cain.

on discovering the northern shore of the Gulf of St Lawrence (now Labrador and Quebec) in 1534; after the murder of Abel, Cain was exiled to the desolate land of Nod (cf. **Bible** *33:16)*

La Première Relation; H. P. Biggar (ed.) The Voyages of Jacques Cartier (1924)

Henri Cartier-Bresson 1908–

2 To me, photography is the simultaneous recognition, in a fraction of a second, of the significance of an event as well as of a precise organisation of forms which give that event its proper expression.

The Decisive Moment (1952)

Barbara Cartland 1901–2000

3 After forty a woman has to choose between losing her figure or her face. My advice is to keep your face, and stay sitting down.

Libby Purves 'Luncheon à la Cartland'; in The Times 6 October 1993; similar remarks have been attributed since c.1980

John Cartwright 1740–1824

4 One man shall have one vote.

The People's Barrier Against Undue Influence (1780) ch. 1 'Principles, maxims, and primary rules of politics' no. 68

Roger Casement 1864–1916

5 Self-government is our right, a thing born in us at birth, a thing no more to be doled out to us, or withheld from us, by another people than the right to life itself—than the right to feel the sun, or smell the flowers, or to love our kind.

statement at the conclusion of his trial, the Old Bailey, London, 29 June 1916

A. M. Cassandre 1901–68

6 A good poster is a visual telegram.

attributed

Barbara Castle 1910–

7 I will fight for what I believe in until I drop dead. And that's what keeps you alive.

in Guardian 14 January 1998

Ted Castle 1907–79

8 In place of strife.

title of Government White Paper, 17 January 1969, suggested by Castle to his wife, Barbara **Castle**, *then Secretary of State for Employment*

Barbara Castle, diary, 15 January 1969

Fidel Castro 1927–

9 History will absolve me.

title of pamphlet (1953)

Edward Caswall 1814–78

10 Jesu, the very thought of Thee
With sweetness fills the breast.

translation of 'Jesu dulcis memoria, dans vera cordis gaudia', *usually attributed to St* **Bernard**

'Jesu, the very thought of thee' (1849 hymn)

11 See, amid the winter's snow,
Born for us on earth below,
See, the Lamb of God appears,
Promised from eternal years!
Hail, thou ever-blessèd morn!
Hail, redemption's happy dawn!

'See, amid the winter's snow' (1858 hymn)

Willa Cather 1873–1947

12 Oh, the Germans classify, but the French arrange!

Death Comes For the Archbishop (1927)

13 I tell you there is such a thing as creative hate!

The Song of the Lark (1915)

Catherine the Great 1729–96

14 I shall be an autocrat: that's my trade. And the good Lord will forgive me: that's his.

attributed

Cato the Elder (or 'the Censor') 234–149 BC

15 *Delenda est Carthago.*
Carthage must be destroyed.

words concluding every speech Cato made in the Senate

Pliny the Elder Naturalis Historia bk. 15, ch. 74

16 *Rem tene; verba sequentur.*
Grasp the subject, the words will follow.

Caius Julius Victor Ars Rhetorica 'De inventione'

Carrie Chapman Catt 1859–1947

17 When a just cause reaches its flood-tide . . . whatever stands in the way must fall before its overwhelming power.

speech at Stockholm, Is Woman Suffrage Progressing? (1911)

Catullus c.84–c.54 BC

18 *Lugete, O Veneres Cupidinesque,*
Et quantum est hominum venustiorum.
Passer mortuus est meae puellae,
Passer, deliciae meae puellae.
Mourn, you powers of Charm and Desire,
and all you who are endowed with charm.
My lady's sparrow is dead, the sparrow
which was my lady's darling.

Carmina no. 3

19 *Vivamus, mea Lesbia, atque amemus.*
Let us live, my Lesbia, and let us love.

Carmina no. 5; cf. **Jonson** 177:23

20 *Da mi basia mille.*
Give me a thousand kisses.

Carmina no. 5

21 *Paene insularum, Sirmio, insularumque Ocelle.*

Sirmio, bright eye of peninsulas and islands.
Carmina no. 31

1 *Nam risu inepto res ineptior nulla est.*
For there is nothing sillier than a silly laugh.
Carmina no. 39; cf. **Congreve** 98:9

2 *Odi et amo: quare id faciam, fortasse requiris.*
Nescio, sed fieri sentio et excrucior.
I hate and I love: why I do so you may well
ask. I do not know, but I feel it happen and
am in agony.
Carmina no. 85

3 *Atque in perpetuum, frater, ave atque vale.*
And so, my brother, hail, and farewell
evermore!
Carmina no. 101 (tr. Sir William Marris)

Charles Causley 1917–

4 Timothy Winters comes to school
With eyes as wide as a football-pool,
Ears like bombs and teeth like splinters:
A blitz of a boy is Timothy Winters.
'Timothy Winters' (1957)

Constantine Cavafy 1863–1933

5 When you set out for Ithaka
ask that your way be long.
'Ithaka' (1911) (tr. E. Keeley and P. Sherrard)

6 And now, what will become of us without
the barbarians?
Those people were a kind of solution.
'Waiting for the Barbarians' (1904)

Edith Cavell 1865–1915

7 Standing, as I do, in view of God and
eternity, I realize that patriotism is not
enough. I must have no hatred or bitterness
towards anyone.
on the eve of her execution
in *The Times* 23 October 1915

Margaret Cavendish (Duchess of Newcastle) *c.*1624–74

8 Marriage is the grave or tomb of wit.
Plays (1662) 'Nature's Three Daughters' pt. 2, act
5, sc. 20

Count Cavour 1810–61

9 We are ready to proclaim throughout Italy
this great principle: a free church in a free
state.
speech, 27 March 1861

William Caxton *c.*1421–91

10 The worshipful father and first founder and
embellisher of ornate eloquence in our
English, I mean Master Geoffrey Chaucer.
Caxton's edition (*c.*1478) of Chaucer's
translation of Boethius *De Consolacione Philosophie*
epilogue

Paul Celan 1920–70

11 *Der Tod ist ein Meister aus Deutschland.*
Death is a master from Germany.
'Deathfugue' (written 1944)

Susannah Centlivre *c.*1669–1723

12 The real Simon Pure.
A Bold Stroke for a Wife (1718) act 5, sc. 1

Cervantes 1547–1616

13 The Knight of the Doleful Countenance.
Don Quixote (1605) pt. 1, ch. 19

14 There are only two families in the world . . .
the haves and the have-nots.
Don Quixote (1605) pt. 2, ch. 20

15 What I say is, patience, and shuffle the
cards.
Don Quixote (1605) pt. 2, ch. 23

Paul Cézanne 1839–1906

16 Treat nature in terms of the cylinder, the
sphere, the cone, all in perspective.
letter to Emile Bernard, 1904; Emile Bernard
Paul Cézanne (1925)

Joseph Chamberlain 1836–1914

17 Provided that the City of London remains,
as it is at present, the clearing-house of the
world, any other nation may be its
workshop.
speech at the Guildhall, 19 January 1904; cf.
Disraeli 112:4

18 The day of small nations has long passed
away. The day of Empires has come.
speech at Birmingham, 12 May 1904

Neville Chamberlain 1869–1940

19 How horrible, fantastic, incredible it is that
we should be digging trenches and trying
on gas-masks here because of a quarrel in a
far away country between people of whom
we know nothing.
on Germany's annexation of the Sudetenland
radio broadcast, 27 September 1938

20 This is the second time in our history that
there has come back from Germany to
Downing Street peace with honour. I
believe it is peace for our time.
speech from 10 Downing Street, 30 September
1938; cf. **Disraeli** 112:14, **Russell** 263:2

21 This morning, the British Ambassador in
Berlin handed the German government a
final Note stating that, unless we heard
from them by eleven o'clock that they were
prepared at once to withdraw their troops
from Poland, a state of war would exist
between us. I have to tell you now that no
such undertaking has been received, and
that consequently this country is at war
with Germany.
radio broadcast, 3 September 1939

22 [Hitler] missed the bus.
speech at Central Hall, Westminster, 4 April
1940

Haddon Chambers 1860–1921

23 The long arm of coincidence.
Captain Swift (1888) act 2

Nicolas-Sébastien Chamfort
1741–94

1 The poor are Europe's blacks.
   Maximes et Pensées (1796) ch. 8

2 *Sois mon frère, ou je te tue.*
   Be my brother, or I kill you.
   his interpretation of 'Fraternité ou la mort
   [Fraternity or death]'
   P. R. Anguis (ed.) *Oeuvres Complètes* (1824) vol. 1
   'Notice Historique sur la Vie et les Écrits de
   Chamfort'

John Chandler 1806–76

3 Conquering kings their titles take
   From the foes they captive make.
   hymn (1837); translation from a Latin original:
   '*Victis sibi cognomina sumant tyranni gentibus* . . . '

Raymond Chandler 1888–1959

4 It was a blonde. A blonde to make a bishop
   kick a hole in a stained glass window.
   Farewell, My Lovely (1940) ch. 13

5 Down these mean streets a man must go
   who is not himself mean, who is neither
   tarnished nor afraid.
   in *Atlantic Monthly* December 1944 'The Simple
   Art of Murder'

6 When I split an infinitive, God damn it, I
   split it so it will stay split.
   letter to Edward Weeks, 18 January 1947

7 When in doubt have a man come through
   the door with a gun in his hand.
   attributed

Coco Chanel 1883–1971

8 You ask if they were happy. This is not a
   characteristic of a European. To be
   contented—that's for the cows.
   A. Madsen *Coco Chanel* (1990) ch. 35

Henry ('Chips') Channon
1897–1958

9 What is more dull than a discreet diary?
   One might just as well have a discreet soul.
   diary, 26 July 1935

10 We saw Queen Mary looking like the
   Jungfrau, white and sparkling in the sun.
   diary, 22 June 1937

11 There is nowhere in the world where sleep
   is so deep as in the libraries of the House of
   Commons.
   diary, 15 January 1939

Charlie Chaplin 1889–1977

12 All I need to make a comedy is a park, a
   policeman and a pretty girl.
   My Autobiography (1964) ch. 10

Arthur Chapman 1873–1935

13 Out where the handclasp's a little stronger,
   Out where the smile dwells a little longer,
   That's where the West begins.
   Out Where the West Begins (1916)

George Chapman c.1559–1634

14 An Englishman,
   Being flattered, is a lamb; threatened, a lion.
   Alphonsus, Emperor of Germany (1654) act 1

15 We have watered our houses in Helicon.
   occasionally misread as, 'We have watered our
   horses in Helicon', *following an 1814 edition*
   May-Day (1611) act 3, sc. 3

16 I am ashamed the law is such an ass.
   Revenge for Honour (1654) act 3, sc. 2; cf. **Dickens**
   110:28

17 Danger, the spur of all great minds.
   The Revenge of Bussy D'Ambois (1613) act 5, sc. 1

18 And let a scholar all Earth's volumes carry,
   He will be but a walking dictionary.
   The Tears of Peace (1609) l. 530

Charles I 1600–49

19 I see all the birds are flown.
   after attempting to arrest five members of the
   *Long Parliament (**Pym**, Hampden, Haselrig,*
   Holles, and Strode)
   in the House of Commons, 4 January 1642

20 You manifestly wrong even the poorest
   ploughman, if you demand not his free
   consent.
   The King's Reasons for declining the
   jurisdiction of the High Court of Justice, 21
   January 1649

21 A subject and a sovereign are clean different
   things.
   speech on the scaffold, 30 January 1649

Charles II 1630–85

22 I am sure no man in England will take away
   my life to make you King.
   to his brother James
   William King *Political & Literary Anecdotes* (1818)

23 It is upon the navy under the good
   Providence of God that the safety, honour,
   and welfare of this realm do chiefly depend.
   'Articles of War' preamble (probably a popular
   paraphrase); Geoffrey Callender *The Naval Side of*
   British History (1952) pt. 1, ch. 8

24 This is very true: for my words are my own,
   and my actions are my ministers'.
   *reply to Lord **Rochester**'s epitaph on him*
   Thomas Hearne: *Remarks and Collections*
   (1885–1921) 17 November 1706; see **Rochester**
   258:10

25 He had been, he said, an unconscionable
   time dying; but he hoped that they would
   excuse it.
   Lord Macaulay *History of England* (1849) vol. 1,
   ch. 4

26 Let not poor Nelly starve.
   *referring to Nell **Gwyn**, his mistress*
   Bishop Gilbert Burnet *History of My Own Time*
   (1724) vol. 1, bk. 3

Charles V 1500–58

27 To God I speak Spanish, to women Italian,
   to men French, and to my horse—German.
   attributed; Lord Chesterfield *Letters to his Son*

Charles, Prince of Wales 1948-

when asked if he was 'in love':
1 Yes . . . whatever that may mean.
after the announcement of his engagement
interview, 24 February 1981; cf. **Duffy** 117:24

2 A monstrous carbuncle on the face of a
much-loved and elegant friend.
on the proposed extension to the National Gallery
speech to the Royal Institute of British
Architects, 30 May 1984; cf. **Spencer** 300:7

Pierre Charron 1541-1603

3 The true science and study of man is man.
De la Sagesse (1601) bk. 1, preface; cf. **Pope**
248:15

Geoffrey Chaucer *c.*1343-1400

4 Whan that Aprill with his shoures soote
The droghte of March hath perced to the
roote.
The Canterbury Tales 'The General Prologue' l. 1

5 And smale foweles maken melodye,
That slepen al the nyght with open ye
(So priketh hem nature in hir corages),
Thanne longen folk to goon on pilgrimages.
The Canterbury Tales 'The General Prologue' l. 9

6 He was a verray, parfit gentil knyght.
The Canterbury Tales 'The General Prologue' l. 72

7 He was as fressh as is the month of May.
The Canterbury Tales 'The General Prologue' l. 92

8 And Frenssh she spak ful faire and fetisly,
After the scole of Stratford atte Bowe,
For Frenssh of Parys was to hire unknowe.
The Canterbury Tales 'The General Prologue' l.
124

9 And theron heng a brooch of gold ful
sheene,
On which ther was first write a crowned A,
And after *Amor vincit omnia.*
The Canterbury Tales 'The General Prologue' l.
160; cf. **Virgil** 325:14

10 A Clerk there was of Oxenford also.
The Canterbury Tales 'The General Prologue' l.
285

11 Housbondes at chirche dore she hadde fyve.
The Canterbury Tales 'The General Prologue' l.
460

12 But Cristes loore and his apostels twelve
He taughte; but first he folwed it hymselve.
The Canterbury Tales 'The General Prologue' l.
527

13 Love wol nat been constreyned by maistrye.
When maistrie comth, the God of Love
anon
Beteth his wynges, and farewel, he is gon!
The Canterbury Tales 'The Franklin's Tale' l. 764

14 The bisy larke, messager of day.
The Canterbury Tales 'The Knight's Tale' l. 1491

15 The smylere with the knyf under the cloke.
The Canterbury Tales 'The Knight's Tale' l. 1999

16 Mordre wol out; that se we day by day.
The Canterbury Tales 'The Nun's Priest's Tale' l.
3052

17 'By God,' quod he, 'for pleynly, at a word,
Thy drasty rymyng is nat worth a toord!'
The Canterbury Tales 'Sir Thopas' l. 929

18 Yblessed be god that I have wedded fyve!
Welcome the sixte, whan that evere he shal.
The Canterbury Tales 'The Wife of Bath's
Prologue' l. 44

19 A likerous mouth moste han a likerous tayl.
The Canterbury Tales 'The Wife of Bath's
Prologue' l. 466

20 But yet I hadde alwey a coltes tooth.
Gat-tothed I was, and that bicam me weel.
The Canterbury Tales 'The Wife of Bath's
Prologue' l. 602

21 Wommen desiren to have sovereynetee
As wel over hir housbond as hir love.
The Canterbury Tales 'The Wife of Bath's Tale' l.
1038

22 Farewel my bok and my devocioun!
The Legend of Good Women 'The Prologue' l. 39

23 And she was fayr as is the rose in May.
The Legend of Good Women 'Cleopatra' l. 613

24 That lyf so short,
the craft so long to lerne.
The Parliament of Fowls l. 1; cf. **Hippocrates**
159:11

25 For I have seyn of a ful misty morwe
Folowen ful ofte a myrie someris day.
Troilus and Criseyde bk. 3, l. 1060

26 For of fortunes sharpe adversitee
The worst kynde of infortune is this,
A man to han ben in prosperitee,
And it remembren, whan it passed is.
Troilus and Criseyde bk. 3, l. 1625; cf. **Boethius**
57:6

27 Ye, fare wel al the snow of ferne yere!
Troilus and Criseyde bk. 5, l. 1176

28 Go, litel bok, go, litel myn tragedye.
Troilus and Criseyde bk. 5, l. 1786; cf. **Stevenson**
304:5

29 O yonge, fresshe folkes, he or she,
In which that love up groweth with youre
age.
Troilus and Criseyde bk. 5, l. 1835

30 O moral Gower, this book I directe
To the.
Troilus and Criseyde bk. 5, l. 1856

Anton Chekhov 1860-1904

31 If a lot of cures are suggested for a disease,
it means that the disease is incurable.
The Cherry Orchard (1904) act 1

32 MEDVEDENKO: Why do you wear black all
the time?
MASHA: I'm in mourning for my life, I'm
unhappy.
The Seagull (1896) act 1

33 Women can't forgive failure.
The Seagull (1896) act 2

34 When a woman isn't beautiful, people
always say, 'You have lovely eyes, you have
lovely hair.'
Uncle Vanya (1897) act 3

1 Medicine is my lawful wife and literature is
my mistress. When I get tired of one I spend
the night with the other.
  letter to A. S. Suvorin, 11 September 1888

2 Brevity is the sister of talent.
  letter to Alexander Chekhov, 11 April 1889

Cher 1946–

3 If grass can grow through cement, love can
find you at every time in your life.
  in *The Times* 30 May 1998

Mary Chesnut 1823–86

4 Atlanta is gone. That agony is over. There is
no hope but we will try to have no fear.
  after the fall of Atlanta to **Sherman**'s *army in
1864*
  Geoffrey C. Ward *The Civil War* (1991) ch. 4

Lord Chesterfield 1694–1773

5 Religion is by no means a proper subject of
conversation in a mixed company.
  Letters . . . to his Godson and Successor (1890) Letter
142

6 An injury is much sooner forgotten than an
insult.
  Letters to his Son (1774) 9 October 1746

7 Take the tone of the company that you are
in.
  Letters to his Son (1774) 16 October 1747

8 I recommend to you to take care of
minutes: for hours will take care of
themselves.
  Letters to his Son (1774) 6 November 1747; cf.
Lowndes 204:4

9 Advice is seldom welcome; and those who
want it the most always like it the least.
  Letters to his Son (1774) 29 January 1748

10 Wear your learning, like your watch in a
private pocket: and do not merely pull it out
and strike it, merely to show that you have
one.
  Letters to his Son (1774) 22 February 1748

11 Women, then, are only children of a larger
growth.
  Letters to his Son (1774) 5 September 1748; cf.
Dryden 116:27

12 It must be owned, that the Graces do not
seem to be natives of Great Britain; and I
doubt, the best of us here have more of
rough than polished diamond.
  Letters to his Son (1774) 18 November 1748

13 It is commonly said, and more particularly
by Lord Shaftesbury, that ridicule is the best
test of truth.
  Letters to his Son (1774) 6 February 1752

14 The chapter of knowledge is a very short,
but the chapter of accidents is a very long
one.
  letter to Solomon Dayrolles, 16 February 1753

15 The pleasure is momentary, the position
ridiculous, and the expense damnable.
  of sex
  attributed

G. K. Chesterton 1874–1936

16 Talk about the pews and steeples
And the Cash that goes therewith!
But the souls of Christian peoples . . .
Chuck it, Smith!
  satirizing F. E. **Smith**'s *response to the Welsh
Disestablishment Bill*
  'Antichrist' (1915)

17 I tell you naught for your comfort,
Yea, naught for your desire,
Save that the sky grows darker yet
And the sea rises higher.
  The Ballad of the White Horse (1911) bk. 1

18 For the great Gaels of Ireland
Are the men that God made mad,
For all their wars are merry,
And all their songs are sad.
  The Ballad of the White Horse (1911) bk. 2

19 Fools! For I also had my hour;
One far fierce hour and sweet:
There was a shout about my ears,
And palms before my feet.
  'The Donkey' (1900)

20 They died to save their country and they
only saved the world.
  'English Graves' (1922)

21 From all that terror teaches,
From lies of tongue and pen,
From all the easy speeches
That comfort cruel men,
From sale and profanation
Of honour and the sword,
From sleep and from damnation,
Deliver us, good Lord!
  'A Hymn' (1915)

22 The cold queen of England is looking in the
glass;
The shadow of the Valois is yawning at the
Mass.
  'Lepanto' (1915)

23 Strong gongs groaning as the guns boom
far,
Don John of Austria is going to the war.
  'Lepanto' (1915)

24 Before the Roman came to Rye or out to
Severn strode,
The rolling English drunkard made the
rolling English road.
  'The Rolling English Road' (1914)

25 A merry road, a mazy road, and such as we
did tread
The night we went to Birmingham by way
of Beachy Head.
  'The Rolling English Road' (1914)

26 For there is good news yet to hear and fine
things to be seen,
Before we go to Paradise by way of Kensal
Green.
  'The Rolling English Road' (1914)

27 Smile at us, pay us, pass us; but do not quite
forget.
For we are the people of England, that
never have spoken yet.
  'The Secret People' (1915)

1 Tea, although an Oriental,
Is a gentleman at least;
Cocoa is a cad and coward,
Cocoa is a vulgar beast.
   'Song of Right and Wrong' (1914)

2 And Noah he often said to his wife when he
sat down to dine,
'I don't care where the water goes if it
doesn't get into the wine.'
   'Wine and Water' (1914)

3 One sees great things from the valley; only
small things from the peak.
   The Innocence of Father Brown (1911)

4 Thieves respect property. They merely wish
the property to become their property that
they may more perfectly respect it.
   The Man who was Thursday (1908) ch. 4

5 Tradition means giving votes to the most
obscure of all classes, our ancestors. It is the
democracy of the dead.
   Orthodoxy (1908) ch. 4

6 They say travel broadens the mind; but you
must have the mind.
   'The Shadow of the Shark' (1921)

7 The Christian ideal has not been tried and
found wanting. It has been found difficult;
and left untried.
   What's Wrong with the World (1910) pt. 1 'The
   Unfinished Temple'

8 Journalism largely consists in saying 'Lord
Jones Dead' to people who never knew that
Lord Jones was alive.
   The Wisdom of Father Brown (1914)

9 Democracy means government by the
uneducated, while aristocracy means
government by the badly educated.
   in *New York Times* 1 February 1931, pt. 5

10 AM IN MARKET HARBOROUGH. WHERE OUGHT
I TO BE?
telegram to his wife in London
   Autobiography (1936)

11 When men stop believing in God they don't
believe in nothing; they believe in anything.
   widely attributed, although not traced in his
   works; first recorded as 'The first effect of not
   believing in God is to believe in anything' in
   Emile Cammaerts *Chesterton: The Laughing
   Prophet* (1937)

Lydia Maria Child 1802–80

12 Woman stock is rising in the market. I shall
not live to see women vote, but I'll come
and rap at the ballot box.
   letter to Sarah Shaw, 3 August 1856

Erskine Childers 1870–1922

13 The riddle of the sands.
   title of novel (1903)

14 Come closer, boys. It will be easier for you.
to the firing squad at his execution
   Burke Wilkinson *The Zeal of the Convert* (1976)
   ch. 26

Charles Chilton *see* Joan Littlewood

Rufus Choate 1799–1859

15 Its constitution the glittering and sounding
generalities of natural right which make up
the Declaration of Independence.
   letter to the Maine Whig State Central
   Committee, 9 August 1856; cf. **Emerson** 124:17

Duc de Choiseul 1719–85

16 A minister who moves about in society is in
a position to read the signs of the times
even in a festive gathering, but one who
remains shut up in his office learns nothing.
   Jack F. Bernard *Talleyrand* (1973)

Noam Chomsky 1928–

17 Colourless green ideas sleep furiously.
   Syntactic Structures (1957) ch. 2

18 The Internet is an élite organization; most
of the population of the world has never
even made a phone call.
on the limitations of the World Wide Web
   in *Observer* 18 February 1996

Agatha Christie 1890–1976

19 He [Hercule Poirot] tapped his forehead.
'These little grey cells. It is "up to them".'
   The Mysterious Affair at Styles (1920) ch. 10

David Christy 1802–*c.*68

20 Cotton is King; or, the economical relations
of slavery.
   title of book, 1855

Chuang Tzu (Zhuangzi) *c.*369–286 BC

21 Once I, Chang Chou, dreamed that I was a
butterfly and was happy as a butterfly. I was
conscious that I was quite pleased with
myself but I did not know that I was Chou.
Suddenly I awoke and there I was, visibly
Chou. I do not know whether it was Chou
dreaming that he was a butterfly or the
butterfly dreaming that it was Chou.
   Chuang Tzu ch. 2; cf. **Basho** 26:3

Francis Pharcellus Church 1839–1906

22 Yes, Virginia, there is a Santa Claus.
*replying to a letter from eight-year-old Virginia
O'Hanlon*
   editorial in New York *Sun*, 21 September 1897

Charles Churchill 1731–64

23 Be England what she will,
With all her faults, she is my country still.
   The Farewell (1764) l. 27; cf. **Cowper** 101:30

24 Just to the windward of the law.
   The Ghost (1763) bk. 3, l. 56

25 Keep up appearances; there lies the test;
The world will give thee credit for the rest.
   Night (1761) l. 311

1 Apt Alliteration's artful aid.

The Prophecy of Famine (1763) l. 86

Lord Randolph Churchill 1849–94

2 The forest laments in order that Mr Gladstone may perspire.

*on **Gladstone**'s hobby of felling trees*

speech on Financial Reform, delivered in Blackpool, 24 January 1884

3 I decided some time ago that if the G. O. M. went for Home Rule, the Orange card would be the one to play. Please God it may turn out the ace of trumps and not the two.

'G. O. M.' = *Grand Old Man* (**Gladstone**)

letter to Lord Justice FitzGibbon, 16 February 1886; cf. **Shapiro** 290:20

4 Ulster will fight; Ulster will be right.

public letter, 7 May 1886

5 An old man in a hurry.

*on **Gladstone***

address to the electors of South Paddington, 19 June 1886

6 I never could make out what those damned dots [decimal points] meant.

W. S. Churchill *Lord Randolph Churchill* (1906) vol. 2

Winston Churchill 1874–1965

7 It cannot in the opinion of His Majesty's Government be classified as slavery in the extreme acceptance of the word without some risk of terminological inexactitude.

speech in the House of Commons, 22 February 1906

8 Business carried on as usual during alterations on the map of Europe.

on the self-adopted 'motto' of the British people

speech at Guildhall, 9 November 1914

9 The whole map of Europe has been changed . . . but as the deluge subsides and the waters fall short we see the dreary steeples of Fermanagh and Tyrone emerging once again.

speech in the House of Commons, 16 February 1922

10 Anyone can rat, but it takes a certain amount of ingenuity to re-rat.

on rejoining the Conservatives twenty years after leaving them for the Liberals, c.1924

Kay Halle *Irrepressible Churchill* (1966)

11 I have waited 50 years to see the boneless wonder sitting on the Treasury Bench.

*of Ramsay **MacDonald***

speech in the House of Commons, 28 January 1931

12 Dictators ride to and fro upon tigers which they dare not dismount. And the tigers are getting hungry.

letter, 11 November 1937

13 I cannot forecast to you the action of Russia. It is a riddle wrapped in a mystery inside an enigma.

radio broadcast, 1 October 1939

14 I have nothing to offer but blood, toil, tears and sweat.

speech in the House of Commons, 13 May 1940; cf. **Byron** 77:22

15 We shall not flag or fail. We shall go on to the end. We shall fight in France, we shall fight on the seas and oceans, we shall fight with growing confidence and growing strength in the air, we shall defend our island, whatever the cost may be. We shall fight on the beaches, we shall fight on the landing grounds, we shall fight in the fields and in the streets, we shall fight in the hills; we shall never surrender.

speech in the House of Commons, 4 June 1940

16 Let us therefore brace ourselves to our duty, and so bear ourselves that, if the British Empire and its Commonwealth lasts for a thousand years, men will still say, 'This was their finest hour.'

speech in the House of Commons, 18 June 1940

17 Never in the field of human conflict was so much owed by so many to so few.

on the Battle of Britain

speech in the House of Commons, 20 August 1940

18 Give us the tools and we will finish the job.

radio broadcast, 9 February 1941

19 When I warned them [the French Government] that Britain would fight on alone whatever they did, their generals told their Prime Minister and his divided Cabinet, 'In three weeks England will have her neck wrung like a chicken.' Some chicken! Some neck!

speech to Canadian Parliament, 30 December 1941

20 Now this is not the end. It is not even the beginning of the end. But it is, perhaps, the end of the beginning.

on the Battle of Egypt

speech at the Mansion House, London, 10 November 1942

21 We make this wide encircling movement in the Mediterranean, having for its primary object the recovery of the command of that vital sea, but also having for its object the exposure of the underbelly of the Axis, especially Italy, to heavy attack.

often quoted as, 'The soft underbelly of Europe'

speech in the House of Commons, 11 November 1942

22 There is no finer investment for any community than putting milk into babies.

radio broadcast, 21 March 1943

23 From Stettin in the Baltic to Trieste in the Adriatic an iron curtain has descended across the Continent.

*'iron curtain' previously had been applied by others to the Soviet Union or her sphere of influence, e.g. Ethel Snowden Through Bolshevik Russia (1920), Dr **Goebbels** Das Reich (25 February 1945), and by Churchill*

*himself in a cable to President **Truman** (4 June 1945)*
speech at Westminster College, Fulton, Missouri, 5 March 1946

1 Democracy is the worst form of Government except all those other forms that have been tried from time to time.
speech in the House of Commons, 11 November 1947

2 This is the sort of English up with which I will not put.
Ernest Gowers *Plain Words* (1948) 'Troubles with Prepositions'

3 Naval tradition?. Monstrous. Nothing but rum, sodomy, prayers, and the lash.
often quoted as 'rum, sodomy, and the lash', as in Peter Gretton Former Naval Person (1968)
Harold Nicolson, diary, 17 August 1950

4 To jaw-jaw is always better than to war-war.
speech at White House, 26 June 1954

5 It was the nation and the race dwelling all round the globe that had the lion's heart. I had the luck to be called upon to give the roar.
speech at Westminster Hall, 30 November 1954

6 I have taken more out of alcohol than alcohol has taken out of me.
Quentin Reynolds *By Quentin Reynolds* (1964) ch. 11

7 In defeat unbeatable: in victory unbearable.
*of Lord **Montgomery***
Edward Marsh *Ambrosia and Small Beer* (1964) ch. 5

8 Like a powerful graceful cat walking delicately and unsoiled across a rather muddy street.
*of **Balfour**'s moving from **Asquith**'s Cabinet to that of **Lloyd George***
Great Contemporaries (1937)

*of the career of Lord **Curzon**:*
9 The morning had been golden; the noontide was bronze; and the evening lead. But all were solid, and each was polished till it shone after its fashion.
Great Contemporaries (1937)

10 It is a good thing for an uneducated man to read books of quotations.
My Early Life (1930) ch. 9

11 In war: resolution. In defeat: defiance. In victory: magnanimity. In peace: goodwill.
The Second World War vol. 1 (1948) epigraph, which according to Edward Marsh in *A Number of People* (1939), occurred to Churchill shortly after the conclusion of the First World War

12 Jellicoe was the only man on either side who could lose the war in an afternoon.
The World Crisis (1927) pt. 1, ch. 5

13 The ability to foretell what is going to happen tomorrow, next week, next month, and next year. And to have the ability afterwards to explain why it didn't happen.
describing the qualifications desirable in a prospective politician
B. Adler *Churchill Wit* (1965)

14 I am fond of pigs. Dogs look up to us. Cats look down on us. Pigs treat us as equals.
attributed, in M. Gilbert *Never Despair* (1988)

15 NANCY ASTOR: If I were your wife I would put poison in your coffee!
CHURCHILL: And if I were your husband I would drink it.
Consuelo Vanderbilt Balsan *Glitter and Gold* (1952)

16 A sheep in sheep's clothing.
*of Clement **Attlee***
Lord Home *The Way the Wind Blows* (1976) ch. 6

Count Galeazzo Ciano 1903–44

17 Victory has a hundred fathers, but defeat is an orphan.
literally 'no-one wants to recognise defeat as his own'
Diary (1946) vol. 2, 9 September 1942

Colley Cibber 1671–1757

18 Oh! how many torments lie in the small circle of a wedding-ring!
The Double Gallant (1707) act 1, sc. 2

19 Off with his head—so much for Buckingham.
Richard III (1700) act 4 (adapted from Shakespeare); cf. **Shakespeare** 286:6

20 Perish the thought!
Richard III (1700) act 5 (adapted from Shakespeare)

21 Conscience avaunt, Richard's himself again.
Richard III (1700) act 5 (adapted from Shakespeare)

Cicero (Marcus Tullius Cicero) 106–43 BC

22 *Salus populi suprema est lex.*
The good of the people is the chief law.
De Legibus bk. 3, ch. 8

23 *'Ipse dixit.' 'Ipse' autem erat Pythagoras.*
'He himself said', and this 'himself' was Pythagoras.
De Natura Deorum bk. 1, ch. 10

24 *Summum bonum.*
The highest good.
De Officiis bk. 1, ch. 5

25 *O tempora, O mores!*
Oh, the times! Oh, the manners!
In Catilinam Speech 1, ch. 1

26 *Civis Romanus sum.*
I am a Roman citizen.
In Verrem Speech 5, ch. 147; **Kennedy** 184:14

27 *Quod di omen avertant.*
May the gods avert this omen.
Third Philippic ch. 35

28 The sinews of war, unlimited money.
Fifth Philippic ch. 5; cf. **Bacon** 21:28, **Farquhar** 126:11

29 Laws are silent in time of war.
Pro Milone ch. 11

1 *Cui bono?*
To whose profit?
Pro Roscio Amerino ch. 84 and *Pro Milone* ch. 12, sect. 32, quoting L. Cassius Longinus Ravilla

2 *Cum dignitate otium.*
Leisure with honour.
Pro Sestio ch. 98

3 O happy Rome, born when I was consul!
Juvenal *Satires* poem 10, l. 122

4 The young man should be praised, decorated, and got rid of.
of Octavian, the future Emperor Augustus
referred to in a letter from Decimus Brutus to Cicero

E. M. Cioran 1911–95

5 I do nothing, granted. But I see the hours pass—which is better than trying to fill them.
in *Guardian* 11 May 1993

Claire Clairmont 1798–1879

6 I shall ever remember the gentleness of your manners and the wild originality of your countenance.
letter to Lord Byron, 16 April 1816

John Clare 1793–1864

7 He could not die when the trees were green, For he loved the time too well.
'The Dying Child'

8 My life hath been one chain of contradictions,
Madhouses, prisons, whore-shops.
'Child Harold' (written 1841) l. 146

9 A quiet, pilfering, unprotected race.
'The Gipsy Camp' (1841)

10 I long for scenes where man hath never trod
A place where woman never smiled or wept
There to abide with my Creator God
And sleep as I in childhood sweetly slept,
Untroubling and untroubled where I lie
The grass below, above, the vaulted sky.
'I Am' (1848)

Edward Hyde, Earl of Clarendon 1609–74

11 Without question, when he first drew the sword, he threw away the scabbard.
of Hampden
The History of the Rebellion (1703, ed. W. D. Macray, 1888) vol. 3

12 He had a head to contrive, a tongue to persuade, and a hand to execute any mischief.
of Hampden
The History of the Rebellion (1703, ed. W. D. Macray, 1888) vol. 3; cf. **Gibbon** 139:5

13 So enamoured on peace that he would have been glad the King should have bought it at any price.
of Falkland
The History of the Rebellion (1703, ed. W. D. Macray, 1888) vol. 3

14 He will be looked upon by posterity as a brave bad man.
of Cromwell
The History of the Rebellion (1703, ed. W. D. Macray, 1888) vol. 6

Alan Clark 1928–99

15 There are no true friends in politics. We are all sharks circling, and waiting, for traces of blood to appear in the water.
diary, 30 November 1990

16 Our old friend economical . . . with the *actualité*.
under cross-examination at the Old Bailey during the Matrix Churchill case
in *Independent* 10 November 1992; cf. **Armstrong** 15:2

17 Safe is spelled D-U-L-L. Politics has got to be a fun activity, otherwise people turn their back on it.
on being selected as parliamentary candidate for Kensington and Chelsea
in *Daily Telegraph* 25 January 1997

Arthur C. Clarke 1917–

18 When a distinguished but elderly scientist states that something is possible, he is almost certainly right. When he states that something is impossible, he is very probably wrong.
Profiles of the Future (1962) ch. 2

19 Any sufficiently advanced technology is indistinguishable from magic.
Profiles of the Future (1962) ch. 2

Austin Clarke 1896–1974

20 And O! She was the Sunday
In every week.
'The Planter's Daughter' (1929)

Claudian 370–c.404

21 *Erret, et extremos alter scrutetur Hiberos:*
Plus habet hic vitae, plus habet ille viae.
Let who will be a wanderer and explore farthest Spain: such may have more of a journey: he of Verona has more of a life.
of the old man of Verona who never left his home
De Sene Veronensi

Appius Claudius Caecus fl. 312–279 BC

22 *Faber est suae quisque fortunae.*
Each man is the smith of his own fortune.
Sallust *Ad Caesarem Senem de Re Publica Oratio* ch. 1, sect. 2

Karl von Clausewitz 1780–1831

1 War is nothing but a continuation of politics with the admixture of other means.
commonly rendered as 'War is the continuation of politics by other means'
  On War (1832–4) bk. 8, ch. 6, sect. B

Henry Clay 1777–1852

2 The gentleman [Josiah Quincy] can not have forgotten his own sentiment, uttered even on the floor of this House, 'peaceably if we can, forcibly if we must'.
  speech in Congress, 8 January 1813; cf. **Quincy** 253:9

3 I had rather be right than be President.
  to Senator Preston of South Carolina, 1839
  attributed; S. W. McCall *Life of Thomas Brackett Reed* (1914) ch. 14

Philip 'Tubby' Clayton 1885–1972

4 CHAIRMAN: What is service?
  CANDIDATE: The rent we pay for our room on earth.
  admission ceremony of Toc H, a society founded after the First World War to provide Christian fellowship and social service
  Tresham Lever *Clayton of Toc H* (1971)

Eldridge Cleaver 1935–98

5 What we're saying today is that you're either part of the solution or you're part of the problem.
  speech in San Francisco, 1968

John Cleland 1710–89

6 Truth! stark naked truth, is the word.
  Memoirs of a Woman of Pleasure a.k.a. *Fanny Hill* (1749) vol. 1

Georges Clemenceau 1841–1929

7 War is too serious a matter to entrust to military men.
  attributed to Clemenceau, but also to Briand and Talleyrand

8 My home policy: I wage war; my foreign policy: I wage war. All the time I wage war.
  speech to French Chamber of Deputies, 8 March 1918

9 It is easier to make war than to make peace.
  speech at Verdun, 20 July 1919

Clement XIII 1693–1769

10 *Sint ut sunt aut non sint.*
  Let them be as they are or not be at all.
  replying to a request for changes in the constitutions of the Society of Jesus
  J. A. M. Crétineau-Joly *Clément XIV et les Jésuites* (1847)

Grover Cleveland 1837–1908

11 I have considered the pension list of the republic a roll of honour.
  Veto of Dependent Pension Bill, 5 July 1888

Harlan Cleveland 1918–

12 The revolution of rising expectations.
  phrase coined, 1950; Arthur Schlesinger *A Thousand Days* (1965) ch. 16

Hillary Rodham Clinton 1947–

13 I am not standing by my man, like Tammy Wynette. I am sitting here because I love him, I respect him, and I honour what he's been through and what we've been through together.
  interview on *60 Minutes*, CBS-TV, 27 January 1992

14 I could have stayed home and baked cookies and had teas. But what I decided was to fulfil my profession, which I entered before my husband was in public life.
  in *Albany Times-Union* 17 March 1992

William Jefferson ('Bill') Clinton 1946–

15 I experimented with marijuana a time or two. And I didn't like it, and I didn't inhale.
  in *Washington Post* 30 March 1992

16 The comeback kid!
  description of himself after coming second in the New Hampshire primary in the 1992 presidential election (since 1952, no presidential candidate had won the election without first winning in New Hampshire)
  Michael Barone and Grant Ujifusa *The Almanac of American Politics 1994*

17 I did not have sexual relations with that woman.
  television interview, in *Daily Telegraph* 27 January 1998

18 Peace is no longer a dream. It is a reality.
  of the Northern Ireland referendum on the Good Friday agreement
  in *Sunday Times* 24 May 1998

Lord Clive 1725–74

19 By God, Mr Chairman, at this moment I stand astonished at my own moderation!
  reply during Parliamentary cross-examination, 1773
  G. R. Gleig *The Life of Robert, First Lord Clive* (1848) ch. 29

Arthur Hugh Clough 1819–61

20 Am I prepared to lay down my life for the British female?
  Really, who knows? . . .
  Ah, for a child in the street I could strike; for the full-blown lady—
  Somehow, Eustace, alas! I have not felt the vocation.
  Amours de Voyage (1858) canto 2, pt. 4

21 Afloat. We move: Delicious! Ah,
  What else is like the gondola?
  Dipsychus (1865) sc. 5

22 How pleasant it is to have money, heigh ho!
  How pleasant it is to have money.
  Dipsychus (1865) sc. 5

1 Thou shalt have one God only; who
Would be at the expense of two?
'The Latest Decalogue' (1862); cf. **Bible** 34:16

2 Thou shalt not kill; but need'st not strive
Officiously to keep alive.
'The Latest Decalogue' (1862)

3 Do not adultery commit;
Advantage rarely comes of it.
'The Latest Decalogue' (1862)

4 Say not the struggle naught availeth,
The labour and the wounds are vain,
The enemy faints not, nor faileth,
And as things have been, things remain.
'Say not the struggle naught availeth' (1855)

5 In front the sun climbs slow, how slowly,
But westward, look, the land is bright.
'Say not the struggle naught availeth' (1855)

Kurt Cobain 1967–94
see also **Young** 344:21

6 I'd rather be dead than cool.
'Stay Away' (1991 song)

William Cobbett 1762–1835

7 Nouns of number, or multitude, such as
Mob, Parliament, Rabble, House of
Commons, Regiment, Court of King's
Bench, Den of Thieves, and the like.
English Grammar (1817) letter 17 'Syntax as
Relating to Pronouns'

8 The great wen of all.
of London
Rural Rides: The Kentish Journal in *Cobbett's Weekly
Political Register* 5 January 1822, vol. 40

Alison Cockburn 1713–94

9 O fickle Fortune, why this cruel sporting?
Why thus torment us poor sons of day?
Nae mair your smiles can cheer me, nae
mair your frowns can fear me,
For the flowers of the forest are a' wade
away.
'*wade*' = weeded (often quoted as 'For the flowers
of the forest are withered away')
'The Flowers of the Forest' (1765)

Claud Cockburn 1904–81

10 Small earthquake in Chile. Not many dead.
*winning entry for a dullest headline competition
at* The Times
In Time of Trouble (1956) ch. 10

Jean Cocteau 1889–1963

11 Life is a horizontal fall.
Opium (1930)

12 If it has to choose who is to be crucified, the
crowd will always save Barabbas.
Le Rappel à l'ordre (1926) 'Le Coq et l'Arlequin'

George M. Cohan 1878–1942

13 Over there, over there,
Send the word, send the word over there

That the Yanks are coming.
The drums rum-tumming everywhere.
'Over There' (1917 song)

14 I'm a Yankee Doodle Dandy,
A Yankee Doodle, do or die;
A real live nephew of my Uncle Sam's,
Born on the fourth of July.
'Yankee Doodle Boy' (1904 song); cf.
Anonymous 11:6

Desmond Coke 1879–1931

15 His blade struck the water a full second
before any other: the lad had started well.
Nor did he flag as the race wore on . . . as
the boats began to near the winning-post,
his oar was dipping into the water nearly
twice as often as any other.
*often misquoted as, 'All rowed fast, but none so
fast as stroke'*
Sandford of Merton (1903) ch. 12

Edward Coke 1552–1634

16 How long soever it hath continued, if it be
against reason, it is of no force in law.
The First Part of the Institutes of the Laws of England
(1628) bk. 1, ch. 10, sect. 80

17 For a man's house is his castle, *et domus sua
cuique est tutissimum refugium* [and each man's
home is his safest refuge].
The Third Part of the Institutes of the Laws of England
(1628) ch. 73

18 They [corporations] cannot commit treason,
nor be outlawed, nor excommunicate, for
they have no souls.
The Reports of Sir Edward Coke (1658) vol. 5, pt. 10
'The case of Sutton's Hospital'; cf. **Thurlow**
318:2

19 Magna Charta is such a fellow, that he will
have no sovereign.
*on the Lords' Amendment to the Petition of Right,
17 May 1628*
J. Rushworth *Historical Collections* (1659) vol. 1

Hartley Coleridge 1796–1849

20 But what is Freedom? Rightly understood,
A universal licence to be good.
'Liberty' (1833)

Samuel Taylor Coleridge
1772–1834

21 O Lady! we receive but what we give,
And in our life alone does Nature live.
'Dejection: an Ode' (1802) st. 4

22 But oh! each visitation
Suspends what nature gave me at my birth,
My shaping spirit of imagination.
'Dejection: an Ode' (1802) st. 6

23 And the Devil did grin, for his darling sin
Is pride that apes humility.
'The Devil's Thoughts' (1799)

1 The frost performs its secret ministry,
Unhelped by any wind.
'Frost at Midnight' (1798) l. 1

2 At this moment he was unfortunately called
out by a person on business from Porlock.
'Kubla Khan' (1816) preliminary note

3 In Xanadu did Kubla Khan
A stately pleasure-dome decree:
Where Alph, the sacred river, ran
Through caverns measureless to man
Down to a sunless sea.
So twice five miles of fertile ground
With walls and towers were girdled round.
'Kubla Khan' (1816)

4 A savage place! as holy and enchanted
As e'er beneath a waning moon was
haunted
By woman wailing for her demon-lover!
And from this chasm, with ceaseless
turmoil seething,
As if this earth in fast thick pants were
breathing,
A mighty fountain momently was forced.
'Kubla Khan' (1816)

5 It was a miracle of rare device,
A sunny pleasure-dome with caves of ice.
'Kubla Khan' (1816)

6 And 'mid this tumult Kubla heard from far
Ancestral voices prophesying war!
'Kubla Khan' (1816)

7 And all who heard should see them there,
And all should cry, Beware! Beware!
His flashing eyes, his floating hair!
Weave a circle round him thrice,
And close your eyes with holy dread,
For he on honey-dew hath fed,
And drunk the milk of Paradise.
'Kubla Khan' (1816)

8 It is an ancient Mariner,
And he stoppeth one of three.
'The Rime of the Ancient Mariner' (1798) pt. 1

9 He holds him with his glittering eye—
The Wedding-Guest stood still.
'The Rime of the Ancient Mariner' (1798) pt. 1

10 And ice, mast-high, came floating by,
As green as emerald.
'The Rime of the Ancient Mariner' (1798) pt. 1

11 'God save thee, ancient Mariner!
From the fiends that plague thee thus!—
Why look'st thou so?'—With my cross-bow
I shot the Albatross.
'The Rime of the Ancient Mariner' (1798) pt. 1

12 We were the first that ever burst
Into that silent sea.
'The Rime of the Ancient Mariner' (1798) pt. 2

13 Water, water, everywhere,
And all the boards did shrink;
Water, water, everywhere,
Nor any drop to drink.
'The Rime of the Ancient Mariner' (1798) pt. 2

14 The Sun's rim dips; the stars rush out;
At one stride comes the dark.
'The Rime of the Ancient Mariner' (1798) pt. 3

15 The hornèd Moon, with one bright star
Within the nether tip.
'The Rime of the Ancient Mariner' (1798) pt. 3;
cf. **Wordsworth** 339:14

16 And a thousand thousand slimy things
Lived on; and so did I.
'The Rime of the Ancient Mariner' (1798) pt. 4

17 Like one, that on a lonesome road
Doth walk in fear and dread,
And having once turned round walks on,
And turns no more his head;
Because he knows, a frightful fiend
Doth close behind him tread.
'The Rime of the Ancient Mariner' (1798) pt. 6

18 He prayeth well, who loveth well
Both man and bird and beast.
He prayeth best, who loveth best
All things both great and small.
'The Rime of the Ancient Mariner' (1798) pt. 7

19 A sadder and a wiser man,
He rose the morrow morn.
'The Rime of the Ancient Mariner' (1798) pt. 7

20 Well, they are gone, and here must I
remain,
This lime-tree bower my prison!
'This Lime-Tree Bower my Prison' (1800) l. 1

21 That willing suspension of disbelief for the
moment, which constitutes poetic faith.
Biographia Literaria (1817) ch. 14

22 The dwarf sees farther than the giant, when
he has the giant's shoulder to mount on.
The Friend (1818) vol. 2 'On the Principles of
Political Knowledge'; cf. **Bernard** 31:4,
Newton 233:14

23 To see him act, is like reading Shakespeare
by flashes of lightning.
of Edmund Kean
Table Talk (1835) 27 April 1823

24 Prose = words in their best order;—poetry =
the *best* words in the best order.
Table Talk (1835) 12 July 1827

25 In politics, what begins in fear usually ends
in folly.
Table Talk (1835) 5 October 1830

26 Youth and Hope—those twin realities of this
phantom world!
Table Talk (1835) 10 July 1834

27 Summer has set in with its usual severity.
letter to Vincent Novello, 9 May 1826

Colette 1873–1954

28 Her childhood, then her adolescence, had
taught her patience, hope, silence and the
easy manipulation of the weapons and
virtues of all prisoners.
Chéri (1920) pt. 2 (translated by Janet Flanner,
1930)

29 If we want to be sincere, we must admit
that there is a well-nourished love and an
ill-nourished love. And the rest is literature.
La Fin de Chéri (1926) (translated by Viola Gerard
Garvin)

William Collingbourne d. 1484

1 The Cat, the Rat, and Lovell our dog
Rule all England under a hog.
*referring to Sir William Catesby (d. 1485), Sir
Richard Ratcliffe (d. 1485), Lord Lovell
(1454–c.1487), whose crest was a dog, and King
Richard III, whose emblem was a wild boar*
> Robert Fabyan *The Concordance of Chronicles* (ed.
> H. Ellis, 1811)

Lord Collingwood 1748–1810

2 Now, gentlemen, let us do something today
which the world may talk of hereafter.
before the Battle of Trafalgar, 21 October 1805
> G. L. Newnham Collingwood (ed.) *A Selection
> from the Correspondence of Lord Collingwood* (1828)
> vol. 1

R. G. Collingwood 1889–1943

3 Perfect freedom is reserved for the man
who lives by his own work and in that work
does what he wants to do.
> *Speculum Mentis* (1924); cf. **Gill** 141:11

Charles Collins

4 Any old iron, any old iron,
Any any old old iron?
You look neat
Talk about a treat,
You look dapper from your napper to your
feet.
> 'Any Old Iron' (1911 song, with E. A. Sheppard
> and Fred Terry); the second line often sung 'Any
> any any old iron?'

5 My old man said, 'Follow the van,
Don't dilly-dally on the way!'
Off went the cart with the home packed in
it,
I walked behind with my old cock linnet,
But I dillied and dallied, dallied and dillied,
Lost the van and don't know where to roam.
You can't trust the 'specials' like the old
time 'coppers'
When you can't find your way home.
> 'Don't Dilly-Dally on the Way' (1919 song, with
> Fred Leigh); popularized by Marie Lloyd

Michael Collins 1890–1922

6 That volley which we have just heard is the
only speech which it is proper to make over
the grave of a dead Fenian.
*at the funeral of Thomas Ashe, who had died in
prison while on hunger strike*
> Glasnevin cemetery, 30th September 1917

7 Think—what I have got for Ireland?
Something which she has wanted these past
seven hundred years. Will anyone be
satisfied at the bargain? Will anyone? I tell
you this—early this morning I signed my
death warrant. I thought at the time how
odd, how ridiculous—a bullet may just as
well have done the job five years ago.
*on signing the treaty establishing the Irish Free
State; he was shot from ambush in the following
year*
> letter, 6 December 1921

8 We've been waiting seven hundred years,
you can have the seven minutes.
*arriving at Dublin Castle for the handover by
British forces on 16 January 1922, and being told
that he was seven minutes late*
> Tim Pat Coogan *Michael Collins* (1990); attributed

9 My own fellow-countrymen won't kill me.
*before leaving for Cork where he was ambushed
and killed, 20 August 1922*
> James Mackay *Michael Collins* (1996)

William Collins 1721–59

10 To fair Fidele's grassy tomb
Soft maids and village hinds shall bring
Each opening sweet of earliest bloom,
And rifle all the breathing spring.
> 'Dirge' (1744); occasionally included in 18th-
> century performances of Shakespeare's
> *Cymbeline*

11 How sleep the brave, who sink to rest,
By all their country's wishes blest!
> 'Ode Written in the Year 1746' (1748)

George Colman, the Elder
1732–94
and **David Garrick** 1717–79

12 Love and a cottage! Eh, Fanny! Ah, give me
indifference and a coach and six!
> *The Clandestine Marriage* (1766) act 1; cf. **Keats**
> 181:23

George Colman, the Younger
1762–1836

13 Oh, London is a fine town,
A very famous city,
Where all the streets are paved with gold,
And all the maidens pretty.
> *The Heir at Law* (performed 1797, published
> 1808) act 1, sc. 2

14 Says he, 'I am a handsome man, but I'm a
gay deceiver.'
> *Love Laughs at Locksmiths* (1808) act 2

Charles Caleb Colton c.1780–1832

15 When you have nothing to say, say nothing.
> *Lacon* (1820) vol. 1, no. 183

16 Examinations are formidable even to the
best prepared, for the greatest fool may ask
more than the wisest man can answer.
> *Lacon* (1820) vol. 1, no. 322

St Colum Cille ?521–597

17 To every cow her calf, to every book its
copy.
> traditionally attributed

Betty Comden 1919–
and **Adolph Green** 1915–

18 New York, New York,—a helluva town.
> *New York, New York* (1945 song)

19 The party's over, it's time to call it a day.
> 'The Party's Over' (1956)

Denis Compton 1918–97

1 I couldn't bat for the length of time required to score 500. I'd get bored and fall over.

to Brian Lara, who had recently scored 501 not out, a world record in first-class cricket

in *Daily Telegraph* 27 June 1994

Ivy Compton-Burnett 1884–1969

2 Well, of course, people are only human . . . But it really does not seem much for them to be.

A Family and a Fortune (1939) ch. 2

3 People don't resent having nothing nearly as much as too little.

A Family and a Fortune (1939) ch. 4

4 A leopard does not change his spots, or change his feeling that spots are rather a credit.

More Women than Men (1933) ch. 4

Marquis de Condorcet 1743–94

5 As one meditates about the nature of the moral sciences one really cannot avoid the conclusion that since, like the physical sciences, they rest upon observation of the facts, they ought to follow the same methods, acquire a language no less exact and precise, and so attain to the same degree of certainty. If some being alien to our species were to set himself to study us he would find no difference between these two studies, and would examine human society as we do that of bees or beavers.

Discours prononcé dans l'Académie Française 21 February 1782

Confucius (K'ung Fu-tzu) 551–479 BC

textual translations are those of Wing-Tsit Chan, 1963

6 A ruler who governs his state by virtue is like the north polar star, which remains in its place while all the other stars revolve around it.

Analects ch. 2, v. 1

7 A man who reviews the old so as to find out the new is qualified to teach others.

Analects ch. 2, v. 11

8 The Way of our Master is none other than conscientiousness and altruism.

the 'one thread' of Confucius' doctrines

Analects ch. 4, v. 15

William Congreve 1670–1729

9 There is nothing more unbecoming a man of quality than to laugh; Jesu, 'tis such a vulgar expression of the passion!

The Double Dealer (1694) act 1, sc. 4; cf. **Catullus** 86:1

10 She lays it on with a trowel.

The Double Dealer (1694) act 3, sc. 10

11 See how love and murder will out.

The Double Dealer (1694) act 4, sc. 6

12 Has he not a rogue's face? . . . a hanging-look to me . . . has a damned Tyburn-face, without the benefit o' the Clergy.

Love for Love (1695) act 2, sc. 7

13 Music has charms to sooth a savage breast.

The Mourning Bride (1697) act 1, sc. 1

14 Heaven has no rage, like love to hatred turned,
Nor Hell a fury, like a woman scorned.

The Mourning Bride (1697) act 3, sc. 8

15 SHARPER: Thus grief still treads upon the heels of pleasure:
Married in haste, we may repent at leisure.
SETTER: Some by experience find those words mis-placed:
At leisure married, they repent in haste.

The Old Bachelor (1693) act 5, sc. 1

16 They come together like the Coroner's Inquest, to sit upon the murdered reputations of the week.

The Way of the World (1700) act 1, sc. 1

17 Say what you will, 'tis better to be left than never to have been loved.

The Way of the World (1700) act 2, sc. 1; cf. **Tennyson** 311:18

18 WITWOUD: Madam, do you pin up your hair with all your letters?
MILLAMANT: Only with those in verse, Mr Witwoud. I never pin up my hair with prose.

The Way of the World (1700) act 2, sc. 4

19 These articles subscribed, if I continue to endure you a little longer, I may by degrees dwindle into a wife.

The Way of the World (1700) act 4, sc. 5

20 I confess freely to you, I could never look long upon a monkey, without very mortifying reflections.

letter to John Dennis, 10 July 1695

Gerry Conlon 1954–

21 The life sentence goes on. It's like a runaway train that you can't just get off.

of life after his conviction was quashed by the Court of Appeal

in *Irish Post* 13 September 1997

James M. Connell 1852–1929

22 The people's flag is deepest red;
It shrouded oft our martyred dead.

'The Red Flag' (1889) in H. E. Piggott *Songs that made History* (1937) ch. 6

23 Then raise the scarlet standard high!
Within its shade we'll live or die.
Tho' cowards flinch and traitors sneer,
We'll keep the red flag flying here.

'The Red Flag' (1889) in H. E. Piggott *Songs that made History* (1937) ch. 6

Billy Connolly 1942–

24 Marriage is a wonderful invention; but, then again, so is a bicycle repair kit.

Duncan Campbell *Billy Connolly* (1976)

Cyril Connolly 1903–74

1 Whom the gods wish to destroy they first call promising.
Enemies of Promise (1938) ch. 13

2 Imprisoned in every fat man a thin one is wildly signalling to be let out.
The Unquiet Grave (1944) pt. 2; cf. **Orwell** 237:8

3 Our memories are card-indexes consulted, and then put back in disorder by authorities whom we do not control.
The Unquiet Grave (1944) pt. 3

James Connolly 1868–1916

4 The worker is the slave of capitalist society, the female worker is the slave of that slave.
The Re-conquest of Ireland (1915)

5 The time for Ireland's battle is NOW, the place for Ireland's battle is HERE.
in *The Workers' Republic* 22 January 1916

Jimmy Connors 1952–

6 New Yorkers love it when you spill your guts out there. Spill your guts at Wimbledon and they make you stop and clean it up.
at Flushing Meadow
in *Guardian* 24 December 1984 'Sports Quotes of the Year'

Joseph Conrad 1857–1924

7 The horror! The horror!
Heart of Darkness (1902) ch. 3

8 Mistah Kurtz—he dead.
Heart of Darkness (1902) ch. 3

9 The terrorist and the policeman both come from the same basket.
The Secret Agent (1907) ch. 4

Shirley Conran 1932–

10 Life is too short to stuff a mushroom.
Superwoman (1975)

John Constable 1776–1837

11 The sound of water escaping from mill-dams, etc., willows, old rotten planks, slimy posts, and brickwork . . . those scenes made me a painter and I am grateful.
letter to John Fisher, 23 October 1821

12 A gentleman's park—is my aversion. It is not beauty because it is not nature.
of Fonthill
letter to John Fisher, 7 October 1822

Benjamin Constant 1767–1834

13 Art for art's sake, with no purpose, for any purpose perverts art. But art achieves a purpose which is not its own.
*describing a conversation with Crabb Robinson about the latter's work on **Kant**'s aesthetics*
Journal intime 11 February 1804; cf. **Cousin** 100:19

Constantine the Great
AD *c.*288–337

14 *In hoc signo vinces.*
In this sign shalt thou conquer.
traditional form of Constantine's vision (AD 312)

Constitution of the United States 1787

15 Congress shall make no law respecting an establishment of religion, or prohibiting the free exercise thereof; or abridging the freedom of speech, or of the press; or the right of the people peaceably to assemble, and to petition the government for a redress of grievances.
First Amendment (1791)

16 A well-regulated militia, being necessary to the security of a free State, the right of the people to keep and bear arms, shall not be infringed.
Second Amendment (1791)

17 Excessive bail shall not be required, nor excessive fines imposed, nor cruel and unusual punishment inflicted.
Eighth Amendment (1791)

A. J. Cook 1885–1931

18 Not a penny off the pay, not a second on the day.
often quoted with 'minute' substituted for 'second'
speech at York, 3 April 1926, in *The Times* 5 April 1926

Eliza Cook 1818–89

19 Better build schoolrooms for 'the boy',
Than cells and gibbets for 'the man'.
'A Song for the Ragged Schools' (1853)

Calvin Coolidge 1872–1933

20 There is no right to strike against the public safety by anybody, anywhere, any time.
telegram to Samuel Gompers, 14 September 1919

21 The chief business of the American people is business.
speech in Washington, 17 January 1925

22 They hired the money, didn't they?
on war debts incurred by England and others
John H. McKee *Coolidge: Wit and Wisdom* (1933)

Duff Cooper 1890–1954

23 Your two stout lovers frowning at one another across the hearth rug, while your small, but perfectly formed one kept the party in a roar.
letter to Lady Diana Manners, later his wife, October 1914

Wendy Cope 1945–

24 Making cocoa for Kingsley Amis.
title of poem (1986)

25 I used to think all poets were Byronic—Mad, bad and dangerous to know.

And then I met a few. Yes it's ironic—
I used to think all poets were Byronic.
They're mostly wicked as a ginless tonic
And wild as pension plans.
'Triolet' (1986); cf. **Lamb** 192:1

Richard Corbet 1582–1635

1 Farewell, rewards and Fairies,
Good housewives now may say,
For now foul sluts in dairies
Do fare as well as they.
'The Fairies' Farewell'

Pierre Corneille 1606–84

2 When there is no peril in the fight, there is
no glory in the triumph.
Le Cid (1637) act 2, sc. 2

3 Do your duty, and leave the outcome to the
Gods.
Horace (1640) act 2, sc. 8

4 A first impulse was never a crime.
Horace (1640) act 5, sc. 3; cf. **Montrond** 226:21

Ralph Cornes

5 Computers are anti-Faraday machines. He
said he couldn't understand anything until
he could count it, while computers count
everything and understand nothing.
in Guardian 28 March 1991

Bernard Cornfeld 1927–

6 Do you sincerely want to be rich?
stock question to salesmen
C. Raw et al. Do You Sincerely Want to be Rich?
(1971)

Frances Cornford 1886–1960

7 How long ago Hector took off his plume,
Not wanting that his little son should cry,
Then kissed his sad Andromache
goodbye—
And now we three in Euston waiting-room.
'Parting in Wartime' (1948)

8 O fat white woman whom nobody loves,
Why do you walk through the fields in
gloves . . .
Missing so much and so much?
'To a Fat Lady seen from the Train' (1910)

Francis M. Cornford 1874–1943

9 Every public action, which is not customary,
either is wrong, or, if it is right, is a
dangerous precedent. It follows that
nothing should ever be done for the first
time.
Microcosmographia Academica (1908) ch. 7

10 That branch of the art of lying which
consists in very nearly deceiving your
friends without quite deceiving your
enemies.
of propaganda
Microcosmographia Academica (1922 ed.)

Mme Cornuel 1605–94

11 No man is a hero to his valet.
Lettres de Mlle Aïssé à Madame C (1787) Letter 13
'De Paris, 1728'; cf. **Byron** 77:24

Coronation Service 1689

12 Here is wisdom; this is the royal Law; these
are the lively Oracles of God.
The Presenting of the Holy Bible; L. G.
Wickham Legge English Coronation Records (1901)

William Cory (born Johnson) 1823–92

13 Jolly boating weather,
And a hay harvest breeze,
Blade on the feather,
Shade off the trees
Swing, swing together
With your body between your knees.
'Eton Boating Song' in Eton Scrap Book (1865)

14 They told me, Heraclitus, they told me you
were dead,
They brought me bitter news to hear and
bitter tears to shed.
I wept as I remembered how often you and I
Had tired the sun with talking and sent him
down the sky.
'Heraclitus' (1858); translation of Callimachus
'Epigram 2'

John Cotton 1584–1652

15 If you pinch the sea of its liberty, though it
be walls of stone or brass, it will beat them
down.
'Limitations of Government'; Perry Miller The
American Puritans (1956)

Baron Pierre de Coubertin
1863–1937

16 The important thing in life is not the
victory but the contest; the essential thing is
not to have won but to have fought well.
speech at a government banquet in London, 24
July 1908

Émile Coué 1857–1926

17 Every day, in every way, I am getting better
and better.
to be said 15 to 20 times, morning and evening
De la suggestion et de ses applications (1915)

Douglas Coupland 1961–

18 Generation X: tales for an accelerated
culture.
title of book (1991)

Victor Cousin 1792–1867

19 We must have religion for religion's sake,
morality for morality's sake, as with art for
art's sake . . . the beautiful cannot be the
way to what is useful, or to what is good, or
to what is holy; it leads only to itself.
Du Vrai, du beau, et du bien [Sorbonne lecture,
1818] (1853) pt. 2; cf. **Constant** 99:13

Jacques Cousteau 1910–97

1 Mankind has probably done more damage to the earth in the 20th century than in all of previous human history.
'Consumer Society is the Enemy' in *New Perspectives Quarterly* Summer 1996

Thomas Coventry 1578–1640

2 The dominion of the sea, as it is an ancient and undoubted right of the crown of England, so it is the best security of the land . . . The wooden walls are the best walls of this kingdom.
'*wooden walls*' = *ships*
speech to the Judges, 17 June 1635; cf. **Blackstone** 55:3, **Themistocles** 315:17

Noël Coward 1899–1973

3 Dance, dance, dance, little lady!
'Dance, Little Lady' (1928 song)

4 Don't let's be beastly to the Germans When our Victory is ultimately won.
'Don't Let's Be Beastly to the Germans' (1943 song)

5 The most I've had is just A talent to amuse.
'If Love Were All' (1929 song)

6 Mad about the boy.
title of song (1932)

7 Mad dogs and Englishmen Go out in the midday sun.
'Mad Dogs and Englishmen' (1931 song)

8 Don't put your daughter on the stage, Mrs Worthington, Don't put your daughter on the stage.
'Mrs Worthington' (1935 song)

9 Poor little rich girl.
title of song (1925)

10 The Stately Homes of England, How beautiful they stand, To prove the upper classes Have still the upper hand.
'The Stately Homes of England' (1938 song); cf. **Hemans** 155:18

11 Very flat, Norfolk.
Private Lives (1930) act 1

12 Extraordinary how potent cheap music is.
Private Lives (1930) act 1

13 Just say the lines and don't trip over the furniture.
advice on acting
D. Richards *The Wit of Noël Coward* (1968)

Abraham Cowley 1618–67

14 God the first garden made, and the first city Cain.
Essays, in Verse and Prose (1668) 'The Garden'; cf. **Cowper** 101:28

15 Life is an incurable disease.
'To Dr Scarborough' (1656) st. 6

Hannah Cowley 1743–1809

16 Vanity, like murder, will out.
The Belle's Stratagem (1780) act 1, sc. 4

17 But what is woman?—only one of Nature's agreeable blunders.
Who's the Dupe? (1779) act 2

William Cowper 1731–1800

18 We perished, each alone: But I beneath a rougher sea, And whelmed in deeper gulfs than he.
'The Castaway' (written 1799) l. 61

19 His wit invites you by his looks to come, But when you knock it never is at home.
'Conversation' (1782) l. 303

20 Damned below Judas; more abhorred than he was.
'Hatred and vengeance, my eternal portion' (written *c.*1774)

21 John Gilpin was a citizen Of credit and renown, A train-band captain eke was he Of famous London town.
'John Gilpin' (1785) l. 1

22 My sister and my sister's child, Myself and children three, Will fill the chaise; so you must ride On horseback after we.
'John Gilpin' (1785) l. 13

23 God moves in a mysterious way His wonders to perform; He plants his footsteps in the sea, And rides upon the storm.
Olney Hymns (1779) 'Light Shining out of Darkness'

24 Oh! for a closer walk with God, A calm and heav'nly frame; A light to shine upon the road That leads me to the Lamb!
Olney Hymns (1779) 'Walking with God'

25 Toll for the brave— The brave! that are no more: All sunk beneath the wave, Fast by their native shore.
'On the Loss of the Royal George' (written 1782)

26 Remorse, the fatal egg by pleasure laid.
'The Progress of Error' (1782) l. 239

27 Thou god of our idolatry, the press . . . Thou ever-bubbling spring of endless lies.
'The Progress of Error' (1782) l. 461

28 God made the country, and man made the town.
The Task (1785) bk. 1 'The Sofa' l. 749; cf. **Cowley** 101:14

29 Slaves cannot breathe in England; if their lungs Receive our air, that moment they are free; They touch our country, and their shackles fall.
The Task (1785) bk. 2 'The Timepiece' l. 40; cf. **Anonymous** 9:7

30 England, with all thy faults, I love thee still— My country!
The Task (1785) bk. 2 'The Timepiece' l. 206; cf. **Churchill** 90:23

1 Variety's the very spice of life,
That gives it all its flavour.
The Task (1785) bk. 2 'The Timepiece' l. 606; cf.
Behn 27:20

2 I was a stricken deer, that left the herd
Long since.
The Task (1785) bk. 3 'The Garden' l. 108; cf.
Shakespeare 272:16

3 Now stir the fire, and close the shutters fast,
Let fall the curtains, wheel the sofa round,
And, while the bubbling and loud-hissing
urn
Throws up a steamy column, and the cups,
That cheer but not inebriate, wait on each,
So let us welcome peaceful evening in.
The Task (1785) bk. 4 'The Winter Evening' l. 34;
cf. **Berkeley** 30:14

4 I crown thee king of intimate delights,
Fire-side enjoyments, home-born happiness.
The Task (1785) bk. 4 'The Winter Evening' l. 139

5 A Roman meal . . .
. . . a radish and an egg.
The Task (1785) bk. 4 'The Winter Evening' l. 168

6 The slope of faces, from the floor to th' roof,
(As if one master-spring controlled them
all),
Relaxed into a universal grin.
of the theatre
The Task (1785) bk. 4 'The Winter Evening' l. 202

7 I would not enter on my list of friends
(Tho' graced with polished manners and
fine sense,
Yet wanting sensibility) the man
Who needlessly sets foot upon a worm.
The Task (1785) bk. 6 'The Winter Walk at Noon'
l. 560

8 As a priest,
A piece of mere church furniture at best.
'Tirocinium' (1785) l. 425

9 I am monarch of all I survey,
My right there is none to dispute;
From the centre all round to the sea
I am lord of the foul and the brute.
'Verses Supposed to be Written by Alexander
Selkirk' (1782)

10 Our severest winter, commonly called the
spring.
letter to the Revd William Unwin, 8 June 1783

George Crabbe 1754–1832

11 Habit with him was all the test of truth,
'It must be right: I've done it from my
youth.'
The Borough (1810) Letter 3 'The Vicar' l. 138

12 With awe, around these silent walks I tread;
These are the lasting mansions of the dead.
'The Library' (1808) l. 105

13 The murmuring poor, who will not fast in
peace.
'The Newspaper' (1785) l. 158

14 A master passion is the love of news.
'The Newspaper' (1785) l. 279

15 'The game,' said he, 'is never lost till won.'
Tales of the Hall (1819) 'Gretna Green' l. 334

16 The face the index of a feeling mind.
Tales of the Hall (1819) 'Lady Barbara' l. 124

17 The cold charities of man to man.
The Village (1783) bk. 1, l. 245

Maurice James Craig 1919–

18 O the bricks they will bleed and the rain it
will weep
And the damp Lagan fog lull the city to
sleep;
It's to hell with the future and live on the
past:
May the Lord in His mercy be kind to Belfast.
*based on the traditional refrain 'May God in His
mercy look down on Belfast'*
'Ballad to a Traditional Refrain' (1974)

Hart Crane 1899–1932

19 Stars scribble on our eyes the frosty sagas,
The gleaming cantos of unvanquished
space.
'Cape Hatteras' (1930)

20 So the 20th Century—so
whizzed the Limited—roared by and left
three men, still hungry on the tracks,
ploddingly
watching the tail lights wizen and converge,
slipping
gimleted and neatly out of sight.
'The River' (1930)

21 Being, of all, least sought for: Emily, hear!
'To Emily Dickinson' (1927)

Stephen Crane 1871–1900

22 The red badge of courage.
title of novel (1895)

Thomas Cranmer 1489–1556

23 This was the hand that wrote it [his
recantation], therefore it shall suffer first
punishment.
at the stake, Oxford, 21 March 1556
John Richard Green *A Short History of the English
People* (1874) ch. 7, sect. 2

Richard Crashaw c.1612–49

24 *Nympha pudica Deum vidit, et erubuit.*
The conscious water saw its God, and
blushed.
*literally, 'the chaste nymph saw . . . '; the
translation above is attributed to **Dryden**, when
a schoolboy*
Epigrammata Sacra (1634) 'Aquae in vinum
versae [Water changed into wine]'; the
translation is discussed in *Notes and Queries* 4th
series (1869) vol. 4

25 Love's passives are his activ'st part.
The wounded is the wounding heart.
'The Flaming Heart upon the Book of Saint
Teresa' (1652) l. 73

26 By all the eagle in thee, all the dove.
'The Flaming Heart upon the Book of Saint
Teresa' (1652) l. 95

1 Love, thou art absolute sole Lord
Of life and death.
'Hymn to the Name and Honour of the
Admirable Saint Teresa' (1652) l. 1

2 Poor World (said I) what wilt thou do
To entertain this starry stranger?
'Hymn of the Nativity' (1652)

3 Welcome, all wonders in one sight!
Eternity shut in a span.
'Hymn of the Nativity' (1652)

4 That not impossible she
That shall command my heart and me.
'Wishes to His (Supposed) Mistress' (1646)

Julia Crawford ?1800–?55

5 Kathleen Mavourneen! the grey dawn is
breaking,
The horn of the hunter is heard on the hill.
'Kathleen Mavourneen' in *Metropolitan Magazine*,
London (1835)

Robert Crawford 1959–

6 In Scotland we live between and across
languages.
Identifying Poets (1993)

Crazy Horse c.1849–77

7 One does not sell the earth upon which the
people walk.
Dee Brown *Bury My Heart at Wounded Knee* (1970)
ch. 12

Mandell Creighton 1843–1901

8 No people do so much harm as those who
go about doing good.
in *The Life and Letters of Mandell Creighton* by his
wife (1904) vol. 2

Michel Guillaume Jean de Crèvecoeur 1735–1813

9 What then is the American, this new man?
He is either a European, or the descendant
of a European, hence that strange mixture
of blood, which you will find in no other
country . . . Here individuals of all nations
are melted into a new race of men, whose
labours and posterity will one day cause
great changes in the world.
Letters from an American Farmer (1782)

Ranulphe Crewe 1558–1646

10 And yet time hath his revolution; there
must be a period and an end to all temporal
things, *finis rerum*, an end of names and
dignities and whatsoever is terrene; and
why not of De Vere? Where is Bohun,
where's Mowbray, where's Mortimer? Nay,
which is more and most of all, where is
Plantagenet? They are entombed in the urns
and sepulchres of mortality. And yet let the
name and dignity of De Vere stand so long
as it pleaseth God.
speech in Oxford Peerage Case, 22 March 1626

Francis Crick 1916–
and James D. Watson 1928–

11 It has not escaped our notice that the
specific pairing we have postulated
immediately suggests a possible copying
mechanism for the genetic material.
*proposing the double helix as the structure of
DNA, and hence the chemical mechanism of
heredity*
in *Nature* 25 April 1953

Quentin Crisp 1908–99

12 There was no need to do any housework at
all. After the first four years the dirt doesn't
get any worse.
The Naked Civil Servant (1968) ch. 15

13 An autobiography is an obituary in serial
form with the last instalment missing.
The Naked Civil Servant (1968) ch. 29

Julian Critchley 1930–2000

14 The only safe pleasure for a parliamentarian
is a bag of boiled sweets.
in *Listener* 10 June 1982

Richmal Crompton 1890–1969

15 I'll thcream and thcream and thcream till
I'm thick.
Violet Elizabeth's habitual threat
Still—William (1925) ch. 8

Oliver Cromwell 1599–1658

16 I would rather have a plain russet-coated
captain that knows what he fights for, and
loves what he knows, than that which you
call 'a gentleman' and is nothing else.
letter to William Spring, September 1643

17 Cruel necessity.
on the execution of **Charles I**
Joseph Spence *Anecdotes* (1820)

18 I beseech you, in the bowels of Christ, think
it possible you may be mistaken.
letter to the General Assembly of the Kirk of
Scotland, 3 August 1650

19 The dimensions of this mercy are above my
thoughts. It is, for aught I know, a crowning
mercy.
letter to William Lenthall, Speaker of the
Parliament of England, 4 September 1651

20 You have sat too long here for any good you
have been doing. Depart, I say, and let us
have done with you. In the name of God, go!
addressing the Rump Parliament, 20 April 1653;
oral tradition; cf. **Amery** 4:16

21 Take away that fool's bauble, the mace.
often quoted as, 'Take away these baubles'
at the dismissal of the Rump Parliament, 20
April 1653

22 Your poor army, those poor contemptible
men, came up hither.
speech to Parliament, 21 April 1657; cf.
Anonymous 6:20

1 Hell or Connaught.

*summary of the choice offered to the Catholic
population of Ireland, transported to the western
counties to make room for settlers*
traditionally attributed

2 Mr Lely, I desire you would use all your skill
to paint my picture truly like me, and not
flatter me at all; but remark all these
roughnesses, pimples, warts, and
everything as you see me; otherwise I will
never pay a farthing for it.

often summarized as, 'Warts and all'
Horace Walpole *Anecdotes of Painting in England*
vol. 3 (1763) ch. 1

3 My design is to make what haste I can to be
gone.

last words; John Morley *Oliver Cromwell* (1900)
bk. 5, ch. 10

Bing Crosby 1903–77

4 Where the blue of the night meets the gold
of the day.

title of song (1931), with Roy Turk and Fred
Ahlert

Douglas Cross

5 I left my heart in San Francisco
High on a hill it calls to me.
To be where little cable cars climb half-way
to the stars,
The morning fog may chill the air—
I don't care!

'I Left My Heart in San Francisco' (1954 song)

Richard Assheton, Lord Cross
1823–1914

6 I hear a smile.

*when the House of Lords laughed at his speech in
favour of Spiritual Peers*
G. W. E. Russell *Collections and Recollections* (1898)
ch. 29

Richard Crossman 1907–74

7 The Civil Service is profoundly deferential
— 'Yes, Minister! No, Minister! If you wish
it, Minister!'

Diaries of a Cabinet Minister vol. 1 (1975) 22
October 1964

Samuel Crossman 1624–83

8 My song is love unknown,
My saviour's love for me,
Love to the loveless shown,
That they might lovely be.
O, who am I,
That for my sake
My Lord should take
Frail flesh and die?

'My song is love unknown' (1664); set to music
as a hymn from 1868, and by John Ireland in
1919

Crowfoot c.1830–90

9 A little while and I will be gone from among
you, whither I cannot tell. From nowhere

we came, into nowhere we go. What is life?
It is a flash of a firefly in the night. It is a
breath of a buffalo in the winter time. It is
as the little shadow that runs across the
grass and loses itself in the sunset.

attributed farewell to his people, 25 April 1890;
cf. **Haggard** 149:2

Aleister Crowley 1875–1947

10 Do what thou wilt shall be the whole of the
Law.

Book of the Law (1909) l. 40; cf. **Rabelais** 253:13

Ralph Cudworth 1617–88

11 Some who are far from atheists, may make
themselves merry with that conceit of
thousands of spirits dancing at once upon a
needle's point.

The True Intellectual System of the Universe (1678)

Richard Cumberland 1631–1718

12 It is better to wear out than to rust out.

George Horne *The Duty of Contending for the Faith*
(1786)

e. e. cummings (Edward Estlin
Cummings) 1894–1962

13 anyone lived in a pretty how town
(with up so floating many bells down)
spring summer autumn winter
he sang his didn't he danced his did.

50 Poems (1949) no. 29

14 'next to of course god america i
love you land of the pilgrims' and so forth.

is 5 (1926) p. 62

15 a politician is an arse upon
which everyone has sat except a man.

1 x 1 (1944) no. 10

16 plato told

him: he couldn't

believe it (jesus

told him; he

wouldn't believe

it) lao

tsze

certainly told

him, and general

(yes

mam)

sherman.

1 x 1 (1944) no. 13

17 pity this busy monster, manunkind,

not. Progress is a comfortable disease.

1 x 1 (1944) no. 14

18 We doctors know

a hopeless case if—listen: there's a hell

of a good universe next door; let's go.

1 x 1 (1944) no. 14

William Thomas Cummings
1903–45

19 There are no atheists in the foxholes.

Carlos P. Romulo *I Saw the Fall of the Philippines*
(1943) ch. 15

Allan Cunningham 1784–1842

1 A wet sheet and a flowing sea,
A wind that follows fast
And fills the white and rustling sail
And bends the gallant mast.
  'A Wet Sheet and a Flowing Sea' (1825)

Mario Cuomo 1932–

2 You campaign in poetry. You govern in prose.
  in *New Republic*, Washington, DC, 8 April 1985

Don Cupitt 1934–

3 Christmas is the Disneyfication of Christianity.
  in *Independent* 19 December 1996

Marie Curie 1867–1934

4 In science, we must be interested in things, not in persons.
  to an American journalist, c.1904, after she and her husband Pierre had shared the Nobel Prize for Physics with A.-H. Becquerel
  Eve Curie *Madame Curie* (1937)

John Philpot Curran 1750–1817

5 The condition upon which God hath given liberty to man is eternal vigilance.
  speech on the right of election of the Lord Mayor of Dublin, 10 July 1790

6 Like the silver plate on a coffin.
  describing Robert Peel's smile
  quoted by Daniel O'Connell, House of Commons, 26 February 1835

Michael Curtiz 1888–1962

7 Bring on the empty horses!
  while directing The Charge of the Light Brigade (1936 film)
  David Niven *Bring on the Empty Horses* (1975) ch. 6

Lord Curzon 1859–1925

8 When a group of Cabinet Ministers begins to meet separately and to discuss independent action, the death-tick is audible in the rafters.
  in November 1922, shortly before the fall of Lloyd George's Coalition Government
  David Gilmour *Curzon* (1994)

9 Not even a public figure. A man of no experience. And of the utmost insignificance.
  of Stanley Baldwin, appointed Prime Minister in 1923 in succession to Bonar Law
  Harold Nicolson *Curzon: the Last Phase* (1934)

St Cyprian c.AD 200–258

10 He cannot have God for his father who has not the church for his mother.
  De Ecclesiae Catholicae Unitate sect. 6; cf. **Augustine** 19:3

11 *Fratres nostros non esse lugendos arcessitione dominica de saeculo liberatos, cum sciamus non amitti sed praemitti.*

Our brethren who have been freed from the world by the summons of the Lord should not be mourned, since we know that they are not lost but sent before.
  De Mortalite ch. 20 (ed. M. L. Hannam, 1933); cf. **Norton** 234:23, **Rogers** 259:2

12 There cannot be salvation for any, except in the Church.
  Epistle Ad Pomponium, De Virginibus sect. 4; cf. **Augustine** 19:3, **Cyprian** 105:10

Hugh Dalton 1887–1962

13 He is loyal to his own career but only incidentally to anything or anyone else.
  of Richard Crossman
  diary, 17 September 1941

Samuel Daniel 1563–1619

14 Care-charmer Sleep, son of the sable Night, Brother to Death, in silent darkness born.
  Delia (1592) Sonnet 54; cf. **Fletcher** 130:8, **Shelley** 293:20

15 Princes in this case
Do hate the traitor, though they love the treason.
  The Tragedy of Cleopatra (1594) act 4, sc. 1; cf. **Dryden** 116:29

Dante Alighieri 1265–1321

16 *Nel mezzo del cammin di nostra vita.*
Midway along the path of our life.
  Divina Commedia 'Inferno' canto 1, l. 1

17 LASCIATE OGNI SPERANZA VOI CH'ENTRATE!
Abandon all hope, you who enter!
  inscription at the entrance to Hell
  Divina Commedia 'Inferno' canto 3, l. 1

18 *Non ragioniam di lor, ma guarda, e passa.*
Let us not speak of them, but look, and pass on.
  Divina Commedia 'Inferno' canto 3, l. 51

19 *Il gran rifiuto.*
The great refusal.
  Divina Commedia 'Inferno' canto 3, l. 60

20 . . . *Nessun maggior dolore,*
Che ricordarsi del tempo felice
Nella miseria.
There is no greater pain than to remember a happy time when one is in misery.
  Divina Commedia 'Inferno' canto 5, l. 121; cf. **Boethius** 57:6

21 *Tu proverai sì come sa di sale*
Lo pane altrui, e com'è duro calle
Lo scendere e'l salir per l'altrui scale.
You shall find out how salt is the taste of another man's bread, and how hard is the way up and down another man's stairs.
  Divina Commedia 'Paradiso' canto 17, l. 58

22 *L'amor che muove il sole e l'altre stelle.*
The love that moves the sun and the other stars.
  Divina Commedia 'Paradiso' canto 33, l. 145

Georges Jacques Danton 1759–94

1 *De l'audace, et encore de l'audace, et toujours de l'audace!*
Boldness, and again boldness, and always boldness!
  speech to the Legislative Committee of General Defence, 2 September 1792

2 Thou wilt show my head to the people: it is worth showing.
  to his executioner, 5 April 1794
    Thomas Carlyle *History of the French Revolution* (1837) vol. 3, bk. 6, ch. 2

Joe Darion 1917–

3 Dream the impossible dream.
  'The Impossible Dream' (1965 song)

Bill Darnell

4 Make it a *green* peace.
  at a meeting of the Don't Make a Wave Committee, which preceded the formation of Greenpeace
    in Vancouver, 1970; Robert Hunter *The Greenpeace Chronicle* (1979); cf. **Hunter** 167:7

Clarence Darrow 1857–1938

5 I do not pretend to know where many ignorant men are sure—that is all that agnosticism means.
  speech at the trial of John Thomas Scopes for teaching Darwin's theory of evolution in school, 15 July 1925

Charles Darwin 1809–82

6 A hairy quadruped, furnished with a tail and pointed ears, probably arboreal in its habits.
  on man's probable ancestors
    The Descent of Man (1871) ch. 21

7 I have called this principle, by which each slight variation, if useful, is preserved, by the term of Natural Selection.
  On the Origin of Species (1859) ch. 3

8 We will now discuss in a little more detail the Struggle for Existence.
  On the Origin of Species (1859) ch. 3

9 The expression often used by Mr Herbert Spencer of the Survival of the Fittest is more accurate [than 'Struggle for Existence'], and is sometimes equally convenient.
  On the Origin of Species (1869 ed.) ch. 3; cf. **Spencer** 300:3

Francis Darwin 1848–1925

10 In science the credit goes to the man who convinces the world, not to the man to whom the idea first occurs.
  in *Eugenics Review* April 1914 'Francis Galton'

Charles D'Avenant 1656–1714

11 Custom, that unwritten law,
By which the people keep even kings in awe.
  Circe (1677) act 2, sc. 3

William D'Avenant 1606–68

12 The lark now leaves his wat'ry nest
And, climbing, shakes his dewy wings.
  'Song: The Lark' (1638)

John Davidson 1857–1909

13 A runnable stag, a kingly crop.
  'A Runnable Stag' (1906)

14 The race is to the swift,
The battle to the strong.
  'War Song' (1899) st. 1; cf. **Bible** 38:27

John Davies 1569–1626

15 This wondrous miracle did Love devise,
For dancing is love's proper exercise.
  'Orchestra, or a Poem of Dancing' (1596) st. 18

Robertson Davies 1913–95

16 I see Canada as a country torn between a very northern, rather extraordinary, mystical spirit which it fears and its desire to present itself to the world as a Scotch banker.
  The Enthusiasms of Robertson Davies (1990)

Scrope Davies c.1783–1852

17 Babylon in all its desolation is a sight not so awful as that of the human mind in ruins.
  ***Addison**, in The Spectator no. 421 (3 July 1712), also remarked of 'a distracted person' that 'Babylon in ruins is not so melancholy a spectacle'*
    letter to Thomas Raikes, May 1835, in *A Portion of the Journal kept by Thomas Raikes* (1856) vol. 2

W. H. Davies 1871–1940

18 It was the Rainbow gave thee birth,
And left thee all her lovely hues.
  'Kingfisher' (1910)

19 What is this life if, full of care,
We have no time to stand and stare.
  'Leisure' (1911)

20 Sweet Stay-at-Home, sweet Well-content,
Thou knowest of no strange continent.
  'Sweet Stay-At-Home' (1913)

Sammy Davis Jnr. 1925–90

21 Being a star has made it possible for me to get insulted in places where the average Negro could never *hope* to go and get insulted.
  Yes I Can (1965) pt. 3, ch. 23

Thomas Davis 1814–45

22 And then I prayed I yet might see
Our fetters rent in twain,
And Ireland, long a province, be
A Nation once again.
  'A Nation Once Again' (1846)

23 But—hark!—some voice like thunder spake:
The West's awake! the West's awake!
  'The West's Asleep' (1846)

Richard Dawkins

1 [Natural selection] has no vision, no foresight, no sight at all. If it can be said to play the role of watchmaker in nature, it is the *blind* watchmaker.
The Blind Watchmaker (1986) ch. 1; cf. **Paley** 239:20

2 The essence of life is statistical improbability on a colossal scale.
The Blind Watchmaker (1986) ch. 11

Lord Dawson of Penn 1864–1945

3 The King's life is moving peacefully towards its close.
bulletin, 20 January 1936

C. Day-Lewis 1904–72

4 It is the logic of our times,
No subject for immortal verse—
That we who lived by honest dreams
Defend the bad against the worse.
'Where are the War Poets?' (1943)

John Dean 1938–

5 We have a cancer within, close to the Presidency, that is growing.
[Nixon] Transcripts, 21 March 1973

Seamus Deane 1940–

6 Meningitis. It was a word you had to bite on to say it. It had a fright and a hiss in it.
Reading in the Dark (1996)

Percy Dearmer 1867–1936

7 Jesu, good above all other,
Gentle Child of gentle Mother,
In a stable born our Brother,
Give us grace to persevere.
'Jesu, good above all other' (1906 hymn)

Simone de Beauvoir 1908–86

8 One is not born a woman: one becomes one.
The Second Sex (1949) vol. 2, pt. 1, ch. 1

Louis de Bernières 1954–

9 The human heart likes a little disorder in its geometry.
Captain Corelli's Mandolin (1994) ch. 26

Eugene Victor Debs 1855–1926

10 While there is a lower class, I am in it; while there is a criminal element, I am of it; while there is a soul in prison, I am not free.
at his trial for sedition, 14 September 1918

Stephen Decatur 1779–1820

11 Our country! In her intercourse with foreign nations, may she always be in the right; but our country, right or wrong.
Decatur's toast at Norfolk, Virginia, April 1816; cf. **Adams** 2:1, **Schurz** 265:21

Daniel Defoe 1660–1731

12 Things as certain as death and taxes, can be more firmly believed.
History of the Devil (1726) bk. 2, ch. 6; cf. **Franklin** 133:9

13 He told me . . . that mine was the middle state, or what might be called the upper station of low life, which he had found by long experience was the best state in the world, the most suited to human happiness.
Robinson Crusoe (1719)

14 My man Friday.
Robinson Crusoe (1719)

15 Necessity makes an honest man a knave.
The Serious Reflections of Robinson Crusoe (1720) ch. 2

16 We loved the doctrine for the teacher's sake.
'Character of the late Dr S. Annesley' (1697)

17 Actions receive their tincture from the times,
And as they change are virtues made or crimes.
A Hymn to the Pillory (1703) l. 29

18 Nature has left this tincture in the blood,
That all men would be tyrants if they could.
The History of the Kentish Petition (1712–13) addenda, l. 11

19 From this amphibious ill-born mob began
That vain, ill-natured thing, an Englishman.
The True Born Englishman (1701) pt.1, l. 132

20 Your Roman-Saxon-Danish-Norman English.
The True-Born Englishman (1701) pt. 1, l. 139

21 Titles are shadows, crowns are empty things,
The good of subjects is the end of kings.
The True-Born Englishman (1701) pt. 2, l. 313

Edgar Degas 1834–1917

22 Art is vice. You don't marry it legitimately, you rape it.
Paul Lafond *Degas* (1918)

Charles de Gaulle 1890–1970

23 France has lost a battle. But France has not lost the war!
proclamation, 18 June 1940

24 Since they whose duty it was to wield the sword of France have let it fall shattered to the ground, I have taken up the broken blade.
speech, 13 July 1940

25 *Europe des patries.*
A Europe of nations.
widely associated with De Gaulle, c.1962, and taken as encapsulating his views, although perhaps not coined by him
J. Lacouture *De Gaulle: the Ruler* (1991)

26 One does not put Voltaire in the Bastille.
*when asked to arrest **Sartre**, in the 1960s*
in *Encounter* June 1975

Thomas Dekker 1570–1641

1 That great fishpond (the sea).
  The Honest Whore (1604) pt. 1, act 1, sc. 2

2 Golden slumbers kiss your eyes,
  Smiles awake you when you rise.
  Patient Grissil (1603) act 4, sc. 2

Walter de la Mare 1873–1956

3 Ann, Ann!
  Come! quick as you can!
  There's a fish that *talks*
  In the frying-pan.
  'Alas, Alack' (1913)

4 Oh, no man knows
  Through what wild centuries
  Roves back the rose.
  'All That's Past' (1912)

5 He is crazed with the spell of far Arabia,
  They have stolen his wits away.
  'Arabia' (1912)

6 Look thy last on all things lovely.
  'Fare Well' (1918)

7 'Is there anybody there?' said the Traveller,
  Knocking on the moonlit door.
  'The Listeners' (1912)

8 'Tell them I came, and no one answered,
  That I kept my word,' he said.
  'The Listeners' (1912)

9 What is the world, O soldiers?
  It is I:
  I, this incessant snow,
  This northern sky;
  Soldiers, this solitude
  Through which we go
  Is I.
  'Napoleon' (1906)

10 Slowly, silently, now the moon
  Walks the night in her silver shoon.
  'Silver' (1913)

Demosthenes *c.*384–*c.*322 BC

11 There is one safeguard known generally to
  the wise, which is an advantage and
  security to all, but especially to democracies
  against despots—suspicion.
  Philippic

12 When asked what was first in oratory, [he]
  replied to his questioner, 'action,' what
  second, 'action,' and again third, 'action'.
  Cicero *Brutus* ch. 37, sect. 142

Jack Dempsey 1895–1983

13 Honey, I just forgot to duck.
  *to his wife, on losing the World Heavyweight title,
  23 September 1926; after a failed attempt on his
  life in 1981, Ronald **Reagan** quipped 'I forgot to
  duck'*
    J. and B. P. Dempsey *Dempsey* (1977)

Deng Xiaoping 1904–97

14 It doesn't matter if a cat is black or white, as
  long as it catches mice.
    *in the early 1960s; in *Daily Telegraph* 20 February
    1997, obituary*

John Denham 1615–69

15 Youth, what man's age is like to be doth
  show;
  We may our ends by our beginnings know.
  'Of Prudence' (1668) l. 225

Lord Denman 1779–1854

16 Trial by jury itself, instead of being a
  security to persons who are accused, will be
  a delusion, a mockery, and a snare.
  *on a case involving the fraudulent omission of
  sixty names from the list of jurors in Dublin*
    speech in the House of Lords, 4 September 1844

Lord Denning 1899–1999

17 The keystone of the rule of law in England
  has been the independence of judges. It is
  the only respect in which we make any real
  separation of powers.
  The Family Story (1981)

John Dennis 1657–1734

18 Damn them! They will not let my play run,
  but they steal my thunder!
  *on hearing his new thunder effects used at a
  performance of* Macbeth, *following the
  withdrawal of one of his own plays after only a
  short run*
    William S. Walsh *A Handy-Book of Literary
    Curiosities* (1893)

Christine de Pisan 1364–*c.*1430

19 Where true love is, it showeth; it will not
  feign.
  'The Epistle of Othea to Hector'

Thomas De Quincey 1785–1859

20 A duller spectacle this earth of ours has not
  to show than a rainy Sunday in London.
  Confessions of an English Opium Eater (1822, ed.
  1856) pt. 2

21 Thou hast the keys of Paradise, oh just,
  subtle, and mighty opium!
  Confessions of an English Opium Eater (1822, ed.
  1856) pt. 2

22 Murder considered as one of the fine arts.
  title of essay in *Blackwood's Magazine* February
  1827

Edward Stanley, 14th Earl of Derby 1799–1869

23 The duty of an Opposition [is] very simple
  . . . to oppose everything, and propose
  nothing.
  quoting 'Mr Tierney, a great Whig authority'
  in the House of Commons, 4 June 1841

Jacques Derrida 1930–

24 *Il n'y a pas de hors-texte.*
  There is nothing outside of the text.
  Of Grammatology (1967)

René Descartes 1596–1650

1 Common sense is the best distributed commodity in the world, for every man is convinced that he is well supplied with it.
Le Discours de la méthode (1637) pt. 1

2 *Je pense, donc je suis.*
I think, therefore I am.
usually quoted as, 'Cogito, ergo sum', *from the 1641 Latin edition*
Le Discours de la méthode (1637) pt. 4

Philippe Néricault Destouches 1680–1754

3 The absent are always in the wrong.
L'Obstacle imprévu (1717) act 1, sc. 6

Buddy De Sylva 1895–1950 and Lew Brown 1893–1958

4 The moon belongs to everyone,
The best things in life are free.
'The Best Things in Life are Free' (1927 song)

Eamonn de Valera 1882–1975

5 Whenever I wanted to know what the Irish people wanted, I had only to examine my own heart and it told me straight off what the Irish people wanted.
speech in Dáil Éireann, 6 January 1922

6 That Ireland which we dreamed of would be the home of a people who valued material wealth only as a basis of right living, of a people who were satisfied with frugal comfort and devoted their leisure to the things of the spirit; a land whose countryside would be bright with cosy homesteads, whose fields and villages would be joyous with sounds of industry, the romping of sturdy children, the contests of athletic youths, the laughter of comely maidens; whose firesides would be the forums of the wisdom of serene old age.
St Patrick's Day broadcast, 17 March 1943

Edward De Vere, Earl of Oxford
see **Oxford**

Robert Devereux, Earl of Essex
see **Essex**

James Dewar 1842–1923

7 Minds are like parachutes. They only function when they are open.
attributed

Lord Dewar 1864–1930

8 [There are] only two classes of pedestrians in these days of reckless motor traffic—the quick, and the dead.
George Robey *Looking Back on Life* (1933) ch. 28

Sergei Diaghilev 1872–1929

9 *Étonne-moi.*
Astonish me.
to Jean **Cocteau**
Wallace Fowlie (ed.) *Journals of Jean Cocteau* (1956) ch. 1

Diana, Princess of Wales 1961–97

10 I'd like to be a queen in people's hearts but I don't see myself being Queen of this country.
interview on *Panorama*, BBC1 TV, 20 November 1995

11 There were three of us in this marriage, so it was a bit crowded.
interview on *Panorama*, BBC1 TV, 20 November 1995

Porfirio Diaz 1830–1915

12 Poor Mexico, so far from God and so close to the United States.
attributed

Charles Dibdin 1745–1814

13 For a soldier I listed, to grow great in fame,
And be shot at for sixpence a-day.
'Charity' (1791)

14 In every mess I finds a friend,
In every port a wife.
'Jack in his Element' (1790)

Thomas Dibdin 1771–1841

15 Oh! what a snug little Island,
A right little, tight little Island!
'The Snug Little Island' (1833)

Charles Dickens 1812–70

16 Jarndyce and Jarndyce still drags its dreary length before the Court, perennially hopeless.
Bleak House (1853) ch. 1

17 This is a London particular . . . A fog, miss.
Bleak House (1853) ch. 3

18 I call them the Wards in Jarndyce. They are caged up with all the others. With Hope, Joy, Youth, Peace, Rest, Life, Dust, Ashes, Waste, Want, Ruin, Despair, Madness, Death, Cunning, Folly, Words, Wigs, Rags, Sheepskin, Plunder, Precedent, Jargon, Gammon, and Spinach!
Miss Flite's birds
Bleak House (1853) ch. 60

19 'Bah,' said Scrooge. 'Humbug!'
A Christmas Carol (1843) stave 1

20 I am the Ghost of Christmas Past.
A Christmas Carol (1843) stave 2

21 'God bless us every one!' said Tiny Tim.
A Christmas Carol (1843) stave 3

22 I am a lone lorn creetur . . . and everythink goes contrairy with me.
Mrs Gummidge
David Copperfield (1850) ch. 3

1 Barkis is willin'.
  David Copperfield (1850) ch. 5

2 I have known him come home to supper
with a flood of tears, and a declaration that
nothing was now left but a jail; and go to
bed making a calculation of the expense of
putting bow-windows to the house, 'in case
anything turned up,' which was his
favourite expression.
  of Mr Micawber
    David Copperfield (1850) ch. 11

3 Annual income twenty pounds, annual
expenditure nineteen nineteen six, result
happiness. Annual income twenty pounds,
annual expenditure twenty pounds nought
and six, result misery.
  Mr Micawber
    David Copperfield (1850) ch. 12

4 Mr. Dick had been for upwards of ten years
endeavouring to keep King Charles the First
out of the Memorial; but he had been
constantly getting into it, and was there
now.
  David Copperfield (1850) ch. 14

5 We are so very 'umble.
  Uriah Heep
    David Copperfield (1850) ch. 17

6 It was as true . . . as taxes is. And nothing's
truer than them.
  Mr Barkis
    David Copperfield (1850) ch. 21

7 What a world of gammon and spinnage it
is, though, ain't it!
  Miss Mowcher
    David Copperfield (1850) ch. 22

8 Accidents will occur in the best-regulated
families.
    David Copperfield (1850) ch. 28 (Mr Micawber)

9 It's only my child-wife.
  of Dora
    David Copperfield (1850) ch. 44

10 None of your live languages for Miss
Blimber. They must be dead—stone
dead—and then Miss Blimber dug them up
like a Ghoul.
  Dombey and Son (1848) ch. 11

11 When found, make a note of.
  Captain Cuttle
    Dombey and Son (1848) ch. 15

12 What the waves were always saying.
  Dombey and Son (1848) title of ch. 16

13 'He calls the knaves, Jacks, this boy,' said
Estella with disdain, before our first game
was out.
  Great Expectations (1861) ch. 8

14 Her bringing me up by hand, gave her no
right to bring me up by jerks.
  Great Expectations (1861) ch. 8

15 Now, what I want is, Facts . . . Facts alone
are wanted in life.
  Mr Gradgrind
    Hard Times (1854) bk. 1, ch. 1

16 Whatever was required to be done, the
Circumlocution Office was beforehand with
all the public departments in the art of
perceiving—HOW NOT TO DO IT.
  Little Dorrit (1857) bk. 1, ch. 10

17 There's milestones on the Dover Road!
  Mr F.'s Aunt
    Little Dorrit (1857) bk. 1, ch. 23

18 The word Papa, besides, gives a pretty form
to the lips. Papa, potatoes, poultry, prunes,
and prism, are all very good words for the
lips: especially prunes and prism.
  Mrs General
    Little Dorrit (1857) bk. 2, ch. 5

19 He'd make a lovely corpse.
  Mrs Gamp
    Martin Chuzzlewit (1844) ch. 25

20 The words she spoke of Mrs Harris, lambs
could not forgive . . . nor worms forget.
  Mrs Gamp
    Martin Chuzzlewit (1844) ch. 49

21 EDUCATION.—At Mr Wackford Squeers's
Academy, Dotheboys Hall, at the delightful
village of Dotheboys, near Greta Bridge in
Yorkshire, Youth are boarded, clothed,
booked, furnished with pocket-money,
provided with all necessaries, instructed in
all languages living and dead, mathematics,
orthography, geometry, astronomy,
trigonometry, the use of the globes, algebra,
single stick (if required), writing, arithmetic,
fortification, and every other branch of
classical literature. Terms, twenty guineas
per annum. No extras, no vacations, and
diet unparalleled.
  Nicholas Nickleby (1839) ch. 3

22 He had but one eye, and the popular
prejudice runs in favour of two.
  Mr Squeers
    Nicholas Nickleby (1839) ch. 4

23 C-l-e-a-n, clean, verb active, to make bright,
to scour. W-i-n, win, d-e-r, der, winder, a
casement. When the boy knows this out of
the book, he goes and does it.
  Mr Squeers
    Nicholas Nickleby (1839) ch. 8

24 Language was not powerful enough to
describe the infant phenomenon.
    Nicholas Nickleby (1839) ch. 23

25 All is gas and gaiters.
  The Gentleman in the Small-clothes
    Nicholas Nickleby (1839) ch. 49

26 Please, sir, I want some more.
  Oliver
    Oliver Twist (1838) ch. 2

27 Known by the *sobriquet* of 'The artful
Dodger'.
    Oliver Twist (1838) ch. 8

28 'If the law supposes that,' said Mr Bumble
. . . 'the law is a ass—a idiot.'
  Bumble
    Oliver Twist (1838) ch. 51; cf. **Chapman** 87:16

1 I think . . . that it is the best club in London.
Mr Twemlow, on the House of Commons
  Our Mutual Friend (1865) bk. 2, ch. 3

2 I want to be something so much worthier than the doll in the doll's house.
Bella
  Our Mutual Friend (1865) bk. 4, ch. 5

3 Kent, sir—everybody knows Kent—apples, cherries, hops, and women.
Jingle
  Pickwick Papers (1837) ch. 2

4 I wants to make your flesh creep.
The Fat Boy
  Pickwick Papers (1837) ch. 8

5 'It's always best on these occasions to do what the mob do.' 'But suppose there are two mobs?' suggested Mr Snodgrass. 'Shout with the largest,' replied Mr Pickwick.
  Pickwick Papers (1837) ch. 13

6 Be wery careful o' vidders all your life.
Mr Weller
  Pickwick Papers (1837) ch. 20

7 'Do you spell it with a "V" or a "W"?' inquired the judge. 'That depends upon the taste and fancy of the speller, my Lord,' replied Sam [Weller].
  Pickwick Papers (1837) ch. 34

8 'You must not tell us what the soldier, or any other man, said, sir,' interposed the judge; 'it's not evidence.'
  Pickwick Papers (1837) ch. 34

9 The have-his-carcase, next to the perpetual motion, is vun of the blessedest things as wos ever made.
Sam Weller
  Pickwick Papers (1837) ch. 43

10 It was the best of times, it was the worst of times.
  A Tale of Two Cities (1859) bk. 1, ch. 1

11 It is a far, far better thing that I do, than I have ever done; it is a far, far better rest that I go to, than I have ever known.
Sydney Carton's thoughts on the scaffold
  A Tale of Two Cities (1859) bk. 3, ch. 15

Emily Dickinson 1830–86

12 Because I could not stop for Death—
He kindly stopped for me—
The Carriage held but just Ourselves—
And Immortality.
  'Because I could not stop for Death' (c.1863)

13 There is no Frigate like a Book
To take us Lands away
Nor any Coursers like a Page
Of prancing Poetry.
  'A Book (2)' (c.1873)

14 The Bustle in a House
The Morning after Death
Is solemnest of industries
Enacted upon Earth—
The Sweeping up the Heart
And putting Love away
We shall not want to use again

Until Eternity.
  'The Bustle in a House' (c.1866)

15 Heaven is what I cannot reach
The apple on the tree
  'Forbidden Fruit' (c.1861)

16 Parting is all we know of heaven,
And all we need of hell.
  'My life closed twice before its close'

17 They shut me up in prose—
As when a little girl
They put me in the closet—
Because they liked me 'still'.
  'They shut me up in prose' (c.1862)

John Dickinson 1732–1808

18 Then join hand in hand, brave Americans all,—
By uniting we stand, by dividing we fall.
  'The Liberty Song' (1768)

Paul Dickson 1939–

19 Rowe's Rule: the odds are five to six that the light at the end of the tunnel is the headlight of an oncoming train.
  in *Washingtonian* November 1978; cf. **Lowell** 204:1

Denis Diderot 1713–84

20 And [with] the guts of the last priest
Let's shake the neck of the last king.
  Dithyrambe sur fête de rois; cf. **Meslier** 217:12

21 *L'esprit de l'escalier.*
Staircase wit.
  the witty riposte one thinks of only when one has left the drawing-room and is already on the way downstairs
  Paradoxe sur le Comédien (written 1773–8, published 1830)

Wentworth Dillon, Lord Roscommon c.1633–1685

22 Choose an author as you choose a friend.
  Essay on Translated Verse (1684) l. 96

23 Immodest words admit of no defence,
For want of decency is want of sense.
  Essay on Translated Verse (1684) l. 113

24 The multitude is always in the wrong.
  Essay on Translated Verse (1684) l. 183; cf. **Ibsen** 168:9

Ernest Dimnet

25 Architecture, of all the arts, is the one which acts the most slowly, but the most surely, on the soul.
  What We Live By (1932) pt. 2, ch. 12

Isak Dinesen 1885–1962

26 A herd of elephant . . . pacing along as if they had an appointment at the end of the world.
  Out of Africa (1937) pt. 1, ch. 1

27 What is man, when you come to think upon him, but a minutely set, ingenious machine

for turning, with infinite artfulness, the red wine of Shiraz into urine?
  Seven Gothic Tales (1934) 'The Dreamers'

Diogenes *c.*400–*c.*325 BC

1 Alexander . . . asked him if he lacked anything. 'Yes,' said he, 'that I do: that you stand out of my sun a little.'
  Plutarch *Parallel Lives* 'Alexander' ch. 14, sect. 4 (translated by T. North, 1579)

Dionysius of Halicarnassus
fl. 30–7 BC

2 History is philosophy from examples.
  Ars Rhetorica ch. 11, sect. 2

Walt Disney 1901–66

3 Fancy being remembered around the world for the invention of a mouse!
  during his last illness
  Leonard Mosley *Disney's World* (1985)

Benjamin Disraeli, Lord
Beaconsfield 1804–81

4 The Continent will [not] suffer England to be the workshop of the world.
  speech, House of Commons, 15 March 1838; cf. **Chamberlain** 86:17

5 Thus you have a starving population, an absentee aristocracy, and an alien Church, and in addition the weakest executive in the world. That is the Irish Question.
  speech, House of Commons, 16 February 1844

6 The noble Lord is the Prince Rupert of Parliamentary discussion.
  of Edward Stanley, later Lord **Derby**
  speech, House of Commons, 24 April 1844; cf. **Bulwer-Lytton** 72:13

7 The right hon. Gentleman caught the Whigs bathing, and walked away with their clothes.
  on Sir Robert **Peel**'s *abandoning protection in favour of free trade, traditionally the policy of the Whig Opposition*
  speech, House of Commons, 28 February 1845

8 A Conservative Government is an organized hypocrisy.
  speech, House of Commons, 17 March 1845

9 Party is organized opinion.
  speech at Oxford, 25 November 1864

10 Is man an ape or an angel? Now I am on the side of the angels.
  speech at Oxford, 25 November 1864

11 You behold a range of exhausted volcanoes.
  of the Treasury Bench
  speech at Manchester, 3 April 1872

12 Coffee house babble.
  on the Bulgarian Atrocities, 1876
  in R. W. Seton-Watson *Britain in Europe 1789–1914* (1955)

13 Cosmopolitan critics, men who are the friends of every country save their own.
  speech at Guildhall, 9 November 1877; cf. **Canning** 81:12

14 Lord Salisbury and myself have brought you back peace—but a peace I hope with honour.
  speech on returning from the Congress of Berlin, 16 July 1878; cf. **Chamberlain** 86:20, **Russell** 263:2

15 A sophistical rhetorician, inebriated with the exuberance of his own verbosity.
  of **Gladstone**
  in *The Times* 29 July 1878

16 I will not go down to posterity talking bad grammar.
  while correcting proofs of his last Parliamentary speech, 31 March 1881
  Robert Blake *Disraeli* (1966) ch. 32

17 No Government can be long secure without a formidable Opposition.
  Coningsby (1844) bk. 2, ch. 1

18 'A sound Conservative government,' said Taper, musingly. 'I understand: Tory men and Whig measures.'
  Coningsby (1844) bk. 2, ch. 6

19 It seems to me a barren thing this Conservatism—an unhappy cross-breed, the mule of politics that engenders nothing.
  Coningsby (1844) bk. 3, ch. 5; cf. **Power** 250:26

20 Read no history: nothing but biography, for that is life without theory.
  Contarini Fleming (1832) pt. 1, ch. 23; cf. **Emerson** 124:12

21 His Christianity was muscular.
  Endymion (1880) ch. 14

22 An insular country, subject to fogs, and with a powerful middle class, requires grave statesmen.
  Endymion (1880) ch. 37

23 As for our majority . . . one is enough.
  Endymion (1880) ch. 64

24 'Sensible men are all of the same religion.' 'And pray what is that?' . . . 'Sensible men never tell.'
  Endymion (1880) ch. 81; cf. **Shaftesbury** 268:7

25 The sweet simplicity of the three per cents.
  Endymion (1880) ch. 91; cf. **Stowell** 304:20

26 The blue ribbon of the turf.
  of the Derby
  Lord George Bentinck (1852) ch. 26

27 'Two nations; between whom there is no intercourse and no sympathy; who are as ignorant of each other's habits, thoughts, and feelings, as if they were dwellers in different zones, or inhabitants of different planets; who are formed by a different breeding, are fed by a different food, are ordered by different manners, and are not governed by the same laws.' 'You speak of—' said Egremont, hesitatingly, 'THE RICH AND THE POOR.'
  Sybil (1845) bk. 2, ch. 5; cf. **Foster** 132:4

28 London is a modern Babylon.
  Tancred (1847) bk. 5, ch. 5

29 All power is a trust.
  Vivian Grey (1826) bk. 6, ch. 7; cf. **Dryden** 116:19

1 Let me die eating ortolans to the sound of soft music!
> *The Young Duke* (1831) bk. 1, ch. 10; cf. **Smith** 298:14

2 Damn your principles! Stick to your party.
> *attributed to Disraeli and believed to have been said to Edward* **Bulwer-Lytton**
> E. Latham *Famous Sayings and their Authors* (1904)

3 Everyone likes flattery; and when you come to Royalty you should lay it on with a trowel.
> *to Matthew* **Arnold**
> G. W. E. Russell *Collections and Recollections* (1898) ch. 23

4 I have climbed to the top of the greasy pole.
> *on becoming Prime Minister*
> W. Monypenny and G. Buckle *Life of Benjamin Disraeli* vol. 4 (1916) ch. 16

5 Never complain and never explain.
> J. Morley *Life of William Ewart Gladstone* (1903) vol. 1; cf. **Fisher** 128:6

6 Pray remember, Mr Dean, no dogma, no Dean.
> W. Monypenny and G. Buckle *Life of Benjamin Disraeli* vol. 4 (1916) ch. 10

7 The school of Manchester.
> *describing the free trade politics of Cobden and* **Bright**
> Robert Blake *Disraeli* (1966) ch. 10

8 There are three kinds of lies: lies, damned lies and statistics.
> attributed to Disraeli in Mark Twain *Autobiography* (1924) vol. 1

9 When I want to read a novel, I write one.
> W. Monypenny and G. Buckle *Life of Benjamin Disraeli* vol. 6 (1920) ch. 17; cf. **Punch** 252:16

William Chatterton Dix 1837–98

10 As with gladness men of old
Did the guiding star behold.
> 'As with gladness men of old' (1861 hymn)

Henry Austin Dobson 1840–1921

11 All passes. Art alone
Enduring stays to us;
The Bust outlasts the throne,—
The Coin, Tiberius.
> 'Ars Victrix' (1876); translation of Gautier's 'L'Art'; cf. **Gautier** 136:20

12 Time goes, you say? Ah no!
Alas, Time stays, *we* go.
> 'The Paradox of Time' (1877)

Ken Dodd 1931–

13 Freud's theory was that when a joke opens a window and all those bats and bogeymen fly out, you get a marvellous feeling of relief and elation. The trouble with Freud is that he never had to play the old Glasgow Empire on a Saturday night after Rangers and Celtic had both lost.
> in *Guardian* 30 April 1991; quoted in many, usually much contracted, forms since the mid-1960s

Philip Doddridge 1702–51

14 O God of Bethel, by whose hand
Thy people still are fed,
Who through this weary pilgrimage
Hast all our fathers led.
> *Hymns* (1755) 'O God of Bethel'

Aelius Donatus

15 Confound those who have said our remarks before us.
> St Jerome *Commentary on Ecclesiastes* bk 1

J. P. Donleavy 1926–

16 When you don't have any money, the problem is food. When you have money, it's sex. When you have both it's health.
> *The Ginger Man* (1955) ch. 5

John Donne 1572–1631
Verse dates are those of composition

17 No spring, nor summer beauty hath such grace,
As I have seen in one autumnal face.
> *Elegies* 'The Autumnal' (*c.*1600)

18 License my roving hands, and let them go,
Behind, before, above, between, below.
O my America, my new found land,
My kingdom, safeliest when with one man manned.
> *Elegies* 'To His Mistress Going to Bed' (*c.*1595)

19 Death be not proud, though some have called thee
Mighty and dreadful, for thou art not so.
> *Holy Sonnets* (1609) no. 6 (ed. J. Carey, 1990)

20 One short sleep past, we wake eternally,
And death shall be no more; Death thou shalt die.
> *Holy Sonnets* (1609) no. 6 (ed. J. Carey, 1990)

21 Batter my heart, three-personed God; for, you
As yet but knock, breathe, shine, and seek to mend.
> *Holy Sonnets* (after 1609) no. 10 (ed. J. Carey, 1990)

22 What if this present were the world's last night?
> *Holy Sonnets* (after 1609) no. 19 (ed. J. Carey, 1990)

23 As thou
Art jealous, Lord, so I am jealous now,
Thou lov'st not, till from loving more, thou free
My soul; who ever gives, takes liberty.
> 'A Hymn to Christ, at the Author's last going into Germany' (1619)

24 Since I am coming to that holy room,
Where, with thy choir of saints for evermore,
I shall be made thy music; as I come
I tune the instrument here at the door,
And what I must do then, think now before.
> 'Hymn to God my God, in my Sickness' (1623)

25 Wilt thou forgive that sin where I begun,
Which is my sin, though it were done before?

Wilt thou forgive those sins, through which
I run
And do them still: though still I do deplore?
When thou hast done, thou hast not done,
For, I have more.
'A Hymn to God the Father' (1623)

1 Nature's great masterpiece, an elephant,
The only harmless great thing.
'The Progress of the Soul' (1601) st. 39

2 On a huge hill,
Cragged, and steep, Truth stands, and he
that will
Reach her, about must, and about must go.
Satire no. 3 (1594–5) l. 79

3 Air and angels.
title of poem, *Songs and Sonnets*

4 All other things, to their destruction draw,
Only our love hath no decay;
This, no tomorrow hath, nor yesterday,
Running it never runs from us away,
But truly keeps his first, last, everlasting
day.
Songs and Sonnets 'The Anniversary'

5 Come live with me, and be my love,
And we will some new pleasures prove
Of golden sands, and crystal brooks,
With silken lines, and silver hooks.
Songs and Sonnets 'The Bait'; cf. **Marlowe** 212:13,
Ralegh 253:24

6 For God's sake hold your tongue, and let me
love.
Songs and Sonnets 'The Canonization'

7 I wonder by my troth, what thou, and I
Did, till we loved, were we not weaned till
then?
But sucked on country pleasures, childishly?
Or snorted we in the seven sleepers den?
Songs and Sonnets 'The Good-Morrow'

8 I long to talk with some old lover's ghost,
Who died before the god of love was born.
Songs and Sonnets 'Love's Deity'

9 'Tis the year's midnight, and it is the day's.
Songs and Sonnets 'A Nocturnal upon St Lucy's
Day'

10 When my grave is broke up again
Some second guest to entertain,
(For graves have learnt that woman-head
To be to more than one a bed)
And he that digs it, spies
A bracelet of bright hair about the bone,
Will he not let us alone?
Songs and Sonnets 'The Relic'

11 Go, and catch a falling star,
Get with child a mandrake root,
Tell me, where all past years are,
Or who cleft the Devil's foot,
Teach me to hear mermaids singing.
Songs and Sonnets 'Song: Go and catch a falling
star'

12 Busy old fool, unruly sun,
Why dost thou thus,
Through windows, and through curtains
call on us?
Must to thy motions lovers' seasons run?
Songs and Sonnets 'The Sun Rising'

13 This bed thy centre is, these walls thy
sphere.
Songs and Sonnets 'The Sun Rising'

14 I have done one braver thing
Than all the Worthies did,
And yet a braver thence doth spring,
Which is, to keep that hid.
Songs and Sonnets 'The Undertaking'

15 Thy firmness makes my circle just,
And makes me end, where I begun.
Songs and Sonnets 'A Valediction: forbidding
mourning'

16 Sir, more than kisses, letters mingle souls.
'To Sir Henry Wotton' (1597–8)

17 But I do nothing upon my self, and yet I am
mine own Executioner.
Devotions upon Emergent Occasions (1624)
'Meditation XII'

18 No man is an Island, entire of it self.
Devotions upon Emergent Occasions (1624)
'Meditation XVII'

19 Any man's death diminishes me, because I
am involved in Mankind; And therefore
never send to know for whom the bell tolls;
it tolls for thee.
Devotions upon Emergent Occasions (1624)
'Meditation XVII'

20 When a whirlwind hath blown the dust of
the Churchyard into the Church, and the
man sweeps out the dust of the Church into
the Churchyard, who will undertake to sift
those dusts again, and to pronounce, This is
the Patrician, this is the noble flower, and
this the yeomanly, this the Plebeian bran.
LXXX Sermons (1640) 8 March 1621/2

21 I throw myself down in my Chamber, and I
call in, and invite God, and his Angels
thither, and when they are there, I neglect
God and his Angels, for the noise of a fly, for
the rattling of a coach, for the whining of a
door.
LXXX Sermons (1640) 12 December 1626 'At the
Funeral of Sir William Cokayne'

22 Poor intricated soul! Riddling, perplexed,
labyrinthical soul!
LXXX Sermons (1640) 25 January 1628/9

23 John Donne, Anne Donne, Un-done.
*in a letter to his wife, on being dismissed from the
service of his father-in-law, Sir George More*
Izaak Walton *The Life of Dr Donne* (first printed in
LXXX Sermons, 1640)

Fedor Dostoevsky 1821–81

24 If you were to destroy in mankind the belief
in immortality, not only love but every
living force maintaining the life of the
world would at once be dried up.
The Brothers Karamazov (1879–80) bk. 2, ch. 6

25 Beauty is mysterious as well as terrible. God
and devil are fighting there, and the
battlefield is the heart of man.
The Brothers Karamazov (1879–80) bk. 3, ch. 3

1 If the devil doesn't exist, but man has created him, he has created him in his own image and likeness.

The Brothers Karamazov (1879–80) bk. 5, ch. 4

Lord Alfred Douglas 1870–1945

2 I am the Love that dare not speak its name.

'Two Loves' (1896)

James Douglas, Earl of Morton
*c.*1516–81

3 Here lies he who neither feared nor flattered any flesh.

*of John **Knox**, said as he was buried, 26 November 1572*

George R. Preedy *The Life of John Knox* (1940) ch. 7

Keith Douglas 1920–44

4 And all my endeavours are unlucky explorers
come back, abandoning the expedition.

'On Return from Egypt, 1943–4' (1946)

5 Remember me when I am dead
And simplify me when I'm dead.

'Simplify me when I'm Dead' (1941)

6 For here the lover and killer are mingled
who had one body and one heart.
And death, who had the soldier singled
has done the lover mortal hurt.

'Vergissmeinnicht, 1943'

O. Douglas 1877–1948

7 It is wonderful how much news there is when people write every other day; if they wait for a month, there is nothing that seems worth telling.

Penny Plain (1920)

Alec Douglas-Home *see* **Lord Home**

Frederick Douglass *c.*1818–95

8 Every tone [of the songs of the slaves] was a testimony against slavery, and a prayer to God for deliverance from chains.

Narrative of the Life of Frederick Douglass (1845) ch. 2

Lorenzo Dow 1777–1834

9 You will be damned if you do—And you will be damned if you don't.

on the Calvinist doctrine of 'Particular Election'
Reflections on the Love of God (1836) ch. 6

Ernest Dowson 1867–1900

10 I have forgot much, Cynara! gone with the wind,
Flung roses, roses, riotously, with the throng,
Dancing, to put thy pale, lost lilies out of mind;

But I was desolate and sick of an old passion,
Yea, all the time, because the dance was long:
I have been faithful to thee, Cynara! in my fashion.

'Non Sum Qualis Eram' (1896) (also known as 'Cynara'); cf. **Horace** 164:18

11 They are not long, the days of wine and roses.

'Vitae Summa Brevis' (1896)

Arthur Conan Doyle 1859–1930

12 It is quite a three-pipe problem.

The Adventures of Sherlock Holmes (1892) 'The Red-Headed League'

13 The giant rat of Sumatra, a story for which the world is not yet prepared.

The Case-Book of Sherlock Homes (1927) 'The Sussex Vampire'

14 'Excellent,' I cried. 'Elementary,' said he.

*often misquoted as, 'Elementary, my dear Watson', a remark attributed to Sherlock Holmes, but not found in any book by Arthur Conan **Doyle**, first found in P.G. **Wodehouse** Psmith Journalist (1915)*

The Memoirs of Sherlock Holmes (1894) 'The Crooked Man'

15 Ex-Professor Moriarty of mathematical celebrity . . . is the Napoleon of crime, Watson.

The Memoirs of Sherlock Holmes (1894) 'The Final Problem'

16 'Is there any other point to which you would wish to draw my attention?'
'To the curious incident of the dog in the night-time.'
'The dog did nothing in the night-time.'
'That was the curious incident,' remarked Sherlock Holmes.

The Memoirs of Sherlock Holmes (1894) 'Silver Blaze'

17 What one man can invent another can discover.

The Return of Sherlock Holmes (1905) 'The Dancing Men'

18 When you have eliminated the impossible, whatever remains, *however improbable*, must be the truth?

The Sign of Four (1890) ch. 6

19 You know my methods. Apply them.

The Sign of Four (1890) ch. 6

20 It is the unofficial force—the Baker Street irregulars.

The Sign of Four (1890) ch. 8

Margaret Drabble 1939–

21 England's not a bad country . . . It's just a mean, cold, ugly, divided, tired, clapped-out, post-imperial, post-industrial slag-heap covered in polystyrene hamburger cartons.

A Natural Curiosity (1989)

Francis Drake *c.*1540–96

1 The singeing of the King of Spain's Beard.
on the expedition to Cadiz, 1587

> Francis Bacon *Considerations touching a War with Spain* (1629)

2 I must have the gentleman to haul and draw with the mariner, and the mariner with the gentleman . . . I would know him, that would refuse to set his hand to a rope, but I know there is not any such here.

> J. S. Corbett *Drake and the Tudor Navy* (1898) vol. 1, ch. 9

3 There is plenty of time to win this game, and to thrash the Spaniards too.

> attributed, in *Dictionary of National Biography* (1917–)

Michael Drayton 1563–1631

4 Ill news hath wings, and with the wind doth go,
Comfort's a cripple and comes ever slow.

> *The Barons' Wars* (1603) canto 2, st. 28

5 Since there's no help, come let us kiss and part,
Nay, I have done: you get no more of me,
And I am glad, yea glad with all my heart,
That thus so cleanly, I myself can free,
Shake hands for ever, cancel all our vows.

> *Idea* (1619) Sonnet 61

6 That shire which we the Heart of England well may call.

> *of Warwickshire*
> *Poly-Olbion* (1612–22) Song 13, l. 2

7 Next these, learn'd Jonson, in this list I bring,
Who had drunk deep of the Pierian spring.

> 'To Henry Reynolds, of Poets and Poesy' (1627) l. 129; cf. **Pope** 247:29

8 Fair stood the wind for France
When we our sails advance,
Nor now to prove our chance
Longer will tarry.

> *To the Cambro-Britons* (1619) 'Agincourt'

William Drennan 1754–1820

9 Nor one feeling of vengeance presume to defile
The cause, or the men, of the Emerald Isle.

> *Erin* (1795) st. 3

John Drinkwater 1882–1937

10 Deep is the silence, deep
On moon-washed apples of wonder.

> 'Moonlit Apples' (1917)

William Driver 1803–86

11 I name thee Old Glory.

> *saluting a new flag hoisted on his ship, the*
> Charles Doggett
> attributed

Thomas Drummond 1797–1840

12 Property has its duties as well as its rights.

> letter to the Earl of Donoughmore, 22 May 1838

William Drummond of Hawthornden 1585–1649

13 Phoebus, arise,
And paint the sable skies,
With azure, white, and red.

> 'Song: Phoebus, arise' (1614)

John Dryden 1631–1700

14 Plots, true or false, are necessary things,
To raise up commonwealths and ruin kings.

> *Absalom and Achitophel* (1681) pt. 1, l. 83

15 Of these the false Achitophel was first,
A name to all succeeding ages curst.

> *Absalom and Achitophel* (1681) pt. 1, l. 150

16 A daring pilot in extremity;
Pleased with the danger, when the waves went high
He sought the storms; but for a calm unfit.

> *Absalom and Achitophel* (1681) pt. 1, l. 159

17 Great wits are sure to madness near allied.

> *Absalom and Achitophel* (1681) pt. 1, l. 163

18 In friendship false, implacable in hate:
Resolved to ruin or to rule the state.

> *Absalom and Achitophel* (1681) pt. 1, l. 173

19 All empire is no more than power in trust.

> *Absalom and Achitophel* (1681) pt. 1, l. 411; cf.
> **Disraeli** 112:29

20 And pity never ceases to be shown
To him, who makes the people's wrongs his own.

> *Absalom and Achitophel* (1681) pt. 1, l. 725

21 Nor is the people's judgement always true:
The most may err as grossly as the few.

> *Absalom and Achitophel* (1681) pt. 1, l. 781

22 Beware the fury of a patient man.

> *Absalom and Achitophel* (1681) pt. 1, l. 1005

23 None but the brave deserves the fair.

> *Alexander's Feast* (1697) l. 7

24 Sweet is pleasure after pain.

> *Alexander's Feast* (1697) l. 60

25 Revenge, revenge! Timotheus cries.

> *Alexander's Feast* (1697) l. 131

26 Errors, like straws, upon the surface flow;
He who would search for pearls must dive below.

> *All for Love* (1678) prologue

27 Men are but children of a larger growth;
Our appetites as apt to change as theirs,
And full as craving too, and full as vain.

> *All for Love* (1678) act 4, sc. 1; cf. **Chesterfield** 89:11

28 I am as free as nature first made man,
Ere the base laws of servitude began,
When wild in woods the noble savage ran.

> *The Conquest of Granada* (1670) pt. 1, act 1, sc. 1

29 T'abhor the makers, and their laws approve,
Is to hate traitors and the treason love.

> *The Hind and the Panther* (1687) pt. 3, l. 706; cf.
> **Augustine** 19:5

30 And love's the noblest frailty of the mind.

> *The Indian Emperor* (1665) act 2, sc. 2; cf.
> **Shadwell** 268:6

1 War is the trade of kings.
King Arthur (1691) act 2, sc. 2

2 Fairest Isle, all isles excelling,
Seat of pleasures, and of loves;
Venus here will choose her dwelling,
And forsake her Cyprian groves.
King Arthur (1691) act 5 'Song of Venus'; cf.
Wesley 332:2

3 The rest to some faint meaning make
pretence,
But Shadwell never deviates into sense.
MacFlecknoe (1682) l. 19

4 But treason is not owned when 'tis descried;
Successful crimes alone are justified.
The Medal (1682) l. 207

5 And Antony, who lost the world for love.
Palamon and Arcite (1700) bk. 2, l. 607

6 But 'tis the talent of our English nation,
Still to be plotting some new reformation.
'The Prologue at Oxford, 1680' (prologue to
Nathaniel Lee *Sophonisba*, 2nd ed., 1681)

7 And this unpolished rugged verse I chose
As fittest for discourse and nearest prose.
Religio Laici (1682) l. 453

8 For secrets are edged tools,
And must be kept from children and from
fools.
Sir Martin Mar-All (1667) act 2, sc. 2

9 What passion cannot Music raise and quell?
A Song for St Cecilia's Day (1687) st. 2

10 There is a pleasure sure,
In being mad, which none but madmen
know!
The Spanish Friar (1681) act 1, sc. 1

11 Wit will shine
Through the harsh cadence of a rugged line.
'To the Memory of Mr Oldham' (1684)

12 Happy the man, and happy he alone,
He, who can call to-day his own:
He who, secure within, can say,
Tomorrow do thy worst, for I have lived
today.
translation of Horace *Odes* bk. 3, no. 29

13 She knows her man, and when you rant and
swear,
Can draw you to her *with a single hair*.
Translation of Persius *Satires* no. 5, l. 246

14 Arms, and the man I sing, who, forced by
fate,
And haughty Juno's unrelenting hate,
Expelled and exiled, left the Trojan shore.
translation of Virgil *Aeneid* (*Aeneis*, 1697) bk. 1, l.
1; cf. **Virgil** 324:9

15 The famous rules, which the French call *Des
Trois Unitez*, or, the Three Unities, which
ought to be observed in every regular play;
namely, of Time, Place, and Action.
An Essay of Dramatic Poesy (1668)

16 He is many times flat, insipid; his comic wit
degenerating into clenches, his serious

swelling into bombast. But he is always
great.
on **Shakespeare**
An Essay of Dramatic Poesy (1668)

17 'Tis sufficient to say, according to the
proverb, that here is God's plenty.
of **Chaucer**
Fables Ancient and Modern (1700) preface

Alexander Dubček 1921–92

18 In the service of the people we followed
such a policy that socialism would not lose
its human face.
in *Rudé Právo* 19 July 1968

Joachim Du Bellay 1522–60

19 *France, mère des arts, des armes et des lois.*
France, mother of arts, of warfare, and of
laws.
Les Regrets (1558) sonnet no. 9

20 *Heureux qui comme Ulysse a fait un beau voyage*
Happy he who like Ulysses has made a great
journey.
Les Regrets (1558) Sonnet no. 31

W. E. B. Du Bois 1868–1963

21 One thing alone I charge you. As you live,
believe in life!
last message, written 26 June, 1957, and read at
his funeral, 1963

Mme Du Deffand 1697–1780

22 *La distance n'y fait rien; il n'y a que le premier
pas qui coûte.*
The distance is nothing; it is only the first
step that is difficult.
*commenting on the legend that St Denis, carrying
his head in his hands, walked two leagues*
letter to Jean Le Rond d'Alembert, 7 July 1763

George Duffield 1818–88

23 Stand up!—stand up for Jesus!
Ye soldiers of the Cross.
'Stand Up, Stand Up for Jesus' (1858 hymn); the
opening line inspired by the dying words of the
American evangelist, Dudley Atkins Tyng

Carol Ann Duffy 1965–

24 Whatever 'in love' means,
true love is talented.
Someone vividly gifted in love has gone.
on the death of **Diana**, *Princess of Wales*
'September, 1997' (1997); cf. **Charles** 88:1

John Foster Dulles 1888–1959

25 The ability to get to the verge without
getting into the war is the necessary art . . .
We walked to the brink and we looked it in
the face.
in *Life* 16 January 1956; cf. **Stevenson** 303:12

Alexandre Dumas 1802–70

1 *Cherchons la femme.*
Let us look for the woman.
*attributed to Joseph Fouché (1763–1820) in the
form 'Cherchez la femme'*
  Les Mohicans de Paris (1854–5) *passim*

2 *Tous pour un, un pour tous.*
All for one, one for all.
  Les Trois Mousquetaires (1844) ch. 9

Daphne Du Maurier 1907–89

3 Last night I dreamt I went to Manderley
again.
  Rebecca (1938) ch. 1; opening words

Charles François du Périer Dumouriez 1739–1823

4 The courtiers who surround him have
forgotten nothing and learnt nothing.
*of Louis XVIII, at the time of the Declaration of
Verona, September 1795; quoted by* **Napoleon** *in
his Declaration to the French on his return from
Elba, 1815*
  Examen impartial d'un Écrit intitulé Déclaration de
  Louis XVIII (1795); cf. **Talleyrand** 309:2

Paul Lawrence Dunbar 1872–1906

5 I know why the caged bird sings!
adopted by Maya **Angelou** *as the title of her
autobiography, 1969*
  'Sympathy' st. 3; cf. **Webster** 330:18

William Dunbar c.1465–c.1513

6 *Timor mortis conturbat me.*
Fear of death troubles me.
  'Lament for the Makaris [makers]'

Isadora Duncan 1878–1927

7 *Adieu, mes amis. Je vais à la gloire.*
Farewell, my friends. I go to glory.
*before her scarf caught in a car wheel, breaking
her neck*
  Mary Desti *Isadora Duncan's End* (1929) ch. 25

Ian Dunlop 1940–

8 The shock of the new: seven historic
exhibitions of modern art.
  title of book (1972)

Douglas Dunn 1942–

9 In a country like this
Our ghosts outnumber us . . .
  'At Falkland Palace' (1988)

10 My poems should be Clyde-built, crude and
sure,
With images of those dole-deployed
To honour the indomitable Reds,
Clydesiders of slant steel and angled cranes.
  'Clydesiders' (1974)

Sean Dunne 1956–97

11 The country wears their going like a scar,
Today their relatives save to support and
Send others in planes for the new diaspora.
  'Letter from Ireland' (1991)

John Dunning 1731–83

12 The influence of the Crown has increased, is
increasing, and ought to be diminished.
  resolution passed in the House of Commons, 6
  April 1780

Richard Duppa 1770–1831

13 In language, the ignorant have prescribed
laws to the learned.
  Maxims (1830) no. 252

John George Lambton, Lord Durham 1792–1840

14 £40,000 a year a moderate income—such a
one as a man *might jog on with.*
  Thomas Creevey, letter to Elizabeth Ord, 13
  September 1821

15 I expected to find a contest between a
government and a people: I found two
nations warring in the bosom of a single
state.
of Canada
  Report of the Affairs of British North America (1839)

Leo Durocher 1906–91

16 I called off his players' names as they came
marching up the steps behind him . . . All
nice guys. They'll finish last. Nice guys.
Finish last.
*casual remark at a practice ground in the
presence of a number of journalists, July 1946,
generally quoted as 'Nice guys finish last'*
  Nice Guys Finish Last (1975) pt. 1

Ian Dury 1942–

17 Sex and drugs and rock and roll.
  title of song (1977)

Andrea Dworkin 1946–

18 Seduction is often difficult to distinguish
from rape. In seduction, the rapist bothers
to buy a bottle of wine.
  speech to women at Harper & Row, 1976

Edward Dyer d. 1607

19 Silence augmenteth grief, writing
increaseth rage,
Staled are my thoughts, which loved and
lost, the wonder of our age.
previously attributed to Fulke **Greville**
  'Elegy on the Death of Sir Philip Sidney' (1593)

20 My mind to me a kingdom is.
  'In praise of a contented mind' (1588),
  attributed

John Dyer 1700–58

21 But transient is the smile of fate:
A little rule, a little sway,
A sunbeam in a winter's day,
Is all the proud and mighty have

Between the cradle and the grave.
Grongar Hill (1726) l. 88

John Dyer

1 And he that will this health deny,
Down among the dead men let him lie.
'Down among the Dead Men' (*c.*1700)

Bob Dylan 1941–

2 How many roads must a man walk down
Before you can call him a man? . . .
The answer, my friend, is blowin' in the
wind,
The answer is blowin' in the wind.
'Blowin' in the Wind' (1962 song)

3 And it's a hard rain's a gonna fall.
'A Hard Rain's A Gonna Fall' (1963 song)

4 Money doesn't talk, it swears.
'It's Alright, Ma (I'm Only Bleeding)' (1965 song)

5 She takes just like a woman, yes, she does
She makes love just like a woman, yes, she
does
And she aches just like a woman
But she breaks like a little girl.
'Just Like a Woman' (1966 song)

6 Hey! Mr Tambourine Man, play a song for
me.
'Mr Tambourine Man' (1965 song)

7 Señor, señor, do you know where we're
headin'?
Lincoln County Road or Armageddon?
'Señor (Tale of Yankee Power)' (1978 song)

8 All that foreign oil controlling American
soil.
'Slow Train' (1979 song)

9 The times they are a-changin'.
title of song (1964)

10 Come mothers and fathers,
Throughout the land
And don't criticize
What you can't understand.
'The Times They Are A-Changing' (1964 song)

Esther Dyson

11 The important thing to remember is that
this is not a new form of life. It is just a new
activity.
of the Internet
in *New York Times* 7 July 1996

Arthur Eddington 1882–1944

12 I shall use the phrase 'time's arrow' to
express this one-way property of time
which has no analogue in space.
The Nature of the Physical World (1928) ch. 4

13 If an army of monkeys were strumming on
typewriters they *might* write all the books in
the British Museum.
The Nature of the Physical World (1928); cf.
Wilensky 335:26

14 If your theory is found to be against the
second law of thermodynamics I can give

you no hope; there is nothing for it but to
collapse in deepest humiliation.
The Nature of the Physical World (1928) ch. 14

15 Science is an edged tool, with which men
play like children, and cut their own
fingers.
attributed in Robert L. Weber *More Random
Walks in Science* (1982)

Mary Baker Eddy 1821–1910

16 Disease is an experience of so-called mortal
mind. It is fear made manifest on the body.
Science and Health with Key to the Scriptures (1875)

Anthony Eden, Earl of Avon
1897–1977

17 We are in an armed conflict; that is the
phrase I have used. There has been no
declaration of war.
on the Suez crisis
speech in the House of Commons, 1 November
1956

Clarissa Eden 1920–

18 For the past few weeks I have really felt as if
the Suez Canal was flowing through my
drawing-room.
speech at Gateshead, 20 November 1956

Marriott Edgar 1880–1951

19 There's a famous seaside place called
Blackpool,
That's noted for fresh air and fun,
And Mr and Mrs Ramsbottom
Went there with young Albert, their son.
'The Lion and Albert' (1932)

Maria Edgeworth 1767–1849

20 Well! some people talk of morality, and
some of religion, but give me a little snug
property.
The Absentee (1812) ch. 2

21 It was her settled purpose to make the Irish
and Ireland ridiculous and contemptible to
Lord Colambre; to disgust him with his
native country . . . To confirm him an
absentee was her object.
The Absentee (1812) ch. 7

Thomas Alva Edison 1847–1931

22 Genius is one per cent inspiration, ninety-
nine per cent perspiration.
said *c.*1903, in *Harper's Monthly Magazine*
September 1932

James Edmeston 1791–1867

23 Lead us, Heavenly Father, lead us
O'er the world's tempestuous sea;
Guard us, guide us, keep us, feed us,
For we have no help but Thee;
Yet possessing every blessing,
If our God our Father be.
'Lead us, heavenly Father, lead us' (1821)

John Maxwell Edmonds
1875–1958

1 When you go home, tell them of us and say,
'For your tomorrows these gave their today.'
*second line often quoted as 'For your tomorrow
we gave our today', as on the Kohima memorial in
the Burma campaign of the Second World War*
Inscriptions Suggested for War Memorials (1919)

Edward III 1312–77

2 Also say to them, that they suffre hym this
day to wynne his spurres, for if god be
pleased, I woll this journey be his, and the
honoure therof.
*speaking of the Black Prince at Crécy, 1346;
commonly quoted 'Let the boy win his spurs'*
The Chronicle of Froissart (tr. Sir John Bourchier,
Lord Berners, 1523–5) ch. 130

Edward VIII, afterwards Duke of Windsor 1894–1972

3 These works brought all these people here.
Something should be done to get them at
work again.
*speaking at the derelict Dowlais Iron and Steel
Works, 18 November 1936; often misquoted as,
'Something must be done'*
in Western Mail 19 November 1936

4 At long last I am able to say a few words of
my own . . . you must believe me when I tell
you that I have found it impossible to carry
the heavy burden of responsibility and to
discharge my duties as King as I would wish
to do without the help and support of the
woman I love.
radio broadcast following his abdication, 11
December 1936

Jonathan Edwards 1703–58

5 Of all Insects no one is more wonderful
than the spider especially with Respect to
their sagacity and admirable way of
working . . . I . . . once saw a very large
spider to my surprise swimming in the air
. . . and others have assured me that they
often have seen spiders fly, the appearance
is truly very pretty and pleasing.
*The Flying Spider—Observations by Jonathan
Edwards when a boy 'Of Insects' in Andover Review
vol. 13 (1890)*

6 The bodies of those that made such a noise
and tumult when alive, when dead, lie as
quietly among the graves of their
neighbours as any others.
Sermon on procrastination in Works (1834) vol.
2

Oliver Edwards 1711–91

7 I have tried too in my time to be a
philosopher; but, I don't know how,
cheerfulness was always breaking in.
James Boswell Life of Samuel Johnson (1791) 17
April 1778

Barbara Ehrenreich 1941–

8 Exercise is the yuppie version of bulimia.
The Worst Years of Our Lives (1991) 'Food Worship'

John Ehrlichman 1925–99

9 I think we ought to let him hang there. Let
him twist slowly, slowly in the wind.
*Richard Nixon had withdrawn his support for
Patrick Gray, nominated as director of the FBI,
although Gray himself had not been informed*
in a telephone conversation with John Dean; in
Washington Post 27 July 1973

Max Ehrmann 1872–1945

10 Go placidly amid the noise and the haste,
and remember what peace there may be
in silence.
*often wrongly dated to 1692, the date of
foundation of a church in Baltimore whose vicar
circulated the poem in 1956*
'Desiderata' (1948)

Albert Einstein 1879–1955

11 Science without religion is lame, religion
without science is blind.
Science, Philosophy and Religion: a Symposium (1941)
ch. 13

12 $E = mc^2$.
*the usual form of Einstein's original statement: 'If
a body releases the energy L in the form of
radiation, its mass is decreased by L/V^2'*
in Annalen der Physik 18 (1905)

13 God is subtle but he is not malicious.
remark made during a week at Princeton
beginning 9 May 1921, later carved above the
fireplace of the Common Room of Fine Hall
(the Mathematical Institute), Princeton
University

14 I am convinced that He [God] does not play
dice.
often quoted as: 'God does not play dice'
letter to Max Born, 4 December 1926; in Einstein
und Born Briefwechsel (1969)

Dwight D. Eisenhower 1890–1969

15 You have broader considerations that might
follow what you might call the 'falling
domino' principle. You have a row of
dominoes set up. You knock over the first
one, and what will happen to the last one is
that it will go over very quickly. So you have
the beginning of a disintegration that would
have the most profound influences.
speech at press conference, 7 April 1954

16 I think that people want peace so much that
one of these days governments had better
get out of the way and let them have it.
broadcast discussion, 31 August 1959

Alfred Eisenstaedt 1898–1995

17 It's more important to click with people
than to click the shutter
in Life 24 August 1995 (electronic edition),
obituary

Eleazar of Worms 1176–1238

1 The highest sacrifice is a broken and contrite heart; the highest wisdom is that which is found in the Torah; the noblest of all ornaments is modesty; and the most beautiful thing that man can do, is to forgive a wrong.
Sefer Rokeah

Edward Elgar 1857–1934

2 To my friends pictured within.
Enigma Variations (1899) dedication

3 There is music in the air.
R. J. Buckley *Sir Edward Elgar* (1905) ch. 4

George Eliot 1819–80

4 A difference of taste in jokes is a great strain on the affections.
Daniel Deronda (1876) bk. 2, ch. 15

5 An election is coming. Universal peace is declared, and the foxes have a sincere interest in prolonging the lives of the poultry.
Felix Holt (1866) ch. 5

6 A woman can hardly ever choose . . . she is dependent on what happens to her. She must take meaner things, because only meaner things are within her reach.
Felix Holt (1866) ch. 27

7 Debasing the moral currency.
The Impressions of Theophrastus Such (1879) essay title

8 He said he should prefer not to know the sources of the Nile, and that there should be some unknown regions preserved as hunting-grounds for the poetic imagination.
Middlemarch (1871–2) bk. 1, ch. 9

9 Fred's studies are not very deep . . . he is only reading a novel.
Middlemarch (1871–2) bk 1, ch. 11

10 If we had a keen vision and feeling of all ordinary human life, it would be like hearing the grass grow and the squirrel's heart beat, and we should die of that roar which lies on the other side of silence.
Middlemarch (1871–2) bk. 2, ch. 20

11 Anger and jealousy can no more bear to lose sight of their objects than love.
The Mill on the Floss (1860) bk. 1, ch. 10

12 The dead level of provincial existence.
The Mill on the Floss (1860) bk. 5, ch. 3

13 'Character' says Novalis, in one of his questionable aphorisms—'character is destiny.'
The Mill on the Floss (1860) bk. 6, ch. 6; cf. **Heraclitus** 156:26, **Novalis** 235:2

T. S. Eliot 1888–1965

14 Because I do not hope to turn again
Because I do not hope
Because I do not hope to turn.
Ash-Wednesday (1930) pt. 1

15 Teach us to care and not to care
Teach us to sit still.
Ash-Wednesday (1930) pt. 1

16 Lady, three white leopards sat under a juniper-tree
In the cool of the day.
Ash-Wednesday (1930) pt. 2

17 What is hell?
Hell is oneself,
Hell is alone, the other figures in it
Merely projections. There is nothing to escape from
And nothing to escape to. One is always alone.
The Cocktail Party (1950) act 1, sc. 3; cf. **Sartre** 264:23

18 Time present and time past
Are both perhaps present in time future,
And time future contained in time past.
Four Quartets 'Burnt Norton' (1936) pt. 1

19 Footfalls echo in the memory
Down the passage which we did not take
Towards the door we never opened
Into the rose-garden.
Four Quartets 'Burnt Norton' (1936) pt. 1

20 Human kind
Cannot bear very much reality.
Four Quartets 'Burnt Norton' (1936) pt. 1.

21 At the still point of the turning world.
Four Quartets 'Burnt Norton' (1936) pt. 2

22 In my beginning is my end.
Four Quartets 'East Coker' (1940) pt. 1; cf. **Mary** 214:14

23 The intolerable wrestle
With words and meanings.
Four Quartets 'East Coker' (1940) pt. 2

24 The houses are all gone under the sea.
The dancers are all gone under the hill.
Four Quartets 'East Coker' (1940) pt. 2

25 O dark dark dark. They all go into the dark,
The vacant interstellar spaces, the vacant into the vacant.
Four Quartets 'East Coker' (1940) pt. 3

26 I think that the river
Is a strong brown god—sullen, untamed and intractable.
Four Quartets 'The Dry Salvages' (1941) pt. 1

27 Speech, and speech impelled us
To purify the dialect of the tribe.
Four Quartets 'Little Gidding' (1942) pt. 2

28 What we call the beginning is often the end
And to make an end is to make a beginning.
The end is where we start from.
Four Quartets 'Little Gidding' (1942) pt. 5

29 So, while the light fails
On a winter's afternoon, in a secluded chapel
History is now and England.
Four Quartets 'Little Gidding' (1942) pt. 5

30 And all shall be well and
All manner of thing shall be well
When the tongues of flame are in-folded
Into the crowned knot of fire

And the fire and the rose are one.
Four Quartets 'Little Gidding' (1942) pt. 5; cf.
Julian 179:10

1 Here I am, an old man in a dry month
Being read to by a boy, waiting for rain.
'Gerontion' (1920)

2 After such knowledge, what forgiveness?
'Gerontion' (1920)

3 Tenants of the house,
Thoughts of a dry brain in a dry season.
'Gerontion' (1920)

4 We are the hollow men.
'The Hollow Men' (1925)

5 *Here we go round the prickly pear*
Prickly pear prickly pear.
Between the idea
And the reality
Between the motion
And the act
Falls the Shadow.
'The Hollow Men' (1925)

6 This is the way the world ends
Not with a bang but a whimper.
'The Hollow Men' (1925)

7 A cold coming we had of it,
Just the worst time of the year
For a journey, and such a long journey:
The ways deep and the weather sharp,
The very dead of winter.
'Journey of the Magi' (1927); cf. **Andrewes** 5:10

8 An alien people clutching their gods.
'Journey of the Magi' (1927)

9 Let us go then, you and I,
When the evening is spread out against the
sky
Like a patient etherized upon a table.
'The Love Song of J. Alfred Prufrock' (1917)

10 I have measured out my life with coffee
spoons.
'The Love Song of J. Alfred Prufrock' (1917)

11 I should have been a pair of ragged claws
Scuttling across the floors of silent seas.
'The Love Song of J. Alfred Prufrock' (1917)

12 No! I am not Prince Hamlet, nor was meant
to be;
Am an attendant lord, one that will do
To swell a progress.
'The Love Song of J. Alfred Prufrock' (1917)

13 I grow old . . . I grow old . . .
I shall wear the bottoms of my trousers
rolled.
'The Love Song of J. Alfred Prufrock' (1917)

14 Shall I part my hair behind? Do I dare to eat
a peach?
I shall wear white flannel trousers, and walk
upon the beach.
I have heard the mermaids singing, each to
each.
I do not think that they will sing to me.
'The Love Song of J. Alfred Prufrock' (1917); cf.
Donne 114:11

15 Yet we have gone on living,
Living and partly living.
Murder in the Cathedral (1935) pt. 1

16 The last temptation is the greatest treason:
To do the right deed for the wrong reason.
Murder in the Cathedral (1935) pt. 1

17 He always has an alibi, and one or two to
spare:
At whatever time the deed took place—
MACAVITY WASN'T THERE!
Old Possum's Book of Practical Cats (1939)
'Macavity: the Mystery Cat'

18 I gotta use words when I talk to you.
Sweeney Agonistes (1932) 'Fragment of an Agon'

19 The nightingales are singing near
The Convent of the Sacred Heart,
And sang within the bloody wood
When Agamemnon cried aloud
And let their liquid siftings fall
To stain the stiff dishonoured shroud.
'Sweeney among the Nightingales' (1919)

20 April is the cruellest month, breeding
Lilacs out of the dead land.
The Waste Land (1922) pt. 1

21 I will show you fear in a handful of dust.
The Waste Land (1922) pt. 1

22 The Chair she sat in, like a burnished
throne,
Glowed on the marble.
The Waste Land (1922) pt. 2; cf. **Shakespeare**
268:17

23 And still she cried, and still the world
pursues,
'Jug Jug' to dirty ears.
The Waste Land (1922) pt. 2; cf. **Lyly** 204:23

24 I think we are in rats' alley
Where the dead men lost their bones.
The Waste Land (1922) pt. 2

25 o o o o that Shakespeherian Rag—
It's so elegant
So intelligent.
The Waste Land (1922) pt. 2; cf. **Buck** 72:2

26 But at my back from time to time I hear
The sound of horns and motors, which shall
bring
Sweeney to Mrs Porter in the spring.
O the moon shone bright on Mrs Porter
And on her daughter
They wash their feet in soda water.
The Waste Land (1922) pt. 3; cf. **Marvell** 213:21

27 I Tiresias, old man with wrinkled dugs.
The Waste Land (1922) pt. 3

28 When lovely woman stoops to folly and
Paces about her room again, alone,
She smoothes her hair with automatic
hand,
And puts a record on the gramophone.
The Waste Land (1922) pt. 3; cf. **Goldsmith** 144:4

29 Shantih, shantih, shantih.
The Waste Land (1922) closing words; cf.
Upanishads 321:22

30 Webster was much possessed by death
And saw the skull beneath the skin.
'Whispers of Immortality' (1919)

1 Immature poets imitate; mature poets steal.
  The Sacred Wood (1920) 'Philip Massinger'

2 In the seventeenth century a dissociation of sensibility set in, from which we have never recovered; and this dissociation, as is natural, was due to the influence of the two most powerful poets of the century, Milton and Dryden.
  Selected Essays (1932) 'The Metaphysical Poets' (1921)

Elizabeth I 1533–1603

3 The queen of Scots is this day leichter of a fair son, and I am but a barren stock.
  to her ladies, June 1566

4 I know what it is to be a subject, what to be a Sovereign, what to have good neighbours, and sometimes meet evil-willers.
  speech to a Parliamentary deputation at Richmond, 12 November 1586, from a report 'which the Queen herself heavily amended in her own hand'

5 In trust I have found treason.
  traditional concluding words of the speech to a Parliamentary deputation at Richmond, 12 November 1586

6 I know I have the body of a weak and feeble woman, but I have the heart and stomach of a king, and of a king of England too; and think foul scorn that Parma or Spain, or any prince of Europe, should dare to invade the borders of my realm.
  speech to the troops at Tilbury on the approach of the Armada, 1588

7 The daughter of debate, that eke discord doth sow.
  on **Mary** *Queen of Scots*
  George Puttenham (ed.) *The Art of English Poesie* (1589) bk. 3, ch. 20

8 Though God hath raised me high, yet this I count the glory of my crown: that I have reigned with your loves.
  The Golden Speech, 1601

9 Must! Is *must* a word to be addressed to princes? Little man, little man! thy father, if he had been alive, durst not have used that word.
  to Robert **Cecil**, *on his saying she must go to bed, shortly before her death*
  J. R. Green *A Short History of the English People* (1874) ch. 7

10 If thy heart fails thee, climb not at all.
  lines after Sir Walter **Ralegh**, *written on a window-pane*
  Thomas Fuller *Worthies of England* vol. 1; cf. **Ralegh** 254:4

11 I would not open windows into men's souls.
  oral tradition, in J. B. Black *Reign of Elizabeth 1558–1603* (1936)

12 All my possessions for a moment of time.
  last words; attributed, but almost certainly apocryphal

Elizabeth II 1926–

13 I declare before you all that my whole life, whether it be long or short, shall be devoted to your service and the service of our great Imperial family to which we all belong.
  broadcast speech, as Princess Elizabeth, to the Commonwealth from Cape Town, 21 April 1947

14 In the words of one of my more sympathetic correspondents, it has turned out to be an 'annus horribilis'.
  speech at Guildhall, London, 24 November 1992

15 I for one believe that there are lessons to be drawn from her life and from the extraordinary and moving reaction to her death.
  broadcast from Buckingham Palace on the evening before the funeral of **Diana**, *Princess of Wales, 5 September 1997*
  in *The Times* 6 September 1997

Queen Elizabeth, the Queen Mother 1900–

16 I'm glad we've been bombed. It makes me feel I can look the East End in the face.
  to a London policeman, 13 September 1940
  John Wheeler-Bennett *King George VI* (1958) pt. 3, ch. 6

17 The Princesses would never leave without me and I couldn't leave without the King, and the King will never leave.
  on the suggestion that the royal family be evacuated during the Blitz
  Penelope Mortimer *Queen Elizabeth* (1986) ch. 25

Alf Ellerton

18 Belgium put the kibosh on the Kaiser.
  title of song (1914)

John Ellerton 1826–93

19 The day Thou gavest, Lord, is ended,
  The darkness falls at Thy behest.
  Hymn (1870), the first line borrowed from an earlier, anonymous hymn

Jane Elliot 1727–1805

20 I've heard them lilting, at the ewe milking,
  Lasses a' lilting, before dawn of day;
  But now they are moaning, on ilka green loaning;
  The flowers of the forest are a' wede away.
  'The Flowers of the Forest' (1769), the most popular version of the traditional lament for the Battle of Flodden in 1513; cf. **Cockburn** 95:9

Charlotte Elliott 1789–1871

21 Just as I am, without one plea.
  Invalid's Hymn Book (1834) 'Just as I am'

22 Watch and pray.
  Morning and Evening Hymns (1836) 'Christian! seek not yet repose'; cf. **Bible** 45:17

Ebenezer Elliott 1781–1849

23 What is a communist? One who hath yearnings

For equal division of unequal earnings.
'Epigram' (1850)

George Ellis 1753–1815

1 Snowy, Flowy, Blowy,
Showery, Flowery, Bowery,
Hoppy, Croppy, Droppy,
Breezy, Sneezy, Freezy.
'The Twelve Months'

Havelock Ellis (Henry Havelock Ellis) 1859–1939

2 What we call 'progress' is the exchange of one nuisance for another nuisance.
Impressions and Comments (1914) 31 July 1912

3 All civilization has from time to time become a thin crust over a volcano of revolution.
Little Essays of Love and Virtue (1922) ch. 7

Friar Elstow

4 With thanks to God we know the way to heaven, to be as ready by water as by land, and therefore we care not which way we go.
when threatened with drowning by Henry VIII
John Stow *The Annals of England* (1615); cf.
Gilbert 139:18

Paul Éluard 1895–1952

5 *L'espoir ne fait pas de poussière.*
Hope raises no dust.
'Ailleurs, ici, partout' (1946)

6 *Adieu tristesse*
Bonjour tristesse
Farewell sadness
Good-day sadness
You are inscribed in the lines of the ceiling.
'À peine défigurée' (1932)

Buchi Emecheta 1944–

7 I am a woman and a woman of Africa. I am a daughter of Nigeria and if she is in shame, I shall stay and mourn with her in shame.
Destination Biafra (1982)

Ralph Waldo Emerson 1803–82

8 If the red slayer think he slays,
Or if the slain think he is slain,
They know not well the subtle ways
I keep, and pass, and turn again.
'Brahma' (1867); cf. **Upanishads** 321:24

9 Here once the embattled farmers stood,
And fired the shot heard round the world.
'Concord Hymn' (1837)

10 When Duty whispers low, *Thou must*,
The youth replies, *I can.*
'Voluntaries' no. 3 (1867)

11 The louder he talked of his honour, the faster we counted our spoons.
The Conduct of Life (1860) 'Worship'; cf. **Johnson**
174:25, **Shaw** 291:13

12 There is properly no history; only biography.
Essays (1841) 'History'; cf. **Disraeli** 112:20

13 A foolish consistency is the hobgoblin of little minds.
Essays (1841) 'Self-Reliance'

14 What is a weed? A plant whose virtues have not been discovered.
Fortune of the Republic (1878)

15 Hitch your wagon to a star.
Society and Solitude (1870) 'Civilization'

16 I hate quotations. Tell me what you know.
Journals and Miscellaneous Notebooks (1961) May 1849

17 Glittering generalities! They are blazing ubiquities.
on Rufus **Choate**
attributed; cf. **Choate** 90:15

18 If a man write a better book, preach a better sermon, or make a better mouse-trap than his neighbour, tho' he build his house in the woods, the world will make a beaten path to his door.
attributed to Emerson in Sarah S. B. Yule *Borrowings* (1889); the quotation was the occasion of a long controversy owing to Elbert Hubbard's claim to its authorship

Robert Emmet 1778–1803

19 Let no man write my epitaph . . . When my country takes her place among the nations of the earth, *then,* and *not till then,* let my epitaph be written.
speech from the dock when condemned to death, 19 September 1803

William Empson 1906–84

20 Waiting for the end, boys, waiting for the end.
'Just a smack at Auden' (1940)

21 Seven types of ambiguity.
title of book (1930)

22 Learning French is some trouble, but after that you have a clear and beautiful language; in English the undergrowth is part of the language.
in *Spectator* 14 June 1935

Friedrich Engels 1820–95

23 *Der Staat wird nicht 'abgeschafft', er stirbt ab.*
The State is not 'abolished', *it withers away.*
Anti-Dühring (1878) pt. 3, ch. 2

Epictetus AD c.50–120

24 Everything has two handles, by one of which it ought to be carried and by the other not.
The Encheiridion sect. 43

Epicurus 341–271 BC

25 Death, therefore, the most awful of evils, is nothing to us, seeing that, when we are death is not come, and when death is come, we are not.
Diogenes Laertius *Lives of Eminent Philosophers* bk. 10

Olaudah Equiano *c.*1745–*c.*1797

1 We are . . . a nation of dancers, singers and poets.
of the Ibo people
Narrative of the Life of Olaudah Equiano (1789) ch. 1

Erasmus *c.*1469–1536

2 *In regione caecorum rex est luscus.*
In the country of the blind the one-eyed man is king.
Adages bk. 3, century 4, no. 96

Robert Devereux, Earl of Essex 1566–1601

3 Reasons are not like garments, the worse for wearing.
letter to Lord Willoughby, 4 January 1599

Henri Estienne 1531–98

4 *Si jeunesse savait; si vieillesse pouvait.*
If youth knew; if age could.
Les Prémices (1594) bk. 4, epigram 4

George Etherege *c.*1635–91

5 I walk within the purlieus of the Law.
Love in a Tub (1664) act 1, sc. 3; cf. **Tennyson** 311:24

Euclid fl. *c.*300 BC

6 *Quod erat demonstrandum.*
Which was to be proved.
often abbreviated to QED
Latin translation from the Greek of *Elementa* bk. 1, proposition 5 and *passim*

7 A line is length without breadth.
Elementa bk. 1, definition 2

8 There is no 'royal road' to geometry.
addressed to Ptolemy I, in Proclus Commentary on the First Book of Euclid's Elementa prologue, pt. 2

Euripides *c.*485–*c.*406 BC

9 My tongue swore, but my mind's unsworn.
Hippolytus lamenting his breaking of an oath
Hippolytus l. 612

10 You mention a slave's condition; not to say what one thinks.
The Phoenician Women l. 392

Abel Evans 1679–1737

11 Under this stone, Reader, survey
Dead Sir John Vanbrugh's house of clay.
Lie heavy on him, Earth! for he
Laid many heavy loads on thee!
'Epitaph on Sir John Vanbrugh, Architect of Blenheim Palace'

Lord Eversley *see* **Charles Shaw-Lefevre**

Gavin Ewart 1916–95

12 So the last date slides into the bracket,
that will appear in all future anthologies—
And in quiet Cornwall and in London's ghastly racket
We are now Betjemanless.
'In Memoriam, Sir John Betjeman (1906–84)' (1985)

William Norman Ewer 1885–1976

13 I gave my life for freedom—This I know:
For those who bade me fight had told me so.
'Five Souls' (1917)

14 How odd
Of God
To choose
The Jews.
Week-End Book (1924); cf. **Browne** 68:19

Frederick William Faber 1814–63

15 Faith of our Fathers! Mary's prayers
Shall win our country back to thee
And by the truth that comes from God
England shall then indeed be free.
'Faith of our Fathers'

16 My God, how wonderful Thou art!
Thy Majesty how bright!
Oratory Hymns (1854) 'The Eternal Father'

Robert Fabyan d. 1513

17 Ranulphe says he took a surfeit by eating of a lamprey, and thereof died.
The New Chronicles of England and France (1516) vol. 1, ch. 229

18 The Duke of Clarence . . . then being a prisoner in the Tower, was secretly put to death and drowned in a barrel of Malmesey wine within the said Tower.
The New Chronicles of England and France (1516) vol. 2 '1478'; 'malvesye' for 'malmesey' in early editions

Clifton Fadiman 1904–

19 Milk's leap toward immortality.
of cheese
Any Number Can Play (1957)

20 The mama of dada.
of Gertrude **Stein**
Party of One (1955)

Émile Faguet 1847–1916

21 It would be equally reasonable to say that sheep are born carnivorous, and everywhere nibble grass.
in response to Rousseau (see **Rousseau** *261:11)*
paraphrasing Joseph de Maistre; *Politiques et Moralistes du Dix-Neuvième Siècle* (1899)

Marianne Faithfull 1946–

22 Maybe the most that you can expect from a relationship that goes bad is to come out of it with a few good songs.
Faithfull (1994) 'Colston Hall'

Lucius Cary, Lord Falkland
1610–43

1 When it is not necessary to change, it is necessary not to change.
Discourses of Infallibility (1660) 'A Speech concerning Episcopacy' delivered in 1641

Frantz Fanon 1925–61

2 The shape of Africa resembles a revolver, and Zaire is the trigger.
attributed

Michael Faraday 1791–1867

3 Nothing is too wonderful to be true, if it be consistent with the laws of nature, and in such things as these, experiment is the best test of such consistency.
diary, 19 March 1849

4 Why sir, there is every possibility that you will soon be able to tax it!
to Gladstone, when asked about the usefulness of electricity
W. E. H. Lecky *Democracy and Liberty* (1899 ed.)

Eleanor Farjeon 1881–1965

5 Morning has broken
Like the first morning,
Blackbird has spoken
Like the first bird.
Children's Bells (1957) 'A Morning Song (for the First Day of Spring)'

Herbert Farjeon 1887–1945

6 For I've danced with a man.
I've danced with a man
Who—well, you'll never guess.
I've danced with a man who's danced with a girl
Who's danced with the Prince of Wales!
'I've danced with a man who's danced with a girl'; first written for Elsa Lanchester and sung at private parties; later sung on stage by Mimi Crawford (1928)

James Farley 1888–1976

7 As Maine goes, so goes Vermont.
after predicting correctly that Franklin Roosevelt would carry all but two states in the election of 1936
statement to the press, 4 November 1936

Edward Farmer c.1809–76

8 I have no pain, dear mother, now;
But oh! I am so dry:
Just moisten poor Jim's lips once more;
And, mother, do not cry!
'The Collier's Dying Child'

Farouk 1920–65

9 The whole world is in revolt. Soon there will be only five Kings left—the King of England, the King of Spades, the King of Clubs, the King of Hearts and the King of Diamonds.
said to Lord Boyd-Orr at a conference in Cairo, 1948

George Farquhar 1678–1707

10 My Lady Bountiful.
The Beaux' Stratagem (1707) act 1, sc. 1

11 Money is the sinews of love, as of war.
Love and a Bottle (1698) act 2, sc. 1; cf. **Cicero** 92:28

12 Poetry's a mere drug, Sir.
Love and a Bottle (1698) act 3, sc. 2; cf. **Lowell** 203:14

13 Hanging and marriage, you know, go by Destiny
The Recruiting Officer (1706) act 3, sc. 2

14 A lady, if undressed at Church, looks silly,
One cannot be devout in dishabilly.
The Stage Coach (1704) prologue

David Glasgow Farragut 1801–70

15 Damn the torpedoes! Full speed ahead.
at the battle of Mobile Bay, 5 August 1864 (torpedoes mines)
A. T. Mahan *Great Commanders: Admiral Farragut* (1892) ch. 10

William Faulkner 1897–1962

16 The past is never dead. It's not even past.
Requiem for a Nun (1951) act 1

Guy Fawkes 1570–1606

17 A desperate disease requires a dangerous remedy.
6 November 1605, in *Dictionary of National Biography* (1917–); cf. **Shakespeare** 272:30

Dianne Feinstein 1933–

18 Toughness doesn't have to come in a pinstripe suit.
in *Time* 4 June 1984

James Fenton 1949–

19 It is not what they built. It is what they knocked down.
It is not the houses. It is the spaces between the houses.
It is not the streets that exist. It is the streets that no longer exist.
German Requiem (1981)

20 Yes
You have come upon the fabled lands where myths
Go when they die.
'The Pitt-Rivers Museum' (1983)

Ferdinand I 1503–64

21 *Fiat justitia et pereat mundus.*
Let justice be done, though the world perish.
motto of Ferdinand I (1503–64), Holy Roman Emperor; cf. **Watson** 329:2

Samuel Ferguson 1810–86

1 As I heard the sweet lark sing
In the clear air of the day.
'The Lark in the Clear Air'

Pierre de Fermat 1601–65

2 *Cuius rei demonstrationem mirabilem sane detexi hanc marginis exiguitas non caperet.*
I have a truly marvellous demonstration of this proposition which this margin is too narrow to contain.
of 'Fermat's last theorem', written in the margin of his copy of Diophantus's *Arithmetica, and subsequently published by his son in 1670 in an edition of the book containing Fermat's annotations*
Simon Singh *Fermat's Last Theorem* (1997)

Enrico Fermi 1901–54

3 Whatever Nature has in store for mankind, unpleasant as it may be, men must accept, for ignorance is never better than knowledge.
Laura Fermi *Atoms in the Family* (1955)

Kathleen Ferrier 1912–53

4 Now I'll have eine kleine Pause.
last words
Gerald Moore *Am I Too Loud?* (1962)

Ludwig Feuerbach 1804–72

5 *Der Mensch ist, was er isst.*
Man is what he eats.
Jacob Moleschott *Lehre der Nahrungsmittel: Für das Volk* (1850) 'Advertisement'; cf. **Brillat-Savarin** 67:3

Richard Phillips Feynman 1918–88

6 For a successful technology, reality must take precedence over public relations, for nature cannot be fooled.
appendix to the *Rogers Commission Report on the Space Shuttle Challenger Accident* 6 June 1986

7 What I cannot create, I do not understand.
attributed

Eugene Field 1850–95

8 Wynken, Blynken, and Nod one night
Sailed off in a wooden shoe—
Sailed on a river of crystal light,
Into a sea of dew.
'Wynken, Blynken, and Nod' (1889)

9 He played the King as though under momentary apprehension that someone else was about to play the ace.
of Creston Clarke as King Lear
review attributed to Field, in the *Denver Tribune* c.1880

Helen Fielding 1958–

10 I will not . . . sulk about having no boyfriend, but develop inner poise and authority and sense of self as woman of substance, complete *without* boyfriend, as best way to obtain boyfriend.
Bridget Jones's Diary (1996)

Henry Fielding 1707–54

11 Oh! The roast beef of England,
And old England's roast beef.
The Grub Street Opera (1731) act 3, sc. 3

12 He in a few minutes ravished this fair creature, or at least would have ravished her, if she had not, by a timely compliance, prevented him.
Jonathan Wild (1743) bk. 3, ch. 7

13 A lottery is a taxation
Upon all the fools in creation
And Heaven be praised
It is easily rais'd,
Credulity's always in fashion.
The Lottery (1732) sc. 1

14 What is commonly called love, namely the desire of satisfying a voracious appetite with a certain quantity of delicate white human flesh.
Tom Jones (1749) bk. 6, ch. 1

15 His designs were strictly honourable, as the phrase is; that is, to rob a lady of her fortune by way of marriage.
Tom Jones (1749) bk. 11, ch. 4

16 All Nature wears one universal grin.
Tom Thumb the Great (1731) act 1, sc. 1

Dorothy Fields 1905–74

17 A fine romance with no kisses.
A fine romance, my friend, this is.
'A Fine Romance' (1936 song)

18 Leave your worry on the doorstep,
Just direct your feet
To the sunny side of the street.
'On the Sunny Side of the Street' (1930 song)

W. C. Fields 1880–1946

19 Never give a sucker an even break.
title of a W. C. Fields film (1941); the catchphrase (Fields's own) is said to have originated in the musical comedy *Poppy* (1923)

20 Some weasel took the cork out of my lunch.
You Can't Cheat an Honest Man (1939 film)

21 It ain't a fit night out for man or beast.
adopted by Fields but claimed by him not to be original; letter, 8 February 1944

22 Hell, I never vote *for* anybody. I always vote *against*.
Robert Lewis Taylor *W. C. Fields* (1950); cf. **Adams** 1:14

23 Here lies W. C. Fields. I would rather be living in Philadelphia.
suggested epitaph for himself, in *Vanity Fair* June 1925

Ronald Firbank 1886–1926

24 'O! help me, heaven,' she prayed, 'to be decorative and to do right!'
The Flower Beneath the Foot (1923) ch. 2

1 There was a pause—just long enough for an angel to pass, flying slowly.
Vainglory (1915) ch. 6

L'Abbé Edgeworth de Firmont
1745–1807

2 *Fils de Saint Louis, montez au ciel.*
Son of Saint Louis, ascend to heaven.
to Louis XVI as he mounted the steps of the guillotine, 1793
attributed

Michael Fish 1944–

3 A woman rang to say she heard there was a hurricane on the way. Well don't worry, there isn't.
weather forecast on the night before serious gales in southern England
BBC TV, 15 October 1987

H. A. L. Fisher 1856–1940

4 Europe is a continent of energetic mongrels.
A History of Europe (1935) ch. 1

John Arbuthnot Fisher 1841–1920

5 Sack the lot!
on government overmanning and overspending
letter to *The Times*, 2 September 1919

6 Never contradict
Never explain
Never apologize.
letter to *The Times*, 5 September 1919; cf.
Disraeli 113:5, **Hubbard** 166:2

7 Yours till Hell freezes.
attributed to Fisher, but not original

Marve Fisher

8 I like Chopin and Bizet, and the voice of Doris Day,
Gershwin songs and old forgotten carols.
But the music that excels is the sound of oil wells
As they slurp, slurp, slurp into the barrels.
'An Old-Fashioned Girl' (1954 song)

9 I want an old-fashioned house
With an old-fashioned fence
And an old-fashioned millionaire.
'An Old-Fashioned Girl' (1954 song)

Gerry Fitt 1926–

10 People [in Northern Ireland] don't march as an alternative to jogging. They do it to assert their supremacy. It is pure tribalism, the cause of troubles all over the world.
referring to the 'marching season' in Northern Ireland, leading up to the anniversary of the Battle of the Boyne on 12 July, when parades by Orange communities traditionally take place
in *The Times* 5 August 1994

11 The people have spoken and the politicians have had to listen.
on the outcome of the referendum on the Good Friday agreement
in *Sunday Telegraph* 24 May 1998

Albert H. Fitz

12 You are my honey, honeysuckle, I am the bee.
'The Honeysuckle and the Bee' (1901 song)

Charles Fitzgeffrey *c.*1575–1638

13 And bold and hard adventures t' undertake,
Leaving his country for his country's sake.
Sir Francis Drake (1596) st. 213

Edward Fitzgerald 1809–83

14 Awake! for Morning in the bowl of night
Has flung the stone that puts the stars to flight:
And Lo! the Hunter of the East has caught
The Sultan's turret in a noose of light.
The Rubáiyát of Omar Khayyám (1859) st. 1

15 Here with a loaf of bread beneath the bough,
A flask of wine, a book of verse—and Thou
Beside me singing in the wilderness—
And wilderness is paradise enow.
The Rubáiyát of Omar Khayyám (1859) st. 11

A book of verses underneath the bough,
A jug of wine, a loaf of bread—and Thou
Beside me singing in the wilderness—
Oh, wilderness were paradise enow!
The Rubáiyát of Omar Khayyám (4th ed., 1879) st. 12

16 Ah, take the cash in hand and waive the rest;
Oh, the brave music of a *distant* drum!
The Rubáiyát of Omar Khayyám (1859) st. 12

Ah, take the cash and let the credit go,
Nor heed the rumble of a distant drum!
The Rubáiyát of Omar Khayyám (4th ed., 1879) st. 13

17 I sometimes think that never blows so red
The rose as where some buried Caesar bled.
The Rubáiyát of Omar Khayyám (1859) st. 19

18 One thing is certain, and the rest is lies;
The flower that once hath blown for ever dies.
The Rubáiyát of Omar Khayyám (1859) st. 26

One thing is certain and the rest is lies;
The flower that once has blown for ever dies.
The Rubáiyát of Omar Khayyám (4th ed., 1879) st. 63

19 The moving finger writes; and, having writ,
Moves on: nor all thy piety nor wit
Shall lure it back to cancel half a line,
Nor all thy tears wash out a word of it.
The Rubáiyát of Omar Khayyám (1859) st. 51; 'all your tears' in 4th ed. (1879) st. 71

20 Who *is* the potter, pray, and who the pot?
The Rubáiyát of Omar Khayyám (1859) st. 60

21 Indeed the idols I have loved so long
Have done my credit in this world much wrong:
Have drowned my glory in a shallow cup
And sold my reputation for a song.
The Rubáiyát of Omar Khayyám (4th ed., 1879) st. 93

1 Alas, that spring should vanish with the
rose!
That youth's sweet-scented manuscript
should close!
The Rubáiyát of Omar Khayyám (1859) st. 72

2 And when Thyself with shining foot shall
pass
Among the guests star-scattered on the
grass,
And in thy joyous errand reach the spot
Where I made one—turn down an empty
glass!
The Rubáiyát of Omar Khayyám (1859) st. 75

And when like her, O Saki, you shall pass
Among the guests star-scattered on the
grass,
And in your joyous errand reach the spot
Where I made one—turn down an empty
glass!
The Rubáiyát of Omar Khayyám (4th ed., 1879) st.
101

3 Taste is the feminine of genius.
letter to J. R. Lowell, October 1877

F. Scott Fitzgerald 1896–1940

4 Let me tell you about the very rich. They are
different from you and me.
*to which Ernest **Hemingway** replied, 'Yes, they
have more money'*
All the Sad Young Men (1926) 'Rich Boy'

5 The beautiful and damned.
title of novel (1922)

6 At eighteen our convictions are hills from
which we look; at forty-five they are caves
in which we hide.
'Bernice Bobs her Hair' (1920)

7 I've been drunk for about a week now, and I
thought it might sober me up to sit in a
library.
The Great Gatsby (1925) ch. 3

8 In a real dark night of the soul it is always
three o'clock in the morning.
'Handle with Care' in *Esquire* March 1936; cf. **St
John of the Cross** 172:14

9 See that little stream—we could walk to it
in two minutes. It took the British a month
to walk it—a whole empire walking very
slowly, dying in front and pushing forward
behind. And another empire walked very
slowly backward a few inches a day, leaving
the dead like a million bloody rugs.
Tender is the Night (1934)

10 There are no second acts in American lives.
Edmund Wilson (ed.) *The Last Tycoon* (1941)
'Hollywood, etc.'

Garret Fitzgerald 1926–

11 Living in history is a bit like finding oneself
in a shuttered mansion to which one has
been brought blindfold, and trying to
imagine what it might look like from the
outside.
in *Irish Times* 9 May 1998

Robert Fitzsimmons 1862–1917

12 The bigger they are, the further they have
to fall.
prior to a fight
in *Brooklyn Daily Eagle* 11 August 1900

Bud Flanagan 1896–1968

13 Underneath the Arches,
I dream my dreams away,
Underneath the Arches,
On cobble-stones I lay.
'Underneath the Arches' (1932 song)

Michael Flanders 1922–75
and Donald Swann 1923–94

14 Have Some Madeira, M'dear.
title of song (*c.*1956)

15 Mud! Mud! Glorious mud!
Nothing quite like it for cooling the blood.
'The Hippopotamus' (1952)

16 Eating people is wrong!
'The Reluctant Cannibal' (1956 song); adopted
as the title of a novel (1959) by Malcolm
Bradbury

Gustave Flaubert 1821–80

17 Human speech is like a cracked kettle on
which we tap crude rhythms for bears to
dance to, while we long to make music that
will melt the stars.
Madame Bovary (1857) pt. 1, ch. 12 (translated by
F. Steegmuller)

18 Poetry is a subject as precise as geometry.
letter to Louise Colet, 14 August 1853

19 Style is life! It is the very life-blood of
thought!
letter to Louise Colet, 7 September 1853

20 Books are made not like children but like
pyramids . . . and they're just as useless! and
they stay in the desert! . . . Jackals piss at
their foot and the bourgeois climb up on
them.
letter to Ernest Feydeau, November/December
1857

James Elroy Flecker 1884–1915

21 West of these out to seas colder than the
Hebrides
I must go
Where the fleet of stars is anchored and the
young
Star captains glow.
'The Dying Patriot' (1913)

22 The dragon-green, the luminous, the dark,
the serpent-haunted sea.
'The Gates of Damascus' (1913)

23 For lust of knowing what should not be
known,
We take the Golden Road to Samarkand.
The Golden Journey to Samarkand (1913) pt. 1,
'Epilogue'

24 I have seen old ships sail like swans asleep
Beyond the village which men still call Tyre,

With leaden age o'ercargoed, dipping deep
For Famagusta and the hidden sun
That rings black Cyprus with a lake of fire.
'Old Ships' (1915)

Ian Fleming 1908–64

1 A medium Vodka dry Martini—with a slice
of lemon peel. Shaken and not stirred.
Dr No (1958) ch. 14

Marjory Fleming 1803–11

2 The most devilish thing is 8 times 8 and 7
times 7 it is what nature itselfe cant endure.
Journals, Letters and Verses (ed. A. Esdaile, 1934)

3 His noses cast is of the roman
He is a very pretty weoman
I could not get a rhyme for roman
And was obliged to call it weoman.
'Sonnet'

Robert, Marquis de Flers
1872–1927
and Arman de Caillavet 1869–1915

4 Democracy is the name we give the people
whenever we need them.
L'habit vert act 1, sc. 12, in *La petite Illustration
série théâtre* 31 May 1913

Andrew Fletcher of Saltoun
1655–1716

5 If a man were permitted to make all the
ballads, he need not care who should make
the laws of a nation.
'An Account of a Conversation concerning a
Right Regulation of Government for the Good
of Mankind. In a Letter to the Marquis of
Montrose' (1704)

John Fletcher 1579–1625

6 Three merry boys, and three merry boys,
And three merry boys are we,
As ever did sing in a hempen string
Under the Gallows-Tree.
The Bloody Brother act 3, sc. 2

7 Death hath so many doors to let out life.
The Custom of the Country (with Massinger) act 2,
sc. 2; cf. **Massinger** 215:1, **Seneca** 267:23,
Webster 330:11

8 Care-charming Sleep, thou easer of all woes,
Brother to Death.
Valentinian (performed *c.*1610–14) act 5, sc. 7
'Song'; cf. **Daniel** 105:14, **Shelley** 293:20

9 Whistle and she'll come to you.
Wit Without Money act 4, sc. 4; cf. **Burns** 75:20

Phineas Fletcher 1582–1650

10 Drop, drop, slow tears,
And bathe those beauteous feet,
Which brought from Heaven
The news and Prince of Peace.
Poetical Miscellanies (1633) 'An Hymn'

11 Love's tongue is in the eyes.
Piscatory Eclogues (1633) no. 5, st. 13

12 Love is like linen often changed, the
sweeter.
Sicelides (performed 1614) act 3, sc. 5

13 The coward's weapon, poison.
Sicelides (performed 1614) act 5, sc. 3

Jean-Pierre Claris de Florian
1755–94

14 *Plaisir d'amour ne dure qu'un moment,
Chagrin d'amour dure toute la vie.*
Love's pleasure lasts but a moment;
Love's sorrow lasts all through life.
Célestine (1784)

Dario Fo 1926–

15 *Non si paga, non si paga.*
We won't pay, we won't pay.
title of play (1975; translated by Lino Pertile in
1978 as 'We Can't Pay? We Won't Pay!' and
performed in London in 1981 as 'Can't Pay?
Won't Pay!')

Ferdinand Foch 1851–1929

16 My centre is giving way, my right is
retreating, situation excellent, I am
attacking.
*message during the first Battle of the Marne,
September 1914*
R. Recouly *Foch* (1919) ch. 6

17 This is not a peace treaty, it is an armistice
for twenty years.
at the signing of the Treaty of Versailles, 1919
Paul Reynaud *Mémoires* (1963) vol. 2

J. Foley 1906–1970

18 Old soldiers never die,
They simply fade away.
'Old Soldiers Never Die' (1920 song);
copyrighted by Foley but possibly a 'folk-song'
from the First World War

Jane Fonda 1937–

19 A man has every season, while a woman has
only the right to spring.
in *Daily Mail* 13 September 1989

Michael Foot 1913–

20 Think of it! A second Chamber selected by
the Whips. A seraglio of eunuchs.
speech in the House of Commons, 3 February
1969

21 It is not necessary that every time he rises
he should give his famous imitation of a
semi-house-trained polecat.
of Norman Tebbit
speech in the House of Commons, 2 March
1978

Samuel Foote 1720–77

22 Born in a cellar . . . and living in a garret.
The Author (1757) act 2

23 So she went into the garden to cut a
cabbage-leaf to make an apple-pie; and at

the same time a great she-bear coming up the street, pops its head into the shop. 'What! no soap?' So he died, and she very imprudently married the barber; and there were present the Picninnies, and the Joblillies, and the Garyulies, and the grand Panjandrum himself, with the little round button at top; and they all fell to playing the game of catch as catch can, till the gun powder ran out at the heels of their boots.

nonsense composed to test the vaunted memory of the actor Charles Macklin (1697?–1797)

Maria Edgeworth *Harry and Lucy* (1825) vol. 2

Miss C. F. Forbes 1817–1911

1 The sense of being well-dressed gives a feeling of inward tranquillity which religion is powerless to bestow.

R. W. Emerson *Letters and Social Aims* (1876)

Gerald Ford 1909–

2 If the Government is big enough to give you everything you want, it is big enough to take away everything you have.

John F. Parker *If Elected* (1960)

3 I am a Ford, not a Lincoln.

on taking the vice-presidential oath, 6 December 1973

in *Washington Post* 7 December 1973

4 Our long national nightmare is over. Our Constitution works; our great Republic is a Government of laws and not of men.

on being sworn in as President, 9 August 1974

G. J. Lankevich *Gerald R. Ford* (1977); cf. **Adams** 1:19

Henry Ford 1863–1947

5 Any customer can have a car painted any colour that he wants so long as it is black.

on the Model T Ford, 1909

Henry Ford with Samuel Crowther *My Life and Work* (1922) ch. 2

6 History is more or less bunk.

in *Chicago Tribune* 25 May 1916

John Ford 1586–after 1639

7 He hath shook hands with time.

The Broken Heart (1633) act 5, sc. 2

8 View but her face, and in that little round, You may observe a world of variety.

'Tis Pity She's a Whore (1633) act 2

Lena Guilbert Ford 1870–1916

9 Keep the Home-fires burning, While your hearts are yearning, Though your lads are far away They dream of Home. There's a silver lining Through the dark cloud shining; Turn the dark cloud inside out, Till the boys come Home.

'Till the Boys Come Home!' (1914 song); music by Ivor Novello

Howell Forgy 1908–83

10 Praise the Lord and pass the ammunition.

at Pearl Harbor, 7 December 1941, while Forgy moved along a line of sailors passing ammunition by hand to the deck

in *New York Times* 1 November 1942; later the title of a song by Frank Loesser, 1942

E. M. Forster 1879–1970

11 Yes—oh dear yes—the novel tells a story.

Aspects of the Novel (1927) ch. 2

12 A dogged attempt to cover the universe with mud, an inverted Victorianism, an attempt to make crossness and dirt succeed where sweetness and light failed.

of James Joyce's Ulysses

Aspects of the Novel (1927) ch. 6; cf. **Arnold** 15:27, **Swift** 306:15

13 It is a period between two wars—the long week-end it has been called.

The Development of English Prose between 1918 and 1939 (1945)

14 Railway termini. They are our gates to the glorious and the unknown. Through them we pass out into adventure and sunshine, to them, alas! we return.

Howards End (1910) ch. 2

15 Only connect! . . . Only connect the prose and the passion.

Howards End (1910) ch. 22

16 The so-called white races are really pinko-grey.

A Passage to India (1924) ch. 7

17 If I had to choose between betraying my country and betraying my friend, I hope I should have the guts to betray my country.

Two Cheers for Democracy (1951) 'What I Believe'

18 So Two cheers for Democracy: one because it admits variety and two because it permits criticism. Two cheers are quite enough: there is no occasion to give three. Only Love the Beloved Republic deserves that.

Two Cheers for Democracy (1951) 'What I Believe'; cf. **Swinburne** 307:25

Venantius Fortunatus

AD *c.*530–*c.*610

19 *Pange, lingua, gloriosi Proelium certaminis.*

Sing, my tongue, of the battle in the glorious struggle.

Passiontide hymn, most commonly sung as: 'Sing, my tongue, the glorious battle'

'Pange lingua gloriosi'; cf. **Thomas Aquinas** 315:22

20 *Vexilla regis prodeunt, Fulget crucis mysterium.*

The banners of the king advance, the mystery of the cross shines bright.

hymn, usually sung as 'The royal banners forward go'

'Vexilla Regis'

1 *Regnavit a ligno Deus.*
God reigned from the wood.
'Vexilla Regis'

Harry Emerson Fosdick 1878–1969

2 I renounce war for its consequences, for the lies it lives on and propagates, for the undying hatred it arouses, for the dictatorships it puts in the place of democracy, for the starvation that stalks after it.
Armistice Day Sermon in New York, 1933

Charles Foster 1828–1904

3 Isn't this a billion dollar country?
responding to a Democratic gibe about a 'million dollar Congress'
at the 51st Congress; also attributed to Thomas B. Reed

John Foster 1770–1843

4 But the two classes [the educated and the uneducated] so beheld in contrast, might they not seem to belong to two different nations?
Essay on the Evils of Popular Ignorance (1820); cf. **Disraeli** 112:27

Stephen Collins Foster 1826–64

5 Beautiful dreamer, wake unto me,
Starlight and dewdrop are waiting for thee.
'Beautiful Dreamer' (1864 song)

6 I'll bet my money on de bobtail nag—
Somebody bet on de bay.
'De Camptown Races' (1850) chorus

7 I dream of Jeanie with the light brown hair,
Floating, like a vapour, on the soft summer air.
'Jeanie with the Light Brown Hair' (1854)

8 Way down upon the Swanee River,
Far, far, away,
There's where my heart is turning ever;
There's where the old folks stay.
'The Old Folks at Home' (1851)

9 All the world is sad and dreary
Everywhere I roam,
Oh! darkies, how my heart grows weary,
Far from the old folks at home.
'The Old Folks at Home' (1851) chorus

Charles Fourier 1772–1837

10 The extension of women's rights is the basic principle of all social progress.
Théorie des Quatre Mouvements (1808) vol. 2, ch. 4

H. W. Fowler 1858–1933

11 The English speaking world may be divided into (1) those who neither know nor care what a split infinitive is; (2) those who do not know, but care very much; (3) those who know and condemn; (4) those who know and approve; and (5) those who know and distinguish. Those who neither know nor care are the vast majority and are a

happy folk, to be envied by most of the minority classes.
Modern English Usage (1926)

Norman Fowler 1938–

12 I have a young family and for the next few years I should like to devote more time to them.
often quoted as 'spend more time with my family'
resignation letter to the Prime Minister, in *Guardian* 4 January 1990; cf. **Thatcher** 315:14

Charles James Fox 1749–1806

13 How much the greatest event it is that ever happened in the world! and how much the best!
on the fall of the Bastille
letter to Richard Fitzpatrick, 30 July 1789

George Fox 1624–91

14 I saw also that there was an ocean of darkness and death, but an infinite ocean of light and love, which flowed over the ocean of darkness.
Journal 1647

15 I . . . espied three steeple-house spires, and they struck at my life.
on seeing the spires of Lichfield
Journal 1651

16 Walk cheerfully over the world, answering that of God in every one.
Journal 1656

Henry Fox *see* Lord Holland

Anatole France 1844–1924

17 In every well-governed state, wealth is a sacred thing; in democracies it is the only sacred thing.
L'Île des pingouins (1908) pt. 6, ch. 2

18 They [the poor] have to labour in the face of the majestic equality of the law, which forbids the rich as well as the poor to sleep under bridges, to beg in the streets, and to steal bread.
Le Lys rouge (1894) ch. 7

Francis I 1494–1547

19 *De toutes choses ne m'est demeuré que l'honneur et la vie qui est saulve.*
Of all I had, only honour and life have been spared.
letter to his mother following his defeat at Pavia, 1525; usually quoted as 'Tout est perdu fors l'honneur [All is lost save honour]'
in *Collection des Documents Inédits sur l'Histoire de France* (1847) vol. 1

St Francis de Sales 1567–1622

20 Big fires flare up in a wind, but little ones are blown out unless they are carried in under cover.
Introduction à la vie dévote (1609) pt. 3, ch. 34; cf. **Bussy-Rabutin** 76:25, **La Rochefoucauld** 193:21

1 It has been well said, that heart speaks to heart, whereas language only speaks to the ears.
   letter to the Archbishop of Bourges, 5 October 1604, in *Oeuvres de Saint François de Sales* (1834) vol. 3

St Francis of Assisi 1181–1226

2 Praised be You, my Lord, with all your creatures,
   especially Sir Brother Sun,
   Who is the day and through whom You give us light.
   'The Canticle of Brother Sun'

3 Lord, make me an instrument of Your peace!
   Where there is hatred let me sow love;
   Where there is injury, pardon;
   Where there is doubt, faith;
   Where there is despair, hope;
   Where there is darkness, light;
   Where there is sadness, joy.
   'Prayer of St Francis' (attributed)

Anne Frank 1929–45

4 I want to go on living even after death!
   diary, 4 April 1944

Benjamin Franklin 1706–90

5 Necessity never made a good bargain.
   Poor Richard's Almanac (1735) April

6 He that lives upon hope will die fasting.
   Poor Richard's Almanac (1758) preface

7 We must indeed all hang together, or, most assuredly, we shall all hang separately.
   at the signing of the Declaration of Independence, 4 July 1776 (possibly not original)

8 There never was a good war, or a bad peace.
   letter to Josiah Quincy, 11 September 1783

9 In this world nothing can be said to be certain, except death and taxes.
   letter to Jean Baptiste Le Roy, 13 November 1789; cf. **Defoe** 107:12

10 Man is a tool-making animal.
   James Boswell *Life of Samuel Johnson* (1791) 7 April 1778

11 What is the use of a new-born child?
   when asked what was the use of a new invention
   J. Parton *Life and Times of Benjamin Franklin* (1864) pt. 4, ch. 17

Lord Franks 1905–92

12 The Pentagon, that immense monument to modern man's subservience to the desk.
   in *Observer* 30 November 1952

Frederick the Great 1712–86

13 My people and I have come to an agreement which satisfies us both. They are to say what they please, and I am to do what I please.
   his interpretation of benevolent despotism
   attributed

14 Rascals, would you live for ever?
   to hesitant Guards at Kolin, 18 June 1757
   attributed

E. A. Freeman 1823–92

15 History is past politics, and politics is present history.
   Methods of Historical Study (1886)

John Freeth c.1731–1808

16 The loss of America what can repay?
   New colonies seek for at Botany Bay.
   'Botany Bay' in *New London Magazine* (1786)

Percy French 1854–1920

17 Where the Mountains of Mourne sweep down to the sea.
   'The Mountains of Mourne'

John Hookham Frere 1769–1846

18 The feathered race with pinions skim the air—
   Not so the mackerel, and still less the bear!
   'The Progress of Man' (1798) canto 1, l. 34

Sigmund Freud 1856–1939

19 Anatomy is destiny.
   Collected Writings (1924) vol. 5

20 The interpretation of dreams is the royal road to a knowledge of the unconscious activities of the mind.
   often misquoted as, 'Dreams are the royal road to the unconscious'
   The Interpretation of Dreams (2nd ed., 1909) ch. 7, sect. E

21 All that matters is love and work.
   attributed

22 Frozen anger.
   his definition of depression
   attributed

Betty Friedan 1921–

23 The problem that has no name.
   being the fact that American women are kept from growing to their full human capacities
   The Feminine Mystique (1963) ch. 14

Milton Friedman 1912–

24 There is an invisible hand in politics that operates in the opposite direction to the invisible hand in the market. In politics, individuals who seek to promote only the public good are led by an invisible hand to promote special interests that it was no part of their intention to promote.
   Bright Promises, Dismal Performance: An Economist's Protest (1983)

Brian Friel 1929–

25 Do you want the whole countryside to be laughing at us?—women of our years?—mature women, *dancing*?
   Dancing at Lughnasa (1990)

Max Frisch 1911–91

1 Technology . . . the knack of so arranging the world that we need not experience it.
Homo Faber (1957) pt. 2

Charles Frohman 1860–1915

2 Why fear death? It is the most beautiful adventure in life.
before drowning in the Lusitania, 7 May 1915
I. F. Marcosson and D. Frohman *Charles Frohman* (1916); cf. **Barrie** 25:15

Erich Fromm 1900–80

3 In the nineteenth century the problem was that *God is dead*; in the twentieth century the problem is that *man is dead*.
The Sane Society (1955) ch. 9

David Frost 1939–

4 Having one child makes you a parent; having two you are a referee.
in *Independent* 16 September 1989

Robert Frost 1874–1963

5 Forgive, O Lord, my little jokes on Thee
And I'll forgive Thy great big one on me.
'Cluster of Faith' (1962)

6 And nothing to look backward to with pride,
And nothing to look forward to with hope.
'The Death of the Hired Man' (1914)

7 'Home is the place where, when you have to go there,
They have to take you in.'
'The Death of the Hired Man' (1914)

8 Some say the world will end in fire,
Some say in ice.
'Fire and Ice' (1923)

9 The land was ours before we were the land's.
She was our land more than a hundred years
Before we were her people.
'The Gift Outright' (1942)

10 Something there is that doesn't love a wall,
That sends the frozen-ground-swell under it.
'Mending Wall' (1914)

11 My apple trees will never get across
And eat the cones under his pines, I tell him.
He only says, 'Good fences make good neighbours.'
'Mending Wall' (1914)

12 I never dared be radical when young
For fear it would make me conservative when old.
'Precaution' (1936)

13 Two roads diverged in a wood, and I—
I took the one less travelled by,
And that has made all the difference.
'The Road Not Taken' (1916)

14 The woods are lovely, dark and deep.
But I have promises to keep,

And miles to go before I sleep,
And miles to go before I sleep.
'Stopping by Woods on a Snowy Evening' (1923)

15 I'd as soon write free verse as play tennis with the net down.
Edward Lathem *Interviews with Robert Frost* (1966)

16 Poetry is what is lost in translation. It is also what is lost in interpretation.
Louis Untermeyer *Robert Frost* (1964)

Christopher Fry 1907–

17 The dark is light enough.
title of play (1954)

18 The lady's not for burning.
title of play (1949); cf. **Thatcher** 315:6

19 Where in this small-talking world can I find
A longitude with no platitude?
The Lady's not for Burning (1949) act 3

Elizabeth Fry 1780–1845

20 Punishment is not for revenge, but to lessen crime and reform the criminal.
note found among her papers; Rachel E. Cresswell and Katharine Fry *Memoir of the Life of Elizabeth Fry* (1848)

Roger Fry 1866–1934

21 Art is significant deformity.
Virginia Woolf *Roger Fry* (1940) ch. 8

J. William Fulbright 1905–95

22 The Soviet Union has indeed been our greatest menace, not so much because of what it has done, but because of the excuses it has provided us for our failures.
in *Observer* 21 December 1958 'Sayings of the Year'

R. Buckminster Fuller 1895–1983

23 God, to me, it seems,
is a verb
not a noun,
proper or improper.
No More Secondhand God (1963) (untitled poem written in 1940); cf. **Hugo** 166:15

24 Now there is one outstandingly important fact regarding Spaceship Earth, and that is that no instruction book came with it.
Operating Manual for Spaceship Earth (1969) ch. 4

Thomas Fuller 1608–61

25 But our captain counts the Image of God nevertheless his image, cut in ebony as if done in ivory.
The Holy State and the Profane State (1642) bk. 2 'The Good Sea-Captain'

26 Anger is one of the sinews of the soul.
The Holy State and the Profane State bk. 3 'Of Anger'

27 Light (God's eldest daughter) is a principal beauty in building.
The Holy State and the Profane State bk. 3 'Of Building'

Thomas Fuller 1654–1734

1 He that plants trees loves others beside himself.
Gnomologia (1732) no. 2247

2 We are all Adam's children but silk makes the difference.
Gnomologia (1732) no. 5425

Alfred Funke b. 1869

3 *Gott strafe England!*
God punish England!
Schwert und Myrte (1914)

David Maxwell Fyfe *see* Lord Kilmuir

Rose Fyleman 1877–1957

4 There are fairies at the bottom of our garden!
Fairies and Chimneys (1918) 'The Fairies' (first published in *Punch* 23 May 1917)

Thomas Gainsborough 1727–88

5 We are all going to Heaven, and Vandyke is of the company.
last words; attributed, William B. Boulton *Thomas Gainsborough* (1905) ch. 9

Hugh Gaitskell 1906–63

6 There are some of us . . . who will fight and fight and fight again to save the Party we love.
speech at Labour Party Conference, 5 October 1960

7 It means the end of a thousand years of history.
on a European federation
speech at Labour Party Conference, 3 October 1962

Gaius (or Caius) AD c.110–c.180

8 *Damnosa hereditas.*
Ruinous inheritance.
The Institutes bk. 2, ch. 163

J. K. Galbraith 1908–

9 The affluent society.
title of book (1958)

10 Trickle-down theory—the less than elegant metaphor that if one feeds the horse enough oats, some will pass through to the road for the sparrows.
The Culture of Contentment (1992)

11 Politics is not the art of the possible. It consists in choosing between the disastrous and the unpalatable.
speech to President Kennedy, 2 March 1962; cf. **Bismarck** 54:13

Galen AD 129–199

12 That which *is* grows, while that which is *not* becomes.
On the Natural Faculties bk. 2, sect. 3

Galileo Galilei 1564–1642

13 *Eppur si muove.*
But it does move.
after his recantation, that the earth moves around the sun, in 1632
attributed; Baretti *Italian Library* (1757) is possibly the earliest appearance of the phrase

John Galsworthy 1867–1933

14 He was afflicted by the thought that where Beauty was, nothing ever ran quite straight, which, no doubt, was why so many people looked on it as immoral.
In Chancery (1920) pt. 1, ch. 13

15 A man of action forced into a state of thought is unhappy until he can get out of it.
Maid in Waiting (1931) ch. 3

John Galt 1779–1839

16 From the lone shieling of the misty island
Mountains divide us, and the waste of seas—
Yet still the blood is strong, the heart is Highland,
And we in dreams behold the Hebrides!
'Canadian Boat Song' translated from the Gaelic in *Blackwoods Edinburgh Magazine* September 1829, and later attributed to Galt

Ray Galton 1930–
and Alan Simpson 1929–

17 I came in here in all good faith to help my country. I don't mind giving a reasonable amount [of blood], but a pint . . . why that's very nearly an armful.
Hancock's Half Hour 'The Blood Donor' (1961 television programme); words spoken by Tony Hancock

Mahatma Gandhi 1869–1948

18 Non-violence is the first article of my faith. It is also the last article of my creed.
speech at Shahi Bag, 18 March 1922, on a charge of sedition

19 Non-cooperation with evil is as much a duty as is cooperation with good.
speech in Ahmadabad, 23 March 1922

Greta Garbo (Greta Lovisa Gustafsson) 1905–90

20 I want to be alone.
Grand Hotel (1932 film), the phrase already being associated with Garbo

Federico García Lorca 1899–1936

21 *A las cinco de la tarde.*
Eran las cinco en punto de la tarde.
Un niño trajo la blanca sábana
a las cinco de la tarde.
At five in the afternoon.
It was exactly five in the afternoon.
A boy brought the white sheet

at five in the afternoon.
Llanto por Ignacio Sánchez Mejías (1935) 'La Cogida y la muerte'

1 *Verde que te quiero verde.*
Verde viento. Verdes ramas.
El barco sobre la mar
y el caballo en la montaña.
Green how I love you green.
Green wind.
Green boughs.
The ship on the sea
and the horse on the mountain.
Romance sonámbulo (1924–7)

Richard Gardiner b. *c.*1533

2 Sowe Carrets in your Gardens, and humbly praise God for them, as for a singular and great blessing.
Profitable Instructions for the Manuring, Sowing and Planting of Kitchen Gardens (1599)

Ed Gardner 1901–63

3 Opera is when a guy gets stabbed in the back and, instead of bleeding, he sings.
in *Duffy's Tavern* (US radio programme, 1940s)

James A. Garfield 1831–81

4 Fellow-citizens: God reigns, and the Government at Washington lives!
speech on the assassination of President Lincoln, 17 April 1865

Giuseppe Garibaldi 1807–82

5 Men, I'm getting out of Rome. Anyone who wants to carry on the war against the outsiders, come with me. I can offer you neither honours nor wages; I offer you hunger, thirst, forced marches, battles and death. Anyone who loves his country, follow me.
Giuseppe Guerzoni *Garibaldi* (1882) vol. 1 (not a verbatim record)

John Nance Garner 1868–1967

6 The vice-presidency isn't worth a pitcher of warm piss.
O. C. Fisher *Cactus Jack* (1978) ch. 11

David Garrick 1717–79

7 Heart of oak are our ships,
Heart of oak are our men:
We always are ready;
Steady, boys, steady;
We'll fight and we'll conquer again and again.
Harlequin's Invasion (1759) 'Heart of Oak' (song)

8 Here lies Nolly Goldsmith, for shortness called Noll,
Who wrote like an angel, but talked like poor Poll.
'Impromptu Epitaph' (written 1773/4); cf. **Goldsmith** 143:17, **Johnson** 176:6

9 Life is a jest; and all things show it.
I thought so once; but now I know it.
'My Own Epitaph' (1720)

10 Heaven sends us good meat, but the Devil sends cooks.
'On Doctor Goldsmith's Characteristical Cookery' (1777)

William Lloyd Garrison 1805–79

11 I am in earnest—I will not equivocate—I will not excuse—I will not retreat a single inch—and I will be heard!
in *The Liberator* 1 January 1831 'Salutatory Address'

12 The compact which exists between the North and the South is 'a covenant with death and an agreement with hell'.
resolution adopted by the Massachusetts Anti-Slavery Society, 27 January 1843; cf. **Bible** 39:27

Samuel Garth 1661–1719

13 All their luxury was doing good.
'Claremont' (1715) l. 148

14 A barren superfluity of words.
The Dispensary (1699) canto 2, l. 82

Elizabeth Gaskell 1810–65

15 A man . . . is *so* in the way in the house!
Cranford (1853) ch. 1

16 I'll not listen to reason . . . Reason always means what someone else has got to say.
Cranford (1853) ch. 14

17 That kind of patriotism which consists in hating all other nations.
Sylvia's Lovers (1863) ch. 1

18 It is a noble grand book, whoever wrote it—but Miss Evans' life taken at the best construction, does so jar against the beautiful book that one cannot help hoping against hope.
on first hearing of the true identity of 'George Eliot', author of Adam Bede
letter to George Smith, 4 August 1859

Paul Gauguin 1848–1903

19 A hint—don't paint too much direct from nature. Art is an abstraction! study nature then brood on it and treasure the creation which will result, which is the only way to ascend towards God—to create like our Divine Master.
letter to Emile Schuffenecker, 14 August 1888

Théophile Gautier 1811–72

20 *Toute passe.—L'art robuste*
Seul à l'éternité,
Le Buste
Survit à la cité.
Everything passes. Robust art alone is eternal, the bust survives the city.
'L'Art' (1857); cf. **Dobson** 113:11

Gavarni (Guillaume Sulpice Chevalier) 1804–66

21 *Les enfants terribles.*
The little terrors.
title of a series of prints (1842)

John Gay 1685–1732

1 Our Polly is a sad slut! nor heeds what we
have taught her.
I wonder any man alive will ever rear a
daughter!
The Beggar's Opera (1728) act 1, sc. 8, air 7

2 Do you think your mother and I should
have lived comfortably so long together, if
ever we had been married?
The Beggar's Opera (1728) act 1, sc. 8

3 The comfortable estate of widowhood, is
the only hope that keeps up a wife's spirits.
The Beggar's Opera (1728) act 1, sc. 10

4 If with me you'd fondly stray.
Over the hills and far away.
The Beggar's Opera (1728) act 1, sc. 13, air 16

5 How happy could I be with either,
Were t'other dear charmer away!
The Beggar's Opera (1728) act 2, sc. 13, air 35

6 And when a lady's in the case,
You know, all other things give place.
Fables (1727) 'The Hare and Many Friends' l. 41

7 An open foe may prove a curse,
But a pretended friend is worse.
Fables (1727) 'The Shepherd's Dog and the Wolf'
l. 33

8 Give me, kind heaven, a private station,
A mind serene for contemplation.
Fables (1738) 'The Vulture, the Sparrow, and
Other Birds' l. 69

9 Behold the bright original appear.
'A Letter to a Lady' (1714) l. 85

10 An inconstant woman, tho' she has no
chance to be very happy, can never be very
unhappy.
'Polly' (1729) act 1, sc. 14

11 All in the Downs the fleet was moored.
The streamers waving in the wind,
When black-eyed Susan came aboard.
'Sweet William's Farewell to Black-Eyed Susan'
(1720)

12 They'll tell thee, sailors, when away,
In ev'ry port a mistress find.
'Sweet William's Farewell to Black-Eyed Susan'
(1720)

Noel Gay 1898–1954

13 I'm leaning on a lamp post at the corner of
the street,
In case a certain little lady comes by.
'Leaning on a Lamp Post' (1937); sung by
George Formby in the film *Father Knew Best*

Eric Geddes 1875–1937

14 The Germans, if this Government is
returned, are going to pay every penny;
they are going to be squeezed as a lemon is
squeezed—until the pips squeak.
speech at Cambridge, 10 December 1918

Bob Geldof 1954–
and Midge Ure 1953–

15 Do they know it's Christmas?
title of song (1984)

Martha Gellhorn 1908–98

16 I had no idea you could be what I became,
an unscathed tourist of wars.
The Face of War (1959)

17 Never believe governments, not any of
them, not a word they say; keep an
untrusting eye on all they do.
in obituary, *Daily Telegraph* 17 February 1998

Jean Genet 1910–86

18 What we need is hatred. From it our ideas
are born.
The Blacks (1959); epigraph

19 Are you there . . . Africa of the millions of
royal slaves, deported Africa, drifting
continent, are you there? Slowly you vanish,
you withdraw into the past, into the tales of
castaways, colonial museums, the works of
scholars.
The Blacks (1959)

Genghis Khan (Temujin) 1162–1227

20 Happiness lies in conquering one's enemies,
in driving them in front of oneself, in
taking their property, in savouring their
despair, in outraging their wives and
daughters.
Witold Rodzinski *The Walled Kingdom: A History
of China* (1979)

George I 1660–1727

21 I hate all Boets and Bainters.
John Campbell *Lives of the Chief Justices* (1849)
'Lord Mansfield'

George II 1683–1760

22 *Non, j'aurai des maîtresses.*
No, I shall have mistresses.
*when Queen **Caroline**, on her deathbed in 1737,
urged him to marry again; the Queen replied,
'Ah! mon dieu! cela n'empêche pas [Oh, my
God! That won't make any difference]'*
John Hervey *Memoirs of the Reign of George II*
(1848) vol. 2.

23 Mad, is he? Then I hope he will *bite* some of
my other generals.
*replying to the Duke of Newcastle, who had
complained that General **Wolfe** was a madman*
Henry Beckles Willson *Life and Letters of James
Wolfe* (1909) ch. 17

George III 1738–1820

24 Born and educated in this country, I glory in
the name of Briton.
The King's Speech on Opening the Session House of
Lords, 18 November 1760

25 Was there ever such stuff as great part of
Shakespeare? Only one must not say so! But

what think you?—what?—Is there not sad
stuff? what? what?—what?

to Fanny Burney, in *Diary and Letters of Madame
d'Arblay* vol. 2 (1842) diary, 19 December 1785

George IV 1762–1830

1 Harris, I am not well; pray get me a glass of
brandy.
*on first seeing Caroline of Brunswick, his future
wife*

Earl of Malmesbury *Diaries and Correspondence*
(1844), 5 April 1795

George V 1865–1936

2 I venture to allude to the impression which
seemed generally to prevail among their
brethren across the seas, that the Old
Country must wake up if she intends to
maintain her old position of pre-eminence
in her Colonial trade against foreign
competitors.

speech at Guildhall, 5 December 1901,
reprinted in 1911 under the title 'Wake up,
England'

3 I pray that my coming to Ireland today may
prove to be the first step towards an end of
strife among her people, whatever their
race or creed. In that hope I appeal to all
Irishmen to pause, to stretch out the hand
of forbearance and conciliation, to forgive
and forget, and to join with me in making
for the land they love a new era of peace,
contentment and goodwill.

speech to the new Ulster Parliament at
Stormont, 22 June 1921

4 I have many times asked myself whether
there can be more potent advocates of
peace upon earth through the years to come
than this massed multitude of silent
witnesses to the desolation of war.

message read at Terlincthun Cemetery,
Boulogne, 13 May 1922

5 After I am dead, the boy will ruin himself in
twelve months.
*of his son, the future **Edward VIII***

Keith Middlemas and John Barnes *Baldwin*
(1969) ch. 34

*on H. G. **Wells**'s comment on 'an alien and
uninspiring court':*
6 I may be uninspiring, but I'll be damned if
I'm an alien!

Sarah Bradford *George VI* (1989); attributed

7 Bugger Bognor.
*on his deathbed in 1936, when someone remarked
'Cheer up, your Majesty, you will soon be at
Bognor again'; alternatively, a comment made in
1929, when it was proposed that the town be
named Bognor Regis on account of the king's
convalescence there after a serious illness*

probably apocryphal; Kenneth Rose *King George
V* (1983) ch. 9

8 How's the Empire?
*said to his private secretary on the morning of his
death*

letter from Lord Wigram, 31 January 1936

George VI 1895–1952

9 I feel happier now that we have no allies to
be polite to and to pamper.

to Queen Mary, 27 June 1940

10 Abroad is bloody.

W. H. Auden *A Certain World* (1970) 'Royalty'; cf.
Mitford 225:2

11 The family firm.
description of the British monarchy
attributed

Daniel George

12 O Freedom, what liberties are taken in thy
name!

The Perpetual Pessimist (1963)

Lloyd George *see* **David Lloyd
George**

Geronimo *c.*1829–1909

13 Once I moved about like the wind. Now I
surrender to you and that is all.

surrendering to General Crook, 25 March 1886

Ira Gershwin 1896–1983

14 I don't think I'll fall in love today.

title of song (1928, from *Treasure Girl*)

15 I got rhythm.

title of song (1930, from *Girl Crazy*)

16 In time the Rockies may crumble,
Gibraltar may tumble,
They're only made of clay,
But our love is here to stay.

'Love is Here to Stay' (1938 song) in *The Goldwyn
Follies*

17 Holding hands at midnight
'Neath a starry sky,
Nice work if you can get it,
And you can get it if you try.

'Nice Work If You Can Get It' (1937 song) in
Damsel in Distress

J. Paul Getty 1892–1976

18 If you can actually count your money, then
you are not really a rich man.

in *Observer* 3 November 1957

Giuseppe Giacosa 1847–1906
and **Luigi Illica** 1857–1919

19 *Che gelida manina.*
Your tiny hand is frozen.
Rodolfo to Mimi

La Bohème (1896) act 1; music by Puccini

Edward Gibbon 1737–94

1 In elective monarchies, the vacancy of the throne is a moment big with danger and mischief.
    The Decline and Fall of the Roman Empire (1776–88) ch. 3

2 History . . . is, indeed, little more than the register of the crimes, follies, and misfortunes of mankind.
    The Decline and Fall of the Roman Empire (1776–88) ch. 3; cf. **Voltaire** 326:7

3 Twenty-two acknowledged concubines, and a library of sixty-two thousand volumes, attested the variety of his inclinations, and from the productions which he left behind him, it appears that the former as well as the latter were designed for use rather than ostentation. [Footnote] By each of his concubines the younger Gordian left three or four children. His literary productions were by no means contemptible.
    The Decline and Fall of the Roman Empire (1776–88) ch. 7

4 Whenever the offence inspires less horror than the punishment, the rigour of penal law is obliged to give way to the common feelings of mankind.
    The Decline and Fall of the Roman Empire (1776–88) ch. 14

5 In every deed of mischief he had a heart to resolve, a head to contrive, and a hand to execute.
    of Comnenus
    The Decline and Fall of the Roman Empire (1776–88) ch. 48; cf. **Clarendon** 93:12

6 To the University of Oxford I acknowledge no obligation; and she will as cheerfully renounce me for a son, as I am willing to disclaim her for a mother. I spent fourteen months at Magdalen College: they proved the fourteen months the most idle and unprofitable of my whole life.
    Memoirs of My Life (1796) ch. 3

7 I sighed as a lover, I obeyed as a son.
    Memoirs of My Life (1796) ch. 4 n.

8 It was at Rome, on the fifteenth of October, 1764, as I sat musing amidst the ruins of the Capitol, while the barefoot friars were singing vespers in the Temple of Jupiter, that the idea of writing the decline and fall of the city first started to my mind.
    Memoirs of My Life (1796) ch. 6 n.

9 My English text is chaste, and all licentious passages are left in the obscurity of a learned language.
    parodied as 'decent obscurity' in the Anti-Jacobin, 1797–8
    Memoirs of My Life (1796) ch. 8

Orlando Gibbons 1583–1625

10 The silver swan, who, living had no note, When death approached unlocked her silent throat.
    The First Set of Madrigals and Motets of Five Parts (1612) 'The Silver Swan'

Stella Gibbons 1902–89

11 When the sukebind hangs heavy from the wains.
    Cold Comfort Farm (1932) ch. 5

12 Something nasty in the woodshed.
    Cold Comfort Farm (1932) ch. 10

Wolcott Gibbs 1902–58

13 Backward ran sentences until reeled the mind.
    satirizing the style of Time *magazine*
    in *New Yorker* 28 November 1936 'Time . . . Fortune . . . Life . . . Luce'

Kahlil Gibran 1883–1931

14 Are you a politician who says to himself: 'I will use my country for my own benefit'? . . . Or are you a devoted patriot, who whispers in the ear of his inner self: 'I love to serve my country as a faithful servant.'
    The New Frontier (1931), tr. Anthony R. Ferris in *The Voice of the Master* (1958); cf. **Kennedy** 184:12

15 Your children are not your children.
    They are the sons and daughters of Life's longing for itself.
    They came through you but not from you
    And though they are with you yet they belong not to you.
    The Prophet (1923) 'On Children'

Wilfrid Wilson Gibson 1878–1962

16 Nor feel the heart-break in the heart of things.
    'Lament' (1918)

André Gide 1869–1951

17 Hugo—alas!
    when asked who was the greatest 19th-century poet
    Claude Martin *La Maturité d'André Gide* (1977)

Humphrey Gilbert c.1537–83

18 We are as near to heaven by sea as by land!
    Richard Hakluyt *Third and Last Volume of the Voyages . . . of the English Nation* (1600); cf. **Elstow** 124:4

W. S. Gilbert 1836–1911

19 That celebrated,
    Cultivated,
    Underrated
    Nobleman,
    The Duke of Plaza Toro!
    The Gondoliers (1889) act 1

20 Of that there is no manner of doubt—
    No probable, possible shadow of doubt—
    No possible doubt whatever.
    The Gondoliers (1889) act 1

21 Take a pair of sparkling eyes.
    The Gondoliers (1889) act 2

22 When every one is somebodee,
    Then no one's anybody.
    The Gondoliers (1889) act 2

1 The Law is the true embodiment
Of everything that's excellent.
It has no kind of fault or flaw,
And I, my Lords, embody the Law.
Iolanthe (1882) act 1

2 I often think it's comical
How Nature always does contrive
That every boy and every gal,
That's born into the world alive,
Is either a little Liberal,
Or else a little Conservative!
Iolanthe (1882) act 2

3 The prospect of a lot
Of dull MPs in close proximity,
All thinking for themselves is what
No man can face with equanimity.
Iolanthe (1882) act 2

4 The House of Peers, throughout the war,
Did nothing in particular,
And did it very well.
Iolanthe (1882) act 2

5 When you're lying awake with a dismal
headache, and repose is taboo'd by
anxiety,
I conceive you may use any language you
choose to indulge in, without
impropriety.
Iolanthe (1882) act 2

6 A wandering minstrel I—
A thing of shreds and patches.
Of ballads, songs and snatches,
And dreamy lullaby!
The Mikado (1885) act 1; cf. **Shakespeare** 272:25

7 I can trace my ancestry back to a
protoplasmal primordial atomic globule.
Consequently, my family pride is something
in-conceivable. I can't help it. I was born
sneering.
The Mikado (1885) act 1

8 As some day it may happen that a victim
must be found,
I've got a little list—I've got a little list
Of society offenders who might well be
under ground
And who never would be missed—who
never would be missed!
The Mikado (1885) act 1

9 The idiot who praises, with enthusiastic
tone,
All centuries but this, and every country but
his own.
The Mikado (1885) act 1

10 Three little maids from school are we.
The Mikado (1885) act 1

11 Modified rapture!
The Mikado (1885) act 1

12 Awaiting the sensation of a short, sharp
shock,
From a cheap and chippy chopper on a big
black block.
The Mikado (1885) act 1

13 Here's a how-de-doo!
The Mikado (1885) act 2

14 Here's a state of things!
The Mikado (1885) act 2

15 My object all sublime
I shall achieve in time—
To let the punishment fit the crime—
The punishment fit the crime.
The Mikado (1885) act 2

16 I have a left shoulder-blade that is a miracle
of loveliness. People come miles to see it.
My right elbow has a fascination that few
can resist.
The Mikado (1885) act 2

17 Something lingering, with boiling oil in it, I
fancy.
The Mikado (1885) act 2

18 Merely corroborative detail, intended to
give artistic verisimilitude to an otherwise
bald and unconvincing narrative.
The Mikado (1885) act 2

19 The flowers that bloom in the spring,
Tra la,
Have nothing to do with the case.
The Mikado (1885) act 2

20 On a tree by a river a little tom-tit
Sang 'Willow, titwillow, titwillow!'
The Mikado (1885) act 2

21 There's a fascination frantic
In a ruin that's romantic;
Do you think you are sufficiently decayed?
The Mikado (1885) act 2

22 If you're anxious for to shine in the high
aesthetic line as a man of culture rare.
Patience (1881) act 1

23 The meaning doesn't matter if it's only idle
chatter of a transcendental kind.
Patience (1881) act 1

24 An attachment à la Plato for a bashful
young potato, or a not too French French
bean!
Patience (1881) act 1

25 If you walk down Piccadilly with a poppy or
a lily in your medieval hand.
Patience (1881) act 1

26 Francesca di Rimini, miminy, piminy,
Je-ne-sais-quoi young man!
Patience (1881) act 2

27 A greenery-yallery, Grosvenor Gallery,
Foot-in-the-grave young man!
Patience (1881) act 2

28 I'm called Little Buttercup—dear Little
Buttercup,
Though I could never tell why.
HMS Pinafore (1878) act 1

29 And so do his sisters, and his cousins and
his aunts!
His sisters and his cousins,
Whom he reckons up by dozens,
And his aunts!
HMS Pinafore (1878) act 1

30 I cleaned the windows and I swept the floor,
And I polished up the handle of the big
front door.
I polished up that handle so carefullee

That now I am the Ruler of the Queen's Navee!
HMS Pinafore (1878) act 1

1 I always voted at my party's call,
And I never thought of thinking for myself at all.
HMS Pinafore (1878) act 1

2 For he himself has said it,
And it's greatly to his credit,
That he is an Englishman!
HMS Pinafore (1878) act 2

3 For he might have been a Roosian,
A French, or Turk, or Proosian,
Or perhaps Ital-ian!
But in spite of all temptations
To belong to other nations,
He remains an Englishman!
HMS Pinafore (1878) act 2

4 It is, it is a glorious thing
To be a Pirate King.
The Pirates of Penzance (1879) act 1

5 I'm very good at integral and differential calculus,
I know the scientific names of beings animalculous;
In short, in matters vegetable, animal, and mineral,
I am the very model of a modern Major-General.
The Pirates of Penzance (1879) act 1

6 When constabulary duty's to be done,
A policeman's lot is not a happy one.
The Pirates of Penzance (1879) act 2

7 He combines the manners of a Marquis with the morals of a Methodist.
Ruddigore (1887) act 1

8 Some word that teems with hidden meaning—like Basingstoke.
Ruddigore (1887) act 2

9 This particularly rapid, unintelligible patter
Isn't generally heard, and if it is it doesn't matter.
Ruddigore (1887) act 2

10 She may very well pass for forty-three
In the dusk with a light behind her!
Trial by Jury (1875)

Eric Gill 1882–1940

11 That state is a state of slavery in which a man does what he likes to do in his spare time and in his working time that which is required of him.
Art-nonsense and Other Essays (1929) 'Slavery and Freedom'; cf. **Collingwood** 97:3

Charlotte Perkins Gilman 1860–1935

12 There is no female mind. The brain is not an organ of sex. As well speak of a female liver.
Women and Economics (1898) ch. 8

Allen Ginsberg 1926–97

13 What if someone gave a war & Nobody came?
Life would ring the bells of Ecstasy and Forever be Itself again.
'Graffiti' (1972); cf. **Sandburg** 264:10

14 I saw the best minds of my generation destroyed by madness, starving hysterical naked,
dragging themselves through the negro streets at dawn looking for an angry fix,
angelheaded hipsters burning for the ancient heavenly connection to the starry dynamo in the machinery of the night.
Howl (1956)

George Gipp 1895–1920

15 Tell them to go in there with all they've got and win just one for the Gipper.
*the catchphrase 'Win one for the Gipper' was later used by Ronald **Reagan**, who played Gipp in the 1940 film* Knute Rockne, All American
Knut Rockne 'Gipp the Great' in *Collier's* 22 November 1930

Jean Giraudoux 1882–1944

16 As soon as war is declared it will be impossible to hold the poets back. Rhyme is still the most effective drum.
La Guerre de Troie n'aura pas lieu (1935) act 2, sc. 4
(tr. Christopher Fry as *Tiger at the Gates*, 1955)

Edna Gladney

17 There are no illegitimate children, only illegitimate parents.
MGM paid her a large sum for the line for the 1941 film based on her life, 'Blossoms in the Dust'
A. Loos *Kiss Hollywood Good-Bye* (1978)

W. E. Gladstone 1809–98

18 My mission is to pacify Ireland.
on receiving news that he was to form his first cabinet, 1st December 1868
H. C. G. Matthew *Gladstone 1809–1874* (1986) ch. 5

19 Swimming for his life, a man does not see much of the country through which the river winds.
diary, 31 December 1868

20 Let the Turks now carry away their abuses in the only possible manner, namely by carrying off themselves . . . one and all, bag and baggage, shall I hope clear out from the province they have desolated and profaned.
Bulgarian Horrors and the Question of the East (1876)

21 [An] Established Clergy will always be a Tory Corps d'Armée.
letter to Bishop Goodwin, 8 September 1881

22 There never was a Churchill from John of Marlborough down that had either morals or principles.
in conversation in 1882, recorded by Captain R. V. Briscoe

1 All the world over, I will back the masses against the classes.
  speech in Liverpool, 28 June 1886

2 The blubbering Cabinet.
  of the colleagues who wept at his final Cabinet meeting
  diary, 10 April 1887

3 The God-fearing and God-sustaining University of Oxford. I served her, perhaps mistakenly, but to the best of my ability.
  farewell message, just before his death, May 1898
  Roy Jenkins *Gladstone* (1995)

4 I absorb the vapour and return it as a flood.
  on public speaking
  Lord Riddell *Some Things That Matter* (1927 ed.)

5 It is not a Life at all. It is a Reticence, in three volumes.
  on J. W. Cross's Life of George Eliot
  E. F. Benson *As We Were* (1930) ch. 6

6 [Money should] fructify in the pockets of the people.
  H. G. C. Matthew *Gladstone 1809–1874* (1986)

Hannah Glasse fl. 1747

7 Take your hare when it is cased.
  '*cased*' = skinned
  The Art of Cookery Made Plain and Easy (1747) ch. 1

William Henry, Duke of Gloucester 1743–1805

8 Another damned, thick, square book! Always scribble, scribble, scribble! Eh! Mr Gibbon?
  Henry Best *Personal and Literary Memorials* (1829); alternatively attributed to the Duke of Cumberland and King George III

Jean-Luc Godard 1930–

9 Photography is truth. The cinema is truth 24 times per second.
  Le Petit Soldat (1960 film)

10 GEORGES FRANJU: Movies should have a beginning, a middle and an end.
  JEAN-LUC GODARD: Certainly, but not necessarily in that order.
  in *Time* 14 September 1981; cf. **Aristotle** 14:15

A. D. Godley 1856–1925

11 What is this that roareth thus?
  Can it be a Motor Bus?
  Yes, the smell and hideous hum
  Indicat Motorem Bum!
  letter to C. R. L. Fletcher, 10 January 1914, in *Reliquiae* (1926) vol. 1

Joseph Goebbels 1897–1945

12 We can manage without butter but not, for example, without guns. If we are attacked we can only defend ourselves with guns not with butter.
  speech in Berlin, 17 January 1936; cf. **Goering** 142:14

13 Making noise is an effective means of opposition.
  Ernest K. Bramsted *Goebbels and National Socialist Propaganda 1925–45* (1965)

Hermann Goering 1893–1946
see also **Johst** 177:6

14 We have no butter . . . but I ask you—would you rather have butter or guns? . . . preparedness makes us powerful. Butter merely makes us fat.
  speech at Hamburg, 1936, in W. Frischauer *Goering* (1951) ch. 10; cf. **Goebbels** 142:12

15 I herewith commission you to carry out all preparations with regard to . . . a *total solution* of the Jewish question in those territories of Europe which are under German influence.
  instructions to Heydrich, 31 July 1941; cf. **Heydrich** 158:18

Johann Wolfgang von Goethe 1749–1832

16 *Es irrt der Mensch, so lang er strebt.*
  Man will err while yet he strives.
  Faust pt. 1 (1808) 'Prolog im Himmel'

17 *Entbehren sollst Du! sollst entbehren!*
  Das ist der ewige Gesang.
  Deny yourself! You must deny yourself! That is the song that never ends.
  Faust pt. 1 (1808) 'Studierzimmer'

18 *Grau, teurer Freund, ist alle Theorie*
  Und grün des Lebens goldner Baum.
  All theory, dear friend, is grey, but the golden tree of actual life springs ever green.
  Faust pt. 1 (1808) 'Studierzimmer'

19 *Meine Ruh' ist hin,*
  Mein Herz ist schwer.
  My peace is gone,
  My heart is heavy.
  Faust pt. 1 (1808) 'Gretchen am Spinnrad'

20 *Die Tat ist alles, nichts der Ruhm.*
  The deed is all, the glory nothing.
  Faust pt. 2 (1832) 'Hochgebirg'

21 *Das Ewig-Weibliche zieht uns hinan.*
  Eternal Woman draws us upward.
  Faust pt. 2 (1832) 'Hochgebirg' closing words

22 *Es bildet ein Talent sich in der Stille,*
  Sich ein Charakter in dem Strom der Welt.
  Talent develops in quiet places, character in the full current of human life.
  Torquato Tasso (1790) act 1, sc. 2

23 *Die Wahlverwandtschaften.*
  Elective affinities.
  title of novel (1809)

24 *Über allen Gipfeln*
  Ist Ruh'.
  Over all the mountain tops is peace.
  Wanderers Nachtlied (1821)

25 *Kennst du das Land, wo die Zitronen blühn?*
  Im dunkeln Laub die Gold-Orangen glühn.
  Know you the land where the lemon-trees

bloom? In the dark foliage the gold oranges
glow.

Wilhelm Meisters Lehrjahre (1795–6) bk. 3, ch. 1

1 *Mehr Licht!*
More light!

abbreviated version of 'Macht doch den
zweiten Fensterladen auch auf, damit mehr
Licht hereinkomme [Open the second
shutter, so that more light can come in]')

K. W. Müller *Goethes letze literarische Thätigkeit*
(1832)

Isaac Goldberg 1887–1938

2 Diplomacy is to do and say
The nastiest thing in the nicest way.

in *The Reflex* October 1927

Whoopi Goldberg 1949–

3 I dislike this idea that if you're a black
person in America then you must be called
an African-American. I'm not an African. I'm
an American. Just call me black, if you want
to call me anything.

in *Irish Times* 25 April 1998 'Quotes of the Week'

William Golding 1911–93

4 Nothing is so impenetrable as laughter in a
language you don't understand.

An Egyptian Journal (1985)

Emma Goldman 1869–1940

5 Anarchism, then, really, stands for the
liberation of the human mind from the
dominion of religion; the liberation of the
human body from the dominion of
property; liberation from the shackles and
restraints of government.

Anarchism and Other Essays (1910)

Oliver Goldsmith 1728–74

6 Sweet Auburn, loveliest village of the plain.

The Deserted Village (1770) l. 1

7 Ill fares the land, to hast'ning ills a prey,
Where wealth accumulates, and men decay;
Princes and lords may flourish, or may fade;
A breath can make them, as a breath has
made;
But a bold peasantry, their country's pride,
When once destroyed, can never be
supplied.

The Deserted Village (1770) l. 51

8 How happy he who crowns in shades like
these,
A youth of labour with an age of ease.

The Deserted Village (1770) l. 99

9 And the loud laugh that spoke the vacant
mind.

The Deserted Village (1770) l. 122

10 A man he was to all the country dear,
And passing rich with forty pounds a year.

The Deserted Village (1770) l. 141

11 Truth from his lips prevailed with double
sway,

And fools, who came to scoff, remained to
pray.

The Deserted Village (1770) l. 179

12 And still they gazed, and still the wonder
grew,
That one small head could carry all he
knew.

The Deserted Village (1770) l. 215

13 How wide the limits stand
Between a splendid and a happy land.

The Deserted Village (1770) l. 267

14 Man wants but little here below,
Nor wants that little long.

'Edwin and Angelina, or the Hermit' (1766); cf.
Young 344:18

15 The doctor found, when she was dead,—
Her last disorder mortal.

'Elegy on Mrs Mary Blaize' (1759)

16 The man recovered of the bite,
The dog it was that died.

'Elegy on the Death of a Mad Dog' (1766)

17 Our Garrick's a salad; for in him we see
Oil, vinegar, sugar, and saltness agree.

Retaliation (1774) l. 11; cf. **Garrick** 136:8

18 Too nice for a statesman, too proud for a
wit.

of Edmund **Burke**
Retaliation (1774) l. 32

19 On the stage he was natural, simple,
affecting;
'Twas only that when he was off he was
acting.

of David **Garrick**
Retaliation (1774) l. 101

20 Such is the patriot's boast, where'er we
roam,
His first, best country ever is, at home.

The Traveller (1764) l. 73

21 And honour sinks where commerce long
prevails.

The Traveller (1764) l. 92

22 Laws grind the poor, and rich men rule the
law.

The Traveller (1764) l. 386

23 How small, of all that human hearts endure,
That part which laws or kings can cause or
cure!

The Traveller (1764) l. 429; cf. **Johnson** 174:3

24 The true use of speech is not so much to
express our wants as to conceal them.

The Bee no. 3 (20 October 1759) 'On the Use of
Language'

25 Measures not men, have always been my
mark.

The Good Natured Man (1768) act 2; cf. **Burke**
74:14, **Canning** 81:15

26 Let schoolmasters puzzle their brain,
With grammar, and nonsense, and learning,
Good liquor, I stoutly maintain,
Gives genius a better discerning.

She Stoops to Conquer (1773) act 1, sc. 1 'Song'

1 The very pink of perfection.
   She Stoops to Conquer (1773) act 1

2 This is Liberty-Hall, gentlemen.
   She Stoops to Conquer (1773) act 2

3 I . . . chose my wife, as she did her wedding gown, not for a fine glossy surface, but such qualities as would wear well.
   The Vicar of Wakefield (1766) ch. 1

4 When lovely woman stoops to folly
   And finds too late that men betray,
   What charm can soothe her melancholy,
   What art can wash her guilt away?
   The Vicar of Wakefield (1766) ch. 29; cf. **Eliot** 122:28

5 There is no arguing with Johnson; for when his pistol misses fire, he knocks you down with the butt end of it.
   James Boswell *Life of Samuel Johnson* (1791) 26 October 1769

Barry Goldwater 1909–98

6 I would remind you that extremism in the defence of liberty is no vice! And let me remind you also that moderation in the pursuit of justice is no virtue!
   accepting the presidential nomination, 16 July 1964

Sam Goldwyn 1882–1974

7 Gentlemen, include me out.
   resigning from the Motion Picture Producers and Distributors of America, October 1933
   Michael Freedland *The Goldwyn Touch* (1986) ch. 10

8 That's the way with these directors, they're always biting the hand that lays the golden egg.
   Alva Johnston *The Great Goldwyn* (1937) ch. 1

9 A verbal contract isn't worth the paper it is written on.
   Alva Johnston *The Great Goldwyn* (1937) ch. 1

10 Pictures are for entertainment, messages should be delivered by Western Union.
   Arthur Marx *Goldwyn* (1976) ch. 15

Ivan Goncharov 1812–91

11 No devastating or redeeming fires have ever burnt in my life . . . My life began by flickering out.
   Oblomov (1859) pt. 2, ch. 4 (tr. David Magarshak)

12 You lost your ability for doing things in childhood . . . It all began with your inability to put on your socks and ended by your inability to live.
   Oblomov (1859) pt. 4, ch. 2 (tr. David Magarshak)

Maud Gonne 1867–1953

13 The Famine Queen.
   of Queen **Victoria**
   in *L'Irlande libre* 1900

Amy Goodman 1957–

14 Go to where the silence is and say something.
   accepting an award from Columbia University for her coverage of the 1991 massacre in East Timor by Indonesian troops
   in *Columbia Journalism Review* March/April 1994

Mikhail Sergeevich Gorbachev 1931–

15 The idea of restructuring [perestroika] . . . combines continuity and innovation, the historical experience of Bolshevism and the contemporaneity of socialism.
   speech on the seventieth anniversary of the Russian Revolution, 2 November 1987

Adam Lindsay Gordon 1833–70

16 Life is mostly froth and bubble,
   Two things stand like stone,
   Kindness in another's trouble,
   Courage in your own.
   Ye Wearie Wayfarer (1866) 'Fytte 8'

Mack Gordon 1904–59

17 Pardon me boy is that the Chattanooga Choo-choo,
   Track twenty nine,
   Boy you can gimme a shine.
   'Chattanooga Choo-choo' (1941 song)

Maxim Gorky 1868–1936

18 The proletarian state must bring up thousands of excellent 'mechanics of culture', 'engineers of the soul'.
   speech at the Writers' Congress 1934; cf. **Kennedy** 184:15, **Stalin** 301:12

Stuart Gorrell 1902–63

19 Georgia, Georgia, no peace I find,
   Just an old sweet song keeps Georgia on my mind.
   'Georgia on my Mind' (1930 song)

George Joachim, Lord Goschen 1831–1907

20 I have the courage of my opinions, but I have not the temerity to give a political blank cheque to Lord Salisbury.
   speech in the House of Commons, 19 February 1884

Stephen Jay Gould 1941–

21 A man does not attain the status of Galileo merely because he is persecuted; he must also be right.
   Ever since Darwin (1977)

22 Science is an integral part of culture. It's not this foreign thing, done by an arcane priesthood. It's one of the glories of human intellectual tradition.
   in *Independent* 24 January 1990

Goya 1746-1828

1 One cannot look at this.

The Disasters of War (1863) title of etching, no. 26

2 The dream of reason produces monsters.

Los Caprichos (1799) plate 43 (title)

Baltasar Gracián 1601-58

3 Never open the door to the least of evils, for many other, greater ones lurk outside.

The Art of Worldly Wisdom (translated by Christopher Maurer, 1994)

4 Renew your brilliance. It is the privilege of the Phoenix. Excellence grows old and so does fame. Custom wears down our admiration, and a mediocre novelty can conquer the greatest eminence in its old age. So be reborn in courage, in intellect, in happiness, and in all else. Dare to renew your brilliance, dawning many times, like the sun, only changing your surroundings. Withhold it and make people miss it; renew it and make them applaud.

The Art of Worldly Wisdom (translated by Christopher Maurer, 1994)

D. M. Graham 1911-99

5 That this House will in no circumstances fight for its King and Country.

motion worded by Graham for a debate at the Oxford Union, of which he was Librarian, 9 February 1933 (passed by 275 votes to 153)

Harry Graham 1874-1936

6 Weep not for little Léonie
Abducted by a French Marquis!
Though loss of honour was a wrench
Just think how it's improved her French.

More Ruthless Rhymes for Heartless Homes (1930) 'Compensation'

7 'There's been an accident,' they said,
'Your servant's cut in half; he's dead!'
'Indeed!' said Mr Jones, 'and please,
Send me the half that's got my keys.'

Ruthless Rhymes for Heartless Homes (1899) 'Mr Jones' (attributed to 'G.W.')

8 Billy, in one of his nice new sashes,
Fell in the fire and was burnt to ashes;
Now, although the room grows chilly,
I haven't the heart to poke poor Billy.

Ruthless Rhymes for Heartless Homes (1899) 'Tender-Heartedness'

James Graham see Marquess of Montrose

Kenneth Grahame 1859-1932

9 There is *nothing*—absolutely nothing—half so much worth doing as simply messing about in boats.

The Wind in the Willows (1908) ch. 1

10 The poetry of motion! The *real* way to travel! The *only* way to travel! Here today—in next week tomorrow! Villages skipped, towns and cities jumped—always somebody else's horizon!

The Wind in the Willows (1908) ch. 2; cf. **Kaufman and Anthony** 180:20

11 O bliss! O poop-poop! O my!

The Wind in the Willows (1908) ch. 2

12 The clever men at Oxford
Know all that there is to be knowed.
But they none of them know one half as much
As intelligent Mr Toad!

The Wind in the Willows (1908) ch. 10

Phil Gramm 1942-

13 I did not come to Washington to be loved, and I have not been disappointed.

Michael Barone and Grant Ujifusa *The American Political Almanac 1994*

Bernie Grant 1944-2000

14 The police were to blame for what happened on Sunday night and what they got was a bloody good hiding.

after a riot in which a policeman was killed
speech as leader of Haringey Council outside Tottenham Town Hall, 8 October 1985

Robert Grant 1785-1838

15 O worship the King, all-glorious above;
O gratefully sing his power and his love:
Our Shield and Defender, the Ancient of Days,
Pavilioned in splendour, and girded with praise.

'O worship the King, all glorious above' (1833 hymn)

Ulysses S. Grant 1822-85

16 No terms except unconditional and immediate surrender can be accepted. I propose to move immediately upon your works.

to Simon Bolivar Buckner, under siege at Fort Donelson, 16 February 1862

17 I purpose to fight it out on this line, if it takes all summer.

dispatch to Washington, from head-quarters in the field, 11 May 1864

18 The war is over—the rebels are our countrymen again.

preventing his men from cheering after Lee's surrender at Appomattox
on 9 April, 1865

19 I know no method to secure the repeal of bad or obnoxious laws so effective as their stringent execution.

inaugural address, 4 March 1869

George Granville, Lord Lansdowne 1666-1735

20 Bright as the day, and like the morning, fair,
Such Cloe is . . . and common as the air.

'Cloe' (1712)

21 Cowards in scarlet pass for men of war.

The She Gallants (1696) act 5

Henry Grattan 1746–1820

1 The thing he proposes to buy is what cannot be sold—liberty.
speech in the Irish Parliament against the proposed union, 16 January 1800
    in *Dictionary of National Biography* (1917–)

Arthur Percival Graves 1846–1931

2 Trottin' to the fair,
Me and Moll Maloney,
Seated, I declare
On a single pony.
    'Ridin' Double'

John Woodcock Graves 1795–1886

3 D'ye ken John Peel with his coat so grey?
D'ye ken John Peel at the break of the day?
D'ye ken John Peel when he's far far away
With his hounds and his horn in the morning?
an alternative version 'coat so gay' is often sung
    'John Peel' (1820)

Robert Graves 1895–1985

4 Beware, madam, of the witty devil,
The arch intriguer who walks disguised
In a poet's cloak, his gay tongue oozing evil.
    'Beware, Madam!'

5 There's a cool web of language winds us in,
Retreat from too much joy or too much fear.
    'The Cool Web' (1927)

6 Truth-loving Persians do not dwell upon
The trivial skirmish fought near Marathon.
    'The Persian Version' (1945)

7 Goodbye to all that.
    title of autobiography (1929)

John Gray 1951–

8 Men are from Mars, women are from Venus.
    title of book (1992)

John Chipman Gray 1839–1915

9 Dirt is only matter out of place; and what is a blot on the escutcheon of the Common Law may be a jewel in the crown of the Social Republic.
    Restraints on the Alienation of Property (2nd ed., 1895) preface

Patrick, Lord Gray d. 1612

10 A dead woman bites not.
*pressing for the execution of **Mary** Queen of Scots in 1587*
    oral tradition

Thomas Gray 1716–71

11 Ruin seize thee, ruthless King!
Confusion on thy banners wait.
    The Bard (1757) l. 1

12 In gallant trim the gilded vessel goes;
Youth on the prow, and Pleasure at the helm.
    'The Bard' (1757) l. 73

13 The curfew tolls the knell of parting day,
The lowing herd wind slowly o'er the lea,
The ploughman homeward plods his weary way,
And leaves the world to darkness and to me.
    Elegy Written in a Country Churchyard (1751) l. 1

14 Beneath those rugged elms, that yew-tree's shade,
Where heaves the turf in many a mouldering heap,
Each in his narrow cell for ever laid,
The rude forefathers of the hamlet sleep.
    Elegy Written in a Country Churchyard (1751) l. 13

15 The paths of glory lead but to the grave.
    Elegy Written in a Country Churchyard (1751) l. 36

16 Full many a gem of purest ray serene,
The dark unfathomed caves of ocean bear:
Full many a flower is born to blush unseen,
And waste its sweetness on the desert air.
    Elegy Written in a Country Churchyard (1751) l. 53

17 Far from the madding crowd's ignoble strife,
Their sober wishes never learned to stray.
    Elegy Written in a Country Churchyard (1751) l. 73

18 Alas, regardless of their doom,
The little victims play!
No sense have they of ills to come,
Nor care beyond to-day.
    Ode on a Distant Prospect of Eton College (1747) l. 51

19 Where ignorance is bliss,
'Tis folly to be wise.
    Ode on a Distant Prospect of Eton College (1747) l. 99

20 Not all that tempts your wand'ring eyes
And heedless hearts, is lawful prize;
Nor all, that glisters, gold.
    'Ode on the Death of a Favourite Cat' (1748)

21 He saw; but blasted with excess of light,
Closed his eyes in endless night.
*of **Milton***
    The Progress of Poesy (1757) l. 101

Horace Greeley 1811–72

22 Go West, young man, and grow up with the country.
    Hints toward Reforms (1850)

Graham Greene 1904–91

23 Catholics and Communists have committed great crimes, but at least they have not stood aside, like an established society, and been indifferent. I would rather have blood on my hands than water like Pilate.
    The Comedians (1966) pt. 3, ch. 4

24 So much of life was a putting-off of unhappiness for another time. Nothing was ever lost by delay.
    The Heart of the Matter (1948) bk. 1, pt. 1, ch. 1

25 What do we ever get nowadays from reading to equal the excitement and the revelation in those first fourteen years?
    The Lost Childhood and Other Essays (1951) title essay

1 There is always one moment in childhood when the door opens and lets the future in.
The Power and the Glory (1940) pt. 1, ch. 1

2 Innocence always calls mutely for protection, when we would be so much wiser to guard ourselves against it: innocence is like a dumb leper who has lost his bell, wandering the world meaning no harm.
The Quiet American (1955) pt. 1, ch. 3

Robert Greene c.1560–92

3 Ah! what is love! It is a pretty thing, As sweet unto a shepherd as a king.
'The Shepherd's Wife's Song' (1590)

4 For there is an upstart crow, beautified with our feathers, that with his tiger's heart wrapped in a player's hide, supposes he is as well able to bumbast out a blank verse as the best of you; and being an absolute *Johannes fac totum*, is in his own conceit the only Shake-scene in a country.
Groatsworth of Wit Bought with a Million of Repentance (1592); cf. **Shakespeare** 275:19

Germaine Greer 1939–

5 The female eunuch.
title of book (1970)

6 Women have very little idea of how much men hate them.
The Female Eunuch (1970)

Pope Gregory the Great

AD c.540–604

7 *Non Angli sed Angeli.*
Not Angles but Angels.
on seeing English slaves in Rome
oral tradition, based on 'Responsum est, quod Angli vocarentur. At ille: 'Bene,' inquit; 'nam et angelicam habent faciem, et tales angelorum in caelis decet esse coheredes [It is well,' he said, 'for they have the faces of angels, and such should be the co-heirs of the angels of heaven]'; Bede *Historia Ecclesiastica* bk. 2

Pope Gregory VII c.1020–85

8 I have loved justice and hated iniquity: therefore I die in exile.
at Salerno, following his conflict with the Emperor Henry IV
J. W. Bowden *The Life and Pontificate of Gregory VII* (1840) vol. 2

Joyce Grenfell 1910–79

9 George—don't do that.
recurring line in monologues about a nursery school, from the 1950s, in *George—Don't Do That* (1977)

Julian Grenfell 1888–1915

10 And Life is Colour and Warmth and Light And a striving evermore for these; And he is dead, who will not fight; And who dies fighting has increase.
'Into Battle' in *The Times* 28 May 1915

Frances Greville c.1724–89

11 Far as distress the soul can wound 'Tis pain in each degree; Bliss goes but to a certain bound, Beyond is agony.
'A Prayer for Indifference' (1759)

Fulke Greville, Lord Brooke

1554–1628
see also **Dyer** 118:19

12 Life is a top which whipping Sorrow driveth.
Caelica (1633) 'The earth with thunder torn, with fire blasted'

Lord Grey of Fallodon 1862–1933

13 The lamps are going out all over Europe; we shall not see them lit again in our lifetime.
on the eve of the First World War
25 Years (1925) vol. 2, ch. 18

Lady Jane Grey 1537–54

14 One of the greatest benefits that God ever gave me is that he sent me so sharp and severe parents and so gentle a schoolmaster.
Roger Ascham *The Schoolmaster* (1570) bk. 1

Arthur Griffith 1871–1922

15 What I have signed I will stand by, in the belief that the end of the conflict of centuries is at hand.
statement to Dáil Éireann before the debate on the Treaty, December 1921

16 We have brought back the flag; we have brought back the evacuation of Ireland after 700 years by British troops and the formation of an Irish army. We have brought back to Ireland her full rights.
when moving acceptance of the Treaty in the Dáil, December 1921

Mervyn Griffith-Jones 1909–79

17 Is it a book you would even wish your wife or your servants to read?
*of D. H. **Lawrence**'s* Lady Chatterley's Lover, while appearing for the prosecution at the Old Bailey, 20 October 1960
in *The Times* 21 October 1960

John Grigg 1924–

18 The personality conveyed by the utterances which are put into her mouth is that of a priggish schoolgirl, captain of the hockey team, a prefect, and a recent candidate for confirmation. It is not thus that she will be able to come into her own as an independent and distinctive character.
*of Queen **Elizabeth II***
in *National and English Review* August 1958

19 Autobiography is now as common as adultery and hardly less reprehensible.
in *Sunday Times* 28 February 1962

Jo Grimond 1913–93

1 In bygone days, commanders were taught that when in doubt, they should march their troops towards the sound of gunfire. I intend to march my troops towards the sound of gunfire.

speech to the Liberal Party Assembly, 14 September 1963

Andrei Gromyko 1909–89

2 Comrades, this man has a nice smile, but he's got iron teeth.

of Mikhail **Gorbachev**

speech to Soviet Communist Party Central Committee, 11 March 1985

George Grossmith 1847–1912

3 You should see me dance the Polka,
You should see me cover the ground,
You should see my coat-tails flying,
As I jump my partner round.

'See me Dance the Polka' (*c.*1887 song)

George and Weedon Grossmith
1847–1912, 1854–1919

4 What's the good of a home if you are never in it?

The Diary of a Nobody (1894) ch. 1

5 I left the room with silent dignity, but caught my foot in the mat.

The Diary of a Nobody (1894) ch. 12

6 I am a poor man, but I would gladly give ten shillings to find out who sent me the insulting Christmas card I received this morning.

The Diary of a Nobody (1894) ch. 13

Andrew Grove 1936–

7 Only the paranoid survive.

dictum on which he has long run his company, the Intel Corporation

in *New York Times* 18 December 1994

Philip Guedalla 1889–1944

8 The little ships, the unforgotten Homeric catalogue of *Mary Jane* and *Peggy IV*, of *Folkestone Belle*, *Boy Billy*, and *Ethel Maud*, of *Lady Haig* and *Skylark* . . . the little ships of England brought the Army home.

on the evacuation of Dunkirk

Mr Churchill (1941) ch. 7

9 The work of Henry James has always seemed divisible by a simple dynastic arrangement into three reigns: James I, James II, and the Old Pretender.

Supers and Supermen (1920) 'Some Critics'

Edgar A. Guest 1881–1959

10 The best of all the preachers are the men who live their creeds.

'Sermons we See' (1926)

Che Guevara 1928–67

11 The Revolution is made by man, but man must forge his revolutionary spirit from day to day.

Socialism and Man in Cuba (1968)

Hervé Guibert 1955–91

12 [Aids was] an illness in stages, a very long flight of steps that led assuredly to death, but whose every step represented a unique apprenticeship. It was a disease that gave death time to live and its victims time to die, time to discover time, and in the end to discover life.

To the Friend who did not Save my Life (1991) ch. 61 (translated by Linda Coverdale)

Dorothy Frances Gurney
1858–1932

13 The kiss of the sun for pardon,
The song of the birds for mirth,
One is nearer God's Heart in a garden
Than anywhere else on earth.

'God's Garden' (1913)

John Hampden Gurney 1802–62

14 My soul, bear thou thy part,
Triumph in God above,
And with a well-tuned heart
Sing thou the songs of love.

'Ye holy angels bright' (1838 hymn)

Woody Guthrie 1912–67

15 This land is your land, this land is my land,
From California to the New York Island.
From the redwood forest to the Gulf Stream waters
This land was made for you and me.

'This Land is Your Land' (1956 song)

Nell Gwyn 1650–87

16 Pray, good people, be civil. I am the Protestant whore.

at Oxford, during the Popish Terror, 1681

Hadrian AD 76–138

17 *Animula vagula blandula,
Hospes comesque corporis.*
Ah! gentle, fleeting, wav'ring sprite,
Friend and associate of this clay!

J. W. Duff (ed.) *Minor Latin Poets* (1934); tr. Byron as 'Adrian's Address to His Soul When Dying'; cf. **Pope** 246:25

Haggadah

18 This is the bread of poverty which our fathers ate in the land of Egypt. Let all who are hungry come and eat; let all who are in need come to our Passover feast. Now we are here; next year may we be in the land of Israel! Now we are slaves; next year may we be free!

The narration

19 Rabban Gamaliel says: 'Whoever does not mention the following three things at

Passover has not fulfilled his duty—the Passover sacrifice, unleavened bread, and bitter herbs.'

The three essentials of the Seder

1 Next year in Jerusalem!

Accepted

H. Rider Haggard 1856–1925

2 Out of the dark we came, into the dark we go . . . Life is nothing. Life is all. It is the hand with which we hold off death. It is the glow-worm that shines in the night-time and is black in the morning; it is the white breath of the oxen in winter; it is the little shadow that runs across the grass and loses itself at sunset.

King Solomon's Mines (1886) ch. 5; cf. **Crowfoot** 104:9

3 She who must be obeyed.

She (1887) ch. 6 and *passim*

William Hague 1961–

4 It was inevitable the Titanic was going to set sail, but that doesn't mean it was a good idea to be on it.

on his opposition to joining the single currency

in *Mail on Sunday* 11 January 1998 'Quotes of the Week'

5 Feather-bedding, pocket-lining, money-grabbing cronies.

on the influence of lobbyists

in the House of Commons, 8 July 1998

Earl Haig 1861–1928

6 A very weak-minded fellow I am afraid, and, like the feather pillow, bears the marks of the last person who has sat on him!

describing Lord **Derby**

letter to Lady Haig, 14 January 1918

7 Every position must be held to the last man: there must be no retirement. With our backs to the wall, and believing in the justice of our cause, each one of us must fight on to the end.

order to British troops, 12 April 1918

Quintin Hogg, Lord Hailsham 1907–

8 A great party is not to be brought down because of a scandal by a woman of easy virtue and a proved liar.

on the Profumo affair, in *The Times* 14 June 1963

9 The elective dictatorship.

title of the Dimbleby Lecture, 19 October 1976

Hakuin 1686–1769

10 If someone claps his hand a sound arises. Listen to the sound of the single hand!

attributed

J. B. S. Haldane 1892–1964

11 Now, my own suspicion is that the universe is not only queerer than we suppose, but queerer than we *can* suppose.

Possible Worlds and Other Essays (1927) 'Possible Worlds'

12 The Creator, if He exists, has a special preference for beetles.

on observing that there are 400,000 species of beetle on this planet, but only 8,000 species of mammals

report of lecture, 7 April 1951, in *Journal of the British Interplanetary Society* (1951) vol. 10

H. R. Haldeman 1929–93

13 Once the toothpaste is out of the tube, it is awfully hard to get it back in.

on the Watergate affair

to John Dean, 8 April 1973

Edward Everett Hale 1822–1909

14 'Do you pray for the senators, Dr Hale?' 'No, I look at the senators and I pray for the country.'

Van Wyck Brooks *New England Indian Summer* (1940)

Matthew Hale 1609–76

15 Christianity is part of the laws of England.

William Blackstone's summary of Hale's words (Taylor's case, 1676) in *Commentaries* (1769); the origin of the expression has been traced to Sir John Prisot (d. 1460)

Nathan Hale 1755–76

16 I only regret that I have but one life to lose for my country.

prior to his execution by the British for spying, 22 September 1776

Henry Phelps Johnston *Nathan Hale, 1776* (1914) ch. 7; cf. **Addison** 2:9

Sarah Josepha Hale 1788–1879

17 Mary had a little lamb,
Its fleece was white as snow,
And everywhere that Mary went
The lamb was sure to go.

Poems for Our Children (1830) 'Mary's Little Lamb'

Judah Ha-Levi c.1075–1141

18 I understand the difference between the God and the Lord and I see how great is the difference between the God of Abraham and the God of Aristotle.

The Kuzari 4.16

George Savile, Lord Halifax ('the Trimmer') 1633–95

19 This innocent word *Trimmer* signifieth no more than this, that if men are together in a boat, and one part of the company would weigh it down on one side, another would make it lean as much to the contrary.

Character of a Trimmer (1685, printed 1688)

1 A known liar should be outlawed in a well-ordered government.
  Political, Moral, and Miscellaneous Thoughts and Reflections (1750) 'Miscellaneous: Lying'

2 Malice is of a low stature, but it hath very long arms.
  Political, Moral, and Miscellaneous Thoughts and Reflections (1750) 'Of Malice and Envy'

3 When the people contend for their liberty, they seldom get anything by their victory but new masters.
  Political, Moral, and Miscellaneous Thoughts and Reflections (1750) 'Of Prerogative, Power and Liberty'

4 Men are not hanged for stealing horses, but that horses may not be stolen.
  Political, Moral, and Miscellaneous Thoughts and Reflections (1750) 'Of Punishment'

5 Wherever a knave is not punished, an honest man is laughed at.
  Political, Moral, and Miscellaneous Thoughts and Reflections (1750) 'Of Punishment'

6 State business is a cruel trade; good nature is a bungler in it.
  Political, Moral, and Miscellaneous Thoughts and Reflections (1750) 'Wicked Ministers'

7 [Halifax] had heard of many kicked down stairs, but never of any that was kicked up stairs before.
  Gilbert Burnet *History of My Own Time* (written 1683–6) vol. 1 (1724)

Joseph Hall 1574–1656

8 Perfection is the child of Time.
  Works (1625)

Radclyffe Hall 1883–1943

9 The well of loneliness
  title of novel (1928)

10 You're neither unnatural, nor abominable, nor mad; you're as much a part of what people call nature as anyone else; only you're unexplained as yet—you've not got your niche in creation.
  of lesbianism
  The Well of Loneliness (1928) bk. 2, ch. 20, sect. 3

Friedrich Halm 1806–71

11 *Zwei Seelen und ein Gedanke,*
  Zwei Herzen und ein Schlag!
  Two souls with but a single thought,
  Two hearts that beat as one.
  Der Sohn der Wildnis (1842) act 2

W. F. ('Bull') Halsey 1882–1959

12 The Third Fleet's sunken and damaged ships have been salvaged and are retiring at high speed toward the enemy.
  on hearing claims that the Japanese had virtually annihilated the US fleet
  report, 14 October 1944; E. B. Potter *Bull Halsey* (1985) ch. 17

Alexander Hamilton c.1755–1804

13 A national debt, if it is not excessive, will be to us a national blessing.
  letter to Robert Morris, 30 April 1781

William Hamilton 1788–1856

14 Truth, like a torch, the more it's shook it shines.
  Discussions on Philosophy (1852) title page (epigram)

15 On earth there is nothing great but man; in man there is nothing great but mind.
  Lectures on Metaphysics and Logic (1859); attributed in a Latin form to Favorinus in Pico di Mirandola (1463–94) *Disputationes Adversus Astrologiam Divinatricem*

Oscar Hammerstein II 1895–1960

16 Fish got to swim and birds got to fly
  I got to love one man till I die,
  Can't help lovin' dat man of mine.
  'Can't Help Lovin' Dat Man of Mine' (1927 song) in *Showboat*

17 Climb ev'ry mountain, ford ev'ry stream
  Follow ev'ry rainbow, till you find your dream.
  'Climb Ev'ry Mountain' (1959 song) in *The Sound of Music*

18 I'm gonna wash that man right outa my hair.
  title of song (1949) from *South Pacific*

19 June is bustin' out all over.
  title of song (1945) in *Carousel*

20 The last time I saw Paris
  Her heart was warm and gay.
  'The Last Time I saw Paris' (1941 song) in *Lady Be Good*

21 The corn is as high as an elephant's eye.
  'Oh, What a Beautiful Mornin' ' (1943 song) in *Oklahoma!*

22 Ol' man river, dat ol' man river,
  He must know sumpin', but don't say nothin',
  He jus' keeps rollin',
  He jus' keeps rollin' along.
  'Ol' Man River' (1927 song) in *Showboat*

23 Some enchanted evening,
  You may see a stranger,
  You may see a stranger,
  Across a crowded room.
  'Some Enchanted Evening' (1949 song) in *South Pacific*

24 The hills are alive with the sound of music,
  With songs they have sung for a thousand years.
  The hills fill my heart with the sound of music,
  My heart wants to sing ev'ry song it hears.
  'The Sound of Music' (1959 title-song in show)

25 There is nothin' like a dame.
  title of song (1949) in *South Pacific*

26 I'm as corny as Kansas in August,
  High as a flag on the Fourth of July!
  'A Wonderful Guy' (1949 song) in *South Pacific*

1 You'll never walk alone.
   title of song (1945) in *Carousel*

Kate Hankey 1834–1911

2 Tell me the old, old story.
   Title of hymn (1867)

Brian Hanrahan 1949–

3 I counted them all out and I counted them
   all back.
   *on the number of British aeroplanes joining the
   raid on Port Stanley in the Falkland Islands*
   BBC broadcast report, 1 May 1982

Lorraine Hansberry 1930–65

4 Though it be a thrilling and marvellous
   thing to be merely young and gifted in such
   times, it is doubly so, doubly dynamic—to
   be young, gifted and *black*.
   *To be young, gifted and black: Lorraine Hansberry in
   her own words* (1969) adapted by Robert
   Nemiroff; cf. **Irvine** 169:9

Edmond Haraucourt 1856–1941

5 *Partir c'est mourir un peu,*
   C'est mourir à ce qu'on aime.
   To go away is to die a little, it is to die to
   that which one loves.
   Seul (1891) 'Rondel de l'Adieu'

Otto Harbach 1873–1963

6 Now laughing friends deride tears I cannot
   hide,
   So I smile and say 'When a lovely flame
   dies,
   Smoke gets in your eyes.'
   'Smoke Gets in your Eyes' (1933 song)

E. Y. ('Yip') Harburg 1898–1981

7 Brother can you spare a dime?
   title of song (1932)

8 Say, it's only a paper moon,
   Sailing over a cardboard sea.
   'It's Only a Paper Moon' (1933 song, with Billy
   Rose)

9 Somewhere over the rainbow
   Way up high,
   There's a land that I heard of
   Once in a lullaby.
   'Over the Rainbow' (1939 song) in *The Wizard of
   Oz*

10 Follow the yellow brick road.
   'We're Off to See the Wizard' (1939 song); cf.
   Baum 26:10, **John** 172:19

William Harcourt 1827–1904

11 We are all socialists now.
   *during the passage of Lord Goschen's 1888
   budget, noted for the reduction of the national
   debt*
   attributed; Hubert Bland 'The Outlook' in G. B.
   Shaw (ed.) *Fabian Essays in Socialism* (1889)

Keir Hardie 1856–1915

12 Woman, even more than the working class,
   is the great unknown quantity of the race.
   speech at Bradford, 11 April 1914

D. W. Harding 1906–

13 Regulated hatred.
   title of an article on the novels of Jane Austen
   in *Scrutiny* March 1940

Godfrey Harold Hardy 1877–1947

14 Beauty is the first test: there is no
   permanent place in the world for ugly
   mathematics.
   A Mathematician's Apology (1940)

Thomas Hardy 1840–1928

15 Done because we are too menny.
   Jude the Obscure (1896) pt. 6, ch. 2

16 Dialect words—those terrible marks of the
   beast to the truly genteel.
   The Mayor of Casterbridge (1886) ch. 20

17 Happiness was but the occasional episode in
   a general drama of pain.
   The Mayor of Casterbridge (1886) ch. 45, closing
   words

18 'Justice' was done, and the President of the
   Immortals (in Aeschylean phrase) had ended
   his sport with Tess.
   Tess of the D'Urbervilles (1891) ch. 59

19 After two thousand years of mass
   We've got as far as poison-gas.
   'Christmas: 1924' (1928)

20 In a solitude of the sea
   Deep from human vanity,
   And the Pride of Life that planned her, stilly
   couches she.
   'Convergence of the Twain' (1914)

21 The Immanent Will that stirs and urges
   everything.
   'Convergence of the Twain' (1914)

22 An aged thrush, frail, gaunt, and small,
   In blast-beruffled plume.
   'The Darkling Thrush' (1902)

23 So little cause for carollings
   Of such ecstatic sound
   Was written on terrestrial things
   Afar or nigh around,
   That I could think there trembled through
   His happy good-night air
   Some blessed Hope, whereof he knew
   And I was unaware.
   'The Darkling Thrush' (1902)

24 I am the family face;
   Flesh perishes, I live on,
   Projecting trait and trace
   Through time to times anon,
   And leaping from place to place
   Over oblivion.
   'Heredity' (1917)

25 What of the faith and fire within us
   Men who march away.
   'Men Who March Away' (1914)

1 In the third-class seat sat the journeying boy
And the roof-lamp's oily flame
Played down on his listless form and face,
Bewrapt past knowing to what he was
  going,
Or whence he came.
  'Midnight on the Great Western' (1917)

2 Woman much missed, how you call to me,
call to me.
  'The Voice' (1914)

3 This is the weather the cuckoo likes,
And so do I.
  'Weathers' (1922)

4 When I set out for Lyonnesse,
A hundred miles away,
The rime was on the spray,
And starlight lit my lonesomeness
When I set out for Lyonnesse
A hundred miles away.
  'When I set out for Lyonnesse' (1914)

5 If this sort of thing continues no more
novel-writing for me. A man must be a fool
to deliberately stand up and be shot at.
  of a hostile review of Tess of the D'Urbervilles,
  1891
    Florence Hardy *The Early Life of Thomas Hardy*
    (1928)

Julius Hare 1795–1855
and Augustus Hare 1792–1834

6 The ancients dreaded death: the Christian
can only fear dying.
  Guesses at Truth (1827) Series 1

Maurice Evan Hare 1886–1967

7 There once was an old man who said,
  'Damn!
It is borne in upon me I am
An engine that moves
In determinate grooves,
I'm not even a bus, I'm a tram.'
  'Limerick' (1905)

W. F. Hargreaves 1846–1919

8 I'm Burlington Bertie
I rise at ten thirty and saunter along like a
  toff,
I walk down the Strand with my gloves on
  my hand,
Then I walk down again with them off.
  'Burlington Bertie from Bow' (1915 song)

9 I acted so tragic the house rose like magic,
The audience yelled 'You're sublime.'
They made me a present of Mornington
  Crescent
They threw it a brick at a time.
  'The Night I Appeared as Macbeth' (1922 song)

John Harington 1561–1612

10 Treason doth never prosper, what's the
reason?
For if it prosper, none dare call it treason.
  Epigrams (1618) bk. 4, no. 5

Lord Harlech 1918–85

11 Britain will be honoured by historians more
for the way she disposed of an empire than
for the way in which she acquired it.
  in *New York Times* 28 October 1962

Harold II *c.*1019–66

12 He will give him seven feet of English
ground, or as much more as he may be
taller than other men.
  *his offer to Harald Hardrada of Norway, invading
  England, before the battle of Stamford Bridge*
    King Harald's Saga 1, in Snorri Sturluson
    Heimskringla (*c.*1260)

Jimmy Harper, Will E. Haines,
and Tommy Connor

13 The biggest aspidistra in the world.
  title of song (1938); popularized by Gracie Fields

Arthur Harris 1892–1984

14 I would not regard the whole of the
remaining cities of Germany as worth the
bones of one British Grenadier.
  *supporting the continued strategic bombing of
  German cities*
    letter to Norman Bottomley, deputy Chief of Air
    Staff, 29 March 1945; cf. **Bismarck** 54:15

Joel Chandler Harris 1848–1908

15 Bred en bawn in a brier-patch!
  Uncle Remus and His Legends of the Old Plantation
  (1881) 'How Mr Rabbit was too Sharp for Mr
  Fox'

16 Tar-baby ain't sayin' nuthin', en Brer Fox, he
lay low.
  Uncle Remus and His Legends of the Old Plantation
  (1881) 'The Wonderful Tar-Baby Story'

Lorenz Hart 1895–1943

17 Bewitched, bothered, and bewildered am I.
  'Bewitched' (1941 song) in *Pal Joey* (1941)

18 When love congeals
It soon reveals
The faint aroma of performing seals.
  'I Wish I Were in Love Again' (1937 song) in
  Babes in Arms

19 I get too hungry for dinner at eight.
I like the theatre, but never come late.
I never bother with people I hate.
That's why the lady is a tramp.
  'The Lady is a Tramp' (1937 song) in *Babes in
  Arms*

20 In a mountain greenery
Where God paints the scenery.
  'Mountain Greenery' (1926 song)

21 Thou swell! Thou witty!
Thou sweet! Thou grand!
Wouldst kiss me pretty?
Wouldst hold my hand?
  'Thou Swell' (1927 song)

Bret Harte 1836–1902

22 If, of all words of tongue and pen,
The saddest are, 'It might have been,'

More sad are these we daily see:
'It is, but hadn't ought to be!'
'Mrs Judge Jenkins' (1867); cf. **Whittier** 334:6

L. P. Hartley 1895–1972

1 The past is a foreign country: they do things differently there.
The Go-Between (1953) prologue; cf. **Morley** 228:8

F. W. Harvey b. 1888

2 From troubles of the world
I turn to ducks
Beautiful comical things.
'Ducks' (1919)

Molly Haskell 1940–

3 Being alone and liking it is, for a woman, an act of treachery, an infidelity far more threatening than adultery.
Love and Other Infectious Diseases (1990)

Minnie Louise Haskins 1875–1957

4 And I said to the man who stood at the gate of the year: 'Give me a light that I may tread safely into the unknown.'
And he replied:
'Go out into the darkness and put your hand into the Hand of God. That shall be to you better than light and safer than a known way.'
quoted by **George VI** *in his Christmas broadcast, 1939*
Desert (1908) 'God Knows'

Edwin Hatch 1835–89

5 Breathe on me, Breath of God,
Fill me with life anew.
'Breathe on me, Breath of God' (1878 hymn)

Helen Hathaway 1893–1932

6 More tears have been shed over men's lack of manners than their lack of morals.
Manners for Men (1928)

Charles Haughey 1925–

7 It was a bizarre happening, an unprecedented situation, a grotesque situation, an almost unbelievable mischance.
on the series of events leading to the resignation of the Attorney General; the acronym GUBU *was subsequently coined by Conor Cruise* **O'Brien** *to describe Haughey's style of government*
at a press conference in 1982

Václav Havel 1936–

8 That special time caught me up in its wild vortex and—in the absence of leisure to reflect on the matter—compelled me to do what had to be done.
on his election to the Presidency of the Czech republic
Summer Meditations (1992)

Stephen Hawes d. c.1523

9 For though the day be never so long,
At last the bells ringeth to evensong.
The Pastime of Pleasure (1509) ch. 42, st. 10

R. S. Hawker 1803–75

10 And have they fixed the where and when?
And shall Trelawny die?
Here's twenty thousand Cornish men
Will know the reason why!
the last three lines have been in existence since the imprisonment by James II, in 1688, of seven bishops, including Trelawny, Bishop of Bristol
'The Song of the Western Men'

Jacquetta Hawkes 1910–96

11 I was conscious of this vanished being and myself as part of an unbroken stream of consciousness . . . With an imaginative effort it is possible to see the eternal present in which all days, all the seasons of the plain, stand in enduring unity.
discovering a Neanderthal skeleton
in *New York Times Biographical Service* 21 March 1996

Stephen Hawking 1942–

12 What is it that breathes fire into the equations and makes a universe for them to describe . . . Why does the universe go to all the bother of existing?
A Brief History of Time (1988)

13 If we find the answer to that [why it is that we and the universe exist], it would be the ultimate triumph of human reason—for then we would know the mind of God.
A Brief History of Time (1988) ch. 11

Nathaniel Hawthorne 1804–64

14 The scarlet letter.
title of novel (1850)

15 America is now given over to a damned mob of scribbling women.
letter, 1855; Caroline Ticknor *Hawthorne and his Publisher* (1913)

Ian Hay 1876–1952

16 War is hell, and all that, but it has a good deal to recommend it. It wipes out all the small nuisances of peace-time.
The First Hundred Thousand (1915)

17 What do you mean, funny? Funny-peculiar or funny ha-ha?
The Housemaster (1938) act 3

Franz Joseph Haydn 1732–1809

18 But all the world understands my language.
on being advised by **Mozart**, *in 1790, not to visit England because he knew too little of the world and too few languages*
Rosemary Hughes *Haydn* (1950) ch. 6

Alfred Hayes 1911–85

19 I dreamed I saw Joe Hill last night
Alive as you and me.

Says I, 'But Joe, you're ten years dead.'
'I never died,' says he.
'I Dreamed I Saw Joe Hill Last Night' (1936 song)

J. Milton Hayes 1884–1940

1 There's a one-eyed yellow idol to the north
of Khatmandu,
There's a little marble cross below the
town,
There's a broken-hearted woman tends the
grave of Mad Carew,
And the Yellow God forever gazes down.
The Green Eye of the Yellow God (1911)

William Hazlitt 1778–1830

2 His sayings are generally like women's
letters; all the pith is in the postscript.
*of Charles **Lamb***
Conversations of James Northcote (1826–7)

3 He talked on for ever; and you wished him
to talk on for ever.
*of **Coleridge***
Lectures on the English Poets (1818) 'On the Living
Poets'

4 There is nothing good to be had in the
country, or if there is, they will not let you
have it.
The Round Table (1817) 'Observations on Mr
Wordsworth's Poem *The Excursion*'

5 We can scarcely hate any one that we know.
Table Talk vol. 2 (1822) 'On Criticism'

6 Well, I've had a happy life.
W. C. Hazlitt *Memoirs of William Hazlitt* (1867)

Bessie Head 1937–86

7 And if the white man thought that Asians
were a low, filthy nation, Asians could still
smile with relief—at least, they were not
Africans. And if the white man thought that
Africans were a low, filthy nation, Africans
in southern Africa could still smile—at least,
they were not bushmen. They all have their
monsters.
Maru (1971) pt. 1

Denis Healey 1917–

8 Like being savaged by a dead sheep.
*on being criticized by Geoffrey **Howe** in the House
of Commons*
in the House of Commons, 14 June 1978

Edna Healey 1918–

9 She has no hinterland; in particular she has
no sense of history.
*of Margaret **Thatcher***
Denis Healey *The Time of My Life* (1989)

Timothy Michael Healy 1855–1931

10 REDMOND: Gladstone is now master of the
Party!
HEALY: Who is to be mistress of the Party?
*at the meeting of the Irish Parliamentary Party on
6 December 1890, when the Party split over
Parnell's involvement in the O'Shea divorce;*

*Healy's reference to Katherine O'Shea was
particularly damaging to Parnell*
Robert Kee *The Laurel and the Ivy* (1993)

Seamus Heaney 1939–

11 Between my finger and my thumb
The squat pen rests.
I'll dig with it.
'Digging' (1966)

12 Don't be surprised
If I demur, for, be advised
My passport's green.
No glass of ours was ever raised
To toast *The Queen*.
rebuking the editors of The Penguin Book of
Contemporary British Poetry *for including
him among its authors*
Open Letter (Field Day pamphlet no. 2, 1983)

13 My heart besieged by anger, my mind a gap
of danger,
I walked among their old haunts, the home
ground where they bled;
And in the dirt lay justice like an acorn in
the winter
Till its oak would sprout in Derry where the
thirteen men lay dead.
of Bloody Sunday, Londonderry, 30 January 1972
'The Road to Derry'

14 The famous
Northern reticence, the tight gag of place
And times: yes, yes. Of the 'wee six' I sing
Where to be saved you only must save face
And whatever you say, you say nothing.
'Whatever You Say Say Nothing' (1975)

15 No death outside my immediate family has
left me more bereft. No death in my
lifetime has hurt poets more.
*funeral oration for Ted **Hughes**, 3 November
1998

William Randolph Hearst 1863–1951

16 You furnish the pictures and I'll furnish the
war.
*message to the artist Frederic Remington in
Havana, Cuba, during the Spanish-American War
of 1898*
attributed

Edward Heath 1916–

17 The unpleasant and unacceptable face of
capitalism.
on the Lonrho affair
in the House of Commons, 15 May 1973

John Heath-Stubbs 1918–

18 Venerable Mother Toothache
Climb down from the white battlements,
Stop twisting in your yellow fingers
The fourfold rope of nerves.
'A Charm Against the Toothache' (1954)

Reginald Heber 1783–1826

19 Brightest and best of the sons of the
morning,

Dawn on our darkness and lend us thine
aid.
'Brightest and best of the sons of the morning'
(1827 hymn)

1 From Greenland's icy mountains,
From India's coral strand.
'From Greenland's icy mountains' (1821 hymn)

2 What though the spicy breezes
Blow soft o'er Ceylon's isle;
Though every prospect pleases,
And only man is vile:
In vain with lavish kindness
The gifts of God are strown;
The heathen in his blindness
Bows down to wood and stone.
'From Greenland's icy mountains' (1821 hymn);
Heber later altered 'Ceylon's isle' to 'Java's isle';
cf. **Kipling** 187:13

3 Holy, Holy, Holy! all the saints adore thee,
Casting down their golden crowns around
the glassy sea,
Cherubim and Seraphim falling down
before thee,
Which wert, and art, and evermore shalt be.
'Holy, Holy, Holy! Lord God Almighty!' (1826
hymn)

G. W. F. Hegel 1770–1831
see also **Marx** 214:6

4 What experience and history teach is
this—that nations and governments have
never learned anything from history, or
acted upon any lessons they might have
drawn from it.
Lectures on the Philosophy of World History:
Introduction (1830, tr. H. B. Nisbet, 1975)
introduction

5 Only in the state does man have a rational
existence . . . Man owes his entire existence
to the state, and has his being within it
alone.
Lectures on the Philosophy of World History:
Introduction (1830, tr. H. B. Nisbet, 1975)

6 When philosophy paints its grey on grey,
then has a shape of life grown old. By
philosophy's grey on grey it cannot be
rejuvenated but only understood. The owl
of Minerva spreads its wings only with the
falling of the dusk.
Philosophy of Right (1821, tr. T. M. Knox, 1952)

Heinrich Heine 1797–1856

7 Dort, wo man Bücher
Verbrennt, verbrennt man auch am Ende
Menschen.
Wherever books will be burned, men also,
in the end, are burned.
Almansor (1823) l. 245

8 Auf Flügeln des Gesanges.
On wings of song.
title of song (1823)

9 Maximilien Robespierre was nothing but
the hand of Jean Jacques Rousseau, the
bloody hand that drew from the womb of

time the body whose soul Rousseau had
created.
Zur Geschichte der Religion und Philosophie in
Deutschland (1834) bk. 3, para. 3

10 Dieu me pardonnera, c'est son métier.
God will pardon me, it is His trade.
on his deathbed
Alfred Meissner Heinrich Heine. Erinnerungen
(1856) ch. 5; cf. **Catherine** 84:14

Werner Heisenberg 1901–76

11 An expert is someone who knows some of
the worst mistakes that can be made in his
subject and who manages to avoid them.
Der Teil und das Ganze (1969) ch. 17 (tr. A. J.
Pomerans as Physics and Beyond, 1971)

Joseph Heller 1923–99

12 There was only one catch and that was
Catch-22, which specified that a concern for
one's own safety in the face of dangers that
were real and immediate was the process of
a rational mind . . . Orr would be crazy to fly
more missions and sane if he didn't, but if
he was sane he had to fly them. If he flew
them he was crazy and didn't have to; but if
he didn't want to he was sane and had to.
Catch-22 (1961) ch. 5

13 Some men are born mediocre, some men
achieve mediocrity, and some men have
mediocrity thrust upon them. With Major
Major it had been all three.
Catch-22 (1961) ch. 9; cf. **Shakespeare** 288:23

14 When I read something saying I've not done
anything as good as Catch-22 I'm tempted to
reply, 'Who has?'
in The Times 9 June 1993

Lillian Hellman 1905–84

15 I cannot and will not cut my conscience to
fit this year's fashions.
letter to John S. Wood, 19 May 1952, in US
Congress Committee Hearing on Un-American
Activities (1952) pt. 8

Leona Helmsley c.1920–

16 Only the little people pay taxes.
comment made to her housekeeper in 1983, and
reported at her trial for tax evasion
in New York Times 12 July 1989

Felicia Hemans 1793–1835

17 The boy stood on the burning deck
Whence all but he had fled.
'Casabianca' (1849)

18 The stately homes of England,
How beautiful they stand!
Amidst their tall ancestral trees,
O'er all the pleasant land.
'The Homes of England' (1849); cf. **Coward**
101:10

Ernest Hemingway 1899–1961
see also **Fitzgerald** 129:4, **Stein** 302:8

1 But did thee feel the earth move?
For Whom the Bell Tolls (1940) ch. 13

2 Paris is a movable feast.
A Movable Feast (1964) epigraph

3 The sun also rises.
title of novel (1926)

4 Grace under pressure.
when asked what he meant by 'guts' in an interview with Dorothy **Parker**
in *New Yorker* 30 November 1929

5 The most essential gift for a good writer is a built-in, shock-proof shit detector.
in *Paris Review* Spring 1958

Arthur W. D. Henley

6 Nobody loves a fairy when she's forty.
title of song (1934)

W. E. Henley 1849–1903

7 Under the bludgeonings of chance
My head is bloody, but unbowed.
'Invictus. In Memoriam R.T.H.B.' (1888)

8 I am the master of my fate:
I am the captain of my soul.
'Invictus. In Memoriam R.T.H.B.' (1888)

9 What have I done for you,
England, my England?
'Pro Rege Nostro' (1900); cf. **MacDonell** 207:9

10 I was a King in Babylon
And you were a Christian slave.
'To W. A.' (1888)

Henri IV 1553–1610

11 I want there to be no peasant in my kingdom so poor that he is unable to have a chicken in his pot every Sunday.
Hardouin de Péréfixe *Histoire de Henry le Grand* (1681); cf. **Hoover** 162:13

12 Paris is well worth a mass.
attributed to Henri IV; alternatively to his minister Sully, in conversation with Henri

13 The wisest fool in Christendom.
of **James I** *of England*
attributed both to Henri IV and Sully

Henry II 1133–89

14 Will no one rid me of this turbulent priest?
of Thomas Becket, Archbishop of Canterbury, murdered in Canterbury Cathedral, December 1170
oral tradition, conflating a number of variant forms

Henry VIII 1491–1547

15 That man hath the sow by the right ear.
of Thomas **Cranmer**, *June 1529*
Acts and Monuments of John Foxe ['Fox's Book of Martyrs'] (1570)

16 The King found her so different from her picture . . . that . . . he swore they had brought him a Flanders mare.
of Anne of Cleves
Tobias Smollett *A Complete History of England* (3rd ed., 1759) vol. 6

Matthew Henry 1662–1714

17 The better day, the worse deed.
An Exposition on the Old and New Testament (1710) Genesis ch. 3, v. 6, gloss 2

18 They that die by famine die by inches.
An Exposition on the Old and New Testament (1710) Psalm 59, v. 15, gloss 5 (referring incorrectly to v. 13)

O. Henry 1862–1910

19 It was beautiful and simple as all truly great swindles are.
Gentle Grafter (1908) 'Octopus Marooned'

20 Turn up the lights; I don't want to go home in the dark.
last words, quoting a song; Charles Alphonso Smith *O. Henry Biography* (1916) ch. 9
I'm afraid to come home in the dark.
Harry Williams (1874–1924) title of song (1907)

Patrick Henry 1736–99

21 Caesar had his Brutus—Charles the First, his Cromwell—and George the Third—('Treason,' cried the Speaker) . . . *may profit by their example. If this* be treason, make the most of it.
speech in the Virginia assembly, May 1765

22 I know not what course others may take; but as for me, give me liberty, or give me death!
speech in Virginia Convention, 23 March 1775

Philip Henry 1631–96

23 All this, and heaven too!
in Matthew Henry *Life of Mr Philip Henry* (1698) ch. 5

Barbara Hepworth 1903–75

24 Carving is interrelated masses conveying an emotion: a perfect relationship between the mind and the colour, light and weight which is the stone, made by the hand which feels.
Herbert Read (ed.) *Unit One* (1934)

Heraclitus *c.*540–*c.*480 BC

25 You can't step twice into the same river.
Plato *Cratylus* 402a

26 A man's character is his fate.
On the Universe fragment 121 (tr. W. H. S. Jones); cf. **Eliot** 121:13, **Novalis** 235:2

27 The road up and the road down are one and the same.
H. Diels and W. Kranz *Die Fragmente der Vorsokratiker* (7th ed., 1954) fragment 60

A. P. Herbert 1890–1971

1 The Farmer will never be happy again;
He carries his heart in his boots;
For either the rain is destroying his grain
Or the drought is destroying his roots.
'The Farmer' (1922)

2 As my poor father used to say
In 1863,
Once people start on all this Art
Goodbye, moralitee!
'Lines for a Worthy Person' (1930)

3 This high official, all allow,
Is grossly overpaid;
There wasn't any Board, and now
There isn't any Trade.
'The President of the Board of Trade' (1922)

4 Holy deadlock.
title of novel (1934)

5 People must not do things for fun. We are
not here for fun. There is no reference to
fun in any Act of Parliament.
Uncommon Law (1935) 'Is it a Free Country?'

6 The critical period in matrimony is
breakfast-time.
Uncommon Law (1935) 'Is Marriage Lawful?'

Lord Herbert of Cherbury
1583–1648

7 Now that the April of your youth adorns
The garden of your face.
'Ditty: Now that the April' (1665)

George Herbert 1593–1633

8 Let all the world in ev'ry corner sing
My God and King.
'Antiphon: Let all the world in ev'ry corner
sing' (1633)

9 I struck the board, and cried, 'No more.
I will abroad.'
'The Collar' (1633)

10 Away; take heed:
I will abroad.
Call in thy death's-head there: tie up thy
fears.
'The Collar' (1633)

11 But as I raved and grew more fierce and
wild
At every word,
Methought I heard one calling, 'Child';
And I replied, 'My Lord.'
'The Collar' (1633)

12 Teach me, my God and King,
In all things Thee to see,
And what I do in any thing
To do it as for Thee.
'The Elixir' (1633)

13 A servant with this clause
Makes drudgery divine:
Who sweeps a room as for Thy laws
Makes that and th' action fine.
'The Elixir' (1633)

14 Lovely enchanting language, sugar-cane,
Honey of roses!
'The Forerunners' (1633)

15 Who says that fictions only and false hair
Become a verse? Is there in truth no beauty?
Is all good structure in a winding stair?
'Jordan (1)' (1633)

16 Love bade me welcome: yet my soul drew
back,
Guilty of dust and sin.
But quick-eyed Love, observing me grow
slack
From my first entrance in,
Drew nearer to me, sweetly questioning,
If I lacked any thing.
'Love: Love bade me welcome' (1633)

17 'You must sit down,' says Love, 'and taste
my meat.'
So I did sit and eat.
'Love: Love bade me welcome' (1633)

18 When God at first made man,
Having a glass of blessings standing by;
Let us (said he) pour on him all we can:
Let the world's riches, which dispersed lie,
Contract into a span.
'The Pulley' (1633)

19 If goodness lead him not, yet weariness
May toss him to My breast.
'The Pulley' (1633)

20 Man stole the fruit, but I must climb the
tree.
'The Sacrifice' (1633) l. 202

21 The God of love my Shepherd is,
And He that doth me feed:
While He is mine, and I am His,
What can I want or need?
'The 23rd Psalm' (1633); cf. **Book of Common
Prayer** 61:6

22 Sweet spring, full of sweet days and roses,
A box where sweets compacted lie.
'Virtue' (1633)

Herodotus *c.*485–*c.*425

23 In peace, children inter their parents; war
violates the order of nature and causes
parents to inter their children.
Histories bk. 1 sect. 87

24 The most hateful torment for men is to
have knowledge of everything but power
over nothing.
Histories bk. 9 sect. 16

Robert Herrick 1591–1674

25 Here a little child I stand,
Heaving up my either hand;
Cold as paddocks though they be,
Here I lift them up to Thee,
For a benison to fall
On our meat, and on us all. Amen.
'Another Grace for a Child' (1647)

26 I sing of brooks, of blossoms, birds, and
bowers:
Of April, May, of June, and July-flowers.
I sing of May-poles, Hock-carts, wassails,
wakes,

Of bride-grooms, brides, and of their bridal-
cakes.
'The Argument of his Book' from *Hesperides*
(1648)

1 And once more yet (ere I am laid out dead)
Knock at a star with my exalted head.
'The Bad Season Makes the Poet Sad' (1648)

2 Cherry-ripe, ripe, ripe, I cry,
Full and fair ones; come and buy:
If so be, you ask me where
They do grow? I answer, there,
Where my Julia's lips do smile;
There's the land, or cherry-isle.
'Cherry-Ripe' (1648)

3 A sweet disorder in the dress
Kindles in clothes a wantonness:
'Delight in Disorder' (1648)

4 Night makes no difference 'twixt the Priest
and Clerk;
Joan as my Lady is as good i' th' dark.
'No Difference i' th' Dark' (1648)

5 Fain would I kiss my Julia's dainty leg,
Which is as white and hairless as an egg.
'On Julia's Legs' (1648)

6 But, for Man's fault, then was the thorn,
Without the fragrant rose-bud, born;
But ne'er the rose without the thorn.
'The Rose' (1647)

7 Fair daffodils, we weep to see
You haste away so soon.
'To Daffodils' (1648)

8 Gather ye rosebuds while ye may,
Old Time is still a-flying:
And this same flower that smiles to-day,
To-morrow will be dying.
'To the Virgins, to Make Much of Time' (1648)

9 Then be not coy, but use your time;
And while ye may, go marry:
For having lost but once your prime,
You may for ever tarry.
'To the Virgins, to Make Much of Time' (1648)

10 Whenas in silks my Julia goes,
Then, then (methinks) how sweetly flows
That liquefaction of her clothes.
Next, when I cast mine eyes and see
That brave vibration each way free;
O how that glittering taketh me!
'Upon Julia's Clothes' (1648)

Lord Hervey 1696–1743

11 Whoever would lie usefully should lie
seldom.
Memoirs of the Reign of George II (ed. J. W. Croker,
1848) vol. 1

12 I am fit for nothing but to carry candles and
set chairs all my life.
letter to Robert Walpole, 1737

Theodor Herzl 1860–1904

13 At Basle I founded the Jewish state.
of the first Zionist congress, held in Basle in 1897
diary, 3 September 1897

Hesiod c.700 BC

14 The half is greater than the whole.
Works and Days l. 40

15 The man who does evil to another does evil
to himself,
and the evil counsel is most evil
for him who counsels it.
Works and Days l. 265, tr. R. Lattimore

Hermann Hesse 1877–1962

16 If you hate a person, you hate something in
him that is part of yourself. What isn't part
of ourselves doesn't disturb us.
Demian (1919) ch. 6

Gordon Hewart 1870–1943

17 A long line of cases shows that it is not
merely of some importance, but is of
fundamental importance that justice should
not only be done, but should manifestly and
undoubtedly be seen to be done.
Rex v Sussex Justices, 9 November 1923

Reinhard Heydrich 1904–42

18 Now the rough work has been done we
begin the period of finer work. We need to
work in harmony with the civil
administration. We count on you gentlemen
as far as the final solution is concerned.
on the planned mass murder of all European Jews;
cf. **Goering** 142:15
speech in Wannsee, 20 January 1942

Du Bose Heyward 1885–1940 and Ira Gershwin 1896–1983

19 It ain't necessarily so,
It ain't necessarily so,
De t'ings dat yo' li'ble
To read in de Bible
It ain't necessarily so.
'It ain't necessarily so' (1935 song) in *Porgy and
Bess*

20 Summer time an' the livin' is easy,
Fish are jumpin' an' the cotton is high.
'Summertime' (1935 song) in *Porgy and Bess*

21 A woman is a sometime thing.
title of song (1935) in *Porgy and Bess*

John Heywood c.1497–c.1580

22 All a green willow, willow;
All a green willow is my garland.
'The Green Willow'

Thomas Heywood c.1574–1641

23 Seven cities warred for Homer, being dead,
Who, living, had no roof to shroud his head.
'The Hierarchy of the Blessed Angels' (1635); cf.
Anonymous 9:19

Aaron Hill 1685–1750

24 Tender-handed stroke a nettle,
And it stings you for your pains;
Grasp it like a man of mettle,

And it soft as silk remains.
'Verses Written on a Window in Scotland'

Damon Hill 1960–

1 Winning is everything. The only ones who remember you when you come second are your wife and your dog.
in *Sunday Times* 18 December 1994 'Quotes of the Year'

Joe Hill 1879–1915

2 You will eat, bye and bye,
In that glorious land above the sky;
Work and pray, live on hay,
You'll get pie in the sky when you die.
'Preacher and the Slave' in *Songs of the Workers* (Industrial Workers of the World, 1911)

3 I will die like a true-blue rebel. Don't waste any time in mourning—organize.
before his death by firing squad
farewell telegram to Bill Haywood, 18 November 1915

Pattie S. Hill 1868–1946

4 Happy birthday to you.
title of song (1935)

Rowland Hill 1744–1833

5 He did not see any reason why the devil should have all the good tunes.
E. W. Broome *The Rev. Rowland Hill* (1881) ch. 7

Edmund Hillary 1919–

6 Well, we knocked the bastard off!
on conquering Mount Everest, 1953
Nothing Venture, Nothing Win (1975) ch. 10

Fred Hillebrand 1893–1963

7 Home James, and don't spare the horses.
title of song (1934)

Hillel 'The Elder' c.60 BC–AD c.9

8 What is hateful to you do not do to your neighbour: that is the whole Torah.
in *Talmud* Shabbat 31a

9 If I am not for myself who is for me? and being for my own self what am I? If not now when?
in *Talmud* Mishnah 'Pirqei Avot' 1:14

James Hilton 1900–54

10 Nothing really wrong with him—only anno domini, but that's the most fatal complaint of all, in the end.
Goodbye, Mr Chips (1934) ch. 1

Hippocrates c.460–357 BC

11 Life is short, the art long.
often quoted as 'Ars longa, vita brevis', *after* **Seneca**'s *rendering in* De Brevitate Vitae *sect. 1*
Aphorisms sect. 1, para. 1 (tr. W. H. S. Jones); cf. **Chaucer** 88:24

Emperor Hirohito 1901–89

12 The war situation has developed not necessarily to Japan's advantage.
announcing Japan's surrender, in a broadcast to his people after atom bombs had destroyed Hiroshima and Nagasaki
on 15 August 1945

Damien Hirst 1965–

13 It's amazing what you can do with an E in A-level art, twisted imagination and a chainsaw.
after winning the 1995 Turner Prize
in *Observer* 3 December 1995 'Sayings of the Week'

Alfred Hitchcock 1899–1980

14 Actors are cattle.
in *Saturday Evening Post* 22 May 1943

15 Television has brought back murder into the home—where it belongs.
in *Observer* 19 December 1965

Adolf Hitler 1889–1945

16 The broad mass of a nation . . . will more easily fall victim to a big lie than to a small one.
Mein Kampf (1925) vol. 1, ch. 10

17 The night of the long knives.
*referring to the massacre of Ernst Roehm and his associates by Hitler on 29–30 June 1934 (subsequently associated with Harold **Macmillan**'s Cabinet dismissals of 13 July 1962)*
S. H. Roberts *The House Hitler Built* (1937) pt. 2, ch. 3

18 I go the way that Providence dictates with the assurance of a sleepwalker.
speech in Munich, 15 March 1936

19 It is the last territorial claim which I have to make in Europe, but it is the claim from which I will not recede and which, God-willing, I will make good.
on the Sudetenland
speech at Berlin Sportpalast, 26 September 1938

20 My patience is now at an end!
speech at Berlin Sportpalast, 26 September 1938,

Lady Ho fl. 300 BC

21 When a pair of magpies fly together
They do not envy the pair of phoenixes.
'A Song of Magpies'; K. Rexroth and Chung (eds.) *The Orchid Boat: Women Poets of China* (1972)

Thomas Hobbes 1588–1679

22 By art is created that great Leviathan, called a commonwealth or state, (in Latin *civitas*) which is but an artificial man . . . and in which, the sovereignty is an artificial soul.
Leviathan (1651); introduction

23 They that approve a private opinion, call it opinion; but they that mislike it, heresy:

and yet heresy signifies no more than private opinion.
Leviathan (1651) pt. 1, ch. 11

1 During the time men live without a common power to keep them all in awe, they are in that condition which is called war; and such a war as is of every man against every man.
Leviathan (1651) pt. 1, ch. 13

2 For as the nature of foul weather, lieth not in a shower or two of rain; but in an inclination thereto of many days together: so the nature of war consisteth not in actual fighting, but in the known disposition thereto during all the time there is no assurance to the contrary.
Leviathan (1651) pt. 1, ch. 13

3 No arts; no letters; no society; and which is worst of all, continual fear and danger of violent death; and the life of man, solitary, poor, nasty, brutish, and short.
Leviathan (1651) pt. 1, ch. 13

4 Liberties . . . depend on the silence of the law.
Leviathan (1651) pt. 2, ch. 16

5 The papacy is not other than the ghost of the deceased Roman Empire, sitting crowned upon the grave thereof.
Leviathan (1651) pt. 4, ch. 47

6 I am about to take my last voyage, a great leap in the dark.
last words; attributed (cf. **Vanbrugh** 322:9), but with no authoritative source

John Cam Hobhouse, Lord Broughton 1786–1869

7 When I invented the phrase 'His Majesty's Opposition' [Canning] paid me a compliment on the fortunate hit.
Recollections of a Long Life (1865) vol. 2, ch. 12; cf. **Bagehot** 22:12

Eric Hobsbawm 1917–

8 This was the kind of war which existed in order to produce victory parades.
of the **Falklands** *War*
in *Marxism Today* January 1983

David Hockney 1937–

9 All painting, no matter what you're painting, is abstract in that it's got to be organized.
David Hockney (1976)

10 The thing with high-tech is that you always end up using scissors.
in *Observer* 10 July 1994 'Sayings of the Week'

Ralph Hodgson 1871–1962

11 'Twould ring the bells of Heaven
The wildest peal for years,
If Parson lost his senses
And people came to theirs,
And he and they together
Knelt down with angry prayers

For tamed and shabby tigers
And dancing dogs and bears,
And wretched, blind, pit ponies,
And little hunted hares.
'Bells of Heaven' (1917)

Al Hoffman 1902–60 and Dick Manning 1912–

12 Takes two to tango.
title of song (1952)

August Heinrich Hoffman (Hoffman von Fallersleben) 1798–1874

13 *Deutschland über alles.*
Germany above all.
title of poem (1841)

Heinrich Hoffmann 1809–94

14 Look at little Johnny there,
Little Johnny Head-In-Air!
Struwwelpeter (1848) 'Johnny Head-In-Air'; cf. **Pudney** 252:2

15 The door flew open, in he ran,
The great, long, red-legged scissor-man.
Struwwelpeter (1848) 'The Little Suck-a-Thumb'

16 Snip! Snap! Snip! They go so fast.
That both his thumbs are off at last.
Struwwelpeter (1848) 'The Little Suck-a-Thumb'

17 The hare sits snug in leaves and grass,
And laughs to see the green man pass.
Struwwelpeter (1848) 'The Man Who Went Out Shooting'

18 And now she's trying all she can,
To shoot the sleepy, green-coat man.
Struwwelpeter (1848) 'The Man Who Went Out Shooting'

19 Anything to me is sweeter
Than to see Shock-headed Peter.
Struwwelpeter (1848) 'Shock-Headed Peter' (title poem)

Gerard Hoffnung 1925–59

20 Standing among savage scenery, the hotel offers stupendous revelations. There is a French widow in every bedroom, affording delightful prospects.
supposedly quoting a letter from a Tyrolean landlord
speech at the Oxford Union, 4 December 1958

Lancelot Hogben 1895–1975

21 This is not the age of pamphleteers. It is the age of the engineers. The spark-gap is mightier than the pen.
Science for the Citizen (1938) epilogue

James Hogg 1770–1835

22 Where the pools are bright and deep
Where the gray trout lies asleep,
Up the river and o'er the lea
That's the way for Billy and me.
'A Boy's Song' (1838)

23 We'll o'er the water, we'll o'er the sea,
We'll o'er the water to Charlie;

Come weel, come wo, we'll gather and go,
And live or die wi' Charlie.
'O'er the Water to Charlie' in *Jacobite Relics of Scotland* Second Series (1821)

1 The private memoirs and confessions of a justified sinner.
title of novel (1824)

Paul Henri, Baron d'Holbach
1723–89

2 If ignorance of nature gave birth to the Gods, knowledge of nature is destined to destroy them.
Système de la Nature (1770) pt. 2, ch. 1

Billie Holiday 1915–59

3 Mama may have, papa may have,
But God bless the child that's got his own!
That's got his own.
'God Bless the Child' (1941 song, with Arthur Herzog Jnr)

4 Southern trees bear strange fruit,
Blood on the leaves and blood at the root,
Black bodies swinging in the Southern breeze,
Strange fruit hanging from the poplar trees.
'Strange Fruit' (1939)

5 Mom and Pop were just a couple of kids when they got married. He was eighteen, she was sixteen, and I was three.
Lady Sings the Blues (1956)

Henry Fox, Lord Holland 1705–74

6 If Mr Selwyn calls again, shew him up: if I am alive I shall be delighted to see him; and if I am dead he would like to see me.
during his last illness
J. H. Jesse *George Selwyn and his Contemporaries* (1844) vol. 3

Henry Scott Holland 1847–1918

7 Death is nothing at all; it does not count. I have only slipped away into the next room.
sermon preached on Whitsunday 1910

John H. Holmes 1879–1964

8 This, now, is the judgement of our scientific age—the third reaction of man upon the universe! This universe is not hostile, nor yet is it friendly. It is simply indifferent.
The Sensible Man's View of Religion (1932) ch. 4

Oliver Wendell Holmes 1809–94

9 It is the province of knowledge to speak and it is the privilege of wisdom to listen.
The Poet at the Breakfast-Table (1872) ch. 10

10 Lean, hungry, savage anti-everythings.
'A Modest Request' (1848)

Oliver Wendell Holmes Jr.
1841–1935

11 We pause to . . . recall what our country has done for each of us and to ask ourselves what we can do for our country in return.
speech, Keene, New Hampshire, 30 May 1884; cf. **Kennedy** 184:12

12 It is better to be seventy years young than forty years old!
reply to invitation from Julia Ward **Howe** *to her seventieth birthday party, 27 May 1889*
Laura Richards and Maud Howe Elliott *Julia Ward Howe* (1916) vol. 2

13 The most stringent protection of free speech would not protect a man falsely shouting fire in a theatre and causing a panic.
sometimes quoted as, 'shouting fire in a crowded theatre'
in *Schenck v. United States* (1919)

John Home 1722–1808

14 My name is Norval; on the Grampian hills My father feeds his flocks.
Douglas (1756) act 2, sc. 1

Alec Douglas-Home, Lord Home
1903–95

15 As far as the fourteenth earl is concerned, I suppose Mr Wilson, when you come to think of it, is the fourteenth Mr Wilson.
replying to Harold **Wilson**'s *remark (on Home's becoming leader of the Conservative party) that 'the whole [democratic] process has ground to a halt with a fourteenth Earl'*
in *Daily Telegraph* 22 October 1963

Homer

16 Achilles' cursed anger sing, O goddess, that son of Peleus, which started a myriad sufferings for the Achaeans.
The Iliad bk. 1, l. 1; cf. **Pope** 248:22

17 Winged words.
The Iliad bk. 1, l. 201

18 Smiling through her tears.
The Iliad bk. 6, l. 484

19 It lies in the lap of the gods.
The Iliad bk. 17, l. 514 and elsewhere

20 Tell me, Muse, of the man of many devices, who wandered far and wide after he had sacked Troy's sacred city, and saw the towns of many men and knew their mind.
of Odysseus
The Odyssey bk. 1, l. 1

21 Rosy-fingered dawn.
The Odyssey bk. 2, l. 1 and *passim*

Thomas Hood 1799–1845

22 The bleak wind of March
Made her tremble and shiver;
But not the dark arch,
Or the black flowing river.
'The Bridge of Sighs' (1844)

1 Mad from life's history,
Glad to death's mystery,
Swift to be hurled.
'The Bridge of Sighs' (1844)

2 And Eugene Aram walked between,
With gyves upon his wrist.
'The Dream of Eugene Aram' (1829)

3 For here I leave my second leg,
And the Forty-second Foot!
'Faithless Nelly Gray' (1826)

4 They went and told the sexton, and
The sexton tolled the bell.
'Faithless Sally Brown' (1826)

5 I remember, I remember,
The house where I was born,
The little window where the sun
Came peeping in at morn.
'I Remember' (1826)

6 She stood breast high amid the corn,
Clasped by the golden light of morn,
'Ruth' (1827); cf. **Keats** 182:14

7 Stitch! stitch! stitch!
In poverty, hunger, and dirt.
And still with a voice of dolorous pitch
She sang the 'Song of the Shirt'.
'The Song of the Shirt' (1843)

8 The sedate, sober, silent, serious, sad-
coloured sect.
of Quakers
Comic Annual (1839) 'The Doves and the Crows'

Richard Hooker *c.*1554–1600

9 Alteration though it be from worse to better
hath in it inconveniences, and those
weighty.
Of the Laws of Ecclesiastical Polity (1593) bk. 4; cf.
Johnson 173:10

Ellen Sturgis Hooper 1816–41

10 I slept, and dreamed that life was beauty;
I woke, and found that life was duty.
'Beauty and Duty' (1840)

Herbert Hoover 1874–1964

11 Our country has deliberately undertaken a
great social and economic experiment,
noble in motive and far-reaching in
purpose.
*on the Eighteenth Amendment enacting
Prohibition*
letter to Senator W. H. Borah, 23 February 1928

12 The American system of rugged
individualism.
speech in New York City, 22 October 1928

13 The slogan of progress is changing from the
full dinner pail to the full garage.
*sometimes paraphrased as, 'a car in every garage
and a chicken in every pot'*
speech, 22 October 1928; cf. **Henri IV** 156:11

14 The grass will grow in the streets of a
hundred cities, a thousand towns.
*on proposals 'to reduce the protective tariff to a
competitive tariff for revenue'*
speech, 31 October 1932

Anthony Hope 1863–1933

15 Economy is going without something you
do want in case you should, some day, want
something you probably won't want.
The Dolly Dialogues (1894) no. 12

16 Oh, for an hour of Herod!
*at the first night of J. M. **Barrie**'s Peter Pan in
1904*
Denis Mackail *The Story of JMB* (1941) ch. 17

Bob Hope 1903–

17 A bank is a place that will lend you money
if you can prove that you don't need it.
In Alan Harrington *Life in the Crystal Palace* (1959)
'The Tyranny of Farms'

18 Well, I'm still here.
*after erroneous reports of his death, marked by
tributes paid to him in Congress*
in Mail on Sunday 7 June 1998 'Quotes of the
Week'

Laurence Hope 1865–1904

19 Pale hands I loved beside the Shalimar,
Where are you now? Who lies beneath your
spell?
The Garden of Kama (1901) 'Kashmiri Song'

20 Less than the dust, beneath thy Chariot
wheel.
The Garden of Kama (1901) 'Less than the Dust'

Gerard Manley Hopkins 1844–89

21 Towery city and branchy between towers;
Cuckoo-echoing, bell-swarmèd, lark-
charmèd, rook-racked, river-rounded.
'Duns Scotus's Oxford' (written 1879)

22 The world is charged with the grandeur of
God.
It will flame out like shining from shook
foil . . .
Generations have trod, have trod, have trod;
And all is seared with trade; bleared,
smeared with toil;
And wears man's smudge and shares man's
smell: the soil
Is bare now, nor can foot feel, being shod.
'God's Grandeur' (written 1877)

23 Because the Holy Ghost over the bent
World broods with warm breast and with
ah! bright wings.
'God's Grandeur' (written 1877)

24 Elected Silence, sing to me
And beat upon my whorlèd ear.
'The Habit of Perfection' (written 1866)

25 What would the world be, once bereft
Of wet and wildness? Let them be left,
O let them be left, wildness and wet;
Long live the weeds and the wilderness yet.
'Inversnaid' (written 1881)

26 O the mind, mind has mountains; cliffs of
fall
Frightful, sheer, no-man-fathomed. Hold
them cheap
May who ne'er hung there.
'No worst, there is none' (written 1885)

1 Glory be to God for dappled things.
'Pied Beauty' (written 1877)

2 All things counter, original, spare, strange;
Whatever is fickle, freckled (who knows
how?)
With swift, slow; sweet, sour; adazzle, dim;
He fathers-forth whose beauty is past
change:
Praise him.
'Pied Beauty' (written 1877)

3 Márgarét, áre you gríeving
Over Goldengrove unleaving?
'Spring and Fall: to a young child' (written
1880)

4 Though worlds of wanwood leafmeal lie.
'Spring and Fall: to a young child' (written
1880)

5 It ís the blight man was born for,
It is Margaret you mourn for.
'Spring and Fall: to a young child' (written
1880)

6 Thou art indeed just, Lord, if I contend
With thee; but, sir, so what I plead is just.
Why do sinners' ways prosper? and why
must
Disappointment all I endeavour end?
'Thou art indeed just, Lord' (written 1889)

7 Birds build—but not I build; no, but strain,
Time's eunuch, and not breed one work
that wakes.
Mine, O thou lord of life, send my roots
rain.
'Thou art indeed just, Lord' (written 1889)

8 I caught this morning morning's minion,
kingdom of daylight's dauphin, dapple-
dawn-drawn Falcon.
'The Windhover' (written 1877)

9 On Saturday sailed from Bremen,
American-outward-bound,
Take settler and seamen, tell men with
women,
Two hundred souls in the round.
'The Wreck of the Deutschland' (written 1876)
pt. 2

10 To lift up the hands in prayer gives God
glory, but a man with a dungfork in his
hand, a woman with a slop-pail, give him
glory too. He is so great that all things give
him glory if you mean they should.
'The Principle or Foundation' (1882)

Horace 65–8 BC

11 *Inceptis gravibus plerumque et magna professis*
Purpureus, late qui splendeat, unus et alter
Adsuitur pannus.
Works of serious purpose and grand
promises often have a purple patch or two
stitched on, to shine far and wide.
Ars Poetica l. 14

12 *Brevis esse laboro,*
Obscurus fio.
I strive to be brief, and I become obscure.
Ars Poetica l. 25

13 *Grammatici certant et adhuc sub iudice lis est.*
Scholars dispute, and the case is still before
the courts.
Ars Poetica l. 78

14 *Proicit ampullas et sesquipedalia verba.*
He throws aside his paint-pots and his
words a foot and a half long.
Ars Poetica l. 97; cf. **Wells** 331:15

15 *Parturient montes, nascetur ridiculus mus.*
Mountains will go into labour, and a silly
little mouse will be born.
Ars Poetica l. 139

16 *Semper ad eventum festinat et in medias res*
Non secus ac notas auditorem rapit.
He always hurries to the main event and
whisks his audience into the middle of
things as though they knew already.
Ars Poetica l. 148

17 *Difficilis, querulus, laudator temporis acti*
Se puero, castigator censorque minorum.
Tiresome, complaining, a praiser of past
times, when he was a boy, a castigator and
censor of the young generation.
Ars Poetica l. 173

18 *Indignor quandoque bonus dormitat Homerus.*
I'm aggrieved when sometimes even
excellent Homer nods.
Ars Poetica l. 359; cf. **Byron** 78:25

19 *Ut pictura poesis.*
A poem is like a painting.
Ars Poetica l. 361

20 *Si possis recte, si non, quocumque modo rem.*
If possible honestly, if not, somehow, make
money.
Epistles bk. 1, no. 1, l. 66; cf. **Pope** 248:24

21 *Nos numerus sumus et fruges consumere nati.*
We are just statistics, born to consume
resources.
Epistles bk. 1, no. 2, l. 27

22 *Ira furor brevis est.*
Anger is a short madness.
Epistles bk. 1, no. 2, l. 62

23 *Nil admirari prope res est una, Numici,*
Solaque quae possit facere et servare beatum.
To marvel at nothing is just about the one
and only thing, Numicius, that can make a
man happy and keep him that way.
Epistles bk. 1, no. 6, l. 1; cf. **Pope** 248:25

24 *Naturam expelles furca, tamen usque recurret.*
You may drive out nature with a pitchfork,
yet she'll be constantly running back.
Epistles bk. 1, no. 10, l. 24

25 *Concordia discors.*
Discordant harmony.
Epistles bk. 1, no. 12, l. 19

26 *Et semel emissum volat irrevocabile verbum.*
And once sent out a word takes wing
beyond recall.
Epistles bk. 1, no. 18, l. 71

1 *Nam tua res agitur, paries cum proximus ardet.*
For it is your business, when the wall next door catches fire.
Epistles bk. 1, no. 18, l. 84

2 *O imitatores, servum pecus.*
O imitators, you slavish herd.
Epistles bk. 1, no. 19, l. 19

3 *Scribimus indocti doctique poemata passim.*
Skilled or unskilled, we all scribble poems.
Epistles bk. 2, no. 1, l. 117; cf. **Pope** 248:27

4 *Atque inter silvas Academi quaerere verum.*
And seek for truth in the groves of Academe.
Epistles bk. 2, no. 2, l. 45

5 *Multa fero, ut placem genus irritabile vatum.*
I have to put up with a lot, to please the touchy breed of poets.
Epistles bk. 2, no. 2, l. 102

6 *Nil desperandum.*
Never despair.
Odes bk. 1, no. 7, l. 27

7 *Dum loquimur, fugerit invida*
Aetas: carpe diem, quam minimum credula postero.
While we're talking, envious time is fleeing: seize the day, put no trust in the future.
Odes bk. 1, no. 11, l. 7

8 *Dulce ridentem Lalagen amabo,*
Dulce loquentem.
I will go on loving Lalage, who laughs so sweetly and talks so sweetly.
Odes bk. 1, no. 22, l. 23

9 *Nunc est bibendum, nunc pede libero*
Pulsanda tellus.
Now for drinking, now the Earth must shake beneath a lively foot.
Odes bk. 1, no. 37, l. 1

10 *Auream quisquis mediocritatem*
Diligit.
Someone who loves the golden mean.
Odes bk. 2, no. 10, l. 5

11 *Eheu fugaces, Postume, Postume,*
Labuntur anni.
Ah me, Postumus, Postumus, the fleeting years are slipping by.
Odes bk. 2, no. 14, l. 1

12 *Credite posteri.*
Believe me, you who come after me!
Odes bk. 2, no. 19, l. 2

13 *Post equitem sedet atra Cura.*
Black Care sits behind the horseman.
Odes bk. 3, no. 1, l. 40

14 *Dulce et decorum est pro patria mori.*
Lovely and honourable it is to die for one's country.
Odes bk. 3, no. 2, l. 13; cf. **Owen** 238:24, **Pound** 250:9

15 *Opaco*
Pelion imposuisse Olympo.
To pile Pelion on top of shady Olympus.
Odes bk. 3, no. 4, l. 52

16 *Exegi monumentum aere perennius.*
I have erected a monument more lasting than bronze.
Odes bk. 3, no. 30, l. 1

17 *Non omnis moriar.*
I shall not altogether die.
Odes bk. 3, no. 30, l. 6

18 *Non sum qualis eram bonae*
Sub regno Cinarae.
I am not as I was when good Cinara was my queen.
Odes bk. 4, no. 1, l. 3; cf. **Dowson** 115:10

19 *Est modus in rebus.*
There is moderation in everything.
Satires bk. 1, no. 1, l. 106

20 *Etiam disiecti membra poetae.*
Even though broken up, the limbs of a poet.
of **Ennius**
Satires bk. 1, no. 4, l. 62

21 *Hoc erat in votis: modus agri non ita magnus,*
Hortus ubi et tecto vicinus iugis aquae fons
Et paulum silvae super his foret.
This was among my prayers: a piece of land not so very large, where a garden should be and a spring of ever-flowing water near the house, and a bit of woodland as well as these.
Satires bk. 2, no. 6, l. 1; cf. **Mallet** 210:7

Samuel Horsley 1733–1806

22 In this country . . . the individual subject . . . 'has nothing to do with the laws but to obey them.'
defending a maxim he had used earlier in committee
speech, House of Lords, 13 November 1795

A. E. Housman 1859–1936

23 Oh who is that young sinner with the handcuffs on his wrists?
And what has he been after that they groan and shake their fists?
And wherefore is he wearing such a conscience-stricken air?
Oh they're taking him to prison for the colour of his hair.
first drafted in summer 1895, following the trial and imprisonment of Oscar **Wilde**
Collected Poems (1939) 'Additional Poems' no. 18

24 The Grizzly Bear is huge and wild;
He has devoured the infant child.
The infant child is not aware
He has been eaten by the bear.
'Infant Innocence' (1938)

25 I, a stranger and afraid
In a world I never made.
Last Poems (1922) no. 12

26 Their shoulders held the sky suspended;
They stood, and earth's foundations stay;
What God abandoned, these defended,
And saved the sum of things for pay.
Last Poems (1922) no. 37 'Epitaph on an Army of Mercenaries'

1 Life, to be sure, is nothing much to lose;
But young men think it is, and we were
young.
More Poems (1936) no. 36

2 Loveliest of trees, the cherry now
Is hung with bloom along the bough,
And stands about the woodland ride
Wearing white for Eastertide.
A Shropshire Lad (1896) no. 2

3 And naked to the hangman's noose
The morning clocks will ring
A neck God made for other use
Than strangling in a string.
A Shropshire Lad (1896) no. 9

4 In summertime on Bredon
The bells they sound so clear;
Round both the shires they ring them
In steeples far and near,
A happy noise to hear.
Here of a Sunday morning
My love and I would lie,
And see the coloured counties,
And hear the larks so high
About us in the sky.
A Shropshire Lad (1896) no. 21

5 On Wenlock Edge the wood's in trouble;
His forest fleece the Wrekin heaves.
A Shropshire Lad (1896) no. 31

6 To-day the Roman and his trouble
Are ashes under Uricon.
A Shropshire Lad (1896) no. 31

7 What are those blue remembered hills,
What spires, what farms are those?
That is the land of lost content,
I see it shining plain,
The happy highways where I went
And cannot come again.
A Shropshire Lad (1896) no. 40

8 Clunton and Clunbury,
Clungunford and Clun,
Are the quietest places
Under the sun.
A Shropshire Lad (1896) no. 50 (epigraph)

9 By brooks too broad for leaping
The lightfoot boys are laid.
A Shropshire Lad (1896) no. 54

10 And malt does more than Milton can
To justify God's ways to man.
A Shropshire Lad (1896) no. 62; cf. **Milton** 221:2

11 Mithridates, he died old.
A Shropshire Lad (1896) no. 62

Samuel Houston 1793–1863

12 The North is determined to preserve this
Union. They are not a fiery, impulsive
people as you are, for they live in colder
climates. But when they begin to move in a
given direction . . . they move with the
steady momentum and perseverance of a
mighty avalanche.
*in 1861, warning the people of Texas against
secession*
Geoffrey C. Ward *The Civil War* (1991) ch. 1

Geoffrey Howe 1926–

13 It is rather like sending your opening
batsmen to the crease only for them to find
the moment that the first balls are bowled
that their bats have been broken before the
game by the team captain.
*on the difficulties caused him as Foreign Secretary
by Margaret **Thatcher**'s anti-European views*
resignation speech as Deputy Prime Minister, in
the House of Commons, 13 November 1990

14 The time has come for others to consider
their own response to the tragic conflict of
loyalties with which I have myself wrestled
for perhaps too long.
resignation speech
in the House of Commons, 13 November 1990

Julia Ward Howe 1819–1910

15 Mine eyes have seen the glory of the
coming of the Lord:
He is trampling out the vintage where the
grapes of wrath are stored;
He hath loosed the fateful lightning of his
terrible swift sword:
His truth is marching on.
'Battle Hymn of the Republic' (1862)

James Howell *c.*1594–1666

16 Some hold translations not unlike to be
The wrong side of a Turkey tapestry.
Familiar Letters (1645–55) bk. 1, no. 6

17 The Netherlands have been for many years,
as one may say, the very cockpit of
Christendom.
Instructions for Foreign Travel (1642)

Frankie Howerd 1922–92

18 Such cruel glasses.
of Robin Day
in *That Was The Week That Was* (BBC television
series, from 1963)

19 It's television, you see. If you are not on the
thing every week, the public think you are
either dead or deported.
attributed

Mary Howitt 1799–1888

20 Buttercups and daisies,
Oh, the pretty flowers;
Coming ere the springtime,
To tell of sunny hours.
'Buttercups and Daisies' (1838)

21 'Will you walk into my parlour?' said a
spider to a fly:
''Tis the prettiest little parlour that ever you
did spy.'
'The Spider and the Fly' (1834)

Edmond Hoyle 1672–1769

22 When in doubt, win the trick.
Hoyle's Games Improved (ed. Charles Jones, 1790)
'Twenty-four Short Rules for Learners'; though
attributed to Hoyle, it is not found in earlier
editions

Fred Hoyle 1915–

1 Space isn't remote at all. It's only an hour's drive away if your car could go straight upwards.

in *Observer* 9 September 1979 'Sayings of the Week'

Elbert Hubbard 1859–1915

2 Never explain—your friends do not need it and your enemies will not believe you anyway.

The Motto Book (1907); cf. **Disraeli** 128:6

3 Life is just one damned thing after another.

Philistine December 1909; often attributed to Frank Ward O'Malley

4 Editor: a person employed by a newspaper, whose business it is to separate the wheat from the chaff, and to see that the chaff is printed.

The Roycroft Dictionary (1914)

Frank McKinney ('Kin') Hubbard 1868–1930

5 Classic music is th'kind that we keep thinkin'll turn into a tune.

Comments of Abe Martin and His Neighbors (1923)

6 It's no disgrace t'be poor, but it might as well be.

Short Furrows (1911)

Jimmy Hughes
and **Frank Lake**

7 You'll get no promotion this side of the ocean,
So cheer up, my lads, Bless 'em all!
Bless 'em all! Bless 'em all! The long and the short and the tall.

'Bless 'Em All' (1940 song)

Langston Hughes 1902–67

8 I, too, sing America.
I am the darker brother.
They send me to eat in the kitchen
When company comes.

'I, Too' in *Survey Graphic* March 1925

9 I've known rivers:
I've known rivers ancient as the world and older than the flow of human blood in human veins.

'The Negro Speaks of Rivers' (1921)

Ted Hughes 1930–98

10 It took the whole of Creation
To produce my foot, my each feather:
Now I hold Creation in my foot.

'Hawk Roosting' (1960)

11 Fourteen centuries have learned,
From charred remains, that what took place
When Alexandria's library burned
Brain-damaged the human race.

'Hear it Again' (1997)

12 . . . With a sudden sharp hot stink of fox,
It enters the dark hole of the head.

'The Thought-Fox' (1957)

13 Ten years after your death
I meet on a page of your journal, as never before,
The shock of your joy.

'Visit' (1998)

Thomas Hughes 1822–96

14 It's more than a game. It's an institution.

of cricket

Tom Brown's Schooldays (1857) pt. 2, ch. 7

Victor Hugo 1802–85

15 The word is the Verb, and the Verb is God.

Contemplations (1856) bk. 1, no. 8

16 A stand can be made against invasion by an army; no stand can be made against invasion by an idea.

Histoire d'un Crime (written 1851–2, published 1877) pt. 5, sect. 10

17 Take away *time is money*, and what is left of England? take away *cotton is king*, and what is left of America?

Les Misérables (1862) 'Marius' bk. 4 ch. 4

David Hume 1711–76

18 Custom, then, is the great guide of human life.

An Enquiry Concerning Human Understanding (1748) sect. 5, pt. 1

19 If we take in our hand any volume; of divinity or school metaphysics, for instance; let us ask, *Does it contain any abstract reasoning concerning quantity or number?* No. *Does it contain any experimental reasoning, concerning matter of fact and existence?* No. Commit it then to the flames: for it can contain nothing but sophistry and illusion.

An Enquiry Concerning Human Understanding (1748) sect. 12, pt. 3

20 Avarice, the spur of industry.

Essays: Moral and Political (1741–2) 'Of Civil Liberty'

21 Money . . . is none of the wheels of trade: it is the oil which renders the motion of the wheels more smooth and easy.

Essays: Moral and Political (1741–2) 'Of Money'

22 Never literary attempt was more unfortunate than my Treatise of Human Nature. It fell *dead-born from the press.*

My Own Life (1777) ch. 1

23 It is not contrary to reason to prefer the destruction of the whole world to the scratching of my finger.

A Treatise upon Human Nature (1739) bk. 2, pt. 3

G. W. Hunt *c.*1829–1904

24 We don't want to fight, but, by jingo if we do,
We've got the ships, we've got the men, we've got the money too.

'We Don't Want to Fight' (1878 music hall song)

Leigh Hunt 1784–1859

1 Abou Ben Adhem (may his tribe increase!)
Awoke one night from a deep dream of
peace.
'Abou Ben Adhem' (1838)

2 Write me as one that loves his fellow-men.
'Abou Ben Adhem' (1838)

3 The laughing queen that caught the world's
great hands.
referring to Cleopatra
'The Nile' (1818)

4 Jenny kissed me when we met,
Jumping from the chair she sat in.
'Rondeau' (1838)

5 This Adonis in loveliness was a corpulent
man of fifty.
of the Prince Regent
in *The Examiner* 22 March 1812

Anne Hunter 1742–1821

6 My mother bids me bind my hair
With bands of rosy hue,
Tie up my sleeves with ribbons rare,
And lace my bodice blue.
'A Pastoral Song' (1794)

Robert Hunter 1941–

7 The word *Greenpeace* had a ring to it—it
conjured images of Eden; it said ecology and
antiwar in two syllables; it fit easily into
even a one-column headline.
Warriors of the Rainbow (1979); cf. **Darnell** 106:4

Herman Hupfeld 1894–1951

8 You must remember this, a kiss is still a
kiss,
A sigh is just a sigh;
The fundamental things apply,
As time goes by.
'As Time Goes By' (1931 song)

Zora Neale Hurston c.1901–60

9 I do not weep at the world—I am too busy
sharpening my oyster knife.
How It Feels to Be Colored Me (1928)

John Huss c.1372–1415

10 *O sancta simplicitas!*
O holy simplicity!
*at the stake, seeing an aged peasant bringing a
bundle of twigs to throw on the pile*
J. W. Zincgreff and J. L. Weidner *Apophthegmata*
(Amsterdam, 1653) pt. 3; cf. **Jerome** 172:3

Saddam Hussein 1937–

11 The mother of battles.
*popular interpretation of his description of the
approaching Gulf War*
speech in Baghdad, 6 January 1991

Francis Hutcheson 1694–1746

12 Wisdom denotes the pursuing of the best
ends by the best means.
*An Inquiry into the Original of our Ideas of Beauty
and Virtue* (1725) Treatise 1

13 That action is best, which procures the
greatest happiness for the greatest
numbers.
*An Inquiry into the Original of our Ideas of Beauty
and Virtue* (1725) Treatise 2; cf. **Bentham** 30:3

Aldous Huxley 1894–1963

14 The proper study of mankind is books.
Crome Yellow (1921) ch. 28; cf. **Pope** 248:15

15 Consistency is contrary to nature, contrary
to life. The only completely consistent
people are the dead.
Do What You Will (1929) 'Wordsworth in the
Tropics'

16 So long as men worship the Caesars and
Napoleons, Caesars and Napoleons will duly
arise and make them miserable.
Ends and Means (1937) ch. 8

17 Chastity—the most unnatural of all the
sexual perversions.
Eyeless in Gaza (1936) ch. 27

18 Beauty for some provides escape,
Who gain a happiness in eyeing
The gorgeous buttocks of the ape
Or Autumn sunsets exquisitely dying.
'Ninth Philosopher's Song' (1920)

Julian Huxley 1887–1975

19 Operationally, God is beginning to resemble
not a ruler but the last fading smile of a
cosmic Cheshire cat.
Religion without Revelation (1957 ed.) ch. 3; cf.
Carroll 83:18

T. H. Huxley 1825–95

20 Most of my colleagues [in the Metaphysical
Society] were -*ists* of one sort or another;
and, however kind and friendly they might
be, I, the man without a rag of a label to
cover himself with, could not fail to have
some of the uneasy feelings which must
have beset the historical fox when, after
leaving the trap in which his tail remained,
he presented himself to his normally
elongated companions. So I took thought,
and invented what I conceived to be the
appropriate title of 'agnostic'.
Collected Essays (1893–4) 'Agnosticism'

21 The great tragedy of Science—the slaying of
a beautiful hypothesis by an ugly fact.
Collected Essays (1893–4) 'Biogenesis and
Abiogenesis'

22 If a little knowledge is dangerous, where is
the man who has so much as to be out of
danger?
Collected Essays vol. 3 (1895) 'On Elementary
Instruction in Physiology' (written 1877)

1 It is the customary fate of new truths to begin as heresies and to end as superstitions.
Science and Culture and Other Essays (1881) 'The Coming of Age of the Origin of Species'

2 Irrationally held truths may be more harmful than reasoned errors.
Science and Culture and Other Essays (1881) 'The Coming of Age of the Origin of Species'

3 Logical consequences are the scarecrows of fools and the beacons of wise men.
Science and Culture and Other Essays (1881) 'On the Hypothesis that Animals are Automata'

4 A man has no reason to be ashamed of having an ape for his grandfather. If there were an ancestor whom I should feel shame in recalling it would rather be a *man*—a man of restless and versatile intellect—who, not content with an equivocal success in his own sphere of activity, plunges into scientific questions with which he has no real acquaintance, only to obscure them by an aimless rhetoric, and distract the attention of his hearers from the real point at issue by eloquent digressions and skilled appeals to religious prejudice.
*replying to Bishop Samuel **Wilberforce** in the debate on **Darwin**'s theory of evolution; see **Wilberforce** 334:16*
meeting of the British Association in Oxford, 30 June 1860

5 I am too much of a sceptic to deny the possibility of anything.
letter to Herbert Spencer, 22 March 1886

Edward Hyde *see* **Earl of Clarendon**

Nicholas Hytner 1956–

6 If you gave him a good script, actors and technicians, Mickey Mouse could direct a movie.
in an interview, *Daily Telegraph* 24 February 1994

Dolores Ibarruri ('La Pasionaria') 1895–1989

7 It is better to die on your feet than to live on your knees.
*also attributed to Emiliano **Zapata***
speech in Paris, 3 September 1936

8 *No pasarán.*
They shall not pass.
radio broadcast, Madrid, 19 July 1936

Henrik Ibsen 1828–1906

9 The majority never has right on its side.
An Enemy of the People (1882) act 4; cf. **Dillon** 111:24

10 You should never have your best trousers on when you go out to fight for freedom and truth.
An Enemy of the People (1882) act 5

11 Mother, give me the sun.
Ghosts (1881) act 3

12 But good God, people don't do such things!
Hedda Gabler (1890) act 4

13 Castles in the air—they are so easy to take refuge in. And easy to build, too.
The Master Builder (1892) act 3

14 On the contrary.
last words, after a nurse had said that he 'seemed to be a little better'
Michael Meyer *Ibsen* (1967)

Ice Cube 1970–

15 If I'm more of an influence to your son as a rapper than you are as a father . . . you got to look at yourself as a parent.
to Mike Sager in *Rolling Stone* 4 October 1990

Ice-T 1958–

16 Passion makes the world go round. Love just makes it a safer place.
The Ice Opinion (as told to Heidi Sigmund, 1994) ch. 4

St Ignatius Loyola 1491–1556

17 Teach us, good Lord, to serve Thee as Thou deservest:
To give and not to count the cost;
To fight and not to heed the wounds;
To toil and not to seek for rest;
To labour and not to ask for any reward
Save that of knowing that we do Thy will.
'Prayer for Generosity' (1548)

Ivan Illich 1926–

18 In a consumer society there are inevitably two kinds of slaves: the prisoners of addiction and the prisoners of envy.
Tools for Conviviality (1973) ch. 3

William Ralph Inge 1860–1954

19 To become a popular religion, it is only necessary for a superstition to enslave a philosophy.
Idea of Progress (Romanes Lecture delivered at Oxford, 27 May 1920)

20 Many people believe that they are attracted by God, or by Nature, when they are only repelled by man.
More Lay Thoughts of a Dean (1931) pt. 4, ch. 1

21 It takes in reality only one to make a quarrel. It is useless for the sheep to pass resolutions in favour of vegetarianism, while the wolf remains of a different opinion.
Outspoken Essays: First Series (1919) 'Patriotism'

22 A man may build himself a throne of bayonets, but he cannot sit on it.
*a similar image was used by Boris **Yeltsin** at the time of the failed military coup in Russia, August 1991*
Philosophy of Plotinus (1923) vol. 2, Lecture 22

Jean Ingelow 1820–97

23 Play uppe 'The Brides of Enderby'.
'The High Tide on the Coast of Lincolnshire, 1571' (1863)

1 But each will mourn her own (she saith)
And sweeter woman ne'er drew breath
Than my sonne's wife, Elizabeth.
'The High Tide on the Coast of Lincolnshire,
1571' (1863)

Robert G. Ingersoll 1833–99

2 An honest God is the noblest work of man.
The Gods (1876) pt. 1; cf. **Pope** 248:20

Bernard Ingham 1932–

3 Blood sport is brought to its ultimate
refinement in the gossip columns.
speech, 5 February 1986

John Kells Ingram 1823–1907

4 They rose in dark and evil days.
'The Memory of the Dead' (1843)

5 Who fears to speak of Ninety-Eight?
Who blushes at the name?
'The Memory of the Dead' (1843)

J. A. D. Ingres 1780–1867

6 Drawing is the true test of art.
Pensées d'Ingres (1922)

Eugène Ionesco 1912–94

7 A civil servant doesn't make jokes.
Tueur sans gages (The Killer, 1958) act 1

St Irenaeus *c.*130–*c.*200 AD

8 The glory of God is a man fully alive.
attributed

Weldon J. Irvine

9 Young, gifted and black.
title of song (1969); cf. **Hansberry** 151:4

Washington Irving 1783–1859

10 A sharp tongue is the only edged tool that
grows keener with constant use.
The Sketch Book (1820) 'Rip Van Winkle'

11 The almighty dollar, that great object of
universal devotion.
Wolfert's Roost (1855) 'The Creole Village'

Christopher Isherwood 1904–86

12 The common cormorant (or shag)
Lays eggs inside a paper bag,
You follow the idea, no doubt?
It's to keep the lightning out.
But what these unobservant birds
Have never thought of, is that herds
Of wandering bears might come with buns
And steal the bags to hold the crumbs.
'The Common Cormorant' (written *c.*1925)

13 I am a camera with its shutter open, quite
passive, recording, not thinking.
Goodbye to Berlin (1939) 'Berlin Diary' Autumn
1930

Alec Issigonis 1906–88

14 A camel is a horse designed by a committee.
on his dislike of working in teams
in *Guardian* 14 January 1991 'Notes and
Queries'; attributed

Alija Izetbegović 1925–

15 And to my people I say, this may not be a
just peace, but it is more just than a
continuation of war.
*after signing the Dayton accord with
representatives of Serbia and Croatia*
in Dayton, Ohio, 21 November 1995

Andrew Jackson 1767–1845

16 Our Federal Union: it must be preserved.
*toast given at the Jefferson Birthday
Celebration, 13 April 1830*

Holbrook Jackson 1874–1948

17 Pedantry is the dotage of knowledge.
Anatomy of Bibliomania (1930) vol. 1

Jesse Jackson 1941–

18 When I look out at this convention, I see
the face of America, red, yellow, brown,
black, and white. We are all precious in
God's sight—the real rainbow coalition.
speech at Democratic National Convention,
Atlanta, 19 July 1988

Michael Jackson 1958–

19 Before you judge me, try hard to love me,
look within your heart
Then ask,—have you seen my childhood?
'Childhood' (1995 song)

Robert H. Jackson 1892–1954

20 That four great nations, flushed with victory
and stung with injury, stay the hands of
vengeance and voluntarily submit their
captive enemies to the judgement of the
law, is one of the most significant tributes
that Power has ever paid to Reason.
*opening statement for the prosecution at
Nuremberg*
before the International Military Tribunal in
Nuremberg, 21 November 1945

Joe Jacobs 1896–1940

21 We was robbed!
*after Jack Sharkey beat Max Schmeling (of whom
Jacobs was manager) in the heavyweight title
fight, 21 June 1932*
Peter Heller *In This Corner* (1975)

22 I should of stood in bed.
*after leaving his sick-bed to attend the World
Baseball Series in Detroit, 1935, and betting on
the losers*
John Lardner *Strong Cigars* (1951)

Jacopone da Todi *c.*1230–1306

23 *Stabat Mater dolorosa,
Iuxta crucem lacrimosa.*

At the cross her station keeping,
Stood the mournful Mother weeping.
'Stabat Mater dolorosa', ascribed also to Pope
Innocent III and others (translation based on
that of E. Caswall in *Lyra Catholica*, 1849)

Mick Jagger 1943-
and Keith Richards 1943-

1 Get off of my cloud.
title of song (1966)

2 And though she's not really ill,
There's a little yellow pill:
She goes running for the shelter
Of a mother's little helper.
'Mother's Little Helper' (1966 song)

3 I can't get no satisfaction
I can't get no girl reaction
'(I Can't Get No) Satisfaction' (1965 song)

4 Ev'rywhere I hear the sound of marching,
charging feet, boy.
'Street Fighting Man' (1968 song)

Richard Jago 1715-81

5 With leaden foot time creeps along
While Delia is away.
'Absence'

Jaina Sutras
textual translations are those of H. Jacobi, 1884

6 This is the quintessence of wisdom: not to
kill anything. Know this to be the legitimate
conclusion from the principle of the
reciprocity with regard to non-killing.
Sūtrakritānga bk. 1, lecture 1, ch. 4, v. 10

7 Exert and control yourself! For it is not easy
to walk on ways where there are minutely
small animals.
Sūtrakritānga bk. 1, lecture 2, ch. 1, v. 11

James I (James VI of Scotland)
1566-1625

8 A custom loathsome to the eye, hateful to
the nose, harmful to the brain, dangerous to
the lungs, and in the black, stinking fume
thereof, nearest resembling the horrible
Stygian smoke of the pit that is bottomless.
A Counterblast to Tobacco (1604)

9 No bishop, no King.
*to a deputation of Presbyterians from the Church
of Scotland, seeking religious tolerance in England*
W. Barlow *Sum and Substance of the Conference*
(1604)

10 The king is truly *parens patriae*, the politique
father of his people.
speech to Parliament, 21 March 1610

11 Dr Donne's verses are like the peace of God;
they pass all understanding.
remark recorded by Archdeacon Plume
(1630-1704); cf. **Bible** 50:27

12 I made the carles lords, but who made the
carlines ladies?
E. Grenville Murray *Embassies and Foreign Courts*
(1855) ch. 14

James V 1512-42

13 It came with a lass, and it will pass with a
lass.
*of the crown of Scotland, on learning of the birth
of **Mary** Queen of Scots, December 1542*
Robert Lindsay of Pitscottie (*c.*1500-65) *History of
Scotland* (1728)

Evan James

14 The land of my fathers, how fair is thy
fame.
'Land of My Fathers' (1856), translated by W. G.
Rothery

Henry James 1843-1916

15 Most English talk is a quadrille in a sentry-
box.
The Awkward Age (1899) bk. 5, ch. 19

16 The black and merciless things that are
behind the great possessions.
The Ivory Tower (1917) notes

17 Cats and monkeys—monkeys and cats—all
human life is there!
The Madonna of the Future (1879) vol. 1

18 We work in the dark—we do what we
can—we give what we have. Our doubt is
our passion and our passion is our task. The
rest is the madness of art.
'The Middle Years' (short story, 1893)

19 What is character but the determination of
incident? What is incident but the
illustration of character?
Partial Portraits (1888) 'The Art of Fiction'

20 The house of fiction has in short not one
window, but a million . . . but they are,
singly or together, as nothing without the
posted presence of the watcher.
The Portrait of a Lady (1908 ed.) preface

21 The note I wanted; that of the strange and
sinister embroidered on the very type of the
normal and easy.
Prefaces (1909) 'The Altar of the Dead'

22 The time-honoured bread-sauce of the
happy ending.
Theatricals (1894) 2nd series

23 The turn of the screw
title of novel (1898)

24 We were alone with the quiet day, and his
little heart, dispossessed, had stopped.
The Turn of the Screw (1898)

25 The war has used up words.
in *New York Times* 21 March 1915

26 Of course, of course.
*on hearing that Rupert **Brooke** had died on a
Greek island*
C. Hassall *Rupert Brooke* (1964) ch. 14

27 Summer afternoon—summer afternoon . . .
the two most beautiful words in the English
language.
Edith Wharton *A Backward Glance* (1934) ch. 10

28 So here it is at last, the distinguished thing!
on experiencing his first stroke
Edith Wharton *A Backward Glance* (1934) ch. 14

P. D. James 1920–

1 What the detective story is about is not murder but the restoration of order.

in *Face* December 1986

2 I had an interest in death from an early age. It fascinated me. When I heard 'Humpty Dumpty sat on a wall,' I thought, 'Did he fall or was he pushed?'

in *Paris Review* 1995

William James 1842–1910

3 There is no worse lie than a truth misunderstood by those who hear it.

The Varieties of Religious Experience (1902)

4 The moral flabbiness born of the exclusive worship of the bitch-goddess *success*.

letter to H. G. Wells, 11 September 1906

5 Hogamus, higamous
Man is polygamous
Higamus, hogamous
Woman monogamous.

in *Oxford Book of Marriage* (1990)

Randall Jarrell 1914–65

6 In bombers named for girls, we burned
The cities we had learned about in school—
Till our lives wore out; our bodies lay among
The people we had killed and never seen.
When we lasted long enough they gave us medals;
When we died they said, 'Our casualties were low.'

'Losses' (1963)

7 It is better to entertain an idea than to take it home to live with you for the rest of your life.

Pictures from an Institution (1954) pt. 1, ch. 4

Douglas Jay 1907–96

8 In the case of nutrition and health, just as in the case of education, the gentleman in Whitehall really does know better what is good for people than the people know themselves.

The Socialist Case (1939) ch. 30

Jean Paul *see* Johann Paul Friedrich Richter

James Jeans 1877–1946

9 If we assume that the last breath of, say, Julius Caesar has by now become thoroughly scattered through the atmosphere, then the chances are that each of us inhales one molecule of it with every breath we take.

now usually quoted as the 'dying breath of Socrates'

An Introduction to the Kinetic Theory of Gases (1940)

10 Life exists in the universe only because the carbon atom possesses certain exceptional properties.

The Mysterious Universe (1930) ch. 1

11 From the intrinsic evidence of his creation, the Great Architect of the Universe now begins to appear as a pure mathematician.

The Mysterious Universe (1930) ch. 5

Thomas Jefferson 1743–1826

12 We hold these truths to be sacred and undeniable; that all men are created equal and independent, that from that equal creation they derive rights inherent and inalienable, among which are the preservation of life, and liberty, and the pursuit of happiness.

'Rough Draft' of the American Declaration of Independence, in J. P. Boyd et al. *Papers of Thomas Jefferson* (1950) vol. 1; cf. **Anonymous** 10:14

13 The tree of liberty must be refreshed from time to time with the blood of patriots and tyrants. It is its natural manure.

letter to W. S. Smith, 13 November 1787

14 If a due participation of office is a matter of right, how are vacancies to be obtained? Those by death are few; by resignation none.

often quoted as, 'Few die and none resign'

letter to E. Shipman and others, 12 July 1801

15 When a man assumes a public trust, he should consider himself as public property.

to Baron von Humboldt, 1807

16 We have the wolf by the ears; and we can neither hold him, nor safely let him go. Justice is in one scale, and self-preservation in the other.

on slavery

letter to John Holmes, 22 April 1820

17 To attain all this [universal republicanism], however, rivers of blood must yet flow, and years of desolation pass over; yet the object is worth rivers of blood, and years of desolation.

letter to John Adams, 4 September 1823; cf. **Powell** 250:23, **Virgil** 324:19

18 Indeed I tremble for my country when I reflect that God is just.

Notes on the State of Virginia (1781–5) Query 18

Francis, Lord Jeffrey 1773–1850

19 This will never do.

on **Wordsworth**'*s* The Excursion *(1814)*

in *Edinburgh Review* November 1814

David Jenkins 1925–

20 I am not clear that God manoeuvres physical things . . . After all, a conjuring trick with bones only proves that it is as clever as a conjuring trick with bones.

on the Resurrection

in 'Poles Apart' (BBC radio, 4 October 1984)

Roy Jenkins 1920–

21 The politics of the left and centre of this country are frozen in an out-of-date mould which is bad for the political and economic health of Britain and increasingly inhibiting for those who live within the mould. Can it be broken?

speech to Parliamentary Press Gallery, 9 June 1980, in *The Times* 10 June 1980

1 Nearly all Prime Ministers are dissatisfied with their successors, perhaps even more so if they come from their own party.

Gladstone (1995)

Elizabeth Jennings 1926–

2 I hate a word like 'pets': it sounds so much Like something with no living of its own.
'My Animals' (1966)

St Jerome *c*.AD 342–420

3 *Venerationi mihi semper fuit non verbosa rusticitas, sed sancta simplicitas.*
I have revered always not crude verbosity, but holy simplicity.
letter 57, To Pammachius; cf. **Huss** 167:10

4 The Roman world is falling, yet we hold our heads erect instead of bowing our necks.
letter 60, To Heliodorus, AD 396

Jerome K. Jerome 1859–1927

5 It is a most extraordinary thing, but I never read a patent medicine advertisement without being impelled to the conclusion that I am suffering from the particular disease therein dealt with in its most virulent form.
Three Men in a Boat (1889) ch. 1

6 I like work: it fascinates me. I can sit and look at it for hours. I love to keep it by me: the idea of getting rid of it nearly breaks my heart.
Three Men in a Boat (1889) ch. 15

William Jerome 1865–1932

7 Any old place I can hang my hat is home sweet home to me.
title of song (1901)

Douglas Jerrold 1803–57

8 The best thing I know between France and England is—the sea.
The Wit and Opinions of Douglas Jerrold (1859) 'The Anglo-French Alliance'

9 Earth is here so kind, that just tickle her with a hoe and she laughs with a harvest.
of Australia
The Wit and Opinions of Douglas Jerrold (1859) 'A Land of Plenty'

John Jewel 1522–71

10 In old time we had treen chalices and golden priests, but now we have treen priests and golden chalices.
Certain Sermons Preached Before the Queen's Majesty (1609)

Pope John XXIII 1881–1963

11 If civil authorities legislate for or allow anything that is contrary to that order and

therefore contrary to the will of God, neither the laws made or the authorizations granted can be binding on the consciences of the citizens, since God has more right to be obeyed than man.
Pacem in Terris (1963)

12 I want to throw open the windows of the Church so that we can see out and the people can see in.
attributed

St John of the Cross 1542–91

13 *Muero porque no muero.*
I die because I do not die.
*the same words occur in St **Teresa** of Ávila 'Versos nacidos del fuego del amor de Dios' (c.1571–3)*
'Coplas del alma que pena por ver a Dios' (c.1578)

14 *Noche oscura.*
Dark night.
often quoted as, 'Faith, the dark night of the soul'; the phrase appears in the chapter heading for the poem in Complete Works *(1864), translated by David Lewis*
title of poem, St John of the Cross (1542–91) *The Ascent of Mount Carmel* (1578–80)

Elton John 1947– and **Bernie Taupin** 1950–

15 Goodbye Norma Jean . . .
It seems to me you lived your life
Like a candle in the wind.
Never knowing who to cling to
When the rain set in.
*of Marilyn **Monroe***
'Candle in the Wind' (song, 1973)

16 The candle burned out long before
Your legend ever did.
'Candle in the Wind' (song, 1973)

17 Goodbye England's rose;
May you ever grow in our hearts.
*rewritten for and sung at the funeral of **Diana**, Princess of Wales, 7 September 1997*
'Candle in the Wind' (song, revised version, 1997)

18 And it seems to me you lived your life
Like a candle in the wind:
Never fading with the sunset
When the rain set in.
And your footsteps will always fall here
On England's greenest hills;
Your candle's burned out long before
Your legend ever will.
'Candle in the Wind' (song, revised version, 1997)

19 Goodbye yellow brick road.
title of song (1973); cf. **Harburg** 151:10

Pope John Paul II 1920–

20 It would be simplistic to say that Divine Providence caused the fall of communism. It fell by itself as a consequence of its own

mistakes and abuses. It fell by itself because of its own inherent weaknesses.

when asked if the fall of the USSR could be ascribed to God

Carl Bernstein and Marco Politi *His Holiness: John Paul II and the Hidden History of our Time* (1996)

Lyndon Baines Johnson 1908–73

1 I am a free man, an American, a United States Senator, and a Democrat, in that order.

in *Texas Quarterly* Winter 1958

2 All I have I would have given gladly not to be standing here today.

following the assassination of J. F. Kennedy

first speech to Congress as President, 27 November 1963

3 In your time we have the opportunity to move not only toward the rich society and the powerful society, but upward to the Great Society.

speech at University of Michigan, 22 May 1964

4 We are not about to send American boys 9 or 10,000 miles away from home to do what Asian boys ought to be doing for themselves.

speech at Akron University, 21 October 1964

5 I don't want loyalty. I want *loyalty*. I want him to kiss my ass in Macy's window at high noon and tell me it smells like roses. I want his pecker in my pocket.

discussing a prospective assistant

David Halberstam *The Best and the Brightest* (1972) ch. 20

6 Better to have him inside the tent pissing out, than outside pissing in.

of J. Edgar Hoover

David Halberstam *The Best and the Brightest* (1972) ch. 20

7 So dumb he can't fart and chew gum at the same time.

of Gerald Ford

Richard Reeves *A Ford, not a Lincoln* (1975) ch. 2

Philander Chase Johnson 1866–1939

8 Cheer up! the worst is yet to come!

in *Everybody's Magazine* May 1920

Philip Johnson 1906–

9 Architecture is the art of how to waste space.

New York Times 27 December 1964

Samuel Johnson 1709–84

10 Change is not made without inconvenience, even from worse to better.

A Dictionary of the English Language (1755) preface; cf. **Hooker** 162:9

11 I am not yet so lost in lexicography as to forget that words are the daughters of earth, and that things are the sons of heaven. Language is only the instrument of science, and words are but the signs of ideas: I wish, however, that the instrument might be less apt to decay, and that signs might be permanent, like the things which they denote.

A Dictionary of the English Language (1755) preface; cf. **Madden** 209:4

12 But these were the dreams of a poet doomed at last to wake a lexicographer.

A Dictionary of the English Language (1755) preface

13 *Lexicographer*. A writer of dictionaries, a harmless drudge.

A Dictionary of the English Language (1755)

14 *Network*. Anything reticulated or decussated at equal distances, with interstices between the intersections.

A Dictionary of the English Language (1755)

15 *Oats*. A grain, which in England is generally given to horses, but in Scotland supports the people.

A Dictionary of the English Language (1755)

16 *Patron*. Commonly a wretch who supports with insolence, and is paid with flattery.

A Dictionary of the English Language (1755)

17 Among the calamities of war may be jointly numbered the diminution of the love of truth, by the falsehoods which interest dictates and credulity encourages.

in *The Idler* no. 30 (11 November 1758)

18 Promise, large promise, is the soul of an advertisement.

The Idler no. 40 (20 January 1759)

19 Language is the dress of thought.

Lives of the English Poets (1779–81) 'Cowley'; cf. **Pope** 248:2, **Wesley** 332:10

20 The father of English criticism.

Lives of the English Poets (1779–81) 'Dryden'

21 I am disappointed by that stroke of death, which has eclipsed the gaiety of nations and impoverished the public stock of harmless pleasure.

on the death of Garrick

Lives of the English Poets (1779–81) 'Edmund Smith'

22 I have always suspected that the reading is right, which requires many words to prove it wrong; and the emendation wrong, that cannot without so much labour appear to be right.

Plays of William Shakespeare . . . (1765) preface

23 No place affords a more striking conviction of the vanity of human hopes, than a public library.

in *The Rambler* no. 106 (23 March 1751)

24 He [the poet] must write as the interpreter of nature, and the legislator of mankind.

Rasselas (1759) ch. 10; cf. **Shelley** 294:6

25 Human life is everywhere a state in which much is to be endured, and little to be enjoyed.

Rasselas (1759) ch. 11

26 Marriage has many pains, but celibacy has no pleasures.

Rasselas (1759) ch. 26

1 Example is always more efficacious than precept.
   Rasselas (1759) ch. 30

2 I consider this mighty structure as a monument of the insufficiency of human enjoyments.
   of the Pyramids
   Rasselas (1759) ch. 32

3 How small of all that human hearts endure,
   That part which laws or kings can cause or cure.
   Still to ourselves in every place consigned,
   Our own felicity we make or find.
   lines added to Oliver Goldsmith's *The Traveller* (1764) l. 429; cf. **Goldsmith** 143:23

4 Let observation with extensive view,
   Survey mankind, from China to Peru.
   The Vanity of Human Wishes (1749) l. 1

5 A frame of adamant, a soul of fire,
   No dangers fright him, and no labours tire.
   of Charles XII of Sweden
   The Vanity of Human Wishes (1749) l. 193

6 He left the name, at which the world grew pale,
   To point a moral, or adorn a tale.
   of Charles XII of Sweden
   The Vanity of Human Wishes (1749) l. 221

7 Hides from himself his state, and shuns to know,
   That life protracted is protracted woe.
   The Vanity of Human Wishes (1749) l. 257

8 Still raise for good the supplicating voice,
   But leave to heaven the measure and the choice.
   The Vanity of Human Wishes (1749) l. 351

9 A lawyer has no business with the justice or injustice of the cause which he undertakes, unless his client asks his opinion, and then he is bound to give it honestly. The justice or injustice of the cause is to be decided by the judge.
   James Boswell *Journal of a Tour to the Hebrides* (1785) 15 August 1773

10 I inherited a vile melancholy from my father, which has made me mad all my life, at least not sober.
   James Boswell *Tour to the Hebrides* (1785) 16 September 1773; cf. **Johnson** 176:16

11 I am always sorry when any language is lost, because languages are the pedigree of nations.
   James Boswell *Tour to the Hebrides* (1785) 18 September 1773

12 I do not much like to see a Whig in any dress; but I hate to see a Whig in a parson's gown.
   James Boswell *Tour to the Hebrides* (1785) 24 September 1773

13 A cucumber should be well sliced, and dressed with pepper and vinegar, and then thrown out, as good for nothing.
   James Boswell *Tour to the Hebrides* (1785) 5 October 1773

14 I am sorry I have not learned to play at cards. It is very useful in life: it generates kindness and consolidates society.
   James Boswell *Tour to the Hebrides* (1785) 21 November 1773

15 JOHNSON: I had no notion that I was wrong or irreverent to my tutor.
   BOSWELL: That, Sir, was great fortitude of mind.
   JOHNSON: No, Sir; stark insensibility.
   James Boswell *Life of Samuel Johnson* (1791) 31 October 1728

16 Sir, we are a nest of singing birds.
   of Pembroke College, Oxford
   James Boswell *Life of Samuel Johnson* (1791) 1730

17 I'll come no more behind your scenes, David; for the silk stockings and white bosoms of your actresses excite my amorous propensities.
   to **Garrick**
   James Boswell *Life of Samuel Johnson* (1791) 1750

18 This man I thought had been a Lord among wits; but, I find, he is only a wit among Lords.
   of Lord **Chesterfield**
   James Boswell *Life of Samuel Johnson* (1791) 1754

19 They teach the morals of a whore, and the manners of a dancing master.
   of the Letters of Lord **Chesterfield**
   James Boswell *Life of Samuel Johnson* (1791) 1754

20 Is not a Patron, my Lord, one who looks with unconcern on a man struggling for life in the water, and, when he has reached ground, encumbers him with help? The notice which you have been pleased to take of my labours, had it been early, had been kind; but it has been delayed till I am indifferent, and cannot enjoy it; till I am solitary, and cannot impart it; till I am known, and do not want it.
   James Boswell *Life of Samuel Johnson* (1791) letter to Lord Chesterfield, 7 February 1755

21 Ignorance, madam, pure ignorance.
   on being asked why he had defined pastern *as the 'knee' of a horse*
   James Boswell *Life of Samuel Johnson* (1791) 1755

22 I did not think he ought to be shut up. His infirmities were not noxious to society. He insisted on people praying with him; and I'd as lief pray with Kit Smart as any one else.
   James Boswell *Life of Samuel Johnson* (1791) 24 May 1763

23 The noblest prospect which a Scotchman ever sees, is the high road that leads him to England!
   James Boswell *Life of Samuel Johnson* (1791) 6 July 1763

24 A man ought to read just as inclination leads him; for what he reads as a task will do him little good.
   James Boswell *Life of Samuel Johnson* (1791) 14 July 1763

25 But if he does really think that there is no distinction between virtue and vice, why,

Sir, when he leaves our houses, let us count our spoons.
James Boswell *Life of Samuel Johnson* (1791) 14 July 1763; cf. **Emerson** 124:11

1 A woman's preaching is like a dog's walking on his hinder legs. It is not done well; but you are surprised to find it done at all.
James Boswell *Life of Samuel Johnson* (1791) 31 July 1763

2 I refute it *thus*.
on Boswell observing of Bishop **Berkeley**'s *theory of the non-existence of matter that though they were satisfied it was not true, they were unable to refute it, Johnson struck his foot against a large stone, till he rebounded from it, with these words*
James Boswell *Life of Samuel Johnson* (1791) 6 August 1763

3 Sir John, Sir, is a very unclubbable man.
of Sir John Hawkins
James Boswell *Life of Samuel Johnson* (1791) Spring 1764

4 In the description of night in Macbeth, the beetle and the bat detract from the general idea of darkness,—inspissated gloom.
James Boswell *Life of Samuel Johnson* (1791) 16 October 1769

5 Most schemes of political improvement are very laughable things.
James Boswell *Life of Samuel Johnson* (1791) 26 October 1769

6 That fellow seems to me to possess but one idea, and that is a wrong one.
of a chance-met acquaintance
James Boswell *Life of Samuel Johnson* (1791) 1770

7 The triumph of hope over experience.
of a man who remarried immediately after the death of a wife with whom he had been unhappy
James Boswell *Life of Samuel Johnson* (1791) 1770

8 Every man has a lurking wish to appear considerable in his native place.
letter to Sir Joshua Reynolds, 17 July 1771

9 He has, indeed, done it very well; but it is a foolish thing well done.
on **Goldsmith**'s *apology in the* London Chronicle *for physically assaulting Thomas Evans*
James Boswell *Life of Samuel Johnson* (1791) 3 April 1773

10 ELPHINSTON: What, have you not read it through?
JOHNSON: No, Sir, do *you* read books *through*?
James Boswell *Life of Samuel Johnson* (1791) 19 April 1773

11 Read over your compositions, and where ever you meet with a passage which you think is particularly fine, strike it out.
quoting a college tutor
James Boswell *Life of Samuel Johnson* (1791) 30 April 1773

12 There are few ways in which a man can be more innocently employed than in getting money.
James Boswell *Life of Samuel Johnson* (1791) 27 March 1775

13 He was dull in a new way, and that made many people think him *great*.
of Thomas **Gray**
James Boswell *Life of Samuel Johnson* (1791) 28 March 1775

14 Fleet-street has a very animated appearance; but I think the full tide of human existence is at Charing-Cross.
James Boswell *Life of Samuel Johnson* (1791) 2 April 1775

15 Patriotism is the last refuge of a scoundrel.
James Boswell *Life of Samuel Johnson* (1791) 7 April 1775

16 Politics are now nothing more than means of rising in the world.
James Boswell *Life of Samuel Johnson* (1791) 18 April 1775

17 In lapidary inscriptions a man is not upon oath.
James Boswell *Life of Samuel Johnson* (1791) 1775

18 We would all be idle if we could.
James Boswell *Life of Samuel Johnson* (1791) 1776

19 No man but a blockhead ever wrote, except for money.
James Boswell *Life of Samuel Johnson* (1791) 5 April 1776

20 BOSWELL: Sir, what is poetry?
JOHNSON: Why Sir, it is much easier to say what it is not. We all *know* what light is; but it is not easy to *tell* what it is.
James Boswell *Life of Samuel Johnson* (1791) 12 April 1776

21 If I had no duties, and no reference to futurity, I would spend my life in driving briskly in a post-chaise with a pretty woman.
James Boswell *Life of Samuel Johnson* (1791) 19 September 1777

22 Depend upon it, Sir, when a man knows he is to be hanged in a fortnight, it concentrates his mind wonderfully.
on the execution of Dr Dodd for forgery, 27 June 1777
James Boswell *Life of Samuel Johnson* (1791) 19 September 1777

23 When a man is tired of London, he is tired of life.
James Boswell *Life of Samuel Johnson* (1791) 20 September 1777

24 All argument is against it; but all belief is for it.
of the existence of ghosts
James Boswell *Life of Samuel Johnson* (1791) 31 March 1778

25 Every man thinks meanly of himself for not having been a soldier, or not having been at sea.
James Boswell *Life of Samuel Johnson* (1791) 10 April 1778

26 Johnson had said that he could repeat a complete chapter of 'The Natural History of Iceland', from the Danish of Horrebow, the whole of which was exactly thus:—'CHAP. LXXII. *Concerning snakes*. There are no snakes

to be met with throughout the whole island.'

James Boswell *Life of Samuel Johnson* (1791) 13 April 1778

1 Sir, the insolence of wealth will creep out.

James Boswell *Life of Samuel Johnson* (1791) 18 April 1778

2 Were it not for imagination, Sir, a man would be as happy in the arms of a chambermaid as of a Duchess.

James Boswell *Life of Samuel Johnson* (1791) 9 May 1778

3 Claret is the liquor for boys; port, for men; but he who aspires to be a hero (smiling) must drink brandy.

James Boswell *Life of Samuel Johnson* (1791) 7 April 1779

4 Worth seeing, yes; but not worth going to see.

on the Giant's Causeway

James Boswell *Life of Samuel Johnson* (1791) 12 October 1779

5 They are forced plants, raised in a hot-bed; and they are poor plants; they are but cucumbers after all.

of Thomas Gray's Odes

James Boswell *Life of Samuel Johnson* (1791) 1780

6 No man was more foolish when he had not a pen in his hand, or more wise when he had.

*of Oliver **Goldsmith***

James Boswell *Life of Samuel Johnson* (1791) 1780; cf. **Garrick** 136:8

7 This merriment of parsons is mighty offensive.

James Boswell *Life of Samuel Johnson* (1791) March 1781

8 We are not here to sell a parcel of boilers and vats, but the potentiality of growing rich, beyond the dreams of avarice.

at the sale of Thrale's brewery

James Boswell *Life of Samuel Johnson* (1791) 6 April 1781; cf. **Moore** 227:4

9 Classical quotation is the *parole* of literary men all over the world.

James Boswell *Life of Samuel Johnson* (1791) 8 May 1781

10 Resolve not to be poor: whatever you have, spend less. Poverty is a great enemy to human happiness; it certainly destroys liberty, and it makes some virtues impracticable, and others extremely difficult.

James Boswell *Life of Samuel Johnson* (1791) letter to Boswell, 7 December 1782

11 How few of his friends' houses would a man choose to be at when he is sick.

James Boswell *Life of Samuel Johnson* (1791) 1783

12 There is a wicked inclination in most people to suppose an old man decayed in his intellects. If a young or middle-aged man, when leaving a company, does not recollect

where he laid his hat, it is nothing; but if the same inattention is discovered in an old man, people will shrug up their shoulders, and say, 'His memory is going.'

James Boswell *Life of Samuel Johnson* (1791) 1783

13 Sir, there is no settling the point of precedency between a louse and a flea.

on the relative merits of two minor poets

James Boswell *Life of Samuel Johnson* (1791) 1783

14 When I observed he was a fine cat, saying, 'Why yes, Sir, but I have had cats whom I liked better than this'; and then as if perceiving Hodge to be out of countenance, adding, 'but he is a very fine cat, a very fine cat indeed.'

James Boswell *Life of Samuel Johnson* (1791) 1783

15 Clear your mind of cant.

James Boswell *Life of Samuel Johnson* (1791) 15 May 1783

16 The black dog I hope always to resist, and in time to drive, though I am deprived of almost all those that used to help me . . . When I rise my breakfast is solitary, the black dog waits to share it, from breakfast to dinner he continues barking, except that Dr Brocklesby for a little keeps him at a distance . . . Night comes at last, and some hours of restlessness and confusion bring me again to a day of solitude. What shall exclude the black dog from a habitation like this?

*on his attacks of melancholia; more recently associated with Winston **Churchill**, who used the phrase 'black dog' when alluding to his own periodic bouts of depression*

letter to Mrs Thrale, 28 June 1783

17 Milton, Madam, was a genius that could cut a Colossus from a rock; but could not carve heads upon cherry-stones.

*to Hannah **More**, who had expressed a wonder that the poet who had written* Paradise Lost *should write such poor sonnets*

James Boswell *Life of Samuel Johnson* (1791) 13 June 1784

18 It might as well be said 'Who drives fat oxen should himself be fat.'

*parodying Henry **Brooke***

James Boswell *Life of Samuel Johnson* (1791) June 1784; cf. **Brooke** 67:18

19 Dictionaries are like watches, the worst is better than none, and the best cannot be expected to go quite true.

letter to Francesco Sastres, 21 August 1784

20 Sir, I look upon every day to be lost, in which I do not make a new acquaintance.

James Boswell *Life of Samuel Johnson* (1791) November 1784

21 Difficult do you call it, Sir? I wish it were impossible.

on the performance of a celebrated violinist

William Seward *Supplement to the Anecdotes of Distinguished Persons* (1797)

1 A man is in general better pleased when he has a good dinner upon his table, than when his wife talks Greek.

    John Hawkins (ed.) *The Works of Samuel Johnson* (1787) 'Apophthegms, Sentiments, Opinions, etc.' vol. 11

2 Of music Dr Johnson used to say that it was the only sensual pleasure without vice.

    in *European Magazine* (1795)

3 What is written without effort is in general read without pleasure.

    William Seward *Biographia* (1799)

Samuel Johnson 1822–82

4 City of God, how broad and far.

    title of hymn (1864)

John Benn Johnstone 1803–91

5 I want you to assist me in forcing her on board the lugger; once there, I'll frighten her into marriage.

    often quoted as, 'Once aboard the lugger and the maid is mine'
    The Gipsy Farmer (performed 1845)

Hanns Johst 1890–1978

6 Whenever I hear the word culture . . . I release the safety-catch of my Browning!

    often attributed to Hermann **Goering**, *and quoted as 'Whenever I hear the word culture, I reach for my pistol!'*
    Schlageter (1933) act 1, sc. 1

Al Jolson 1886–1950

7 You think that's noise—you ain't heard nuttin' yet!

    in a café, competing with the din from a neighbouring building site, in 1906; subsequently an aside in the 1927 film The Jazz Singer
    Martin Abramson *The Real Story of Al Jolson* (1950) (*later the title of a Jolson song, 1919, in the form 'You Ain't Heard Nothing Yet'*)

Henry Arthur Jones 1851–1929 and Henry Herman 1832–94

8 O God! Put back Thy universe and give me yesterday.

    The Silver King (1907) act 2, sc. 4

John Paul Jones 1747–92

9 I have not yet begun to fight.

    when asked whether he had lowered his flag, as his ship was sinking, 23 September 1779
    Mrs Reginald De Koven *Life and Letters of John Paul Jones* (1914) vol. 1

LeRoi Jones *see* Imamu Amiri Baraka

Mary Harris 'Mother' Jones 1830–1930

10 Pray for the dead and fight like hell for the living!

    The Autobiography of Mother Jones (1925)

Steve Jones 1944–

11 Sex and taxes are in many ways the same. Tax does to cash what males do to genes. It dispenses assets among the population as a whole. Sex, not death, is the great leveller.

    speech to the Royal Society; in *Independent* 25 January 1997

Ben Jonson *c.*1573–1637

12 Neither do thou lust after that tawney weed tobacco.

    Bartholomew Fair (1614) act 2, sc. 6

13 The voice of Rome is the consent of heaven!

    Catiline his Conspiracy (1611) act 3, sc. 1

14 Queen and huntress, chaste and fair,
Now the sun is laid to sleep,
Seated in thy silver chair,
State in wonted manner keep:
Hesperus entreats thy light,
Goddess, excellently bright.

    Cynthia's Revels (1600) act 5, sc. 3

15 This is Mab, the Mistress-Fairy
That doth nightly rob the dairy.

    The Entertainment at Althorpe (1603)

16 Still to be neat, still to be drest,
As you were going to a feast;
Still to be powdered, still perfumed,
Lady, it is to be presumed,
Though art's hid causes are not found,
All is not sweet, all is not sound.

    Epicene (1609) act 1, sc. 1

17 Such sweet neglect more taketh me,
Than all the adulteries of art;
They strike mine eyes, but not my heart.

    Epicene (1609) act 1, sc. 1

18 Blind Fortune still
Bestows her gifts on such as cannot use them.

    Every Man out of His Humour (1599) act 2, sc. 2

19 Ramp up my genius, be not retrograde;
But boldly nominate a spade a spade.

    The Poetaster (1601) act 5, sc. 1

20 I glory
More in the cunning purchase of my wealth
Than in the glad possession.

    Volpone (1606) act 1, sc. 1

21 I have been at my book, and am now past the craggy paths of study, and come to the flowery plains of honour and reputation.

    Volpone (1606) act 2, sc. 1

22 Suns, that set, may rise again;
But if once we lose this light,
'Tis with us perpetual night.

    Volpone (1606) act 3, sc. 5; cf. **Catullus** 85:19

23 Come, my Celia, let us prove,
While we can, the sports of love.

    Volpone (1606) act 3, sc. 5; cf. **Catullus** 85:19

24 You have a gift, sir, (thank your education),
Will never let you want, while there are men,
And malice, to breed causes.

    to a lawyer
    Volpone (1606) act 5, sc. 1

1 Rest in soft peace, and, asked, say here doth
lie
Ben Jonson his best piece of poetry.
  'On My First Son' (1616)

2 This figure that thou here seest put,
It was for gentle Shakespeare cut,
Wherein the graver had a strife
With Nature, to out-do the life.
  on the portrait of **Shakespeare**
  First Folio Shakespeare (1623) 'To the Reader'

3 Reader, look
Not on his picture, but his book.
  on the portrait of **Shakespeare**
  First Folio Shakespeare (1623) 'To the Reader'

4 Drink to me only with thine eyes,
And I will pledge with mine;
Or leave a kiss but in the cup,
And I'll not look for wine.
  'To Celia' (1616)

5 Soul of the Age!
The applause, delight, the wonder of our
stage!
  'To the Memory of My Beloved, the Author, Mr
  William Shakespeare' (1623)

6 How far thou didst our Lyly outshine,
Or sporting Kyd, or Marlowe's mighty line.
  'To the Memory of . . . Shakespeare' (1623)

7 Thou hadst small Latin, and less Greek.
  'To the Memory of . . . Shakespeare' (1623)

8 He was not of an age, but for all time!
  'To the Memory of . . . Shakespeare' (1623)

9 Sweet Swan of Avon!
  'To the Memory of . . . Shakespeare' (1623)

10 Donne, for not keeping of accent, deserved
hanging . . . Shakespeare wanted art.
  *in Conversations with William Drummond of
  Hawthornden* (written 1619) no. 3

11 Whatsoever he [Shakespeare] penned, he
never blotted out a line. My answer hath
been 'Would he had blotted a thousand' . . .
But he redeemed his vices with his virtues.
There was ever more in him to be praised
than to be pardoned.
  Timber, or Discoveries made upon Men and Matter
  (1641) l. 658 'De Shakespeare Nostrati'; cf. **Pope**
  248:28

Janis Joplin 1943–70

12 Fourteen heart attacks and he had to die in
my week.
  when ex-President **Eisenhower**'s *death prevented
  her photograph appearing on the cover of
  Newsweek*
  in *New Musical Express* 12 April 1969

John Jortin 1698–1770

13 *Palmam qui meruit, ferat.*
Let him who has won it bear the palm.
  adopted by Lord **Nelson** *as his motto*
  Lusus Poetici (3rd ed., 1748) 'Ad Ventos'

Joseph II 1741–90

14 Too beautiful for our ears, and much too
many notes, dear Mozart.
  of The Abduction from the Seraglio *(1782)*
  attributed; Franz Xaver Niemetschek *Life of
  Mozart* (1798)

Chief Joseph *c.*1840–1904

15 From where the sun now stands I will fight
no more forever.
  speech at the end of the Nez Percé war in 1877

Jenny Joseph 1932–

16 When I am an old woman I shall wear
purple
With a red hat which doesn't go, and
doesn't suit me.
And I shall spend my pension on brandy
and summer gloves
And satin sandals, and say we've got no
money for butter.
  'Warning' (1974)

Benjamin Jowett 1817–93

17 The lie in the soul is a true lie.
  introduction to his translation (1871) of Plato's
  Republic bk. 2

James Joyce 1882–1941

18 Dear, dirty Dublin.
  Dubliners (1914) 'A Little Cloud'

19 riverrun, past Eve and Adam's, from swerve
of shore to bend of bay, brings us by a
commodious vicus of recirculation back to
Howth Castle and Environs.
  Finnegans Wake (1939) pt. 1

20 All moanday, tearsday, wailsday, thumpsday,
frightday, shatterday till the fear of the Law.
  Finnegans Wake (1939) pt. 2

21 Three quarks for Muster Mark!
  Finnegans Wake (1939) pt. 2

22 A portrait of the artist as a young man.
  title of book (1916)

23 Once upon a time and a very good time it
was there was a moocow coming down
along the road and this moocow that was
down along the road met a nicens little boy
named baby tuckoo.
  A Portrait of the Artist as a Young Man (1916);
  opening words

24 Poor Parnell! he cried loudly. My dead king!
  A Portrait of the Artist as a Young Man (1916) ch. 1

25 Ireland is the old sow that eats her farrow.
  A Portrait of the Artist as a Young Man (1916) ch. 5

26 Stately, plump Buck Mulligan came from
the stairhead, bearing a bowl of lather on
which a mirror and a razor lay crossed.
  Ulysses (1922); opening words

27 The snotgreen sea. The scrotumtightening
sea.
  Ulysses (1922)

1 It is a symbol of Irish art. The cracked
lookingglass of a servant.
Ulysses (1922)

2 I fear those big words, Stephen said, which
make us so unhappy.
Ulysses (1922)

3 History, Stephen said, is a nightmare from
which I am trying to awake.
Ulysses (1922)

4 The heaventree of stars hung with humid
nightblue fruit.
Ulysses (1922)

5 O, father forsaken,
Forgive your son!
'Ecce Puer'

William Joyce (Lord Haw-Haw) 1906–46

6 Germany calling! Germany calling!
habitual introduction to propaganda broadcasts
to Britain during the Second World War

Juan Carlos I 1938–

7 I will neither abdicate the Crown nor leave
Spain. Whoever rebels will provoke a new
civil war and will be responsible.
on the occasion of the attempted coup in 1981
television broadcast at 1.15 a.m., 24 February
1981

Jack Judge 1878–1938 and Harry Williams 1874–1924

8 It's a long way to Tipperary,
It's a long way to go;
It's a long way to Tipperary,
To the sweetest girl I know!
Goodbye, Piccadilly,
Farewell, Leicester Square,
It's a long, long way to Tipperary,
But my heart's right there!
'It's a Long Way to Tipperary' (1912 song)

Julian of Norwich 1343–after 1416

9 He showed me something small, no bigger
than a hazelnut, lying in the palm of my
hand, as it seemed to me, and it was as
round as a ball. I looked at it with the eye of
my understanding, and thought: What can
this be? I was amazed that it could last, for I
thought that because of its littleness it
would suddenly have fallen into nothing.
And I was answered in my understanding: It
lasts and always will, because God loves it;
and thus every thing has being through the
love of God.
Revelations of Divine Love (the long text) ch. 5

10 Sin is behovely, but all shall be well and all
shall be well and all manner of thing shall
be well.
Revelations of Divine Love (the long text) ch. 27,
Revelation 13; cf. **Eliot** 121:30

Julian the Apostate AD *c.*332–363

11 *Vicisti, Galilaee.*
You have won, Galilean.
supposed dying words
a late embellishment of Theodoret *Ecclesiastical
History* (AD *c.*450); cf. **Swinburne** 308:1

Carl Gustav Jung 1875–1961

12 The contents of the personal unconscious
are chiefly the *feeling-toned complexes* . . . The
contents of the collective unconscious, on
the other hand, are known as *archetypes.*
Eranos Jahrbuch (1934)

13 A man who has not passed through the
inferno of his passions has never overcome
them.
Memories, Dreams, Reflections (1962) ch. 9

14 As far as we can discern, the sole purpose of
human existence is to kindle a light in the
darkness of mere being.
Memories, Dreams, Reflections (1962) ch. 11

15 Every form of addiction is bad, no matter
whether the narcotic be alcohol or
morphine or idealism.
Memories, Dreams, Reflections (1962) ch. 12

Jung Chang 1952–

16 At the age of fifteen my grandmother
became the concubine of a warlord general.
Wild Swans (1991)

'Junius'

17 The liberty of the press is the *Palladium* of all
the civil, political, and religious rights of an
Englishman.
The Letters of Junius (1772 ed.) 'Dedication to the
English Nation'

18 There is a holy mistaken zeal in politics as
well as in religion. By persuading others, we
convince ourselves.
in *Public Advertiser* 19 December 1769, letter 35

Juvenal AD *c.*60–*c.*130

19 Honesty is praised and left to shiver.
Satires no. 1, l. 74 (translation by G. G. Ramsay)

20 Even if nature says no, indignation makes
me write verse.
Satires no. 1, l. 79

21 The misfortunes of poverty carry with them
nothing harder to bear than that it makes
men ridiculous.
Satires no. 3, l. 152

22 *. . . Omnia Romae*
Cum pretio.
Everything in Rome has its price.
Satires no. 3, l. 183

23 *Rara avis in terris nigroque simillima cycno.*
A rare bird on this earth, like nothing so
much as a black swan.
Satires no. 6, l. 165

24 *Sed quis custodiet ipsos*
Custodes?

But who is to guard the guards themselves?
> *Satires* no. 6, l. 347

1 *Tenet insanabile multos*
Scribendi cacoethes et aegro in corde senescit.
Many suffer from the incurable disease of writing, and it becomes chronic in their sick minds.
> *Satires* no. 7, l. 51

2 Travel light and you can sing in the robber's face.
> *Satires* no. 10, l. 22

3 . . . *Duas tantum res anxius optat,*
Panem et circenses.
Only two things does he [the modern citizen] anxiously wish for—bread and circuses.
> *Satires* no. 10, l. 80

4 *Mens sana in corpore sano.*
A sound mind in a sound body.
> *Satires* no. 10, l. 356

5 . . . *Prima est haec ultio, quod se*
Iudice nemo nocens absolvitur.
This is the first of punishments, that no guilty man is acquitted if judged by himself.
> *Satires* no. 13, l. 2

6 *Maxima debetur puero reverentia, siquid*
Turpe paras, nec tu pueri contempseris annos.
A child is owed the greatest respect; if you ever have something disgraceful in mind, don't ignore your son's tender years.
> *Satires* no. 14, l. 47

Franz Kafka 1883–1924

7 When Gregor Samsa awoke one morning from uneasy dreams he found himself transformed in his bed into a gigantic insect.
> *The Metamorphosis* (1915) ch. 1; cf. **Austin** 20:6

8 Someone must have traduced Joseph K., for without having done anything wrong he was arrested one fine morning.
> *The Trial* (1925) ch. 1

9 You may object that it is not a trial at all; you are quite right, for it is only a trial if I recognize it as such.
> *The Trial* (1925) ch. 2

10 It's often better to be in chains than to be free.
> *The Trial* (1925) ch. 8

Gus Kahn 1886–1941
and Raymond B. Egan 1890–1952

11 There's nothing surer,
The rich get rich and the poor get children.
> 'Ain't We Got Fun' (1921 song)

Immanuel Kant 1724–1804

12 Two things fill the mind with ever new and increasing wonder and awe, the more often and the more seriously reflection concentrates upon them: the starry heaven above me and the moral law within me.
> *Critique of Practical Reason* (1788)

13 There is an imperative which commands a certain conduct immediately, without having as its condition any other purpose to be attained by it. This imperative is Categorical . . . This imperative may be called that of Morality.
> *Fundamental Principles of the Metaphysics of Ethics* (1785) sect. 2 (translated by T. K. Abbott)

14 Happiness is not an ideal of reason but of imagination.
> *Fundamental Principles of the Metaphysics of Ethics* (1785) sect. 2 (translated by T. K. Abbott)

15 Out of the crooked timber of humanity no straight thing can ever be made.
> *Idee zu einer allgemeinen Geschichte in weltbürgerlicher Absicht* (1784) proposition 6

Alphonse Karr 1808–90

16 If we are to abolish the death penalty, let the murderers take the first step.
> *Les Guêpes* January 1849 (6th series, 1859)

17 *Plus ça change, plus c'est la même chose.*
The more things change, the more they are the same.
> *Les Guêpes* January 1849 (6th series, 1859)

George S. Kaufman 1889–1961

18 Satire is what closes Saturday night.
> Scott Meredith *George S. Kaufman and his Friends* (1974) ch. 6

Gerald Kaufman 1930–

19 The longest suicide note in history.
> *on the Labour Party manifesto* New Hope for Britain *(1983)*
> Denis Healey *The Time of My Life* (1989) ch. 23

Paul Kaufman
and Mike Anthony

20 Poetry in motion.
> title of song (1960); cf. **Grahame** 145:10

Christoph Kaufmann 1753–95

21 *Sturm und Drang.*
Storm and stress.
> title suggested by Kaufmann for a romantic drama of the American War of Independence by the German dramatist, F. M. Klinger (1775), and thereafter given to a period of literary ferment which prevailed in Germany during the latter part of the 18th century

Kenneth Kaunda 1924–

22 Westerners have aggressive problem-solving minds; Africans experience people.
> attributed, 1990

Patrick Kavanagh 1904–67

23 The weak, washy way of true tragedy—
A sick horse nosing around the meadow for a clean place to die.
> 'The Great Hunger' (1947)

Paul Keating 1944-

1 Even as it [Great Britain] walked out on you and joined the Common Market, you were still looking for your MBEs and your knighthoods, and all the rest of the regalia that comes with it. You would take Australia right back down the time tunnel to the cultural cringe where you have always come from.

addressing Australian Conservative supporters of Great Britain

speech, House of Representatives (Australia) 27 February 1992

John Keats 1795–1821

2 A thing of beauty is a joy for ever.
Endymion (1818) bk. 1, l. 1

3 St Agnes' Eve—Ah, bitter chill it was!
The owl, for all his feathers, was a-cold;
The hare limped trembling through the frozen grass,
And silent was the flock in woolly fold.
'The Eve of St Agnes' (1820) st. 1

4 The silver, snarling trumpets 'gan to chide.
'The Eve of St Agnes' (1820) st. 4

5 By degrees
Her rich attire creeps rustling to her knees.
'The Eve of St Agnes' (1820) st. 26

6 Trembling in her soft and chilly nest.
'The Eve of St Agnes' (1820) st. 27

7 As though a rose should shut, and be a bud again.
'The Eve of St Agnes' (1820) st. 27

8 And still she slept an azure-lidded sleep,
In blanchèd linen, smooth, and lavendered,
While he from forth the closet brought a heap
Of candied apple, quince, and plum, and gourd;
With jellies soother than the creamy curd,
And lucent syrops, tinct with cinnamon.
'The Eve of St Agnes' (1820) st. 30

9 He played an ancient ditty, long since mute,
In Provence called, 'La belle dame sans mercy.'
'The Eve of St Agnes' (1820) st. 33

10 And they are gone: aye, ages long ago
These lovers fled away into the storm.
'The Eve of St Agnes' (1820) st. 42

11 Ever let the fancy roam,
Pleasure never is at home.
'Fancy' (1820) l. 1

12 I had a dove and the sweet dove died;
And I have thought it died of grieving:
O, what could it grieve for? Its feet were tied,
With a silken thread of my own hand's weaving.
'I had a dove and the sweet dove died' (written 1818)

13 In drear nighted December
Too happy, happy tree
Thy branches ne'er remember
Their green felicity.
'In drear nighted December' (written 1817)

14 So the two brothers and their murdered man
Rode past fair Florence.
'Isabella; or, The Pot of Basil' (1820) st. 27

15 'For cruel 'tis,' said she,
'To steal my Basil-pot away from me.'
'Isabella; or, The Pot of Basil' (1820) st. 62

16 Here are sweet peas, on tip-toe for a flight.
'I stood tip-toe upon a little hill' (1817) l. 57

17 Oh, what can ail thee knight at arms
Alone and palely loitering?
The sedge has withered from the lake
And no birds sing!
'La belle dame sans merci' (1820) st. 1

18 I see a lily on thy brow
With anguish moist and fever dew,
And on thy cheeks a fading rose
Fast withereth too.
'La belle dame sans merci' (1820) st. 3

19 I met a lady in the meads
Full beautiful, a faery's child
Her hair was long, her foot was light
And her eyes were wild.
'La belle dame sans merci' (1820) st. 4

20 . . . La belle dame sans merci
Thee hath in thrall.
'La belle dame sans merci' (1820) st. 10

21 I saw their starved lips in the gloam
With horrid warning gapèd wide
And I awoke and found me here
On the cold hill's side.
'La belle dame sans merci' (1820) st. 11

22 She was a gordian shape of dazzling hue,
Vermilion-spotted, golden, green, and blue;
Striped like a zebra, freckled like a pard,
Eyed like a peacock, and all crimson barred.
'Lamia' (1820) pt. 1, l. 47

23 Love in a hut, with water and a crust,
Is—Love, forgive us!—cinders, ashes, dust.
'Lamia' (1820) pt. 2, l. 1; cf. **Colman** 97:12

24 Do not all charms fly
At the mere touch of cold philosophy?
'Lamia' (1820) pt. 2, l. 229

25 Philosophy will clip an Angel's wings.
'Lamia' (1820) pt. 2, l. 234

26 Souls of poets dead and gone,
What Elysium have ye known,
Happy field or mossy cavern,
Choicer than the Mermaid Tavern?
'Lines on the Mermaid Tavern' (1820)

27 Thou still unravished bride of quietness,
Thou foster-child of silence and slow time.
'Ode on a Grecian Urn' (1820) st. 1

28 What men or gods are these? What maidens loth?
What mad pursuit? What struggle to escape?
'Ode on a Grecian Urn' (1820) st. 1

29 Heard melodies are sweet, but those unheard

Are sweeter.
'Ode on a Grecian Urn' (1820) st. 2

1 For ever wilt thou love, and she be fair!
'Ode on a Grecian Urn' (1820) st. 2

2 For ever piping songs for ever new.
'Ode on a Grecian Urn' (1820) st. 3

3 For ever warm and still to be enjoyed,
For ever panting, and for ever young.
'Ode on a Grecian Urn' (1820) st. 3

4 O Attic shape! Fair attitude!
'Ode on a Grecian Urn' (1820) st. 5

5 'Beauty is truth, truth beauty,'—that is all
Ye know on earth, and all ye need to know.
'Ode on a Grecian Urn' (1820) st. 5

6 No, no, go not to Lethe, neither twist
Wolf's-bane, tight-rooted, for its poisonous
wine.
'Ode on Melancholy' (1820) st. 1

7 But when the melancholy fit shall fall
Sudden from heaven like a weeping cloud,
That fosters the droop-headed flowers all,
And hides the green hill in an April shroud;
Then glut thy sorrow on a morning rose,
Or on the rainbow of the salt sand-wave,
Or on the wealth of globèd peonies.
'Ode on Melancholy' (1820) st. 2

8 She dwells with Beauty—Beauty that must
die;
And Joy, whose hand is ever at his lips
Bidding adieu.
'Ode on Melancholy' (1820) st. 3

9 My heart aches, and a drowsy numbness
pains
My sense, as though of hemlock I had
drunk,
Or emptied some dull opiate to the drains.
'Ode to a Nightingale' (1820) st. 1

10 O, for a draught of vintage! that hath been
Cooled a long age in the deep-delvèd earth,
Tasting of Flora and the country green.
'Ode to a Nightingale' (1820) st. 2

11 O for a beaker full of the warm South,
Full of the true, the blushful Hippocrene,
With beaded bubbles winking at the brim,
And purple-stainèd mouth.
'Ode to a Nightingale' (1820) st. 2

12 Away! away! for I will fly to thee,
Not charioted by Bacchus and his pards,
But on the viewless wings of Poesy,
Though the dull brain perplexes and
retards:
Already with thee! tender is the night.
'Ode to a Nightingale' (1820) st. 4

13 Darkling I listen; and, for many a time
I have been half in love with easeful Death,
Called him soft names in many a musèd
rhyme,
To take into the air my quiet breath;
Now more than ever seems it rich to die,
To cease upon the midnight with no pain.
'Ode to a Nightingale' (1820) st. 6

14 Thou wast not born for death, immortal
bird!
No hungry generations tread thee down;

The voice I hear this passing night was
heard
In ancient days by emperor and clown:
Perhaps the self-same song that found a
path
Through the sad heart of Ruth, when, sick
for home,
She stood in tears amid the alien corn;
The same that oft-times hath
Charmed magic casements, opening on the
foam
Of perilous seas, in faery lands forlorn.
'Ode to a Nightingale' (1820) st. 7; cf. **Hood**
162:6

15 Forlorn! the very word is like a bell
To toll me back from thee to my sole self!
Adieu! the fancy cannot cheat so well
As she is famed to do, deceiving elf.
'Ode to a Nightingale' (1820) st. 8

16 Was it a vision, or a waking dream?
Fled is that music:—do I wake or sleep?
'Ode to a Nightingale' (1820) st. 8

17 'Mid hushed, cool-rooted flowers, fragrant-
eyed,
Blue, silver-white, and budded Tyrian.
'Ode to Psyche' (1820) st. 1

18 Much have I travelled in the realms of gold,
And many goodly states and kingdoms seen.
'On First Looking into Chapman's Homer'
(1817)

19 Then felt I like some watcher of the skies
When a new planet swims into his ken;
Or like stout Cortez when with eagle eyes
He stared at the Pacific—and all his men
Looked at each other with a wild surmise—
Silent, upon a peak in Darien.
'On First Looking into Chapman's Homer'
(1817)

20 Turn the key deftly in the oilèd wards,
And seal the hushèd casket of my soul.
'Sonnet to Sleep' (written 1819)

21 Season of mists and mellow fruitfulness,
Close bosom-friend of the maturing sun;
Conspiring with him how to load and bless
With fruit the vines that round the thatch-
eaves run.
'To Autumn' (1820) st. 1

22 Where are the songs of Spring? Ay, where
are they?
Think not of them, thou hast thy music too.
'To Autumn' (1820) st. 3

23 Then in a wailful choir the small gnats
mourn
Among the river sallows, borne aloft
Or sinking as the light wind lives or dies.
'To Autumn' (1820) st. 3

24 It is a flaw
In happiness, to see beyond our bourn.
'To J. H. Reynolds, Esq.' (written 1818)

25 To one who has been long in city pent,
'Tis very sweet to look into the fair
And open face of heaven.
'To one who has been long in city pent' (1817);
cf. **Milton** 222:15

1 When I behold, upon the night's starred
face
Huge cloudy symbols of a high romance.
'When I have fears that I may cease to be'
(written 1818)

2 Then on the shore
Of the wide world I stand alone and think
Till love and fame to nothingness do sink.
'When I have fears that I may cease to be'
(written 1818)

3 A long poem is a test of invention which I
take to be the polar star of poetry, as fancy
is the sails, and imagination the rudder.
letter to Benjamin Bailey, 8 October 1817

4 I am certain of nothing but the holiness of
the heart's affections and the truth of
imagination—what the imagination seizes
as beauty must be truth—whether it existed
before or not.
letter to Benjamin Bailey, 22 November 1817;
cf. **Keats** 182:5

5 O for a life of sensations rather than of
thoughts!
letter to Benjamin Bailey, 22 November 1817

6 Negative Capability, that is when man is
capable of being in uncertainties, mysteries,
doubts, without any irritable reaching after
fact and reason—Coleridge, for instance,
would let go by a fine isolated verisimilitude
caught from the penetralium of mystery,
from being incapable of remaining content
with half knowledge.
letter to George and Thomas Keats, 21
December 1817

7 If poetry comes not as naturally as the
leaves to a tree it had better not come at all.
letter to John Taylor, 27 February 1818

8 It is impossible to live in a country which is
continually under hatches . . . Rain! Rain!
Rain!
letter to J. H. Reynolds from Devon, 10 April
1818

9 I am in that temper that if I were under
water I would scarcely kick to come to the
top.
letter to Benjamin Bailey, 25 May 1818

10 O the flummery of a birth place! Cant! Cant!
Cant! It is enough to give a spirit the guts-
ache.
letter to John Hamilton Reynolds, 11 July 1818

11 The Wordsworthian or egotistical sublime.
letter to Richard Woodhouse, 27 October 1818

12 The roaring of the wind is my wife and the
stars through the window pane are my
children.
letter to George and Georgiana Keats, 24
October 1818

13 I have met with women whom I really think
would like to be married to a poem and to
be given away by a novel.
letter to Fanny Brawne, 8 July 1819

14 Fine writing is next to fine doing the top
thing in the world.
letter to J. H. Reynolds, 24 August 1819

15 If you should have a boy do not christen
him John . . . 'Tis a bad name and goes
against a man. If my name had been
Edmund I should have been more fortunate.
letter to George and Georgiana Keats, 13
January 1820

16 'Load every rift' of your subject with ore.
letter to Shelley, August 1820; cf. **Spenser**
300:15

17 Here lies one whose name was writ in
water.
epitaph for himself
Richard Monckton Milnes *Life, Letters and
Literary Remains of John Keats* (1848) vol. 2; cf.
Shakespeare 275:27

John Keble 1792–1866

18 Blessed are the pure in heart,
For they shall see our God,
The secret of the Lord is theirs,
Their soul is Christ's abode.
The Christian Year (1827) 'Blessed are the pure in
heart'

19 New every morning is the love
Our wakening and uprising prove.
The Christian Year (1827) 'Morning'

20 The trivial round, the common task,
Would furnish all we ought to ask.
The Christian Year (1827) 'Morning'

21 The voice that breathed o'er Eden,
That earliest wedding-day.
'Holy Matrimony' (1857 hymn)

22 If the Church of England were to fail, it
would be found in my parish.
D. Newsome *The Parting of Friends* (1966) ch. 8,
pt. 3

Garrison Keillor 1942–

23 Years ago, manhood was an opportunity for
achievement, and now it is a problem to be
overcome.
The Book of Guys (1994)

Helen Keller 1880–1968

24 The mystery of language was revealed to
me. I knew then that 'w-a-t-e-r' meant the
wonderful cool something that was flowing
over my hand. That living word awakened
my soul, gave it light, joy, set it free!
The Story of My Life (1902) ch. 4

Frank B. Kellogg *see* Aristide Briand

Thomas Kelly 1769–1855

25 The head that once was crowned with
thorns
Is crowned with glory now.
'The head that once was crowned with thorns'
(1820 hymn)

Lord Kelvin 1824–1907

26 When you can measure what you are
speaking about, and express it in numbers,

you know something about it; but when you cannot measure it, when you cannot express it in numbers, your knowledge is of a meagre and unsatisfactory kind: it may be the beginning of knowledge, but you have scarcely, in your thoughts, advanced to the stage of *science*, whatever the matter may be.
often quoted as 'If you cannot measure it, then it is not science'
    Popular Lectures and Addresses vol. 1 (1889) 'Electrical Units of Measurement', delivered 3 May 1883

Thomas à Kempis *see* **Thomas**

Thomas Ken 1637–1711

1 Awake, my soul, and with the sun
Thy daily stage of duty run.
Shake off dull sloth, and joyful rise
To pay thy morning sacrifice.
    'Morning Hymn' in Winchester College *Manual of Prayers* (1695) but already in use by 1674

2 Redeem thy mis-spent time that's past,
And live this day as if thy last.
    'Morning Hymn' (1709 ed.) v. 2

3 Teach me to live, that I may dread
The grave as little as my bed.
    'Evening Hymn' (1695) v. 3

Jaan Kenbrovin
and **William Kellette**

4 I'm forever blowing bubbles.
    title of song (1919)

Florynce Kennedy 1916–

5 If men could get pregnant, abortion would be a sacrament.
    in *Ms.* March 1973

Jimmy Kennedy
and **Michael Carr**

6 We're gonna hang out the washing on the Siegfried Line.
    title of song (1939)

John F. Kennedy 1917–63

7 We stand today on the edge of a new frontier.
    speech accepting the Democratic nomination in Los Angeles, 15 July 1960

8 We shall pay any price, bear any burden, meet any hardship, support any friend, oppose any foe to assure the survival and the success of liberty.
    inaugural address, 20 January 1961

9 If a free society cannot help the many who are poor, it cannot save the few who are rich.
    inaugural address, 20 January 1961

10 Let us never negotiate out of fear. But let us never fear to negotiate.
    inaugural address, 20 January 1961

11 All this will not be finished in the first 100 days. Nor will it be finished in the first 1,000 days, nor in the life of this Administration, nor even perhaps in our lifetime on this planet. But let us begin.
    inaugural address, 20 January 1961

12 And so, my fellow Americans: ask not what your country can do for you—ask what you can do for your country.
    inaugural address, 20 January 1961; cf. **Gibran** 139:14, **Holmes** 161:11

13 There are no 'white' or 'coloured' signs on the foxholes or graveyards of battle.
    Message to Congress on proposed Civil Rights Bill, 19 June 1963

14 *Ich bin ein Berliner.*
I am a Berliner.
    speech in West Berlin, 26 June 1963; cf. **Cicero** 92:26

15 In free society art is not a weapon . . . Artists are not engineers of the soul.
    speech at Amherst College, Mass., 26 October 1963; cf. **Gorky** 144:18, **Stalin** 301:12

16 It was involuntary. They sank my boat.
    on being asked how he became a war hero
    Arthur M. Schlesinger Jr. *A Thousand Days* (1965) ch. 4

Joseph P. Kennedy 1888–1969

17 We're going to sell Jack like soapflakes.
    when his son John made his bid for the Presidency
    John H. Davis *The Kennedy Clan* (1984) ch. 23

18 When the going gets tough, the tough get going.
    also attributed to Knute Rockne
    J. H. Cutler *Honey Fitz* (1962)

Rose Kennedy 1890–1995

19 Now Teddy must run.
    *to her daughter, on hearing of the assassination of Robert **Kennedy***
    in *The Times* 24 January 1995 (obituary); attributed, perhaps apocryphal

Jomo Kenyatta 1891–1978

20 The African is conditioned, by the cultural and social institutions of centuries, to a freedom of which Europe has little conception, and it is not in his nature to accept serfdom forever. He realizes that he must fight unceasingly for his own emancipation; for without this he is doomed to remain the prey of rival imperialisms.
    Facing Mount Kenya (1938); conclusion

Jack Kerouac 1922–69

21 The beat generation.
    phrase coined in the course of a conversation; in *Playboy* June 1959

Jean Kerr 1923–

22 I feel about airplanes the way I feel about diets. It seems to me that they are wonderful things for other people to go on.
    The Snake Has All the Lines (1958)

1 I'm tired of all this nonsense about beauty
being only skin-deep. That's deep enough.
What do you want—an adorable pancreas?
The Snake has all the Lines (1958)

William Kethe d. 1594

2 All people that on earth do dwell,
Sing to the Lord with cheerful voice.
'All people that on earth do dwell' in *Fourscore
and Seven Psalms of David* (Geneva, 1561; later
known as the Geneva Psalter); usually sung to
the tune 'Old Hundredth', and often known by
that name

3 O enter then his gates with praise,
Approach with joy his courts unto.
'All people that on earth do dwell' in *Fourscore
and Seven Psalms of David* (Geneva, 1561; later
known as the Geneva Psalter)

Thomas Kettle 1880-1916

4 My only programme for Ireland consists, in
equal parts, of Home Rule and the Ten
Commandments. My only counsel to Ireland
is, that in order to become deeply Irish, she
must become European.
'Apology'

5 Ireland is a small but insuppressible island
half an hour nearer the sunset than Great
Britain.
'On Crossing the Irish Sea'

Francis Scott Key 1779-1843

6 'Tis the star-spangled banner; O long may it
wave
O'er the land of the free, and the home of
the brave!
'The Star-Spangled Banner' (1814)

Marian Keyes

7 My biological clock is ticking so loud I'm
nearly deafened by it. They search me going
into planes.
'Late Opening at the Last Chance Saloon' (1997)

John Maynard Keynes 1883-1946

8 I work for a Government I despise for ends I
think criminal.
letter to Duncan Grant, 15 December 1917

9 Lenin was right. There is no subtler, no
surer means of overturning the existing
basis of society than to debauch the
currency.
The Economic Consequences of the Peace (1919) ch. 6

10 I do not know which makes a man more
conservative—to know nothing but the
present, or nothing but the past.
The End of Laissez-Faire (1926) pt. 1

11 If the Treasury were to fill old bottles with
banknotes, bury them at suitable depths in
disused coalmines which are then filled up
to the surface with town rubbish, and leave
it to private enterprise on well-tried
principles of *laissez-faire* to dig the notes up
again (the right to do so being obtained, of
course, by tendering for leases of the note-
bearing territory) there need be no more
unemployment and, with the help of the
repercussions, the real income of the
community, and its capital wealth also,
would probably become a good deal greater
than it actually is.
General Theory (1936) bk. 3, ch. 10

12 Madmen in authority, who hear voices in
the air, are distilling their frenzy from some
academic scribbler of a few years back.
General Theory (1947 ed.) ch. 24

13 *In the long run* we are all dead.
A Tract on Monetary Reform (1923) ch. 3

14 We threw good housekeeping to the winds.
But we saved ourselves and helped save the
world.
of Britain in the Second World War
A. J. P. Taylor *English History, 1914-1945* (1965)

Ruhollah Khomeini 1900-89

15 If laws are needed, Islam has established
them all. There is no need . . . after
establishing a government, to sit down and
draw up laws.
*Islam and Revolution: Writings and Declarations of
Imam Khomeini* (1981) 'Islamic Government'

16 I would like to inform all the intrepid
Muslims in the world that the author of the
book entitled *The Satanic Verses*, which has
been compiled, printed and published in
opposition to Islam, the Prophet and the
Qur'an, as well as those publishers who
were aware of its contents, have been
declared *madhur el dam* [those whose blood
must be shed]. I call on all zealous Muslims
to execute them quickly, wherever they find
them, so that no-one will dare to insult
Islam again. Whoever is killed in this path
will be regarded as a martyr.
fatwa against Salman **Rushdie**, issued 14
February 1989; cf. **Wesker** 331:21

Nikita Khrushchev 1894-1971

17 If anyone believes that our smiles involve
abandonment of the teaching of Marx,
Engels and Lenin he deceives himself. Those
who wait for that must wait until a shrimp
learns to whistle.
speech in Moscow, 17 September 1955

18 Whether you like it or not, history is on our
side. We will bury you.
speech to Western diplomats at reception in
Moscow for Polish leader Mr Gomulka, 18
November 1956

19 If one cannot catch the bird of paradise,
better take a wet hen.
in *Time* 6 January 1958

20 If you start throwing hedgehogs under me, I
shall throw a couple of porcupines under
you.
in *New York Times* 7 November 1963

Kitty Kiernan d. 1945

21 I felt, if we were ever to part, it would be
easier for us both, especially for me, to do it

soon, because later it would be bitter for me. But I'd love you just the same.
letter to Michael Collins, 1921

Joyce Kilmer 1886–1918

1 I think that I shall never see
A poem lovely as a tree.
'Trees' (1914); cf. Nash 231:17

2 Poems are made by fools like me,
But only God can make a tree.
'Trees' (1914)

David Maxwell Fyfe, Lord Kilmuir 1900–67

3 Loyalty is the Tory's secret weapon.
Anthony Sampson *Anatomy of Britain* (1962) ch. 6

Francis Kilvert 1840–79

4 Of all noxious animals, too, the most noxious is a tourist. And of all tourists the most vulgar, ill-bred, offensive and loathsome is the British tourist.
diary, 5 April 1870

Benjamin Franklin King 1857–94

5 Nothing to do but work,
Nothing to eat but food,
Nothing to wear but clothes
To keep one from going nude.
'The Pessimist'

Henry King 1592–1669

6 Sleep on (my Love!) in thy cold bed
Never to be disquieted.
My last Good-night! Thou wilt not wake
Till I thy fate shall overtake:
Till age, or grief, or sickness must
Marry my body to that dust
It so much loves; and fill the room
My heart keeps empty in thy tomb.
Stay for me there: I will not fail
To meet thee in that hollow vale.
'An Exequy' (1657) l. 81 (written for his wife Anne, d. 1624)

7 But hark! My pulse, like a soft drum
Beats my approach, tells thee I come.
'An Exequy' (1657) l. 111

Martin Luther King 1929–68

8 I want to be the white man's brother, not his brother-in-law.
in *New York Journal-American* 10 September 1962

9 Injustice anywhere is a threat to justice everywhere.
letter from Birmingham Jail, Alabama, 16 April 1963

10 If a man hasn't discovered something he will die for, he isn't fit to live.
speech in Detroit, 23 June 1963

11 I have a dream that one day on the red hills of Georgia the sons of former slaves and the sons of former slave owners will be able to sit down together at the table of brotherhood.
speech at Civil Rights March in Washington, 28 August 1963

12 I just want to do God's will. And he's allowed me to go up to the mountain. And I've looked over, and I've seen the promised land . . . So I'm happy tonight. I'm not worried about anything. I'm not fearing any man.
on the day before his assassination
speech in Memphis, 3 April 1968

13 A riot is at bottom the language of the unheard.
Where Do We Go From Here? (1967) ch. 4

Stoddard King 1889–1933

14 There's a long, long trail awinding
Into the land of my dreams.
'There's a Long, Long Trail' (1913 song)

William Lyon Mackenzie King 1874–1950

15 If some countries have too much history, we have too much geography.
speech, Canadian House of Commons, 18 June 1936

Stephen King 1947–

16 Terror . . . often arises from a pervasive sense of disestablishment; that things are in the unmaking.
Danse Macabre (1981)

Charles Kingsley 1819–75

17 Be good, sweet maid, and let who will be clever;
Do noble things, not dream them, all day long.
'A Farewell' (1858)

18 Do the work that's nearest,
Though it's dull at whiles,
Helping, when we meet them,
Lame dogs over stiles.
'The Invitation. To Tom Hughes' (1856)

19 O Mary, go and call the cattle home,
And call the cattle home,
And call the cattle home,
Across the sands of Dee.
'The Sands of Dee' (1858)

20 And never home came she.
'The Sands of Dee' (1858)

21 For men must work, and women must weep,
And there's little to earn, and many to keep,
'The Three Fishers' (1858)

22 When all the world is young, lad,
And all the trees are green;
And every goose a swan, lad,
And every lass a queen;
Then hey for boot and horse, lad,
And round the world away:
Young blood must have its course, lad,
And every dog his day.
'Young and Old' (from *The Water Babies*, 1863)

1 We have used the Bible as if it was a
constable's handbook—an opium-dose for
keeping beasts of burden patient while they
are being overloaded.

Letters to the Chartists no. 2; cf. **Marx** 214:4

Hugh Kingsmill (Hugh Kingsmill Lunn) 1889–1949

2 What still alive at twenty-two,
A clean upstanding chap like you?
Sure, if your throat 'tis hard to slit,
Slit your girl's, and swing for it.

'Two Poems, after A. E. Housman' (1933) no. 1

Neil Kinnock 1942–

3 If Margaret Thatcher wins on Thursday, I
warn you not to be ordinary, I warn you not
to be young, I warn you not to fall ill, and I
warn you not to grow old.

on the prospect of a Conservative re-election
speech at Bridgend, 7 June 1983

Alfred Kinsey 1894–1956

4 The only unnatural sex act is that which
you cannot perform.

in *Time* 21 January 1966

Rudyard Kipling 1865–1936

5 When you've shouted 'Rule Britannia';
when you've sung 'God save the Queen'—
When you've finished killing Kruger with
your mouth.

'The Absent-Minded Beggar' (1899) st. 1

6 England's on the anvil—hear the hammers
ring—
Clanging from the Severn to the Tyne!

'The Anvil' (1927)

7 Seek not to question other than
The books I leave behind.

'The Appeal' (1940)

8 Oh, East is East, and West is West, and
never the twain shall meet,
Till Earth and Sky stand presently at God's
great Judgement Seat;
But there is neither East nor West, Border,
nor Breed, nor Birth,
When two strong men stand face to face,
tho' they come from the ends of earth!

'The Ballad of East and West' (1892)

9 Foot—foot—foot—foot—sloggin' over
Africa—
(Boots—boots—boots—boots—movin' up
and down again!)

'Boots' (1903)

10 If any question why we died,
Tell them, because our fathers lied.

'Common Form' (1919)

11 It's clever, but is it Art?

'The Conundrum of the Workshops' (1892)

12 They've taken of his buttons off an' cut his
stripes away,
An' they're hangin' Danny Deever in the
mornin'.

'Danny Deever' (1892)

13 The 'eathen in 'is blindness bows down to
wood an' stone;
'E don't obey no orders unless they is 'is
own.

'The 'Eathen' (1896); cf. **Heber** 155:2

14 And what should they know of England
who only England know?

'The English Flag' (1892)

15 The female of the species is more deadly
than the male.

'The Female of the Species' (1919)

16 So 'ere's to you, Fuzzy-Wuzzy, at your 'ome
in the Soudan;
You're a pore benighted 'eathen but a first-
class fightin' man.

'Fuzzy-Wuzzy' (1892)

17 Gentlemen-rankers out on the spree,
Damned from here to Eternity,
God ha' mercy on such as we,
Baa! Yah! Bah!

'Gentlemen-Rankers' (1892)

18 Our England is a garden, and such gardens
are not made
By singing:—'Oh, how beautiful!' and sitting
in the shade.

'The Glory of the Garden' (1911)

19 You're a better man than I am, Gunga Din!

'Gunga Din' (1892)

20 If you can keep your head when all about
you
Are losing theirs and blaming it on you . . .
If you can meet with triumph and disaster
And treat those two impostors just the
same.

'If—' (1910)

21 If you can talk with crowds and keep your
virtue,
Or walk with Kings—nor lose the common
touch . . .
Yours is the Earth and everything that's in
it,
And—which is more—you'll be a Man, my
son!

'If—' (1910)

22 There are nine and sixty ways of
constructing tribal lays,
And—every—single—one—of—them—is—
right!

'In the Neolithic Age' (1893)

23 Then ye returned to your trinkets; then ye
contented your souls
With the flannelled fools at the wicket or
the muddied oafs at the goals.

'The Islanders' (1903)

24 For the Colonel's Lady an' Judy O'Grady
Are sisters under their skins!

'The Ladies' (1896)

25 Down to Gehenna or up to the Throne,
He travels the fastest who travels alone.

L'Envoi to *The Story of the Gadsbys* (1890), 'The
Winners'

26 On the road to Mandalay,
Where the flyin'-fishes play,

An' the dawn comes up like thunder outer
China 'crost the Bay!
'Mandalay' (1892)

1 Ship me somewheres east of Suez, where
the best is like the worst.
'Mandalay' (1892)

2 'Have you news of my boy Jack?'
Not this tide.
'When d'you think that he'll come back?'
Not with this wind blowing, and this tide.
'My Boy Jack' (1916)

3 The toad beneath the harrow knows
Exactly where each tooth-point goes;
The butterfly upon the road
Preaches contentment to that toad.
'Pagett, MP' (1886)

4 Brothers and Sisters, I bid you beware
Of giving your heart to a dog to tear.
'The Power of the Dog' (1909)

5 The tumult and the shouting dies—
The captains and the kings depart—
Still stands Thine ancient Sacrifice,
An humble and a contrite heart.
Lord God of Hosts, be with us yet,
Lest we forget—lest we forget!
'Recessional' (1897)

6 Lo, all our pomp of yesterday
Is one with Nineveh, and Tyre!
'Recessional' (1897)

7 Such boasting as the Gentiles use,
Or lesser breeds without the Law.
'Recessional' (1897)

8 How far is St. Helena from the field of
Austerlitz?
'A St. Helena Lullaby' (1910)

9 Five and twenty ponies,
Trotting through the dark—
Brandy for the Parson,
'Baccy for the Clerk;
Laces for a lady, letters for a spy,
Watch the wall, my darling, while the
Gentlemen go by!
'A Smuggler's Song' (1906)

10 If blood be the price of admiralty,
Lord God, we ha' paid in full!
'The Song of the Dead' (1896)

11 Then it's Tommy this, an' Tommy that, an'
'Tommy 'ow's yer soul?'
But it's 'Thin red line of 'eroes' when the
drums begin to roll.
'Tommy' (1892); cf. **Russell** 263:3

12 Of all the trees that grow so fair,
Old England to adorn,
Greater are none beneath the Sun,
Than Oak, and Ash, and Thorn.
'A Tree Song' (1906)

13 A fool there was and he made his prayer
(Even as you and I!)
To a rag and a bone and a hank of hair
(We called her the woman who did not care)
But the fool he called her his lady fair—
(Even as you and I!)
'The Vampire' (1897) st. 1

14 They shut the road through the woods
Seventy years ago.
Weather and rain have undone it again,
And now you would never know
There was once a road through the woods.
'The Way through the Woods' (1910)

15 And that is called paying the Dane-geld;
But we've proved it again and again,
That if once you have paid him the Dane-
geld
You never get rid of the Dane.
'What Dane-geld means' (1911)

16 When 'Omer smote 'is bloomin' lyre,
He'd 'eard men sing by land an' sea;
An' what he thought 'e might require,
'E went an' took—the same as me!
'When 'Omer smote 'is bloomin' lyre' (1896)

17 Take up the White Man's burden—
Send forth the best ye breed—
Go, bind your sons to exile
To serve your captives' need.
'The White Man's Burden' (1899)

18 Lalun is a member of the most ancient
profession in the world.
In Black and White (1888) 'On the City Wall'; cf.
Reagan 255:1

19 They settled things by making up a saying,
'What the Bandar-log think now the Jungle
will think later': and that comforted them a
great deal.
The Jungle Book (1894) 'Kaa's Hunting'

20 The motto of all the mongoose family is,
'Run and find out.'
The Jungle Book (1894) 'Rikki-Tikki-Tavi'

21 He walked by himself, and all places were
alike to him.
Just So Stories (1902) 'The Cat that Walked by
Himself'

22 An Elephant's Child—who was full of
'satiable curtiosity.
Just So Stories (1902) 'The Elephant's Child'

23 The great grey-green, greasy, Limpopo River,
all set about with fever trees.
Just So Stories (1902) 'The Elephant's Child'

24 Little Friend of all the World.
Kim's nickname
Kim (1901) ch. 1

25 The man who would be king.
title of short story (1888)

26 He swathed himself in quotations—as a
beggar would enfold himself in the purple
of Emperors.
Many Inventions (1893) 'The Finest Story in the
World'

27 The silliest woman can manage a clever
man; but it takes a very clever woman to
manage a fool.
Plain Tales from the Hills (1888) 'Three and—an
Extra'

28 Now this is the Law of the Jungle—as old
and as true as the sky;

And the Wolf that shall keep it may prosper,
but the Wolf that shall break it must die.

The Second Jungle Book (1895) 'The Law of the
Jungle'

1 'Tisn't beauty, so to speak, nor good talk
necessarily. It's just It. Some women'll stay
in a man's memory if they once walked
down a street.

Traffics and Discoveries (1904) 'Mrs Bathurst'

2 Power without responsibility: the
prerogative of the harlot throughout the
ages.

*summing up Lord **Beaverbrook**'s political
standpoint vis-à-vis the* Daily Express, *and
quoted by Stanley **Baldwin**, 18 March 1931*

in *Kipling Journal* vol. 38, no. 180, December
1971; cf. **Stoppard** 304:14

Henry Kissinger 1923–

3 Power is the great aphrodisiac.
in *New York Times* 19 January 1971

4 We are the President's men.
M. and B. Kalb *Kissinger* (1974) ch. 7

5 For other nations, Utopia is a blessed past
never to be recovered; for Americans it is
just beyond the horizon.
attributed

Lord Kitchener 1850–1916

6 You are ordered abroad as a soldier of the
King . . . While treating all women with
perfect courtesy, you should avoid any
intimacy. Do your duty bravely. Fear God.
Honour the King.
message to soldiers of the British Expeditionary
Force (1914), in *The Times* 19 August 1914

7 I don't mind your being killed, but I object
to your being taken prisoner.
to the Prince of Wales during the First World War
in *Journals and Letters of Reginald Viscount Esher*
(1938) vol. 3, 18 December 1914

Paul Klee 1879–1940

8 Art does not reproduce the visible; rather, it
makes visible.
Inward Vision (1958) 'Creative Credo' (1920)

9 An active line on a walk, moving freely
without a goal. A walk for walk's sake. The
agent is a point that shifts position.
Pedagogical Sketchbook (1925)

Friedrich Klopstock 1724–1803

10 God and I both knew what it meant once;
now God alone knows.
C. Lombroso *The Man of Genius* (1891) pt. 1, ch. 2;
cf. **Browning** 71:13

Charles Knight
and Kenneth Lyle

11 When there's trouble brewing,
When there's something doing,
Are we downhearted?
No! Let 'em all come!
'Here we are! Here we are again!!' (1914 song)

Frank H. Knight 1885–1973

12 Costs merely register competing attractions.
Risk, Uncertainty and Profit (1921)

L. C. Knights 1906–97

13 How many children had Lady Macbeth?
satirizing an over-realistic approach to criticism
title of essay (1933)

Mary Knowles 1733–1807

14 He gets at the substance of a book directly;
he tears out the heart of it.
*on Samuel **Johnson***
James Boswell *The Life of Samuel Johnson* (1791) 15
April 1778

John Knox c.1505–72

15 The first blast of the trumpet against the
monstrous regiment of women.
'*regiment*' = *rule*
title of pamphlet (1558)

Ronald Knox 1888–1957

16 When suave politeness, tempering bigot
zeal,
Corrected *I believe* to *One does feel.*
'Absolute and Abitofhell' (1913)

17 There once was a man who said, 'God
Must think it exceedingly odd
If he finds that this tree
Continues to be
When there's no one about in the Quad.'
Langford Reed *Complete Limerick Book* (1924), to
which came the anonymous reply:
Dear Sir,
Your astonishment's odd:
I am always about in the Quad.
And that's why the tree
Will continue to be,
Since observed by
Yours faithfully,
God.

18 A loud noise at one end and no sense of
responsibility at the other.
definition of a baby
attributed

Vicesimus Knox 1752–1821

19 Can anything be more absurd than keeping
women in a state of ignorance, and yet so
vehemently to insist on their resisting
temptation?
Mary Wollstonecraft *A Vindication of the Rights of
Woman* (1792) ch. 7

Ted Koehler

20 Stormy weather,
Since my man and I ain't together.
'Stormy Weather' (1933 song)

Arthur Koestler 1905–83

21 One may not regard the world as a sort of
metaphysical brothel for emotions.
Darkness at Noon (1940) 'The Second Hearing' pt.
7

1 God seems to have left the receiver off the hook, and time is running out.
The Ghost in the Machine (1967) ch. 18

Helmut Kohl 1930–

2 The policy of European integration is in reality a question of war and peace in the 21st century.
speech at Louvain University, 2 February 1996

Käthe Kollwitz 1867–1945

3 As you, the children of my body, have been my tasks, so too are my other works.
letter to her son Hans, 21 February 1915

4 I have never done any work cold . . . I have always worked with my blood, so to speak.
letter to her son Hans, 16 April 1917

The Koran
textual translations are those of A. J. Arberry, 1964

5 In the Name of God, the Merciful, the Compassionate.
sura 1

6 That is the Book [the Koran], wherein is no doubt,
a guidance to the godfearing
who believe in the Unseen.
sura 2

7 The month of Ramadan, wherein the Koran was sent down to be a guidance
to the people, and as clear signs
of the Guidance and the Salvation
So let those of you, who are present
at the month, fast it.
sura 2

8 No compulsion is there in religion.
sura 2

9 God has
permitted trafficking, and forbidden usury.
sura 2

10 Say to the unbelievers: 'You shall be overthrown, and mustered into Gehenna—an evil cradling!'
sura 3

11 The true religion with God is Islam.
sura 3

12 Every soul shall taste of death; you shall surely
be paid in full your wages on the Day
of Resurrection.
sura 3

13 Men are the managers of the affairs of women.
sura 4

14 Whatever good visits thee, it is of God; whatever evil visits thee is of thyself.
sura 4

15 To God belongs all that is in the heavens and in the earth, and God encompasses everything.
sura 4

16 Souls are very
prone to avarice. If you do good

and are godfearing, surely God is aware of the things you do.
sura 4;
Men's souls are naturally inclined to covetousness; but if ye be kind towards women and fear to wrong them, God is well acquainted with what ye do.
in George Sale's translation, 1734

17 And we have sent down to thee the Book with the truth, confirming the Book
that was before it, and assuring it.
sura 5

18 Glory be to Him, who carried His servant by night
from the Holy Mosque to the Further Mosque
the precincts of which We have blessed,
that We might show him some of Our signs.
sura 17

19 Perform the prayer
at the sinking of the sun to the darkening of the night
and the recital of dawn.
sura 17

20 He
named you Muslims
aforetime and in this, that the Messenger might be a witness against you, and that you might be witnesses against mankind.
sura 22

21 Muhammad is not the father of any one of your men, but the Messenger of God, and the Seal of the Prophets
sura 33

22 It belongs not to any mortal that
God should speak to him, except
by revelation, or from behind
a veil.
sura 42

23 Surely,
unto God all things come home.
sura 42

24 He is God
the Creator, the Maker, the Shaper,
To Him belong the Names Most Beautiful.
sura 59

Jiddu Krishnamurti d. 1986

25 Religion is the frozen thought of men out of which they build temples.
in *Observer* 22 April 1928 'Sayings of the Week'

Kris Kristofferson 1936–

26 Freedom's just another word for nothin' left to lose,
Nothin' ain't worth nothin', but it's free.
'Me and Bobby McGee' (1969 song, with Fred Foster)

Stanley Kubrick 1928–99

27 The great nations have always acted like gangsters, and the small nations like prostitutes.
in *Guardian* 5 June 1963

Satish Kumar 1937–

1 Lead me from death to life, from falsehood to truth.
Lead me from despair to hope, from fear to trust.
Lead me from hate to love, from war to peace.
Let peace fill our heart, our world, our universe.
'Prayer for Peace' (1981); adapted from the **Upanishads**; cf. **Upanishads** 321:21

Milan Kundera 1929–

2 The unbearable lightness of being.
title of novel (1984)

Thomas Kyd 1558–94

3 My son—and what's a son? A thing begot
Within a pair of minutes, thereabout,
A lump bred up in darkness.
The Spanish Tragedy (1592) act 3, sc. 11, The Third Addition (1602 ed.) l. 5

4 It grew a gallows and did bear our son,
It bore thy fruit and mine.
The Spanish Tragedy (1592) act 3, sc. 12, The Fourth Addition (1602 ed.) l. 70

5 Hieronimo is mad again.
alternative title given to *The Spanish Tragedy* in 1615

Henry Labouchere 1831–1912

6 He [Labouchere] did not object to the old man always having a card up his sleeve, but he did object to his insinuating that the Almighty had placed it there.
*on **Gladstone**'s 'frequent appeals to a higher power'*
Earl Curzon *Modern Parliamentary Eloquence* (1913)

Jean de la Bruyère 1645–96

7 The people have little intelligence, the great no heart . . . if I had to choose I should have no hesitation: I would be of the people.
Les Caractères ou les moeurs de ce siècle (1688) 'Des Grands'

8 Man has but three events in his life: to be born, to live, and to die. He is not conscious of his birth, he suffers at his death and he forgets to live.
Les Caractères ou les moeurs de ce siècle (1688) 'De l'homme'

Nivelle de la Chaussée 1692–1754

9 When everyone is wrong, everyone is right.
La Gouvernante (1747) act 1, sc. 3

Pierre Choderlos de Laclos 1741–1803

10 Our intentions make blackguards of us all; our weakness in carrying them out we call probity.
Les Liaisons Dangereuses (1782) letter 66

11 He cannot rate me very high if he thinks he is worth my fidelity!
Les Liaisons Dangereuses (1782) letter 113

12 A man enjoys the happiness he feels, a woman the happiness she gives.
Les Liaisons Dangereuses (1782) letter 130

Christian Lacroix 1951–

13 Haute Couture should be fun, foolish and almost unwearable.
in *Observer* 27 December 1987 'Sayings of the Year'

Jean de la Fontaine 1621–95

14 I bend and I break not.
Fables bk. 1 (1668) 'Le Chêne et le Roseau'

15 *La mort ne surprend point le sage,*
Il est toujours prêt à partir.
Death never takes the wise man by surprise; he is always ready to go.
Fables bk. 8 (1678–9) 'La Mort et le Mourant'; cf. **Montaigne** 226:8

Madame de La Fayette 1634–93

16 One reproaches a lover, but can one reproach a husband, when his only fault is that he no longer loves?
The Princess of Clèves (1678) pt. 4

Jules Laforgue 1860–87

17 *Ah! que la vie est quotidienne.*
Oh, what a day-to-day business life is.
Complainte sur certains ennuis (1885)

Fiorello La Guardia 1882–1947

18 When I make a mistake, it's a beaut!
on the appointment of Herbert O'Brien as a judge in 1936
William Manners *Patience and Fortitude* (1976)

John Lahr 1941–

19 Criticism is a life without risk.
Light Fantastic (1996)

20 Society drives people crazy with lust and calls it advertising.
in *Guardian* 2 August 1989

R. D. Laing 1927–89

21 The divided self.
title of book (1960) on schizophrenia

22 Madness need not be all breakdown. It may also be break-through.
The Politics of Experience (1967) ch. 6

Alphonse de Lamartine 1790–1869

23 *Ô temps! suspend ton vol, et vous, heures propices! Suspendez votre cours.*
O Time! arrest your flight, and you, propitious hours, stay your course.
Le Lac (1820) st. 6

Lady Caroline Lamb 1785–1828

1 Mad, bad, and dangerous to know.
of Byron, after their first meeting at a ball
diary, March 1812; in Elizabeth Jenkins *Lady
Caroline Lamb* (1932)

Charles Lamb 1775–1834

2 Presents, I often say, endear Absents.
Essays of Elia (1823) 'A Dissertation upon Roast
Pig'

3 Your *borrowers of books*—those mutilators of
collections, spoilers of the symmetry of
shelves, and creators of odd volumes.
Essays of Elia (1823) 'The Two Races of Men'

4 Not many sounds in life . . . exceed in
interest a knock at the door.
Essays of Elia (1823) 'Valentine's Day'

5 [A pun] is a pistol let off at the ear; not a
feather to tickle the intellect.
Last Essays of Elia (1833) 'Popular Fallacies' no. 9

6 Gone before
To that unknown and silent shore.
'Hester' (1803) st. 7

7 I have had playmates, I have had
companions,
In my days of childhood, in my joyful
school-days,—
All, all are gone, the old familiar faces.
'The Old Familiar Faces'

8 A child's a plaything for an hour.
'Parental Recollections' (1809); often attributed
to Lamb's sister Mary

9 I have something more to do than feel.
*on the death of his mother, at his sister Mary's
hands*
letter to S. T. Coleridge, 27 September 1796

10 Cultivate simplicity, Coleridge.
letter to S. T. Coleridge, 8 November 1796

11 This very night I am going to leave off
tobacco! Surely there must be some other
world in which this unconquerable purpose
shall be realized.
letter to Thomas Manning, 26 December 1815

12 An Archangel a little damaged.
of Coleridge
letter to Wordsworth, 26 April 1816

13 When my sonnet was rejected, I exclaimed,
'Damn the age; I will write for Antiquity!'
letter to B. W. Proctor, 22 January 1829

John George Lambton *see* Lord Durham

George Lamming b. 1927

14 In the castle of my skin.
title of novel (1953)

Norman Lamont 1942–

15 Rising unemployment and the recession
have been the price that we've had to pay to
get inflation down. [Labour shouts] That is a
price well worth paying.
speech in the House of Commons, 16 May 1991

16 The green shoots of economic spring are
appearing once again.
often misquoted as, 'the green shoots of recovery'
speech at Conservative Party Conference, 9
October 1991

17 We give the impression of being in office
but not in power.
as a backbencher
speech in the House of Commons, 9 June 1993

Giuseppe di Lampedusa 1896–1957

18 If we want things to stay as they are, things
will have to change.
The Leopard (1957)

19 Love. Of course, love. Flames for a year,
ashes for thirty.
The Leopard (1957)

Osbert Lancaster 1908–86

20 Fan-vaulting . . . from an aesthetic
standpoint frequently belongs to the 'Last-
supper-carved-on-a-peach-stone' class of
masterpiece.
Pillar to Post (1938) 'Perpendicular'

Walter Savage Landor 1775–1864

21 I strove with none; for none was worth my
strife;
Nature I loved, and, next to Nature, Art.
'Dying Speech of an Old Philosopher' (1853)

22 Ah, what avails the sceptred race!
Ah, what the form divine!
'Rose Aylmer' (1806)

23 George the First was always reckoned
Vile, but viler George the Second;
And what mortal ever heard
Any good of George the Third?
When from earth the Fourth descended
God be praised the Georges ended!
epigram in *The Atlas*, 28 April 1855

Andrew Lang 1844–1912

24 They hear like ocean on a western beach
The surge and thunder of the Odyssey.
'The Odyssey' (1881)

25 He uses statistics as a drunken man uses
lamp posts—for support rather than
illumination.
Alan L. Mackay *Harvest of a Quiet Eye* (1977);
attributed

William Langland c.1330–c.1400

26 In a somer seson, whan softe was the sonne.
The Vision of Piers Plowman B text (ed. A. V. C.
Schmidt, 1987) prologue l. 1

27 Ac on a May morwenynge on Malverne
hilles
Me bifel a ferly, of Fairye me thoghte.
The Vision of Piers Plowman B text (ed. A. V. C.
Schmidt, 1987) prologue l. 5

Ac on a May mornyng on Maluerne hulles
Me biful for to slepe, for werynesse of-
walked.

The Vision of Piers Plowman C text (ed. D. Pearsall,
1978) prologue l. 6)

1 A faire feeld ful of folk fond I ther bitwene.

The Vision of Piers Plowman B text (ed. A. V. C.
Schmidt, 1987) prologue l. 17

2 Grammer, the ground of al.

The Vision of Piers Plowman B text (ed. A. V. C.
Schmidt, 1987) Passus 15, l. 370

Stephen Langton d. 1228

3 *Veni, Sancte Spiritus,*
Et emitte coelitus
Lucis tuae radium.

Come, Holy Spirit, and send out from
heaven the beam of your light.

The 'Golden Sequence' for Whit Sunday (also
attributed to several others, notably Pope
Innocent III)

Lao Tzu *c.*604–*c.*531 BC

textual translations are those of Wing-Tsit Chan,
1963

4 Heaven and earth are not humane
They regard all things as straw dogs.
The sage is not humane.
He regards all people as straw dogs.

Tao-te Ching ch. 5

5 The best [rulers] are those whose existence
is [merely] known by the people.
The next best are those who are loved and
praised.
The next are those who are feared.
And the next are those who are reviled . . .
[The great rulers] accomplish their task;
they complete their work.
Nevertheless their people say that they
simply follow Nature.

Tao-te Ching ch. 17

6 There is nothing softer and weaker than
water,
And yet there is nothing better for attacking
hard and strong things.
For this reason there is no substitute for it.
All the world knows that the weak
overcomes the strong and the soft
overcomes the hard.
But none can practice it.

Tao-te Ching ch. 78

Dionysius Lardner 1793–1859

7 Men might as well project a voyage to the
moon as attempt to employ steam
navigation against the stormy North
Atlantic Ocean.

speech to the British Association for the
Advancement of Science, 1838

Ring Lardner 1885–1933

8 Are you lost daddy I arsked tenderly.
Shut up he explained.

The Young Immigrunts (1920) ch. 10

James Larkin 1867–1947

9 Hell has no terror for me. I have lived there.
Thirty six years of hunger and poverty have
been my portion. They cannot terrify me
with hell. Better to be in hell with Dante
and Davitt than to be in heaven with Carson
and Murphy.

in 1913, during the 'Dublin lockout' labour
dispute

Ulick O'Connor *The Troubles* (rev. ed., 1996)

Philip Larkin 1922–1985

10 Sexual intercourse began
In nineteen sixty-three
(Which was rather late for me) —
Between the end of the *Chatterley* ban
And the Beatles' first LP.

'Annus Mirabilis' (1974)

11 What will survive of us is love.

'An Arundel Tomb' (1964)

12 And that will be England gone,
The shadows, the meadows, the lanes,
The guildhalls, the carved choirs.
There'll be books; it will linger on
In galleries; but all that remains
For us will be concrete and tyres.

'Going, Going' (1974)

13 Nothing, like something, happens
anywhere.

'I Remember, I Remember' (1955)

14 They fuck you up, your mum and dad.
They may not mean to, but they do.
They fill you with the faults they had
And add some extra, just for you.

'This Be The Verse' (1974)

15 Why should I let the toad *work*
Squat on my life?
Can't I use my wit as a pitchfork
And drive the brute off?

'Toads' (1955)

16 Give me your arm, old toad;
Help me down Cemetery Road.

'Toads Revisited' (1964)

17 A beginning, a muddle, and an end.

on the 'classic formula' for a novel

in *New Fiction* no. 15, January 1978; cf. **Aristotle**
14:15

Duc de la Rochefoucauld 1613–80

18 We are all strong enough to bear the
misfortunes of others.

Maximes (1678) no. 19

19 There are good marriages, but no delightful
ones.

Maximes (1678) no. 113

20 Hypocrisy is a tribute which vice pays to
virtue.

Maximes (1678) no. 218

21 Absence diminishes commonplace passions
and increases great ones, as the wind
extinguishes candles and kindles fire.

Maximes (1678) no. 276; cf. **Bussy-Rabutin**
76:25, **Francis de Sales** 132:20

1 In most of mankind gratitude is merely a secret hope for greater favours.
  Maximes (1678) no. 298; cf. **Walpole** 327:23

2 In the misfortune of our best friends, we always find something which is not displeasing to us.
  Réflexions ou Maximes Morales (1665) maxim 99

Duc de la Rochefoucauld-Liancourt 1747–1827

3 LOUIS XVI: *C'est une grande révolte.*
LA ROCHEFOUCAULD-LIANCOURT: *Non, Sire, c'est une grande révolution.*

LOUIS XVI: It is a big revolt.
LA ROCHEFOUCAULD-LIANCOURT: No, Sir, it is a big revolution.
  on a report reaching Versailles of the Fall of the Bastille, 1789
  F. Dreyfus *La Rochefoucauld-Liancourt* (1903) ch. 2, sect. 3

Hugh Latimer c.1485–1555

4 *Gutta cavat lapidem, non vi sed saepe cadendo.*
The drop of rain maketh a hole in the stone, not by violence, but by oft falling.
  The Second Sermon preached before the King's Majesty (19 April 1549); cf. **Ovid** 238:13

5 Be of good comfort Master Ridley, and play the man. We shall this day light such a candle by God's grace in England, as (I trust) shall never be put out.
  prior to being burned for heresy, 16 October 1555
  John Foxe *Actes and Monuments* (1570 ed.)

Harry Lauder 1870–1950

6 Keep right on to the end of the road,
Keep right on to the end.
Tho' the way be long, let your heart be strong,
Keep right on round the bend.
  'The End of the Road' (1924 song)

7 I love a lassie, a bonnie, bonnie lassie,
She's as pure as the lily in the dell.
She's as sweet as the heather, the bonnie bloomin' heather—
Mary, ma Scotch Bluebell.
  'I Love a Lassie' (1905 song)

8 Roamin' in the gloamin'.
  'Roamin' in the Gloamin'' (1911 song)

Stan Laurel 1890–1965

9 Another nice mess you've gotten me into.
  often 'another fine mess'
  Another Fine Mess (1930 film) and many other Laurel and Hardy films; spoken by Oliver Hardy

Wilfrid Laurier 1841–1919

10 The nineteenth century was the century of the United States. I think we can claim that it is Canada that shall fill the twentieth century.
  speech in Ottawa, 18 January 1904

D. H. Lawrence 1885–1930

11 To the Puritan all things are impure, as somebody says.
  Etruscan Places (1932) 'Cerveteri'; cf. **Bible** 51:14

12 It was in 1915 the old world ended.
  Kangaroo (1923)

13 John Thomas says good-night to Lady Jane, a little droopingly, but with a hopeful heart.
  Lady Chatterley's Lover (1928) ch. 19

14 Pornography is the attempt to insult sex, to do dirt on it.
  Phoenix (1936) 'Pornography and Obscenity' ch. 3

15 Never trust the artist. Trust the tale. The proper function of a critic is to save the tale from the artist who created it.
  Studies in Classic American Literature (1923) ch. 1

16 Be a good animal, true to your instincts.
  The White Peacock (1911) pt. 2, ch. 2

17 Don't you find it a beautiful clean thought, a world empty of people, just uninterrupted grass, and a hare sitting up?
  Women in Love (1920) ch. 11

18 Men! The only animal in the world to fear!
  'Mountain Lion' (1923)

19 I never saw a wild thing
Sorry for itself.
  'Self-Pity' (1929)

20 Now it is autumn and the falling fruit
And the long journey towards oblivion . . .
Have you built your ship of death, O have you?
O build your ship of death, for you will need it.
  'Ship of Death' (1932)

21 Not I, not I, but the wind that blows through me!
  'Song of a Man who has Come Through' (1917)

22 When I read Shakespeare I am struck with wonder
That such trivial people should muse and thunder
In such lovely language.
  'When I Read Shakespeare' (1929)

23 Tragedy ought really to be a great kick at misery.
  letter to A. W. McLeod, 6 October 1912

24 The dead don't die. They look on and help.
  letter to J. Middleton Murry, 2 February 1923

T. E. Lawrence 1888–1935

25 Many men would take the death-sentence without a whimper to escape the life-sentence which fate carries in her other hand.
  The Mint (1955) pt. 1, ch. 4

26 I loved you, so I drew these tides of men into my hands and wrote my will across the sky in stars.
  The Seven Pillars of Wisdom (1926) dedication

Nigel Lawson 1932–

1 It represented the tip of a singularly ill-concealed iceberg, with all the destructive potential that icebergs possess.
of an article by Alan Walters, Margaret **Thatcher**'s *economic adviser, criticizing the Exchange Rate Mechanism*
in the House of Commons following his resignation as Chancellor, 31 October 1989

Emma Lazarus 1849–87

2 Give me your tired, your poor,
Your huddled masses yearning to breathe free.
inscription on the Statue of Liberty, New York
'The New Colossus' (1883)

Stephen Leacock 1869–1944

3 Advertising may be described as the science of arresting human intelligence long enough to get money from it.
Garden of Folly (1924) 'The Perfect Salesman'

4 I am what is called a *professor emeritus*—from the Latin *e*, 'out', and *meritus*, 'so he ought to be'.
Here are my Lectures (1938) ch. 14

5 A sportsman is a man who, every now and then, simply has to get out and kill something. Not that he's cruel. He wouldn't hurt a fly. It's not big enough.
My Remarkable Uncle (1942)

Mary Leapor 1722–46

6 In spite of all romantic poets sing,
This gold, my dearest, is an useful thing.
'Mira to Octavia'

Edward Lear 1812–88

7 Who, or why, or which, or what,
Is the Akond of Swat?
'The Akond of Swat' (1888)

8 There was an Old Man with a beard,
Who said, 'It is just as I feared!—
Two Owls and a Hen,
Four Larks and a Wren,
Have all built their nests in my beard!'
A Book of Nonsense (1846)

9 On the coast of Coromandel
Where the early pumpkins blow,
In the middle of the woods,
Lived the Yonghy-Bonghy-Bò.
'The Courtship of the Yonghy-Bonghy-Bò' (1871)

10 The Dong with a luminous nose.
title of poem (1871)

11 Far and few, far and few,
Are the lands where the Jumblies live;
Their heads are green, and their hands are blue,
And they went to sea in a Sieve.
'The Jumblies' (1871)

12 There was an old man of Thermopylae,
Who never did anything properly.
More Nonsense (1872) 'One Hundred Nonsense Pictures and Rhymes'

13 'How pleasant to know Mr Lear!'
Who has written such volumes of stuff!
Some think him ill-tempered and queer,
But a few think him pleasant enough.
Nonsense Songs (1871) preface

14 The Owl and the Pussy-Cat went to sea
In a beautiful pea-green boat.
They took some honey, and plenty of money,
Wrapped up in a five-pound note.
'The Owl and the Pussy-Cat' (1871)

15 Pussy said to the Owl, 'You elegant fowl!
How charmingly sweet you sing!
O let us be married! too long we have tarried:
But what shall we do for a ring?'
They sailed away for a year and a day,
To the land where the Bong-tree grows,
And there in a wood a Piggy-wig stood
With a ring at the end of his nose.
'The Owl and the Pussy-Cat' (1871)

16 They dined on mince, and slices of quince,
Which they ate with a runcible spoon;
And hand in hand, on the edge of the sand,
They danced by the light of the moon.
'The Owl and the Pussy-Cat' (1871)

17 The Pobble who has no toes
Had once as many as we;
When they said, 'Some day you may lose them all';—
He replied,—'Fish fiddle de-dee!'
'The Pobble Who Has No Toes' (1871)

18 He has gone to fish, for his Aunt Jobiska's
Runcible Cat with crimson whiskers!
'The Pobble Who Has No Toes' (1871)

Timothy Leary 1920–96

19 If you take the game of life seriously, if you take your nervous system seriously, if you take your sense organs seriously, if you take the energy process seriously, you must turn on, tune in and drop out.
lecture, June 1966, in *The Politics of Ecstasy* (1968) ch. 21

20 The PC is the LSD of the '90s.
remark made in the early 1990s; in *Guardian* 1 June 1996

21 Why not? Why not? Why not? Yeah.
last words; in *Independent* 1 June 1996

Mary Elizabeth Lease 1853–1933

22 Kansas had better stop raising corn and begin raising hell.
E. J. James et al. *Notable American Women 1607–1950* (1971) vol. 2

F. R. Leavis 1895–1978

23 The common pursuit.
title of book (1952)

24 The few really great—the major novelists . . . are significant in terms of the human awareness they promote; awareness of the possibilities of life.
The Great Tradition (1948) ch. 1

1 Self-contempt, well-grounded.
on the foundation of T. S. Eliot's work
in *Times Literary Supplement* 21 October 1988
(quoted by Christopher Ricks in a BBC radio
talk); cf. **Milton** 222:13

Fran Lebowitz 1946–

2 There is no such thing as inner peace. There
is only nervousness or death.
Metropolitan Life (1978)

3 The best fame is a writer's fame: it's enough
to get a table at a good restaurant, but not
enough that you get interrupted when you
eat.
in *Observer* 30 May 1993 'Sayings of the Week'

Stanislaw Lec 1909–66

4 Is it progress if a cannibal uses knife and
fork?
Unkempt Thoughts (1962)

John le Carré 1931–

5 The spy who came in from the cold.
title of novel (1963)

Le Corbusier 1887–1965

6 A house is a machine for living in.
Vers une architecture (1923); cf. **Tolstoy** 318:16

Alexandre Auguste Ledru-Rollin
1807–74

7 Ah well! I am their leader, I really had to
follow them!
E. de Mirecourt *Les Contemporains* vol. 14 (1857)
'Ledru-Rollin'

Gypsy Rose Lee 1914–70

8 God is love, but get it in writing.
attributed

Harper Lee 1926–

9 Shoot all the bluejays you want, if you can
hit 'em, but remember it's a sin to kill a
mockingbird.
To Kill a Mockingbird (1960) ch. 10

Henry Lee ('Light-Horse Harry')
1756–1818

10 A citizen, first in war, first in peace, and
first in the hearts of his countrymen.
Funeral Oration on the death of General Washington
(1800)

Laurie Lee 1914–97

11 I was set down from the carrier's cart at the
age of three; and there with a sense of
bewilderment and terror my life in the
village began.
Cider with Rosie (1959)

Nathaniel Lee c.1653–92

12 When Greeks joined Greeks, then was the
tug of war!
The Rival Queens (1677) act 4, sc. 2

13 They called me mad, and I called them mad,
and damn them, they outvoted me.
attributed

Robert E. Lee 1807–70

14 It is well that war is so terrible. We should
grow too fond of it.
after the battle of Fredericksburg, December 1862
attributed

refusing an offer to write his memoirs:
15 I should be trading on the blood of my men.
attributed, perhaps apocryphal

Lynda Lee-Potter

16 Powerful men often succeed through the
help of their wives. Powerful women only
succeed in spite of their husbands.
in *Daily Mail* 16 May 1984

Richard Le Gallienne 1866–1947

17 The cry of the Little Peoples goes up to God
in vain,
For the world is given over to the cruel sons
of Cain.
'The Cry of the Little Peoples' (1899)

Tom Lehrer 1928–

18 Plagiarize! Let no one else's work evade
your eyes,
Remember why the good Lord made your
eyes.
'Lobachevski' (1953 song)

19 Poisoning pigeons in the park.
song title, 1953

20 It is sobering to consider that when Mozart
was my age he had already been dead for a
year.
N. Shapiro (ed.) *An Encyclopedia of Quotations
about Music* (1978)

Gottfried Wilhelm Leibniz
1646–1716

21 *Nihil est sine ratione.*
There is nothing without a reason.
Studies in Physics and the Nature of Body (1671)

22 *Eadem sunt quorum unum potest substitui alteri
salva veritate.*
Two things are identical if one can be
substituted for the other without affecting
the truth.
'Table de définitions' (1704) in L. Coutourat (ed.)
Opuscules et fragments inédits de Leibniz (1903)

Fred W. Leigh d. 1924

23 Can't get away to marry you today,
My wife won't let me!
'Waiting at the Church (My Wife Won't Let Me)'
(1906 song)

24 Why am I always the bridesmaid,
Never the blushing bride?
'Why Am I Always the Bridesmaid?' (1917 song,
with Charles Collins and Lily Morris)

Curtis E. LeMay 1906-90

1 They've got to draw in their horns and stop their aggression, or we're going to bomb them back into the Stone Age.
on the North Vietnamese
   Mission with LeMay (1965)

Lenin 1870-1924

2 While the State exists, there can be no freedom. When there is freedom there will be no State.
   State and Revolution (1919) ch. 5

3 What is to be done?
   title of pamphlet (1902); originally the title of a novel (1863) by N. G. Chernyshevsky

4 Communism is Soviet power plus the electrification of the whole country.
   Report to 8th Congress, 1920

5 Who? Whom? [i.e. Who masters whom?]
   definition of political science, meaning 'Who will outstrip whom?'
   in *Polnoe Sobranie Sochinenii* vol. 44 (1970) 17 October 1921 and elsewhere

6 A good man fallen among Fabians.
   of George Bernard **Shaw**
   Arthur Ransome *Six Weeks in Russia in 1919* (1919) 'Notes of Conversations with Lenin'

7 Liberty is precious—so precious that it must be rationed.
   Sidney and Beatrice Webb *Soviet Communism* (1936)

John Lennon 1940-80
see also **Lennon and McCartney**

8 Happiness is a warm gun.
   title of song (1968)

9 Will the people in the cheaper seats clap your hands? All the rest of you, if you'll just rattle your jewellery.
   at the Royal Variety Performance, 4 November 1963

John Lennon 1940-1980
and Paul McCartney 1942-
see also **Lennon, McCartney**

10 For I don't care too much for money,
   For money can't buy me love.
   'Can't Buy Me Love' (1964 song)

11 All the lonely people, where do they all come from?
   'Eleanor Rigby' (1966 song)

12 Give peace a chance.
   title of song (1969)

13 It's been a hard day's night,
   And I've been working like a dog.
   'A Hard Day's Night' (1964 song)

14 Strawberry fields forever.
   title of song (1967)

15 She's got a ticket to ride, but she don't care.
   'Ticket to Ride' (1965 song)

16 Will you still need me, will you still feed me,

When I'm sixty four?
   'When I'm Sixty Four' (1967 song)

17 Oh I get by with a little help from my friends,
   Mm, I get high with a little help from my friends.
   'With a Little Help From My Friends' (1967 song)

Dan Leno (George Galvin) 1860-1904

18 Ah! what is man? Wherefore does he why? Whence did he whence? Whither is he withering?
   Dan Leno Hys Booke (1901) ch. 1

William Lenthall 1591-1662

19 I have neither eye to see, nor tongue to speak here, but as the House is pleased to direct me.
   to **Charles I,** *on being asked if he had seen any of the five MPs whom the King had ordered to be arrested, 4 January 1642*
   John Rushworth *Historical Collections. The Third Part* vol. 2 (1692); cf. **Lincoln** 199:12

Leonardo da Vinci 1452-1519

20 In her [Nature's] inventions nothing is lacking, and nothing is superfluous.
   Edward McCurdy (ed. and trans.) *Leonardo da Vinci's Notebooks* (1906) bk. 1

21 The poet ranks far below the painter in the representation of visible things, and far below the musician in that of invisible things.
   Irma A. Richter (ed.) *Selections from the Notebooks of Leonardo da Vinci* (1952)

Mikhail Lermontov 1814-41

22 Of two close friends, one is always the slave of the other.
   A Hero of our Time (1840) 'Princess Mary' (translated by Philip Longworth)

23 I am like a man yawning at a ball; the only reason he does not go home to bed is that his carriage has not arrived yet.
   A Hero of our Time (1840) 'Princess Mary' (translated by Philip Longworth)

Alan Jay Lerner 1918-86

24 Don't let it be forgot
   That once there was a spot
   For one brief shining moment that was known
   As Camelot.
   now particularly associated with the White House of John Fitzgerald **Kennedy**
   'Camelot' (1960 song)

25 Why can't a woman be more like a man? Men are so honest, so thoroughly square.
   'A Hymn to Him' (1956 song) in *My Fair Lady*

26 The rain in Spain stays mainly in the plain.
   'The Rain in Spain' (1956 song) in *My Fair Lady*

Doris Lessing 1919–

1 When old settlers say 'One has to
understand the country,' what they mean is,
'You have to get used to our ideas about the
native.'
The Grass is Singing (1950) ch. 1

2 What of October, that ambiguous month,
the month of tension, the unendurable
month?
Martha Quest (1952) pt. 4, sect. 1

G. E. Lessing 1729–81

3 One single grateful thought raised to
heaven is the most perfect prayer.
Minna von Barnhelm (1767) act 2, sc. 7

Lord Leverhulme 1851–1925

4 Half the money I spend on advertising is
wasted, and the trouble is I don't know
which half.
David Ogilvy *Confessions of an Advertising Man*
(1963)

Ada Leverson 1865–1936

5 He seemed at ease and to have the look of
the last gentleman in Europe.
of Oscar **Wilde**
Letters to the Sphinx (1930)

Primo Levi 1919–87

6 Our language lacks words to express this
offence, the demolition of a man.
of a year spent in Auschwitz
If This is a Man (1958)

Bernard Levin 1928–

7 The Stag at Bay with the mentality of a fox
at large.
of Harold **Macmillan**
The Pendulum Years (1970) ch. 12

8 Whom the mad would destroy, they first
make gods.
of **Mao** *Zedong in 1967*
Levin quoting himself in *The Times* 21
September 1987

Duc de Lévis 1764–1830

9 *Noblesse oblige.*
Nobility has its obligations.
Maximes et Réflexions (1812 ed.) 'Morale: Maximes
et Préceptes' no. 73

10 *Gouverner, c'est choisir.*
To govern is to choose.
Maximes et Réflexions (1812 ed.) 'Politique:
Maximes de Politique' no. 19

C. S. Lewis 1898–1963

11 No one ever told me that grief felt so like
fear.
A Grief Observed (1961)

12 She's the sort of woman who lives for
others—you can always tell the others by
their hunted expression.
The Screwtape Letters (1942) no. 26

13 Often when I pray I wonder if I am not
posting letters to a non-existent address.
letter to Arthur Greeves, 24 December 1930

14 He that but looketh on a plate of ham and
eggs to lust after it, hath already committed
breakfast with it in his heart.
letter, 10 March 1954

Esther Lewis (later Clark) fl. 1747–89

15 Why are the needle and the pen
Thought incompatible by men?
'A Mirror for Detractors' (1754) l. 146

George Cornewall Lewis 1806–63

16 Life would be tolerable but for its
amusements.
in *The Times* 18 September 1872; cf. **Surtees**
306:10

Sam M. Lewis 1885–1959
and Joe Young 1889–1939

17 How 'ya gonna keep 'em down on the farm
(after they've seen Paree)?
title of song (1919)

Sinclair Lewis 1885–1951

18 Our American professors like their
literature clear and cold and pure and very
dead.
The American Fear of Literature (Nobel Prize
Address, 12 December 1930)

19 She did her work with the thoroughness of
a mind which reveres details and never
quite understands them.
Babbitt (1922) ch. 18

20 It can't happen here.
title of novel (1935)

Wyndham Lewis 1882–1957

21 Angels in jumpers.
describing the figures in Stanley **Spencer's**
paintings
attributed

George Leybourne d. 1884

22 He'd fly through the air with the greatest of
ease,
A daring young man on the flying trapeze.
'The Flying Trapeze' (1868 song)

Liberace 1919–87

23 When the reviews are bad I tell my staff
that they can join me as I cry all the way to
the bank.
Autobiography (1973) ch. 2

Georg Christoph Lichtenberg
1742–99

24 The journalists have constructed for
themselves a little wooden chapel, which
they also call the Temple of Fame, in which
they put up and take down portraits all day

long and make such a hammering you can't hear yourself speak.

A. Leitzmann *Georg Christoph Lichtenberg Aphorismen* (1904)

1 There is a great deal of difference between *still* believing something, and *again* believing it.

Notebook E no. 8 1775–6 in *Aphorisms* (1990)

A. J. Liebling 1904–63

2 Freedom of the press is guaranteed only to those who own one.

'The Wayward Press: Do you belong in Journalism?' (1960)

Charles-Joseph, Prince de Ligne 1735–1814

3 *Le congrès ne marche pas, il danse.*
The Congress makes no progress; it dances.

Auguste de la Garde-Chambonas *Souvenirs du Congrès de Vienne* (1820) ch. 1

George Lillo 1693–1739

4 There's sure no passion in the human soul, But finds its food in music.

The Fatal Curiosity (1736) act 1, sc. 2

Abraham Lincoln 1809–65

5 To give victory to the right, not bloody bullets, but peaceful ballots only, are necessary.

often quoted as, 'The ballot is stronger than the bullet'

speech, 18 May 1858

6 'A house divided against itself cannot stand.' I believe this government cannot endure permanently, half slave and half free.

speech, 16 June 1858; cf. **Bible** 45:25

7 In giving freedom to the slave, we assure freedom to the free—honourable alike in what we give and what we preserve. We shall nobly save, or meanly lose, the last, best hope of earth.

Annual Message to Congress, 1 December 1862

8 Fourscore and seven years ago our fathers brought forth upon this continent a new nation, conceived in liberty, and dedicated to the proposition that all men are created equal . . . In a larger sense we cannot dedicate, we cannot consecrate, we cannot hallow this ground. The brave men, living and these dead, who struggled here, have consecrated it far above our power to add or detract. The world will little note, nor long remember, what we say here, but it can never forget what they did here. It is for us, the living, rather to be dedicated here to the unfinished work which they who fought here have thus far so nobly advanced . . . we here highly resolve that the dead shall not have died in vain, that this nation, under God, shall have a new birth of freedom; and that government of the people, by the

people, and for the people, shall not perish from the earth.

the Lincoln Memorial inscription reads 'by the people, for the people'

address at the dedication of the National Cemetery at Gettysburg, 19 November 1863, as reported the following day, in R. P. Basler (ed.) *Collected Works . . .* (1953) vol. 7; cf. **Webster** 330:5

9 I claim not to have controlled events, but confess plainly that events have controlled me.

letter to A. G. Hodges, 4 April 1864

10 It is not best to swap horses when crossing streams.

reply to National Union League, 9 June 1864

11 With malice toward none; with charity for all; with firmness in the right, as God gives us to see the right, let us strive on to finish the work we are in: to bind up the nation's wounds; to care for him who shall have borne the battle, and for his widow and his orphan, to do all which may achieve and cherish a just and lasting peace among ourselves, and with all nations.

second inaugural address, 4 March 1865

12 As President, I have no eyes but constitutional eyes; I cannot see you.

attributed reply to the South Carolina Commissioners; cf. **Lenthall** 197:19

13 People who like this sort of thing will find this the sort of thing they like.

judgement of a book

G. W. E. Russell *Collections and Recollections* (1898) ch. 30

14 So you're the little woman who wrote the book that made this great war!

*on meeting Harriet Beecher **Stowe**, author of* Uncle Tom's Cabin

Carl Sandburg *Abraham Lincoln: The War Years* (1936) vol. 2, ch. 39

15 You may fool all the people some of the time; you can even fool some of the people all the time; but you can't fool all of the people all the time.

*also attributed to Phineas **Barnum***

Alexander K. McClure *Lincoln's Yarns and Stories* (1904)

Vachel Lindsay 1879–1931

16 Booth led boldly with his big bass drum— (Are you washed in the blood of the Lamb?)

'General William Booth Enters into Heaven' (1913); cf. **Bible** 52:10

Graham Linehan and **Arthur Mathews**

17 It's great being a priest, isn't it, Ted?

'Good Luck, Father Ted' (1994), episode from *Father Ted* (Channel 4 TV, 1994–8)

18 Careful now!

placard alerting Craggy Island to a banned film

'The Passion of St Tibulus' (1994), episode from *Father Ted* (Channel 4 TV, 1994–8)

Gary Lineker 1960–

1 The nice aspect about football is that, if things go wrong, it's the manager who gets the blame.

remark before his first match as captain of England
in *Independent* 12 September 1990

Eric Linklater 1899–1974

2 'There won't be any revolution in America,' said Isadore. Nikitin agreed. 'The people are all too clean. They spend all their time changing their shirts and washing themselves. You can't feel fierce and revolutionary in a bathroom.'
Juan in America (1931) bk. 5, pt. 3

Art Linkletter 1912–

3 The four stages of man are infancy, childhood, adolescence and obsolescence.
A Child's Garden of Misinformation (1965) ch. 8

George Linley 1798–1865

4 Among our ancient mountains,
And from our lovely vales,
Oh, let the prayer re-echo:
'God bless the Prince of Wales!'
'God Bless the Prince of Wales' (1862 song); translated from the Welsh original by J. C. Hughes (1837–87)

Lin Yutang 1895–1976

5 [The traveller can] get the greatest joy of travel even without going to the mountains, by staying at home and watching and going about the field to watch a sailing cloud, or a dog, or a hedge, or a lonely tree.
The Importance of Living (1938) ch. 11

Richard Littledale 1833–90

6 Let holy charity
Mine outward vesture be,
And lowliness become mine inner clothing.
'Come down, O Love divine' (1867 hymn)

Joan Littlewood 1914–
and **Charles Chilton** 1914–

7 Oh what a lovely war.
title of stage show (1963)

Maxim Litvinov 1876–1951

8 Peace is indivisible.
note to the Allies, 25 February 1920; A. U. Pope *Maxim Litvinoff* (1943)

Penelope Lively 1933–

9 Language tethers us to the world; without it we spin like atoms.
Moon Tiger (1987)

10 We are walking lexicons. In a single sentence of idle chatter we preserve Latin, Anglo-Saxon, Norse; we carry a museum inside our heads, each day we

commemorate peoples of whom we have never heard.
Moon Tiger (1987)

Ken Livingstone 1945–

11 If voting changed anything, they'd abolish it.
title of book, 1987

Livy 59 BC–AD 17

12 *Vae victis.*
Down with the defeated!
cry (already proverbial) of the Gallic King, Brennus, on capturing Rome in 390 BC
Ab Urbe Condita bk. 5, ch. 48, sect. 9

13 *Pugna magna victi sumus.*
We were defeated in a great battle.
announcement of disaster for the Romans in Hannibal's ambush at Lake Trasimene in 217 BC
Ab Urbe Condita bk. 22, ch. 7, sect. 8

Richard Llewellyn (Richard Llewellyn Lloyd) 1907–83

14 How green was my valley.
title of book (1939)

Robert Lloyd

15 Alone from Jargon born to rescue Law,
From precedent, grave hum, and formal saw!
To strip chicanery of its vain pretence,
And marry Common Law to Common Sense!
'The Law-Student' (1762); on Lord Mansfield, Lord Chief Justice, 1756–88

16 While all the art of Imitation,
Is pilf'ring from the first creation.
'Shakespeare' (1762)

David Lloyd George 1863–1945

17 The leal and trusty mastiff which is to watch over our interests, but which runs away at the first snarl of the trade unions . . . A mastiff? It is the right hon. Gentleman's poodle.
on the House of Lords and A. J. Balfour respectively
in the House of Commons, 26 June 1907

18 A fully-equipped duke costs as much to keep up as two Dreadnoughts; and dukes are just as great a terror and they last longer.
speech at Newcastle, 9 October 1909, in *The Times* 11 October 1909

19 At eleven o'clock this morning came to an end the cruellest and most terrible war that has ever scourged mankind. I hope we may say that thus, this fateful morning, came to an end all wars.
speech in the House of Commons, 11 November 1918; cf. **Wells** 331:18

20 What is our task? To make Britain a fit country for heroes to live in.
speech at Wolverhampton, 23 November 1918

1 Unless I am mistaken, by the steps we have taken [in Ireland] we have murder by the throat.
  speech at the Mansion House, 9 November 1920

2 Negotiating with de Valera . . . is like trying to pick up mercury with a fork.
  to which **de Valera** *replied, 'Why doesn't he use a spoon?'*
  M. J. MacManus *Eamon de Valera* (1944) ch. 6

John Locke 1632–1704

3 New opinions are always suspected, and usually opposed, without any other reason but because they are not already common.
  An Essay concerning Human Understanding (1690) 'Dedicatory Epistle'

4 No man's knowledge here can go beyond his experience.
  An Essay concerning Human Understanding (1690) bk. 2, ch. 1, sect. 19

5 Crooked things may be as stiff and unflexible as straight: and men may be as positive in error as in truth.
  An Essay concerning Human Understanding (1690) bk. 4, ch. 19, sect. 11

6 All men are liable to error; and most men are, in many points, by passion or interest, under temptation to it.
  An Essay concerning Human Understanding (1690) bk. 4, ch. 20, sect. 17

7 The end of law is, not to abolish or restrain, but to preserve and enlarge freedom.
  Second Treatise of Civil Government (1690) ch. 6, sect. 57

8 The great and chief end, therefore, of men's uniting into commonwealths, and putting themselves under government, is the preservation of their property.
  Second Treatise of Civil Government (1690) ch. 9, sect. 124

Frederick Locker-Lampson 1821–95

9 And many are afraid of God—
  And more of Mrs Grundy.
  'The Jester's Plea' (1868); cf. **Morton** 229:11

John Gibson Lockhart 1794–1854

10 It is a better and a wiser thing to be a starved apothecary than a starved poet; so back to the shop Mr John, back to 'plasters, pills, and ointment boxes.'
  reviewing Keats's Endymion
  in *Blackwood's Edinburgh Magazine* August 1818

David Lodge 1935–

11 Literature is mostly about having sex and not much about having children. Life is the other way round.
  The British Museum is Falling Down (1965) ch. 4

Frank Loesser 1910–69

12 See what the boys in the back room will have

And tell them I'm having the same.
  'Boys in the Back Room' (1939 song)

13 Isn't it grand! Isn't it fine! Look at the cut, the style, the line!
  The suit of clothes is altogether, but altogether it's altogether
  The most remarkable suit of clothes that I have ever seen.
  'The King's New Clothes' (1952 song); from the film *Hans Christian Andersen*

Jack London 1876–1916

14 The call of the wild.
  title of novel (1903)

Huey Long 1893–1935

15 For the present you can just call me the Kingfish.
  Every Man a King (1933)

16 Oh hell, say that I am *sui generis* and let it go at that.
  to journalists attempting to analyse his political personality
  T. Harry Williams *Huey Long* (1969)

Henry Wadsworth Longfellow 1807–82

17 I shot an arrow into the air,
  It fell to earth, I knew not where.
  'The Arrow and the Song' (1845)

18 Thou, too, sail on, O Ship of State!
  Sail on, O Union, strong and great!
  'The Building of the Ship' (1849)

19 Between the dark and the daylight,
  When the night is beginning to lower,
  Comes a pause in the day's occupations,
  That is known as the Children's Hour.
  'The Children's Hour' (1859)

20 The cares that infest the day
  Shall fold their tents, like the Arabs,
  And as silently steal away.
  'The Day is Done' (1844)

21 This is the forest primeval.
  Evangeline (1847) introduction

22 A youth, who bore, 'mid snow and ice,
  A banner with the strange device,
  Excelsior!
  'Excelsior' (1841)

23 Giotto's tower,
  The lily of Florence blossoming in stone.
  'Giotto's Tower' (1866)

24 I like that ancient Saxon phrase, which calls
  The burial-ground God's-Acre!
  'God's-Acre' (1841)

25 Life is real! Life is earnest!
  And the grave is not its goal;
  Dust thou art, to dust returnest,
  Was not spoken of the soul.
  'A Psalm of Life' (1838); cf. **Bible** 33:13

26 Lives of great men all remind us
  We can make our lives sublime,
  And, departing, leave behind us
  Footprints on the sands of time.
  'A Psalm of Life' (1838)

1 Though the mills of God grind slowly, yet
they grind exceeding small;
Though with patience He stands waiting,
with exactness grinds He all.
'Retribution' (1870), translation of Friedrich von
Logau (1604–55) *Sinnegedichte* (1654) no. 3224

2 A Lady with a Lamp shall stand
In the great history of the land,
A noble type of good,
Heroic womanhood.
on Florence **Nightingale**
'Santa Filomena' (1857)

3 By the shore of Gitche Gumee,
By the shining Big-Sea-Water,
Stood the wigwam of Nokomis.
The Song of Hiawatha (1855) 'Hiawatha's
Childhood'

4 Listen, my children, and you shall hear
Of the midnight ride of Paul Revere,
On the eighteenth of April in Seventy-five.
Tales of a Wayside Inn pt. 1 (1863) 'The Landlord's
Tale: Paul Revere's Ride'

5 One if by land and two if by sea;
And I on the opposite shore will be,
Ready to ride and sound the alarm.
Tales of a Wayside Inn pt. 1 (1863) 'The Landlord's
Tale: Paul Revere's Ride'; cf. **Revere** 256:2

6 Ships that pass in the night, and speak each
other in passing;
Only a signal shown and a distant voice in
the darkness.
Tales of a Wayside Inn pt. 3 (1874) 'The
Theologian's Tale: Elizabeth' pt. 4

7 Under a spreading chestnut tree
The village smithy stands;
The smith, a mighty man is he,
With large and sinewy hands.
'The Village Blacksmith' (1839)

8 Something attempted, something done,
Has earned a night's repose.
'The Village Blacksmith' (1839)

9 It was the schooner Hesperus,
That sailed the wintry sea;
And the skipper had taken his little
daughter,
To bear him company.
'The Wreck of the Hesperus' (1839)

10 There was a little girl
Who had a little curl
Right in the middle of her forehead,
When she was good
She was very, very good,
But when she was bad she was horrid.
*composed for, and sung to, his second daughter
while a babe in arms, c.1850*
B. R. Tucker-Macchetta *The Home Life of Henry W.
Longfellow* (1882) ch. 5

Lord Longford 1905–

11 In 1969 I published a small book on
Humility. It was a pioneering work which
has not, to my knowledge, been superseded.
in *Tablet* 22 January 1994

Longinus on the Sublime

12 Sublimity is the echo of a noble mind.
sect. 9

Alice Roosevelt Longworth 1884–1980

13 If you haven't got anything good to say
about anyone come and sit by me.
maxim embroidered on a cushion in her home
Michael Teague *Mrs L: Conversations with Alice
Roosevelt Longworth* (1981)

Anita Loos 1893–1981

14 Gentlemen prefer blondes.
title of book (1925)

15 So I really think that American gentlemen
are the best after all, because kissing your
hand may make you feel very very good but
a diamond and safire bracelet lasts forever.
Gentlemen Prefer Blondes (1925) ch. 4; cf. **Robin**
257:20

Frederico García Lorca *see* **García Lorca**

Edward N. Lorenz 1917–

16 Predictability: Does the flap of a butterfly's
wings in Brazil set off a tornado in Texas?
title of paper given to the American Association
for the Advancement of Science, Washington,
29 December 1979; James Gleick *Chaos* (1988)

Konrad Lorenz 1903–89

17 It is a good morning exercise for a research
scientist to discard a pet hypothesis every
day before breakfast. It keeps him young.
Das Sogenannte Böse (1963; tr. Marjorie Latzke as
On Aggression, 1966) ch. 2

Louis XIV (the 'Sun King') 1638–1715

18 *L'État c'est moi.*
I am the State.
before the Parlement de Paris, 13 April 1655
probably apocryphal; J. A. Dulaure *Histoire de
Paris* (1834) vol. 6

19 Every time I create an appointment, I create
a hundred malcontents and one ingrate.
Voltaire *Siècle de Louis XIV* (1768 ed.) vol. 2, ch. 26

20 *Il n'y a plus de Pyrénées.*
The Pyrenees are no more.
*on the accession of his grandson to the throne of
Spain, 1700*
attributed to Louis by Voltaire in *Siècle de Louis
XIV* (1753) ch. 26, but to the Spanish
Ambassador to France in the *Mercure Galant*
(Paris) November 1700

Louis XVI 1754–93

*diary entry for 14 July 1789, the day of the
storming of the Bastille:*
21 *Rien.*
Nothing.
Simon Schama *Citizens* (1989) ch. 10

Louis XVIII 1755–1824

1 Remember that there is not one of you who does not carry in his cartridge-pouch the marshal's baton of the duke of Reggio; it is up to you to bring it forth.

speech to Saint-Cyr cadets, 9 August 1819

2 *L'exactitude est la politesse des rois.*
Punctuality is the politeness of kings.

attributed in *Souvenirs de J. Lafitte* (1844) bk. 1, ch. 3

Louis Philippe 1773–1850

3 Died, has he? Now I wonder what he meant by that?

of Talleyrand

attributed, perhaps apocryphal

Joe Louis 1914–81

4 He can run. But he can't hide.

of Billy Conn, his opponent, before a heavyweight title fight, 19 June 1946
Louis: My Life Story (1947)

Ada Lovelace 1815–52

5 The Analytical Engine weaves algebraic patterns just as the Jacquard loom weaves flowers and leaves.

of Babbage's mechanical computer

Luigi Menabrea *Sketch of the Analytical Engine invented by Charles Babbage* (1843), translated and annotated by Ada Lovelace, Note A

Richard Lovelace 1618–58

6 Stone walls do not a prison make,
Nor iron bars a cage;
Minds innocent and quiet take
That for an hermitage.

'To Althea, From Prison' (1649)

7 I could not love thee, Dear, so much,
Loved I not honour more.

'To Lucasta, Going to the Wars' (1649)

James Lovell 1928–

8 Houston, we've had a problem.

on Apollo 13 space mission, 14 April 1970
in *The Times* 15 April 1970

Samuel Lover 1797–1868

9 When once the itch of literature comes over a man, nothing can cure it but the scratching of a pen.

Handy Andy (1842) ch. 36

10 Young Rory O'More courted Kathaleen bawn,
He was bold as a hawk, and she soft as the dawn.

'Rory O'More'' (1837 song); cf. **Thurber** 318:1

David Low 1891–1963

11 Colonel Blimp.

Cartoon creation, proponent of reactionary establishment opinions

Robert Lowe, Lord Sherbrooke 1811–92

12 The Chancellor of the Exchequer is a man whose duties make him more or less of a taxing machine. He is intrusted with a certain amount of misery which it is his duty to distribute as fairly as he can.

speech, House of Commons, 11 April 1870

Amy Lowell 1874–1925

13 And the softness of my body will be guarded by embrace
By each button, hook, and lace.
For the man who should loose me is dead,
Fighting with the Duke in Flanders,
In a pattern called a war.
Christ! What are patterns for?

'Patterns' (1916)

14 All books are either dreams or swords,
You can cut, or you can drug, with words.

'Sword Blades and Poppy Seed' (1914); cf.
Farquhar 126:12

James Russell Lowell 1819–91

15 An' you've got to git up airly
Ef you want to take in God.

The Biglow Papers (First Series, 1848) no. 1 'A Letter'

16 There comes Poe with his raven like Barnaby Rudge,
Three-fifths of him genius, and two-fifths sheer fudge.

'A Fable for Critics' (1848) l. 1215; cf. **Poe** 246:13

17 Blessèd are the horny hands of toil!

'A Glance Behind the Curtain' (1844); cf.
Salisbury 263:21

18 Once to every man and nation comes the moment to decide,
In the strife of Truth with Falsehood, for the good or evil side.

'The Present Crisis' (1845)

19 Truth forever on the scaffold, Wrong forever on the throne.

'The Present Crisis' (1845)

Robert Lowell 1917–77

20 Their monument sticks like a fishbone in the city's throat.

'For the Union Dead' (1964)

21 These are the tranquillized *Fifties*,
and I am forty. Ought I to regret my seed-time?

'Memories of West Street and Lepke' (1956)

22 At forty-five,
What next, what next?
At every corner,
I meet my Father,
my age, still alive.

'Middle Age' (1964)

23 This is death.
To die and know it. This is the Black Widow, death.

'Mr Edwards and the Spider' (1950)

1 If we see light at the end of the tunnel,
It's the light of the oncoming train.
  'Since 1939' (1977); cf. **Dickson** 111:19

2 But I suppose even God was born
too late to trust the old religion.
  'Tenth Muse' (1964)

3 the present, yes,
we are in it,
it's the infection
of things gone.
  'We Took Our Paradise' (1977)

William Lowndes 1652–1724

4 Take care of the pence, and the pounds will
take care of themselves.
  Lord Chesterfield *Letters to his Son* (1774) 5
  February 1750; cf. **Carroll** 83:22, **Chesterfield**
  89:8

L. S. Lowry 1887–1976

5 I'm a simple man, and I use simple
materials.
  Mervyn Levy *Paintings of L. S. Lowry* (1975)

Malcolm Lowry 1909–57

6 How alike are the groans of love to those of
the dying.
  Under the Volcano (1947) ch. 12

Lucan AD 39–65

7 There stands the ghost of a great name.
  of Pompey
  Pharsalia bk. 1, l. 135

8 Thinking nothing done while anything
remained to be done.
  Pharsalia bk. 2, l. 657; cf. **Rogers** 259:1

9 I have a wife, I have sons: we have given so
many hostages to the fates.
  Pharsalia bk. 6, l. 661; cf. **Bacon** 21:17

Clare Booth Luce 1903–87

10 Much of . . . his global thinking is, no matter
how you slice it, still globaloney.
  speech to the House of Representatives,
  February 1943

Lucilius c.180–102 BC

11 *Maior erat natu; non omnia possumus omnes.*
He was greater in years; we cannot all do
everything.
  Macrobius *Saturnalia* bk. 6, ch. 1, sect. 35; cf.
  Virgil 325:12

Lucretius c.94–55 BC

12 *Tantum religio potuit suadere malorum.*
So much wrong could religion induce.
  De Rerum Natura bk. 1, l. 101

13 . . . *Nil posse creari*
De nilo.
Nothing can be created out of nothing.
  De Rerum Natura bk. 1, l. 155

14 *Inque brevi spatio mutantur saecla animantum
Et quasi cursores vitai lampada tradunt.*

Some races increase, others are reduced,
and in a short while the generations of
living creatures are changed and like
runners relay the torch of life.
  De Rerum Natura bk. 2, l. 8

Fray Luis de León c.1527–91

15 We were saying yesterday . . .
  *on resuming a lecture at Salamanca University in
  1577, after five years' imprisonment*
  attributed, among others, by A. F. G. Bell in *Luis
  de León* (1925) ch. 8

Martin Luther 1483–1546

16 Here stand I. I can do no other. God help
me. Amen.
  speech at the Diet of Worms, 18 April 1521;
  attributed

17 For, where God built a church, there the
devil would also build a chapel . . . In such
sort is the devil always God's ape.
  Colloquia Mensalia (1566) ch. 2 (tr. H. Bell as
  Martin Luther's Divine Discourses, 1652)

18 A safe stronghold our God is still,
A trusty shield and weapon.
  'Eine feste Burg ist unser Gott' (1529); tr.
  Thomas Carlyle

19 Who loves not woman, wine, and song
Remains a fool his whole life long.
  attributed (later inscribed in the Luther room in
  the Wartburg, but with no proof of authorship)

Rosa Luxemburg 1871–1919

20 Freedom is always and exclusively freedom
for the one who thinks differently.
  Die Russische Revolution (1918) sect. 4

John Lydgate c.1370–c.1451

21 Sithe off oure language he was the
lodesterre.
  of Chaucer
  The Fall of Princes (1431–8) prologue l. 252

22 Woord is but wynd; leff woord and tak the
dede.
  Secrets of Old Philosophers l. 1224

John Lyly c.1554–1606

23 What bird so sings, yet so does wail?
O 'tis the ravished nightingale.
Jug, jug, jug, jug, tereu, she cries,
And still her woes at midnight rise.
  Campaspe (1584) act 5, sc. 1; cf. **Eliot** 122:23

24 Night hath a thousand eyes.
  The Maydes Metamorphosis (1600) act 3, sc. 1

25 If all the earth were paper white
And all the sea were ink
'Twere not enough for me to write
As my poor heart doth think.
  'If all the earth were paper white'

Lord Lyndhurst 1772–1863

1 Campbell has added another terror to death.

on Lord Campbell's Lives of the Lord Chancellors being written without the consent of heirs or executors

E. Bowen-Rowlands *Seventy-Two Years At the Bar* (1924) ch. 10; cf. **Wetherell** 332:22

Jonathan Lynn 1943–
and Antony Jay 1930–

2 I think it will be a clash between the political will and the administrative won't.

Yes Prime Minister (1987) vol. 2

Lysander d. 395 BC

3 Deceive boys with toys, but men with oaths.

Plutarch *Parallel Lives* 'Lysander' ch. 8; cf. **Plutarch** 246:10

Henry Francis Lyte 1793–1847

4 Abide with me: fast falls the eventide;
The darkness deepens; Lord, with me abide.

'Abide with Me' (probably written in 1847)

5 Change and decay in all around I see;
O Thou, who changest not, abide with me.

'Abide with Me' (probably written in 1847)

6 Praise my soul, the King of heaven;
To his feet thy tribute bring.
Ransomed, healed, restored, forgiven,
Who like me his praise should sing?

'Praise, my soul, the King of heaven' (1834 hymn)

7 Father-like, he tends and spares us.

'Praise, my soul, the King of heaven' (1834 hymn)

E. R. Bulwer, Lord Lytton *see* Owen Meredith

Douglas MacArthur 1880–1964

8 I came through and I shall return.

on reaching Australia, 20 March 1942, having broken through Japanese lines en route from Corregidor

in *New York Times* 21 March 1942

Rose Macaulay 1881–1958

9 Love's a disease. But curable.

Crewe Train (1926)

10 'Take my camel, dear,' said my aunt Dot, as she climbed down from this animal on her return from High Mass.

The Towers of Trebizond (1956)

Thomas Babington Macaulay 1800–59

11 In order that he might rob a neighbour whom he had promised to defend, black men fought on the coast of Coromandel, and red men scalped each other by the Great Lakes of North America.

Biographical Essays (1857) 'Frederic the Great'

12 The gallery in which the reporters sit has become a fourth estate of the realm.

Essays Contributed to the Edinburgh Review (1843) vol. 1 'Hallam'

13 The gigantic body, the huge massy face, seamed with the scars of disease, the brown coat, the black worsted stockings, the grey wig with the scorched foretop, the dirty hands, the nails bitten and pared to the quick.

Essays Contributed to the Edinburgh Review (1843) vol. 1 'Samuel Johnson'

14 If men are to wait for liberty till they become wise and good in slavery, they may indeed wait for ever.

Essays Contributed to the Edinburgh Review (1843) vol. 1 'Milton'

15 We know no spectacle so ridiculous as the British public in one of its periodical fits of morality.

Essays Contributed to the Edinburgh Review (1843) vol. 1 'Moore's *Life of Lord Byron*'

16 On the day of the accession of George the Third, the ascendancy of the Whig party terminated; and on that day the purification of the Whig party began.

Essays Contributed to the Edinburgh Review (1843) vol. 2 'William Pitt, Earl of Chatham'

17 Every schoolboy knows who imprisoned Montezuma, and who strangled Atahualpa.

Essays Contributed to the Edinburgh Review (1843) vol. 3 'Lord Clive'; cf. **Taylor** 310:1

18 She [the Roman Catholic Church] may still exist in undiminished vigour when some traveller from New Zealand shall, in the midst of a vast solitude, take his stand on a broken arch of London Bridge to sketch the ruins of St Paul's.

Essays Contributed to the Edinburgh Review (1843) vol. 3 'Von Ranke'; cf. **Walpole** 327:12

19 She [the Church of Rome] thoroughly understands what no other church has ever understood, how to deal with enthusiasts.

Essays Contributed to the Edinburgh Review (1843) vol. 3 'Von Ranke'

20 It was a crime in a child to read by the bedside of a sick parent one of those beautiful collects which had soothed the griefs of forty generations of Christians.

History of England vol. 1 (1849) ch. 2

21 The Puritan hated bear-baiting, not because it gave pain to the bear, but because it gave pleasure to the spectators.

History of England vol. 1 (1849) ch. 2

22 The English Bible, a book which, if everything else in our language should perish, would alone suffice to show the whole extent of its beauty and power.

T. F. Ellis (ed.) *Miscellaneous Writings of Lord Macaulay* (1860) 'John Dryden' (1828)

23 His imagination resembled the wings of an ostrich. It enabled him to run, though not to soar.

T. F. Ellis (ed.) *Miscellaneous Writings of Lord Macaulay* (1860) 'John Dryden' (1828)

1 This province of literature is a debatable line. It lies on the confines of two distinct territories . . . It is sometimes fiction. It is sometimes theory.

of history
T. F. Ellis (ed.) *Miscellaneous Writings of Lord Macaulay* (1860) vol. 1 'History' (1828)

2 Till Skiddaw saw the fire that burned on Gaunt's embattled pile,
And the red glare on Skiddaw roused the burghers of Carlisle.
'The Armada' (1833)

3 And the Man of Blood was there, with his long essenced hair,
And Astley, and Sir Marmaduke, and Rupert of the Rhine.
'The Battle of Naseby' (1824)

4 The priest who slew the slayer,
And shall himself be slain.
Lays of Ancient Rome (1842) 'The Battle of Lake Regillus' st. 10

5 Let no man stop to plunder,
But slay, and slay, and slay;
The Gods who live for ever
Are on our side to-day.
Lays of Ancient Rome (1842) 'The Battle of Lake Regillus' st. 35

6 Lars Porsena of Clusium
By the nine gods he swore
That the great house of Tarquin
Should suffer wrong no more.
Lays of Ancient Rome (1842) 'Horatius' st. 1

7 And how can man die better
Than facing fearful odds,
For the ashes of his fathers,
And the temples of his Gods?
Lays of Ancient Rome (1842) 'Horatius' st. 27

8 Now who will stand on either hand,
And keep the bridge with me?
Lays of Ancient Rome (1842) 'Horatius' st. 29

9 Then none was for a party;
Then all were for the state.
Lays of Ancient Rome (1842) 'Horatius' st. 32

10 But hark! the cry is Astur
And lo! the ranks divide,
And the great Lord of Luna
Comes with his stately stride.
Lays of Ancient Rome (1842) 'Horatius' st. 42

11 Was none who would be foremost
To lead such dire attack;
But those behind cried 'Forward!'
And those before cried 'Back!'
Lays of Ancient Rome (1842) 'Horatius' st. 50

12 Oh, Tiber! father Tiber
To whom the Romans pray,
A Roman's life, a Roman's arms,
Take thou in charge this day!
Lays of Ancient Rome (1842) 'Horatius' st. 59

13 And even the ranks of Tuscany
Could scarce forbear to cheer.
Lays of Ancient Rome (1842) 'Horatius' st. 60

14 Thank you, madam, the agony is abated.
aged four, having had hot coffee spilt over his legs
G. O. Trevelyan *Life and Letters of Lord Macaulay* (1876) ch. 1

Anthony McAuliffe 1898–1975

15 Nuts!
replying to the German demand for surrender at Bastogne, Belgium, 22 December 1944
in *New York Times* 28 December 1944

Norman McCaig 1910–96

16 Who owns this landscape?
The millionaire who bought it or
the poacher staggering downhill in the early morning
with a deer on his back?
'A Man in Assynt' (1969)

Joseph McCarthy 1908–57

17 I have here in my hand a list of two hundred and five [people] that were known to the Secretary of State as being members of the Communist Party and who nevertheless are still working and shaping the policy of the State Department.
speech at Wheeling, West Virginia, 9 February 1950

18 McCarthyism is Americanism with its sleeves rolled.
speech in Wisconsin, 1952

Mary McCarthy 1912–89

19 Europe is the unfinished negative of which America is the proof.
On the Contrary (1961) 'America the Beautiful'

20 If someone tells you he is going to make a 'realistic decision', you immediately understand that he has resolved to do something bad.
On the Contrary (1961) 'American Realist Playwrights'

21 Every word she writes is a lie, including 'and' and 'the'.
*on Lillian **Hellman***
in *New York Times* 16 February 1980

Paul McCartney 1942–
*see also **Lennon and McCartney***

22 Ballads and babies. That's what happened to me.
on reaching the age of fifty
in *Time* 8 June 1992

George B. McClellan 1826–85

23 All quiet along the Potomac.
said at the time of the American Civil War
attributed; cf. **Beers** 27:14

Ewen MacColl 1915–89

24 And I used to sleep standing on my feet
As we hunted for the shoals of herring.
'The Shoals of Herring' (1960 song, from the BBC Radio broadcast *Singing the Fishing*)

David McCord 1897-

1 By and by
God caught his eye.
'Remainders' (1935); epitaph for a waiter

Horace McCoy 1897-1955

2 They shoot horses don't they.
title of novel (1935)

John McCrae 1872-1918

3 In Flanders fields the poppies blow
Between the crosses, row on row.
'In Flanders Fields' (1915)

Hugh MacDiarmid 1892-1978

4 Scotland small? Our multiform, our infinite
Scotland *small*?
Only as a patch of hillside may be a cliché
corner
To a fool who cries 'Nothing but heather!'
...
Direadh 1 (1974)

5 The rose of all the world is not for me.
I want for my part
Only the little white rose of Scotland
That smells sharp and sweet—and breaks
the heart.
'The Little White Rose' (1934)

George MacDonald 1824-1905

6 Where did you come from, baby dear?
Out of the everywhere into here.
At the Back of the North Wind (1871) ch. 33 'Song'

Ramsay MacDonald 1866-1937

7 Tomorrow every Duchess in London will be
wanting to kiss me!
*after forming the National Government, 25
August 1931*
Viscount Snowden *An Autobiography* (1934) vol. 2

Trevor McDonald 1939-

8 I am a West Indian peasant who has drifted
into this business and who has survived. If I
knew the secret, I would bottle it and sell it.
in *Independent* 20 April 1996 'Quote Unquote'

A. G. MacDonell 1889-1941

9 England, their England.
title of novel (1933); cf. **Henley** 156:9

William McGonagall c.1825-1902

10 Beautiful Railway Bridge of the Silv'ry Tay!
Alas, I am very sorry to say
That ninety lives have been taken away
On the last Sabbath day of 1879,
Which will be remembered for a very long
time.
'The Tay Bridge Disaster'

Patrick McGoohan 1928-, George Markstein, and David Tomblin

11 I am not a number, I am a free man!
Number Six, in *The Prisoner* (TV series 1967-68);
additional title sequence from the second
episode onwards

Roger McGough 1937-

12 Let me die a youngman's death
Not a clean & in-between-
The-sheets, holy-water death.
'Let Me Die a Youngman's Death' (1967)

13 I could never begin a poem; 'When I am
dead'
In case it tempted Fate, and Fate gave way.
'When I am Dead' (1982)

Jimmie McGregor 1932-

14 Oh, he's football crazy, he's football mad
And the football it has robbed him o' the
wee bit sense he had.
And it would take a dozen skivvies, his
clothes to wash and scrub,
Since our Jock became a member of that
terrible football club.
'Football Crazy' (1960 song)

Niccolò Machiavelli 1469-1527

15 Men should be either treated generously or
destroyed, because they take revenge for
slight injuries—for heavy ones they cannot.
The Prince (written 1513) ch. 3 (tr. Allan Gilbert)

16 It is much safer for a prince to be feared
than loved, if he is to fail in one of the two.
The Prince (written 1513) ch. 8 (tr. Allan Gilbert)

17 The prince must be a fox, therefore, to
recognize the traps and a lion to frighten
the wolves.
The Prince (written 1513) ch. 18 (tr. Allan Gilbert)

Kelvin Mackenzie 1946-

18 We are surfing food.
of cable television
in *Trouble at the Top* (BBC2) 12 February 1997

James Mackintosh 1765-1832

19 The Commons, faithful to their system,
remained in a wise and masterly inactivity.
Vindiciae Gallicae (1791) sect. 1

Alexander Maclaren 1826-1910

20 'The Church is an anvil which has worn out
many hammers', and the story of the first
collision is, in essentials, the story of all.
Expositions of Holy Scripture: Acts of the Apostles
(1907) ch. 4

Don McLean 1945-

21 Something touched me deep inside
The day the music died.
on the death of Buddy Holly
'American Pie' (1972 song)

1 So, bye, bye, Miss American Pie,
Drove my Chevy to the levee
But the levee was dry.
Them good old boys was drinkin' whiskey
    and rye
Singin' 'This'll be the day that I die.'
    'American Pie' (1972 song)

Archibald MacLeish 1892–1982

2 A poem should not mean
But be.
    'Ars Poetica' (1926)

Iain Macleod 1913–70

3 It is some measure of the tightness of the
magic circle on this occasion that neither
the Chancellor of the Exchequer nor the
Leader of the House of Commons had any
inkling of what was happening.
    *of the 'evolvement' of Alec Douglas-**Home** as*
    Conservative leader after the resignation of
    *Harold **Macmillan***
        in *The Spectator* 17 January 1964

Marshall McLuhan 1911–80

4 The new electronic interdependence
recreates the world in the image of a global
village.
    The Gutenberg Galaxy (1962)

5 The medium is the message.
    Understanding Media (1964) ch. 1 (title)

6 Gutenberg made everybody a reader. Xerox
makes everybody a publisher.
    in *Guardian Weekly* 12 June 1977

Comte de MacMahon 1808–93

7 *J'y suis, j'y reste.*
Here I am, and here I stay.
    at the taking of the Malakoff fortress during the
    Crimean War, 8 September 1855
        G. Hanotaux *Histoire de la France Contemporaine*
        (1903–8) vol. 2

Harold Macmillan 1894–1986

8 Let us be frank about it: most of our people
have never had it so good.
    'You Never Had It So Good' was the Democratic
    Party slogan during the 1952 US election
    campaign
        speech at Bedford, 20 July 1957

9 I thought the best thing to do was to settle
up these little local difficulties, and then
turn to the wider vision of the
Commonwealth.
    on leaving for a Commonwealth tour, following
    the resignation of the Chancellor of the Exchequer
    and others
        statement at London airport, 7 January 1958

10 The wind of change is blowing through this
continent, and, whether we like it or not,
this growth of [African] national
consciousness is a political fact.
    speech at Cape Town, 3 February 1960

11 There are three bodies no sensible man
directly challenges: the Roman Catholic
Church, the Brigade of Guards and the
National Union of Mineworkers.
    in *Observer* 22 February 1981; cf. **Baldwin** 23:13

12 First of all the Georgian silver goes, and
then all that nice furniture that used to be
in the saloon. Then the Canalettos go.
    on privatization; often quoted as, 'Selling off the
    family silver'
        speech to the Tory Reform Group, 8 November
        1985

13 Events, dear boy. Events.
    when asked what his biggest problem was
    attributed

Robert McNamara 1916–

14 I don't object to it's being called
'McNamara's War' . . . It is a very important
war and I am pleased to be identified with it
and do whatever I can to win it.
    in *New York Times* 25 April 1964

15 We . . . acted according to what we thought
were the principles and traditions of this
nation. We were wrong. We were terribly
wrong.
    of the conduct of the Vietnam War by the
    ***Kennedy** and **Johnson** administrations*
        in *Daily Telegraph* (electronic edition) 10 April
        1995

Louis MacNeice 1907–63

16 It's no go the merrygoround, it's no go the
rickshaw,
All we want is a limousine and a ticket for
the peepshow.
    'Bagpipe Music' (1938)

17 The glass is falling hour by hour, the glass
will fall for ever,
But if you break the bloody glass you won't
hold up the weather.
    'Bagpipe Music' (1938)

18 So they were married—to be the more
together—
And found they were never again so much
together,
    'Les Sylphides' (1941)

19 I am not yet born; O fill me
With strength against those who would
freeze my
humanity.
    'Prayer Before Birth' (1944)

20 Let them not make me a stone and let them
not spill me,
Otherwise kill me.
    'Prayer Before Birth' (1944)

21 By a high star our course is set,
Our end is Life. Put out to sea.
    'Thalassa' (1964)

22 I would have a poet able-bodied, fond of
talking, a reader of the newspapers, capable
of pity and laughter, informed in
economics, appreciative of women,
involved in personal relationships, actively
interested in politics, susceptible to physical
impressions.
    Modern Poetry (1938)

Geoffrey Madan 1895–1947

1 The great tragedy of the classical languages is to have been born twins.

Geoffrey Madan's Notebooks (1981)

2 The dust of exploded beliefs may make a fine sunset.

Livre sans nom: Twelve Reflections (privately printed 1934) no. 12

Salvador de Madariaga 1886–1978

3 Since, in the main, it is not armaments that cause wars but wars (or the fears thereof) that cause armaments, it follows that every nation will at every moment strive to keep its armament in an efficient state as required by its fear, otherwise styled security.

Morning Without Noon (1974) pt. 1, ch. 9

Samuel Madden 1686–1765

4 Words are men's daughters, but God's sons are things.

Boulter's Monument (1745) l. 377; cf. **Johnson** 173:11

Madonna 1958–

5 Being blonde is definitely a different state of mind. I can't really put my finger on it, but the artifice of being blonde has some incredible sort of sexual connotation.

in *Rolling Stone* 23 March 1989

6 Many people see Eva Perón as either a saint or the incarnation of Satan. That means I can definitely identify with her.

on playing the starring role in the film Evita
in *Newsweek* 5 February 1996

Maurice Maeterlinck 1862–1949

7 *Il n'y a pas de morts.*
There are no dead.

L'Oiseau bleu (1909) act 4

John Gillespie Magee 1922–41

8 Oh! I have slipped the surly bonds of earth And danced the skies on laughter-silvered wings.

'High Flight' (1943); cf. **Reagan** 255:3

9 And, while with silent lifting mind I've trod The high, untrespassed sanctity of space, Put out my hand and touched the face of God.

'High Flight' (1943); cf. **Reagan** 255:3

Magna Carta

10 That the English Church shall be free.

Clause 1

11 No free man shall be taken or imprisoned or dispossessed, or outlawed or exiled, or in any way destroyed, nor will we go upon him, nor will we send against him except by the lawful judgement of his peers or by the law of the land.

Clause 39

12 To no man will we sell, or deny, or delay, right or justice.

Clause 40

Mahāyāna Buddhist texts

13 Where there is no perception, appellation, conception, or conventional expression, there one speaks of 'perfect wisdom'.

Perfect Wisdom in 8,000 Lines (*c.*100 BC–100 AD) ch. 7, v. 177

14 Form is emptiness and the very emptiness is form; emptiness does not differ from form, nor does form differ from emptiness; whatever is form, that is emptiness, whatever is emptiness, that is form.

Heart Sutra (4th century AD) v. 3

Gustav Mahler 1860–1911

15 Fortissimo at last!

on seeing Niagara Falls
K. Blaukopf *Gustav Mahler* (1973) ch. 8

16 The symphony must be like the world. It must embrace everything.

remark to Sibelius, Helsinki, 1907

Norman Mailer 1923–

17 So we think of Marilyn who was every man's love affair with America, Marilyn Monroe who was blonde and beautiful and had a sweet little rinky-dink of a voice and all the cleanliness of all the clean American backyards.

Marilyn (1973)

18 All the security around the American president is just to make sure the man who shoots him gets caught.

in *Sunday Telegraph* 4 March 1990

Maimonides (Moses ben Maimon) 1135–1204

19 When I find the road narrow, and can see no other way of teaching a well established truth except by pleasing one intelligent man and displeasing ten thousand fools—I prefer to address myself to the man.

The Guide for the Perplexed, introduction

Joseph de Maistre 1753–1821

20 *Toute nation a le gouvernement qu'elle mérite.*
Every country has the government it deserves.

Lettres et Opuscules Inédits (1851) vol. 1, letter 53 (15 August 1811)

John Major 1943–

21 If the policy isn't hurting, it isn't working.

on controlling inflation
speech in Northampton, 27 October 1989

22 Society needs to condemn a little more and understand a little less.

interview with *Mail on Sunday* 21 February 1993

23 Fifty years on from now, Britain will still be the country of long shadows on county

[cricket] grounds, warm beer, invincible green suburbs, dog lovers, and—as George Orwell said—old maids bicycling to Holy Communion through the morning mist.
> speech to the Conservative Group for Europe, 22 April 1993; cf. **Orwell** 237:11

1 It is time to get back to basics: to self-discipline and respect for the law, to consideration for others, to accepting responsibility for yourself and your family, and not shuffling it off on the state.
> speech to the Conservative Party Conference, 8 October 1993

2 So right. OK. We lost.
on election night
> in *Guardian* 3 May 1997

Bernard Malamud 1914–86

3 There's no such thing as an unpolitical man, especially a Jew.
> *The Fixer* (1966) ch. 9

Malcolm X 1925–65

4 If you're born in America with a black skin, you're born in prison.
> in an interview, June 1963

Stéphane Mallarmé 1842–98

5 *La chair est triste, hélas! et j'ai lu tous les livres.*
The flesh, alas, is wearied; and I have read all the books there are.
> 'Brise Marin' (1887)

6 *Prélude à l'après-midi d'un faune.*
Prelude to the afternoon of a faun.
> title of poem (*c.*1865)

David Mallet (or Malloch) *c.*1705–65

7 O grant me, Heaven, a middle state,
Neither too humble nor too great;
More than enough, for nature's ends,
With something left to treat my friends.
> 'Imitation of Horace'; cf. **Horace** 164:21

George Leigh Mallory 1886–1924

8 Because it's there.
on being asked why he wanted to climb Mount Everest (Mallory was lost on Everest in the following year)
> in *New York Times* 18 March 1923

Thomas Malory d. 1471

9 Whoso pulleth out this sword of this stone and anvil is rightwise King born of all England.
> *Le Morte D'Arthur* (finished 1470, printed by Caxton 1485) bk. 1, ch. 4

10 The questing beast . . . had in shape like a serpent's head and a body like a leopard, buttocked like a lion and footed like a hart. And in his body there was such a noise as it had been twenty couple of hounds questing.
'questing' = yelping
> *Le Morte D'Arthur* (1485) bk. 9, ch. 12

11 Thus endeth the story of the Sangreal, that was briefly drawn out of French into English, the which is a story chronicled for one of the truest and the holiest that is in this world.
> *Le Morte D'Arthur* (1485) bk. 17, ch. 23

12 And many men say that there is written upon his tomb this verse: *Hic iacet Arthurus, rex quondam rexque futurus* [Here lies Arthur, the once and future king].
> *Le Morte d'Arthur* (1485) bk. 31, ch. 7

André Malraux 1901–76

13 *La condition humaine.*
The human condition.
> title of book (1933)

14 *L'art est un anti-destin.*
Art is a revolt against fate.
> *Les Voix du silence* (1951) pt. 4, ch. 7

Thomas Robert Malthus 1766–1834

15 Population, when unchecked, increases in a geometrical ratio. Subsistence only increases in an arithmetical ratio.
> *Essay on the Principle of Population* (1798) ch. 1

16 The perpetual struggle for room and food.
> *Essay on the Principle of Population* (1798) ch. 3

Lord Mancroft 1914–87

17 Cricket—a game which the English, not being a spiritual people, have invented in order to give themselves some conception of eternity.
> *Bees in Some Bonnets* (1979)

W. R. Mandale

18 Up and down the City Road,
In and out the Eagle,
That's the way the money goes—
Pop goes the weasel!
> 'Pop Goes the Weasel' (1853 song); also attributed to Charles Twiggs

Nelson Mandela 1918–

19 I have dedicated my life to this struggle of the African people. I have fought against white domination, and I have fought against black domination. I have cherished the ideal of a democratic and free society in which all persons live together in harmony with equal opportunities. It is an ideal which I hope to live for, and to see realized. But if needs be, it is an ideal for which I am prepared to die.
> speech at his trial in Pretoria, 20 April 1964

20 No one is born hating another person because of the colour of his skin, or his background, or his religion. People must learn to hate, and if they can learn to hate, they can be taught to love, for love comes more naturally to the human heart than its opposite.
> *Long Walk to Freedom* (1994)

1 True reconciliation does not consist in merely forgetting the past.
speech, 7 January 1996

Winnie Mandela 1934–

2 With that stick of matches, with our necklace, we shall liberate this country.
speech in black townships, 14 April 1986, in Guardian 15 April 1986

3 Maybe there is no rainbow nation after all because it does not have the colour black.
at the funeral of a black child reportedly shot dead by a white farmer
in Irish Times 25 April 1998 'Quotes of the Week'

Osip Mandelstam 1892–1938

4 The age is rocking the wave
with human grief
to a golden beat, and an adder
is breathing in time with it in the grass.
'The Age' (1923) (tr. C. M. Bowra)

Manilius (Marcus Manilius) 1st century AD

5 *Eripuitque Jovi fulmen viresque tonandi,*
et sonitum ventis concessit, nubibus ignem.
And snatched from Jove the lightning shaft and power to thunder, and attributed the noise to the winds, the flame to the clouds.
of human intelligence
Astronomica bk. 1, l. 104; cf. Turgot 320:18

Thomas Mann 1875–1955

6 We come out of the dark and go into the dark again, and in between lie the experiences of our life.
The Magic Mountain (1924) ch. 6, sect. 8 (tr. H. T. Lowe-Porter)

7 A man's dying is more the survivors' affair than his own.
The Magic Mountain (1924) ch. 6, sect. 8 (tr. H. T. Lowe-Porter)

Katherine Mansfield 1888–1923

8 Whenever I prepare for a journey I prepare as though for death. Should I never return, all is in order.
Journal (1927) 29 January 1922

William Murray, Lord Mansfield 1705–93

9 Consider what you think justice requires, and decide accordingly. But never give your reasons; for your judgement will probably be right, but your reasons will certainly be wrong.
advice to a newly appointed colonial governor ignorant in the law
John Lord Campbell The Lives of the Chief Justices of England (1849) vol. 2, ch. 40

Richard Mant 1776–1848

10 Bright the vision that delighted
Once the sight of Judah's seer;

Sweet the countless tongues united
To entrance the prophet's ear.
'Bright the vision that delighted' (1837 hymn)

Mao Zedong 1893–1976

11 Politics is war without bloodshed while war is politics with bloodshed.
lecture, 1938

12 Every Communist must grasp the truth, 'Political power grows out of the barrel of a gun'.
speech, 6 November 1938

13 The atom bomb is a paper tiger which the United States reactionaries use to scare people. It looks terrible, but in fact it isn't . . . All reactionaries are paper tigers.
interview, 1946

14 Letting a hundred flowers blossom and a hundred schools of thought contend is the policy for promoting progress in the arts and the sciences and a flourishing socialist culture in our land.
speech in Peking, 27 February 1957,

Diego Maradona 1960–

15 The goal was scored a little bit by the hand of God, another bit by head of Maradona.
on his controversial goal against England in the 1986 World Cup
in Guardian 1 July 1986

William Learned Marcy 1786–1857

16 The politicians of New York . . . see nothing wrong in the rule, that to the victor belong the spoils of the enemy.
speech to the Senate, 25 January 1832

Lynn Margulis 1938–

17 Gaia is a tough bitch. People think the earth is going to die and they have to save it, that's ridiculous . . . There's no doubt that Gaia can compensate for our output of greenhouse gases, but the environment that's left will not be happy for any people.
in New York Times Biographical Service January 1996

Marie-Antoinette 1755–93

18 *Qu'ils mangent de la brioche.*
Let them eat cake.
on being told that her people had no bread
attributed, but much older; in his *Confessions* (1740) Rousseau refers to a similar remark being a well-known saying; another version is 'Que ne mangent-ils de la croûte de pâté? [Why don't they eat pastry?]', attributed to Marie-Thérèse (1638–83), wife of Louis XIV

Edwin Markham 1852–1940

19 A thing that grieves not and that never hopes,
Stolid and stunned, a brother to the ox?
'The Man with the Hoe' (1899)

Johnny Marks 1909–85

1 Rudolph, the Red-Nosed Reindeer
Had a very shiny nose.
'Rudolph, the Red-Nosed Reindeer' (1949 song)

Sarah, Duchess of Marlborough 1660–1744

2 The Duke returned from the wars today and
did pleasure me in his top-boots.
oral tradition

Bob Marley 1945–81

3 Get up, stand up
Stand up for your rights
Get up, stand up
Never give up the fight.
'Get up, Stand up' (1973 song)

4 I shot the sheriff
But I swear it was in self-defence
I shot the sheriff
And they say it is a capital offence.
'I Shot the Sheriff' (1974 song)

Christopher Marlowe 1564–93

5 Why, this is hell, nor am I out of it.
Doctor Faustus (1604) act 1, sc. 3

6 Was this the face that launched a thousand
ships,
And burnt the topless towers of Ilium?
Doctor Faustus (1604) act 5, sc. 1

7 *O lente lente currite noctis equi.*
The stars move still, time runs, the clock
will strike,
The devil will come, and Faustus must be
damned.
O I'll leap up to my God: who pulls me
down?
See, see, where Christ's blood streams in
the firmament.
One drop would save my soul, half a drop,
ah my Christ.
Doctor Faustus (1604) act 5, sc. 2; cf. **Ovid** 238:10

8 My men, like satyrs grazing on the lawns,
Shall with their goat feet dance an antic
hay.
Edward II (1593) act 1, sc. 1

9 Where both deliberate, the love is slight;
Who ever loved that loved not at first sight?
Hero and Leander (1598) First Sestiad, l. 175

10 I count religion but a childish toy,
And hold there is no sin but ignorance.
The Jew of Malta (c.1592) prologue

11 Thus methinks should men of judgement
frame
Their means of traffic from the vulgar trade,
And, as their wealth increaseth, so enclose
Infinite riches in a little room.
The Jew of Malta (c.1592) act 1, sc. 1

12 BARNARDINE: Thou hast committed—
BARABAS: Fornication? But that was in
another country: and besides, the wench is
dead.
The Jew of Malta (c.1592) act 4, sc. 1

13 Come live with me, and be my love,
And we will all the pleasures prove,
That valleys, groves, hills and fields,
Woods or steepy mountain yields.
'The Passionate Shepherd to his Love'; cf.
Donne 114:5, **Ralegh** 253:24

14 Our swords shall play the orators for us.
Tamburlaine the Great (1590) pt. 1, act 1, sc. 2

15 Is it not passing brave to be a king,
And ride in triumph through Persepolis?
Tamburlaine the Great (1590) pt. 1, act 2, sc. 5

16 The ripest fruit of all,
That perfect bliss and sole felicity,
The sweet fruition of an earthly crown.
Tamburlaine the Great (1590) pt. 1, act 2, sc. 7

17 Virtue is the fount whence honour springs.
Tamburlaine the Great (1590) pt. 1, act 4, sc. 4

18 Now walk the angels on the walls of
heaven,
As sentinels to warn th' immortal souls,
To entertain divine Zenocrate.
Tamburlaine the Great (1590) pt. 2, act 2, sc. 4

19 Holla, ye pampered jades of Asia!
What, can ye draw but twenty miles a
day . . . ?
Tamburlaine the Great (1590) pt. 2, act 4, sc. 3; cf.
Shakespeare 274:18

Don Marquis 1878–1937

20 procrastination is the
art of keeping
up with yesterday.
archy and mehitabel (1927) 'certain maxims of
archy'

21 it s cheerio
my deario that
pulls a lady through.
archy and mehitabel (1927) 'cheerio, my deario'

22 but wotthehell archy wotthehell
jamais triste archy jamais triste
that is my motto.
archy and mehitabel (1927) 'mehitabel sees paris'

23 did you ever
notice that when
a politician
does get an idea
he usually
gets it all wrong.
archys life of mehitabel (1933) 'archygrams'

24 Writing a book of poetry is like dropping a
rose petal down the Grand Canyon and
waiting for the echo.
E. Anthony *O Rare Don Marquis* (1962)

25 The art of newspaper paragraphing is to
stroke a platitude until it purrs like an
epigram.
E. Anthony *O Rare Don Marquis* (1962)

John Marriot 1780–1825

26 Thou, whose eternal Word
Chaos and darkness heard,
And took their flight,
Hear us, we humbly pray,
And, where the Gospel-day

Sheds not its glorious ray,
Let there be light!

'almighty' substituted for 'eternal' from 1861
'Thou, whose eternal Word' (hymn written
*c.*1813)

Frederick Marryat 1792–1848

1 If you please, ma'am, it was a very little one.
the nurse, excusing her illegitimate baby
Mr Midshipman Easy (1836) ch. 3

2 All zeal . . . all zeal, Mr Easy.
Mr Midshipman Easy (1836) ch. 9

Arthur Marshall 1910–89

3 What, knocked a tooth out? Never mind,
dear, laugh it off, laugh it off; it's all part of
life's rich pageant.
The Games Mistress (recorded monologue, 1937)

John Marshall 1755–1835

4 The power to tax involves the power to
destroy.
in *McCulloch v. Maryland* (1819)

5 The people made the Constitution, and the
people can unmake it. It is the creature of
their own will, and lives only by their will.
in *Cohens v. Virginia* (1821)

Thomas R. Marshall 1854–1925

6 What this country needs is a really good
5-cent cigar.
in *New York Tribune* 4 January 1920, pt. 7

Martial AD *c.*40–*c.*104

7 *Non amo te, Sabidi, nec possum dicere quare:*
Hoc tantum possum dicere, non amo te.
I don't love you, Sabidius, and I can't tell
you why; all I can tell you is this, that I
don't love you.
Epigrammata bk. 1, no. 32; cf. **Brown** 68:18

8 *Laudant illa sed ista legunt.*
They praise those works, but read these.
Epigrammata bk. 4, no. 49

9 *Non est vivere, sed valere vita est.*
Life's not just being alive, but being well.
Epigrammata bk. 6, no. 70

10 *Difficilis facilis, iucundus acerbus es idem:*
Nec tecum possum vivere nec sine te.
Difficult or easy, pleasant or bitter, you are
the same you: I cannot live with you—or
without you.
Epigrammata bk. 12, no. 46(47)

11 *Rus in urbe.*
Country in the town.
Epigrammata bk. 12, no. 57

Andrew Marvell 1621–78

12 Where the remote Bermudas ride
In the ocean's bosom unespied.
'Bermudas' (*c.*1653)

13 Echo beyond the Mexique Bay.
'Bermudas' (*c.*1653)

14 My love is of a birth as rare
As 'tis for object strange and high:

It was begotten by Despair
Upon Impossibility.
Magnanimous Despair alone
Could show me so divine a thing,
Where feeble Hope could ne'er have flown
But vainly flapped its tinsel wing.
'The Definition of Love' (1681)

15 How vainly men themselves amaze
To win the palm, the oak, or bays.
'The Garden' (1681) st. 1

16 What wondrous life is this I lead!
Ripe apples drop about my head;
The luscious clusters of the vine
Upon my mouth do crush their wine;
The nectarine, and curious peach,
Into my hands themselves do reach;
Stumbling on melons, as I pass,
Ensnared with flowers, I fall on grass.
'The Garden' (1681) st. 5

17 Annihilating all that's made
To a green thought in a green shade.
'The Garden' (1681) st. 6

18 *He* nothing common did or mean
Upon that memorable scene:
But with his keener eye
The axe's edge did try.
on the execution of **Charles I**
'An Horatian Ode upon Cromwell's Return from
Ireland' (written 1650) l. 57

19 Had we but world enough, and time,
This coyness, lady, were no crime.
'To His coy Mistress' (1681) l. 1

20 I would
Love you ten years before the flood:
And you should, if you please, refuse
Till the conversion of the Jews.
My vegetable love should grow
Vaster than empires, and more slow.
'To His coy Mistress' (1681) l. 7

21 But at my back I always hear
Time's wingèd chariot hurrying near:
And yonder all before us lie
Deserts of vast eternity.
'To His Coy Mistress' (1681) l. 21; cf. **Eliot**
122:26

22 The grave's a fine and private place,
But none, I think, do there embrace.
'To His Coy Mistress' (1681) l. 27

23 Let us roll all our strength, and all
Our sweetness, up into one ball:
And tear our pleasures with rough strife,
Thorough the iron gates of life.
Thus, though we cannot make our sun
Stand still, yet we will make him run.
'To His Coy Mistress' (1681) l. 41

Holt Marvell

24 A cigarette that bears a lipstick's traces,
An airline ticket to romantic places;
And still my heart has wings
These foolish things
Remind me of you.
'These Foolish Things Remind Me of You' (1935
song)

Chico Marx 1891–1961

1 I wasn't kissing her, I was just whispering in her mouth.

on being discovered by his wife with a chorus girl
Groucho Marx and Richard J. Anobile *Marx Brothers Scrapbook* (1973) ch. 24

Groucho Marx 1895–1977

2 PLEASE ACCEPT MY RESIGNATION. I DON'T WANT TO BELONG TO ANY CLUB THAT WILL ACCEPT ME AS A MEMBER.
Groucho and Me (1959) ch. 26

3 I never forget a face, but in your case I'll be glad to make an exception.
Leo Rosten *People I have Loved, Known or Admired* (1970) 'Groucho'

Karl Marx 1818–83

4 Religion is . . . the opium of the people.
A Contribution to the Critique of Hegel's Philosophy of Right (1843–4) introduction; cf. **Kingsley** 187:1

5 From each according to his abilities, to each according to his needs.
Critique of the Gotha Programme (written 1875, but of earlier origin); cf. **Blanc** 56:18, **Morelly** 228:6, and 'The formula of Communism, as propounded by Cabet, may be expressed thus:—"the duty of each is according to his faculties; his right according to his wants" ' in *North British Review* (1849) vol 10

6 Hegel says somewhere that all great events and personalities in world history reappear in one fashion or another. He forgot to add: the first time as tragedy, the second as farce.
The Eighteenth Brumaire of Louis Bonaparte (1852) sect. 1; cf. **Hegel** 155:4

7 The class struggle necessarily leads to the dictatorship of the proletariat.
the phrase 'dictatorship of the proletariat' had been used earlier in the Constitution of the World Society of Revolutionary Communists (1850), signed by Marx and others
letter to Georg Weydemeyer 5 March 1852; Marx claimed that the phrase had been coined by Auguste Blanqui (1805–81), but it has not been found in this form in Blanqui's work

Karl Marx 1818–83 and Friedrich Engels 1820–95

8 A spectre is haunting Europe—the spectre of Communism.
The Communist Manifesto (1848) opening words

9 The history of all hitherto existing society is the history of class struggles.
The Communist Manifesto (1848) pt. 1

10 The proletarians have nothing to lose but their chains. They have a world to win. WORKING MEN OF ALL COUNTRIES, UNITE!
commonly rendered as 'Workers of the world, unite!'
The Communist Manifesto (1848) closing words (from the 1888 translation by Samuel Moore, edited by Engels)

Queen Mary 1867–1953

11 All this thrown away for *that*.
*on returning home to Marlborough House, London after the abdication of her son, King **Edward VIII**, December 1936*
David Duff *George and Elizabeth* (1983) ch. 10

12 I do not think you have ever realised the shock, which the attitude you took up caused your family and the whole nation. It seemed inconceivable to those who had made such sacrifices during the war that you, as their King, refused a lesser sacrifice.
letter to the Duke of Windsor (formerly **Edward VIII**), July 1938

Mary, Queen of Scots 1542–87

13 Look to your consciences and remember that the theatre of the world is wider than the realm of England.
to the commissioners appointed to try her at Fotheringhay, 13 October 1586
Antonia Fraser *Mary Queen of Scots* (1969) ch. 25

14 *En ma fin git mon commencement.*
In my end is my beginning.
*motto embroidered with an emblem of her mother, Mary of Guise, and quoted in a letter from William Drummond of Hawthornden to Ben Jonson in 1619; cf. **Eliot** 121:22*

Mary Tudor 1516–58

15 When I am dead and opened, you shall find 'Calais' lying in my heart.
Holinshed's Chronicles vol. 4 (1808)

John Masefield 1878–1967

16 Quinquireme of Nineveh from distant Ophir
Rowing home to haven in sunny Palestine,
With a cargo of ivory,
And apes and peacocks,
Sandalwood, cedarwood, and sweet white wine.
'Cargoes' (1903); cf. **Bible** 36:4

17 I must go down to the sea again, to the lonely sea and the sky,
And all I ask is a tall ship and a star to steer her by.
'I must down to the seas' in the original of 1902, possibly a misprint
'Sea Fever' (1902)

Donald Mason 1913–

18 Sighted sub, sank same.
on sinking a Japanese submarine in the Atlantic region (the first US naval success in the war)
radio message, 28 January 1942

Philip Massinger 1583–1640

19 Ambition, in a private man a vice,
Is in a prince the virtue.
The Bashful Lover (licensed 1636, published 1655) act 1, sc. 2

20 Pray enter
You are learned Europeans and we worse

Than ignorant Americans.
The City Madam (licensed 1632, published 1658)
act 3, sc. 3

1 Death has a thousand doors to let out life:
I shall find one.
A Very Woman (licensed 1634, published 1655)
act 5, sc. 4; cf. **Fletcher** 130:7, **Seneca** 267:23,
Webster 330:11

Cotton Mather 1662–1728

2 I write the wonders of the Christian
religion, flying from the depravations of
Europe, to the American strand: and,
assisted by the Holy Author of that religion,
I do . . . report the wonderful displays of His
infinite power, wisdom, goodness, and
faithfulness, wherewith His Divine
Providence hath irradiated an Indian
wilderness.
introduction to *Magnalia Christi Americana*
(1702), opening line

3 That there is a Devil is a thing doubted by
none but such as are under the influences of
the Devil. For any to deny the being of a
Devil must be from an ignorance or
profaneness worse than diabolical.
The Wonders of the Invisible World (1693)

Increase Mather 1639–1723

4 Thunder is the voice of God, and, therefore,
to be dreaded.
Remarkable Providences (1684)

James Mathew 1830–1908

5 In England, justice is open to all—like the
Ritz Hotel.
R. E. Megarry *Miscellany-at-Law* (1955)

Henri Matisse 1869–1954

6 What I dream of is an art of balance, of
purity and serenity devoid of troubling or
depressing subject matter . . . a soothing,
calming influence on the mind, rather like a
good armchair which provides relaxation
from physical fatigue.
Notes d'un peintre (1908)

Leonard Matlovich d. 1988

7 When I was in the military, they gave me a
medal for killing two men and a discharge
for loving one.
attributed

W. Somerset Maugham 1874–1965

8 The most useful thing about a principle is
that it can always be sacrificed to
expediency.
The Circle (1921) act 3

9 Money is like a sixth sense without which
you cannot make a complete use of the
other five.
Of Human Bondage (1915) ch. 51

10 I [Death] was astonished to see him in
Baghdad, for I had an appointment with
him tonight in Samarra.
Sheppey (1933) act 3

11 Dying is a very dull, dreary affair. And my
advice to you is to have nothing whatever to
do with it.
to his nephew Robin, in 1965
Robin Maugham *Conversations with Willie* (1978)

Bill Mauldin 1921–

12 I feel like a fugitive from th' law of
averages.
cartoon caption in *Up Front* (1945)

James Maxton 1885–1946

13 All I say is, if you cannot ride two horses you
have no right in the circus.
*opposing disaffiliation of the Scottish Independent
Labour Party from the Labour Party; usually
quoted as, ' . . . no right in the bloody circus'*
in *Daily Herald* 12 January 1931

Vladimir Mayakovsky 1893–1930

14 If you wish—
. . . I'll be irreproachably tender;
not a man, but—a cloud in trousers!
'The Cloud in Trousers' (1915) (tr. Samuel
Charteris)

15 Not a sound. The universe sleeps, resting a
huge ear on its paw with mites of stars.
'The Cloud in Trousers' (1915) (tr. Samuel
Charteris)

16 Oh for just
one
more conference
regarding the eradication of all conferences!
'In Re Conferences'; Herbert Marshall (ed.)
Mayakovsky (1965)

Shepherd Mead 1914–

17 How to succeed in business without really
trying.
title of book (1952)

Hughes Mearns 1875–1965

18 As I was walking up the stair
I met a man who wasn't there.
He wasn't there again today.
I wish, I wish he'd stay away.
lines written for *The Psycho-ed*, an amateur play,
in Philadelphia, 1910 (set to music in 1939 as
'The Little Man Who Wasn't There')

Peter Medawar 1915–87

19 If politics is the art of the possible, research
is surely the art of the soluble. Both are
immensely practical-minded affairs.
in *New Statesman* 19 June 1964; cf. **Bismarck**
54:13

Catherine de' Medici 1518–89

20 A false report, if believed during three days,
may be of great service to a government.
Isaac D'Israeli *Curiosities of Literature* 2nd series
(1849) vol. 2; perhaps apocryphal

Cosimo de' Medici 1389–1464

1 We read that we ought to forgive our enemies; but we do not read that we ought to forgive our friends.
*speaking of what **Bacon** refers to as 'perfidious friends'*
> Francis Bacon *Apophthegms* (1625) no. 206

Golda Meir 1898–1978

2 Those that perished in Hitler's gas chambers were the last Jews to die without standing up to defend themselves.
> speech to United Jewish Appeal Rally, New York, 11 June 1967

Nellie Melba 1861–1931

3 Sing 'em muck! It's all they can understand!
advice to Dame Clara Butt, prior to her departure for Australia
> W. H. Ponder *Clara Butt* (1928) ch. 12

William Lamb, Lord Melbourne 1779–1848

4 God help the Minister that meddles with art!
> Lord David Cecil *Lord M* (1954) ch. 3

5 I wish I was as cocksure of anything as Tom Macaulay is of everything.
> Lord Cowper's preface to *Lord Melbourne's Papers* (1889)

6 Now, is it to lower the price of corn, or isn't it? It is not much matter which we say, but mind, we must all say *the same*.
> attributed; Walter Bagehot *The English Constitution* (1867) ch. 1

7 What I want is men who will support me when I am in the wrong.
replying to a politician who said 'I will support you as long as you are in the right'
> Lord David Cecil *Lord M* (1954) ch. 4

David Mellor 1949–

8 I do believe the popular press is drinking in the last chance saloon.
> interview on *Hard News* (Channel 4), 21 December 1989

Herman Melville 1819–91

9 Call me Ishmael.
> *Moby Dick* (1851), opening words

10 A whaleship was my Yale College and my Harvard.
> *Moby Dick* (1851) ch. 24

11 Towards thee I roll, thou all-destroying but unconquering whale . . . from hell's heart I stab at thee.
> *Moby Dick* (1851) ch. 135

Menander 342–c.292 BC

12 Whom the gods love dies young.
> *Dis Exapaton* fragment 4, in F. H. Sandbach (ed.) *Menandri Reliquiae Selectae* (1990)

Mencius *see* Meng-tzu

H. L. Mencken 1880–1956

13 Puritanism. The haunting fear that someone, somewhere, may be happy.
> *Chrestomathy* (1949) ch. 30

14 Democracy is the theory that the common people know what they want, and deserve to get it good and hard.
> *A Little Book in C major* (1916)

15 Conscience: the inner voice which warns us that someone may be looking.
> *A Little Book in C major* (1916)

Moses Mendelssohn 1729–86

16 To put it in one word: I believe that Judaism knows nothing of revealed religion, in the sense in which this is understood by Christians. The Israelites possess divine legislation.
> *Jerusalem* (1783) pt. 2

Meng-tzu (Mencius) 371–289 BC

17 All men have the mind which cannot bear [to see the suffering of] others.
> *The Book of Mencius* bk. 2, pt. A, v. 6

18 Moral principles please our minds as beef and mutton and pork please our mouths.
> *The Book of Mencius* bk. 6, pt. A, v. 7

Robert Gordon Menzies 1894–1978

19 What Great Britain calls the Far East is to us the near north.
> in *Sydney Morning Herald* 27 April 1939

David Mercer 1928–80

20 A suitable case for treatment.
> title of television play (1962); later filmed as *Morgan—A Suitable Case for Treatment* (1966)

Johnny Mercer 1909–76

21 You've got to ac-cent-tchu-ate the positive
Elim-my-nate the negative
Latch on to the affirmative
Don't mess with Mister In-between.
> 'Ac-cent-tchu-ate the Positive' (1944 song)

22 Jeepers Creepers—where you get them peepers?
> 'Jeepers Creepers' (1938 song)

23 Make it one for my baby
And one more for the road.
> 'One For My Baby' (1943 song)

24 That old black magic.
> title of song (1942)

George Meredith 1828–1909

25 'Tis Ireland gives England her soldiers, her generals too.
> *Diana of the Crossways* (1885) ch. 2

26 A dainty rogue in porcelain.
> *The Egoist* (1879) ch. 5

1 Kissing don't last: cookery do!
   The Ordeal of Richard Feverel (1859) ch. 28

2 The lark ascending.
   title of poem (1881)

3 She whom I love is hard to catch and conquer,
   Hard, but O the glory of the winning were she won!
   'Love in the Valley' st. 2

4 On a starred night Prince Lucifer uprose.
   Tired of his dark dominion swung the fiend.
   'Lucifer in Starlight' (1883)

5 Around the ancient track marched, rank on rank,
   The army of unalterable law.
   'Lucifer in Starlight' (1883)

6 Ah, what a dusty answer gets the soul
   When hot for certainties in this our life!
   Modern Love (1862) st. 50

7 Enter these enchanted woods,
   You who dare.
   'The Woods of Westermain' (1883)

Owen Meredith (Lord Lytton) 1831–91

8 Genius does what it must, and Talent does what it can.
   'Last Words of a Sensitive Second-Rate Poet' (1868)

Bob Merrill 1921–98

9 How much is that doggie in the window?
   title of song (1953)

10 People who need people are the luckiest people in the world.
   'People who Need People' (1964 song)

Dixon Lanier Merritt 1879–1972

11 Oh, a wondrous bird is the pelican!
   His beak holds more than his belican.
   He takes in his beak
   Food enough for a week.
   But I'll be darned if I know how the helican.
   in *Nashville Banner* 22 April 1913

Jean Meslier c.1664–1733

12 An ignorant, uneducated man . . . said he wished . . . that all the great men in the world and all the nobility could be hanged, and strangled with the guts of priests.
   often quoted 'I should like . . . the last of the kings to be strangled with the guts of the last priest'
   Testament (ed. R. Charles, 1864) vol. 1, ch. 2; cf. **Diderot** 111:20

Methodist Service Book 1975

13 I am no longer my own, but yours. Put me to what you will, rank me with whom you will; put me to doing, put me to suffering.
   The Covenant Prayer (based on the words of Richard Alleine in the First Covenant Service, 1782)

Prince Metternich 1773–1859

14 Italy is a geographical expression.
   discussing the Italian question with **Palmerston** *in 1847*
   Mémoires, Documents, etc. de Metternich publiés par son fils (1883) vol. 7

15 Citizens of a dream-world, nothing is altered. On 14 March 1848, there was merely one man fewer.
   of his own downfall
   Aus Metternich's Nachgelassenen Papieren (1880) vol. 8

16 Error has never approached my spirit.
   addressed to Guizot in 1848

Anthony Meyer 1920–

17 I question the right of that great Moloch, national sovereignty, to burn its children to save its pride.
   speaking against the Falklands War, 1982
   in *Listener* 27 September 1990

Michelangelo 1475–1564

18 I've finished that chapel I was painting. The Pope is quite satisfied.
   on completing the ceiling of the Sistine chapel
   letter to his father, October 1512; E. H. Ramsden (ed.) *The Letters of Michelangelo* (1963)

Thomas Middleton c.1580–1627

19 Anything for a quiet life.
   title of play (written c.1620, possibly with John Webster)

20 My study's ornament, thou shell of death,
   Once the bright face of my betrothèd lady.
   The Revenger's Tragedy (1607) act 1, sc. 1 (previously attributed to Cyril Tourneur, c.1575–1626)

21 Nine coaches waiting—hurry, hurry, hurry.
   The Revenger's Tragedy (1607) act 2, sc. 1

Bette Midler 1945–

22 When it's three o'clock in New York, it's still 1938 in London.
   attributed

Midrash

23 The Holy One, blessed be He, makes ladders by which He makes one go up, and another go down.
   Leviticus Rabbah 8:1

24 A man cannot say to the Angel of Death, 'Wait for me until I make up my accounts.'
   Ecclesiastes Rabbah 8:8

George Mikes 1912–

25 On the Continent people have good food; in England people have good table manners.
   How to be an Alien (1946)

26 An Englishman, even if he is alone, forms an orderly queue of one.
   How to be an Alien (1946) p. 44

John Stuart Mill 1806–73

1 Ask yourself whether you are happy, and
you cease to be so.
Autobiography (1873) ch. 5

2 The Conservatives . . . being by the law of
their existence the stupidest party.
Considerations on Representative Government (1861)
ch. 7 n.

3 The only purpose for which power can be
rightfully exercised over any member of a
civilized community, against his will, is to
prevent harm to others. His own good,
either physical or moral, is not a sufficient
warrant.
On Liberty (1859) ch. 1

4 Liberty consists in doing what one desires.
On Liberty (1859) ch. 5

5 What is now called the nature of women is
an eminently artificial thing—the result of
forced repression in some directions,
unnatural stimulation in others.
The Subjection of Women (1869) ch. 1

Edna St Vincent Millay 1892–1950

6 Childhood is the kingdom where nobody
dies.
Nobody that matters, that is.
'Childhood is the Kingdom where Nobody dies'
(1934)

7 Down, down, down into the darkness of the
grave
Gently they go, the beautiful, the tender,
the kind;
Quietly they go, the intelligent, the witty,
the brave.
I know. But I do not approve. And I am not
resigned.
'Dirge Without Music' (1928)

8 My candle burns at both ends;
It will not last the night;
But ah, my foes, and oh, my friends—
It gives a lovely light.
A Few Figs From Thistles (1920) 'First Fig'

9 Justice denied in Massachusetts.
*relating to the trial of Sacco and **Vanzetti** and
their execution on 22 August 1927*
title of poem (1928)

10 We shall die in darkness, and be buried in
the rain.
'Justice Denied in Massachusetts' (1928)

Alice Duer Miller 1874–1942

11 I am American bred,
I have seen much to hate here—much to
forgive,
But in a world where England is finished
and dead,
I do not wish to live.
The White Cliffs (1940)

Arthur Miller 1915–

12 A suicide kills two people, Maggie, that's
what it's for!
After the Fall (1964) act 2

13 Death of a salesman.
title of play (1949)

14 He's a man way out there in the blue, riding
on a smile and a shoeshine. And when they
start not smiling back—that's an
earthquake . . . A salesman is got to dream,
boy. It comes with the territory.
Death of a Salesman (1949) 'Requiem'

15 This is Red Hook, not Sicily . . . This is the
gullet of New York swallowing the tonnage
of the world.
A View from the Bridge (1955) act 1

16 A good newspaper, I suppose, is a nation
talking to itself.
in *Observer* 26 November 1961

Henry Miller 1891–1980

17 Every man with a bellyful of the classics is
an enemy to the human race.
Tropic of Cancer (1934)

Jonathan Miller 1934–

18 In fact, I'm not really a *Jew*. Just Jew-*ish*. Not
the whole hog, you know.
Beyond the Fringe (1960 review) 'Real Class'

Spike Milligan 1918–

19 Money couldn't buy friends but you got a
better class of enemy.
Puckoon (1963) ch. 6

A. J. Mills, Fred Godfrey, and Bennett Scott

20 Take me back to dear old Blighty.
title of song (1916)

Irving Mills 1894–1985

21 It don't mean a thing
If it ain't got that swing.
'It Don't Mean a Thing' (1932 song; music by
Duke **Ellington**)

Henry Hart Milman 1791–1868

22 Ride on! ride on in majesty!
The wingèd squadrons of the sky
Look down with sad and wond'ring eyes
To see the approaching sacrifice.
'Ride on! ride on in majesty!' (1827 hymn)

A. A. Milne 1882–1956

23 The more he looked inside the more Piglet
wasn't there.
The House at Pooh Corner (1928) ch. 1

24 'I don't *want* him,' said Rabbit. 'But it's
always useful to know where a friend-and-
relation *is*, whether you want him or
whether you don't.'
The House at Pooh Corner (1928) ch. 3

25 A Bear of Very Little Brain.
The House at Pooh Corner (1928) ch. 6

26 They're changing guard at Buckingham
Palace—
Christopher Robin went down with Alice.

Alice is marrying one of the guard.
'A soldier's life is terrible hard,'
Says Alice.
When We Were Very Young (1924) 'Buckingham Palace'

1 James James
Morrison Morrison
Weatherby George Dupree
Took great
Care of his Mother,
Though he was only three.
James James
Said to his Mother,
'Mother,' he said, said he;
'You must never go down to the end of the town, if you don't go down with me.'
When We Were Very Young (1924) 'Disobedience'

2 The King asked
The Queen, and
The Queen asked
The Dairymaid:
'Could we have some butter for
The Royal slice of bread?'
When We Were Very Young (1924) 'The King's Breakfast'

3 Hush! Hush! Whisper who dares!
Christopher Robin is saying his prayers.
When We Were Very Young (1924) 'Vespers'; cf.
Morton 229:6

4 Isn't it funny
How a bear likes honey?
Buzz! Buzz! Buzz!
I wonder why he does?
Winnie-the-Pooh (1926) ch. 1

5 Time for a little something.
Winnie-the-Pooh (1926) ch. 6

6 My spelling is Wobbly. It's good spelling but it Wobbles, and the letters get in the wrong places.
Winnie-the-Pooh (1926) ch. 6

Lord Milner 1854–1925

7 If we believe a thing to be bad, and if we have a right to prevent it, it is our duty to try to prevent it and to damn the consequences.
speech in Glasgow, 26 November 1909

John Milton 1608–74

8 Such sweet compulsion doth in music lie.
'Arcades' (1645) l. 68

9 Blest pair of Sirens, pledges of heaven's joy,
Sphere-born harmonious sisters, Voice, and Verse.
'At a Solemn Music' (1645)

10 An old and haughty nation proud in arms.
Comus (1637) l. 33

11 Come, knit hands, and beat the ground,
In a light fantastic round.
Comus (1637) l. 143

12 He that has light within his own clear breast
May sit i' the centre, and enjoy bright day,
But he that hides a dark soul, and foul thoughts

Benighted walks under the midday sun;
Himself is his own dungeon.
Comus (1637) l. 381

13 'Tis chastity, my brother, chastity:
She that has that, is clad in complete steel.
Comus (1637) l. 420

14 How charming is divine philosophy!
Not harsh and crabbèd, as dull fools suppose,
But musical as is Apollo's lute.
Comus (1637) l. 475

15 Storied of old in high immortal verse
Of dire chimeras and enchanted isles,
And rifted rocks whose entrance leads to hell.
Comus (1637) l. 516

16 And filled the air with barbarous dissonance.
Comus (1637) l. 550

17 Against the threats
Of malice or of sorcery, or that power
Which erring men call chance, this I hold firm,
Virtue may be assailed, but never hurt,
Surprised by unjust force, but not enthralled.
Comus (1637) l. 586

18 Sabrina fair,
Listen where thou art sitting
Under the glassy, cool, translucent wave,
In twisted braids of lilies knitting
The loose train of thy amber-dropping hair.
Comus (1637) l. 859 'Song'

19 Thus I set my printless feet
O'er the cowslip's velvet head,
That bends not as I tread.
Comus (1637) l. 897

20 Hence, vain deluding joys,
The brood of folly without father bred.
'Il Penseroso' (1645) l. 1

21 Come, pensive nun, devout and pure,
Sober, steadfast, and demure.
'Il Penseroso' (1645) l. 31

22 Where glowing embers through the room
Teach light to counterfeit a gloom,
Far from all resort of mirth,
Save the cricket on the hearth.
'Il Penseroso' (1645) l. 79

23 Hide me from day's garish eye.
'Il Penseroso' (1645) l. 141

24 And storied windows richly dight,
Casting a dim religious light.
'Il Penseroso' (1645) l. 159

25 Hence, loathèd Melancholy,
Of Cerberus, and blackest Midnight born,
In Stygian cave forlorn
'Mongst horrid shapes, and shrieks, and sights unholy.
'L'Allegro' (1645) l. 1

26 So buxom, blithe, and debonair.
of Euphrosyne [Mirth], *one of the three Graces*
'L'Allegro' (1645) l. 24

1 Nods, and becks, and wreathèd smiles.
   'L'Allegro' (1645) l. 28

2 Come, and trip it as ye go
   On the light fantastic toe.
   'L'Allegro' (1645) l. 33

3 Meadows trim with daisies pied,
   Shallow brooks, and rivers wide.
   'L'Allegro' (1645) l. 75

4 Where perhaps some beauty lies,
   The cynosure of neighbouring eyes.
   'L'Allegro' (1645) l. 79

5 Then to the spicy nut-brown ale.
   'L'Allegro' (1645) l. 100

6 Towered cities please us then,
   And the busy hum of men.
   'L'Allegro' (1645) l. 117

7 Such sights as youthful poets dream
   On summer eves by haunted stream.
   Then to the well-trod stage anon,
   If Jonson's learnèd sock be on,
   Or sweetest Shakespeare fancy's child,
   Warble his native wood-notes wild.
   'L'Allegro' (1645) l. 129

8 Let us with a gladsome mind
   Praise the Lord, for he is kind,
   For his mercies ay endure,
   Ever faithful, ever sure.
   'Let us with a gladsome mind' (1645);
   paraphrase of Psalm 136; cf. **Book of
   Common Prayer** 63:22

9 Yet once more, O ye laurels, and once more
   Ye myrtles brown, with ivy never sere.
   'Lycidas' (1638) l. 1

10 For Lycidas is dead, dead ere his prime,
   Young Lycidas, and hath not left his peer.
   'Lycidas' (1638) l. 8

11 For we were nursed upon the self-same hill.
   'Lycidas' (1638) l. 23

12 To sport with Amaryllis in the shade,
   Or with the tangles of Neaera's hair.
   'Lycidas' (1638) l. 68

13 Fame is the spur.
   'Lycidas' (1638) l. 70

14 Comes the blind Fury with th' abhorrèd
   shears,
   And slits the thin-spun life.
   'Lycidas' (1638) l. 75

15 The hungry sheep look up, and are not fed.
   'Lycidas' (1638) l. 125

16 But that two-handed engine at the door
   Stands ready to smite once, and smite no
   more.
   'Lycidas' (1638) l. 130

17 Bring the rathe primrose that forsaken dies,
   The tufted crow-toe, and pale jessamine.
   'Lycidas' (1638) l. 142

18 Look homeward angel now, and melt with
   ruth.
   'Lycidas' (1638) l. 163

19 So sinks the day-star in the ocean bed,
   And yet anon repairs his drooping head,
   And tricks his beams, and with new
   spangled ore,

Flames in the forehead of the morning sky.
   'Lycidas' (1638) l. 168

20 Through the dear might of Him that walked
   the waves.
   'Lycidas' (1638) l. 173

21 At last he rose, and twitched his mantle
   blue:
   Tomorrow to fresh woods, and pastures
   new.
   'Lycidas' (1638) l. 192

22 For what can war, but endless war still
   breed?
   'On the Lord General Fairfax at the Siege of
   Colchester' (written 1648)

23 The star-led wizards haste with odours
   sweet.
   'On the Morning of Christ's Nativity' (1645) st. 4

24 It was the winter wild,
   While the heaven-born-child
   All meanly wrapped in the rude manger
   lies;
   Nature in awe to him
   Had doffed her gaudy trim,
   With her great master so to sympathize.
   'On the Morning of Christ's Nativity' (1645)
   'The Hymn' st. 1

25 Time will run back, and fetch the age of
   gold.
   'On the Morning of Christ's Nativity' (1645)
   'The Hymn' st. 14

26 So when the sun in bed,
   Curtained with cloudy red,
   Pillows his chin upon an orient wave.
   'On the Morning of Christ's Nativity' (1645)
   'The Hymn' st. 26

27 Time is our tedious song should here have
   ending.
   'On the Morning of Christ's Nativity' (1645)
   'The Hymn' st. 27

28 New *Presbyter* is but old *Priest* writ large.
   'On the New Forcers of Conscience under the
   Long Parliament' (1646)

29 Fly envious Time, till thou run out thy race,
   Call on the lazy leaden-stepping hours.
   'On Time' (1645)

30 If any ask for him, it shall be said,
   Hobson has supped, and's newly gone to
   bed.
   'On the University Carrier' (1645)

31 Rhyme being ... but the invention of a
   barbarous age, to set off wretched matter
   and lame metre.
   Paradise Lost (1667) 'The Verse' (preface, added
   1668)

32 The troublesome and modern bondage of
   rhyming.
   Paradise Lost (1667) 'The Verse' (preface, added
   1668)

33 Of man's first disobedience, and the fruit
   Of that forbidden tree, whose mortal taste
   Brought death into the world, and all our
   woe,
   With loss of Eden.
   Paradise Lost (1667) bk. 1, l. 1

1 Things unattempted yet in prose or rhyme.
  Paradise Lost (1667) bk. 1, l. 16

2   What in me is dark
  Illumine, what is low raise and support;
  That to the height of this great argument
  I may assert eternal providence,
  And justify the ways of God to men.
  Paradise Lost (1667) bk. 1, l. 22; cf. **Housman**
  165:10, **Pope** 248:8

3 No light, but rather darkness visible
  Served only to discover sights of woe.
  Paradise Lost (1667) bk. 1, l. 63

4   What though the field be lost?
  All is not lost; the unconquerable will,
  And study of revenge, immortal hate,
  And courage never to submit or yield.
  Paradise Lost (1667) bk. 1, l. 105

5 And out of good still to find means of evil.
  Paradise Lost (1667) bk. 1, l. 165

6 The mind is its own place, and in itself
  Can make a heaven of hell, a hell of heaven.
  Paradise Lost (1667) bk. 1, l. 254

7 Better to reign in hell, than serve in heaven.
  Paradise Lost (1667) bk. 1, l. 263

8   A wand,
  He walked with to support uneasy steps
  Over the burning marl.
  Paradise Lost (1667) bk. 1, l. 292

9 Thick as autumnal leaves that strew the
      brooks
  In Vallombrosa, where the Etrurian shades
  High overarched imbower.
  Paradise Lost (1667) bk. 1, l. 302

10 First Moloch, horrid king besmeared with
       blood
  Of human sacrifice, and parents' tears.
  Paradise Lost (1667) bk. 1, l. 392

11   And when night
  Darkens the streets, then wander forth the
       sons
  Of Belial, flown with insolence and wine.
  Paradise Lost (1667) bk. 1, l. 500

12 A shout that tore hell's concave, and beyond
  Frighted the reign of Chaos and old Night.
  Paradise Lost (1667) bk. 1, l. 542

13   Mammon led them on,
  Mammon, the least erected spirit that fell
  From heaven.
  Paradise Lost (1667) bk. 1, l. 678

14   Let none admire
  That riches grow in hell; that soil may best
  Deserve the precious bane.
  Paradise Lost (1667) bk. 1, l. 690

15   From morn
  To noon he fell, from noon to dewy eve,
  A summer's day; and with the setting sun
  Dropped from the zenith like a falling star.
  Paradise Lost (1667) bk. 1, l. 742

16   Pandemonium, the high capital
  Of Satan and his peers.
  Paradise Lost (1667) bk. 1, l. 756

17 Belial, in act more graceful and humane;
  A fairer person lost not heaven; he seemed

For dignity composed and high exploit:
But all was false and hollow; though his
     tongue
Dropped manna, and could make the worse
     appear
The better reason.
  Paradise Lost (1667) bk. 2, l. 109; cf.
  Aristophanes 14:9

18   With grave
  Aspect he rose, and in his rising seemed
  A pillar of state; deep on his front engraven
  Deliberation sat and public care;
  And princely counsel in his face yet shone,
  Majestic though in ruin.
  Paradise Lost (1667) bk. 2, l. 300

19   To sit in darkness here
  Hatching vain empires.
  Paradise Lost (1667) bk. 2, l. 377

20   Long is the way
  And hard, that out of hell leads up to light.
  Paradise Lost (1667) bk. 2, l. 432

21 For eloquence the soul, song charms the
  sense.
  Paradise Lost (1667) bk. 2, l. 556

22   Black it stood as night,
  Fierce as ten Furies, terrible as hell,
  And shook a dreadful dart.
  Paradise Lost (1667) bk. 2, l. 670

23   Chaos umpire sits,
  And by decision more embroils the fray.
  Paradise Lost (1667) bk. 2, l. 907

24 Sable-vested Night, eldest of things.
  Paradise Lost (1667) bk. 2, l. 962

25 With ruin upon ruin, rout on rout,
  Confusion worse confounded.
  Paradise Lost (1667) bk. 2, l. 995

26 Die he or justice must.
  Paradise Lost (1667) bk. 3, l. 210

27 Dark with excessive bright.
  Paradise Lost (1667) bk. 3, l. 380

28 Hypocrisy, the only evil that walks
  Invisible, except to God alone.
  Paradise Lost (1667) bk. 3, l. 683

29 Me miserable! which way shall I fly
  Infinite wrath, and infinite despair?
  Which way I fly is hell; myself am hell.
  Paradise Lost (1667) bk. 4, l. 73

30 Evil, be thou my good.
  Paradise Lost (1667) bk. 4, l. 110

31 Flowers of all hue, and without thorn the
  rose.
  Paradise Lost (1667) bk. 4, l. 256

32   Not that fair field
  Of Enna, where Proserpine gathering
       flowers
  Herself a fairer flower by gloomy Dis
  Was gathered, which cost Ceres all that
  pain.
  Paradise Lost (1667) bk. 4, l. 268

33 He for God only, she for God in him.
  Paradise Lost (1667) bk. 4, l. 299

1 Adam, the goodliest man of men since born
His sons, the fairest of her daughters Eve.
Paradise Lost (1667) bk. 4, l. 323

2 These two
Emparadised in one another's arms
The happier Eden, shall enjoy their fill
Of bliss on bliss.
Paradise Lost (1667) bk. 4, l. 505

3 With thee conversing I forget all time.
Paradise Lost (1667) bk. 4, l. 639

4 Millions of spiritual creatures walk the earth
Unseen, both when we wake, and when we sleep.
Paradise Lost (1667) bk. 4, l. 677

5 Sleep on
Blest pair; and O yet happiest if ye seek
No happier state, and know to know no more.
Paradise Lost (1667) bk. 4, l. 773

6 Him there they found
Squat like a toad, close at the ear of Eve.
Paradise Lost (1667) bk. 4, l. 799

7 But wherefore thou alone? Wherefore with thee
Came not all hell broke loose?
Paradise Lost (1667) bk. 4, l. 917

8 My fairest, my espoused, my latest found,
Heaven's last best gift, my ever new delight.
Paradise Lost (1667) bk. 5, l. 18

9 Best image of myself and dearer half.
Paradise Lost (1667) bk. 5, l. 95

10 What if earth
Be but the shadow of heaven, and things therein
Each to other like, more than on earth is thought?
Paradise Lost (1667) bk. 5, l. 574

11 Hear all ye angels, progeny of light,
Thrones, dominations, princedoms, virtues, powers.
Paradise Lost (1667) bk. 5, l. 600; cf. **Bible** 51:1

12 There Leviathan
Hugest of living creatures, on the deep
Stretched like a promontory sleeps or swims.
Paradise Lost (1667) bk. 7, l. 412

13 Oft-times nothing profits more
Than self esteem, grounded on just and right
Well managed.
Paradise Lost (1667) bk. 8, l. 571; cf. **Leavis** 196:1

14 The serpent subtlest beast of all the field.
Paradise Lost (1667) bk. 9, l. 86

15 As one who long in populous city pent,
Where houses thick and sewers annoy the air,
Forth issuing on a summer's morn to breathe
Among the pleasant villages and farms
Adjoined, from each thing met conceives delight.
Paradise Lost (1667) bk. 9, l. 445; cf. **Keats** 182:25

16 She fair, divinely fair, fit love for gods.
Paradise Lost (1667) bk. 9, l. 489

17 God so commanded, and left that command
Sole daughter of his voice; the rest, we live
Law to our selves, our reason is our law.
Paradise Lost (1667) bk. 9, l. 652

18 Earth felt the wound, and Nature from her seat
Sighing through all her works gave signs of woe
That all was lost.
Paradise Lost (1667) bk. 9, l. 782

19 O fairest of creation, last and best
Of all God's works.
Paradise Lost (1667) bk. 9, l. 896

20 Flesh of flesh,
Bone of my bone thou art, and from thy state
Mine never shall be parted, bliss or woe.
Paradise Lost (1667) bk. 9, l. 914; cf. **Bible** 33:4

21 . . . Yet I shall temper so
Justice with mercy.
Paradise Lost (1667) bk. 10, l. 77

22 This novelty on earth, this fair defect
Of nature?
Paradise Lost (1667) bk. 10, l. 891

23 Demoniac frenzy, moping melancholy
And moon-struck madness.
Paradise Lost (1667) bk. 11, l. 485

24 The evening star,
Love's harbinger.
Paradise Lost (1667) bk. 11, l. 588

25 The world was all before them, where to choose
Their place of rest, and Providence their guide:
They hand in hand, with wandering steps and slow,
Through Eden took their solitary way.
Paradise Lost (1667) bk. 12, l. 646

26 But on occasion's forelock watchful wait.
Paradise Regained (1671) bk. 3, l. 173

27 He who seeking asses found a kingdom.
of Saul
Paradise Regained (1671) bk. 3, l. 242; cf. **Bible** 35:16

28 Athens, the eye of Greece, mother of arts
And eloquence . . .
See there the olive grove of Academe,
Plato's retirement, where the Attic bird
Trills her thick-warbled notes the summer long.
Paradise Regained (1671) bk. 4, l. 240

29 The first and wisest of them all professed
To know this only, that he nothing knew.
Paradise Regained (1671) bk. 4, l. 293; cf. **Socrates** 298:21

30 Deep-versed in books and shallow in himself.
Paradise Regained (1671) bk. 4, l. 327

31 But headlong joy is ever on the wing.
'The Passion' (1645) st. 1

32 Ask for this great deliverer now, and find him

Eyeless in Gaza at the mill with slaves.
Samson Agonistes (1671) l. 40

1 O dark, dark, dark, amid the blaze of noon,
Irrecoverably dark, total eclipse
Without all hope of day!
Samson Agonistes (1671) l. 80

2 The sun to me is dark
And silent as the moon,
When she deserts the night
Hid in her vacant interlunar cave.
Samson Agonistes (1671) l. 86

3 To live a life half dead, a living death.
Samson Agonistes (1671) l. 100

4 Just are the ways of God,
And justifiable to men;
Unless there be who think not God at all.
Samson Agonistes (1671) l. 293

5 Nothing is here for tears, nothing to wail.
Samson Agonistes (1671) l. 1721

6 And calm of mind, all passion spent.
Samson Agonistes (1671) l. 1758

7 Time the subtle thief of youth.
Sonnet 7 'How soon hath time' (1645)

8 Licence they mean when they cry liberty;
For who loves that, must first be wise and
good.
Sonnet 12 'I did but prompt the age' (1673)

9 When I consider how my light is spent,
E're half my days, in this dark world and
wide,
And that one talent which is death to hide
Lodged with me useless.
Sonnet 16 'When I consider how my light is
spent' (1673)

10 They also serve who only stand and wait.
Sonnet 16 'When I consider how my light is
spent' (1673)

11 Methought I saw my late espousèd saint
Brought to me like Alcestis from the grave.
Sonnet 19 'Methought I saw my late espousèd
saint' (1673)

12 Cromwell, our chief of men.
'To the Lord General Cromwell' (written 1652)

13 Peace hath her victories
No less renowned than war.
'To the Lord General Cromwell' (written 1652)

14 A good book is the precious life-blood of a
master spirit, embalmed and treasured up
on purpose to a life beyond life.
Areopagitica (1644)

15 I cannot praise a fugitive and cloistered
virtue, unexercised and unbreathed, that
never sallies out and sees her adversary, but
slinks out of the race, where that immortal
garland is to be run for, not without dust
and heat . . . that which purifies us is trial,
and trial is by what is contrary.
Areopagitica (1644)

16 Here the great art lies, to discern in what
the law is to be to restraint and
punishment, and in what things persuasion
only is to work.
Areopagitica (1644)

17 If we think to regulate printing, thereby to
rectify manners, we must regulate all
recreations and pastimes, all that is
delightful to man.
Areopagitica (1644)

18 What does he [God] then but reveal Himself
to his servants, and as his manner is, first to
his Englishmen?
Areopagitica (1644)

19 A city of refuge, the mansion-house of
liberty.
of London
Areopagitica (1644)

20 Opinion in good men is but knowledge in
the making.
Areopagitica (1644) p. 31

21 Let not England forget her precedence of
teaching nations how to live.
The Doctrine and Discipline of Divorce (1643) 'To the
Parliament of England'

22 What I have spoken, is the language of that
which is not called amiss *The good old Cause.*
*The Ready and Easy Way to Establish a Free
Commonwealth* (2nd ed., 1660); cf. **Wordsworth**
340:16

Comte de Mirabeau 1749–91

23 War is the national industry of Prussia.
attributed to Mirabeau by Albert Sorel
(1842–1906), based on Mirabeau's introduction
to *De la monarchie prussienne sous Frédéric le Grand*
(1788)

The Missal

24 *Dominus vobiscum.*
Et cum spiritu tuo.
The Lord be with you.
And with thy spirit.
The Ordinary of the Mass

25 *In Nomine Patris, et Filii, et Spiritus Sancti.*
In the Name of the Father, and of the Son,
and of the Holy Ghost.
The Ordinary of the Mass

26 *Quia peccavi nimis cogitatione, verbo, et opere,
mea culpa, mea culpa, mea maxima culpa.*
I have sinned exceedingly in thought, word,
and deed, through my fault, through my
fault, through my most grievous fault.
The Ordinary of the Mass

27 *Kyrie eleison . . . Christe eleison.*
Lord, have mercy upon us . . . Christ, have
mercy upon us.
The Ordinary of the Mass

28 *Gloria in excelsis Deo, et in terra pax hominibus
bonae voluntatis.*
Glory be to God on high, and on earth peace
to men of good will.
The Ordinary of the Mass; cf. **Bible** 46:5

29 *Deo gratias.*
Thanks be to God.
The Ordinary of the Mass

1 *Credo in unum Deum.*
I believe in one God.
> *The Ordinary of the Mass* 'The Nicene Creed'; cf.
> **Book of Common Prayer** 59:22

2 *Et homo factus est.*
And was made man.
> *The Ordinary of the Mass* 'The Nicene Creed'

3 *Sursum corda.*
Lift up your hearts.
> *The Ordinary of the Mass*; cf. **Book of Common Prayer** 60:1

4 *Sanctus, sanctus, sanctus, Dominus Deus Sabaoth. Pleni sunt coeli et terra gloria tua. Hosanna in excelsis. Benedictus qui venit in nomine Domini.*
Holy, holy, holy, Lord God of Hosts. Heaven and earth are full of thy glory. Hosanna in the highest. Blessed is he that cometh in the name of the Lord.
> *The Ordinary of the Mass*; cf. **Bible** 52:8, **Book of Common Prayer** 60:3

5 *Pater noster, qui es in coelis, sanctificetur nomen tuum; adveniat regnum tuum; fiat voluntas tua sicut in coelo, et in terra . . . sed libera nos a malo.*
Our Father, who art in heaven, hallowed be thy name; thy kingdom come; thy will be done on earth, as it is in heaven . . . but deliver us from evil.
> *The Ordinary of the Mass*; cf. **Bible** 42:23

6 *Agnus Dei, qui tollis peccata mundi, miserere nobis.*
Lamb of God, who takest away the sins of the world, have mercy on us.
> *The Ordinary of the Mass*; cf. **Bible** 47:23

7 *Domine, non sum dignus ut intres sub tectum meum; sed tantum dic verbo, et sanabitur anima mea.*
Lord, I am not worthy that thou shouldst enter under my roof; but say only the word, and my soul shall be healed.
> *The Ordinary of the Mass*; cf. **Bible** 43:13

8 *Ite missa est.*
Go, you are dismissed.
> *commonly interpreted as 'Go, the Mass is ended'*
> *The Ordinary of the Mass*

9 *Verbum caro factum est.*
The word was made flesh.
> *The Ordinary of the Mass*; cf. **Bible** 47:21

10 *Requiem aeternam dona eis, Domine: et lux perpetua luceat eis.*
Grant them eternal rest, O Lord; and let perpetual light shine on them.
> *Order of Mass for the Dead*

11 *Dies irae, dies illa,*
Solvet saeclum in favilla,
Teste David cum Sibylla.
That day, the day of wrath, will turn the universe to ashes, as David foretells (and the Sibyl too).
> *Order of Mass for the Dead* 'Sequentia' l. 1;
> commonly known as *Dies Irae* and sometimes
> attributed to Thomas of Celano (*c.*1190–1260)

12 *Rex tremendae maiestatis,*
Qui salvandos salvas gratis,
Salva me, fons pietatis!
O King of tremendous majesty, who freely saves those who should be saved, save me, O source of pity!
> *Order of Mass for the Dead* 'Sequentia' l. 22

13 *Requiescant in pace.*
May they rest in peace.
> *Order of Mass for the Dead*

14 *O felix culpa, quae talem ac tantum meruit habere Redemptorem.*
O happy fault, which has earned such a mighty Redeemer.
> 'Exsultet' on Holy Saturday

Adrian Mitchell 1932–

15 Most people ignore most poetry
because
most poetry ignores most people.
> *Poems* (1964)

George Mitchell 1933–

16 Nobody ever said it would be easy—and that was an understatement.
> *on the peace talks*
> in *Times* 19 February 1998

17 I am pleased to announce that the two governments and the political parties in Northern Ireland have reached agreement.
> *announcing the Good Friday agreement*
> in *Times* 11 April 1998

John Mitchell 1785–1859

18 The most important political question on which modern times have to decide is the policy that must now be pursued, in order to maintain the security of Western Europe against the overgrown power of Russia.
> *Thoughts on Tactics* (1838)

Joni Mitchell (Roberta Joan Anderson) 1945–

19 They paved paradise
And put up a parking lot,
With a pink hotel,
A boutique, and a swinging hot spot.
> 'Big Yellow Taxi' (1970 song)

20 We are stardust,
We are golden,
And we got to get ourselves
Back to the garden.
> 'Woodstock' (1969 song)

Margaret Mitchell 1900–49

21 Death and taxes and childbirth! There's never any convenient time for any of them.
> *Gone with the Wind* (1936) ch. 38

22 I wish I could care what you do or where you go but I can't . . . My dear, I don't give a damn.
> *Gone with the Wind* (1936) ch. 57

23 After all, tomorrow is another day.
> *Gone with the Wind* (1936), closing words

Nancy Mitford 1904–73

1 Love in a cold climate.
   title of book (1949); cf. **Southey** 299:19

2 Frogs . . . are slightly better than Huns or
   Wops, but abroad is unutterably bloody and
   foreigners are fiends.
   The Pursuit of Love (1945) ch. 15; cf. **George VI**
   138:10

François Mitterrand 1916–96

3 She has the eyes of Caligula, but the mouth
   of Marilyn Monroe.
   of Margaret **Thatcher**, *briefing his new European
   Minister Roland Dumas*
   in *Observer* 25 November 1990

Wilson Mizner 1876–1933

4 Be nice to people on your way up because
   you'll meet 'em on your way down.
   Alva Johnston *The Legendary Mizners* (1953) ch. 4

5 If you steal from one author, it's plagiarism;
   if you steal from many, it's research.
   Alva Johnston *The Legendary Mizners* (1953) ch. 4

6 A trip through a sewer in a glass-bottomed
   boat.
   *of Hollywood; reworked by Mayor Jimmy Walker
   into 'A reformer is a guy who rides through a
   sewer in a glass-bottomed boat'*
   Alva Johnston *The Legendary Mizners* (1953) ch. 4

Ariane Mnouchkine 1934–

7 A cultural Chernobyl.
   of Euro Disney
   in *Harper's Magazine* July 1992; cf. **Ballard** 24:17

Emilio Mola 1887–1937

8 Fifth column.
   *an extra body of supporters claimed by General
   Mola in a broadcast as being within Madrid when
   he besieged the city with four columns of
   Nationalist forces*
   in *New York Times* 16 and 17 October 1936

Molière 1622–73

9 One should eat to live, and not live to eat.
   L'Avare (1669) act 3, sc. 1

10 All that is not prose is verse; and all that is
    not verse is prose.
    Le Bourgeois Gentilhomme (1671) act 2, sc. 4

11 Good heavens! For more than forty years I
    have been speaking prose without knowing
    it.
    Le Bourgeois Gentilhomme (1671) act 2, sc. 4

12 *Que diable allait-il faire dans cette galère?*
    What the devil was he doing in that galley?
    Les Fourberies de Scapin (1671) act 2, sc. 11

13 GÉRONTE: It seems to me you are locating
    them wrongly: the heart is on the left and
    the liver is on the right.
    SGANARELLE: Yes, in the old days that was so,
    but we have changed all that, and we now
    practise medicine by a completely new
    method.
    Le Médecin malgré lui (1667) act 2, sc. 4

14 Here [in Paris] they hang a man first, and try
    him afterwards.
    Monsieur de Pourceaugnac (1670) act 1, sc. 5

15 *L'homme est, je vous l'avoue, un méchant animal.*
    Man, I can assure you, is a nasty creature.
    Le Tartuffe (1669) act 5, sc. 6

Helmuth von Moltke 1800–91

16 Everlasting peace is a dream, and not even a
    pleasant one; and war is a necessary part of
    God's arrangement of the world . . . Without
    war the world would deteriorate into
    materialism.
    letter to Dr J. K. Bluntschli, 11 December 1880

Walter Mondale 1928–

17 When I hear your new ideas I'm reminded
    of that ad, 'Where's the beef?'
    in a televised debate with Gary Hart, 11 March
    1984

James, Duke of Monmouth
1649–85

18 Do not hack me as you did my Lord Russell.
    to his executioner
    T. B. Macaulay *History of England* vol. 1 (1849) ch.
    5

Jean Monnet 1888–1979

19 We should not create a nation Europe
    instead of a nation France.
    François Duchêne *Jean Monnet* (1994)

Marilyn Monroe 1926–62

on being asked what she wore in bed:
20 Chanel No. 5.
    Pete Martin *Marilyn Monroe* (1956)

James Monroe 1758–1831

21 We owe it . . . to the amicable relations
    existing between the United States and
    those [European] powers to declare that we
    should consider any attempt on their part to
    extend their system to any portion of this
    hemisphere as dangerous to our peace and
    safety.
    *principle that became known as the 'Monroe
    Doctrine'*
    annual message to Congress, 2 December 1823

John Samuel Bewley Monsell
1811–75

22 Fight the good fight with all thy might.
    'The Fight for Faith' (1863 hymn); cf. **Bible**
    51:12

23 O worship the Lord in the beauty of
    holiness,
    Bow down before him, his glory proclaim.
    'O Worship the Lord' (1863 hymn)

Lady Mary Wortley Montagu
1689–1762

1 And we meet with champagne and a chicken at last.

   Six Town Eclogues (1747) 'The Lover' l. 25

2 Men are vile inconstant toads.

   letter to Anne Justice, *c.*12 June 1710

3 I have too much indulged my sedentary humour and have been a rake in reading.

   letter to her daughter Lady Bute, 11 April 1759

4 Civility costs nothing and buys everything.

   letter to her daughter Lady Bute, 30 May 1756

5 People wish their enemies dead—but I do not; I say give them the gout, give them the stone!

   W. S. Lewis et al. (eds.) *Horace Walpole's Correspondence* (1973) vol. 35

C. E. Montague 1867–1928

6 War hath no fury like a non-combatant.

   Disenchantment (1922) ch. 16

Montaigne 1533–92

7 I want death to find me planting my cabbages, but caring little for it, and even less about the imperfections of my garden.

   Essais (1580, ed. M. Rat, 1958) bk. 1, ch. 20

8 The ceaseless labour of your life is to build the house of death.

   Essais (1580, ed. M. Rat, 1958) bk. 1, ch. 20

9 It should be noted that children at play are not playing about; their games should be seen as their most serious-minded activity.

   Essais (1580, ed. M. Rat, 1958) bk. 1, ch. 23

10 There is scarcely any less bother in the running of a family than in that of an entire state. And domestic business is no less importunate for being less important.

   Essais (1580, ed. M. Rat, 1958) bk. 1, ch. 39

11 The greatest thing in the world is to know how to be oneself.

   Essais (1580, ed. M. Rat, 1958) bk. 1, ch. 39

12 When I play with my cat, who knows whether she isn't amusing herself with me more than I am with her?

   Essais (1580, ed. M. Rat, 1958) bk. 2, ch. 12

13 *Que sais-je?*
   What do I know?
   on the position of the sceptic
   Essais (1580, ed. M. Rat, 1958) bk. 2, ch. 12

14 It could be said of me that in this book I have only made up a bunch of other men's flowers, providing of my own only the string that ties them together.

   Essais (1580, ed. M. Rat, 1958) bk. 3, ch. 12

Montesquieu 1689–1755

15 If the triangles were to make a God they would give him three sides.

   Lettres Persanes (1721) no. 59 (tr. J. Ozell, 1722)

16 The English are busy; they don't have time to be polite.

   Pensées et fragments inédits . . . vol. 2 (1901) no. 1428

17 Happy the people whose annals are blank in history-books!

   attributed to Montesquieu by Thomas Carlyle in *History of Frederick the Great* bk. 16, ch. 1

Lord Montgomery of Alamein
1887–1976

18 *Here* we will stand and fight; there will be no further withdrawal. I have ordered that all plans and instructions dealing with further withdrawal are to be burnt, and at once. We will stand and fight *here*. If we can't stay here alive, then let us stay here dead.

   speech in Cairo, 13 August 1942

19 Rule 1, on page 1 of the book of war, is: 'Do not march on Moscow' . . . [Rule 2] is: 'Do not go fighting with your land armies in China.'

   speech in the House of Lords, 30 May 1962

Robert Montgomery 1807–55

20 The solitary monk who shook the world.

   Luther: a Poem (1842) ch. 3 'Man's Need and God's Supply'

Casimir, Comte de Montrond
1768–1843

21 Have no truck with first impulses for they are always generous ones.

   attributed; cf. **Corneille** 100:4

James Graham, Marquess of Montrose 1612–50

22 Let them bestow on every airth a limb.

   'Lines written on the Window of his Jail the Night before his Execution'

23 He either fears his fate too much,
   Or his deserts are small,
   That puts it not unto the touch
   To win or lose it all.

   'My Dear and Only Love' (written *c.*1642)

Percy Montrose

24 In a cavern, in a canyon,
   Excavating for a mine,
   Dwelt a miner, Forty-niner,
   And his daughter, Clementine.
   Oh, my darling, oh my darling, oh my darling Clementine!
   Thou art lost and gone for ever, dreadful sorry, Clementine.

   'Clementine' (1884 song)

Monty Python's Flying Circus
1969–74

25 It's *not* pining—it's passed on! This parrot is no more! It has ceased to be! It's expired and gone to meet its maker! This is a late parrot! It's a stiff! Bereft of life it rests in peace—if

you hadn't nailed it to the perch it would be pushing up the daisies! It's rung down the curtain and joined the choir invisible! THIS IS AN EX-PARROT!

Monty Python's Flying Circus (1969)

1 Nobody expects the Spanish Inquisition!
Monty Python's Flying Circus (1970)

Clement C. Moore 1779–1863

2 'Twas the night before Christmas, when all through the house
Not a creature was stirring, not even a mouse.
'A Visit from St Nicholas' (December 1823)

Edward Moore 1712–57

3 This is adding insult to injuries.
The Foundling (1748) act 5, sc. 5

4 I am rich beyond the dreams of avarice.
The Gamester (1753) act 2, sc. 2; cf. **Johnson** 176:8

George Moore 1852–1933

5 All reformers are bachelors.
The Bending of the Bough (1900) act 1

6 A man travels the world in search of what he needs and returns home to find it.
The Brook Kerith (1916) ch. 11

Henry Moore 1898–1986

7 Sculpture in stone should look honestly like stone . . . to make it look like flesh and blood, hair and dimples is coming down to the level of the stage conjuror.
in *Architectural Association Journal* May 1930

8 The first hole made through a piece of stone is a revelation.
in *Listener* 18 August 1937

Marianne Moore 1887–1972

9 Imaginary gardens with real toads in them.
'Poetry' (1935)

10 My father used to say,
'Superior people never make long visits, have to be shown Longfellow's grave or the glass flowers at Harvard.'
'Silence' (1935)

11 I am troubled, I'm dissatisfied, I'm Irish.
'Spenser's Ireland' (1941)

Thomas Moore 1779–1852

12 Though an angel should write, still 'tis *devils* must print.
The Fudges in England (1835) Letter 3, l. 65

13 Believe me, if all those endearing young charms,
Which I gaze on so fondly today,
Were to change by tomorrow, and fleet in my arms,
Like fairy gifts fading away!
Irish Melodies (1807) 'Believe me, if all those endearing young charms'

14 'Twas from Kathleen's eyes he flew,
Eyes of most unholy blue!
Irish Melodies (1807) 'By that Lake'

15 The harp that once through Tara's halls
The soul of music shed,
Now hangs as mute on Tara's walls
As if that soul were fled.
Irish Melodies (1807) 'The harp that once through Tara's halls'

16 No, there's nothing half so sweet in life
As love's young dream.
Irish Melodies (1807) 'Love's Young Dream'

17 The Minstrel Boy to the war is gone,
In the ranks of death you'll find him;
His father's sword he has girded on,
And his wild harp slung behind him.
Irish Melodies (1807) 'The Minstrel Boy'

18 'Tis the last rose of summer
Left blooming alone;
All her lovely companions
Are faded and gone.
Irish Melodies (1807) ''Tis the last rose of summer'

19 I never nursed a dear gazelle,
To glad me with its soft black eye,
But when it came to know me well,
And love me, it was sure to die!
Lalla Rookh (1817) 'The Fire-Worshippers' pt. 1, l. 283; cf. **Payn** 242:9

20 Oft, in the stilly night,
Ere Slumber's chain has bound me,
Fond Memory brings the light
Of other days around me.
National Airs (1815) 'Oft in the Stilly Night'

Thomas Osbert Mordaunt 1730–1809

21 One crowded hour of glorious life
Is worth an age without a name.
'A Poem, said to be written by Major Mordaunt during the last German War', in *The Bee, or Literary Weekly Intelligencer* 12 October 1791

Hannah More 1745–1833

22 For you'll ne'er mend your fortunes, nor help the just cause,
By breaking of windows, or breaking of laws.
'An Address to the Meeting in Spa Fields' (1817); cf. **Pankhurst** 240:12

23 He liked those literary cooks
Who skim the cream of others' books;
And ruin half an author's graces
By plucking bon-mots from their places.
Florio (1786) pt. 1, l. 123

Thomas More 1478–1535

24 Your sheep, that were wont to be so meek and tame, and so small eaters, now, as I hear say, be become so great devourers, and so wild, that they eat up and swallow down the very men themselves.
Utopia (1516) bk. 1

25 If the parties will at my hands call for justice, then, all were it my father stood on the one side, and the Devil on the other, his cause being good, the Devil should have right.

William Roper *Life of Sir Thomas More*

1 Is not this house as nigh heaven as my own?

of the Tower of London

William Roper *Life of Sir Thomas More*

2 Fare well my dear child and pray for me, and I shall for you and all your friends that we may merrily meet in heaven.

last letter to his daughter Margaret Roper, 5 July 1535, on the eve of his execution

3 I pray you, master Lieutenant, see me safe up, and my coming down let me shift for my self.

of mounting the scaffold

William Roper *Life of Sir Thomas More*

4 This hath not offended the king.

lifting his beard aside after laying his head on the block

Francis Bacon *Apophthegms New and Old* (1625) no. 22

Thomas Morell 1703–84

5 See, the conquering hero comes!
Sound the trumpets, beat the drums!

Judas Maccabeus (1747) 'A chorus of youths' and *Joshua* (1748) pt. 3 (to music by Handel)

Morelly

6 Every citizen will make his own contribution to the activities of the community according to his strength, his talent, and his age: it is on this basis that his duties will be determined, conforming with the distributive laws.

Code de la Nature (1755) pt. 4; cf. **Blanc** 56:18, **Marx** 214:5

Robin Morgan 1941–

7 Sisterhood is powerful.

title of book (1970)

Christopher Morley 1890–1957

8 Life is a foreign language: all men mispronounce it.

Thunder on the Left (1925) ch. 14; cf. **Hartley** 153:1

Lord Morley 1838–1923

9 The golden Gospel of Silence is effectively compressed in thirty fine volumes.

on **Carlyle***'s* History of Frederick the Great *(1858–65), Carlyle having written of his subject as 'that strong, silent man'*

Critical Miscellanies (1886) 'Carlyle'

10 You have not converted a man, because you have silenced him.

On Compromise (1874) ch. 5

Countess Morphy (Marcelle Azra Forbes) fl. 1930–50

11 The tragedy of English cooking is that 'plain' cooking cannot be entrusted to 'plain' cooks.

English Recipes (1935)

Charles Morris 1745–1838

12 But a house is much more to my mind than a tree,
And for groves, O! a good grove of chimneys for me.

'Country and Town' (1840)

Desmond Morris 1928–

13 The city is not a concrete jungle, it is a human zoo.

The Human Zoo (1969) introduction

14 There are one hundred and ninety-three living species of monkeys and apes. One hundred and ninety-two of them are covered with hair. The exception is a naked ape self-named *Homo sapiens*.

The Naked Ape (1967) introduction

George Pope Morris 1802–64

15 Woodman, spare that tree!
Touch not a single bough!
In youth it sheltered me,
And I'll protect it now.

'Woodman, Spare That Tree' (1830); cf. **Campbell** 81:1

William Morris 1834–96

16 The idle singer of an empty day.

The Earthly Paradise (1868–70) 'An Apology'

17 Dreamer of dreams, born out of my due time,
Why should I strive to set the crooked straight?

The Earthly Paradise (1868–70) 'An Apology'

18 Forget the spreading of the hideous town;
Think rather of the pack-horse on the down,
And dream of London, small and white and clean,
The clear Thames bordered by its gardens green.

The Earthly Paradise (1868–70) 'Prologue: The Wanderers' l. 3

19 Have nothing in your houses that you do not know to be useful, or believe to be beautiful.

Hopes and Fears for Art (1882) 'Making the Best of It'

Jim Morrison 1943–71

20 C'mon, baby, light my fire.

'Light My Fire' (1967 song, with Robby Krieger)

21 We want the world and we want it now!

'When the Music's Over' (1967 song)

R. F. Morrison

22 Just a wee deoch-an-doris,
Just a wee yin, that's a'.

Just a wee deoch-an-doris,
Before we gang awa'.
There's a wee wifie waitin',
In a wee but-an-ben;
If you can say
'It's a braw bricht moonlicht nicht',
Ye're a' richt, ye ken.
'Just a Wee Deoch-an-Doris' (1911 song);
popularized by Harry Lauder

Samuel Morse 1791–1872

1 What hath God wrought.
Samuel Morse, in the first electric telegraph
message, 24 May 1844; cf. **Bible** 34:25

Owen Morshead 1893–1977

2 The House of Hanover, like ducks, produce
bad parents—they trample on their young.
as Royal Librarian, in conversation with Harold
Nicolson, *biographer of* **George V**
Harold Nicolson, letter to Vita Sackville-West, 7
January 1949

John Mortimer 1923–

3 No brilliance is needed in the law. Nothing
but common sense, and relatively clean
fingernails.
A Voyage Round My Father (1971) act 1

4 The worst fault of the working classes is
telling their children they're not going to
succeed, saying: 'There is life, but it's not
for you.'
in *Daily Mail* 31 May 1988

J. B. Morton ('Beachcomber') 1893–1975

5 One disadvantage of being a hog is that at
any moment some blundering fool may try
to make a silk purse out of your wife's ear.
By the Way (1931)

6 Hush, hush,
Nobody cares!
Christopher Robin
Has
Fallen
Down-
Stairs.
By the Way (1931); cf. **Milne** 218:3

7 Dr Strabismus (Whom God Preserve) of
Utrecht.
Morton's Folly (1933)

Jelly Roll Morton 1885–1941

8 Jazz music is to be played sweet, soft, plenty
rhythm.
Mister Jelly Roll (1950)

Rogers Morton 1914–79

9 I'm not going to rearrange the furniture on
the deck of the Titanic.
*having lost five of the last six primaries as
President* **Ford**'s *campaign manager*
in *Washington Post* 16 May 1976

Thomas Morton c.1764–1838

10 Approbation from Sir Hubert Stanley is
praise indeed.
A Cure for the Heartache (1797) act 5, sc. 2

11 Always ding, dinging Dame Grundy into my
ears—what will Mrs Grundy zay? What will
Mrs Grundy think?
Speed the Plough (1798) act 1, sc. 1; cf. **Locker-
Lampson** 201:9

Edwin Moses 1955–

12 I don't really see the hurdles. I sense them
like a memory.
attributed

John Lothrop Motley 1814–77

13 As long as he lived, he was the guiding-star
of a whole brave nation, and when he died
the little children cried in the streets.
of **William** *of Orange*
The Rise of the Dutch Republic (1856) pt. 6, ch. 7; cf.
Auden 18:1

Lord Mountbatten 1900–79

14 Right, now I understand people think
you're the Forgotten Army on the Forgotten
Front. I've come here to tell you you're
quite wrong. You're not the Forgotten Army
on the Forgotten Front. No, make no
mistake about it. Nobody's ever *heard* of
you.
*encouragement to troops when taking over as
Supreme Allied Commander South-East Asia in
late 1943*
R. Hough *Mountbatten* (1980)

Marjorie ('Mo') Mowlam 1949–

15 It takes courage to push things forward.
*on her decision to visit Loyalist prisoners in The
Maze*
in *Guardian* 8 January 1998

Wolfgang Amadeus Mozart 1756–91

16 Melody is the essence of music. I compare a
good melodist to a fine racer, and
counterpoints to hack post-horses.
remark to Michael Kelly, 1786

Malcolm Muggeridge 1903–90

17 Something beautiful for God.
title of book (1971); see **Teresa** 314:10

Edwin Muir 1887–1959

18 And without fear the lawless roads
Ran wrong through all the land.
'Hölderlin's Journey' (1937)

Frank Muir 1920–98

19 The thinking man's crumpet.
of Joan **Bakewell**
attributed

Lewis Mumford 1895–1990

1 Our national flower is the concrete
cloverleaf.
  in *Quote Magazine* 8 October 1961

Edvard Munch 1863–1944

2 You should not paint the chair, but only
what someone has felt about it.
  written *c.*1891

Murasaki Shikibu *c.*978–*c.*1031

3 Anything whatsoever may become the
subject of a novel, provided only that it
happens in this mundane life and not in
some fairyland beyond our human ken.
  The Tale of Genji

Iris Murdoch 1919–99

4 Dora Greenfield left her husband because
she was afraid of him. She decided six
months later to return to him for the same
reason.
  The Bell (1958) ch. 1

5 One doesn't have to get anywhere in a
marriage. It's not a public conveyance.
  A Severed Head (1961) ch. 3

6 Love is the extremely difficult realisation
that something other than oneself is real.
Love, and so art and morals, is the discovery
of reality.
  'The Sublime and the Good' in *Chicago Review* 13
  (1959)

Rupert Murdoch 1931–

asked why he had allowed Page 3 to develop:
7 I don't know. The editor did it when I was
away.
  in *Guardian* 25 February 1994

C. W. Murphy
and Will Letters

8 Has anybody here seen Kelly?
Kelly from the Isle of Man?
  'Has Anybody Here Seen Kelly?' (1909 song)

Fred Murray

9 Ginger, you're balmy!
  title of song (1910)

James Augustus Henry Murray
1837–1915

10 I feel that in many respects I and my
assistants are simply pioneers, pushing our
way experimentally through an untrodden
forest, where no white man's axe has been
before us.
  'Report on the Philological Society's Dictionary'
  (1884)

Ed Murrow 1908–65

11 No one can terrorize a whole nation, unless
we are all his accomplices.
  of Joseph McCarthy
  'See It Now', broadcast, 7 March 1954

12 He mobilized the English language and sent
it into battle to steady his fellow
countrymen and hearten those Europeans
upon whom the long dark night of tyranny
had descended.
  of Winston Churchill
  broadcast, 30 November 1954, in *In Search of
  Light* (1967)

13 Anyone who isn't confused doesn't really
understand the situation.
  on the Vietnam War
  Walter Bryan *The Improbable Irish* (1969) ch. 1

Alfred de Musset 1810–57

14 *Malgré moi l'infini me tourmente.*
I can't help it, the idea of the infinite
torments me.
  'L'Espoir en Dieu' (1838)

15 *Le seul bien qui me reste au monde
Est d'avoir quelquefois pleuré.*
The only good thing left to me is that I have
sometimes wept.
  'Tristesse' (1841)

Benito Mussolini 1883–1945

16 We must leave exactly on time . . . From
now on everything must function to
perfection.
  to a station-master
  Giorgio Pini *Mussolini* (1939) vol. 2, ch. 6

Vladimir Nabokov 1899–1977

17 Lolita, light of my life, fire of my loins. My
sin, my soul. Lo-lee-ta: the tip of the tongue
taking a trip of three steps down the palate
to tap, at three, on the teeth. Lo. Lee. Ta.
  Lolita (1955) ch. 1

18 You can always count on a murderer for a
fancy prose style.
  Lolita (1955) ch. 1

Ralph Nader 1934–

19 Unsafe at any speed.
  title of book (1965)

Ian Nairn 1930–

20 If what is called development is allowed to
multiply at the present rate, then by the
end of the century Great Britain will consist
of isolated oases of preserved monuments
in a desert of wire, concrete roads, cosy
plots and bungalows . . . Upon this new
Britain the *Review* bestows a name in the
hope that it will stick—SUBTOPIA.
  in *Architectural Review* June 1955

Lewis Namier 1888–1960

21 No number of atrocities however horrible
can deprive a nation of its right to
independence, nor justify its being put
under the heel of its worst enemies and
persecutors.
  in 1919; Julia Namier *Lewis Namier* (1971)

Fridtjof Nansen 1861–1930

1 Never stop because you are afraid—you are
never so likely to be wrong. Never keep a
line of retreat: it is a wretched invention.
The difficult is what takes a little time; the
impossible is what takes a little longer.

in *Listener* 14 December 1939; cf. **Anonymous**
6:12, **Calonne** 80:12

Napoleon I 1769–1821

2 Think of it, soldiers; from the summit of
these pyramids, forty centuries look down
upon you.

before the Battle of the Pyramids
speech to the Army of Egypt on 21 July 1798

3 It [the Channel] is a mere ditch, and will be
crossed as soon as someone has the courage
to attempt it.

letter to Consul Cambacérès, 16 November
1803

4 I want the whole of Europe to have one
currency; it will make trading much easier.

letter to his brother Louis, 6 May 1807

5 There is only one step from the sublime to
the ridiculous.

*to De Pradt, Polish ambassador, after the retreat
from Moscow in 1812*

D. G. De Pradt *Histoire de l'Ambassade dans le
grand-duché de Varsovie en 1812* (1815); cf. **Paine**
239:6

6 As to moral courage, I have very rarely met
with two o'clock in the morning courage: I
mean instantaneous courage.

E. A. de Las Cases *Mémorial de Ste-Hélène* (1823)
vol. 1, pt. 2, 4–5 December 1815; cf. **Thoreau**
317:20

7 An army marches on its stomach.

attributed, but probably condensed from a long
passage in E. A. de Las Cases *Mémorial de Ste-
Hélène* (1823) vol. 4, 14 November 1816; also
attributed to **Frederick the Great**

8 As though he had 200,000 men.

when asked how to deal with the Pope
J. M. Robinson *Cardinal Consalvi* (1987); cf. **Stalin**
301:13

9 *La carrière ouverte aux talents.*
The career open to the talents.

Barry E. O'Meara *Napoleon in Exile* (1822) vol. 1

10 England is a nation of shopkeepers.

Barry E. O'Meara *Napoleon in Exile* (1822) vol. 2;
cf. **Adams** 2:3, **Smith** 297:9

11 Not tonight, Josephine.

attributed, but probably apocryphal; the phrase
does not appear in contemporary sources, but
was current by the early twentieth century

Ogden Nash 1902–71

12 The turtle lives 'twixt plated decks
Which practically conceal its sex.
I think it clever of the turtle
In such a fix to be so fertile.

'Autres Bêtes, Autres Moeurs' (1931)

13 The cow is of the bovine ilk;
One end is moo, the other, milk.

'The Cow' (1931)

14 Beneath this slab
John Brown is stowed.
He watched the ads,
And not the road.

'Lather as You Go' (1942)

15 Candy
Is dandy
But liquor
Is quicker.

'Reflections on Ice-breaking' (1931)

16 I test my bath before I sit,
And I'm always moved to wonderment
That what chills the finger not a bit
Is so frigid upon the fundament.

'Samson Agonistes' (1942)

17 I think that I shall never see
A billboard lovely as a tree.
Perhaps, unless the billboards fall,
I'll never see a tree at all.

'Song of the Open Road' (1933); cf. **Kilmer**
186:1

18 Sure, deck your lower limbs in pants;
Yours are the limbs, my sweeting.
You look divine as you advance—
Have you seen yourself retreating?

'What's the Use?' (1940)

Thomas Nashe 1567–1601

19 O, tis a precious apothegmatical Pedant,
who will find matter enough to dilate a
whole day of the first invention of *Fy, fa,
fum*, I smell the blood of an English-man.

Have with you to Saffron-walden (1596); cf.
Shakespeare 277:28

20 Brightness falls from the air;
Queens have died young and fair;
Dust hath closed Helen's eye.
I am sick, I must die.
Lord have mercy on us.

Summer's Last Will and Testament (1600) l. 1590

21 From winter, plague and pestilence, good
lord, deliver us!

Summer's Last Will and Testament (1600) l. 1878

James Ball Naylor 1860–1945

22 King David and King Solomon
Led merry, merry lives,
With many, many lady friends,
And many, many wives;
But when old age crept over them—
With many, many qualms!—
King Solomon wrote the Proverbs
And King David wrote the Psalms.

'King David and King Solomon' (1935)

John Mason Neale 1818–66

23 All glory, laud, and honour
To thee, Redeemer, King,
To whom the lips of children
Made sweet hosannas ring.

'All glory, laud, and honour' (1851 hymn)

1 Good King Wenceslas looked out,
On the feast of Stephen;
When the snow lay round about,
Deep and crisp and even.
   'Good King Wenceslas'

2 Jerusalem the golden,
With milk and honey blessed.
   'Jerusalem the golden' (1858 hymn); translated
   from the Latin of St Bernard of Cluny (b. *c.*1100)

Jawaharlal Nehru 1889–1964

3 At the stroke of the midnight hour, while
the world sleeps, India will awake to life
and freedom.
   immediately prior to Independence
   speech to the Indian Constituent Assembly, 14
   August 1947

4 The light has gone out of our lives and there
is darkness everywhere.
   *following **Gandhi**'s assassination*
   broadcast, 30 January 1948; Richard J. Walsh
   Nehru on Gandhi (1948) ch. 6

5 There is no easy walk-over to freedom
anywhere, and many of us will have to pass
through the valley of the shadow again and
again before we reach the mountain-tops of
our desire.
   'From Lucknow to Tripuri' (1939)

A. S. Neill 1883–1973

6 If we have to have an exam at 11, let us
make it one for humour, sincerity,
imagination, character—and where is the
examiner who could test such qualities.
   letter to *Daily Telegraph* 1957

Horatio, Lord Nelson 1758–1805

7 I have only one eye,—I have a right to be
blind sometimes . . . I really do not see the
signal!
   at the battle of Copenhagen, 1801
   Robert Southey *Life of Nelson* (1813) ch. 7

8 When I came to explain to them the *'Nelson
touch'*, it was like an electric shock.
   letter to Lady Hamilton, 1 October 1805

9 England expects that every man will do his
duty.
   at the battle of Trafalgar, 21 October 1805
   Robert Southey *Life of Nelson* (1813) ch. 9

10 This is too warm work, Hardy, to last long.
   at the battle of Trafalgar, 21 October 1805
   Robert Southey *Life of Nelson* (1813) ch. 9

11 Thank God, I have done my duty.
   at the battle of Trafalgar, 21 October 1805
   Robert Southey *Life of Nelson* (1813) ch. 9

12 Kiss me, Hardy.
   at the battle of Trafalgar, 21 October 1805
   Robert Southey *Life of Nelson* (1813) ch. 9

Nero AD 37–68

13 *Qualis artifex pereo!*
What an artist dies with me!
   Suetonius *Lives of the Caesars* 'Nero'

Gérard de Nerval 1808–55

14 *Je suis le ténébreux,—le veuf,—l'inconsolé,*
Le prince d'Aquitaine à la tour abolie.
I am the darkly shaded, the bereaved, the
inconsolate, the prince of Aquitaine, with
the blasted tower.
   Les Chimères (1854) 'El Desdichado'

Edith Nesbit 1858–1924

15 It is a curious thing that people only ask if
you are enjoying yourself when you aren't.
   Five of Us, and Madeline (1925)

Allan Nevins 1890–1971

16 Offering Germany too little, and offering
even that too late, until finally Nazi
Germany had become a menace to all
mankind.
   in *Current History* (New York) May 1935

Henry Newbolt 1862–1938

17 'Take my drum to England, hang et by the
shore,
Strike et when your powder's runnin' low;
If the Dons sight Devon, I'll quit the port o'
Heaven,
An' drum them up the Channel as we
drummed them long ago.'
   'Drake's Drum' (1897)

18 Drake he's in his hammock till the great
Armadas come.
(Capten, art tha sleepin' there below?)
   'Drake's Drum' (1897)

19 Now the sunset breezes shiver,
And she's fading down the river,
But in England's song for ever
She's the Fighting Téméraire.
   'The Fighting Téméraire' (1897)

20 There's a breathless hush in the Close to-
night—
Ten to make and the match to win—
A bumping pitch and a blinding light,
An hour to play and the last man in.
And it's not for the sake of a ribboned coat,
Or the selfish hope of a season's fame,
But his Captain's hand on his shoulder
smote—
'Play up! play up! and play the game!'
   'Vitaï Lampada' (1897)

Anthony Newley 1931–
and Leslie Bricusse 1931–

21 Stop the world, I want to get off.
   title of musical (1961)

John Henry Newman 1801–90

22 Two and two only supreme and luminously
self-evident beings, myself and my Creator.
   Apologia pro Vita Sua (1864) 'History of My
   Religious Opinions to the Year 1833'

23 Ten thousand difficulties do not make one
doubt.
   Apologia pro Vita Sua (1864) 'Position of my Mind
   since 1845'

1 It is almost a definition of a gentleman to say that he is one who never inflicts pain.
The Idea of a University (1852) 'Knowledge and Religious Duty'

2 She [the Catholic Church] holds that it were better for sun and moon to drop from heaven, for the earth to fail, and for all the many millions who are upon it to die of starvation in extremest agony, as far as temporal affliction goes, than that one soul, I will not say, should be lost, but should commit one single venial sin.
Lectures on Anglican Difficulties (1852) Lecture 8

3 If I am obliged to bring religion into after-dinner toasts (which indeed does not seem quite the thing) I shall drink—to the Pope, if you please—still, to Conscience first, and to the Pope afterwards.
A Letter Addressed to the Duke of Norfolk . . . (1875) sect. 5

4 May He support us all the day long, till the shades lengthen, and the evening comes, and the busy world is hushed, and the fever of life is over, and our work is done! Then in His mercy may He give us a safe lodging, and a holy rest, and peace at the last.
'Wisdom and Innocence' (19 February 1843)

5 Firmly I believe and truly
God is Three, and God is One;
And I next acknowledge duly
Manhood taken by the Son.
The Dream of Gerontius (1865)

6 Praise to the Holiest in the height,
And in the depth be praise;
In all his words most wonderful,
Most sure in all His ways.
The Dream of Gerontius (1865)

7 Lead, kindly Light, amid the encircling gloom,
Lead thou me on.
'Lead, kindly Light' (1834)

8 *We can believe what we choose.* We are answerable for what we choose to believe.
letter to Mrs William Froude, 27 June 1848

9 *Cor ad cor loquitur.*
Heart speaks to heart.
motto of Newman; cf. **Francis** 133:1

Huey Newton 1942–

10 I suggested [in 1966] that we use the panther as our symbol and call our political vehicle the Black Panther Party. The panther is a fierce animal, but he will not attack until he is backed into a corner; then he will strike out.
Revolutionary Suicide (1973) ch. 16

Isaac Newton 1642–1727

11 Every body continues in its state of rest, or of uniform motion in a right line, unless it is compelled to change that state by forces impressed upon it.
Principia Mathematica (1687) Laws of Motion 1 (tr. Andrew Motte, 1729)

12 To every action there is always opposed an equal reaction: or, the mutual actions of two bodies upon each other are always equal, and directed to contrary parts.
Principia Mathematica (1687) Laws of Motion 3 (tr. Andrew Motte, 1729)

13 *Hypotheses non fingo.*
I do not feign hypotheses.
Principia Mathematica (1713 ed.) 'Scholium Generale'

14 If I have seen further it is by standing on the shoulders of giants.
letter to Robert Hooke, 5 February 1676; cf. **Bernard** 31:4, **Coleridge** 96:22

15 I don't know what I may seem to the world, but as to myself, I seem to have been only like a boy playing on the sea-shore and diverting myself in now and then finding a smoother pebble or a prettier shell than ordinary, whilst the great ocean of truth lay all undiscovered before me.
Joseph Spence *Anecdotes* (ed. J. Osborn, 1966) no. 1259

16 O Diamond! Diamond! thou little knowest the mischief done!
to a dog, who knocked over a candle which set fire to some papers and thereby 'destroyed the almost finished labours of some years'
Thomas Maude *Wensley-Dale* . . . *a Poem* (1772) st. 23 n.; probably apocryphal

John Newton 1725–1807

17 Amazing grace! how sweet the sound
That saved a wretch like me!
Olney Hymns (1779) 'Amazing grace'

18 Glorious things of thee are spoken,
Zion, city of our God!
Olney Hymns (1779) 'Glorious things of thee are spoken'

19 How sweet the name of Jesus sounds
In a believer's ear!
Olney Hymns (1779) 'How sweet the name of Jesus sounds'

Nicholas I 1796–1855

20 Turkey is a dying man. We may endeavour to keep him alive, but we shall not succeed. He will, he must die.
F. Max Müller (ed.) *Memoirs of Baron Stockmar* (tr. G. A. M. Müller, 1873) vol. 2

21 Russia has two generals in whom she can confide—Generals Janvier [January] and Février [February].
attributed; in *Punch* 10 March 1855

Nicias *c.*470–413 BC

22 For a city consists in men, and not in walls nor in ships empty of men.
speech to the defeated Athenian army at Syracuse, 413 BC
Thucydides *History of the Peloponnesian Wars* bk. 7, sect. 77

Harold Nicolson 1886–1968

1 Ponderous and uncertain is that relation between pressure and resistance which constitutes the balance of power. The arch of peace is morticed by no iron tendons.
Public Faces (1932) ch. 6

2 To be a good diarist one must have a little snouty, sneaky mind.
of Samuel **Pepys**
diary, 9 November 1947

3 For seventeen years he did nothing at all but kill animals and stick in stamps.
of King **George V**
diary, 17 August 1949

Reinhold Niebuhr 1892–1971

4 Man's capacity for justice makes democracy possible, but man's inclination to injustice makes democracy necessary.
Children of Light and Children of Darkness (1944) foreword

Martin Niemöller 1892–1984

5 When Hitler attacked the Jews I was not a Jew, therefore, I was not concerned. And when Hitler attacked the Catholics, I was not a Catholic, and therefore, I was not concerned. And when Hitler attacked the unions and the industrialists, I was not a member of the unions and I was not concerned. Then, Hitler attacked me and the Protestant church—and there was nobody left to be concerned.
often quoted in the form 'In Germany they came first for the Communists, and I didn't speak up because I wasn't a Communist . . . ' and so on
in *Congressional Record* 14 October 1968

Friedrich Nietzsche 1844–1900

6 I teach you the superman. Man is something to be surpassed.
Also Sprach Zarathustra (1883) prologue, sect. 3

7 You are going to women? Do not forget the whip!
Also Sprach Zarathustra (1883) bk. 1 'Von Alten und jungen Weiblein'

8 God is dead: but considering the state the species Man is in, there will perhaps be caves, for ages yet, in which his shadow will be shown.
Die fröhliche Wissenschaft (1882) bk. 3, sect. 108; cf. **Plato** 246:2

9 He who fights with monsters might take care lest he thereby become a monster.
Jenseits von Gut und Böse (1886) ch. 4, no. 146

10 Master-morality and slave-morality.
Jenseits von Gut und Böse (1886) ch. 9, no. 260

11 At the base of all these aristocratic races the predator is not to be mistaken, the splendorous *blond beast*, avidly rampant for plunder and victory.
Zur Genealogie der Moral (1887) 1st treatise, no. 11

Florence Nightingale 1820–1910

12 It may seem a strange principle to enunciate as the very first requirement in a Hospital that it should do the sick no harm.
Notes on Hospitals (1863 ed.) preface

13 Too kind, too kind.
on the Order of Merit being brought to her at her home, 5 December 1907
E. Cook *Life of Florence Nightingale* (1913) vol. 2, pt. 7, ch. 9

Richard Milhous Nixon 1913–94

14 There can be no whitewash at the White House.
on Watergate
television speech, 30 April 1973

15 I brought myself down. I gave them a sword. And they stuck it in.
television interview, 19 May 1977

16 When the President does it, that means that it is not illegal.
David Frost *I Gave Them a Sword* (1978) ch. 8

Kwame Nkrumah 1900–72

17 Freedom is not something that one people can bestow on another as a gift. They claim it as their own and none can keep it from them.
speech in Accra, 10 July 1953

Caroline Maria Noel 1817–77

18 At the name of Jesus
Every knee shall bow,
Every tongue confess him
King of glory now.
'At the name of Jesus' (1861 hymn); cf. **Bible** 50:24

Thomas Noel 1799–1861

19 Rattle his bones over the stones;
He's only a pauper, whom nobody owns!
'The Pauper's Drive' (1841)

Christopher North 1785–1854

20 His Majesty's dominions, on which the sun never sets.
Blackwood's Magazine (April 1829) 'Noctes Ambrosianae' no. 42; cf. **Schiller** 265:12

Alfred Harmsworth, Lord Northcliffe 1865–1922

21 The power of the press is very great, but not so great as the power of suppress.
office message, *Daily Mail* 1918

22 When I want a peerage, I shall buy it like an honest man.
Tom Driberg *Swaff* (1974) ch. 2

Caroline Norton 1808–77

23 And all our calm is in that balm—
Not lost but gone before.
'Not Lost but Gone Before'; cf. **Cyprian** 105:11, **Rogers** 259:2

Jack Norworth 1879–1959

1 Oh, shine on, shine on, harvest moon
Up in the sky.
I ain't had no lovin'
Since April, January, June, or July.
'Shine On, Harvest Moon' (1908 song)

Novalis 1772–1801

2 I often feel, and ever more deeply I realize,
that Fate and character are the same
conception.
*often quoted as 'Character is destiny' or
'Character is fate'*
Heinrich von Ofterdingen (1802) bk. 2; cf. **Eliot**
121:13, **Heraclitus** 156:26

3 A God-intoxicated man.
of Spinoza
attributed

Alfred Noyes 1880–1958

4 Go down to Kew in lilac-time, in lilac-time,
in lilac-time,
Go down to Kew in lilac-time (it isn't far
from London!).
'The Barrel-Organ' (1904)

5 Look for me by moonlight;
Watch for me by moonlight;
I'll come to thee by moonlight, though hell
should bar the way!
'The Highwayman' (1907)

Lord Nuffield 1877–1963

on seeing the Morris Minor prototype in 1945:
6 It looks like a poached egg—we can't make
that.
attributed

Sam Nunn 1938–

7 Don't ask, don't tell.
summary of the **Clinton** administration's
compromise policy on homosexuals serving in
the armed forces, in *New York Times* 12 May 1993

Bill Nye 1850–96

8 I have been told that Wagner's music is
better than it sounds.
Mark Twain *Autobiography* (1924) vol. 1

Julius Nyerere 1922–99

9 Should we really let our people starve so we
can pay our debts?
in *Guardian* 21 March 1985

Charles Edward Oakley 1832–65

10 Hills of the North, rejoice:
Rivers and mountain-spring,
Hark to the advent voice!
Valley and lowland, sing!
'Hills of the North, rejoice' (1870 hymn)

Lawrence Oates 1880–1912

11 I am just going outside and may be some
time.
Robert Falcon **Scott** diary entry, 16–17 March
1912

Conor Cruise O'Brien 1917–

12 If I saw Mr Haughey buried at midnight at a
crossroads, with a stake driven through his
heart—politically speaking—I should
continue to wear a clove of garlic round my
neck, just in case.
in *Observer* 10 October 1982

Edna O'Brien 1932–

13 August is a wicked month.
title of novel (1965)

Flann O'Brien 1911–66

14 The conclusion of your syllogism, I said
lightly, is fallacious, being based upon
licensed premises.
At Swim-Two-Birds (1939) ch. 1

15 A pint of plain is your only man.
At Swim-Two-Birds (1939) 'The Workman's
Friend'

Sean O'Casey 1880–1964

16 I killin' meself workin', an' he shruttin'
about from mornin' till night like a
paycock!
Juno and the Paycock (1925) act 1

17 He's an oul' butty o' mine—oh, he's a
darlin' man, a daarlin' man.
Juno and the Paycock (1925) act 1

18 The whole worl's in a state o' chassis!
Juno and the Paycock (1925) act 1

William of Occam c.1285–1349

19 *Entia non sunt multiplicanda praeter
necessitatem.*
No more things should be presumed to exist
than are absolutely necessary.
*'Occam's Razor', an ancient philosophical principle
often attributed to Occam but earlier in origin*
not found in this form in his writings, although
he frequently used similar expressions.

David Ogilvy 1911–99

20 The consumer isn't a moron; she is your
wife.
Confessions of an Advertising Man (1963) ch. 5

James Ogilvy, Lord Seafield
1664–1730

21 Now there's ane end of ane old song.
*as he signed the engrossed exemplification of the
Act of Union, 1706*
in *The Lockhart Papers* (1817) vol. 1

Theodore O'Hara 1820–67

22 The bivouac of the dead.
title of poem (1847)

23 Sons of the dark and bloody ground.
'The Bivouac of the Dead' (1847) st. 1

John O'Keeffe 1747–1833

24 Amo, amas, I love a lass,
As a cedar tall and slender;

Sweet cowslip's grace
Is her nom'native case,
And she's of the feminine gender.
The Agreeable Surprise (1781) act 2, sc. 2

1 Fat, fair and forty were all the toasts of the young men.
The Irish Mimic (1795) sc. 2

Dennis O'Kelly *c.*1720–87

2 Eclipse first, the rest nowhere.
comment at Epsom on the occasion of the horse Eclipse's first race, 3 May 1769; the Dictionary of National Biography *gives the occasion as the Queen's Plate at Winchester, 1769*
in *Annals of Sporting* vol. 2 (1822)

Abraham Okpik

3 There are very few Eskimos, but millions of Whites, just like mosquitoes. It is something very special and wonderful to be an Eskimo—they are like the snow geese. If an Eskimo forgets his language and Eskimo ways, he will be nothing but just another mosquito.
attributed, 1966

Bruce Oldfield 1950–

4 Fashion is more usually a gentle progression of revisited ideas.
in *Independent* 9 September 1989

Laurence Olivier 1907–89

5 Shakespeare—the nearest thing in incarnation to the eye of God.
in *Kenneth Harris Talking To* (1971) 'Sir Laurence Olivier'

6 Acting is a masochistic form of exhibitionism. It is not quite the occupation of an adult.
in *Time* 3 July 1978

Frank Ward O'Malley *see* Elbert Hubbard

Omar *c.*581–644

7 If these writings of the Greeks agree with the book of God, they are useless and need not be preserved; if they disagree, they are pernicious and ought to be destroyed.
on burning the library of Alexandria, AD c.641
Edward Gibbon *The Decline and Fall of the Roman Empire* (1776–88) ch. 51

Jacqueline Kennedy Onassis 1929–94

8 If you bungle raising your children I don't think whatever else you do well matters very much.
Theodore C. Sorenson *Kennedy* (1965)

9 The one thing I do not want to be called is First Lady. It sounds like a saddle horse.
Peter Colier and David Horowitz *The Kennedys* (1984)

Eugene O'Neill 1888–1953

10 For de little stealin' dey gits you in jail soon or late. For de big stealin' dey makes you Emperor and puts you in de Hall o' Fame when you croaks.
The Emperor Jones (1921) sc. 1

11 The iceman cometh.
title of play (1946)

12 A long day's journey into night.
title of play (written 1940–1)

13 Mourning becomes Electra
title of play (1931)

Yoko Ono 1933–

14 Woman is the nigger of the world.
remark made in a 1968 interview for *Nova* magazine and adopted by her husband John **Lennon** as the title of a song (1972)

Brian O'Nolan *see* Flann O'Brien

John Opie 1761–1807

15 I mix them with my brains, sir.
on being asked with what he mixed his colours
Samuel Smiles *Self-Help* (1859) ch. 4

J. Robert Oppenheimer 1904–67

16 I remembered the line from the Hindu scripture, the *Bhagavad Gita* . . . 'I am become death, the destroyer of worlds.'
on the explosion of the first atomic bomb near Alamogordo, New Mexico, 16 July 1945
Len Giovannitti and Fred Freed *The Decision to Drop the Bomb* (1965); cf. **Bhagavadgita** 32:17

17 The physicists have known sin; and this is a knowledge which they cannot lose.
lecture at Massachusetts Institute of Technology, 25 November 1947

Susie Orbach 1946–

18 Fat is a feminist issue.
title of book (1978)

Roy Orbison 1936–88 and Joe Melsom

19 Only the lonely (know the way I feel).
title of song (1960)

Baroness Orczy 1865–1947

20 We seek him here, we seek him there,
Those Frenchies seek him everywhere.
Is he in heaven?—Is he in hell?
That demmed, elusive Pimpernel?
The Scarlet Pimpernel (1905) ch. 12

Meta Orred

21 In the gloaming, Oh my darling!
When the lights are dim and low,
And the quiet shadows falling
Softly come and softly go.
'In the Gloaming' (1877 song)

José Ortega y Gasset 1883–1955

22 *Yo soy yo y mi circunstancia, y si no la salvo a ella no me salvo yo.*

I am I plus my surroundings, and if I do not preserve the latter I do not preserve myself.
  Meditaciones del Quijote (1914)

1 *La civilización no es otra cosa que el ensayo de reducir la fuerza a ultima ratio.*
Civilization is nothing more than the effort to reduce the use of force to the last resort.
  La Rebelión de las Masas (1930)

Joe Orton 1933–67

2 I'd the upbringing a nun would envy . . . Until I was fifteen I was more familiar with Africa than my own body.
  Entertaining Mr Sloane (1964) act 1

3 It's all any reasonable child can expect if the dad is present at the conception.
  Entertaining Mr Sloane (1964) act 3

George Orwell 1903–50

4 Four legs good, two legs bad.
  Animal Farm (1945) ch. 3

5 All animals are equal but some animals are more equal than others.
  Animal Farm (1945) ch. 10

6 The creatures outside looked from pig to man, and from man to pig, and from pig to man again, but already it was impossible to say which was which.
  Animal Farm (1945); closing words

7 Good prose is like a window-pane.
  Collected Essays (1968) vol. 1 'Why I Write'

8 I'm fat, but I'm thin inside. Has it ever struck you that there's a thin man inside every fat man, just as they say there's a statue inside every block of stone?
  Coming up For Air (1939) pt. 1, ch. 3; cf. **Connolly** 99:2

9 Down and out in Paris and London.
  title of book (1933)

10 Keep the aspidistra flying.
  title of novel (1936)

11 Old maids biking to Holy Communion through the mists of the autumn mornings . . . these are not only fragments, but *characteristic* fragments, of the English scene.
  The Lion and the Unicorn (1941) pt. 1 'England Your England'; cf. **Major** 209:23

12 Probably the battle of Waterloo *was* won on the playing-fields of Eton, but the opening battles of all subsequent wars have been lost there.
  The Lion and the Unicorn (1941) pt. 1 'England Your England'; cf. **Wellington** 331:12

13 It was a bright cold day in April, and the clocks were striking thirteen.
  Nineteen Eighty-Four (1949) pt. 1, ch. 1

14 BIG BROTHER IS WATCHING YOU.
  Nineteen Eighty-Four (1949) pt. 1, ch. 1

15 Freedom is the freedom to say that two plus two make four. If that is granted, all else follows.
  Nineteen Eighty-Four (1949) pt. 1, ch. 7

16 The Lottery, with its weekly pay-out of enormous prizes, was the one public event to which the proles paid serious attention . . . It was their delight, their folly, their anodyne, their intellectual stimulant . . . the prizes were largely imaginary. Only small sums were actually paid out, the winners of the big prizes being non-existent persons.
  Nineteen Eighty-Four (1949) pt. 1, ch. 8

17 *Doublethink* means the power of holding two contradictory beliefs in one's mind simultaneously, and accepting both of them.
  Nineteen Eighty-Four (1949) pt. 2, ch. 9

18 If you want a picture of the future, imagine a boot stamping on a human face—for ever.
  Nineteen Eighty-Four (1949) pt. 3, ch. 3

19 Political language . . . is designed to make lies sound truthful and murder respectable, and to give an appearance of solidity to pure wind.
  Shooting an Elephant (1950) 'Politics and the English Language'

20 Whatever is funny is subversive, every joke is ultimately a custard pie . . . A dirty joke is a sort of mental rebellion.
  in *Horizon* September 1941 'The Art of Donald McGill'

21 The quickest way of ending a war is to lose it.
  in *Polemic* May 1946 'Second Thoughts on James Burnham'

22 At 50, everyone has the face he deserves.
  last words in his notebook, 17 April 1949

23 Advertising is the rattling of a stick inside a swill bucket.
  attributed

Dorothy Osborne 1627–95

24 All letters, methinks, should be free and easy as one's discourse, not studied as an oration, nor made up of hard words like a charm.
  letter to William Temple, September 1653

John Osborne 1929–94

25 Don't clap too hard—it's a very old building.
  The Entertainer (1957) no. 7

26 But I have a go, lady, don't I? I 'ave a go. I do.
  The Entertainer (1957) no. 7

27 Look back in anger.
  title of play (1956); cf. **Paul** 242:6

28 They spend their time mostly looking forward to the past.
  Look Back in Anger (1956) act 2, sc. 1

29 Royalty is the gold filling in a mouthful of decay.
  'They call it cricket' in T. Maschler (ed.) *Declaration* (1957)

30 This is a letter of hate. It is for you my countrymen, I mean those men of my country who have defiled it. The men with manic fingers leading the sightless, feeble, betrayed body of my country to its death . . . damn you England.
  in *Tribune* 18 August 1961

Arthur O'Shaughnessy 1844–81

1 We are the music makers,
We are the dreamers of dreams . . .
We are the movers and shakers
Of the world for ever, it seems.
'Ode' (1874)

2 For each age is a dream that is dying,
Or one that is coming to birth.
'Ode' (1874)

William Osler 1849–1919

3 One finger in the throat and one in the
rectum makes a good diagnostician.
Aphorisms from his Bedside Teachings (1961)

4 The desire to take medicine is perhaps the
greatest feature which distinguishes man
from animals.
H. Cushing Life of Sir William Osler (1925) vol. 1,
ch. 14

John L. O'Sullivan 1813–95

5 The best government is that which governs
least.
in United States Magazine and Democratic Review
(1837) introduction

6 A torchlight procession marching down
your throat.
describing certain kinds of whisky
G. W. E. Russell Collections and Recollections (1898)
ch. 19

James Otis 1725–83

7 Taxation without representation is tyranny.
associated with his attack on writs of
assistance, 1761, and later a watchword of the
American Revolution

Thomas Otway 1652–85

8 And for an apple damn'd mankind.
The Orphan (1680) act 3

9 No praying, it spoils business.
Venice Preserved (1682) act 2, sc. 1

Ovid 43 BC–AD c.17

10 Lente currite noctis equi.
Run slowly, horses of the night.
Amores bk. 1, no. 13, l. 40; cf. **Marlowe** 212:7

11 Iuppiter ex alto periuria ridet amantum.
Jupiter from on high laughs at lovers'
perjuries.
Ars Amatoria bk. 1, l. 633

12 Expedit esse deos, et, ut expedit, esse putemus.
It is convenient that there be gods, and, as it
is convenient, let us believe that there are.
Ars Amatoria bk. 1, l. 637; cf. **Voltaire** 326:5

13 Gutta cavat lapidem, consumitur anulus usu.
Dripping water hollows out a stone, a ring is
worn away by use.
Epistulae Ex Ponto bk. 4, no. 10, l. 5; cf. **Latimer**
194:4

14 Medio tutissimus ibis.
You will go most safely by the middle way.
Metamorphoses bk. 2, l. 137

15 Video meliora, proboque;
Deteriora sequor.
I see the better things, and approve; I follow
the worse.
Metamorphoses bk. 7, l. 20; cf. **Bible** 49:15

16 Tempus edax rerum.
Time the devourer of everything.
Metamorphoses bk. 15, l. 234

17 Teque, rebellatrix, tandem, Germania, magni
Triste caput pedibus supposuisse ducis!
How you, rebellious Germany, laid your
wretched head beneath the feet of the great
general.
Tristia bk. 3, no. 12, l. 47

John Owen c.1563–1622

18 God and the doctor we alike adore
But only when in danger, not before;
The danger o'er, both are alike requited,
God is forgotten, and the Doctor slighted.
Epigrams; cf. **Quarles** 253:3

Robert Owen 1771–1858

19 All the world is queer save thee and me, and
even thou art a little queer.
to his partner W. Allen, on severing business
relations at New Lanark, 1828
attributed

Wilfred Owen 1893–1918

20 My subject is War, and the pity of War.
The Poetry is in the pity.
Preface (written 1918) in Poems (1963)

21 What passing-bells for these who die as
cattle?
Only the monstrous anger of the guns.
'Anthem for Doomed Youth' (written 1917)

22 The shrill, demented choirs of wailing
shells;
And bugles calling for them from sad shires.
'Anthem for Doomed Youth' (written 1917)

23 The pallor of girls' brows shall be their pall;
Their flowers the tenderness of patient
minds,
And each slow dusk a drawing-down of
blinds.
'Anthem for Doomed Youth' (written 1917)

24 If you could hear, at every jolt, the blood
Come gargling from the froth-corrupted
lungs,
Obscene as cancer, bitter as the cud
Of vile, incurable sores on innocent
tongues,—
My friend, you would not tell with such
high zest
To children ardent for some desperate glory,
The old Lie: Dulce et decorum est
Pro patria mori.
'Dulce et Decorum Est' (1963 ed.); cf. **Horace**
164:14

25 Was it for this the clay grew tall?
'Futility' (written 1918)

26 I am the enemy you killed, my friend.
'Strange Meeting' (written 1918)

1 Let us sleep now.

'Strange Meeting' (written 1918)

Count Oxenstierna 1583–1654

2 Dost thou not know, my son, with how little wisdom the world is governed?

letter to his son, 1648, in J. F. af Lundblad *Svensk Plutark* (1826) pt. 2; an alternative attribution quotes 'a certain Pope' (possibly Julius III, 1487–1555) saying, 'Thou little thinkest what *a little foolery governs the whole world!*'

Vance Packard 1914–97

3 The hidden persuaders.

title of a study of the advertising industry (1957)

Lord George Paget 1818–80

4 As far as it engendered excitement the finest run in Leicestershire could hardly bear comparison.

the second-in-command's view of the charge of the Light Brigade
The Light Cavalry Brigade in the Crimea (1881) ch. 5

Camille Paglia 1947–

5 There is no female Mozart because there is no female Jack the Ripper.

in *International Herald Tribune* 26 April 1991

Thomas Paine 1737–1809

6 The sublime and the ridiculous are often so nearly related, that it is difficult to class them separately. One step above the sublime, makes the ridiculous; and one step above the ridiculous, makes the sublime again.

The Age of Reason pt. 2 (1795); cf. **Napoleon** 231:5

7 Though we have been wise enough to shut and lock a door against absolute Monarchy, we at the same time have been foolish enough to put the crown in possession of the key.

Common Sense (1776) ch. 1

8 These are the times that try men's souls. The summer soldier and the sunshine patriot will, in this crisis, shrink from the service of their country; but he that stands it *now*, deserves the love and thanks of men and women.

The Crisis (December 1776) introduction

9 The religion of humanity.

The Crisis (November 1778)

10 As he rose like a rocket, he fell like the stick.

*on Edmund **Burke**'s losing the debate on the French Revolution to Charles James **Fox**, in the House of Commons*
Letter to the Addressers on the late Proclamation (1792)

11 Lay then the axe to the root, and teach governments humanity. It is their sanguinary punishments which corrupt mankind.

The Rights of Man (1791)

12 The idea of hereditary legislators is as inconsistent as that of hereditary judges, or hereditary juries; and as absurd as an hereditary mathematician, or an hereditary wise man; and as ridiculous as an hereditary poet laureate.

The Rights of Man (1791)

13 I compare it to something kept behind a curtain, about which there is a great deal of bustle and fuss, and a wonderful air of seeming solemnity; but when, by any accident, the curtain happens to be open, and the company see what it is, they burst into laughter.

of monarchy
The Rights of Man pt. 2 (1792)

14 The Minister, whoever he at any time may be, touches it as with an opium wand, and it sleeps obedience.

of Parliament
The Rights of Man pt. 2 (1792)

15 When, in countries that are called civilized, we see age going to the workhouse and youth to the gallows, something must be wrong in the system of government.

The Rights of Man pt. 2 (1792)

16 My country is the world, and my religion is to do good.

The Rights of Man pt. 2 (1792)

17 A share in two revolutions is living to some purpose.

Eric Foner *Tom Paine and Revolutionary America* (1976) ch. 7

Ian Paisley 1926–

18 The mother of all treachery.

on the Good Friday agreement
in *Times* 16 April 1998

José de Palafox 1780–1847

19 *Guerra a cuchillo.*

War to the knife.

on 4 August 1808, at the siege of Saragossa, the French general Verdier sent a one-word suggestion: 'Capitulation'. Palafox replied 'Guerra y cuchillo [War and the knife]', *later reported as above; it subsequently appeared, at the behest of Palafox himself, on survivors' medals*
José Gòmez de Arteche y Moro *Guerra de la Independencia* (1875) vol. 2, ch. 4

William Paley 1743–1805

20 Suppose I had found a *watch* upon the ground, and it should be enquired how the watch happened to be in that place . . . the inference, we think, is inevitable; that the watch must have had a maker, that there must have existed, at some time and at some place or other, an artificer or artificers, who formed it for the purpose which we find it actually to answer; who

comprehended its construction, and
designed its use.

Natural Theology (1802) ch. 1; cf. **Dawkins** 107:1

1 Who can refute a sneer?

Principles of Moral and Political Philosophy (1785)
bk. 5, ch. 9

Pali Tripitaka

2 It is called Nirvana because of the getting
rid of craving.

Samyutta-nikāya [Kindred Sayings] pt. 1, p. 39

3 The Noble Truth of the Path leading to the
Cessation of suffering is this: It is simply the
Noble Eightfold Path, namely right view;
right thought; right speech; right action;
right livelihood; right effort; right
mindfulness; right concentration.

First Sermon of the Buddha
Samyutta-nikāya [Kindred Sayings] pt. 56, p. 11

4 For hate is not conquered by hate: hate is
conquered by love. This is a law eternal.

Dhammapada v. 5

5 Even as rain breaks not through a well-
thatched house, passions break not through
a well-guarded mind.

Dhammapada v. 14

Lord Palmerston 1784–1865

6 We have no eternal allies and we have no
perpetual enemies. Our interests are eternal
and perpetual, and those interests it is our
duty to follow.

speech, House of Commons, 1 March 1848

7 You may call it combination, you may call it
the accidental and fortuitous concurrence of
atoms.

on a projected Palmerston–Disraeli coalition
speech, House of Commons, 5 March 1857

8 Lord Palmerston, with characteristic levity
had once said that only three men in
Europe had ever understood [the Schleswig-
Holstein question], and of these the Prince
Consort was dead, a Danish statesman
(unnamed) was in an asylum, and he
himself had forgotten it.

R. W. Seton-Watson *Britain in Europe 1789–1914*
(1937) ch. 11

9 Die, my dear Doctor, that's the last thing I
shall do!

last words; E. Latham *Famous Sayings and their*
Authors (1904)

Christabel Pankhurst 1880–1958

10 Never lose your temper with the Press or
the public is a major rule of political life.

Unshackled (1959) ch. 5

11 We are here to claim our right as women,
not only to be free, but to fight for freedom.
That it is our right as well as our duty.

in *Votes for Women* 31 March 1911

Emmeline Pankhurst 1858–1928

12 The argument of the broken window pane
is the most valuable argument in modern
politics.

George Dangerfield *The Strange Death of Liberal*
England (1936); cf. **More** 227:22

Mitchell Parish

13 When the deep purple falls over sleepy
garden walls.

'Deep Purple' (1939); words added to music
(1934) by Peter de Rose

Dorothy Parker 1893–1967

14 Oh, life is a glorious cycle of song,
A medley of extemporanea;
And love is a thing that can never go wrong;
And I am Marie of Roumania.

'Comment' (1937)

15 Four be the things I'd been better without:
Love, curiosity, freckles, and doubt.

'Inventory' (1937)

16 Men seldom make passes
At girls who wear glasses.

'News Item' (1937)

17 Why is it no one ever sent me yet
One perfect limousine, do you suppose?
Ah no, it's always just my luck to get
One perfect rose.

'One Perfect Rose' (1937)

18 Guns aren't lawful;
Nooses give;
Gas smells awful;
You might as well live.

'Résumé' (1937)

19 Where's the man could ease a heart like a
satin gown?

'The Satin Dress' (1937)

20 By the time you say you're his,
Shivering and sighing
And he vows his passion is
Infinite, undying—
Lady, make a note of this:
One of you is lying.

'Unfortunate Coincidence' (1937)

21 Excuse my dust.

suggested epitaph for herself (1925)
Alexander Woollcott *While Rome Burns* (1934)
'Our Mrs Parker'

22 Sorrow is tranquillity remembered in
emotion.

Here Lies (1939) 'Sentiment'; cf. **Wordsworth**
341:20

23 She ran the whole gamut of the emotions
from A to B.

of Katharine Hepburn at a Broadway first night,
1933
attributed

24 Wit has truth in it; wise-cracking is simply
callisthenics with words.

in *Paris Review* Summer 1956

1 How do they know?
*on being told that Calvin **Coolidge** had died*
Malcolm Cowley *Writers at Work* 1st Series
(1958)

2 Hollywood money isn't money. It's
congealed snow, melts in your hand, and
there you are.
Malcolm Cowley *Writers at Work* 1st Series
(1958)

Martin Parker d. *c.*1656

3 You gentlemen of England
Who live at home at ease,
How little do you think
On the dangers of the seas.
'The Valiant Sailors'.

4 The times will not mend
Till the King enjoys his own again.
'Upon Defacing of Whitehall' (1671)

Ross Parker 1914–74
and Hugh Charles 1907–

5 There'll always be an England
While there's a country lane.
'There'll always be an England' (1939 song)

C. Northcote Parkinson 1909–93

6 Expenditure rises to meet income.
The Law and the Profits (1960) ch. 1

7 Work expands so as to fill the time available
for its completion.
Parkinson's Law (1958) ch. 1

8 Time spent on any item of the agenda will
be in inverse proportion to the sum
involved.
Parkinson's Law (1958) ch. 3

Charles Stewart Parnell 1846–91

9 My policy is not a policy of conciliation, but
a policy of retaliation.
*in 1877, on his parliamentary tactics in the House
of Commons as leader of the Irish party*
in *Dictionary of National Biography* (1917–)

10 No man has a right to fix the boundary of
the march of a nation; no man has a right to
say to his country—thus far shalt thou go
and no further.
speech at Cork, 21 January 1885

Matthew Parris 1949–

*of Lady **Thatcher** in the House of Lords:*
11 A big cat detained briefly in a poodle
parlour, sharpening her claws on the velvet.
Look Behind You! (1993)

12 Being an MP feeds your vanity and starves
your self-respect.
in *The Times* 9 February 1994

Tony Parsons 1953–

13 I never saw a beggar yet who would
recognise guilt if it bit him on his unwashed
ass.
Dispatches from the Front Line of Popular Culture
(1994)

Blaise Pascal 1623–62

14 I have made this [letter] longer than usual,
only because I have not had the time to
make it shorter.
Lettres Provinciales (1657) no. 16; cf. **Thoreau**
317:17

15 When we see a natural style, we are quite
surprised and delighted, for we expected to
see an author and we find a man.
Pensées (1670, ed. L. Brunschvicg, 1909) sect. 1,
no. 29

16 Had Cleopatra's nose been shorter, the
whole face of the world would have
changed.
Pensées (1670, ed. L. Brunschvicg, 1909) sect. 2,
no. 162

17 The eternal silence of these infinite spaces
[the heavens] terrifies me.
Pensées (1670, ed. L. Brunschvicg, 1909) sect. 2,
no. 206

18 The heart has its reasons which reason
knows nothing of.
Pensées (1670, ed. L. Brunschvicg, 1909) sect. 4,
no. 277

19 Man is only a reed, the weakest thing in
nature; but he is a thinking reed.
Pensées (1670, ed. L. Brunschvicg, 1909) sect. 6,
no. 347

Boris Pasternak 1890–1960

20 Man is born to live, not to prepare for life.
Doctor Zhivago (1958) pt. 2, ch. 9, sect. 14 (tr. Max
Hayward and Manya Harari)

21 Yet the order of the acts is planned
And the end of the way inescapable.
I am alone; all drowns in the Pharisees'
hypocrisy.
To live your life is not as simple as to cross a
field.
Doctor Zhivago (1958) 'Zhivago's Poems: Hamlet'

Louis Pasteur 1822–95

22 Where observation is concerned, chance
favours only the prepared mind.
address given on the inauguration of the
Faculty of Science, University of Lille, 7
December 1854

23 There are no such things as applied
sciences, only applications of science.
address, 11 September 1872

Walter Pater 1839–94

24 She is older than the rocks among which
she sits.
of the Mona Lisa
Studies in the History of the Renaissance (1873)
'Leonardo da Vinci'

25 To burn always with this hard, gemlike
flame, to maintain this ecstasy, is success in
life.
Studies in the History of the Renaissance (1873)
'Conclusion'

'Banjo' Paterson 1864–1941

1 Once a jolly swagman camped by a
billabong,
Under the shade of a coolibah tree;
And he sang as he watched and waited till
his 'Billy' boiled:
'You'll come a-waltzing, Matilda, with me.'
'Waltzing Matilda' (1903 song)

Coventry Patmore 1823–96

2 The angel in the house.
title of poem (1854–62)

3 Some dish more sharply spiced than this
Milk-soup men call domestic bliss.
'Olympus' l. 15

Alan Paton 1903–88

4 Cry, the beloved country.
title of novel (1948)

St Patrick fl. 5th cent.

5 Christ beside me,
Christ before me,
Christ behind me,
Christ within me,
Christ beneath me,
Christ above me.
'St Patrick's Breastplate'

Leslie Paul 1905–85

6 Angry young man.
the phrase was later associated with John
Osborne's *play* Look Back in Anger *(1956)*
title of book (1951)

Wolfgang Pauli 1900–58

7 I don't mind your thinking slowly: I mind
your publishing faster than you think.
attributed

Jeremy Paxman 1950–

8 No government in history has been as
obsessed with public relations as this one
. . . Speaking for myself, if there is a
message I want to be off it.
after criticism from Alastair Campbell of
interviewing tactics in The World at One *and*
Newsnight
in *Daily Telegraph* 3 July 1998

James Payn 1830–98

9 I had never had a piece of toast
Particularly long and wide,
But fell upon the sanded floor,
And always on the buttered side.
in *Chambers's Journal* 2 February 1884; cf. **Moore**
227:19

J. H. Payne 1791–1852

10 Home, sweet home.
title of song, from *Clari, or, The Maid of Milan*
(1823 opera)

11 Mid pleasures and palaces though we may
roam,

Be it ever so humble, there's no place like
home.
Clari, or, The Maid of Milan (1823 opera) 'Home,
Sweet Home'

Thomas Love Peacock 1785–1866

12 My house has been broken open on the
most scientific principles.
Crotchet Castle (1831) ch. 17

13 'I distinguish the picturesque and the
beautiful, and I add to them, in the laying
out of grounds, a third and distinct
character, which I call *unexpectedness*.'
'Pray, sir,' said Mr Milestone, 'by what name
do you distinguish this character, when a
person walks round the grounds for the
second time?'
Headlong Hall (1816) ch. 4

14 Marriage may often be a stormy lake, but
celibacy is almost always a muddy
horsepond.
Melincourt (1817) ch. 7

15 Laughter is pleasant, but the exertion is too
much for me.
Nightmare Abbey (1818) ch. 5

Norman Vincent Peale 1898–

16 The power of positive thinking.
title of book (1952)

Patrick Pearse 1879–1916

17 The fools, the fools, the fools, they have left
us our Fenian dead, and while Ireland holds
these graves Ireland unfree shall never be at
peace.
oration over the grave of the Fenian Jeremiah
O'Donovan Rossa, 1 August 1915

Lester Pearson 1897–1972

18 The grim fact is that we prepare for war like
precocious giants and for peace like
retarded pygmies.
speech in Toronto, 14 March 1955

Robert Peel 1788–1850

19 All my experience in public life is in favour
of the employment of what the world
would call young men instead of old ones.
to Wellington in 1829

20 The hasty inordinate demand for peace
might be just as dangerous as the clamour
for war.
in the House of Commons, 1832

21 I see no dignity in persevering in error.
in the House of Commons, 1833

22 Of all vulgar arts of government, that of
solving every difficulty which might arise
by thrusting the hand into the public purse
is the most delusory and contemptible.
in the House of Commons, 1834

George Peele c.1556–96

23 When as the rye reach to the chin,
And chopcherry, chopcherry ripe within,

Strawberries swimming in the cream,
And schoolboys playing in the stream,
Then O, then O, then O, my true love said,
Till that time come again,
She could not live a maid.
The Old Wive's Tale (1595) l. 75 'Song'

1 His golden locks time hath to silver turned;
O time too swift, O swiftness never ceasing!
Polyhymnia (1590) 'Sonnet'

2 Goddess, allow this aged man his right,
To be your beadsman now that was your knight.
Polyhymnia (1590) 'Sonnet'

Charles Péguy 1873–1914

3 Tyranny is always better organised than freedom.
Basic Verities (1943) 'War and Peace'

Pelé 1940–

4 Football? It's the beautiful game.
attributed

Lord Pembroke c.1501–70

5 Out ye whores, to work, to work, ye whores, go spin.
Andrew Clark (ed.) *'Brief Lives' . . . by John Aubrey* (1898)

Lord Pembroke c.1534–1601

6 A parliament can do any thing but make a man a woman, and a woman a man.
quoted by his son, the 4th Earl, in a speech on 11 April 1648, proving himself Chancellor of Oxford in *Harleian Miscellany* (1745) vol. 5

Henry Herbert, Lord Pembroke 1734–94

7 Dr Johnson's sayings would not appear so extraordinary, were it not for his bow-wow way.
James Boswell *Life of Samuel Johnson* (1791) 27 March 1775; cf. **Scott** 266:27

Vladimir Peniakoff 1897–1951

8 A message came on the wireless for me. It said: 'SPREAD ALARM AND DESPONDENCY'. So the time had come, I thought, Eighth Army was taking the offensive. The date was, I think, May 18th, 1942.
Private Army (1950) pt. 2, ch. 5; the Army Act (1879) says that anyone who 'spreads reports calculated to create unnecessary alarm or despondency' is liable to penal servitude

William Penn 1644–1718

9 No pain, no palm; no thorns, no throne; no gall, no glory; no cross, no crown.
No Cross, No Crown (1669 pamphlet)

10 Men are generally more careful of the breed of their horses and dogs than of their children.
Some Fruits of Solitude (1693) pt. 1, no. 85

Roger Penrose 1931–

11 Consciousness . . . is the phenomenon whereby the universe's very existence is made known.
The Emperor's New Mind (1989) ch. 10 'Conclusion'

Samuel Pepys 1633–1703

12 And so to bed.
Diary 20 April 1660

13 I went out to Charing Cross, to see Major-general Harrison hanged, drawn, and quartered; which was done there, he looking as cheerful as any man could do in that condition.
Diary 13 October 1660

14 Pretty witty Nell.
of Nell **Gwyn**
Diary 3 April 1665

15 Strange to say what delight we married people have to see these poor fools decoyed into our condition.
Diary 25 December 1665

16 Music and women I cannot but give way to, whatever my business is.
Diary 9 March 1666

17 And so I betake myself to that course, which is almost as much as to see myself go into my grave—for which, and all the discomforts that will accompany my being blind, the good God prepare me!
Diary 31 May 1669 closing lines

18 Memoirs are true and useful stars, whilst studied histories are those stars joined in constellations, according to the fancy of the poet.
J. R. Tanner (ed.) *Samuel Pepys's Naval Minutes* (1926)

S. J. Perelman 1904–79

19 Crazy like a fox.
title of book (1944)

Shimon Peres 1923–

20 Television has made dictatorship impossible, but democracy unbearable.
at a Davos meeting, in *Financial Times* 31 January 1995

Pericles c.495–429 BC

21 For famous men have the whole earth as their memorial.
Thucydides *History of the Peloponnesian War* bk. 2

22 Your great glory is not to be inferior to what God has made you, and the greatest glory of a woman is to be least talked about by men, whether they are praising you or criticizing you.
Thucydides *History of the Peloponnesian War* bk. 2

Eva Perón 1919–52

1 Keeping books on charity is capitalist
nonsense! I just use the money for the poor.
I can't stop to count it.
   Fleur Cowles *Bloody Precedent: the Peron Story*
   (1952)

2 I will return. And I will be millions.
   inscription on the tomb of Eva **Perón**, Buenos
   Aires

Charles Perrault 1628–1703

3 *Anne, ma sœur Anne, ne vois-tu rien venir?*
Anne, sister Anne, do you see nothing
coming?
   Histoires et contes du temps passé (1697) 'La barbe
   bleue'

Edward Perronet 1726–92

4 All hail the power of Jesus' Name;
Let Angels prostrate fall;
Bring forth the royal diadem
To crown Him Lord of all.
   'All hail the power of Jesus' Name' (1780 hymn)

Jimmy Perry

5 Who do you think you are kidding, Mister
Hitler?
If you think we're on the run?
   'Who do you think you are kidding, Mister
   Hitler' (theme song of *Dad's Army*, BBC
   television, 1968–77)

Ted Persons

6 Things ain't what they used to be.
   title of song (1941)

Henri Philippe Pétain 1856–1951

7 To write one's memoirs is to speak ill of
everybody except oneself.
   in *Observer* 26 May 1946

Laurence J. Peter 1919–90

8 In a hierarchy every employee tends to rise
to his level of incompetence.
   The Peter Principle (1969) ch. 1

Petronius Arbiter d. AD 65

9 *Cave canem.*
Beware of the dog.
   Satyricon 'Cena Trimalchionis' ch. 29

10 *Abiit ad plures.*
He's gone to join the majority.
   meaning the dead
   Satyricon 'Cena Trimalchionis' ch. 42; cf. **Young**
   344:19

11 *Nam Sibyllam quidem Cumis ego ipse oculis meis*
vidi in ampulla pendere, et cum illi pueri dicerent:
Σίβυλλα, τί θέλεις; respondebat illa: ἀποθανεῖν
θέλω.
I myself with my own eyes saw the Sibyl at
Cumae hanging in a flask; and when the
boys cried at her: ' Sibyl, Sibyl, what do you
want?' 'I would that I were dead,' she used
to answer.
   Satyricon 'Cena Trimalchionis' ch. 48, sect. 8; cf.
   Rossetti 260:20

Edward John Phelps 1822–1900

12 The man who makes no mistakes does not
usually make anything.
   speech at the Mansion House, London, 24
   January 1889

Kim Philby 1912–88

13 To betray, you must first belong.
   in *Sunday Times* 17 December 1967

Prince Philip, Duke of Edinburgh 1921–

14 Gentlemen, I think it is about time we
'pulled our fingers out' . . . If we want to be
more prosperous we've simply got to get
down to it and work for it. The rest of the
world does not owe us a living.
   speech in London, 17 October 1961

Jack Philip 1840–1900

15 Don't cheer, men; those poor devils are
dying.
   at the Battle of Santiago, 4 July 1898
   in *Dictionary of American Biography* vol. 14 (1934)
   'John Woodward Philip'

Ambrose Philips c.1675–1749

16 The flowers anew, returning seasons bring;
But beauty faded has no second spring.
   The First Pastoral (1708) 'Lobbin' l. 47

17 There solid billows of enormous size,
Alps of green ice, in wild disorder rise.
   'A Winter-Piece' in *The Tatler* 7 May 1709

Pablo Picasso 1881–1973

18 No, painting is not made to decorate
apartments. It's an offensive and defensive
weapon against the enemy.
   interview with Simone Téry, 24 March 1945, in
   Alfred H. Barr *Picasso* (1946)

19 God is really only another artist. He
invented the giraffe, the elephant, and the
cat. He has no real style. He just goes on
trying other things.
   F. Gilot and C. Lake *Life With Picasso* (1964) pt. 1

20 Every positive value has its price in negative
terms . . . The genius of Einstein leads to
Hiroshima.
   F. Gilot and C. Lake *Life With Picasso* (1964) pt. 2

John Pilger 1939–

21 I used to see Vietnam as a war, rather than a
country.
   in *Sunday Times* 1 December 1996

Ben Pimlott 1945–

1 If you have a Royal Family you have to make the best of whatever personalities the genetic lottery comes up with.
in *Independent* 13 September 1997 'Quote Unquote'

Pindar 518–438 BC

2 Water is best. But gold shines like fire blazing in the night, supreme of lordly wealth.
Olympian Odes bk. 1, l. 1

Harold Pinter 1930–

3 If only I could get down to Sidcup! I've been waiting for the weather to break. He's got my papers, this man I left them with, it's got it all down there, I could prove everything.
The Caretaker (1960) act 1

4 The weasel under the cocktail cabinet.
on being asked what his plays were about
J. Russell Taylor *Anger and After* (1962)

Luigi Pirandello 1867–1936

5 Six characters in search of an author.
title of play (1921)

Robert M. Pirsig 1928–

6 Zen and the art of motorcycle maintenance.
title of book (1974)

7 That's the classical mind at work, runs fine inside but looks dingy on the surface.
Zen and the Art of Motorcycle Maintenance (1974) pt. 3, ch. 26

Walter B. Pitkin 1878–1953

8 Life begins at forty.
title of book (1932)

William Pitt, Earl of Chatham 1708–78

9 The atrocious crime of being a young man ... I shall neither attempt to palliate nor deny.
speech, House of Commons, 2 March 1741

10 Unlimited power is apt to corrupt the minds of those who possess it.
speech, House of Lords, 9 January 1770; cf. **Acton** 1:8

11 I invoke the genius of the Constitution!
speech, House of Lords, 18 November 1777

12 The parks are the lungs of London.
quoted by William Windham in the House of Commons, 30 June 1808

William Pitt 1759–1806

13 England has saved herself by her exertions, and will, as I trust, save Europe by her example.
replying to a toast in which he had been described as the saviour of his country in the wars with France
R. Coupland *War Speeches of William Pitt* (1915)

14 Roll up that map; it will not be wanted these ten years.
of a map of Europe, on hearing of Napoleon's victory at Austerlitz, December 1805
Earl Stanhope *Life of the Rt. Hon. William Pitt* vol. 4 (1862) ch. 43

15 Oh, my country! how I leave my country!
also variously reported as 'How I love my country'; and 'My country! oh, my country!'
Earl Stanhope *Life of the Rt. Hon. William Pitt* vol. 3 (1879) ch. 43; Earl Stanhope *Life of the Rt. Hon. William Pitt* (1st ed.), vol. 4 (1862) ch. 43; and G. Rose *Diaries and Correspondence* (1860) vol. 2, 23 January 1806; oral tradition reports, 'I think I could eat one of Bellamy's veal pies'

Pius VII 1742–1823

16 We are prepared to go to the gates of Hell—but no further.
attempting to reach an agreement with **Napoleon**, *c.1800–1*
J. M. Robinson *Cardinal Consalvi* (1987)

Pius XII 1876–1958

17 One Galileo in two thousand years is enough.
on being asked to proscribe the works of **Teilhard de Chardin**
attributed; Stafford Beer *Platform for Change* (1975)

Max Planck 1858–1947

18 A new scientific truth does not triumph by convincing its opponents and making them see the light, but rather because its opponents eventually die, and a new generation grows up that is familiar with it.
A Scientific Autobiography (1949, translated by F. Gaynor)

Sylvia Plath 1932–63

19 Every woman adores a Fascist,
The boot in the face, the brute
Brute heart of a brute like you.
'Daddy' (1963)

20 Dying,
Is an art, like everything else.
'Lady Lazarus' (1963)

21 Out of the ash
I rise with my red hair
And I eat men like air.
'Lady Lazarus' (1963)

22 Love set you going like a fat gold watch.
'Morning Song' (1965)

Plato 429–347 BC

23 Socrates, he says, breaks the law by corrupting young men and not recognizing the gods that the city recognizes, but some other new deities.
Apologia 24b

24 Is that which is holy loved by the gods because it is holy, or is it holy because it is loved by the gods?
Euthyphro 10

1 This was the end, Echekrates, of our friend;
a man of whom we may say that of all
whom we met at that time he was the
wisest and justest and best.
on the death of **Socrates**
Phaedo 118a

2 Behold! human beings living in a
underground den . . . Like ourselves . . . they
see only their own shadows, or the
shadows of one another, which the fire throws on
the opposite wall of the cave.
The Republic bk. 7, 515b; cf. **Nietzsche** 234:8

Plautus *c.*250–184 BC

3 *Dictum sapienti sat est.*
A sentence is enough for a sensible man.
proverbially: 'Verbum sapienti sat est [A word
is enough for the wise]', *and abbreviated to*
'verb. sap.'
Persa l. 729

Pliny the Elder AD 23–79

4 *Semper aliquid novi Africam adferre.*
Africa always brings [us] something new.
often quoted as 'Ex Africa semper aliquid novi
[Always something new out of Africa]'
Historia Naturalis bk. 8, sect. 42

5 *Addito salis grano.*
With the addition of a grain of salt.
commonly quoted as 'Cum grano salis [With a
grain of salt]'
Historia Naturalis bk. 23, sect. 149

William Plomer 1903–73

6 Out of that bungled, unwise war
An alp of unforgiveness grew.
'The Boer War' (1960)

7 With first-rate sherry flowing into second-
rate whores,
And third-rate conversation without one
single pause:
Just like a young couple
Between the wars.
'Father and Son: 1939' (1945)

Plutarch AD *c.*46–*c.*120

8 For we are told that when a certain man
was accusing both of them to him, he
[Caesar] said that he had no fear of those fat
and long-haired fellows, but rather of those
pale and thin ones.
Parallel Lives 'Anthony' sect. 11; cf.
Shakespeare 276:1

9 The man who is thought to have been the
first to see beneath the surface of Caesar's
public policy and to fear it, as one might
fear the smiling surface of the sea.
of **Cicero**
Parallel Lives 'Julius Caesar' sect. 4

10 He who cheats with an oath acknowledges
that he is afraid of his enemy, but that he
thinks little of God.
Parallel Lives 'Lysander' ch. 8; cf. **Lysander** 205:3

Edgar Allan Poe 1809–49

11 I was a child and she was a child,
In this kingdom by the sea;
But we loved with a love which was more
than love—
I and my Annabel Lee.
'Annabel Lee' (1849)

12 To the tintinnabulation that so musically
wells
From the bells, bells, bells, bells.
'The Bells' (1849) st. 1

13 Ghastly, grim and ancient raven wandering
from the Nightly shore—
Tell me what thy lordly name is on the
Night's Plutonian shore!
'The Raven' (1845) st. 8

14 Quoth the Raven, 'Nevermore'.
'The Raven' (1845) st. 17

15 The glory that was Greece
And the grandeur that was Rome.
'To Helen' (1831)

Henri Poincaré 1854–1912

16 Science is built up of facts, as a house is
built of stones; but an accumulation of facts
is no more a science than a heap of stones is
a house.
Science and Hypothesis (1905) ch. 9

Madame de Pompadour 1721–64

17 *Après nous le déluge.*
After us the deluge.
Madame du Hausset *Mémoires* (1824)

Alexander Pope 1688–1744

18 Poetic Justice, with her lifted scale.
The Dunciad (1742) bk. 1, l. 52

19 All crowd, who foremost shall be damned to
Fame.
The Dunciad (1742) bk. 3, l. 158

20 A wit with dunces, and a dunce with wits.
The Dunciad (1742) bk. 4, l. 90

21 The Right Divine of Kings to govern wrong.
The Dunciad (1742) bk. 4, l. 187

22 Stretched on the rack of a too easy chair.
The Dunciad (1742) bk. 4, l. 343

23 Thy truffles, Perigord! thy hams, Bayonne!
The Dunciad (1742) bk. 4, l. 558

24 Lo! thy dread empire, Chaos! is restored;
Light dies before thy uncreating word:
Thy hand, great Anarch! lets the curtain fall;
And universal darkness buries all.
The Dunciad (1742) bk. 4, l. 653

25 Vital spark of heav'nly flame!
Quit, oh quit this mortal frame:
Trembling, hoping, ling'ring, flying,
Oh the pain, the bliss of dying!
'The Dying Christian to his Soul' (1730); cf.
Hadrian 148:17

1 On all the line a sudden vengeance waits,
And frequent hearses shall besiege your
gates.
'Elegy to the Memory of an Unfortunate Lady'
(1717) l. 37

2 How shall I lose the sin, yet keep the sense,
And love th'offender, yet detest th'offence?
'Eloisa to Abelard' (1717) l. 191; cf. **Augustine**
19:5

3 You beat your pate, and fancy wit will come:
Knock as you please, there's nobody at
home.
'Epigram: You beat your pate' (1732)

4 I am his Highness' dog at Kew;
Pray, tell me sir, whose dog are you?
'Epigram Engraved on the Collar of a Dog
which I gave to his Royal Highness' (1738)

5 Sir, I admit your gen'ral rule
That every poet is a fool:
But you yourself may serve to show it,
That every fool is not a poet.
'Epigram from the French' (1732)

6 You think this cruel? take it for a rule,
No creature smarts so little as a fool.
'An Epistle to Dr Arbuthnot' (1735) l. 83

7 As yet a child, nor yet a fool to fame,
I lisped in numbers, for the numbers came.
'An Epistle to Dr Arbuthnot' (1735) l. 127

8 The Muse but served to ease some friend,
not wife,
To help me through this long disease, my
life.
'An Epistle to Dr Arbuthnot' (1735) l. 131

9 And he, whose fustian's so sublimely bad,
It is not poetry, but prose run mad.
'An Epistle to Dr Arbuthnot' (1735) l. 187

10 Damn with faint praise, assent with civil
leer,
And without sneering, teach the rest to
sneer;
Willing to wound, and yet afraid to strike.
of **Addison**
'An Epistle to Dr Arbuthnot' (1735) l. 201; cf.
Wycherley 342:4

11 'Satire or sense, alas! can Sporus feel?
Who breaks a butterfly upon a wheel?'
of Lord **Hervey**
'An Epistle to Dr Arbuthnot' (1735) l. 307

12 Unlearn'd, he knew no schoolman's subtle
art,
No language, but the language of the heart.
of his own father
'An Epistle to Dr Arbuthnot' (1735) l. 398

13 Chaste to her husband, frank to all beside,
A teeming mistress, but a barren bride.
Epistles to Several Persons 'To a Lady' (1735) l. 71

14 See how the world its veterans rewards!
A youth of frolics, an old age of cards.
Epistles to Several Persons 'To a Lady' (1735) l. 243

15 And mistress of herself, though china fall.
Epistles to Several Persons 'To a Lady' (1735) l. 268

16 Who shall decide, when doctors disagree?
Epistles to Several Persons 'To Lord Bathurst' (1733)
l. 1

17 Die, and endow a college, or a cat.
Epistles to Several Persons 'To Lord Bathurst' (1733)
l. 98

18 The ruling passion, be it what it will,
The ruling passion conquers reason still.
Epistles to Several Persons 'To Lord Bathurst' (1733)
l. 155; cf. **Pope** 247:23

19 Consult the genius of the place in all.
Epistles to Several Persons 'To Lord Burlington'
(1731) l. 57; cf. **Virgil** 325:3

20 To rest, the cushion and soft Dean invite,
Who never mentions Hell to ears polite.
Epistles to Several Persons 'To Lord Burlington'
(1731) l. 149

21 Deep harvests bury all his pride has
planned,
And laughing Ceres re-assume the land.
Epistles to Several Persons 'To Lord Burlington'
(1731) l. 175

22 'Tis use alone that sanctifies expense.
Epistles to Several Persons 'To Lord Burlington'
(1731) l. 179

23 Search then the Ruling Passion: There,
alone,
The wild are constant, and the cunning
known;
The fool consistent, and the false sincere.
Epistles to Several Persons 'To Lord Cobham' (1734)
l. 174; cf. **Pope** 247:18

24 Odious! in woollen! 'twould a saint provoke!
Epistles to Several Persons 'To Lord Cobham' (1734)
l. 242

25 Old politicians chew on wisdom past,
And totter on in business to the last.
Epistles to Several Persons 'To Lord Cobham' (1734)
l. 248

26 She went, to plain-work, and to purling
brooks,
Old-fashioned halls, dull aunts, and
croaking rooks.
'Epistle to Miss Blount, on her leaving the
Town, after the Coronation [of King George I,
1715]' (1717)

27 Or o'er cold coffee trifle with the spoon,
Court the slow clock, and dine exact at
noon.
'Epistle to Miss Blount, on her leaving the
Town, after the Coronation [of King George I,
1715]' (1717)

28 Nature, and Nature's laws lay hid in night.
God said, Let Newton be! and all was light.
'Epitaph: Intended for Sir Isaac Newton' (1730);
cf. **Squire** 301:8

29 A little learning is a dangerous thing;
Drink deep, or taste not the Pierian spring:
There shallow draughts intoxicate the
brain,
And drinking largely sobers us again.
An Essay on Criticism (1711) l. 215; cf. **Drayton**
116:7

30 Hills peep o'er hills, and Alps on Alps arise!
An Essay on Criticism (1711) l. 232

1 True wit is Nature to advantage dressed,
What oft was thought, but ne'er so well
expressed.
An Essay on Criticism (1711) l. 297

2 Expression is the dress of thought.
An Essay on Criticism (1711) l. 318; cf. **Johnson**
173:19, **Wesley** 332:10

3 As some to church repair,
Not for the doctrine, but the music there.
An Essay on Criticism (1711) l. 342

4 A needless Alexandrine ends the song,
That, like a wounded snake, drags its slow
length along.
An Essay on Criticism (1711) l. 356

5 Some praise at morning what they blame at
night;
But always think the last opinion right.
An Essay on Criticism (1711) l. 430

6 To err is human; to forgive, divine.
An Essay on Criticism (1711) l. 525

7 For fools rush in where angels fear to tread.
An Essay on Criticism (1711) l. 625

8 Eye Nature's walks, shoot Folly as it flies,
And catch the Manners living as they rise.
Laugh where we must, be candid where we
can;
But vindicate the ways of God to man.
An Essay on Man Epistle 1 (1733) l. 13; cf. **Milton**
221:2

9 Pleased to the last, he crops the flowery
food,
And licks the hand just raised to shed his
blood.
An Essay on Man Epistle 1 (1733) l. 83

10 Hope springs eternal in the human breast:
Man never Is, but always To be blest.
An Essay on Man Epistle 1 (1733) l. 95

11 Lo! the poor Indian, whose untutored mind
Sees God in clouds, or hears him in the
wind.
An Essay on Man Epistle 1 (1733) l. 99

12 Why has not man a microscopic eye?
For this plain reason, man is not a fly.
An Essay on Man Epistle 1 (1733) l. 193

13 The spider's touch, how exquisitely fine!
Feels at each thread, and lives along the
line.
An Essay on Man Epistle 1 (1733) l. 217

14 And, spite of Pride, in erring Reason's spite,
One truth is clear, 'Whatever IS, is RIGHT.'
An Essay on Man Epistle 1 (1733) l. 293

15 Know then thyself, presume not God to
scan;
The proper study of mankind is man.
An Essay on Man Epistle 2 (1733) l. 1; cf.
Charron 88:3, **Huxley** 167:14

16 Created half to rise, and half to fall;
Great lord of all things, yet a prey to all;
Sole judge of truth, in endless error hurled;
The glory, jest, and riddle of the world!
An Essay on Man Epistle 2 (1733) l. 15

17 Behold the child, by Nature's kindly law
Pleased with a rattle, tickled with a straw.
An Essay on Man Epistle 2 (1733) l. 275

18 For forms of government let fools contest;
Whate'er is best administered is best.
An Essay on Man Epistle 3 (1733) l. 303

19 Thus God and nature linked the gen'ral
frame,
And bade self-love and social be the same.
An Essay on Man Epistle 3 (1733) l. 317; *An Essay
on Man* Epistle 4 (1734) l. 396 is similar

20 An honest man's the noblest work of God.
An Essay on Man Epistle 4 (1734) l. 248; cf.
Ingersoll 169:2

21 All our knowledge is, ourselves to know.
An Essay on Man Epistle 4 (1734) l. 398

22 Achilles' wrath, to Greece the direful spring
Of woes unnumbered, heavenly goddess,
sing!
translation of *The Iliad* (1715) bk. 1, l. 1; cf.
Homer 161:16

23 For I, who hold sage Homer's rule the best,
Welcome the coming, speed the going
guest.
Imitations of Horace Horace bk. 2, Satire 2 (1734)
l. 159; Pope's translation of *The Odyssey* (1725–6)
bk. 15, l. 84, has 'Speed the parting guest'

24 Get place and wealth, if possible, with
grace;
If not, by any means get wealth and place.
Imitations of Horace Horace bk. 1, Epistle 1 (1738)
l. 103; cf. **Horace** 163:20

25 Not to admire, is all the art I know,
To make men happy, and to keep them so.
Imitations of Horace Horace bk. 1, Epistle 6 (1738)
l. 1; cf. **Horace** 163:23

26 The people's voice is odd,
It is, and it is not, the voice of God.
Imitations of Horace Horace bk. 2, Epistle 1 (1737)
l. 89; cf. **Alcuin** 3:10

27 But those who cannot write, and those who
can,
All rhyme, and scrawl, and scribble, to a
man.
Imitations of Horace Horace bk. 2, Epistle 1 (1737)
l. 187; cf. **Horace** 164:3

28 Ev'n copious Dryden, wanted, or forgot,
The last and greatest art, the art to blot.
Imitations of Horace Horace bk. 2, Epistle 1 (1737)
l. 280; cf. **Jonson** 178:11

29 There still remains, to mortify a wit,
The many-headed monster of the pit.
Imitations of Horace Horace bk. 2, Epistle 1 (1737)
l. 304

30 Let humble Allen, with an awkward shame,
Do good by stealth, and blush to find it
fame.
Imitations of Horace Epilogue to the Satires (1738)
Dialogue 1, l. 135

31 Where'er you walk, cool gales shall fan the
glade,
Trees, where you sit, shall crowd into a
shade.
Pastorals (1709) 'Summer' l. 73

32 They shift the moving toyshop of their
heart.
The Rape of the Lock (1714) canto 1, l. 100

1 Fair tresses man's imperial race insnare,
And beauty draws us with a single hair.
The Rape of the Lock (1714) canto 2, l. 27

2 Belinda smiled, and all the world was gay.
The Rape of the Lock (1714) canto 2, l. 52

3 Here thou, great Anna! whom three realms obey,
Dost sometimes counsel take—and sometimes tea.
The Rape of the Lock (1714) canto 3, l. 7

4 At ev'ry word a reputation dies.
The Rape of the Lock (1714) canto 3, l. 16; cf.
Sheridan 294:18

5 The hungry judges soon the sentence sign,
And wretches hang that jury-men may dine.
The Rape of the Lock (1714) canto 3, l. 21

6 Coffee, (which makes the politician wise,
And see thro' all things with his half-shut eyes).
The Rape of the Lock (1714) canto 3, l. 117

7 Not louder shrieks to pitying heav'n are cast,
When husbands or when lapdogs breathe their last.
The Rape of the Lock (1714) canto 3, l. 157

8 Party-spirit, which at best is but the madness of many for the gain of a few.
letter to Edward Blount, 27 August 1714

9 To endeavour to work upon the vulgar with fine sense, is like attempting to hew blocks with a razor.
Miscellanies (1727) vol. 2 'Thoughts on Various Subjects'

10 All gardening is landscape-painting.
Joseph Spence *Anecdotes* (ed. J. Osborn, 1966) no. 606

11 Here am I, dying of a hundred good symptoms.
to George, Lord Lyttelton, 15 May 1744

Karl Popper 1902–94

12 We may become the makers of our fate when we have ceased to pose as its prophets.
The Open Society and its Enemies (1945) introduction

13 Science must begin with myths, and with the criticism of myths.
'The Philosophy of Science' in C. A. Mace (ed.)
British Philosophy in the Mid-Century (1957)

Cole Porter 1891–1964

14 But I'm always true to you, darlin', in my fashion.
Yes I'm always true to you, darlin', in my way.
'Always True to You in my Fashion' (1949 song)

15 In olden days a glimpse of stocking
Was looked on as something shocking
Now, heaven knows,
Anything goes.
'Anything Goes' (1934 song)

16 When they begin the Beguine.
'Begin the Beguine' (1935 song)

17 I get no kick from champagne,
Mere alcohol doesn't thrill me at all,
So tell me why should it be true
That I get a kick out of you?
'I Get a Kick Out of You' (1934 song) in *Anything Goes*

18 Birds do it, bees do it,
Even educated fleas do it.
Let's do it, let's fall in love.
'Let's Do It' (1954 song; words added to the 1928 original)

19 Miss Otis regrets (she's unable to lunch today).
title of song (1934)

20 What a swell party this is.
'Well, Did You Evah?' (1940 song; revived for the film *High Society*, 1956)

21 You're the top! You're the Coliseum,
You're the top! You're the Louvre Museum,
'You're the Top' (1934 song) in *Anything Goes*

Beilby Porteus 1731–1808

22 . . . One murder made a villain,
Millions a hero.
Death (1759) l. 154; cf. **Rostand** 261:3

23 War its thousands slays, Peace its ten thousands.
Death (1759) l. 179; cf. **Bible** 35:23

Francis Pott 1832–1909

24 The strife is o'er, the battle done;
Now is the Victor's triumph won;
O let the song of praise be sung:
Alleluia!
'The strife is o'er, the battle done' (1861 hymn);
translation of 'Finita iam sunt praelia' (c.1695)

Beatrix Potter 1866–1943

25 It is said that the effect of eating too much lettuce is 'soporific'.
The Tale of the Flopsy Bunnies (1909)

26 Don't go into Mr McGregor's garden: your father had an accident there, he was put into a pie by Mrs McGregor.
The Tale of Peter Rabbit (1902)

Dennis Potter 1935–94

27 Below my window . . . the blossom is out in full now . . . I *see* it is the whitest, frothiest, blossomiest blossom that there ever could be, and I can see it . . . The nowness of everything is absolutely wondrous.
on his heightened awareness of things, in the face of his imminent death
interview with Melvyn Bragg on Channel 4, March 1994

28 Religion to me has always been the wound, not the bandage.
interview with Melvyn Bragg on Channel 4, March 1994

Stephen Potter 1900–69

1 *How to be one up*—how to make the other man feel that something has gone wrong, however slightly.
Lifemanship (1950)

2 'Yes, but not in the South', with slight adjustments, will do for any argument about any place, if not about any person.
Lifemanship (1950) p. 43

3 A good general rule is to state that the bouquet is better than the taste, and vice versa.
on wine-tasting
One-Upmanship (1952) ch. 14

4 The theory and practice of gamesmanship or The art of winning games without actually cheating.
title of book (1947)

Ezra Pound 1885–1972

5 Winter is icummen in,
Lhude sing Goddamm,
Raineth drop and staineth slop,
And how the wind doth ramm!
Sing: Goddamm.
'Ancient Music' (1917); cf. **Anonymous** 10:3

6 Tching prayed on the mountain and wrote MAKE IT NEW
on his bath tub.
Cantos (1954) no. 53; cf. **Bible** 52:25

7 Hang it all, Robert Browning,
There can be but the one 'Sordello'.
Draft of XXX Cantos (1930) no. 2

8 And even I can remember
A day when the historians left blanks in their writings,
I mean for things they didn't know.
Draft of XXX Cantos (1930) no. 13

9 Died some, pro patria,
non 'dulce' non 'et decor' . . .
walked eye-deep in hell
believing in old men's lies, the unbelieving
came home, home to a lie.
Hugh Selwyn Mauberley (1920) 'E. P. Ode . . . ' pt. 4; cf. **Horace** 164:14

10 There died a myriad,
And of the best, among them,
For an old bitch gone in the teeth,
For a botched civilization.
Hugh Selwyn Mauberley (1920) 'E. P. Ode . . . ' pt. 5

11 The ant's a centaur in his dragon world.
Pisan Cantos (1948) no. 81

12 Pull down thy VANITY
Thou art a beaten dog beneath the hail,
A swollen magpie in a fitful sun,
Half black half white
Nor knowst'ou wing from tail.
Pisan Cantos (1948) no. 81

13 Music begins to atrophy when it departs too far from the dance; that poetry begins to atrophy when it gets too far from music.
The ABC of Reading (1934) 'Warning'

14 Literature is news that STAYS news.
The ABC of Reading (1934) ch. 2

15 Poetry must be *as well written as prose*.
letter to Harriet Monroe, January 1915

Nicolas Poussin 1594–1665

16 An imitation in lines and colours on any surface of all that is to be found under the sun.
of painting
letter to M. de Chambray, 1665

Anthony Powell 1905–2000

17 Books do furnish a room.
title of novel (1971); cf. **Smith** 298:9

18 A dance to the music of time.
title of novel sequence (1951–75), after 'Le 4 stagioni che ballano al suono del tempo [The four seasons dancing to the sound of time]', title given by Giovanni Pietro Bellori to a painting by Nicolas **Poussin**

19 He's so wet you could shoot snipe off him.
A Question of Upbringing (1951) ch. 1

20 Growing old is like being increasingly penalized for a crime you haven't committed.
Temporary Kings (1973) ch. 1

Colin Powell 1937–

21 First, we are going to cut it off, and then, we are going to kill it.
strategy for dealing with the Iraqi Army in the Gulf War
at a press conference, 23 January 1991

Enoch Powell 1912–98

22 History is littered with the wars which everybody knew would never happen.
speech to the Conservative Party Conference, 19 October 1967

23 As I look ahead, I am filled with foreboding. Like the Roman, I seem to see 'the River Tiber foaming with much blood'.
speech in Birmingham, 20 April 1968; cf. **Virgil** 324:19

24 For a politician to complain about the press is like a ship's captain complaining about the sea.
in *Guardian* 3 December 1984

25 All political lives, unless they are cut off in midstream at a happy juncture, end in failure, because that is the nature of politics and of human affairs.
Joseph Chamberlain (1977)

John O'Connor Power 1848–1919

26 The mules of politics: without pride of ancestry, or hope of posterity.
of the Liberal Unionists
H. H. Asquith *Memories and Reflections* (1928) vol. 1, ch. 16; cf. **Disraeli** 112:19

Terry Pratchett 1948–

27 Most modern fantasy just rearranges the furniture in Tolkien's attic.
Stan Nicholls (ed.) *Wordsmiths of Wonder* (1993)

John Prescott 1938-

1 People like me were branded, pigeon-holed, a ceiling put on our ambitions.
on failing his 11-plus
speech at Ruskin College, Oxford, 13 June 1996

2 We did it! Let's wallow in our victory!
*on Tony **Blair**'s warning that the Labour Party should not be triumphalist in victory*
speech to the Labour Party Conference, 29 September 1997

Keith Preston 1884-1927

3 Of all the literary scenes
Saddest this sight to me:
The graves of little magazines
Who died to make verse free.
'The Liberators'

Jacques Prévert 1900-77

4 *C'est tellement simple, l'amour.*
Love is so simple.
Les Enfants du Paradis (1945 film)

Richard Price 1723-91

5 Now, methinks, I see the ardour for liberty catching and spreading; a general amendment beginning in human affairs; the dominion of kings changed for the dominion of laws, and the dominion of priests giving way to the dominion of reason and conscience.
A Discourse on the Love of our Country (1790)

J. B. Priestley 1894-1984

6 First you take their faces from 'em by calling 'em the masses and then you accuse 'em of not having any faces.
Saturn Over the Water (1961) ch. 2

7 Our great-grand-children, when they learn how we began this war by snatching glory out of defeat, and then swept on to victory, may also learn how the little holiday steamers made an excursion to hell and came back glorious.
radio broadcast, 5 June 1940

Matthew Prior 1664-1721

8 Be to her virtues very kind;
Be to her faults a little blind;
Let all her ways be unconfined;
And clap your padlock—on her mind.
'An English Padlock' (1705) l. 79

9 Euphelia serves to grace my measure;
But Chloe is my real flame.
'An Ode' (1709)

10 Cured yesterday of my disease,
I died last night of my physician.
'The Remedy Worse than the Disease' (1727)

11 No, no; for my virginity,
When I lose that, says Rose, I'll die:
Behind the elms last night, cried Dick,
Rose, were you not extremely sick?
'A True Maid' (1718)

V. S. Pritchett 1900-97

12 The principle of procrastinated rape is said to be the ruling one in all the great best-sellers.
The Living Novel (1946) 'Clarissa'

Adelaide Ann Procter 1825-64

13 A lost chord.
title of poem (1858)

14 It may be that Death's bright Angel
Will speak in that chord again
It may be that only in Heaven
I shall hear that grand Amen.
'A Lost Chord' (1858)

Protagoras b. *c.*485 BC

15 That man is the measure of all things.
Plato *Theaetetus* 160d

Pierre-Joseph Proudhon 1809-65

16 *La propriété c'est le vol.*
Property is theft.
Qu'est-ce que la propriété? (1840) ch. 1

Marcel Proust 1871-1922

Textual translations are those of C. K. Scott-Moncrieff and S. Hudson, revised by T. Kilmartin, 1981

17 And suddenly the memory revealed itself. The taste was that of the little piece of madeleine which on Sunday mornings at Combray . . . my aunt Léonie used to give me, dipping it first in her own cup of tea or tisane.
Du côté de chez Swann (Swann's Way, 1913) vol. 1

18 I have a horror of sunsets, they're so romantic, so operatic.
Sodome et Gomorrhe (Cities of the Plain, 1922) vol. 1

19 We are healed of a suffering only by experiencing it to the full.
Albertine disparue (The Sweet Cheat Gone, 1925) ch. 1

20 The true paradises are the paradises that we have lost.
Le Temps retrouvé (Time Regained, 1926) ch. 3

Publilius Syrus

21 A beautiful face is a mute recommendation.
Sententiae no. 199, in J. and A. Duff *Minor Latin Poets* (Loeb ed., 1934); translated by Thomas Tenison in *Baconiana* (1679) 'Ornamenta Rationalia' no. 12

22 *Inopi beneficium bis dat qui dat celeriter.*
He gives the poor man twice as much good who gives quickly.
proverbially 'Bis dat qui cito dat [He gives twice who gives soon]'
Sententiae no. 274, in J. and A. Duff *Minor Latin Poets*

1 *Necessitas dat legem non ipsa accipit.*
Necessity gives the law without itself
acknowledging one.
proverbially 'Necessitas non habet legem
[Necessity has no law]'
   Sententiae no. 444, in J. and A. Duff *Minor Latin Poets*

John Pudney 1909–77

2 Do not despair
For Johnny-head-in-air;
He sleeps as sound
As Johnny underground.
   'For Johnny' (1942); cf. **Hoffmann** 160:14

Augustus Welby Pugin 1812–52

3 There is nothing worth living for but
Christian Architecture and a boat.
   in *The Builder* 1852 vol. 10

4 Nothing can be more dangerous than
looking at prints of buildings, and trying to
imitate bits of them. These architectural
books are as bad as the Scriptures in the
hands of the Protestants.
   J. Mordaunt Crook *Dilemma of Style* (1987)

Joseph Pulitzer 1847–1911

5 A cynical, mercenary, demagogic, corrupt
press will produce in time a people as base
as itself.
   *inscribed on the gateway to the Columbia School
of Journalism in New York*
   W. J. Granberg *The World of Joseph Pulitzer* (1965)

William Pulteney, Earl of Bath
1684–1764

6 For Sir Ph—p well knows
That innuendos
Will serve him no longer in verse or in
   prose,
Since twelve honest men have decided the
   cause,
And were judges of fact, tho' not judges of
   laws.
   on the unsuccessful prosecution of The
Craftsman, *1729 by Philip Yorke, later Lord*
Hardwicke
   'The Honest Jury' (1729) st. 3

Punch 1841–1992

7 Advice to persons about to marry.—'Don't.'
   4 January 1845; cf. **Bacon** 21:18

8 You pays your money and you takes your
choice.
   3 January 1846

9 Never do to-day what you can put off till to-
morrow.
   22 December 1849

10 Who's 'im, Bill?
A stranger!
'Eave 'arf a brick at 'im.
   25 February 1854

11 What is Matter?—Never mind.
What is Mind?—No matter.
   14 July 1855

12 Mun, a had na' been the-erre abune two
hours when—*bang*—went saxpence!!!
   5 December 1868

13 Cats is 'dogs' and rabbits is 'dogs' and so's
Parrats, but this 'ere 'Tortis' is a insect, and
there ain't no charge for it.
   6 March 1869

14 Go directly—see what she's doing, and tell
her she mustn't.
   16 November 1872

15 There was one poor tiger that hadn't *got* a
Christian.
   3 April 1875

16 I never read books—I *write* them.
   11 May 1878; cf. **Disraeli** 113:9

17 WIFE OF TWO YEARS' STANDING: Oh yes! I'm
sure he's not so fond of me as at first. He's
away so much, neglects me dreadfully, and
he's so cross when he comes home. What
shall I do?
WIDOW: Feed the brute!
   31 October 1885

18 I'm afraid you've got a bad egg, Mr Jones.
Oh no, my Lord, I assure you! Parts of it are
excellent!
   11 May 1895

19 Look here, Steward, if this is coffee, I want
tea; but if this is tea, then I wish for coffee.
   23 July 1902

20 Sometimes I sits and thinks, and then again
I just sits.
   24 October 1906

Alexander Pushkin 1799–1837

21 A tedious season they await
Who hear November at the gate.
   Eugene Onegin (1833) ch. 4, st. 40 (translated by
Babette Deutsch)

22 Moscow: those syllables can start
A tumult in the Russian heart.
   Eugene Onegin (1833) ch. 7, st. 36 (translated by
Babette Deutsch)

23 A green oak grows by a curving shore;
And round that oak hangs a golden chain.
   Ruslan and Lyudmila (1820) 'Prologue' (translated
by Elisaveta Fen)

Israel Putnam 1718–90

24 Don't one of you fire until you see the white
of their eyes.
   also attributed to William Prescott (1726–95)
   at Bunker Hill, 1775, in R. Frothingham *History
of the Siege of Boston* (1873) ch. 5

Mario Puzo 1920–99

25 I'll make him an offer he can't refuse.
   The Godfather (1969) ch. 1

26 A lawyer with his briefcase can steal more
than a hundred men with guns.
   The Godfather (1969) ch. 1

Pyrrhus 319–272 BC

1 One more such victory and we are lost.
on defeating the Romans at Asculum, 279 BC
Plutarch *Parallel Lives* 'Pyrrhus' ch. 21, sect. 9

Mary Quant 1934–

2 Being young is greatly overestimated . . .
Any failure seems so total. Later on you
realize you can have another go.
interview in *Observer* 5 May 1996

Francis Quarles 1592–1644

3 Our God and soldiers we alike adore
Ev'n at the brink of danger; not before:
After deliverance, both alike requited,
Our God's forgotten, and our soldiers
slighted.
Divine Fancies (1632) 'Of Common Devotion'; cf.
Owen 238:18

4 We spend our midday sweat, our midnight
oil;
We tire the night in thought, the day in toil.
Emblems (1635) bk. 2, no. 2, l. 33

5 Man is man's A.B.C. There is none that can
Read God aright, unless he first spell Man.
Hieroglyphics of the Life of Man (1638) no. 1, l. 1

6 We'll cry both arts and learning down,
And hey! then up go we!
The Shepherd's Oracles (1646) Eclogue 11 'Song of
Anarchus'

Arthur Quiller-Couch ('Q')
1863–1944

7 The best is the best, though a hundred
judges have declared it so.
Oxford Book of English Verse (1900) preface

8 All the old statues of Victory have wings:
but Grief has no wings. She is the
unwelcome lodger that squats on the
hearthstone between us and the fire and
will not move or be dislodged.
Armistice Day anniversary sermon, Cambridge,
November 1923

Josiah Quincy 1772–1864

9 As it will be the right of all, so it will be the
duty of some, definitely to prepare for a
separation, amicably if they can, violently if
they must.
speech, 14 January 1811; cf. **Clay** 94:2

W. V. O. Quine 1908–

10 It is the tension between the scientist's laws
and his own attempted breaches of them
that powers the engines of science and
makes it forge ahead.
Quiddities (1987) p. 8 'Anomaly'

The Qur'an *see* **The Koran**

François Rabelais c.1494–c.1553

11 The appetite grows by eating.
Gargantua (1534) bk. 1, ch. 5

12 Nature abhors a vacuum.
quoting, in Latin, an article of ancient wisdom
Gargantua (1534) bk. 1, ch. 5

13 *Fay ce que vouldras.*
Do what you like.
Gargantua (1534) bk. 1, ch. 57; cf. **Crowley**
104:10

14 A child is not a vase to be filled, but a fire to
be lit.
attributed

15 I am going to seek a great perhaps . . . Bring
down the curtain, the farce is played out.
last words; attributed, but probably apocryphal

Yitzhak Rabin 1922–95

16 We say to you today in a loud and a clear
voice: enough of blood and tears. Enough.
to the Palestinians, at the signing of the
Israel–Palestine Declaration
in Washington, 13 September, 1993

Jean Racine 1639–99

17 I have loved him too much not to feel any
hatred for him.
Andromaque (1667) act 2, sc. 1

18 She floats, she hesitates; in a word, she's a
woman.
Athalie (1691) act 3, sc. 3

19 *C'est Vénus tout entière à sa proie attachée.*
It's Venus entire latched onto her prey.
Phèdre (1677) act 1, sc. 3

20 *Dans le fond des forêts votre image me suit.*
Deep in the forest glade your picture chases
me.
Phèdre (1677) act 2, sc. 2

James Rado 1939–
and **Gerome Ragni** 1942–

21 When the moon is in the seventh house,
And Jupiter aligns with Mars . . .
This is the dawning of the age of Aquarius.
'Aquarius' (1967 song) in *Hair*

Thomas Rainborowe d. 1648

22 The poorest he that is in England hath a life
to live as the greatest he.
during the Army debates at Putney, 29 October
1647

Kathleen Raine 1908–

23 He has married me with a ring, a ring of
bright water.
'The Marriage of Psyche' (1952)

Walter Ralegh c.1552–1618

24 If all the world and love were young,
And truth in every shepherd's tongue,
These pretty pleasures might me move
To live with thee, and be thy love.
'Answer to Marlow'; cf. **Donne** 114:5, **Marlowe**
212:13

1 Say to the court, it glows
And shines like rotten wood;
Say to the church, it shows
What's good, and doth no good:
If church and court reply,
Then give them both the lie.
　'The Lie' (1608)

2 Give me my scallop-shell of quiet,
My staff of faith to walk upon,
My scrip of joy, immortal diet,
My bottle of salvation,
My gown of glory, hope's true gage,
And thus I'll take my pilgrimage.
　'The Passionate Man's Pilgrimage' (1604)

3 But true love is a durable fire,
In the mind ever burning.
　'Walsinghame'

4 Fain would I climb, yet fear I to fall.
　　line written on a window-pane, in Thomas
　　Fuller *History of the Worthies of England* (1662)
　　'Devonshire'; cf. **Elizabeth I** 123:10

5 Even such is Time, which takes in trust
Our youth, our joys, and all we have,
And pays us but with age and dust;
Who in the dark and silent grave,
When we have wandered all our ways,
Shuts up the story of our days:
And from which earth, and grave, and dust,
The Lord shall raise me up, I trust.
　　written the night before his death, and found
　　in his Bible in the Gate-house at Westminster

6 O eloquent, just, and mighty Death! . . . thou
hast drawn together all the farstretched
greatness, all the pride, cruelty, and
ambition of man, and covered it all over
with these two narrow words, *Hic jacet* [Here
lies].
　　The History of the World (1614) bk. 5, ch. 6

7 'Tis a sharp remedy, but a sure one for all
ills.
　*on feeling the edge of the axe prior to his
　execution*
　　D. Hume *History of Great Britain* (1754) vol. 1, ch.
　　4

8 So the heart be right, it is no matter which
way the head lies.
　*at his execution, on being asked which way he
　preferred to lay his head*
　　W. Stebbing *Sir Walter Raleigh* (1891) ch. 30

Walter Raleigh 1861–1922

9 In examinations those who do not wish to
know ask questions of those who cannot
tell.
　　Laughter from a Cloud (1923) 'Some Thoughts on
　　Examinations'

10 I wish I loved the Human Race;
I wish I loved its silly face.
　　'Wishes of an Elderly Man' (1923)

11 An anthology is like all the plums and
orange peel picked out of a cake.
　　letter to Mrs Robert Bridges, 15 January 1915

John Randolph 1773–1833

12 Never were abilities so much below
mediocrity so well rewarded; no, not when
Caligula's horse was made Consul.
　*on the appointment of Richard Rush as US
　Secretary of the Treasury*
　　speech, 1 February 1828

13 He is a man of splendid abilities but utterly
corrupt. He shines and stinks like rotten
mackerel by moonlight.
　of Edward Livingston
　　W. Cabell Bruce *John Randolph of Roanoke* (1923)
　　vol. 2

Arthur Ransome 1884–1967

14 BETTER DROWNED THAN DUFFERS IF NOT
DUFFERS WONT DROWN.
　　Arthur Ransome *Swallows and Amazons* (1930) ch.
　　1

Gerald Ratner 1949–

15 We even sell a pair of earrings for under £1,
which is cheaper than a prawn sandwich
from Marks & Spencers. But I have to say
the earrings probably won't last as long.
　　speech to the Institute of Directors, Albert Hall,
　　23 April 1991

Terence Rattigan 1911–77

16 You can be in the Horseguards and still be
common, dear.
　　Separate Tables (1954) 'Table Number Seven' sc. 1

Derek Raymond 1931–94

17 The psychopath is the furnace that gives no
heat.
　　The Hidden Files (1992)

Herbert Read 1893–1968

18 Art is . . . pattern informed by sensibility.
　　The Meaning of Art (1955) ch. 1

19 I saw him stab
And stab again
A well-killed Boche.
This is the happy warrior,
This is he . . .
　　Naked Warriors (1919) 'The Scene of War, 4. The
　　Happy Warrior'; cf. **Wordsworth** 339:17

Charles Reade 1814–84

20 *Courage, mon ami, le diable est mort!*
Take courage, my friend, the devil is dead!
　　The Cloister and the Hearth (1861) ch. 24, and
　　passim

21 Sow an act, and you reap a habit. Sow a
habit and you reap a character. Sow a
character, and you reap a destiny.
　　attributed; in *Notes and Queries* (9th Series) vol.
　　12, 17 October 1903

Nancy Reagan 1923–

22 If the President has a bully pulpit, then the
First Lady has a white glove pulpit . . . more

refined, restricted, ceremonial, but it's a pulpit all the same.

in *New York Times* 10 March 1988; cf. **Roosevelt** 260:6

Ronald Reagan 1911–

1 Politics is supposed to be the second oldest profession. I have come to realize that it bears a very close resemblance to the first.

at a conference in Los Angeles, 2 March 1977; cf. **Kipling** 188:18

2 An evil empire.

of the Soviet Union

speech to the National Association of Evangelicals, 8 March 1983

3 We will never forget them, nor the last time we saw them this morning, as they prepared for the journey and waved goodbye and 'slipped the surly bonds of earth' to 'touch the face of God.'

after the loss of the space shuttle Challenger *with all its crew*

broadcast from the Oval Office, 28 January 1986; cf. **Magee** 209:8

4 I now begin the journey that will lead me into the sunset of my life.

statement to the American people revealing that he had Alzheimer's disease

in *Daily Telegraph* 5 January 1995

Erell Reaves

5 Lady of Spain, I adore you.
Right from the night I first saw you,
My heart has been yearning for you,
What else could any heart do?
'Lady of Spain' (1913 song)

Red Cloud 1822–1909

6 You have heard the sound of the white soldier's axe upon the Little Piney. His presence here is . . . an insult to the spirits of our ancestors. Are we then to give up their sacred graves to be ploughed for corn? Dakotas, I am for war!

speech at council at Fort Laramie, 1866; Charles A. Eastman *Indian Heroes and Great Chieftains* (1918)

Henry Reed 1914–86

7 As we get older we do not get any younger.
Seasons return, and today I am fifty-five,
And this time last year I was fifty-four,
And this time next year I shall be sixty-two.
'Chard Whitlow (Mr Eliot's Sunday Evening Postscript)' (1946)

8 Today we have naming of parts. Yesterday,
We had daily cleaning. And tomorrow morning,
We shall have what to do after firing. But today,
Today we have naming of parts. Japonica
Glistens like coral in all of the neighbour gardens,
And today we have naming of parts.
'Lessons of the War: 1, Naming of Parts' (1946)

9 They call it easing the Spring: it is perfectly easy
If you have any strength in your thumb: like the bolt,
And the breech, and the cocking-piece, and the point of balance,
Which in our case we have not got; and the almond blossom
Silent in all of the gardens and the bees going backwards and forwards,
For today we have naming of parts.
'Lessons of the War: 1, Naming of Parts' (1946)

10 And the sooner the tea's out of the way, the sooner we can get out the gin, eh?

Private Life of Hilda Tablet (1954 radio play) in *Hilda Tablet and Others* (1971)

11 Modest? My word, no . . . He was an all-the-lights-on man.

A Very Great Man Indeed (1953 radio play) in *Hilda Tablet and Others* (1971)

12 I have known her pass the whole evening without mentioning a single book, or *in fact anything unpleasant*, at all.

A Very Great Man Indeed (1953 radio play) in *Hilda Tablet and Others* (1971)

John Reed 1887–1920

13 Ten days that shook the world.

title of book (1919)

Max Reger 1873–1916

14 I am sitting in the smallest room of my house. I have your review before me. In a moment it will be behind me.

responding to a savage review by Rudolph Louis in München Neueste Nachrichten, *7 February 1906*

Nicolas Slonimsky *Lexicon of Musical Invective* (1953)

Keith Reid 1946–

15 Her face, at first . . . just ghostly
Turned a whiter shade of pale.
'A Whiter Shade of Pale' (1967 song)

Erich Maria Remarque 1898–1970

16 All quiet on the western front.

English title of *Im Westen nichts Neues* (1929 novel); cf. **Beers** 27:14, **McClellan** 206:23

Montague John Rendall 1862–1950

17 Nation shall speak peace unto nation.

motto of the BBC; cf. **Bible** 39:11

Pierre Auguste Renoir 1841–1919

18 I paint with my prick.

perhaps an inversion of 'It's with my brush that I make love'

A. André *Renoir* (1919)

Walter Reuther 1907-70

1 If it looks like a duck, walks like a duck and quacks like a duck, then it just may be a duck.
*as a test, during the **McCarthy** era, of Communist affiliations*
attributed

Paul Revere 1735-1818

2 [We agreed] that if the British went out by water, we would show two lanterns in the North Church steeple; and if by land, one as a signal.
*signals to be used if the British troops moved out of Boston; cf. **Longfellow** 202:5*
arrangements agreed with the Charlestown Committee of Safety on 16 April, 1775

Charles Revson 1906-75

3 In the factory we make cosmetics; in the store we sell hope.
A. Tobias *Fire and Ice* (1976)

Frederic Reynolds 1764-1841

4 It is better to have written a damned play, than no play at all—it snatches a man from obscurity.
The Dramatist (1789) act 1, sc. 1

Joshua Reynolds 1723-92

5 If you have great talents, industry will improve them: if you have but moderate abilities, industry will supply their deficiency.
Discourses on Art (ed. R. Wark, 1975) no. 2 (11 December 1769)

6 Genius . . . is the child of imitation.
Discourses on Art (ed. R. Wark, 1975) no. 6 (10 December 1774)

Malvina Reynolds 1900-78

7 Little boxes on the hillside . . .
And they're all made out of ticky-tacky
And they all look just the same.
on the tract houses in the hills to the south of San Francisco
'Little Boxes' (1962 song)

Cecil Rhodes 1853-1902

8 Ask any man what nationality he would prefer to be, and ninety-nine out of a hundred will tell you that they would prefer to be Englishmen.
Gordon Le Sueur *Cecil Rhodes* (1913)

9 So little done, so much to do.
on the day of his death
Lewis Michell *Life of Rhodes* (1910) vol. 2, ch. 39; cf. **Tennyson** 311:22

Jean Rhys *c.*1890-1979

10 The perpetual hunger to be beautiful and that thirst to be loved which is the real curse of Eve.
The Left Bank (1927) 'Illusion'

11 Love was a terrible thing. You poisoned it and stabbed at it and knocked it down into the mud—well down—and it got up and staggered on, bleeding and muddy and awful. Like—like Rasputin.
Quartet (1928)

12 A doormat in a world of boots.
describing herself
in *Guardian* 6 December 1990

David Ricardo 1772-1823

13 Rent is that portion of the earth, which is paid to the landlord for the use of the original and indestructible powers of the soil.
On the Principles of Political Economy and Taxation (1817) ch. 2

Grantland Rice 1880-1954

14 For when the One Great Scorer comes to mark against your name,
He writes—not that you won or lost—but how you played the Game.
'Alumnus Football' (1941)

15 All wars are planned by old men
In council rooms apart.
'The Two Sides of War' (1955)

Stephen Rice 1637-1715

16 I will drive a coach and six horses through the Act of Settlement.
W. King *State of the Protestants of Ireland* (1672) ch. 3, sect. 8

Mandy Rice-Davies 1944-

17 He would, wouldn't he?
on hearing that Lord Astor denied her allegations, concerning himself and his house parties at Cliveden
at the trial of Stephen Ward, 29 June 1963

Ann Richards 1933-

18 Poor George, he can't help it—he was born with a silver foot in his mouth.
*of George **Bush***
keynote speech at the Democratic convention, 1988

Frank Richards (Charles Hamilton) 1876-1961

19 The fat greedy owl of the Remove.
'Billy Bunter' in the *Magnet* (1909) vol. 3, no. 72 'The Greyfriars Photographer'

Samuel Richardson 1689-1761

20 Mine is the most plotting heart in the world.
Clarissa (1747-8) vol. 3, letter 76

21 The affair is over. Clarissa lives.
announcement by Lovelace of his successful seduction of Clarissa
Clarissa (1747-8) vol. 5, letter 22

22 His spurious brat, Tom Jones.
*of **Fielding***
letter to Thomas Edwards, 21 February 1752

1 Instruction, Madam, is the pill; amusement is the gilding.

letter to Lady Echlin, 22 September 1755

Duc de Richelieu 1585–1642

2 If you give me six lines written by the hand of the most honest of men, I will find something in them which will hang him.

attributed

Hans Richter 1843–1916

3 Up with your damned nonsense will I put twice, or perhaps once, but sometimes always, by God, never.

attributed

Johann Paul Friedrich Richter

('Jean Paul') 1763–1825

4 Providence has given to the French the empire of the land, to the English that of the sea, and to the Germans that of—the air!

Thomas Carlyle 'Jean Paul Friedrich Richter' in *Edinburgh Review* no. 91 (1827)

Nicholas Ridley 1929–93

of the European community:

5 This is all a German racket, designed to take over the whole of Europe.

in *Spectator* 14 July 1990

Rig Veda

6 Whence this creation has arisen—perhaps it formed itself, or perhaps it did not—the one who looks down on it, in the highest heaven, only he knows—or perhaps he does not know.

Creation Hymn bk. 10, hymn 129, v. 7

7 When they divided the Man, into how many parts did they apportion him? What did they call his mouth, his two arms and thighs and feet?

His mouth became the Brahman; his arms were made into the Warrior, his thighs the People, and from his feet the Servants were born.

Hymn of Man bk. 10, hymn 190, v. 11

Rainer Maria Rilke 1875–1926

8 *So leben wir und nehmen immer Abschied.*
We live our lives, for ever taking leave.

Duineser Elegien (tr. J. B. Leishman and Stephen Spender, 1948) no. 8

9 *Wir haben, wo wir lieben, ja nur dies:*
einander lassen; denn dass wir uns halten,
das fällt uns leicht und ist nicht erst zu lernen.
We need in love to practise only this: letting each other go. For holding on comes easily; we do not need to learn it.

Requiem für eine Freundin ('Requiem for a Friend')

Arthur Rimbaud 1854–91

10 . . . *Je me suis baigné dans le Poème*
De la Mer.

I have bathed in the Poem of the Sea.

'Le Bâteau ivre' (1883)

11 *Je regrette l'Europe aux anciens parapets!*
I pine for Europe of the ancient parapets!

'Le Bâteau ivre' (1883)

12 *Ô saisons, ô châteaux!*
Quelle âme est sans défauts?
O seasons, O castles! What soul is without fault?

'Ô saisons, ô châteaux' (1872)

13 *A noir, E blanc, I rouge, U vert, O bleu: voyelles,*
Je dirais quelque jour vos naissances latentes.
A black, E white, I red, U green, O blue: vowels, some day I will tell of the births that may be yours.

'Voyelles' (1870)

César Ritz 1850–1918

14 The customer is never wrong.

R. Nevill and C. E. Jerningham *Piccadilly to Pall Mall* (1908)

Antoine de Rivarol 1753–1801

15 *Ce qui n'est pas clair n'est pas français.*
What is not clear is not French.

Discours sur l'Universalité de la Langue Française (1784)

Lord Robbins 1898–1984

16 Economics is the science which studies human behaviour as a relationship between ends and scarce means which have alternative uses.

Essay on the Nature and Significance of Economic Science (1932) ch. 1, sect. 3

Maximilien Robespierre 1758–94

17 Any law which violates the inalienable rights of man is essentially unjust and tyrannical; it is not a law at all.

Déclaration des droits de l'homme 24 April 1793, article 6

18 Any institution which does not suppose the people good, and the magistrate corruptible, is evil.

Déclaration des droits de l'homme 24 April 1793, article 25

19 Intimidation without virtue is disastrous; virtue without intimidation is powerless.

J. M. Thompson *The French Revolution* (1943); attributed

Leo Robin 1900–84

20 A kiss on the hand may be quite continental,
But diamonds are a girl's best friend.

'Diamonds are a Girl's Best Friend' (1949 song) from the film *Gentlemen Prefer Blondes*; cf. **Loos** 202:15

21 Thanks for the memory.

title of song (with Ralph Rainger, 1937)

Elizabeth Robins 1862–1952

22 To say in print what she thinks is the last thing the woman novelist or journalist is so rash as to attempt . . . Her publishers are not women.

in 1908, as first president of the Women Writers' Suffrage League

Edwin Arlington Robinson
1869–1935

1 I shall have more to say when I am dead.
'John Brown' (1920)

2 Go to the western gate, Luke Havergal,
There where the vines cling crimson on the wall,
And in the twilight wait for what will come.
'Luke Havergal' (1896)

3 And Richard Cory, one calm summer night,
Went home and put a bullet through his head.
'Richard Cory' (1897)

John Robinson 1919–83

4 Honest to God.
title of book (1963)

Mary Robinson 1758–1800

5 Pavement slippery, people sneezing,
Lords in ermine, beggars freezing;
Titled gluttons dainties carving,
Genius in a garret starving.
'January, 1795'

Mary Robinson 1944–

6 Instead of rocking the cradle, they rocked the system.
in her victory speech, paying tribute to the women of Ireland
in *The Times* 10 November 1990; cf. **Wallace** 327:3

Boyle Roche 1743–1807

7 A disorderly set of people whom no king can govern and no God can please.
of the Ulster Protestants
attributed

8 Mr Speaker, I smell a rat; I see him forming in the air and darkening the sky; but I'll nip him in the bud.
attributed

Lord Rochester 1647–80

9 'Is there then no more?'
She cries. 'All this to love and rapture's due;
Must we not pay a debt to pleasure too?'
'The Imperfect Enjoyment' (1680)

10 Here lies a great and mighty king
Whose promise none relies on;
He never said a foolish thing,
Nor ever did a wise one.
of **Charles II***; an alternative first line reads:*
'*Here lies our sovereign lord the King*'
John Wilmot, Earl of Rochester 'The King's Epitaph'; cf. **Charles II** 87:24

11 Natural freedoms are but just:
There's something generous in mere lust.
'A Ramble in St James' Park' (1680)

12 Reason, an *ignis fatuus* of the mind,
Which leaves the light of nature, sense, behind.
'A Satire against Mankind' (1679) l. 11

13 Then Old Age, and Experience, hand in hand,
Lead him to Death, and make him understand . . .
Huddled in dirt the reasoning engine lies,
Who was so proud, so witty and so wise.
'A Satire against Mankind' (1679) l. 25

14 For all men would be cowards if they durst.
'A Satire against Mankind' (1679) l. 158

15 A merry monarch, scandalous and poor.
'A Satire on King Charles II' (1697)

16 Ancient person, for whom I
All the flattering youth defy,
Long be it ere thou grow old,
Aching, shaking, crazy, cold;
But still continue as thou art,
Ancient person of my heart.
'A Song of a Young Lady to her Ancient Lover' (1691)

John D. Rockefeller 1839–1937

17 The growth of a large business is merely a survival of the fittest . . . The American beauty rose can be produced in the splendour and fragrance which bring cheer to its beholder only by sacrificing the early buds which grow up around it.
W. J. Ghent *Our Benevolent Feudalism* (1902); 'American Beauty Rose' became the title of a 1950 song by Hal David and others; cf. **Darwin** 106:9, **Spencer** 300:3

Gene Roddenberry 1921–91

18 These are the voyages of the starship *Enterprise*. Its five-year mission . . . to boldly go where no man has gone before.
Star Trek (television series, from 1966)

19 Beam us up, Mr Scott.
often misquoted as, 'Beam me up, Scotty'
Star Trek (1966 onwards) 'Gamesters of Triskelion'

Anita Roddick 1942–

20 I think that business practices would improve immeasurably if they were guided by 'feminine' principles—qualities like love and care and intuition.
Body and Soul (1991)

Theodore Roethke 1908–63

21 I have known the inexorable sadness of pencils,
Neat in their boxes, dolour of pad and paper-weight,
All the misery of manilla folders and mucilage,
Desolation in immaculate public places.
'Dolour' (1948)

22 O who can be
Both moth and flame? The weak moth blundering by.

Whom do we love? I thought I knew the truth;
Of grief I died, but no one knew my death.
'The Sequel' (1964)

Samuel Rogers 1763-1855

1 Think nothing done while aught remains to do.
'Human Life' (1819) l. 49; cf. **Lucan** 204:8

2 But there are moments which he calls his own,
Then, never less alone than when alone,
Those whom he loved so long and sees no more,
Loved and still loves—not dead—but gone before,
He gathers round him.
'Human Life' (1819) l. 755; cf. **Cyprian** 105:11,
Norton 234:23

3 It doesn't much signify whom one marries, for one is sure to find next morning that it was someone else.
Alexander Dyce (ed.) *Table Talk of Samuel Rogers* (1860)

Will Rogers 1879-1935

4 Income Tax has made more Liars out of the American people than Golf.
The Illiterate Digest (1924) 'Helping the Girls with their Income Taxes'

5 Everything is funny as long as it is happening to Somebody Else.
The Illiterate Digest (1924) 'Warning to Jokers: lay off the prince'

6 Well, all I know is what I read in the papers.
in *New York Times* 30 September 1923

7 You can't say civilization don't advance, however, for in every war they kill you in a new way.
in *New York Times* 23 December 1929

Mies van der Rohe 1886-1969

8 God is in the details.
in *New York Times* 19 August 1969

Mme Roland 1754-93

9 *Ô liberté! Ô liberté! que de crimes on commet en ton nom!*
O liberty! O liberty! what crimes are committed in thy name!
before being guillotined
A. de Lamartine *Histoire des Girondins* (1847) bk. 51, ch. 8

Richard Rolle de Hampole
*c.*1290-1349

10 When Adam dalfe and Eve spane
Go spire if thou may spede,
Where was than the pride of man
That now merres his mede?
G. G. Perry *Religious Pieces* (Early English Text Society, Original Series no. 26, revised ed. 1914)

Pierre de Ronsard 1524-85

11 *Quand vous serez bien vieille, au soir, à la chandelle,
Assise auprès du feu, dévidant et filant,
Direz, chantant mes vers, en vous émerveillant,
Ronsard me célébrait du temps que j'étais belle.*
When you are very old, and sit in the candle-light at evening spinning by the fire, you will say, as you murmur my verses, a wonder in your eyes, 'Ronsard sang of me in the days when I was fair.'
Sonnets pour Hélène (1578) bk. 2, no. 42

Eleanor Roosevelt 1884-1962

12 No one can make you feel inferior without your consent.
in *Catholic Digest* August 1960

Franklin D. Roosevelt 1882-1945

13 The forgotten man at the bottom of the economic pyramid.
radio address, 7 April 1932

14 I pledge you, I pledge myself, to a new deal for the American people.
speech to the Democratic Convention in Chicago, 2 July 1932, accepting the presidential nomination

15 The only thing we have to fear is fear itself.
inaugural address, 4 March 1933

16 In the field of world policy I would dedicate this Nation to the policy of the good neighbour.
inaugural address, 4 March 1933

17 I have seen war . . . I hate war.
speech at Chautauqua, NY, 14 August 1936

18 I see one-third of a nation ill-housed, ill-clad, ill-nourished.
second inaugural address, 20 January 1937

19 We must be the great arsenal of democracy.
'Fireside Chat' radio broadcast, 29 December 1940

20 We look forward to a world founded upon four essential human freedoms. The first is freedom of speech and expression—everywhere in the world. The second is freedom of every person to worship God in his own way—everywhere in the world. The third is freedom from want . . . The fourth is freedom from fear.
message to Congress, 6 January 1941

21 Yesterday, December 7, 1941—a date which will live in infamy—the United States of America was suddenly and deliberately attacked by naval and air forces of the Empire of Japan.
address to Congress, 8 December 1941

Theodore Roosevelt 1858-1919

22 Speak softly and carry a big stick; you will go far.
speech in Chicago, 3 April 1903

1 A man who is good enough to shed his blood for the country is good enough to be given a square deal afterwards.

   speech at the Lincoln Monument, Springfield, Illinois, 4 June 1903

2 The men with the muck-rakes are often indispensable to the well-being of society; but only if they know when to stop raking the muck.

   speech in Washington, 14 April 1906; cf. **Bunyan** 73:7

3 It is not the critic who counts; not the man who points out how the strong man stumbles, or where the doer of deeds could have done better. The credit belongs to the man who is actually in the arena.

   'Citizenship in a Republic', speech at the Sorbonne, Paris, 23 April 1910

4 There is no room in this country for hyphenated Americanism.

   speech in New York, 12 October 1915

5 One of our defects as a nation is a tendency to use what have been called 'weasel words'. When a weasel sucks eggs the meat is sucked out of the egg. If you use a 'weasel word' after another, there is nothing left of the other.

   speech in St Louis, 31 May 1916

6 I have got such a bully pulpit!

   his personal view of the presidency
   in *Outlook* (New York) 27 February 1909; cf. **Reagan** 254:22

Lord Rosebery 1847–1929

7 I have never known the sweets of place with power, but of place without power, of place with the minimum of power—that is a purgatory, and if not a purgatory it is a hell.

   in *Spectator* 6 July 1895

8 There are two supreme pleasures in life. One is ideal, the other real. The ideal is when a man receives the seals of office from his Sovereign. The real pleasure comes when he hands them back.

   Sir Robert Peel (1899)

Ethel Rosenberg 1916–53 and Julius Rosenberg 1918–53

9 We are innocent . . . To forsake this truth is to pay too high a price even for the priceless gift of life.

   petition for executive clemency, filed 9 January 1953

Christina Rossetti 1830–94

10 My heart is like a singing bird
Whose nest is in a watered shoot.

   'A Birthday' (1862)

11 Come to me in the silence of the night;
Come in the speaking silence of a dream.

   'Echo' (1862)

12 In the bleak mid-winter
Frosty wind made moan,

Earth stood hard as iron,
Water like a stone;
Snow had fallen, snow on snow,
Snow on snow,
In the bleak mid-winter,
Long ago.

   'Mid-Winter' (1875)

13 Better by far you should forget and smile
Than that you should remember and be sad.

   'Remember' (1862)

14 Does the road wind up-hill all the way?
Yes, to the very end.
Will the day's journey take the whole long day?
From morn to night, my friend.

   'Up-Hill' (1862)

15 Our Indian Crown is in great measure the trapping of a splendid misery.

   letter to Amelia Heimann, 29 July 1880

Dante Gabriel Rossetti 1828–82

16 The blessed damozel leaned out
From the gold bar of Heaven;
Her eyes were deeper than the depth
Of waters stilled at even;
She had three lilies in her hand,
And the stars in her hair were seven.

   'The Blessed Damozel' (1870) st. 1

17 Look in my face; my name is Might-have-been;
I am also called No-more, Too-late, Farewell.

   The House of Life (1881) pt. 2 'A Superscription'

18 Sleepless with cold commemorative eyes.

   The House of Life (1881) pt. 2 'A Superscription'

19 I have been here before,
But when or how I cannot tell:
I know the grass beyond the door,
The sweet keen smell,
The sighing sound, the lights around the shore.

   'Sudden Light' (1870)

20 'I saw the Sibyl at Cumae'
(One said) 'with mine own eye.
She hung in a cage, and read her rune
To all the passers-by.
Said the boys, "What wouldst thou, Sibyl?"
She answered, "I would die." '

   translation of Petronius *Satyricon* 'Cena Trimalchionis' ch. 48, sect. 8; cf. **Petronius** 244:11

Gioacchino Rossini 1792–1868

21 Wagner has lovely moments but awful quarters of an hour.

   to Emile Naumann, April 1867, in E. Naumann *Italienische Tondichter* (1883) vol. 4

Edmond Rostand 1868–1918

22 A large nose is in fact the sign of an affable man, good, courteous, witty, liberal, courageous, such as I am.

   Cyrano de Bergerac (1897) act 1, sc. 1

1 There is, in spite of you, something which I
shall take with me . . . and it's . . . My
panache!
Cyrano de Bergerac (1897) act 5, sc. 4

Jean Rostand 1894–1977

2 The biologist passes, the frog remains.
*sometimes quoted as 'Theories pass. The frog
remains'*
Inquiétudes d'un biologiste (1967)

3 Kill a man, and you are an assassin. Kill
millions of men, and you are a conqueror.
Kill everyone, and you are a god.
Pensées d'un biologiste (1939) p. 116; cf. **Porteus**
249:22, **Young** 344:12

Leo Rosten 1908–97

4 Any man who hates dogs and babies can't
be all bad.
of W. C. Fields, and often attributed to him
speech at Masquers' Club dinner, 16 February
1939

Philip Roth 1933–

5 A Jewish man with parents alive is a fifteen-
year-old boy, and will remain a fifteen-year-
old boy until *they die!*
Portnoy's Complaint (1967)

6 Doctor, my doctor, what do you say, LET'S
PUT THE ID BACK IN YID!
Portnoy's Complaint (1967)

Lord Rothschild 1910–90

7 The promises and panaceas that gleam like
false teeth in the party manifestoes.
Meditations of a Broomstick (1977)

Claude-Joseph Rouget de Lisle
1760–1836

8 *Allons, enfants de la patrie,
Le jour de gloire est arrivé . . .
Aux armes, citoyens!
Formez vos battaillons!*
Come, children of our country, the day of
glory has arrived . . . To arms, citizens! Form
your battalions!
'La Marseillaise' (25 April 1792)

Charles Roupell

9 To play billiards well is a sign of an ill-spent
youth.
attributed, in D. Duncan *Life of Herbert Spencer*
(1908) ch. 20

Jean-Jacques Rousseau 1712–78

10 The social contract.
title of book, *Du contrat social* (1762)

11 Man was born free, and everywhere he is in
chains.
Du Contrat social (1762) ch. 1

Martin Joseph Routh 1755–1854

12 You will find it a very good practice always
to verify your references, sir!
John William Burgon *Lives of Twelve Good Men*
(1888 ed.) vol. 1

Matthew Rowbottom, Richard
Stannard, and The Spice Girls

13 Yo I'll tell you what I want, what I really
really want
so tell me what you want, what you really
really want.
'Wannabe' (1996 song)

Nicholas Rowe 1674–1718

14 Is this that haughty, gallant, gay Lothario?
The Fair Penitent (1703) act 5, sc. 1

Helen Rowland 1875–1950

15 A husband is what is left of a lover, after the
nerve has been extracted.
A Guide to Men (1922)

Richard Rowland c.1881–1947

16 The lunatics have taken charge of the
asylum.
*on the take-over of United Artists by Charles
Chaplin and others*
Terry Ramsaye *A Million and One Nights* (1926)
vol. 2, ch. 79

Maude Royden 1876–1956

17 The Church should go forward along the
path of progress and be no longer satisfied
only to represent the Conservative Party at
prayer.
address at Queen's Hall, London, 16 July 1917

Naomi Royde-Smith c.1875–1964

18 I know two things about the horse
And one of them is rather coarse.
Weekend Book (1928)

Paul Alfred Rubens 1875–1917

19 Oh! we don't want to lose you but we think
you ought to go
For your King and your Country both need
you so.
'Your King and Country Want You' (1914 song);
cf. **Anonymous** 11:7

Richard Rumbold c.1622–85

20 I never could believe that Providence had
sent a few men into the world, ready booted
and spurred to ride, and millions ready
saddled and bridled to be ridden.
on the scaffold
T. B. Macaulay *History of England* vol. 1 (1849) ch.
1

Robert Runcie 1921–2000

21 People are mourning on both sides of this
conflict. In our prayers we shall quite

rightly remember those who are bereaved in our own country and the relations of the young Argentinian soldiers who were killed. Common sorrow could do something to reunite those who were engaged in this struggle. A shared anguish can be a bridge of reconciliation. Our neighbours are indeed like us.

service of thanksgiving at the end of the Falklands war, St. Paul's Cathedral, London, 26 July 1982

Damon Runyon 1884–1946

1 Guys and dolls.
title of book (1931)

2 'My boy,' he says, 'always try to rub up against money, for if you rub up against money long enough, some of it may rub off on you.'
in *Cosmopolitan* August 1929, 'A Very Honourable Guy'

3 I long ago come to the conclusion that all life is 6 to 5 against.
in *Collier's* 8 September 1934, 'A Nice Price'

Salman Rushdie 1947–

4 One of the things a writer is for is to say the unsayable, speak the unspeakable and ask difficult questions.
in *Independent on Sunday* 10 September 1995 'Quotes of the Week'

5 It means everything—it means freedom.
on the news that the fatwa had effectively been lifted
in *Mail on Sunday* 27 September 1998

Dean Rusk 1909–94

6 We're eyeball to eyeball, and I think the other fellow just blinked.
on the Cuban missile crisis, 24 October 1962
in *Saturday Evening Post* 8 December 1962

John Ruskin 1819–1900

7 I have seen, and heard, much of Cockney impudence before now; but never expected to hear a coxcomb ask two hundred guineas for flinging a pot of paint in the public's face.
*on **Whistler**'s Nocturne in Black and Gold*
Fors Clavigera (1871–84) Letter 79, 18 June 1877; cf. **Whistler** 333:5

8 Life without industry is guilt, and industry without art is brutality.
Lectures on Art (1870) Lecture 3 'The Relation of Art to Morals' sect. 95

9 All violent feelings . . . produce in us a falseness in all our impressions of external things, which I would generally characterize as the 'Pathetic Fallacy'.
Modern Painters (1856) vol. 3, pt. 4, ch. 12

10 To see clearly is poetry, prophecy, and religion—all in one.
Modern Painters (1856) vol. 3, pt. 4 'Of Modern Landscape'

11 Mountains are the beginning and the end of all natural scenery.
Modern Painters (1856) vol. 4, pt. 5, ch. 20

12 All books are divisible into two classes, the books of the hour, and the books of all time.
Sesame and Lilies (1865) 'Of Kings' Treasuries'

13 How long most people would look at the best book before they would give the price of a large turbot for it.
Sesame and Lilies (1865) 'Of Kings' Treasuries'

14 We call ourselves a rich nation, and we are filthy and foolish enough to thumb each other's books out of circulating libraries!
Sesame and Lilies (1865) 'Of Kings' Treasuries'

15 When we build, let us think that we build for ever.
Seven Lamps of Architecture (1849) 'The Lamp of Memory' sect. 10

16 Remember that the most beautiful things in the world are the most useless; peacocks and lilies for instance.
Stones of Venice vol. 1 (1851) ch. 2, sect. 17

17 Labour without joy is base. Labour without sorrow is base. Sorrow without labour is base. Joy without labour is base.
Time and Tide (1867) Letter 5

18 The first duty of a State is to see that every child born therein shall be well housed, clothed, fed and educated, till it attain years of discretion.
Time and Tide (1867) Letter 13

Bertrand Russell 1872–1970

19 One of the symptoms of approaching nervous breakdown is the belief that one's work is terribly important, and that to take a holiday would bring all kinds of disaster.
The Conquest of Happiness (1930) ch. 5

20 To be able to fill leisure intelligently is the last product of civilization.
The Conquest of Happiness (1930) ch. 14

21 Work is of two kinds: first, altering the position of matter at or near the earth's surface relatively to other such matter; second, telling other people to do so. The first kind is unpleasant and ill paid; the second is pleasant and highly paid.
In Praise of Idleness and Other Essays (1986) title essay (1932)

22 Mathematics may be defined as the subject in which we never know what we are talking about, nor whether what we are saying is true.
Mysticism and Logic (1918) ch. 4

23 Mathematics, rightly viewed, possesses not only truth, but supreme beauty—a beauty cold and austere, like that of sculpture.
Philosophical Essays (1910) no. 4

24 It is obvious that 'obscenity' is not a term capable of exact legal definition; in the practice of the Courts, it means 'anything that shocks the magistrate'.
Sceptical Essays (1928) 'The Recrudescence of Puritanism'

George William Russell *see* Æ

Lord John Russell 1792–1878

1 It is impossible that the whisper of a faction should prevail against the voice of a nation.
reply to an Address from a meeting of 150,000 persons at Birmingham on the defeat of the second Reform Bill, October 1831
S. Walpole *Life of Lord John Russell* (1889) vol. 1, ch. 7

2 If peace cannot be maintained with honour, it is no longer peace.
speech at Greenock, 19 September 1853; cf. **Chamberlain** 86:20, **Disraeli** 112:14

William Howard Russell 1820–1907

3 They dashed on towards that thin red line tipped with steel.
of the Russians charging the British at the battle of Balaclava, 1854
The British Expedition to the Crimea (1877); Russell's original dispatch read, 'That thin red streak topped with a line of steel'

Ernest Rutherford 1871–1937

4 All science is either physics or stamp collecting.
J. B. Birks *Rutherford at Manchester* (1962)

5 We haven't got the money, so we've got to think!
in *Bulletin of the Institute of Physics* (1962) vol. 13 (as recalled by R. V. Jones)

Gilbert Ryle 1900–76

6 Philosophy is the replacement of category-habits by category-disciplines.
The Concept of Mind (1949) introduction

7 The dogma of the Ghost in the Machine.
on the mental-conduct concepts of **Descartes**
The Concept of Mind (1949) ch. 1

Vita Sackville-West 1892–1962

8 The greater cats with golden eyes
Stare out between the bars.
The King's Daughter (1929) pt. 2, no. 1

Anwar al-Sadat 1918–81

9 Peace is much more precious than a piece of land.
speech in Cairo, 8 March 1978

Françoise Sagan 1935–

10 To jealousy, nothing is more frightful than laughter.
La Chamade (1965) ch. 9

Charles-Augustin Sainte-Beuve 1804–69

11 Et Vigny plus secret,
Comme en sa tour d'ivoire, avant midi rentrait.
And Vigny more discreet, as if in his ivory tower, returned before noon.
Les Pensées d'Août, à M. Villemain (1837)

Antoine de Saint-Exupéry 1900–44

12 Grown-ups never understand anything for themselves, and it is tiresome for children to be always and forever explaining things to them.
Le Petit Prince (1943) ch. 1

Saki 1870–1916

13 Waldo is one of those people who would be enormously improved by death.
Beasts and Super-Beasts (1914) 'The Feast of Nemesis'

14 The cook was a good cook, as cooks go; and as cooks go, she went.
Reginald (1904) 'Reginald on Besetting Sins'

15 I always say beauty is only sin deep.
Reginald (1904) 'Reginald's Choir Treat'

16 We all know that Prime Ministers are wedded to the truth, but like other married couples they sometimes live apart.
The Unbearable Bassington (1912) ch. 13

J. D. Salinger 1919–

17 I keep picturing all these little kids playing some game in this big field of rye and all . . . I mean if they're running and they don't look where they're going I have to come out from somewhere and catch them. That's all I'd do all day. I'd just be the catcher in the rye.
The Catcher in the Rye (1951) ch. 22

Lord Salisbury (3rd Marquess of Salisbury) 1830–1903

18 Too clever by half.
of **Disraeli**'s *amendment on Disestablishment*
speech, House of Commons, 30 March 1868; cf. **Salisbury** 263:23

19 English policy is to float lazily downstream, occasionally putting out a diplomatic boathook to avoid collisions.
letter to Lord Lytton, 9 March 1877

20 We are part of the community of Europe and we must do our duty as such.
speech at Caernarvon, 10 April 1888

21 Horny-handed sons of toil.
in *Quarterly Review* October 1873; later popularized in the US by Denis Kearney (1847–1907); cf. **Lowell** 203:17

22 By office boys for office boys.
of the Daily Mail
H. Hamilton Fyfe *Northcliffe, an Intimate Biography* (1930) ch. 4

Lord Salisbury (5th Marquess of Salisbury) 1893–1972

23 Too clever by half.
of Iain Macleod, Colonial Secretary 'in his relationship to the white communities of Africa'
in the House of Lords, 7 March 1961; cf. **Salisbury** 263:18

Sallust 86–35 BC

1 A venal city ripe to perish, if a buyer can be found.
of Rome
Jugurtha ch. 35

2 *Punica fide.*
With Carthaginian trustworthiness.
meaning treachery
Jugurtha ch. 108, sect. 3

Lord Samuel 1870–1963

3 A library is thought in cold storage.
A Book of Quotations (1947)

Paul A. Samuelson 1915–

4 The consumer, so it is said, is the king . . . each is a voter who uses his money as votes to get the things done that he wants done.
Economics (8th ed., 1970)

George Sand 1804–76

5 We cannot tear out a single page of our life, but we can throw the book in the fire.
Mauprat (1837)

6 There is only one happiness in life, to love and be loved.
letter to Lina Calamatta, 31 March 1862

Carl Sandburg 1878–1967

7 Hog Butcher for the World,
Tool Maker, Stacker of Wheat,
Player with Railroads and the Nation's
Freight Handler;
Stormy, husky, brawling,
City of the Big Shoulders.
'Chicago' (1916)

8 The fog comes
on little cat feet.
It sits looking
over harbour and city
on silent haunches
and then moves on.
'Fog' (1916)

9 Pile the bodies high at Austerlitz and Waterloo.
Shovel them under and let me work—
I am the grass; I cover all.
'Grass' (1918)

10 Little girl . . . Sometime they'll give a war and nobody will come.
The People, Yes (1936); cf. **Ginsberg** 141:13

11 Poetry is the achievement of the synthesis of hyacinths and biscuits.
in *Atlantic Monthly* March 1923 'Poetry Considered'

12 Slang is a language that rolls up its sleeves, spits on its hands and goes to work.
in *New York Times* 13 February 1959

Henry 'Red' Sanders

13 Sure, winning isn't everything. It's the only thing.
in *Sports Illustrated* 26 December 1955; often attributed to Vince Lombardi

Lord Sandwich 1718–92

14 If any man will draw up his case, and put his name at the foot of the first page, I will give him an immediate reply. Where he compels me to turn over the sheet, he must wait my leisure.
N. W. Wraxall *Memoirs* (1884) vol. 1

Martha Sansom 1690–1736

15 Foolish eyes, thy streams give over,
Wine, not water, binds the lover.
'Song' (written c.1726)

George Santayana 1863–1952

16 Fanaticism consists in redoubling your effort when you have forgotten your aim.
The Life of Reason (1905) vol. 1, introduction

17 Those who cannot remember the past are condemned to repeat it.
The Life of Reason (1905) vol. 1, ch. 12

Sappho

18 Just as the sweet-apple reddens on the high branch, high on the highest, and the apple-pickers missed it, or rather did not miss it out, but could not reach it.
describing a girl before her marriage
D. L. Page (ed.) *Lyrica Graeca Selecta* (1968) no. 224

John Singer Sargent 1856–1925

19 Every time I paint a portrait I lose a friend.
N. Bentley and E. Esar *Treasury of Humorous Quotations* (1951)

Leslie Sarony 1897–1985

20 Ain't it grand to be blooming well dead?
title of song (1932)

Patrick Sarsfield c.1655–93

21 Would to God this wound had been for Ireland.
on being mortally wounded at the battle of Landen, 19 August 1693, while fighting for France
attributed

Jean-Paul Sartre 1905–80

22 I am condemned to be free.
L'Être et le néant (1943) pt. 4, ch. 1

23 Hell is other people.
Huis Clos (1944) sc. 5; cf. **Eliot** 121:17

24 Human life begins on the far side of despair.
Les Mouches (1943) act 3, sc. 2

25 I hate victims who respect their executioners.
Les Séquestrés d'Altona (1960) act 1, sc. 1

Siegfried Sassoon 1886–1967

26 If I were fierce, and bald, and short of breath,
I'd live with scarlet Majors at the Base,
And speed glum heroes up the line to death.
'Base Details' (1918)

1 Does it matter?—losing your sight? . . .
There's such splendid work for the blind;
And people will always be kind,
As you sit on the terrace remembering
And turning your face to the light.
  'Does it Matter?' (1918)

2 Everyone suddenly burst out singing;
And I was filled with such delight
As prisoned birds must find in freedom.
  'Everyone Sang' (1919)

3 'He's a cheery old card,' grunted Harry to Jack
As they slogged up to Arras with rifle and pack.
But he did for them both by his plan of attack.
  'The General' (1918)

4 Here was the world's worst wound. And here with pride
'Their name liveth for ever' the Gateway claims.
  'On Passing the New Menin Gate' (1928); cf. **Anonymous** 10:5

Cicely Saunders 1916–

5 Deception is not as creative as truth. We do best in life if we look at it with clear eyes, and I think that applies to coming up to death as well.
  of the Hospice movement
    in *Time* 5 September 1988

George Savile *see* Lord Halifax

Dorothy L. Sayers 1893–1957

6 I admit it is better fun to punt than to be punted, and that a desire to have all the fun is nine-tenths of the law of chivalry.
  Gaudy Night (1935) ch. 14

7 I always have a quotation for everything—it saves original thinking.
  Have His Carcase (1932)

Gerald Scarfe 1936–

8 I find a particular delight in taking the caricature as far as I can. It satisfies me to stretch the human frame about and recreate it and yet keep a likeness.
  Scarfe by Scarfe (1986)

Arthur Scargill 1938–

9 Parliament itself would not exist in its present form had people not defied the law.
  evidence to House of Commons Select Committee on Employment, 2 April 1980

Friedrich von Schelling 1775–1854

10 Architecture in general is frozen music.
  Philosophie der Kunst (1809)

Friedrich von Schiller 1759–1805

11 *Freude, schöner Götterfunken,*
Tochter aus Elysium,
Wir betreten feuertrunken,
Himmlische, dein Heiligtum.
Deine Zauber binden wieder,
Was die Mode streng geteilt.

Joy, beautiful radiance of the gods, daughter of Elysium, we set foot in your heavenly shrine dazzled by your brilliance. Your charms re-unite what common use has harshly divided.
  'An die Freude' (1785)

12 The sun does not set in my dominions.
  Philip II
    Don Carlos (1787) act 1, sc. 6; cf. **North** 234:20

13 With stupidity the gods themselves struggle in vain.
  The Maid of Orleans (1801) act 3, sc. 6

14 The world's history is the world's judgement.
  'Resignation' (1786) st. 19

Moritz Schlick 1882–1936

15 The meaning of a proposition is the method of its verification.
  Philosophical Review (1936) vol. 45

Artur Schnabel 1882–1951

16 The notes I handle no better than many pianists. But the pauses between the notes—ah, that is where the art resides!
  in *Chicago Daily News* 11 June 1958

Budd Schulberg 1914–

17 What makes Sammy run?
  title of book (1941)

E. F. Schumacher 1911–77

18 Small is beautiful. A study of economics as if people mattered.
  title of book (1973)

Robert Schumann 1810–56

19 Hats off, gentlemen—a genius!
  of Chopin
    'An Opus 2' (1831); H. Pleasants (ed.) *Schumann on Music* (1965)

J. A. Schumpeter 1883–1950

20 The cold metal of economic theory is in Marx's pages immersed in such a wealth of steaming phrases as to acquire a temperature not naturally its own.
  Capitalism, Socialism and Democracy (1942)

Carl Schurz 1829–1906

21 My country, right or wrong; if right, to be kept right; and if wrong, to be set right!
  speech, US Senate, 29 February 1872; cf. **Decatur** 107:11

Kurt Schwitters 1887–1948

22 I am a painter and I nail my pictures together.
  R. Hausmann *Am Anfang war Dada* (1972)

C. P. Scott 1846–1932

1 Comment is free, but facts are sacred.
  in *Manchester Guardian* 5 May 1921; cf.
  Stoppard 304:16

2 *Television?* The word is half Greek, half Latin.
  No good can come of it.
  Asa Briggs *The BBC: the First Fifty Years* (1985)

Robert Falcon Scott 1868–1912

3 Great God! this is an awful place.
  of the South Pole
  diary, 17 January 1912

4 For God's sake look after our people.
  last diary entry, 29 March 1912

Sir Walter Scott 1771–1832

5 But answer came there none.
  The Bridal of Triermain (1813) canto 3, st. 10; cf.
  Carroll 84:7

6 Come open the West Port, and let me gang
  free,
  And it's room for the bonnets of Bonny
  Dundee!'
  The Doom of Devorgoil (1830) act 2, sc. 2 'Bonny
  Dundee'

7 Yet seemed that tone, and gesture bland,
  Less used to sue than to command.
  The Lady of the Lake (1810) canto 1, st. 21; cf.
  Shakespeare 285:8

8 And the stern joy which warriors feel
  In foemen worthy of their steel.
  The Lady of the Lake (1810) canto 5, st. 10

9 If thou would'st view fair Melrose aright,
  Go visit it by the pale moonlight.
  The Lay of the Last Minstrel (1805) canto 2, st. 1

10 Breathes there the man, with soul so dead,
  Who never to himself hath said,
  This is my own, my native land!
  The Lay of the Last Minstrel (1805) canto 6, st. 1

11 Unwept, unhonoured, and unsung.
  The Lay of the Last Minstrel (1805) canto 6, st. 1

12 O Caledonia! stern and wild,
  Meet nurse for a poetic child!
  The Lay of the Last Minstrel (1805) canto 6, st. 2

13 O! many a shaft, at random sent,
  Finds mark the archer little meant!
  And many a word, at random spoken,
  May soothe or wound a heart that's broken.
  The Lord of the Isles (1813) canto 5, st. 18

14 Had'st thou but lived, though stripped of
  power,
  A watchman on the lonely tower.
  Marmion (1808) introduction to canto 1, st. 8

15 And come he slow, or come he fast,
  It is but Death who comes at last.
  Marmion (1808) canto 2, st. 30

16 O, young Lochinvar is come out of the west,
  Through all the wide Border his steed was
  the best.
  Marmion (1808) canto 5, st. 12 ('Lochinvar' st. 1)

17 So faithful in love, and so dauntless in war,
  There never was knight like the young
  Lochinvar.
  Marmion (1808) canto 5, st. 12 ('Lochinvar' st. 1)

18 O what a tangled web we weave,
  When first we practise to deceive!
  Marmion (1808) canto 6, st. 17

19 O Woman! in our hours of ease,
  Uncertain, coy, and hard to please,
  And variable as the shade
  By the light quivering aspen made;
  When pain and anguish wring the brow,
  A ministering angel thou!
  Marmion (1808) canto 6, st. 30; cf. **Shakespeare**
  273:13

20 Vacant heart and hand, and eye,—
  Easy live and quiet die.
  The Bride of Lammermoor (1819) ch. 2

21 Touch not the cat but a glove.
  '*but*' = *without*
  The Fair Maid of Perth (1828) ch. 34

22 And three wild lads were we;
  Thou on the land, and I on the sand,
  And Jack on the gallows-tree!
  Guy Mannering (1815) ch. 34

23 The hour is come, but not the man.
  The Heart of Midlothian (1818) ch. 4, title

24 March, march, Eskdale and Liddesdale,
  All the Blue Bonnets are bound for the
  Border.
  The Monastery (1820) ch. 25

25 There's a gude time coming.
  Rob Roy (1817) ch. 32

26 The play-bill, which is said to have
  announced the tragedy of Hamlet, the
  character of the Prince of Denmark being
  left out.
  *commonly alluded to as 'Hamlet without the
  Prince'*
  The Talisman (1825) introduction; W. J. Parke
  Musical Memories (1830) vol. 1 gives a similar
  anecdote from 1787

27 The Big Bow-Wow strain I can do myself like
  any now going; but the exquisite touch,
  which renders ordinary commonplace
  things and characters interesting, from the
  truth of the description and the sentiment,
  is denied to me.
  on Jane **Austen**
  W. E. K. Anderson (ed.) *Journals of Sir Walter Scott*
  (1972) 14 March 1826; cf. **Pembroke** 243:7

Scottish Metrical Psalms 1650

28 The Lord's my shepherd, I'll not want.
  He makes me down to lie
  In pastures green: he leadeth me
  the quiet waters by.
  Psalm 23, v. 1; cf. **Book of Common Prayer**
  61:6

29 My head thou dost with oil anoint,
  and my cup overflows.
  Psalm 23, v. 1; cf. **Book of Common Prayer**
  61:7

1 I to the hills will lift mine eyes
from whence doth come mine aid.
Psalm 121, v. 1; cf. **Book of Common Prayer**
63:12

Edmund Hamilton Sears 1810–76

2 It came upon the midnight clear,
That glorious song of old,
From Angels bending near the earth
To touch their harps of gold.
The Christian Register (1850) 'That Glorious Song
of Old'

John Sedgwick d. 1864

3 They couldn't hit an elephant at this
distance.
*comment of a Union general, immediately prior to
being killed by enemy fire at the battle of
Spotsylvania in the American Civil War*
Robert Denney *The Civil War Years* (1992)

Charles Sedley c.1639–1701

4 Phyllis, without frown or smile,
Sat and knotted all the while.
'Phyllis Knotting' (1694)

Alan Seeger 1888–1916

5 I have a rendezvous with Death
At some disputed barricade.
'I Have a Rendezvous with Death' (1916)

Pete Seeger 1919–

6 Where have all the flowers gone?
title of song (1961)

John Seeley 1834–95

7 We [the English] seem, as it were, to have
conquered and peopled half the world in a
fit of absence of mind.
The Expansion of England (1883) Lecture 1

Erich Segal 1937–

8 Love means not ever having to say you're
sorry.
Love Story (1970)

Sei Shōnagon c.966–c.1013

9 If writing did not exist, what terrible
depressions we should suffer from.
The Pillow Book

John Selden 1584–1654

10 *Scrutamini scripturas* [Let us look at the
scriptures]. These two words have undone
the world.
Table Talk (1689) 'Bible Scripture'

11 Ignorance of the law excuses no man; not
that all men know the law, but because 'tis
an excuse every man will plead, and no
man can tell how to confute him.
Table Talk (1689) 'Law'

12 There never was a merry world since the
fairies left off dancing, and the Parson left
conjuring.
Table Talk (1689) 'Parson'

13 Syllables govern the world.
Table Talk (1689) 'Power: State'

Arthur Seldon 1916–

14 Government of the busy by the bossy for
the bully.
on over-government
Capitalism (1990)

W. C. Sellar 1898–1951
and R. J. Yeatman 1898–1968

15 1066 and all That
title of book (1930)

16 History is not what you thought. *It is what
you can remember.*
1066 and All That (1930) 'Compulsory Preface'

17 'Honi soie qui mal y pense' ('Honey, your
silk stocking's hanging down').
1066 and All That (1930) ch. 24; cf. **Anonymous**
11:12

18 The Cavaliers (Wrong but Wromantic) and
the Roundheads (Right but Repulsive).
1066 and All That (1930) ch. 35

19 The National Debt is a very Good Thing and
it would be dangerous to pay it off, for fear
of Political Economy.
1066 and All That (1930) ch. 38

20 Gladstone . . . spent his declining years
trying to guess the answer to the Irish
Question; unfortunately whenever he was
getting warm, the Irish secretly changed the
Question.
1066 and All That (1930) ch. 57

21 AMERICA was thus clearly top nation, and
History came to a .
1066 and All That (1930) ch. 62

Seneca ('the Younger') c.4 BC–AD 65

22 *Homines dum docent discunt.*
Even while they teach, men learn.
Epistulae Morales no. 7, sect. 8

23 Anyone can stop a man's life, but no one his
death; a thousand doors open on to it.
Phoenissae l. 152; cf. **Massinger** 215:1, **Webster**
330:11

Gitta Sereny 1923–

*to Albert Speer, who having always denied
knowledge of the Holocaust had said that he was
at fault in having 'looked away':*
24 You cannot look away from something you
don't know. If you looked away, then you
knew.
recalled on BBC2 *Reputations*, 2 May 1996

Robert W. Service 1874–1958

25 A promise made is a debt unpaid, and the
trail has its own stern code.
'The Cremation of Sam McGee' (1907)

26 Ah! the clock is always slow;
It is later than you think.
'It Is Later Than You Think' (1921)

1 This is the law of the Yukon, that only the
Strong shall thrive;
That surely the Weak shall perish, and only
the Fit survive.
'The Law of the Yukon' (1907)

2 When we, the Workers, all demand: 'What
are WE fighting for?' . . .
Then, then we'll end that stupid crime, that
devil's madness—War.
'Michael' (1921)

3 Back of the bar, in a solo game, sat
Dangerous Dan McGrew,
And watching his luck was his light-o'-love,
the lady that's known as Lou.
'The Shooting of Dan McGrew' (1907)

Edward Sexby d. 1658

4 Killing no murder briefly discourst in three
questions.
an apology for tyrannicide
title of pamphlet (1657)

Anne Sexton 1928–74

5 In a dream you are never eighty.
'Old' (1962)

Thomas Shadwell *c.*1642–92

6 And wit's the noblest frailty of the mind.
A True Widow (1679) act 2, sc. 1; cf. **Dryden**
116:30

1st Lord Shaftesbury 1621–83

7 'Men of sense are really but of one religion.'
. . . 'Pray, my lord, what religion is that
which men of sense agree in?' 'Madam,'
says the earl immediately, 'men of sense
never tell it.'
Bishop Gilbert Burnet *History of My Own Time*
(1724) vol. 1; cf. **Disraeli** 112:24

3rd Lord Shaftesbury 1671–1713

8 How comes it to pass, then, that we appear
such cowards in reasoning, and are so afraid
to stand the test of ridicule?
A Letter Concerning Enthusiasm (1708) sect. 2

William Shakespeare 1564–1616
*The line number is given without brackets where
the scene is all verse up to the quotation and the
line number is certain, and in square brackets
where prose makes it variable. All references are
to the Oxford Standard Authors edition in one
volume*

All's Well that Ends Well
9 That I should love a bright particular star
And think to wed it.
All's Well that Ends Well (1603–4) act 1, sc. 1, l. [98]

10 It is like a barber's chair that fits all
buttocks.
All's Well that Ends Well (1603–4) act 2, sc. 2, l. [18]

11 A young man married is a man that's
marred.
All's Well that Ends Well (1603–4) act 2, sc. 3, l.
[315]

Antony and Cleopatra

12 CLEOPATRA: I'll set a bourn how far to be
beloved.
ANTONY: Then must thou needs find out
new heaven, new earth.
Antony and Cleopatra (1606–7) act 1, sc. 1, l. 16

13 Let Rome in Tiber melt, and the wide arch
Of the ranged empire fall.
Antony and Cleopatra (1606–7) act 1, sc. 1, l. 33

14 A Roman thought hath struck him.
Antony and Cleopatra (1606–7) act 1, sc. 2, l. [91]

15 Where's my serpent of old Nile?
Antony and Cleopatra (1606–7) act 1, sc. 5, l. 24

16 My salad days,
When I was green in judgment.
Antony and Cleopatra (1606–7) act 1, sc. 5, l. 73

17 The barge she sat in, like a burnished
throne,
Burned on the water.
Antony and Cleopatra (1606–7) act 2, sc. 2, l. [199];
cf. **Eliot** 122:22

18 For her own person,
It beggared all description.
Antony and Cleopatra (1606–7) act 2, sc. 2, l. [205]

19 I saw her once
Hop forty paces through the public street;
And having lost her breath, she spoke, and
panted
That she did make defect perfection,
And, breathless, power breathe forth.
Antony and Cleopatra (1606–7) act 2, sc. 2, l. [236]

20 Age cannot wither her, nor custom stale
Her infinite variety; other women cloy
The appetites they feed, but she makes
hungry
Where most she satisfies.
Antony and Cleopatra (1606–7) act 2, sc. 2, l. [243]

21 I' the east my pleasure lies.
Antony and Cleopatra (1606–7) act 2, sc. 3, l. 40

22 Let's have one other gaudy night: call to me
All my sad captains; fill our bowls once
more;
Let's mock the midnight bell.
Antony and Cleopatra (1606–7) act 3, sc. 11, l. 182

23 O infinite virtue! com'st thou smiling from
The world's great snare uncaught?
Antony and Cleopatra (1606–7) act 4, sc. 8, l. 17

24 The hearts
That spanieled me at heels, to whom I gave
Their wishes, do discandy, melt their sweets
On blossoming Caesar.
Antony and Cleopatra (1606–7) act 4, sc. 10, l. 33

25 Unarm, Eros; the long day's task is done,
And we must sleep.
Antony and Cleopatra (1606–7) act 4, sc. 12, l. 35

26 I am dying, Egypt, dying.
Antony and Cleopatra (1606–7) act 4, sc. 13, l. 18

27 A Roman by a Roman
Valiantly vanquished.
Antony and Cleopatra (1606–7) act 4, sc. 13, l. 57

28 O! withered is the garland of the war,
The soldier's pole is fall'n; young boys and
girls

Are level now with men; the odds is gone,
And there is nothing left remarkable
Beneath the visiting moon.

Antony and Cleopatra (1606–7) act 4, sc. 13, l. 64

1 Let's do it after the high Roman fashion,
And make death proud to take us.

Antony and Cleopatra (1606–7) act 4, sc. 13, l. 87

2 He words me, girls, he words me.

Antony and Cleopatra (1606–7) act 5, sc. 2, l. 190

3 Finish, good lady; the bright day is done,
And we are for the dark.

Antony and Cleopatra (1606–7) act 5, sc. 2, l. 192

4 I shall see
Some squeaking Cleopatra boy my
greatness
I' the posture of a whore.

Antony and Cleopatra (1606–7) act 5, sc. 2, l. 218

5 I wish you all joy of the worm.

Antony and Cleopatra (1606–7) act 5, sc. 2, l. [260]

6 Give me my robe, put on my crown; I have
Immortal longings in me.

Antony and Cleopatra (1606–7) act 5, sc. 2, l. [282]

7 I am fire and air; my other elements
I give to baser life.

Antony and Cleopatra (1606–7) act 5, sc. 2, l. [291]

8 CHARMIAN: O eastern star!
CLEOPATRA: Peace! peace!
Dost thou not see my baby at my breast,
That sucks the nurse asleep?

Antony and Cleopatra (1606–7) act 5, sc. 2, l. [309]

9 Now boast thee, death, in thy possession
lies
A lass unparalleled.

Antony and Cleopatra (1606–7) act 5, sc. 2, l. [317]

10 She looks like sleep,
As she would catch a second Antony
In her strong toil of grace.

Antony and Cleopatra (1606–7) act 5, sc. 2, l. [347]

11 She hath pursued conclusions infinite
Of easy ways to die.

Antony and Cleopatra (1606–7) act 5, sc. 2, l. [356]

As You Like It

12 Fleet the time carelessly, as they did in the
golden world.

As You Like It (1599) act 1, sc. 1, l. [126]

13 O, how full of briers is this working-day
world!

As You Like It (1599) act 1, sc. 3, l. [12]

14 Sweet are the uses of adversity,
Which like the toad, ugly and venomous,
Wears yet a precious jewel in his head;
And this our life, exempt from public
haunt,
Finds tongues in trees, books in the running
brooks,
Sermons in stones, and good in everything.

As You Like It (1599) act 2, sc. 1, l. 12; cf. **Bernard**
31:5

15 Ay, now am I in Arden; the more fool I.
When I was at home I was in a better place;
but travellers must be content.

As You Like It (1599) act 2, sc. 4, l. [16]

16 Under the greenwood tree
Who loves to lie with me,
And turn his merry note
Unto the sweet bird's throat,
Come hither, come hither, come hither:
Here shall he see
No enemy
But winter and rough weather.

As You Like It (1599) act 2, sc. 5, l. 1

17 I can suck melancholy out of a song as a
weasel sucks eggs.

As You Like It (1599) act 2, sc. 5, l. [12]

18 And so, from hour to hour, we ripe and ripe,
And then from hour to hour, we rot and rot:
And thereby hangs a tale.

As You Like It (1599) act 2, sc. 7, l. 26

19 A worthy fool! Motley's the only wear.

As You Like It (1599) act 2, sc. 7, l. 34

20 All the world's a stage,
And all the men and women merely players:
They have their exits and their entrances;
And one man in his time plays many parts,
His acts being seven ages.

As You Like It (1599) act 2, sc. 7, l. 139

21 At first the infant,
Mewling and puking in the nurse's arms.
And then the whining schoolboy, with his
satchel,
And shining morning face, creeping like
snail
Unwillingly to school.

As You Like It (1599) act 2, sc. 7, l. 143

22 Then a soldier,
Full of strange oaths, and bearded like the
pard,
Jealous in honour, sudden and quick in
quarrel,
Seeking the bubble reputation
Even in the cannon's mouth.

As You Like It (1599) act 2, sc. 7, l. 149

23 The sixth age shifts
Into the lean and slippered pantaloon.

As You Like It (1599) act 2, sc. 7, l. 157

24 Second childishness, and mere oblivion,
Sans teeth, sans eyes, sans taste, sans
everything.

As You Like It (1599) act 2, sc. 7, l. 165

25 Blow, blow, thou winter wind,
Thou art not so unkind
As man's ingratitude.

As You Like It (1599) act 2, sc. 7, l. 174

26 Most friendship is feigning, most loving
mere folly.

As You Like It (1599) act 2, sc. 7, l. 181

27 Run, run, Orlando: carve on every tree
The fair, the chaste, and unexpressive she.

As You Like It (1599) act 3, sc. 2, l. 9

28 O wonderful, wonderful, and most
wonderful wonderful! and yet again
wonderful, and after that, out of all
whooping!

As You Like It (1599) act 3, sc. 2, l. [202]

1 There was no thought of pleasing you when
she was christened.
As You Like It (1599) act 3, sc. 2, l. [284]

2 Thank heaven, fasting, for a good man's
love.
As You Like It (1599) act 3, sc. 5, l. 58

3 Men are April when they woo, December
when they wed: maids are May when they
are maids, but the sky changes when they
are wives.
As You Like It (1599) act 4, sc. 1, l. [153]

4 It was a lover and his lass,
With a hey, and a ho, and a hey nonino,
That o'er the green cornfield did pass,
In the spring time, the only pretty ring
time,
When birds do sing, hey ding a ding, ding;
Sweet lovers love the spring.
As You Like It (1599) act 5, sc. 3, l. [18]

5 A poor virgin, sir, an ill-favoured thing, sir,
but mine own.
As You Like It (1599) act 5, sc. 4, l. [60]

6 The retort courteous . . . the quip modest . . .
the reply churlish . . . the reproof valiant . . .
the countercheck quarrelsome . . . the lie
circumstantial . . . the lie direct.
of the degrees of a lie
As You Like It (1599) act 5, sc. 4, l. [96]

7 Your 'if' is the only peace-maker; much
virtue in 'if'.
As You Like It (1599) act 5, sc. 4, l. [108]

8 He uses his folly like a stalking-horse, and
under the presentation of that he shoots his
wit.
As You Like It (1599) act 5, sc. 4, l. [112]

Coriolanus

9 My gracious silence, hail!
Coriolanus (1608) act 2, sc. 1, l. [194]

10 Hear you this Triton of the minnows? mark
you
His absolute 'shall'?
Coriolanus (1608) act 3, sc. 1, l. 88

11 What is the city but the people?
Coriolanus (1608) act 3, sc. 1, l. 198

12 There is a world elsewhere.
Coriolanus (1608) act 3, sc. 3, l. 133

13 The beast
With many heads butts me away.
Coriolanus (1608) act 4, sc. 1, l. 1

14 O! a kiss
Long as my exile, sweet as my revenge!
Coriolanus (1608) act 5, sc. 3, l. 44

15 Chaste as the icicle
That's curdied by the frost from purest
snow,
And hangs on Dian's temple.
Coriolanus (1608) act 5, sc. 3, l. 65

16 If you have writ your annals true, 'tis there,
That, like an eagle in a dove-cote, I
Fluttered your Volscians in Corioli:
Alone I did it.
Coriolanus (1608) act 5, sc. 5, l. 114

Cymbeline

17 Boldness be my friend!
Arm me, audacity.
Cymbeline (1609–10) act 1, sc. 6, l. 18

18 Hark! hark! the lark at heaven's gate sings.
Cymbeline (1609–10) act 2, sc. 3, l. [22]

19 Fear no more the heat o' the sun,
Nor the furious winter's rages;
Thou thy worldly task hast done,
Home art gone and ta'en thy wages:
Golden lads and girls all must,
As chimney-sweepers, come to dust.
Cymbeline (1609–10) act 4, sc. 2, l. 258

20 Hang there like fruit, my soul,
Till the tree die.
Cymbeline (1609–10) act 5, sc. 5, l. 263

Hamlet

21 You come most carefully upon your hour.
Hamlet (1601) act 1, sc. 1, l. 6

22 For this relief much thanks.
Hamlet (1601) act 1, sc. 1, l. 8

23 The graves stood tenantless and the sheeted
dead
Did squeak and gibber in the Roman streets.
Hamlet (1601) act 1, sc. 1, l. 115

24 And then it started like a guilty thing
Upon a fearful summons.
Hamlet (1601) act 1, sc. 1, l. 148

25 Some say that ever 'gainst that season
comes
Wherein our Saviour's birth is celebrated,
The bird of dawning singeth all night long;
And then, they say, no spirit can walk
abroad.
Hamlet (1601) act 1, sc. 1, l. 158

26 But, look, the morn, in russet mantle clad,
Walks o'er the dew of yon high eastern hill.
Hamlet (1601) act 1, sc. 1, l. 166

27 A little more than kin, and less than kind.
Hamlet (1601) act 1, sc. 2, l. 65

28 Not so, my lord; I am too much i' the sun.
Hamlet (1601) act 1, sc. 2, l. 67

29 O! that this too too solid flesh would melt,
Thaw, and resolve itself into a dew.
Hamlet (1601) act 1, sc. 2, l. 129

30 How weary, stale, flat, and unprofitable
Seem to me all the uses of this world.
Hamlet (1601) act 1, sc. 2, l. 133

31 So excellent a king; that was, to this,
Hyperion to a satyr.
Hamlet (1601) act 1, sc. 2, l. 139

32 Frailty, thy name is woman!
A little month; or ere those shoes were old
With which she followed my poor father's
body,
Like Niobe, all tears; why she, even she,—
O God! a beast, that wants discourse of
reason,
Would have mourned longer.
Hamlet (1601) act 1, sc. 2, l. 146

33 No more like my father
Than I to Hercules.
Hamlet (1601) act 1, sc. 2, l. 152

1 It is not, nor it cannot come to good;
But break, my heart, for I must hold my
tongue!
Hamlet (1601) act 1, sc. 2, l. 158

2 Thrift, thrift, Horatio! the funeral baked
meats
Did coldly furnish forth the marriage tables.
Hamlet (1601) act 1, sc. 2, l. 180

3 He was a man, take him for all in all,
I shall not look upon his like again.
Hamlet (1601) act 1, sc. 2, l. 187

4 But answer made it none.
Hamlet (1601) act 1, sc. 2, l. 215

5 A countenance more in sorrow than in
anger.
Hamlet (1601) act 1, sc. 2, l. 231

6 Himself the primrose path of dalliance
treads,
And recks not his own rede.
Hamlet (1601) act 1, sc. 3, l. 50

7 For the apparel oft proclaims the man.
Hamlet (1601) act 1, sc. 3, l. 72

8 Neither a borrower, nor a lender be.
Hamlet (1601) act 1, sc. 3, l. 75

9 This above all: to thine own self be true,
And it must follow, as the night the day,
Thou canst not then be false to any man.
Hamlet (1601) act 1, sc. 3, l. 78; cf. **Bacon** 21:33

10 Ay, springes to catch woodcocks.
Hamlet (1601) act 1, sc. 3, l. 115

11 It is a nipping and an eager air.
Hamlet (1601) act 1, sc. 4, l. 2

12 But to my mind,—though I am native here,
And to the manner born,—it is a custom
More honoured in the breach than the
observance.
Hamlet (1601) act 1, sc. 4, l. 14

13 Angels and ministers of grace defend us!
Hamlet (1601) act 1, sc. 4, l. 39

14 Something is rotten in the state of
Denmark.
Hamlet (1601) act 1, sc. 4, l. 90

15 List, list, O, list!
Hamlet (1601) act 1, sc. 5, l. 13

16 I could a tale unfold whose lightest word
Would harrow up thy soul, freeze thy young
blood,
Make thy two eyes, like stars, start from
their spheres,
Thy knotted and combinèd locks to part,
And each particular hair to stand on end,
Like quills upon the fretful porpentine.
Hamlet (1601) act 1, sc. 5, l. 15

17 Murder most foul, as in the best it is;
But this most foul, strange, and unnatural.
Hamlet (1601) act 1, sc. 5, l. 27

18 O my prophetic soul!
My uncle!
Hamlet (1601) act 1, sc. 5, l. 40

19 O, horrible! O, horrible! most horrible!
Hamlet (1601) act 1, sc. 5, l. 80

20 O villain, villain, smiling, damnèd villain!
My tables,—meet it is I set it down,

That one may smile, and smile, and be a
villain.
Hamlet (1601) act 1, sc. 5, l. 106

21 There are more things in heaven and earth,
Horatio,
Than are dreamt of in your philosophy.
Hamlet (1601) act 1, sc. 5, l. 166; cf. **Haldane**
149:11

22 To put an antic disposition on.
Hamlet (1601) act 1, sc. 5, l. 172

23 Rest, rest, perturbèd spirit.
Hamlet (1601) act 1, sc. 5, l. 182

24 The time is out of joint; O cursèd spite,
That ever I was born to set it right!
Hamlet (1601) act 1, sc. 5, l. 188

25 Brevity is the soul of wit.
Hamlet (1601) act 2, sc. 2, l. 90

26 More matter with less art.
Hamlet (1601) act 2, sc. 2, l. 95

27 POLONIUS: What do you read, my lord?
HAMLET: Words, words, words.
Hamlet (1601) act 2, sc. 2, l. [195]

28 Though this be madness, yet there is
method in't.
Hamlet (1601) act 2, sc. 2, l. [211]

29 There is nothing either good or bad, but
thinking makes it so.
Hamlet (1601) act 2, sc. 2, l. [259]

30 O God! I could be bounded in a nut-shell,
and count myself a king of infinite space,
were it not that I have bad dreams.
Hamlet (1601) act 2, sc. 2, l. [263]

31 What a piece of work is a man! How noble
in reason! how infinite in faculty! in form,
in moving, how express and admirable! in
action how like an angel! in apprehension
how like a god! the beauty of the world! the
paragon of animals! And yet, to me, what is
this quintessence of dust? man delights not
me; no, nor woman neither, though, by
your smiling, you seem to say so.
Hamlet (1601) act 2, sc. 2, l. [323]

32 I am but mad north-north-west; when the
wind is southerly, I know a hawk from a
handsaw.
Hamlet (1601) act 2, sc. 2, l. [405]

33 The play, I remember, pleased not the
million; 'twas caviare to the general.
Hamlet (1601) act 2, sc. 2, l. [465]

34 Use every man after his desert, and who
should 'scape whipping?
Hamlet (1601) act 2, sc. 2, l. [561]

35 O, what a rogue and peasant slave am I.
Hamlet (1601) act 2, sc. 2, l. [584]

36 For Hecuba!
What's Hecuba to him or he to Hecuba
That he should weep for her?
Hamlet (1601) act 2, sc. 2, l. [592]

37 The play's the thing
Wherein I'll catch the conscience of the
king.
Hamlet (1601) act 2, sc. 2, l. [641]

1 To be, or not to be: that is the question:
Whether 'tis nobler in the mind to suffer
The slings and arrows of outrageous
    fortune,
Or to take arms against a sea of troubles,
And by opposing end them? To die: to sleep;
No more; and, by a sleep to say we end
The heart-ache and the thousand natural
    shocks
That flesh is heir to, 'tis a consummation
Devoutly to be wished. To die, to sleep;
To sleep: perchance to dream: ay, there's
    the rub;
For in that sleep of death what dreams may
    come
When we have shuffled off this mortal coil,
Must give us pause.
  Hamlet (1601) act 3, sc. 1, l. 56

2 For who would bear the whips and scorns of
    time,
The oppressor's wrong, the proud man's
    contumely,
The pangs of disprized love, the law's delay
    . . .
When he himself might his quietus make
With a bare bodkin?
  Hamlet (1601) act 3, sc. 1, l. 70

3 Nymph, in thy orisons
Be all my sins remembered.
  Hamlet (1601) act 3, sc. 1, l. 89

4 Get thee to a nunnery.
  Hamlet (1601) act 3, sc. 1, l. [124]

5 Be thou as chaste as ice, as pure as snow,
thou shalt not escape calumny. Get thee to a
nunnery, go; farewell.
  Hamlet (1601) act 3, sc. 1, l. [142]

6 I say, we will have no more marriages.
  Hamlet (1601) act 3, sc. 1, l. [156]

7 O! what a noble mind is here o'erthrown:
The courtier's, soldier's, scholar's, eye,
    tongue, sword;
The expectancy and rose of the fair state,
The glass of fashion, and the mould of form,
The observèd of all observers, quite, quite,
    down!
  Hamlet (1601) act 3, sc. 1, l. [159]

8 Now see that noble and most sovereign
    reason,
Like sweet bells jangled, out of tune and
    harsh.
  Hamlet (1601) act 3, sc. 1, l. [166]

9 Speak the speech, I pray you, as I
pronounced it to you, trippingly on the
tongue.
  Hamlet (1601) act 3, sc. 2, l. 1

10 I would have such a fellow whipped for
o'erdoing Termagant; it out-herods Herod.
  Hamlet (1601) act 3, sc. 2, l. 14

11 Suit the action to the word, the word to the
action.
  Hamlet (1601) act 3, sc. 2, l. [20]

12 To hold, as 'twere, the mirror up to nature.
  Hamlet (1601) act 3, sc. 2, l. [25]

13 The lady doth protest too much, methinks.
  Hamlet (1601) act 3, sc. 2, l. [242]

14 HAMLET: No, no, they do but jest, poison in
    jest; no offence i' the world.
KING: What do you call the play?
HAMLET: The Mouse-trap.
  Hamlet (1601) act 3, sc. 2, l. [247]

15 Let the galled jade wince, our withers are
unwrung.
  Hamlet (1601) act 3, sc. 2, l. [256]

16 Why, let the stricken deer go weep,
The hart ungallèd play;
For some must watch, while some must
    sleep:
So runs the world away.
  Hamlet (1601) act 3, sc. 2, l. [287]; cf. **Cowper**
  102:2

17 You would play upon me; you would seem
to know my stops; you would pluck out the
heart of my mystery; you would sound me
from my lowest note to the top of my
compass.
  Hamlet (1601) act 3, sc. 2, l. [387]

18 Very like a whale.
  Hamlet (1601) act 3, sc. 2, l. [406]

19 They fool me to the top of my bent.
  Hamlet (1601) act 3, sc. 2, l. [408]

20 'Tis now the very witching time of night,
When churchyards yawn.
  Hamlet (1601) act 3, sc. 2, l. [413]

21 Now might I do it pat, now he is praying.
  Hamlet (1601) act 3, sc. 3, l. 73

22 My words fly up, my thoughts remain
    below:
Words without thoughts never to heaven
    go.
  Hamlet (1601) act 3, sc. 3, l. 97

23 How now! a rat? Dead, for a ducat, dead!
  Hamlet (1601) act 3, sc. 4, l. 23

24 Thou wretched, rash, intruding fool,
    farewell!
I took thee for thy better.
  Hamlet (1601) act 3, sc. 4, l. 31

25 A king of shreds and patches.
  Hamlet (1601) act 3, sc. 4, l. 102; cf. **Gilbert**
  140:6

26 Assume a virtue, if you have it not.
  Hamlet (1601) act 3, sc. 4, l. 160

27 I must be cruel only to be kind.
  Hamlet (1601) act 3, sc. 4, l. 178

28 Hoist with his own petar.
  Hamlet (1601) act 3, sc. 4, l. 207

29 I'll lug the guts into the neighbour room.
  Hamlet (1601) act 3, sc. 4, l. 212

30 Diseases desperate grown,
By desperate appliances are relieved,
Or not at all.
  Hamlet (1601) act 4, sc. 2, l. 9; cf. **Fawkes** 126:17

31 How all occasions do inform against me,
And spur my dull revenge!
  Hamlet (1601) act 4, sc. 4, l. 32

32 How should I your true love know
From another one?

By his cockle hat and staff,
And his sandal shoon.
Hamlet (1601) act 4, sc. 5, l. [23]

1 He is dead and gone, lady,
He is dead and gone,
At his head a grass-green turf;
At his heels a stone.
Hamlet (1601) act 4, sc. 5, l. [29]

2 Come, my coach! Good-night, ladies; good-night, sweet ladies; good-night, good-night.
Hamlet (1601) act 4, sc. 5, l. [72]

3 When sorrows come, they come not single spies,
But in battalions.
Hamlet (1601) act 4, sc. 5, l. [78]

4 There's such divinity doth hedge a king,
That treason can but peep to what it would.
Hamlet (1601) act 4, sc. 5, l. [123]

5 There's rosemary, that's for remembrance;
pray, love, remember: and there is pansies,
that's for thoughts.
Hamlet (1601) act 4, sc. 5, l. [174]

6 There's rue for you; and here's some for me;
we may call it herb of grace o' Sundays. O!
you must wear your rue with a difference.
There's a daisy; I would give you some
violets, but they withered all when my
father died.
Hamlet (1601) act 4, sc. 5, l. [179]

7 And where the offence is let the great axe
fall.
Hamlet (1601) act 4, sc. 5, l. [218]

8 There is a willow grows aslant a brook,
That shows his hoar leaves in the glassy
stream.
Hamlet (1601) act 4, sc. 7, l. 167

9 There with fantastic garlands did she come,
Of crow-flowers, nettles, daisies, and long
purples,
That liberal shepherds give a grosser name,
But our cold maids do dead men's fingers
call them.
Hamlet (1601) act 4, sc. 7, l. 169

10 There, on the pendent boughs her coronet
weeds
Clambering to hang, an envious sliver
broke,
When down her weedy trophies and herself
Fell in the weeping brook.
Hamlet (1601) act 4, sc. 7, l. 173

11 Alas, poor Yorick. I knew him, Horatio; a
fellow of infinite jest.
Hamlet (1601) act 5, sc. 1, l. [201]

12 Imperious Caesar, dead, and turned to clay,
Might stop a hole to keep the wind away.
Hamlet (1601) act 5, sc. 1, l. [235]

13 A ministering angel shall my sister be,
When thou liest howling.
Hamlet (1601) act 5, sc. 1, l. [263]; cf. **Scott**
266:19

14 Sweets to the sweet: farewell!
Hamlet (1601) act 5, sc. 1, l. [265]

15 There's a divinity that shapes our ends,
Rough-hew them how we will.

Hamlet (1601) act 5, sc. 2, l. 10

16 Not a whit, we defy augury; there's a special
providence in the fall of a sparrow. If it be
now, 'tis not to come; if it be not to come, it
will be now; if it be not now, yet it will
come: the readiness is all.
Hamlet (1601) act 5, sc. 2, l. [232]

17 A hit, a very palpable hit.
Hamlet (1601) act 5, sc. 2, l. [295]

18 Why, as a woodcock to mine own springe,
Osric;
I am justly killed with my own treachery.
Hamlet (1601) act 5, sc. 2, l. [320]

19 This fell sergeant, death,
Is swift in his arrest.
Hamlet (1601) act 5, sc. 2, l. [350]

20 I am more an antique Roman than a Dane.
Hamlet (1601) act 5, sc. 2, l. [355]

21 Absent thee from felicity awhile,
And in this harsh world draw thy breath in
pain,
To tell my story.
Hamlet (1601) act 5, sc. 2, l. [361]

22 The rest is silence.
Hamlet (1601) act 5, sc. 2, l. [372]

23 Now cracks a noble heart. Good-night,
sweet prince,
And flights of angels sing thee to thy rest!
Hamlet (1601) act 5, sc. 2, l. [373]

24 Rosencrantz and Guildenstern are dead.
Hamlet (1601) act 5, sc. 2, l. [385]

Henry IV, Part 1

25 Let us be Diana's foresters, gentlemen of the
shade, minions of the moon.
Henry IV, Part 1 (1597) act 1, sc. 2, l. [28]

26 The rusty curb of old father antick, the law.
Henry IV, Part 1 (1597) act 1, sc. 2, l. [68]

27 To put down Richard, that sweet lovely rose,
And plant this thorn, this canker,
Bolingbroke.
Henry IV, Part 1 (1597) act 1, sc. 3, l. 175

28 By heaven methinks it were an easy leap
To pluck bright honour from the pale-faced
moon.
Henry IV, Part 1 (1597) act 1, sc. 3, l. 201

29 Go hang thyself in thine own heir-apparent
garters!
Henry IV, Part 1 (1597) act 2, sc. 2, l. [49]

30 It would be argument for a week, laughter
for a month, and a good jest for ever.
Henry IV, Part 1 (1597) act 2, sc. 2, l. [104]

31 Falstaff sweats to death
And lards the lean earth as he walks along.
Henry IV, Part 1 (1597) act 2, sc. 2, l. [119]

32 Out of this nettle, danger, we pluck this
flower, safety.
Henry IV, Part 1 (1597) act 2, sc. 3, l. [11]

33 Nay that's past praying for.
Henry IV, Part 1 (1597) act 2, sc. 4, l. [214]

34 That roasted Manningtree ox with the
pudding in his belly.
Henry IV, Part 1 (1597) act 2, sc. 4, l. [504]

1 Banish not him thy Harry's company:
banish plump Jack and banish all the world.
Henry IV, Part 1 (1597) act 2, sc. 4, l. [533]

2 O monstrous! but one half-pennyworth of
bread to this intolerable deal of sack!
Henry IV, Part 1 (1597) act 2, sc. 4, l. [598]

3 GLENDOWER: I can call spirits from the vasty
deep.
HOTSPUR: Why, so can I, or so can any man;
But will they come when you do call for
them?
Henry IV, Part 1 (1597) act 3, sc. 1, l. [53]

4 Now I perceive the devil understands
Welsh.
Henry IV, Part 1 (1597) act 3, sc. 1, l. [233]

5 I saw young Harry, with his beaver on.
Henry IV, Part 1 (1597) act 4, sc. 1, l. 104

6 Rebellion lay in his way, and he found it.
Henry IV, Part 1 (1597) act 5, sc. 1, l. 28

7 I would it were bed-time, Hal, and all well.
Henry IV, Part 1 (1597) act 5, sc. 1, l. [125]

8 Thou owest God a death.
Henry IV, Part 1 (1597) act 5, sc. 1, l. [126]; cf.
Shakespeare 274:23

9 What is honour? A word. What is that word,
honour? Air. A trim reckoning! Who hath
it? He that died o' Wednesday.
Henry IV, Part 1 (1597) act 5, sc. 1, l. [136]

10 Two stars keep not their motion in one
sphere.
Henry IV, Part 1 (1597) act 5, sc. 4, l. 65

11 Thy ignominy sleep with thee in the grave,
But not remembered in thy epitaph!
Henry IV, Part 1 (1597) act 5, sc. 4, l. [100]

12 Poor Jack, farewell!
I could have better spared a better man.
Henry IV, Part 1 (1597) act 5, sc. 4, l. [103]

Henry IV, Part 2

13 I am not only witty in myself, but the cause
that wit is in other men.
Henry IV, Part 2 (1597) act 1, sc. 2, l. [10]

14 It is the disease of not listening, the malady
of not marking, that I am troubled withal.
Henry IV, Part 2 (1597) act 1, sc. 2, l. [139]

15 I am as poor as Job, my lord, but not so
patient.
Henry IV, Part 2 (1597) act 1, sc. 2, l. [145]

16 CHIEF JUSTICE: God send the prince a better
companion!
FALSTAFF: God send the companion a better
prince!
Henry IV, Part 2 (1597) act 1, sc. 2, l. [227]

17 I can get no remedy against this
consumption of the purse: borrowing only
lingers and lingers it out, but the disease is
incurable.
Henry IV, Part 2 (1597) act 1, sc. 2, l. [268]

18 Pack-horses,
And hollow pampered jades of Asia,
Which cannot go but thirty miles a day.
Henry IV, Part 2 (1597) act 2, sc. 4, l. [176]; cf.
Marlowe 212:19

19 Is it not strange that desire should so many
years outlive performance?
Henry IV, Part 2 (1597) act 2, sc. 4, l. [283]

20 Uneasy lies the head that wears a crown.
Henry IV, Part 2 (1597) act 3, sc. 1, l. 31

21 Most forcible Feeble.
Henry IV, Part 2 (1597) act 3, sc. 2, l. [181]

22 We have heard the chimes at midnight.
Henry IV, Part 2 (1597) act 3, sc. 2, l. [231]

23 I care not; a man can die but once; we owe
God a death.
Henry IV, Part 2 (1597) act 3, sc. 2, l. [253]; cf.
Shakespeare 274:8

24 Thy wish was father, Harry, to that thought.
Henry IV, Part 2 (1597) act 4, sc. 5, l. 91

25 This is the English, not the Turkish court;
Not Amurath an Amurath succeeds,
But Harry, Harry.
Henry IV, Part 2 (1597) act 5, sc. 2, l. 47

Henry V

26 O! for a Muse of fire, that would ascend
The brightest heaven of invention.
Henry V (1599) chorus, l. 1

27 Can this cockpit hold
The vasty fields of France? or may we cram
Within this wooden O the very casques
That did affright the air at Agincourt?
Henry V (1599) chorus, l. 11

28 Consideration like an angel came,
And whipped the offending Adam out of
him.
Henry V (1599) act 1, sc. 1, l. 28

29 When we have matched our rackets to
these balls,
We will in France, by God's grace, play a set
Shall strike his father's crown into the
hazard.
Henry V (1599) act 1, sc. 2, l. 261

30 Now all the youth of England are on fire,
And silken dalliance in the wardrobe lies.
Henry V (1599) act 2, chorus, l. 1

31 He's in Arthur's bosom, if ever man went to
Arthur's bosom.
Henry V (1599) act 2, sc. 3, l. [9]

32 His nose was as sharp as a pen, and a'
babbled of green fields.
Henry V (1599) act 2, sc. 3, l. [17]

33 Once more unto the breach, dear friends,
once more;
Or close the wall up with our English dead!
Henry V (1599) act 3, sc. 1, l. 1

34 The game's afoot:
Follow your spirit; and, upon this charge
Cry 'God for Harry! England and Saint
George!'
Henry V (1599) act 3, sc. 1, l. 32

35 A little touch of Harry in the night.
Henry V (1599) act 4, chorus, l. 47

36 The king's a bawcock, and a heart of gold,
A lad of life, an imp of fame,
Of parents good, of fist most valiant:
I kiss his dirty shoe, and from my heart-
string

I love the lovely bully.
Henry V (1599) act 4, sc. 1, l. 44

1 I think the king is but a man, as I am: the violet smells to him as it doth to me.
Henry V (1599) act 4, sc. 1, l. [106]

2 I am afeard there are few die well that die in a battle; for how can they charitably dispose of any thing when blood is their argument?
Henry V (1599) act 4, sc. 1, l. [149]

3 Every subject's duty is the king's; but every subject's soul is his own.
Henry V (1599) act 4, sc. 1, l. [189]

4 Upon the king! let us our lives, our souls, Our debts, our careful wives, Our children, and our sins lay on the king!
Henry V (1599) act 4, sc. 1, l. [250]

5 And what have kings that privates have not too, Save ceremony, save general ceremony?
Henry V (1599) act 4, sc. 1, l. [258]

6 O God of battles! steel my soldiers' hearts.
Henry V (1599) act 4, sc. 1, l. [309]

7 If we are marked to die, we are enow To do our country loss; and if to live, The fewer men, the greater share of honour.
Henry V (1599) act 4, sc. 3, l. 20

8 He which hath no stomach to this fight, Let him depart.
Henry V (1599) act 4, sc. 3, l. 35

9 This day is called the feast of Crispian: He that outlives this day and comes safe home, Will stand a tip-toe when this day is named, And rouse him at the name of Crispian.
Henry V (1599) act 4, sc. 3, l. 40

10 Then will he strip his sleeve and show his scars, And say, 'These wounds I had on Crispin's day.' Old men forget: yet all shall be forgot, But he'll remember with advantages What feats he did that day.
Henry V (1599) act 4, sc. 3, l. 47

11 We few, we happy few, we band of brothers; For he to-day that sheds his blood with me Shall be my brother; be he ne'er so vile This day shall gentle his condition: And gentlemen in England, now a-bed Shall think themselves accursed they were not here, And hold their manhoods cheap whiles any speaks That fought with us upon Saint Crispin's day.
Henry V (1599) act 4, sc. 3, l. 60

Henry VI, Part 1

12 Expect Saint Martin's summer, halcyon days.
Henry VI, Part 1 (1592) act 1, sc. 2, l. 131

13 From off this brier pluck a white rose with me.
Plantagenet
Henry VI, Part 1 (1592) act 2, sc. 4, l. 30

14 Pluck a red rose from off this thorn with me.
Somerset
Henry VI, Part 1 (1592) act 2, sc. 4, l. 33

Henry VI, Part 2

15 Thrice is he armed that hath his quarrel just.
Henry VI, Part 2 (1592) act 3, sc. 2, l. 233

16 The first thing we do, let's kill all the lawyers.
Henry VI, Part 2 (1592) act 4, sc. 2, l. [86]

17 And Adam was a gardener.
Henry VI, Part 2 (1592) act 4, sc. 2, l. [146]

18 Away with him! away with him! he speaks Latin.
Henry VI, Part 2 (1592) act 4, sc. 7, l. [62]

Henry VI, Part 3

19 O tiger's heart wrapped in a woman's hide!
Henry VI, Part 3 (1592) act 1, sc. 4, l. 137

Henry VIII

20 As the long divorce of steel falls on me, Make of your prayers one sweet sacrifice, And lift my soul to heaven.
Henry VIII (1613) act 2, sc. 1, l. 76

21 Heaven will one day open The king's eyes, that so long have slept upon This bold bad man.
Henry VIII (1613) act 2, sc. 2, l. [42]

22 Orpheus with his lute made trees, And the mountain-tops that freeze, Bow themselves when he did sing.
Henry VIII (1613) act 3, sc. 1, l. 3

23 Farewell! a long farewell, to all my greatness!
Henry VIII (1613) act 3, sc. 2, l. 352

24 When he falls, he falls like Lucifer, Never to hope again.
Henry VIII (1613) act 3, sc. 2, l. 372

25 Cromwell, I charge thee, fling away ambition: By that sin fell the angels.
Henry VIII (1613) act 3, sc. 2, l. 441

26 Had I but served my God with half the zeal I served my king, he would not in mine age Have left me naked to mine enemies.
Henry VIII (1613) act 3, sc. 2, l. 456; cf. **Wolsey** 338:26

27 Men's evil manners live in brass; their virtues We write in water.
Henry VIII (1613) act 4, sc. 2, l. 45; cf. **Keats** 183:17

Julius Caesar

28 O you hard hearts, you cruel men of Rome, Knew you not Pompey?
Julius Caesar (1599) act 1, sc. 1, l. [40]

29 Beware the ides of March.
Julius Caesar (1599) act 1, sc. 2, l. 18

30 Why, man, he doth bestride the narrow world

Like a Colossus; and we petty men
Walk under his huge legs, and peep about
To find ourselves dishonourable graves.
Men at some time are masters of their fates:
The fault, dear Brutus, is not in our stars,
But in ourselves, that we are underlings.
Julius Caesar (1599) act 1, sc. 2, l. 134

1 Let me have men about me that are fat;
Sleek-headed men and such as sleep o'
nights;
Yond' Cassius has a lean and hungry look;
He thinks too much: such men are
dangerous.
Julius Caesar (1599) act 1, sc. 2, l. 191; cf.
Plutarch 246:8

2 'Tis very like: he hath the falling sickness.
Julius Caesar (1599) act 1, sc. 2, l. [255]

3 It is the bright day that brings forth the
adder.
Julius Caesar (1599) act 2, sc. 1, l. 14

4 Let's carve him as a dish fit for the gods,
Not hew him as a carcass fit for hounds.
Julius Caesar (1599) act 2, sc. 1, l. 173

5 When beggars die, there are no comets
seen;
The heavens themselves blaze forth the
death of princes.
Julius Caesar (1599) act 2, sc. 2, l. 30

6 Cowards die many times before their
deaths;
The valiant never taste of death but once.
Julius Caesar (1599) act 2, sc. 2, l. 32

7 But I am constant as the northern star,
Of whose true-fixed and resting quality
There is no fellow in the firmament.
Julius Caesar (1599) act 3, sc. 1, l. 60

8 *Et tu, Brute?* Then fall, Caesar!
Julius Caesar (1599) act 3, sc. 1, l. 77

9 Live a thousand years,
I shall not find myself so apt to die:
No place will please me so, no mean of
death,
As here by Caesar, and by you cut off,
The choice and master spirits of this age.
Julius Caesar (1599) act 3, sc. 1, l. 159

10 O! pardon me, thou bleeding piece of earth,
That I am meek and gentle with these
butchers.
Julius Caesar (1599) act 3, sc. 1, l. 254

11 Cry, 'Havoc!' and let slip the dogs of war.
Julius Caesar (1599) act 3, sc. 1, l. 273

12 Not that I loved Caesar less, but that I loved
Rome more.
Julius Caesar (1599) act 3, sc. 2, l. [22]

13 As he was valiant, I honour him: but, as he
was ambitious, I slew him.
Julius Caesar (1599) act 3, sc. 2, l. [27]

14 Who is here so base that would be a
bondman? If any, speak; for him have I
offended . . . I pause for a reply.
Julius Caesar (1599) act 3, sc. 2, l. [31]

15 Friends, Romans, countrymen, lend me
your ears;

I come to bury Caesar, not to praise him.
The evil that men do lives after them,
The good is oft interrèd with their bones.
Julius Caesar (1599) act 3, sc. 2, l. [79]

16 For Brutus is an honourable man.
Julius Caesar (1599) act 3, sc. 2, l. [88]

17 He was my friend, faithful and just to me.
Julius Caesar (1599) act 3, sc. 2, l. [91]

18 When that the poor have cried, Caesar hath
wept;
Ambition should be made of sterner stuff.
Julius Caesar (1599) act 3, sc. 2, l. [97]

19 If you have tears, prepare to shed them
now.
Julius Caesar (1599) act 3, sc. 2, l. [174]

20 This was the most unkindest cut of all.
Julius Caesar (1599) act 3, sc. 2, l. [188]

21 O! what a fall was there, my countrymen.
Julius Caesar (1599) act 3, sc. 2, l. [195]

22 I am no orator, as Brutus is;
But, as you know me all, a plain, blunt man.
Julius Caesar (1599) act 3, sc. 2, l. [221]

23 But were I Brutus,
And Brutus Antony, there were an Antony
Would ruffle up your spirits, and put a
tongue
In every wound of Caesar, that should move
The stones of Rome to rise and mutiny.
Julius Caesar (1599) act 3, sc. 2, l. [230]

24 Here was a Caesar! when comes such
another?
Julius Caesar (1599) act 3, sc. 2, l. [257]

25 Now let it work; mischief, thou art afoot.
Julius Caesar (1599) act 3, sc. 2, l. [265]

26 Tear him for his bad verses, tear him for his
bad verses.
Julius Caesar (1599) act 3, sc. 3, l. [34]

27 He shall not live; look, with a spot I damn
him.
Julius Caesar (1599) act 4, sc. 1, l. 6

28 Let me tell you, Cassius, you yourself
Are much condemned to have an itching
palm.
Julius Caesar (1599) act 4, sc. 3, l. 7

29 There is a tide in the affairs of men,
Which, taken at the flood, leads on to
fortune.
Julius Caesar (1599) act 4, sc. 3, l. 217

30 O Julius Caesar! thou art mighty yet!
Thy spirit walks abroad, and turns our
swords
In our own proper entrails.
Julius Caesar (1599) act 5, sc. 3, l. 94

31 Thy life hath had some smatch of honour in
it.
Julius Caesar (1599) act 5, sc. 5, l. 46

32 This was the noblest Roman of them all.
Julius Caesar (1599) act 5, sc. 5, l. 68

33 Nature might stand up
And say to all the world, 'This was a man!'
Julius Caesar (1599) act 5, sc. 5, l. 74

King John

1 Grief fills the room up of my absent child,
Lies in his bed, walks up and down with me.
King John (1591–8) act 3, sc. 4, l. 93

2 To gild refinèd gold, to paint the lily,
To throw a perfume on the violet,
To smooth the ice, or add another hue
Unto the rainbow, or with taper light
To seek the beauteous eye of heaven to
garnish,
Is wasteful and ridiculous excess.
King John (1591–8) act 4, sc. 2, l. 11

3 Heaven take my soul, and England keep my
bones!
King John (1591–8) act 4, sc. 3, l. 10

4 Come the three corners of the world in
arms,
And we shall shock them: nought shall
make us rue,
If England to itself do rest but true.
King John (1591–8) act 5, sc. 7, l. 116

King Lear

5 Nothing will come of nothing: speak again.
King Lear (1605–6) act 1, sc. 1, l. [92]

6 LEAR: So young, and so untender?
CORDELIA: So young, my lord, and true.
King Lear (1605–6) act 1, sc. 1, l. [108]

7 I want that glib and oily art
To speak and purpose not.
King Lear (1605–6) act 1, sc. 1, l. [227]

8 Why bastard? wherefore base?
When my dimensions are as well compact,
My mind as generous, and my shape as true,
As honest madam's issue?
King Lear (1605–6) act 1, sc. 2, l. 6

9 I grow, I prosper;
Now, gods, stand up for bastards!
King Lear (1605–6) act 1, sc. 2, l. 21

10 This is the excellent foppery of the world,
that, when we are sick in fortune,—often
the surfeit of our own behaviour,— we
make guilty of our own disasters the sun,
the moon, and the stars; as if we were
villains by necessity, fools by heavenly
compulsion, knaves, thieves, and treachers
by spherical predominance, drunkards,
liars, and adulterers by an enforced
obedience of planetary influence.
King Lear (1605–6) act 1, sc. 2, l. [132]

11 How sharper than a serpent's tooth it is
To have a thankless child!
King Lear (1605–6) act 1, sc. 4, l. [312]

12 O! let me not be mad, not mad, sweet
heaven;
Keep me in temper; I would not be mad!
King Lear (1605–6) act 1, sc. 5, l. [51]

13 Thou whoreson zed! thou unnecessary
letter!
King Lear (1605–6) act 2, sc. 2, l. [68]

14 O, sir! you are old;
Nature in you stands on the very verge
Of her confine.
King Lear (1605–6) act 2, sc. 4, l. [148]

15 O reason not the need! Our basest beggars
Are in the poorest thing superfluous.
King Lear (1605–6) act 2, sc. 4, l. 264

16 I will do such things,—
What they are yet I know not,—but they
shall be
The terrors of the earth.
King Lear (1605–6) act 2, sc. 4, l. [283]

17 Contending with the fretful elements;
Bids the wind blow the earth into the sea,
Or swell the curlèd waters 'bove the main,
That things might change or cease.
King Lear (1605–6) act 3, sc. 1, l. 4

18 Blow, winds, and crack your cheeks! rage!
blow!
You cataracts and hurricanoes, spout
Till you have drenched our steeples,
drowned the cocks!
You sulphurous and thought-executing fires,
Vaunt-couriers to oak-cleaving thunderbolts,
Singe my white head!
King Lear (1605–6) act 3, sc. 2, l. 1

19 Rumble thy bellyful! Spit, fire! Spout, rain!
Nor rain, wind, thunder, fire, are my
daughters:
I tax not you, you elements, with
unkindness.
King Lear (1605–6) act 3, sc. 2, l. 14

20 I am a man
More sinned against than sinning.
King Lear (1605–6) act 3, sc. 2, l. [59]

21 O! that way madness lies; let me shun that.
King Lear (1605–6) act 3, sc. 4, l. 21

22 Take physic, pomp;
Expose thyself to feel what wretches feel.
King Lear (1605–6) act 3, sc. 4, l. 33

23 Thou art the thing itself; unaccommodated
man is no more but such a poor, bare,
forked animal as thou art.
King Lear (1605–6) act 3, sc. 4, l. [109]

24 This is the foul fiend Flibbertigibbet: he
begins at curfew, and walks till the first
cock.
King Lear (1605–6) act 3, sc. 4, l. [118]

25 The green mantle of the standing pool.
King Lear (1605–6) act 3, sc. 4, l. [136]

26 The prince of darkness is a gentleman.
King Lear (1605–6) act 3, sc. 4, l. [148]

27 Poor Tom's a-cold.
King Lear (1605–6) act 3, sc. 4, l. [151]

28 Child Roland to the dark tower came,
His word was still, Fie, foh, and fum,
I smell the blood of a British man.
King Lear (1605–6) act 3, sc. 4, l. [185]; cf.
Browning 69:27, **Nashe** 231:19

29 Out, vile jelly!
Where is thy lustre now?
King Lear (1605–6) act 3, sc. 7, l. [83]

30 As flies to wanton boys, are we to the gods;
They kill us for their sport.
King Lear (1605–6) act 4, sc. 1, l. 36

1 GLOUCESTER: Is't not the king?
LEAR: Ay, every inch a king.
King Lear (1605–6) act 4, sc. 6, l. [110]

2 Die: die for adultery! No:
The wren goes to't, and the small gilded fly
Does lecher in my sight.
King Lear (1605–6) act 4, sc. 6, l. [115]

3 Get thee glass eyes;
And, like a scurvy politician, seem
To see the things thou dost not.
King Lear (1605–6) act 4, sc. 6, l. [175]

4 When we are born we cry that we are come
To this great stage of fools.
King Lear (1605–6) act 4, sc. 6, l. [187]

5 Mine enemy's dog,
Though he had bit me, should have stood
that night
Against my fire.
King Lear (1605–6) act 4, sc. 7, l. 36

6 Thou art a soul in bliss; but I am bound
Upon a wheel of fire.
King Lear (1605–6) act 4, sc. 7, l. 46

7 I am a very foolish, fond old man,
Fourscore and upward, not an hour more or
less;
And, to deal plainly,
I fear I am not in my perfect mind.
King Lear (1605–6) act 4, sc. 7, l. 60

8 Men must endure
Their going hence, even as their coming
hither:
Ripeness is all.
King Lear (1605–6) act 5, sc. 2, l. 9

9 Come, let's away to prison;
We two alone will sing like birds i' the cage:
When thou dost ask me blessing, I'll kneel
down,
And ask of thee forgiveness.
King Lear (1605–6) act 5, sc. 3, l. 8; cf. **Webster**
330:18

10 The gods are just, and of our pleasant vices
Make instruments to plague us.
King Lear (1605–6) act 5, sc. 3, l. [172]

11 The wheel is come full circle.
King Lear (1605–6) act 5, sc. 3, l. [176]

12 Howl, howl, howl, howl! O! you are men of
stones:
Had I your tongue and eyes, I'd use them so
That heaven's vaults should crack. She's
gone for ever!
King Lear (1605–6) act 5, sc. 3, l. [259]

13 Her voice was ever soft,
Gentle and low, an excellent thing in
woman.
King Lear (1605–6) act 5, sc. 3, l. [274]

14 And my poor fool is hanged! No, no, no life!
Why should a dog, a horse, a rat, have life,
And thou no breath at all? Thou'lt come no
more,
Never, never, never, never, never!
King Lear (1605–6) act 5, sc. 3, l. [307]

15 Vex not his ghost: O! let him pass; he hates
him

That would upon the rack of this tough
world
Stretch him out longer.
King Lear (1605–6) act 5, sc. 3, l. [314]

16 The oldest hath borne most: we that are
young,
Shall never see so much, nor live so long.
King Lear (1605–6) act 5, sc. 3, l. [327]

Love's Labour's Lost

17 Cormorant devouring Time.
Love's Labour's Lost (1595) act 1, sc. 1, l. 4

18 A wightly wanton with a velvet brow,
With two pitch balls stuck in her face for
eyes.
Love's Labour's Lost (1595) act 3, sc. 1, l. [206]

19 From women's eyes this doctrine I derive:
They are the ground, the books, the
academes,
From whence doth spring the true
Promethean fire.
Love's Labour's Lost (1595) act 4, sc. 3, l. [302]

20 Taffeta phrases, silken terms precise.
Love's Labour's Lost (1595) act 5, sc. 2, l. 407

21 Henceforth my wooing mind shall be
expressed
In russet yeas and honest kersey noes.
Love's Labour's Lost (1595) act 5, sc. 2, l. 413

22 When daisies pied and violets blue
And lady-smocks all silver-white
And cuckoo-buds of yellow hue
Do paint the meadows with delight,
The cuckoo then, on every tree,
Mocks married men.
Love's Labour's Lost (1595) act 5, sc. 2, l. [902]

23 When icicles hang by the wall,
And Dick the shepherd, blows his nail,
And Tom bears logs into the hall,
And milk comes frozen home in pail,
When blood is nipped and ways be foul,
Then nightly sings the staring owl,
Tu-who;
Tu-whit, tu-who—a merry note,
While greasy Joan doth keel the pot.
Love's Labour's Lost (1595) act 5, sc. 2, l. [920]

24 The words of Mercury are harsh after the
songs of Apollo.
Love's Labour's Lost (1595) act 5, sc. 2, l. [938]

Macbeth

25 FIRST WITCH: When shall we three meet
again
In thunder, lightning, or in rain?
SECOND WITCH: When the hurly-burly's
done,
When the battle's lost and won.
Macbeth (1606) act 1, sc. 1, l. 1

26 Fair is foul, and foul is fair:
Hover through the fog and filthy air.
Macbeth (1606) act 1, sc. 1, l. 11

27 What bloody man is that?
Macbeth (1606) act 1, sc. 2, l. 1

28 And munched, and munched, and
munched: 'Give me,' quoth I:

'Aroint thee, witch!' the rump-fed ronyon
cries.
Her husband's to Aleppo gone, master o' the
Tiger:
But in a sieve I'll thither sail,
And, like a rat without a tail,
I'll do, I'll do, and I'll do.

Macbeth (1606) act 1, sc. 3, l. 6

1 Sleep shall neither night nor day
Hang upon his pent-house lid.
He shall live a man forbid.
Weary se'nnights nine times nine
Shall he dwindle, peak, and pine:
Though his bark cannot be lost,
Yet it shall be tempest-tost.

Macbeth (1606) act 1, sc. 3, l. 19

2 The weird sisters, hand in hand,
Posters of the sea and land,
Thus do go about, about.

Macbeth (1606) act 1, sc. 3, l. 32

3 So foul and fair a day I have not seen.

Macbeth (1606) act 1, sc. 3, l. 38

4 If you can look into the seeds of time,
And say which grain will grow and which
will not.

Macbeth (1606) act 1, sc. 3, l. 58

5 Say, from whence
You owe this strange intelligence? or why
Upon this blasted heath you stop our way
With such prophetic greeting?

Macbeth (1606) act 1, sc. 3, l. 72

6 What! can the devil speak true?

Macbeth (1606) act 1, sc. 3, l. 107

7 Two truths are told,
As happy prologues to the swelling act
Of the imperial theme.

Macbeth (1606) act 1, sc. 3, l. 127

8 Present fears
Are less than horrible imaginings.

Macbeth (1606) act 1, sc. 3, l. 137

9 Come what come may,
Time and the hour runs through the
roughest day.

Macbeth (1606) act 1, sc. 3, l. 146

10 MALCOLM: Nothing in his life
Became him like the leaving it.

Macbeth (1606) act 1, sc. 4, l. 7

11 There's no art
To find the mind's construction in the face.

Macbeth (1606) act 1, sc. 4, l. 11

12 Glamis thou art, and Cawdor; and shalt be
What thou art promised. Yet I do fear thy
nature;
It is too full o' the milk of human kindness
To catch the nearest way; thou wouldst be
great,
Art not without ambition; but without
The illness should attend it; what thou
wouldst highly,
That thou wouldst holily; wouldst not play
false,
And yet wouldst wrongly win.

Macbeth (1606) act 1, sc. 5, l. [16]

13 The raven himself is hoarse
That croaks the fatal entrance of Duncan
Under my battlements.

Macbeth (1606) act 1, sc. 5, l. [38]

14 Unsex me here,
And fill me from the crown to the toe top
full
Of direst cruelty.

Macbeth (1606) act 1, sc. 5, l. [38]

15 Come to my woman's breasts,
And take my milk for gall, you murdering
ministers.

Macbeth (1606) act 1, sc. 5, l. [47]

16 Your face, my thane, is as a book where
men
May read strange matters.

Macbeth (1606) act 1, sc. 5, l. [63]

17 Look like the innocent flower,
But be the serpent under't.

Macbeth (1606) act 1, sc. 5, l. [66]

18 This guest of summer,
The temple-haunting martlet.

Macbeth (1606) act 1, sc. 6, l. 3

19 If it were done when 'tis done, then 'twere
well
It were done quickly: if the assassination
Could trammel up the consequence, and
catch
With his surcease success; that but this
blow
Might be the be-all and the end-all here,
But here, upon this bank and shoal of time,
We'd jump the life to come.

Macbeth (1606) act 1, sc. 7, l. 1

20 Bloody instructions, which, being taught,
return,
To plague the inventor.

Macbeth (1606) act 1, sc. 7, l. 9

21 Besides, this Duncan
Hath borne his faculties so meek, hath been
So clear in his great office, that his virtues
Will plead like angels trumpet-tongued,
against
The deep damnation of his taking-off.

Macbeth (1606) act 1, sc. 7, l. 16

22 I have no spur
To prick the sides of my intent, but only
Vaulting ambition, which o'erleaps itself,
And falls on the other.

Macbeth (1606) act 1, sc. 7, l. 25

23 He hath honoured me of late; and I have
bought
Golden opinions from all sorts of people.

Macbeth (1606) act 1, sc. 7, l. 32

24 Was the hope drunk,
Wherein you dressed yourself?

Macbeth (1606) act 1, sc. 7, l. 35

25 Letting 'I dare not' wait upon 'I would,'
Like the poor cat i' the adage?

Macbeth (1606) act 1, sc. 7, l. 44

26 I dare do all that may become a man;
Who dares do more is none.

Macbeth (1606) act 1, sc. 7, l. 46

1 LADY MACBETH: I have given suck, and know
How tender 'tis to love the babe that milks
me:
I would, while it was smiling in my face,
Have plucked my nipple from his boneless
gums,
And dash'd the brains out, had I so sworn as
you
Have done to this.
MACBETH: If we should fail,—
LADY MACBETH: We fail!
But screw your courage to the sticking-
place,
And we'll not fail.
  Macbeth (1606) act 1, sc. 7, l. 54

2 Bring forth men-children only.
  Macbeth (1606) act 1, sc. 7, l. 72

3 False face must hide what the false heart
doth know.
  Macbeth (1606) act 1, sc. 7, l. 82

4 There's husbandry in heaven;
Their candles are all out.
  Macbeth (1606) act 2, sc. 1, l. 4

5 Is this a dagger which I see before me,
The handle toward my hand? Come, let me
clutch thee:
I have thee not, and yet I see thee still.
  Macbeth (1606) act 2, sc. 1, l. 33

6 The bell invites me.
Hear it not, Duncan; for it is a knell
That summons thee to heaven or to hell.
  Macbeth (1606) act 2, sc. 1, l. 62

7 It was the owl that shrieked, the fatal
bellman,
Which gives the stern'st good-night.
  Macbeth (1606) act 2, sc. 2, l. 4

8 Had he not resembled
My father as he slept I had done't.
  Macbeth (1606) act 2, sc. 2, l. 14

9 Methought I heard a voice cry, 'Sleep no
more!
Macbeth does murder sleep,' the innocent
sleep,
Sleep that knits up the ravelled sleave of
care.
  Macbeth (1606) act 2, sc. 2, l. 36

10 Glamis hath murdered sleep, and therefore
Cawdor
Shall sleep no more, Macbeth shall sleep no
more!
  Macbeth (1606) act 2, sc. 2, l. 43

11 Infirm of purpose!
Give me the daggers. The sleeping and the
dead
Are but as pictures; 'tis the eye of childhood
That fears a painted devil.
  Macbeth (1606) act 2, sc. 2, l. 55

12 Will all great Neptune's ocean wash this
blood
Clean from my hand? No, this my hand will
rather
The multitudinous seas incarnadine,
Making the green one red.
  Macbeth (1606) act 2, sc. 2, l. 61

13 A little water clears us of this deed.
  Macbeth (1606) act 2, sc. 2, l. 68

14 Drink, sir, is a great provoker . . . Lechery,
sir, it provokes, and unprovokes; it
provokes the desire, but it takes away the
performance.
  Macbeth (1606) act 2, sc. 3, l. [28]

15 The labour we delight in physics pain.
  Macbeth (1606) act 2, sc. 3, l. [56]

16 Confusion now hath made his masterpiece!
  Macbeth (1606) act 2, sc. 3, l. [72]

17 Shake off this downy sleep, death's
counterfeit,
And look on death itself!
  Macbeth (1606) act 2, sc. 3, l. [83]

18 MACDUFF: Our royal master's murdered!
LADY MACBETH: Woe, alas!
What! in our house?
  Macbeth (1606) act 2, sc. 3, l. [95]

19 Had I but died an hour before this chance,
I had lived a blessed time.
  Macbeth (1606) act 2, sc. 3, l. [98]

20 There's daggers in men's smiles: the near in
blood,
The nearer bloody.
  Macbeth (1606) act 2, sc. 3, l. [147]

21 A falcon, towering in her pride of place,
Was by a mousing owl hawked at and killed.
  Macbeth (1606) act 2, sc. 4, l. 12

22 BANQUO: Go not my horse the better,
I must become a borrower of the night
For a dark hour or twain.
MACBETH: Fail not our feast.
  Macbeth (1606) act 3, sc. 1, l. 26

23 We have scotched the snake, not killed it.
  Macbeth (1606) act 3, sc. 2, l. 13

24 Duncan is in his grave;
After life's fitful fever he sleeps well;
Treason has done his worst: nor steel, nor
poison,
Malice domestic, foreign levy, nothing,
Can touch him further.
  Macbeth (1606) act 3, sc. 2, l. 22

25 Come, seeling night,
Scarf up the tender eye of pitiful day,
And with thy bloody and invisible hand,
Cancel and tear to pieces that great bond
Which keeps me pale!
  Macbeth (1606) act 3, sc. 2, l. 46

26 Now spurs the lated traveller apace
To gain the timely inn.
  Macbeth (1606) act 3, sc. 3, l. 6

27 But now I am cabined, cribbed, confined,
bound in
To saucy doubts and fears.
  Macbeth (1606) act 3, sc. 4, l. 24

28 Now good digestion wait on appetite,
And health on both!
  Macbeth (1606) act 3, sc. 4, l. 38

29 Thou canst not say I did it: never shake
Thy gory locks at me.
  Macbeth (1606) act 3, sc. 4, l. 50

1 Stand not upon the order of your going.
Macbeth (1606) act 3, sc. 4, l. 119

2 It will have blood, they say; blood will have blood.
Macbeth (1606) act 3, sc. 4, l. 122

3 I am in blood
Stepped in so far that, should I wade no more,
Returning were as tedious as go o'er.
Macbeth (1606) act 3, sc. 4, l. 136

4 Double, double toil and trouble;
Fire burn and cauldron bubble.
Macbeth (1606) act 4, sc. 1, l. 10

5 Eye of newt, and toe of frog,
Wool of bat, and tongue of dog,
Adder's fork, and blind-worm's sting,
Lizard's leg, and howlet's wing,
For a charm of powerful trouble,
Like a hell-broth boil and bubble.
Macbeth (1606) act 4, sc. 1, l. 14

6 By the pricking of my thumbs,
Something wicked this way comes.
Macbeth (1606) act 4, sc. 1, l. 44

7 How now, you secret, black, and midnight hags!
Macbeth (1606) act 4, sc. 1, l. 48

8 Be bloody, bold, and resolute.
Macbeth (1606) act 4, sc. 1, l. 79

9 But yet, I'll make assurance double sure,
And take a bond of fate.
Macbeth (1606) act 4, sc. 1, l. 83

10 Macbeth shall never vanquished be until
Great Birnam wood to high Dunsinane hill
Shall come against him.
Macbeth (1606) act 4, sc. 1, l. 92

11 Stands Scotland where it did?
Macbeth (1606) act 4, sc. 3, l. 164

12 Give sorrow words: the grief that does not speak
Whispers the o'er-fraught heart, and bids it break.
Macbeth (1606) act 4, sc. 3, l. 209

13 He has no children. All my pretty ones?
Did you say all? O hell-kite! All?
What! all my pretty chickens and their dam,
At one fell swoop?
Macbeth (1606) act 4, sc. 3, l. 216

14 Out, damned spot!
Macbeth (1606) act 5, sc. 1, l. [38]

15 Who would have thought the old man to have had so much blood in him?
Macbeth (1606) act 5, sc. 1, l. [42]

16 The Thane of Fife had a wife: where is she now?
Macbeth (1606) act 5, sc. 1, l. [46]

17 All the perfumes of Arabia will not sweeten this little hand.
Macbeth (1606) act 5, sc. 1, l. [56]

18 What's done cannot be undone.
Macbeth (1606) act 5, sc. 1, l. [74]

19 The devil damn thee black, thou cream-faced loon!

Where gott'st thou that goose look?
Macbeth (1606) act 5, sc. 3, l. 11

20 I have lived long enough: my way of life
Is fall'n into the sear, the yellow leaf.
Macbeth (1606) act 5, sc. 3, l. 22; cf. **Byron** 78:26

21 Canst thou not minister to a mind diseased?
Macbeth (1606) act 5, sc. 3, l. 37

22 Throw physic to the dogs; I'll none of it.
Macbeth (1606) act 5, sc. 3, l. 47

23 I have supped full with horrors.
Macbeth (1606) act 5, sc. 5, l. 13

24 She should have died hereafter;
There would have been a time for such a word,
To-morrow, and to-morrow, and to-morrow,
Creeps in this petty pace from day to day,
To the last syllable of recorded time;
And all our yesterdays have lighted fools
The way to dusty death. Out, out, brief candle!
Life's but a walking shadow, a poor player,
That struts and frets his hour upon the stage,
And then is heard no more; it is a tale
Told by an idiot, full of sound and fury,
Signifying nothing.
Macbeth (1606) act 5, sc. 5, l. 16

25 Macduff was from his mother's womb
Untimely ripped.
Macbeth (1606) act 5, sc. 7, l. 44

26 Lay on, Macduff;
And damned be him that first cries, 'Hold, enough!'
Macbeth (1606) act 5, sc. 7, l. 62

Measure for Measure

27 And liberty plucks justice by the nose.
Measure for Measure (1604) act 1, sc. 3, l. 29

28 A man whose blood
Is very snow-broth.
Measure for Measure (1604) act 1, sc. 4, l. 57

29 O! it is excellent
To have a giant's strength, but it is tyrannous
To use it like a giant.
Measure for Measure (1604) act 2, sc. 2, l. 107

30 Man, proud man,
Drest in a little brief authority,
Most ignorant of what he's most assured,
His glassy essence, like an angry ape,
Plays such fantastic tricks before high heaven,
As make the angels weep.
Measure for Measure (1604) act 2, sc. 2, l. 117

31 Be absolute for death; either death or life
Shall thereby be the sweeter.
Measure for Measure (1604) act 3, sc. 1, l. 5

32 If I must die,
I will encounter darkness as a bride,
And hug it in mine arms.
Measure for Measure (1604) act 3, sc. 1, l. 81

33 CLAUDIO: Ay, but to die, and go we know not where;

To lie in cold obstruction and to rot.
Measure for Measure (1604) act 3, sc. 1, l. 116

1 There, at the moated grange, resides this dejected Mariana.
Measure for Measure (1604) act 3, sc. 1, l. [279]; cf. **Tennyson** 312:18

The Merchant of Venice
2 God made him, and therefore let him pass for a man.
The Merchant of Venice (1596–8) act 1, sc. 2, l. [59]

3 I will buy with you, sell with you, talk with you, walk with you, and so following; but I will not eat with you, drink with you, nor pray with you. What news on the Rialto?
The Merchant of Venice (1596–8) act 1, sc. 3, l. [36]

4 If I can catch him once upon the hip, I will feed fat the ancient grudge I bear him.
The Merchant of Venice (1596–8) act 1, sc. 3, l. [47]

5 The devil can cite Scripture for his purpose.
The Merchant of Venice (1596–8) act 1, sc. 3, l. [99]

6 Still have I borne it with a patient shrug, For sufferance is the badge of all our tribe.
The Merchant of Venice (1596–8) act 1, sc. 3, l. [110]

7 You call me misbeliever, cut-throat dog, And spit upon my Jewish gabardine.
The Merchant of Venice (1596–8) act 1, sc. 3, l. [112]

8 It is a wise father that knows his own child.
The Merchant of Venice (1596–8) act 2, sc. 2, l. [83]

9 Truth will come to light; murder cannot be hid long.
The Merchant of Venice (1596–8) act 2, sc. 2, l. [86]

10 My daughter! O my ducats! O my daughter!
The Merchant of Venice (1596–8) act 2, sc. 8, l. 15

11 The portrait of a blinking idiot.
The Merchant of Venice (1596–8) act 2, sc. 9, l. 54

12 Let him look to his bond.
The Merchant of Venice (1596–8) act 3, sc. 1, l. [51]

13 If you prick us, do we not bleed? if you tickle us, do we not laugh? if you poison us, do we not die? and if you wrong us, shall we not revenge?
The Merchant of Venice (1596–8) act 3, sc. 1, l. [69]

14 The villainy you teach me I will execute, and it shall go hard but I will better the instruction.
The Merchant of Venice (1596–8) act 3, sc. 1, l. [76]

15 He makes a swan-like end, Fading in music.
The Merchant of Venice (1596–8) act 3, sc. 2, l. 44

16 Tell me where is fancy bred, Or in the heart or in the head?
The Merchant of Venice (1596–8) act 3, sc. 2, l. 63

17 ... An unlessoned girl, unschooled, unpractised; Happy in this, she is not yet so old But she may learn; happier than this, She is not bred so dull but she can learn.
The Merchant of Venice (1596–8) act 3, sc. 2, l. 160

18 I am a tainted wether of the flock, Meetest for death: the weakest kind of fruit Drops earliest to the ground.
The Merchant of Venice (1596–8) act 4, sc. 1, l. 114

19 I never knew so young a body with so old a head.
The Merchant of Venice (1596–8) act 4, sc. 1, l. [163]

20 The quality of mercy is not strained, It droppeth as the gentle rain from heaven Upon the place beneath.
The Merchant of Venice (1596–8) act 4, sc. 1, l. [182]

21 Though justice be thy plea, consider this, That in the course of justice none of us Should see salvation: we do pray for mercy, And that same prayer doth teach us all to render The deeds of mercy.
The Merchant of Venice (1596–8) act 4, sc. 1, l. [197]

22 Wrest once the law to your authority: To do a great right, do a little wrong.
The Merchant of Venice (1596–8) act 4, sc. 1, l. [215]

23 A Daniel come to judgement! yea, a Daniel!
The Merchant of Venice (1596–8) act 4, sc. 1, l. [223]

24 The court awards it, and the law doth give it.
The Merchant of Venice (1596–8) act 4, sc. 1, l. [301]

25 He is well paid that is well satisfied.
The Merchant of Venice (1596–8) act 4, sc. 1, l. [416]

26 The moon shines bright: in such a night as this ...
Troilus methinks mounted the Troyan walls, And sighed his soul toward the Grecian tents, Where Cressid lay that night.
The Merchant of Venice (1596–8) act 5, sc. 1, l. 1

27 In such a night Stood Dido with a willow in her hand Upon the wild sea-banks, and waft her love To come again to Carthage.
The Merchant of Venice (1596–8) act 5, sc. 1, l. 9

28 How sweet the moonlight sleeps upon this bank!
Here will we sit, and let the sounds of music Creep in our ears; soft stillness and the night Become the touches of sweet harmony.
The Merchant of Venice (1596–8) act 5, sc. 1, l. 54

29 Look, how the floor of heaven Is thick inlaid with patines of bright gold.
The Merchant of Venice (1596–8) act 5, sc. 1, l. 58

30 How far that little candle throws his beams! So shines a good deed in a naughty world.
The Merchant of Venice (1596–8) act 5, sc. 1, l. 90

The Merry Wives of Windsor
31 Why, then the world's mine oyster, Which I with sword will open.
The Merry Wives of Windsor (1597) act 2, sc. 2, l. 2

32 There is divinity in odd numbers, either in nativity, chance or death.
The Merry Wives of Windsor (1597) act 5, sc. 1, l. 3

A Midsummer Night's Dream
33 The course of true love never did run smooth.
A Midsummer Night's Dream (1595–6) act 1, sc. 1, l. 134

1 So quick bright things come to confusion.
A Midsummer Night's Dream (1595–6) act 1, sc. 1,
l. 149

2 Love looks not with the eyes, but with the
mind,
And therefore is winged Cupid painted
blind.
A Midsummer Night's Dream (1595–6) act 1, sc. 1,
l. 234

3 I could play Ercles rarely, or a part to tear a
cat in, to make all split.
A Midsummer Night's Dream (1595–6) act 1, sc. 2,
l. [31]

4 I will roar you as gently as any sucking
dove; I will roar you as 'twere any
nightingale.
A Midsummer Night's Dream (1595–6) act 1, sc. 2,
l. [85]

5 Pyramus is a sweet-faced man; a proper
man, as one shall see in a summer's day.
A Midsummer Night's Dream (1595–6) act 1, sc. 2,
l. [89]

6 Over hill, over dale,
Thorough bush, thorough brier,
Over park, over pale,
Thorough flood, thorough fire.
A Midsummer Night's Dream (1595–6) act 2, sc. 1,
l. 2

7 I must go seek some dew-drops here,
And hang a pearl in every cowslip's ear.
A Midsummer Night's Dream (1595–6) act 2, sc. 1,
l. 14

8 Ill met by moonlight, proud Titania.
A Midsummer Night's Dream (1595–6) act 2, sc. 1,
l. 60

9 The nine men's morris is filled up with
mud.
A Midsummer Night's Dream (1595–6) act 2, sc. 1,
l. 98

10 The seasons alter: hoary-headed frosts
Fall in the fresh lap of the crimson rose.
A Midsummer Night's Dream (1595–6) act 2, sc. 1,
l. 107

11 I'll put a girdle round about the earth
In forty minutes.
A Midsummer Night's Dream (1595–6) act 2, sc. 1,
l. 175

12 I know a bank whereon the wild thyme
blows,
Where oxlips and the nodding violet grows
Quite over-canopied with luscious
woodbine,
With sweet musk-roses, and with eglantine.
A Midsummer Night's Dream (1595–6) act 2, sc. 1,
l. 249

13 You spotted snakes with double tongue,
Thorny hedge-hogs, be not seen.
A Midsummer Night's Dream (1595–6) act 2, sc. 2,
l. 9

14 Weaving spiders come not here;
Hence you long-legged spinners, hence!
A Midsummer Night's Dream (1595–6) act 2, sc. 2,
l. 20

15 Look in the almanack; find out moonshine,
find out moonshine.
A Midsummer Night's Dream (1595–6) act 3, sc. 1,
l. [55]

16 What hempen home-spuns have we
swaggering here,
So near the cradle of the fairy queen?
A Midsummer Night's Dream (1595–6) act 3, sc. 1,
l. [82]

17 Lord, what fools these mortals be!
A Midsummer Night's Dream (1595–6) act 3, sc. 2,
l. 115

18 She was a vixen when she went to school:
And though she be but little, she is fierce.
A Midsummer Night's Dream (1595–6) act 3, sc. 2,
l. 324

19 Ghosts, wandering here and there,
Troop home to churchyards.
A Midsummer Night's Dream (1595–6) act 3, sc. 2,
l. 381

20 Let us have the tongs and the bones.
A Midsummer Night's Dream (1595–6) act 4, sc. 1,
l. [33]

21 The lunatic, the lover, and the poet,
Are of imagination all compact.
A Midsummer Night's Dream (1595–6) act 5, sc. 1,
l. 7

22 The poet's eye, in a fine frenzy rolling,
Doth glance from heaven to earth, from
earth to heaven;
And, as imagination bodies forth
The forms of things unknown, the poet's
pen
Turns them to shapes, and gives to airy
nothing
A local habitation and a name.
A Midsummer Night's Dream (1595–6) act 5, sc. 1,
l. 12

23 The best in this kind are but shadows, and
the worst are no worse, if imagination
amend them.
A Midsummer Night's Dream (1595–6) act 5, sc. 1,
l. [215]

24 The iron tongue of midnight hath told
twelve;
Lovers, to bed; 'tis almost fairy time.
A Midsummer Night's Dream (1595–6) act 5, sc. 1,
l. [372]

25 Not a mouse
Shall disturb this hallowed house:
I am sent with broom before,
To sweep the dust behind the door.
A Midsummer Night's Dream (1595–6) act 5, sc. 2,
l. 17

Much Ado About Nothing

26 He is a very valiant trencher-man.
Much Ado About Nothing (1598–9) act 1, sc. 1, l.
[52]

27 There was a star danced, and under that was
I born.
Much Ado About Nothing (1598–9) act 2, sc. 1, l.
[351]

1 Sigh no more, ladies, sigh no more,
Men were deceivers ever.
Much Ado About Nothing (1598–9) act 2, sc. 3, l. [65]

2 Sits the wind in that corner?
Much Ado About Nothing (1598–9) act 2, sc. 3, l. [108]

3 Comparisons are odorous.
Much Ado About Nothing (1598–9) act 3, sc. 5, l. [18]

4 You have stayed me in a happy hour.
Much Ado About Nothing (1598–9) act 4, sc. 1, l. [283]

5 O God, that I were a man! I would eat his heart in the market-place.
Much Ado About Nothing (1598–9) act 4, sc. 1, l. [311]

6 No, I was not born under a rhyming planet.
Much Ado About Nothing (1598–9) act 5, sc. 2, l. [40]

Othello

7 But I will wear my heart upon my sleeve
For daws to peck at: I am not what I am.
Othello (1602–4) act 1, sc. 1, l. 64

8 Even now, now, very now, an old black ram
Is tupping your white ewe.
Othello (1602–4) act 1, sc. 1, l. 88

9 Your daughter and the Moor are now making the beast with two backs.
Othello (1602–4) act 1, sc. 1, l. [117]

10 Keep up your bright swords, for the dew will rust them.
Othello (1602–4) act 1, sc. 2, l. 59

11 I will a round unvarnished tale deliver.
Othello (1602–4) act 1, sc. 3, l. 90

12 And of the Cannibals that each other eat,
The Anthropophagi, and men whose heads
Do grow beneath their shoulders.
Othello (1602–4) act 1, sc. 3, l. 143

13 She loved me for the dangers I had passed,
And I loved her that she did pity them.
Othello (1602–4) act 1, sc. 3, l. 167

14 I do perceive here a divided duty.
Othello (1602–4) act 1, sc. 3, l. 181

15 Our great captain's captain.
Othello (1602–4) act 2, sc. 1, l. 74

16 To suckle fools and chronicle small beer.
Othello (1602–4) act 2, sc. 1, l. 163

17 O! I have lost my reputation. I have lost the immortal part of myself, and what remains is bestial.
Othello (1602–4) act 2, sc. 3, l. [264]

18 O! thereby hangs a tail.
Othello (1602–4) act 3, sc. 1, l. [8]

19 Excellent wretch! Perdition catch my soul
But I do love thee! and when I love thee not,
Chaos is come again.
Othello (1602–4) act 3, sc. 3, l. 90

20 Who steals my purse steals trash; 'tis something, nothing;
'Twas mine, 'tis his, and has been slave to thousands;

But he that filches from me my good name
Robs me of that which not enriches him,
And makes me poor indeed.
Othello (1602–4) act 3, sc. 3, l. 157

21 O! beware, my lord, of jealousy;
It is the green-eyed monster which doth mock
The meat it feeds on.
Othello (1602–4) act 3, sc. 3, l. 165

22 If I do prove her haggard,
Though that her jesses were my dear heart-strings,
I'd whistle her off and let her down the wind,
To prey at fortune.
Othello (1602–4) act 3, sc. 3, l. 260

23 I had rather be a toad,
And live upon the vapour of a dungeon,
Than keep a corner in the thing I love
For others' uses.
Othello (1602–4) act 3, sc. 3, l. 270

24 Trifles light as air
Are to the jealous confirmations strong
As proofs of holy writ.
Othello (1602–4) act 3, sc. 3, l. 323

25 Farewell the tranquil mind; farewell content!
Farewell the plumèd troop and the big wars
That make ambition virtue!
Othello (1602–4) act 3, sc. 3, l. 349

26 Pride, pomp, and circumstance of glorious war!
Othello (1602–4) act 3, sc. 3, l. 355

27 Othello's occupation's gone!
Othello (1602–4) act 3, sc. 3, l. 358

28 That handkerchief
Did an Egyptian to my mother give.
Othello (1602–4) act 3, sc. 4, l. 56

29 A sibyl, that had numbered in the world
The sun to course two hundred compasses,
In her prophetic fury sewed the work;
The worms were hallowed that did breed the silk.
Othello (1602–4) act 3, sc. 4, l. 71

30 But yet the pity of it, Iago! O! Iago, the pity of it, Iago!
Othello (1602–4) act 4, sc. 1, l. [205]

31 Those that do teach young babes
Do it with gentle means and easy tasks;
He might have chid me so; for, in good faith,
I am a child to chiding.
Othello (1602–4) act 4, sc. 2, l. 111

32 The poor soul sat sighing by a sycamore tree,
Sing all a green willow;
Her hand on her bosom, her head on her knee,
Sing willow, willow, willow.
Othello (1602–4) act 4, sc. 3, l. [41]

33 It is the cause, it is the cause, my soul;
Let me not name it to you, you chaste stars!
It is the cause.
Othello (1602–4) act 5, sc. 2, l. 1

1 Put out the light, and then put out the light.
Othello (1602–4) act 5, sc. 2, l. 7

2 Murder's out of tune,
And sweet revenge grows harsh.
Othello (1602–4) act 5, sc. 2, l. 113

3 Here is my journey's end, here is my butt,
And very sea-mark of my utmost sail.
Othello (1602–4) act 5, sc. 2, l. 266

4 I have done the state some service, and they
know 't;
No more of that. I pray you, in your letters,
When you shall these unlucky deeds relate,
Speak of me as I am; nothing extenuate,
Nor set down aught in malice: then, must
you speak
Of one that loved not wisely but too well;
Of one not easily jealous, but, being
wrought,
Perplexed in the extreme; of one whose
hand,
Like the base Indian, threw a pearl away
Richer than all his tribe.
Othello (1602–4) act 5, sc. 2, l. 338

5 I kissed thee ere I killed thee, no way but
this,
Killing myself to die upon a kiss.
Othello (1602–4) act 5, sc. 2, l. 357

Richard II

6 Old John of Gaunt, time-honoured
Lancaster.
Richard II (1595) act 1, sc. 1, l. 1

7 The purest treasure mortal times afford
Is spotless reputation; that away,
Men are but gilded loam or painted clay.
Richard II (1595) act 1, sc. 1, l. 177

8 We were not born to sue, but to command.
Richard II (1595) act 1, sc. 1, l. 196; cf. **Scott**
266:7

9 How long a time lies in one little word!
Four lagging winters and four wanton
springs
End in a word; such is the breath of kings.
Richard II (1595) act 1, sc. 3, l. 213

10 There is no virtue like necessity.
Richard II (1595) act 1, sc. 3, l. 278

11 As the last taste of sweets, is sweetest last,
Writ in remembrance more than things
long past.
Richard II (1595) act 2, sc. 1, l. 13

12 This royal throne of kings, this sceptered
isle,
This earth of majesty, this seat of Mars,
This other Eden, demi-paradise,
This fortress built by Nature for herself
Against infection and the hand of war,
This happy breed of men, this little world,
This precious stone set in the silver sea.
Richard II (1595) act 2, sc. 1, l. 40

13 This blessèd plot, this earth, this realm, this
England.
Richard II (1595) act 2, sc. 1, l. 50

14 Grace me no grace, nor uncle me no uncle.
Richard II (1595) act 2, sc. 3, l. 87

15 The caterpillars of the commonwealth.
Richard II (1595) act 2, sc. 3, l. 166

16 Things past redress are now with me past
care.
Richard II (1595) act 2, sc. 3, l. 171

17 Not all the water in the rough rude sea
Can wash the balm from an anointed king.
Richard II (1595) act 3, sc. 2, l. 54

18 O! call back yesterday, bid time return.
Richard II (1595) act 3, sc. 2, l. 69

19 Let's talk of graves, of worms, and epitaphs;
Make dust our paper, and with rainy eyes
Write sorrow on the bosom of the earth.
Let's choose executors, and talk of wills.
Richard II (1595) act 3, sc. 2, l. 145

20 For God's sake, let us sit upon the ground
And tell sad stories of the death of kings.
Richard II (1595) act 3, sc. 2, l. 155

21 Within the hollow crown
That rounds the mortal temples of a king
Keeps Death his court.
Richard II (1595) act 3, sc. 2, l. 160

22 What must the king do now? Must he
submit?
The king shall do it: must he be deposed?
The king shall be contented.
Richard II (1595) act 3, sc. 3, l. 143

23 I'll give my jewels for a set of beads,
My gorgeous palace for a hermitage,
My gay apparel for an almsman's gown,
My figured goblets for a dish of wood,
My sceptre for a palmer's walking staff.
Richard II (1595) act 3, sc. 3, l. 147

24 Go, bind thou up yon dangling apricocks.
Richard II (1595) act 3, sc. 4, l. 29

25 Here, in this place,
I'll set a bank of rue, sour herb of grace.
Richard II (1595) act 3, sc. 4, l. 104

26 God save the king! Will no man say, amen?
Richard II (1595) act 4, sc. 1, l. 172

27 With mine own tears I wash away my balm,
With mine own hands I give away my
crown.
Richard II (1595) act 4, sc. 1, l. 207

28 That were some love but little policy.
Richard II (1595) act 5, sc. 1, l. 84

29 Who are the violets now
That strew the green lap of the new come
spring?
Richard II (1595) act 5, sc. 2, l. 46

30 How sour sweet music is,
When time is broke, and no proportion
kept!
So is it in the music of men's lives.
Richard II (1595) act 5, sc. 5, l. 42

31 I wasted time, and now doth time waste me.
Richard II (1595) act 5, sc. 5, l. 49

Richard III

32 Now is the winter of our discontent
Made glorious summer by this sun of York.
Richard III (1591) act 1, sc. 1, l. 1

1 This weak piping time of peace.
Richard III (1591) act 1, sc. 1, l. 24

2 Was ever woman in this humour wooed?
Was ever woman in this humour won?
Richard III (1591) act 1, sc. 2, l. 229

3 Clarence is come,—false, fleeting, perjured
Clarence.
Richard III (1591) act 1, sc. 4, l. 55

4 Woe to the land that's governed by a child!
Richard III (1591) act 2, sc. 3, l. 11; cf. **Bible**
38:29

5 So wise so young, they say, do never live
long.
Richard III (1591) act 3, sc. 1, l. 79

6 Talk'st thou to me of 'ifs'? Thou art a traitor:
Off with his head!
Richard III (1591) act 3, sc. 4, l. 74; cf. **Cibber**
92:19

7 I am not in the giving vein to-day.
Richard III (1591) act 4, sc. 2, l. 115

8 Harp not on that string.
Richard III (1591) act 4, sc. 4, l. 365

9 True hope is swift, and flies with swallow's
wings;
Kings it makes gods, and meaner creatures
kings.
Richard III (1591) act 5, sc. 2, l. 23

10 The king's name is a tower of strength.
Richard III (1591) act 5, sc. 3, l. 12

11 A horse! a horse! my kingdom for a horse!
Richard III (1591) act 5, sc. 4, l. 7

Romeo and Juliet

12 A pair of star-crossed lovers.
Romeo and Juliet (1595) prologue

13 Younger than she are happy mothers made.
Romeo and Juliet (1595) act 1, sc. 2, l. 12

14 O! then, I see, Queen Mab hath been with
you . . .
She is the fairies' midwife, and she comes
In shape no bigger than an agate-stone.
Romeo and Juliet (1595) act 1, sc. 4, l. 53

15 You and I are past our dancing days.
Romeo and Juliet (1595) act 1, sc. 5, l. [35]

16 O! she doth teach the torches to burn
bright.
It seems she hangs upon the cheek of night
Like a rich jewel in an Ethiop's ear;
Beauty too rich for use, for earth too dear.
Romeo and Juliet (1595) act 1, sc. 5, l. [48]

17 My only love sprung from my only hate!
Too early seen unknown, and known too
late!
Romeo and Juliet (1595) act 1, sc. 5, l. [142]

18 He jests at scars, that never felt a wound.
But, soft! what light through yonder
window breaks?
It is the east, and Juliet is the sun.
Romeo and Juliet (1595) act 2, sc. 2, l. 1

19 O Romeo, Romeo! wherefore art thou
Romeo?
Romeo and Juliet (1595) act 2, sc. 2, l. 33

20 What's in a name? that which we call a rose
By any other name would smell as sweet.
Romeo and Juliet (1595) act 2, sc. 2, l. 43

21 It is too rash, too unadvised, too sudden.
Romeo and Juliet (1595) act 2, sc. 2, l. 118

22 O! for a falconer's voice,
To lure this tassel-gentle back again.
Romeo and Juliet (1595) act 2, sc. 2, l. 158

23 Good-night, good-night! parting is such
sweet sorrow.
Romeo and Juliet (1595) act 2, sc. 2, l. 184

24 I am the very pink of courtesy.
Romeo and Juliet (1595) act 2, sc. 4, l. [63]

25 No, 'tis not so deep as a well, nor so wide as
a church door; but 'tis enough, 'twill serve.
Romeo and Juliet (1595) act 3, sc. 1, l. [100]

26 A plague o' both your houses!
Romeo and Juliet (1595) act 3, sc. 1, l. [112]

27 O! I am Fortune's fool.
Romeo and Juliet (1595) act 3, sc. 1, l. [142]

28 Gallop apace, you fiery-footed steeds,
Towards Phoebus' lodging.
Romeo and Juliet (1595) act 3, sc. 2, l. 1

29 Give me my Romeo: and, when he shall die,
Take him and cut him out in little stars,
And he will make the face of heaven so fine
That all the world will be in love with night,
And pay no worship to the garish sun.
Romeo and Juliet (1595) act 3, sc. 2, l. 21

30 Adversity's sweet milk, philosophy.
Romeo and Juliet (1595) act 3, sc. 3, l. 54

31 It was the nightingale, and not the lark,
That pierced the fearful hollow of thine ear.
Romeo and Juliet (1595) act 3, sc. 5, l. 2

32 Night's candles are burnt out, and jocund
day
Stands tiptoe on the misty mountain tops.
Romeo and Juliet (1595) act 3, sc. 5, l. 9

33 Thank me no thankings, nor proud me no
prouds.
Romeo and Juliet (1595) act 3, sc. 5, l. 153

34 Death lies on her like an untimely frost.
Romeo and Juliet (1595) act 4, sc. 5, l. 28

35 Tempt not a desperate man.
Romeo and Juliet (1595) act 5, sc. 3, l. 59

36 How oft when men are at the point of death
Have they been merry! which their keepers
call
A lightning before death.
Romeo and Juliet (1595) act 5, sc. 3, l. 88

The Taming of the Shrew

37 Kiss me Kate, we will be married o' Sunday.
The Taming of the Shrew (1592) act 2, sc. 1, l. 318

38 This is the way to kill a wife with kindness.
The Taming of the Shrew (1592) act 4, sc. 1, l. [211]

39 A woman moved is like a fountain troubled,
Muddy, ill-seeming, thick, bereft of beauty.
The Taming of the Shrew (1592) act 5, sc. 2, l. 143

The Tempest

1 He hath no drowning mark upon him; his complexion is perfect gallows.
The Tempest (1611) act 1, sc. 1, l. [33]

2 What seest thou else
In the dark backward and abysm of time?
The Tempest (1611) act 1, sc. 2, l. 49

3 My library
Was dukedom large enough.
The Tempest (1611) act 1, sc. 2, l. 109

4 The still-vexed Bermoothes.
The Tempest (1611) act 1, sc. 2, l. 229

5 You taught me language; and my profit on't
Is, I know how to curse.
The Tempest (1611) act 1, sc. 2, l. 363

6 Come unto these yellow sands,
And then take hands.
The Tempest (1611) act 1, sc. 2, l. 375

7 Full fathom five thy father lies;
Of his bones are coral made:
Those are pearls that were his eyes:
Nothing of him that doth fade,
But doth suffer a sea-change
Into something rich and strange.
The Tempest (1611) act 1, sc. 2, l. 394

8 What's past is prologue.
The Tempest (1611) act 2, sc. 1, l. [261]

9 A very ancient and fish-like smell.
The Tempest (1611) act 2, sc. 2, l. [27]

10 Misery acquaints a man with strange bedfellows.
The Tempest (1611) act 2, sc. 2, l. [42]

11 'Ban, 'Ban, Ca-Caliban,
Has a new master—Get a new man.
The Tempest (1611) act 2, sc. 2, l. [197]

12 Thou deboshed fish thou.
The Tempest (1611) act 3, sc. 2, l. [30]

13 He that dies pays all debts.
The Tempest (1611) act 3, sc. 2, l. [143]

14 Be not afeard: the isle is full of noises,
Sounds and sweet airs, that give delight,
and hurt not.
The Tempest (1611) act 3, sc. 2, l. [147]

15 Our revels now are ended. These our actors,
As I foretold you, were all spirits and
Are melted into air, into thin air:
And, like the baseless fabric of this vision,
The cloud-capped towers, the gorgeous palaces,
The solemn temples, the great globe itself,
Yea, all which it inherit, shall dissolve
And, like this insubstantial pageant faded,
Leave not a rack behind. We are such stuff
As dreams are made on, and our little life
Is rounded with a sleep.
The Tempest (1611) act 4, sc. 1, l. 148

16 I do begin to have bloody thoughts.
The Tempest (1611) act 4, sc. 1, l. [221]

17 But this rough magic
I here abjure.
The Tempest (1611) act 5, sc. 1, l. 50

18 I'll break my staff,
Bury it certain fathoms in the earth,
And, deeper than did ever plummet sound,
I'll drown my book.
The Tempest (1611) act 5, sc. 1, l. 54

19 Where the bee sucks, there suck I
In a cowslip's bell I lie;
There I couch when owls do cry.
On the bat's back I do fly
After summer merrily:
Merrily, merrily shall I live now
Under the blossom that hangs on the bough.
The Tempest (1611) act 5, sc. 1, l. 88

20 How beauteous mankind is! O brave new world,
That has such people in't.
The Tempest (1611) act 5, sc. 1, l. 183

Timon of Athens

21 Men shut their doors against a setting sun.
Timon of Athens (*c.*1607) act 1, sc. 2, l. [152]

22 You fools of fortune, trencher-friends, time's flies.
Timon of Athens (*c.*1607) act 3, sc. 6, l. [107]

23 We have seen better days.
Timon of Athens (*c.*1607) act 4, sc. 2, l. 27

24 The moon's an arrant thief,
And her pale fire she snatches from the sun.
Timon of Athens (*c.*1607) act 4, sc. 3, l. 437

25 Timon hath made his everlasting mansion
Upon the beachèd verge of the salt flood.
Timon of Athens (*c.*1607) act 5, sc. 1, l. [220]

Titus Andronicus

26 She is a woman, therefore may be wooed;
She is a woman, therefore may be won;
Titus Andronicus (1590) act 2, sc. 1, l. 82

27 Come, and take choice of all my library,
And so beguile thy sorrow.
Titus Andronicus (1590) act 4, sc. 1, l. 34

Troilus and Cressida

28 Take but degree away, untune that string,
And, hark! what discord follows.
Troilus and Cressida (1602) act 1, sc. 3, l. 109

29 To be wise, and love,
Exceeds man's might.
Troilus and Cressida (1602) act 3, sc. 2, l. [163]

30 Time hath, my lord, a wallet at his back,
Wherein he puts alms for oblivion.
Troilus and Cressida (1602) act 3, sc. 3, l. 145

31 Perseverance, dear my lord,
Keeps honour bright.
Troilus and Cressida (1602) act 3, sc. 3, l. 150

32 One touch of nature makes the whole world kin.
Troilus and Cressida (1602) act 3, sc. 3, l. 175

33 There's language in her eye, her cheek, her lip,
Nay, her foot speaks; her wanton spirits look out
At every joint and motive of her body.
Troilus and Cressida (1602) act 4, sc. 5, l. 55

34 The end crowns all,
And that old common arbitrator, Time,

Will one day end it.
Troilus and Cressida (1602) act 4, sc. 5, l. 223

1 Words, words, mere words, no matter from the heart.
Troilus and Cressida (1602) act 5, sc. 3, l. [109]

Twelfth Night

2 If music be the food of love, play on.
Twelfth Night (1601) act 1, sc. 1, l. 1

3 That strain again! it had a dying fall.
Twelfth Night (1601) act 1, sc. 1, l. 4

4 I am a great eater of beef, and I believe that does harm to my wit.
Twelfth Night (1601) act 1, sc. 3, l. [92]

5 I would I had bestowed that time in the tongues that I have in fencing, dancing, and bear-baiting. O! had I but followed the arts!
Twelfth Night (1601) act 1, sc. 3, l. [99]

6 Many a good hanging prevents a bad marriage.
Twelfth Night (1601) act 1, sc. 5, l. [20]

7 A plague o' these pickle herring!
Twelfth Night (1601) act 1, sc. 5, l. [127]

8 He is very well-favoured, and he speaks very shrewishly: one would think his mother's milk were scarce out of him.
Twelfth Night (1601) act 1, sc. 5, l. [170]

9 Make me a willow cabin at your gate.
Twelfth Night (1601) act 1, sc. 5, l. [289]

10 Halloo your name to the reverberate hills.
Twelfth Night (1601) act 1, sc. 5, l. [293]

11 Not to be a-bed after midnight is to be up betimes.
Twelfth Night (1601) act 2, sc. 3, l. 1

12 O mistress mine! where are you roaming?
O! stay and hear; your true love's coming,
That can sing both high and low.
Trip no further, pretty sweeting;
Journeys end in lovers meeting,
Every wise man's son doth know.
Twelfth Night (1601) act 2, sc. 3, l. [42]

13 What is love? 'tis not hereafter;
Present mirth hath present laughter;
What's to come is still unsure:
In delay there lies no plenty;
Then come kiss me, sweet and twenty,
Youth's a stuff will not endure.
Twelfth Night (1601) act 2, sc. 3, l. [50]

14 He does it with a better grace, but I do it more natural.
Twelfth Night (1601) act 2, sc. 3, l. [91]

15 Dost thou think, because thou art virtuous, there shall be no more cakes and ale?
Twelfth Night (1601) act 2, sc. 3, l. [124]

16 My purpose is, indeed, a horse of that colour.
Twelfth Night (1601) act 2, sc. 3, l. [184]

17 I was adored once too.
Twelfth Night (1601) act 2, sc. 3, l. [200]

18 Let still the woman take
An elder than herself, so wears she to him,
So sways she level in her husband's heart.
Twelfth Night (1601) act 2, sc. 4, l. 29

19 Come away, come away, death,
And in sad cypress let me be laid.
Twelfth Night (1601) act 2, sc. 4, l. 51

20 Now, the melancholy god protect thee, and the tailor make thy doublet of changeable taffeta, for thy mind is a very opal.
Twelfth Night (1601) act 2, sc. 4, l. [74]

21 She never told her love,
But let concealment, like a worm i' the bud,
Feed on her damask cheek: she pined in thought;
And with a green and yellow melancholy,
She sat like patience on a monument,
Smiling at grief.
Twelfth Night (1601) act 2, sc. 4, l. [112]

22 I am all the daughters of my father's house,
And all the brothers too.
Twelfth Night (1601) act 2, sc. 4, l. [122]

23 But be not afraid of greatness: some men are born great, some achieve greatness, and some have greatness thrust upon them.
Twelfth Night (1601) act 2, sc. 5, l. [158]; cf.
Heller 155:13

24 Remember who commended thy yellow stockings, and wished to see thee ever cross-gartered.
Twelfth Night (1601) act 2, sc. 5, l. [168]

25 In the south suburbs, at the Elephant,
Is best to lodge.
Twelfth Night (1601) act 3, sc. 3, l. 39

26 I think we do know the sweet Roman hand.
Twelfth Night (1601) act 3, sc. 4, l. [31]

27 Why, this is very midsummer madness.
Twelfth Night (1601) act 3, sc. 4, l. [62]

28 If this were played upon a stage now, I could condemn it as an improbable fiction.
Twelfth Night (1601) act 3, sc. 4, l. [142]

29 More matter for a May morning.
Twelfth Night (1601) act 3, sc. 4, l. [158]

30 Still you keep o' the windy side of the law.
Twelfth Night (1601) act 3, sc. 4, l. [183]

31 Thus the whirligig of time brings in his revenges.
Twelfth Night (1601) act 5, sc. 1, l. [388]

32 I'll be revenged on the whole pack of you.
Twelfth Night (1601) act 5, sc. 1, l. [390]

33 When that I was and a little tiny boy,
With hey, ho, the wind and the rain;
A foolish thing was but a toy,
For the rain it raineth every day.
Twelfth Night (1601) act 5, sc. 1, l. [401]

The Two Gentlemen of Verona

34 O! how this spring of love resembleth
The uncertain glory of an April day.
The Two Gentlemen of Verona (1592–3) act 1, sc. 3, l. 84

35 Who is Silvia? what is she,
That all our swains commend her?
The Two Gentlemen of Verona (1592–3) act 4, sc. 2, l. 40

The Winter's Tale

1 A sad tale's best for winter.
I have one of sprites and goblins.
The Winter's Tale (1610–11) act 2, sc. 1, l. 24

2 I have drunk, and seen the spider.
The Winter's Tale (1610–11) act 2, sc. 1, l. 45

3 What's gone and what's past help
Should be past grief.
The Winter's Tale (1610–11) act 3, sc. 2, l. [223]

4 Exit, pursued by a bear.
stage direction
The Winter's Tale (1610–11) act 3, sc. 3

5 When daffodils begin to peer,
With heigh! the doxy, over the dale,
Why, then comes in the sweet o' the year.
The Winter's Tale (1610–11) act 4, sc. 2, l. 1

6 While we lie tumbling in the hay.
The Winter's Tale (1610–11) act 4, sc. 2, l. 12

7 My father named me Autolycus; who being,
as I am, littered under Mercury, was
likewise a snapper-up of unconsidered
trifles.
The Winter's Tale (1610–11) act 4, sc. 2, l. [24]

8 Jog on, jog on the foot-path way,
And merrily hent the stile-a:
A merry heart goes all the day,
Your sad tires in a mile-a.
The Winter's Tale (1610–11) act 4, sc. 2, l. [133]

9 For you there's rosemary and rue; these
keep
Seeming and savour all the winter long.
The Winter's Tale (1610–11) act 4, sc. 3, l. 74

10 The marigold, that goes to bed wi' the sun,
And with him rises weeping.
The Winter's Tale (1610–11) act 4, sc. 3, l. 105

11 Daffodils,
That come before the swallow dares, and
take
The winds of March with beauty.
The Winter's Tale (1610–11) act 4, sc. 3, l. 121

12 Pale prime-roses,
That die unmarried, ere they can behold
Bright Phoebus in his strength,.
The Winter's Tale (1610–11) act 4, sc. 3, l. 122

13 The queen of curds and cream.
The Winter's Tale (1610–11) act 4, sc. 3, l. 161

14 Though I am not naturally honest, I am so
sometimes by chance.
The Winter's Tale (1610–11) act 4, sc. 3, l. [734]

15 Stars, stars!
And all eyes else dead coals.
The Winter's Tale (1610–11) act 5, sc. 1, l. 67

16 O! she's warm.
If this be magic, let it be an art
Lawful as eating.
The Winter's Tale (1610–11) act 5, sc. 3, l. 109

The Passionate Pilgrim (attribution doubtful)

17 Crabbed age and youth cannot live together:
Youth is full of pleasance, age is full of care.
The Passionate Pilgrim (1599) no. 12

18 Age, I do abhor thee, youth, I do adore thee.
The Passionate Pilgrim (1599) no. 12

The Rape of Lucrece

19 Beauty itself doth of itself persuade
The eyes of men without an orator.
The Rape of Lucrece (1594) l. 29

20 And now this pale swan in her watery nest
Begins the sad dirge of her certain ending.
The Rape of Lucrece (1594) l. 1611

Sonnets

21 To the onlie begetter of these insuing
sonnets, Mr. W. H.
also attributed to Thomas Thorpe, the publisher
Sonnets (1609) dedication

22 From fairest creatures we desire increase,
That thereby beauty's rose might never die.
Sonnet 1

23 Shall I compare thee to a summer's day?
Thou art more lovely and more temperate:
Rough winds do shake the darling buds of
May,
And summer's lease hath all too short a
date.
Sonnet 18

24 But thy eternal summer shall not fade.
Sonnet 18

25 Desiring this man's art, and that man's
scope,
With what I most enjoy contented least.
Sonnet 29

26 Haply I think on thee,—and then my state,
Like to the lark at break of day arising
From sullen earth, sings hymns at heaven's
gate.
Sonnet 29

27 When to the sessions of sweet silent
thought
I summon up remembrance of things past.
Sonnet 30

28 Full many a glorious morning have I seen
Flatter the mountain-tops with sovereign
eye.
Sonnet 33

29 Not marble, nor the gilded monuments
Of princes, shall outlive this powerful
rhyme.
Sonnet 55

30 Like as the waves make towards the pebbled
shore,
So do our minutes hasten to their end.
Sonnet 60

31 Bare ruined choirs, where late the sweet
birds sang.
Sonnet 73

32 So all my best is dressing old words new,
Spending again what is already spent.
Sonnet 76

33 Time's thievish progress to eternity.
Sonnet 77

34 Farewell! thou art too dear for my
possessing.
Sonnet 87

35 Thus have I had thee, as a dream doth
flatter,

In sleep a king, but, waking, no such matter.
Sonnet 87

1 Lilies that fester smell far worse than
weeds.
Sonnet 94

2 When in the chronicle of wasted time
I see descriptions of the fairest wights.
Sonnet 106

3 For we, which now behold these present
days,
Have eyes to wonder, but lack tongues to
praise.
Sonnet 106

4 Alas! 'tis true I have gone here and there,
And made myself a motley to the view.
Sonnet 110

5 My nature is subdued
To what it works in, like the dyer's hand.
Sonnet 111

6 Let me not to the marriage of true minds
Admit impediments. Love is not love
Which alters when it alteration finds.
Sonnet 116

7 Love alters not with his brief hours and
weeks,
But bears it out even to the edge of doom.
If this be error, and upon me proved,
I never writ, nor no man ever loved.
Sonnet 116

8 The expense of spirit in a waste of shame
Is lust in action.
Sonnet 129

9 My mistress' eyes are nothing like the sun;
Coral is far more red than her lips' red:
If snow be white, why then her breasts are
dun;
If hairs be wires, black wires grow on her
head.
Sonnet 130

10 Whoever hath her wish, thou hast thy *Will*,
And *Will* to boot, and *Will* in over-plus.
Sonnet 135

11 Two loves I have of comfort and despair,
Which like two spirits do suggest me still:
The better angel is a man right fair,
The worser spirit a woman, coloured ill.
Sonnet 144

12 For I have sworn thee fair, and thought thee
bright,
Who art as black as hell, as dark as night.
Sonnet 147

Venus and Adonis

13 Love is a spirit all compact of fire,
Not gross to sink, but light, and will aspire.
Venus and Adonis (1593) l. 145

14 Love comforteth like sunshine after rain.
Venus and Adonis (1593) l. 799

15 For he being dead, with him is beauty slain,
And, beauty dead, black chaos comes again.
Venus and Adonis (1593) l. 1019

16 Item, I give unto my wife my second best
bed, with the furniture.
will, 1616; E. K. Chambers *William Shakespeare*
(1930) vol. 2

17 Good friend, for Jesu's sake forbear
To dig the dust enclosed here.
Blest be the man that spares these stones,
And curst be he that moves my bones.
inscription on his grave, Stratford upon Avon,
probably composed by himself

Shammai *c.*1st century BC–1st century
AD

18 Say little and do much. Receive all men with
a cheerful countenance.
in *Talmud* Mishnah 'Pirqei Avot' 1:15

Bill Shankly 1914–81

19 Some people think football is a matter of
life and death . . . I can assure them it is
much more serious than that.
in *Sunday Times* 4 October 1981

Robert Shapiro 1942–

20 Not only did we play the race card, we
played it from the bottom of the deck.
*on the defence team's change of strategy at the
trial of O. J. Simpson*
in *The Times* 5 October 1995; cf. **Churchill** 91:3

George Bernard Shaw 1856–1950

21 All great truths begin as blasphemies.
Annajanska (1919)

22 Oh, you are a very poor soldier—a chocolate
cream soldier!
Arms and the Man (1898) act 1

23 I'm only a beer teetotaller, not a champagne
teetotaller.
Candida (1898) act 3

24 The British soldier can stand up to anything
except the British War Office.
The Devil's Disciple (1901) act 3

25 Stimulate the phagocytes.
The Doctor's Dilemma (1911) act 1

26 All professions are conspiracies against the
laity.
The Doctor's Dilemma (1911) act 1

27 The one point on which all women are in
furious secret rebellion against the existing
law is the saddling of the right to a child
with the obligation to become the servant
of a man.
Getting Married (1911) preface 'The Right to
Motherhood'

28 A man who has no office to go to—I don't
care who he is—is a trial of which you can
have no conception.
The Irrational Knot (1905) ch. 18

29 John Bull's other island.
title of play (1907)

30 There are only two qualities in the world:
efficiency and inefficiency, and only two

sorts of people: the efficient and the inefficient.
John Bull's Other Island (1907) act 4

1 The greatest of evils and the worst of crimes is poverty.
Major Barbara (1907) preface

2 I am a Millionaire. That is my religion.
Major Barbara (1907) act 2

3 I can't talk religion to a man with bodily hunger in his eyes.
Major Barbara (1907) act 2

4 Alcohol is a very necessary article . . . It enables Parliament to do things at eleven at night that no sane person would do at eleven in the morning.
Major Barbara (1907) act 2

5 He knows nothing; and he thinks he knows everything. That points clearly to a political career.
Major Barbara (1907) act 3

6 Nothing is ever done in this world until men are prepared to kill one another if it is not done.
Major Barbara (1907) act 3

7 But a lifetime of happiness! No man alive could bear it: it would be hell on earth.
Man and Superman (1903) act 1

8 The more things a man is ashamed of, the more respectable he is.
Man and Superman (1903) act 1

9 Of all human struggles there is none so treacherous and remorseless as the struggle between the artist man and the mother woman.
Man and Superman (1903) act 1

10 You think that you are Ann's suitor; that you are the pursuer and she the pursued . . . Fool: it is you who are the pursued, the marked down quarry, the destined prey.
Man and Superman (1903) act 2

11 Hell is full of musical amateurs: music is the brandy of the damned.
Man and Superman (1903) act 3

12 Englishmen never will be slaves: they are free to do whatever the Government and public opinion allow them to do.
Man and Superman (1903) act 3

13 When the military man approaches, the world locks up its spoons and packs off its womankind.
Man and Superman (1903) act 3; cf. **Emerson** 124:11

14 What is virtue but the Trade Unionism of the married?
Man and Superman (1903) act 3

15 Liberty means responsibility. That is why most men dread it.
Man and Superman (1903) 'Maxims: Liberty and Equality'

16 He who can, does. He who cannot, teaches.
Man and Superman (1903) 'Maxims: Education'

17 Marriage is popular because it combines the maximum of temptation with the maximum of opportunity.
Man and Superman (1903) 'Maxims: Marriage'

18 If you strike a child take care that you strike it in anger, even at the risk of maiming it for life. A blow in cold blood neither can nor should be forgiven.
Man and Superman (1903) 'Maxims: How to Beat Children'

19 Youth, which is forgiven everything, forgives itself nothing: age, which forgives itself everything, is forgiven nothing.
Man and Superman (1903) 'Maxims: Stray Sayings'

20 Take care to get what you like or you will be forced to like what you get.
Man and Superman (1903) 'Maxims: Stray Sayings'

21 Beware of the man who does not return your blow: he neither forgives you nor allows you to forgive yourself.
Man and Superman (1903) 'Maxims: Stray Sayings'

22 You will never find an Englishman in the wrong. He does everything on principle. He . . . supports his king on loyal principles and cuts off his king's head on republican principles.
The Man of Destiny (1898)

23 Anarchism is a game at which the police can beat you.
Misalliance (1914)

24 A great devotee of the Gospel of Getting On.
Mrs Warren's Profession (1898) act 4

25 You'll never have a quiet world till you knock the patriotism out of the human race.
O'Flaherty V.C. (1919)

26 A perpetual holiday is a good working definition of hell.
Parents and Children (1914) 'Children's Happiness'

27 There is only one religion, though there are a hundred versions of it.
Plays Pleasant and Unpleasant (1898) vol. 2, preface

28 It is impossible for an Englishman to open his mouth without making some other Englishman hate or despise him.
Pygmalion (1916) preface

29 I don't want to talk grammar, I want to talk like a lady.
Pygmalion (1916) act 2

30 Gin was mother's milk to her.
Pygmalion (1916) act 3

31 Walk! Not bloody likely.
Pygmalion (1916) act 3

32 No Englishman is ever fairly beaten.
Saint Joan (1924) sc. 4

33 Must then a Christ perish in torment in every age to save those that have no imagination?
Saint Joan (1924) epilogue

1 Assassination is the extreme form of censorship.
  The Showing-Up of Blanco Posnet (1911) 'Limits to Toleration'

2 The younger generation is knocking at the door, and as I open it there steps spritely in the incomparable Max.
  *on handing over the theatre review column to Max **Beerbohm***
    in *Saturday Review* 21 May 1898 'Valedictory'

3 The photographer is like the cod which produces a million eggs in order that one may reach maturity.
    introduction to the catalogue for Alvin Langdon Coburn's exhibition at the Royal Photographic Society, 1906

4 The trouble, Mr Goldwyn, is that you are only interested in art and I am only interested in money.
  *telegraphed version of the outcome of a conversation between Shaw and Sam **Goldwyn***
    Alva Johnson *The Great Goldwyn* (1937) ch. 3

5 [Dancing is] a perpendicular expression of a horizontal desire.
    in *New Statesman* 23 March 1962

6 England and America are two countries divided by a common language.
    attributed in this and other forms to George Bernard **Shaw**, but not found in Shaw's published writings; cf. **Wilde** 334:21

Hartley Shawcross 1902–

7 'But,' said Alice, 'the question is whether you can make a word mean different things.' 'Not so,' said Humpty-Dumpty, 'the question is which is to be the master. That's all.' We are the masters at the moment, and not only at the moment, but for a very long time to come.
  often quoted as, 'We are the masters now'
    speech in the House of Commons, 2 April 1946; cf. **Carroll** 84:11

Charles Shaw-Lefevre 1794–1888

8 What is that fat gentleman in such a passion about?
  *as a child, on hearing Charles James **Fox** speak in Parliament*
    G. W. E. Russell *Collections and Recollections* (1898) ch. 11

Patrick Shaw-Stewart 1888–1917

9 I saw a man this morning
  Who did not wish to die.
    poem (1916)

10 Stand in the trench, Achilles,
  Flame-capped, and shout for me.
    poem (1916)

Mary Shelley 1797–1851

11 I beheld the wretch—the miserable monster whom I had created.
    Frankenstein (1818) ch. 5

12 Teach him to think for himself? Oh, my God, teach him rather to think like other people!
  on her son's education
    Matthew Arnold *Essays in Criticism* Second Series (1888) 'Shelley'

Percy Bysshe Shelley 1792–1822

13 The cemetery is an open space among the ruins, covered in winter with violets and daisies. It might make one in love with death, to think that one should be buried in so sweet a place.
    Adonais (1821) preface

14 I weep for Adonais—he is dead!
    Adonais (1821) st. 1

15 Winter is come and gone,
  But grief returns with the revolving year.
    Adonais (1821) st. 18

16 Alas! that all we loved of him should be,
  But for our grief, as if it had not been,
  And grief itself be mortal!
    Adonais (1821) st. 21

17 A pardlike Spirit, beautiful and swift.
    Adonais (1821) st. 32

18 He has out-soared the shadow of our night;
  Envy and calumny and hate and pain,
  And that unrest which men miscall delight,
  Can touch him not and torture not again;
  From the contagion of the world's slow stain
  He is secure.
    Adonais (1821) st. 40

19 He is a portion of the loveliness
  Which once he made more lovely.
    Adonais (1821) st. 43

20 Life, like a dome of many-coloured glass,
  Stains the white radiance of Eternity.
    Adonais (1821) st. 52

21 A widow bird sat mourning for her love
  Upon a wintry bough.
    Charles the First (1822) sc. 5, l. 9

22 That orbèd maiden, with white fire laden,
  Whom mortals call the Moon.
    'The Cloud' (1819)

23 I never was attached to that great sect,
  Whose doctrine is that each one should select
  Out of the crowd a mistress or a friend,
  And all the rest, though fair and wise, commend
  To cold oblivion.
    'Epipsychidion' (1821) l. 149

24 Let there be light! said Liberty,
  And like sunrise from the sea,
  Athens arose!
    Hellas (1822) l. 682

25 The world's great age begins anew,
  The golden years return.
    Hellas (1822) l. 1060

26 Thou Paradise of exiles, Italy!
    'Julian and Maddalo' (1818) l. 57

27 Most wretched men
  Are cradled into poetry by wrong:

They learn in suffering what they teach in
song.
'Julian and Maddalo' (1818) l. 544

1 A cloud-encircled meteor of the air,
A hooded eagle among blinking owls.
of Samuel Taylor **Coleridge**
'Letter to Maria Gisborne' (1820) l. 207

2 When the lamp is shattered
The light in the dust lies dead—
When the cloud is scattered
The rainbow's glory is shed.
'Lines: When the lamp' (1824)

3 Beneath is spread like a green sea
The waveless plain of Lombardy.
'Lines written amongst the Euganean Hills'
(1818) l. 90

4 Sun-girt city, thou hast been
Ocean's child, and then his queen.
of Venice
'Lines written amongst the Euganean Hills'
(1818) l. 115

5 I met Murder on the way—
He had a mask like Castlereagh—
Very smooth he looked, yet grim,
Seven bloodhounds followed him.
'The Mask of Anarchy' (1819) st. 2

6 His big tears, for he wept well,
Turned to mill-stones as they fell.
of 'Fraud' [Lord Eldon]
'The Mask of Anarchy' (1819) st. 4

7 O wild West Wind, thou breath of Autumn's
being,
Thou, from whose unseen presence the
leaves dead
Are driven, like ghosts from an enchanter
fleeing,
Yellow, and black, and pale, and hectic red,
Pestilence-stricken multitudes.
'Ode to the West Wind' (1819) l. 1

8 Oh, lift me as a wave, a leaf, a cloud!
I fall upon the thorns of life! I bleed!
'Ode to the West Wind' (1819) l. 53

9 Make me thy lyre, even as the forest is.
'Ode to the West Wind' (1819) l. 57

10 If Winter comes, can Spring be far behind?
'Ode to the West Wind' (1819) l. 70

11 I met a traveller from an antique land
Who said: Two vast and trunkless legs of
stone
Stand in the desert.
'Ozymandias' (1819)

12 'My name is Ozymandias, king of kings:
Look on my works, ye Mighty, and despair!'
'Ozymandias' (1819)

13 Hell is a city much like London.
'Peter Bell the Third' (1819) pt. 3, st. 1

14 Ere Babylon was dust,
The Magus Zoroaster, my dead child,
Met his own image walking in the garden.
Prometheus Unbound (1819) act 1, l. 191

15 Grief for awhile is blind, and so was mine.
Prometheus Unbound (1820) act 1, l. 304

16 The dust of creeds outworn.
Prometheus Unbound (1820) act 1, l. 697

17 He gave man speech, and speech created
thought,
Which is the measure of the universe.
Prometheus Unbound (1820) act 2, sc. 4, l. 72

18 My soul is an enchanted boat,
Which, like a sleeping swan, doth float
Upon the silver waves of thy sweet singing.
Prometheus Unbound (1820) act 2, sc. 5, l. 72

19 A traveller from the cradle to the grave
Through the dim night of this immortal
day.
Prometheus Unbound (1820) act 4, l. 551

20 How wonderful is Death,
Death and his brother Sleep!
Queen Mab (1813) canto 1, l. 1; cf. **Daniel** 105:14,
Fletcher 130:8

21 Daisies, those pearled Arcturi of the earth,
The constellated flower that never sets.
'The Question' (1822)

22 A Sensitive Plant in a garden grew.
'The Sensitive Plant' (1820) pt. 1, l. 1

23 And the jessamine faint, and the sweet
tuberose,
The sweetest flower for scent that blows.
'The Sensitive Plant' (1820) pt. 1, l. 37

24 Rarely, rarely, comest thou,
Spirit of Delight!
'Song' (1824); epigraph to **Elgar**'s Second
Symphony

25 Men of England, wherefore plough
For the lords who lay ye low?
'Song to the Men of England' (written 1819)

26 An old, mad, blind, despised, and dying
king.
of **George III**
'Sonnet: England in 1819' (written 1819)

27 Music, when soft voices die,
Vibrates in the memory—
Odours, when sweet violets sicken,
Live within the sense they quicken.
'To—: Music, when soft voices die' (1824)

28 The desire of the moth for the star,
Of the night for the morrow,
The devotion to something afar
From the sphere of our sorrow.
'To—: One word is too often profaned' (1824)

29 Hail to thee, blithe Spirit!
Bird thou never wert.
'To a Skylark' (1819)

30 And singing still dost soar, and soaring ever
singest.
'To a Skylark' (1819)

31 Thou art unseen, but yet I hear thy shrill
delight.
'To a Skylark' (1819)

32 Our sincerest laughter
With some pain is fraught;
Our sweetest songs are those that tell of
saddest thought.
'To a Skylark' (1819)

1 Teach me half the gladness
That thy brain must know,
Such harmonious madness
From my lips would flow
The world should listen then—as I am
listening now.
    'To a Skylark' (1819)

2 Swiftly walk o'er the western wave,
Spirit of Night!
    'To Night' (1824)

3 And like a dying lady, lean and pale,
Who totters forth, wrapped in a gauzy veil.
    'The Waning Moon' (1824)

4 A lovely lady, garmented in light
From her own beauty.
    'The Witch of Atlas' (written 1820) st. 5

5 Poetry is the record of the best and happiest
moments of the happiest and best minds.
    A Defence of Poetry (written 1821)

6 Poets are the unacknowledged legislators of
the world.
    A Defence of Poetry (written 1821); cf. **Johnson**
    173:24

7 Monarchy is only the string that ties the
robber's bundle.
    A Philosophical View of Reform (written 1819–20)
    ch. 2

William Shenstone 1714–63

8 The world may be divided into people that
read, people that write, people that think,
and fox-hunters.
    Works . . . (1764) vol. 2 'On Writing and Books'

Philip Henry Sheridan 1831–88

9 The only good Indians I ever saw were dead.
    in response to the Comanche chief Toch-a-way,
    who described himself as a 'good Indian'
    at Fort Cobb, January 1869; attributed but
    denied by Sheridan

Richard Brinsley Sheridan 1751–1816

10 O Lord, Sir—when a heroine goes mad she
always goes into white satin.
    The Critic (1779) act 3, sc. 1

11 Illiterate him, I say, quite from your
memory.
    The Rivals (1775) act 1, sc. 2

12 Madam, a circulating library in a town is as
an evergreen tree of diabolical knowledge.
    The Rivals (1775) act 1, sc. 2

13 He is the very pineapple of politeness!
    The Rivals (1775) act 3, sc. 3

14 If I reprehend any thing in this world, it is
the use of my oracular tongue, and a nice
derangement of epitaphs!
    The Rivals (1775) act 3, sc. 3

15 She's as headstrong as an allegory on the
banks of the Nile.
    The Rivals (1775) act 3, sc. 3

16 No caparisons, Miss, if you
please!—Caparisons don't become a young
woman.
    The Rivals (1775) act 4, sc. 2

17 You shall see them on a beautiful quarto
page where a neat rivulet of text shall
meander through a meadow of margin.
    The School for Scandal (1777) act 1, sc. 1

18 Here is the whole set! a character dead at
every word.
    The School for Scandal (1777) act 2, sc. 2; cf. **Pope**
    249:4

19 Here's to the maiden of bashful fifteen
Here's to the widow of fifty
Here's to the flaunting, extravagant quean;
And here's to the housewife that's thrifty.
    The School for Scandal (1777) act 3, sc. 3

20 An unforgiving eye, and a damned
disinheriting countenance!
    The School for Scandal (1777) act 4, sc. 1

21 There is no trusting appearances.
    The School for Scandal (1777) act 5, sc. 2

22 You write with ease, to show your breeding,
But easy writing's vile hard reading.
    'Clio's Protest' (written 1771, published 1819)

23 A man may surely be allowed to take a glass
of wine by his own fireside.
    on being encountered drinking a glass of wine in
    the street, while watching his theatre, the Drury
    Lane, burn down
    T. Moore Life of Sheridan (1825) vol. 2

Sidney Sherman 1805–73

24 Remember the Alamo!
    battle cry at San Jacinto, 21 April 1836,
    traditionally attributed to General Sherman

William Tecumsah Sherman 1820–91

25 Hold out. Relief is coming.
    usually quoted as 'Hold the fort! I am coming!'
    flag signal from Kennesaw Mountain to General
    John Murray Corse at Allatoona Pass, 5 October
    1864; cf. **Bliss** 56:20

26 There is many a boy here to-day who looks
on war as all glory, but, boys, it is all hell.
    speech at Columbus, Ohio, 11 August 1880, in
    Lloyd Lewis Sherman, Fighting Prophet (1932)

James Shirley 1596–1666

27 The glories of our blood and state
Are shadows, not substantial things;
There is no armour against fate;
Death lays his icy hand on kings.
    The Contention of Ajax and Ulysses (1659) act 1, sc.
    3

28 Only the actions of the just
Smell sweet, and blossom in their dust.
    The Contention of Ajax and Ulysses (1659) act 1, sc.
    3

Mikhail Sholokhov 1905–84

29 And quiet flows the Don.
    title of novel (1934)

Clare Short 1946–

contrasting political advisers with elected politicians:

1 I sometimes call them the people who live in the dark. Everything they do is in hiding ... Everything we do is in the light. They live in the dark.

in *New Statesman* 9 August 1996

2 It will be golden elephants next.

suggesting that the government of Montserrat was 'talking mad money' in claiming assistance for evacuating the island

in *Observer* 24 August 1997

The Shorter Catechism (1647)

3 'What is the chief end of man?'
'To glorify God and to enjoy him for ever'.

The Siddur

4 Hear, O Israel: the Lord our God, the Lord is One.

The Shema; cf. **Bible** 34:27

Algernon Sidney 1622–83

5 'Tis not necessary to light a candle to the sun.

Discourses concerning Government (1698) ch. 2, sect. 23; cf. **Burton** 76:17, **Young** 344:13

6 The law is established, which no passion can disturb. 'Tis void of desire and fear, lust and anger ... 'Tis deaf, inexorable, inflexible.

Discourses concerning Government (1698) ch. 3, sect. 15

Philip Sidney 1554–86

7 My true love hath my heart and I have his, By just exchange one for the other giv'n.

Arcadia ('Old Arcadia', completed 1581) bk. 3

8 Biting my truant pen, beating myself for spite,
'Fool,' said my Muse to me; 'look in thy heart and write.'

Astrophil and Stella (1591) sonnet 1

9 With how sad steps, O Moon, thou climb'st the skies;
How silently, and with how wan a face.

Astrophil and Stella (1591) sonnet 31

10 Dumb swans, not chattering pies, do lovers prove;
They love indeed who quake to say they love.

Astrophil and Stella (1591) sonnet 54

11 I am no pick-purse of another's wit.

Astrophil and Stella (1591) sonnet 74

12 Poetry ... A speaking picture, with this end: to teach and delight.

The Defence of Poetry (1595)

13 [The poet] cometh unto you, with a tale which holdeth children from play, and old men from the chimney corner.

The Defence of Poetry (1595)

14 Comedy is an imitation of the common errors of our life.

The Defence of Poetry (1595)

15 Delight hath a joy in it either permanent or present. Laughter hath only a scornful tickling.

The Defence of Poetry (1595)

16 Thy necessity is yet greater than mine.

on giving his water-bottle to a dying soldier on the battle-field of Zutphen, 1586; commonly quoted as 'thy need is greater than mine'

Fulke Greville *Life of Sir Philip Sidney* (1652) ch. 12

Emmanuel Joseph Sieyès 1748–1836

17 J'ai vécu.
I survived.

when asked what he had done during the French Revolution

F. A. M. Mignet *Notice historique sur la vie et les travaux de M. le Comte de Sieyès* (1836)

Maurice Sigler 1901–61
and Al Hoffman 1902–60

18 Little man, you've had a busy day.

title of song (1934)

Sikh Scriptures
translated by W. H. McLeod, 1984

19 The light which shone from each of the ten Masters shines now from the sacred pages of the Guru Granth Sahib. Turn your thoughts to its message and call on God, saying, *Vahiguru!*

Ardas

20 You must always wear the Five Ks. These are uncut hair [*kes*], a sword or dagger [*kirpan*], a pair of shorts [*kachh*], a comb [*kangha*], and a steel bangle [*kara*].

Sikh Rahit Maryada

21 After three days and three nights had passed he [Guru Nanak] emerged from the stream, and having done so he declared: 'There is neither Hindu nor Muslim'

Mahima Prakas Varatak

Alan Sillitoe 1928–

22 The loneliness of the long-distance runner.

title of novel (1959)

Georges Simenon 1903–89

23 Writing is not a profession but a vocation of unhappiness.

interview in *Paris Review* Summer 1955

Paul Simon 1942–

24 Like a bridge over troubled water
I will lay me down.

'Bridge over Troubled Water' (1970 song)

25 And here's to you, Mrs Robinson
Jesus loves you more than you will know.

'Mrs Robinson' (1967 song, from the film *The Graduate*)

1 Improvisation is too good to leave to chance.

in *International Herald Tribune* 12 October 1990

Simonides *c.*556–468 BC

2 Go, tell the Spartans, thou who passest by,
That here obedient to their laws we lie.

epitaph for the 300 Spartans killed at Thermopylae, 480 BC

Herodotus *Histories* bk. 7; attributed

3 Painting is silent poetry, poetry is eloquent painting.

Plutarch *Moralia* 'De Gloria Atheniensium' sect. 3

Harold Simpson

4 Down in the forest something stirred:
It was only the note of a bird.

'Down in the Forest' (1906 song)

John Simpson 1944–

5 I'm sick to death of the 'I'm going to tell you everything about me and what I think' school of journalism. You don't watch the BBC for polemic.

interview in *Radio Times* 9 August 1997

Kirke Simpson 1881–1972

6 [Warren] Harding of Ohio was chosen by a group of men in a smoke-filled room early today as Republican candidate for President.

often attributed to Harry Daugherty, one of Harding's supporters, who appears merely to have concurred with this version of events, when pressed for comment by Simpson

news report, filed 12 June 1920; William Safire *New Language of Politics* (1968)

George R. Sims 1847–1922

7 It is Christmas Day in the Workhouse.

'In the Workhouse—Christmas Day' (1879)

C. H. Sisson 1914–

8 Here lies a civil servant. He was civil
To everyone, and servant to the devil.

The London Zoo (1961)

Sitting Bull *c.*1831–90

9 What law have I broken? Is it wrong for me to love my own? Is it wicked for me because my skin is red, because I am Sioux, because I was born where my fathers lived, because I would die for my people and my country?

to Major Brotherton, recorded July 1881

10 The Black Hills belong to me. If the whites try to take them, I will fight.

Dee Brown *Bury My Heart at Wounded Knee* (1970) ch. 12

Edith Sitwell 1887–1964

11 Jane, Jane,
Tall as a crane,
The morning light creaks down again.

Façade (1923) 'Aubade'

12 The fire was furry as a bear.

Façade (1923) 'Dark Song'

13 I enjoyed talking to her, but thought *nothing* of her writing. I considered her 'a beautiful little knitter'.

of Virginia **Woolf**

letter to Geoffrey Singleton, 11 July 1955

Osbert Sitwell 1892–1969

14 In reality, killing time
Is only the name for another of the multifarious ways
By which Time kills us.

'Milordo Inglese' (1958); cf. **Boucicault** 65:4

15 On the coast of Coromandel
Dance they to the tunes of Handel.

'On the Coast of Coromandel' (1943)

John Skelton *c.*1460–1529

16 Far may be sought
Erst that ye can find
So courteous, so kind,
As Merry Margaret,
This midsummer flower,
Gentle as falcon
Or hawk of the tower.

The Garland of Laurel (1523) 'To Mistress Margaret Hussey'

17 With margerain gentle,
The flower of goodlihead,
Embroidered the mantle
Is of your maidenhead.

The Garland of Laurel (1523) 'To Mistress Margery Wentworth'

Noel Skelton 1880–1935

18 To state as clearly as may be what means lie ready to develop a property-owning democracy, to bring the industrial and economic status of the wage-earner abreast of his political and educational, to make democracy stable and four-square.

in *The Spectator* 19 May 1923

B. F. Skinner 1904–90

19 The real question is not whether machines think but whether men do.

Contingencies of Reinforcement (1969) ch. 9

20 Education is what survives when what has been learned has been forgotten.

New Scientist 21 May 1964

Gillian Slovo 1952–

21 In most families it is the children who leave home. In mine it was the parents.

of her anti-apartheid activist parents, Joe Slovo and Ruth First

Every Secret Thing (1997)

Christopher Smart 1722–71

22 For I will consider my Cat Jeoffrey.
For he is the servant of the Living God duly and daily serving him.

Jubilate Agno (c.1758–63) Fragment B, l. 695

1 For he counteracts the powers of darkness
  by his electrical skin and glaring eyes.
For he counteracts the Devil, who is death,
  by brisking about the life.
  Jubilate Agno (c.1758–63) Fragment B, l. 721

2 Beauteous the garden's umbrage mild,
  Walk, water, meditated wild,
  And all the bloomy beds.
  A Song to David (1763) st. 81

3 Glorious the northern lights astream;
  Glorious the song, when God's the theme;
  Glorious the thunder's roar.
  A Song to David (1763) st. 85

4 And now the matchless deed's achieved,
  Determined, dared, and done.
  A Song to David (1763) st. 95

Samuel Smiles 1812–1904

5 We each day dig our graves with our teeth.
  Duty (1880) ch. 16

6 The spirit of self-help is the root of all
  genuine growth in the individual.
  Self-Help (1859) ch. 1

Adam Smith 1723–90

7 People of the same trade seldom meet
  together, even for merriment and diversion,
  but the conversation ends in a conspiracy
  against the public, or in some contrivance
  to raise prices.
  Wealth of Nations (1776) bk. 1, ch. 10, pt. 2

8 The chief enjoyment of riches consists in
  the parade of riches.
  Wealth of Nations (1776) bk. 1, ch. 11

9 To found a great empire for the sole
  purpose of raising up a people of customers,
  may at first sight appear a project fit only
  for a nation of shopkeepers. It is, however, a
  project altogether unfit for a nation of
  shopkeepers; but extremely fit for a nation
  whose government is influenced by
  shopkeepers.
  Wealth of Nations (1776) bk. 4, ch. 7, pt. 3; cf.
  Adams 2:3, **Napoleon** 231:10

10 Consumption is the sole end and purpose of
  production; and the interest of the producer
  ought to be attended to only so far as it may
  be necessary for promoting that of the
  consumer.
  Wealth of Nations (1776) bk. 4, ch. 8

11 There is no art which one government
  sooner learns of another than that of
  draining money from the pockets of the
  people.
  Wealth of Nations (1776) bk. 5, ch. 2

Alfred Emanuel Smith 1873–1944

12 All the ills of democracy can be cured by
  more democracy.
  speech in Albany, 27 June 1933, in *New York
  Times* 28 June 1933

Delia Smith

13 Football and cookery are the two most
  important subjects in the country.
  *having been appointed a director of Norwich City
  football club*
  in *Observer* 23 February 1997 'Said and Done'

Dodie Smith 1896–1990

14 The family—that dear octopus from whose
  tentacles we never quite escape.
  Dear Octopus (1938)

Edgar Smith 1857–1938

15 You may tempt the upper classes
  With your villainous demi-tasses,
  But; Heaven will protect a working-girl!
  'Heaven Will Protect the Working-Girl' (1909
  song)

F. E. Smith, Lord Birkenhead
1872–1930

16 The world continues to offer glittering
  prizes to those who have stout hearts and
  sharp swords.
  rectorial address, Glasgow University, 7
  November 1923

17 JUDGE: You are extremely offensive, young
  man.
  SMITH: As a matter of fact, we both are, and
  the only difference between us is that I am
  trying to be, and you can't help it.
  2nd Earl of Birkenhead *Earl of Birkenhead* (1933)
  vol. 1, ch. 9

Godfrey Smith 1926–

18 In a world full of audio visual marvels, may
  words matter to you and be full of magic.
  letter to a new grandchild, in *Sunday Times* 5
  July 1987

Ian Smith 1919–

19 I don't believe in black majority rule in
  Rhodesia—not in a thousand years.
  broadcast speech, 20 March 1976

Logan Pearsall Smith 1865–1946

20 There is more felicity on the far side of
  baldness than young men can possibly
  imagine.
  Afterthoughts (1931) 'Age and Death'

21 A best-seller is the gilded tomb of a
  mediocre talent.
  Afterthoughts (1931) 'Art and Letters'

22 People say that life is the thing, but I prefer
  reading.
  Afterthoughts (1931) 'Myself'

Samuel Francis Smith 1808–95

23 My country, 'tis of thee,
  Sweet land of liberty,
  Of thee I sing:
  Land where my fathers died,
  Land of the pilgrims' pride,

From every mountain-side
Let freedom ring.
'America' (1831)

Stevie Smith 1902–71

1 Oh I am a cat that likes to
Gallop about doing good.
'The Galloping Cat' (1972)

2 A good time was had by all.
title of book (1937)

3 I was much too far out all my life
And not waving but drowning.
'Not Waving but Drowning' (1957)

4 This Englishwoman is so refined
She has no bosom and no behind.
'This Englishwoman' (1937)

Sydney Smith 1771–1845

5 A Curate—there is something which excites
compassion in the very name of a Curate!!!
'Persecuting Bishops' in *Edinburgh Review* (1822)

6 I have no relish for the country; it is a kind
of healthy grave.
letter to Miss G. Harcourt, 1838

7 That knuckle-end of England—that land of
Calvin, oat-cakes, and sulphur.
of Scotland
Lady Holland *Memoir* (1855) vol. 1, ch. 2

8 Take short views, hope for the best, and
trust in God.
Lady Holland *Memoir* (1855) vol. 1, ch. 6

9 No furniture so charming as books.
Lady Holland *Memoir* (1855) vol. 1, ch. 9; cf.
Powell 250:17

10 My definition of marriage . . . it resembles a
pair of shears, so joined that they cannot be
separated; often moving in opposite
directions, yet always punishing anyone
who comes between them.
Lady Holland *Memoir* (1855) vol. 1, ch. 11

11 Deserves to be preached to death by wild
curates.
Lady Holland *Memoir* (1855) vol. 1, ch. 11

12 Brighton Pavilion looks as if St Paul's had
slipped down to Brighton and pupped.
attributed; Alan Bell (ed.) *The Sayings of Sydney
Smith* (1993)

13 I never read a book before reviewing it; it
prejudices a man so.
H. Pearson *The Smith of Smiths* (1934) ch. 3

14 My idea of heaven is, eating *pâté de foie gras*
to the sound of trumpets.
view ascribed by Smith to his friend Henry Luttrell
H. Pearson *The Smith of Smiths* (1934) ch. 10; cf.
Disraeli 113:1

Walter Chalmers Smith 1824–1908

15 Immortal, invisible, God only wise.
'God, All in All' (1867 hymn)

Tobias Smollett 1721–71

16 That great Cham of literature, Samuel
Johnson.
letter to John Wilkes, 16 March 1759

Jan Christiaan Smuts 1870–1950

17 Mankind is once more on the move. The
very foundations have been shaken and
loosened, and things are again fluid. The
tents have been struck, and the great
caravan of humanity is once more on the
march.
*on the setting up of the League of Nations, in the
wake of the First World War*
W. K. Hancock *Smuts* (1968)

C. P. Snow 1905–80

18 The official world, the corridors of power.
Homecomings (1956) ch. 22

19 The two cultures and the scientific
revolution.
title of The Rede Lecture (1959)

Socrates 469–399 BC

20 How many things I can do without!
*on looking at a multitude of goods exposed for
sale*
Diogenes Laertius *Lives of the Philosophers* bk. 2,
ch. 25

21 I know nothing except the fact of my
ignorance.
Diogenes Laertius *Lives of the Philosophers* bk. 2,
sect. 32; cf. **Milton** 222:29

22 It is never right to do wrong or to requite
wrong with wrong, or when we suffer evil
to defend ourselves by doing evil in return.
Plato *Crito* 49d

23 But, my dearest Agathon, it is truth which
you cannot contradict; you can without any
difficulty contradict Socrates.
Plato *Symposium* 201d

24 Crito, we owe a cock to Aesculapius; please
pay it and don't forget it.
last words; Plato *Phaedo* 118

Solon c.640–after 556 BC

25 I grow old ever learning many things.
Theodor Bergk (ed.) *Poetae Lyrici Graeci* (1843) no.
18

26 Call no man happy before he dies, he is at
best but fortunate.
Herodotus *Histories* bk. 1, ch. 32; cf. **Bible** 41:25

Alexander Solzhenitsyn 1918–

27 You only have power over people as long as
you don't take *everything* away from them.
But when you've robbed a man of *everything*
he's no longer in your power — he's free
again.
The First Circle (1968) ch. 17

28 The Gulag archipelago.
title of book (1973–5)

29 The Iron Curtain did not reach the ground
and under it flowed liquid manure from the
West.
speaking at Far Eastern Technical University,
Vladivostok, 30 May 1994; cf. **Churchill** 91:23

William Somerville 1675–1742

1 The chase, the sport of kings;
Image of war, without its guilt.
The Chase (1735) bk. 1, l. 14; cf. **Surtees** 306:8

Anastasio Somoza 1925–80

2 You won the elections, but I won the count.
replying to an accusation of ballot-rigging
in *Guardian* 17 June 1977; cf. **Stoppard** 304:13

Stephen Sondheim 1930–

3 I like to be in America!
O.K. by me in America!
Ev'rything free in America
For a small fee in America!
'America' (1957 song) in *West Side Story*

4 Everything's coming up roses.
title of song (1959) in *Gypsy*

5 Where are the clowns?
Send in the clowns.
'Send in the Clowns' (1973 song) in *A Little Night Music*

Susan Sontag 1933–

6 Societies need to have one illness which becomes identified with evil, and attaches blame to its 'victims'.
AIDS and its Metaphors (1989)

7 What pornography is really about, ultimately, isn't sex but death.
in *Partisan Review* Spring 1967

Donald Soper 1903–98

8 It is, I think, good evidence of life after death.
on the quality of debate in the House of Lords
in *Listener* 17 August 1978

Sophocles c.496–406 BC

9 There are many wonderful things, and nothing is more wonderful than man.
Antigone l. 333

10 Not to be born is, past all prizing, best.
Oedipus Coloneus l. 1225 (translation by R. C. Jebb); cf. **Auden** 17:28, **Yeats** 342:24

11 Someone asked Sophocles, 'How is your sex-life now? Are you still able to have a woman?' He replied, 'Hush, man; most gladly indeed am I rid of it all, as though I had escaped from a mad and savage master.'
Plato *Republic* bk. 1, 329b

Robert Southey 1774–1843

12 Now tell us all about the war,
And what they fought each other for.
'The Battle of Blenheim' (1800)

13 'But what good came of it at last?'
Quoth little Peterkin.
'Why that I cannot tell,' said he,
'But 'twas a famous victory.'
'The Battle of Blenheim' (1800)

14 And then they knew the perilous rock,
And blessed the Abbot of Aberbrothock.
'The Inchcape Rock' (1802)

15 My name is Death: the last best friend am I.
'The Lay of the Laureate' (1816) st. 87

16 You are old, Father William, the young man cried,
The few locks which are left you are grey;
You are hale, Father William, a hearty old man,
Now tell me the reason, I pray.
'The Old Man's Comforts' (1799); cf. **Carroll** 83:16

17 The arts babblative and scribblative.
Colloquies on the Progress and Prospects of Society (1829) no. 10, pt. 2

18 Men started at the intelligence, and turned pale, as if they had heard of the loss of a dear friend.
on the death of **Nelson**
The Life of Nelson (1813) ch. 9

19 She has made me in love with a cold climate, and frost and snow, with a northern moonlight.
on Mary **Wollstonecraft***'s letters from Sweden and Norway*
letter to his brother Thomas, 28 April 1797; cf. **Mitford** 225:1

20 Literature cannot be the business of a woman's life: and it ought not to be.
letter to Charlotte Brontë, 12 March 1837

Robert Southwell c.1561–95

21 As I in hoary winter night stood shivering in the snow,
Surprised was I with sudden heat which made my heart to glow;
And lifting up a fearful eye to view what fire was near
A pretty Babe all burning bright did in the air appear.
'The Burning Babe' (c.1590)

Muriel Spark 1918–

22 I am a hoarder of two things: documents and trusted friends.
Curriculum Vitae (1992)

23 I am putting old heads on your young shoulders . . . all my pupils are the crème de la crème.
The Prime of Miss Jean Brodie (1961) ch. 1

24 One's prime is elusive. You little girls, when you grow up, must be on the alert to recognise your prime at whatever time of your life it may occur.
The Prime of Miss Jean Brodie (1961) ch. 1

John Sparrow 1906–92

25 That indefatigable and unsavoury engine of pollution, the dog.
letter to *The Times* 30 September 1975

Herbert Spencer 1820–1903

26 Science is organized knowledge.
Education (1861) ch. 2

1 People are beginning to see that the first requisite to success in life is to be a good animal.
  Education (1861) ch. 2

2 Absolute morality is the regulation of conduct in such a way that pain shall not be inflicted.
  Essays (1891) vol. 3 'Prison Ethics'

3 This survival of the fittest which I have here sought to express in mechanical terms, is that which Mr Darwin has called 'natural selection, or the preservation of favoured races in the struggle for life.
  Principles of Biology (1865) pt. 3, ch. 12; cf. **Darwin** 106:9

4 A clever theft was praiseworthy amongst the Spartans; and it is equally so amongst Christians, provided it be on a sufficiently large scale.
  Social Statics (1850) pt. 2, ch. 16, sect. 3

Lord Spencer 1964–

5 Every proprietor and editor of every publication that has paid for intrusive and exploitative photographs of her . . . has blood on their hands today.
  *on the death of his sister, **Diana**, Princess of Wales, in a car crash while being pursued by photographers, 31 August 1997*
  in *Daily Telegraph* 1 September 1997

6 She needed no royal title to continue to generate her particular brand of magic.
  *tribute at the funeral of his sister, **Diana**, Princess of Wales, 7 September 1997*
  in *Guardian* 8 September 1997

Raine, Countess Spencer 1929–

7 Alas, for our towns and cities. Monstrous carbuncles of concrete have erupted in gentle Georgian Squares.
  The Spencers on Spas (1983) p. 14; cf. **Charles** 88:2

Stanley Spencer 1891–1959

8 Painting is saying 'Ta' to God.
  letter from Spencer's daughter Shirin, in *Observer* 7 February 1988

Stephen Spender 1909–95

9 I think continually of those who were truly great.
  'I think continually of those who were truly great' (1933)

10 Born of the sun they travelled a short while towards the sun,
  And left the vivid air signed with their honour.
  'I think continually of those who were truly great' (1933)

11 Pylons, those pillars
  Bare like nude, giant girls that have no secret.
  'The Pylons' (1933)

Edmund Spenser *c.*1552–99

12 Ah! when will this long weary day have end,
  And lend me leave to come unto my love?
  'Epithalamion' (1595) l. 278

13 A gentle knight was pricking on the plain.
  The Faerie Queen (1596) bk. 1, canto 1, st. 1

14 Sleep after toil, port after stormy seas,
  Ease after war, death after life does greatly please.
  The Faerie Queen (1596) bk. 1, canto 9, st. 40

15 And with rich metal loaded every rift.
  The Faerie Queen (1596) bk. 2, canto 7, st. 28; cf. **Keats** 183:16

16 And all for love, and nothing for reward.
  The Faerie Queen (1596) bk. 2, canto 8, st. 2

17 Be bold, be bold, and everywhere Be bold
      . . .
  Be not too bold.
  The Faerie Queen (1596) bk. 3, canto 11, st. 54

18 Dan Chaucer, well of English undefiled.
  The Faerie Queen (1596) bk. 4, canto 2, st. 32

19 Ill can he rule the great, that cannot reach the small.
  The Faerie Queen (1596) bk. 5, canto 2, st. 43

20 O sacred hunger of ambitious minds.
  The Faerie Queen (1596) bk. 5, canto 12, st. 1

21 A monster, which the Blatant beast men call.
  The Faerie Queen (1596) bk. 5, canto 12, st. 37

22 Of such deep learning little had he need,
  Ne yet of Latin, ne of Greek that breed
  Doubts 'mongst Divines, and difference of texts,
  From whence arise diversity of sects,
  And hateful heresies.
  'Prosopopoia or Mother Hubbard's Tale' (1591) l. 385

23 With that, I saw two swans of goodly hue,
  Come softly swimming down along the Lee.
  Prothalamion (1596) l. 37

24 Sweet Thames, run softly, till I end my song.
  Prothalamion (1596) l. 54

25 Uncouth unkist, said the old famous poet Chaucer.
  The Shepherd's Calendar (1579) 'Letter to Gabriel Harvey'

26 So now they have made our English tongue a gallimaufry or hodgepodge of all other speeches.
  The Shepherd's Calendar (1579) 'Letter to Gabriel Harvey'

Baruch Spinoza 1632–77

27 There is no hope without fear, and no fear without hope.
  Ethics (1677) pt. 2, para. 178

Benjamin Spock 1903–98

28 You know more than you think you do.
  Common Sense Book of Baby and Child Care (1946)

William Archibald Spooner
1844–1930

1 You will find as you grow older that the weight of rages will press harder and harder upon the employer.
William Hayter *Spooner* (1977) ch. 6

2 Her late husband, you know, a very sad death—eaten by missionaries—poor soul!
William Hayter *Spooner* (1977) ch. 6

Cecil Spring-Rice 1859–1918

3 I vow to thee, my country—all earthly things above—
Entire and whole and perfect, the service of my love,
The love that asks no question: the love that stands the test,
That lays upon the altar the dearest and the best:
The love that never falters, the love that pays the price,
The love that makes undaunted the final sacrifice.
'I Vow to Thee, My Country' (written on the eve of his departure from Washington, 12 January 1918)

Bruce Springsteen 1949–

4 Born in the USA.
title of song (1984)

5 We gotta get out while we're young,
'Cause tramps like us, baby, we were born to run.
'Born to Run' (1974 song)

C. H. Spurgeon 1834–92

6 If you want truth to go round the world you must hire an express train to pull it; but if you want a lie to go round the world, it will fly: it is as light as a feather, and a breath will carry it. It is well said in the old proverb, 'a lie will go round the world while truth is pulling its boots on'.
Gems from Spurgeon (1859)

J. C. Squire 1884–1958

7 But I'm not so think as you drunk I am.
'Ballade of Soporific Absorption' (1931)

8 It did not last: the Devil howling 'Ho!
Let Einstein be!' restored the status quo.
'In continuation of Pope on Newton' (1926); see **Pope** 247:28

Mme de Staël 1766–1817

9 *Tout comprendre rend très indulgent.*
To be totally understanding makes one very indulgent.
Corinne (1807) bk. 18, ch. 5

10 A man can brave opinion, a woman must submit to it.
Delphine (1802) epigraph

11 Speech happens not to be his language.
on being asked what she found to talk about with her new lover, a hussar
attributed

Joseph Stalin 1879–1953

12 There are various forms of production: artillery, automobiles, lorries. You also produce 'commodities', 'works', 'products'. Such things are highly necessary. Engineering things. For people's souls. 'Products' are highly necessary too. 'Products' are very important for people's souls. You are engineers of human souls.
speech to writers at **Gorky**'s house, 26 October 1932; cf. **Gorky** 144:18

13 The Pope! How many divisions has *he* got?
on being asked to encourage Catholicism in Russia by way of conciliating the Pope, 13 May 1935
W. S. Churchill *The Gathering Storm* (1948) ch. 8; cf. **Napoleon** 231:8

14 There is one eternally true legend—that of Judas.
at the trial of Radek in 1937
Robert Payne *The Rise and Fall of Stalin* (1966)

15 One death is a tragedy, a million deaths a statistic.
attributed

Henry Morton Stanley 1841–1904

16 Dr Livingstone, I presume?
How I found Livingstone (1872) ch. 11

Charles E. Stanton 1859–1933

17 *Lafayette, nous voilà!*
Lafayette, we are here.
at the tomb of Lafayette in Paris, 4 July 1917; in New York Tribune 6 September 1917

Edwin Mcmasters Stanton
1814–69

18 Now he belongs to the ages.
*of Abraham **Lincoln**, following his assassination, 15 April 1865*
I. M. Tarbell *Life of Abraham Lincoln* (1900) vol. 2

Elizabeth Cady Stanton 1815–1902

19 Woman's degradation is in man's idea of his sexual rights. Our religion, laws, customs, are all founded on the belief that woman was made for man.
letter to Susan B. Anthony, 14 June 1860

Frank L. Stanton 1857–1927

20 Sweetes' li'l' feller,
Everybody knows;
Dunno what to call him,
But he's mighty lak' a rose!
'Mighty Lak' a Rose' (1901 song)

John Stark 1728–1822

21 We beat them to-day or Molly Stark's a widow.
before the Battle of Bennington, 16 August 1777

Christina Stead 1902–83

22 A self-made man is one who believes in luck and sends his son to Oxford.
House of All Nations (1938) 'Credo'

David Steel 1938–

1 I have the good fortune to be the first Liberal leader for over half a century who is able to say to you at the end of our annual assembly: go back to your constituencies and prepare for government.

speech to the Liberal Party Assembly, 18 September 1981

Richard Steele 1672–1729

2 A woman seldom writes her mind but in her postscript.

in *The Spectator* no. 79 (31 May 1711); cf. **Bacon** 21:8

3 To love her is a liberal education.

of Lady Elizabeth Hastings

in *The Tatler* no. 49 (2 August 1709)

4 It was very prettily said, that we may learn the little value of fortune by the persons on whom heaven is pleased to bestow it.

in *The Tatler* no. 203 (27 July 1710)

Lincoln Steffens 1866–1936

5 I have seen the future; and it works.

following a visit to the Soviet Union in 1919
letter to Marie Howe, 3 April 1919

Edward Steichen 1879–1973

6 The mission of photography is to explain man to man and each man to himself.

Cornell Capa (ed.) *The Concerned Photographer* (1972)

Gertrude Stein 1874–1946

7 Rose is a rose is a rose is a rose.

Sacred Emily (1913)

8 You are all a lost generation.

of the young who served in the First World War
subsequently taken by Ernest **Hemingway** as his epigraph to *The Sun Also Rises* (1926)

9 'What *is* the answer?' No answer came. She laughed and said, 'In that case what is the question?'

last words; Donald Sutherland *Gertrude Stein, A Biography of her Work* (1951)

John Steinbeck 1902–68

10 Okie use' ta mean you was from Oklahoma. Now it means you're a dirty son-of-a-bitch. Okie means you're scum. Don't mean nothing itself, it's the way they say it.

The Grapes of Wrath (1939) ch. 18

Gloria Steinem 1934–

11 We are becoming the men we wanted to marry.

in *Ms* July/August 1982

12 A woman without a man is like a fish without a bicycle.

attributed

Stendhal 1783–1842

13 A novel is a mirror which passes over a highway. Sometimes it reflects to your eyes the blue of the skies, at others the churned-up mud of the road.

Le Rouge et le noir (1830) bk. 2, ch. 19

14 I know of only one rule: style cannot be too *clear*, too *simple*.

letter to Balzac, 30 October 1840

J. K. Stephen 1859–92

15 When the Rudyards cease from kipling And the Haggards ride no more.

'To R.K.' (1891)

Leslie Stephen 1832–1904

16 The editor of such a work must, by the necessity of the case, be autocratic. He will do his best to be a considerate autocrat.

of the compilation of a dictionary of national biography

in *Athenaeum* 23 December 1882

James Stephens 1882–1950

17 Finality is death. Perfection is finality. Nothing is perfect. There are lumps in it.

The Crock of Gold (1912) bk. 1, ch. 4

18 I hear a sudden cry of pain!
There is a rabbit in a snare:
Now I hear the cry again,
But I cannot tell from where . . .
Little one! Oh, little one!
I am searching everywhere.

'The Snare' (1915)

Laurence Sterne 1713–68

19 They order, said I, this matter better in France.

A Sentimental Journey (1768) opening words

20 'Pray, my dear,' quoth my mother, 'have you not forgot to wind up the clock?'—'Good G—!' cried my father, making an exclamation, but taking care to moderate his voice at the same time,—'Did ever woman, since the creation of the world, interrupt a man with such a silly question?'

Tristram Shandy (1759–67) bk. 1, ch. 1

21 I should have no objection to this method, but that I think it must smell too strong of the lamp.

Tristram Shandy (1759–67) bk. 1, ch. 23

22 'Tis better in battle than in bed', said my uncle Toby.

of death

Tristram Shandy (1759–67) bk. 5, ch. 3

23 There is a North-west passage to the intellectual World.

Tristram Shandy (1759–67) bk. 5, ch. 42

24 'The poor soul will die:—' 'He shall not die, by G—', cried my uncle Toby.—The Accusing Spirit, which flew up to heaven's chancery with the oath, blushed as he gave it in;—and the Recording Angel, as he wrote it down, dropped a tear upon the word, and blotted it out for ever.

Tristram Shandy (1759–67) bk. 6, ch. 8

25 'A soldier,' cried my Uncle Toby, interrupting the corporal, 'is no more

exempt from saying a foolish thing, Trim, than a man of letters.'—'But not so often, an' please your honour,' replied the corporal.
Tristram Shandy (1759–67) bk. 8, ch. 19

1 —d! said my mother, 'what is all this story about?'— 'A Cock and a Bull,' said Yorick.
Tristram Shandy (1759–67) bk. 9, ch. 33

Brooks Stevens 1911–

2 Our whole economy is based on planned obsolescence.
Vance Packard *The Waste Makers* (1960) ch. 6

Wallace Stevens 1879–1955

3 Let be be finale of seem.
The only emperor is the emperor of ice-cream.
'The Emperor of Ice-Cream' (1923)

4 Frogs Eat Butterflies. Snakes Eat Frogs. Hogs Eat Snakes. Men Eat Hogs.
title of poem (1923)

5 Poetry is the supreme fiction, madame.
'A High-Toned old Christian Woman' (1923)

6 They said, 'You have a blue guitar,
You do not play things as they are.'
The man replied, 'Things as they are
Are changed upon the blue guitar.'
'The Man with the Blue Guitar' (1937)

7 I do not know which to prefer,
The beauty of inflections
Or the beauty of innuendoes,
The blackbird whistling
Or just after.
'Thirteen Ways of Looking at a Blackbird' (1923)

Adlai Stevenson 1900–65

8 I suppose flattery hurts no one, that is, if he doesn't inhale.
television broadcast, 30 March 1952

9 Let's talk sense to the American people. Let's tell them the truth, that there are no gains without pains.
speech of acceptance at the Democratic National Convention, Chicago, 26 July 1952

10 In America any boy may become President and I suppose it's just one of the risks he takes!
speech in Indianapolis, 26 September 1952

11 The young man who asks you to set him one heart-beat from the Presidency of the United States.
*of Richard **Nixon** as Vice-Presidential nominee*
speech at Cleveland, Ohio, 23 October 1952

12 We hear the Secretary of State boasting of his brinkmanship—the art of bringing us to the edge of the abyss.
speech at Hartford, Connecticut, 25 February 1956; see **Dulles** 117:25

13 She would rather light a candle than curse the darkness, and her glow has warmed the world.
*of Eleanor **Roosevelt***
in *New York Times* 8 November 1962

Anne Stevenson 1933–

14 Blackbirds are the cellos of the deep farms.
'Green Mountain, Black Mountain' (1982)

Robert Louis Stevenson 1850–94

15 Am I no a bonny fighter?
Kidnapped (1886) ch. 10

16 I've a grand memory for forgetting, David.
Kidnapped (1886) ch. 18

17 I have thus played the sedulous ape to Hazlitt, to Lamb, to Wordsworth, to Sir Thomas Browne, to Defoe, to Hawthorne, to Montaigne, to Baudelaire and to Obermann.
Memories and Portraits (1887) ch. 4 'A College Magazine'

18 The strange case of Dr Jekyll and Mr Hyde.
title of novel, 1886

19 I travel not to go anywhere, but to go. I travel for travel's sake. The great affair is to move.
Travels with a Donkey (1879) 'Cheylard and Luc'

20 If landscapes were sold, like the sheets of characters of my boyhood, one penny plain and twopence coloured, I should go the length of twopence every day of my life.
Travels with a Donkey (1879) 'Father Apollinaris'

21 Fifteen men on the dead man's chest
Yo-ho-ho, and a bottle of rum!
Drink and the devil had done for the rest—
Yo-ho-ho, and a bottle of rum!
Treasure Island (1883) ch. 1

22 Tip me the black spot.
Treasure Island (1883) ch. 3

23 Pieces of eight, pieces of eight, pieces of eight!
Treasure Island (1883) ch. 10

24 Many's the long night I've dreamed of cheese—toasted, mostly.
Treasure Island (1883) ch. 15

25 To travel hopefully is a better thing than to arrive, and the true success is to labour.
Virginibus Puerisque (1881) 'El Dorado'

26 What hangs people . . . is the unfortunate circumstance of guilt.
The Wrong Box (with Lloyd Osbourne, 1889) ch. 7

27 If you are going to make a book end badly, it must end badly from the beginning.
letter to J. M. Barrie, November 1892

28 The world is so full of a number of things, I'm sure we should all be as happy as kings.
A Child's Garden of Verses (1885) 'Happy Thought'

29 I was the giant great and still
That sits upon the pillow-hill,
And sees before him, dale and plain,
The pleasant land of counterpane.
A Child's Garden of Verses (1885) 'The Land of Counterpane'

30 I have a little shadow that goes in and out with me.
A Child's Garden of Verses (1885) 'My Shadow'

31 I will make you brooches and toys for your delight

Of bird-song at morning and star-shine at night.
Songs of Travel (1896) 'I will make you brooches and toys for your delight'

1 Trusty, dusky, vivid, true,
With eyes of gold and bramble-dew,
Steel-true and blade-straight,
The great artificer
Made my mate.
Songs of Travel (1896) 'My Wife'

2 Sing me a song of a lad that is gone,
Say, could that lad be I?
Merry of soul he sailed on a day
Over the sea to Skye.
Songs of Travel (1896) 'Sing me a song of a lad that is gone'

3 Give to me the life I love,
Let the lave go by me,
Give the jolly heaven above
And the byway nigh me.
Songs of Travel (1896) 'The Vagabond'

4 All I seek, the heaven above
And the road below me.
Songs of Travel (1896) 'The Vagabond'

5 Go, little book, and wish to all
Flowers in the garden, meat in the hall,
A bin of wine, a spice of wit,
A house with lawns enclosing it.
Underwoods (1887) 'Envoy'; cf. **Chaucer** 88:28

6 Under the wide and starry sky
Dig the grave and let me lie.
Underwoods (1887) 'Requiem'

7 This be the verse you grave for me:
'Here he lies where he longed to be;
Home is the sailor, home from sea,
And the hunter home from the hill.'
Underwoods (1887) 'Requiem'

Ian Stewart 1945–

8 Genes are not like engineering blueprints; they are more like recipes in a cookbook. They tell us what ingredients to use, in what quantities, and in what order—but they do not provide a complete, accurate plan of the final result.
Life's Other Secret (1998) preface

Sting 1951–

9 If I were a Brazilian without land or money or the means to feed my children, I would be burning the rain forest too.
in *International Herald Tribune* 14 April 1989

Caskie Stinnett 1911–

10 A diplomat . . . is a person who can tell you to go to hell in such a way that you actually look forward to the trip.
Out of the Red (1960) ch. 4

Samuel John Stone 1839–1900

11 The Church's one foundation
Is Jesus Christ, her Lord;
She is his new creation

By water and the word.
Lyra Fidelium (1866) 'The Church's one foundation'

Marie Stopes 1880–1958

12 An impersonal and scientific knowledge of the structure of our bodies is the surest safeguard against prurient curiosity and lascivious gloating.
Married Love (1918) ch. 5

Tom Stoppard 1937–

13 It's not the voting that's democracy, it's the counting.
Jumpers (1972) act 1; cf. **Somoza** 299:2

14 The House of Lords, an illusion to which I have never been able to subscribe—responsibility without power, the prerogative of the eunuch throughout the ages.
Lord Malquist and Mr Moon (1966) pt. 6; cf. **Kipling** 189:2

15 I'm with you on the free press. It's the newspapers I can't stand.
Night and Day (1978) act 1

16 Comment is free but facts are on expenses.
Night and Day (1978) act 2; cf. **Scott** 266:1

17 The bad end unhappily, the good unluckily. That is what tragedy means.
Rosencrantz and Guildenstern are Dead (1967) act 2; cf. **Wilde** 335:2

William Stoughton 1631–1701

18 God hath sifted a nation that he might send choice grain into this wilderness.
sermon in Boston, 29 April 1669

Harriet Beecher Stowe 1811–96

19 I s'pect I growed. Don't think nobody never made me.
Topsy
Uncle Tom's Cabin (1852) ch. 20

William Scott, Lord Stowell 1745–1836

20 The elegant simplicity of the three per cents.
Lord Campbell *Lives of the Lord Chancellors* (1857); cf. **Disraeli** 112:25

21 A precedent embalms a principle.
an opinion, while Advocate-General, 1788

Lytton Strachey 1880–1932

22 Francis Bacon . . . was no striped frieze; he was shot silk.
Elizabeth and Essex (1928) ch. 5

23 CHAIRMAN OF MILITARY TRIBUNAL: What would you do if you saw a German soldier trying to violate your sister?
STRACHEY: I would try to get between them.
otherwise rendered as, 'I should interpose my body'
Robert Graves *Good-bye to All That* (1929) ch. 23

1 Discretion is not the better part of biography.

Michael Holroyd *Lytton Strachey* vol. 1 (1967) preface

2 If this is dying, then I don't think much of it.

on his deathbed

Michael Holroyd *Lytton Strachey* vol. 2 (1968) pt. 2, ch. 6

Thomas Wentworth, Lord Strafford 1593–1641

3 The authority of a King is the keystone which closeth up the arch of order and government which, once shaken, all the frame falls together in a confused heap of foundation and battlement.

Hugh Trevor-Roper *Historical Essays* (1952) 'The Outbreak of the Great Rebellion'

William L. Strauss and A. J. E. Cave

4 Notwithstanding, if he could be reincarnated and placed in a New York subway—provided that he were bathed, shaved, and dressed in modern clothing—it is doubtful whether he would attract any more attention than some of its other denizens.

of Neanderthal man

in *Quarterly Review of Biology* Winter 1957

Jack Straw 1946–

5 It's not because ageing wrinklies have tried to stop people having fun. It's because . . . these so-called soft drugs are potentially very dangerous.

asserting his opposition to the legalization of cannabis

on *Breakfast with Frost*, BBC1 TV, 4 January 1998

Janet Street-Porter 1946–

6 A terminal blight has hit the TV industry nipping fun in the bud and stunting our growth. This blight is management—the dreaded Four M's: male, middle class, middle-aged and mediocre.

MacTaggart Lecture, Edinburgh Television Festival, 25 August 1995

August Strindberg 1849–1912

7 Family! . . . the home of all social evil, a charitable institution for comfortable women, an anchorage for house-fathers, and a hell for children.

The Son of a Servant (1886)

Jan Struther 1901–53

8 Lord of all hopefulness, Lord of all joy, Whose trust, ever childlike, no cares could destroy, Be there at our waking, and give us, we pray,

Your bliss in our hearts, Lord, at the break of the day.

'All Day Hymn' (1931 hymn)

G. A. Studdert Kennedy 1883–1929

9 When Jesus came to Birmingham they simply passed Him by, They never hurt a hair of Him, they only let Him die.

Peace Rhymes of a Padre (1921) 'Indifference'

John Suckling 1609–42

10 Why so pale and wan, fond lover? Prithee, why so pale?

Aglaura (1637) act 4, sc. 1 'Song'

11 Her feet beneath her petticoat, Like little mice, stole in and out.

'A Ballad upon a Wedding' (1646) st. 8

12 Love is the fart Of every heart: It pains a man when 'tis kept close, And others doth offend, when 'tis let loose.

'Love's Offence' (1646)

13 Out upon it, I have loved Three whole days together.

'A Poem with the Answer' (1659)

Annie Sullivan 1866–1936

14 Language grows out of life, out of its needs and experiences . . . *Language* and *knowledge* are indissolubly connected; they are interdependent. Good work in language presupposes and depends on a real knowledge of things

speech to the American Association to Promote the Teaching of Speech to the Deaf, July 1894

Louis Henri Sullivan 1856–1924

15 Form follows function.

The Tall Office Building Artistically Considered (1896)

Terry Sullivan

*see also Harry **Bedford** and Terry **Sullivan***

16 She sells sea-shells on the sea-shore.

'She Sells Sea-Shells' (1908 song)

Timothy Daniel Sullivan 1827–1914

17 'God save Ireland!' said the heroes; 'God save Ireland', say they all: Whether on the scaffold high Or the battlefield we die, Oh, what matter when for Erin dear we fall.

'God Save Ireland' (1867)

Maximilien de Béthune, Duc de Sully 1559–1641

18 Tilling and grazing are the two breasts by which France is fed.

Mémoires (1638) pt. 1, ch. 15

1 The English take their pleasures sadly after the fashion of their country.
    attributed

Arthur Hays Sulzberger
1891–1968

2 We tell the public which way the cat is jumping. The public will take care of the cat.
on journalism
    in *Time* 8 May 1950

Edith Summerskill 1901–80

3 Nagging is the repetition of unpalatable truths.
    speech to the Married Women's Association, House of Commons, 14 July 1960

Charles Sumner 1811–74

4 Where Slavery is, there Liberty cannot be; and where Liberty is, there Slavery cannot be.
    'Slavery and the Rebellion'; speech at Cooper Institute 5 November 1864

5 There is the national flag. He must be cold, indeed, who can look upon its folds rippling in the breeze without pride of country.
    Are We a Nation? 19 November 1867

Henry Howard, Earl of Surrey
*c.*1517–47

6 So cruel prison how could betide, alas,
As proud Windsor? Where I in lust and joy
With a king's son my childish years did pass
In greater feast than Priam's sons of Troy.
    'So cruel prison' (1557)

7 Wyatt resteth here, that quick could never rest;
Whose heavenly gifts increased by disdain,
And virtue sank the deeper in his breast;
Such profit he of envy could obtain.
    'Wyatt resteth here' (1557)

R. S. Surtees 1805–64

8 'Unting is all that's worth living for . . . it's the sport of kings, the image of war without its guilt, and only five-and-twenty per cent of its danger.
    Handley Cross (1843) ch. 7; cf. **Somerville** 299:1

9 It ar'n't that I loves the fox less, but that I loves the 'ound more.
    Handley Cross (1843) ch. 16

10 Life would be very pleasant if it were not for its enjoyments.
    Mr Facey Romford's Hounds (1865) ch. 32; cf. **Lewis** 198:16

11 Everyone knows that the real business of a ball is either to look out for a wife, to look after a wife, or to look after somebody else's wife.
    Mr Facey Romford's Hounds (1865) ch. 56

12 He was a gentleman who was generally spoken of as having nothing a-year, paid quarterly.
    Mr Sponge's Sporting Tour (1853) ch. 24

Hannen Swaffer 1879–1962

13 Freedom of the press in Britain means freedom to print such of the proprietor's prejudices as the advertisers don't object to.
    Tom Driberg *Swaff* (1974) ch. 2

Jonathan Swift 1667–1745

14 Satire is a sort of glass, wherein beholders do generally discover everybody's face but their own.
    The Battle of the Books (1704) preface

15 Instead of dirt and poison we have rather chosen to fill our hives with honey and wax; thus furnishing mankind with the two noblest of things, which are sweetness and light.
    The Battle of the Books (1704); cf. **Arnold** 15:27, **Forster** 131:12

16 It is the folly of too many, to mistake the echo of a London coffee-house for the voice of the kingdom.
    The Conduct of the Allies (1711)

17 Laws are like cobwebs, which may catch small flies, but let wasps and hornets break through.
    A Critical Essay upon the Faculties of the Mind (1709); cf. **Anacharsis** 5:3

18 I have heard of a man who had a mind to sell his house, and therefore carried a piece of brick in his pocket, which he shewed as a pattern to encourage purchasers.
    The Drapier's Letters (1724) no. 2

19 And he gave it for his opinion, that whoever could make two ears of corn or two blades of grass to grow upon a spot of ground where only one grew before, would deserve better of mankind, and do more essential service to his country than the whole race of politicians put together.
    Gulliver's Travels (1726) 'A Voyage to Brobdingnag' ch. 7

20 He had been eight years upon a project for extracting sun-beams out of cucumbers, which were to be put into vials hermetically sealed, and let out to warm the air in raw inclement summers.
    Gulliver's Travels (1726) 'A Voyage to Laputa, etc.' ch. 5

21 Proper words in proper places, make the true definition of a style.
    Letter to a Young Gentleman lately entered into Holy Orders (9 January 1720)

22 Not die here in a rage, like a poisoned rat in a hole.
    letter to Bolingbroke, 21 March 1730

23 I have been assured by a very knowing American of my acquaintance in London, that a young healthy child well nursed is at a year old a most delicious, nourishing, and wholesome food, whether stewed, roasted,

baked, or boiled, and I make no doubt that it will equally serve in a fricassee, or a ragout.

A Modest Proposal for Preventing the Children of Ireland from being a Burden to their Parents or Country (1729)

1 We have just enough religion to make us hate, but not enough to make us love one another.

Thoughts on Various Subjects (1711)

2 When a true genius appears in the world, you may know him by this sign, that the dunces are all in confederacy against him.

Thoughts on Various Subjects (1711)

3 The stoical scheme of supplying our wants, by lopping off our desires, is like cutting off our feet when we want shoes.

Thoughts on Various Subjects (1711)

4 Every man desires to live long; but no man would be old.

Thoughts on Various Subjects (1727 ed.)

5 How haughtily he lifts his nose, To tell what every schoolboy knows.

'The Journal' (1727) l. 81

6 Hail, fellow, well met, All dirty and wet: Find out, if you can, Who's master, who's man.

'My Lady's Lamentation' (written 1728) l. 165

7 Philosophy! the lumber of the schools.

'Ode to Sir W. Temple' (written 1692)

8 As learned commentators view In Homer more than Homer knew.

'On Poetry' (1733) l. 103

9 So geographers, in Afric-maps, With savage-pictures fill their gaps; And o'er unhabitable downs Place elephants for want of towns.

'On Poetry' (1733) l. 177

10 Hobbes clearly proves, that every creature Lives in a state of war by nature.

'On Poetry' (1733) l. 319

11 So, naturalists observe, a flea Hath smaller fleas that on him prey; And these have smaller fleas to bite 'em, And so proceed *ad infinitum*.

'On Poetry' (1733) l. 337

12 Good God! what a genius I had when I wrote that book.

of A Tale of a Tub

Sir Walter Scott (ed.) *Works of Swift* (1814) vol. 1

13 I shall be like that tree, I shall die at the top.

Sir Walter Scott (ed.) *Works of Swift* (1814) vol. 1

14 A stick and a string, with a fly at one end and a fool at the other.

description of angling; the remark has also been attributed to Samuel **Johnson**, *in the form 'a stick and a string, with a worm at one end and a fool at the other'*

in *The Indicator* 27 October 1819

15 *Ubi saeva indignatio ulterius cor lacerare nequit.* Where fierce indignation can no longer tear his heart.

epitaph; Shane Leslie *The Skull of Swift* (1928) ch. 15; cf. **Yeats** 343:25

Algernon Charles Swinburne
1837–1909

16 Maiden, and mistress of the months and stars Now folded in the flowerless fields of heaven.

Atalanta in Calydon (1865) l. 1

17 When the hounds of spring are on winter's traces, The mother of months in meadow or plain Fills the shadows and windy places With lisp of leaves and ripple of rain.

Atalanta in Calydon (1865) chorus 'When the hounds of spring'

18 For winter's rains and ruins are over, And all the season of snows and sins; The days dividing lover and lover, The light that loses, the night that wins; And time remembered is grief forgotten, And frosts are slain and flowers begotten, And in green underwood and cover Blossom by blossom the spring begins.

Atalanta in Calydon (1865) chorus 'When the hounds of spring'

19 Villon, our sad bad glad mad brother's name.

'Ballad of François Villon' (1878)

20 We shift and bedeck and bedrape us, Thou art noble and nude and antique.

'Dolores' (1866) st. 7

21 Change in a trice The lilies and languors of virtue For the raptures and roses of vice.

'Dolores' (1866) st. 9

22 O splendid and sterile Dolores, Our Lady of Pain.

'Dolores' (1866) st. 9

23 As a god self-slain on his own strange altar, Death lies dead.

'A Forsaken Garden' (1878)

24 From too much love of living, From hope and fear set free, We thank with brief thanksgiving Whatever gods may be That no man lives forever, That dead men rise up never; That even the weariest river Winds somewhere safe to sea.

'The Garden of Proserpine' (1866)

25 Even love, the beloved Republic, that feeds upon freedom lives.

'Hertha' (1871); cf. **Forster** 131:18

26 Yea, is not even Apollo, with hair and harpstring of gold, A bitter God to follow, a beautiful God to behold?

'Hymn to Proserpine' (1866)

1 Thou hast conquered, O pale Galilean; the
world has grown grey from Thy breath.
'Hymn to Proserpine' (1866); cf. **Julian** 179:11

2 Swallow, my sister, O sister swallow,
How can thine heart be full of the spring?
A thousand summers are over and dead.
What hast thou found in the spring to
follow?
'Itylus' (1864)

3 O sister, sister, thy first-begotten!
The hands that cling and the feet that
follow,
The voice of the child's blood crying yet
Who hath remembered me? Who hath forgotten?
Thou hast forgotten, O summer swallow,
But the world shall end when I forget.
'Itylus' (1864)

4 Apples of gold for the king's daughter.
'The King's Daughter'

5 If love were what the rose is,
And I were like the leaf,
Our lives would grow together
In sad or singing weather,
Blown fields or flowerful closes,
Green pleasure or grey grief.
'A Match' (1866)

Thomas Sydenham 1624–89

6 Almighty God hath not bestowed on
mankind a remedy of so universal an extent
and so efficacious in curing divers maladies
as opiates.
manuscript version of published text,
Observationes Medicae (1676, G. G. Meynell (ed.)
1991)

John Millington Synge 1871–1909

7 But we do be afraid of the sea, and we do
only be drownded now and again.
The Aran Islands (1907) pt. 2

8 Oh my grief, I've lost him surely. I've lost
the only Playboy of the Western World.
The Playboy of the Western World (1907) act 3

Thomas Szasz 1920–

9 Happiness is an imaginary condition,
formerly often attributed by the living to
the dead, now usually attributed by adults
to children, and by children to adults.
The Second Sin (1973) 'Emotions'

10 If you talk to God, you are praying; if God
talks to you, you have schizophrenia. If the
dead talk to you, you are a spiritualist; if
God talks to you, you are a schizophrenic.
The Second Sin (1973) 'Schizophrenia'

11 Formerly, when religion was strong and
science weak, men mistook magic for
medicine; now, when science is strong and
religion weak, men mistake medicine for
magic.
The Second Sin (1973) 'Science and Scientism'

Albert von Szent-Györgyi
1893–1986

12 Discovery consists of seeing what everybody
has seen and thinking what nobody has
thought.
Irving Good (ed.) *The Scientist Speculates* (1962)

Tacitus AD c.56–after 117

13 He [Nerva] has united things long
incompatible, the principate and liberty.
Agricola ch. 3

14 They make a wilderness and call it peace.
Agricola ch. 30

15 It is part of human nature to hate the man
you have hurt.
Agricola ch. 42

16 *Sine ira et studio.*
With neither anger nor partiality.
Annals bk. 1, ch. 1

17 *Elegantiae arbiter.*
The arbiter of taste.
of **Petronius**
Annals bk. 16, ch. 18

18 He seemed much greater than a private
citizen while he still was a private citizen,
and by everyone's consent capable of
reigning if only he had not reigned.
of the Emperor Galba
Histories bk. 1, ch. 49

19 *Deos fortioribus adesse.*
The gods are on the side of the stronger.
Histories bk. 4, ch. 17; cf. **Bussy-Rabutin** 77:1

20 *Experientia docuit.*
Experience has taught.
commonly quoted as 'Experientia docet
[experience teaches]'
The Histories bk. 5, ch. 6

Rabindranath Tagore 1861–1941

21 Bigotry tries to keep truth safe in its hand
With a grip that kills it.
Fireflies (1928)

22 Touch my life with the magic of thy fire.
sung at the funeral of Mother **Teresa** *in Calcutta,
13 September 1997*
'The Magic of thy Fire'

Nellie Talbot

23 Jesus wants me for a sunbeam.
title of hymn (1921) in *CSSM Choruses* No. 1

Charles-Maurice de Talleyrand
1754–1838

24 This is the beginning of the end.
*on the announcement of Napoleon's Pyrrhic
victory at Borodino, 1812*
attributed; Sainte-Beuve *M. de Talleyrand* (1870)
ch. 3

25 It is not an event, it is an item of news.
on hearing of the death of **Napoleon** *in 1821*
Philip Henry Stanhope *Notes of Conversations with
the Duke of Wellington* (1888) 1 November 1831

1 *Surtout, Messieurs, point de zèle.*

Above all, gentlemen, not the slightest zeal.

P. Chasles *Voyages d'un critique à travers la vie et les livres* (1868) vol. 2

2 *Ils n'ont rien appris, ni rien oublié.*

They have learnt nothing, and forgotten nothing.

of the Bourbons in exile

oral tradition, attributed to Talleyrand by the Chevalier de Panat; cf. **Dumouriez** 118:4

3 That, Sire, is a question of dates.

often quoted as, 'treason is a matter of dates'; replying to the Tsar's criticism of those who 'betrayed the cause of Europe'

Duff Cooper *Talleyrand* (1932)

The Talmud
see also **Hillel**, **Shammai**

Mishnah

4 The tradition is a fence around the Law.

Mishnah Pirqei Avot 3:14

5 Turn it [Torah] and turn it again, for everything is in it.

Mishnah Pirqei Avot 5:22

Gemara

6 Even an iron partition cannot interpose between Israel and their Father in Heaven.

Babylonian Talmud Pesahim 85b

7 *He shall live by them* [the laws of the Torah], but he shall not die because of them.

Babylonian Talmud Yoma 85b

8 If the soft [water] can wear away the hard [stone], how much more can the words of the Torah, which are hard like iron, carve a way into my heart which is of flesh and blood!

Babylonian Talmud Avot de Rabbi Nathan 20b

Tantric Buddhist texts

9 By the enjoyment of all desires, to which one devotes oneself just as one pleases, it is by such practice as this that one may speedily gain Buddhahood.

With the enjoyment of all desires, to which one devotes oneself just as one pleases, in union with one's chosen divinity, one worships oneself, the Supreme One.

Guhyasamāja Tantra v. 7

Booth Tarkington 1869–1946

10 There are two things that will be believed of any man whatsoever, and one of them is that he has taken to drink.

Penrod (1914) ch. 10

Nahum Tate 1652–1715

11 As pants the hart for cooling streams When heated in the chase.

New Version of the Psalms (1696) Psalm 42 (with Nicholas Brady); cf. **Book of Common Prayer** 61:21

12 Through all the changing scenes of life, In trouble and in joy,

The praises of my God shall still My heart and tongue employ.

New Version of the Psalms (1696) Psalm 34 (with Nicholas Brady)

13 While shepherds watched their flocks by night,

All seated on the ground,

The angel of the Lord came down,

And glory shone around.

Supplement to the New Version of the Psalms (1700) 'While Shepherds Watched'

R. H. Tawney 1880–1962

14 Militarism . . . is fetish worship. It is the prostration of men's souls and the laceration of their bodies to appease an idol.

The Acquisitive Society (1921) ch. 4

15 Freedom for the pike is death for the minnows.

Equality (ed. 4, rev. ed., 1938) ch. 5, sect. 2

16 Private property is a necessary institution, at least in a fallen world; men work more and dispute less when goods are private than when they are common. But it is to be tolerated as a concession to human frailty, not applauded as desirable in itself.

Religion and the Rise of Capitalism (1926) ch. 1, sect. 1

17 What harm have I ever done to the Labour Party?

declining the offer of a peerage

in *Evening Standard* 18 January 1962

A. J. P. Taylor 1906–90

18 History gets thicker as it approaches recent times.

English History 1914–45 (1965); bibliography

19 The First World War had begun—imposed on the statesmen of Europe by railway timetables. It was an unexpected climax to the railway age.

The First World War (1963) ch. 1

Ann Taylor 1782–1866
and Jane Taylor 1783–1824

20 Who ran to help me when I fell,

And would some pretty story tell,

Or kiss the place to make it well?

My Mother.

Original Poems for Infant Minds (1804) 'My Mother'

21 Twinkle, twinkle, little star,

How I wonder what you are!

Up above the world so high,

Like a diamond in the sky!

Rhymes for the Nursery (1806) 'The Star'; cf. **Carroll** 83:20

Bayard Taylor 1825–78

22 Till the sun grows cold,

And the stars are old,

And the leaves of the Judgement Book unfold.

'Bedouin Song'

Jeremy Taylor 1613–67

1 This thing ... that can be understood and not expressed, may take a neuter gender;—and every schoolboy knows it.
The Real Presence ... (1654) sect. 5; cf. **Macaulay** 205:17

2 The union of hands and hearts.
XXV Sermons Preached at Golden Grove (1653) 'The Marriage Ring' pt. 1

Tom Taylor 1817–80

3 Hawkshaw, the detective.
usually quoted as 'I am Hawkshaw, the detective'
The Ticket-of-leave Man (1863) act 4, sc. 1

Norman Tebbit 1931–

4 I grew up in the Thirties with our unemployed father. He did not riot, he got on his bike and looked for work.
speech at Conservative Party Conference, 15 October 1981, in *Daily Telegraph* 16 October 1981

5 The cricket test—which side do they cheer for? ... Are you still looking back to where you came from or where you are?
on the loyalties of Britain's immigrant population
interview in *Los Angeles Times*, reported in *Daily Telegraph* 20 April 1990

Tecumseh 1768–1813

6 Where today are the Pequot? Where are the Narragansett, the Mohican, the Pokanoket, and many other once powerful tribes of our people? They have vanished before the avarice and oppression of the white man, as snow before the summer sun.
Dee Brown *Bury My Heart at Wounded Knee* (1970) ch. 1

Pierre Teilhard de Chardin 1881–1955

7 The history of the living world can be summarised as the elaboration of ever more perfect eyes within a cosmos in which there is always something more to be seen.
The Phenomenon of Man (1959)

William Temple 1881–1944

8 It is a mistake to suppose that God is only, or even chiefly, concerned with religion.
R. V. C. Bodley *In Search of Serenity* (1955) ch. 12

9 Personally, I have always looked on cricket as organized loafing.
attributed

John Tenniel 1820–1914

10 Dropping the pilot.
*on **Bismarck**'s departure from office*
cartoon caption, and title of poem, in *Punch* 29 March 1890

Alfred, Lord Tennyson 1809–92

11 Break, break, break,
On thy cold grey stones, O Sea!

And I would that my tongue could utter
The thoughts that arise in me.
'Break, Break, Break' (1842)

12 And the stately ships go on
To their haven under the hill;
But O for the touch of a vanished hand,
And the sound of a voice that is still!
'Break, Break, Break' (1842)

13 I come from haunts of coot and hern,
I make a sudden sally
And sparkle out among the fern,
To bicker down a valley.
'The Brook' (1855) l. 23

14 For men may come and men may go,
But I go on for ever.
'The Brook' (1855) l. 33

15 Half a league, half a league,
Half a league onward,
All in the valley of Death
Rode the six hundred.
'The Charge of the Light Brigade' (1854)

16 'Forward, the Light Brigade!'
Was there a man dismayed?
Not though the soldier knew
Some one had blundered:
Their's not to make reply,
Their's not to reason why,
Their's but to do and die:
Into the valley of Death
Rode the six hundred.
Cannon to right of them,
Cannon to left of them,
Cannon in front of them
Volleyed and thundered.
'The Charge of the Light Brigade' (1854)

17 Into the jaws of Death,
Into the mouth of Hell.
'The Charge of the Light Brigade' (1854)

18 Sunset and evening star,
And one clear call for me!
And may there be no moaning of the bar,
When I put out to sea.
'Crossing the Bar' (1889)

19 For though from out our bourne of time and place
The flood may bear me far,
I hope to see my pilot face to face
When I have crossed the bar.
'Crossing the Bar' (1889)

20 A dream of fair women.
title of poem (1832)

21 A daughter of the gods, divinely tall,
And most divinely fair.
'A Dream of Fair Women' (1832) l. 87

22 He clasps the crag with crookèd hands;
Close to the sun in lonely lands,
Ringed with the azure world, he stands.
The wrinkled sea beneath him crawls;
He watches from his mountain walls,
And like a thunderbolt he falls.
'The Eagle' (1851)

23 And when they buried him the little port
Had seldom seen a costlier funeral.
'Enoch Arden' (1864)

1 More black than ashbuds in the front of
  March.
  'The Gardener's Daughter' (1842) l. 28

2 I waited for the train at Coventry.
  'Godiva' (1842) l. 1

3 Wearing the white flower of a blameless
  life,
  Before a thousand peering littlenesses,
  In that fierce light which beats upon a
  throne,
  And blackens every blot.
  of Prince **Albert**
  Idylls of the King (1862 ed.) dedication l. 24

4 Clothed in white samite, mystic, wonderful.
  Idylls of the King 'The Coming of Arthur' (1869) l.
  284; 'The Passing of Arthur' (1869) l. 199

5 From the great deep to the great deep he
  goes.
  Idylls of the King 'The Coming of Arthur' (1869) l.
  410

6 We needs must love the highest when we
  see it.
  Idylls of the King 'Guinevere' (1859) l. 655

7 Elaine the fair, Elaine the loveable,
  Elaine, the lily maid of Astolat.
  Idylls of the King 'Lancelot and Elaine' (1859) l. 1

8 His honour rooted in dishonour stood,
  And faith unfaithful kept him falsely true.
  Idylls of the King 'Lancelot and Elaine' (1859) l.
  871

9 It is the little rift within the lute,
  That by and by will make the music mute.
  Idylls of the King 'Merlin and Vivien' (1859) l. 388

10 And trust me not at all or all in all.
  Idylls of the King 'Merlin and Vivien' (1859) l. 396

11 Man dreams of fame while woman wakes to
  love.
  Idylls of the King 'Merlin and Vivien' (1859) l. 458

12 So all day long the noise of battle rolled
  Among the mountains by the winter sea.
  Idylls of the King 'The Passing of Arthur' (1869) l.
  170

13 Authority forgets a dying king.
  Idylls of the King 'The Passing of Arthur' (1869) l.
  289

14 The old order changeth, yielding place to
  new,
  And God fulfils himself in many ways,
  Lest one good custom should corrupt the
  world.
  Idylls of the King 'The Passing of Arthur' (1869) l.
  408

15 More things are wrought by prayer
  Than this world dreams of.
  Idylls of the King 'The Passing of Arthur' (1869) l.
  415

16 To the island-valley of Avilion;
  Where falls not hail, or rain, or any snow,
  Nor ever wind blows loudly; but it lies
  Deep-meadowed, happy, fair with orchard
  lawns.
  Idylls of the King 'The Passing of Arthur' (1869) l.
  427

17 The last red leaf is whirled away,
  The rooks are blown about the skies.
  In Memoriam A. H. H. (1850) canto 15

18 'Tis better to have loved and lost
  Than never to have loved at all.
  In Memoriam A. H. H. (1850) canto 27; cf.
  Congreve 98:17

19 But what am I?
  An infant crying in the night:
  An infant crying for the light:
  And with no language but a cry.
  In Memoriam A. H. H. (1850) canto 54

20 So careful of the type she seems,
  So careless of the single life.
  of Nature
  In Memoriam A. H. H. (1850) canto 55

21 Nature, red in tooth and claw.
  In Memoriam A. H. H. (1850) canto 56

22 So many worlds, so much to do,
  So little done, such things to be.
  In Memoriam A. H. H. (1850) canto 73; cf. **Rhodes**
  256:9

23 Laburnums, dropping-wells of fire.
  In Memoriam A. H. H. (1850) canto 83

24 Fresh from brawling courts
  And dusty purlieus of the law.
  In Memoriam A. H. H. (1850) canto 89; cf.
  Etherege 125:5

25 You tell me, doubt is Devil-born.
  In Memoriam A. H. H. (1850) canto 96

26 There lives more faith in honest doubt,
  Believe me, than in half the creeds.
  In Memoriam A. H. H. (1850) canto 96

27 Their meetings made December June,
  Their every parting was to die.
  In Memoriam A. H. H. (1850) canto 97

28 He seems so near and yet so far.
  In Memoriam A. H. H. (1850) canto 97

29 Ring out, wild bells, to the wild sky.
  In Memoriam A. H. H. (1850) canto 106

30 Ring out the old, ring in the new,
  Ring, happy bells, across the snow:
  The year is going, let him go;
  Ring out the false, ring in the true.
  In Memoriam A. H. H. (1850) canto 106

31 Ring out the darkness of the land;
  Ring in the Christ that is to be.
  In Memoriam A. H. H. (1850) canto 106

32 Not the schoolboy heat,
  The blind hysterics of the Celt.
  In Memoriam A. H. H. (1850) canto 109

33 And drowned in yonder living blue
  The lark becomes a sightless song.
  In Memoriam A. H. H. (1850) canto 115

34 Wearing all that weight
  Of learning lightly like a flower.
  In Memoriam A. H. H. (1850) canto 131

35 There hath he lain for ages and will lie
  Battening upon huge seaworms in his sleep,
  Until the latter fire shall heat the deep.
  'The Kraken' (1830)

1 Kind hearts are more than coronets,
  And simple faith than Norman blood.
    'Lady Clara Vere de Vere' (1842) st. 7

2 On either side the river lie
  Long fields of barley and of rye,
  That clothe the wold and meet the sky;
  And through the field the road runs by
  To many-towered Camelot.
    'The Lady of Shalott' (1832, revised 1842) pt. 1

3 Willows whiten, aspens quiver,
  Little breezes dusk and shiver.
    'The Lady of Shalott' (1832, revised 1842) pt. 1

4 'I am half sick of shadows,' said
  The Lady of Shalott.
    'The Lady of Shalott' (1832, revised 1842) pt. 2

5 She left the web, she left the loom,
  She made three paces through the room,
  She saw the water-lily bloom,
  She saw the helmet and the plume,
  She looked down to Camelot.
  Out flew the web and floated wide;
  The mirror cracked from side to side;
  'The curse is come upon me,' cried
  The Lady of Shalott.
    'The Lady of Shalott' (1832, revised 1842) pt. 3

6 Airy, fairy Lilian.
    'Lilian' (1830)

7 In the spring a livelier iris changes on the
    burnished dove;
  In the spring a young man's fancy lightly
    turns to thoughts of love.
    'Locksley Hall' (1842) l. 19

8 He will hold thee, when his passion shall
    have spent its novel force,
  Something better than his dog, a little
    dearer than his horse.
    'Locksley Hall' (1842) l. 49

9 Men, my brothers, men the workers, ever
    reaping something new:
  That which they have done but earnest of
    the things that they shall do:
    'Locksley Hall' (1842) l. 117

10 Pilots of the purple twilight, dropping down
     with costly bales.
    'Locksley Hall' (1842) l. 122

11 Heard the heavens fill with shouting, and
     there rained a ghastly dew
   From the nations' airy navies grappling in
     the central blue;
    'Locksley Hall' (1842) l. 123

12 Till the war-drum throbbed no longer, and
     the battle-flags were furled
   In the Parliament of man, the Federation of
     the world.
    'Locksley Hall' (1842) l. 127

13 Science moves, but slowly slowly, creeping
     on from point to point.
    'Locksley Hall' (1842) l. 134

14 I the heir of all the ages, in the foremost
     files of time.
    'Locksley Hall' (1842) l. 178

15 Forward, forward let us range,
   Let the great world spin for ever down the
     ringing grooves of change.
    'Locksley Hall' (1842) l. 181

16 Better fifty years of Europe than a cycle of
     Cathay.
    'Locksley Hall' (1842) l. 184

17 Music that gentlier on the spirit lies,
   Than tired eyelids upon tired eyes.
    'The Lotos-Eaters' (1832) Choric Song, st. 1

18 Weeded and worn the ancient thatch
   Upon the lonely moated grange.
   She only said, 'My life is dreary,
   He cometh not,' she said;
   She said, 'I am aweary, aweary,
   I would that I were dead!'
    'Mariana' (1830) st. 1; cf. **Shakespeare** 282:1

19 I hate that dreadful hollow behind the little
     wood.
    Maud (1855) pt. 1, sect. 1

20 Faultily faultless, icily regular, splendidly
     null,
   Dead perfection, no more.
    Maud (1855) pt. 1, sect. 2

21 Come into the garden, Maud,
   For the black bat, night, has flown,
   Come into the garden, Maud,
   I am here at the gate alone.
   And the woodbine spices are wafted abroad,
   And the musk of the rose is blown.
    Maud (1855) pt. 1, sect. 22, st. 1

22 Queen rose of the rosebud garden of girls.
    Maud (1855) pt. 1, sect. 22, st. 9

23 She is coming, my dove, my dear;
   She is coming, my life, my fate;
   The red rose cries, 'She is near, she is near;'
   And the white rose weeps, 'She is late.'
    Maud (1855) pt. 1, sect. 22, st. 10

24 She is coming, my own, my sweet;
   Were it ever so airy a tread,
   My heart would hear her and beat,
   Were it earth in an earthy bed.
    Maud (1855) pt. 1, sect. 22, st. 11

25 You must wake and call me early, call me
     early, mother dear;
   Tomorrow 'ill be the happiest time of all the
     glad New-year;
   Of all the glad New-year, mother, the
     maddest merriest day;
   For I'm to be Queen o' the May, mother, I'm
     to be Queen o' the May.
    'The May Queen' (1832)

26 After it, follow it,
   Follow The Gleam.
    'Merlin and The Gleam' (1889) st. 9

27 God-gifted organ-voice of England,
   Milton, a name to resound for ages.
    'Milton: Alcaics' (1863)

28 The last great Englishman is low.
    'Ode on the Death of the Duke of Wellington'
    (1852) st. 3

29 That world-earthquake, Waterloo!
    'Ode on the Death of the Duke of Wellington'
    (1852) st. 6

1 Who never sold the truth to serve the hour,
Nor paltered with Eternal God for power.
'Ode on the Death of the Duke of Wellington'
(1852) st. 7

2 With prudes for proctors, dowagers for
deans,
And sweet girl-graduates in their golden
hair.
The Princess (1847) 'Prologue' l. 141

3 And blessings on the falling out
That all the more endears,
When we fall out with those we love
And kiss again with tears!
The Princess (1847) pt. 2, song (added 1850)

4 Sweet and low, sweet and low,
Wind of the western sea,
Low, low, breathe and blow,
Wind of the western sea!
The Princess (1847) pt. 3, song (added 1850)

5 The splendour falls on castle walls
And snowy summits old in story:
The long light shakes across the lakes,
And the wild cataract leaps in glory.
Blow, bugle, blow, set the wild echoes
flying,
Blow, bugle; answer, echoes, dying, dying,
dying.
The Princess (1847) pt. 4, song (added 1850)

6 O sweet and far from cliff and scar
The horns of Elfland faintly blowing!
The Princess (1847) pt. 4, song (added 1850)

7 Tears, idle tears, I know not what they
mean,
Tears from the depth of some divine despair
Rise in the heart, and gather to the eyes,
In looking on the happy autumn-fields,
And thinking of the days that are no more.
The Princess (1847) pt. 4, l. 21, song (added 1850)

8 Dear as remembered kisses after death.
The Princess (1847) pt. 4, l. 36, song (added 1850)

9 O tell her, Swallow, thou that knowest each,
That bright and fierce and fickle is the
South,
And dark and true and tender is the North.
The Princess (1847) pt. 4, l. 78, song (added 1850)

10 Man is the hunter; woman is his game.
The Princess (1847) pt. 5, l. 147

11 Home they brought her warrior dead.
She nor swooned, nor uttered cry:
All her maidens, watching said,
'She must weep or she will die.'
The Princess (1847) pt. 6, song (added 1850)

12 Rose a nurse of ninety years,
Set his child upon her knee.
The Princess (1847) pt. 6, song (added 1850)

13 Like summer tempest came her tears.
The Princess (1847) pt. 6, song (added 1850)

14 Now sleeps the crimson petal, now the
white;
Nor waves the cypress in the palace walk.
The Princess (1847) pt. 7, l. 161, song (added 1850)

15 Now lies the Earth all Danaë to the stars,
And all thy heart lies open unto me.
The Princess (1847) pt. 7, l. 167, song (added 1850)

16 Now folds the lily all her sweetness up,
And slips into the bosom of the lake:
So fold thyself, my dearest, thou, and slip
Into my bosom and be lost in me.
The Princess (1847) pt. 7, l. 171, song (added 1850)

17 Come down, O maid, from yonder
mountain height:
What pleasure lives in height?
The Princess (1847) pt. 7, l. 177, song (added 1850)

18 For Love is of the valley, come thou down
And find him.
The Princess (1847) pt. 7, l. 184, song (added 1850)

19 The moan of doves in immemorial elms,
And murmuring of innumerable bees.
The Princess (1847) pt. 7, l. 206, song (added 1850)

20 No little lily-handed baronet he.
The Princess (1847) 'Conclusion' l. 84

21 At Flores in the Azores Sir Richard Grenville
lay.
'The Revenge' (1878) st. 1

22 And the sun went down, and the stars came
out far over the summer sea,
But never a moment ceased the fight of the
one and the fifty-three.
'The Revenge' (1878) st. 9

23 Sink me the ship, Master Gunner—sink her,
split her in twain!
Fall into the hands of God, not into the
hands of Spain!
'The Revenge' (1878) st. 11

24 My strength is as the strength of ten,
Because my heart is pure.
'Sir Galahad' (1842)

25 Alone and warming his five wits,
The white owl in the belfry sits.
'Song—The Owl' (1830)

26 The gods themselves cannot recall their
gifts.
'Tithonus' (1860, revised 1864) l. 52

27 All the charm of all the Muses
often flowering in a lonely word.
'To Virgil' (1882) st. 3

28 It little profits that an idle king,
By this still hearth, among these barren
crags,
Matched with an agèd wife, I mete and dole
Unequal laws unto a savage race.
'Ulysses' (1842) l. 1

29 Much have I seen and known; cities of men
And manners, climates, councils,
governments,
Myself not least, but honoured of them all;
And drunk delight of battle with my peers,
Far on the ringing plains of windy Troy.
'Ulysses' (1842) l. 18

30 This is my son, mine own Telemachus.
'Ulysses' (1842) l. 33

31 Death closes all: but something ere the end,
Some work of noble note, may yet be done,
Not unbecoming men that strove with gods.
'Ulysses' (1842) l. 58

32 It may be that the gulfs will wash us down:
It may be we shall touch the Happy Isles,

And see the great Achilles, whom we knew.
'Ulysses' (1842) l. 69

1 That which we are, we are;
One equal temper of heroic hearts,
Made weak by time and fate, but strong in
will
To strive, to seek, to find, and not to yield.
'Ulysses' (1842) l. 74

2 Every moment dies a man,
Every moment one is born.
'The Vision of Sin' (1842) pt. 4, st. 9; cf.
Babbage 20:15

3 In the end I accepted the honour, because
during dinner Venables told me that, if I
became Poet Laureate, I should always
when I dined out be offered the liver-wing
of a fowl.
on being made Poet Laureate in 1850
in *Alfred Lord Tennyson: A Memoir by his Son* (1897)
vol. 1

4 It is the height of luxury to sit in a hot bath
and read about little birds.
*having had running hot water installed in his new
house*
Hallam Tennyson *Tennyson and his Friends* (1911)

5 A louse in the locks of literature.
of Churton Collins
Evan Charteris *Life and Letters of Sir Edmund Gosse*
(1931) ch. 14

Terence *c.*190–159 BC

6 *Hinc illae lacrimae.*
Hence those tears.
Andria l. 126

7 I am a man, I count nothing human foreign
to me.
Heauton Timorumenos l. 77

8 *Fortis fortuna adiuvat.*
Fortune assists the brave.
Phormio l. 203; cf. **Virgil** 325:5

9 *Quot homines tot sententiae: suus cuique mos.*
There are as many opinions as there are
people: each has his own correct way.
Phormio l. 454

Mother Teresa 1910–97

10 Now let us do something beautiful for God.
letter to Malcolm Muggeridge before making a
BBC TV programme about the Missionaries of
Charity, 1971; cf. **Muggeridge** 229:17

11 The biggest disease today is not leprosy or
tuberculosis, but rather the feeling of being
unwanted, uncared for and deserted by
everybody.
in *The Observer* 3 October 1971

St Teresa of Ávila 1512–82
see also **John** 172:13

12 Alas, O Lord, to what a state dost Thou bring
those who love Thee!
Interior Castle Mansion 6, ch. 11, para. 6 (tr. the
Benedictines of Stanbrook, 1921)

St Teresa of Lisieux 1873–97

13 I will spend my heaven doing good on earth.
T. N. Taylor (ed.) *Soeur Thérèse of Lisieux* (1912)
epilogue

14 After my death I will let fall a shower of
roses.
T. N. Taylor (ed.) *Soeur Thérèse of Lisieux* (1912)
epilogue

Tertullian AD *c.*160–*c.*225

15 As often as we are mown down by you, the
more we grow in numbers; the blood of
Christians is the seed.
traditionally 'The blood of the martyrs is the seed
of the Church'
Apologeticus ch. 50, sect. 13

16 *Certum est quia impossibile est.*
It is certain because it is impossible.
often quoted as 'Credo quia impossibile'
De Carne Christi ch. 5

A. S. J. Tessimond 1902–62

17 Cats, no less liquid than their shadows,
Offer no angles to the wind.
Cats (1934) p. 20

William Makepeace Thackeray
1811–63

18 Business first; pleasure afterwards.
The Rose and the Ring (1855) ch. 1

19 A woman with fair opportunities and
without a positive hump, may marry whom
she likes.
Vanity Fair (1847–8) ch. 4

20 Whenever he met a great man he grovelled
before him, and my-lorded him as only a
free-born Briton can do.
Vanity Fair (1847–8) ch. 13

21 If a man's character is to be abused, say
what you will, there's nobody like a relation
to do the business.
Vanity Fair (1847–8) ch. 19

22 Them's my sentiments!
Fred Bullock
Vanity Fair (1847–8) ch. 21

23 Darkness came down on the field and city:
and Amelia was praying for George, who
was lying on his face, dead, with a bullet
through his heart.
Vanity Fair (1847–8) ch. 32

24 How to live well on nothing a year.
Vanity Fair (1847–8) ch. 36 (title)

25 I think I could be a good woman if I had five
thousand a year.
Vanity Fair (1847–8) ch. 36

26 Come, children, let us shut up the box and
the puppets, for our play is played out.
Vanity Fair (1847–8) ch. 67

27 Werther had a love for Charlotte
Such as words could never utter;
Would you know how first he met her?
She was cutting bread and butter.
'Sorrows of Werther' (1855)

1 Charlotte, having seen his body
Borne before her on a shutter,
Like a well-conducted person
Went on cutting bread and butter.
'Sorrows of Werther' (1855)

Margaret Thatcher 1925–

2 No woman in my time will be Prime
Minister or Chancellor or Foreign
Secretary—not the top jobs. Anyway I
wouldn't want to be Prime Minister. You
have to give yourself 100%.
*on her appointment as Shadow Education
Spokesman*
  in *Sunday Telegraph* 26 October 1969

3 In politics if you want anything said, ask a
man. If you want anything done, ask a
woman.
  in *People* (New York) 15 September 1975

4 I stand before you tonight in my red chiffon
evening gown, my face softly made up, my
fair hair gently waved . . . the Iron Lady of
the Western World! Me? A cold war warrior?
Well, yes—if that is how they wish to
interpret my defence of values and
freedoms fundamental to our way of life.
  speech at Finchley, 31 January 1976; 'The Iron
  Lady' was the name given to her by the Soviet
  defence ministry newspaper *Red Star*, which
  accused her of trying to revive the cold war

5 No one would remember the Good
Samaritan if he'd only had good intentions.
He had money as well.
  television interview, 6 January 1980

6 To those waiting with bated breath for that
favourite media catchphrase, the U-turn, I
have only this to say. 'You turn if you want;
the lady's not for turning.'
  speech at Conservative Party Conference in
  Brighton, 10 October 1980; cf. **Fry** 134:18

7 Just rejoice at that news and congratulate
our armed forces and the Marines. Rejoice!
*on the recapture of South Georgia, usually quoted
as, 'Rejoice, rejoice!'*
  to newsmen outside 10 Downing Street, 25
  April 1982

8 I was asked whether I was trying to restore
Victorian values. I said straight out I was.
And I am.
  speech to the British Jewish Community, 21
  July 1983, referring to an interview earlier that
  year

9 Now it must be business as usual.
*on the steps of Brighton police station a few hours
after the bombing of the Grand Hotel, Brighton;
often quoted as 'We shall carry on as usual'*
  in *The Times* 13 October 1984

10 We can do business together.
*of Mikhail **Gorbachev***
  in *The Times* 18 December 1984

11 We must try to find ways to starve the
terrorist and the hijacker of the oxygen of
publicity on which they depend.
  speech to American Bar Association in London,
  15 July 1985

12 There is no such thing as Society. There are
individual men and women, and there are
families.
  in *Woman's Own* 31 October 1987

13 We have become a grandmother.
  in *The Times* 4 March 1989

14 I am naturally very sorry to see you go, but
understand . . . your wish to be able to
spend more time with your family.
*reply to Norman **Fowler**'s resignation letter*
  in *Guardian* 4 January 1990; cf. **Fowler** 132:12

15 No! No! No!
*making clear her opposition to a single European
currency, and more centralized controls from
Brussels*
  in the House of Commons, 30 October 1990

William Roscoe Thayer 1859–1923

16 Log-cabin to White House.
  title of biography (1910) of James **Garfield**

Themistocles *c*.528–*c*.462 BC

17 The wooden wall is your ships.
*interpreting the words of the Delphic oracle to the
Athenians, before the battle of Salamis in 480 BC,
'That the wooden wall only shall not fall, but help
you and your children'*
  Plutarch *Parallel Lives* 'Themistocles' bk. 2, ch. 1

Thomas à Kempis *c*.1380–1471

18 *O quam cito transit gloria mundi.*
Oh how quickly the glory of the world
passes away!
  De Imitatione Christi bk. 1, ch. 3, sect. 6; cf.
  Anonymous 12:22

19 For man proposes, but God disposes.
  De Imitatione Christi bk. 1, ch. 19, sect. 2

20 Would that we had spent one whole day
well in this world!
  De Imitatione Christi bk. 1, ch. 23, sect. 2

21 If you bear the cross gladly, it will bear you.
  De Imitatione Christi bk. 2, ch. 12, sect. 5

St Thomas Aquinas *c*.1225–74

22 *Pange, lingua, gloriosi
Corporis mysterium.*
Now, my tongue, the mystery telling
Of the glorious Body sing.
  'Pange Lingua Gloriosi' (Corpus Christi hymn,
  tr. J. M. Neale, E. Caswall, and others); cf.
  Fortunatus 131:19

23 *Tantum ergo sacramentum
Veneremur cernui;
Et antiquum documentum
Novo cedat ritui.*
Therefore we, before him bending,
This great Sacrament revere;
Types and shadows have their ending,
For the newer rite is here.
  'Pange Lingua Gloriosi' (Corpus Christi hymn,
  tr. J. M. Neale, E. Caswall, and others)

24 Moral science is better occupied when
treating of friendship than of justice.
  Exposition of Aristotle's Ethics (*c*.1271) bk. 8, lecture
  1

Brandon Thomas 1856–1914

1 I'm Charley's aunt from Brazil—where the nuts come from.
Charley's Aunt (1892) act 1

Dylan Thomas 1914–53

2 Though lovers be lost love shall not;
And death shall have no dominion.
'And death shall have no dominion' (1936); cf.
Bible 49:12

3 Do not go gentle into that good night,
Old age should burn and rave at close of day;
Rage, rage against the dying of the light.
'Do Not Go Gentle into that Good Night' (1952)

4 The force that through the green fuse drives the flower
Drives my green age.
'The force that through the green fuse drives the flower' (1934)

5 The hand that signed the paper felled a city;
Five sovereign fingers taxed the breath,
Doubled the globe of dead and halved a country;
These five kings did a king to death.
'The hand that signed the paper felled a city' (1936)

6 It was my thirtieth year to heaven.
'Poem in October' (1946)

7 After the first death, there is no other.
'A Refusal to Mourn the Death, by Fire, of a Child in London' (1946)

8 Books that told me everything about the wasp, except why.
A Child's Christmas in Wales (1954)

9 To begin at the beginning: It is spring, moonless night in the small town, starless and bible-black.
Under Milk Wood (1954)

10 I want, above all, to work like a fiend, a *good* fiend.
letter to Edith **Sitwell**, 11 April 1947

11 The land of my fathers. My fathers can have it.
of Wales
in *Adam* December 1953; cf. **James** 170:14

12 A man you don't like who drinks as much as you do.
definition of an alcoholic
Constantine Fitzgibbon *Life of Dylan Thomas* (1965) ch. 6

13 Poetry is not the most important thing in life . . . I'd much rather lie in a hot bath reading Agatha Christie and sucking sweets.
Joan Wyndham *Love is Blue* (1986) 6 July 1943

Edward Thomas 1878–1917

14 Yes; I remember Adlestrop—
The name, because one afternoon
Of heat the express-train drew up there
Unwontedly. It was late June.
'Adlestrop' (1917)

15 I have come to the borders of sleep,
The unfathomable deep

Forest where all must lose
Their way.
'Lights Out' (1917)

16 I see and hear nothing;
Yet seem, too, to be listening, lying in wait
For what I should, yet never can, remember.
'Old Man' (1917)

17 Out in the dark over the snow
The fallow fawns invisible go.
'Out in the dark' (1917)

Elizabeth Thomas 1675–1731

18 From marrying in haste, and repenting at leisure;
Not liking the person, yet liking his treasure:
Libera nos.
'A New Litany, occasioned by an invitation to a wedding' (1722)

Gwyn Thomas 1913–81

19 There are still parts of Wales where the only concession to gaiety is a striped shroud.
in *Punch* 18 June 1958

Irene Thomas

20 Protestant women may take the pill. Roman Catholic women must keep taking The Tablet.
in *Guardian* 28 December 1990

R. S. Thomas 1913–2000

21 Doctors in verse
Being scarce now, most poets
Are their own patients.
'The Cure' (1958)

22 There is no love
For such, only a willed gentleness.
'They' (1968)

23 Hate takes a long time
To grow in, and mine
Has increased from birth;
Not for the brute earth . . .
. . . I find
This hate's for my own kind . . .
'Those Others' (1961)

24 There is no present in Wales,
And no future;
There is only the past,
Brittle with relics . . .
And an impotent people,
Sick with inbreeding,
Worrying the carcase of an old song.
'Welsh Landscape' (1955)

Francis Thompson 1859–1907

25 As the run-stealers flicker to and fro,
To and fro:—
O my Hornby and my Barlow long ago!
'At Lord's' (1913)

26 I fled Him, down the nights and down the days;
I fled Him, down the arches of the years;

I fled Him, down the labyrinthine ways
Of my own mind; and in the mist of tears
I hid from Him, and under running
laughter.
'The Hound of Heaven' (1913) pt. 1

1 Lo, all things fly thee, for thou fliest Me!'
'The Hound of Heaven' (1913) pt. 5

2 'Tis ye, 'tis your estrangèd faces,
That miss the many-splendoured thing.
'The Kingdom of God' (1913)

3 Upon thy so sore loss
Shall shine the traffic of Jacob's ladder
Pitched betwixt Heaven and Charing Cross.
'The Kingdom of God' (1913)

4 And lo, Christ walking on the water
Not of Gennesareth, but Thames!
'The Kingdom of God' (1913)

5 Look for me in the nurseries of heaven.
'To My Godchild Francis M.W.M.' (1913)

6 Insculped and embossed,
With His hammer of wind,
And His graver of frost.
'To a Snowflake' (1913)

Julian Thompson 1934–

7 You don't mind dying for Queen and
country, but you certainly don't want to die
for politicians.
'The Falklands War—the Untold Story'
(Yorkshire Television) 1 April 1987

James Thomson 1700–48

8 When Britain first, at heaven's command,
Arose from out the azure main,
This was the charter of the land,
And guardian angels sung this strain:
'Rule, Britannia, rule the waves;
Britons never will be slaves.'
Alfred: a Masque (1740) act 2

9 Delightful task! to rear the tender thought,
To teach the young idea how to shoot.
The Seasons (1746) 'Spring' l. 1152

10 An elegant sufficiency, content,
Retirement, rural quiet, friendship, books.
The Seasons (1746) 'Spring' l. 1161

11 Sighed and looked unutterable things.
The Seasons (1746) 'Summer' l. 1188

James Thomson 1834–82

12 The city of dreadful night.
title of poem, written 1870–3

13 As we rush, as we rush in the train,
The trees and the houses go wheeling back,
But the starry heavens above that plain
Come flying on our track.
'Sunday at Hampstead' (written 1863–5) st. 10

14 Give a man a horse he can ride,
Give a man a boat he can sail.
'Sunday up the River' (written 1865) st. 15

Roy Thomson 1894–1976

15 Like having your own licence to print
money.
on the profitability of commercial television in
Britain
R. Braddon Roy Thomson (1965) ch. 32

Henry David Thoreau 1817–62

16 Some circumstantial evidence is very
strong, as when you find a trout in the milk.
Journal 11 November 1850

17 Not that the story need be long, but it will
take a long while to make it short.
letter to Harrison Blake, 16 November 1857; cf.
Pascal 241:14

18 I have travelled a good deal in Concord.
Walden (1854) 'Economy'

19 The mass of men lead lives of quiet
desperation.
Walden (1854) 'Economy'

20 The three-o'-clock in the morning courage,
which Bonaparte thought was the rarest.
Walden (1854) 'Sounds'; cf. **Napoleon** 231:6

21 It is not worthwhile to go around the world
to count the cats in Zanzibar.
Walden (1854) 'Conclusion'

22 If a man does not keep pace with his
companions, perhaps it is because he hears
a different drummer. Let him step to the
music which he hears, however measured
or far away.
Walden (1854) 'Conclusion'

Robert Thorne d. 1527

23 There is no land unhabitable nor sea
innavigable.
Richard Hakluyt The Principal Navigations,
Voyages, and Discoveries of the English Nation (1589)

Jeremy Thorpe 1929–

24 Greater love hath no man than this, that he
lay down his friends for his life.
on Harold **Macmillan**'s sacking seven of his
Cabinet on 13 July 1962
D. E. Butler and Anthony King The General
Election of 1964 (1965) ch. 1; cf. **Bible** 48:8

Thucydides c.455–c.400 BC

25 Happiness depends on being free, and
freedom depends on being courageous.
Thucydides History of the Peloponnesian War bk. 2,
ch. 4, sect. 43 (tr. Rex Warner)

James Thurber 1894–1961

26 Her own mother lived the latter years of her
life in the horrible suspicion that electricity
was dripping invisibly all over the house.
My Life and Hard Times (1933) ch. 2

27 It's a naïve domestic Burgundy without any
breeding, but I think you'll be amused by its
presumption.
cartoon caption in New Yorker 27 March 1937

28 Well, if I called the wrong number, why did
you answer the phone?
cartoon caption in New Yorker 5 June 1937

1 It's our *own* story *exactly*! He bold as a hawk,
she soft as the dawn.
cartoon caption in *New Yorker* 25 February 1939;
cf. **Lover** 203:10

Edward, Lord Thurlow 1731–1806

2 Corporations have neither bodies to be
punished, nor souls to be condemned, they
therefore do as they like.
*usually quoted as 'Did you ever expect a
corporation to have a conscience, when it has no
soul to be damned, and no body to be kicked?'*
John Poynder *Literary Extracts* (1844) vol. 1; cf.
Coke 95:18

Chidiock Tichborne c.1558–86

3 My prime of youth is but a frost of cares;
My feast of joy is but a dish of pain;
My crop of corn is but a field of tares;
And all my good is but vain hope of gain.
The day is past, and yet I saw no sun;
And now I live, and now my life is done.
'Elegy' (composed in the Tower of London prior
to his execution)

Thomas Tickell 1686–1740

4 There taught us how to live; and (oh! too
high
The price for knowledge) taught us how to
die.
'To the Earl of Warwick. On the Death of Mr
Addison' (1721) l. 76

Lionel Tiger 1937–

5 Male bonding.
Men in Groups (1969)

Paul Tillich 1886–1965

6 Neurosis is the way of avoiding non-being
by avoiding being.
The Courage To Be (1952) pt. 2, ch. 3

Tipu Sultan c.1750–99

7 In this world I would rather live two days
like a tiger, than two hundred years like a
sheep.
Alexander Beatson *A View of the Origin and
Conduct of the War with Tippoo Sultan* (1800) ch. 10

Titus AD 39–81

8 *Amici, diem perdidi.*
Friends, I have lost a day.
*on reflecting that he had done nothing to help
anybody all day*
Suetonius *Lives of the Caesars* 'Titus' ch. 8, sect. 1

Alexis de Tocqueville 1805–59

9 Despots themselves do not deny that
freedom is excellent; only they desire it for
themselves alone, and they maintain that
everyone else is altogether unworthy of it.
L'Ancien régime (1856)

10 History is a gallery of pictures in which
there are few originals and many copies.
L'Ancien régime (1856)

11 What is understood by republican
government in the United States is the slow
and quiet action of society upon itself.
De la Démocratie en Amérique (1835–40) vol. 1

Alvin Toffler 1928–

12 Culture shock is relatively mild in
comparison with a much more serious
malady that might be called 'future shock'.
Future shock is the dizzying disorientation
brought on by the premature arrival of the
future.
in *Horizon* Summer 1965; the book *Future Shock*
was published 1970

J. R. R. Tolkien 1892–1973

13 One Ring to rule them all, One Ring to find
them
One Ring to bring them all and in the
darkness bind them.
The Fellowship of the Ring (1954) epigraph

14 In a hole in the ground there lived a hobbit.
The Hobbit (1937)

Leo Tolstoy 1828–1910

15 All happy families resemble one another,
but each unhappy family is unhappy in its
own way.
Anna Karenina (1875–7) pt. 1, ch. 1 (tr. A. and L.
Maude)

16 Our body is a machine for living. It is
organized for that, it is its nature. Let life go
on in it unhindered and let it defend itself,
it will do more than if you paralyse it by
encumbering it with remedies.
War and Peace (1865–9) bk. 10, ch. 29 (tr. A. and
L. Maude); cf. **Le Corbusier** 196:6

17 All newspaper and journalistic activity is an
intellectual brothel from which there is no
retreat.
letter to Prince V. P. Meshchersky, 22 August
1871

Wolfe Tone 1763–98

18 I find, then, I am but a bad anatomist.
*Wolfe Tone (1763–98), who in trying to cut his
throat in prison severed his windpipe instead of
his jugular, and lingered for several days*
Oliver Knox *Rebels and Informers* (1998)

Augustus Montague Toplady 1740–78

19 Rock of Ages, cleft for me,
Let me hide myself in Thee.
Let the water and the blood,
From Thy riven side which flowed,
Be of sin the double cure,
Cleanse me from its guilt and power.
'Rock of Ages, cleft for me' (1776 hymn)

Cyril Tourneur *see* Thomas Middleton

Pete Townshend 1945–

1 Hope I die before I get old.
'My Generation' (1965 song)

Polly Toynbee 1946–

2 It is Stupidvision . . . It patronises. It talks to the vacuum cleaner and the washing machine and the microwave without much contact with the human brain.
of daytime television
in *Radio Times* 11 May 1996

Thomas Traherne *c.*1637–74

3 The corn was orient and immortal wheat, which never should be reaped, nor was ever sown. I thought it had stood from everlasting to everlasting.
Centuries of Meditations 'Third Century' sect. 3

4 O what venerable creatures did the aged seem! Immortal cherubims! And young men glittering and sparkling angels, and maids strange seraphic pieces of life and beauty!
Centuries of Meditations 'Third Century' sect. 3

Joseph Trapp 1679–1747

5 The King, observing with judicious eyes
The state of both his universities,
To Oxford sent a troop of horse, and why?
That learned body wanted loyalty;
To Cambridge books, as very well discerning
How much that loyal body wanted learning.
lines written on **George I**'s *donation of the Bishop of Ely's Library to Cambridge University*
John Nichols *Literary Anecdotes* (1812–16) vol. 3; cf. **Browne** 69:11

Merle Travis 1917–83

6 Sixteen tons, what do you get?
Another day older and deeper in debt.
Say brother, don't you call me 'cause I can't go
I owe my soul to the company store.
'Sixteen Tons' (1947 song)

G. M. Trevelyan 1876–1962

7 Disinterested intellectual curiosity is the life-blood of real civilization.
English Social History (1942) introduction

8 If the French noblesse had been capable of playing cricket with their peasants, their chateaux would never have been burnt.
English Social History (1942) ch. 8

9 [Education] has produced a vast population able to read but unable to distinguish what is worth reading, an easy prey to sensations and cheap appeals.
English Social History (1942) ch. 18

Calvin Trillin 1935–

10 The shelf life of the modern hardback writer is somewhere between the milk and the yoghurt.
in *Sunday Times* 9 June 1991; attributed

David Trimble 1944–

11 We are not here to negotiate with them, but to confront them.
on entering the Mitchell talks on Northern Ireland with Sinn Feinn
in *Guardian* 18 September 1997

12 The fundamental Act of Union is there, intact.
of the Northern Ireland settlement
in *Daily Telegraph* 11 April 1998

Tommy Trinder 1909–89

13 Overpaid, overfed, oversexed, and over here.
of American troops in Britain during the Second World War
associated with Trinder, but probably not his invention

Anthony Trollope 1815–82

14 Three hours a day will produce as much as a man ought to write.
Autobiography (1883) ch. 15

15 The end of a novel, like the end of a children's dinner-party, must be made up of sweetmeats and sugar-plums.
Barchester Towers (1857) ch. 53

16 When taken in the refreshing waters of office any . . . pill can be swallowed.
The Bertrams (1859) ch. 16

17 There is no road to wealth so easy and respectable as that of matrimony.
Doctor Thorne (1858) ch. 16

18 She knew how to allure by denying, and to make the gift rich by delaying it.
Phineas Finn (1869) ch. 57

19 Newspaper editors sport daily with the names of men of whom they do not hesitate to publish almost the severest words that can be uttered; but let an editor be himself attacked, even without his name, and he thinks that the thunderbolt of heaven should fall upon the offender.
Phineas Redux (1874) ch. 27

20 The tenth Muse, who now governs the periodical press.
The Warden (1855) ch. 14

21 Love is like any other luxury. You have no right to it unless you can afford it.
The Way We Live Now (1875) ch. 84

Frances Trollope 1780–1863

22 I draw from life—but I always pulp my acquaintance before serving them up. You would never recognize a pig in a sausage.
remark, *c.*1848; S. Baring-Gould *Early Reminiscences 1834–1864* (1923)

Leon Trotsky 1879–1940

1 Old age is the most unexpected of all things that happen to a man.
   Diary in Exile (1959) 8 May 1935

2 Civilization has made the peasantry its pack animal. The bourgeoisie in the long run only changed the form of the pack.
   History of the Russian Revolution (1933) vol. 3, ch. 1

3 You [the Mensheviks] are pitiful isolated individuals; you are bankrupts; your role is played out. Go where you belong from now on — into the dustbin of history!
   History of the Russian Revolution (1933) vol. 3, ch. 10; cf. **Birrell** 54:8

Pierre Trudeau 1919–

4 The state has no place in the nation's bedrooms.
   interview, Ottawa, 22 December 1967

5 Living next to you is in some ways like sleeping with an elephant. No matter how friendly and even-tempered the beast, one is affected by every twitch and grunt.
   on relations between Canada and the US
   speech at National Press Club, Washington D. C., 25 March 1969

Harry S. Truman 1884–1972

6 If you can't stand the heat, get out of the kitchen.
   associated with Truman, but attributed by him to Harry Vaughan, his 'military jester'; in *Time* 28 April 1952

7 I never give them [the public] hell. I just tell the truth, and they think it is hell.
   in *Look* 3 April 1956

8 A statesman is a politician who's been dead 10 or 15 years.
   in *New York World Telegram and Sun* 12 April 1958

9 It's a recession when your neighbour loses his job; it's a depression when you lose yours.
   in *Observer* 13 April 1958

10 The buck stops here.
   unattributed motto on Truman's desk

Donald Trump 1946–

11 Deals are my art form. Other people paint beautifully on canvas or write wonderful poetry. I like making deals, preferably big deals. That's how I get my kicks.
   Donald Trump and Tony Schwartz *The Art of the Deal* (1987)

Sojourner Truth c.1797–1883

12 That man . . . says that women need to be helped into carriages, and lifted over ditches . . . Nobody ever helps me into carriages, or over mud puddles, or gives me any best place, and aren't I a woman? . . . I have ploughed, and planted, and gathered into barns, and no man could head me—and aren't I a woman?
   speech at Women's Rights Convention, Akron, Ohio, 1851

Barbara W. Tuchman 1912–89

13 For one August in its history Paris was French—and silent.
   August 1914 (1962) ch. 20

Sophie Tucker 1884–1966

14 From birth to 18 a girl needs good parents. From 18 to 35, she needs good looks. From 35 to 55, good personality. From 55 on, she needs good cash.
   Michael Freedland *Sophie* (1978)

Ivan Turgenev 1818–83

15 Nature is not a temple, but a workshop, and man's the workman in it.
   Fathers and Sons (1862) ch. 9 (tr. Rosemary Edmonds)

16 Just try and set death aside. It sets you aside, and that's the end of it!
   Fathers and Sons (1862) ch. 27 (tr. Rosemary Edmonds)

17 Whatever a man prays for, he prays for a miracle. Every prayer reduces itself to this: Great God, grant that twice two be not four.
   Poems in Prose (1881) 'Prayer'

A. R. J. Turgot 1727–81

18 *Eripuit coelo fulmen, sceptrumque tyrannis.*
   He snatched the lightning shaft from heaven, and the sceptre from tyrants.
   inscription for a bust of Benjamin **Franklin**, inventor of the lightning conductor; cf. **Manilius** 211:5

Alan Turing 1912–54

19 We are not interested in the fact that the brain has the consistency of cold porridge.
   A. P. Hodges *Alan Turing: the Enigma* (1983)

Charles Tennyson Turner 1808–79

20 Bright over Europe fell her golden hair.
   'Letty's Globe' (1880)

J. M. W. Turner 1775–1851

21 He *sees* more in my pictures than I ever painted!
   of John **Ruskin**
   Mary Lloyd *Sunny Memories* (1879) vol. 1

22 If I could find anything blacker than black, I'd use it.
   when a friend complained of the blackness of the sails in 'Peace—Burial at Sea' (1844)
   in *Dictionary of National Biography* (1917–)

Walter James Redfern Turner 1889–1946

23 When I was but thirteen or so
   I went into a golden land,
   Chimborazo, Cotopaxi
   Took me by the hand.
   'Romance' (1916)

John Tusa 1936–

1 Management that wants to change an institution must first show it loves that institution.

in *Observer* 27 February 1994 'Sayings of the Week'

Mark Twain 1835–1910

2 There was things which he stretched, but mainly he told the truth.

The Adventures of Huckleberry Finn (1884) ch. 1

3 Hain't we got all the fools in town on our side? and ain't that a big enough majority in any town?

The Adventures of Huckleberry Finn (1884) ch. 26

4 Soap and education are not as sudden as a massacre, but they are more deadly in the long run.

A Curious Dream (1872) 'Facts concerning the Recent Resignation'

5 Truth is the most valuable thing we have. Let us economize it.

Following the Equator (1897) ch. 7; cf. **Armstrong** 15:2

6 It takes your enemy and your friend, working together, to hurt you to the heart: the one to slander you and the other to get the news to you.

Following the Equator (1897) ch. 45

7 The innocents abroad.

title of book (1869)

8 There are laws to protect the freedom of the press's speech, but none that are worth anything to protect the people from the press.

'License of the Press' (1873)

9 What a good thing Adam had. When he said a good thing he knew nobody had said it before.

Notebooks (1935)

10 Cauliflower is nothing but cabbage with a college education.

Pudd'nhead Wilson (1894) ch. 5

11 When angry, count four; when very angry, swear.

Pudd'nhead Wilson (1894) ch. 10

12 As to the Adjective: when in doubt, strike it out.

Pudd'nhead Wilson (1894) ch. 11

13 The report of my death was an exaggeration.

usually quoted as 'Reports of my death have been greatly exaggerated'

in *New York Journal* 2 June 1897

Kenneth Tynan 1927–80

14 A critic is a man who knows the way but can't drive the car.

in *New York Times Magazine* 9 January 1966

15 'Sergeant Pepper'—a decisive moment in the history of Western Civilization.

in 1967; Howard Elson *McCartney* (1986)

16 A neurosis is a secret you don't know you're keeping.

Kathleen Tynan *Life of Kenneth Tynan* (1987) ch. 19

William Tyndale c.1494–1536

17 If God spare my life, ere many years I will cause a boy that driveth the plough shall know more of the scripture than thou doest!

to an opponent

in *Dictionary of National Biography* (1917–)

18 Lord, open the King of England's eyes!

at the stake

John Foxe *Actes and Monuments* (1570)

Ulpian d. 228

19 *Nulla iniuria est, quae in volentem fiat.*
No injustice is done to someone who wants that thing done.

usually quoted as 'Volenti non fit iniuria'

Corpus Iuris Civilis Digests bk. 47, ch. 10, sect. 1, subsect. 5 (usually quoted 'Volenti non fit iniuria')

Miguel de Unamuno 1864–1937

20 *La vida es duda,*
y la fe sin la duda es sólo muerte.
Life is doubt,
And faith without doubt is nothing but death.

Poesías (1907) 'Salmo II'

The Upanishads

21 From delusion lead me to Truth.
From darkness lead me to Light.
from death lead me to immortality.

Brihadāranyaka Upanishad ch. 1, pt. 3, v. 28; cf. **Kumar** 191:1

22 *Shantih, shantih, shantih.*
Peace! Peace! Peace!

Taittiriya Upanishad ch. 1, pt. 1, mantra; cf. **Eliot** 122:17

23 Abiding in the midst of ignorance, thinking themselves wise and learned, fools go aimlessly hither and thither, like blind led by the blind.

Katha Upanishad ch. 2, v. 5; cf. **Bible** 44:7

24 If any man thinks he slays, and if another thinks he is slain, neither knows the ways of truth. The Eternal in man cannot kill: the Eternal in man cannot die.

Katha Upanishad ch. 2, v. 19; cf. **Bhagavadgita** 32:16, **Emerson** 124:8

John Updike 1932–

25 A soggy little island huffing and puffing to keep up with Western Europe.

of England

Picked Up Pieces (1976) 'London Life' (written 1969)

26 America is a vast conspiracy to make you happy.

Problems (1980) 'How to love America and Leave it at the Same Time'

1 Celebrity is a mask that eats into the face.
   Self-Consciousness: Memoirs (1989)

Peter Ustinov 1921–

2 Laughter . . . the most civilized music in the
   world.
   Dear Me (1977) ch. 3

3 I do not believe that friends are necessarily
   the people you like best, they are merely
   the people who got there first.
   Dear Me (1977) ch. 5

4 At the age of four with paper hats and
   wooden swords we're all Generals. Only
   some of us never grow out of it.
   Romanoff and Juliet (1956) act 1

Paul Valéry 1871–1945

5 Science means simply the aggregate of all
   the recipes that are always successful. The
   rest is literature.
   Moralités (1932) p. 41; cf. **Verlaine** 323:11

6 God created man and, finding him not
   sufficiently alone, gave him a companion to
   make him feel his solitude more keenly.
   Tel Quel 1 (1941) 'Moralités'

7 Politics is the art of preventing people from
   taking part in affairs which properly
   concern them.
   Tel Quel 2 (1943) 'Rhumbs'

John Vanbrugh 1664–1726

8 BELINDA: Ay, but you know we must return
   good for evil.
   LADY BRUTE: That may be a mistake in the
   translation.
   The Provoked Wife (1697) act 1, sc. 1

9 So, now I am in for Hobbes's voyage, a great
   leap in the dark.
   'Heartfree' on marriage
   The Provoked Wife (1697) act 5, sc. 5; cf. **Hobbes**
   160:6

10 When once a woman has given you her
   heart, you can never get rid of the rest of
   her body.
   The Relapse (1696) act 3, sc. 1

Vivian van Damm c.1889–1960

11 We never closed.
   *of the Windmill Theatre, London, during the
   Second World War*
   Tonight and Every Night (1952) ch. 18

William Henry Vanderbilt
1821–85

12 The public be damned!
   *on whether the public should be consulted about
   luxury trains*
   letter from A. W. Cole to *New York Times* 25
   August 1918

Laurens van der Post 1906–96

13 Human beings are perhaps never more
   frightening than when they are convinced
   beyond doubt that they are right.
   Lost World of the Kalahari (1958)

14 I don't think a man who has watched the
   sun going down could walk away and
   commit a murder.
   in *Daily Telegraph* 17 December 1996; obituary

Henry Van Dyke 1852–1933

15 Time is
   Too slow for those who wait,
   Too swift for those who fear,
   Too long for those who grieve,
   Too short for those who rejoice;
   But for those who love,
   Time is eternity.
   'Time is too slow for those who wait' (1905),
   read at the funeral of **Diana**, Princess of Wales;
   Nigel Rees in 'Quote . . . Unquote' October 1997
   notes that the original form of the last line is
   'Time is not'

Vincent Van Gogh 1853–90

16 I cannot help it that my pictures do not sell.
   Nevertheless the time will come when
   people will see that they are worth more
   than the price of the paint.
   letter to his brother Theo, 20 October 1888

Bartolomeo Vanzetti 1888–1927

17 Sacco's name will live in the hearts of the
   people and in their gratitude when
   Katzmann's and yours bones will be
   dispersed by time, when your name, his
   name, your laws, institutions, and your false
   god are but a deem rememoring of a cursed
   past in which man was wolf to the man.
   *statement disallowed at his trial, with Nicola
   Sacco, for murder and robbery; both were
   sentenced to death on 9 April 1927, and executed
   on 23 August 1927*
   M. D. Frankfurter and G. Jackson *Letters of Sacco
   and Vanzetti* (1928)

Michel Vaucaire

18 *Non! rien de rien,*
   Non! je ne regrette rien.
   No, no regrets,
   No, we will have no regrets.
   'Non, je ne regrette rien' (1960 song); sung by
   Edith Piaf

Henry Vaughan 1622–95

19 Wise Nicodemus saw such light
   As made him know his God by night.
   Silex Scintillans (1650–5) 'The Night'

20 My soul, there is a country
   Far beyond the stars,
   Where stands a wingèd sentry
   All skilful in the wars.
   Silex Scintillans (1650–5) 'Peace'

21 Happy those early days, when I
   Shined in my angel-infancy.

Before I understood this place
Appointed for my second race,
Or taught my soul to fancy aught
But a white, celestial thought.
Silex Scintillans (1650–5) 'The Retreat'

1 And in those weaker glories spy
Some shadows of eternity.
Silex Scintillans (1650–5) 'The Retreat'

2 They are all gone into the world of light,
And I alone sit lingering here.
Silex Scintillans (1650–5) 'They are all gone'

3 Dear, beauteous death! the jewel of the just,
Shining nowhere but in the dark.
Silex Scintillans (1650–5) 'They are all gone'

4 I saw Eternity the other night,
Like a great ring of pure and endless light,
All calm, as it was bright.
Silex Scintillans (1650–5) 'The World'

Janet-Maria Vaughan 1899–1993

5 I am here—trying to do science in hell.
working as a doctor in Belsen at the end of the war
letter to a friend, 12 May 1945

Thomas, Lord Vaux 1510–56

6 For age with stealing steps
Hath clawed me with his clutch.
'The Aged Lover Renounceth Love' (1557); a garbled version is sung by the gravedigger in *Hamlet*

Thorstein Veblen 1857–1929

7 Conspicuous consumption of valuable goods is a means of reputability to the gentleman of leisure.
Theory of the Leisure Class (1899) ch. 4

Vegetius fl. AD 379–95

8 *Qui desiderat pacem, praeparet bellum.*
Let him who desires peace, prepare for war.
usually quoted as 'Si vis pacem, para bellum [If you want peace, prepare for war]'
Epitoma Rei Militaris bk. 3, prologue; cf. **Aristotle** 14:13

Robert Venturi 1925–

9 Less is a bore.
Complexity and Contradiction in Architecture (1966) ch. 2

Pierre Vergniaud 1753–93

10 There was reason to fear that the Revolution, like Saturn, might devour in turn each one of her children.
Alphonse de Lamartine *Histoire des Girondins* (1847) bk. 38, ch. 20

Paul Verlaine 1844–96

11 *Et tout le reste est littérature.*
All the rest is mere fine writing.
'Art poétique' (1882); cf. **Valéry** 322:5

12 *Et, Ô ces voix d'enfants chantants dans la coupole!*
And oh those children's voices, singing beneath the dome!
'Parsifal' A Jules Tellier (1886)

13 *Il pleure dans mon coeur*
Comme il pleut sur la ville.
Tears are shed in my heart like the rain on the town.
Romances sans paroles (1874) 'Ariettes oubliées' no. 3

Hendrik Frensch Verwoerd
1901–66

14 It is abundantly clear that unplanned education creates many problems, disrupts the communal life of the Bantu and endangers the communal life of the European.
speech in South African Senate, 7 June 1954

Vespasian AD 9–79

15 *Pecunia non olet.*
Money has no smell.
upon **Titus**'s *objecting to his tax on public lavatories, Vespasian held a coin to Titus's nose; on being told it didn't smell, he replied,* 'Atque e lotio est [Yes, that's made from urine]'
traditional summary of Suetonius *Lives of the Caesars* 'Vespasian' sect. 23

16 *Vae, puto deus fio.*
Woe is me, I think I am becoming a god.
when fatally ill
Suetonius *Lives of the Caesars* 'Vespasian' sect. 23, subsect. 4

17 An emperor ought to die standing.
Vespasian (AD 9–79)
Suetonius *Lives of the Caesars* 'Vespasian' sect. 24

Queen Victoria 1819–1901

18 I will be good.
on being shown a chart of the line of succession, 11 March 1830
Theodore Martin *The Prince Consort* (1875) vol. 1, ch. 2

19 It was with some emotion . . . that I beheld Albert—who is beautiful.
of her first meeting with Prince **Albert**, *c.1838*
attributed; Stanley Weintraub *Albert: Uncrowned King* (1997)

20 He speaks to Me as if I was a public meeting.
of **Gladstone**
G. W. E. Russell *Collections and Recollections* (1898) ch. 14

21 We are not interested in the possibilities of defeat; they do not exist.
on the Boer War during 'Black Week', December 1899
Lady Gwendolen Cecil *Life of Robert, Marquis of Salisbury* (1931) vol. 3, ch. 6

22 We are not amused.
attributed, in Caroline Holland *Notebooks of a Spinster Lady* (1919) ch. 21, 2 January 1900

Gore Vidal 1925–

1 Whenever a friend succeeds, a little
something in me dies.
   in *Sunday Times Magazine* 16 September 1973

José Antonio Viera Gallo 1943–

2 Socialism can only arrive by bicycle.
   Ivan Illich *Energy and Equity* (1974) epigraph

Alfred de Vigny 1797–1863

3 *J'aime le son du cor, le soir, au fond des bois.*
   I love the sound of the horn, at night, in the
   depth of the woods.
   'Le Cor' (1826)

4 *Seul le silence est grand; tout le reste est faiblesse.*
   Silence alone is great; all else is feebleness.
   'La mort du loup' (1843) pt. 3

Philippe-Auguste Villiers de L'Isle-Adam 1838–89

5 Living? The servants will do that for us.
   Axël (1890) pt. 4, sect. 2

François Villon b. 1431

6 *Mais où sont les neiges d'antan?*
   But where are the snows of yesteryear?
   Le Grand Testament (1461) 'Ballade des dames du
   temps jadis' (tr. D. G. Rossetti)

7 *En cette foi je veux vivre et mourir.*
   In this faith I wish to live and to die.
   Le Grand Testament (1461) 'Ballade pour prier
   Nostre Dame'

St Vincent of Lerins d. AD c.450

8 *Quod ubique, quod semper, quod ab omnibus
   creditum est.*
   What is everywhere, what is always, what is
   by all people believed.
   Commonitorium Primum sect. 2

Virgil 70–19 BC

9 *Arma virumque cano, Troiae qui primus ab oris
   Italiam fato profugus Laviniaque venit
   Litora, multum ille et terris iactatus et alto
   Vi superum, saevae memorem Iunonis ob iram.*
   I sing of arms and the man who first from
   the shores of Troy came destined an exile to
   Italy and the Lavinian beaches, a man much
   buffeted on land and on the deep by force of
   the gods because of fierce Juno's never-
   forgetting anger.
   Aeneid bk. 1, l. 1; cf. **Dryden** 117:14

10 *Forsan et haec olim meminisse iuvabit.*
   Maybe one day it will be cheering to
   remember even these things.
   Aeneid bk. 1, l. 203

11 *Et vera incessu patuit dea.*
   And her true godhead was evident from her
   walk.
   Aeneid bk. 1, l. 408

12 *Sunt lacrimae rerum et mentem mortalia
   tangunt.*
   There are tears shed for things even here
   and mortality touches the heart.
   Aeneid bk. 1, l. 463

13 *Equo ne credite, Teucri.
   Quidquid id est, timeo Danaos et dona ferentes.*
   Do not trust the horse, Trojans. Whatever it
   is, I fear the Greeks even when they bring
   gifts.
   Aeneid bk. 2, l. 48

14 *Dis aliter visum.*
   The gods thought otherwise.
   Aeneid bk. 2, l. 428

15 *Quid non mortalia pectora cogis,
   Auri sacra fames!*
   To what do you not drive human hearts,
   cursed craving for gold!
   Aeneid bk. 3, l. 56

16 *Varium et mutabile semper
   Femina.*
   Fickle and changeable always is woman.
   Aeneid bk. 4, l. 569; see below

17 *Exoriare aliquis nostris ex ossibus ultor.*
   Rise up from my dead bones, avenger!
   Aeneid bk. 4, l. 625 (translation by C. Day-Lewis)

18 *Hos successus alit: possunt, quia posse videntur.*
   These success encourages: they can because
   they think they can.
   Aeneid bk. 5, l. 231

19 *Bella, horrida bella,
   Et Thybrim multo spumantem sanguine cerno.*
   I see wars, horrible wars, and the Tiber
   foaming with much blood.
   Aeneid bk. 6, l. 86; cf. **Powell** 250:23

20 *Facilis descensus Averno:
   Noctes atque dies patet atri ianua Ditis;
   Sed revocare gradum superasque evadere ad
   auras,
   Hoc opus, hic labor est.*
   Easy is the way down to the Underworld: by
   night and by day dark Hades' door stands
   open; but to retrace one's steps and to make
   a way out to the upper air, that's the task,
   that is the labour.
   Aeneid bk. 6, l. 126

21 *Ibant obscuri sola sub nocte.*
   Darkling they went under the lonely night.
   Aeneid bk. 6, l. 268

22 *Stabant orantes primi transmittere cursum
   Tendebantque manus ripae ulterioris amore.*
   They stood begging to be the first to make
   the voyage over and they reached out their
   hands in longing for the further shore.
   Aeneid bk. 6, l. 313

23 *Tu regere imperio populos, Romane, memento
   (Hae tibi erunt artes), pacique imponere morem,
   Parcere subiectis et debellare superbos.*
   You, Roman, make your task to rule nations
   by your government (these shall be your
   skills), to impose ordered ways upon a state
   of peace, to spare those who have submitted
   and to subdue the arrogant.
   Aeneid bk. 6, l. 851

1 *Manibus date lilia plenis.*
Give me lilies in armfuls.
Aeneid bk. 6, l. 884

2 *Sunt geminae Somni portae, quarum altera fertur Cornea, qua veris facilis datur exitus umbris, Altera candenti perfecta nitens elephanto, Sed falsa ad caelum mittunt insomnia Manes.*
There are two gates of Sleep, one of which it is held is made of horn and by it easy egress is given to real ghosts; the other shining, fashioned of gleaming white ivory, but the shades send deceptive visions that way to the light.
Aeneid bk. 6, l. 893

3 *Geniumque loci primamque deorum Tellurem Nymphasque et adhuc ignota precatur Flumina.*
He prays to the spirit of the place and to Earth, the first of the gods, and to the Nymphs and as yet unknown rivers.
*Aeneid bk. 7, l. 136; cf. **Pope** 247:19*

4 *Macte nova virtute, puer, sic itur ad astra.*
Blessings on your young courage, boy; that's the way to the stars.
Aeneid bk. 9, l. 641

5 *Audentis Fortuna iuvat.*
Fortune assists the bold.
often quoted as 'Fortune favours the brave'
*Aeneid bk. 10, l. 284; cf. **Terence** 314:8*

6 *Et dulcis moriens reminiscitur Argos.*
And dying remembers his sweet Argos.
Aeneid bk. 10, l. 782

7 *Experto credite.*
Trust one who has gone through it.
Aeneid bk. 11, l. 283

8 *Tityre, tu patulae recubans sub tegmine fagi Silvestrem tenui Musam meditaris avena.*
Tityrus, you who lie under cover of the spreading beech-tree, you are practising your pastoral music on a thin stalk.
Eclogues no. 1, l. 1

9 *Latet anguis in herba.*
There's a snake hidden in the grass.
Eclogues no. 3, l. 93

10 *Ultima Cumaei venit iam carminis aetas; Magnus ab integro saeclorum nascitur ordo. Iam redit et virgo, redeunt Saturnia regna, Iam nova progenies caelo demittitur alto.*
Now has come the last age according to the oracle at Cumae; the great series of lifetimes starts anew. Now too the virgin goddess returns, the golden days of Saturn's reign return, now a new race is sent down from high heaven.
Eclogues no. 4, l. 4

11 *Ambo florentes aetatibus, Arcades ambo, Et cantare pares et respondere parati.*
Both in the flower of their youth, Arcadians both, and matched and ready alike to start a song and to respond.
Eclogues no. 7, l. 4

12 *Non omnia possumus omnes.*
We can't all do everything.
*Eclogues no. 8, l. 63; cf. **Lucilius** 204:11*

13 *Nam neque adhuc Vario videor nec dicere Cinna Digna, sed argutos inter strepere anser olores.*
For I don't seem yet to write things as good either as Varius or as Cinna, but to be a goose honking amongst tuneful swans.
Eclogues no. 9, l. 32

14 *Omnia vincit Amor: et nos cedamus Amori.*
Love conquers all things: let us too give in to Love.
*Eclogues no. 10, l. 69; cf. **Chaucer** 88:9*

15 *Ultima Thule.*
Farthest Thule.
Georgics no. 1, l. 30

16 *Ter sunt conati imponere Pelio Ossam Scilicet atque Ossae frondosum involvere Olympum; Ter pater exstructos disiecit fulmine montis.*
Three times they endeavoured to pile Ossa on Pelion, no less, and to roll leafy Olympus on top of Ossa; three times our Father broke up the towering mountains with a thunderbolt.
Georgics no. 1, l. 281

17 *O fortunatos nimium, sua si bona norint, Agricolas!*
O farmers excessively fortunate if only they recognized their blessings!
Georgics no. 2, l. 458

18 *Felix qui potuit rerum cognoscere causas.*
Lucky is he who has been able to understand the causes of things.
*of **Lucretius***
Georgics no. 2, l. 490

19 *Sed fugit interea, fugit inreparabile tempus.*
But meanwhile it is flying, irretrievable time is flying.
usually quoted as 'tempus fugit [time flies]'
Georgics no. 3, l. 284

Voltaire 1694–1778

20 *Dans ce meilleur des mondes possibles . . . tout est au mieux.*
In this best of possible worlds . . . all is for the best.
usually quoted 'All is for the best in the best of all possible worlds'
Candide (1759) ch. 1

21 These two nations have been at war over a few acres of snow near Canada, and . . . they are spending on this fine struggle more than Canada itself is worth.
of the struggle between the French and the British for the control of colonial north Canada
Candide (1759) ch. 23

22 *Dans ce pays-ci il est bon de tuer de temps en temps un amiral pour encourager les autres.*

In this country [England] it is thought well to kill an admiral from time to time to encourage the others.

referring to the contentious execution of Admiral Byng (1704–57) for neglect of duty in failing to relieve Minorca

Candide (1759) ch. 23; cf. **Walpole** 326:18

1 *Il faut cultiver notre jardin.*
We must cultivate our garden.

Candide (1759) ch. 30

2 [Men] use thought only to justify their injustices, and speech only to conceal their thoughts.

Dialogues (1763) 'Le Chapon et la poularde'

3 *Le mieux est l'ennemi du bien.*
The best is the enemy of the good.

Contes (1772) 'La Begueule' l. 2; though often attributed to Voltaire, the notion in fact derives from an Italian proverb quoted in his Dictionnaire philosophique (1770 ed.) 'Art Dramatique': '*Le meglio è l'inimico del bene*'

4 Superstition sets the whole world in flames; philosophy quenches them.

Dictionnaire philosophique (1764) 'Superstition'

5 *Si Dieu n'existait pas, il faudrait l'inventer.*
If God did not exist, it would be necessary to invent him.

Épîtres no. 96 'A l'Auteur du livre des trois imposteurs'; cf. **Ovid** 238:12

6 This agglomeration which was called and which still calls itself the Holy Roman Empire was neither holy, nor Roman, nor an empire.

Essai sur l'histoire générale et sur les moeurs et l'esprit des nations (1756) ch. 70

7 History is nothing more than a tableau of crimes and misfortunes.

L'Ingénu (1767) ch. 10; cf. **Gibbon** 139:2

8 Governments need both shepherds and butchers.

'The Piccini Notebooks' (c.1735–50) in T. Besterman (ed.) Voltaire's Notebooks (2nd ed., 1968) vol. 2

9 God is on the side not of the heavy battalions, but of the best shots.

'The Piccini Notebooks' (c.1735–50) in T. Besterman (ed.) Voltaire's Notebooks (2nd ed., 1968) vol. 2; cf. **Anouilh** 13:7, **Bussy-Rabutin** 77:1

10 We owe respect to the living; to the dead we owe only truth.

'Première Lettre sur Oedipe' in Oeuvres (1785) vol. 1

11 The composition of a tragedy requires testicles.

on being asked why no woman had ever written 'a tolerable tragedy'

letter from Byron to John Murray, 2 April 1817

12 The English plays are like their English puddings: nobody has any taste for them but themselves.

Joseph Spence Anecdotes (ed. J. M. Osborn, 1966) no. 1033

13 I disapprove of what you say, but I will defend to the death your right to say it.

*to **Helvétius**, following the burning of De l'esprit in 1759*

attributed to **Voltaire**, but in fact a later summary of his attitude by S. G. Tallentyre in The Friends of Voltaire (1907); cf. **Voltaire** 326:14

14 What a fuss about an omelette!

what Voltaire apparently said on the burning of De l'esprit

James Parton Life of Voltaire (1881) vol. 2, ch. 25; cf. **Voltaire** 326:13

15 This is no time for making new enemies.

on being asked to renounce the Devil, on his deathbed

attributed

Derek Walcott 1930–

16 I who have cursed
The drunken officer of British rule, how choose
Between this Africa and the English tongue I love?

'A Far Cry From Africa' (1962)

17 I come from a backward place: your duty is supplied by life around you. One guy plants bananas; another plants cocoa; I'm a writer, I plant lines. There's the same clarity of occupation, and the sense of devotion.

in Guardian 12 July 1997

Lech Wałęsa 1943–

18 You have riches and freedom here but I feel no sense of faith or direction. You have so many computers, why don't you use them in the search for love?

in Paris, on his first journey outside the Soviet area, in Daily Telegraph 14 December 1988

Alice Walker 1944–

19 Did this happen to your mother? Did your sister throw up a lot?

title of poem (1979)

20 Expect nothing. Live frugally on surprise.

'Expect nothing' (1973)

21 The quietly pacifist peaceful always die
to make room for men who shout.

'The QPP' (1973)

22 I think it pisses God off if you walk by the colour purple in a field somewhere and don't notice it.

The Colour Purple (1982)

Felix Walker fl. 1820

23 I'm talking to Buncombe ['bunkum'].

excusing a long, dull, irrelevant speech in the House of Representatives, c.1820 (Buncombe being his constituency)

W. Safire New Language of Politics (2nd ed., 1972); cf. **Carlyle** 82:23

George Wallace 1919-98

1 Segregation now, segregation tomorrow and segregation forever!
   inaugural speech as Governor of Alabama, January 1963, in *Birmingham World* 19 January 1963

Henry Wallace 1888-1965

2 The century on which we are entering—the century which will come out of this war—can be and must be the century of the common man.
   speech, 8 May 1942

William Ross Wallace d. 1881

3 For the hand that rocks the cradle
   Is the hand that rules the world.
   'What rules the world' (1865); cf. **Robinson** 258:6

Graham Wallas 1858-1932

4 The little girl had the making of a poet in her who, being told to be sure of her meaning before she spoke, said, 'How can I know what I think till I see what I say?'
   The Art of Thought (1926) ch. 4

Edmund Waller 1606-87

5 Go, lovely rose!
   Tell her, that wastes her time and me,
   That now she knows,
   When I resemble her to thee,
   How sweet and fair she seems to be.
   'Go, lovely rose!' (1645)

Horace Walpole 1717-97

6 Our supreme governors, the mob.
   letter to Horace Mann, 7 September 1743

7 [Strawberry Hill] is a little plaything-house that I got out of Mrs Chenevix's shop, and is the prettiest bauble you ever saw. It is set in enamelled meadows, with filigree hedges.
   letter to Hon. Henry Conway, 8 June 1747

8 Every drop of ink in my pen ran cold.
   letter to George Montagu, 30 July 1752

9 One of the greatest geniuses that ever existed, Shakespeare, undoubtedly wanted taste.
   letter to Christopher Wren, 9 August 1764

10 It is charming to totter into vogue.
   letter to George Selwyn, 2 December 1765

11 The way to ensure summer in England is to have it framed and glazed in a comfortable room.
   letter to Revd William Cole, 28 May 1774

12 The next Augustan age will dawn on the other side of the Atlantic. There will, perhaps, be a Thucydides at Boston, a Xenophon at New York, and, in time, a Virgil at Mexico, and a Newton at Peru. At last, some curious traveller from Lima will visit England and give a description of the ruins of St Paul's, like the editions of Balbec and Palmyra.
   letter to Horace Mann, 24 November 1774; cf. **Macaulay** 205:18

13 This world is a comedy to those that think, a tragedy to those that feel.
   letter to Anne, Countess of Upper Ossory, 16 August 1776

14 It is the story of a mountebank and his zany.
   *of **Boswell**'s Tour of the Hebrides*
   letter to Hon. Henry Conway, 6 October 1785

15 All his own geese are swans, as the swans of others are geese.
   *of Joshua **Reynolds***
   letter to Anne, Countess of Upper Ossory, 1 December 1786

16 How should such a fellow as Sheridan, who has no diamonds to bestow, fascinate all the world?—yet witchcraft, no doubt there has been, for when did simple eloquence ever convince a majority?
   letter to Lady Ossory, 9 February 1787

17 That hyena in petticoats, Mrs Wollstonecraft.
   letter to Hannah More, 26 January 1795

18 While he felt like a victim, he acted like a hero.
   of Admiral Byng, on the day of his execution
   Memoirs of the Reign of King George II (ed. Lord Holland, 1846) vol. 2, 1757; cf. **Voltaire** 325:22

Robert Walpole, Lord Orford 1676-1745

19 They now *ring* the bells, but they will soon *wring* their hands.
   on the declaration of war with Spain, 1739
   W. Coxe *Memoirs of Sir Robert Walpole* (1798) vol. 1

20 All those men have their price.
   of fellow parliamentarians
   W. Coxe *Memoirs of Sir Robert Walpole* (1798) vol. 1

21 Madam, there are fifty thousand men slain this year in Europe, and not one Englishman.
   *to Queen **Caroline**, 1734, on the war of the Polish succession, in which the English had refused to participate*
   John Hervey *Memoirs* (written 1734-43, published 1848) vol. 1

22 We must muzzle this terrible young cornet of horse.
   *of the elder William **Pitt**, who had held a cornetcy before his election to Parliament, c.1736*
   in *Dictionary of National Biography* (1917-)

23 [Gratitude of place-expectants] is a lively sense of future favours.
   W. Hazlitt *Lectures on the English Comic Writers* (1819) 'On Wit and Humour'; cf. **La Rochefoucauld** 194:1

William Walsh 1663–1708

1 I can endure my own despair,
But not another's hope.
'Song: Of All the Torments'

Izaak Walton 1593–1683

2 As no man is born an artist, so no man is
born an angler.
The Compleat Angler (1653) 'Epistle to the Reader'

3 I am, Sir, a Brother of the Angle.
The Compleat Angler (1653) pt. 1, ch. 1

4 I love such mirth as does not make friends
ashamed to look upon one another next
morning.
The Compleat Angler (1653) pt. 1, ch. 5

5 I love any discourse of rivers, and fish and
fishing.
The Compleat Angler (1653) pt. 1, ch. 18

6 But God, who is able to prevail, wrestled
with him, as the Angel did with Jacob, and
marked him; marked him for his own.
Life of Donne (1670 ed.)

7 The great Secretary of Nature and all
learning, Sir Francis Bacon.
Life of Herbert (1670 ed.)

William Warburton 1698–1779

8 Orthodoxy is my doxy; heterodoxy is
another man's doxy.
to Lord Sandwich, in Joseph Priestley *Memoirs*
(1807) vol. 1

Artemus Ward 1834–67

9 Let us all be happy, and live within our
means, even if we have to borrer the money
to do it with.
Artemus Ward in London (1867) ch. 7

10 Why is this thus? What is the reason of this
thusness?
Artemus Ward's Lecture (1869) 'Heber C. Kimball's
Harem'

Barbara Ward 1914–81

11 We cannot cheat on DNA. We cannot get
round photosynthesis. We cannot say I am
not going to give a damn about
phytoplankton. All these tiny mechanisms
provide the preconditions of our planetary
life. To say we do not care is to say in the
most literal sense that 'we choose death'.
Only One Earth (1972)

Andy Warhol 1927–87

12 In the future everybody will be world
famous for fifteen minutes.
Andy Warhol (1968) (volume released to mark his
exhibition in Stockholm, February–March,
1968)

13 Being good in business is the most
fascinating kind of art.
*Philosophy of Andy Warhol (From A to B and Back
Again)* (1975)

Sylvia Townsend Warner
1893–1978

14 One need not write in a diary what one is to
remember for ever.
diary, 22 October 1930

15 Total grief is like a minefield. No knowing
when one will touch the tripwire.
diary, 11 December 1969

Earl Warren 1891–1974

16 In civilized life, law floats in a sea of ethics.
in *New York Times* 12 November 1962

Booker T. Washington 1856–1915

17 No race can prosper till it learns that there
is as much dignity in tilling a field as in
writing a poem.
Up from Slavery (1901)

18 You can't hold a man down without staying
down with him.
attributed

George Washington 1732–99

19 Few men have virtue to withstand the
highest bidder.
letter, 17 August 1779

20 'Tis our true policy to steer clear of
permanent alliances, with any portion of
the foreign world.
President's Address . . . retiring from Public Life 17
September 1796

21 Let me . . . warn you in the most solemn
manner against the baneful effects of the
spirit of party.
President's Address . . . 17 September 1796

22 I can't tell a lie, Pa; you know I can't tell a
lie. I did cut it with my hatchet.
M. L. Weems *Life of George Washington* (10th ed.,
1810) ch. 2

23 Liberty, when it begins to take root, is a
plant of rapid growth.
attributed

Ned Washington 1901–76

24 Hi diddle dee dee (an actor's life for me).
title of song (1940) from the film *Pinocchio*

25 The night is like a lovely tune,
Beware my foolish heart!
'My Foolish Heart' (1949 song)

James Dewey Watson 1928–

26 No *good* model ever accounted for *all* the
facts, since some data was bound to be
misleading if not plain wrong.
Francis Crick *Some Mad Pursuit* (1988)

27 Some day a child is going to sue its parents
for being born. They will say, my life is so
awful with these terrible genetic defects
and you just callously didn't find out.
on the question of genetic screening of foetuses
interview in *Sunday Telegraph* 16 February 1997

Thomas Watson Snr. 1874–1956

1 You cannot be a success in any business
without believing that it is the greatest
business in the world . . . You have to put
your heart in the business and the business
in your heart.

   Robert Sobel *IBM: Colossus in Transition* (1981)

William Watson *c.*1559–1603

2 *Fiat justitia et ruant coeli.*
Let justice be done though the heavens fall.

   *A Decacordon of Ten Quodlibeticall Questions
Concerning Religion and State* (1602), being the
first citation in an English work of a famous
maxim; cf. **Ferdinand** 126:21

William Watson 1858–1936

3 April, April,
Laugh thy girlish laughter.
'April'

4 My hand will miss the insinuated nose,
Mine eyes the tail that wagged contempt at
Fate.
'An Epitaph'

Isaac Watts 1674–1748

5 How doth the little busy bee
Improve each shining hour.

   Divine Songs for Children (1715) 'Against Idleness
and Mischief'; cf. **Carroll** 83:15

6 For Satan finds some mischief still
For idle hands to do.

   Divine Songs for Children (1715) 'Against Idleness
and Mischief'

7 Let dogs delight to bark and bite,
For God hath made them so.

   Divine Songs for Children (1715) 'Against
Quarrelling'

8 Birds in their little nests agree.

   Divine Songs for Children (1715) 'Love between
Brothers and Sisters'

9 Come, let us join our cheerful songs
With angels round the throne;
Ten thousand thousand are their tongues,
But all their joys are one.

   Hymns and Spiritual Songs (1707) 'Come, let us
join our cheerful songs'

10 When I survey the wondrous cross
On which the prince of glory died,
My richest gain I count but loss,
And pour contempt on all my pride.

   Hymns and Spiritual Songs (1707) 'Crucifixion to
the World, by the Cross of Christ'

11 There is a land of pure delight,
Where saints immortal reign.

   Hymns and Spiritual Songs (1707) 'A Prospect of
Heaven makes Death easy'

12 Jesus shall reign where'er the sun
Does his successive journeys run;
His kingdom stretch from shore to shore,
Till moons shall wax and wane no more.

   The Psalms of David Imitated (1719) Psalm 72

13 Our God, our help in ages past
Our hope for years to come,

Our shelter from the stormy blast,
And our eternal home.

   'Our God' altered to 'O God' by John **Wesley**,
1738

   The Psalms of David Imitated (1719) Psalm 90

14 A thousand ages in Thy sight
Are like an evening gone;
Short as the watch that ends the night
Before the rising sun.

   The Psalms of David Imitated (1719) Psalm 90

15 Time, like an ever-rolling stream,
Bears all its sons away.

   The Psalms of David Imitated (1719) Psalm 90

Evelyn Waugh 1903–66

16 I am not I: thou art not he or she: they are
not they.

   Brideshead Revisited (1945) 'Author's Note'

17 The sound of English county families baying
for broken glass.

   Decline and Fall (1928) 'Prelude'; cf. **Belloc** 28:22

18 I expect you'll be becoming a schoolmaster,
sir. That's what most of the gentlemen does,
sir, that gets sent down for indecent
behaviour.

   Decline and Fall (1928) 'Prelude'

19 Any one who has been to an English public
school will always feel comparatively at
home in prison. It is the people brought up
in the gay intimacy of the slums, Paul
learned, who find prison so soul-destroying.

   Decline and Fall (1928) pt. 3, ch. 4

20 *The Beast* stands for strong mutually
antagonistic governments everywhere . . .
Self-sufficiency at home, self-assertion
abroad.

   Scoop (1938) bk. 1, ch. 1

21 Up to a point, Lord Copper.

   Scoop (1938) bk. 1, ch. 1

22 'Feather-footed through the plashy fen
passes the questing vole' . . . 'Yes,' said the
Managing Editor. 'That must be good style.'

   Scoop (1938) bk. 1, ch. 1

23 To see him fumbling with our rich and
delicate language is to experience all the
horror of seeing a Sèvres vase in the hands
of a chimpanzee.

   of Stephen **Spender**

   in *The Tablet* 5 May 1951

24 A typical triumph of modern science to find
the only part of Randolph that was not
malignant and remove it.

   *on hearing that Randolph Churchill's lung, when
removed, proved non-malignant*

   Michael Davie (ed.) *Diaries of Evelyn Waugh* (1976)
'Irregular Notes 1960–65', March 1964

Frederick Weatherly 1848–1929

25 Where are the boys of the old Brigade,
Who fought with us side by side?
'The Old Brigade' (1886 song)

26 Roses are flowering in Picardy,
But there's never a rose like you.
'Roses of Picardy' (1916 song)

Sidney Webb 1859–1947

1 The inevitability of gradualness.
> presidential address to the annual conference of the Labour Party, 26 June 1923

Max Weber 1864–1920

2 The protestant ethic and the spirit of capitalism.
> *Archiv für Sozialwissenschaft Sozialpolitik* vol. 20 (1904–5) (title of article)

3 The concept of the 'official secret' is its [bureaucracy's] specific invention.
> 'Politik als Beruf' (1919)

Daniel Webster 1782–1852

4 It is, Sir, as I have said, a small college. And yet *there are those who love it*!
> argument in the case of the Trustees of Dartmouth College v. Woodward, 10 March 1818

5 The people's government, made for the people, made by the people, and answerable to the people.
> second speech in the Senate on Foote's Resolution, 26 January 1830; cf. **Lincoln** 199:8

6 Liberty *and* Union, now and forever, one and inseparable!
> second speech in the Senate on Foote's Resolution, 26 January 1830

7 There is always room at the top.
> *on being advised against joining the overcrowded legal profession*
> attributed

John Webster *c.*1580–*c.*1625

8 Vain the ambition of kings
Who seek by trophies and dead things,
To leave a living name behind,
And weave but nets to catch the wind.
> *The Devil's Law-Case* (1623) act 5, sc. 4

9 O, that it were possible,
We might but hold some two days'
conference
With the dead!
> *The Duchess of Malfi* (1623) act 4, sc. 2

10 I am Duchess of Malfi still.
> *The Duchess of Malfi* (1623) act 4, sc. 2

11 I know death hath ten thousand several doors
For men to take their exits.
> *The Duchess of Malfi* (1623) act 4, sc. 2; cf. **Fletcher** 130:7, **Massinger** 215:1, **Seneca** 267:23

12 Cover her face; mine eyes dazzle: she died young.
> *The Duchess of Malfi* (1623) act 4, sc. 2

13 Strangling is a very quiet death.
> *The Duchess of Malfi* (1623) act 5, sc. 4

14 We are merely the stars' tennis-balls, struck and bandied
Which way please them.
> *The Duchess of Malfi* (1623) act 5, sc. 4

15 'Tis just like a summer birdcage in a garden; the birds that are without despair to get in, and the birds that are within despair, and are in a consumption, for fear they shall never get out.
> *The White Devil* (1612) act 1, sc. 2

16 A mere tale of a tub, my words are idle.
> *The White Devil* (1612) act 2, sc. 1

17 Call for the robin-red-breast and the wren,
Since o'er shady groves they hover,
And with leaves and flowers do cover
The friendless bodies of unburied men.
> *The White Devil* (1612) act 5, sc. 4

18 We think caged birds sing, when indeed they cry.
> *The White Devil* (1612) act 5, sc. 4; cf. **Dunbar** 118:5, **Shakespeare** 278:9

19 My soul, like to a ship in a black storm,
Is driven, I know not whither.
> *The White Devil* (1612) act 5, sc. 6

20 I have caught
An everlasting cold; I have lost my voice
Most irrecoverably.
> *The White Devil* (1612) act 5, sc. 6

Josiah Wedgwood 1730–95

21 Am I not a man and a brother.
> *legend on Wedgwood cameo, depicting a kneeling Negro slave in chains*
> reproduced in facsimile in E. Darwin *The Botanic Garden* pt. 1 (1791)

Simone Weil 1909–43

22 All sins are attempts to fill voids.
> *La Pesanteur et la grâce* (1948)

23 What a country calls its vital economic interests are not the things which enable its citizens to live, but the things which enable it to make war.
> W. H. Auden *A Certain World* (1971)

Victor Weisskopf 1908–

24 It was absolutely marvellous working for Pauli. You could ask him anything. There was no worry that he would think a particular question was stupid, since he thought *all* questions were stupid.
> in *American Journal of Physics* 1977

Johnny Weissmuller 1904–84

25 Me Tarzan, you Jane.
> *summing up his role in* Tarzan, the Ape Man *(1932 film)*
> in *Photoplay Magazine* June 1932; the words do not occur in the film or in the original novel by Edgar Rice Burroughs

Chaim Weizmann 1874–1952

26 Something had been done for us which, after two thousand years of hope and yearning, would at last give us a resting-place in this terrible world.
> *of the Balfour declaration*
> speech in Jerusalem, 25 November 1936; cf. **Balfour** 23:14

Thomas Earle Welby 1881–1933

1 'Turbot, Sir,' said the waiter, placing before
me two fishbones, two eyeballs, and a bit of
black mackintosh.
The Dinner Knell (1932) 'Birmingham or Crewe?'

Fay Weldon 1931–

2 The life and loves of a she-devil.
title of novel (1984)

3 Every time you open your wardrobe, you
look at your clothes and you wonder what
you are going to wear. What you are really
saying is 'Who am I going to be today?'
in *New Yorker* 26 June 1995

Orson Welles 1915–85

4 The biggest electric train set any boy ever
had!
of the RKO studios
Peter Noble *The Fabulous Orson Welles* (1956) ch. 7

Duke of Wellington 1769–1852

5 As Lord Chesterfield said of the generals of
his day, 'I only hope that when the enemy
reads the list of their names, he trembles as
I do.'
*usually quoted as, 'I don't know what effect these
men will have upon the enemy, but, by God, they
frighten me'*
letter, 29 August 1810, in *Supplementary
Despatches . . .* (1860) vol. 6

6 Up Guards and at them!
letter from an officer in the Guards, 22 June
1815, in *The Battle of Waterloo* by a Near
Observer [J. Booth] (1815); later denied by
Wellington

7 Next to a battle lost, the greatest misery is a
battle gained.
in *Diary of Frances, Lady Shelley 1787–1817* (ed. R.
Edgcumbe, 1912) vol. 1

8 Publish and be damned.
*replying to a blackmail threat prior to the
publication of Harriette* **Wilson**'s *Memoirs
(1825)*
attributed; Elizabeth Longford *Wellington: The
Years of the Sword* (1969) ch. 10

9 I used to say of him that his presence on the
field made the difference of forty thousand
men.
of **Napoleon**
Philip Henry Stanhope *Notes of Conversations with
the Duke of Wellington* (1888) 2 November 1831

10 Ours is composed of the scum of the
earth—the mere scum of the earth.
of the army
Philip Henry Stanhope *Notes of Conversations with
the Duke of Wellington* (1888) 4 November 1831

11 I never saw so many shocking bad hats in
my life.
on seeing the first Reformed Parliament, 1832
William Fraser *Words on Wellington* (1889)

12 The battle of Waterloo was won on the
playing fields of Eton.
oral tradition, but probably apocryphal; the
earliest reference is a remark said to have been
made when revisiting Eton; cf. **Orwell** 237:12

13 An extraordinary affair. I gave them their
orders and they wanted to stay and discuss
them.
of his first Cabinet meeting as Prime Minister
attributed; Peter Hennessy *Whitehall* (1990)

H. G. Wells 1866–1946

14 He had read Shakespeare and found him
weak in chemistry.
Complete Short Stories (1927) 'Lord of the
Dynamos'

15 'Sesquippledan,' he would say.
'Sesquippledan verboojuice.'
The History of Mr Polly (1909) ch. 1, pt. 5; cf.
Horace 163:14

16 The Social Contract is nothing more or less
than a vast conspiracy of human beings to
lie to and humbug themselves and one
another for the general Good. Lies are the
mortar that bind the savage individual man
into the social masonry.
Love and Mr Lewisham (1900) ch. 23

17 The shape of things to come.
title of book (1933)

18 The war that will end war.
title of book (1914); cf. **Lloyd George** 200:19

19 God damn you all: I told you so.
*suggestion for his own epitaph, in conversation
with Ernest Barker, 1939*
Ernest Barker *Age and Youth* (1953)

Arnold Wesker 1932–

20 Chips with every damn thing. You breed
babies and you eat chips with everything.
Chips with Everything (1962) act 1, sc. 2

21 The Khomeini cry for the execution of
Rushdie is an infantile cry. From the
beginning of time we have seen that. To
murder the thinker does not murder the
thought.
in *Weekend Guardian* 3 June 1989; cf. **Khomeini**
185:16

Charles Wesley 1707–88

22 Amazing love! How can it be
That thou, my God, shouldst die for me?
'And can it be' (1738 hymn)

23 Hark! how all the welkin rings,
Glory to the King of kings.
Peace on earth and mercy mild,
God and sinners reconciled.
Hymns and Sacred Poems (1739) 'Hymn for
Christmas'; the first two lines altered to 'Hark!
the herald-angels sing Glory to the new born
King' in George Whitefield *Hymns for Social
Worship* (1753)

24 O for a thousand tongues to sing.
Hymns and Sacred Poems (1740) 'For the
Anniversary Day of one's Conversion'

1 Jesu, lover of my soul,
Let me to thy bosom fly.
Hymns and Sacred Poems (1740) 'In Temptation'

2 Love divine, all loves excelling,
Joy of heav'n, to earth come down,
Fix in us thy humble dwelling,
All thy faithful mercies crown.
Hymns for those that seek . . . Redemption (1747)
'Love divine', based on Dryden; cf. **Dryden**
117:2

3 Lo! He comes with clouds descending,
Once for favoured sinners slain.
Hymns of Intercession for all Mankind (1758) 'Lo! He
comes'

John Wesley 1703-91

4 The Gospel of Christ knows of no religion
but social; no holiness but social holiness.
Hymns and Sacred Poems (1739) Preface

5 I design plain truth for plain people.
Sermons on Several Occasions (1746)

6 I went to America to convert the Indians;
but oh, who shall convert me?
Journal (ed. N. Curnock) 24 January 1738

7 I look upon all the world as my parish.
Journal (ed. N. Curnock) 11 June 1739

8 Time has shaken me by the hand and death
is not far behind.
letter to Ezekiel Cooper, 1 February 1791

Mary Wesley 1912-

9 In my day, I would only have sex with a
man if I found him extremely attractive.
These days, girls seem to choose them in
much the same way as they might choose to
suck on a boiled sweet.
in *Independent* 18 October 1997 'Quote Unquote'

Samuel Wesley 1662-1735

10 Style is the dress of thought; a modest dress,
Neat, but not gaudy, will true critics please.
'An Epistle to a Friend concerning Poetry'
(1700); cf. **Johnson** 173:19, **Pope** 248:2

Mae West 1892-1980

11 I always say, keep a diary and some day it'll
keep you.
Every Day's a Holiday (1937 film)

12 Beulah, peel me a grape.
I'm No Angel (1933 film)

13 It's not the men in my life that counts—it's
the life in my men.
I'm No Angel (1933 film)

14 'Goodness, what beautiful diamonds!'
'Goodness had nothing to do with it.'
Night After Night (1932 film)

15 Why don't you come up sometime, and see
me?
often altered to, 'Why don't you come up and see
me sometime?'
She Done Him Wrong (1933 film)

16 Is that a gun in your pocket, or are you just
glad to see me?
usually quoted as 'Is that a pistol in your pocket
. . .'
Joseph Weintraub *Peel Me a Grape* (1975)

Rebecca West 1892-1983

17 Having watched the form of our traitors for
a number of years, I cannot think that
espionage can be recommended as a
technique for building an impressive
civilization. It's a lout's game.
The Meaning of Treason (1982 ed.), introduction

18 I myself have never been able to find out
precisely what feminism is: I only know
that people call me a feminist whenever I
express sentiments that differentiate me
from a doormat or a prostitute.
in *The Clarion* 14 November 1913

19 People would rather be led to *perdition* by a
man, than to *victory* by a woman.
in conversation in 1979, just before Margaret
Thatcher*'s first election victory*
in *Sunday Telegraph* 17 January 1988

John Fane, Lord Westmorland
1759-1841

20 *Merit,* indeed! . . . We are come to a pretty
pass if they talk of *merit* for a bishopric.
noted in Lady Salisbury's diary, 9 December
1835

R. P. Weston 1878-1936
and **Bert Lee** 1880-1947

21 Good-bye-ee!—Good-bye-ee!
Wipe the tear, baby dear, from your eye-ee.
'Good-bye-ee!' (*c*.1915 song)

Charles Wetherell 1770-1846

22 Then there is my noble and biographical
friend who has added a new terror to death.
of Lord Campbell
Lord St Leonards *Misrepresentations in Campbell's
Lives of Lyndhurst and Brougham* (1869); cf.
Lyndhurst 205:1

Edith Wharton 1862-1937

23 An unalterable and unquestioned law of the
musical world required that the German
text of French operas sung by Swedish
artists should be translated into Italian for
the clearer understanding of English-
speaking audiences.
The Age of Innocence (1920) bk. 1, ch. 1

24 Mrs Ballinger is one of the ladies who
pursue Culture in bands, as though it were
dangerous to meet it alone.
Xingu and Other Stories (1916) 'Xingu'

Thomas, Lord Wharton 1648-1715

25 Ara! but why does King James stay behind?
Lilli burlero bullen a la
Ho! by my shoul 'tis a Protestant wind.
'A New Song' (written 1687)

1 I sang a king out of three kingdoms.
said to have been Wharton's boast after 'A New Song' became an propaganda weapon against James II
in *Dictionary of National Biography* (1917-)

Richard Whately 1787–1863

2 It is not that pearls fetch a high price *because* men have dived for them; but on the contrary, men dive for them because they fetch a high price.
Introductory Lectures on Political Economy (1832) p. 253

William Whewell 1794–1866

3 Hence no force however great can stretch a cord however fine into an horizontal line which is accurately straight: there will always be a bending downwards.
often cited as an example of accidental metre and rhyme, and changed in later editions
Elementary Treatise on Mechanics (1819) ch. 4, problem 2

James McNeill Whistler 1834–1903

4 I maintain that two and two would continue to make four, in spite of the whine of the amateur for three, or the cry of the critic for five.
Whistler v. Ruskin. Art and Art Critics (1878)

5 No, I ask it for the knowledge of a lifetime.
in his case against **Ruskin**, *replying to the question: 'For two days' labour, you ask two hundred guineas?'*
D. C. Seitz *Whistler Stories* (1913)

6 OSCAR WILDE: How I wish I had said that.
WHISTLER: You will, Oscar, you will.
R. Ellman *Oscar Wilde* (1987) pt. 2, ch. 5

E. B. White 1899–1985

7 Commuter—one who spends his life
In riding to and from his wife;
A man who shaves and takes a train,
And then rides back to shave again.
'The Commuter' (1982)

8 MOTHER: It's broccoli, dear.
CHILD: I say it's spinach, and I say the hell with it.
cartoon caption in *New Yorker* 8 December 1928

H. Kirke White 1785–1806

9 Oft in danger, oft in woe,
Onward, Christians, onward go.
'Oft in danger, oft in woe' (1812 hymn)

Patrick White 1912–90

10 Conversation is imperative if gaps are to be filled, and old age, it is the last gap but one.
The Tree of Man (1955) ch. 22

11 So that, in the end, there was no end.
The Tree of Man (1955); closing words

Theodore H. White 1915–86

12 The flood of money that gushes into politics today is a pollution of democracy.
in *Time* 19 November 1984

Alfred North Whitehead 1861–1947

13 There are no whole truths; all truths are half-truths. It is trying to treat them as whole truths that plays the devil.
Dialogues (1954) prologue

14 Intelligence is quickness to apprehend as distinct from ability, which is capacity to act wisely on the thing apprehended.
Dialogues (1954) 15 December 1939

15 Civilization advances by extending the number of important operations which we can perform without thinking about them.
Introduction to Mathematics (1911) ch. 5

Katharine Whitehorn 1928–

16 I wouldn't say when you've seen one Western you've seen the lot; but when you've seen the lot you get the feeling you've seen one.
Sunday Best (1976) 'Decoding the West'

George Whiting

17 When you're all dressed up and have no place to go.
title of song (1912)

William Whiting 1825–78

18 Eternal Father, strong to save,
Whose arm doth bind the restless wave,
Who bidd'st the mighty ocean deep
Its own appointed limits keep:
O hear us when we cry to thee,
For those in peril on the sea.
'Eternal Father, Strong to Save' (1869 hymn)

Walt Whitman 1819–92

19 I sing the body electric.
title of poem (1855)

20 O Captain! my Captain! our fearful trip is done,
The ship has weathered every rack, the prize we sought is won.
'O Captain! My Captain!' (1871)

21 Exult O shores, and ring O bells! But I with mournful tread
Walk the deck my Captain lies, Fallen cold and dead.
'O Captain! My Captain!' (1871)

22 Pioneers! O pioneers!
title of poem (1881)

23 Camerado, this is no book,
Who touches this touches a man.
'So Long!' (1881)

24 I think I could turn and live with animals, they are so placid and self-contained,
I stand and look at them long and long.
They do not sweat and whine about their condition,

They do not lie awake in the dark and weep
  for their sins,
They do not make me sick discussing their
  duty to God.
  'Song of Myself' (written 1855) pt. 32

1 Do I contradict myself?
  Very well then I contradict myself,
  (I am large, I contain multitudes.)
  'Song of Myself' (written 1855) pt. 51

2 When lilacs last in the dooryard bloomed,
  And the great star early drooped in the
    western sky in the night,
  I mourned, and yet shall mourn with ever-
    returning spring.
  'When lilacs last in the dooryard bloomed'
  (1881) st. 1

3 The United States themselves are essentially
  the greatest poem.
  Leaves of Grass (1855) preface

John Greenleaf Whittier 1807–92

4 'Shoot, if you must, this old grey head,
  But spare your country's flag,' she said.
  'Barbara Frietchie' (1863)

5 Dear Lord and Father of mankind,
  Forgive our foolish ways!
  Re-clothe us in our rightful mind,
  In purer lives thy service find,
  In deeper reverence praise.
  'The Brewing of Soma' (1872)

6 For of all sad words of tongue or pen,
  The saddest are these: 'It might have been!'
  'Maud Muller' (1854); cf. **Harte** 152:22

Robert Whittington

7 As time requireth, a man of marvellous
  mirth and pastimes, and sometime of as sad
  gravity, as who say: a man for all seasons.
  of Sir Thomas **More**
    Vulgaria (1521) pt. 2 'De constructione
    nominum'; Erasmus had applied the idea
    earlier in the prefatory letter to In Praise of Folly
    (1509), saying that More played 'Omnium
    horarum hominem [A man of all hours]'

Charlotte Whitton 1896–1975

8 Whatever women do they must do twice as
  well as men to be thought half as good.
  in Canada Month June 1963

Cornelius Whur

9 While lasting joys the man attend
  Who has a faithful female friend.
  'The Female Friend' (1837)

William H. Whyte 1917–

10 The organization man.
  title of book (1956)

George John Whyte-Melville
1821–78

11 But I freely admit that the best of my fun
  I owe it to horse and hound.
  'The Good Grey Mare' (1933)

Ann Widdecombe 1947–

12 He has something of the night in him.
  of Michael Howard as a contender for the
  Conservative leadership
    in Sunday Times 11 May 1997 (electronic edition)

Elie Wiesel 1928–

13 Take sides. Neutrality helps the oppressor,
  never the victim. Silence encourages the
  tormentor, never the tormented.
  accepting the Nobel Peace Prize
    in New York Times 11 December 1986

14 God of forgiveness, do not forgive those
  murderers of Jewish children here.
  at Auschwitz
    in The Times 27 January 1995

Samuel Wilberforce 1805–73

15 If I were a cassowary
  On the plains of Timbuctoo,
  I would eat a missionary,
  Cassock, band, and hymn-book too.
  impromptu verse (attributed)

16 Was it through his grandfather or his
  grandmother that he claimed his descent
  from a monkey?
  addressed to T. H. Huxley at a meeting of the
  British Association for the Advancement of
  Science, Oxford, June 1860; cf. **Huxley** 168:4

Richard Wilbur 1921–

17 There is a poignancy in all things clear,
  In the stare of the deer, in the ring of a
  hammer in the morning.
  'Clearness' (1950)

18 We milk the cow of the world, and as we do
  We whisper in her ear, 'You are not true.'
  'Epistemology' (1950)

19 The good grey guardians of art
  Patrol the halls on spongy shoes.
  'Museum Piece' (1950)

Ella Wheeler Wilcox 1855–1919

20 Laugh and the world laughs with you;
  Weep, and you weep alone.
  'Solitude'

Oscar Wilde 1854–1900

21 We have really everything in common with
  America nowadays except, of course,
  language.
  The Canterville Ghost (1887)

22 The truth is rarely pure, and never simple.
  The Importance of Being Earnest (1895) act 1

23 In married life three is company and two
  none.
  The Importance of Being Earnest (1895) act 1

24 To lose one parent, Mr Worthing, may be
  regarded as a misfortune; to lose both looks
  like carelessness.
  The Importance of Being Earnest (1895) act 1

25 LADY BRACKNELL: A handbag?
  The Importance of Being Earnest (1895) act 1

1 All women become like their mothers. That is their tragedy. No man does. That's his.
The Importance of Being Earnest (1895) act 1

2 The good ended happily, and the bad unhappily. That is what fiction means.
The Importance of Being Earnest (1895) act 2; cf. **Stoppard** 304:17

3 I never travel without my diary. One should always have something sensational to read in the train.
The Importance of Being Earnest (1895) act 2

4 Every great man nowadays has his disciples, and it is always Judas who writes the biography.
Intentions (1891) 'The Critic as Artist' pt. 1

5 I can resist everything except temptation.
Lady Windermere's Fan (1892) act 1

6 We are all in the gutter, but some of us are looking at the stars.
Lady Windermere's Fan (1892) act 3

7 A man who knows the price of everything and the value of nothing.
definition of a cynic
Lady Windermere's Fan (1892) act 3

8 There is no such thing as a moral or an immoral book. Books are well written, or badly written.
The Picture of Dorian Gray (1891) preface

9 A thing is not necessarily true because a man dies for it.
The Portrait of Mr W. H. (1901)

10 MRS ALLONBY: They say, Lady Hunstanton, that when good Americans die they go to Paris.
LADY HUNSTANTON: Indeed? And when bad Americans die, where do they go to?
LORD ILLINGWORTH: Oh, they go to America.
A Woman of No Importance (1893) act 1; cf. **Appleton** 13:13

11 The English country gentleman galloping after a fox—the unspeakable in full pursuit of the uneatable.
A Woman of No Importance (1893) act 1

12 LORD ILLINGWORTH: The Book of Life begins with a man and a woman in a garden.
MRS ALLONBY: It ends with Revelations.
A Woman of No Importance (1893) act 1

13 Children begin by loving their parents; after a time they judge them; rarely, if ever, do they forgive them.
A Woman of No Importance (1893) act 2

14 You should study the Peerage, Gerald . . . It is the best thing in fiction the English have ever done.
A Woman of No Importance (1893) act 3

15 I never saw a man who looked
With such a wistful eye
Upon that little tent of blue
Which prisoners call the sky.
The Ballad of Reading Gaol (1898) pt. 1, st. 3

16 Yet each man kills the thing he loves,
By each let this be heard,
Some do it with a bitter look,

Some with a flattering word.
The coward does it with a kiss,
The brave man with a sword!
The Ballad of Reading Gaol (1898) pt. 1, st. 7

17 For he who lives more lives than one
More deaths than one must die.
The Ballad of Reading Gaol (1898) pt. 3, st. 37

18 And alien tears will fill for him
Pity's long-broken urn,
For his mourners will be outcast men,
And outcasts always mourn.
inscribed on Wilde's tomb in Père Lachaise cemetery
The Ballad of Reading Gaol (1898) pt. 4, st. 23

19 When I ask for a watercress sandwich, I do not mean a loaf with a field in the middle of it.
to a waiter
Max Beerbohm, letter to Reggie Turner, 15 April 1893

20 Ah, well, then, I suppose that I shall have to die beyond my means.
at the mention of a huge fee for a surgical operation
R. H. Sherard *Life of Oscar Wilde* (1906) ch. 18

21 Shaw has not an enemy in the world; and none of his friends like him.
letter from Bernard Shaw to Archibald Henderson, 22 February 1911

22 I have nothing to declare except my genius.
at the New York Custom House
Frank Harris *Oscar Wilde* (1918)

23 One of us must go.
of the wallpaper in the room where he was dying
attributed, probably apocryphal

Billy Wilder 1906–

24 Hindsight is always twenty-twenty.
J. R. Columbo *Wit and Wisdom of the Moviemakers* (1979) ch. 7

Thornton Wilder 1897–1975

25 Literature is the orchestration of platitudes.
in *Time* 12 January 1953

Robert Wilensky 1951–

26 We've all heard that a million monkeys banging on a million typewriters will eventually reproduce the entire works of Shakespeare. Now, thanks to the Internet, we know this is not true.
in *Mail on Sunday* 16 February 1997 'Quotes of the Week'; cf. **Eddington** 119:13

Wilhelm II ('Kaiser Bill') 1859–1941

27 We have . . . fought for our place in the sun and have won it. It will be my business to see that we retain this place in the sun unchallenged, so that the rays of that sun may exert a fructifying influence upon our foreign trade and traffic.
speech in Hamburg, 18 June 1901; in *The Times* 20 June 1901; cf. **Bülow** 72:11

John Wilkes 1727-97

1 EARL OF SANDWICH: 'Pon my soul, Wilkes, I don't know whether you'll die upon the gallows or of the pox.
WILKES: That depends, my Lord, whether I first embrace your Lordship's principles, or your Lordship's mistresses.
Charles Petrie *The Four Georges* (1935); probably apocryphal

Emma Hart Willard 1787-1870

2 Rocked in the cradle of the deep.
title of song (1840), inspired by a prospect of the Bristol Channel

William III (William of Orange)
1650-1702

3 'Do you not see your country is lost?' asked the Duke of Buckingham. 'There is one way never to see it lost' replied William, 'and that is to die in the last ditch.'
Bishop Gilbert Burnet *History of My Own Time* (1838 ed.)

4 Every bullet has its billet.
John Wesley *Journal* (1827) 6 June 1765

Isaac Williams 1802-65

5 Be thou my Guardian and my Guide.
title of hymn (1842)

Peter Williams

6 Guide me, O thou great Jehovah,
Pilgrim through this barren land;
I am weak, but thou art mighty;
Hold me with thy powerful hand;
Bread of heaven, bread of heaven,
Feed me till I want no more.
first line frequently in the form 'O thou great Redeemer'
'Praying for Strength' (1771); translation of 'Arglwydd, arwain trwy'r anialwch' (1745) by William Williams (1717-91)

Shirley Williams 1930-

7 No test tube can breed love and affection. No frozen packet of semen ever read a story to a sleepy child.
in *Daily Mirror* 2 March 1978

Tennessee Williams 1911-83

8 What is the victory of a cat on a hot tin roof?—I wish I knew . . . Just staying on it, I guess, as long as she can.
Cat on a Hot Tin Roof (1955) act 1

9 I have always depended on the kindness of strangers.
A Streetcar Named Desire (1947) sc. 11

William Carlos Williams
1883-1963

10 Minds like beds always made up,
(more stony than a shore)
unwilling or unable.
Paterson (1946) bk. 1, preface

Marianne Williamson 1953-

11 Our deepest fear is not that we are inadequate. Our deepest fear is that we are powerful beyond measure. It is our light, not our darkness, that most frightens us.
A Return to Love (1992) ch. 7

Roy Williamson 1936-90

12 O flower of Scotland, when will we see your like again,
that fought and died for your bit hill and glen
and stood against him, proud Edward's army,
and sent him homeward tae think again.
unofficial Scottish Nationalist anthem
'O Flower of Scotland' (1968)

Love Maria Willis 1824-1908

13 Father, hear the prayer we offer:
Not for ease that prayer shall be.
'Father, hear the prayer we offer' (1864 hymn)

Wendell Willkie 1892-1944

14 The constitution does not provide for first and second class citizens.
An American Programme (1944) ch. 2

Angus Wilson 1913-91

15 Once a Catholic always a Catholic.
The Wrong Set (1949) p. 168

Charles E. Wilson 1890-1961

16 For years I thought what was good for our country was good for General Motors and vice versa. The difference did not exist. Our company is too big. It goes with the welfare of the country.
testimony to the Senate Armed Services Committee on his proposed nomination for Secretary of Defence, 15 January 1953

Harold Wilson 1916-95

17 The Britain that is going to be forged in the white heat of this revolution will be no place for restrictive practices or for outdated methods on either side of industry.
often quoted as, 'the white heat of technology'
speech at the Labour Party Conference, 1 October 1963

18 A week is a long time in politics.
probably first said at the time of the 1964 sterling crisis
Nigel Rees *Sayings of the Century* (1984)

19 From now the pound abroad is worth 14 per cent or so less in terms of other currencies. It does not mean, of course, that the pound here in Britain, in your pocket or purse or in your bank, has been devalued.
often quoted as 'the pound in your pocket'
ministerial broadcast, 19 November 1967

20 Get your tanks off my lawn, Hughie.
to the trade union leader Hugh Scanlon, at Chequers in June 1969
Peter Jenkins *The Battle of Downing Street* (1970)

Harriette Wilson 1789–1846

1 I shall not say why and how I became, at the age of fifteen, the mistress of the Earl of Craven.
Memoirs (1825) opening words

Sandy Wilson 1924–

2 We've got to have
We plot to have
For it's so dreary not to have
That certain thing called the Boy Friend.
The Boyfriend (1954) title song

Woodrow Wilson 1856–1924

3 It is like writing history with lightning. And my only regret is that it is all so terribly true.
on seeing D. W. Griffith's film The Birth of a Nation
at the White House, 18 February 1915

4 No nation is fit to sit in judgement upon any other nation.
speech in New York, 20 April 1915

5 There is such a thing as a man being too proud to fight.
speech in Philadelphia, 10 May 1915

6 We have stood apart, studiously neutral.
speech to Congress, 7 December 1915

7 It must be a peace without victory . . . Only a peace between equals can last.
speech to US Senate, 22 January 1917

8 The world must be made safe for democracy.
speech to Congress, 2 April 1917

Anne Finch, Lady Winchilsea 1661–1720

9 Poetry's the feverish fit,
Th' o'erflowing of unbounded wit.
'Enquiry after Peace' (1713) l. 42

10 Now the jonquil o'ercomes the feeble brain;
We faint beneath the aromatic pain.
'The Spleen' (1701)

11 My hand delights to trace unusual things,
And deviates from the known and common way;
Nor will in fading silks compose
Faintly the inimitable rose.
'The Spleen' (1701) l. 82

Duchess of Windsor (Wallis Simpson) 1896–1986

12 You can never be too rich or too thin.
attributed

Duke of Windsor *see* Edward VIII

Catherine Winkworth 1827–78

13 Now thank we all our God,
With heart and hands and voices.
Lyra Germanica (1858) 'Now thank we all our God' (translation of Martin Rinkart's 'Nun danket alle Gott', *c.*1636)

14 Praise to the Lord! the Almighty, the King of creation!
title of hymn (1863); translated from the German of Joachim Neander (1650–80)

15 *Peccavi*—I have Sindh.
of Sir Charles Napier's conquest of Sindh, 1843, supposedly sent by Napier to Lord Ellenborough; '*peccavi*' = *I have sinned*
in *Punch* 18 May 1844; attributed

John Winthrop 1588–1649

16 We must consider that we shall be a city upon a hill, the eyes of all people are on us; so that if we shall deal falsely with our God in this work we have undertaken, and so cause Him to withdraw His present help from us, we shall be made a story and a byword through the world.
Christian Charity, A Model Hereof (sermon, 1630)

Robert Charles Winthrop 1809–94

17 A Star for every State, and a State for every Star.
speech on Boston Common, 27 August 1862, in *Addresses and Speeches* vol. 2 (1867)

Owen Wister 1860–1938

18 When you call me that, *smile*!
'*that*' being 'you son-of-a—'
The Virginian (1902) ch. 2

George Wither 1588–1667

19 I loved a lass, a fair one,
As fair as e'er was seen;
She was indeed a rare one,
Another Sheba queen.
A Description of Love (1620) 'I loved a lass, a fair one'

Ludwig Wittgenstein 1889–1951

20 What is your aim in philosophy?—To show the fly the way out of the fly-bottle.
Philosophische Untersuchungen (1953) pt. 1, sect. 309

21 What can be said at all can be said clearly; and whereof one cannot speak thereof one must be silent.
Tractatus Logico-Philosophicus (1922) preface

22 The world is everything that is the case.
Tractatus Logico-Philosophicus (1922)

23 The limits of my language mean the limits of my world.
Tractatus Logico-Philosophicus (1922)

24 Tell them I've had a wonderful life.
to his doctor's wife, before losing consciousness, 28 April 1951
Ray Monk *Ludwig Wittgenstein* (1990)

P. G. Wodehouse 1881–1975

25 Chumps always make the best husbands . . . All the unhappy marriages come from the husbands having brains.
The Adventures of Sally (1920) ch. 10

1 He spoke with a certain what-is-it in his voice, and I could see that, if not actually disgruntled, he was far from being gruntled.
The Code of the Woosters (1938) ch. 1

2 It is no use telling me that there are bad aunts and good aunts. At the core, they are all alike. Sooner or later, out pops the cloven hoof.
The Code of the Woosters (1938) ch. 2

3 I turned to Aunt Agatha, whose demeanour was now rather like that of one who, picking daisies on the railway, has just caught the down express in the small of the back.
The Inimitable Jeeves (1923) ch. 4

4 When Aunt is calling to Aunt like mastodons bellowing across primeval swamps.
The Inimitable Jeeves (1923) ch. 16

5 It was my Uncle George who discovered that alcohol was a food well in advance of medical thought.
The Inimitable Jeeves (1923) ch. 16

6 What with excellent browsing and sluicing and cheery conversation and what-not, the afternoon passed quite happily.
My Man Jeeves (1919) 'Jeeves and the Unbidden Guest'

7 Ice formed on the butler's upper slopes.
Pigs Have Wings (1952) ch. 5

Terry Wogan 1938–

8 Television contracts the imagination and radio expands it.
in *Observer* 30 December 1984 'Sayings of the Year'

Naomi Wolf 1962–

9 To ask women to become unnaturally thin is to ask them to relinquish their sexuality.
The Beauty Myth (1990)

Charles Wolfe 1791–1823

10 Not a drum was heard, not a funeral note, As his corse to the rampart we hurried.
'The Burial of Sir John Moore at Corunna' (1817)

11 We buried him darkly at dead of night, The sods with our bayonets turning.
'The Burial of Sir John Moore at Corunna' (1817)

12 We carved not a line, and we raised not a stone—
But we left him alone with his glory.
'The Burial of Sir John Moore at Corunna' (1817)

Humbert Wolfe 1886–1940

13 You cannot hope
to bribe or twist,
thank God! the
British journalist.
But, seeing what
the man will do

unbribed, there's
no occasion to.
'Over the Fire' (1930)

James Wolfe 1727–59

14 The General . . . repeated nearly the whole of Gray's Elegy . . . adding, as he concluded, that he would prefer being the author of that poem to the glory of beating the French to-morrow.
J. Playfair *Biographical Account of J. Robinson* in *Transactions of the Royal Society of Edinburgh* vol. 7 (1815)

15 Now God be praised, I will die in peace.
J. Knox *Historical Journal of the Campaigns in North America* (ed. A. G. Doughty, 1914) vol. 2

Thomas Wolfe 1900–38

16 Which of us has not remained forever prison-pent? Which of us is not forever a stranger and alone?
foreword to *Look Homeward, Angel* (1929)

17 You can't go home again.
title of book, 1940

Tom Wolfe 1931–

18 The bonfire of the vanities.
title of novel (1987); deriving from Savonarola's 'burning of the vanities' in Florence, 1497

19 A liberal is a conservative who has been arrested.
The Bonfire of the Vanities (1987) ch. 24

20 Electric Kool-Aid Acid test.
title of novel on hippy culture (1968)

21 Radical Chic . . . is only radical in Style; in its heart it is part of Society and its tradition—Politics, like Rock, Pop, and Camp, has its uses.
in *New York* 8 June 1970

Mary Wollstonecraft 1759–97

22 To give a sex to mind was not very consistent with the principles of a man [Rousseau] who argued so warmly, and so well, for the immortality of the soul.
often quoted as, 'Mind has no sex'
A Vindication of the Rights of Woman (1792) ch. 3

23 I do not wish them [women] to have power over men; but over themselves.
A Vindication of the Rights of Woman (1792) ch. 4

24 A slavish bondage to parents cramps every faculty of the mind.
A Vindication of the Rights of Woman (1792) ch. 11

Thomas Wolsey c.1475–1530

25 Father Abbot, I am come to lay my bones amongst you.
George Cavendish *Negotiations of Thomas Wolsey* (1641)

26 Had I but served God as diligently as I have served the King, he would not have given me over in my grey hairs.
George Cavendish *Negotiations of Thomas Wolsey* (1641); cf. **Shakespeare** 275:26

Kenneth Wolstenholme

1 They think it's all over—it is now.
   television commentary in closing moments of
   the World Cup Final, 30 July 1966

Mrs Henry Wood 1814–87

2 Dead! and . . . never called me mother.
   East Lynne (dramatized by T. A. Palmer, 1874, the
   words do not occur in the novel of 1861)

George Woodcock 1912–95

3 Canadians do not like heroes, and so they
   do not have them.
   Canada and the Canadians (1970)

Thomas Woodrooffe 1899–1978

4 At the present moment, the whole Fleet's lit
   up. When I say 'lit up', I mean lit up by fairy
   lamps.
   *live outside broadcast, Spithead Review, 20 May
   1937*
   Asa Briggs *History of Broadcasting in the UK* (1965)
   vol. 2

Harry Woods

5 Oh we ain't got a barrel of money,
   Maybe we're ragged and funny,
   But we'll travel along
   Singin' a song,
   Side by side.
   'Side by Side' (1927 song)

Virginia Woolf 1882–1941

6 Examine for a moment an ordinary mind
   on an ordinary day.
   The Common Reader (1925) 'Modern Fiction'

7 A woman must have money and a room of
   her own if she is to write fiction.
   A Room of One's Own (1929) ch. 1

8 This is an important book, the critic
   assumes, because it deals with war. This is
   an insignificant book because it deals with
   the feelings of women in a drawing-room.
   A Room of One's Own (1929) ch. 4

9 The scratching of pimples on the body of
   the bootboy at Claridges.
   *of James **Joyce**'s Ulysses*
   letter to Lytton Strachey, 24 April 1922

10 I read the book of Job last night. I don't
   think God comes well out of it.
   letter to Lady Robert Cecil, 12 November 1922

11 As an experience, madness is terrific . . . and
   in its lava I still find most of the things I
   write about.
   letter to Ethel Smyth, 22 June 1930

Alexander Woollcott 1887–1943

12 She was like a sinking ship firing on the
   rescuers.
   *of Mrs Patrick **Campbell***
   While Rome Burns (1944) 'The First Mrs
   Tanqueray'

13 All the things I really like to do are either
   illegal, immoral, or fattening.
   R. E. Drennan *Wit's End* (1973)

Dorothy Wordsworth 1771–1855

14 A beautiful evening, very starry, the horned
   moon.
   'Alfoxden Journal' 23 March 1798; cf.
   Coleridge 96:15

15 I never saw daffodils so beautiful. They grew
   among the mossy stones about and about
   them; some rested their heads upon these
   stones as on a pillow for weariness; and the
   rest tossed and reeled and danced, and
   seemed as if they verily laughed with the
   wind that blew upon them over the lake.
   'Grasmere Journal' 15 April 1802; cf.
   Wordsworth 340:1

Elizabeth Wordsworth 1840–1932

16 If all the good people were clever,
   And all clever people were good,
   The world would be nicer than ever
   We thought that it possibly could.
   But somehow, 'tis seldom or never
   The two hit it off as they should;
   The good are so harsh to the clever,
   The clever so rude to the good!
   'Good and Clever'

William Wordsworth 1770–1850

17 Who is the happy Warrior? Who is he
   Whom every man in arms should wish to
   be?
   'Character of the Happy Warrior' (1807); cf.
   Read 254:19

18 Earth has not anything to show more fair:
   Dull would he be of soul who could pass by
   A sight so touching in its majesty:
   This City now doth like a garment wear
   The beauty of the morning.
   'Composed upon Westminster Bridge' (1807)

19 Dear God! the very houses seem asleep;
   And all that mighty heart is lying still!
   'Composed upon Westminster Bridge' (1807)

20 The light that never was, on sea or land,
   The consecration, and the Poet's dream.
   on a picture of Peele Castle in a storm
   'Elegiac Stanzas' (1807)

21 Bliss was it in that dawn to be alive,
   But to be young was very heaven!
   'The French Revolution, as it Appeared to
   Enthusiasts' (1809); also *The Prelude* (1850) bk. 9,
   l. 108

22 The moving accident is not my trade;
   To freeze the blood I have no ready arts.
   'Hart-Leap Well' (1800) pt. 2, l. 1

23 All shod with steel
   We hissed along the polished ice.
   'Influence of Natural Objects' (1809); also *The
   Prelude* (1850) bk. 1, l. 414

24 It is a beauteous evening, calm and free.
   'It is a beauteous evening, calm and free' (1807)

25 We must be free or die, who speak the
   tongue

That Shakespeare spake.
'It is not to be thought of that the Flood' (1807)

1 I wandered lonely as a cloud
That floats on high o'er vales and hills,
When all at once I saw a crowd,
A host, of golden daffodils;
Beside the lake, beneath the trees,
Fluttering and dancing in the breeze.
'I wandered lonely as a cloud' (1815 ed.); cf.
Wordsworth 339:15

2 For oft, when on my couch I lie
In vacant or in pensive mood,
They flash upon that inward eye
Which is the bliss of solitude;
And then my heart with pleasure fills,
And dances with the daffodils.
'I wandered lonely as a cloud' (1815 ed.)

3 The still, sad music of humanity,
Nor harsh nor grating, though of ample
power
To chasten and subdue.
'Lines composed . . . above Tintern Abbey'
(1798) l. 91

4 Milton! thou shouldst be living at this hour:
England hath need of thee: she is a fen
Of stagnant waters.
'Milton! thou shouldst be living at this hour'
(1807)

5 My heart leaps up when I behold
A rainbow in the sky:
'My heart leaps up when I behold' (1807)

6 The Child is father of the Man.
'My heart leaps up when I behold' (1807)

7 There was a time when meadow, grove, and
stream,
The earth, and every common sight,
To me did seem
Apparelled in celestial light,
The glory and the freshness of a dream.
'Ode. Intimations of Immortality' (1807) st. 1

8 The rainbow comes and goes,
And lovely is the rose.
'Ode. Intimations of Immortality' (1807) st. 2

9 Whither is fled the visionary gleam?
Where is it now, the glory and the dream?
'Ode. Intimations of Immortality' (1807) st. 4

10 Our birth is but a sleep and a forgetting:
The Soul that rises with us, our life's Star,
Hath had elsewhere its setting,
And cometh from afar:
Not in entire forgetfulness,
And not in utter nakedness,
But trailing clouds of glory do we come
From God, who is our home:
Heaven lies about us in our infancy!
Shades of the prison-house begin to close
Upon the growing boy.
'Ode. Intimations of Immortality' (1807) st. 5

11 And by the vision splendid
Is on his way attended;
At length the man perceives it die away,
And fade into the light of common day.
'Ode. Intimations of Immortality' (1807) st. 5

12 But for those obstinate questionings
Of sense and outward things,

Fallings from us, vanishings;
Blank misgivings of a creature
Moving about in worlds not realised,
High instincts before which our mortal
nature
Did tremble like a guilty thing surprised.
'Ode. Intimations of Immortality' (1807) st. 9

13 Though nothing can bring back the hour
Of splendour in the grass, of glory in the
flower.
'Ode. Intimations of Immortality' (1807) st. 10

14 To me the meanest flower that blows can
give
Thoughts that do often lie too deep for
tears.
'Ode. Intimations of Immortality' (1807) st. 11

15 Stern daughter of the voice of God!
'Ode to Duty' (1807)

16 Plain living and high thinking are no more:
The homely beauty of the good old cause
Is gone.
'O friend! I know not which way I must look'
(1807); cf. **Milton** 223:22

17 Once did she hold the gorgeous East in fee,
And was the safeguard of the West.
'On the Extinction of the Venetian Republic'
(1807)

18 Some sipping punch, some sipping tea,
But as you by their faces see
All silent, and all damned?
Peter Bell pt. 1, l. 543 in 1819 MS (subsequently
deleted so as 'not to offend the pious')

19 A reasoning, self-sufficing thing,
An intellectual All-in-all!
'A Poet's Epitaph' (1800)

20 In common things that round us lie
Some random truths he can impart,—
The harvest of a quiet eye
That broods and sleeps on his own heart.
'A Poet's Epitaph' (1800)

21 Unprofitably travelling toward the grave.
The Prelude (1850) bk. 1, l. 267

22 Made one long bathing of a summer's day.
The Prelude (1850) bk. 1, l. 290

23 All things have second birth;
The earthquake is not satisfied at once.
The Prelude (1850) bk. 10, l. 83

24 There is
One great society alone on earth,
The noble Living, and the noble Dead.
The Prelude (1850) bk. 11, l. 393

25 I thought of Chatterton, the marvellous boy,
The sleepless soul that perished in its pride.
'Resolution and Independence' (1807) st. 7

26 We poets in our youth begin in gladness;
But thereof comes in the end despondency
and madness.
'Resolution and Independence' (1807) st. 7

27 Still glides the Stream, and shall for ever
glide;
The Form remains, the Function never dies.
'The River Duddon' (1820) no. 34 'After-
Thought'

1 We feel that we are greater than we know.
'The River Duddon' (1820) no. 34 'After-Thought'

2 Scorn not the Sonnet; Critic, you have frowned,
Mindless of its just honours; with this key
Shakespeare unlocked his heart.
'Scorn not the Sonnet' (1827); cf. **Browning** 70:12

3 She dwelt among the untrodden ways
Beside the springs of Dove,
A maid whom there were none to praise
And very few to love.
'She dwelt among the untrodden ways' (1800)

4 A violet by a mossy stone.
'She dwelt among the untrodden ways' (1800)

5 She lived unknown, and few could know
When Lucy ceased to be;
But she is in her grave, and, oh,
The difference to me!
'She dwelt among the untrodden ways' (1800)

6 She was a phantom of delight.
title of poem (1807)

7 A perfect woman; nobly planned,
To warn, to comfort, and command.
'She was a phantom of delight' (1807)

8 A slumber did my spirit seal;
I had no human fears:
She seemed a thing that could not feel
The touch of earthly years.
'A slumber did my spirit seal' (1800)

9 Behold her, single in the field,
Yon solitary Highland lass!
'The Solitary Reaper' (1807)

10 For old, unhappy, far-off things,
And battles long ago.
'The Solitary Reaper' (1807)

11 What, you are stepping westward?
'Stepping Westward' (1807)

12 Surprised by joy—impatient as the wind.
'Surprised by joy—impatient as the wind' (1815)

13 Our meddling intellect
Mis-shapes the beauteous forms of things:—
We murder to dissect.
'The Tables Turned' (1798)

14 Two Voices are there; one is of the sea,
One of the mountains; each a mighty Voice:
In both from age to age thou didst rejoice,
They were thy chosen music, Liberty!
'Thought of a Briton on the Subjugation of Switzerland' (1807)

15 O Cuckoo! Shall I call thee bird,
Or but a wandering voice?
'To the Cuckoo' (1807)

16 Thy friends are exultations, agonies,
And love, and man's unconquerable mind.
'To Toussaint L'Ouverture' (1807)

17 We are seven.
title of poem (1798)

18 The world is too much with us; late and soon,
Getting and spending, we lay waste our powers.
'The world is too much with us' (1807)

19 Great God! I'd rather be
A Pagan suckled in a creed outworn;
So might I, standing on this pleasant lea,
Have glimpses that would make me less forlorn;
Have sight of Proteus rising from the sea;
Or hear old Triton blow his wreathèd horn.
'The world is too much with us' (1807)

20 Poetry is the spontaneous overflow of powerful feelings: it takes its origin from emotion recollected in tranquillity.
Lyrical Ballads (2nd ed., 1802) preface; cf. **Parker** 240:22

21 Never forget what I believe was observed to you by Coleridge, that every great and original writer, in proportion as he is great and original, must himself create the taste by which he is to be relished.
letter to Lady Beaumont, 21 May 1807

Henry Wotton 1568–1639

22 You meaner beauties of the night,
That poorly satisfy our eyes,
More by your number, than your light;
You common people of the skies,
What are you when the moon shall rise?
'On His Mistress, the Queen of Bohemia' (1624)

23 He first deceased; she for a little tried
To live without him: liked it not, and died.
'Upon the Death of Sir Albertus Moreton's Wife' (1651)

24 Well building hath three conditions.
Commodity, firmness, and delight.
Elements of Architecture (1624) pt. 1

25 An ambassador is an honest man sent to lie abroad for the good of his country.
written in the album of Christopher Fleckmore in 1604

Frank Lloyd Wright 1867–1959

26 The physician can bury his mistakes, but the architect can only advise his client to plant vines—so they should go as far as possible from home to build their first buildings.
in *New York Times* 4 October 1953, sect. 6

Lady Mary Wroth c.1586–c.1652

27 Love, a child, is ever crying:
Please him and he straight is flying,
Give him, he the more is craving,
Never satisfied with having.
'Love, a child, is ever crying' (1621)

Harry Wu 1937–

28 I want to see the word laogai in every dictionary in every language in the world. I want to see the laogai ended. Before 1974, the word 'gulag' did not appear in any dictionary. Today, this single word conveys the meaning of Soviet political violence and

its labour camp system. 'Laogai' also deserves a place in our dictionaries.
the laogai *are Chinese labour camps*
in *Washington Post* 26 May 1996

Thomas Wyatt *c.*1503–42

1 They flee from me, that sometime did me seek
With naked foot, stalking in my chamber.
'They flee from me' (1557)

2 When her loose gown from her shoulders did fall,
And she me caught in her arms long and small;
Therewith all sweetly did me kiss,
And softly said, 'Dear heart, how like you this?'
'They flee from me' (1557)

William Wycherley *c.*1640–1716

3 Go to your business, I say, pleasure, whilst I go to my pleasure, business.
The Country Wife (1675) act 2

4 And with faint praises one another damn.
of drama critics
The Plain Dealer (1677) prologue; cf. **Pope** 247:10

5 A man without money needs no more fear a crowd of lawyers than a crowd of pickpockets.
The Plain Dealer (1677) act 3, sc. 1

Tammy Wynette 1942–98
and Billy Sherrill *c.*1938–

6 Stand by your man.
title of song (1968)

Xenophon *c.*428–*c.*354 BC

7 The sea! the sea!
Anabasis bk. 4, ch. 7, sect. 24

Augustin, Marquis de Ximénèz 1726–1817

8 *Attaquons dans ses eaux*
La perfide Albion!
Let us attack in her own waters perfidious Albion!
'L'Ère des Français' (October 1793); cf. **Bossuet** 64:19

William Yancey 1814–63

9 The man and the hour have met.
of Jefferson **Davis**, *President-elect of the Confederacy, in 1861*
Shelby Foote *The Civil War: Fort Sumter to Perryville* (1991)

W. F. Yeames 1835–1918

10 And when did you last see your father?
a Roundhead officer addressing the child of a Cavalier family
title of painting (1878), now in the Walker Art Gallery, Liverpool

W. B. Yeats 1865–1939

11 O body swayed to music, O brightening glance,
How can we know the dancer from the dance?
'Among School Children' (1928)

12 Tell me of that lady
The poet stubborn with his passion sang us
When age might well have chilled his blood.'
'Broken Dreams' (1914)

13 That dolphin-torn, that gong-tormented sea.
'Byzantium' (1933)

14 I must lie down where all the ladders start,
In the foul rag-and-bone shop of the heart.
'The Circus Animals' Desertion' (1939) pt. 3

15 We were the last romantics.
'Coole Park and Ballylee, 1931' (1933)

16 The years like great black oxen tread the world.
The Countess Cathleen (1895) act 4

17 Love has pitched his mansion in
The place of excrement;
For nothing can be sole or whole
That has not been rent.
'Crazy Jane Talks with the Bishop' (1932)

18 Down by the salley gardens my love and I did meet;
She passed the salley gardens with little snow-white feet.
She bid me take love easy, as the leaves grow on the tree;
But I, being young and foolish, with her would not agree.
'Down by the Salley Gardens' (1889)

19 I have met them at close of day
Coming with vivid faces
From counter or desk among grey
Eighteenth-century houses.
I have passed with a nod of the head
Or polite meaningless words.
'Easter, 1916' (1921)

20 All changed, changed utterly:
A terrible beauty is born.
'Easter, 1916' (1921)

21 Too long a sacrifice
Can make a stone of the heart.
'Easter, 1916' (1921)

22 I write it out in a verse—
MacDonagh and MacBride
And Connolly and Pearse
Now and in time to be,
Wherever green is worn,
Are changed, changed utterly:
A terrible beauty is born.
'Easter, 1916' (1921)

23 The fascination of what's difficult
Has dried the sap of my veins, and rent
Spontaneous joy and natural content
Out of my heart.
'The Fascination of What's Difficult' (1910)

24 Never to have lived is best, ancient writers say;

Never to have drawn the breath of life,
  never to have looked into the eye of day.
  'From *Oedipus at Colonus*' (1928); cf. **Sophocles**
  299:10

1 The ghost of Roger Casement
  Is beating on the door.
  'The Ghost of Roger Casement' (1939)

2 I have spread my dreams under your feet;
  Tread softly because you tread on my
    dreams.
  'He Wishes for the Cloths of Heaven' (1899)

3 The light of evening, Lissadell,
  Great windows open to the south,
  Two girls in silk kimonos, both
  Beautiful, one a gazelle.
  'In Memory of Eva Gore Booth and Con
  Markiewicz' (1933)

4 My country is Kiltartan Cross;
  My countrymen Kiltartan's poor.
  'An Irish Airman Foresees his Death' (1919)

5 Nor law, nor duty bade me fight,
  Nor public men, nor cheering crowds.
  'An Irish Airman Foresees his Death' (1919)

6 I will arise and go now, and go to Innisfree,
  And a small cabin build there, of clay and
    wattles made;
  Nine bean rows will I have there, a hive for
    the honey-bee,
  And live alone in the bee-loud glade.
  'The Lake Isle of Innisfree' (1893)

7 I hear lake water lapping with low sounds
    by the shore . . .
  I hear it in the deep heart's core.
  'The Lake Isle of Innisfree' (1893)

8 A shudder in the loins engenders there
  The broken wall, the burning roof and
    tower
  And Agamemnon dead.
  'Leda and the Swan' (1928)

9 Did that play of mine send out
  Certain men the English shot?
  'The Man and the Echo' (1939)

10 We had fed the heart on fantasies,
  The heart's grown brutal from the fare.
  'Meditations in Time of Civil War' no. 6 'The
  Stare's Nest by my Window' (1928)

11 And say my glory was I had such friends.
  'The Municipal Gallery Re-visited' (1939)

12 Why, what could she have done, being what
    she is?
  Was there another Troy for her to burn?
  'No Second Troy' (1910)

13 I think it better that at times like these
  A poet's mouth be silent, for in truth
  We have no gift to set a statesman right.
  'On being asked for a War Poem' (1919)

14 A pity beyond all telling,
  Is hid in the heart of love.
  'The Pity of Love' (1893)

15 Out of Ireland have we come.
  Great hatred, little room,
  Maimed us at the start.
  I carry from my mother's womb

A fanatic heart.
  'Remorse for Intemperate Speech' (1933)

16 That is no country for old men. The young
  In one another's arms, birds in the trees
  —Those dying generations—at their song,
  The salmon-falls, the mackerel-crowded
    seas.
  'Sailing to Byzantium' (1928)

17 An aged man is but a paltry thing.
  'Sailing to Byzantium' (1928)

18 And therefore I have sailed the seas and
    come
  To the holy city of Byzantium.
  'Sailing to Byzantium' (1928)

19 Things fall apart; the centre cannot hold;
  Mere anarchy is loosed upon the world,
  The blood-dimmed tide is loosed, and
    everywhere
  The ceremony of innocence is drowned;
  The best lack all conviction, while the worst
  Are full of passionate intensity.
  'The Second Coming' (1921)

20 And what rough beast, its hour come round
    at last,
  Slouches towards Bethlehem to be born?
  'The Second Coming' (1921)

21 Far-off, most secret and inviolate Rose.
  'The Secret Rose' (1899)

22 A woman of so shining loveliness
  That men threshed corn at midnight by a
    tress,
  A little stolen tress.
  'The Secret Rose' (1899)

23 Romantic Ireland's dead and gone,
  It's with O'Leary in the grave.
  'September, 1913' (1914)

24 And pluck till time and times are done
  The silver apples of the moon,
  The golden apples of the sun.
  'Song of Wandering Aengus' (1899)

25 Swift has sailed into his rest;
  Savage indignation there
  Cannot lacerate his breast.
  'Swift's Epitaph' (1933); cf. **Swift** 307:15

26 But was there ever dog that praised his
    fleas?
  'To a Poet, Who would have Me Praise certain
  bad Poets, Imitators of His and of Mine' (1910)

27 Michael Angelo left a proof
  On the Sistine Chapel roof,
  Where but half-awakened Adam
  Can disturb globe-trotting Madam.
  'Under Ben Bulben' (1939) pt. 4

28 Irish poets, learn your trade,
  Sing whatever is well made.
  'Under Ben Bulben' (1939) pt. 5

29 Cast your mind on other days
  That we in coming days may be
  Still the indomitable Irishry.
  'Under Ben Bulben' (1939) pt. 5

30 On limestone quarried near the spot
  By his command these words are cut:
  Cast a cold eye

On life, on death.
Horseman, pass by!
'Under Ben Bulben' (1939) pt. 6

1 When you are old and grey and full of sleep,
And nodding by the fire, take down this
book,
And slowly read.
'When You Are Old' (1893)

2 We make out of the quarrel with others,
rhetoric, but of the quarrel with ourselves,
poetry.
Essays (1924) 'Anima Hominis' sect. 5

of the Anglo-Irish:

3 We . . . are no petty people. We are one of
the great stocks of Europe. We are the
people of Burke; we are the people of Swift,
the people of Emmet, the people of Parnell.
We have created most of the modern
literature of this country. We have created
the best of its political intelligence.
speech in the Irish Senate, 11 June 1925

Boris Yeltsin 1931–

4 You can make a throne of bayonets, but you
can't sit on it for long.
*from the top of a tank, during the attempted
military coup against* **Gorbachev**
in *Independent* 24 August 1991; cf. **Inge** 168:22

5 Today is the last day of an era past.
*at a Berlin ceremony to end the Soviet military
presence*
in *Guardian* 1 September 1994

Yevgeny Yevtushenko 1933–

6 Over Babiy Yar
There are no memorials.
The steep hillside like a rough inscription.
'Babiy Yar' (1961) (tr. Robin Milner-Gulland)

7 Life is a rainbow which also includes black.
in *Guardian* 11 August 1987

Shoichi Yokoi 1915–97

8 It is a terrible shame for me—I came back,
still alive, without having won the war.
*on returning to Japan after surviving for 28 years
in the jungles of Guam before surrendering to the
Americans in 1972*
in *Independent* 26 September 1997

Andrew Young 1932–

9 Nothing is illegal if one hundred well-placed
business men decide to do it.
Morris K. Udall *Too Funny to be President* (1988)

Edward Young 1683–1765

10 Be wise with speed;
A fool at forty is a fool indeed.
The Love of Fame (1725–8) Satire 2, l. 282

11 Hot, envious, noisy, proud, the scribbling
fry
Burn, hiss, and bounce, waste paper, stink,
and die.
The Love of Fame (1725–8) Satire 3, l. 65

12 One to destroy, is murder by the law;
And gibbets keep the lifted hand in awe;
To murder thousands, takes a specious
name,
'War's glorious art', and gives immortal
fame.
The Love of Fame (1725–8) Satire 7, l. 55; cf.
Porteus 249:22, **Rostand** 261:3

13 How science dwindles, and how volumes
swell,
How commentators each dark passage
shun,
And hold their farthing candle to the sun.
The Love of Fame (1725–8) Satire 7, l. 96; cf.
Burton 76:17, **Sidney** 295:5

14 Procrastination is the thief of time.
Night Thoughts (1742–5) 'Night 1' l. 393

15 At thirty a man suspects himself a fool;
Knows it at forty, and reforms his plan.
Night Thoughts (1742–5) 'Night 1' l. 417

16 By night an atheist half believes a God.
Night Thoughts (1742–5) 'Night 5' l. 176

17 [The senses] Take in at once the landscape of
the world,
At a small inlet, which a grain might close,
And half create the wondrous world they
see.
Night Thoughts (1742–5) 'Night 6' l. 425

18 To know the world, not love her, is thy
point,
She gives but little, nor that little, long.
Night Thoughts (1742–5) 'Night 8' l. 1276; cf.
Goldsmith 143:14

19 Life is the desert, life the solitude;
Death joins us to the great majority.
The Revenge (1721) act 4; cf. **Petronius** 244:10

George W. Young 1846–1919

20 The lips that touch liquor must never touch
mine.
title of poem (c..1870); also attributed, in a
different form, to Harriet A. Glazebrook, 1874

Neil Young 1945–
and Jeff Blackburn

21 It's better to burn out
Than to fade away.
quoted by Kurt **Cobain** *in his suicide note, 8 April
1994*
'My My, Hey Hey (Out of the Blue) (1978 song)

Yevgeny Zamyatin 1884–1937

22 Heretics are the only bitter remedy against
the entropy of human thought.
'Literature, Revolution and Entropy' quoted in
The Dragon and other Stories (1967, tr. M.
Ginsberg) introduction

Israel Zangwill 1864–1926

23 America is God's Crucible, the great
Melting-Pot where all the races of Europe
are melting and re-forming!
The Melting Pot (1908) act 1

Emiliano Zapata 1879–1919

1 Many of them, so as to curry favour with
tyrants, for a fistful of coins, or through
bribery or corruption, are shedding the
blood of their brothers.
*on the maderistas who, in Zapata's view, had
betrayed the revolutionary cause*
   Plan de Ayala 28 November 1911, para. 10

Frank Zappa 1940–93

2 Rock journalism is people who can't write
interviewing people who can't talk for
people who can't read.
   Linda Botts *Loose Talk* (1980); cf. **Capp** 82:1

Zeno of Citium *c*.335–*c*.263 BC

3 The reason why we have two ears and only
one mouth is that we may listen the more
and talk the less.
to a youth who was talking nonsense
   Diogenes Laertius *Lives of the Philosophers* 'Zeno'
   ch. 7

Zhuangzi *see* Chuang Tzu

Ronald L. Ziegler 1939–

4 [Mr Nixon's latest statement] is the
Operative White House Position . . . and all
previous statements are inoperative.
   in *Boston Globe* 18 April 1973

Grigori Zinoviev 1883–1936

5 Armed warfare must be preceded by a
struggle against the inclinations to
compromise which are embedded among
the majority of British workmen, against
the ideas of evolution and peaceful
extermination of capitalism. Only then will
it be possible to count upon complete
success of an armed insurrection.
   letter to the British Communist Party, 15
   September 1924, in *The Times* 25 October 1924;
   the 'Zinoviev Letter', later shown to be a
   forgery

Hiller B. Zobel

6 Asking the ignorant to use the
incomprehensible to decide the
unknowable.
   'The Jury on Trial' in *American Heritage*
   July–August 1995

7 Judges must follow their oaths and do their
duty, heedless of editorials, letters,
telegrams, threats, petitions, panellists and
talk shows.
   judicial ruling reducing the conviction of Louise
   Woodward from murder to manslaughter, 10
   November 1997

Émile Zola 1840–1902

8 One forges one's style on the terrible anvil
of daily deadlines.
   Le Figaro 1881

9 J'accuse.
   I accuse.
*title of an open letter to the President of the
French Republic, in connection with the Dreyfus
affair*
   in *L'Aurore* 13 January 1898

Zoroastrian Scriptures
translations by M. Boyce, 1984

10 We worship Mithra of wide pastures,
possessing a thousand ears, possessing ten
thousand eyes, the divinity worshipped
with spoken name.
   The Yashts yasht 10: Avestan Hymn to Mithra, v.1

11 Truly there are two primal Spirits, twins
renowned to be in conflict. In thought and
word, in act they are two: the better and the
bad. And those who act well have chosen
rightly between these two, not so the
evildoers.
   The Gathas yasna 30, v. 3

12 I am Zarathustra, Were I able, I should be a
true foe to the Deceiver, but a strong
support to the Just One.
   The Gathas yasna 43, v. 8

Index

A *A noir, E blanc, I rouge*   RIMB 257:13
  from A to B   PARK 240:23
abandon A. all hope   DANT 105:17
abased shall be a.   BIBL 46:25
abated agony is a.   MACA 206:14
abbot blessed the A.   SOUT 299:14
A.B.C. Man is man's A.   QUAR 253:5
a-bed a. after midnight   SHAK 288:11
Aberbrothock Abbot of A.   SOUT 299:14
Aberdour half-owre to A.   BALL 24:10
abgeschafft *Der Staat wird nicht 'a.'* ENGE 124:23
abhorrence my heart's a.   BROW 71:5
abide A. with me   LYTE 205:4
  a. with my Creator God   CLAR 93:10
  Others a. our question   ARNO 15:20
abiding there is none a.   BIBL 36:34
abiit *A. at plures*   PETR 244:10
abilities according to his a.   MARX 214:5
  God has given you good a.   ARAB 13:17
  instincts and a.   BALZ 24:21
ability a. for doing things   GONC 144:12
  according to his a.   BLAN 56:18
  as distinct from a.   WHIT 333:14
abjure rough magic I here a.   SHAK 287:17
able have a poet a.-bodied   MACN 208:22
aboard Once a. the lugger   JOHN 177:5
abolish a. or restrain   LOCK 201:7
  a. serfdom   ALEX 3:15
  a. the death penalty   KARR 180:16
abolished State is not 'a.'   ENGE 124:23
abomination a. of desolation   BIBL 44:35
  a. unto the Lord   ANON 5:12
  Lying lips are a.   BIBL 37:28
abominations A. OF THE EARTH   BIBL 52:21
abortion a. would be a sacrament   KENN 184:5
Abou Ben Adhem A. (may his tribe increase!)
                                    HUNT 167:1
abound that grace may a.   BIBL 49:10
about a. must go   DONN 114:2
above a., between, below   DONN 113:18
Abraham God of A.   HA-L 149:18
abroad A. is bloody   GEOR 138:10
  A. is unutterably bloody   MITF 225:2
  I will a.   HERB 157:9
  I will a.   HERB 157:10
  sent to lie a.   WOTT 341:25
  You are ordered a.   KITC 189:6
Absalom O A., my son, my son   BIBL 35:33
absence A. diminishes commonplace passions
                                    LA R 193:21
  A. is to love   BUSS 76:25
  a. of mind   SEEL 267:7
  shoot me in my a.   BEHA 27:17
absent a. are always in the wrong   DEST 109:3
  A. in body   BIBL 49:24
  a. one from another   BIBL 33:32
  A. thee from felicity   SHAK 273:21
  my a. child   SHAK 277:1
absentee a. aristocracy   DISR 112:5
  confirm him an a.   EDGE 119:21
absents endear A.   LAMB 192:2
absolute a. power corrupts   ACTO 1:8
  Be a. for death   SHAK 281:31
absolutism a. moderated by assassination ANON 6:17
absolve History will a. me   CAST 85:9
abstract a. reasoning   HUME 166:19
  all painting is a.   HOCK 160:9

abundance he shall have a.   BIBL 45:7
abused character is to be a.   THAC 314:21
abuses attended with considerable a.   BURK 73:22
  carry away their a.   GLAD 141:20
abysm a. of time   SHAK 287:2
academe groves of A.   HORA 164:4
  olive grove of A.   MILT 222:28
academes books, the a.   SHAK 278:19
academia a. in Oxford   AUNG 19:10
academic some a. scribbler   KEYN 185:12
accent for not keeping of a.   JONS 178:10
accents caught his clear a.   BROW 70:17
accentuate a. the positive   MERC 216:21
acceptable a. unto God   BIBL 49:19
accident moving a. is not my trade   WORD 339:22
  There's been an a.   GRAH 145:7
accidents A. will occur   DICK 110:8
  chapter of a.   CHES 89:14
accomplices we are all his a.   MURR 230:11
accord with one a.   BOOK 58:22
according a. to his abilities   MARX 214:5
  a. to his strength   MORE 228:6
accounts make up my a.   MIDR 217:24
accuse *J'a.*   ZOLA 345:9
ace about to play the a.   FIEL 127:9
achieve I shall a. in time   GILB 140:15
  some a. greatness   SHAK 288:23
Achilles A.' cursed anger sing   HOME 161:16
  A.' wrath   POPE 248:22
  in the trench, A.   SHAW 292:10
  name A. assumed   BROW 68:21
  see the great A.   TENN 313:32
aching A., shaking, crazy   ROCH 258:16
Achitophel false A. was first   DRYD 116:15
acid Electric Kool-Aid A. test   WOLF 338:20
acknowledge a. thee to be the Lord   BOOK 58:10
acquaintance auld a. be forgot   BURN 75:4
  make a new a.   JOHN 176:20
acquainted a. with grief   BIBL 40:16
acres few a. of snow   VOLT 325:21
act A. of Union is there   TRIM 319:12
  Between the motion And the a.   ELIO 122:5
  in any A. of Parliament   HERB 157:5
  To see him a.   COLE 96:23
  within the meaning of the A.   ANON 9:10
acted I a. so tragic   HARG 152:9
acting A. a masochistic form   OLIV 236:6
  when he was off he was a.   GOLD 143:19
action A. this day   ANON 5:13
  a. to the word   SHAK 272:11
  again third, 'a.'   DEMO 108:12
  Makes that and th' a. fine   HERB 157:13
  man of a.   GALS 135:15
  Place, and A.   DRYD 117:15
actions a. of the just   SHIR 294:28
  a. of two bodies   NEWT 233:12
  A. receive their tincture   DEFO 107:17
  my a. are my ministers'   CHAR 87:24
active a. line on a walk   KLEE 189:9
activity just a new a.   DYSO 118:11
actor a.'s life for me   WASH 328:24
actors A. are cattle   HITC 159:14
acts no second a. in American lives   FITZ 129:10
actualité economical with the *a.*   CLAR 93:16
actum *Nil a. credens*   LUCA 204:8
ad reminded of that a.   MOND 225:17

adage poor cat i' the a.	SHAK 279:25
Adam A. Had 'em	ANON 5:14
A., the goodliest man	MILT 222:1
A. was a gardener	SHAK 275:17
good thing A. had	TWAI 321:9
half-awakened A.	YEAT 343:27
in A. all die	BIBL 50:2
old A. in this Child	BOOK 60:7
riverrun, past Eve and A.'s	JOYC 178:19
When A. dalfe	ROLL 259:10
whipped the offending A.	SHAK 274:28
adamant frame of a.	JOHN 174:5
adazzle sweet, sour; a., dim	HOPK 163:2
adder a. is breathing in time with it	MAND 211:4
brings forth the a.	SHAK 276:3
deaf as an a.	ADAM 1:18
like the deaf a.	BOOK 62:4
addicted a. to prayers	ASHF 16:13
addiction a. is bad	JUNG 179:15
prisoners of a.	ILLI 168:18
Addison Cato did, and A. approved	BUDG 72:6
address non-existent a.	LEWI 198:13
adeste A., fideles	ANON 12:6
adieu Bidding a.	KEAT 182:8
ad infinitum proceed a.	SWIF 307:11
adjective As to the A.	TWAI 321:12
Adlestrop Yes; I remember A.	THOM 316:14
administered Whate'er is best a.	POPE 248:18
administration criticism of a.	BAGE 22:12
administrative a. won't	LYNN 205:2
admiral kill an a. from time to time	VOLT 325:22
admiralty price of a.	KIPL 188:10
admirari Nil a.	HORA 163:23
admire Not to a., is all the art	POPE 248:25
adolescence a. and obsolescence	LINK 200:3
Adonais I weep for A.	SHEL 292:14
Adonis A. in loveliness	HUNT 167:5
adored I was a. once	SHAK 288:17
adorn a. a tale	JOHN 174:6
ads watched the a.	NASH 231:14
adsuitur Purpureus A. pannus	HORA 163:11
Adullam cave A.	BIBL 35:24
political Cave of A.	BRIG 67:2
adult not the occupation of an a.	OLIV 236:6
adulteration adultery, but a.	BYRO 79:4
adulteries a. of art	JONS 177:17
adultery as common as a.	GRIG 147:19
call gallantry, and gods a.	BYRO 78:16
committed a. in my heart	CART 84:23
die for a.	SHAK 278:2
Do not a. commit	CLOU 95:3
Not quite a.	BYRO 79:4
Thou shalt not commit a.	BIBL 34:16
woman taken in a.	BIBL 47:33
adults by a. to children	SZAS 308:9
advance When we our sails a.	DRAY 116:8
advantage A. rarely comes of it	CLOU 95:3
Japan's a.	HIRO 159:12
undertaking of Great A.	ANON 6:9
with equal a. content	CANN 81:11
advent Hark to the a. voice	OAKL 235:10
adventure awfully big a.	BARR 25:15
most beautiful a. in life	FROH 134:2
pass out into a.	FORS 131:14
adventures bold and hard a.	FITZ 128:13
adversity A.'s sweet milk	SHAK 286:30
bread of a.	BIBL 40:1
fortunes sharpe a.	CHAU 88:26
Sweet are the uses of a.	SHAK 269:14
advertisement soul of an a.	JOHN 173:18
advertisers a. don't object to	SWAF 306:13
advertising A. may be described	LEAC 195:3
A. the rattling of a stick	ORWE 237:23
lust and calls it a.	LAHR 191:20
money I spend on a.	LEVE 198:4
advice A. is seldom welcome	CHES 89:9
advise STREETS FLOODED. PLEASE A.	BENC 29:8
advisers political a.	SHOR 295:1
aere Exegi monumentum a. perennius	HORA 164:16
Aesculapius owe a cock to A.	SOCR 298:24
aesthetic high a. line	GILB 140:22
aetas fugerit invida A.	HORA 164:7
afeared Be not a.	SHAK 287:14
affable sign of an a. man	ROST 260:22
affair a. is over	RICH 256:21
affairs taking part in a.	VALÉ 322:7
tide in the a.	SHAK 276:29
affections holiness of the heart's a.	KEAT 183:4
affinities Elective a.	GOET 142:23
affliction bread of a.	BIBL 36:17
mine a. and my misery	BIBL 40:28
waters of a.	BIBL 40:1
affluent a. society	GALB 135:9
afford unless you can a. it	TROL 319:21
afloat A. We move: Delicious	CLOU 94:21
afraid a. of his enemy	PLUT 246:10
a. of the sea	SYNG 308:7
a. of Virginia Woolf	ALBE 3:9
because she was a. of him	MURD 230:4
I, a stranger and a.	HOUS 164:25
many are a. of God	LOCK 201:9
not that I'm a. to die	ALLE 4:8
Afric in A.-maps	SWIF 307:9
Africa A. and her prodigies	BROW 69:4
A. than my own body	ORTO 237:2
choose between this A.	WALC 326:16
deported A.	GENE 137:19
new out of A.	PLIN 246:4
shape of A.	FANO 126:2
sloggin' over A.	KIPL 187:9
African A. is conditioned	KENY 184:20
[A.] national consciousness	MACM 208:10
I'm not an A.	GOLD 143:3
struggle of the A. people	MAND 210:19
Africans A. experience people	KAUN 180:22
A. were a low, filthy nation	HEAD 154:7
after A. the first death	THOM 316:7
happily ever a.	ANON 5:18
one damned thing a. another	HUBB 166:3
Or just a.	STEV 303:7
afternoon At five in the a.	GARC 135:21
lose the war in an a.	CHUR 92:12
summer a.	JAME 170:27
aftersight a. and foresight	ELIO 121:27
Afton Flow gently, sweet A.	BURN 75:3
again believing it a.	LICH 199:1
against a. every man	BIBL 33:24
always vote a.	FIEL 127:22
life is 6 to 5 a.	RUNY 262:3
not with me is a. me	BIBL 43:33
somewhat a. thee	BIBL 52:4
vote a. somebody	ADAM 1:14
who can be a. us	BIBL 49:17
Agamemnon And A. dead	YEAT 343:8
When A. cried aloud	ELIO 122:19
agate bigger than an a.-stone	SHAK 286:14
age A. cannot wither her	SHAK 268:20
a. going to the workhouse	PAIN 239:15
A., I do abhor thee	SHAK 289:18
a. is a dream that is dying	O'SH 238:2
a. is rocking the wave	MAND 211:4
a. might well have chilled	YEAT 342:12
a. of chivalry	BURK 74:7
a. of ease	GOLD 143:8
a., which forgives itself	SHAW 291:19
A. will not be defied	BACO 21:22

age (cont.)

a. with stealing steps	VAUX 323:6
Crabbed a. and youth	SHAK 289:17
dawning of the a. of Aquarius	RADO 253:21
days of our a.	BOOK 62:15
fetch the a. of gold	MILT 220:25
He was not of an a.	JONS 178:8
if a. could	ESTI 125:4
I meet my Father, my a.	LOWE 203:22
invention of a barbarous a.	MILT 220:31
old a. always fifteen years older	BARU 25:21
Old A., and Experience	ROCH 258:13
Old a. is the most unexpected	TROT 320:1
Soul of the A.	JONS 178:5
when Mozart was my a.	LEHR 196:20
with a. and dust	RALE 254:5
With leaden a. o'ercargoed	FLEC 129:24
worth an a. without a name	MORD 227:21

aged a. man is but a paltry thing — YEAT 343:17
a. thrush — HARD 151:22
allow this a. man his right — PEEL 243:2
did the a. seem — TRAH 319:4
means Certainly a. — BYRO 79:1

agenda any item of the a. — PARK 241:8
agendum *quid superessit a.* — LUCA 204:8
ages belongs to the a. — STAN 301:18
God, our help in a. past — WATT 329:13
heir of all the a. — TENN 312:14
Rock of A. — TOPL 318:19
Agnes St A.' Eve — KEAT 181:3
agnostic title of 'a.' — HUXL 167:20
agnosticism all a. means — DARR 106:5
agnus *A. Dei* — MISS 224:6
agonies exultations, a. — WORD 341:16
agony a. is abated — MACA 206:14
am in a. — CATU 86:2
Beyond is a. — GREV 147:11
most extreme a. — BETT 32:6
agree a. with the book of God — OMAR 236:7
colours will a. — BACO 21:31
agreement a. with hell — GARR 136:12
have reached a. — MITC 224:17
with hell are we at a. — BIBL 39:30
a-hunting We daren't go a. — ALLI 4:12
aids [A. was] an illness in stages — GUIB 148:12
ail Oh, what can a. thee — KEAT 181:17
aim when you have forgotten your a. — SANT 264:16
ain't a. necessarily so — HEYW 158:19
Say it a. so — ANON 9:17
air A. and angels — DONN 114:3
England was too pure an A. — ANON 9:7
fly through the a. — LEYB 198:22
I am fire and a. — SHAK 269:7
In the clear a. — FERG 127:1
lands hatless from the a. — BETJ 31:20
music in the a. — ELGA 121:3
nipping and an eager a. — SHAK 271:11
to the Germans that of—the a. — RICH 257:4
with pinions skim the a. — FRER 133:18
airline a. ticket to romantic places — MARV 213:24
airplanes feel about a. — KERR 184:22
airy A., fairy Lilian — TENN 312:6
nations' a. navies — TENN 312:11
Akond A. of Swat — LEAR 195:7
Alamo Remember the A. — SHER 294:24
alarm little a. now and then — BURN 74:25
SPREAD A. AND DESPONDENCY — PENI 243:8
alas A. but cannot pardon — AUDE 18:21
A., poor Yorick — SHAK 273:11
Hugo—a. — GIDE 139:17
albatross I shot the A. — COLE 96:11
Albert A. is beautiful — VICT 323:19
Went there with young A. — EDGA 119:19

Albion perfidious A. — XIMÉ 342:8
alcohol A. a very necessary article — SHAW 291:4
a. doesn't thrill me — PORT 249:17
a. or morphine — JUNG 179:15
a. was a food — WODE 338:5
taken more out of a. — CHUR 92:6
Aldershot burnish'd by A. sun — BETJ 32:3
ale no more cakes and a. — SHAK 288:15
spicy nut-brown a. — MILT 220:5
Alexander gane, like A. — BURN 75:7
not A. — ALEX 3:13
Some talk of A. — ANON 9:22
Alexandria A.'s library burned — HUGH 166:11
Alexandrine needless A. — POPE 248:4
algebraic weaves a. patterns — LOVE 203:5
alibi always has an a. — ELIO 122:17
Alice Christopher Robin went down with A.
— MILN 218:26
alien a. people clutching their gods — ELIO 122:8
a. tears will fill for him — WILD 335:18
amid the a. corn — KEAT 182:14
blame the a. — AESC 2:24
damned if I'm an a. — GEOR 138:6
alike all places were a. to him — KIPL 188:21
aliter *Dis a. visum* — VIRG 324:14
alive a. and well — ANON 8:3
a. I shall be delighted — HOLL 161:6
came back, still a. — YOKO 344:8
Half dead and half a. — BETJ 31:18
If we can't stay here a. — MONT 226:18
man fully a. — IREN 169:8
noise and tumult when a. — EDWA 120:6
not just being a. — MART 213:9
Not while I'm a. — BEVI 32:15
Officiously to keep a. — CLOU 95:2
still a. at twenty-two — KING 187:2
was dead, and is a. — BIBL 46:35
what keeps you a. — CAST 85:7
all 1066 and a. that — SELL 267:15
a. for love — SPEN 300:16
A. for one, one for all — DUMA 118:2
a. hell broke loose — MILT 222:7
a. shall be well — ELIO 121:30
a. shall be well — JULI 179:10
A. that a man hath — BIBL 36:38
a. the world is young — KING 186:22
a. things to all men — BIBL 49:27
A. things were made by him — BIBL 47:16
given Her a. on earth — BYRO 78:12
have a. in all — CARE 82:5
Jack — I'm a. right — BONE 58:1
man for a. seasons — WHIT 334:7
or a. in all — TENN 311:10
we should at a. times — BOOK 60:3
you were a. to me — BROW 71:12
allegiance a. to the flag — BELL 28:4
allegory headstrong as an a. — SHER 294:15
Allen love of Barbara A. — BALL 23:16
alley lives in our a. — CARE 82:10
rats' a. — ELIO 122:24
alliance A., n. In international politics — BIER 53:18
alliances clear of permanent a. — WASH 328:20
allies no a. to be polite to — GEOR 138:9
no eternal a. — PALM 240:6
alliteration A.'s artful aid — CHUR 91:1
allons *A., enfants de la patrie* — ROUG 261:8
allow Government and public opinion a. — SHAW 291:12
allure a. by denying — TROL 319:18
almanack Look in the a. — SHAK 283:15
almighty a. dollar — IRVI 169:11
A. had placed it there — LABO 191:6
A.'s orders to perform — ADDI 2:6
A., the King of Creation — WINK 337:14

almost A. thou persuadest me BIBL 49:4
alms a. and oblations BOOK 59:25
a. may be in secret BIBL 42:22
puts a. for oblivion SHAK 287:30
alone a. against smiling enemies BOWE 65:12
A. and palely loitering KEAT 181:17
A. I did it SHAK 270:16
Being a. and liking it HASK 153:3
dangerous to meet it a. WHAR 332:24
I want to be a. GARB 135:20
never less a. ROGE 259:2
never walk a. HAMM 151:1
not sufficiently a. VALÉ 322:6
One is always a. ELIO 121:17
One is one and all a. ANON 7:17
stranger and a. WOLF 338:16
that the man should be a. BIBL 33:2
We were a. JAME 170:24
who travels a. KIPL 187:25
along All a., down along BALL 24:16
aloud Angels cry a. BOOK 58:10
alp a. of unforgiveness PLOM 246:6
Alph A., the sacred river, ran COLE 96:3
Alpha A. and Omega BIBL 52:3
alpine through an A. village LONG 201:22
alps A. of green ice PHIL 244:17
A. on Alps arise POPE 247:30
altar a. with this inscription BIBL 48:34
on his own strange a. SWIN 307:23
alteration A. though it be HOOK 162:9
alters when it a. finds SHAK 290:6
alternatives a. that are not their own BONH 58:3
altogether righteous a. BOOK 61:4
altruism conscientiousness and a. CONF 98:8
alway I am with you a. BIBL 45:22
always a. be an England PARK 241:5
sometimes a. RICH 257:3
Alzheimer he had A.'s disease REAG 255:4
am I A. THAT I AM BIBL 34:3
I think, therefore I a. DESC 109:2
Ama A. et fac quod vis AUGU 19:4
Amaryllis sport with A. MILT 220:12
amateur a. is a man who can't AGAT 3:2
whine of the a. for three WHIS 333:4
amavi Sero te a. AUGU 19:2
amaze vainly men themselves a. MARV 213:15
amazing A. grace NEWT 233:17
A. love WESL 331:22
ambassador a. is an honest man WOTT 341:25
ambiguity Seven types of a. EMPS 124:21
ambition A. can creep BURK 74:11
A., in a private man a vice MASS 214:19
A. should be made SHAK 276:18
fling away a. SHAK 275:25
make a. virtue SHAK 284:25
Vain the a. of kings WEBS 330:8
Vaulting a. SHAK 279:22
ambitions ceiling put on our a. PRES 251:1
ambitious as he was a., I slew him SHAK 276:13
of a. minds SPEN 300:20
ambo Arcades a. VIRG 325:11
Ambree Mary A. BALL 24:2
ambrosial a. hair VIRG 324:11
âme â. est sans défauts RIMB 257:12
amen Will no man say, a. SHAK 285:26
America America! A. BATE 26:5
A. is a vast conspiracy UPDI 321:26
A. is God's Crucible ZANG 344:23
a. is now given over HAWT 153:15
A. is the proof MCCA 206:19
A., thou half-brother BAIL 23:1
A. thus top nation SELL 267:21
born in A. MALC 210:4

England and A. divided SHAW 292:6
every man's love affair with A. MAIL 209:17
glorious morning for A. ADAM 2:2
God bless A. BERL 30:17
I like to be in A. SOND 299:3
in common with A. WILD 334:21
I, too, sing A. HUGH 166:8
loss of A. FREE 133:16
next to god a. CUMM 104:14
O my A. DONN 113:18
to A. to convert the Indians WESL 332:6
American A. as cherry pie BROW 68:13
A. beauty rose ROCK 258:17
A.-outward-bound HOPK 163:9
A., this new man CEÈV 103:8
chief business of the A. people COOL 99:21
free man, an A. JOHN 173:1
I am A. bred MILL 218:11
I'm an A. GOLD 143:3
in love with A. names BENÉ 29:10
Miss A. Pie MCLE 208:1
no second acts in A. lives FITZ 129:10
oil controlling A. soil DYLA 119:8
send A. boys JOHN 173:4
truth, justice and the A. way ANON 6:21
Americanism A. with its sleeves rolled MCCA 206:18
hyphenated A. ROOS 260:4
Americans for A. it is just beyond KISS 189:5
Good A., when they die APPL 13:13
ignorant A. MASS 214:20
my fellow A. KENN 184:12
when bad A. die WILD 335:10
Americas off for the A. BARR 25:18
amicably a. if they can QUIN 253:9
amicus A. Plato ARIS 14:20
Amis cocoa for Kingsley A. COPE 99:24
amitti non a. sed praemitti CYPR 105:11
ammunition pass the a. FORG 131:10
amo A., amas O'KE 235:24
Non a. te MART 213:7
Odi et a. CATU 86:2
amor a. che muove il sole DANT 105:22
A. vincit omnia CHAU 88:9
Omnia vincit A. VIRG 325:14
amorous my a. propensities JOHN 174:17
amour beginning of an A. BEHN 27:19
ampullas Proicit a. HORA 163:14
Amurath Not A. an Amurath succeeds SHAK 274:25
amuse talent to a. COWA 101:5
amused a. by its presumption THUR 317:27
We are not a. VICT 323:22
amusements but for its a. LEWI 198:16
analytical A. Engine weaves LOVE 203:5
anarch Thy hand, great A. POPE 246:24
anarchism A. is a game SHAW 291:23
A. stands for the liberation GOLD 143:5
anarchy Mere a. is loosed YEAT 343:19
anatomist am but a bad a. TONE 318:18
anatomy A. is destiny FREU 133:19
ancestor If there were an a. HUXL 168:4
ancestral A. voices prophesying war COLE 96:6
ancestry pride of a. POWE 250:26
trace my a. GILB 140:7
anchor a. to let fall ASKE 16:16
ancient a. and fish-like smell SHAK 287:9
A. of days BIBL 41:10
A. of Days GRAN 145:15
A. person of my heart ROCH 258:16
A. times BACO 20:21
Beauty so a. AUGU 19:2
feet in a. time BLAK 55:27
It is an a. Mariner COLE 96:8
most a. profession KIPL 188:18

ancient (*cont.*)
rivers a. as the world   HUGH 166:9
ancients a. dreaded death   HARE 152:6
and including 'a.'   MCCA 206:21
Andromache kissed his sad A.   CORN 100:7
angel a. from your door   BLAK 56:7
a. in the house   PATM 242:2
a. of death   BRIG 66:20
A. of Death   BYRO 78:14
a. of the Lord came down   TATE 309:13
a. of the Lord came upon them   BIBL 46:3
a. should write   MOOR 227:12
ape or an a.   DISR 112:10
as the A. did with Jacob   WALT 328:6
beautiful and ineffectual a.   ARNO 16:1
better a. is a man   SHAK 290:11
clip an A.'s wings   KEAT 181:25
Death's bright a.   PROC 251:14
for an a. to pass   FIRB 128:1
Look homeward a.   MILT 220:18
ministering a.   SHAK 273:13
ministering a. thou   SCOT 266:19
Recording A., as he wrote it down   STER 302:24
say to the A. of Death   MIDR 217:24
Shined in my a.-infancy   VAUG 322:21
White as an a.   BLAK 56:9
wrote like an a.   GARR 136:8
angeli *Non Angli sed A.*   GREG 147:7
angels Air and a.   DONN 114:3
A. and ministers of grace   SHAK 271:13
A. bending near the earth   SEAR 267:2
A. cry aloud   BOOK 58:10
a. fear to tread   POPE 248:7
A. in jumpers   LEWI 198:21
a., nor principalities   BIBL 49:18
a. on the walls   MARL 212:18
behold the a. of God   BIBL 33:30
By that sin fell the a.   SHAK 275:25
entertained a. unawares   BIBL 51:18
flights of a.   SHAK 273:23
Four a. round my head   ANON 8:17
Hear all ye a.   MILT 222:11
make the a. weep   SHAK 281:30
Michael and his a.   BIBL 52:14
neglect God and his A.   DONN 114:21
Not Angles but A.   GREG 147:7
plead like a.   SHAK 279:21
saw a treefull of a.   BENÉ 29:13
tongues of men and of a.   BIBL 49:30
With a. round the throne   WATT 329:9
women are a.   BYRO 79:18
anger Achilles' cursed a. sing   HOME 161:16
A. and jealousy   ELIO 121:11
A. is a short madness   HORA 163:22
A. is one of the sinews   FULL 134:26
A. makes dull men   BACO 22:6
Frozen a.   FREU 133:22
Juno's never-forgetting a.   VIRG 324:9
Look back in a.   OSBO 237:27
monstrous a. of the guns   OWEN 238:21
more in sorrow than in a.   SHAK 271:5
neither a. nor partiality   TACI 308:16
strike it in a.   SHAW 291:18
angle Brother of the A.   WALT 328:3
angler no man is born an a.   WALT 328:2
angles Not A. but Angels   GREG 147:7
Offer no a.   TESS 314:17
Angli *Non A. sed Angeli*   GREG 147:7
Anglo-Irishman He was an A.   BEHA 27:16
angry a. with my friend   BLAK 56:11
A. young man   PAUL 242:6
Be ye a.   BIBL 50:19
when very a., swear   TWAI 321:11

anguis *Latet a. in herba*   VIRG 325:9
anguish With a. moist   KEAT 181:18
animal Be a good a.   LAWR 194:16
be a good a.   SPEN 300:1
every a. is sad   ANON 12:18
Man is a noble a.   BROW 69:2
only a. in the world to fear   LAWR 194:18
political a.   ARIS 14:17
vegetable, a., and mineral   GILB 141:5
animals All a. are equal   ORWE 237:5
distinguish us from other a.   BEAU 26:12
man from a.   OSLE 238:4
minutely small a.   JAIN 170:7
not over-fond of a.   ATTE 17:8
turn and live with a.   WHIT 333:24
animula *A. vagula blandula*   HADR 148:17
Anna Here thou, great A.   POPE 249:3
Annabel Lee I and my A.   POE 246:11
annals a. are blank   MONT 226:17
Anne of A. of Cleves   HENR 156:16
sister A., do you see nothing   PERR 244:3
annihilating A. all that's made   MARV 213:17
Anno Domini only a.   HILT 159:10
annoy only does it to a.   CARR 83:17
annus a. horribilis   ELIZ 123:14
anointed balm from an a. king   SHAK 285:17
another a. fine mess   LAUR 194:9
in a. country   MARL 212:12
members one of a.   BIBL 50:18
when come such a.   SHAK 276:24
answer A. a fool   BIBL 38:5
a. came there none   CARR 84:7
a. came there none   SCOT 266:5
a. is blowin' in the wind   DYLA 119:2
a. made it none   SHAK 271:4
a. the phone   THUR 317:28
a. to the Irish Question   SELL 267:20
on the way to a pertinent a.   BRON 67:6
soft a.   BIBL 37:32
stay for an a.   BACO 21:30
what a dusty a.   MERE 217:6
What *is* the a.   STEI 302:9
wisest man can a.   COLT 97:16
answerable a. for what we choose   NEWM 233:8
answered no one a.   DE L 108:8
answering a. that of God   FOX 132:16
ant a.'s a centaur   POUN 250:11
Go to the a.   BIBL 37:21
anthology a. is like all   RALE 254:11
Anthropophagi A., and men   SHAK 284:12
anti savage a.-everythings   HOLM 161:10
antic a. disposition   SHAK 271:22
dance an a. hay   MARL 212:8
antick old father a., the law   SHAK 273:26
anti-destin *L'art est un a.*   MALR 210:14
antique group that's quite a.   BYRO 78:21
noble and nude and a.   SWIN 307:20
traveller from an a. land   SHEL 293:11
antiquity write for A.   LAMB 192:13
antiwar ecology and a.   HUNT 167:7
Antony catch a second A.   SHAK 269:10
anvil a. of daily deadlines   ZOLA 345:8
Church is an a.   MACL 207:20
England's on the a.   KIPL 187:6
anxiety taboo'd by a.   GILB 140:5
any A. old iron   COLL 97:4
anybody Is there a. there   DE L 108:7
no one's a.   GILB 139:22
anything A. for a quiet life   MIDD 217:19
A. goes   PORT 249:15
believe in a.   CHES 90:11
anywhere get a. in a marriage   MURD 230:5
apart have stood a.   WILS 337:6

of man's life a thing a.	BYRO 78:18	**Arcadians** A. both	VIRG 325:11
ape a. for his grandfather	HUXL 168:4	**arch** a. of order	STRA 305:3
gorgeous buttocks of the a.	HUXL 167:18	**archangel** A. a little damaged	LAMB 192:12
Is man an a.	DISR 112:10	**archbishop** My Lord A.	BULL 72:10
naked a.	MORR 228:14	**archer** mark the a. little meant	SCOT 266:13
played the sedulous a.	STEV 303:17	**arches** down the a. of the years	THOM 316:26
apes a. and peacocks	MASE 214:16	Underneath the A.	FLAN 129:13
ivory, and a.	BIBL 36:4	**archetypes** known as a.	JUNG 179:12
aphrodisiac Power is the great a.	KISS 189:3	**archipelago** Gulag a.	SOLZ 298:28
Apollo songs of A.	SHAK 278:24	**architect** a. can only advise	WRIG 341:26
Yea, is not even A.	SWIN 307:26	A. of the Universe	JEAN 171:11
Apollyon his name is A.	BUNY 73:1	**architectural** a. books	PUGI 252:4
apologize Never a.	FISH 128:6	**architecture** A. acts the most slowly	DIMN 111:25
apology a. for the Devil	BUTL 77:12	A. in general	SCHE 265:10
apostles A.: praise thee	BOOK 58:11	A. is the art	JOHN 173:9
I am the least of the a.	BIBL 50:1	Christian A.	PUGI 252:3
apostolic Catholick and A. Church	BOOK 59:23	rise and fall of English a.	BETJ 32:5
apothecary starved a.	LOCK 201:10	**Arcturi** Daisies, those pearled A.	SHEL 293:21
apparel a. oft proclaims the man	SHAK 271:7	**Arden** Ay, now am I in A.	SHAK 269:15
apparition Anno 1670, was an a.	AUBR 17:17	**ardet** *paries cum proximus a.*	HORA 164:1
appeal a. unto Caesar	BIBL 49:1	**ardua** A. *ad astra*	ANON 12:17
appear a. considerable	JOHN 175:8	**are** be as they a.	CLEM 94:10
appearance outward a.	BIBL 35:20	**arena** actually in the a.	ROOS 260:3
appearances Keep up a.	CHUR 90:25	**Argentinian** young A. soldiers	RUNC 261:21
no trusting a.	SHER 294:21	**Argos** remembers his sweet A.	VIRG 325:6
appetite a. grows by eating	RABE 253:11	**argue** cannot a. with	AUCT 17:19
good digestion wait on a.	SHAK 280:28	**arguing** will be much a.	MILT 223:20
voracious a.	FIEL 127:14	**argument** All a. is against it	JOHN 175:24
appetites carnal lusts and a.	BOOK 60:15	a. for a week	SHAK 273:30
Our a. as apt to change	DRYD 116:27	a. of the broken window	PANK 240:12
apple a. of his eye	BIBL 34:29	height of this great a.	MILT 221:2
a. on the tree	DICK 111:15	no a. but force	BROW 69:11
cabbage-leaf to make an a.-pie	FOOT 130:23	no force but a.	BROW 69:11
for an a. damn'd mankind	OTWA 238:8	**arise** A., shine	BIBL 40:20
sweet-a. reddens	SAPP 264:18	**aristocracy** a. means government by	CHES 90:9
apples a., cherries, hops	DICK 111:3	a. of Great Britain	BRIG 66:21
a. of gold	BIBL 38:1	A. of the moneybag	CARL 82:21
A. of gold	SWIN 308:4	**aristocratic** a. class	ARNO 15:28
golden a. of the sun	YEAT 343:24	**Aristotle** God of A.	HA-L 149:18
moon-washed a. of wonder	DRIN 116:10	**arithmetical** a. ratio	MALT 210:15
Ripe a. drop	MARV 213:16	**ark** into the A.	BIBL 33:19
applied no such things as a. sciences	PAST 241:23	**arm** auld moon in her a.	BALL 24:9
appointment a. at the end of the world	DINE 111:26	did not put your a. around it	BLAC 54:21
a. with him in Samarra	MAUG 215:10	long a. of coincidence	CHAM 86:23
create an a.	LOUI 202:19	strength with his a.	BIBL 45:34
approbation A. from Sir Hubert	MORT 229:10	**arma** A. *virumque cano*	VIRG 324:9
approve I do not a.	MILL 218:7	*leges inter a.*	CICE 92:29
après A. *nous le déluge*	POMP 246:17	**armadas** till the great A. come	NEWB 232:18
apricocks dangling a.	SHAK 285:24	**Armageddon** called in the Hebrew tongue A.	
April A., April, Laugh	WATS 329:3		BIBL 52:20
A. is the cruellest month	ELIO 122:20	Lincoln County Road or A.	DYLA 119:7
A. of your youth	HERB 157:7	**armaments** not a. that cause wars	MADA 209:3
A. shroud	KEAT 182:7	**armchair** like a good a.	MATI 215:6
bright cold day in A.	ORWE 237:13	**armed** a. conflict	EDEN 119:17
glory of an A. day	SHAK 288:34	A. warfare must be preceded	ZINO 345:5
Men are A. when they woo	SHAK 270:3	a. with more than complete steel	ANON 7:18
Now that A.'s there	BROW 70:8	**Armenteers** Mademoiselle from A.	ANON 8:14
Whan that A.	CHAU 88:4	**armes** *Aux a., citoyens*	ROUG 261:8
aprons made themselves a.	BIBL 33:7	**armful** very nearly an a.	GALT 136:17
apt A. Alliteration	CHUR 91:1	**armies** a. clash by night	ARNO 15:5
a. to die	SHAK 276:9	money and large a.	ANOU 13:7
Aquarius dawning of the age of A.	RADO 253:21	stronger than all the a.	ANON 10:7
Aquitaine prince of A.	NERV 232:14	**armistice** It is an a. for twenty years	FOCH 130:17
Arabia perfumes of A.	SHAK 281:17	**armour** a. of God	BIBL 50:22
spell of far A.	DE L 108:5	a. of light	BIBL 49:21
Arabs like the A.	LONG 201:20	a. of light	BOOK 59:12
Aram Eugene A. walked between	HOOD 162:2	**armoured** a. cars of dreams	BISH 54:10
Arbeit A. *macht frei*	ANON 11:21	**arms** a. against a sea of troubles	SHAK 272:1
arbiter *Elegantiae a.*	TACI 308:17	a. and the man	VIRG 324:9
arbitrator old common a., Time	SHAK 287:34	A., and the man I sing	DRYD 117:14
arboreal a. in its habits	DARW 106:6	a. of a chambermaid	JOHN 176:2
Arcades A. *ambo*	VIRG 325:11	a. were made the Warrior	RIG 257:7
Arcadia *Et in A. ego*	ANON 12:12	caught in her a.	WYAT 342:2

arms (cont.)
Emparadised in one another's a. — MILT 222:2
everlasting a. — BIBL 34:30
it hath very long a. — HALI 150:2
keep and bear a. — CONS 99:16
proud in a. — MILT 219:10
army a. marches on its stomach — NAPO 231:7
a. of Martyrs — BOOK 58:11
a. of unalterable law — MERE 217:5
contemptible little a. — ANON 6:20
Forgotten A. — MOUN 229:14
formation of an Irish a. — GRIF 147:16
invasion by an a. — HUGO 166:16
little ships brought the A. home — GUED 148:8
Your poor a. — CROM 103:22
aroint A. thee, witch — SHAK 278:28
aroma a. of performing seals — HART 152:18
aromatic beneath the a. pain — WINC 337:10
a-roving go no more a. — ANON 7:16
arrange French a. — CATH 85:12
arrest a. all beauty — CAME 80:17
swift in his a. — SHAK 273:19
arrested a. one fine morning — KAFK 180:8
conservative been a. — WOLF 338:19
arrive a. where I am — BUNY 73:11
arrogant subdue the a. — VIRG 324:23
arrow a. that flieth by day — BOOK 62:17
shot an a. — LONG 201:17
time's a. — EDDI 119:12
arrows a. of desire — BLAK 55:27
Like as the a. — BOOK 63:19
slings and a. — SHAK 272:1
ars A. longa, vita brevis — HIPP 159:11
arse politician is an a. upon — CUMM 104:15
arsenal great a. of democracy — ROOS 259:19
art adulteries of a. — JONS 177:17
A. alone Enduring stays — DOBS 113:11
A. a revolt against fate — MALR 210:14
a. can wash her guilt away — GOLD 144:4
A. does not reproduce the visible — KLEE 189:8
A. for art's sake — CONS 99:13
a. for art's sake — COUS 100:19
A. is an abstraction — GAUG 136:19
A. is born of humiliation — AUDE 18:23
A. is meant to disturb — BRAQ 66:4
a. is not a weapon — KENN 184:15
A. is pattern informed by sensibility — READ 254:18
A. is significant deformity — FRY 134:21
A. is vice — DEGA 107:22
a. of balance — MATI 215:6
a. of the possible — BISM 54:13
a. of the possible — GALB 135:11
a. of the soluble — MEDA 215:19
a. which one government sooner — SMIT 297:11
clever, but is it A. — KIPL 187:11
Deals are my a. form — TRUM 320:11
Desiring this man's a. — SHAK 289:25
Dying is an a. — PLAT 245:20
E in A-level a. — HIRS 159:13
fascinating kind of a. — WARH 328:13
glib and oily a. — SHAK 277:7
good grey guardians of a. — WILB 334:19
Here the great a. lies — MILT 223:16
industry without a. — RUSK 262:8
last and greatest a. — POPE 248:28
Life is short, the a. long — HIPP 159:11
Minister that meddles with a. — MELB 216:4
More matter with less a. — SHAK 271:26
nature is the a. of God — BROW 69:5
necessary a. — DULL 117:25
next to Nature, A. — LAND 192:21
only interested in a. — SHAW 292:4
people start on all this A. — HERB 157:2

Robust a. alone is eternal — GAUT 136:20
Shakespeare wanted a. — JONS 178:10
symbol of Irish a. — JOYC 179:1
true test of a. — INGR 169:6
where the a. resides — SCHN 265:16
artful A. Dodger — DICK 110:27
Arthur in A.'s bosom — SHAK 274:31
article first a. of my faith — GAND 135:18
articles These a. subscribed — CONG 98:19
articulate made a. all that I saw — BROW 68:12
artificer great a. Made my mate — STEV 304:1
artificial All things are a. — BROW 69:5
but an a. man — HOBB 159:22
artisan employment to the a. — BELL 28:21
artist a. man and the mother woman — SHAW 291:9
God only another a. — PICA 244:19
Never trust the a. — LAWR 194:15
no man is born an a. — WALT 328:2
portrait of the a. — JOYC 178:22
What an a. dies — NERO 232:13
artistic a. verisimilitude — GILB 140:18
artists A. not engineers of the soul — KENN 184:15
arts a. babblative and scribblative — SOUT 299:17
cry both a. and learning — QUAR 253:6
followed the a. — SHAK 288:5
France, famed in all great a. — ARNO 15:25
France, mother of a. — DU B 117:19
interested in the a. — AYCK 20:9
mother of a. — MILT 222:28
one of the fine a. — DE Q 108:22
ascendancy a. of the Whig party — MACA 205:16
ascendeth a. up for ever and ever — BIBL 52:18
ascending angels of God a. — BIBL 33:30
lark a. — MERE 217:2
ash Oak, and A., and Thorn — KIPL 188:12
Out of the a. — PLAT 245:21
ashamed a. to look upon one another — WALT 328:4
more things a man is a. of — SHAW 291:8
ashbuds a. in the front of March — TENN 311:1
ashes a. for thirty — LAMP 192:19
a. of his fathers — MACA 206:7
a. to ashes — BOOK 60:25
a. under Uricon — HOUS 165:6
burnt to a. — GRAH 145:8
universe to a. — MISS 224:11
Asia churches which are in A. — BIBL 52:2
not in A. — ARDR 14:3
pampered jades of A. — MARL 212:19
Asian A. boys ought to be — JOHN 173:4
Asians A. could still smile — HEAD 154:7
aside set death a. — TURG 320:16
ask a. and cannot answer — SHAW 292:9
A., and it shall be given — BIBL 43:5
a. if you are enjoying — NESB 232:15
A. me no more — CARE 82:7
a. not what your country — KENN 184:12
could a. him anything — WEIS 330:24
Don't a., don't tell — NUNN 235:7
if you gotta a. — ARMS 14:26
Would this man a. why — AUDE 17:29
asking a. too much — CANN 81:11
time of a. — BOOK 60:13
asleep men were all a. — BRID 66:19
very houses seem a. — WORD 339:19
asp hole of the a. — BIBL 39:23
aspens Willows whiten, a. quiver — TENN 312:3
aspidistra biggest a. in the world — HARP 152:13
Keep the a. flying — ORWE 237:10
ass firstborn the greatest a. — CARO 83:10
kiss my a. in Macy's window — JOHN 173:5
law is a a. — DICK 110:28
law is such an a. — CHAP 87:16
not covet his a. — BIBL 34:16

on his unwashed a.	PARS 241:13
with the jawbone of an a.	BIBL 35:9
assassin you are an a.	ROST 261:3
assassination absolutism moderated by a.	ANON 6:17
A. is the extreme form	SHAW 292:1
asserted boldly a.	BURR 76:3
asses go seek the a.	BIBL 35:16
seeking a. found	MILT 222:27
assume A. a virtue	SHAK 272:26
assurance make a. double sure	SHAK 281:9
Assyrian A. came down	BYRO 78:13
Astolat lily maid of A.	TENN 311:7
astonish A. me	DIAG 109:9
a. the bourgeois	BAUD 26:9
astonished a. at my own moderation	CLIV 94:19
astonishment Your a.'s odd	KNOX 189:17
astounded a. by them	ATTE 17:8
astra *ardua ad a.*	ANON 12:17
sic itur ad a.	VIRG 325:4
astray like sheep have gone a.	BIBL 40:17
Astur cry is A.	MACA 206:10
asunder let no man put a.	BOOK 60:20
let not man put a.	BIBL 44:18
asylum taken charge of the a.	ROWL 261:16
was in an a.	PALM 240:8
atheism inclineth man's mind to a.	BACO 21:2
atheist a. half believes a God	YOUN 344:16
a. is a man	BUCH 71:25
I am still an a.	BUÑU 72:20
atheists far from a.	CUDW 104:11
no a. in the foxholes	CUMM 104:19
Athens A. arose	SHEL 292:24
A., the eye of Greece	MILT 222:28
athirst give unto him that is a.	BIBL 52:26
Atlanta A. is gone	CHES 89:4
Atlantic stormy North A. Ocean	LARD 193:7
atom carbon a.	JEAN 171:10
grasped the mystery of the a.	BRAD 65:23
atomic primordial a. globule	GILB 140:7
win an a. war	BRAD 65:22
atoms a. of Democritus	BLAK 56:1
concurrence of a.	PALM 240:7
atrocities a. however horrible	NAMI 230:21
attack by his plan of a.	SASS 265:3
lead such dire a.	MACA 206:11
attacked when a. it defends itself	ANON 11:10
attacking I am a.	FOCH 130:16
attempted Something a.	LONG 202:8
attendant a. lord, one that will do	ELIO 122:12
attic Beauty crieth in an a.	BUTL 77:15
furniture in Tolkien's a.	PRAT 250:27
glory of the A. stage	ARNO 15:24
O A. shape	KEAT 182:4
Where the A. bird	MILT 222:28
attire Her rich a.	KEAT 181:5
attitude Fair a.	KEAT 182:4
attracted a. by God	INGE 168:20
attractions Costs register competing a.	KNIG 189:12
auburn Sweet A., loveliest village	GOLD 143:6
audace *toujours de l'a.*	DANT 106:1
audacity Arm me, a.	SHAK 270:17
audience whisks his a.	HORA 163:16
audiences English-speaking a.	WHAR 332:23
audio-visual full of a. marvels	SMIT 297:18
auditorem *notas a. rapit*	HORA 163:16
augury we defy a.	SHAK 273:16
august A. for the people	AUDE 17:27
A. is a wicked month	O'BR 235:13
corny as Kansas in A.	HAMM 150:26
recommence in A.	BYRO 79:6
Augustan next A. age	WALP 327:12
auld For a. lang syne	BURN 75:5
aunt A. is calling to Aunt	WODE 338:4

Charley's a. from Brazil	THOM 316:1
aunts bad a. and good aunts	WODE 338:2
dull a., and croaking rooks	POPE 247:26
his cousins and his a.	GILB 140:29
auream *A. quisquis mediocritatem*	HORA 164:10
auri *A. sacra fames*	VIRG 324:15
Auschwitz saved one Jew from A.	AUDE 18:24
write a poem after A.	ADOR 2:21
year spent in A.	LEVI 198:6
austere beauty cold and a.	RUSS 262:23
Austerlitz A. and Waterloo	SAND 264:9
field of A.	KIPL 188:8
Australia take A. right back	KEAT 181:1
Austria Don John of A. is going	CHES 89:23
author a. of peace	BOOK 58:18
Choose an a.	DILL 111:22
expected to see an a.	PASC 241:15
half an a.'s graces	MORE 227:23
in search of an a.	PIRA 245:5
authority A. forgets a dying king	TENN 311:13
little brief a.	SHAK 281:30
man under a.	BIBL 43:14
autobiography a. is an obituary	CRIS 103:13
A. is now as common	GRIG 147:19
autocrat a.: that's my trade	CATH 85:14
considerate a.	STEP 302:16
autres *encourager les a.*	VOLT 325:22
autumn happy a. fields	TENN 313:7
mists of the a. mornings	ORWE 237:11
Now it is a.	LAWR 194:20
autumnal one a. face	DONN 113:17
availeth struggle naught a.	CLOU 95:4
avalanche perseverance of a mighty a.	HOUS 165:12
avarice A., the spur	HUME 166:20
dreams of a.	JOHN 176:8
dreams of a.	MOOR 227:4
very prone to a.	KORA 190:16
ave *a. atque vale*	CATU 86:3
A. Maria	ANON 12:9
A. verum corpus	ANON 12:10
avenge a. even a look	BURK 74:6
avenger from my dead bones, a.	VIRG 324:17
Time, the a.	BYRO 79:6
averages fugitive from th' law of a.	MAUL 215:12
Averno *Facilis descensus A.*	VIRG 324:20
avertant *di omen a.*	CICE 92:27
Avilion island-valley of A.	TENN 311:16
avis *Rara a.*	JUVE 179:23
avoiding a. being	TILL 318:6
Avon Sweet Swan of A.	JONS 178:9
awake A., my soul	KEN 184:1
West's a.	DAVI 106:23
When you're lying a.	GILB 140:5
aware surely God is a.	KORA 190:16
away a.! for I will fly	KEAT 182:12
WHEN I'M A.	ASQU 17:3
awe wonder and a.	KANT 180:12
aweary I am a., aweary	TENN 312:18
awful bleeding and muddy and a.	RHYS 256:11
this is an a. place	SCOT 266:3
awfully a. big adventure	BARR 25:15
awkward a. squad fire over me	BURN 76:1
awoke a. one morning	BYRO 79:24
So I a., and behold	BUNY 73:6
When Gregor Samsa a. one morning	KAFK 180:7
axe a.'s edge did try	MARV 213:18
a. to the root	PAIN 239:11
let the great a. fall	SHAK 273:7
Lizzie Borden took an a.	ANON 8:10
axes no a. being ground	BROU 68:10
axle fly sat upon the a.-tree	BACO 21:32
Azores Flores in the A.	TENN 313:21

azure a., white, and red — DRUM 116:13
slept an a.-lidded sleep — KEAT 181:8

B

babblative b. and scribblative — SOUT 299:17
babble Coffee house b. — DISR 112:12
babbled b. of green fields — SHAK 274:32
babe love the b. — SHAK 280:1
pretty B. all burning — SOUT 299:21
babes b. and sucklings — BOOK 60:27
babies Ballads and b. — MCCA 206:22
hates dogs and b. — ROST 261:4
putting milk into b. — CHUR 91:22
Babiy Yar Over B. there are no memorials — YEVT 344:6
Bab-lock-hithe Thames at B. — ARNO 15:16
baby B. in an ox's stall — BETJ 31:17
come from, b. dear — MACD 207:6
my b. at my breast — SHAK 269:8
one for my b. — MERC 216:23
Babylon B. in all its desolation — DAVI 106:17
B. is fallen — BIBL 52:17
By the waters of B. — BOOK 63:23
Ere B. was dust — SHEL 293:14
King in B. — HENL 156:10
modern b. — DISR 112:28
MYSTERY, B. THE GREAT — BIBL 52:21
Bacchus charioted by B. — KEAT 182:12
baccy B. for the Clerk — KIPL 188:9
Bach of J. S. B. — BEEC 27:9
bachelors reformers are b. — MOOR 227:5
back at my b. from time to time I hear — ELIO 122:26
at my b. I always hear — MARV 213:21
boys in the b. room — LOES 201:12
boys in the b. rooms — BEAV 26:16
counted them all b. — HANR 151:3
in the small of the b. — WODE 338:3
looking b. — BIBL 46:13
those before cried 'B.!' — MACA 206:11
time to get b. to basics — MAJO 210:1
backs beast with two b. — SHAK 284:9
With our b. to the wall — HAIG 149:7
backward B. ran sentences — GIBB 139:13
backyards clean American b. — MAIL 209:17
bad and the b. unhappily — WILD 335:2
b. aunts and good aunts — WODE 338:2
b. end unhappily — STOP 304:17
b. in the best of us — ANON 10:8
b. publicity — BEHA 27:18
B. women never take the blame — BROO 68:1
brave b. man — CLAR 93:14
Defend the b. against the worse — DAY- 107:4
either good or b. — SHAK 271:29
How sad and b. — BROW 69:28
Mad, b., and dangerous — LAMB 192:1
neither good nor b. — BALZ 24:21
sad b. glad mad — SWIN 307:19
shocking b. hats — WELL 331:11
This bold b. man — SHAK 275:21
When b. men combine — BURK 74:13
when she was b. — LONG 202:10
badge red b. of courage — CRAN 102:22
badly end b. — STEV 303:27
bag b. and baggage — GLAD 141:20
Lays eggs inside a paper b. — ISHE 169:12
baggage bag and b. — GLAD 141:20
bah 'B.,' said Scrooge — DICK 109:19
Bailey come home Bill B. — CANN 81:18
Bainters hate all Boets and B. — GEOR 137:21
baked b. cookies and had teas — CLIN 94:14
Baker Street B. irregulars — DOYL 115:20
balance art of b. — MATI 215:6

b. of power — NICO 234:1
b. of the Old — CANN 81:16
balances weighed in the b. — BIBL 41:8
bald b., and short of breath — SASS 264:26
b. and unconvincing — GILB 140:18
fight between two b. men — BORG 64:14
Go up, thou b. head — BIBL 36:21
baldness far side of b. — SMIT 297:20
Balfour of the B. declaration — WEIZ 330:26
Balkans damned silly thing in the B. — BISM 54:19
ball real business of a b. — SURT 306:11
wind it into a b. — BLAK 55:19
yawning at a b. — LERM 197:23
ballad met with a b. — CALV 80:13
ballads B. and babies — MCCA 206:22
permitted to make all the b. — FLET 130:5
ballot b. is stronger than — LINC 199:5
rap at the b. box — CHIL 90:12
ballots peaceful b. — LINC 199:5
balls B. will be lost always — BERR 31:11
rackets to these b. — SHAK 274:29
With two pitch b. — SHAK 278:18
balm no b. in Gilead — BIBL 40:24
balmy Ginger, you're b. — MURR 230:9
banal b. Eldorado — BAUD 26:8
banality b. of evil — AREN 14:4
band we b. of brothers — SHAK 275:11
bandage wound, not the b. — POTT 249:28
bandaged death b. my eyes — BROW 71:2
Bandar-log What the B. think — KIPL 188:19
bandied struck and b. — WEBS 330:14
bands b. of Orion — BIBL 37:13
bane Deserve the precious b. — MILT 221:14
baneful b. effects — WASH 328:21
bang b.—went saxpence — PUNC 252:12
Not with a b. but a whimper — ELIO 122:6
banish B. not him — SHAK 274:1
banished Alone, a b. man — BALL 24:4
bank b. and shoal of time — SHAK 279:19
b. will lend you money — HOPE 162:17
cry all the way to the b. — LIBE 198:23
I know a b. — SHAK 283:12
robbing a b. — BREC 66:12
sleeps upon this b. — SHAK 282:28
banker as a Scotch b. — DAVI 106:16
banknotes fill old bottles with b. — KEYN 185:11
banks Ye b. and braes — BURN 75:6
banner b. with the strange device — LONG 201:22
star-spangled b. — KEY 185:6
banners b. of the king advance — FORT 131:20
Confusion on thy b. wait — GRAY 146:11
Bantu communal life of the B. — VERW 323:14
baptism in my B. — BOOK 60:8
bar no moaning of the b. — TENN 310:18
When I have crossed the b. — TENN 310:19
Barabbas B. was a publisher — CAMP 81:4
B. was a robber — BIBL 48:10
crowd will always save B. — COCT 95:12
Barbara love of B. Allen — BALL 23:16
barbarians in my own mind the B. — ARNO 15:28
without the b. — CAVA 86:6
young b. all at play — BYRO 78:6
barbarous b. dissonance — MILT 219:16
b. to write a poem — ADOR 12:5
invention of a b. age — MILT 220:31
barber like a b.'s chair — SHAK 268:10
bare B. like nude, giant girls — SPEN 300:11
B. ruined choirs — SHAK 289:31
barefoot b. friars — GIBB 139:8
bargain made a good b. — FRAN 133:5
barge b. she sat in — SHAK 268:17
Barkis B. is willin' — DICK 110:1
barley Corn rigs, an' b. rigs — BURN 75:13

fields of b. and of rye	TENN 312:2	**Bayonne** hams, B.	POPE 246:23
barleycorn bold John B.	BURN 75:25	**bays** oak, or b.	MARV 213:15
Barlow Hornby and my B.	THOM 316:25	**BBC** don't watch B. for polemic	SIMP 296:5
Barnaby like B. Rudge	LOWE 203:16	**be** b. as they are	CLEM 94:10
baronet No little lily-handed b.	TENN 313:20	Let b. be finale of seem	STEV 303:3
barrel ain't got a b. of money	WOOD 339:5	poem should not mean but b.	MACL 208:2
drowned in a b. of Malmesey	FABY 125:18	that which shall b.	BIBL 38:14
grows out of the b. of a gun	MAO 211:12	To b., or not to be	SHAK 272:1
meal in a b.	BIBL 36:9	**beaches** fight on the b.	CHUR 91:15
barren b. superfluity of words	GART 136:14	**beacons** b. of wise men	HUXL 168:3
I am but a b. stock	ELIZ 123:3	**beaded** With b. bubbles	KEAT 182:11
barricade some disputed b.	SEEG 267:5	**beadsman** be your b.	PEEL 243:2
base Labour without joy is b.	RUSK 262:17	**beak** b. from out my heart	POE 246:14
people as b. as itself	PULI 252:5	in his b. Food enough	MERR 217:11
Why bastard? wherefore b.	SHAK 277:8	**beaker** O for a b. full	KEAT 182:11
baser fellows of the b. sort	BIBL 48:32	**Beale** Miss Buss and Miss B.	ANON 8:19
basia Da mi b. mille	CATU 85:20	**beam** B. me up, Scotty	RODD 258:19
basics time to get back to b.	MAJO 210:1	b. that is in thine own eye	BIBL 43:3
basil steal my B.-pot	KEAT 181:15	**beamish** But oh, b. nephew	CARR 84:15
Basingstoke hidden meaning—like B.	GILB 141:8	my b. boy	CARR 84:4
basket come from the same b.	CONR 99:9	**bean** b. and the cod	BOSS 64:18
Basle At B. I founded	HERZ 158:13	Nine b. rows	YEAT 343:6
bastard we knocked the b. off	HILL 159:6	not too French French b.	GILB 140:24
Why b.? wherefore base	SHAK 277:8	**bear** B. of Very Little Brain	MILN 218:25
bastards stand up for b.	SHAK 277:9	b. very much reality	ELIO 121:20
Bastille Voltaire in the B.	DE G 107:26	Exit, pursued by a b.	SHAK 289:4
bat beetle and the b.	JOHN 175:4	fire was furry as a b.	SITW 296:12
black b., night, has flown	TENN 312:21	fitted by nature to b.	AURE 19:3
couldn't b. for the time	COMP 98:1	Grizzly B. is huge and wild	HOUS 164:24
Twinkle, twinkle, little b.	CARR 83:20	How a b. likes honey	MILN 219:4
Wool of b.	SHAK 281:5	Puritan hated b.-baiting	MACA 205:21
bath rather lie in a hot b.	THOM 316:13	so b. ourselves that	CHUR 91:16
sit in a hot b.	TENN 314:4	still less the b.	FRER 133:18
test my b. before I sit	NASH 231:16	**beard** King of Spain's B.	DRAK 116:1
bathe b. those beauteous feet	FLET 130:10	Old Man with a b.	LEAR 195:8
bathing caught the Whigs b.	DISR 112:7	**bearded** b. like the pard	SHAK 269:22
one long b. of a summer's day	WORD 340:22	**beareth** B. all things	BIBL 49:31
bathroom can't feel revolutionary in a b.	LINK 200:2	b. up things light	BACO 21:21
baton marshal's b.	LOUI 203:1	**bears** b. the marks of the last person	HAIG 149:6
bats b. have been broken	HOWE 165:13	Teddy B. have their Picnic	BRAT 66:6
batsmen opening b. to the crease	HOWE 165:13	**beast** b. or a god	ARIS 14:18
battalions not of the heavy b.	VOLT 326:9	b. With many heads	SHAK 270:13
battening B. upon huge seaworms	TENN 311:35	b. with two backs	SHAK 284:9
batter B. my heart	DONN 113:21	Blatant b. men call	SPEN 300:21
battle b. and murder	BOOK 59:6	blond b.	NIET 234:11
b. done	POTT 249:24	but a just b.	ANON 6:1
b. flags were furled	TENN 312:12	fit night out for man or b.	FIEL 127:21
b., n. A method	BIER 53:19	life of his b.	BIBL 37:27
b.'s lost and won	SHAK 278:25	mark, or the name of the b.	BIBL 52:15
b. to the strong	BIBL 38:27	marks of the b.	HARD 151:16
b. to the strong	DAVI 106:14	more subtil than any b.	BIBL 33:6
better in b. than in bed	STER 302:22	number of the b.	BIBL 52:16
defeated in a great b.	LIVY 200:13	questing b.	MALO 210:10
die in a b.	SHAK 275:2	serpent subtlest b.	MILT 222:14
France has lost a b.	DE G 107:23	What rough b.	YEAT 343:20
glorious b.	FORT 131:19	who worship the b.	BIBL 52:18
Ireland's b.	CONN 99:5	**beastie** cow'rin', tim'rous b.	BURN 75:30
Next to a b. lost	WELL 331:7	**beastly** b. to the Germans	COWA 101:4
noise of b. rolled	TENN 311:12	**beasts** b. at Ephesus	BIBL 50:4
smelleth the b. afar off	BIBL 37:14	b. of the forest	BOOK 62:24
battlefield b. is the heart	DOST 114:25	like brute b.	BOOK 60:15
battlements down from the white b.	HEAT 154:18	**beat** b. generation	KERO 184:21
battles b. long ago	WORD 341:10	b. their swords	BIBL 39:11
mother of all b.	HUSS 167:11	We b. them today	STAR 301:21
O God of b.	SHAK 275:6	**beaten** b. path to his door	EMER 124:18
opening b. of subsequent wars	ORWE 237:12	No Englishman is ever fairly b.	SHAW 291:32
baubles Take away these b.	CROM 103:21	**beating** driven by b.	ASCH 16:10
Baum Lebens goldner B.	GOET 142:18	glory of b. the French	WOLF 338:14
bawcock king's a b.	SHAK 274:36	hearts b.	BROW 70:20
bay flourishing like a green b.-tree	BOOK 61:17	**Beatles** B.' first LP	LARK 193:10
bayonets throne of b.	INGE 168:22	**beatus** B. vir qui timet Dominum	BIBL 52:32
throne of b.	YELT 344:4	**beaut** it's a b.	LA G 191:18
with our b. turning	WOLF 338:11	**beauteous** B. the garden's umbrage	SMAR 297:2

beauteous (*cont.*)
It is a b. evening — WORD 339:24
beauties meaner b. of the night — WOTT 341:22
beautiful Albert is b. — VICT 323:19
All things bright and b. — ALEX 3:16
b. and damned — FITZ 129:5
b. and ineffectual angel — ARNO 16:1
b. and simple — HENR 156:19
b. cannot be the way — COUS 100:19
B. dreamer — FOST 132:5
b. face is a mute — PUBL 251:21
b. game — PELÉ 243:4
believe to be b. — MORR 228:19
hunger to be b. — RHYS 256:10
most b. things — RUSK 262:16
Names Most B. — KORA 190:24
singing:—'Oh, how b.!' — KIPL 187:18
Small is b. — SCHU 265:18
Something b. for God — MUGG 229:17
something b. for God — TERE 314:10
When a woman isn't b. — CHEK 88:34
beauty American b. rose — ROCK 258:17
arrest all b. — CAME 80:17
b. being only skin-deep — KERR 185:1
B. crieth in an attic — BUTL 77:15
B. draws us — POPE 249:1
b. faded — PHIL 244:16
B. for some provides escape — HUXL 167:18
B. is mysterious — DOST 114:25
b. is only sin deep — SAKI 263:15
b. is past change — HOPK 163:2
B. is the first test — HARD 151:14
b. is truth — KEAT 182:5
B. itself doth of itself — SHAK 289:19
b. of holiness — BOOK 62:20
b. of holiness — MONS 225:23
b. of inflections — STEV 303:7
b. of Israel — BIBL 35:26
B. so ancient — AUGU 19:2
b.'s rose — SHAK 289:22
B. that must die — KEAT 182:8
b. without vanity — BYRO 79:20
dreamed that life was b. — HOOP 162:10
England, home and b. — ARNO 16:6
If you get simple b. — BROW 70:5
imagination seizes as b. — KEAT 183:4
no excellent b. — BACO 21:4
Of its own b. — BYRO 78:4
order and b. — BAUD 26:7
principal b. in building — FULL 134:27
She walks in b. — BYRO 79:14
some b. lies — MILT 220:4
supreme b. — RUSS 262:23
terrible b. is born — YEAT 342:20
thick, bereft of b. — SHAK 286:39
thing of b. — KEAT 181:2
Where B. was — GALS 135:14
winds of March with b. — SHAK 289:11
with him is b. slain — SHAK 290:15
your b.'s orient deep — CARE 82:7
beaver Harry, with his b. on — SHAK 274:5
because B. I do not hope to turn — ELIO 121:14
B. it's there — MALL 210:8
B. We're here — ANON 10:15
becks Nods, and b. — MILT 220:1
become all that may b. a man — SHAK 279:26
becomes that which *is not* b. — GALE 135:12
bed And so to b. — PEPY 243:12
as little as my b. — KEN 184:3
b. be blest that I lie on — ANON 8:17
better in battle than in b. — STER 302:22
found out thy b. — BLAK 56:13
mind is not a b. — AGAT 3:1

(my Love!) in thy cold b. — KING 186:6
my second best b. — SHAK 290:16
newly gone to b. — MILT 220:30
on the lawn I lie in b. — AUDE 18:13
should of stood in b. — JACO 169:22
take up thy b., and walk — BIBL 47:30
This b. thy centre is — DONN 114:13
wore in b. — MONR 225:20
bedfellows strange b. — SHAK 287:10
bedroom French widow in every b. — HOFF 160:20
what you do in the b. — CAMP 80:20
bedrooms in the nation's b. — TRUD 320:4
beds Minds like b. always made up — WILL 336:10
bedtime I would it were b., Hal — SHAK 274:7
bee b.-loud glade — YEAT 343:6
How doth the little busy b. — WATT 329:5
I am the b. — FITZ 128:12
sting like a b. — ALI 4:5
Where the b. sucks — SHAK 287:19
beech spreading b.-tree — VIRG 325:8
beef great eater of b. — SHAK 288:4
roast b. of England — FIEL 127:11
roast b. of old England — BURK 74:12
Where's the b. — MOND 225:17
been as if it had not b. — SHEL 292:16
beer chronicle small b. — SHAK 284:16
only a b. teetotaller — SHAW 290:23
warm b., invincible suburbs — MAJO 209:23
Beersheba Dan even to B. — BIBL 35:11
bees b. do it — PORT 249:18
innumerable b. — TENN 313:19
of b. or beavers — COND 98:5
was it his b.-winged eyes — BETJ 31:15
beetle b. and the bat — JOHN 175:4
beetles special preference for b. — HALD 149:12
before B. we were her people — FROS 134:9
Not lost but gone b. — NORT 234:23
not lost but sent b. — CYPR 105:11
begetter To the onlie b. — SHAK 289:21
beggar b. would enfold himself — KIPL 188:26
b. would recognise guilt — PARS 241:13
beggared b. all description — SHAK 268:18
beggars b. freezing — ROBI 258:5
Our basest b. — SHAK 277:15
When b. die — SHAK 276:5
begged living HOMER b. his bread — ANON 9:19
begging his seed b. their bread — BOOK 61:16
begin B. at the beginning — CARR 83:26
b. at the beginning — THOM 316:9
b. the Beguine — PORT 249:16
b. with certainties — BACO 20:18
But let us b. — KENN 184:11
beginning As it was in the b. — BOOK 58:9
badly from the b. — STEV 303:27
begin at the b. — THOM 316:9
b., a middle — ARIS 14:15
b., a muddle — LARK 193:17
b. is often the end — ELIO 121:28
b. of an Amour — BEHN 27:19
b. of the end — TALL 308:24
b. of wisdom — BOOK 63:4
end of the b. — CHUR 91:20
In my b. is my end — ELIO 121:22
In my end is my b. — MARY 214:14
In the b. — BIBL 32:21
In the b. was the Word — BIBL 47:15
Movies should have a b. — GODA 142:10
told you from the b. — BIBL 40:10
beginnings ends by our b. know — DENH 108:15
begot thing b. — KYD 191:3
begotten b. by Despair — MARV 213:14
B., not made — BOOK 59:22
only b. of the Father — BIBL 47:21

beguile b. thy sorrow — SHAK 287:27
beguiled serpent b. me — BIBL 33:9
Beguine begin the B. — PORT 249:16
begun b. to fight — JONE 177:9
behaviour studies human b. — ROBB 257:16
behemoth Behold now b. — BIBL 37:15
behind b. your scenes — JOHN 174:17
Get thee b. me, Satan — BIBL 44:11
it will be b. me — REGE 255:14
let them go, B., before — DONN 113:18
no bosom and no b. — SMIT 298:4
those b. cried 'Forward!' — MACA 206:11
with a light b. her — GILB 141:10
behold B. an Israelite — BIBL 47:25
B. the man — BIBL 53:11
being avoiding b. — TILL 318:6
darkness of mere b. — JUNG 179:14
have our b. — BIBL 48:35
unbearable lightness of b. — KUND 191:2
Belfast be kind to B. — CRAI 102:18
belfry while owl in the b. — TENN 313:25
Belgium B. put the kibosh on the Kaiser — ELLE 123:18
Belial B., in act more graceful — MILT 221:17
sons Of B., flown with insolence — MILT 221:11
belief all b. is for it — JOHN 175:24
beliefs dust of exploded b. — MADA 209:2
believe b. in life — DU B 117:21
B. me, you who come after — HORA 164:12
b. what we choose — NEWM 233:8
Corrected *I b.* — KNOX 189:16
don't b. in fairies — BARR 25:14
fight for what I b. in — CAST 85:7
Firmly I b. — NEWM 233:5
he couldn't b. it — CUMM 104:16
I b. in God the Father — BOOK 58:16
If you b., clap your hands — BARR 25:16
I will not b. — BIBL 48:20
Lord, I b. — BIBL 45:29
ye will not b. — BIBL 47:29
believed b. in hope — BIBL 49:9
b. of any man — TARK 309:10
by all people b. — VINC 324:8
if b. during three days — MEDI 215:20
not seen, and yet have b. — BIBL 48:21
believer In a b.'s ear — NEWT 233:19
believers all b. — BOOK 58:12
Light half-b. in our casual creeds — ARNO 15:18
believeth He that b. on me — BIBL 47:32
whosoever b. in him — BIBL 47:28
believing b. something — LICH 199:1
stop b. in God — CHES 90:11
Belinda B. smiled — POPE 249:2
bell b. invites me — SHAK 280:6
Cuckoo-echoing, b.-swarmèd — HOPK 162:21
dinner b. — BYRO 78:27
for whom the b. tolls — DONN 114:19
sexton tolled the b. — HOOD 162:4
word is like a b. — KEAT 182:15
bella *B., horrida bella* — VIRG 324:19
Bellamy B.'s veal pies — PITT 245:15
belle b. dame sans merci — KEAT 181:9
j'étais b. — RONS 259:11
bellman fatal b. — SHAK 280:7
bells b. of Hell — ANON 9:4
b. ringeth to evensong — HAWE 153:9
floating many b. down — CUMM 104:13
From the b., bells, bells — POE 246:12
Like sweet b. jangled — SHAK 272:8
now ring the b. — WALP 327:19
Ring out, wild b. — TENN 311:29
ring the b. of Ecstasy — GINS 141:13
ring the b. of Heaven — HODG 160:11
bellyful Rumble thy b. — SHAK 277:19

belong b. not to you — GIBR 139:15
don't want to b. to any club — MARX 214:2
To betray, you must first b. — PHIL 244:13
beloved Cry, the b. country — PATO 242:4
how far to be b. — SHAK 268:12
man greatly b. — BIBL 41:11
My b. is mine — BIBL 39:5
This is my b. Son — BIBL 42:9
below above, between, b. — DONN 113:18
belt b. without hitting below it — ASQU 17:2
bend b. and I break not — LA F 191:14
right on round the b. — LAUD 194:6
bending always be a b. downwards — WHEW 333:3
beneath married b. me — ASTO 17:6
benedicite *B., omnia opera Domini* — BIBL 53:6
benedictus *B. qui venit* — MISS 224:4
benighted B. walks under the midday sun — MILT 219:12
poor b. 'eathen — KIPL 187:16
bent top of my b. — SHAK 272:19
bereft b. Of wet — HOPK 162:25
Berliner *Ich bin ein B.* — KENN 184:14
Bermoothes still-vexed B. — SHAK 287:4
Bermudas remote B. ride — MARV 213:12
berry made a better b. — BUTL 77:16
Bertie Burlington B. — HARG 152:8
beside b. thyself — BIBL 49:3
Christ b. me — PATR 242:5
best all the great b.-sellers — PRIT 251:12
bad in the b. of us — ANON 10:8
b. chosen language — AUST 19:19
b. in this kind — SHAK 283:23
b. is like the worst — KIPL 188:1
b. is the best — QUIL 253:7
b. is the enemy of the good — VOLT 326:3
b. is yet to be — BROW 71:3
b. of all possible worlds — BRAD 65:21
b. of all possible worlds — CABE 79:26
b. of all possible worlds — VOLT 325:20
b. rulers — LAO 193:5
b.-seller is the gilded tomb — SMIT 297:21
b. thing God invents — BROW 70:5
b. things in life are free — DE S 109:4
It was the b. of times — DICK 111:10
justest and b. — PLAT 246:1
past all prizing, b. — SOPH 299:10
poetry = the b. words — COLE 96:24
pursuing of the b. ends — HUTC 167:12
record of the b. — SHEL 294:5
Send forth the b. — KIPL 188:17
that is the b. — AUST 19:22
Whate'er is b. administered — POPE 248:18
bestow b. on every airth a limb — MONT 226:22
bestride b. the narrow world — SHAK 275:30
betake b. myself to that course — PEPY 243:17
Bethel O God of B. — DODD 113:14
Bethlehem But thou, B. — BIBL 41:16
little town of B. — BROO 68:5
Slouches towards B. — YEAT 343:20
Betjemanless We are now B. — EWAR 125:12
betray guts to b. my country — FORS 131:17
To b., you must first belong — PHIL 244:13
betrayed night that he was b. — BOOK 60:5
betrothed of my b. lady — MIDD 217:20
better appear the b. reason — MILT 221:17
B. by far you should forget — ROSS 260:13
b. day, the worse deed — HENR 156:17
b. man than I am — KIPL 187:19
better spared a b. man — SHAK 274:12
b. than a thousand — BOOK 62:12
b. than it sounds — NYE 235:8
b. the instruction — SHAK 282:14
b. to have loved and lost — TENN 311:18
Every day, I am getting b. — COUÉ 100:17

better (*cont.*)
Fail b. BECK 27:2
far, far b. thing DICK 111:11
for b. for worse BOOK 60:18
from worse to b. HOOK 162:9
from worse to b. JOHN 173:10
Gad! she'd b. CARL 83:4
He is not b. ANON 5:17
I took thee for thy b. SHAK 272:24
I was in a b. place SHAK 269:15
make a b. mouse-trap EMER 124:18
much b. than likely BRON 67:16
seemed a little b. IBSE 168:14
see the b. things OVID 238:15
We have seen b. days SHAK 287:23
between 'ouses in b. BATE 26:4
try to get b. them STRA 304:23
beware B., madam GRAV 146:4
B. my foolish heart WASH 328:25
B. of the dog PETR 244:9
B. the ides of March SHAK 275:29
bid you b. KIPL 188:4
bewildered Bewitched, bothered, and b. HART 152:17
to the utterly b. CAPP 82:1
bewitched B., bothered, and bewildered HART 152:17
bewrapt B. past knowing HARD 152:1
biases critic is a bundle of b. BALL 24:18
bibendum *Nunc est b.* HORA 164:9
Bible English B. MACA 205:22
have used the B. KING 187:1
read in de B. HEYW 158:19
starless and b.-black THOM 316:9
bicycle arrive by b. VIER 324:2
b.-pump the human heart AMIS 4:21
fish without a b. STEI 302:12
so is a b. repair kit CONN 98:24
bicycling old maids b. MAJO 209:23
bidder withstand the highest b. WASH 328:19
bien *mieux est l'ennemi du b.* VOLT 326:3
big b. enough to take away everything FORD 131:2
b. squadrons against the small BUSS 77:1
fall victim to a b. lie HITL 159:16
shining B.-Sea-Water LONG 202:3
bigamy B. is having ANON 6:4
bigger b. they are FITZ 129:12
biggest b. aspidistra in the world HARP 152:13
b. electric train set WELL 331:4
bigotry B. tries to keep truth TAGO 308:21
bike got on his b. TEBB 310:4
billabong swagman camped by a b. PATE 242:1
billboard lovely as a tree NASH 231:1
billet bullet has its b. WILL 336:4
billiards play b. well ROUP 261:9
billion b. dollar country FOST 132:3
billow Fierce was the wild b. ANAT 5:4
billows b. of enormous size PHIL 244:17
billy B., in one of his sashes GRAH 145:8
That's the way for B. HOGG 160:22
till his 'B.' boiled PATE 242:1
bind b. my hair HUNT 167:6
b. their kings in chains BOOK 63:29
b. the sweet influences BIBL 37:13
b. your sons to exile KIPL 188:17
binds b. to himself a joy BLAK 56:2
biographers picklocks of b. BENÉ 29:12
biographical noble and b. friend WETH 332:22
biography better part of b. STRA 305:1
B. is about Chaps BENT 30:7
Judas who writes the b. WILD 335:4
no history; only b. EMER 124:12
nothing but b. DISR 112:20
biological b. clock is ticking KEYE 185:7
biologist b. passes ROST 261:2

bird b.-haunted English lawn ARNO 15:9
b. of dawning SHAK 270:25
b. on the wing BOUL 65:6
B. thou never wert SHEL 293:29
Both man and b. COLE 96:18
cannot catch the b. of paradise KHRU 185:19
escaped even as a b. BOOK 63:16
immortal b. KEAT 182:14
It's a b. ANON 6:21
like a singing b. ROSS 260:10
only the note of a b. SIMP 296:4
rare b. on this earth JUVE 179:23
Shall I call thee b. WORD 341:15
sight of any b. BIBL 37:17
What b. so sings LYLY 204:23
why the caged b. sings DUNB 118:5
birdcage like a summer b. WEBS 330:15
birds b., and Prime Ministers BALD 23:9
b. are flown CHAR 87:19
B. build HOPK 163:7
b. got to fly HAMM 150:16
B. in their little nests agree WATT 329:8
b. of the air have nests BIBL 43:16
b. that are without despair WEBS 330:15
late the sweet b. sang SHAK 289:31
nest of singing b. JOHN 174:16
no b. sing KEAT 181:17
prisoned b. must find SASS 265:2
read about little b. TENN 314:4
singing of b. BIBL 39:4
sing like b. i' the cage SHAK 278:9
think caged b. sing WEBS 330:18
birdsong b. at morning STEV 303:31
Birmingham B. by way of Beachy Head CHES 89:25
no great hopes from B. AUST 19:17
When Jesus came to B. STUD 305:9
Birnam Great B. wood SHAK 281:10
birth b. is but a sleep WORD 340:10
flummery of a b. place KEAT 183:10
give b. astride of a grave BECK 27:1
not conscious of his b. LA B 191:8
one that is coming to b. O'SH 238:2
present at the b. ORTO 237:3
Rainbow gave thee b. DAVI 106:18
Saviour's b. is celebrated SHAK 270:25
birthday Happy b. to you HILL 159:4
birthright Esau selleth his b. BIBL 33:27
births tell of the b. RIMB 257:13
bis *B. dat qui cito dat* PUBL 251:22
biscuits hyacinths and b. SAND 264:11
bisexuality b. doubles your chances ALLE 4:9
bishop B. of Rome BOOK 64:5
make a b. kick a hole CHAN 87:4
No b., no King JAME 170:9
bishopric merit for a b. WEST 332:20
bit b. the babies BROW 70:26
Though he had b. me SHAK 278:5
bitch b.-goddess success JAME 171:4
Gaia is a tough b. MARG 211:17
old b. gone in the teeth POUN 250:10
bite b. some of my other generals GEOR 137:23
man recovered of the b. GOLD 143:16
bites dead woman b. not GRAY 146:10
biting b. the hand that lays GOLD 144:8
bitter be not b. against them BIBL 51:2
b. God to follow SWIN 307:26
b. herbs BIBL 34:6
b. tears to shed CORY 100:14
bitterness b. of his soul BIBL 41:24
bivouac b. of the dead O'HA 235:22
bizarre b. happening HAUG 153:7
Bizet Chopin and B. FISH 128:8
black art as b. as hell SHAK 290:12

b. against may	BUNT 72:19
b. and merciless things	JAME 170:16
b. as if bereaved of light	BLAK 56:9
b. black oxen	YEAT 342:16
b., but comely	BIBL 39:2
b. chaos comes again	SHAK 290:15
b. dog	JOHN 176:16
blacker than b.	TURN 320:22
B. Hills belong to me	SITT 296:10
B. it stood as night	MILT 221:22
b. majority rule	SMIT 297:19
b. men fought	MACA 205:11
B. Panther Party	NEWT 233:10
B. Widow, death	LOWE 203:23
devil damn thee b.	SHAK 281:19
growth of b. consciousness	BIKO 53:22
Just call me b.	GOLD 143:3
looking for a b. hat	BOWE 65:14
More b. than ashbuds	TENN 311:1
not b. and white	BOY 65:18
not have the colour b.	MAND 211:3
old b. magic	MERC 216:24
old b. ram	SHAK 284:8
rainbow which includes b.	YEVT 344:7
sad, b. isle	BAUD 26:8
so long as it is b.	FORD 131:5
Tip me the b. spot	STEV 303:22
Why do you wear b.	CHEK 88:32
with a b. skin	MALC 210:4
young, gifted and b.	HANS 151:4
Young, gifted and b.	IRVI 169:9
blackbird B. has spoken	FARJ 126:5
b. whistling	STEV 303:7
blackbirds B. are the cellos	STEV 303:14
blacker b. than black	TURN 320:22
blackguards intentions make b.	LACL 191:10
Blackpool famous seaside place called B.	EDGA 119:19
blacks poor are Europe's b.	CHAM 87:1
blade Steel-true and b.-straight	STEV 304:1
blame Bad women never take the b.	BROO 68:1
b. at night	POPE 248:5
b. the alien	AESC 2:24
manager who gets the b.	LINE 200:1
blameless Fearless, b. knight	ANON 11:11
flower of a b. life	TENN 311:3
blaming b. it on you	KIPL 187:20
blanch when counsellors b.	BACO 21:7
blandula Animula vagula b.	HADR 148:17
blank b., my lord	SHAK 288:21
political b. cheque	GOSC 144:20
blasphemies truths being as b.	SHAW 290:21
blasphemy b. against the Holy Ghost	BIBL 43:34
blast b.-beruffled plume	HARD 151:22
blasted b. with excess	GRAY 146:21
Upon this b. heath	SHAK 279:5
blatant B. beast men call	SPEN 300:21
bleak In the b. mid-winter	ROSS 260:12
bleed b. a while	BALL 24:6
do we not b.	SHAK 282:13
thorns of life! I b.	SHEL 293:8
bleeding b. piece of earth	SHAK 276:10
instead of b., he sings	GARD 136:3
bless B. 'em all	HUGH 166:7
B. the Lord	BIBL 53:6
b. ye the Lord	BOOK 58:15
God b. us every one	DICK 109:21
load and b. With fruit	KEAT 182:21
blessed B. are the poor	BIBL 42:14
B. are the pure in heart	KEBL 183:18
b. art thou among women	BIBL 45:32
B. be he that cometh	BOOK 63:11
b. be the name of the Lord	BIBL 36:37
b. damozel	ROSS 260:16

B. is the man	BOOK 62:11
Judge none b.	BIBL 41:25
more b. to give	BIBL 48:38
This b. plot	SHAK 285:13
blessing b. to the country	BISM 54:12
national b.	HAMI 150:13
Yet possessing every b.	EDME 119:23
blessings b. on the falling out	TENN 313:3
glass of b.	HERB 157:18
blest always to be b.	ARMS 14:24
always To be b.	POPE 248:10
B. pair of Sirens	MILT 219:9
b. that I lie on	ANON 8:17
blight b. man was born for	HOPK 163:5
Blighty back to dear old B.	MILL 218:20
blimp Colonel B.	LOW 203:11
blind accompany my being b.	PEPY 243:17
b. guides	BIBL 44:31
b. lead the blind	BIBL 44:7
b. led by the blind	UPAN 321:23
b. man in a dark room	BOWE 65:14
b. watchmaker	DAWK 107:1
country of the b.	ERAS 125:2
Cupid painted b.	SHAK 283:2
Grief for awhile is b.	SHEL 293:15
halt, and the b.	BIBL 46:27
Justice, though she's painted b.	BUTL 77:9
old, mad, b.	SHEL 293:26
religion without science is b.	EINS 120:11
right to be b. sometimes	NELS 232:7
splendid work for the b.	SASS 265:1
blindness 'eathen in 'is b.	KIPL 187:13
heathen in his b.	HEBE 155:2
Love comes from b.	BUSS 76:24
blinds drawing-down of b.	OWEN 238:23
blinked other fellow just b.	RUSK 262:6
blinking portrait of a b. idiot	SHAK 282:11
bliss B. goes but to a certain bound	GREV 147:11
b. or woe	MILT 222:20
B. was it in that dawn	WORD 339:21
men call domestic b.	PATM 242:3
Of b. on bliss	MILT 222:2
soul in b.	SHAK 278:6
Where ignorance is b.	GRAY 146:19
blithe b. Spirit	SHEL 293:29
buxom, b., and debonair	MILT 219:26
blitz b. of a boy is Timothy Winters	CAUS 86:4
blizzard walked to his death in a b.	ANON 7:8
block old b. itself	BURK 74:19
blockhead No man but a b.	JOHN 175:19
blocks hew b. with a razor	POPE 249:9
blond b. beast	NIET 234:11
blonde Being b. is definitely	MADO 209:5
b. to make a bishop kick	CHAN 87:4
blondes Gentlemen prefer b.	LOOS 202:14
blood b. and iron	BISM 54:18
b. be the price	KIPL 188:10
b. come gargling	OWEN 238:24
b. his blood	YEAT 342:12
b. is their argument	SHAK 275:2
b. Is very snow-broth	SHAK 281:28
b. of Christians is the seed	TERT 314:15
b. Of human sacrifice	MILT 221:10
b. of patriots	JEFF 171:13
b. on their hands	SPEN 300:5
B. sport brought	INGH 169:3
B., sweat, and tear-wrung	BYRO 77:22
b., toil, tears and sweat	CHUR 91:14
b. will have blood	SHAK 281:2
but with b.	BROW 68:14
Christ's b. streams	MARL 212:7
Deliver me from b.-guiltiness	BOOK 61:29
enough of b. and tears	RABI 253:16

blood (*cont.*)

flesh and b.	BIBL 50:23
flow of human b.	HUGH 166:9
foaming with much b.	POWE 250:23
for cooling the b.	FLAN 129:15
glories of our b. and state	SHIR 294:27
in b. Stepped in	SHAK 281:3
innocent of the b.	BIBL 45:19
I smell the b.	NASH 231:19
I smell the b.	SHAK 277:28
Man of B. was there	MACA 206:3
near in b.	SHAK 280:20
one glorious b.-red	BROW 70:10
on the b. of my men	LEE 196:15
raised to shed his b.	POPE 248:9
rather have b. on my hands	GREE 146:23
rivers of b.	JEFF 171:17
shall his b. be shed	BIBL 33:21
show business with b.	BRUN 71:20
so much b. in him	SHAK 281:15
Tiber foaming with much b.	VIRG 324:19
tincture in the b.	DEFO 107:18
voice of the child's b.	SWIN 308:3
waded thro' red b.	BALL 24:12
washed in the b. of the Lamb	LIND 199:16
wash this b. Clean	SHAK 280:12
white in the b. of the Lamb	BIBL 52:10
worked with my b.	KOLL 190:4
Young b. must have its course	KING 186:22
bloodhounds Seven b. followed	SHEL 293:5
bloodshed war without b.	MAO 211:11
bloody Abroad is b.	GEOR 138:10
b., bold, and resolute	SHAK 281:8
b., but unbowed	HENL 156:7
dark and b. ground	O'HA 235:23
have b. thoughts	SHAK 287:16
no right in the b. circus	MAXT 215:13
Not b. likely	SHAW 291:31
teach B. instructions	SHAK 279:20
under the b. past	AHER 3:4
What b. man	SHAK 278:27
bloom b. in the spring	GILB 140:19
How can ye b. sae fresh	BURN 75:8
hung with b.	HOUS 165:2
with the b. go I	ARNO 15:23
blooming grand to be b. well dead	SARO 264:20
bloomy all the b. beds	SMAR 297:2
blossom b. as the rose	BIBL 40:4
b. in the dust	SHIR 294:28
b. that hangs on the bough	SHAK 287:19
frothiest, blossomiest b.	POTT 249:27
hundred flowers b.	MAO 211:14
blossoms b., birds, and bowers	HERR 157:26
blot art to b.	POPE 248:28
b. on the escutcheon	GRAY 146:9
blotted b. a thousand	JONS 178:11
b. it out for ever	STER 302:24
blow Blow, b., thou winter wind	SHAK 269:25
B., bugle, blow	TENN 313:5
B. out, you bugles	BROO 67:19
B., winds, and crack	SHAK 277:18
not return your b.	SHAW 291:21
when will thou b.	ANON 10:18
bloweth wind b. where it listeth	BIBL 47:27
blowing answer is b. in the wind	DYLA 119:2
I'm forever b. bubbles	KENB 184:4
blown flower that once hath b.	FITZ 128:18
blows b. so red The rose	FITZ 128:17
blubbering b. Cabinet	GLAD 142:2
blue B. Bonnets are bound	SCOT 266:24
b. guitar	STEV 303:6
b. of the night	CROS 104:4
b. remembered hills	HOUS 165:7

B., silver-white	KEAT 182:17
Eyes of most unholy b.	MOOR 227:14
little tent of b.	WILD 335:15
yonder living b.	TENN 311:33
bluebell mary, ma Scotch B.	LAUD 194:7
bluebirds b. over the white cliffs	BURT 76:7
blueprints Genes not like a.	STEW 304:8
blunder frae mony a b. free us	BURN 75:29
it is a b.	BOUL 66:5
so grotesque a b.	BENT 30:8
blunders Nature's agreeable b.	COWL 101:17
blunt plain, b. man	SHAK 276:22
blush born to b. unseen	GRAY 146:16
blushed saw its God, and b.	CRAS 102:24
blushful b. Hippocrene	KEAT 182:11
board I struck the b.	HERB 157:9
There wasn't any B.	HERB 157:3
boast Such is the patriot's b.	GOLD 143:20
boat Architecture and a b.	PUGI 252:3
b. he can sail	THOM 317:14
if men are together in a b.	HALI 149:19
sank my b.	KENN 184:16
sewer in a glass-bottomed b.	MIZN 225:6
boathook diplomatic b.	SALI 263:19
boating Jolly b. weather	CORY 100:13
boats messing about in b.	GRAH 145:9
bobtail money on de b. nag	FOST 132:6
Boche well-killed B.	READ 254:19
bodies b. are buried in peace	BIBL 41:30
b. of those	EDWA 120:6
b. of unburied men	WEBS 330:17
One soul inhabiting two b.	ARIS 14:21
Pile the b. high	SAND 264:9
present your b.	BIBL 49:19
structure of our b.	STOP 304:12
bodkin With a bare b.	SHAK 272:2
body Absent in b.	BIBL 49:24
Africa than my own b.	ORTO 237:2
b. between your knees	CORY 100:13
b. Borne before her	THAC 315:1
b. continues in its state of rest	NEWT 233:11
b. is a machine	TOLS 318:16
b. of a weak and feeble woman	ELIZ 123:6
b. swayed to music	YEAT 342:11
commit his b. to the deep	BOOK 64:1
gigantic b.	MACA 205:13
Gin a body meet a b.	BURN 75:8
in a sound b.	JUVE 180:4
in mind, b., or estate	BOOK 59:10
interpose my b.	STRA 304:23
John Brown's b.	ANON 8:4
Marry my b. to that dust	KING 186:6
my useless b.	BROW 68:12
no b. to be kicked	THUR 318:2
Of the glorious B. sing	THOM 315:22
rid of the rest of her b.	VANB 322:10
sing the b. electric	WHIT 333:19
so young a b.	SHAK 282:19
this is my b.	BIBL 45:13
with my b. I thee worship	BOOK 60:19
Boets hate all B. and Bainters	GEOR 137:21
Bognor Bugger B.	GEOR 138:7
boilers b. and vats	JOHN 176:8
bois au fond du b.	VIGN 324:3
Nous n'irons plus aux b.	ANON 11:18
bold Be b., be bold	SPEN 300:17
b. as a hawk	LOVE 203:10
b. as a hawk	THUR 318:1
b. as a lion	BIBL 38:7
Fortune assists the b.	VIRG 325:5
This b. bad man	SHAK 275:21
boldly to b. go	RODD 258:18
boldness B., and again boldness	DANT 106:1

B. be my friend — SHAK 270:17
what first? b. — BACO 21:6
Bolingbroke this canker, B. — SHAK 273:27
bolt b., and the breech — REED 255:9
bomb atom b. is a paper tiger — MAO 211:13
b. them back into the Stone Age — LEMA 197:1
bombed glad we've been b. — ELIZ 123:16
bomber b. will always get through — BALD 23:10
bombers b. named for girls — JARR 171:6
bombs Come, friendly b. — BETJ 32:2
bond look to his b. — SHAK 282:12
take a b. of fate — SHAK 281:9
bondage b. of rhyming — MILT 220:32
b. to parents — WOLL 338:24
bonding male b. — TIGE 318:5
bondman so base that would be a b. — SHAK 276:14
bonds surly b. of earth — MAGE 209:8
surly b. of earth — REAG 255:3
bone B. of my bone — MILT 222:20
B. of my bones — BIBL 33:4
hair about the b. — DONN 114:10
rag and a b. — KIPL 188:13
boneless b. wonder — CHUR 91:11
bones b. of a single Pomeranian — BISM 54:15
b. of one British Grenadier — HARR 152:14
Can these b. live — BIBL 41:5
conjuring trick with b. — JENK 171:20
dead men lost their b. — ELIO 122:24
England keep my b. — SHAK 277:3
from my dead b., avenger — VIRG 324:17
he that moves my b. — SHAK 290:17
lay my b. amongst you — WOLS 338:25
O ye dry b. — BIBL 41:6
Rattle his b. — NOEL 234:19
tongs and the b. — SHAK 283:20
valley full of b. — BIBL 41:4
bonfire b. of the vanities — WOLF 338:18
bonjour B. tristesse — ÉLUA 124:6
bon-mots b. from their places — MORE 227:23
bonnets Blue B. are bound — SCOT 266:24
b. of Bonny Dundee — SCOT 266:6
bonny Am I no a b. fighter — STEV 303:15
bonnets of B. Dundee — SCOT 266:6
b., bonnie banks — ANON 9:9
saw ye b. Lesley — BURN 75:7
bono Cui b. — CICE 93:1
bonum Summum b. — CICE 92:24
Boojum Snark was a B. — CARR 84:16
book agree with the b. of God — OMAR 236:7
b. is the precious life-blood — MILT 223:14
B. of Life begins — WILD 335:12
B. wherein is no doubt — KORA 190:6
but his b. — JONS 178:3
Camerado, this is no b. — WHIT 333:23
damned, thick, square b. — GLOU 142:8
Farewel my b. — CHAU 88:22
Go, litel b. — CHAU 88:28
Go, little b. — STEV 304:5
great b. — CALL 80:11
I'll drown my b. — SHAK 287:18
knows this out of the b. — DICK 110:23
leaves of the Judgement B. unfold — TAYL 309:22
look at the best b. — RUSK 262:13
noble grand b. — GASK 136:18
no Frigate like a B. — DICK 111:13
oldest rule in the b. — CARR 84:1
read a b. before reviewing it — SMIT 298:13
sent down to thee the B. — KORA 190:17
substance of a b. directly — KNOW 189:14
this b. I directe To the — CHAU 88:30
throw the b. in the fire — SAND 264:5
throw this b. about — BELL 28:6
to every b. its copy — COLU 97:17

use of a b. — CARR 83:13
when I wrote that b. — SWIF 307:12
without mentioning a single b. — REED 255:12
writing a b. — BRON 67:16
wrote the b. — LINC 199:14
Your face, my thane, is as a b. — SHAK 279:16
books b. are divisible — RUSK 262:12
b. are either dreams or swords — LOWE 203:14
B. are made — FLAU 129:20
b. are to be tasted — BACO 21:26
B. are well written — WILD 335:8
B. do furnish a room — POWE 250:17
B. from Boots' and country lanes — BETJ 31:22
b. I leave behind — KIPL 187:7
B. say: she did this because — BARN 25:8
b., the academes — SHAK 278:19
b. to gather facts from — CARL 83:3
b. undeservedly forgotten — AUDE 18:22
B. will speak plain — BACO 21:7
borrowers of b. — LAMB 192:3
collection of b. — CARL 82:22
cream of others' b. — MORE 227:23
Deep-versed in b. — MILT 222:30
God has written all the b. — BUTL 77:12
his b. were read — BELL 28:24
I never read b. — PUNC 252:16
Keeping b. on charity — PERÓ 244:1
making many b. — BIBL 38:35
more in woods than b. — BERN 31:5
proper study of mankind is b. — HUXL 167:14
quiet, friendship, b. — THOM 317:10
read all the b. — MALL 210:5
read b. *through* — JOHN 175:10
so charming as b. — SMIT 298:9
thumb each other's b. — RUSK 262:9
to Cambridge b. he sent — BROW 69:11
Wherever b. will be burned — HEIN 155:7
boot b. in the face — PLAT 245:19
B., saddle, to horse — BROW 69:23
b. stamping on a human face — ORWE 237:18
bootboy body of the b. at Claridges — WOOL 339:9
booted b. and spurred — RUMB 261:20
boots Books from B.' and country lanes — BETJ 31:22
boots—b.—movin' — KIPL 187:9
doormat in a world of b. — RHYS 256:12
in his top-b. — MARL 212:2
truth is pulling its b. on — SPUR 301:6
boozes tell a man who "b." — BURT 76:5
Borden Lizzie B. took an axe — ANON 8:10
border B., nor Breed — KIPL 187:8
bound for the B. — SCOT 266:24
crossing the B. — AUDE 18:11
gaed o'er the B. — BURN 75:7
borders b. of sleep — THOM 316:15
bore Less is a b. — VENT 323:9
bored I'd get b. and fall over — COMP 98:1
born blight man was b. for — HOPK 163:5
b. free — ANON 5:15
B. in a cellar — FOOT 130:22
B. in the USA — SPRI 301:4
b. of a woman — BIBL 37:6
B. of the sun — SPEN 300:10
B. of the Virgin Mary — BOOK 58:16
b. out of due time — BIBL 50:1
b. out of my due time — MORR 228:17
b. to run — SPRI 301:5
b. to set it right — SHAK 271:24
b. under a rhyming planet — SHAK 284:6
b. where my fathers lived — SITT 296:9
Every moment one is b. — TENN 314:2
for being b. — WATS 328:27
had not been b. — BIBL 45:12
house where I was b. — HOOD 162:5

born (*cont.*)
I am not yet b. — MACN 208:19
I was free b. — BIBL 48:40
Man is b. to live — PAST 241:20
Man is b. unto trouble — BIBL 37:5
Man that is b. of a woman — BOOK 60:23
Man was b. free — ROUS 261:11
Not to be b. — BACO 22:8
Not to be b. — SOPH 299:10
not to be b. is best — AUDE 17:28
One is not b. a woman — DE B 107:8
some men are b. great — SHAK 288:23
sucker b. every minute — BARN 25:12
time to be b. — BIBL 38:16
took the trouble to be b. — BEAU 26:13
to the manner b. — SHAK 271:12
under that was I b. — SHAK 283:27
unto us a child is b. — BIBL 39:19
We were not b. to sue — SHAK 285:8
When we are b. — SHAK 278:4
wherein I was b. — BIBL 37:2
borne It is b. in upon me — HARE 152:7
Still have I b. it — SHAK 282:6
borogoves mimsy were the b. — CARR 84:3
borrow have to b. the money — WARD 328:9
borrower b., nor a lender be — SHAK 271:8
b. of the night — SHAK 280:22
borrowers b. of books — LAMB 192:3
borrowing b. only lingers — SHAK 274:17
bosom b. of a single state — DURH 118:15
Close b.-friend — KEAT 182:21
in Arthur's b. — SHAK 274:31
no b. and no behind — SMIT 298:4
slip Into my b. — TENN 313:16
bosoms white b. — JOHN 174:17
bossy by the b. for the bully — SELD 267:14
Boston B. man is the east wind — APPL 13:14
good old B. — BOSS 64:18
Botany Bay New colonies seek for at B. — FREE 133:16
botch make a b. — BELL 28:23
bother young whom I hope to b. — AUDE 18:19
bothered Bewitched, b., and bewildered — HART 152:17
bottle bothers to buy a b. — DWOR 118:18
b. it and sell it — MCDO 207:8
way out of the b.-bottle — WITT 337:20
bottles fill with banknotes — KEYN 185:11
new wine into old b. — BIBL 43:21
bottom fairies at the b. of our garden — FYLE 135:4
forgotten man at the b. — ROOS 259:13
bottomless Law is a b. pit — ARBU 13:21
pit that is b. — JAME 170:8
boue *nostalgie de la b.* — AUGI 18:25
bough bloom along the b. — HOUS 165:2
bread beneath the b. — FITZ 128:15
boundary right to fix the b. — PARN 241:10
bounded b. in a nut-shell — SHAK 271:30
bounden b. duty — BOOK 60:3
bountiful My Lady b. — FARQ 126:10
bouquet b. is better than the taste — POTT 250:3
bourgeois astonish the b. — BAUD 26:9
b. climb up on them — FLAU 129:20
bourgeoisie b. in the long run — TROT 320:2
bourn see beyond our b. — KEAT 182:24
set a b. how far — SHAK 268:12
bourne b. of time and place — TENN 310:19
bow B. down before him — MONS 225:23
b. myself — BIBL 36:25
b. of burning gold — BLAK 55:27
drew a b. at a venture — BIBL 36:18
every knee should b. — BIBL 50:24
set my b. in the cloud — BIBL 33:22
bowels in the b. of Christ — CROM 103:18
bower lime-tree b. my prison — COLE 96:20

bowl golden b. be broken — BIBL 38:34
Morning in the b. of night — FITZ 128:14
bows B. down to wood and stone — HEBE 155:2
bow windows putting b. to the house — DICK 110:2
bow-wow Big B. strain — SCOT 266:27
his b. way — PEMB 243:7
box b. where sweets lie — HERB 157:22
twelve good men into a b. — BROU 68:8
boxes Little b. on the hillside — REYN 256:7
boxing B.'s just showbusiness — BRUN 71:20
boy Alas, pitiable b. — VIRG 325:1
any b. may become President — STEV 303:10
Being read to by a b. — ELIO 122:1
b. brought in the white sheet — GARC 135:21
b. my greatness — SHAK 269:4
b. on the sea-shore — NEWT 233:15
b. stood on the burning deck — HEMA 155:17
b. will ruin himself — GEOR 138:5
Chatterton, the marvellous b. — WORD 340:25
Let the b. win — EDWA 120:2
little tiny b. — SHAK 288:33
Mad about the b. — COWA 101:6
Minstrel B. to the war — MOOR 227:17
remain a fifteen-year-old b. — ROTH 261:5
sat the journeying b. — HARD 152:1
schoolrooms for 'the b.' — COOK 99:19
Upon the growing b. — WORD 340:10
boyfriend best way to obtain b. — FIEL 127:10
certain thing called the B. — WILS 337:2
boyhood b. of Judas — Æ 2:22
boys As flies to wanton b. — SHAK 277:30
b. in the back room — LOES 201:12
b. in the back rooms — BEAV 26:16
b. of the old Brigade — WEAT 329:25
Christian b. — ARNO 16:7
Deceive b. with toys — LYSA 205:3
for office b. — SALI 263:22
lightfoot b. are laid — HOUS 165:9
send American b. — JOHN 173:4
three merry b. are we — FLET 130:6
Till the b. come home — FORD 131:9
bracelet b. of bright hair — DONN 114:10
bracket date slides into the b. — EWAR 125:12
braes among thy green b. — BURN 75:3
Ye banks and b. — BURN 75:6
braids b. of lilies knitting — MILT 219:18
brain Bear of Very Little B. — MILN 218:25
b. has the consistency — TURI 320:19
dry b. in a dry season — ELIO 122:3
harmful to the b. — JAME 170:8
petrifactions of a plodding b. — BYRO 79:9
schoolmasters puzzle their b. — GOLD 143:26
brains mix them with my b. — OPIE 236:15
branch b. shall grow — BIBL 39:21
on the high b. — SAPP 264:18
branchy b. between towers — HOPK 162:21
brandy B. for the parson — KIPL 188:9
b. of the damned — SHAW 291:11
drink b. — JOHN 176:3
get me a glass of b. — GEOR 138:1
brass evil manners live in b. — SHAK 275:27
brat spurious b., Tom Jones — RICH 256:22
brave b. bad man — CLAR 93:14
Fortune assists the b. — TERE 314:8
Fortune favours the b. — VIRG 325:5
home of the b. — KEY 185:6
How sleep the b. — COLL 97:11
None but the b. — DRYD 116:23
O b. new world — SHAK 287:20
Oh, the b. music — FITZ 128:16
Toll for the b. — COWP 101:25
to-morrow to be b. — ARMS 14:25
braver done one b. thing — DONN 114:14

braw b. bricht moonlicht	MORR 228:22
Brazil Charley's aunt from B.	THOM 316:1
Brazilian If I were a B.	STIN 304:9
breach More honoured in the b.	SHAK 271:12
Once more unto the b.	SHAK 274:33
bread b. and circuses	JUVE 180:3
b. beneath the bough	FITZ 128:15
b. of adversity	BIBL 40:1
b. of affliction	BIBL 36:17
B. of heaven	WILL 336:6
b. of poverty	HAGG 148:18
b.-sauce of the happy ending	JAME 170:22
Cast thy b. upon the waters	BIBL 38:31
cutting b. and butter	THAC 314:27
eat dusty b.	BOGA 57:7
I am the b. of life	BIBL 47:31
if his son ask b.	BIBL 43:6
live by b. alone	BIBL 42:10
one half-pennyworth of b.	SHAK 274:2
our daily b.	BIBL 42:23
Royal slice of b.	MILN 219:2
shalt thou eat b.	BIBL 33:12
taste of another man's b.	DANT 105:21
took B.	BOOK 60:5
took b., and blessed it	BIBL 45:13
unleavened b.	BIBL 34:6
we did eat b.	BIBL 34:11
break bend and I b. not	LA F 191:14
B., break, break	TENN 310:11
But b., my heart	SHAK 271:1
if you b. the bloody glass	MACN 208:17
lark at b. of day	SHAK 289:26
Never give a sucker an even b.	FIEL 127:19
shall he not b.	BIBL 40:12
breakdown approaching nervous b.	RUSS 262:19
Madness need not be all b.	LAIN 191:22
breakfast committed b. with it	LEWI 198:14
critical period is b.-time	HERB 157:6
impossible things before b.	CARR 84:9
breakfasted b. with you	BRUC 71:15
breaking b. of windows	MORE 227:22
breast b. high amid the corn	HOOD 162:6
broods with warm b.	HOPK 162:23
parts of the b.	BYRD 77:18
sooth a savage b.	CONG 98:13
weariness May toss him to My b.	HERB 157:19
breastie panic's in thy b.	BURN 75:30
breasts b. by which France is fed	SULL 305:18
breath Breathe on me, B. of God	HATC 153:5
drawn the b. of life	YEAT 342:24
every thing that hath b.	BOOK 63:30
having lost her b., she spoke	SHAK 268:19
last b. of Julius Caesar	JEAN 171:9
love thee with the b.	BROW 69:15
sweeter woman ne'er drew b.	INGE 169:1
thou no b. at all	SHAK 278:14
breathe B. on me, Breath of God	HATC 153:5
summer's morn to b.	MILT 222:15
yearning to b. free	LAZA 195:2
breathes B. there the man	SCOT 266:10
breathless b. hush in the Close	NEWB 232:20
bred B. en bawn in a brier-patch	HARR 152:15
Bredon In summertime on B.	HOUS 165:4
breed Border, nor B.	KIPL 187:8
b. of their horses	PENN 243:10
breeding without any b.	THUR 317:27
breeze dancing in the b.	WORD 340:1
breezes b. dusk and shiver	TENN 312:3
breezy B., Sneezy, Freezy	ELLI 124:1
brekekekex B. koax koax	ARIS 14:11
brethren Dearly beloved b.	BOOK 58:4
least of these my b.	BIBL 45:10
brevis Ars longa, vita b.	HIPP 159:11

B. esse laboro	HORA 163:12
brevity B. is the sister	CHEK 89:2
B. is the soul of wit	SHAK 271:25
bribe cannot hope to b. or twist	WOLF 338:13
bricht braw b. moonlicht	MORR 228:22
brick carried a piece of b.	SWIF 306:18
'Eave arf a b. at 'im	PUNC 252:10
Follow the yellow b. road	HARB 151:10
Goodbye yellow b. road	JOHN 172:19
inherited it b.	AUGU 19:9
paved with yellow b.	BAUM 26:10
threw it a b. at a time	HARG 152:9
bride barren b.	POPE 247:13
encounter darkness as a b.	SHAK 281:32
Never the blushing b.	LEIG 196:24
unravished b. of quietness	KEAT 181:27
bridegroom Like a b.	AYTO 20:13
bridegrooms Of b., brides	HERR 157:26
brides of Enderby	INGE 168:23
Of bride-grooms, b.	HERR 157:26
bridesmaid always the b.	LEIG 196:24
bridge Beautiful Railway B.	MCGO 207:10
b. over troubled water	SIMO 295:24
going a b. too far	BROW 69:16
keep the b. with me	MACA 206:8
On the B. of Toome	CARB 82:3
brief little b. authority	SHAK 281:30
strive to be b.	HORA 163:12
brier bawn in a b.-patch	HARR 152:15
briers O, how full of b.	SHAK 269:13
brigade boys of the old B.	WEAT 329:25
bright All things b. and beautiful	ALEX 3:16
Behold the b. original	GAY 137:9
b. and fierce and fickle	TENN 313:9
B. as the day	GRAN 146:30
b. day is done	SHAK 269:3
b. day that brings forth	SHAK 276:3
b. particular star	SHAK 268:9
B. the vision	MANT 211:10
dark and b.	BYRO 79:14
Death's b. angel	PROC 251:14
excessive b.	MILT 221:27
Keep up your b. swords	SHAK 284:10
look, the land is b.	CLOU 95:5
quick b. things	SHAK 283:1
thought thee b.	SHAK 290:12
torches to burn b.	SHAK 286:16
Tyger, burning b.	BLAK 56:14
young lady named B.	BULL 72:9
brightest B. and best	HEBE 154:19
brightness B. falls from the air	NASH 231:20
Brighton B. Pavilion looks as if	SMIT 298:12
brilliance Renew your b.	GRAC 145:4
brillig 'Twas b.	CARR 84:3
brim winking at the b.	KEAT 182:11
bring B. me my arrows of desire	BLAK 55:27
bringing b. me up by hand	DICK 110:14
brink walked to the b.	DULL 117:25
brinkmanship boasting of his b.	STEV 303:12
brioche mangent de la b.	MARI 211:18
Britain B. a fit country	LLOY 200:20
B. will be honoured by historians	HARL 152:11
B. will still be	MAJO 209:23
speak for B.	BOOT 64:10
When B. first	THOM 317:8
Britannia Rule, B.	THOM 317:8
shouted 'Rule B.'	KIPL 187:5
think of Cool B.	BENN 29:18
British as the B. public	MACA 205:15
blood of a B. man	SHAK 277:28
bones of one B. Grenadier	HARR 152:14
B. female	CLOU 94:20
B. Grenadier	ANON 9:22

British (*cont.*)
drunken officer of B. rule — WALC 326:16
thank God! the B. journalist — WOLF 338:13
Briton free-born B. can — THAC 314:20
glory in the name of B. — GEOR 137:24
No good man is a B. — AUSO 19:15
Britons B. never will be slaves — THOM 317:8
broad b. is the way — BIBL 43:8
how b. and far — JOHN 177:4
too b. for leaping — HOUS 165:9
broadens travel b. the mind; but — CHES 90:6
broccoli b., dear — WHIT 333:8
broken bats have been b. — HOWE 165:13
Can it be b. — JENK 171:21
house has been b. open — PEAC 242:12
Morning has b. — FARJ 126:5
not quickly b. — BIBL 38:19
taken up the b. blade — DE G 107:24
broker honest b. — BISM 54:17
bronze monument more lasting than b. — HORA 164:16
noontide was b. — CHUR 92:9
brooches b. and toys — STEV 303:31
brood b. of folly — MILT 219:20
broods b. with warm breast — HOPK 162:23
brook grows aslant a b. — SHAK 273:8
brooks By b. too broad — HOUS 165:9
broom sent with b. before — SHAK 283:25
brothel intellectual b. — TOLS 318:17
metaphysical b. for the emotions — KOES 189:21
brothels b. with bricks of religion — BLAK 55:24
brother Be my b. — CHAM 87:2
BIG B. IS WATCHING YOU — ORWE 237:14
B. can you spare a dime — HARB 151:7
b., hail, and farewell — CATU 86:3
B. of the Angle — WALT 328:3
b. sin against me — BIBL 44:17
B. to Death — DANI 105:14
b. to dragons — BIBL 37:12
closer than a b. — BIBL 37:37
dear b. here departed — BOOK 60:25
Death and his b. — SHEL 293:20
especially Sir B. Sun — FRAN 133:2
hateth his b. — BIBL 51:35
man and a b. — WEDG 330:21
my b. is a hairy man — BIBL 33:28
my b. Jonathan — BIBL 35:29
my b.'s keeper — BIBL 33:14
my likeness—my b. — BAUD 26:6
want to be the white man's b. — KING 186:8
brotherhood crown thy good with b. — BATE 26:5
Love the b. — BIBL 51:27
sit down at the table of b. — KING 186:11
brothers all the b. too — SHAK 288:22
So the two b. — KEAT 181:14
we band of b. — SHAK 275:11
brow b. of labour — BRYA 71:22
with a velvet b. — SHAK 278:18
Your bonny b. was brent — BURN 75:14
brown b. coat — MACA 205:13
falling on the city b. — BRID 66:19
Jeanie with the light b. hair — FOST 132:7
John B.'s body — ANON 8:4
river Is a strong b. god — ELIO 121:26
Browning God and Robert B. — BROW 71:13
Hang it all, Robert B. — POUN 250:7
safety-catch of my B. — JOHS 177:6
brows pallor of girls' b. — OWEN 238:23
browsing b. and sluicing — WODE 338:6
bruise It shall b. thy head — BIBL 33:10
bruised b. reed — BIBL 36:33
b. reed — BIBL 40:12
brush so fine a b. — AUST 20:3
with my b. I make love — RENO 255:18

brutal heart's grown b. from the fare — YEAT 343:10
brutality without art is b. — RUSK 262:8
brute Et tu, B.? — SHAK 276:8
Feed the b. — PUNC 252:17
heart of a b. like you — PLAT 245:19
like b. beasts — BOOK 60:15
brutish nasty, b., and short — HOBB 160:3
Brutus B. is an honourable man — SHAK 276:16
You too, B. — CAES 80:4
bubble mostly froth and b. — GORD 144:16
Seeking the b. reputation — SHAK 269:22
world's a b. — BACO 22:7
bubbles I'm forever blowing b. — KENB 184:4
With beaded b. — KEAT 182:11
Bücher wo man B. Verbrennt — HEIN 155:7
buck b. stops here — TRUM 320:10
bucket stick inside a swill b. — ORWE 237:23
Buckingham so much for B. — CIBB 92:19
Buckingham Palace changing guard at B. — MILN 218:26
bud be a b. again — KEAT 181:7
nip him in the b. — ROCH 258:8
Buddhahood speedily gain B. — TANT 309:9
buds darling b. of May — SHAK 289:23
buffalo breath of a b. — CROW 104:9
bugger B. Bognor — GEOR 138:7
bugle Blow, b., blow — TENN 313:5
bugles Blow out, you b. — BROO 67:19
b. calling from sad shires — OWEN 238:22
build Birds b. — HOPK 163:7
b. the house of death — MONT 226:8
easy to b. — IBSE 168:13
Lord b. the house — BOOK 63:18
think we b. for ever — RUSK 262:15
building principal beauty in b. — FULL 134:27
very old b. — OSBO 237:25
built not what they b. — FENT 126:19
Till we have b. Jerusalem — BLAK 55:27
bulimia yuppie version of b. — EHRE 120:8
bull Cock and a B. — STER 303:1
Dance tiptoe, b. — BUNT 72:19
bullet b. has its billet — WILL 336:4
b. through his head — ROBI 258:3
b. through his heart — THAC 314:23
stronger than the b. — LINC 199:5
bullets bloody b. — LINC 199:5
b. made of platinum — BELL 28:7
bully by the bossy for the b. — SELD 267:14
love the lovely b. — SHAK 274:36
such a b. pulpit — ROOS 260:6
bulwark floating b. of the island — BLAC 55:3
bum Indicat Motorem B. — GODL 142:11
bump go b. in the night — ANON 7:1
Buncombe talking to B. — WALK 326:23
through reporters to B. — CARL 82:23
bungler good nature is a b. — HALI 150:6
bunk History more or less b. — FORD 131:6
burden bear any b. — KENN 184:8
borne the b. — BIBL 44:23
b. of them is intolerable — BOOK 59:27
my b. is light — BIBL 43:32
White Man's B. — KIPL 188:17
bureaucracy [b.'s] specific invention — WEBE 330:3
bureaucrats Guidelines for b. — BORE 64:12
burghers b. of Carlisle — MACA 206:2
burgundy naive domestic B. — THUR 317:27
burial b.-ground God's-Acre — LONG 201:24
buried all b. here — BRON 67:11
bodies are b. in peace — BIBL 41:30
b. at midnight — O'BR 235:12
b. him darkly — WOLF 338:11
b. in so sweet a place — SHEL 292:13
b. in the rain — MILL 218:10
when they b. him — TENN 310:23

where some b. Caesar bled   FITZ 128:17
Burlington B. Bertie   HARG 152:8
burn another Troy for her to b.   YEAT 343:12
   better to b. out   YOUN 344:21
   better to marry than to b.   BIBL 49:26
   b. always with this hard, gemlike   PATE 241:25
   b. its children to save   MEYE 217:17
   sun shall not b. thee   BOOK 63:13
burned Alexandria's library b.   HUGH 166:11
   B. on the water   SHAK 268:17
   b. women   BRAN 66:2
   bush b. with fire   BIBL 33:39
   men also, in the end, are b.   HEIN 155:7
burning boy stood on the b. deck   HEMA 155:17
   b. fiery furnace   BIBL 41:7
   b. of the leaves   BINY 54:5
   b. roof and tower   YEAT 343:8
   b. the rain forest   STIN 304:9
   Keep the Home-fires b.   FORD 131:9
   lady's not for b.   FRY 134:18
   out of the b.   BIBL 41:15
   pretty Babe all b.   SOUT 299:21
   Tyger, b. bright   BLAK 56:14
burnished Furnish'd and b.   BETJ 32:3
   like a b. throne   ELIO 122:22
burns candle b. at both ends   MILL 218:8
burps History just b.   BARN 25:9
bury B. my heart at Wounded Knee   BENÉ 29:11
   dead b. their dead   BIBL 43:17
   physician can b. his mistakes   WRIG 341:26
   We will b. you   KHRU 185:18
bus Can it be a Motor B.   GODL 142:11
   missed the b.   CHAM 86:22
   not even a b., I'm a tram   HARE 152:7
bush Behold, the b. burned   BIBL 33:39
   Thorough b., thorough brier   SHAK 283:6
bushel neither under a b.   BIBL 46:20
bushmen they were not b.   HEAD 154:7
business about my Father's b.   BIBL 46:8
   Being good in b.   WARH 328:13
   b. as usual   THAT 315:9
   B. carried on as usual   CHUR 91:8
   B. first   THAC 314:18
   b. like show business   BERL 30:20
   b. practices improve   RODD 258:20
   do b. together   THAT 315:10
   go to my pleasure, b.   WYCH 342:3
   growth of a large b.   ROCK 258:17
   heart in the b.   WATS 329:1
   How to succeed in b.   MEAD 215:17
   In civil b.   BACO 21:6
   it is your b.   HORA 164:1
   it spoils b.   OTWA 238:9
   Liberty is unfinished b.   ANON 8:6
   occupy their b.   BOOK 63:1
   of the American people is b.   COOL 99:21
   spring of b.   BAGE 22:11
   totter on in b.   POPE 247:25
businessmen well-placed b. decide   YOUN 344:9
Buss Miss B. and Miss Beale   ANON 8:19
bust b. survives the city   GAUT 136:20
buste Le B. Survit à la cité   GAUT 136:20
busting June is b. out   HAMM 150:19
bustle B. in a House   DICK 111:14
busy B. old fool   DONN 114:12
   Government of the b.   SELD 267:14
   had a b. day   SIGL 295:18
   how b. I must be   ASTL 17:5
butcher Hog B. for the World   SAND 264:7
butchered B. to make a Roman holiday   BYRO 78:6
butchers gentle with these b.   SHAK 276:10
   shepherds and b.   VOLT 326:8
butler b.'s upper slopes   WODE 338:7

butt here is my b.   SHAK 285:3
   knocks you down with the b.   GOLD 144:5
butter B. and eggs   CALV 80:13
   B. and honey   BIBL 39:17
   b. for the Royal slice of bread   MILN 219:2
   cutting bread and b.   THAC 314:27
   manage without b.   GOEB 142:12
   no money for b.   JOSE 178:16
   rather have b. or guns   GOER 142:14
   She brought forth b.   BIBL 35:3
buttercup I'm called Little B.   GILB 140:28
buttercups B. and daisies   HOWI 165:20
buttered always on the b. side   PAYN 242:9
butterflies Frogs eat B.   STEV 303:4
butterfly breaks a b.   POPE 247:11
   b. dreaming that   CHUA 90:21
   b. upon the road   KIPL 188:3
   flap of a b.'s wings   LORE 202:16
   Float like a b.   ALI 4:5
   You, the b.   BASH 26:3
buttock boiling his b.   AUBR 17:16
buttocks chair that fits all b.   SHAK 268:10
   gorgeous b. of the ape   HUXL 167:18
button each b., hook, and lace   LOWE 203:13
   little round b. at top   FOOT 130:23
butts b. me away   SHAK 270:13
butty oul' b. o' mine   O'CA 235:17
buxom b., blithe, and debonair   MILT 219:26
buy b. it like an honest man   NORT 234:22
   I will b. with you   SHAK 282:3
   money can't b. me love   LENN 197:10
   no man might b. or sell   BIBL 52:15
buyer b. can be found   SALL 264:1
buys b. everything   MONT 226:4
buzz B.! Buzz! Buzz!   MILN 219:4
by B. and by   MCCO 207:1
bymatter been a b.   BACO 21:8
Byronic think all poets were B.   COPE 99:25
byword b. among all people   BIBL 36:1
   story and a b.   WINT 337:16
Byzantium holy city of B.   YEAT 343:18

C

ça Ç. ira   ANON 11:9
cabbage c.-leaf to make an apple-pie   FOOT 130:23
   c. with a college education   TWAI 321:10
cabbages Of c.—and kings   CARR 84:6
   planting my c.   MONT 226:7
cabin Make me a willow c.   SHAK 288:9
cabined c., cribbed, confined   SHAK 280:27
cabinet another to mislead the C.   ASQU 16:20
   blubbering C.   GLAD 142:2
   group of C. Ministers   CURZ 105:8
cable little c. cars climb   CROS 104:5
   of c. television   MACK 207:18
Cabots Lowells talk to the C.   BOSS 64:18
   C.'s wife   CURZ 105:8
cacoethes Scribendi c.   JUVE 180:1
cad Cocoa is a c. and coward   CHES 90:1
cadence harsh c. of a rugged line   DRYD 117:11
Cadiz reeking into C. Bay   BROW 70:10
Caesar appeal unto C.   BIBL 49:1
   Aut C., aut nihil   BORG 64:15
   Ave C., morituri te salutant   ANON 12:8
   C.'s laurel crown   BLAK 55:14
   C.'s public policy   PLUT 246:9
   decree from C. Augustus   BIBL 46:2
   Hail C.   ANON 12:8
   Here was a C.   SHAK 276:24
   Imperious C., dead   SHAK 273:12

Caesar (*cont.*)
loved C. less   SHAK 276:12
Render unto C.   BIBL 44:27
unto C. shalt thou go   BIBL 49:2
where some buried C. bled   FITZ 128:17
Caesars C. and Napoleons   HUXL 167:16
cage Nor iron bars a c.   LOVE 203:6
red breast in a c.   BLAK 55:12
sing like birds i' the c.   SHAK 278:9
caged think c. birds sing   WEBS 330:18
why the c. bird sings   DUNB 118:5
Cain cruel sons of C.   LE G 196:17
first city C.   COWL 101:14
land God gave to C.   CART 85:1
mark upon C.   BIBL 33:15
cake Let them eat c.   MARI 211:18
picked out of a c.   RALE 254:11
cakes no more c. and ale   SHAK 288:15
Calais 'C.' lying in my heart   MARY 214:13
calculus integral and differential c.   GILB 141:5
Caledonia O C.! stern and wild   SCOT 266:12
calf c. and the young lion   BIBL 39:22
fatted c.   BIBL 46:34
Caliban C., Has a new master   SHAK 287:11
California C. to the New York Island   GUTH 148:15
Caligula C.'s horse was made Consul   RAND 254:12
eyes of C.   MITT 225:3
call c. it a day   COMD 97:19
c. me early, mother dear   TENN 312:25
C. me Ishmael   MELV 216:9
c. of the wild   LOND 201:14
c. the cattle home   KING 186:19
Go, for they c. you   ARNO 15:13
how you c. to me   HARD 152:2
O! c. back yesterday   SHAK 285:18
When you c. me that   WIST 337:18
called c. unto thee, O Lord   BOOK 63:21
many are c.   BIBL 44:26
calling Germany c.   JOYC 179:6
callisthenics c. with words   PARK 240:24
calm c., as it was bright   VAUG 323:4
famous c. and dead   BROW 70:8
calumny thou shalt not escape c.   SHAK 272:5
Cambridge To C. books   TRAP 319:5
to C. books he sent   BROW 69:11
came c. first for the Communists   NIEM 234:5
c. unto his own   BIBL 47:20
I c., I saw, I conquered   CAES 80:3
I c. through   MACA 205:8
Tell them I c.   DE L 108:8
camel c. is a horse   ISSI 169:14
easier for a c.   BIBL 44:20
raiment of c.'s hair   BIBL 42:7
swallow a c.   BIBL 44:31
Take my c., dear   MACA 205:10
Camelot known as C.   LERN 197:24
many-towered C.   TENN 312:2
camera I am a c.   ISHE 169:13
camerado C., this is no book   WHIT 333:23
cammin c. di nostra vita   DANT 105:16
campaign c. in poetry   CUOM 105:2
can He who c., does   SHAW 291:16
they c. because they think they can   VIRG 324:18
youth replies, I c.   EMER 124:10
Canada C. that shall fill   LAUR 194:10
I see C.   DAVI 106:16
more than C. itself is worth   VOLT 325:21
Canadians C. do not like heroes   WOOD 339:3
cancer c. close to the Presidency   DEAN 107:5
Obscene as c.   OWEN 238:24
candid be c. where we can   POPE 248:8
c. friend   CANN 81:13
candied c. apple, quince   KEAT 181:8

candle c. burned out   JOHN 172:16
c. burns at both ends   MILL 218:8
c. in the wind   JOHN 172:15
c. in the wind   JOHN 172:18
c. to the sun   SIDN 295:5
c. to the sun   YOUN 344:13
Fire and fleet and c.-lighte   BALL 24:1
lighted a c.   BIBL 46:20
light such a c.   LATI 194:5
little c. throws his beams   SHAK 282:30
rather light a c.   STEV 303:13
set a c. in the sun   BURT 76:17
candles c. are all out   SHAK 280:4
carry c. and set chairs   HERV 158:12
Night's c.   SHAK 286:32
wind extinguishes c.   LA R 193:21
candy C. is dandy   NASH 231:15
canem *Cave c.*   PETR 244:9
canker this c., Bolingbroke   SHAK 273:27
cannibal c. uses knife and fork   LEC 196:4
cannibals C. that each other eat   SHAK 284:12
cannon C. to right of them   TENN 310:16
in the c.'s mouth   SHAK 269:22
cano *Arma virumque c.*   VIRG 324:9
canoe coffin clapt in a c.   BYRO 77:23
Canossa not go to C.   BISM 54:14
cant c. of *Not men*   BURK 74:14
Clear your mind of c.   JOHN 176:15
cantate C. *Domino canticum novum*   BIBL 52:30
Cantuar how full of C.   BULL 72:10
capability Negative C.   KEAT 183:6
capable c. of reigning   TACI 308:18
caparisons No c., Miss   SHER 294:16
cape Nobly, nobly C. Saint Vincent   BROW 70:10
capital high c. Of Satan   MILT 221:16
capitalism extermination of c.   ZINO 345:5
spirit of c.   WEBE 330:2
unacceptable face of c.   HEAT 154:17
capitalist slave of the c. society   CONN 99:4
captain broken by the team c.   HOWE 165:13
c. of my soul   HENL 156:8
my C. lies, Fallen   WHIT 333:21
O C.! my Captain   WHIT 333:20
Our great captain's c.   SHAK 284:15
plain russet-coated c.   CROM 103:16
ship's c. complaining   POWE 250:24
train-band c. eke was he   COWP 101:21
captains All my sad c.   SHAK 268:22
c. and the kings   KIPL 188:5
c. courageous   BALL 24:2
C. of industry   CARL 82:26
Star c. glow   FLEC 129:21
thunder of the c.   BIBL 37:14
captives all prisoners and c.   BOOK 59:8
car can't drive the c.   TYNA 321:14
c. could go straight upwards   HOYL 166:1
c. in every garage   HOOV 162:13
caravan great c. of humanity   SMUT 298:17
carbon c. atom   JEAN 171:10
carbuncle monstrous c.   CHAR 88:2
carbuncles Monstrous c.   SPEN 300:7
carcase Wheresoever the c. is   BIBL 45:1
card c. up his sleeve   LABO 191:6
memories are c.-indexes   CONN 99:3
Orange c.   CHUR 91:3
play the race c.   SHAP 290:20
cardboard over a c. sea   HARB 151:8
cardinal on the C.'s chair   BARH 25:2
cards c. with a man called Doc   ALGR 4:2
learned to play at c.   JOHN 174:14
old age of c.   POPE 247:14
shuffle the c.   CERV 86:15
care age is full of c.   SHAK 289:17

better c. of myself — BLAK 55:10
Black C. sits behind — HORA 164:13
c. for nobody — BICK 53:16
don't c. too much for money — LENN 197:10
if, full of c. — DAVI 106:19
Nor c. beyond to-day — GRAY 146:18
she don't c. — LENN 197:15
take c. of minutes — CHES 89:8
Teach us to c. — ELIO 121:15
Took great C. of his Mother — MILN 219:1
To say we do not c. — WARD 328:11
wish I could c. what you do — MITC 224:22
with me past c. — SHAK 285:16
career C. open to the talents — CARL 82:15
c. open to the talents — NAPO 231:9
loyal to his own c. — DALT 105:13
careful C. now — LINE 199:18
c. of the type — TENN 311:20
carefully You come most c. — SHAK 270:21
careless c. of the single life — TENN 311:20
first fine c. rapture — BROW 70:9
carelessness both looks like c. — WILD 334:24
cares c. that infest the day — LONG 201:20
Nobody c. — MORT 229:6
Carew grave of Mad C. — HAYE 154:1
caricature c. as far as I can — SCAR 265:8
carlines made the c. ladies — JAME 170:12
Carlisle burghers of C. — MACA 206:2
carnal c. lusts and appetites — BOOK 60:15
carnivorous sheep born c. — FAGU 125:21
caro verbum c. factum est — MISS 224:9
carollings little cause for c. — HARD 151:23
carpe c. diem — HORA 164:7
carping each c. tongue — BRAD 65:25
carriage C. held but just Ourselves — DICK 111:12
carried ought to be c. — EPIC 124:24
carrier down from the c.'s cart — LEE 196:11
carrots Sowe C. in your Gardens — GARD 136:2
carry c. a big stick — ROOS 259:22
c. nothing out — BIBL 51:10
cars c. the great Gothic cathedrals — BART 25:19
Carthage C. must be destroyed — CATO 85:15
Carthaginian C. trustworthiness — SALL 264:2
carve c. heads upon cherry-stones — JOHN 176:17
Let's c. him — SHAK 276:4
carved c. not a line — WOLF 338:12
carving C. is interrelated — HEPW 156:24
case c. is concluded — AUGU 19:6
corpse in the c. — BARH 25:4
everything that is the c. — WITT 337:22
in our c. we have not got — REED 255:9
lady's in the c. — GAY 137:6
nothing to do with the c. — GILB 140:19
casements magic c. — KEAT 182:14
cash c. payment — CARL 82:12
needs good c. — TUCK 320:14
take the c. in hand — FITZ 128:16
casket seal the hushèd c. — KEAT 182:20
cassock C. band, and hymn-book — WILB 334:15
cassowary If I were a c. — WILB 334:15
cast C. a cold eye — YEAT 343:30
c. off the works of darkness — BIBL 49:21
C. thy bread — BIBL 38:31
C. your mind on other days — YEAT 343:29
die is c. — CAES 80:2
let him first c. a stone — BIBL 47:34
Satan c. out Satan — BIBL 45:24
castle c. of my skin — LAMM 192:14
falls on c. walls — TENN 313:5
house is his c. — COKE 95:17
Castlereagh had a mask like C. — SHEL 293:5
castles C. in the air — IBSE 168:13
casualties c. were low — JARR 171:6

casualty is the first c. — ANON 11:2
cat big c. in a poodle parlour — PARR 241:11
c. on a hot tin roof — WILL 336:8
c. that likes to gallop — SMIT 298:1
C., the Rat, and Lovell — COLL 97:1
C. with crimson whiskers — LEAR 195:18
consider my C. Jeoffrey — SMAR 296:22
cosmic Cheshire c. — HUXL 167:19
endow a college, or a c. — POPE 247:17
Had Tiberius been a c. — ARNO 15:11
if a c. is black or white — DENG 108:14
Like a powerful graceful c. — CHUR 92:8
part to tear a c. in — SHAK 283:3
play with my c. — MONT 226:12
poor c. i' the adage — SHAK 279:25
Touch not the c. — SCOT 266:21
very fine c. — JOHN 176:14
which way the c. is jumping — SULZ 306:2
wildest of all wild animals was the C. — KIPL 188:21
cataracts You c. and hurricanoes — SHAK 277:18
catch catch as c. can — FOOT 130:23
hard to c. and conquer — MERE 217:3
If I can c. him once — SHAK 282:4
Catch-22 anything as good as C. — HELL 155:14
only one catch and that was C. — HELL 155:12
catcher c. in the rye — SALI 263:17
catching poverty's c. — BEHN 27:21
categorical imperative is C. — KANT 180:13
category replacement of c.-habits — RYLE 263:6
caterpillars c. of the commonwealth — SHAK 285:15
Cathay cycle of C. — TENN 312:16
cathedrals cars the great Gothic c. — BART 25:19
Catherine child of Karl Marx and C. — ATTL 17:11
catholic C. and Apostolick Church — BOOK 59:23
C. Faith — BOOK 59:2
Once a C. — WILS 336:15
Roman C. Church — MACM 208:11
Roman C. women must — THOM 316:20
She [the C. Church] — NEWM 233:2
Catholics C. and Communists — GREE 146:23
When Hitler attacked the C. — NIEM 234:5
Cato Voice of C. — JONS 177:13
What C. did — BUDG 72:6
cats C. and monkeys — JAME 170:17
c. is 'dogs' — PUNC 252:13
C. look down on us — CHUR 92:14
C., no less liquid — TESS 314:17
count the c. in Zanzibar — THOR 317:21
greater c. with golden eyes — SACK 263:8
killed the c. — BROW 70:26
cattle Actors are c. — HITC 159:14
call the c. home — KING 186:19
thousands of great c. — BURK 74:9
caught man who shoots him gets c. — MAIL 209:18
cauldron Fire burn and c. bubble — SHAK 281:4
cauliflower C. is nothing but cabbage — TWAI 321:10
causas rerum cognoscere c. — VIRG 325:18
cause c. may be inconvenient — BENN 29:24
c., or just impediment — BOOK 60:13
c. that wit is — SHAK 274:13
good old C. — MILT 223:22
good old c. — WORD 340:16
great c. of cheering — BENN 29:23
his c. being good — MORE 227:25
it is the c., my soul — SHAK 284:33
judge thou my c. — BIBL 40:29
little c. for carollings — HARD 151:23
shew any just c. — BOOK 60:16
causes Home of lost c. — ARNO 15:29
malice, to breed c. — JONS 177:24
Tough on the c. of crime — BLAI 55:6
cautiously do c., and look to the end — ANON 12:19
cavaliero perfect c. — BYRO 77:24

cavaliers C. (Wrong but Wromantic) | SELL 267:18
cave C. *canem* | PETR 244:9
political C. of Adullam | BRIG 67:2
vacant interlunar c. | MILT 223:2
wall of the c. | PLAT 246:2
caves c. in which we hide | FITZ 129:6
c. of ice | COLE 96:5
dark unfathomed c. of ocean | GRAY 146:16
there will be c. | NIET 234:8
caviare c. to the general | SHAK 271:33
Cawdor Glamis thou art, and C. | SHAK 279:12
cease c. from mental fight | BLAK 55:27
c. upon the midnight | KEAT 182:13
ceasing Remembering without c. | BIBL 51:4
ceiling lines of the c. | ÉLUA 124:6
celebrity C. is a mask | UPDI 322:1
of mathematical c. | DOYL 115:15
celestial Apparelled in c. light | WORD 340:7
Celia Come, my C. | JONS 177:23
celibacy c. has no pleasures | JOHN 173:26
c. is almost always | PEAC 242:14
cell Each in his narrow c. | GRAY 146:14
hot c. of their hearts | BOGA 57:7
cellar Born in a c. | FOOT 130:22
cellos c. of the deep farms | STEV 303:14
cells c. and gibbets | COOK 99:19
little grey c. | CHRI 90:19
Celt hysterics of the C. | TENN 311:32
cement grass can grow through c. | CHER 89:3
cemetery c. is an open space | SHEL 292:13
Help me down C. Road | LARK 193:16
censor c. of the young | HORA 163:17
censorship extreme form of c. | SHAW 292:1
centaur ant's a c. | POUN 250:11
centre c. cannot hold | YEAT 343:19
c. is everywhere | ANON 8:21
My c. is giving way | FOCH 130:16
This bed thy c. is | DONN 114:13
cents simplicity of the three per c. | DISR 112:25
centuries All c. but this | GILB 140:9
forty c. look down | NAPO 231:2
Through what wild c. | DE L 108:4
century c. of light | BAHA 22:23
c. of the common man | WALL 327:2
sad, glittering c. | BURC 73:14
So the 20th C. | CRAN 102:20
Cerberus C., and blackest Midnight | MILT 219:25
ceremony c. of innocence is drowned | YEAT 343:19
general c. | SHAK 275:5
Ceres C. re-assume the land | POPE 247:21
certain c. because it is impossible | TERT 314:16
c. of nothing | KEAT 183:4
c. thing called the Boy Friend | WILS 337:2
her c. ending | SHAK 289:20
lady of a 'c. age' | BYRO 79:1
sure and c. hope | BOOK 60:25
certainties begin with c. | BACO 20:18
hot for c. | MERE 217:6
certified that I may be c. | BOOK 61:19
chaff wheat from the c. | HUBB 166:4
chagrin C. *d'amour* | FLOR 130:14
chain hangs a golden c. | PUSH 252:23
chainless spirit of the c. mind | BYRO 79:15
chains better to be in c. | KAFK 180:10
bind their kings in c. | BOOK 63:29
deliverance from c. | DOUG 115:8
everywhere he is in c. | ROUS 261:11
lose but their c. | MARX 214:10
chainsaw imagination and a c. | HIRS 159:13
chair c. *est triste* | MALL 210:5
C. she sat in | ELIO 122:22
like a barber's c. | SHAK 268:10
on the Cardinal's c. | BARH 25:2

should not paint the c. | MUNC 230:2
chairs carry candles and set c. | HERV 158:12
chaise longue hurly-burly of the c. | CAMP 80:19
chalices golden c. | JEWE 172:10
Cham great C. of literature | SMOL 298:16
chamber stalking in my c. | WYAT 342:1
chambermaid arms of a c. | JOHN 176:2
champagne c. and a chicken | MONT 226:1
c. or high heels | BENN 29:24
get no kick from c. | PORT 249:17
not a c. teetotaller | SHAW 290:23
chance c. favours only the prepared | PAST 241:22
C. has appointed her | BUNT 72:18
erring men call c. | MILT 219:17
Give peace a c. | LENN 197:12
in the last c. saloon | MELL 216:8
too good to leave to c. | SIMO 296:1
Chancellor C. of the Exchequer | LOWE 203:12
chances changes and c. | BOOK 60:6
Chanel C. No. 5 | MONR 225:20
change C. and decay | LYTE 205:5
c. the past | AGAT 3:3
c. the people who teach | BYAT 77:17
C. without inconvenience | JOHN 173:10
compelled to c. that state | NEWT 233:11
Management that wants to c. | TUSA 321:1
more things c. | KARR 180:17
necessary not to c. | FALK 126:1
things will have to c. | LAMP 192:18
wind of c. is blowing | MACM 208:10
changeable c. always is woman | VIRG 324:16
changed changed, c. utterly | YEAT 342:20
changed, c. utterly | YEAT 342:22
c. upon the blue guitar | STEV 303:6
If voting c. anything | LIVI 200:11
we shall all be c. | BIBL 50:7
changes c. and chances | BOOK 60:6
changing c. scenes of life | TATE 309:12
times they are a-c. | DYLA 119:9
channel [C.] is a mere ditch | NAPO 231:3
Fog in C. | BROC 67:5
chaos black c. comes again | SHAK 290:15
C. and darkness | MARR 212:26
C. and old Night | MILT 221:12
C. is come again | SHAK 284:19
C. umpire sits | MILT 221:23
dread empire, C. | POPE 246:24
chapel also build a c. | LUTH 204:17
c. I was painting | MICH 217:18
chaps Biography is about C. | BENT 30:7
chapter c. of accidents | CHES 89:14
repeat a complete c. | JOHN 175:26
character c. dead at every word | SHER 294:18
c. in the full current | GOET 142:22
c. is destiny | ELIO 121:13
c. is his fate | HERA 156:26
c. is to be abused | THAC 314:21
Fate and c. | NOVA 235:2
reap a c. | READ 254:21
What is c. | JAME 170:19
characters Six c. in search | PIRA 245:5
charge Take thou in c. | MACA 206:12
charging marching, c. feet | JAGG 170:4
Charing Cross existence is at C. | JOHN 175:14
Heaven and C. | THOM 317:3
chariot axle-tree of the c.-wheel | BACO 21:32
c. of fire | BLAK 55:27
Swing low, sweet c. | ANON 10:4
Time's wingèd c. | MARV 213:21
charioted c. by Bacchus | KEAT 182:12
chariots wheels of his c. | BIBL 35:4
charities cold c. | CRAB 102:17
charity c. for all | LINC 199:11

C. shall cover — BIBL 51:29
C. suffereth long — BIBL 49:31
have not c. — BIBL 49:30
Keeping books on c. — PERÓ 244:1
Let holy c. — LITT 200:6
Charles keep King C. the First out — DICK 110:4
Charley C.'s aunt from Brazil — THOM 316:1
Charlie o'er the water to C. — HOGG 160:23
Charlotte C. has been writing — BRON 67:16
charm c. of all the Muses — TENN 313:27
hard words like a c. — OSBO 237:24
What c. can soothe — GOLD 144:4
what c. is — CAMU 81:6
charmer voice of the c. — BOOK 62:4
Were t'other dear c. away — GAY 137:5
charms Do not all c. fly — KEAT 181:24
endearing young c. — MOOR 227:13
Music has c. — CONG 98:13
charter c. of the land — THOM 317:8
chases your picture c. me — RACI 253:20
chassis worl's in a state o' c. — O'CA 235:18
chaste as c. as ice — SHAK 272:5
c. and fair — JONS 177:14
C. as the icicle — SHAK 270:15
C. to her husband — POPE 247:13
My English text is c. — GIBB 139:9
chasten and subdue — WORD 340:3
chasteneth he c. — BIBL 51:17
chastised c. you with whips — BIBL 36:7
chastity and continency — AUGU 18:26
C.—the most unnatural — HUXL 167:17
'Tis c., my brother — MILT 219:13
chateaux ô c. — RIMB 257:12
Chattanooga C. Choo-choo — GORD 144:17
chatter only idle c. — GILB 140:23
chattering not c. pies — SIDN 295:10
Chatterley Between the end of the C. ban — LARK 193:10
Chatterton C., the marvellous boy — WORD 340:25
cheap how potent c. music is — COWA 101:12
in c. shoes — AMIE 4:18
cheaper c. than a prawn sandwich — RATN 254:15
in the c. seats — LENN 197:9
cheat cannot c. on DNA — WARD 328:11
cheated Old men who never c. — BETJ 31:20
cheating period of c. — BIER 53:21
cheats c. with an oath — PLUT 246:10
cheek dancing c.-to-cheek — BERL 30:16
smite thee on thy right c. — BIBL 42:18
cheeks crack your c.! rage! blow — SHAK 277:18
on thy c. — KEAT 181:18
cheer Be of good c. — BIBL 44:5
c. but not inebriate — BERK 30:14
c. but not inebriate — COWP 102:3
Don't c., men — PHIL 244:15
scarce forbear to c. — MACA 206:13
So c. up, my lads — HUGH 166:7
which side do they c. for — TEBB 310:5
cheerful as c. as any man could — PEPY 243:13
c. countenance — BIBL 37:33
c. giver — BIBL 50:11
join our c. songs — WATT 329:9
with a c. countenance — SHAM 290:18
cheerfulness c. was always breaking in — EDWA 120:7
cheeriness Chintzy, Chintzy c. — BETJ 31:18
cheering c. us all up — BENN 29:23
cheerio c. my deario — MARQ 212:21
cheers Two c. for Democracy — FORS 131:18
cheese I've dreamed of c. — STEV 303:24
like some valley c. — AUDE 18:20
of c. — FADI 125:19
pound of c. — CALV 80:13
chemistry found him weak in c. — WELL 331:14
cheque political blank c. — GOSC 144:20

cherchez C. la femme — DUMA 118:1
Chernobyl cultural C. — MNOU 225:7
cherries apples, c., hops — DICK 111:3
Life is just a bowl of c. — BROW 68:15
cherry American as c. pie — BROW 68:13
carve heads upon c.-stones — JOHN 176:17
c. now — HOUS 165:2
C. ripe — CAMP 81:5
C.-ripe, ripe, ripe — HERR 158:2
cherubim C. and Seraphim — HEBE 155:3
cherubims Immortal c. — TRAH 319:4
Cheshire cosmic C. cat — HUXL 167:19
chest on the dead man's c. — STEV 303:21
Chesterton dared attack my C. — BELL 28:17
chestnut spreading c. tree — LONG 202:7
chevalier *c. sans peur et sans reproche* — ANON 11:1
Chevy Drove my C. to the levee — MCLE 208:1
chew can't fart and c. gum — JOHN 173:7
chewing gum c. for the eyes — ANON 10:1
chic Radical C. . . . only radical in Style — WOLF 338:21
chicken champagne and a c. — MONT 226:1
c. in every pot — HOOV 162:13
c. in his pot — HENR 156:11
Some c.! Some neck — CHUR 91:19
chickens all my pretty c. — SHAK 281:13
chiding I am a child to c. — SHAK 284:31
chief c. end of man — SHOR 295:3
Cromwell, our c. of men — MILT 223:12
Sinners; of whom I am c. — BIBL 51:7
chieftain c. o' the puddin'-race — BURN 75:28
child As yet a c. — POPE 247:7
C.! do not throw — BELL 28:6
C. is father — WORD 340:6
c.is not a vase — RABE 253:14
c. is owed the greatest — JUVE 180:6
c. of Time — HALL 150:8
c.'s a plaything — LAMB 192:8
devoured the infant c. — HOUS 164:24
English c. — BLAK 56:9
every c. born therein — RUSK 262:18
God bless the c. — HOLI 161:3
governed by a c. — SHAK 286:4
have a thankless c. — SHAK 277:11
healthy c. well nursed — SWIF 306:23
I am a c. to chiding — SHAK 284:31
If you strike a c. — SHAW 291:18
I heard one calling, 'C.' — HERB 157:11
Is it well with the c. — BIBL 36:22
I was a c. — POE 246:11
knows his own c. — SHAK 282:8
little c. I stand — HERR 157:25
Love, a c. — WROT 341:27
Magus Zoroaster, my dead c. — SHEL 293:14
my absent c. — SHAK 277:1
On a cloud I saw a c. — BLAK 56:4
one c. makes you a parent — FROS 134:4
receive one such little c. — BIBL 44:14
right to a c. — SHAW 290:27
spare the rod, and spoil the c. — BUTL 77:7
sucking c. shall play — BIBL 39:23
thy king is a c. — BIBL 38:29
Train up a c. — BIBL 37:39
unto us a c. is born — BIBL 39:19
use of a new-born c. — FRAN 133:11
voice of the c.'s blood — SWIN 308:3
When I was a c. — BIBL 49:33
childbirth Death and taxes and c. — MITC 224:21
childhood C. is the kingdom — MILL 218:6
have you seen my c. — JACK 169:19
lost your ability in c. — GONC 144:12
moment in c. — GREE 147:1
childish put away c. things — BIBL 49:33
children as c. fear — BACO 21:9

children (*cont.*)
become as little c. — BIBL 44:13
bring forth c. — BIBL 33:11
burn its c. to save — MEYE 217:17
by c. to adults — SZAS 308:9
c. are not your children — GIBR 139:15
c. at play — MONT 226:9
C. begin by loving — WILD 335:13
c. died in the streets — AUDE 18:1
c. inter their parents — HERO 157:23
c. like the olive-branches — BOOK 63:20
c. love their parents — AUCT 17:22
c. of a larger growth — CHES 89:11
c. of a larger growth — DRYD 116:27
c. of light — BIBL 46:36
c. of my body — KOLL 190:3
c. only scream — BYRO 79:22
c. sooner allured by love — ASCH 16:10
c. sweeten labours — BACO 21:20
c. who leave home — SLOV 296:21
Come, dear c. — ARNO 15:6
committed by c. on children — BOWE 65:10
each one of her c. — VERG 323:10
first class, and with c. — BENC 29:7
hell for c. — STRI 305:7
holdeth c. from play — SIDN 295:13
How many c. — KNIG 189:13
kept from c. and from fools — DRYD 117:8
known as the C.'s Hour — LONG 201:19
little c. cried — MOTL 229:13
made c. laugh — AWDR 20:8
Myself and c. three — COWP 101:22
not much about having c. — LODG 201:11
oh those c.'s voices — VERL 323:12
poor get c. — KAHN 180:11
provoke not your c. to wrath — BIBL 50:21
raising your c. — ONAS 236:8
so are the young c. — BOOK 63:19
stars are my c. — KEAT 183:12
Suffer the little c. — BIBL 45:30
than of their c. — PENN 243:10
tiresome for c. — SAIN 263:12
upon the c. — BIBL 34:13
weeping for her c. — BIBL 42:4
wife and c. — BACO 21:17
wrong name of innocent c. — BINC 54:2
child-wife only my c. — DICK 110:9
Chile Small earthquake in C. — COCK 95:10
chill bitter c. it was — KEAT 181:3
chilly c. and grown old — BROW 71:11
chimaera c. of my age — BERN 31:6
Chimborazo C., Cotopaxi — TURN 320:23
chimeras dire c. and enchanted isles — MILT 219:15
chimes c. at midnight — SHAK 274:22
chimney c.-sweepers, come to dust — SHAK 270:19
old men from the c. corner — SIDN 295:13
chimneys grove of c. — MORR 228:12
Your c. I sweep — BLAK 56:5
chimpanzee vase in the hands of a c. — WAUG 329:23
china C. to Peru — JOHN 174:4
land armies in C. — MONT 226:19
outer C. 'crost the Bay — KIPL 187:26
though c. fall — POPE 247:15
chintzy Chintzy, C. cheeriness — BETJ 31:18
chip c. of the old 'block' — BURK 74:19
chips c. with everything — WESK 331:20
chivalry age of c. — BURK 74:7
nine-tenths of the law of c. — SAYE 265:6
chocolate c. cream soldier — SHAW 290:22
choice c. of all my library — SHAK 287:27
measure and the c. — JOHN 174:4
you takes your c. — PUNC 252:8
choir in a wailful c. — KEAT 182:23

choirs Bare ruined c. — SHAK 289:31
C. and Places — BOOK 58:20
c. of wailing shells — OWEN 238:22
choisir *Gouverner, c'est c.* — LÉVI 198:10
choo-choo Chattanooga C. — GORD 144:17
choose *believe what we c.* — NEWM 233:8
C. an author — DILL 111:22
to govern is to c. — LÉVI 198:10
woman can hardly ever c. — ELIO 121:6
chopcherry c. ripe within — PEEL 242:23
Chopin C. and Bizet — FISH 128:8
chopper cheap and chippy c. — GILB 140:12
chord lost c. — PROC 251:13
chortled c. in his joy — CARR 84:4
chose c. him five smooth stones — BIBL 35:22
chosen best c. language — AUST 19:19
c. generation — BIBL 51:26
few are c. — BIBL 44:26
Mary hath c. — BIBL 46:19
Christ all things through C. — BIBL 50:29
C. and His saints — ANON 13:6
C. being raised from the dead — BIBL 49:12
C. beside me — PATR 242:5
C. perish in torment — SHAW 291:33
C. receive thy saule — BALL 24:1
C. risen from the dead — BIBL 50:2
C.'s blood streams — MARL 212:7
C. that is to be — TENN 311:31
C. walking on the water — THOM 317:4
in C. Church hall — ARNO 15:17
Jesus C. — BIBL 51:19
Jesus C. his only Son — BOOK 58:16
lady of C.'s College — AUBR 17:14
We preach C. crucified — BIBL 49:23
Christe *C. eleison* — MISS 223:27
christened when she was c. — SHAK 270:1
Christian C. Architecture — PUGI 252:3
C. boys — ARNO 16:7
C. can die — ADDI 2:16
C. can only fear dying — HARE 152:6
C. ideal has not been tried — CHES 90:7
hadn't *got* a C. — PUNC 252:15
Onward, C. soldiers — BARI 25:5
persuadest me to be a C. — BIBL 49:4
wonders of the c. religion — MATH 215:2
you were a C. slave — HENL 156:10
Christianity C. is part of the laws — HALE 149:15
Disneyfication of C. — CUPI 105:3
His C. was muscular — DISR 112:21
Christians blood of C. is the seed — TERT 314:15
C., awake — BYRO 77:19
generations of C. — MACA 205:20
Christmas C. Day in the Workhouse — SIMS 296:7
C. is the Disneyfication — CUPI 105:3
C.-morning bells say 'Come!' — BETJ 31:16
Do they know it's C. — GELD 137:15
Ghost of C. Past — DICK 109:20
insulting C. card — GROS 148:6
night before C. — MOOR 227:2
well that C. should fall — ADDI 2:13
white C. — BERL 30:21
Christopher Robin C. has fallen — MORT 229:6
C. is saying his prayers — MILN 219:3
chronicle c. of wasted time — SHAK 290:2
c. small beer — SHAK 284:16
Chuang Tzu C.'s dreaming heart — BASH 26:3
chuck C. it, Smith — CHES 89:16
chumps C. make the best husbands — WODE 337:25
church Catholick and Apostolick C. — BOOK 59:23
Christ's C. militant — BOOK 59:24
c. for his mother — CYPR 105:10
c. furniture at best — COWP 102:8
C. is an anvil — MACL 207:20

C. is 'one generation' — CARE 82:8
C. of [England] should — ROYD 261:17
C. of England were to fail — KEBL 183:22
[C. of Rome] thoroughly — MACA 205:19
C. shall be free — MAGN 209:10
C.'s one foundation — STON 304:11
except in the C. — CYPR 105:12
free c. — CAVO 86:9
God built a c. — LUTH 204:17
Housbondes at c. dore — CHAU 88:11
I will build my c. — BIBL 44:10
no salvation outside the c. — AUGU 19:3
open the windows of the C. — JOHN 172:12
Say to the c., it shows — RALE 254:1
She [the Catholic C.] — NEWM 233:2
some to c. repair — POPE 248:3
Stands the C. clock — BROO 67:21
there must be the C. — AMBR 4:13
churches John to the seven c. — BIBL 52:2
Churchill never was a C. — GLAD 141:22
churchyard dust of the C. — DONN 114:20
churchyards Troop home to c. — SHAK 283:19
When c. yawn — SHAK 272:20
ciel *montez au c.* — FIRM 128:2
cigar really good 5-cent c. — MARS 213:6
cigarette c. that bears a lipstick's traces — MARV 213:24
Cinara C. was my queen — HORA 164:18
Cinarae *bonae Sub regno C.* — HORA 164:18
Cincinnatus C. of the West — BYRO 79:12
cinders c., ashes, dust — KEAT 181:23
cinema c. is truth 24 times per second — GODA 142:9
circenses *Panem et c.* — JUVE 180:3
circle God is a c. — ANON 8:21
makes by c. just — DONN 114:15
tightness of the magic c. — MACL 208:3
wheel is come full c. — SHAK 278:11
circumference c. is nowhere — ANON 8:21
circumlocution C. Office — DICK 110:16
circumspectly walk c. — BIBL 50:20
circumspice *Si monumentum requiris, c.* — ANON 13:1
circumstance Pride, pomp, and c. — SHAK 284:26
circumstantial c. evidence — THOR 317:16
circumstancia *Yo soy yo y mi c.* — ORTE 236:22
circus no right in the c. — MAXT 215:13
circuses bread and c. — JUVE 180:3
cities c. we had learned about — JARR 171:6
flower of c. — ANON 8:12
hell to c. — AESC 2:23
Seven c. warred — HEYW 158:23
streets of a hundred c. — HOOV 162:14
Towered c. please us — MILT 220:6
citizen c., first in war — LEE 196:10
c. of no mean city — BIBL 48:39
c. of the world — BACO 21:14
c. of the world — BOSW 64:20
c. or the police — AUDE 18:17
Every c. will make — MORE 228:6
greater than a private c. — TACI 308:18
I am a Roman c. — CICE 92:26
John Gilpin was a c. — COWP 101:21
zealous c. — BURK 74:10
citizens first and second class c. — WILL 336:14
cito *Bis dat qui c. dat* — PUBL 251:22
city citizen of no mean c. — BIBL 48:39
c. consists in men — NICI 233:22
c. is not a concrete jungle — MORR 228:13
C. now doth like a garment wear — WORD 339:18
c. of dreadful night — THOM 317:12
C. of God — JOHN 177:4
c. of refuge — MILT 223:19
C. of the Big Shoulders — SAND 264:7
c. that is set on an hill — BIBL 42:16
c. upon a hill — WINT 337:16

first c. Cain — COWL 101:14
Hell is a c. — SHEL 293:13
in populous c. pent — MILT 222:15
long in c. pent — KEAT 182:25
no continuing c. — BIBL 51:20
peper felled a c. — THOM 316:5
rose-red c. — BURG 73:18
Sun-girt c. — SHEL 293:4
that great c. — BIBL 52:17
What is the c. but the people — SHAK 270:11
Without a c. wall — ALEX 3:18
civil c. discord — ADDI 2:11
c. to everyone — SISS 296:8
In c. business — BACO 21:6
Pray, good people, be c. — GWYN 148:16
civility C. costs nothing — MONT 226:4
civilization can't say c. don't advance — ROGE 259:7
C. advances by extending — WHIT 333:15
c. has from time to time — ELLI 124:3
C. has made the peasantry — TROT 320:2
C. nothing more than — ORTE 237:1
elements of modern c. — CARL 82:16
For a botched c. — POUN 250:10
history of Western C. — TYNA 321:15
last product of c. — RUSS 262:20
life-blood of real c. — TREV 319:7
civilized that are called c. — PAIN 239:15
civil servant c. doesn't make jokes — IONE 169:7
Here lies a c. — SISS 296:8
civil servants of c. — BRID 66:17
Civil Service C. is deferential — CROS 104:7
civis *C. Romanus sum* — CICE 92:26
claim last territorial c. — HITL 159:19
clair *n'est pas c.* — RIVA 257:15
clamour c. for war — PEEL 242:20
clap Don't c. too hard — OSBO 237:25
If you believe, c. your hands — BARR 25:16
in the cheaper seats c. your hands — LENN 197:9
Clapham man on the C. omnibus — BOWE 65:13
clapped-out c., post-imperial — DRAB 115:21
claps If someone c. his hand — HAKU 149:10
Clarence perjured C. — SHAK 286:3
claret c. is the liquor for boys — JOHN 176:3
Claridges body of the bootboy at C. — WOOL 339:9
Clarissa C. lives — RICH 256:21
clasped C. by the golden light — HOOD 162:6
class c. struggle — MARX 214:7
first and second c. citizens — WILL 336:14
history of c. struggles — MARX 214:9
While there is a lower c. — DEBS 107:10
classes But the two c. — FOST 132:4
masses against the c. — GLAD 142:1
two c. of travel — BENC 29:7
classic C. music is th'kind — HUBB 166:5
classical c. mind at work — PIRS 245:7
C. quotation — JOHN 176:9
tragedy of the c. languages — MADA 209:1
classics bellyful of the c. — MILL 218:17
classify Germans c. — CATH 85:12
Claudel pardon Paul C. — AUDE 18:5
claw red in tooth and c. — TENN 311:21
clawed c. me with his clutch — VAUX 323:6
claws pair of ragged c. — ELIO 122:11
clay associate of this c. — HADR 148:17
for this the c. grew tall — OWEN 238:25
clean c. American backyards — MAIL 209:17
c. place to die — KAVA 180:23
c., verb active — DICK 110:23
Make me a c. heart — BOOK 61:28
Not a c. & in-between-the-sheets — MCGO 207:12
cleansed doors of perception were c. — BLAK 55:26
clear C. your mind of cant — JOHN 176:15
In the c. air — FERG 127:1

clear (*cont.*)
poignancy in all things c. — WILB 334:17
too c., too simple — STEN 302:14
What is not c. — RIVA 257:15
clearing-house c. of the world — CHAM 86:17
clears little water c. us — SHAK 280:13
cleave c. the wood — ANON 9:15
c. unto his wife — BIBL 33:5
cleft c. for me — TOPL 318:19
clementine his daughter, C. — MONT 226:24
Cleopatra C.'s nose been shorter — PASC 241:16
squeaking C. — SHAK 269:4
clercs *trahison des c.* — BEND 29:9
clergy benefit o' the C. — CONG 98:12
Established C. — GLAD 141:21
cleric neither c. nor layman — BERN 31:6
clerk C. there was of Oxenford — CHAU 88:10
clerks treason of all c. — AUDE 17:26
clever c., but is it Art — KIPL 187:11
c. men at Oxford — GRAH 145:12
c. theft was praiseworthy — SPEN 300:4
c. to a fault — BROW 69:21
good people were c. — WORD 339:16
let who will be c. — KING 186:17
manage a c. man — KIPL 188:27
Too c. by half — SALI 263:18
Too c. by half — SALI 263:23
click c. with people — EISE 120:17
cliffs bluebirds over the white c. — BURT 76:7
c. of fall — HOPK 162:26
climate in love with a cold c. — SOUT 299:19
Love in a cold c. — MITF 225:1
climb C. ev'ry mountain — HAMM 150:17
c. not at all — ELIZ 123:10
c. up into the heaven — BOOK 63:25
Fain would I c. — RALE 254:4
climbing c., shakes his dewy wings — D'AV 106:12
cloak knyf under the c. — CHAU 88:15
clock biological c. is ticking — KEYE 185:7
c. is always slow — SERV 267:26
Court the slow c. — POPE 247:27
forgot to wind up the c. — STER 302:20
Stands the Church c. — BROO 67:21
clocks c. were striking thirteen — ORWE 237:13
clockwork c. orange — BURG 73:15
cloistered fugitive and c. virtue — MILT 223:15
close breathless hush in the C. — NEWB 232:20
c. the wall up — SHAK 274:33
Doth c. behind him tread — COLE 96:17
not c. enough — CAPA 81:20
peacefully towards its c. — DAWS 107:3
closed We never c. — VAN 322:11
closer c. walk with God — COWP 101:24
Come c., boys — CHIL 90:14
friend that sticketh c. — BIBL 37:37
closet from forth the c. — KEAT 181:8
put me in the c. — DICK 111:17
cloth fair white linen c. — BOOK 59:17
trick of wearing a c. coat — BALM 24:20
clothed C. in white samite — TENN 311:4
woman c. with the sun — BIBL 52:13
clothes Emperor's new c. — ANDE 5:5
in c. a wantonness — HERR 158:3
liquefaction of her c. — HERR 158:10
remarkable suit of c. — LOES 201:13
clothing c. is of wrought gold — BOOK 61:24
in sheep's c. — BIBL 43:10
sheep in sheep's c. — CHUR 92:16
cloud c. in trousers — MAYA 215:14
c. of unknowing — ANON 6:5
c. of witnesses — BIBL 51:16
each c. contains pennies — BURK 74:23
fiend hid in a c. — BLAK 56:10

Get off my c. — JAGG 170:1
lonely as a c. — WORD 340:1
On a c. I saw a child — BLAK 56:4
pillar of a c. — BIBL 34:10
set my bow in the c. — BIBL 33:22
There ariseth a little c. — BIBL 36:11
watch a sailing c. — LIN 200:5
cloudcuckooland How about 'C.' — ARIS 14:8
clouded upon our c. hills — BLAK 55:27
clouds c. rain down righteousness — BIBL 53:5
comes with c. descending — WESL 332:3
O c., unfold! — BLAK 55:27
trailing c. of glory — WORD 340:10
cloven out pops the c. hoof — WODE 338:2
cloverleaf concrete c. — MUMF 230:1
clowns Send in the c. — SOND 299:5
club best c. in London — DICK 111:1
don't want to belong to any c. — MARX 214:2
that terrible football c. — MCGR 207:14
Clun Clungunford and C. — HOUS 165:8
Clunbury Clunton and C. — HOUS 165:8
Clungunford C. and Clun — HOUS 165:8
Clunton C. and Clunbury — HOUS 165:8
clutch clawed me with his c. — VAUX 323:6
clutching alien people c. their gods — ELIO 122:8
Clyde poems should be C.-built — DUNN 118:10
CMG C. (Call Me God) — ANON 8:18
coach c. and six horses — RICE 256:16
indifference and a c. and six — COLM 97:12
rattling of a c. — DONN 114:21
coaches Nine c. waiting — MIDD 217:21
coal island made mainly of c. — BEVA 32:7
like miners' c. dust — BOOT 64:11
coalition rainbow c. — JACK 169:18
coals all eyes else dead c. — SHAK 289:15
c. of fire — BIBL 38:3
coarse one of them is rather c. — ROYD 261:18
coast c. of Coromandel — SITW 296:15
On the c. of Coromandel — LEAR 195:9
coat c. of many colours — BIBL 33:33
stick in his c. — BROW 70:16
cobble On c.-stones I lay — FLAN 129:13
Cobbleigh Uncle Tom C. — BALL 24:16
cobwebs Laws are like c. — SWIF 306:17
cocaine C. habit-forming — BANK 24:23
cock before the c. crow — BIBL 45:14
C. and a Bull — STER 303:1
c. crowing on its own dunghill — ALDI 3:11
Our c. won't fight — BEAV 26:18
owe a c. to Aesculapius — SOCR 298:24
cockatrice hand on the c.' den — BIBL 39:23
cockle c. hat and staff — SHAK 272:32
Cockney C. impudence — RUSK 262:7
cockpit Can this c. hold — SHAK 274:27
c. of Christendom — HOWE 165:17
cocksure c. of anything — MELB 216:5
cocktail weasel under the c. cabinet — PINT 245:4
cocoa c. for Kingsley Amis — COPE 99:24
C. is a cad and coward — CHES 90:1
cod bean and the c. — BOSS 64:18
photographer is like the c. — SHAW 292:3
coeli *Rorate, c.* — BIBL 53:5
coeur *Il pleure dans mon c.* — VERL 323:13
coffee c.-house — SWIF 306:16
C. house babble — DISR 112:12
C., (which makes the politician wise) — POPE 249:6
if this is c. — PUNC 252:19
measured out my life with c. spoons — ELIO 122:10
o'er cold c. — POPE 247:27
put poison in your c. — CHUR 92:15
coffin c. clapt in a canoe — BYRO 77:23
silver plate on a c. — CURR 105:6
cogito *C., ergo sum* — DESC 109:2

cognoscere *rerum c. causas*   VIRG 325:18
cohorts his c. were gleaming   BYRO 78:13
coin C., Tiberius   DOBS 113:11
coincidence long arm of c.   CHAM 86:23
coins for a fistful of c.   ZAPA 345:1
coition way of c.   BROW 69:7
coitum *Post c.*   ANON 12:18
cold Cast a c. eye   YEAT 343:30
   caught An everlasting c.   WEBS 330:20
   c. charities   CRAB 102:17
   c. coming they had of it   ANDR 5:10
   c. coming we had of it   ELIO 122:7
   c. grave   BALL 24:14
   C. in the earth   BRON 67:13
   c. metal of economic theory   SCHU 265:20
   c. relation   BURK 74:10
   c. war   BARU 25:20
   c. war warrior   THAT 315:4
   Fallen c. and dead   WHIT 333:21
   ink in my pen ran c.   WALP 327:8
   in love with a c. climate   SOUT 299:19
   i' the c. o' the moon   BROW 69:26
   lie in c. obstruction   SHAK 281:33
   Love in a c. climate   MITF 225:1
   neither c. nor hot   BIBL 52:6
   past the common c.   AYRE 20:12
   Poor Tom's a-c.   SHAK 277:27
   spy who came in from the c.   LE C 196:5
   To c. oblivion   SHEL 292:23
   waxeth c.   BALL 24:15
Coliseum While stands the C.   BYRO 78:7
   You're the C.   PORT 249:21
collapse c. in deepest humiliation   EDDI 119:14
   C. of Stout Party   ANON 6:6
collections mutilators of c.   LAMB 192:3
collective c. unconscious   JUNG 179:12
collects beautiful c.   MACA 205:20
college cabbage with a c. education   TWAI 321:10
   endow a c.   POPE 247:17
   Master of this c.   BEEC 27:10
   small c.   WEBS 330:4
colonel C. Blimp   LOW 203:11
   C.'s Lady   KIPL 187:24
colonies New c. seek   FREE 133:16
colossus C. from a rock   JOHN 176:17
   Like a C.   SHAK 275:30
colour any c. that he wants   FORD 131:5
   c. of his hair   HOUS 164:23
   c. purple   WALK 326:22
   horse of that c.   SHAK 288:16
   I know the c. rose   ABSE 1:3
   Life is C.   GREN 147:10
coloured no 'white' or 'c.' signs   KENN 184:13
   penny plain and twopence c.   STEV 303:20
colourless C. green ideas   CHOM 90:17
colours coat of many c.   BIBL 33:33
   c. will agree   BACO 21:31
   lines and c.   POUS 250:16
column Fifth c.   MOLA 225:8
comb two bald men over a c.   BORG 64:14
combination call it c.   PALM 240:7
combine When bad men c.   BURK 74:13
come better not c. at all   KEAT 183:7
   C., and he cometh   BIBL 43:14
   C. away, come away, death   SHAK 288:19
   C., dear children   ARNO 15:6
   C., Holy Spirit   LANG 193:3
   C. in the speaking silence   ROSS 260:11
   C. into the garden   TENN 312:21
   C., let us join our cheerful songs   WATT 329:9
   c., let us sing   BOOK 62:18
   c., Lord Jesus   BIBL 52:28
   C. mothers and fathers   DYLA 119:10

C. unto me   BIBL 43:31
C. unto my love   SPEN 300:12
C. unto these yellow sands   SHAK 287:6
C. what come may   SHAK 279:9
he that should c.   BIBL 43:29
King of glory shall c. in   BOOK 61:9
men may c.   TENN 310:14
mine hour is not yet c.   BIBL 47:26
Mr Watson, c. here   BELL 28:2
nobody will c.   SAND 264:10
O c., all ye faithful   ANON 12:6
shape of things to c.   WELL 331:17
Sumer is c. in   ANON 10:3
therefore I cannot c.   BIBL 46:26
'tis not to c.   SHAK 273:16
wheel is c. full circle   SHAK 278:11
when death is c., we are not   EPIC 124:25
where do they all c. from   LENN 197:11
whistle, an' I'll c.   BURN 75:20
Why don't you c. up   WEST 332:15
comeback c. kid   CLIN 94:16
comedy All I need to make a c.   CHAP 87:12
   C. is an imitation   SIDN 295:14
   c. to those that think   WALP 327:13
comely black, but c.   BIBL 39:2
comes conquering hero c.   MORE 228:5
   nobody c.   BECK 26:21
comest c. into thy kingdom   BIBL 47:12
cometh Blessed be he that c.   BOOK 63:11
   c. unto the Father   BIBL 48:6
   He c. not   TENN 312:18
comets no c. seen   SHAK 276:5
comfort c. and despair   SHAK 290:11
   c. and relieve them   BOOK 59:10
   C.'s a cripple   DRAY 116:4
   c. ye my people   BIBL 40:6
   good c., Master Ridley   LATI 194:5
   love her, c. her   BOOK 60:17
   naught for your c.   CHES 89:17
   to c., and command   WORD 341:7
   waters of c.   BOOK 61:6
comfortable c. estate of widowhood   GAY 137:3
   c. words   BOOK 59:28
comfortably lived c. so long together   GAY 137:2
   Speak ye c.   BIBL 40:6
comforted c. his people   BIBL 40:15
   they shall be c.   BIBL 42:14
   would not be c.   BIBL 42:4
comforters Miserable c.   BIBL 37:7
comical Beautiful c. things   HARV 153:2
   I often think it's c.   GILB 140:2
coming cold c. we had of it   ELIO 122:7
   c. for us that night   BALD 23:7
   C. in on a wing and a pray'r   ADAM 2:5
   C. thro' the rye   BURN 75:8
   c. to that holy room   DONN 113:24
   Everything's c. up roses   SOND 299:4
   good time c.   SCOT 266:25
   He is c.   AYTO 20:13
   my c. down   MORE 228:3
   She is c., my dove   TENN 312:23
   their c. hither   SHAK 278:8
   Yanks are c.   COHA 95:13
command c. success   ADDI 2:7
   left that c.   MILT 222:17
   not born to sue, but to c.   SHAK 285:8
   sue than to c.   SCOT 266:7
   to comfort, and c.   WORD 341:7
commandment first and great c.   BIBL 44:20
commandments keep his c.   BIBL 39:1
commend c. my spirit   BIBL 47:14
   c. my spirit   BOOK 61:12
   virtue to c.   CONG 98:20

comment C. is free — SCOT 266:1
  C. is free — STOP 304:16
commentators c. each dark passage — YOUN 344:13
  learned c. view — SWIF 307:8
commerce In matters of c. — CANN 81:11
  where c. long prevails — GOLD 143:21
commit c. his body to the deep — BOOK 64:1
committed c. breakfast with it — LEWI 198:14
committee C.—a group of men — ALLE 4:7
  c. is a group of the unwilling — ANON 6:7
  horse designed by a c. — ISSI 169:14
commodity C., firmness, and delight — WOTT 341:24
common and still be c. — RATT 254:16
  century of the c. man — WALL 327:2
  c. as the air — GRAN 145:20
  c. pursuit — LEAV 195:23
  c. things that round us — WORD 340:20
  light of c. day — WORD 340:11
  nor lose the c. touch — KIPL 187:21
  not already c. — LOCK 201:3
  nothing c. did or mean — MARV 213:18
  steals the c. — ANON 10:12
  trivial round, the c. task — KEBL 183:20
commoner persistent c. — BENN 29:14
common law marry C. — LLOY 200:15
commonplace ordinary c. things — SCOT 266:27
commons C., faithful to their system — MACK 207:19
  libraries of the C. — CHAN 87:11
  on the House of C. — DICK 111:1
common sense C. is the best distributed — DESC 109:1
  marry Common Law to C. — LLOY 200:15
  Nothing but c. — MORT 229:3
commonwealth caterpillars of the c. — SHAK 285:15
commonwealths raise up c. — DRYD 116:14
  uniting into c. — LOCK 201:8
communicated C. monthly — BETJ 31:20
communications Evil c. — BIBL 50:5
communion Table, at the C.-time — BOOK 59:17
communism caused the fall of c. — JOHN 172:20
  C. is Soviet power — LENI 197:4
  Russian C. the illegitimate child — ATTL 17:11
  spectre of C. — MARX 214:8
communist call me a c. — CAMA 80:15
  I wasn't a C. — NIEM 234:5
  members of the C. Party — MCCA 206:17
  What is a c. — ELLI 123:23
communists Catholics and C. — GREE 146:23
community part of the c. of Europe — SALI 263:20
commuter C.—one who spends — WHIT 333:7
compact c. which exists — GARR 136:12
compacted sweets c. lie — HERB 157:22
companion c. to owls — BIBL 37:12
  even thou, my c. — BOOK 62:2
  gave him a c. — VALÉ 322:6
  send the prince a better c. — SHAK 274:16
company C. for carrying on — ANON 6:9
  c. he chooses — BURT 76:5
  not good c. — AUST 19:22
  owe my soul to the c. store — TRAV 319:6
  three is c. — WILD 334:23
  tone of the c. — CHES 89:7
compare Shall I c. thee — SHAK 289:23
comparisons C. are odorous — SHAK 284:3
compass mariner's needle [c.] — BACO 22:5
  top of my c. — SHAK 272:17
compassed c. me round — BOOK 63:8
  we also are compassed about — BIBL 51:16
compassion something which excites c. — SMIT 298:5
compassionate Merciful, the C. — KORA 190:5
compel c. thee to go a mile — BIBL 42:19
competing Costs register c. attractions — KNIG 189:12
competition rigour of c. — ANON 6:8
complain Never c. and never explain — DISR 113:5

complaint most fatal c. of all — HILT 159:10
complete clad in c. steel — MILT 219:13
complexes feeling-toned c. — JUNG 179:12
compliance timely c. — FIEL 127:12
complies c. against his will — BUTL 77:8
composing C.'s not voluntary — BIRT 54:9
comprehended darkness c. it not — BIBL 47:17
comprendre Tout c. rend très indulgent — STAÉ 301:9
compulsion No c. in religion — KORA 190:8
  Such sweet c. — MILT 219:8
computer modern c. hovers — BREN 66:14
computers C. are anti-Faraday — CORN 100:5
  so many c. — WALĘ 326:18
conceal c. our wants — GOLD 143:24
conceit folly and c. — AUST 19:25
  wise in his own c. — BIBL 38:5
conceits accepted for c. — BACO 20:19
conceive virgin shall c. — BIBL 39:17
conceived c. by the Holy Ghost — BOOK 58:16
  my mother c. me — BOOK 61:27
concentrates c. his mind — JOHN 175:22
conception present at the c. — ORTO 237:3
concerned nobody left to be c. — NIEM 234:5
conciliation not a policy of c. — PARN 241:9
concluded case is c. — AUGU 19:6
conclusions pursued c. infinite — SHAK 269:11
concord lover of c. — BOOK 58:18
  travelled a good deal in C. — THOR 317:18
  truth, unity, and c. — BOOK 59:26
concordia C. discors — HORA 163:25
concrete city is not a c. jungle — MORR 228:13
  c. and tyres — LARK 193:12
  c. cloverleaf — MUMF 230:1
concubine c. of a warlord — JUNG 179:16
condemn c. a little more — MAJO 209:22
  Neither do I c. thee — BIBL 47:35
condemned c. to be free — SART 264:22
  you yourself Are much c. — SHAK 276:28
condition c. upon which God — CURR 105:5
  could do in that c. — PEPY 243:13
conditions c. of men — BOOK 59:9
conduct c. unbecoming — ANON 5:19
  regulation of c. — SPEN 300:2
cone sphere, the c. — CÉZA 86:16
cones eat the c. under his pines — FROS 134:11
confederacy dunces are all in c. — SWIF 307:2
conference c. a ready man — BACO 21:27
  hold some two days' c. — WEBS 330:9
  naked into the c. chamber — BEVA 32:9
conferences eradication of c. — MAYA 215:16
confess c. to almighty God — MISS 223:26
confessions c. of a justified sinner — HOGG 161:1
confident glad c. morning — BROW 70:18
confine verge Of her c. — SHAK 277:14
confined cabined, cribbed, c. — SHAK 280:27
conflict armed c. — EDEN 119:17
  end of the c. of centuries — GRIF 147:15
  Never in the field of human c. — CHUR 91:17
  tragic c. of loyalties — HOWE 165:14
conflicts all disputes or c. — BRIA 66:16
confounded Confusion worse c. — MILT 221:25
  let me never be c. — BOOK 58:14
confront to c. them — TRIM 319:11
confused anyone who isn't c. — MURR 230:13
confusion come to c. — SHAK 283:1
  C. now hath made — SHAK 280:16
  C. on thy banners wait — GRAY 146:11
  C. worse confounded — MILT 221:25
congeals When love c. — HART 152:18
congregation face of this c. — BOOK 60:14
congress C. makes no progress — LIGN 199:3
conjecture not beyond all c. — BROW 68:21
conjuring c. trick with bones — JENK 171:20

conjuror level of the stage c.	MOOR 227:7
Connaught Hell or C.	CROM 104:1
connect Only c.	FORS 131:15
conquer hard to catch and c.	MERE 217:3
shalt thou c.	CONS 99:14
we will c.	BEE 27:7
conquered c. and peopled	SEEL 267:7
I came, I saw, I c.	CAES 80:3
Thou has c.	SWIN 308:1
conquering c. hero comes	MORE 228:5
C. kings	CHAN 87:3
c. one's enemies	GENG 137:20
conqueror you are a c.	ROST 261:3
conquests spread her c.	BURN 75:7
conscience C. avaunt	CIBB 92:21
c. of the king	SHAK 271:37
C.: the inner voice	MENC 216:15
corporation to have a c.	THUR 318:2
cut my c.	HELL 155:15
reason and c.	PRIC 251:5
to C. first	NEWM 233:3
consciences binding on the c.	JOHN 172:11
Look to your c.	MARY 214:13
conscientiousness c. and altruism	CONF 98:8
consciousness C. . . . . is the phenomenon	PENR 243:11
consecrated c. obstruction	BAGE 22:17
consecration c., and the Poet's	WORD 339:20
consent demand not his free c.	CHAR 87:20
whispering 'I will ne'er c.'	BYRO 78:17
without your c.	ROOS 259:12
consequences damn the c.	MILN 219:7
conservative c. been arrested	WOLF 338:19
C. Government	DISR 112:8
C. Party at prayer	ROYD 261:17
make me c. when old	FROS 134:12
makes a man more c.	KEYN 185:10
Or else a little C.	GILB 140:2
sound C. government	DISR 112:18
conservatives C. . . . . being by the law	MILL 218:2
consider c. her ways, and be wise	BIBL 37:21
c. how my light is spent	MILT 223:9
considerable appear c.	JOHN 175:8
considerate c. autocrat	STEP 302:16
consideration C. like an angel came	SHAK 274:28
consistency foolish c.	EMER 124:13
consistent completely c. are the dead	HUXL 167:15
c. with the laws of nature	FARA 126:3
conspicuous C. consumption	VEBL 323:7
Vega c. overhead	AUDE 18:13
conspiracies c. against the laity	SHAW 290:26
conspiracy c. against the public	SMIT 297:7
c. to make you happy	UPDI 321:26
conspiring C. with him	KEAT 182:21
constable c.'s handbook	KING 187:1
constabulary c. duty's to be done	GILB 141:6
constant c. as the northern star	SHAK 276:7
One here will c. be	BUNY 73:9
constellated c. flower	SHEL 293:21
constituencies go back to your c.	STEE 302:1
constitution c. does not provide	WILL 336:14
establishment of C.	CARD 82:4
Every country has its own c.	ANON 6:17
genius of the C.	PITT 245:11
people made the C.	MARS 213:5
principle of the English c.	BLAC 55:4
constitutional c. eyes	LINC 199:12
construction mind's c.	SHAK 279:11
consul born when I was c.	CICE 93:3
horse was made C.	RAND 254:12
consult C. the genius	POPE 247:19
consulted right to be c.	BAGE 22:21
consume born to c. resources	HORA 163:21
consumed bush was not c.	BIBL 33:39
consumer c. isn't a moron	OGIL 235:20
c. is the king	SAMU 264:4
c. society	ILLI 168:18
consumere *fruges c. nati*	HORA 163:21
consummation c. Devoutly to be wished	SHAK 272:1
consummatum C. *est*	BIBL 53:12
consumption Conspicuous c.	VEBL 323:7
C. is the sole end	SMIT 297:10
c. of the purse	SHAK 274:17
contagion c. of the world's slow stain	SHEL 292:18
contemplation mind serene for c.	GAY 137:8
contempt c. on all my pride	WATT 329:10
contemptible c. little army	ANON 6:20
poor c. men	CROM 103:22
contending C. with the fretful	SHAK 277:17
content land of lost c.	HOUS 165:7
sweet Well-c.	DAVI 106:20
contented c. least	SHAK 289:25
king shall be c.	SHAK 285:22
contentment Preaches c. to the toad	KIPL 188:3
contest not the victory but the c.	COUB 100:16
continency chastity and c.	AUGU 18:26
continent Africa, drifting c.	GENE 137:19
brought forth upon this c.	LINC 199:8
C. isolated	BROC 67:5
knowest of no strange c.	DAVI 106:20
continental may be quite c.	ROBI 257:20
continually think c. of those	SPEN 300:9
continuance c. in well doing	BIBL 49:5
continuation c. of politics	CLAU 94:1
continued How long soever it hath c.	COKE 95:16
continuing no c. city	BIBL 51:20
contract C. into a span	HERB 157:18
social c.	ROUS 261:1
Social C. is nothing more	WELL 331:16
verbal c. isn't worth	GOLD 144:9
contradict Do I c. myself	WHIT 334:1
Never c.	FISH 128:6
truth which you cannot c.	SOCR 298:23
contradictions chain of c.	CLAR 93:8
contrary directed to c. parts	NEWT 233:12
everythin goes c. with me	DICK 109:22
On the c.	IBSE 168:14
trial is by what is c.	MILT 223:15
contribution make his own c.	MORE 228:6
contrite broken and c. heart	ELEA 121:1
control Ground c. to Major Tom	BOWI 65:16
convenient c. that there be gods	OVID 238:12
convent C. of the Sacred Heart	ELIO 122:19
conversation C. is imperative	WHIT 333:10
subject of c.	CHES 89:5
third-rate c.	PLOM 246:7
conversations without pictures or c.	CARR 83:13
conversing With thee c.	MILT 222:3
conversion c. of the Jews	MARV 213:20
convert who shall c. me	WESL 332:6
converted Except ye be c.	BIBL 44:13
have not c. a man	MORL 228:10
convictions c. are hills	FITZ 129:6
convince we c. ourselves	JUNI 179:18
convinces man who c. the world	DARW 106:10
cookery c. do	MERE 217:1
Football and c.	SMIT 297:13
cookies baked c. and had teas	CLIN 94:14
cooking 'plain' c. cannot be entrusted	MORP 228:11
cooks as good c. go	SAKI 263:14
Devil sends c.	GARR 136:10
literary c.	MORE 227:23
cool c. web of language	GRAV 146:5
in the c. of the day	BIBL 33:7
rather be dead than c.	COBA 95:6
think of C. Britannia	BENN 29:18
cooled C. a long age	KEAT 182:10

cooling for c. the blood — FLAN 129:15
cooperation partnership and c. — ANON 6:8
coot haunts of c. and hern — TENN 310:13
copies few originals and many c. — TOCQ 318:10
copy to every book its c. — COLU 97:17
cor C. ad cor loquitur — NEWM 233:9
J'aime le son du c. — VIGN 324:3
coral C. is far more red — SHAK 290:9
India's c. strand — HEBE 155:1
corbies twa c. — BALL 24:13
cord silver c. be loosed — BIBL 38:34
stretch a c. however fine — WHEW 333:3
threefold c. — BIBL 38:19
triple c. — BURK 73:20
corda Sursum c. — MISS 224:3
core c. of a world's culture — BOLD 57:11
deep heart's c. — YEAT 343:7
cork c. out of my lunch — FIEL 127:20
corkscrews crooked as c. — AUDE 17:28
cormorant common c. (or shag) — ISHE 169:12
C. devouring Time — SHAK 278:17
corn amid the alien c. — KEAT 182:14
breast high amid the c. — HOOD 162:6
c. as high as an elephant's eye — HAMM 150:21
C. rigs, an' barley rigs — BURN 75:13
c. was orient — TRAH 319:3
lower the price of c. — MELB 216:6
stop raising c. — LEAS 195:22
there was c. in Egypt — BIBL 33:34
two ears of c. — SWIF 306:19
corner At every c., I meet my Father — LOWE 203:22
c. in the thing I love — SHAK 284:23
c. of a foreign field — BROO 67:23
in a c., some untidy spot — AUDE 18:9
wind in that c. — SHAK 284:2
corners three c. of the world — SHAK 277:4
cornet young c. of horse — WALP 327:22
Cornish twenty thousand C. men — HAWK 153:10
corny c. as Kansas in August — HAMM 150:26
Coromandel coast of C. — SITW 296:15
On the coast of C. — LEAR 195:9
coronets more than c. — TENN 312:1
corporation c. to have a conscience — THUR 318:2
corporations [c.] cannot commit treason — COKE 95:18
corpore Mens sana in c. sano — JUVE 180:4
corpse c. in the case — BARH 25:4
make a lovely c. — DICK 110:19
corpulent c. man of fifty — HUNT 167:5
corpus Ave verum c. — ANON 12:10
correct All present and c. — ANON 5:16
correcteth he c. — BIBL 37:18
corridors c. of power — SNOW 298:18
corroborative c. detail — GILB 140:18
corrupt c. good manners — BIBL 50:5
moth and rust doth c. — BIBL 42:24
power is apt to c. — PITT 245:10
corrupts absolute power c. — ACTO 1:8
corse c. to the rampart — WOLF 338:10
Cortez like stout C. — KEAT 182:19
cosmetics we make c. — REVS 256:3
cost count the c. — IGNA 168:17
costs C. register competing attractions — KNIG 189:12
Cotopaxi Chimborazo, C. — TURN 320:23
cottage Love and a c. — COLM 97:12
cotton c. is high — HEYW 158:20
C. is King — CHRI 90:20
c. is king — HUGO 166:17
couch when on my c. I lie — WORD 340:2
counsel evil c. is most evil — HESI 158:15
princely c. in his face — MILT 221:18
sometimes c. take — POPE 249:3
took sweet c. — BOOK 62:2
counsellors when c. blanch — BACO 21:7

counsels all good c. — BOOK 58:23
count c. everything — CORN 100:5
c. the cost — IGNA 168:17
if you can c. your money — GETT 138:18
I won the c. — SOMO 299:2
Let me c. the ways — BROW 69:14
let us c. our spoons — JOHN 174:25
When angry, c. four — TWAI 321:11
counted c. our spoons — EMER 124:11
c. them all out — HANR 151:3
countenance cheerful c. — BIBL 37:33
C. Divine — BLAK 55:27
disinheriting c. — SHER 294:20
Knight of the Doleful C. — CERV 86:13
originality of your c. — CLAI 93:6
counter All things c. — HOPK 163:2
counterfeit c. a gloom — MILT 219:22
sleep, death's c. — SHAK 280:17
counterpane land of c. — STEV 303:29
counterpoint Too much c. — BEEC 27:9
counterpoints c. to hack post-horses — MOZA 229:16
counties Forget six c. — MORR 228:18
counting it's the c. — STOP 304:13
country all their c.'s wishes — COLL 97:11
Anyone who loves his c. — GARI 136:5
ask not what your c. — KENN 184:12
betraying my c. — FORS 131:17
billion dollar c. — FOST 132:3
Britain a fit c. — LLOY 200:20
c. be always successful — ADAM 2:1
c. has the government — MAIS 209:20
C. in the town — MART 213:11
c. is lost — WILL 336:9
c. is the world — PAIN 239:16
c. takes her place — EMME 124:19
Cry, the beloved c. — PATO 242:4
died to save their c. — CHES 89:20
die for one's c. — HORA 164:14
every c. but his own — GILB 140:9
fight for its King and C. — GRAH 145:5
first, best c. — GOLD 143:20
for his c.'s sake — FITZ 128:13
for our c.'s good — CART 84:21
friend of every c. — CANN 81:12
friends of every c. — DISR 112:13
God made the c. — COWP 101:28
good news from a far c. — BIBL 38:4
good of his c. — WOTT 341:25
grow up with the c. — GREE 146:22
how I leave my c. — PITT 245:15
I love thee still— My c. — COWP 101:30
impossible to live in a c. — KEAT 183:8
in a c. village — AUST 20:2
in another c. — MARL 212:12
I pray for the c. — HALE 149:14
King and c. need you — ANON 11:7
lose for my c. — HALE 149:16
love to serve my c. — GIBR 139:14
My c. is Kiltartan Cross — YEAT 343:4
My c., right or wrong — SCHU 265:21
My c., 'tis of thee — SMIT 297:23
My soul, there is a c. — VAUG 322:20
no c. for old men — YEAT 343:16
no relish for the c. — SMIT 298:6
our c., right or wrong — DECA 107:11
past is a foreign c. — HART 153:1
quarrel in a far away c. — CHAM 86:19
Queen and c. — THOM 317:7
rather than a c. — PILG 244:21
see much of the c. — GLAD 141:19
serve our c. — ADDI 2:9
service of their c. — PAIN 239:8
she is my c. still — CHUR 90:23

to all the c. dear — GOLD 143:10
to be had in the c. — HAZL 154:4
tremble for my c. — JEFF 171:18
understand the c. — LESS 198:1
vow to thee, my c. — SPRI 301:3
we can do for our c. — HOLM 161:11
what was good for our c. — WILS 336:16
While there's a c. lane — PARK 241:5
win our c. back — FABE 125:15
your King and your C. — RUBE 261:19
countrymen Friends, Romans, c. — SHAK 276:15
hearts of his c. — LEE 196:10
rebels are our c. — GRAN 145:18
county English c. families — WAUG 329:17
countymen fellow-c. won't kill me — COLL 97:9
couple young c. between the wars — PLOM 246:7
courage C., mon ami — READ 254:20
c. never to submit — MILT 221:4
c. without ferocity — BYRO 79:20
in the morning c. — THOR 317:20
It takes c. — MOWL 229:15
red badge of c. — CRAN 102:22
screw your c. — SHAK 280:1
two o'clock in the morning c. — NAPO 231:6
with a good c. — BOOK 61:14
courageous captains c. — BALL 24:2
freedom depends on being c. — THUC 317:25
cours Suspendez votre c. — LAMA 191:23
course c. of true love — SHAK 282:33
finished my c. — BIBL 51:13
myself to that c. — PEPY 243:17
Of c., of course — JAME 170:26
court c. awards it — SHAK 282:24
c. for owls — BIBL 40:3
not having a C. — BAGE 22:18
Say to the c., it glows — RALE 254:1
courteous c. to strangers — BACO 21:14
courtesy very pink of c. — SHAK 286:24
women with perfect c. — KITC 189:6
courtmartialled c. in my absence — BEHA 27:17
courts Approach with joy his c. — KETH 185:3
case is still before the c. — HORA 163:13
Fresh from brawling c. — TENN 311:24
one day in thy c. — BOOK 62:12
cousins his c. and his aunts — GILB 140:29
couture Haute C. should be fun — LACR 191:13
covenant c. with death — BIBL 39:30
c. with death — GARR 136:12
token of a c. — BIBL 33:22
covenanted c. with him — BIBL 45:11
Coventry for the train at C. — TENN 311:2
cover C. her face — WEBS 330:12
I c. all — SAND 264:9
covered c. his face — BIBL 39:14
covet Thou shalt not c. — BIBL 34:16
covetousness inclined to c. — KORA 190:16
cow c. is of the bovine ilk — NASH 231:13
milk the c. of the world — WILB 334:18
never saw a Purple C. — BURG 73:17
To every c. her calf — COLU 97:17
coward c.'s weapon, poison — FLET 130:13
No c. soul is mine — BRON 67:12
cowards all men would be c. — ROCH 258:14
C. die many times — SHAK 276:6
c. in reasoning — SHAF 268:8
C. in scarlet — GRAN 145:21
cows contented—that's for the c. — CHAN 87:8
cowslip O'er the c.'s velvet head — MILT 219:19
cowslips c. tall her pensioners be — SHAK 283:7
coy Then be not c. — HERR 158:9
coyness This c., lady — MARV 213:19
crabbed C. age and youth — SHAK 289:17
crack c. in the tea-cup opens — AUDE 17:25

cracked c. from side to side — TENN 312:5
crackling c. of thorns — BIBL 38:21
cradle c. and the grave — DYER 118:21
c. of the deep — WILL 336:2
c. of the fairy queen — SHAK 283:16
c. to the grave — SHEL 293:19
hand that rocks the c. — WALL 327:3
rocking the c. — ROBI 258:6
cradling evil c. — KORA 190:10
craft c. so long to lerne — CHAU 88:24
craggy c. paths of study — JONS 177:21
crane tall as a c. — SITW 296:11
crankum crinkum c. — AUBR 17:13
craving full as c. too — DRYD 116:27
getting rid of c. — PALI 240:2
crazed c. with the spell of far Arabia — DE L 108:5
crazy C. like a fox — PERE 243:19
c. to fly more missions — HELL 155:12
he's football c. — MCGR 207:14
creaks morning light c. down again — SITW 296:11
cream c.-faced loon — SHAK 281:19
queen of curds and c. — SHAK 289:13
create c. the taste — WORD 341:21
c. the wondrous world — YOUN 344:17
What I cannot c. — FEYN 127:7
created all men are c. equal — ANON 10:14
c. him in his own image — DOST 115:1
monster whom I had c. — SHEL 292:11
Nothing can be c. — LUCR 204:13
creation from the first c. — LLOY 200:16
I hold C. in my foot — HUGH 166:10
present at the C. — ALFO 3:20
this c. has arisen — RIG 257:6
your niche in c. — HALL 150:10
creative c. hate — CATH 85:13
c. urge — BAKU 23:5
Deception is not as c. — SAUN 265:5
creator abide with my C. God — CLAR 93:10
C., if He exists — HALD 149:12
image of the C. — BONA 57:21
myself and my C. — NEWM 232:22
Remember now thy C. — BIBL 38:33
creature God's first C. — BACO 22:3
'lone lorn c. — DICK 109:22
creatures c. great and small — ALEX 3:16
credit greatly to his c. — GILB 141:2
In science the c. goes — DARW 106:10
let the c. go — FITZ 128:16
credite Experto c. — VIRG 325:7
credo C. in unum Deum — MISS 224:1
C. quia impossibile — TERT 314:16
creed last article of my c. — GAND 135:18
Sapping a solemn c. — BYRO 78:1
creeds dust of c. outworn — SHEL 293:16
Light half-believers in our casual c. — ARNO 15:18
live their c. — GUES 148:10
than in half the c. — TENN 311:10
creep Ambition can c. — BURK 74:11
bade me c. past — BROW 71:2
make your flesh c. — DICK 111:4
creeps c. rustling to her knees — KEAT 181:5
crème c. de la crème — SPAR 299:23
cribbed cabined, c., confined — SHAK 280:27
cricket C.—a game which the English — MANC 210:17
c. as organized loafing — TEMP 310:9
c. on the hearth — MILT 219:22
c. test — TEBB 310:5
c. with their peasants — TREV 319:8
everything lost but c. — CARD 82:4
cried little children c. — MOTL 229:13
when he c. — AUDE 18:1
crieth c. in the wilderness — BIBL 40:7
crime c. of being a young man — PITT 245:9

crime (cont.)
c. you haven't committed — POWE 250:20
Napoleon of c. — DOYL 115:15
never a c. — CORN 100:4
punishment fit the c. — GILB 140:15
Tough on c. — BLAI 55:6
worse than a c. — BOUL 65:5
crimes c. are committed in thy name — ROLA 259:9
c., follies, and misfortunes — GIBB 139:2
c. of this guilty land — BROW 68:14
Successful c. alone — DRYD 117:4
virtues made or c. — DEFO 107:17
worst of c. — SHAW 291:1
criminal ends I think c. — KEYN 185:8
while there is a c. element — DEBS 107:10
crimson Cat with c. whiskers — LEAR 195:18
Now sleeps the c. petal — TENN 313:14
cringe to the cultural c. — KEAT 181:1
crinkum c. crankum — AUBR 17:13
crisp Deep and c. and even — NEAL 232:1
Crispian feast of C. — SHAK 275:9
crisps like eating c. — BOY 65:18
critic c. is a bundle of biases — BALL 24:18
c. is a man who knows the way — TYNA 321:14
C., you have frowned — WORD 341:2
cry of the c. for five — WHIS 333:4
important book, the c. assumes — WOOL 339:8
not the c. who counts — ROOS 260:3
criticism C. is a life without risk — LAHR 191:19
c. of life — ARNO 16:2
father of English c. — JOHN 173:20
criticize c. What you can't understand — DYLA 119:10
croaks c. the fatal entrance — SHAK 279:13
crocodile How doth the little c. — CARR 83:15
crocodiles wisdom of the c. — BACO 21:35
Cromwell C., I charge thee — SHAK 275:25
ruin that C. knocked about — BEDF 27:6
cronies money-grabbing c. — HAGU 149:5
crooked crag with c. hands — TENN 310:22
c. as corkscrews — AUDE 17:28
C. things may be as stiff — LOCK 201:5
c. timber of humanity — KANT 180:15
set the c. straight — MORR 228:17
croppy Hoppy, C., Droppy — ELLI 124:1
crops c. the flowery food — POPE 248:9
cross bear the c. gladly — THOM 315:21
c. of gold — BRYA 71:22
c. of Jesus — BARI 25:5
no c., no crown — PENN 243:9
old rugged c. — BENN 29:19
see thee ever c.-gartered — SHAK 288:24
survey the wondrous c. — WATT 329:10
crossbow With my c. I shot — COLE 96:11
crosses Between the c., row on row — MCCR 207:3
crossness make c. and dirt succeed — FORS 131:12
crow before the cock c. — BIBL 45:14
upstart c. — GREE 147:4
crowd will always save Barabbas — COCT 95:12
Far from the madding c.'s — GRAY 146:17
crowded Across a c. room — HAMM 150:23
c. hour of glorious life — MORD 227:21
crowds talk with c. — KIPL 187:21
crown abdicate the C. — JUAN 179:7
Caesar's laurel c. — BLAK 55:14
c. in possession — PAIN 239:7
C. is, according to the saying — BAGE 22:11
c. of life — BIBL 52:5
c. of thorns — BRYA 71:22
c. of twelve stars — BIBL 52:13
c. thy good with brotherhood — BATE 26:5
c. to her husband — BIBL 37:26
glory of my c. — ELIZ 123:8
head that wears a c. — SHAK 274:20

I give away my c. — SHAK 285:27
Indian c. — ROSS 260:15
influence of the C. — DUNN 118:12
no cross, no c. — PENN 243:9
of an earthly c. — MARL 212:16
put on my c. — SHAK 269:6
strike his father's c. — SHAK 274:29
Within the hollow c. — SHAK 285:21
crowned c. with thorns — KELL 183:25
crowner C.'s Quest — BARH 25:4
crowning c. mercy — CROM 103:19
crowns Casting down their golden c. — HEBE 155:3
c. are empty things — DEFO 107:21
crucible America is God's C. — ZANG 344:23
crucified c., dead, and buried — BOOK 58:16
when they c. my Lord — ANON 10:16
crucify mankind — BRYA 71:22
cruel c. and unusual punishment — CONS 99:17
C., but composed — ARNO 15:11
C. necessity — CROM 103:17
c. only to be kind — SHAK 272:27
jealousy is c. as the grave — BIBL 39:8
State business is a c. trade — HALI 150:6
Such c. glasses — HOWE 165:18
cruellest April is the c. month — ELIO 122:20
cruelty C. has a human heart — BLAK 56:16
full Of direst c. — SHAK 279:14
crumbs dogs eat of the c. — BIBL 44:8
fed with the c. — BIBL 47:3
crumpet thinking man's c. — MUIR 229:19
cruse oil in a c. — BIBL 36:9
cry c. all the way to the bank — LIBE 198:23
c. come unto thee — BOOK 60:12
c. of the Little Peoples — LE G 196:17
C., the beloved country — PATO 242:4
his little son should c. — CORN 100:7
indeed they c. — WEBS 330:18
no language but a c. — TENN 311:19
we c. that we are come — SHAK 278:4
we still should c. — BACO 22:8
crying child is ever c. — WROT 341:27
c. in the wilderness — BIBL 42:6
cuckoo C.-echoing, bell-swarmèd — HOPK 162:21
C.! Shall I call thee bird — WORD 341:15
c. then, on every tree — SHAK 278:22
Lhude sing c. — ANON 10:3
weather the c. likes — HARD 152:3
cucumber c. should be well sliced — JOHN 174:13
cucumbers but c. after all — JOHN 176:5
sun-beams out of c. — SWIF 306:20
cui C. bono — CICE 93:1
culpa mea c. — MISS 223:26
O felix c. — MISS 224:14
cultivate c. our garden — VOLT 326:1
C. simplicity — LAMB 192:10
cultiver Il faut c. notre jardin — VOLT 326:1
cultural c. Chernobyl — MNOU 225:7
c. Stalingrad — BALL 24:17
culture core of a world's c. — BOLD 57:11
hear the word c. — JOHS 177:6
integral part of c. — GOUL 144:22
man of c. rare — GILB 140:22
pursue C. in bands — WHAR 332:24
cultures two c. — SNOW 298:19
Cumae saw the Sibyl at C. — ROSS 260:20
Cumaei Ultima C. — VIRG 325:10
cumbered c. about much serving — BIBL 46:18
cunning right hand forget her c. — BOOK 63:24
cup death in the c. — BURN 75:12
let this c. pass — BIBL 45:15
my c. overflows — SCOT 266:29
tak a c. o' kindness yet — BURN 75:5

Cupid C. painted blind	SHAK 283:2
C.'s darts do not feel	ANON 8:19
Cupidinesque *Veneres C.*	CATU 85:18
cups c., That cheer	COWP 102:3
cura *sedet atra C.*	HORA 164:13
curable disease. But c.	MACA 205:9
curantur *Similia similibus c.*	ANON 12:23
curate name of a C.	SMIT 298:5
curates preached to death by wild c.	SMIT 298:11
curb use the snaffle and the c.	CAMP 80:21
curds queen of c. and cream	SHAK 289:13
cure c. of all diseases	BROW 69:8
C. the disease	BACO 21:11
no C. for this Disease	BELL 28:10
cured c. by more democracy	SMIT 297:12
C. yesterday of my disease	PRIO 251:10
cures c. are suggested	CHEK 88:31
Like c. like	ANON 12:23
curfew c. tolls the knell	GRAY 146:13
curiosity c., freckles, and doubt	PARK 240:15
c. of individuals	ARTS 16:9
Disinterested intellectual c.	TREV 319:7
curiouser C. and curiouser	CARR 83:14
curl had a little c.	LONG 202:10
currency Debasing the moral c.	ELIO 121:7
debauch the c.	KEYN 185:9
one c.	NAPO 231:4
curse C. God, and die	BIBL 37:1
c. is come upon me	TENN 312:5
I know how to c.	SHAK 287:5
open foe may prove a c.	GAY 137:7
real c. of Eve	RHYS 256:10
curst c. be he that moves my bones	SHAK 290:17
to all succeeding ages c.	DRYD 116:15
curtain Bring down the c.	RABE 253:15
iron c.	CHUR 91:23
Iron C. did not reach	SOLZ 298:29
kept behind a c.	PAIN 239:13
lets the c. fall	POPE 246:24
curtained C. with cloudy red	MILT 220:26
curtiosity full of 'satiable c.	KIPL 188:22
cushion c. and soft Dean	POPE 247:20
custodes *quis custodiet ipsos C.*	JUVE 179:24
custodiet *quis c. ipsos Custodes*	JUVE 179:24
custom C. is the great guide	HUME 166:18
c. loathsome to the eye	JAME 170:8
C. reconciles us	BURK 74:4
C., that unwritten law	D'AV 106:11
follow the c.	AMBR 4:14
Lest one good c.	TENN 311:14
customer c. is never wrong	RITZ 257:14
customers people of c.	SMIT 297:9
cut c. him out in little stars	SHAK 286:29
c. my conscience to fit	HELL 155:15
Look at the c.	LOES 201:13
man who c. his country's	BYRO 79:11
most unkindest c. of all	SHAK 276:20
we are going to c. it off	POWE 250:21
will I c. off Israel	BIBL 36:1
Cutty-sark Weel done, C.	BURN 75:27
cycle c. of Cathay	TENN 312:16
cylinder in terms of the c.	CÉZA 86:16
cymbals well-tuned c.	BOOK 63:30
Cynara faithful to thee, C.	DOWS 115:10
cynic definition of a c.	WILD 335:7
cynosure c. of neighbouring eyes	MILT 220:4
cypress in sad c.	SHAK 288:19
Cythera C., so they say	BAUD 26:8

D

dad girls in slacks remember D.	BETJ 31:16
if the d. is present	ORTO 237:3
They fuck you up, your mum and d.	LARK 193:14
dada mama of d.	FADI 125:20
daffodils d., That come before	SHAK 289:11
dances with the d.	WORD 340:2
Fair d., we weep	HERR 158:7
host, of golden d.	WORD 340:1
never saw d. so beautiful	WORD 339:15
When d. begin to peer	SHAK 289:5
dagger Is this a d.	SHAK 280:5
daggers d. in men's smiles	SHAK 280:20
Give me the d.	SHAK 280:11
daily our d. bread	BIBL 42:23
daintily I must have things d. served	BETJ 31:21
dainty d. rogue in porcelain	MERE 216:26
dairy doth nightly rob the d.	JONS 177:15
dairymaid Queen asked the D.	MILN 219:2
daisies Buttercups and d.	HOWI 165:20
d. pied and violets blue	SHAK 278:22
D., those pearled Arcturi	SHEL 293:21
Meadows trim with d. pied	MILT 220:3
Dakotas D., I am for war	RED 255:6
dalliance primrose path of d.	SHAK 271:6
dam pretty chickens and their d.	SHAK 281:13
damage d. to the earth	COUS 101:1
damaged Archangel a little d.	LAMB 192:12
damages d. his mind	ANON 12:4
Damascus rivers of D.	BIBL 36:24
dame belle d. sans merci	KEAT 181:20
belle d. sans mercy	KEAT 181:9
nothin' like a d.	HAMM 150:25
damn D. the age	LAMB 192:13
d. the consequences	MILN 219:7
D. the torpedoes	FARR 126:15
D. with faint praise	POPE 247:10
d. you England	OSBO 237:30
don't give a d.	MITC 224:22
one another d.	WYCH 342:4
with a spot I d. him	SHAK 276:27
damnation d. of his taking-off	SHAK 279:21
damnations Twenty-nine distinct d.	BROW 71:6
damned All silent, and all d.	WORD 340:18
beautiful and d.	FITZ 129:5
brandy of the d.	SHAW 291:11
D. below Judas	COWP 101:20
D. from here to Eternity	KIPL 187:17
d. if you don't	DOW 115:9
d. to Fame	POPE 246:19
Faustus must be d.	MARL 212:7
for an apple d. mankind	OTWA 238:8
lies, d. lies and statistics	DISR 113:8
public be d.	VAND 322:12
Publish and be d.	WELL 331:8
written a d. play	REYN 256:4
damnosa *D. hereditas*	GAIU 135:8
damozel blessed d.	ROSS 260:16
Dan D. even to Beer-sheba	BIBL 35:11
Dangerous D. McGrew	SERV 268:3
Danaë all D. to the stars	TENN 313:15
Danaos *timeo D. et dona ferentes*	VIRG 324:13
dance D., dance, dance, little lady	COWA 101:3
d. is a measured pace	BACO 20:20
D. tiptoe, bull	BUNT 72:19
d. to the music of time	POWE 250:18
d. wyt me, in irlaunde	ANON 7:13
know the dancer from the d.	YEAT 342:11
Let's face the music and d.	BERL 30:18
Lord of the D.	CART 84:24
On with the d.	BYRO 77:26

dance (*cont.*)
  see me d. the Polka — GROS 148:3
  too far from the d. — POUN 250:13
  will you join the d. — CARR 83:24
danced d. by the light of the moon — LEAR 195:16
  d. in the morning — CART 84:24
  d. with the Prince of Wales — FARJ 126:6
  reeled and d. — WORD 339:15
  There was a star d. — SHAK 283:27
dancer know the d. from the dance — YEAT 342:11
dancers d. are all gone under the hill — ELIO 121:24
  nation of d. — EQUI 125:1
dances d. with the daffodils — WORD 340:2
  it d. — LIGN 199:3
dancing [D.] a perpendicular expression — SHAW 292:5
  d. cheek-to-cheek — BERL 30:16
  d. is love's proper exercise — DAVI 106:15
  Fluttering and d. — WORD 340:1
  manners of a d. master — JOHN 174:19
  mature women, *d.* — FRIE 133:25
  past our d. days — SHAK 286:15
dandy Yankee Doodle D. — COHA 95:14
Dane paying the D.-geld — KIPL 188:15
  Roman than a D. — SHAK 273:20
danger big with d. and mischief — GIBB 139:1
  D., the spur — CHAP 87:17
  Oft in d. — WHIT 333:9
  only when in d. — OWEN 238:18
  Out of this nettle, d. — SHAK 273:32
  run into any kind of d. — BOOK 58:19
  so much as to be out of d. — HUXL 167:22
dangerous d. to know — LAMB 192:1
  d. to meet it alone — WHAR 332:24
  knowledge is d. — HUXL 167:22
  many a d. thing — BISH 54:10
  more d. than an idea — ALAI 3:8
  such men are d. — SHAK 276:1
dangers D. by being despised — BURK 74:21
  d. of the seas — PARK 241:3
  d. of this night — BOOK 59:1
  d. thou canst make us scorn — BURN 75:25
  No d. fright him — JOHN 174:5
  She loved me for the d. — SHAK 284:13
dangling d. apricocks — SHAK 285:24
Daniel D. come to judgement — SHAK 282:23
Danish fame of D. kings — ANON 13:4
Danny hangin' D. Deever — KIPL 187:12
dapple d.-dawn-drawn Falcon — HOPK 163:8
dappled d. things — HOPK 163:1
dare I d. not — SHAK 279:25
  none d. call it treason — HARI 152:10
  You who d. — MERE 217:7
dared d., and done — SMAR 297:4
dares Who d. do more is none — SHAK 279:26
  Who d. wins — ANON 11:1
Darien Silent, upon a peak in D. — KEAT 182:19
daring d. pilot in extremity — DRYD 116:16
  d. young man — LEYB 198:22
dark agree in the d. — BACO 21:31
  as good i' th' d. — HERR 158:4
  blind man in a d. room — BOWE 65:14
  come out of the d. — MANN 211:6
  comes the d. — COLE 96:14
  d. and bloody ground — O'HA 235:23
  d. and bright — BYRO 79:14
  d. and evil days — INGR 169:4
  d. and stormy night — BULW 72:12
  d. and true and tender — TENN 313:9
  d. as night — SHAK 290:12
  d., dark, dark — MILT 223:1
  d. is light enough — FRY 134:17
  d. night of the soul — FITZ 129:8
  d. night of the soul — JOHN 172:14

d. Satanic mills — BLAK 55:27
D. with excessive bright — MILT 221:27
d. world of sin — BICK 53:17
go home in the d. — HENR 156:20
great leap in the d. — VANB 322:9
hides a d. soul — MILT 219:12
In the d. backward — SHAK 287:2
leap in the d. — HOBB 160:6
leap into the d. — BROW 68:17
O d. dark dark — ELIO 121:25
Out in the d. — THOM 316:17
people who live in the d. — SHOR 295:1
Tired of his d. dominion — MERE 217:4
we are for the d. — SHAK 269:3
We work in the d. — JAME 170:18
What in me is d. — MILT 221:2
darker I am the d. brother — HUGH 166:8
darkies Oh! d., how my heart — FOST 132:9
darkling D. I listen — KEAT 182:13
  d. plain — ARNO 15:5
darkly through a glass, d. — BIBL 49:33
darkness cast off the works of d. — BIBL 49:21
  Chaos and old — MARR 212:26
  counteracts the powers of d. — SMAR 297:1
  curse the d. — STEV 303:13
  d. comprehended it not — BIBL 47:17
  d. falls at Thy behest — ELLE 123:19
  d. of mere being — JUNG 179:14
  d. of the land — TENN 311:31
  d. visible — MILT 221:3
  d. was upon the face — BIBL 32:21
  Dawn on our d. — HEBE 154:19
  encounter d. as a bride — SHAK 281:32
  In me d. — BONH 58:2
  in the d. bind them — TOLK 318:13
  into outer d. — BIBL 43:15
  Lighten our d. — BOOK 59:1
  light to them that sit in d. — BIBL 46:1
  lump bred up in d. — KYD 191:3
  ocean of d. — FOX 132:14
  people that walked in d. — BIBL 39:18
  pestilence that walketh in d. — BOOK 62:17
  prince of d. — SHAK 277:26
  rulers of the d. — BIBL 50:23
  sit in d. — BOOK 62:28
  sit in d. here — MILT 221:19
  there is d. everywhere — NEHR 232:4
  Thou makest d. — BOOK 62:24
  universal d. buries all — POPE 246:24
  works of d. — BOOK 59:12
darling call you d. after sex — BARN 25:10
  d. buds of May — SHAK 289:23
  d. man, a daarlin' man — O'CA 235:17
  my d. from the lions — BOOK 61:15
dart shook a dreadful d. — MILT 221:22
data some d. was bound to be — WATS 328:26
date d. which will live in infamy — ROOS 259:21
  doubles your chances for a d. — ALLE 4:9
  last d. slides — EWAR 125:12
  Standards are always out of d. — BENN 29:20
dates matter of d. — TALL 309:3
daughter d. of debate — ELIZ 123:7
  d. of the gods — TENN 310:21
  d. went through the river — BUNY 73:10
  Don't put your d. on the stage — COWA 101:8
  ever rear a d. — GAY 137:1
  farmer's d. — CALV 80:13
  for the d.'s daughter — SWIN 308:4
  King's d. — BOOK 61:24
  O my ducats! O my d. — SHAK 282:10
  so is her d. — BIBL 40:30
  Sole d. of his voice — MILT 222:17
  taken his little d. — LONG 202:9

daughters d. of my father's house — SHAK 288:22
d. of the Philistines — BIBL 35:27
thunder, fire, are my d. — SHAK 277:19
Words are men's d. — MADD 209:4
words are the d. — JOHN 173:11
dauntless D. the slug-horn — BROW 69:27
so d. in war — SCOT 266:17
dauphin kingdom of daylight's d. — HOPK 163:8
David D. his ten thousands — BIBL 35:23
D. wrote the Psalms — NAYL 231:22
royal D.'s city — ALEX 3:17
dawn d. comes up like thunder — KIPL 187:26
D. on our darkness — HEBE 154:19
grey d. is breaking — CRAW 103:5
in that d. to be alive — WORD 339:21
redemption's happy d. — CASW 85:11
Rosy-fingered d. — HOME 161:21
dawning bird of d. — SHAK 270:25
d. of the age of Aquarius — RADO 253:21
day Action this D. — ANON 5:13
arrow that flieth by d. — BOOK 62:17
bright d. is done — SHAK 269:3
burn thee by d. — BOOK 63:13
D. by day — BOOK 58:13
d. is at hand — BIBL 49:21
d. of small nations — CHAM 86:18
d. of wrath — MISS 224:11
d.'s at the morn — BROW 70:27
d.'s garish eye — MILT 219:23
d. that I die — MCLE 208:1
d. the music died — MCLE 207:21
d. Thou gavest, Lord — ELLE 123:19
d.-to-day business — LAFO 191:17
end of a perfect d. — BOND 57:22
every d. to be lost — JOHN 176:20
first d. — BIBL 32:22
first, last, everlasting d. — DONN 114:4
gold of the d. — CROS 104:4
heat of the d. — BIBL 44:23
I have lost a d. — TITU 318:8
knell of parting d. — GRAY 146:13
lark at break of d. — SHAK 289:26
Let the d. perish — BIBL 37:2
long d.'s journey — O'NE 236:12
met them at close of d. — YEAT 342:19
murmur of a summer's d. — ARNO 15:14
night and d., brother — BORR 64:16
not a second on the d. — COOK 99:18
of this immortal d. — SHEL 293:19
one d. in thy courts — BOOK 62:12
seize the d. — HORA 164:7
sinks the d.-star — MILT 220:19
So foul and fair a d. — SHAK 279:3
spent one whole d. — THOM 315:20
Sufficient unto the d. — BIBL 43:1
this d. as if thy last — KEN 184:2
through her busy d. — JAGG 170:2
to a summer's d. — SHAK 289:23
tomorrow is another d. — MITC 224:23
Until the d. break — BIBL 39:5
weary d. have end — SPEN 300:12
Without all hope of d. — MILT 223:1
write every other d. — DOUG 115:7
daylight d. in upon magic — BAGE 22:20
kingdom of d.'s dauphin — HOPK 163:8
days behold these present d. — SHAK 290:3
d. are evil — BIBL 50:20
d. grow short — ANDE 5:7
d. of wine and roses — DOWS 115:11
d. on the earth are as a shadow — BIBL 36:34
d. that are no more — TENN 313:7
E'er half my d. — MILT 223:9
first 1,000 d. — KENN 184:11

number of my d. — BOOK 61:19
of few d. — BIBL 37:6
Ten d. that shook the world — REED 255:13
that thy d. may be long — BIBL 34:16
Three whole d. together — SUCK 305:13
two d. like a tiger — TIPU 318:7
We have seen better d. — SHAK 287:23
daytime d. television — TOYN 319:2
dazzle mine eyes d. — WEBS 330:12
dea *vera incessu patuit d.* — VIRG 324:11
dead and Guildenstern are d. — SHAK 273:24
and the noble D. — WORD 340:24
bivouac of the d. — O'HA 235:22
character d. at every word — SHER 294:18
cold and pure and very d. — LEWI 198:18
completely consistent are the d. — HUXL 167:15
conference With the d. — WEBS 330:9
cut in half; he's d. — GRAH 145:7
D.! and never called me — WOOD 339:2
d.-born from the press. — HUME 166:22
d. bury their dead — BIBL 43:17
d. don't die — LAWR 194:24
D., for a ducat — SHAK 272:23
d. for the duration — ASQU 16:17
d. he would like to see me — HOLL 161:6
d. level — ELIO 121:12
d. lion — BIBL 38:25
d. men lost their bones — ELIO 122:24
d. shall not have died in vain — LINC 199:8
d. woman bites not — GRAY 146:10
democracy of the d. — CHES 90:5
Down among the d. — DYER 119:1
ere I am laid out d. — HERR 158:1
Evelyn Hope is d. — BROW 70:4
face of the d. — BEER 27:14
famous calm and d. — BROW 70:6
found, when she was d. — GOLD 143:15
God is d. — FROM 134:3
grand to be blooming well d. — SARO 264:20
had already been d. a year — LEHR 196:20
He is d. and gone, lady — SHAK 273:1
HOMER d. — ANON 9:19
if the d. rise not — BIBL 50:4
If the d. talk to you — SZAS 308:10
lang time d. — ANON 6:2
Lilacs out of the d. land — ELIO 122:20
Lycidas is d. — MILT 220:10
mansions of the d. — CRAB 102:12
Mistah Kurtz—he d. — CONR 99:8
more to say when I am d. — ROBI 258:1
My d. king — JOYC 178:24
not d.—but gone — ROGE 259:2
not d., but sleepeth — BIBL 43:23
Not many d. — COCK 95:10
on the d. man's chest — STEV 303:21
our English d. — SHAK 274:33
past never d. — FAUL 126:16
quick, and the d. — DEWA 109:8
rather be d. than cool — COBA 95:6
saying 'Lord Jones D.' — CHES 90:8
sea gave up the d. — BIBL 52:23
Sea shall give up her d. — BOOK 64:1
simplify me when I'm d. — DOUG 115:5
There are no d. — MAET 209:7
they're a' d. — ANON 7:10
think you are d. or deported — HOWE 165:19
thirteen men lay d. — HEAN 154:13
told me you were d. — CORY 100:14
to the d. we owe only truth — VOLT 326:10
very d. of winter — ELIO 122:7
was alive and is d. — ANON 7:9
was d., and is alive — BIBL 46:35
we are all d. — KEYN 185:13

dead (*cont.*)
wench is d. — MARL 212:12
When I am d. — MCGO 207:13
without works is d. — BIBL 51:21
you're ten years d. — HAYE 153:19
deadlines daily d. — ZOLA 345:8
deadlock Holy d. — HERB 157:4
deadly more d. in the long run — TWAI 321:4
more d. than the male — KIPL 187:15
deaf d. as an adder — ADAM 1:18
d., inexorable — SIDN 295:6
deal new d. for the American people — ROOS 259:14
square d. afterwards — ROOS 260:1
deals D. are my art form — TRUM 320:11
dean cushion and soft D. — POPE 247:20
no dogma, no D. — DISR 113:6
deans dowagers for d. — TENN 313:2
dear D. dead women — BROW 71:11
D., dirty Dublin — JOYC 178:18
Plato is d. to me — ARIS 14:20
too d. for my possession — SHAK 289:34
deario cheerio my d. — MARQ 212:21
dearly D. beloved brethren — BOOK 58:4
death abolish the d. penalty — KARR 180:16
After the first d. — THOM 316:7
ancients dreaded d. — HARE 152:6
angel of d. — BRIG 66:20
Angel of D. — BYRO 78:14
another terror to d. — LYND 205:1
any man's d. diminishes me — DONN 114:19
at the point of d. — SHAK 286:36
Be absolute for d. — SHAK 281:31
before his d. — BIBL 41:25
Black Widow, d. — LOWE 203:23
Brother to D. — DANI 105:14
Brother to D. — FLET 130:8
Brought d. into the world — MILT 220:33
build the house of d. — MONT 226:8
build your ship of d. — LAWR 194:20
Call in thy d.'s-head there — HERB 157:10
Come away, come away, d. — SHAK 288:19
coming up to d. — SAUN 265:5
could not stop for D. — DICK 111:12
covenant with d. — BIBL 39:30
covenant with d. — GARR 136:12
Dear, beauteous d. — VAUG 323:3
d. after life — SPEN 300:14
D. and his brother — SHEL 293:20
d. and taxes — DEFO 107:12
d. and taxes — FRAN 133:9
D. and taxes and childbirth — MITC 224:21
d. bandaged my eyes — BROW 71:2
D. be not proud — DONN 113:19
D. closes all — TENN 313:31
D. has a thousand doors — MASS 215:1
d. hath no more dominion — BIBL 49:12
D. hath so many doors — FLET 130:7
d. hath ten thousand — WEBS 330:11
d. in the cup — BURN 75:12
d. in the pot — BIBL 36:23
D. is a master from Germany — CELA 86:11
[D. is] nature's way — ANON 6:11
d. is not far behind — WESL 332:8
D. is nothing at all — HOLL 161:7
D. is the cure — BROW 69:8
D. joins us to — YOUN 344:19
D. lies dead — SWIN 307:23
D. lies on her — SHAK 286:34
D. never takes the wise man — LA F 191:15
d., nor life — BIBL 49:18
D. of a salesman — MILL 218:13
d. of kings — SHAK 285:20
d. part thee and me — BIBL 35:13

D.'s bright angel — PROC 251:14
d. shall have no dominion — THOM 316:2
D., the most awful of evils — EPIC 124:25
D. thou shalt die — DONN 113:20
d.-tick is audible — CURZ 105:8
d., where is thy sting — BIBL 50:8
D., where is thy sting-a-ling — ANON 9:4
D. who comes at last — SCOT 266:15
d., who had the soldier singled — DOUG 115:6
easeful D. — KEAT 182:13
evidence of life after d. — SOPE 299:8
faithful unto d. — BIBL 52:5
Finality is d. — STEP 302:17
forced marches, battles and d. — GARI 136:5
from d. lead me to — UPAN 321:21
gave d. time to live — GUIB 148:12
Glad to d.'s mystery — HOOD 162:1
go on living even after d. — FRAN 133:4
her own d.-warrant — BAGE 22:19
his name that sat on him was d. — BIBL 52:9
hour of d. — BOOK 59:7
I am become d. — OPPE 236:16
improved by d. — SAKI 263:13
interest in d. — JAME 171:2
in that sleep of d. — SHAK 272:1
in their d. not divided — BIBL 35:28
in the shadow of d. — BIBL 46:1
in the valley of D. — TENN 310:15
Into the jaws of D. — TENN 310:17
I signed my d. warrant — COLL 97:7
isn't sex but d. — SONT 299:7
just, and mighty D. — RALE 254:6
Keeps D. his court — SHAK 285:21
Lead me from d. to life — KUMA 191:1
liberty, or give me d. — HENR 156:22
life went through with d. — FORT 131:20
living d. — MILT 223:3
Love is strong as d. — BIBL 39:8
love thee better after d. — BROW 69:15
make d. proud — SHAK 269:1
make one in love with d. — SHEL 292:13
matter of life and d. — SHAN 290:19
Men fear d. — BACO 21:9
Morning after D. — DICK 111:14
much possessed by d. — ELIO 122:30
My name is D. — SOUT 299:15
new terror to d. — WETH 332:22
No d. in my lifetime — HEAN 154:15
no one his d. — SENE 267:23
no one knew my d. — ROET 258:22
nothing but d. — UNAM 321:20
Now boast thee, d. — SHAK 269:9
one fear, D.'s shadow — BLUN 57:2
only nervousness or d. — LEBO 196:2
owe God a d. — SHAK 274:23
owest God a d. — SHAK 274:8
preached to d. by wild curates — SMIT 298:11
prepare as though for d. — MANS 211:8
reaction to her d. — ELIZ 123:15
rendezvous with D. — SEEG 267:5
Reports of my d. — TWAI 321:13
Revenge triumphs over d. — BACO 21:10
say to the Angel of D. — MIDR 217:24
set d. aside — TURG 320:16
shadow of d. — BOOK 62:28
shall be destroyed is d. — BIBL 50:3
sharpness of d. — BOOK 58:12
sleep, d.'s counterfeit — SHAK 280:17
snares of d. — BOOK 63:8
soul shall taste of d. — KORA 190:12
stroke of d. — JOHN 173:21
sudden d. — BOOK 59:6
suffers at his d. — LA B 191:8

suicide 25 years after his d.   BEAV 26:17
swallow up d. in victory   BIBL 39:28
Ten years after your d.   HUGH 166:13
there shall be no more d.   BIBL 52:25
This fell sergeant, d.   SHAK 273:19
Those by d. are few   JEFF 171:14
thou shell of d.   MIDD 217:20
up the line to d.   SASS 264:26
valley of the shadow of d.   BOOK 61:7
very quiet d.   WEBS 330:13
wages of sin is d.   BIBL 49:13
way to dusty d.   SHAK 281:24
we are in d.   BOOK 60:24
When d. approached   GIBB 139:10
Why fear d.   FROH 134:2
deaths million d. a statistic   STAL 301:15
  More d. than one must die   WILD 335:17
death sentence take the d. without a whimper
                                                 LAWR 194:25
debasing D. the moral currency   ELIO 121:7
debatable d. line   MACA 206:1
debate daughter of d.   ELIZ 123:7
  Rupert of d.   BULW 72:13
debonair blithe, and d.   MILT 219:26
deboshed Thou d. fish   SHAK 287:12
debt deeper in d.   TRAV 319:6
  national d.   HAMI 150:13
  National D. is a very Good Thing   SELL 267:19
  pay a d. to pleasure   ROCH 258:9
debts forgive us our d.   BIBL 42:23
  pays all d.   SHAK 287:13
  so we can pay our d.   NYER 235:9
decay Change and d.   LYTE 205:5
  our love hath no d.   DONN 114:4
decayed sufficiently d.   GILB 140:21
deceased He first d.   WOTT 341:23
deceitful heart is d.   BIBL 40:26
deceits d. of the world   BOOK 59:5
deceive D. boys with toys   LYSA 205:3
  d. ourselves   BIBL 51:32
  Oh, don't d. me   ANON 6:15
deceiver foe to the D.   ZORO 345:12
  gay d.   COLM 97:14
deceivers Men were d. ever   SHAK 284:1
deceiving d. elf   KEAT 182:15
  nearly d. your friends   CORN 100:10
December D. when they wed   SHAK 270:3
  drear nighted D.   KEAT 181:13
  May to D.   ANDE 5:7
  meetings made D. June   TENN 311:27
Decembers fifteen wild D.   BRON 67:13
decency want of d.   DILL 111:23
decent d. obscurity   GIBB 139:9
decently d. and in order   BIBL 49:34
deception D. is not as creative   SAUN 265:5
decide moment to d.   LOWE 203:18
decision make a 'realistic d.'   MCCA 206:20
deck boy stood on the burning d.   HEMA 155:17
  from the bottom of the d.   SHAP 290:20
  Walk the d. my Captain lies   WHIT 333:21
declaration no d. of war   EDEN 119:17
declare the glory of God   BOOK 61:3
  nothing to d.   WILD 335:22
  ye are to d. it   BOOK 60:13
decline writing the d. and fall   GIBB 139:8
decorate painting not made to d.   PICA 244:18
decorated d., and got rid of   CICE 93:4
decorative to be d. and to do right   FIRB 127:24
decorum *Dulce et d. est*   HORA 164:14
  Dulce et d. est   OWEN 238:24
decoyed d. into our condition   PEPY 243:15
decree d. from Caesar Augustus   BIBL 46:2
  establish the d.   BIBL 41:9

Dee Across the sands of D.   KING 186:19
deed better day, the worse d.   HENR 156:17
  d. is all, the glory nothing   GOET 142:20
  right d. for the wrong reason   ELIO 122:16
  tak the d.   LYDG 204:22
deep cradle of the d.   WILL 336:2
  D. and crisp and even   NEAL 232:1
  d. as a well   SHAK 286:25
  D.-versed in books   MILT 222:30
  From the great d.   TENN 311:5
  Not d. the Poet sees   ARNO 15:12
  Out of the d.   BOOK 63:21
  spirits from the vasty d.   SHAK 274:3
  too d. for tears   WORD 340:14
  wonders in the d.   BOOK 63:1
deeper In d. reverence praise   WHIT 334:5
deer a-chasing the d.   BURN 75:18
  I was a stricken d.   COWP 102:2
  stare of the d.   WILB 334:17
  stricken d.   SHAK 272:16
Deever hangin' Danny D.   KIPL 187:12
défauts *âme est sans d.*   RIMB 257:12
defeat d. is an orphan   CIAN 92:17
  In d.; defiance   CHUR 92:11
  In d. unbeatable   CHUR 92:7
  possibilities of d.   VICT 323:21
defeated d. in a great battle   LIVY 200:13
  Down with the d.   LIVY 200:12
  history to the d.   AUDE 18:21
defect fair d. of nature   MILT 222:22
  she did make d. perfection   SHAK 268:19
defence only d. is in offence   BALD 23:10
defend d. ourselves with guns   GOEB 142:12
  d. to the death your right   VOLT 326:13
  d. us from all perils   BOOK 59:1
defended God abandoned, these d.   HOUS 164:26
defends when attacked it d. itself   ANON 11:10
defiance In defeat;   CHUR 92:11
defied Age will not be d.   BACO 21:22
defiled shall be d.   BIBL 41:26
definition d. is the enclosing   BUTL 77:13
  working d. of hell   SHAW 291:26
deformity Art is significant d.   FRY 134:21
dei *D. gloriam*   ANON 12:7
  vox D.   ALCU 3:10
deities some other new d.   PLAT 245:23
déjà d. vu all over again   BERR 31:10
delay deny, or d.   MAGN 209:12
  Nothing lost by d.   GREE 146:24
delayed d. till I am indifferent   JOHN 174:20
delaying rich by d.   TROL 319:18
delegate When in trouble, d.   BORE 64:12
delenda *D. est Carthago*   CATO 85:15
deleted Expletive d.   ANON 6:19
Delia While D. is away   JAGO 170:5
deliberate Where both d.   MARL 212:9
deliberates woman who d.   ADDI 2:8
deliberation D. sat and public care   MILT 221:18
delicious Afloat. We move: D.   CLOU 94:21
delight D. hath a joy   SIDN 295:15
  Energy is Eternal D.   BLAK 55:20
  ever new d.   MILT 222:8
  firmness, and d.   WOTT 341:24
  hear thy shrill d.   SHEL 293:31
  labour we d. in   SHAK 280:15
  land of pure d.   WATT 329:11
  Let dogs d.   WATT 329:7
  men miscall d.   SHEL 292:18
  phantom of d.   WORD 341:6
  Spirit of D.   SHEL 293:24
  thing met conceives d.   MILT 222:15
delightful no d. ones   LA R 193:19
delights king of intimate d.   COWP 102:4

delitabill Storys to rede ar d.   BARB 24:25
deliver d. us from evil   MISS 224:5
  O d. my soul   BOOK 61:15
deliverance d. from chains   DOUG 115:8
delivered God hath d. him   BIBL 35:25
deluge Après nous le d.   POMP 246:17
delusion d., a mockery   DENM 108:16
democracies d. against despots   DEMO 108:11
  in d. it is the only sacred   FRAN 132:17
democracy cured by more d.   SMIT 297:12
  D. is the name we give   FLER 130:4
  D. is the theory   MENC 216:14
  D. is the worst form   CHUR 92:1
  d. means government   ATTL 17:12
  D. means government by   CHES 90:9
  d. of the dead   CHES 90:5
  d. unbearable   PERE 243:20
  great arsenal of d.   ROOS 259:19
  justice makes d. possible   NIEB 234:4
  less d. to save   ATKI 17:7
  made safe for d.   WILS 337:8
  not the voting that's d.   STOP 304:13
  pollution of d.   WHIT 333:12
  property-owning d.   SKEL 296:18
  Russia an empire or d.   BRZE 71:23
  Two cheers for D.   FORS 131:18
democrat Senator, and a D.   JOHN 173:1
demolition d. of a man   LEVI 198:6
demon wailing for her d.-lover   COLE 96:4
demonstrandum Quod erat d.   EUCL 125:6
den d. of thieves   BIBL 44:25
denied Justice d.   MILL 218:9
Denmark in the state of D.   SHAK 271:14
deny d. me thrice   BIBL 45:14
  d., or delay   MAGN 209:12
  d. the being of a devil   MATH 215:3
  You must d. yourself   GOET 142:17
denying allure by d.   TROL 319:18
Deo D. gratias   MISS 223:29
  Jubilate D., omnis terra   BIBL 52:31
deoch-an-doris Just a wee d.   MORR 228:22
depart servant d. in peace   BIBL 46:7
  will not d.   BIBL 37:39
departed glory is d.   BIBL 35:15
departing and at my d.   ANON 7:4
deported think you are dead or d.   HOWE 165:19
depression d. when you lose yours   TRUM 320:9
depressions terrible d.   SEI 267:9
derangement nice d. of epitaphs   SHER 294:14
Derry oak would sprout in D.   HEAN 154:13
descending comes with clouds d.   WESL 332:3
descensus Facilis d. Averno   VIRG 324:20
descent d. from a monkey   WILB 334:16
description beggared all d.   SHAK 268:18
desert d. shall rejoice   BIBL 40:4
  in a d. land   BIBL 34:29
  Life is the d.   YOUN 344:19
  make straight in the d.   BIBL 40:7
  on the d. air   GRAY 146:16
  Stand in the d.   SHEL 293:11
  Use every man after his d.   SHAK 271:34
deserts D. of vast eternity   MARV 213:21
  his d. are small   MONT 226:23
  she d. the night   MILT 223:2
deserve and d. to get it   MENC 216:14
deserves gets what he d.   ANON 12:1
designs d. were strictly honourable   FIEL 127:15
desire d. of the moth   SHEL 293:28
  d. should so many years   SHAK 274:19
  gratified d.   BLAK 56:3
desired More to be d.   BOOK 61:4
desires all d. known   BOOK 59:18
  all holy d.   BOOK 58:23

d. of our own hearts   BOOK 58:5
d. of the heart   AUDE 17:28
doing what one d.   MILL 218:4
enjoyment of all d.   TANT 309:9
lopping off our d.   SWIF 307:3
desireth as the hart d.   BOOK 61:21
desiring D. this man's art   SHAK 289:35
desk modern man's subservience to the d.   FRAN 133:12
desolation abomination of d.   BIBL 44:35
  D. in immaculate public places   ROET 258:21
  Magnificent d.   ALDR 3:12
  years of d.   JEFF 171:17
despair begotten by D.   MARV 213:14
  comfort and d.   SHAK 290:11
  Do not d.   PUDN 252:2
  endure my own d.   WALS 328:1
  far side of d.   SART 264:24
  some divine d.   TENN 313:7
  ye Mighty, and d.   SHEL 293:12
desperandum Nil d.   HORA 164:6
desperate Diseases d. grown   SHAK 272:30
  Tempt not a d. man   SHAK 286:35
desperation lives of quiet d.   THOR 317:19
despise work for a Government I d.   KEYN 185:8
despised Dangers by being d.   BURK 74:21
  d. and rejected   BIBL 40:16
despond slough was D.   BUNY 72:22
despondency d. and madness   WORD 340:26
  last words of Mr D.   BUNY 73:10
  SPREAD ALARM AND D.   PENI 243:8
despotism d. tempered by epigrams   CARL 82:20
despots against d.—suspicion   DEMO 108:11
  D. themselves do not deny   TOCQ 318:9
destiny Anatomy is d.   FREU 133:19
  character is d.   ELIO 121:13
destroy d. the town to save it   ANON 8:2
  gods wish to d.   CONN 99:1
  One to d.   YOUN 344:12
  power to d.   MARS 213:4
  Whom the mad would d.   LEVI 198:8
  winged life d.   BLAK 56:2
  worms d. this body   BIBL 37:9
destroyed Carthage must be d.   CATO 85:15
  enemy that shall be d.   BIBL 50:3
  ought to be d.   OMAR 236:7
  treated generously or d.   MACH 207:15
destroyer d. of worlds   OPPE 236:16
destroyeth d. in the noon-day   BOOK 62:17
destroys Time which d. all things   BHAG 32:9
destruction d. of the whole world   HUME 166:23
  leadeth to d.   BIBL 43:8
  Pride goeth before d.   BIBL 37:36
  to their d. draw   DONN 114:4
  urge for d.   BAKU 23:5
detail corroborative d.   GILB 140:18
details God is in the d.   ROHE 259:8
  mind which reveres d.   LEWI 198:19
detective d. story is about   JAME 171:1
  Hawkshaw, the d.   TAYL 310:3
deteriora D. sequor   OVID 238:15
determination d. of incident   JAME 170:19
determined D., dared, and done   SMAR 297:4
detest d. at leisure   BYRO 79:5
deus puto d. fio   VESP 323:16
Deutschland D. über alles   HOFF 160:13
devastating d. or redeeming fires   GONC 144:11
development what is called d.   NAIR 230:20
De Vere name and dignity of D.   CREW 103:10
deviates d. into sense   DRYD 117:3
device with the strange d.   LONG 201:22
devices d. and desires   BOOK 58:5
  man of many d.   HOME 161:20
devil apology for the D.   BUTL 77:12

can the d. speak true — SHAK 279:6
d. and all his works — BOOK 60:9
d. can cite Scripture — SHAK 282:5
d. damn thee black — SHAK 281:19
d. doesn't exist — DOST 115:1
D. howling 'Ho' — SQUI 301:8
d. is dead — READ 254:20
D. sends cooks — GARR 136:10
d. should have all — HILL 159:5
D. should have right — MORE 227:25
d.'s madness—War — SERV 268:2
d. taketh him up — BIBL 42:12
d. understands Welsh — SHAK 274:4
d. would also build — LUTH 204:17
doubt is D.-born — TENN 311:25
face the d. — BURN 75:25
fears a painted d. — SHAK 280:11
flesh, and the d. — BOOK 59:5
God and d. — DOST 114:25
laughing d. — BYRO 78:11
of the D.'s party — BLAK 55:21
of the witty d. — GRAV 146:4
there is a D. — MATH 215:3
wedlock's the d. — BYRO 79:18
What the d. was he doing — MOLI 225:12
your adversary the d. — BIBL 51:30
devilish most d. thing — FLEM 130:2
devils d. must print — MOOR 227:12
lighting d. — BINC 54:2
Devon If the Dons sight D. — NEWB 232:17
devotion my bok and my d. — CHAU 88:22
object of universal d. — IRVI 169:11
devour d. in turn each one — VERG 323:10
seeking whom he may d. — BIBL 51:30
when they would d. — BACO 21:35
devourer Time the d. — OVID 238:16
devourers become so great d. — MORE 227:24
devout d. in dishabilly — FARQ 126:14
dew d. will rust them — SHAK 284:10
Drop down d., heavens — BIBL 53:5
fades awa' like morning d. — BALL 24:15
resolve itself into a d. — SHAK 270:29
Walks o'er the d. — SHAK 270:26
dewdrop Starlight and d. — FOST 132:5
dewdrops seek some d. here — SHAK 283:7
dewy shakes his d. wings — D'AV 106:12
di d. omen avertant — CICE 92:27
diable d. est mort — READ 254:20
diabolical tree of d. knowledge — SHER 294:12
diagnostician makes a good d. — OSLE 238:3
dialect D. words — HARD 151:16
purify the d. of the tribe — ELIO 121:27
diamond d. and safire bracelet — LOOS 202:15
d. in the sky — TAYL 309:21
O D.! Diamond — NEWT 233:16
polished d. — CHES 89:12
diamonds d. a girl's best friend — ROBI 257:20
has no d. — WALP 327:16
what beautiful d. — WEST 332:14
Dian hangs on D.'s temple — SHAK 270:15
Diana D.'s foresters — SHAK 273:25
Great is D. — BIBL 48:37
diarist To be a good d. — NICO 234:2
diary discreet d. — CHAN 87:9
keep a d. and some day — WEST 332:11
never travel without my d. — WILD 335:3
write in a d. — WARN 328:14
diaspora for the new d. — DUNN 118:11
dic sed tantum d. verbo — MISS 224:7
dice God does not play d. — EINS 120:14
Dick D. the shepherd — SHAK 278:23
Mr. D. had been for upwards of ten years — DICK 110:4
dictator Every d. uses religion — BHUT 32:19

dictators D. ride to and fro upon tigers — CHUR 91:12
dictatorship d. impossible — PERE 243:20
d. of the proletariat — MARX 214:7
elective d. — HAIL 149:9
dictionaries D. are like watches — JOHN 176:19
Lexicographer. A writer of d. — JOHN 173:13
dictionary but a walking d. — CHAP 87:18
dictum D. sapienti — PLAU 246:3
did d. for them both — SASS 265:3
Dido Stood D. with a willow — SHAK 282:27
die And shall Trelawny d. — HAWK 153:10
apt to d. — SHAK 276:9
Ay, but to d., and go — SHAK 281:33
being born, to d. — BACO 22:8
better to d. on your feet — IBAR 168:7
Christian can d. — ADDI 2:16
clean place to d. — KAVA 180:23
Cowards d. many times — SHAK 276:6
Curse God, and d. — BIBL 37:1
day that I d. — MCLE 208:1
Death thou shalt d. — DONN 113:20
determine to d. here — BEE 27:7
did not wish to d. — SHAW 292:9
D., and endow a college — POPE 247:17
d. before I wake — ANON 9:3
d. beyond my means — WILD 335:20
d. but do not surrender — CAMB 80:16
d. but once — ADDI 2:9
d. eating ortolans — DISR 113:1
d. for adultery — SHAK 278:2
d. for one's country — HORA 164:14
d. for politicians — THOM 317:7
d. for the people — BIBL 48:2
D. he or justice must — MILT 221:26
d. here in a rage — SWIF 306:22
d. in my week — JOPL 178:12
d. in peace — WOLF 338:15
d. in the last ditch — WILL 336:3
d. is cast — CAES 80:2
d. like a true-blue rebel — HILL 159:3
D., my dear Doctor — PALM 240:9
d. of that roar — ELIO 121:10
d. upon a kiss — SHAK 285:5
d. when the body dies — BHAG 32:16
d. when the trees were green — CLAR 93:7
Easy live and quiet d. — SCOT 266:20
easy ways to d. — SHAK 269:11
Few d. and none resign — JEFF 171:14
few d. well — SHAK 275:2
frogs don't d. for 'fun' — BION 54:6
gave its victims time to d. — GUIB 148:12
Good Americans, when they d. — APPL 13:13
he must d. — NICH 233:20
He shall not d. — STER 302:24
Hope I d. before — TOWN 319:1
how can man d. better — MACA 206:7
I did not d. — ANON 6:14
I die because I do not d. — JOHN 172:13
If I should d. — BROO 67:23
I'll d. young — BRUC 71:14
in Adam all d. — BIBL 50:2
I shall d. at the top — SWIF 307:13
I shall not altogether d. — HORA 164:17
it was sure to d. — MOOR 227:19
I would d. — ROSS 260:20
last Jews to d. — MEIR 216:2
Let me d. a youngman's death — MCGO 207:12
Let us do—or d. — BURN 75:23
love her till I d. — ANON 10:6
love one another or d. — AUDE 18:17
man can d. but once — SHAK 274:23
marked to d. — SHAK 275:7
not d. because of them — TALM 309:7

die (cont.)
not that I'm afraid to d. — ALLE 4:8
Old soldiers never d. — FOLE 130:18
only let Him d. — STUD 305:9
ought to d. standing — VESP 323:17
something he will d. — KING 186:10
taught us how to d. — TICK 318:4
Their's but to do and d. — TENN 310:16
these who d. as cattle — OWEN 238:21
They that d. by famine — HENR 156:18
those who are about to d. — ANON 12:8
thou shalt surely d. — BIBL 33:1
time to d. — BIBL 38:16
To d. and know it — LOWE 203:23
To d. will be an awfully big — BARR 25:15
To go away is to d. — HARA 151:5
to live and to d. — VILL 324:7
to morrow we shall d. — BIBL 39:27
weep or she will d. — TENN 313:11
we needs must d. — BIBL 35:32
When beggars d. — SHAK 276:5
when you d. — HILL 159:2
where myths Go when they d. — FENT 126:20
who would wish to d. — BORR 64:16
died d. an hour before — SHAK 280:19
D., has he — LOUI 203:3
d. hereafter — SHAK 281:24
d. last night of my physician — PRIO 251:10
d. of grieving — KEAT 181:12
D. some, pro patria — POUN 250:9
d. to save their country — CHES 89:20
dog it was that d. — GOLD 143:16
He that d. o' Wednesday — SHAK 274:9
'I never d.,' says he — HAYE 153:19
liked it not, and d. — WOTT 341:23
Mithridates, he d. old — HOUS 165:11
question why we d. — KIPL 187:10
she d. young — WEBS 330:12
would God I had d. for thee — BIBL 35:33
Would to God we had d. — BIBL 34:11
diem carpe d. — HORA 164:7
d. perdidi — TITU 318:8
dies because a man d. for it — WILD 335:9
before he d. — SOLO 298:26
D. irae — MISS 224:11
d. young — MENA 216:12
Every moment d. a man — BABB 20:15
He that d. — SHAK 287:13
kingdom where nobody d. — MILL 218:6
king never d. — BLAC 55:2
man who d. . . . . rich — CARN 83:7
moment d. a man — TENN 314:2
once hath blown for ever d. — FITZ 128:18
something in me d. — VIDA 324:1
diest Where thou d., will I die — BIBL 35:13
diet d. unparalleled — DICK 110:21
diets feel about d. — KERR 184:22
Dieu Si D. n'existait pas — VOLT 326:5
difference d. of forty thousand — WELL 331:9
made all the d. — FROS 134:13
oh, The d. to me — WORD 341:5
wear your rue with a d. — SHAK 273:6
different hears a d. drummer — THOR 317:22
How d. from us — ANON 8:19
how very d. — ANON 7:12
rich are d. from you and me — FITZ 129:4
differential integral and d. calculus — GILB 141:5
differently do things d. there — HART 153:1
freedom for the one who thinks d. — LUXE 204:20
difficult d.; and left untried — CHES 90:7
D. do you call it, Sir — JOHN 176:21
d. takes a little time — NANS 231:1
d. we do immediately — ANON 6:12

fascination of what's d. — YEAT 342:23
first step that is d. — DU D 117:22
difficulties d. do not make one doubt — NEWM 232:23
little local d. — MACM 208:9
difficulty solving every d. — PEEL 242:22
with great d. I am got hither — BUNY 73:11
dig I'll d. with it — HEAN 154:11
digest learn, and inwardly d. — BOOK 59:13
digestion good d. wait on appetite — SHAK 280:28
diggeth He that d. a pit — BIBL 38:28
dignified d. parts — BAGE 22:10
dignitate Cum d. otium — CICE 93:2
dignity d. in tilling a field — WASH 328:17
d. which His Majesty — BALD 23:12
no d. in persevering in error — PEEL 242:21
with silent d. — GROS 148:5
dignus non sum d. — MISS 224:7
digressions eloquent d. — HUXL 168:4
dilige D. et quod vis fac — AUGU 19:4
dilly-dally Don't d. on the way — COLL 97:5
dim d. religious light — MILT 219:24
dime Brother can you spare a d. — HARB 151:7
dimensions my d. are as well compact — SHAK 277:8
diminished ought to be d. — DUNN 118:12
dimittis Nunc d. — BIBL 53:8
dine d. exact at noon — POPE 247:27
gang and d. — BALL 24:13
dinner d. bell — BYRO 78:27
d. of herbs — BIBL 37:34
good d. upon his table — JOHN 177:1
hungry for d. at eight — HART 152:19
Diogenes would be D. — ALEX 3:13
diplomacy D. is to do and say — GOLD 143:2
diplomat d. . . . . is a person — STIN 304:10
diplomatic d. boathook — SALI 263:19
direct could d. a movie — HYTN 168:6
d. and rule our hearts — BOOK 59:14
direction move in a given d. — HOUS 165:12
directors way with these d. — GOLD 144:8
direful d. in the sound — AUST 19:17
to Greece the d. spring — POPE 248:22
dirge Begins the sad d. — SHAK 289:20
dirt d. doesn't get any worse — CRIS 103:12
D. is only matter — GRAY 146:9
in d. the reasoning engine — ROCH 258:13
in the d. lay justice — HEAN 154:13
make crossness and d. succeed — FORS 131:12
dirty Dear, d. Dublin — JOYC 178:18
'Jug Jug' to d. ears — ELIO 122:23
dis D. aliter visum — VIRG 324:14
disagree if they d. — OMAR 236:7
when doctors d. — POPE 247:16
disappointed d. by that stroke — JOHN 173:21
you have d. us — BELL 28:12
disappointment D. all I endeavour end — HOPK 163:6
disapprove d. of what you say — VOLT 326:13
disaster triumph and d. — KIPL 187:20
disastrous d. and the unpalatable — GALB 135:11
disbelief willing suspension of d. — COLE 96:21
discandy d., melt their sweets — SHAK 268:24
discharge d. for loving one — MATL 215:7
no d. in that war — BIBL 38:23
disciples great man has his d. — WILD 335:4
discipline order and military d. — ANON 6:10
disciplines by category-d. — RYLE 263:6
disclaim d. her for a mother — GIBB 139:6
discontent winter of d. — CALL 80:10
winter of our d. — SHAK 285:32
discontented every one that was d. — BIBL 35:24
discord civil d. — ADDI 2:11
d. doth sow — ELIZ 123:7
hark! what d. follows — SHAK 287:28
discors Concordia d. — HORA 163:25

discouragement There's no d. — BUNY 73:9
discourse d. of rivers — WALT 328:5
discover another can d. — DOYL 115:17
discovery D. consists of seeing — SZEN 308:12
d. of a new dish — BRIL 67:4
Medicinal d. — AYRE 20:12
discreet d. diary — CHAN 87:9
discretion D. is not the better part — STRA 305:1
discuss stay and d. them — WELL 331:13
discussion government by d. — ATTL 17:12
disease biggest d. today — TERE 314:11
Cured yesterday of my d. — PRIO 251:10
Cure the d. — BACO 21:11
desperate d. — FAWK 126:17
D., Ignorance, and Idleness — BEVE 32:12
D. is an experience — EDDY 119:16
d. is incurable — CHEK 88:31
d. is incurable — SHAK 274:17
d. of not listening — SHAK 274:14
incurable d. of writing — JUVE 180:1
Life is an incurable d. — COWL 101:15
Love's a d. — MACA 205:9
no Cure for this D. — BELL 28:10
Progress is a comfortable d. — CUMM 104:17
remedy is worse than the d. — BACO 21:25
suffering from the particular d. — JERO 172:5
this long d., my life — POPE 247:8
diseased mind d. — BYRO 78:4
minister to a mind d. — SHAK 281:21
diseases cure of all d. — BROW 69:8
D. desperate grown — SHAK 272:30
disestablishment sense of d. — KING 186:16
disgrace no d. t'be poor — HUBB 166:6
private life is a d. — ANON 9:14
disgraced dies . . . rich dies d. — CARN 83:7
disgraceful something d. in mind — JUVE 180:6
disgruntled if not actually d. — WODE 338:1
disguise better go in d. — BRAT 66:6
dish discovery of a new d. — BRIL 67:4
d. fit for the gods — SHAK 276:4
in a lordly d. — BIBL 35:3
dishabilly devout in d. — FARQ 126:14
dishonour rooted in d. — TENN 311:8
disiecti Etiam d. membra poetae — HORA 164:20
disinheriting d. countenance — SHER 294:20
disinterested D. intellectual curiosity — TREV 319:7
dismal beset him round With d. stories — BUNY 73:9
D. Science — CARL 82:24
dismiss Lord, d. us — BUCK 72:4
Disney of Euro D. — BALL 24:17
of Euro D. — MNOU 225:7
Disneyfication D. of Christianity — CUPI 105:3
disobedience man's first d. — MILT 220:33
disorder d. in its geometry — DE B 107:9
sweet d. in the dress — HERR 158:3
displeasing not d. to us — LA R 194:2
disposes God d. — THOM 315:19
disposition antic d. — SHAK 271:22
dispossessed imprisoned or d. — MAGN 209:11
dissatisfied I'm a — MOOR 227:11
dissect murder to d. — WORD 341:13
dissonance barbarous d. — MILT 219:16
distance d. is nothing — DU D 117:22
d. lends enchantment — CAMP 81:3
distinction think that there is no d. — JOHN 174:25
distinctive man's d. mark — BROW 70:1
distinguished d. thing — JAME 170:28
distress every one that was in d. — BIBL 35:24
Far as d. — GREV 147:11
distressed afflicted, or d. — BOOK 59:10
I am d. for thee — BIBL 35:29
distressful most d. country — ANON 8:1
distribute d. as fairly as he can — LOWE 203:12

ditch [Channel] is a mere ditch — NAPO 231:3
die in the last d. — WILL 336:3
fall into the d. — BIBL 44:7
ditty played an ancient d. — KEAT 181:9
dive must d. below — DRYD 116:26
diversity some d. — BARC 25:1
divided d. by a common language — SHAW 292:6
d. duty — SHAK 284:14
d. into three parts — CAES 79:28
d. self — LAIN 191:21
has harshly d. — SCHI 265:11
If a house be d. — BIBL 45:25
in their death not d. — BIBL 35:28
dividing by d. we fall — DICK 111:18
divine human form d. — BLAK 56:6
possess d. legislation — MEND 216:16
Right D. of Kings — POPE 246:21
say that D. providence — JOHN 172:20
some d. despair — TENN 313:7
To forgive, is . . . — POPE 248:6
what the form d. — LAND 192:2
divinely most d. fair — TENN 310:21
divinity d. doth hedge a king — SHAK 273:4
d. in odd numbers — SHAK 282:32
d. that shapes our ends — SHAK 273:15
divisions How many d. has he got — STAL 301:13
divorce long d. of steel — SHAK 275:20
dixit Ipse d. — CICE 92:23
DNA cannot cheat on D. — WARD 328:11
do can't all d. everything — VIRG 325:12
damned if you d. — DOW 115:9
d. not do to your neighbour — HILL 159:8
d. what had to be done — HAVE 153:8
d. what I please — FRED 133:13
D. what thou wilt — CROW 104:10
d. ye even so to them — BIBL 43:7
George—don't d. that — GREN 147:9
HOW NOT TO D. IT — DICK 110:16
I can d. no other — LUTH 204:16
I'll do, I'll do, and I'll d. — SHAK 278:28
know not what they d. — BIBL 47:11
Let's d. it — PORT 249:18
Let us d.—or die — BURN 75:23
Love and d. what you will — AUGU 19:4
so much to d. — RHOD 256:9
to my servant, D. this — BIBL 43:14
what I d. in any thing — HERB 157:12
What must I d. to be saved — BIBL 48:31
doc cards with a man called D. — ALGR 4:2
docent dum d. discunt — SENE 267:22
doctor d. found, when she was dead — GOLD 143:15
God and the d. — OWEN 238:18
doctors D. in verse — THOM 316:21
d. know a hopeless case — CUMM 104:18
when d. disagree — POPE 247:16
doctrine loved the d. — DEFO 107:16
not for the d. — POPE 248:3
documents d. and friends — SPAR 299:22
dodger artful D. — DICK 110:27
dog beaten d. beneath the hail — POUN 250:12
better than his d. — TENN 312:8
Beware of the d. — PETR 244:9
black d. — JOHN 176:16
d. in the night-time — DOYL 115:16
d. is turned to his own vomit — BIBL 51:31
d. it was that died — GOLD 143:16
d. returneth to his vomit — BIBL 38:6
d.'s walking on his hinder legs — JOHN 175:1
engine of pollution, the d. — SPAR 299:25
every d. his day — KING 186:22
heart to a d. to tear — KIPL 188:4
Is thy servant a d. — BIBL 36:27
living d. — BIBL 38:25

dog (*cont.*)
Lovell our d.	COLL 97:1
man bites a d.	BOGA 57:8
Mine enemy's d.	SHAK 278:5
over the lazy d.	ANON 9:13
poor d. Tray	CAMP 81:2
tongue of d.	SHAK 281:5
was there ever d.	YEAT 343:26
whose d. are you	POPE 247:4
working like a d.	LENN 197:13
your wife and your d.	HILL 159:1

doggie How much is that d. — MERR 217:9
dogma no d., no Dean — DISR 113:6

dogs all things as straw d.
	LAO 193:4
d. eat of the crumbs	BIBL 44:8
d. go on with their doggy life	AUDE 18:9
D. look up to us	CHUR 92:14
fought the d.	BROW 70:26
hates d. and babies	ROST 261:4
Lame d. over stiles	KING 186:18
Let d. delight	WATT 329:7
let slip the d. of war	SHAK 276:11
Mad d. and Englishmen	COWA 101:7
Throw physic to the d.	SHAK 281:22

doing continuance in well d.
	BIBL 49:5
d. in that galley	MOLI 225:12
not be weary in well d.	BIBL 50:16
put me to d.	METH 217:13
see what she's d.	PUNC 252:14
This is the Lord's d.	BOOK 63:10

doleful Knight of the D. Countenance — CERV 86:13
doll d. in the doll's house — DICK 111:2
dollar almighty d. — IRVI 169:11
billion d. country — FOST 132:3
dolore *Nessun maggior d.* — DANT 105:20
Dolores splendid and sterile D. — SWIN 307:22
dolour d. of pad and paper-weight — ROET 258:21
dolphin d.-torn, that gong-tormented — YEAT 342:13
dome d. of many-coloured glass — SHEL 292:20
singing beneath the d. — VERL 323:12
domestic d. business — MONT 226:10
Malice d. — SHAK 280:24
men call d. bliss — PATM 242:3
dominant Hark, the d.'s persistence — BROW 71:9
domination against white d. — MAND 210:19
dominations Thrones, and — MILT 222:11
dominion death hath no more d. — BIBL 49:12
death shall have no d. — THOM 316:2
d. of kings changed — PRIC 251:5
d. of religion — GOLD 143:5
dominions His Majesty's d. — NORT 234:20
not set in my d. — SCHI 265:12
domino 'falling d.' principle — EISE 120:15
dominus *D. illuminatio mea* — ANON 12:11
D. illuminatio mea — BIBL 52:29
D. vobiscum — MISS 223:24
Nisi D. — BIBL 53:2
don D. John of Austria is going — CHES 89:23
quiet flows the D. — SHOL 294:29
Remote and ineffectual D. — BELL 28:17
dona *Requiem aeternam d. eis* — MISS 224:10
done decide that d. can be done — ALLE 4:7
D. because we are too menny — HARD 151:15
d. very well out of the war — BALD 23:8
d. when 'tis done — SHAK 279:19
he d. her wrong — ANON 7:11
If you want anything d. — THAT 315:3
Inasmuch as ye have d. — BIBL 45:10
remained to be d. — LUCA 204:8
something d. — LONG 202:8
surprised to find it d. — JOHN 175:1
that which is d. — BIBL 38:14
we have d. those things — BOOK 58:6

What could she have d.	YEAT 343:12
What is to be d.	LENI 197:3
What's d. cannot be undone	SHAK 281:18
what's d. is done	SHAK 280:23

dong D. with a luminous nose — LEAR 195:10
donkeys Lions led by d. — ANON 8:8
Donne John D., Anne Donne — DONN 114:23
dons If the D. sight Devon — NEWB 232:17
don't about to marry.—'d.' — PUNC 252:7
damned if you d. — DOW 115:9
doodle Yankee D. — ANON 11:6
doom regardless of their d. — GRAY 146:18
to the edge of d. — SHAK 290:7
Doon braes o' bonny D. — BURN 75:6
door angel from your d. — BLAK 56:7
beating on the d. — YEAT 343:1
coming in at one d. — BEDE 27:5
Death's shadow at the d. — BLUN 57:2
d. flew open — HOFF 160:15
d. we never opened — ELIO 121:19
I am the d. — BIBL 47:37
knock at the d. — LAMB 192:4
knocking at Preferment's d. — ARNO 15:15
knocking at the d. — SHAW 292:2
lights around the d. — ROSS 260:19
Never open the d. — GRAC 145:3
stand at the d., and knock — BIBL 52:7
through the d. with a gun — CHAN 87:7
when the d. opens — GREE 147:1
whining of a d. — DONN 114:21
wide as a church d. — SHAK 286:25
doorkeeper d. in the house of my God — BOOK 62:12
doormat d. in a world of boots — RHYS 256:12
d. or a prostitute — WEST 332:18
doors Death has a thousand d. — MASS 215:1
Death hath so many d. — FLET 130:7
d. of perception — BLAK 55:26
Men shut their d. — SHAK 287:21
ten thousand several d. — WEBS 330:11
thousand d. open on to it — SENE 267:23
ye everlasting d. — BOOK 61:9
dooryard last in the d. bloomed — WHIT 334:2
Dorcas D.: this woman — BIBL 48:29
dormitat *bonus d. Homerus* — HORA 163:18
dotage Pedantry is the d. — JACK 169:17
Dotheboys D. Hall — DICK 110:21
dots damned d. meant — CHUR 91:6
double Double, d. toil and trouble — SHAK 281:4
peace of the d.-bed — CAMP 80:19
doubles d. your chances for a date — ALLE 4:9
doublet tailor make thy d. — SHAK 288:20
doublethink D. means the power — ORWE 237:17
doubt Book wherein is no d. — KORA 190:6
curiosity, freckles, and d. — PARK 240:15
do not make one d. — NEWM 232:23
d. and sorrow — BARI 25:6
d. is Devil-born — TENN 311:25
in d., strike it out — TWAI 321:12
let us never, never d. — BELL 28:20
Life is d. — UNAM 321:20
more faith in honest d. — TENN 311:26
No possible d. whatever — GILB 139:20
Our d. is our passion — JAME 170:18
wherefore didst thou d. — BIBL 44:6
doubts end in d. — BACO 20:18
dove all the d. — CRAS 102:26
d. found no rest — BIBL 33:20
on the burnished d. — TENN 312:7
sweet d. died — KEAT 181:12
wings like a d. — BOOK 62:1
dovecote eagle in a d. — SHAK 270:16
Dover milestones on the D. Road — DICK 110:17
white cliffs of D. — BURT 76:7

doves harmless as d.	BIBL 43:25	d. of avarice	JOHN 176:8
moan of d.	TENN 313:19	d. of avarice	MOOR 227:4
dowagers d. for deans	TENN 313:2	d. out of the ivory gate	BROW 69:10
down D. among the dead	DYER 119:1	d. to sell	BEDD 27:4
D. and out in Paris	ORWE 237:9	I have bad d.	SHAK 271:30
d. express in the small of the back	WODE 338:3	interpretation of d.	FREU 133:20
D. in the forest	SIMP 296:4	land of my d.	KING 186:14
d. into the darkness	MILL 218:7	old men shall dream d.	BIBL 41:14
D. to Gehenna	KIPL 187:25	scream for help in d.	CANE 81:10
fled Him, d. the nights	THOM 316:26	tread on my d.	YEAT 343:2
go d. to the sea	BOOK 63:1	**dreamt** d. I went to Manderley	DU M 118:3
He that is d.	BUNY 73:8	d. of in your philosophy	SHAK 271:21
kicked d. stairs	HALI 150:7	**dreary** drags its d. length	DICK 109:16
meet 'em on your way d.	MIZN 225:4	**dress** d. of thought	POPE 248:2
staying d. with him	WASH 328:18	Peace, the human d.	BLAK 56:6
downhearted Are we d.	ANON 5:21	sweet disorder in the d.	HERR 158:3
Are we d.	KNIG 189:11	**dressed** all d. up	BURT 76:6
downs in the D. the fleet was moored	GAY 137:11	all d. up	WHIT 333:17
downstairs kick me d.	BICK 53:15	d. in modern clothing	STRA 305:4
downwards look no way but d.	BUNY 73:7	impossible to be well d.	AMIE 4:18
dozens Whom he reckons up by d.	GILB 140:29	**dressing** d. old words new	SHAK 289:32
dragon d.-green, the luminous	FLEC 129:22	**drest** D. in a little brief authority	SHAK 281:30
fought against the d.	BIBL 52:14	**Dr Fell** do not love thee, D.	BROW 68:18
dragons brother to d.	BIBL 37:12	**dried** at once be d. up	DOST 114:24
D. in their pleasant palaces	BIBL 39:24	**drink** D. and the devil	STEV 303:21
habitation of d.	BIBL 40:3	D. deep, or taste not	POPE 247:29
drains opiate to the d.	KEAT 182:9	D., sir, is a great provoker	SHAK 280:14
drake D. he's in his hammock	NEWB 232:18	D. to me only	JONS 178:4
Drang Sturm und D.	KAUF 180:21	eat, d., and be merry	BIBL 46:22
draw d. you to her	DRYD 117:13	he has taken to d.	TARK 309:10
drawers d. of water	BIBL 34:32	Let us eat and d.	BIBL 39:27
drawing D. is the true test	INGR 169:6	Nor any drop to d.	COLE 96:13
no d. back	BRON 67:17	to eat, and to d.	BIBL 38:24
drawing-room through my d.	EDEN 119:18	your husband I would d. it	CHUR 92:15
dreadful city of d. night	THOM 317:12	**drinking** D. the blude-red wine	BALL 24:7
dreadnoughts as much as to keep up as two D.		D. when we are not thirsty	BEAU 26:12
	LLOY 200:18	Now for d.	HORA 164:9
dream as a d. doth flatter	SHAK 289:35	**drinks** d. as much as you do	THOM 316:12
behold it was a d.	BUNY 73:6	**dripping** D. water hollows out	OVID 238:13
children d. not	BROW 69:10	electricity was d.	THUR 317:26
d. my dreams away	FLAN 129:13	**drive** can't d. the car	TYNA 321:14
d. of fair women	TENN 310:20	**drives** Who d. fat oxen	JOHN 176:18
d. of peace	HUNT 167:1	**driveth** d. furiously	BIBL 36:28
d. of reason	GOYA 145:2	**driving** d. briskly in a post-chaise	JOHN 175:21
d. that is dying	O'SH 238:2	like the d. of Jehu	BIBL 36:28
D. the impossible	DARI 106:3	**droopingly** d., but with a hopeful heart	LAWR 194:13
freshness of a d.	WORD 340:7	**drop** Drop, d., slow tears	FLET 130:10
glory and the d.	WORD 340:9	Nor any d. to drink	COLE 96:13
I have a d.	KING 186:11	turn on, tune in and d. out	LEAR 195:19
In a d. you are never eighty	SEXT 268:5	**dropping** D. the pilot	TENN 310:10
love's young d.	MOOR 227:16	**drops** Little d. of water	CARN 83:9
no longer a d.	CLIN 94:18	**drought** d. is destroying his roots	HERB 157:1
not d. them	KING 186:17	d. of March	CHAU 88:4
peace is a d.	MOLT 225:16	**drown** I'll d. my book	SHAK 287:18
salesman is got to d.	MILL 218:14	**drownded** d. now and again	SYNG 308:7
silence of a d.	ROSS 260:11	**drowned** BETTER D. THAN DUFFERS	RANS 254:14
till you find your d.	HAMM 150:17	d. in the depth of the sea	BIBL 44:14
waking d.	KEAT 182:16	d. in yonder living blue	TENN 311:33
dreamed d. I saw Joe Hill	HAYE 153:19	**drowning** no d. mark	SHAK 287:1
d. that I dwelt	BUNN 72:17	not waving but d.	SMIT 298:3
d. that life was beauty	HOOP 162:10	**drowns** d. things weighty	BACO 21:21
he d., and behold	BIBL 33:30	**drowsy** d. numbness pains	KEAT 182:9
I've d. of cheese	STEV 303:24	**drudge** Lexicographer. A harmless d.	JOHN 173:13
dreamer Beautiful d.	FOST 132:5	**drudgery** Makes d. divine	HERB 157:13
d. of dreams	BIBL 34:28	**drug** Poetry's a mere d.	FARQ 126:12
D. of dreams	MORR 228:17	you can d., with words	LOWE 203:14
dreamers We are the d. of dreams	O'SH 238:1	**drugs** Sex and d. and rock and roll	DURY 118:17
dreaming butterfly d. that	CHUA 90:21	so-called soft d.	STRA 305:5
d. of a white Christmas	BERL 30:21	**drum** big bass d.	LIND 199:16
d. spires	ARNO 15:22	My pulse, like a soft d.	KING 186:7
dreams armoured cars of d.	BISH 54:10	Not a d. was heard	WOLF 338:10
books are either d. or swords	LOWE 203:14	Rhyme still the most effective d.	GIRA 141:16
d. of a poet	JOHN 173:12	Take my d. to England	NEWB 232:17

drummer hears a different d. — THOR 317:22
drumming in the valley d. — AUDE 18:14
drums d. begin to roll — KIPL 188:11
drunk d. for about a week — FITZ 129:7
from Philip d. — ANON 5:20
I have d. — SHAK 289:2
not so think as you d. — SQUI 301:7
Was the hope d. — SHAK 279:24
drunken d. man uses lampposts — LANG 192:25
stagger like a d. man — BOOK 63:2
dry But oh! I am so d. — FARM 126:8
d. brain in a dry season — ELIO 122:3
keep your powder d. — BLAC 55:1
old man in a d. month — ELIO 122:1
O ye d. bones — BIBL 41:6
Dublin Dear, dirty D. — JOYC 178:18
ducat Dead, for a d. — SHAK 272:23
ducats O my d.! O my daughter — SHAK 282:10
duchess chambermaid as of a D. — JOHN 176:2
every D. in London — MACD 207:7
I am D. of Malfi still — WEBS 330:10
That's my last D. — BROW 70:22
duck just forgot to d. — DEMP 108:13
looks like a d. — REUT 256:1
ducks d., produce bad parents — MORS 229:2
I turn to d. — HARV 153:2
stealing d. — ARAB 13:17
duffers BETTER DROWNED THAN D. — RANS 254:14
dugs old man with wrinkled d. — ELIO 122:7
duke D. of Plaza Toro — GILB 139:19
fully-equipped d. — LLOY 200:18
dukedom d. large enough — SHAK 287:3
dulce D. et decorum est — HORA 164:14
D. et decorum est — OWEN 238:24
D. ridentem — HORA 164:8
dull d. in a new way — JOHN 175:13
D. would he be of soul — WORD 339:18
some d. opiate — KEAT 182:9
very d., dreary affair — MAUG 215:11
dumb as a sheep is d. — BIBL 40:18
So d. he can't fart — JOHN 173:7
Duncan fatal entrance of D. — SHAK 279:13
dunce d. with wits — POPE 246:20
dunces d. are all in confederacy — SWIF 307:2
Dundee bonnets of Bonny D. — SCOT 266:6
Dunfermline D. town — BALL 24:7
dungeon Himself is his own d. — MILT 219:12
dungeons Brightest in d., Liberty — BYRO 79:15
dungfork man with a d. — HOPK 163:10
dunghill cock crowing on its own d. — ALDI 3:11
Dunsinane high D. hill — SHAK 281:10
durable true love is a d. fire — RALE 254:3
duration d. of the war — ASQU 16:17
dusk each slow d. — OWEN 238:23
falling of the d. — HEGE 155:6
forty-three In the d. — GILB 141:10
dust blossom in the d. — SHIR 294:28
chimney-sweepers, come to d. — SHAK 270:19
D. hath closed Helen's eye — NASH 231:20
d. of creeds outworn — SHEL 293:16
d. of exploded beliefs — MADA 209:2
d. of the Churchyard — DONN 114:20
d. thou art — BIBL 33:13
D. thou art — LONG 201:25
d. to dust — BOOK 60:25
Excuse my d. — PARK 240:21
fear in a handful of d. — ELIO 122:21
forbear To dig the d. — SHAK 290:17
Hope raises no d. — ÉLUA 124:5
Less than the d. — HOPE 162:20
Marry my body to that d. — KING 186:6
not without d. and heat — MILT 223:15
shake off the d. — BIBL 43:24

sweep the d. — SHAK 283:25
what a d. do I raise — BACO 21:32
with age and d. — RALE 254:5
dustbin d. of history — TROT 320:3
dustheap d. called 'history' — BIRR 54:8
dusty what a d. answer — MERE 217:6
Dutch fault of the D. — CANN 81:11
duties d. as well as its rights — DRUM 116:12
d. will be determined — MORE 228:6
If I had no d. — JOHN 175:21
duty as much a d. as cooperation — GAND 135:19
daily stage of d. — KEN 184:1
divided d. — SHAK 284:14
do our d. as such — SALI 263:20
Do your d. — CORN 100:3
d. of an Opposition — DERB 108:23
every man will do his d. — NELS 232:9
Every subject's d. — SHAK 275:3
first d. of a State — RUSK 262:18
I have done my d. — NELS 232:11
life was d. — HOOP 162:10
Nor law, nor d. — YEAT 343:5
When D. whispers low — EMER 124:10
whole d. of man — BIBL 39:1
dwarf d. sees farther — COLE 96:22
dwarfs d. on the shoulders — BERN 31:4
dwell people that on earth do d. — KETH 185:2
dwells She d. with Beauty — KEAT 182:8
dwelt d. among the untrodden ways — WORD 341:3
d. among us — BIBL 47:21
dwindle d. into a wife — CONG 98:19
dyer like the d.'s hand — SHAK 290:5
dying achieve it through not d. — ALLE 4:10
Autumn sunsets exquisitely d. — HUXL 167:18
bliss of d. — POPE 246:25
Christian can only fear d. — HARE 152:6
D. a very dull, dreary — MAUG 215:11
d. breath of Socrates — JEAN 171:9
D. is an art — PLAT 245:20
d. of a hundred good symptoms — POPE 249:11
d. remembers — VIRG 325:6
feel that he is d. — CALI 80:8
groans of love to those of the d. — LOWR 204:6
he hung, the d. Lord — JACO 169:23
I am d., Egypt — SHAK 268:26
If this is d. — STRA 305:2
like a d. lady — SHEL 294:3
lips of d. men — ARNO 15:21
man's d. is more the survivors' affair — MANN 211:7
poor devils are d. — PHIL 244:15
Those d. generations — YEAT 343:16
Turkey is a d. man — NICH 233:20
unconscionable time d. — CHAR 87:25
dyke auld fail d. — BALL 24:13

E

E E = mc² — EINS 120:12
each beating each to e. — BROW 70:20
eagle all the e. in thee — CRAS 102:26
e. among blinking owls — SHEL 293:1
e. in a dove-cote — SHAK 270:16
e. in the air — BIBL 38:10
Fate is not an e. — BOWE 65:11
with e. eyes — KEAT 182:19
eagles e. be gathered — BIBL 45:1
with wings as e. — BIBL 40:11
ear close at the e. of Eve — MILT 222:6
hath the sow by the right e. — HENR 156:15
out of your wife's e. — MORT 229:5
upon my whorlèd e. — HOPK 162:24

earl As far as the fourteenth e.   HOME 161:15
e. and a knight of the garter   ATTL 17:10
E. of Fitzdotterel's eldest   BROU 68:7
early E. one morning   ANON 6:15
get up e.   LOWE 203:15
had it been e.   JOHN 174:20
earnest I am in e.   GARR 136:11
Life is e.   LONG 201:25
earrings e. for under £1   RATN 254:15
ears e., and hear not   BOOK 63:7
hath e. to hear   BIBL 45:26
lend me your e.   SHAK 276:15
stoppeth her e.   BOOK 62:4
we have two e.   ZENO 345:3
earth all the e. were paper   LYLY 204:25
bleeding piece of e.   SHAK 276:10
Cold in the e.   BRON 67:13
damage to the e.   COUS 101:1
deep-delvèd e.   KEAT 182:10
E. all Danaë to the stars   TENN 313:15
e. breaks up   BROW 69:24
E. felt the wound   MILT 222:18
E. has not anything to show   WORD 339:18
e. in an earthy bed   TENN 312:24
e. is all the home I have   AYTO 20:14
e. is the Lord's   BIBL 49:28
e. is the Lord's   BOOK 61:8
E., receive an honoured guest   AUDE 18:4
E. stood hard as iron   ROSS 260:12
famous men have the whole e.   PERI 243:21
feel the e. move   HEMI 156:1
giants in the e.   BIBL 33:18
girdle round about the e.   SHAK 283:11
given Her all on e.   BYRO 78:12
going to and fro in the e.   BIBL 36:36
heaven and the e.   BIBL 32:21
if e. Be but the shadow   MILT 222:10
inherit the e.   BIBL 42:14
It fell to e.   LONG 201:17
Lie heavy on him, E.   EVAN 125:11
move the e.   ARCH 14:2
new heaven and a new e.   BIBL 52:24
new heavens and a new e.   BIBL 40:22
not for the brute e.   THOM 316:23
of the e., earthy   BIBL 50:6
on e. peace   BIBL 46:5
On e. there is nothing great   HAMI 150:15
One does not sell the e.   CRAZ 103:7
salt of the e.   BIBL 42:15
sleepers in that quiet e.   BRON 67:15
surly bonds of e.   MAGE 209:8
surly bonds of e.   REAG 255:3
way of all the e.   BIBL 34:33
Yours is the E.   KIPL 187:21
earthquake e. is not satisfied   WORD 340:23
Lord was not in the e.   BIBL 36:13
Small e. in Chile   COCK 95:10
world-e., Waterloo   TENN 312:29
earthy of the earth, e.   BIBL 50:6
ease age of e.   GOLD 143:8
Not for e. that prayer   WILL 336:13
take thine e.   BIBL 46:22
easeful e. Death   KEAT 182:13
easer e. of all woes   FLET 130:8
easier will be e. for you   CHIL 90:14
easing e. the Spring   REED 255:9
east Britain calls the Far E.   MENZ 216:19
E. is East   KIPL 187:8
E. of Suez   KIPL 188:1
e. wind made flesh   APPL 13:14
gorgeous E. in fee   WORD 340:17
I' the e. my pleasure lies   SHAK 268:21
It is the e.   SHAK 286:18

look the E. End in the face   ELIZ 123:16
neither from the e.   BOOK 62:8
on the e. of Eden   BIBL 33:16
wise men from the e.   BIBL 42:2
Eastertide Wearing white for E.   HOUS 165:2
eastward garden e. in Eden   BIBL 32:24
easy E. live and quiet die   SCOT 266:20
e. to take refuge in   IBSE 168:13
e. ways to die   SHAK 269:11
e. writing's vile hard reading   SHER 294:22
every said it would be e.   MITC 224:16
normal and e.   JAME 170:21
rack of a too e. chair   POPE 246:22
should be free and e.   OSBO 237:24
Summer time an' the livin' is e.   HEYW 158:20
woman of e. virtue   HAIL 149:8
eat e., drink, and be merry   BIBL 46:22
e. the fat of the land   BIBL 33:36
e. to live   MOLI 225:9
e. up and swallow down   MORE 227:24
have meat and cannot e.   BURN 75:15
I did e.   BIBL 33:8
I would e. his heart   SHAK 284:5
Let them e. cake   MARI 211:18
Let us e. and drink   BIBL 39:27
neither should he e.   BIBL 51:6
see what I e.   CARR 83:19
shalt thou e. bread   BIBL 33:12
Take, e.   BIBL 45:13
Take, e., this is my Body   BOOK 60:5
Tell me what you e.   BRIL 67:3
thou shalt not e. of it   BIBL 33:1
to e., and to drink   BIBL 38:24
Ye shall e. it in haste   BIBL 34:7
eaten e. by missionaries   SPOO 301:2
e. by the bear   HOUS 164:24
we've already e.   BENN 29:15
eater great e. of beef   SHAK 288:4
Out of the e.   BIBL 35:7
eateth e. grass as an ox   BIBL 37:15
Why e. your Master   BIBL 43:18
eating appetite grows by e.   RABE 253:11
E. people is wrong   FLAN 129:16
eats Man is what he e.   FEUE 127:5
Ebenezer Pale E. thought it wrong   BELL 28:25
ebony his image, cut in e.   FULL 134:25
ecce E. homo   BIBL 53:11
ecclesia *Ubi Petrus, ibi ergo e.*   AMBR 4:13
Ecclesiastes *Vanitas vanitatum, dixit E.*   BIBL 53:4
echo E. beyond the Mexique Bay   MARV 213:13
e. of a noble mind   LONG 202:12
Footfalls e. in the memory   ELIO 121:19
waiting for the e.   MARQ 212:24
echoes wild e. flying   TENN 313:5
eclipse E. first   O'KE 236:2
total e.   MILT 223:1
eclipsed e. the gaiety   JOHN 173:21
ecology e. and antiwar   HUNT 167:7
economic cold metal of e. theory   SCHU 265:20
vital e. interests   WEIL 330:23
economical e. with the *actualité*   CLAR 93:16
e. with the truth   ARMS 15:2
economics E. is the science   ROBB 257:16
study of e.   SCHU 265:18
economists e., and calculators   BURK 74:7
economize Let us e. it   TWAI 321:5
economy E. is going without   HOPE 162:15
e. of truth   BURK 74:16
ecstasy What wild e.   KEAT 181:28
ecstatic such e. sound   HARD 151:23
Eden garden eastward in E.   BIBL 32:24
happier E.   MILT 222:2
loss of E.   MILT 220:33

Eden (cont.)

on the east of E.	BIBL 33:16
other E.	SHAK 285:12
Through E. took	MILT 222:25
voice that breathed o'er E.	KEBL 183:21
edge teeth are set on e.	BIBL 41:1
edged Science is an e. tool	EDDI 119:15
editions e. of Balbec and Palmyra	WALP 327:12
editor E.: a person employed	HUBB 166:4
e. did it when I was away	MURD 230:7
e. himself be attacked	TROL 319:19
e. of such a work	STEP 302:16
Edom over E. will I cast out	BOOK 62:5
educated clothed, fed, and e.	RUSK 262:18
e. and the uneducated	FOST 132:4
government by the badly e.	CHES 90:9
education cabbage with a college e.	TWAI 321:10
e., education, and education	BLAI 55:7
E. has been theirs	AUST 19:23
[E.] has produced	TREV 319:9
e. is so astonishing	ADAM 1:17
E. is what survives	SKIN 296:20
is a liberal e.	STEE 302:3
part of e.	BACO 21:29
poor e. I have received	BOTT 65:3
Soap and e.	TWAI 321:24
thank your e.	JONS 177:24
unplanned e. creates	VERW 323:14
eels e. boil'd in broo	BALL 23:20
effect little e. after much labour	AUST 20:3
efficient e. and the inefficient	SHAW 290:30
e. parts	BAGE 22:10
effort redoubling your e.	SANT 264:16
written without e.	JOHN 177:3
egg e. boiled very soft	AUST 19:16
e. by pleasure laid	COWP 101:26
got a bad e.	PUNC 252:18
hairless as an e.	HERR 158:5
looks like a poached e.	NUFF 235:6
radish and an e.	COWP 102:5
eggs as a weasel sucks e.	SHAK 269:17
Lays e. inside a paper bag	ISHE 169:12
roast their e.	BACO 21:34
eglantine with e.	SHAK 283:12
ego Et in Arcadia e.	ANON 12:12
egotistical e. sublime	KEAT 183:11
Egypt firstborn in the land of E.	BIBL 34:8
there was corn in E.	BIBL 33:34
wonders in the land of E.	BIBL 34:4
Egyptian E. to my mother	SHAK 284:28
Egyptians spoiled the E.	BIBL 34:9
eheu E. fugaces Labuntur anni	HORA 164:11
eight Pieces of e.	STEV 303:23
We want e.	ANON 10:17
eightfold E. Path	PALI 240:3
eighty In a dream you are never e.	SEXT 268:5
Einstein Let E. be	SQUI 301:8
either happy could I be with e.	GAY 137:5
Elaine E., the lily maid	TENN 311:7
élan é. vital	BERG 30:12
elbow e. has a fascination	GILB 140:16
elder take An e. than herself	SHAK 288:18
elderly e. man of 42	ASHF 16:12
Eldorado E. of all the old fools	BAUD 26:8
election e. is coming	ELIO 121:5
elections e. are won	ADAM 1:14
You won the e.	SOMO 299:2
elective E. affinities	GOET 142:23
e. dictatorship	HAIL 149:9
Electra Mourning becomes E.	O'NE 236:13
electric biggest e. train set	WELL 331:4
E. Kool-Aid Acid test	WOLF 338:20
sing the body e.	WHIT 333:19

tried to mend the E. Light	BELL 28:21
electrical e. skin and glaring eyes	SMAR 297:1
electricity e. was dripping	THUR 317:26
usefulness of e.	FARA 126:4
electrification e. of the whole country	LENI 197:4
electronic new e. interdependence	MCLU 208:4
elegant e. simplicity	STOW 304:20
e. sufficiency	THOM 317:10
Most intelligent, very e.	BUCK 72:2
so e.	ELIO 122:25
You e. fowl	LEAR 195:15
elegy whole of Gray's E.	WOLF 338:14
eleison Kyrie e.	MISS 223:27
elementary E., my dear Watson	DOYL 115:14
'E.,' said he	DOYL 115:14
elements with the fretful e.	SHAK 277:17
elephant at the E.	SHAK 288:25
corn as high as an e.'s eye	HAMM 150:21
couldn't hit an e.	SEDG 267:3
E.'s Child	KIPL 188:22
herd of e. pacing	DINE 111:26
masterpiece, an e.	DONN 114:1
sleeping with an e.	TRUD 320:5
elephants e. for want of towns	SWIF 307:9
golden e. next	SHOR 295:2
eleven failing his e.-plus	PRES 251:1
elf deceiving e.	KEAT 182:15
elfland horns of E.	TENN 313:6
Eli Eli, E., lama sabachthani	BIBL 45:21
Elijah E. passed by him	BIBL 36:14
E. went up by a whirlwind	BIBL 36:19
spirit of E.	BIBL 36:20
eliminated the impossible	DOYL 115:18
Elisha rest on E.	BIBL 36:20
Elizabeth my sonne's wife, E.	INGE 169:1
elms Behind the e. last night	PRIO 251:11
Beneath those rugged e.	GRAY 146:14
in immemorial e.	TENN 313:19
eloquence e. the soul	MILT 221:21
ornate e. in our English	CAXT 86:10
simple e. ever convince	WALP 327:16
else happening to Somebody E.	ROGE 259:5
elsewhere There is a world e.	SHAK 270:12
Elysium What E. have ye known	KEAT 181:26
embarras e. des richesses	ALLA 4:6
embarrassment e. of riches	ALLA 4:6
embers glowing e. through the room	MILT 219:22
embrace do there e.	MARV 213:22
e. your Lordship's principles	WILK 336:1
embraceth mercy e. him	BOOK 61:13
emendation e. wrong	JOHN 173:22
emerald green as e.	COLE 96:10
men, of the E. Isle	DREN 116:9
emeritus called a professor e.	LEAC 195:4
Emily E., hear	CRAN 102:21
emotion e. recollected in tranquillity	WORD 341:20
masses conveying an e.	HEPW 156:24
morality touched by e.	ARNO 16:4
tranquillity remembered in e.	PARK 240:22
emotions gamut of the e.	PARK 240:23
metaphysical brothel for the e.	KOES 189:21
emparadised E. in one another's arms	MILT 222:2
emperor dey makes you E.	O'NE 236:10
E. has nothing on	ANDE 5:6
e. of ice-cream	STEV 303:3
e. to die standing	VESP 323:17
empire All e. is no more	DRYD 116:19
arch Of the ranged e.	SHAK 268:13
course of e.	BERK 30:15
e. walking very slowly	FITZ 129:9
evil e.	REAG 255:2
found a great e.	SMIT 297:9
How's the E.	GEOR 138:8

lost an e. ACHE 1:6
metropolis of the e. COBB 95:8
nor Roman, nor an e. VOLT 326:6
Russia an e. or democracy BRZE 71:23
way she disposed of an e. HARL 152:11
empires day of E. CHAM 86:18
Hatching vain e. MILT 221:19
Vaster than e. MARV 213:20
employed innocently e. JOHN 175:12
employee In a hierarchy every e. PETE 244:8
employer harder upon the e. SPOO 301:1
employment e. to the artisan BELL 28:21
emptiness Form is e. MahÂ 209:14
empty Bring on the e. horses CURT 105:7
e., swept, and garnished BIBL 43:36
rich he hath sent e. away BIBL 45:34
singer of an e. day MORR 228:16
turn down an e. glass FITZ 129:2
enamelled e. meadows WALP 327:7
enamoured So e. on peace CLAR 93:13
enchanted e. isles MILT 219:15
Enter these e. woods MERE 217:7
holy and e. COLE 96:4
Some e. evening HAMM 150:23
enchantment distance lends e. CAMP 81:3
enchantments e. of the Middle Age ARNO 15:29
e. of the Middle Age BEER 27:12
encircling amid the e. gloom NEWM 233:7
encompasses God e. everything KORA 190:15
encounter e. darkness as a bride SHAK 281:32
encourage right to e. BAGE 22:21
to e. the others VOLT 325:22
encourager e. les autres VOLT 325:22
end a ne e. of ane old song OGIL 235:21
appointment at the e. of the world DINE 111:26
beginning of the e. TALL 308:24
came to an e. all wars LLOY 200:19
e. badly STEV 303:27
e. crowns all SHAK 287:34
e. in doubts BACO 20:18
e. is where we start from ELIO 121:28
e. justifies the means BUSE 76:19
e. of a novel TROL 319:15
e. of a thousand years of history GAIT 135:7
e. of the beginning CHUR 91:20
e. of the way inescapable PAST 241:21
e. where I began DONN 114:15
In my beginning is my e. ELIO 121:22
In my e. is my beginning MARY 214:14
let me know mine e. BOOK 61:19
look to the e. ANON 12:19
middle, and an e. ARIS 14:15
muddle, and an e. LARK 193:17
on to the e. of the road LAUD 194:6
Our e. is Life MACN 208:21
there was no e. WHIT 333:11
This was the e. PLAT 246:1
till you come to the e. CARR 83:26
unto the e. of the world BIBL 45:22
Waiting for the e. EMPS 124:20
war that will e. war WELL 331:18
world will e. in fire FROS 134:8
world without e. BOOK 58:9
endearing e. young charms MOOR 227:13
endeavours e. are unlucky explorers DOUG 115:4
ended Georges e. LAND 192:23
in 1915 the old world e. LAWR 194:12
Mass is e. MISS 224:8
Enderby Brides of E. INGE 168:23
ending bread-sauce of the happy e. JAME 170:22
her certain e. SHAK 289:20
way of e. a war ORWE 237:21
endless in e. night GRAY 146:21

ends between e. and scarce means ROBB 257:16
divinity that shapes our e. SHAK 273:15
e. by our beginnings know DENH 108:15
pursuing of the best e. HUTC 167:12
endure e. for a night BOOK 61:11
e. my own despair WALS 328:1
e. them AURE 19:14
human hearts e. JOHN 174:3
nature itselfe cant e. FLEM 130:2
stuff will not e. SHAK 288:13
endured state to be e. JOHN 173:25
endureth mercy e. for ever BOOK 63:22
enemies alone against smiling e. BOWE 65:12
conquering one's e. GENG 137:20
e. be scattered BOOK 62:6
e. will not believe HUBB 166:2
left me naked to mine e. SHAK 275:26
Love your e. BIBL 46:10
making new e. VOLT 326:15
no perpetual e. PALM 240:6
wish their e. dead MONT 226:5
enemy afraid of his e. PLUT 246:10
better class of e. MILL 218:19
e. that shall be destroyed BIBL 50:3
e. to the human race MILL 218:17
greatest e. is inclination BAHY 22:24
high speed toward the e. HALS 150:12
I am the e. you killed OWEN 238:26
If thine e. be hungry BIBL 38:3
life, its e. ANOU 13:8
Mine e.'s dog SHAK 278:5
not an e. in the world WILD 335:21
O mine e. BIBL 36:15
one e. ALI 4:3
Our friends, the e. BÉRA 30:11
sometimes his own worst e. BEVI 32:15
spoils of the e. MARC 211:16
will have upon the e. WELL 331:5
your e. and your friend TWAI 321:6
energy E. is Eternal Delight BLAK 55:20
enfants e. de la patrie ROUG 261:8
Les e. terribles GAVA 136:21
engine be a Really Useful E. AWDR 20:7
e. of pollution, the dog SPAR 299:25
I am An e. HARE 152:7
in dirt reasoning e. ROCH 258:13
two-handed e. MILT 220:16
engineers age of the e. HOGB 160:21
e. of human souls STAL 301:12
e. of the soul GORK 144:18
not e. of the soul KENN 184:15
engines e. to play a little BURK 74:5
England ah, faithless E. BOSS 64:19
always be an E. PARK 241:5
Be E. what she will CHUR 90:23
between France and E. JERR 172:8
damn you E. OSBO 237:30
E. and America divided SHAW 292:6
E. and Saint George SHAK 274:34
E. expects NELS 232:9
E. has saved herself PITT 245:13
E. hath need of thee WORD 340:4
E., home and beauty ARNO 16:6
E. invented the phrase BAGE 22:12
E. is a garden KIPL 187:18
E. is a nation of shopkeepers NAPO 231:10
E. keep my bones SHAK 277:3
E., my England HENL 156:9
E.'s green and pleasant land BLAK 55:27
E.'s native people BURN 76:2
E.'s not a bad country DRAB 115:21
E.'s on the anvil KIPL 187:6
E.'s winding sheet BLAK 55:15

England (*cont.*)

E., their England	MACD 207:9
E. then indeed be free	FABE 125:15
E. to be the workshop	DISR 112:4
E. was too pure an Air	ANON 9:7
E. will have her neck wrung	CHUR 91:19
E., with all thy faults	COWP 101:30
ensure summer in E.	WALP 327:11
gentlemen of E.	PARK 241:3
gives E. her soldiers	MERE 216:25
God punish E.	FUNK 135:3
Goodbye, E.'s rose	JOHN 172:17
Gott strafe E.	FUNK 135:3
Heart of E.	DRAY 116:6
here did E. help me	BROW 70:11
History is now and E.	ELIO 121:29
in E. people have	MIKE 217:25
in E.'s song for ever	NEWB 232:19
leads him to E.	JOHN 174:23
Let not E. forget	MILT 223:21
Oh, to be in E.	BROW 70:8
roast beef of old E.	BURK 74:12
Rule all E.	COLL 97:1
Slaves cannot breathe in E.	COWP 101:29
Speak for E.	AMER 4:15
stately homes of E.	HEMA 155:18
That is for ever E.	BROO 67:23
that will be E. gone	LARK 193:12
this Realm of E.	BOOK 64:5
this realm, this E.	SHAK 285:13
Wake up, E.	GEOR 138:2
we are the people of E.	CHES 89:27
who only E. know	KIPL 187:14
world where E. is finished	MILL 218:11
youth of E.	SHAK 274:30
Englanders Little E.	ANON 8:9
English as an angel is the E. child	BLAK 56:9
bird-haunted E. lawn	ARNO 15:9
Certain men the E. shot	YEAT 343:9
Cricket—a game which the E.	MANC 210:17
E. are busy	MONT 226:16
E. Bible	MACA 205:22
E. child	BLAK 56:9
E. Church shall be free	MAGN 209:10
E., not the Turkish court	SHAK 274:25
E. plays are like	VOLT 326:12
E. take their pleasures	SULL 306:1
E. tongue I love	WALC 326:16
E. unofficial rose	BROO 67:20
E. up with which I will not put	CHUR 92:2
fragments of the E. scene	ORWE 237:11
in E. the undergrowth	EMPS 124:22
in the E. language	JAME 170:27
made our E. tongue	SPEN 300:26
mobilized the E. language	MURR 230:12
Most E. talk	JAME 170:15
rolling E. road	CHES 89:24
Saxon-Danish-Norman E.	DEFO 107:20
seven feet of E. ground	HARO 152:12
talent of our E. nation	DRYD 117:6
to the E. that of the sea	RICH 257:4
well of E. undefiled	SPEN 300:18
Englishman blood of an E.	NASH 231:19
E., Being flattered	CHAP 87:14
E., even if he is alone	MIKE 217:26
E. in the wrong	SHAW 291:22
E. to open his mouth	SHAW 291:28
for E. or Jew	BLAK 55:17
he is an E.	GILB 141:2
He remains an E.	GILB 141:3
last great E.	TENN 312:28
No E. is ever fairly beaten	SHAW 291:32
not one E.	WALP 327:21

rights of an E.	JUNI 179:17
thing, an E.	DEFO 107:19
Englishmen E. never will be slaves	SHAW 291:12
first to his E.	MILT 223:18
prefer to be E.	RHOD 256:8
Englishness all the eternal E.	CARD 82:4
Englishwoman E. is so refined	SMIT 298:4
Princess leave the E.	BISM 54:12
enigma mystery inside an e.	CHUR 91:13
enjoy e. him for ever	SHOR 295:3
what I most e.	SHAK 289:25
enjoyed little to be e.	JOHN 173:25
still to be e.	KEAT 182:3
enjoying if you are e.	NESB 232:15
enjoyment chief e. of riches	SMIT 297:8
e. of all desires	TANT 309:9
enjoyments Fire-side e.	COWP 102:4
if it were not for its e.	SURT 306:10
insufficiency of human e.	JOHN 174:2
Enoch E. walked with God	BIBL 33:17
enough e. for everyone's need	BUCH 72:1
e. of blood and tears	RABI 253:16
Hold, e.	SHAK 281:26
Patriotism is not e.	CAVE 86:7
two thousand years is e.	PIUS 245:17
Entbehren *E. sollst Du*	GOET 142:17
enter Let no one e.	ANON 12:5
shall not e.	BIBL 44:13
you who e.	DANT 105:17
entered iron e. into his soul	BOOK 62:26
enterprise leave it to private e.	KEYN 185:11
voyages of the starship *E.*	RODD 258:18
entertain better to e. an idea	JARR 171:7
e. divine Zenocrate	MARL 212:18
e. this starry stranger	CRAS 103:2
entertained e. angels unawares	BIBL 51:18
enthralled but not e.	MILT 219:17
enthusiasts how to deal with e.	MACA 205:19
entia *E. non sunt multiplicanda*	OCCA 235:19
entire E. and whole and perfect	SPRI 301:3
entropy e. of human thought	ZAMY 344:22
envious Hot, e., noisy	YOUN 344:11
environmental any e. group	BRUN 71:19
envy e., hatred, and malice	BOOK 59:4
e. the pair of phoenixes	HO 159:21
moved with e.	BIBL 48:32
prisoners of e.	ILLI 168:18
épater *é. le bourgeois*	BAUD 26:9
Ephesians Diana of the E.	BIBL 48:37
Ephesus beasts at E.	BIBL 50:4
epigram purrs like an e.	MARQ 212:25
epigrams despotism tempered by e.	CARL 82:20
episode but the occasional e.	HARD 151:17
epitaph no man write my e.	EMME 124:19
not remembered in thy e.	SHAK 274:11
epitaphs nice derangement of e.	SHER 294:14
of worms, and e.	SHAK 285:19
eppur *E. si muove*	GALI 135:13
equal all men are created e.	LINC 199:8
e. division of unequal earnings	ELLI 123:23
e. in dignity and rights	ANON 5:15
faith shines in e.	BRON 67:12
more e. than others	ORWE 237:5
equality e. in the servants' hall	BARR 25:13
majestic e. of the law	FRAN 132:18
not e. or fairness	BERL 31:1
equals peace between e.	WILS 337:7
Pigs treat us as e.	CHUR 92:14
equanimity face with e.	GILB 140:3
equations fire into the e.	HAWK 153:12
equi *currite noctis e.*	MARL 212:7
currite noctis e.	OVID 238:10
equivocate I will not e.	GARR 136:11

eradication e. of conferences   MAYA 215:16
erected least e. spirit   MILT 221:13
Erin for E. dear we fall   SULL 305:17
eripuit *E. coelo fulmen*   TURG 320:18
eripuitque *E. Jovi*   MANI 211:5
err Man will e.   GOET 142:16
   most may e.   DRYD 116:21
   prefer To e.   ANON 11:5
   To e. is human   POPE 248:6
erred e., and strayed from thy ways   BOOK 58:5
error E. has never approached   METT 217:16
   e. is immense   BOLI 57:14
   limit to infinite e.   BREC 66:8
   men are liable to e.   LOCK 201:6
   no dignity in persevering in e.   PEEL 242:21
   positive in e. as in truth   LOCK 201:5
   stalking-horse to e.   BOLI 57:13
errors common e. of our life   SIDN 295:14
   E., like straws   DRYD 116:26
   reasoned e.   HUXL 168:2
Esau E. my brother   BIBL 33:28
   E. selleth his birthright   BIBL 33:27
   hands are the hands of E.   BIBL 33:29
escalier *esprit de l'e.*   DIDE 111:21
escape Beauty for some provides e.   HUXL 167:18
   What struggle to e.   KEAT 181:28
escaped e. with the skin of my teeth   BIBL 37:8
   Our soul is e.   BOOK 63:16
escutcheon blot on the e.   GRAY 146:9
Eskimo E. forgets his language   OKPI 236:3
espionage e. can be recommended   WEST 332:17
espoused My fairest, my e.   MILT 222:8
   my late e. saint   MILT 223:11
esprit *e. de l'escalier*   DIDE 111:21
essenced long e. hair   MACA 206:3
estate fourth e. of the realm   MACA 205:12
   in mind, body, or e.   BOOK 59:10
estranging unplumbed, salt, e. sea   ARNO 15:26
état *L'É. c'est moi*   LOUI 202:18
eternal E. Father, strong to save   WHIT 333:18
   E. in man cannot kill   BHAG 32:16
   E. in man cannot kill   UPAN 321:24
   E. Passion   ARNO 15:10
   e. rocks beneath   BRON 67:14
   e. silence   PASC 241:17
   e. triangle   ANON 6:16
   Grant them e. rest   MISS 224:10
   Hope springs e.   POPE 248:10
   our e. home   WATT 329:13
   Robust art alone is e.   GAUT 136:20
   thy e. summer   SHAK 289:24
   whose e. Word   MARR 212:26
eternity Deserts of vast e.   MARV 213:21
   E. shut in a span   CRAS 103:3
   E.'s sunrise   BLAK 56:2
   progress to e.   SHAK 289:33
   saw E. the other night   VAUG 323:4
   shadows of e.   VAUG 323:1
   some conception of e.   MANC 210:17
   white radiance of E.   SHEL 292:20
   who love, time is e.   VAN 322:15
etherized patient e. upon a table   ELIO 122:9
ethic protestant e.   WEBE 330:2
ethics law floats in a sea of e.   WARR 328:16
Ethiopian E. change his skin   BIBL 40:25
Eton playing-fields of E.   ORWE 237:12
   playing fields of E.   WELL 331:12
étonne *É.-moi*   DIAG 109:9
Etrurian where the E. shades   MILT 221:9
Eugene Aram E., though a thief   CALV 80:14
eunuch female e.   GREE 147:5
   prerogative of the e.   STOP 304:14
   strain, Time's e.   HOPK 163:7

eunuchs seraglio of e.   FOOT 130:20
Eureka E.! [I've got it!]   ARCH 14:1
Europe another war in E.   BISM 54:19
   Bright over E.   TURN 320:20
   create a nation E.   MONN 225:19
   depravations of E.   MATH 215:2
   dogs of E. bark   AUDE 18:4
   E. a continent of energetic mongrels   FISH 128:4
   E. by her example   PITT 245:13
   E. of nations   DE G 107:25
   E. the unfinished negative   MCCA 206:19
   fifty years of E.   TENN 312:16
   glory of E.   BURK 74:7
   great stocks of E.   YEAT 344:3
   I pine for E.   RIMB 257:11
   keep up with Western E.   UPDI 321:25
   lamps are going out all over E.   GREY 147:13
   last gentleman in E.   LEVE 198:5
   map of E. has been changed   CHUR 91:9
   part of the community of E.   SALI 263:20
   poor are E.'s blacks   CHAM 87:1
   security of E.   MITC 224:18
   spectre is haunting E.   MARX 214:8
   take over the whole of E.   RIDL 257:5
   Whoever speaks of E.   BISM 54:16
   whole of E.   NAPO 231:4
European become E.   KETT 185:4
   communal life of the E.   VERW 323:14
   not a characteristic of a E.   CHAN 87:8
   policy of E. integration   KOHL 190:2
Europeans You are learned E.   MASS 214:20
Euston in E. waiting-room   CORN 100:7
eve and E. spane   ROLL 259:10
   fairest of her daughters E.   MILT 222:1
   real curse of E.   RHYS 256:10
   riverrun, past E. and Adam's   JOYC 178:19
Evelyn E. Hope is dead   BROW 70:4
even E. as you and I   KIPL 188:13
evening e. and the morning   BIBL 32:22
   e. is spread out against the sky   ELIO 122:9
   e. star   MILT 222:24
   It is a beauteous e.   WORD 339:24
   light of e., Lissadell   YEAT 343:3
   like an e. gone   WATT 329:14
   Some enchanted e.   HAMM 150:23
   welcome peaceful e. in   COWP 102:3
evensong bells ringeth to e.   HAWE 153:9
event greatest e. it is   FOX 132:13
   hurries to the main e.   HORA 163:16
   not an e.   TALL 308:25
eventide fast falls the e.   LYTE 205:4
events E., dear boy   MACM 208:13
   e. have controlled me   LINC 199:9
ever For e. panting   KEAT 182:3
evergreen e. tree   SHER 294:12
everlasting caught An e. cold   WEBS 330:20
   e. arms   BIBL 34:30
   e. life   BIBL 47:28
   e. life   BIBL 47:32
   e. No   CARL 83:2
evermore for e.   BOOK 63:14
   name liveth for e.   ANON 10:5
   name liveth for e.   BIBL 41:30
every E. day, I am getting better   COUÉ 100:11
   To e. thing   BIBL 38:16
Everyman E., I will go with thee   ANON 6:18
everyone E. burst out singing   SASS 265:2
   When e. is wrong   LA C 191:9
everything E. cannot all do e.   LUCI 204:11
   can't all do e.   VIRG 325:12
   chips with e.   WESK 331:20
   e. is in it   TALM 309:5
   E. passes   ANON 11:20

everything (*cont.*)
e. that is the case — WITT 337:22
God encompasses e. — KORA 190:15
knowledge of e. — HERO 157:24
Life, the Universe and E. — ADAM 1:11
Macaulay is of e. — MELB 216:5
robbed a man of *e.* — SOLZ 298:27
sans taste, sans e. — SHAK 269:24
everywhere centre is e. — ANON 8:21
Out of the e. — MACD 207:6
Water, water, e. — COLE 96:13
evidence circumstantial e. — THOR 317:16
it's not e. — DICK 111:8
evil banality of e. — AREN 14:4
dark and e. days — INGR 169:4
days are e. — BIBL 50:20
deliver us from e. — MISS 224:5
Do e. in return — AUDE 18:16
do e., that good may come — BIBL 49:7
doing e. in return — SOCR 298:22
E., be thou my good — MILT 221:30
E. be to him who evil thinks — ANON 11:12
E. communications — BIBL 50:5
e. counsel is most evil — HESI 158:15
e. cradling — KORA 190:10
e. empire — REAG 255:2
e. manners live in brass — SHAK 275:27
e. thereof — BIBL 43:1
e. which I would not — BIBL 49:15
face of 'e.' — BURR 76:4
fear nae e. — BURN 75:25
find means of e. — MILT 221:5
for e. to triumph — BURK 74:22
God prepares e. — ANON 12:4
he that doeth e. — BIBL 52:1
Hypocrisy, the only e. — MILT 221:28
illness identified with e. — SONT 299:6
like great e. — CALL 80:11
meet e.-willers — ELIZ 123:4
necessary e. — BRAD 65:21
non-cooperation with e. — GAND 135:19
on the e. and on the good — BIBL 42:20
open and notorious e. liver — BOOK 59:16
punishment in itself is e. — BENT 30:4
refuse the e. — BIBL 39:17
Resist not e. — BIBL 42:18
return good for e. — VANB 322:8
root of all e. — BIBL 51:11
unruly e. — BIBL 51:22
whatever e. visits thee — KORA 190:14
evils expect new e. — BACO 21:16
greatest of e. — SHAW 291:1
least of e. — GRAC 145:3
evolution Some call it e. — CARR 84:17
ewe one little e. lamb — BIBL 35:30
tupping your white e. — SHAK 284:8
Ewig-Weibliche E. *zieht uns hinan* — GOET 142:21
exact not to be e. — BURK 73:22
writing an e. man — BACO 21:27
exactitude *L'e. est la politesse* — LOUI 203:2
exaggerated have been greatly e. — TWAI 321:13
exalted e. among the heathen — BOOK 61:26
e. them of low degree — BIBL 45:34
valley shall be e. — BIBL 40:7
exalteth whosoever e. himself — BIBL 46:25
exam have an e. at 11 — NEIL 232:6
examinations E. are formidable — COLT 97:16
In e., those who do not wish — RALE 254:9
examine E. for a moment — WOOL 339:6
example Europe by her e. — PITT 245:13
E. is always more efficacious — JOHN 174:1
examples philosophy from e. — DION 112:2
exceed e. his grasp — BROW 69:17

excel thou shalt not e. — BIBL 33:37
excellent e. thing in woman — SHAK 278:13
excelling all loves e. — WESL 332:2
Excelsior strange device E. — LONG 201:22
excelsis *Gloria in e.* — MISS 223:28
except E. the Lord build — BOOK 63:18
exception glad to make an e. — MARX 214:3
excess e. of light — GRAY 146:21
Nothing in e. — ANON 12:3
road of e. — BLAK 55:22
excessive e. bright — MILT 221:27
exchange By just e. one for the other — SIDN 295:7
excite e. my amorous propensities — JOHN 174:17
excitement equal the e. — GREE 146:25
it engendered e. — PAGE 239:4
exciting films are too e. — BERR 31:13
excrement in the place of e. — YEAT 342:17
excursion made an e. to hell — PRIE 251:7
excuse E. my dust — PARK 240:21
excuses e. for our failures — FULB 134:22
execute zealous Muslims to e. — KHOM 185:16
execution stringent e. — GRAN 145:19
executioner I am mine own E. — DONN 114:17
executioners victims who respect their e. — SART 264:25
executors Let's choose e. — SHAK 285:19
exercise E. is the yuppie version — EHRE 120:8
love's proper e. — DAVI 106:15
exertion e. is too much for me — PEAC 242:15
exertions saved herself by her e. — PITT 245:13
exile destined as an e. — VIRG 324:9
die in e. — GREG 147:8
exiled outlawed or e. — MAGN 209:11
exiles Paradise of e. — SHEL 292:26
exist presumed to e. — OCCA 235:19
existence purpose of human e. — JUNG 179:14
Struggle for E. — DARW 106:8
woman's whole e. — BYRO 78:18
existing bother of e. — HAWK 153:12
exit E., pursued by a bear — SHAK 289:4
exits men to take their exits — WEBS 330:11
exoriare E. *aliquis nostris* — VIRG 324:17
ex-parrot THIS IS AN E. — MONT 226:25
expect E. nothing — WALK 326:20
expectations revolution of rising e. — CLEV 94:12
expects England e. — NELS 232:9
Nobody e. — MONT 227:1
expediency be sacrificed to e. — MAUG 215:8
expedient e. for us — BIBL 48:2
most e. for them — BOOK 58:22
expedit E. *esse deos* — OVID 238:12
expedition abandoning the e. — DOUG 115:4
expelles *Naturam e. furca* — HORA 163:24
expenditure annual e. nineteen — DICK 110:3
E. rises to meet income — PARK 241:6
expense at the e. of two — CLOU 95:1
e. damnable — CHES 89:15
e. of spirit — SHAK 290:8
sanctifies e. — POPE 247:22
expenses facts are on e. — STOP 304:16
experience can go beyond his e. — LOCK 201:4
E. has taught — TACI 308:20
know it from e. — ARAB 13:18
man of no e. — CURZ 105:9
Old Age, and E. — ROCH 258:13
one year's e. 30 times — CARR 83:12
part of e. — BACO 21:29
triumph of hope over e. — JOHN 175:7
trying every e. once — ANON 11:8
we need not e. it — FRIS 134:1
experiences lie the e. of our life — MANN 211:6
experiencing only by e. it — PROU 251:19
experiment e. is the best test — FARA 126:3
social and economic e. — HOOV 162:11

experimental e. reasoning HUME 166:19
expert e. is one who knows more and more BUTL 77:3
e. is someone who knows HEIS 155:11
experto E. credite VIRG 325:7
explain e. his explanation BYRO 78:15
e. man to man STEI 302:6
e. why it didn't happen CHUR 92:13
Never complain and never e. DISR 113:5
Never e. FISH 128:6
Never e. HUBB 166:2
explained Shut up he e. LARD 193:8
explaining forever e. things SAIN 263:12
expletive E. deleted ANON 6:19
explore E. farthest Spain CLAU 93:21
explorers endeavours are unlucky e. DOUG 115:4
express down e. in the small of the back WODE 338:3
e. our wants GOLD 143:24
Never e. yourself more BOHR 57:10
expressed ne'er so well e. POPE 248:1
expression conventional e. MahÂ 209:13
E. is the dress POPE 248:2
extend attempt to e. their system MONR 225:21
extermination e. of capitalism ZINO 345:5
extinction one generation from e. CARE 82:8
extra add some e., just for you LARK 193:14
extras No e., no vacations DICK 110:21
extremism e. in the defence of liberty GOLD 144:6
extremity daring pilot in e. DRYD 116:16
exultations e., agonies WORD 341:16
eye apple of his e. BIBL 34:29
beam that is in thine own e. BIBL 43:3
bright e. of peninsulas CATU 85:21
Cast a cold e. YEAT 343:30
custom loathsome to the e. JAME 170:8
day's garish e. MILT 219:23
e. for eye BIBL 34:17
e. of a needle BIBL 44:20
Green E. HAYE 154:1
had but one e. DICK 110:22
harvest of a quiet e. WORD 340:20
If thine e. offend thee BIBL 44:15
in the twinkling of an e. BIBL 50:7
language in her e. SHAK 287:33
looked into the e. of day YEAT 342:24
man a microscopic e. POPE 248:12
mild and magnificent e. BROW 70:17
neither e. to see LENT 197:19
see e. to eye BIBL 40:15
soft black e. MOOR 227:19
to the e. of God OLIV 236:5
unforgiving e. SHER 294:20
untrusting e. on all they do GELL 137:17
with his glittering e. COLE 96:9
eyeball e. to eyeball RUSK 262:6
eyeless E. in Gaza MILT 222:32
eyelids tired e. upon tired eyes TENN 312:17
eyes all e. else dead coals SHAK 289:15
And her e. were wild KEAT 181:19
bodily hunger in his e. SHAW 291:3
chewing gum for the e. ANON 10:1
Closed his e. GRAY 146:21
cold commemorative e. ROSS 260:18
constitutional e. LINC 199:12
cynosure of neighbouring e. MILT 220:4
death bandaged my e. BROW 71:2
drew his e. along AUGU 18:27
electrical skin and glaring e. SMAR 297:1
ever more perfect e. TEIL 310:7
e. as wide as a football-pool CAUS 86:4
e. have they, and see not BOOK 63:7
e. of Caligula MITT 225:3
E. of most unholy blue MOOR 227:14
e. to wonder SHAK 290:3

Foolish e. SANS 264:15
Get thee glass e. SHAK 278:3
King of England's e. TYND 321:18
Love looks not with the e. SHAK 283:2
Love's tongue is in the e. FLET 130:11
marvellous in our e. BOOK 63:10
Mine e. have seen HOWE 165:15
My mistress' e. SHAK 290:9
night has a thousand e. BOUR 65:8
Night hath a thousand e. LYLY 204:24
Smoke gets in your e. HARB 151:6
Stars scribble on our e. CRAN 102:19
stuck in her face for e. SHAK 278:18
Take a pair of sparkling e. GILB 139:21
tempts your wand'ring e. GRAY 146:20
was it his bees-winged e. BETJ 31:15
why the good Lord made your e. LEHR 196:18
will lift mine e. SCOT 267:1
with his half-shut e. POPE 249:6
with thine e. JONS 178:4
You have lovely e. CHEK 88:34

F

faber F. est suae CLAU 93:22
Fabians good man fallen among F. LENI 197:6
fabill nocht bot f. BARB 24:25
fables profane and old wives' f. BIBL 51:8
fac Dilige et quod vis f. AUGU 19:4
face beautiful f. is a mute PUBL 251:21
Coming with vivid f. YEAT 342:19
construction in the f. SHAK 279:11
covered his f. BIBL 39:14
Cover her f. WEBS 330:12
f. of 'evil' BURR 76:4
f. so pleased my mind ANON 10:6
f. the index CRAB 102:16
False f. must hide SHAK 280:3
garden in her f. CAMP 81:5
garden of your f. HERB 157:7
has the f. he deserves ORWE 237:22
honest, sonsie f. BURN 75:28
I am the family f. HARD 151:4
in the public's f. RUSK 262:7
keep your f. CART 85:3
Look in my f. ROSS 260:17
Lord make his f. shine BIBL 34:23
lying on his f., dead THAC 314:23
mask that eats into the f. UPDI 322:1
men stand f. to face KIPL 187:8
never forget a f. MARX 214:3
night's starred f. KEAT 183:1
Once the bright f. MIDD 217:20
painted her f. BIBL 36:29
Pity a human f. BLAK 56:6
rabbit has a charming f. ANON 9:14
rogue's f. CONG 98:12
shining morning f. SHAK 269:21
sing in the robber's f. JUVE 180:2
socialism would not lose its human f. DUBČ 117:18
spirit passed before my f. BIBL 37:4
stamping on a human f. ORWE 237:18
touched the f. of God MAGE 209:9
unacceptable f. of capitalism HEAT 154:17
View but her f. FORD 131:8
Was this the f. MARL 212:6
Your f., my thane SHAK 279:16
faces grind the f. of the poor BIBL 39:12
not having any f. PRIE 251:6
old familiar f. LAMB 192:7
Private f. in public places AUDE 18:12

faces (*cont.*)
slope of f. COWP 102:6
facilis *F. descensus Averno* VIRG 324:20
fact irritable reaching after f. KEAT 183:6
judges of f. PULT 252:6
ugly f. HUXL 167:21
faction whisper of a f. RUSS 263:1
factions Old religious f. BURK 74:20
facts accounted for *all* the f. WATS 328:26
built up of f. POIN 246:16
f. are on expenses STOP 304:16
f. are sacred SCOT 266:1
give you all the f. AUDE 18:18
inert f. ADAM 1:17
politics consists in ignoring f. ADAM 1:16
what I want is, F. DICK 110:15
faculty f. of the mind WOLL 338:24
fade f. into the light WORD 340:11
Than to f. away YOUN 344:21
They simply f. away FOLE 130:18
fades f. awa' like morning dew BALL 24:15
faery f. lands forlorn KEAT 182:14
f.'s child KEAT 181:19
fail F. better BECK 27:2
F. not our feast SHAK 280:22
shall not flag or f. CHUR 91:15
we'll not SHAK 280:1
words f. us AUST 20:6
fails One sure, if another f. BROW 71:6
failure Any f. seems so total QUAN 253:2
political lives end in f. POWE 250:25
Women can't forgive f. CHEK 88:33
fain F. would I climb RALE 254:4
faint F., yet pursuing BIBL 35:5
reap, if we f. not BIBL 50:16
walk, and not f. BIBL 40:11
with f. praises WYCH 342:4
fainted should utterly have f. BOOK 61:10
fair anything to show more f. WORD 339:18
deserves the f. DRYD 116:23
dream of f. women TENN 310:20
f. as is the rose CHAU 88:23
f. defect of nature MILT 222:22
F. is foul SHAK 278:26
F. stood the wind DRAY 116:8
f. white linen cloth BOOK 59:17
Fat, f. and forty O'KE 236:1
I have sworn thee f. SHAK 290:12
Sabrina f. MILT 219:18
she be f. KEAT 182:1
She f., divinely fair MILT 222:16
so f. that they called him AUBR 17:14
So foul and f. a day SHAK 279:3
sweet and f. she seems WALL 327:5
thou art f., my love BIBL 39:6
Trottin' to the f. GRAV 146:2
With you f. maid ANON 7:16
fairest F. Isle DRYD 117:2
f. of creation MILT 222:19
From f. creatures SHAK 289:22
fairies don't believe in f. BARR 25:14
Do you believe in f. BARR 25:16
f. at the bottom of our garden FYLE 135:4
f. left off dancing SELD 267:12
f.' midwife SHAK 286:14
rewards and F. CORB 100:1
fairy believes it was a f. AUBR 17:17
cradle of the f. queen SHAK 283:16
f. when she's forty HENL 156:6
Like f. gifts fading MOOR 227:13
'tis almost f. time SHAK 283:24
faith Catholic F. BOOK 59:2
f. as a grain of mustard seed BIBL 44:12

f. hath made thee whole BIBL 43:22
f. shall be my shield ASKE 16:16
f. shines equal BRON 67:12
f. unfaithful TENN 311:8
f. without doubt UNAM 321:20
F. without works BIBL 51:21
first article of my f. GAND 135:18
good fight of f. BIBL 51:12
In this f. I wish to live VILL 324:7
kept the f. BIBL 51:13
more f. in honest doubt TENN 311:26
O thou of little f. BIBL 44:6
scientific f.'s absurd BROW 70:3
Sea of F. ARNO 15:4
though I have all f. BIBL 49:30
What of the f. HARD 151:25
work of f. BIBL 51:4
faithful Ever f., ever sure MILT 220:8
f. and just to me SHAK 276:17
f. female friend WHUR 334:9
f. in that which is least BIBL 47:2
f. to thee, Cynara DOWS 115:10
f. unto death BIBL 52:5
good and f. servant BIBL 45:5
O come, all ye f. ANON 12:6
So f. in love SCOT 266:17
faithless Human on my f. arm AUDE 18:7
falcon dapple-dawn-drawn F. HOPK 163:8
f., towering in her pride SHAK 280:21
Gentle as f. SKEL 296:16
falconer O! for a f.'s voice SHAK 286:22
Falklands F. thing was a fight BORG 64:14
fall and half to f. POPE 248:16
by dividing we f. DICK 111:18
did he f. JAME 171:2
f. in love today GERS 138:14
f. into it BIBL 38:28
f. into the hands BIBL 51:15
F. into the hands of God TENN 313:23
f. into the hands of the Lord BIBL 41:23
f. out with those we love TENN 313:3
f. to rise BROW 69:19
fear no f. BUNY 73:8
further they have to f. FITZ 129:12
hard rain's a gonna f. DYLA 119:3
it had a dying f. SHAK 288:3
Life is a horizontal f. COCT 95:11
O! what a f. was there SHAK 276:21
Things f. apart YEAT 343:19
yet I fear to f. RALE 254:4
fallacy Pathetic F. RUSK 262:9
fallen Babylon is f. BIBL 52:17
Christopher Robin has f. MORT 229:6
F. cold and dead WHIT 333:21
f. from grace BIBL 50:14
f. from heaven BIBL 39:25
f. into the midst of it BOOK 62:3
good man f. among Fabians LENI 197:6
how are the mighty f. BIBL 35:26
How are the mighty f. BIBL 35:29
lot is f. unto me BOOK 61:2
falleth where the tree f. BIBL 38:32
falling catch a f. star DONN 114:11
'f. domino' principle EISE 120:15
f. sickness SHAK 276:2
fallings F. from us, vanishings WORD 340:12
falls F. the Shadow ELIO 122:5
false all was f. and hollow MILT 221:17
bear f. witness BIBL 34:16
Beware of f. prophets BIBL 43:10
F. face must hide SHAK 280:3
f., fleeting, perjured SHAK 286:3
f. report, if believed MEDI 215:20

f. sincere POPE 247:23
f. to any man SHAK 271:9
f. to others BACO 21:33
Ring out the f. TENN 311:30
falsehood F. has a perennial spring BURK 73:23
falsehoods f. which interest dictates JOHN 173:17
falseness produce in us a f. RUSK 262:9
Falstaff F. sweats to death SHAK 273:31
Famagusta F. and the hidden sun FLEC 129:24
fame best f. is a writer's fame LEBO 196:3
blush to find it f. POPE 248:30
call the Temple of F. LICH 198:24
damned to F. POPE 246:19
F. is like a river BACO 21:21
F. is the spur MILT 220:13
love and f. KEAT 183:2
Man dreams of f. TENN 311:11
nor yet a fool to f. POPE 247:7
Physicians of the Utmost F. BELL 28:10
famed France, f. in all great arts ARNO 15:25
fames *Aura sacra f.* VIRG 324:15
familiar f. friend BOOK 61:20
mine own f. friend BOOK 62:2
old f. faces LAMB 192:7
families best-regulated f. DICK 110:8
f. in a country village AUST 20:2
f. last not three oaks BROW 69:1
happy f. resemble TOLS 318:15
mothers of large f. BELL 28:8
there are f. THAT 315:12
family f. firm GEOR 138:11
f.—that dear octopus SMIT 297:14
F.! . . . the home of all STRI 305:7
have a young f. FOWL 132:12
I am the f. face HARD 151:24
running of a f. MONT 226:10
Selling off the f. silver MACM 208:12
spend more time with f. THAT 315:14
famine F. Queen GONN 144:13
feed her f. fat BYRO 79:2
They that die by f. HENR 156:18
famous f. calm and dead BROW 70:6
f. for fifteen minutes WARH 328:12
f. men have the whole earth PERI 243:21
found myself f. BYRO 79:24
praise f. men BIBL 41:29
'twas a f. victory SOUT 299:13
fan F.-vaulting . . . from an aesthetic LANC 192:20
fanatic f. is a great leader BROU 68:11
fanaticism f. consists in SANT 264:16
fancies heart of furious f. ANON 11:4
fancy f. is the sails KEAT 183:3
let the f. roam KEAT 181:11
Now my sere f. BYRO 78:26
where is f. bred SHAK 282:16
young man's f. TENN 312:7
fantasies fed the heart on f. YEAT 343:10
fantastic light f. round MILT 219:11
light f. toe MILT 220:2
fantasy Most modern f. PRAT 250:27
far F. and few LEAR 195:11
f., far better thing DICK 111:11
F. from the madding crowd's GRAY 146:17
f. side of despair SART 264:24
going a bridge too f. BROW 69:16
good news from a f. country BIBL 38:4
hills and f. away GAY 137:4
How f. is KIPL 188:3
Mexico, so f. from God DIAZ 109:12
much too f. out all my life SMIT 298:3
quarrel in a f. away country CHAM 86:19
so near and yet so f. TENN 311:28
unhappy, f.-off things WORD 341:10

Faraday anti-F. machines CORN 100:5
farce f. is played out RABE 253:15
second as f. MARX 214:6
second time as f. BARN 25:9
farewell Ae f., and then for ever BURN 75:2
F.! a long farewell SHAK 275:23
f. content SHAK 284:25
f., he is gon CHAU 88:13
F. my bok CHAU 88:22
F., my friends DUNC 118:7
F. night BUNY 73:10
F., rewards CORB 100:1
Too-late, F. ROSS 260:17
farm down on the f. LEWI 198:17
farmer f. will never be happy again HERB 157:1
farmers embattled f. stood EMER 124:9
f. excessively fortunate VIRG 325:17
farms cellos of the deep f. STEV 303:14
farrow old sow that eats her f. JOYC 178:25
fart can't f. and chew gum JOHN 173:7
Love is the f. SUCK 305:12
farthest F. Thule VIRG 325:15
farthing f. candle to the sun YOUN 344:13
farthings sold for two f. BIBL 46:21
fascinates I like work: it f. me JERO 172:6
fascination f. frantic GILB 140:21
f. of what's difficult YEAT 342:23
Fascist Every woman adores a F. PLAT 245:19
fashion F. is more usually OLDF 236:4
glass of f. SHAK 272:7
in my f. DOWS 115:10
in my f. PORT 249:14
fashions fit this year's f. HELL 155:15
fast at least twice as f. CARR 84:5
come he f. SCOT 266:15
grew f. and furious BURN 75:26
none so f. as stroke COKE 95:15
Snip! They go so f. HOFF 160:16
will not f. in peace CRAB 102:13
faster F. than a speeding bullet ANON 6:21
fastest travels the f. KIPL 187:25
fasting die f. FRAN 133:6
Thank heaven, f. SHAK 270:2
fat Butter merely makes us f. GOER 142:14
f. and long-haired PLUT 246:8
F., fair and forty O'KE 236:1
f. friend BRUM 71:17
f. greedy owl RICH 256:19
F. is a feminist issue ORBA 236:18
f. of the land BIBL 33:36
f. white woman CORN 100:8
in every f. man CONN 99:2
men about me that are f. SHAK 276:1
outside every f. man AMIS 4:20
should himself be f. JOHN 176:13
that f. gentleman SHAW 292:8
thin man inside every f. man ORWE 237:8
fatal f. bellman SHAK 280:7
most f. complaint of all HILT 159:10
fate Art a revolt against f. MALR 210:14
character is his f. HERA 156:26
F. and character NOVA 235:2
F. is not an eagle BOWE 65:11
F. wrote her a tragedy BEER 27:13
fears his f. too much MONT 226:23
makers of our f. POPP 249:12
master of my f. HENL 156:8
smile of f. DYER 118:21
take a bond of f. SHAK 281:9
tempted F. MCGO 207:13
thy f. shall overtake KING 186:6
father about my F.'s business BIBL 46:8
cometh unto the f. BIBL 48:6

father (*cont.*)
Eternal F., strong to save — WHIT 333:18
f. had an accident there — POTT 249:26
F., hear the prayer — WILL 336:13
F.-like, he tends — LYTE 205:7
f. of English criticism — JOHN 173:20
f. of many nations — BIBL 49:9
f. of the Man — WORD 340:6
F. which is in heaven — BIBL 42:21
glad f. — BIBL 37:25
Glory be to the F. — BOOK 58:9
God the F. Almighty — BOOK 59:22
have God for his f. — CYPR 105:10
Honour thy f. and thy mother — BIBL 34:16
I meet my F., my age — LOWE 203:22
In my F.'s house — BIBL 48:5
last see your F. — YEAM 342:10
Lloyd George knew my f. — ANON 8:11
Lord and F. of mankind — WHIT 334:5
Muhammad is not the f. — KORA 190:21
My f. feeds his flocks — HOME 161:14
My f. wept — BLAK 56:10
No more like my f. — SHAK 270:33
O, f. forsaken — JOYC 179:5
old f. antick, the law — SHAK 273:26
only begotten of the f. — BIBL 47:21
Our F. — BIBL 42:23
politique f. — JAME 170:10
resembled My f. as he slept — SHAK 280:8
sash my f. wore — ANON 10:2
shall a man leave his f. — BIBL 33:5
than you are as a f. — ICE 168:15
thicker than my f.'s loins — BIBL 36:6
when my f. died — SHAK 273:6
will say unto him, F. — BIBL 46:33
wise f. that knows — SHAK 282:8
wish was f., Harry — SHAK 274:24
without f. bred — MILT 219:20
worshipful f. — CAXT 86:10
You are old, F. William — CARR 83:16
fatherly commend to thy f. goodness — BOOK 59:10
fathers because our f. lied — KIPL 187:10
f., provoke not — BIBL 50:21
He f.-forth whose beauty — HOPK 163:2
I am going to my F. — BUNY 73:11
land of my f. — JAME 170:14
My f. can have it — THOM 316:11
sins of the f. — BOOK 59:19
sojourners, as were all our f. — BIBL 36:34
Victory has a hundred f. — CIAN 92:17
years ago our f. brought forth — LINC 199:8
Father William You are old, F. — SOUT 299:16
fathom Full f. five — SHAK 287:7
fathoms fifty f. deep — BALL 24:10
fatted f. calf — BIBL 46:34
fattening illegal, immoral, or f. — WOOL 339:13
fault clever to a f. — BROW 69:21
most grievous f. — MISS 223:26
no kind of f. or flaw — GILB 140:1
O happy f. — MISS 224:14
soul is without f. — RIMB 257:12
think it is their f. — BROO 68:1
faultless Faultily f. — TENN 312:20
faults England, with all thy f. — COWP 101:30
f. a little blind — PRIO 251:8
fill you with the f. they had — LARK 193:14
Jesus! with all thy f. — BUTL 77:14
With all her f. — CHUR 90:23
faune *après-midi d'un f.* — MALL 210:6
favilla *Solvet saeclum in f.* — MISS 224:11
favoured Hail, thou that art highly f. — BIBL 45:32
favours hope for greater f. — LA R 194:1
sense of future f. — WALP 327:23

fawns fallow f. invisible — THOM 316:17
fay *F. ce que vouldras* — RABE 253:13
fear begins in f. — COLE 96:25
by means of pity and f. — ARIS 14:14
f. and trembling — BIBL 50:25
F. God — BIBL 39:1
F. God — BIBL 51:27
F. God. Honour the King — KITC 189:6
f. in a handful of dust — ELIO 122:21
f. made manifest — EDDY 119:16
f. my name — BIBL 41:19
f. no evil — BOOK 61:7
f. no fall — BUNY 73:8
f. of the Law — JOYC 178:20
f. of the Lord — BOOK 63:4
f. those big words — JOYC 179:2
f. to negotiate — KENN 184:10
For f. of finding something worse — BELL 28:11
fourth is freedom from f. — ROOS 259:20
From hope and f. set free — SWIN 307:24
grief felt so like f. — LEWI 198:11
Men f. death — BACO 21:9
no hope without f. — SPIN 300:27
one f., Death's shadow — BLUN 57:2
only thing we have to f. — ROOS 259:15
Our deepest f. is not — WILL 336:11
so long as they f. — ACCI 1:4
There is no f. in love — BIBL 51:34
too much joy or too much f. — GRAV 146:5
travel in the direction of our f. — BERR 31:12
try to have no f. — CHES 89:4
without f. the lawless roads — MUIR 229:18
feared neither f. nor flattered — DOUG 115:3
prince to be f. — MACH 207:16
fearful f. symmetry — BLAK 56:14
f. thing — BIBL 51:15
f. trip is done — WHIT 333:20
fearfully f. and wonderfully made — BOOK 63:26
fearless F., blameless knight — ANON 11:11
fears f. his fate too much — MONT 226:23
f. to speak of Ninety-Eight — INGR 169:5
from sudden f. — BYRO 79:13
man who f. the Lord — BIBL 52:32
Present f. — SHAK 279:8
tie up thy f. — HERB 157:10
feast going to a f. — JONS 177:16
Paris is a movable f. — HEMI 156:2
feather f.-footed through the plashy fen — WAUG 329:22
f. in his cap — ANON 11:6
f. to tickle — LAMB 192:5
my each f. — HUGH 166:10
feathered f. race — FRER 133:18
federal Our F. Union — JACK 169:16
federation F. of the world — TENN 312:12
fee For a small f. in America — SOND 299:3
gorgeous East in f. — WORD 340:17
feeble Most forcible F. — SHAK 274:21
o'ercomes the f. brain — WINC 337:10
feebleness all else is f. — VIGN 324:4
feed f. his flock — BIBL 40:9
f. me in a green pasture — BOOK 61:6
F. my sheep — BIBL 48:22
F. the brute — PUNC 252:17
will you still f. me — LENN 197:16
feel f. it happen — CATU 86:2
f. that he is dying — CALI 80:8
f. the heart-break — GIBS 139:16
f. what wretches feel — SHAK 277:22
more to do than f. — LAMB 192:9
to One does f. — KNOX 189:16
tragedy to those that f. — WALP 327:13
feelings overflow of powerful f. — WORD 341:20
feeling-toned f. complexes — JUNG 179:12

feels happiness he f.   LACL 191:12
fees answered, as they took their F.   BELL 28:10
feet bathe those beauteous f.   FLET 130:10
better to die on your f.   IBAR 168:7
cutting off our f.   SWIF 307:3
dust of your f.   BIBL 43:24
f. beneath her petticoat   SUCK 305:11
f. have they, and walk not   BOOK 63:7
f. in ancient time   BLAK 55:27
f. of him that bringeth   BIBL 40:14
fog comes on little cat f.   SAND 264:8
from his f. the Servants   RIG 257:7
Its f. were tied   KEAT 181:12
marching, charging f.   JAGG 170:4
moon under her f.   BIBL 52:13
palms before my f.   CHES 89:19
set my printless f.   MILT 219:19
seven f. of English ground   HARO 152:12
shoes from off thy f.   BIBL 34:1
skull, and the f.   BIBL 36:32
feign it will not f.   DE P 108:19
felicity Absent thee from f.   SHAK 273:21
Our own f. we make   JOHN 174:3
felix F. qui potuit rerum   VIRG 325:18
O f. culpa   MISS 224:14
fell At one f. swoop   SHAK 281:13
f. among thieves   BIBL 46:15
From morn to noon he f.   MILT 221:15
It f. by itself   JOHN 172:20
feller Sweetes' li'l' f.   STAN 301:20
fellow loves his f-men   HUNT 167:2
felt has f. about it   MUNC 230:2
female British f.   CLOU 94:20
faithful f. friend   WHUR 334:9
f. eunuch   GREE 147:5
f. of the species   KIPL 187:15
f. worker slave of that slave   CONN 99:4
male and the f.   BIBL 33:19
no f. mind   GILM 141:12
no f. Mozart   PAGL 239:5
feminine 'f.' principles   RODD 258:20
Taste is the f.   FITZ 129:3
feminist call me a f.   WEST 332:18
Fat is a f. issue   ORBA 236:18
femme Cherchez la f.   DUMA 118:1
fen f. Of stagnant waters   WORD 340:4
through the plashy f.   WAUG 329:22
fence tradition is a f.   TALM 309:4
fences Good f. make good neighbours   FROS 134:11
Fenian grave of a dead F.   COLL 97:6
left us our F. dead   PEAR 242:17
Fermanagh dreary steeples of F.   CHUR 91:9
Fermat F.'s last theorem   FERM 127:2
fertile In such a fix to be so f.   NASH 231:12
festal line of f. light   ARNO 15:17
fester Lilies that f.   SHAK 290:1
festina F. lente   AUGU 19:8
fetish Militarism . . . is f. worship   TAWN 309:14
fetters F. of gold   ASTE 17:4
f. rent in twain   DAVI 106:22
Milton wrote in f.   BLAK 55:21
fever f. of life is done   NEWM 233:4
Février Janvier and F.   NICH 233:21
few as grossly as the f.   DRYD 116:21
Far and f.   LEAR 195:11
f. are chosen   BIBL 44:26
Gey f.   ANON 7:10
so much owed by so many to so f.   CHUR 91:17
We few, we happy f.   SHAK 275:11
fewer one man f.   METT 217:15
fiat F. justitia   FERD 126:21
F. justitia   WATS 329:2
f. voluntas   MISS 224:5

fickle f. is the South   TENN 313:9
Whatever is f., freckled   HOPK 163:2
fiction best thing in f.   WILD 335:14
continuous f.   BEVA 32:10
house of f.   JAME 170:20
improbable f.   SHAK 288:28
Poetry is the supreme f.   STEV 303:5
sometimes f.   MACA 206:1
Stranger than f.   BYRO 79:7
That is what f. means   WILD 335:2
fictions f. only and false hair   HERB 157:15
Fidele fair F.'s grassy tomb   COLL 97:10
fideles Adeste, f.   ANON 12:6
fidelity thinks he is worth my f.   LACL 191:11
field corner of a foreign f.   BROO 67:23
fair f. full of folk   LANG 193:1
lay f. to field   BIBL 39:13
lilies of the f.   BIBL 42:27
not as simple as to cross a f.   PAST 241:21
Not that fair f. Of Enna   MILT 221:32
only inhabitants of the f.   BURK 74:9
presence on the f.   WELL 331:9
single in the f.   WORD 341:9
What though the f. be lost   MILT 221:4
fields plough the f.   CAMP 80:18
fiend f. Flibbertigibbet   SHAK 277:24
f. hid in a cloud   BLAK 56:10
foul F.   BUNY 73:1
frightful f.   COLE 96:17
swung the f.   MERE 217:4
work like a f.   THOM 316:10
fierce as I raved and grew more f.   HERB 157:11
but little, she is f.   SHAK 283:18
F. as ten Furies   MILT 221:22
f. light which beats   TENN 311:3
F. was the wild billow   ANAT 5:4
fiery burning f. furnace   BIBL 41:7
throne was like the f. flame   BIBL 41:10
fife Thane of F. had a wife   SHAK 281:16
fifteen At the age of f.   JUNG 179:16
at the age of f.   WILS 337:1
famous for f. minutes   WARH 328:12
F. men on the dead man's chest   STEV 303:21
f. wild Decembers   BRON 67:13
old age always f. years older   BARU 25:21
fifth F. column   MOLA 225:8
fifties tranquillized F.   LOWE 203:21
fifty At f., everyone   ORWE 237:22
corpulent man of f.   HUNT 167:5
fig sewed f. leaves together   BIBL 33:7
fight begun to f.   JONE 177:9
don't want to f.   HUNT 166:24
f. and fight again   GAIT 135:6
f. and not to heed the wounds   IGNA 168:17
f. for freedom   PANK 240:11
f. for freedom and truth   IBSE 168:10
f. for its King and Country   GRAH 145:5
f. for the living   JONE 177:10
f. for what I believe in   CAST 85:7
f. it out on this line   GRAN 145:17
f. no more   JOSE 178:15
f. on the beaches   CHUR 91:15
f. on to the end   HAIG 149:7
F. the good fight   BIBL 51:12
F. the good fight   MONS 225:22
fought a good f.   BIBL 51:13
I will f.   SITT 296:10
never a moment ceased the f.   TENN 313:22
Never give up the f.   MARL 212:3
nor duty bade me f.   YEAT 343:5
no stomach to this f.   SHAK 275:8
peril in the f.   CORN 100:2
rise and f. againe   BALL 24:6

fight *(cont.)*
those who bade me f. — EWER 125:13
thought it wrong to f. — BELL 28:25
too proud to f. — WILS 337:5
Ulster will f. — CHUR 91:4
fighter Am I no a bonny f. — STEV 303:15
I was ever a f. — BROW 71:2
fighting first-class f. man — KIPL 187:16
What are WE f. for — SERV 268:2
figure f. that thou here seest — JONS 178:2
losing her f. or her face — CART 85:3
filigree f. hedges — WALP 327:7
fill F. me with life anew — HATC 153:5
O f. me — MACN 208:19
trying to f. them — CIOR 93:5
films seldom go to f. — BERR 31:13
fils *F. de Saint Louis* — FIRM 128:2
final f. solution — HEYD 158:18
finality F. is death — STEP 302:17
find f. it after many days — BIBL 38:31
returns home to f. it — MOOR 227:6
Run and f. out — KIPL 188:20
strive, to seek, to f. — TENN 314:1
thou shalt f. me — ANON 9:15
findeth f. his life — BIBL 43:28
fine f. romance with no kisses — FIEL 127:17
F. writing — KEAT 183:14
passage which is particularly f. — JOHN 175:11
very f. cat — JOHN 176:14
fine arts one of the f. — STEI 302:6
finem *respice f.* — ANON 12:19
finest f. hour — CHUR 91:16
finger chills the f. not a bit — NASH 231:16
little f. shall be thicker — BIBL 36:6
moving f. writes — FITZ 128:19
my f. and my thumb — HEAN 154:11
One f. in the throat — OSLE 238:1
scratching of my f. — HUME 166:23
fingernails relatively clean f. — MORT 229:3
fingers cut their own f. — EDDI 119:15
dead men's f. — SHAK 273:9
pulled our f. out — PHIL 244:14
twisting in your yellow f. — HEAT 154:18
finish f. the job — CHUR 91:18
Nice guys f. last — DURO 118:16
start together and f. — BEEC 27:8
finished f. in the first 100 days — KENN 184:11
f. my course — BIBL 51:13
It is f. — BIBL 48:15
world where England is f. — MILL 218:11
finite f. quantities — BERK 30:13
fire all compact of f. — SHAK 290:13
bound Upon a wheel of f. — SHAK 278:6
bush burned with f. — BIBL 33:39
chariot of f. — BLAK 55:27
coals of f. — BIBL 38:3
don't f. until you see — PUTN 252:24
dropping-wells of f. — TENN 311:23
faith and f. within us — HARD 151:25
Fell in the f. — GRAH 145:8
F. and fleet — BALL 24:1
f. and the rose are one — ELIO 121:30
f. into the equations — HAWK 153:12
f. of my loins — NABO 230:17
f. to be lit — RABE 253:14
f. was furry as a bear — SITW 296:12
gold shines like f. — PIND 245:2
I am f. and air — SHAK 269:7
jewel of your f. — TAGO 308:22
kindles f. — LA R 193:21
light my f. — MORR 228:20
Lord was not in the f. — BIBL 36:13
neighbour's house is on f. — BURK 74:5

nodding by the f. — YEAT 344:1
Now stir the f. — COWP 102:3
O! for a Muse of f. — SHAK 274:26
pale f. she snatches — SHAK 287:24
set a house on f. — BACO 21:34
shouted 'F.' — BELL 28:13
shouting f. in a theatre — HOLM 161:13
soul of f. — JOHN 174:5
Thorough flood, thorough f. — SHAK 283:6
tongues like as of f. — BIBL 48:24
true love is a durable f. — RALE 254:3
wind is to f. — BUSS 76:25
world will end in f. — FROS 134:8
youth of England are on f. — SHAK 274:30
firebrand Ye were as a f. — BIBL 41:15
firefly f. in the night — CROW 104:9
fires Big f. flare up — FRAN 132:20
devastating or redeeming f. — GONC 144:11
fireside at his own f. — SHER 294:23
F. enjoyments — COWP 102:4
firm family f. — GEOR 138:11
firmament f. sheweth his handy-work — BOOK 61:3
streams in the f. — MARL 212:7
firmly F. I believe — NEWM 233:5
firmness f., and delight — WOTT 341:24
f. makes my circle — DONN 114:15
first Eclipse f. — O'KE 236:2
f. article of my faith — GAND 135:18
f. fruits of them that slept — BIBL 50:2
f. in a village — CAES 80:1
f. in the hearts — LEE 196:10
f. man — BIBL 50:6
f. step that is difficult — DU D 117:22
f. that ever burst — COLE 96:12
last shall be f. — BIBL 44:22
nothing should be done for the f. time — CORN 100:9
no truck with f. impulses — MONT 226:21
people who got there f. — USTI 322:3
to be called F. Lady — ONAS 236:9
firstborn f. the greatest ass — CARO 83:10
smite all the f. — BIBL 34:8
fish f. and fishing — WALT 328:5
F. are jumpin' — HEYW 158:20
F. fiddle-de-dee — LEAR 195:17
F. got to swim — HAMM 150:16
f. that *talks* — DE L 108:3
f. without a bicycle — STEI 302:12
Phone for the f.-knives — BETJ 31:21
surrounded by f. — BEVA 32:7
Thou deboshed f. — SHAK 287:12
fishbone monument sticks like a f. — LOWE 203:20
fishbones two f., two eyeballs — WELB 331:1
fishers f. of men — BIBL 42:13
fishlike ancient and f. smell — SHAK 287:9
fishpond great f. (the sea) — DEKK 108:1
fistful for a f. of coins — ZAPA 345:1
fit I am f. for nothing — HERV 156:12
fittest Survival of the F. — DARW 106:9
survival of the f. — SPEN 300:3
five At f. in the afternoon — GARC 135:21
Full fathom f. — SHAK 287:7
had f. thousand a year — THAC 314:25
I have wedded f. — CHAU 88:18
in a f.-pound note — LEAR 195:14
she hadde f. — CHAU 88:11
warming his f. wits — TENN 313:25
fixed great gulf f. — BIBL 47:4
flag allegiance to the f. — BELL 28:4
brought back the f. — GRIF 147:16
High as a f. — HAMM 150:26
keep the red f. flying — CONN 98:23
national f. — SUMN 306:5

people's f. is deepest red	CONN 98:22
shall not f. or fail	CHUR 91:15
spare your country's f.	WHIT 334:4
flame Both moth and f.	ROET 258:22
Chloe is my real f.	PRIO 251:9
F.-capped, and shout	SHAW 292:10
f. out like shining	HOPK 162:22
hard, gemlike f.	PATE 241:25
tongues of f. are in-folded	ELIO 121:30
When a lovely f. dies	HARB 151:6
flames Commit it then to the f.	HUME 166:19
f. in the forehead	MILT 220:19
love. F. for a year	LAMP 192:19
Flanders brought him a F. mare	HENR 156:16
In F. fields the poppies blow	MCCR 207:3
flashing His f. eyes	COLE 96:7
flat Very f., Norfolk	COWA 101:11
flatter F. the mountain-tops	SHAK 289:28
flattered Englishman, Being f.	CHAP 87:14
neither feared nor f.	DOUG 115:3
flattery Everyone likes f.	DISR 113:3
f. hurts no one	STEV 303:8
paid with f.	JOHN 173:16
flaunting f., extravagant quean	SHER 294:19
flaw no kind of fault or f.	GILB 140:1
flax smoking f.	BIBL 40:12
flea louse and a f.	JOHN 176:13
naturalists observe, a f.	SWIF 307:11
fleas educated f. do it	PORT 249:18
praised his f.	YEAT 343:26
fled F. is that music	KEAT 182:16
I f. Him	THOM 316:26
flee f. away, and be at rest	BOOK 62:1
f. from the wrath to come	BIBL 42:8
f. when no man pursueth	BIBL 38:7
They f. from me	WYAT 342:1
fleece f. was white as snow	HALE 149:17
His forest f.	HOUS 165:5
fleet Fire and f.	BALL 24:1
F. in which we serve	BOOK 63:31
F. the time carelessly	SHAK 269:12
in the Downs the f. was moored	GAY 137:11
whole F.'s lit up	WOOD 339:4
fleets Ten thousand f.	BYRO 78:9
flesh All f. is grass	BIBL 40:8
delicate white human f.	FIEL 127:14
east wind made f.	APPL 13:14
flattered any f.	DOUG 115:3
f., alas, is wearied	MALL 210:5
f. and blood	BIBL 50:23
f., and the devil	BOOK 59:5
f. is as grass	BIBL 51:25
f. is weak	BIBL 45:17
F. of flesh	MILT 222:20
f. of my flesh	BIBL 33:4
F. perishes, I live on	HARD 151:24
in my f. shall I see God	BIBL 37:9
lusts of the f.	BOOK 60:9
make your f. creep	DICK 111:4
my heart and my f.	BOOK 62:10
they shall be one f.	BIBL 33:5
this too too solid f.	SHAK 270:29
thorn in the f.	BIBL 50:13
Word was made f.	BIBL 47:21
word was made f.	MISS 224:9
flesh pots we sat by the f.	BIBL 34:11
Flibbertigibbet fiend F.	SHAK 277:24
flies As f. to wanton boys	SHAK 277:30
catch small f.	SWIF 306:17
joy as it f.	BLAK 56:2
fliest for thou f. Me	THOM 317:1
fling f. the ringleaders	ARNO 16:8
flirtation innocent f.	BYRO 79:4

float f. lazily downstream	SALI 263:19
F. like a butterfly	ALI 4:5
floating f. bulwark of the island	BLAC 55:3
his f. hair	COLE 96:7
floats She f., she hesitates	RACI 253:18
flock feed his f.	BIBL 40:9
keeping watch over their f.	BIBL 46:3
tainted wether of the f.	SHAK 282:18
flocks My father feeds his f.	HOME 161:14
shepherds watched their f.	TATE 309:13
flog f. the rank and file	ARNO 16:8
flood just cause reaches its f.-tide	CATT 85:17
return it as a f.	GLAD 142:4
taken at the f.	SHAK 276:29
ten years before the f.	MARV 213:20
Thorough f., thorough fire	SHAK 283:6
verge of the salt f.	SHAK 287:25
flooded STREETS F.	BENC 29:8
floods f. drown it	BIBL 39:9
floor fell upon the sanded f.	PAYN 242:9
floors Scuttling across the f. of silent seas	ELIO 122:11
Flora Tasting of F.	KEAT 182:10
floraisons mois des f.	ARAG 13:19
Florence lily of F.	LONG 201:23
Rode past fair F.	KEAT 181:14
Flores F. in the Azores	TENN 313:21
flourisheth f. as a flower	BOOK 62:23
flourishing f. like a green bay-tree	BOOK 61:17
flow blood must yet f.	JEFF 171:17
F. gently, sweet Afton	BURN 75:3
flower as the f. of the field	BIBL 40:8
cometh forth like a f.	BIBL 37:6
drives the f.	THOM 316:4
flourisheth as a f.	BOOK 62:23
f. fadeth	BIBL 40:8
f. of goodlihead	SKEL 296:17
f. of Scotland	WILL 336:12
f. that once hath blown	FITZ 128:18
f. thereof falleth	BIBL 51:25
Full many a f. is born	GRAY 146:16
Herself a fairer f.	MILT 221:32
lightly like a f.	TENN 311:34
like the innocent f.	SHAK 279:17
London, thou art the f.	ANON 8:12
meanest f. that blows	WORD 340:14
pluck this f., safety	SHAK 273:32
sweetest f. for scent	SHEL 293:23
this same f. that smiles	HERR 158:8
flowerpots your damned f.	BROW 71:5
flowers cool-rooted f.	KEAT 182:17
droop-headed f.	KEAT 182:7
Ensnared with f.	MARV 213:16
F. in the garden	STEV 304:5
F. of all hue	MILT 221:31
f. of the forest	COCK 95:9
f. of the forest	ELLI 123:20
f. that bloom in the spring	GILB 140:19
f. the tenderness of patient minds	OWEN 238:23
hundred f. blossom	MAO 211:14
No f., by request	AING 3:5
other men's f.	MONT 226:14
Where have all the f. gone	SEEG 267:6
wild f., and Prime Ministers	BALD 23:9
flowery crops the f. food	POPE 248:9
f. plains of honour	JONS 177:21
flowing f. sea	CUNN 105:1
f. with milk and honey	BIBL 34:2
flown birds are f.	CHAR 87:19
flummery f. of a birth place	KEAT 183:10
flutter F. and bear him up	BETJ 31:19
fluttering F. and dancing	WORD 340:1
fly all things F. thee	THOM 317:1
f. at one end	SWIF 307:14

fly *(cont.)*
F. envious Time   MILT 220:29
f. sat upon the axletree   BACO 21:32
f. through the air   LEYB 198:22
for I will f. to thee   KEAT 182:12
man is not a f.   POPE 248:12
noise of a f.   DONN 114:21
said a spider to a f.   HOWI 165:21
seen spiders f.   EDWA 120:5
show the f. the way out   WITT 337:20
small gilded f. Does lecher   SHAK 278:2
which way shall I f.   MILT 221:29
wouldn't hurt a f.   LEAC 195:5
flying on the f. trapeze   LEYB 198:22
time is f.   VIRG 325:19
flying-fishes f. play   KIPL 187:26
foam f. Of perilous seas   KEAT 182:14
To Noroway o'er the f.   BALL 24:8
foaming f. with much blood   POWE 250:23
foe angry with my f.   BLAK 56:11
erect and manly f.   CANN 81:13
f. outstretched   BLAK 56:12
open f. may prove a curse   GAY 137:7
willing f. and sea room   ANON 11:3
wish my deadly f.   BRET 66:15
fog f. and filthy air   SHAK 278:26
f. comes on little cat feet   SAND 264:8
F. in Channel   BROC 67:5
London particular . . . A f.   DICK 109:17
fogs insular country, subject to f.   DISR 112:22
foi *En cette f. je veux vivre*   VILL 324:7
foil shining from shook f.   HOPK 162:22
fold Do not f.   ANON 6:13
like the wolf on the f.   BYRO 78:13
folding f. of the hands   BIBL 37:22
folds f. rippling   SUMN 306:5
folk incest and f.-dancing   ANON 11:8
folks O yonge, fresshe f.   CHAU 88:29
where the old f. stay   FOST 132:8
follies crimes, f., and misfortunes   GIBB 139:2
follow F. me   BIBL 42:13
F. The Gleam   TENN 312:26
F. the van   COLL 97:5
f. the worse   OVID 238:15
I really had to f. them   LEDR 196:7
Pay, pack, and f.   BURT 76:8
followed first he f. it hymselve   CHAU 88:12
folly accordyng to his f.   BIBL 38:5
brood of f.   MILT 219:20
f. and conceit   AUST 19:25
fool returneth to his f.   BIBL 38:6
lovely woman stoops to f.   ELIO 122:28
lovely woman stoops to f.   GOLD 144:4
most loving mere f.   SHAK 269:26
persist in his f.   BLAK 55:23
shoot F. as it flies   POPE 248:8
'Tis f. to be wise   GRAY 146:19
uses his f.   SHAK 270:8
usually ends in f.   COLE 96:25
fond *au f. des bois*   VIGN 324:3
grow too f. of it   LEE 196:14
fons *aquae f.*   HORA 164:21
f. *pietatis*   MISS 224:12
food alcohol was a f.   WODE 338:5
Continent have good f.   MIKE 217:25
finds its f. in music   LILL 199:4
F. enough for a week   MERR 217:11
give f. to the poor   CAMA 80:15
music be the f. of love   SHAK 288:2
problem is f.   DONL 113:16
room and f.   MALT 210:16
wholesome f.   SWIF 306:23
fool Answer a f.   BIBL 38:5

Busy old f.   DONN 114:12
every f. is not a poet   POPE 247:5
f. all the people   LINC 199:15
f. at forty   YOUN 344:10
f. at the other   SWIF 307:14
f. consistent   POPE 247:23
f. hath said in his heart   BOOK 61:1
f. his whole life long   LUTH 204:19
f. returneth to his folly   BIBL 38:6
'F.,' said my Muse   SIDN 295:8
f.'s bauble, the mace   CROM 103:21
f. there was   KIPL 188:13
f. would persist   BLAK 55:23
greatest f. may ask   COLT 97:16
laughter of a f.   BIBL 38:21
smarts so little as a f.   POPE 247:6
suspects himself a f.   YOUN 344:15
They f. me   SHAK 272:19
Thou f.   BIBL 46:23
to manage a f.   KIPL 188:27
wisest f. in Christendom   HENR 156:13
foolery *little f.*   OXEN 239:2
foolish Beware my f. heart   WASH 328:25
f., fond old man   SHAK 278:7
f. thing well done   JOHN 175:9
Forgive our f. ways   WHIT 334:5
never said a f. thing   ROCH 258:10
No man was more f.   JOHN 176:6
saying a f. thing   STER 302:25
These f. things   MARV 213:24
young and f.   YEAT 342:18
foolishest f. act a wise man commits   BROW 69:7
foolishness to the Greeks f.   BIBL 49:23
fools all the f. in town   TWAI 321:3
flannelled f. at the wicket   KIPL 187:23
F.! For I also had my hour   CHES 89:19
f. go aimlessly   UPAN 321:23
f. rush in   POPE 248:7
f., the fools, the fools   PEAR 242:17
f., who came to scoff   GOLD 143:11
kept from children and from f.   DRYD 117:8
let f. contest   POPE 248:18
millions mostly f.   CARL 82:23
poor f. decoyed   PEPY 243:15
scarecrows of f.   HUXL 168:3
suffer f. gladly   BIBL 50:12
this great stage of f.   SHAK 278:4
what f. these mortals be   SHAK 283:17
foot caught my f. in the mat   GROS 148:5
foot—f.—sloggin'   KIPL 187:9
F.-in-the-grave young man   GILB 140:27
Forty-second F.   HOOD 162:3
her f. was light   KEAT 181:19
I hold Creation in my f.   HUGH 166:10
Nay, her f. speaks   SHAK 287:33
sets f. upon a worm   COWP 102:7
silver f. in his mouth   RICH 256:18
sole of her f.   BIBL 33:20
Withdraw thy f.   BIBL 38:2
football f. a matter of life and death   SHAN 290:19
F. and cookery   SMIT 297:13
F.? the beautiful game   PELÉ 243:4
he's f. crazy   MCGR 207:14
owe to f.   CAMU 81:9
footfalls F. echo in the memory   ELIO 121:19
footpath jog on the f.   SHAK 289:8
footprints F. on the sands   LONG 201:26
foppery f. of the world   SHAK 277:10
for F. ever panting   KEAT 182:3
who is f. me   HILL 159:9
forasmuch f. as without thee   BOOK 59:14
forbid f. them not   BIBL 45:30
He shall live a man f.   SHAK 279:1

forbidden Of that f. tree · MILT 220:33
force every living f. · DOST 114:24
f. that through the green · THOM 316:4
no argument but f. · BROW 69:11
no f. however great · WHEW 333:3
reduce the use of f. to · ORTE 237:1
Surprised by unjust f. · MILT 219:17
forces f. impressed upon it · NEWT 233:11
forcible Most f. Feeble · SHAK 274:21
forcibly f. if we must · CLAY 94:2
ford I am a F., not a Lincoln · FORD 131:3
forefathers f. of the hamlet sleep · GRAY 146:14
Think of your f. · ADAM 1:22
forehead Flames in the f. · MILT 220:19
foreign corner of a f. field · BROO 67:23
f. policy: I wage war · CLEM 94:8
Life is a f. language · MORL 228:8
nothing human f. to me · TERE 314:7
past is a f. country · HART 153:1
portion of the f. world · WASH 328:20
foreigners more f. I saw · BELL 29:5
Foreign Secretary F. naked into the conference · BEVA 32:9
forelock occasion's f. watchful · MILT 222:26
foremost none who would be f. · MACA 206:11
foresight aftersight and f. · ELIO 121:27
forest beasts of the f. · BOOK 62:24
burning the rain f. · STIN 304:9
Deep in the f. · RACI 253:20
Down in the f. · SIMP 296:4
flowers of the f. · COCK 95:9
flowers of the f. · ELLI 123:20
f. laments · CHUR 91:2
f. primeval · LONG 201:21
through an untrodden f. · MURR 230:10
unfathomable deep f. · THOM 316:15
forests f. of the night · BLAK 56:14
foretell ability to f. · CHUR 92:13
for ever f. hold his peace · BOOK 60:16
mercy endureth f. · BOOK 63:22
forget Better by far you should f. · ROSS 260:13
do not thou f. me · ASTL 17:5
F. six counties · MORR 228:18
f. thee, O Jerusalem · BOOK 63:24
Lest we f. · KIPL 188:5
never f. a face · MARX 214:3
nor worms f. · DICK 110:20
Old men f. · SHAK 275:10
forgetting consist in merely f. · MAND 211:1
grand memory for f. · STEV 303:16
sleep and a f. · WORD 340:10
forgive allows you to f. yourself · SHAW 291:21
do not f. those murderers · WIES 334:14
do they f. them · WILD 335:13
Father, f. them · BIBL 47:11
f. him · BIBL 44:17
F., O Lord, my little jokes · FROS 134:5
F. our foolish ways · WHIT 334:5
f. our friends · MEDI 216:1
f. us our debts · BIBL 42:23
f. us our trespasses · BOOK 58:8
lambs could not f. · DICK 110:20
Lord will f. me · CATH 85:14
to f. a wrong · ELEA 121:1
To f., divine · POPE 248:6
Wilt thou f. that sin · DONN 113:25
Women can't f. failure · CHEK 88:33
forgiven f. everything · SHAW 291:19
Her sins are f. · BIBL 46:12
restored, f. · LYTE 205:6
forgiveness After such knowledge, what f. · ELIO 122:2
forgot auld acquaintance be f. · BURN 75:4
just f. to duck · DEMP 108:13

forgotten been learned has been f. · SKIN 296:20
books undeservedly f. · AUDE 18:22
F. Army · MOUN 229:14
f. man at the bottom · ROOS 259:13
f. nothing and learnt nothing · DUMO 118:4
he himself had f. it · PALM 240:8
injury is much sooner f. · CHES 89:6
learnt nothing and f. nothing · TALL 309:2
not one of them is f. · BIBL 46:21
ruins of f. times · BROW 68:20
things one has f. · CANE 81:10
Thou hast f. · SWIN 308:3
fork pick up mercury with a f. · LLOY 201:2
forked poor, bare, f. animal · SHAK 277:23
forlorn faery lands f. · KEAT 182:14
F.! the very word · KEAT 182:15
form F. follows function · SULL 305:15
f. from off my door · POE 246:14
F. is emptiness · MahÄ 209:14
F. remains · WORD 340:27
human f. divine · BLAK 56:16
lick it into f. · BURT 76:11
formed perhaps it f. itself · RIG 257:6
small, but perfectly f. · COOP 99:23
former f. and the latter · BOOK 59:11
forms f. of government · POPE 248:18
forsaken never the righteous f. · BOOK 61:16
O, father f. · JOYC 179:5
primrose that f. dies · MILT 220:17
utterly f. · BETT 32:6
why hast thou f. me · BIBL 45:21
forsaking f. all other · BOOK 60:17
fort Hold the f. · BLIS 56:20
Hold the f. · SHER 294:25
fortissimo F. at last · MAHL 209:15
fortuna *Audentis F. iuvat* · VIRG 325:5
fortunate at best but f. · SOLO 298:26
farmers excessively f. · VIRG 325:17
fortune Blind F. still Bestows · JONS 177:18
F. assists the brave · TERE 314:8
f.s sharpe adversitee · CHAU 88:26
hostages to f. · BACO 21:17
I am F.'s fool · SHAK 286:27
leads on to f. · SHAK 276:29
little value of f. · STEE 302:4
possession of a good f. · AUST 19:24
rob a lady of her f. · FIEL 127:15
smith of his own f. · CLAU 93:22
You fools of f. · SHAK 287:22
forty fairy when she's f. · HENL 156:6
Fat, fair and f. · O'KE 236:1
fool at f. · YOUN 344:10
F. years on · BOWE 65:9
In f. minutes · SHAK 283:11
Knows it at f. · YOUN 344:15
Life begins at f. · PITK 245:8
miner, F.-niner · MONT 226:24
forty-five At f., what next · LOWE 203:22
forty-three pass for f. · GILB 141:10
forward F., forward let us range · TENN 312:15
from this day f. · BOOK 60:18
looking f. to the past · OSBO 237:28
nothing to look f. to · FROS 134:6
those behind cried 'F.!' · MACA 206:11
to push things f. · MOWL 229:15
foster f.-child of silence · KEAT 181:27
fou I wasna f. · BURN 75:9
fought f. against Sisera · BIBL 35:2
f. a good fight · BIBL 51:13
f. each other for · SOUT 299:12
to have f. well · COUB 100:16
foul f. Fiend · BUNY 73:1
f. is fair · SHAK 278:26

foul (cont.)
Murder most f. — SHAK 271:17
So f. and fair a day — SHAK 279:3
found awoke and f. me here — KEAT 181:21
f. a kingdom — MILT 222:27
f. my sheep which was lost — BIBL 46:30
f. no more of her — BIBL 36:32
Hast thou f. me — BIBL 36:15
was lost, and is f. — BIBL 46:35
When f., make a note — DICK 110:11
foundation Church's one f. — STON 304:11
founded f. the Jewish state — HERZ 158:13
founder f. and embellisher — CAXT 86:10
founding f. a bank — BREC 66:12
fount f. whence honour springs — MARL 212:17
fountain f. of all goodness — BOOK 58:21
f. of honour — BACO 21:1
f. of the water of life — BIBL 52:26
f. sealed — BIBL 39:7
like a f. troubled — SHAK 286:39
four At the age of f. — USTI 322:4
F. lagging winters — SHAK 285:9
f.-legged friend — BROO 68:4
F. legs good — ORWE 237:4
say that two plus two make f. — ORWE 237:15
twice two be not f. — TURG 320:17
fourscore come to f. years — BOOK 62:15
fourteen first f. years — GREE 146:25
fourteenth f. Mr Wilson — HOME 161:15
fourth f. estate of the realm — MACA 205:12
fowl liver-wing of a f. — TENN 314:3
fowler snare of the f. — BOOK 63:16
fowls smale f. maken melodye — CHAU 88:5
fox beset the historical f. — HUXL 167:20
Crazy like a f. — PERE 243:19
f. knows many things — ARCH 13:22
galloping after a f. — WILD 335:11
loves the f. less — SURT 306:9
mentality of a f. at large — LEVI 198:7
people that think, and f.-hunters — SHEN 294:8
prince must be a f. — MACH 207:17
quick brown f. — ANON 9:13
sharp hot stink of f. — HUGH 166:12
They've shot our f. — BIRC 54:7
foxes f. have a sincere interest — ELIO 121:5
f. have holes — BIBL 43:16
second to the f. — BERL 30:23
foxholes no atheists in the f. — CUMM 104:19
signs on the f. — KENN 184:13
frabjous O f. day — CARR 84:4
frailty concession to human f. — TAWN 309:16
f. of the mind — SHAD 268:6
F., thy name is woman — SHAK 270:32
love's the noblest f. — DRYD 116:30
frame f. of adamant — JOHN 174:5
framed f. and glazed — WALP 327:11
français n'est pas f. — RIVA 257:15
France better in F. — STER 302:19
between F. and England — JERR 172:8
by which F. is fed — SULL 305:18
F., famed in all great arts — ARNO 15:25
F. has lost a battle — DE G 107:23
F., mother of arts — DU B 117:19
F. was long a despotism — CARL 82:20
stood the wind for F. — DRAY 116:8
vasty fields of F. — SHAK 274:27
wield the sword of F. — DE G 107:24
Francesca di Rimini F., miminy — GILB 140:26
frankincense f., and myrrh — BIBL 42:3
frantic fascination f. — GILB 140:21
frater f., ave atque vale — CATU 86:3
frauds all great men are f. — BONA 57:20
freckled f. like a pard — KEAT 181:22

Whatever is fickle, f. — HOPK 163:2
freckles curiosity, f., and doubt — PARK 240:15
In those f. — SHAK 283:7
Fred Here lies F. — ANON 7:9
free as soon write f. verse — FROS 134:15
best things in life are f. — DE S 109:4
born f. — ANON 5:15
but it's f. — KRIS 190:26
Church shall be f. — MAGN 209:10
Comment is f. — SCOT 266:1
condemned to be f. — SART 264:22
Ev'rything f. in America — SOND 299:3
favours f. speech — BROU 68:10
f. again — SOLZ 298:27
f. as nature first made man — DRYD 116:28
f. church — CAVO 86:9
freedom to the f. — LINC 199:7
f. man, an American — JOHN 173:1
Greece might still be f. — BYRO 78:24
half f. — LINC 199:6
I am a f. man — MCGO 207:11
I am not f. — DEBS 107:10
in chains than to be f. — KAFK 180:10
I was f. born — BIBL 48:40
land of the f. — KEY 185:6
Man was born f. — ROUS 261:11
Mother of the F. — BENS 29:27
No f. man shall be taken — MAGN 209:11
not only to be f. — PANK 240:11
protection of f. speech — HOLM 161:13
should themselves be f. — BROO 67:18
that moment they are f. — COWP 101:29
Thou art f. — ARNO 15:20
truth makes men f. — AGAR 2:25
truth shall make you f. — BIBL 47:36
We must be f. or die — WORD 339:25
freedom abridging the f. of speech — CONS 99:15
better organised than f. — PÉGU 243:3
But what is F. — COLE 95:20
conditioned to a f. — KENY 184:20
fight for f. and truth — IBSE 168:10
first is f. of speech — ROOS 259:20
f. depends on being courageous — THUC 317:25
f. for the one who thinks differently — LUXE 204:20
f. for the pike — TAWN 309:15
f. is a noble thing — BARB 24:26
f. is excellent — TOCQ 318:9
F. is not a gift — NKRU 234:17
F. is the freedom to say — ORWE 237:15
F. of the press guaranteed — LIEB 199:2
F. of the press in Britain — SWAF 306:13
f. of the press's speech — TWAI 321:8
F.'s just another word — KRIS 190:26
f. to the slave — LINC 199:7
gave my life for f. — EWER 125:13
it means f. — RUSH 262:5
Let f. ring — SMIT 297:23
no easy walk-over to f. — NEHR 232:5
obtained I this f. — BIBL 48:40
O F., what liberties are taken — GEOR 138:12
Perfect f. is reserved — COLL 97:3
preserve and enlarge f. — LOCK 201:7
riches and f. — WALĘ 326:18
there can be no f. — LENI 197:2
freedoms four essential human f. — ROOS 259:20
freemen rule o'er f. — BROO 67:18
freeze f. my humanity — MACN 208:19
freezes Yours till Hell f. — FISH 128:7
frei Arbeit macht f. — ANON 11:21
French drawn out of F. — MALO 210:11
F. are with equal advantage — CANN 81:11
F. arrange — CATH 85:12
F. of Parys — CHAU 88:8

F., or Turk GILB 141:3
F. widow in every bedroom HOFF 160:20
glory of beating the F. WOLF 338:14
how it's improved her F. GRAH 145:6
If the F. noblesse TREV 319:8
Learning F. is some trouble EMPS 124:22
no more F. ANON 9:1
not clear is not F. RIVA 257:15
not too French F. bean GILB 140:24
Paris was F.—and silent TUCH 320:13
to men F. CHAR 87:27
to the F. the empire of the land RICH 257:4
Frenchmen Fifty million F. ANON 6:22
frenzy Demoniac f. MILT 222:23
poet's eye, in a fine f. SHAK 283:22
frequent f. hearses POPE 247:1
frère *Sois mon f.* CHAM 87:2
fresh ancient and so f. AUGU 19:2
f. air and fun EDGA 119:19
f. as is the month of May CHAU 88:7
f. lap of the crimson rose SHAK 283:10
O yonge, f. folkes CHAU 88:29
Freud trouble with F. DODD 113:13
Freude *F., schöner Götterfunken* SCHI 265:11
friars f. were singing vespers GIBB 139:8
fricassee f., or a ragout SWIF 306:23
Friday My man F. DEFO 107:14
friend angry with my f. BLAK 56:11
as you choose a f. DILL 111:22
betraying my f. FORS 131:17
Boldness be my f. SHAK 270:17
candid f. CANN 81:13
diamonds a girl's best f. ROBI 257:20
ease some f. POPE 247:8
faithful female f. WHUR 334:9
familiar f. BOOK 61:20
fat f. BRUM 71:17
four-legged f. BROO 68:4
F. and associate of this clay HADR 148:17
f.-and-relation MILN 218:24
F., go up higher BIBL 46:24
f. in power ADAM 1:15
f. of every country CANN 81:12
f. that sticketh closer BIBL 37:37
He was my f. SHAK 276:17
I finds a f. DIBD 109:14
I lose a f. SARG 264:19
last best f. am I SOUT 299:15
Little F. of all the World KIPL 188:24
loss of a dear f. SOUT 299:18
mine own familiar f. BOOK 62:2
pretended f. is worse GAY 137:7
What is a f. ARIS 14:21
Whenever a f. succeeds VIDA 324:1
your enemy and your f. TWAI 321:6
friendless f. bodies of unburied men WEBS 330:17
friends documents and f. SPAR 299:22
forgive our f. MEDI 216:1
f. are necessarily USTI 322:3
f. do not need it HUBB 166:2
f.' houses JOHN 176:11
f. of every country DISR 112:13
F., Romans, countrymen SHAK 276:15
I had such f. YEAT 343:11
in the house of God as f. BOOK 62:2
lay down his f. for his life THOR 317:24
life for his f. BIBL 48:8
love of f. BELL 29:1
Make to yourselves f. BIBL 47:1
misfortune of our best f. LA R 194:2
Money couldn't buy f. MILL 218:19
my f. pictured within ELGA 121:2
my list of f. COWP 102:7

nearly deceiving your f. CORN 100:10
none of his f. like him WILD 335:21
no true f. in politics CLAR 93:15
Our f., the enemy BÉRA 30:11
thousand f. ALI 4:3
treat my f. MALL 210:7
two close f. LERM 197:22
want of f. BRET 66:15
win f. and influence people CARN 83:8
with a little help from my f. LENN 197:17
friendship F. from knowledge BUSS 76:24
F. is Love BYRO 79:10
In f. false DRYD 116:18
Most f. is feigning SHAK 269:26
treating of f. THOM 315:24
frieze no striped f. STRA 304:22
frigate no F. like a Book DICK 111:13
fright f. and a hiss DEAN 107:6
frighten by God, they f. me WELL 331:5
f. the horses CAMP 80:20
frightening never more f. VAN 322:13
frog f. remains ROST 261:2
leap-splash—a f. BASH 26:2
toe of f. SHAK 281:5
frogs F. are slightly better MITF 225:2
f. don't die for 'fun' BION 54:6
F. eat Butterflies STEV 303:4
frontier f. of my Person AUDE 18:15
new f. KENN 184:7
frost but a f. of cares TICH 318:3
f. performs its secret ministry COLE 96:1
His graver of f. THOM 317:6
like an untimely f. SHAK 286:34
frosts hoary-headed f. SHAK 283:10
froth mostly f. and bubble GORD 144:16
frown without f. or smile SEDL 267:4
frozen F. anger FREU 133:22
f. in an out-of-date mould JENK 171:21
f. music SCHE 265:10
sends the f.-ground-swell FROS 134:10
through the f. grass KEAT 181:3
Your tiny hand is f. GIAC 138:19
fructify [Money should] f. GLAD 142:6
fruit bore thy f. and mine KYD 191:4
f. Of that forbidden tree MILT 220:33
Hang there like f. SHAK 270:20
Man stole the f. HERB 157:20
trees bear strange f. HOLI 161:4
fruitful as the f. vine BOOK 63:20
fruitfulness mellow f. KEAT 182:21
fruition f. of an earthly crown MARL 212:16
fruits By their f. BIBL 43:11
first f. of them that slept BIBL 50:2
frustra *Nisi Dominus f.* ANON 12:15
frustrate each f. ghost BROW 71:8
fry scribbling f. YOUN 344:11
frying-pan *talks* In the f. DE L 108:3
fuck They f. you up, your mum and dad LARK 193:14
fudge two-fifths sheer f. LOWE 203:16
fugaces *Eheu f. Labuntur anni* HORA 164:11
fugit *f. irreparabile tempus* VIRG 325:19
fugitive f. and cloistered virtue MILT 223:15
f. from th' law of averages MAUL 215:12
Fuji F. through mist BASH 26:1
full F. fathom five SHAK 287:7
F. speed ahead FARR 126:15
f. tide of human existence JOHN 175:14
fulmen *Eripuit coelo f.* TURG 320:18
fulness f. thereof BIBL 49:28
fum *Fy, fa, f.* NASH 231:19
fume black, stinking f. JAME 170:8
fun desire to have all the f. SAYE 265:6
frogs don't die for 'f.' BION 54:6

fun (*cont.*)
Haute Couture should be f. — LACR 191:13
no reference to f. — HERB 157:5
noted for fresh air and f. — EDGA 119:19
Politics has got to be f. — CLAR 93:17
stop people having f. — STRA 305:5
function Form follows f. — SULL 305:15
F. never dies — WORD 340:27
fundament frigid on the f. — NASH 231:16
funeral costlier f. — TENN 310:23
f. baked meats — SHAK 271:2
not a f. note — WOLF 338:10
funny Everything is f. — ROGE 259:5
F.-peculiar or funny ha-ha — HAY 153:17
Isn't it f. — MILN 219:4
Whatever is f. is subversive — ORWE 237:20
fur On some other f. — ANON 11:5
furca *Naturam expelles f.* — HORA 163:24
furies Fierce as ten F. — MILT 221:22
furious grew fast and f. — BURN 75:26
furiously driveth f. — BIBL 36:28
heathen so f. rage — BOOK 60:26
furnace burning fiery f. — BIBL 41:7
furnish Books do f. a room — POWE 250:17
f. all we ought to ask — KEBL 183:20
f. the war — HEAR 154:16
furnished F. and burnish'd — BETJ 32:3
furniture church f. at best — COWP 102:8
don't trip over the f. — COWA 101:13
f. on the deck of the Titanic — MORT 229:9
No f. so charming — SMIT 298:9
rearranges the f. — PRAT 250:27
furor *Ira f. brevis est* — HORA 163:22
furry fire was f. as a bear — SITW 296:12
further but no f. — PIUS 245:16
f. they have to fall — FITZ 129:12
fury Comes the blind F. — MILT 220:14
f., like a woman scorned — CONG 98:14
f. of a patient man — DRYD 116:22
In her prophetic f. — SHAK 284:29
sound and f. — SHAK 281:24
War hath no f. — MONT 226:6
fuse through the green f. — THOM 316:4
fuss f. about an omelette — VOLT 326:14
fustian f.'s so sublimely bad — POPE 247:9
future f. ain't what it used to be — BERR 31:8
F. shock — TOFF 318:12
lets the f. in — GREE 147:1
no trust in the f. — HORA 164:7
once and f. king — MALO 210:12
perhaps present in time f. — ELIO 121:18
picture of the f. — ORWE 237:18
promise of a bright f. — AHER 3:4
seen the f. and it works — STEF 302:5
sense of f. favours — WALP 327:23
fuzzy-wuzzy 'ere's *to* you, F. — KIPL 187:16

G

gabardine my Jewish g. — SHAK 282:7
Gaels great G. of Ireland — CHES 89:18
gag tight g. of place — HEAN 154:14
Gaia G. is a tough bitch — MARG 211:17
gaiety eclipsed the g. — JOHN 173:21
only concession to g. — THOM 316:19
gaily G. into Ruislip gardens — BETJ 32:1
gain g. of a few — POPE 249:8
g. the whole world — BIBL 45:28
gained misery is a battle g. — WELL 331:7
gains no g. without pains — STEV 303:9
gaiters gas and g. — DICK 110:25

Galatians great text in G. — BROW 71:6
galère *dans cette g.* — MOLI 225:12
gales cool g. shall fan the glade — POPE 248:31
Galilean O pale G. — SWIN 308:1
You have won, G. — JULI 179:11
Galileo G. in two thousand years — PIUS 245:17
status of G. — GOUL 144:21
gall take my milk for g. — SHAK 279:15
wormwood and the g. — BIBL 40:28
gallant died a very g. gentleman — ANON 7:8
gallantry What men call g. — BYRO 78:16
galley doing in that g. — MOLI 225:12
Gallia *G. est omnis divisa* — CAES 79:28
gallimaufry g. or hodgepodge — SPEN 300:26
gallop G. about doing good — SMIT 298:1
G. apace — SHAK 286:28
galloped we g. all three — BROW 70:14
gallow grew a g. — KYD 191:4
gallows die upon the g. — WILK 336:1
g. in every one — CARL 83:3
Jack on the g.-tree — SCOT 266:22
nothing but the g. — BURK 74:8
perfect g. — SHAK 287:1
Under the G.-Tree — FLET 130:6
gambler whore and the g. — BLAK 55:15
game Anarchism is a g. — SHAW 291:23
beautiful g. — PELÉ 243:4
g.'s afoot — SHAK 274:34
how you played the G. — RICE 256:14
play the g. — NEWB 232:20
'The g.,' said he — CRAB 102:15
time to win this g. — DRAK 116:3
woman is his g. — TENN 313:10
games G. people play — BERN 31:7
g. should be seen — MONT 226:9
gamesmanship theory and practice of g. — POTT 250:4
gammon world of g. and spinnage — DICK 110:7
gamut g. of the emotions — PARK 240:23
gangsters great nations acted like g. — KUBR 190:27
gap last g. but one — WHIT 333:10
garage to the full g. — HOOV 162:13
Garde *La G. meurt* — CAMB 80:16
garden Back to the g. — MITC 224:20
Come into the g. — TENN 312:21
England is a g. — KIPL 187:18
fairies at the bottom of our g. — FYLE 135:4
g. eastward in Eden — BIBL 32:24
g. inclosed — BIBL 39:7
g. in her face — CAMP 81:5
g. is a lovesome thing — BROW 68:16
g. of your face — HERB 157:7
g.'s umbrage mild — SMAR 297:2
God the first g. made — COWL 101:14
imperfections of my g. — MONT 226:7
Lord God walking in the g. — BIBL 33:7
man and a woman in a g. — WILD 335:12
nearer God's Heart in a g. — GURN 148:13
planted a g. — BACO 21:12
rosebud g. of girls — TENN 312:22
where a g. should be — HORA 164:21
gardener Adam was a g. — SHAK 275:17
supposing him to be the g. — BIBL 48:18
gardening g. is but landscape-painting — POPE 249:10
gardens Sowe Carrets in your G. — GARD 136:2
garish day's g. eye — MILT 219:23
garland green willow is my g. — HEYW 158:22
O! withered is the g. — SHAK 268:28
garlic clove of g. round my neck — O'BR 235:12
garment g. was white as snow — BIBL 41:10
garmented in light — SHEL 294:4
garments part my g. — BOOK 61:5
Reasons are not like g. — ESSE 125:3
garnished empty, swept, and g. — BIBL 43:36

garret Genius in a g. — ROBI 258:5
living in a g. — FOOT 130:22
garter knight of the g. — ATTL 17:10
garters own heir-apparent g. — SHAK 273:29
gas g. and gaiters — DICK 110:25
G. smells awful — PARK 240:18
got as far as poison-g. — HARD 151:19
gasp last g. — BIBL 42:1
gate cabin at your g. — SHAK 288:9
lead you to Heaven's g. — BLAK 55:19
man at the g. of the year — HASK 153:4
November at the g. — PUSH 252:21
out of the ivory g. — BROW 69:10
Wide is the g. — BIBL 43:8
gates besiege your g. — POPE 247:1
enter then his g. — KETH 185:3
g. of hell — BIBL 44:10
g. to the glorious and unknown — FORS 131:14
O ye g. — BOOK 61:9
to the g. of Hell — PIUS 245:16
two g. of Sleep — VIRG 325:2
Gath Tell it not in G. — BIBL 35:27
gather G. ye rosebuds — HERR 158:8
gathered g. together in my name — BIBL 44:16
gathering g. where thou hast not strawed — BIBL 45:6
gat-toothed G. I was — CHAU 88:20
gaudeamus G. igitur, Juvenes dum sumus — ANON 12:13
gaudy Neat, but not g. — WESL 332:10
one other g. night — SHAK 268:22
Gaul G. as a whole is divided — CAES 79:28
Gaunt Old John of G. — SHAK 285:6
gauzy wrapped in a g. veil — SHEL 294:3
gave Lord g., and the Lord — BIBL 36:37
she g. me of the tree — BIBL 33:8
gay g. deceiver — COLM 97:14
g. Lothario — ROWE 261:14
g. man trapped — BOY 65:17
Gaza Eyeless in G. — MILT 222:32
gazelle nursed a dear g. — MOOR 227:19
one a g. — YEAT 343:3
gazing g. up into heaven — BIBL 48:23
geese Like g. about the sky — AUDE 17:24
swans of others are g. — WALP 327:15
Gehazi Whence comest thou, G. — BIBL 36:26
Gehenna Down to G. — KIPL 187:25
gem g. of purest ray serene — GRAY 146:16
gemlike hard, g. flame — PATE 241:25
gender of the feminine g. — O'KE 235:24
general caviare to the g. — SHAK 271:33
feet of the great g. — OVID 238:17
generalities glittering and sounding g. — CHOA 90:15
Glittering g. — EMER 124:17
General Motors good for G. — WILS 336:16
generals bite some of my other g. — GEOR 137:23
Russia has two g. — NICH 233:21
we're all G. — USTI 322:4
generation beat g. — KERO 184:21
best minds of my g. — GINS 141:14
G. X — COUP 100:18
in their g. wiser — BIBL 46:36
lost g. — STEI 302:8
O g. of vipers — BIBL 42:8
one g. from extinction — CARE 82:8
third and fourth g. — BIBL 34:13
generations g. have trod — HOPK 162:22
G. pass — BROW 69:1
hungry g. — KEAT 182:14
Those dying g. — YEAT 343:16
generous always g. ones — MONT 226:21
generously treated g. or destroyed — MACH 207:15
genes G. not like blueprints — STEW 304:8
what males do to g. — JONE 177:11
genetic g. lottery comes up with — PIML 245:1

mechanism for g. material — CRIC 103:11
terrible g. defects — WATS 328:27
geniumque G. loci — VIRG 325:3
genius except my g. — WILD 335:22
feminine g. — FITZ 129:3
G. does what it must — MERE 217:8
G. in a garret — ROBI 258:5
G. is one per cent inspiration — EDIS 119:22
G. is only a greater aptitude — BUFF 72:8
G. is the child — REYN 256:6
g. of Einstein leads to Hiroshima — PICA 244:20
g. of the Constitution — PITT 245:11
g. of the place — POPE 247:19
'G.' which means — CARL 82:17
gentlemen—a g. — SCHU 265:19
great g. — BEAU 26:13
Milton, Madam, was a g. — JOHN 176:17
Ramp up my g. — JONS 177:19
Three-fifths of him g. — LOWE 203:16
true g. appears — SWIF 307:2
what a g. I had — SWIF 307:12
geniuses One of the greatest g. — WALP 327:9
genteel to the truly g. — HARD 151:16
gentil verray, parfit g. knyght — CHAU 88:6
Gentiles boasting as the G. use — KIPL 188:7
gentle Do not go g. — THOM 316:3
G. as falcon — SKEL 296:16
G. Child of gentle Mother — DEAR 107:7
g. rain from heaven — SHAK 282:20
gentleman definition of a g. — NEWM 233:1
died a very gallant g. — ANON 7:8
g. in Whitehall — JAY 171:8
g.'s park — CONS 99:12
g. who was generally spoken — SURT 306:12
last g. in Europe — LEVE 198:5
mariner with the g. — DRAK 116:2
prince of darkness is a g. — SHAK 277:26
gentlemen G. go by — KIPL 188:9
g. in England — SHAK 275:11
g. of England — PARK 241:3
G. prefer blondes — LOOS 202:14
G.-rankers — KIPL 187:17
gentleness only a willed g. — THOM 316:22
gently roar you as g. — SHAK 283:4
geographers g., in Afric-maps — SWIF 307:9
geographical g. concept — BISM 54:16
g. expression — METT 217:14
geography G. is about Maps — BENT 30:7
too much g. — KING 186:15
geometrical g. ratio — MALT 210:15
geometry as precise as g. — FLAU 129:18
disorder in its g. — DE B 107:9
does not know g. — ANON 12:5
'royal road' to g. — EUCL 125:8
George accession of G. the Third — MACA 205:16
G.—don't do that — GREN 147:9
Georges G. ended — LAND 192:23
Georgia G. on my mind — GORR 144:19
red hills of G. — KING 186:11
geriatric years in a g. home — AMIS 5:1
German all a G. racket — RIDL 257:5
Germans beastly to the G. — COWA 101:4
G. . . . are going to be squeezed — GEDD 137:14
G. classify — CATH 85:12
to the G. that of—the air — RICH 257:4
Germany at war with G. — CHAM 86:21
Death is a master from G. — CELA 86:11
G. above all — HOFF 160:13
G. calling — JOYC 179:6
Offering G. too little — NEVI 232:16
rebellious G. — OVID 238:17
remaining cities of G. — HARR 152:14
Gershwin G. songs — FISH 128:8

Gesang *Das ist der ewige G.* — GOET 142:17
Weib und G. — LUTH 204:19
get G. thee behind me, Satan — BIBL 44:11
g. up airly — LOWE 203:15
g. what you like — SHAW 291:20
getting G. and spending — WORD 341:18
Gospel of G. On — SHAW 291:24
ghastly G. good taste — BETJ 32:5
G., grim and ancient — POE 246:13
ghost each frustrate g. — BROW 71:8
G. in the Machine — RYLE 263:7
g. of a great name — LUCA 204:7
g. of Roger Casement — YEAT 343:1
g. of the deceased — HOBB 160:5
some old lover's g. — DONN 114:8
ghosties ghoulies and g. — ANON 7:1
ghosts egress is given to real g. — VIRG 325:2
g. of departed quantities — BERK 30:13
g. outnumber us — DUNN 118:9
G., wandering here and there — SHAK 283:19
ghoul dug them up like a G. — DICK 110:10
ghoulies g. and ghosties — ANON 7:1
giant g. great and still — STEV 303:29
g.'s strength — SHAK 281:29
hand of the g. — BOOK 63:19
like a g. — BOOK 62:9
sees farther than the g. — COLE 96:22
giants for war like precocious g. — PEAR 242:18
g. in the earth — BIBL 33:18
on the shoulders of g. — NEWT 233:14
shoulders of g. — BERN 31:4
Want one of five g. — BEVE 32:12
gibber squeak and g. — SHAK 270:23
gibbets cells and g. — COOK 99:15
g. keep the lifted hand in awe — YOUN 344:12
Gibbon Eh! Mr G. — GLOU 142:8
Gibraltar G. may tumble — GERS 138:16
gift Freedom is not a g. — NKRU 234:17
last best g. — MILT 222:8
make the g. rich — TROL 319:18
You have a g. — JONS 177:24
gifted vividly g. in love — DUFF 117:24
young, g. and black — HANS 151:4
Young, g. and black — IRVI 169:9
giftie g. gie us — BURN 75:29
gifts Bestows her g. — JONS 177:18
cannot recall their g. — TENN 313:26
even when they bring g. — VIRG 324:13
presented unto him g. — BIBL 42:3
gigantic g. body — MACA 205:13
gild g. refinèd gold — SHAK 277:2
gilded g. loam — SHAK 285:7
gilding amusement is the g. — RICH 257:1
Gilead no balm in G. — BIBL 40:24
Gilpin John G. was a citizen — COWP 101:21
gin get out the g. — REED 255:10
G. was mother's milk — SHAW 291:30
ginger G., you're balmy — MURR 230:9
ginless wicked as a g. tonic — COPE 99:25
Giotto G.'s tower — LONG 201:23
Gipfeln *Über allen G. Ist Ruh'* — GOET 142:24
Gipper Win just one for the G. — GIPP 141:15
girded g. up his loins — BIBL 36:12
girdle g. round about the earth — SHAK 283:11
girl can't get no g. reaction — JAGG 170:3
danced with a g. — FARJ 126:6
diamonds a g.'s best friend — ROBI 257:20
g. needs good parents — TUCK 320:14
Poor little rich g. — COWA 101:9
pretty g. is like a melody — BERL 30:19
unlessoned g. — SHAK 282:17
was a little g. — LONG 202:10
girlish Laugh thy g. laughter — WATS 329:3

girls bombers named for g. — JARR 171:6
g. in slacks remember Dad — BETJ 31:16
g. that are so smart — CARE 82:10
g. who wear glasses — PARK 240:16
rosebud garden of g. — TENN 312:22
Gitche Gumee By the shore of G. — LONG 202:3
give G., and it shall be given — BIBL 46:11
g. and not to count — IGNA 168:17
g. me back my legions — AUGU 19:7
G. me my Romeo — SHAK 286:29
G. to me the life I love — STEV 304:3
g. to the poor — BIBL 44:19
more blessed to g. — BIBL 48:38
not as the world giveth, g. I — BIBL 48:7
peace which the world cannot g. — BOOK 58:23
receive but what we g. — COLE 95:21
given g. away by a novel — KEAT 183:13
I would have g. gladly — JOHN 173:2
shall be g. — BIBL 45:7
giver cheerful g. — BIBL 50:11
gives happiness she g. — LACL 191:12
who g. soon — PUBL 251:22
giving not in the g. vein — SHAK 286:7
glad g. confident morning — BROW 70:18
just g. to see me — WEST 332:16
too soon made g. — BROW 70:23
gladly bear the cross g. — THOM 315:21
I would have given g. — JOHN 173:2
gladness As with g. men of old — DIX 113:10
oil of g. — BOOK 61:23
serve the Lord with g. — BOOK 62:22
Teach me half the g. — SHEL 294:1
gladsome Let us with a g. mind — MILT 220:8
Glamis G. hath murdered sleep — SHAK 280:10
G. thou art, and Cawdor — SHAK 279:12
glare red g. on Skiddaw — MACA 206:2
Glasgow G. Empire on a Saturday night — DODD 113:13
glass baying for broken g. — WAUG 329:17
dome of many-coloured g. — SHEL 292:20
Get thee g. eyes — SHAK 278:3
g. of blessings — HERB 157:18
if you break the bloody g. — MACN 208:17
liked the Sound of Broken G. — BELL 28:22
No g. of ours was raised — HEAN 154:12
Satire is a sort of g. — SWIF 306:14
take a g. of wine — SHER 294:23
through a g., darkly — BIBL 49:33
turn down an empty g. — FITZ 129:2
glasses girls who wear g. — PARK 240:16
ladder and some g. — BATE 26:4
Such cruel g. — HOWE 165:18
glassy around the g. sea — HEBE 155:3
g., cool, translucent — MILT 219:18
in the g. stream — SHAK 273:8
gleam Follow The G. — TENN 312:26
glen Down the rushy g. — ALLI 4:12
glib g. and oily art — SHAK 277:7
glittering g. and sounding generalities — CHOA 90:15
g. prizes — SMIT 297:16
how that g. taketh me — HERR 158:10
with his g. eye — COLE 96:9
gloaming In the g. — ORRE 236:21
Roamin' in the g. — LAUD 194:8
global g. thinking — LUCE 204:10
image of a g. village — MCLU 208:4
globaloney still g. — LUCE 204:10
globe g.-trotting Madam — YEAT 343:27
great g. itself — SHAK 287:15
globule primordial atomic g. — GILB 140:7
gloom counterfeit a g. — MILT 219:22
inspissated g. — JOHN 175:4
gloomy by g. Dis Was gathered — MILT 221:32
gloria *G. in excelsis* — MISS 223:28

Sic transit g. mundi — ANON 12:22
gloriam *Dei g.* — ANON 12:7
glories g. of our blood and state — SHIR 294:27
in those weaker g. spy — VAUG 323:1
glorious all-g. above — GRAN 145:15
all g. within — BOOK 61:24
G. things of thee — NEWT 233:18
Mud! G. mud — FLAN 129:15
What a g. morning — ADAM 2:2
glory all things give him g. — HOPK 163:10
alone with his g. — WOLF 338:12
crowned with g. now — KELL 183:25
day of g. has arrived — ROUG 261:8
declare the g. of God — BOOK 61:3
deed is all, the g. nothing — GOET 142:20
g. and the dream — WORD 340:9
g. and the freshness — WORD 340:7
g. and the nothing — BYRO 78:10
g. as of the only begotten — BIBL 47:21
G. be to God — HOPK 163:1
g. be to the Father — BOOK 58:9
g. in the name of Briton — GEOR 137:24
g. in the triumph — CORN 100:2
g. is departed — BIBL 35:15
g., laud, and honour — NEAL 231:23
g. of Europe — BURK 74:7
g. of God is a man — IREN 169:8
g. of man as the flower — BIBL 51:25
g. of my crown — ELIZ 123:8
g. of the Attic stage — ARNO 15:24
g. of the coming — HOWE 165:15
g. of the Lord — BIBL 40:20
g. of the Lord shone — BIBL 46:3
g. of them — BIBL 42:12
g. of the winning — MERE 217:3
g. of the world — ANON 12:22
g. of this world passes — THOM 315:18
g. shone around — TATE 309:13
g. that was Greece — POE 246:15
G. to God in the highest — BIBL 46:5
g. to her — BIBL 49:29
greater g. of God — ANON 12:7
greatest g. of a woman — PERI 243:22
I felt it was g. — BYRO 79:17
I go to g. — DUNC 118:7
King of g. — BOOK 61:9
Land of Hope and G. — BENS 29:27
looks on war as all g. — SHER 294:26
name thee Old G. — DRIV 116:11
paths of g. — GRAY 146:15
say my g. was — YEAT 343:11
Solomon in all his g. — BIBL 42:27
some desperate g. — OWEN 238:24
trailing clouds of g. — WORD 340:10
uncertain g. — SHAK 288:34
What price g. — ANDE 5:8
glove white g. pulpit — REAG 254:22
gloves through the fields in g. — CORN 100:8
with my g. on my hand — HARG 152:8
glow g. has warmed the world — STEV 303:13
made my heart to g. — SOUT 299:21
glow-worm g. that shines — HAGG 149:2
glut g. thy sorrow — KEAT 182:7
Glyn With Elinor G. — ANON 11:5
gnashing g. of teeth — BIBL 43:15
gnat strain at a g. — BIBL 44:31
gnats small g. mourn — KEAT 182:23
go G., and do thou likewise — BIBL 46:17
g., and sin no more — BIBL 47:35
G., and the Lord be with thee — BIBL 35:21
g. anywhere I damn well please — BEVI 32:13
G. down, Moses — ANON 10:20
G., for they call you — ARNO 15:13

G., litel bok — CHAU 88:28
G., little book — STEV 304:5
G., lovely rose — WALL 327:5
g. no more a-roving — BYRO 79:16
G. to jail — ANON 7:6
G. to the ant — BIBL 37:21
G. West, young man — GREE 146:22
G. ye into all the world — BIBL 45:31
I g. on for ever — TENN 310:14
I have a g. — OSBO 237:26
In the name of God, g. — AMER 4:16
In the name of God, g. — CROM 103:20
I say to this man, G. — BIBL 43:14
Let my people g. — BIBL 34:5
no place to g. — WHIT 333:17
no place to g. — BURT 76:6
not g. to Canossa — BISM 54:14
One of us must g. — WILD 335:23
thus far shalt thou g. — PARN 241:10
to boldly g. — RODD 258:18
To g. away is to die — HARA 151:5
unto Caesar shalt thou g. — BIBL 49:2
you can have another g. — QUAN 253:2
goal moving freely, without a g. — KLEE 189:9
goals muddied oafs at the g. — KIPL 187:23
goat fleecy hairy g. — BELL 28:19
with their g. feet — MARL 212:8
goats g. on the left — BIBL 45:8
goblins sprites and g. — SHAK 289:1
God acceptable unto G. — BIBL 49:19
armour of G. — BIBL 50:22
As a g. self-slain — SWIN 307:23
attracted by G. — INGE 168:20
beast or a g. — ARIS 14:18
becoming a g. — VESP 323:16
best thing G. invents — BROW 70:5
bitter G. to follow — SWIN 307:26
burial-ground G.'s-acre — LONG 201:24
But for the grace of G. — BRAD 65:19
by the hand of G. — MARA 211:15
choose a Jewish G. — BROW 68:19
closer walk with G. — COWP 101:24
CMG (Call Me G.) — ANON 8:18
conscious water saw its G. — CRAS 102:24
daughter of the voice of G. — WORD 340:15
discussing their duty to G. — WHIT 333:24
don't think G. comes well out of it — WOOL 339:10
Enoch walked with G. — BIBL 33:17
even G. was born too late — LOWE 204:2
Fear G. — BIBL 39:1
Fear G. — BIBL 51:27
Fellow-citizens: G. reigns — GARF 136:4
For G.'s sake, look after our people — SCOT 266:4
forgotten before G. — BIBL 46:21
G. Almighty first planted — BACO 21:12
G. and devil — DOST 114:25
G. and I both knew — KLOP 189:10
G. and mammon — BIBL 42:26
G. and nature — AUCT 17:20
G. and Robert Browning — BROW 71:13
G. and the doctor — OWEN 238:18
G. beginning to resemble — HUXL 167:19
G. be in my head — ANON 7:4
G. be merciful — BIBL 47:8
G. be praised — WOLF 338:15
G. be thanked — BROO 67:22
G. bless America — BERL 30:17
G. bless the child — HOLI 161:3
G. bless the Prince — LINL 200:4
G. bless us every one — DICK 109:21
g. cannot change the past — AGAT 3:3
G. caught his eye — MCCO 207:1
G. disposes — THOM 315:19

God (*cont.*)

G. does not play dice	EINS 120:14
G. has given you good abilities	ARAB 13:17
G. has more right	JOHN 172:11
G. has written all the books	BUTL 77:12
G. hath joined together	BIBL 44:18
G. hath made them so	WATT 329:7
G. help the Minister	MELB 216:4
G. in His mercy	CRAI 102:18
G.-intoxicated man	NOVA 235:3
G. is dead	FROM 134:3
G. is dead	NIET 234:8
G. is in the details	ROHE 259:8
G. is just	JEFF 171:18
G. is love	BIBL 51:33
G. is love, but	LEE 196:8
G. is no respecter	BIBL 48:30
G. is not mocked	BIBL 50:15
G. is on everyone's side	ANOU 13:7
G. is on the side	VOLT 326:9
G. is our hope	BOOK 61:25
G. is subtle but not malicious	EINS 120:13
G. is Three	NEWM 233:5
G. is usually on the side	BUSS 77:1
G. is working his purpose out	AING 3:6
G. made the country	COWP 101:28
G. moves in a mysterious	COWP 101:23
G. must think it exceedingly odd	KNOX 189:17
G. of Abraham	HA-L 149:18
G. of love	HERB 157:21
G. only another artist	PICA 244:19
G., our help in ages past	WATT 329:13
G. paints the scenery	HART 152:20
G. prepares evil	ANON 12:4
G. punish England	FUNK 135:3
G. reigned from the wood	FORT 132:1
G. save king Solomon	BIBL 35:36
G. save our gracious king	ANON 7:5
G. save the king	BIBL 35:18
G. save the king	SHAK 285:26
G. saw that it was good	BIBL 32:23
G. seems to have left the receiver	KOES 190:1
G.'s first Creature	BACO 22:3
G. shall wipe away	BIBL 52:11
G. shall wipe away	BIBL 52:25
G.'s in his heaven	BROW 70:27
G. so commanded	MILT 222:17
G. so loved the world	BIBL 47:28
G.-sustaining University	GLAD 142:3
G. the Father Almighty	BOOK 58:16
G. the first garden made	COWL 101:14
G. to be his guide	BUNY 73:8
G., to me, it seems	FULL 134:23
G. took him	BIBL 33:17
G. whom he hath not seen	BIBL 51:35
G. will pardon me	HEIN 155:10
grandeur of G.	HOPK 162:22
greater glory of G.	ANON 12:7
great g. Pan	BROW 69:13
Had I but served G.	WOLS 338:26
half believes a G.	YOUN 344:16
hands of the living G.	BIBL 51:15
hath not seen G.	BIBL 52:1
have G. for his father	CYPR 105:10
He for G. only	MILT 221:33
here is G.'s plenty	DRYD 117:17
honest G.	INGE 169:2
Honest to G.	ROBI 258:4
house of my G.	BOOK 62:12
How odd Of G.	EWER 125:14
If G. be for us	BIBL 49:17
if G. did not exist	VOLT 326:5
if G. talks to you	SZAS 308:10

if there be a G.	ANON 9:5
In the name of G., go	AMER 4:16
In the name of G., go	CROM 103:20
in the sight of G.	BOOK 60:14
into the Hand of G.	HASK 153:4
it is not, the voice of G.	POPE 248:26
Just are the ways of G.	MILT 223:4
justify G.'s ways	HOUS 165:10
justify the ways of G.	MILT 221:2
kingdom of G. is within you	BIBL 47:5
know his G. by night	VAUG 322:19
known unto G.	ANON 9:21
know the mind of G.	HAWK 153:13
land G. gave to Cain	CART 85:1
like kissing G.	BRUC 71:14
love the Lord thy G.	BIBL 44:29
man sent from G.	BIBL 47:18
many are afraid of G.	LOCK 201:9
mills of G. grind slowly	LONG 202:1
My God, my G.	BIBL 45:21
Name of G., the Merciful	KORA 190:5
nature is the art of G.	BROW 69:5
nature of G.	ANON 8:21
Nearer, my G., to thee	ADAM 2:4
neglect Gs and his Angels	DONN 114:21
next to g. america	CUMM 104:14
no G. can please	ROCH 258:7
Now thank we all our G.	WINK 337:13
Of all G.'s works	MILT 222:19
of such is the kingdom of G.	BIBL 45:30
O G. of Bethel	DODD 113:14
one G. only	CLOU 95:1
only G. can make a tree	KILM 186:2
others call it G.	CARR 84:17
our G. is still	LUTH 204:18
Our G.'s forgotten	QUAR 253:3
out of the mouth of G.	BIBL 42:10
owe G. a death	SHAK 274:23
paltered with Eternal G.	TENN 313:1
peace of G.	JAME 170:11
presume not G. to scan	POPE 248:15
put your trust in G.	BLAC 55:1
Read G. aright	QUAR 253:5
river Is a strong brown g.	ELIO 121:26
saying 'Ta' to G.	SPEN 300:8
see G. in the ordinary things	AWDR 20:8
Sees G. in clouds	POPE 248:11
shall I see G.	BIBL 37:9
sing My G. and King	HERB 157:8
Something beautiful for G.	MUGG 229:17
something beautiful for G.	TERE 314:10
stop believing in G.	CHES 90:11
sung 'G. the Queen'	KIPL 187:5
suppose that G. is only	TEMP 310:8
Teach me, my G. and King	HERB 157:12
Thanks to G.	BUÑU 72:20
that of G. in every one	FOX 132:16
them that love G.	BIBL 49:16
There is no G.	BOOK 61:1
thinks little of G.	PLUT 246:10
three-personed G.	DONN 113:21
Thunder is the voice of G.	MATH 215:4
thy God my G.	BIBL 35:13
To glorify G.	SHOR 295:3
To G. belongs all that is	KORA 190:15
To G. I speak Spanish	CHAR 87:27
to the eye of G.	OLIV 236:5
to the unknown g.	BIBL 48:34
touched the face of G.	MAGE 209:9
touch the face of G.	REAG 255:3
triangles were to make a G.	MONT 226:15
unto G.	BIBL 44:27
unto G. all things come home	KORA 190:23

Verb is G. HUGO 166:15
Very God of very G. BOOK 59:22
voice of G. ALCU 3:10
want to take in G. LOWE 203:15
ways of G. to man POPE 248:8
What G. abandoned HOUS 164:26
What hath G. wrought BIBL 34:25
What hath G. wrought MORS 229:1
When G. at first made man HERB 157:18
when G.'s the theme SMAR 297:3
whom G. hath joined BOOK 60:20
With G. all things are possible BIBL 44:21
Word was with G. BIBL 47:15
you are a g. ROST 261:3
godamm Lhude sing G. POUN 250:5
goddess bitch-g. success JAME 171:4
godfathers G. and Godmothers BOOK 60:8
godhead true g. was evident VIRG 324:11
godly g., righteous, and sober life BOOK 58:7
godmothers Godfathers and G. BOOK 60:8
Godot waiting for G. BECK 26:20
gods alien people clutching their g. ELIO 122:8
By the nine g. MACA 206:6
convenient that there be g. OVID 238:12
daughter of the g. TENN 310:21
dish fit for the g. SHAK 276:4
fit love for g. MILT 222:16
gave birth to the G. HOLB 161:2
g. are on the side of the stronger TACI 308:19
g. avert this omen CICE 92:27
g. themselves cannot recall TENN 313:26
g. themselves struggle SCHI 265:13
g. thought otherwise VIRG 324:14
G. who live for ever MACA 206:5
g. wish to destroy CONN 99:1
in the lap of the g. HOME 161:19
Kings it makes g. SHAK 286:9
loved by the g. PLAT 245:24
not recognizing the g. PLAT 245:23
outcome to the G. CORN 100:3
These be thy g., O Israel BIBL 34:18
they first make g. LEVI 198:8
Thou shalt have no other g. BIBL 34:12
What men or g. KEAT 181:28
Whom the g. love MENA 216:12
goest whither thou g., I will go BIBL 35:13
going At the g. down of the sun BINY 54:4
country wears their g. DUNN 118:11
endure Their g. hence SHAK 278:8
g. gets tough KENN 184:18
g. the way of all the earth BIBL 34:33
g. to a feast JONS 177:16
g. to and fro in the earth BIBL 36:36
order of your g. SHAK 281:1
to what he was g. HARD 152:1
gold apples of g. BIBL 38:1
Apples of g. SWIN 308:4
bringing g., and silver BIBL 36:4
clothing is of wrought g. BOOK 61:24
cross of g. BRYA 71:22
cursed craving for g. VIRG 324:15
fetch the age of g. MILT 220:25
gild refinèd g. SHAK 277:2
g., and frankincense BIBL 42:3
g. filling in a mouthful of decay OSBO 237:29
g. of the day CROS 104:4
g. shines like fire PIND 245:2
g., yea, than much fine gold BOOK 61:4
harpstring of g. SWIN 307:26
in purple and g. BYRO 78:13
Nor all, that glisters, g. GRAY 146:20
patines of bright g. SHAK 282:29
realms of g. KEAT 182:18

streets are paved with g. COLM 97:13
stuffed their mouths with g. BEVA 32:11
This g., my dearest LEAP 195:6
what's become of all the g. BROW 71:11
golden Casting down their g. crowns HEBE 155:3
Clasped by the g. light HOOD 162:6
end of a g. string BLAK 55:19
fell her g. hair TURN 320:20
g. bowl be broken BIBL 38:34
g. days of Saturn's reign VIRG 325:10
g. elephants next SHOR 295:2
G. lads and girls SHAK 270:19
G. opinions SHAK 279:23
g. priests JEWE 172:10
G. Road to Samarkand FLEC 129:23
G. slumbers kiss your eyes DEKK 108:2
g. years return SHEL 292:25
hand that lays the g. egg GOLD 144:8
hangs a g. chain PUSH 252:23
His g. locks PEEL 243:1
in the g. world SHAK 269:12
in their g. hair TENN 313:2
Jerusalem the g. NEAL 232:2
love in a g. bowl BLAK 55:16
loves the g. mean HORA 164:10
morning had been g. CHUR 92:9
We are g. MITC 224:20
went into a g. land TURN 320:23
Goldengrove G. unleaving HOPK 163:3
golf made more Liars than G. ROGE 259:4
Golgotha in the Hebrew G. BIBL 48:11
gondola Did'st ever see a g. BYRO 77:23
What else is like the g. CLOU 94:21
gone All, all are g. LAMB 192:7
And they are g. KEAT 181:10
G. before LAMB 192:6
g. from original righteousness BOOK 64:3
g. into the world of light VAUG 323:2
g. with the wind DOWS 115:10
not dead—but g. ROGE 259:2
She's g. for ever SHAK 278:12
what haste I can to be g. CROM 104:3
What's g. SHAK 289:3
gong that g-tormented sea YEAT 342:13
gongs Strong g. groaning CHES 89:23
good Address to the unco g. BURN 75:1
and doth no g. RALE 254:1
Any g. of George the Thirds LAND 192:23
any g. thing BIBL 47:24
anything g. to say LONG 202:13
be a g. animal SPEN 300:1
Be g., sweet maid KING 186:17
best is the enemy of the g. VOLT 326:3
better than the G. Old Days BINC 54:3
choose the g. BIBL 39:17
could be a g. woman THAC 314:25
do evil, that g. may come BIBL 49:7
Do g. by stealth POPE 248:30
do g. to them BIBL 46:10
either g. or bad SHAK 271:29
Evil, be thou my g. MILT 221:30
for our country's g. CART 84:21
Gallop about doing g. SMIT 298:1
go about doing g. CREI 103:8
God saw that it was g. BIBL 32:23
g. and faithful servant BIBL 45:5
g. ended happily WILD 335:2
g. fences make good neighbours FROS 134:11
g. in the worst of us ANON 10:8
g. man to do nothing BURK 74:22
g. news from Ghent to Aix BROW 70:13
g. of subjects DEFO 107:21
g. of the people CICE 92:22

good (cont.)
g. old Cause	MILT 223:22
g. old cause	WORD 340:16
g. people were clever	WORD 339:16
g. that I would I do not	BIBL 49:15
g. time coming	SCOT 266:25
g. time was had by all	SMIT 298:2
g. unluckily	STOP 304:17
g. will toward men	BIBL 46:5
G. women always think	BROO 68:1
had been g. for that man	BIBL 45:12
Hanging is too g. for him	BUNY 73:3
heaven doing g. on earth	TERE 314:13
highest g.	CICE 92:24
His own g.	MILL 218:3
hold fast that which is g.	BIBL 51:5
I will be g.	VICT 323:18
like a g. fiend	THOM 316:10
luxury was doing g.	GART 136:13
neither g. nor bad	BALZ 24:21
never had it so g.	MACM 208:8
No g. man is a Briton	AUSO 19:15
not g. company	AUST 19:22
nothing g. to be had	HAZL 154:4
of g. report	BIBL 50:28
only g. Indians	SHER 294:9
only g. thing left	MUSS 230:15
on the evil and on the g.	BIBL 42:20
or be thought half as g.	WHIT 334:8
out of g. still to find	MILT 221:5
policy of the g. neighbour	ROOS 259:16
possibility of g. times	BRAN 66:3
return g. for evil	VANB 322:8
said a g. thing	TWAI 321:9
thy g. with brotherhood	BATE 26:5
universal licence to be g.	COLE 95:20
Whatever g. visits thee	KORA 190:14
what g. came of it	SOUT 299:13
what was g. for our country	WILS 336:16
When she was g.	LONG 202:10
woman was full of g. works	BIBL 48:29
work together for g.	BIBL 49:16
your g. works	BIBL 42:17

goodbye G.!—Good-bye-ee
	WEST 332:21
G., moralitee	HERB 157:2
G. to all that	GRAV 146:7

goodlihead flower of g.
	SKEL 296:17

goodly I have a g. heritage
	BOOK 61:2

goodness fountain of all g.
	WEST 332:14
G. had nothing to do with it	BOOK 58:21
g. of the Lord	BOOK 61:10
If g. lead him not	HERB 157:19

goodnight g., sweet ladies
	SHAK 273:2
G., sweet prince	SHAK 273:23
John Thomas says g.	LAWR 194:13
My last G.	KING 186:6

goodwill In peace; g.
	CHUR 92:11

goose every g. a swan
	KING 186:22
g. honking amongst tuneful swans	VIRG 325:13
steal a g.	ANON 10:12
that g. look	SHAK 281:19

gordian She was a g. shape
	KEAT 181:22

gored you tossed and g.
	BOSW 65:1

gorgeous g. East in fee
	WORD 340:17

gory never shake Thy g. locks
	SHAK 280:29
Welcome to your g. bed	BURN 75:22

gospel G. of Christ
	WESL 332:4
G. of Getting On	SHAW 291:24
preach the g.	BIBL 45:31

gossip in the g. columns
	INGH 169:3

got I g. rhythm
	GERS 138:15
in our case we have not g.	REED 255:9

Gothic cars the great G. cathedrals
	BART 25:19

gotta g. use words when I talk to you
	ELIO 122:18

gout give them the g.
	MONT 226:5

gouverner *G. c'est choisir*
	LÉVI 198:10

govern g. in prose
	CUOM 105:2
g. New South Wales	BELL 28:12
of Kings to g. wrong	POPE 246:21
to g. is to choose	LÉVI 198:10

governess Be a g.
	BRON 67:10

government at g. expense
	ARTS 16:9
best g.	O'SU 238:5
forms of g.	POPE 248:18
G. and public opinion	SHAW 291:12
g. as an adversary	BRUN 71:19
G. at Washington lives	GARF 136:4
g. by discussion	ATTL 17:12
g. by the uneducated	CHES 90:9
g. is influenced by	SMIT 297:3
g. it deserves	MAIS 209:20
g. of laws	ADAM 1:19
G. of laws and not of men	FORD 131:4
g. of the people	LINC 199:3
g. shall be upon his shoulder	BIBL 39:19
great service to a g.	MEDI 215:20
If the G. is big enough	FORD 131:2
No G. can be long secure	DISR 112:17
one g. sooner learns	SMIT 297:11
people's g.	WEBS 330:5
prepare for g.	STEE 302:1
rule nations by your g.	VIRG 324:23
understood by republican g.	TOCQ 318:11
vulgar arts of g.	PEEL 242:22
well-ordered g.	HALI 150:1
work for a G. I despise	KEYN 185:8
worst form of G.	CHUR 92:1

governments g. had better get out of the way
	EISE 120:16
g. need both shepherds	VOLT 326:8
Never believe g.	GELL 137:17
that the two g.	MITC 224:17

governors supreme g., the mob
	WALP 327:6

governs g. his state by virtue
	CONF 98:6
that which g. least	O'SU 238:5

Gower O moral G.
	CHAU 88:30

grace Amazing g.
	NEWT 233:17
Angels and ministers of g.	SHAK 271:13
But for the g. of God	BRAD 65:19
by the g. of God	BIBL 50:1
fallen from g.	BIBL 50:14
G. me no grace	SHAK 285:14
g. of a boy	BETJ 32:4
G. under pressure	HEMI 156:4
inward and spiritual g.	BOOK 60:11
speech be alway with g.	BIBL 51:3
strong toil of g.	SHAK 269:10
that g. may abound	BIBL 49:10
with a better g.	SHAK 288:14
wordy o' a g.	BURN 75:28

graces G. do not seem to be natives
	CHES 89:12

gracious he is g.
	BOOK 63:22

gradualness inevitability of g.
	WEBB 330:1

graduates sweet girl-g.
	TENN 313:2

grain choice g.
	STOU 304:18
g. of salt	PLIN 246:5
rain is destroying his g.	HERB 157:1
world in a g. of sand	BLAK 55:11

grammar don't want to talk g.
	SHAW 291:29
g., and nonsense	GOLD 143:26
G., the ground of al	LANG 193:2
Heedless of g.	BARH 25:3
talking bad g.	DISR 112:16

grammatici *G. certant*
	HORA 163:13

gramophone puts a record on the g.
	ELIO 122:28

grand down the G. Canyon
	MARQ 212:24

g. Perhaps | BROW 69:20
g. to be blooming well dead | SARO 264:20
grandeur charged with the g. | HOPK 162:22
g. that was Rome | POE 246:15
grandfather ape for his g. | HUXL 168:4
g. or his grandmother | WILB 334:16
grandmother grandfather or his g. | WILB 334:16
We have become a g. | THAT 315:13
grange at the moated g. | SHAK 282:1
lonely moated g. | TENN 312:18
Granth Guru G. Sahib | SIKH 295:19
grape peel me a g. | WEST 332:12
grapes g. of wrath | HOWE 165:15
sour g. | BIBL 41:1
grapeshot whiff of g. | CARL 82:18
grasp exceed his g. | BROW 69:17
G. it like a man of mettle | HILL 158:24
grass All flesh is g. | BIBL 40:8
but as g. | BOOK 62:23
eateth g. as an ox | BIBL 37:15
everywhere nibble g. | FAGU 125:21
flesh is as g. | BIBL 51:25
g. beyond the door | ROSS 260:19
g. can grow through cement | CHER 89:3
g. will grow in the streets | HOOV 162:14
green g. shorn | BACO 21:13
hearing the g. grow | ELIO 121:10
I am the g. | SAND 264:9
I fall on g. | MARV 213:16
snake hidden in the g. | VIRG 325:9
splendour in the g. | WORD 340:13
two blades of g. | SWIF 306:19
grasshoppers half a dozen g. | BURK 74:9
grassy fair Fidele's g. tomb | COLL 97:10
grateful single g. thought | LESS 198:3
gratefully O g. sing | GRAN 145:11
gratias Deo g. | MISS 223:29
gratified g. desire | BLAK 56:3
gratitude g. is merely a secret hope | LA R 194:1
grau G. ist alle Theorie | GOET 142:18
grave cold g. | BALL 24:14
cradle and the g. | DYER 118:21
cradle to the g. | SHEL 293:19
Dig the g. and let me lie | STEV 304:6
dread The g. as little | KEN 184:3
give birth astride of a g. | BECK 27:1
go into my g. | PEPY 243:17
g. is not its goal | LONG 201:25
g. of a dead Fenian | COLL 97:6
g.'s a fine and private | MARV 213:22
g., where is thy victory | BIBL 50:8
g., whither thou goest | BIBL 38:26
into the darkness of the g. | MILL 218:7
jealousy is cruel as the g. | BIBL 39:8
kind of healthy g. | SMIT 298:6
lead but to the g. | GRAY 146:15
Marriage is the g. | CAVE 86:8
pompous in the g. | BROW 69:2
requires g. statesmen | DISR 112:22
she is in her g. | WORD 341:5
shown Longfellow's g. | MOOR 227:10
stand at my g. and cry | ANON 6:14
travelling toward the g. | WORD 340:21
with sorrow to the g. | BIBL 33:35
graved G. inside of it | BROW 70:2
graves dig our g. with our teeth | SMIL 297:5
g. of little magazines | PRES 251:3
g. of their neighbours | EDWA 120:6
g. stood tenantless | SHAK 270:23
Let's talk of g. | SHAK 285:19
grazing Tilling and g. | SULL 305:18
greasy grey-green, g., Limpopo | KIPL 188:23
top of the g. pole | DISR 113:4

great all g. men are frauds | BONA 57:20
both g. and small | COLE 96:18
From the g. deep | TENN 311:5
g. book | CALL 80:11
g. gulf fixed | BIBL 47:4
g. have no heart | LA B 191:7
g. illusion | ANGE 5:11
G. is Diana | BIBL 48:37
g. is truth | BROO 68:6
g. life if you don't weaken | BUCH 71:24
g. man has his disciples | WILD 335:4
G. Society | JOHN 173:3
g.—the major novelists | LEAV 195:24
g. things from the valley | CHES 90:3
he is always g. | DRYD 117:16
Ill can he rule the g. | SPEN 300:19
Lives of g. men | LONG 201:26
many people think him g. | JOHN 175:13
nothing g. but man | HAMI 150:15
some men are born g. | SHAK 288:23
those who were truly g. | SPEN 300:9
Great Britain G. has lost an empire | ACHE 1:6
natives of G. | CHES 89:12
greater G. love hath no man | BIBL 48:8
g. than a private citizen | TACI 308:18
g. than Solomon | BIBL 43:35
g. than the whole | HESI 158:14
g. than we know | WORD 341:1
thy need is g. | SIDN 295:16
greatest firstborn the g. ass | CARO 83:10
g. event it is | FOX 132:13
g. happiness | HUTC 167:13
g. thing in the world | MONT 226:11
happiness of the g. number | BENT 30:3
I'm the g. | ALI 4:4
life to live as the g. he | RAIN 253:22
greatly g. to his credit | GILB 141:2
greatness farewell, to all my g. | SHAK 275:23
g. thrust upon them | SHAK 288:23
nature of all g. | BURK 73:22
Greece glory that was G. | POE 246:15
G. might still be free | BYRO 78:24
isles of G. | BYRO 78:23
greed G. is all right | BOES 57:5
not enough for everyone's g. | BUCH 72:1
Greek half G., half Latin | SCOT 266:2
loving, natural, and G. | BYRO 78:21
small Latin, and less G. | JONS 178:7
wife talks G. | JOHN 177:1
Greeks G. had a word | AKIN 3:7
G. joined Greeks | LEE 196:12
G. seek after wisdom | BIBL 49:22
I fear the G. | VIRG 324:13
unto the G. foolishness | BIBL 49:23
writings of the G. | OMAR 236:7
green bordered by its gardens g. | MORR 228:18
Colourless g. ideas | CHOM 90:17
die when the trees were g. | CLAR 93:7
drives my g. age | THOM 316:4
feed me in a g. pasture | BOOK 61:6
Flora and the country g. | KEAT 182:10
g. and pleasant land | BLAK 55:27
g. as emerald | COLE 96:10
g. banks of Shannon | CAMP 81:2
G. Eye | HAYE 154:1
g.-eyed monster | SHAK 284:21
g. grass shorn | BACO 21:13
G. grow the rashes, O | BURN 75:11
G. grow the rushes O | ANON 7:17
g. hill far away | ALEX 3:18
G. how I love you | GARC 136:1
g. in judgment | SHAK 268:16
g. shoots of recovery | LAMO 192:16

green (cont.)

How g. was my valley	LLEW 200:14
laughs to see the g. man	HOFF 160:17
life springs ever g.	GOET 142:18
Make it a g. peace	DARN 106:4
Making the g. one red	SHAK 280:12
My passport's g.	HEAN 154:12
Praise the g. earth	BUNT 72:18
shoot the sleepy, g.-coat man	HOFF 160:18
strew the g. lap	SHAK 285:29
Their g. felicity	KEAT 181:13
To a g. thought	MARV 213:17
wearin' o' the G.	ANON 8:1
Wherever g. is worn	YEAT 342:22

greenery In a mountain g. — HART 152:20
greenery-yallery g., Grosvenor Gallery — GILB 140:27
greenhouse g. gases — MARG 211:17
Greenland From G.'s icy mountains — HEBE 155:1
Greenpeace G. had a ring to it — HUNT 167:7
Greensleeves G. was all my joy — ANON 7:7
greenwood to the g. go — BALL 24:4

Under the g. tree	SHAK 269:16

greet How should I g. thee — BYRO 79:19
grenadier British G. — ANON 9:22
Pomeranian g. — BISM 54:15
Grenville Richard G. lay — TENN 313:21
grey bring down my g. hairs — BIBL 33:35

Green pleasure or g. grief	SWIN 308:5
g.-green, greasy, Limpopo	KIPL 188:23
hair is g.	BYRO 79:13
in my g. hairs	WOLS 338:26
lend me your g. mare	BALL 24:16
little g. cells	CHRI 90:19
philosophy paints its g.	HEGE 155:6
this old g. head	WHIT 334:4
world has grown g.	SWIN 308:1
you are old and g.	YEAT 344:1

grief acquainted with g. — BIBL 40:16

But g. returns	SHEL 292:15
Green pleasure or grey g.	SWIN 308:5
g. felt so like fear	LEWI 198:11
G. fills the room up	SHAK 277:1
G. for awhile is blind	SHEL 292:16
g. forgotten	SWIN 307:18
G. has no wings	QUIL 253:8
g. is like a minefield	WARN 328:15
g. itself be mortall	SHEL 292:16
g. that does not speak	SHAK 281:12
Of g. I died	ROET 258:22
pain and g.	BOOK 61:18
Should be past g.	SHAK 289:3
Silence augmenteth g.	DYER 118:19

griefs soothed the g. — MACA 205:20
grieve what could it g. for — KEAT 181:12
grieves thing that g. not — MARK 211:19
grieving áre you g. — HOPK 163:3
grievous most g. fault — MISS 223:26
remembrance of them is g. — BOOK 59:27
grin ending with the g. — CARR 83:18
one universal g. — FIEL 127:16
Relaxed into a universal g. — COWP 102:6
grind g. the faces of the poor — BIBL 39:12
Laws g. the poor — GOLD 143:22
mills of God g. slowly — LONG 202:1
grinders incisors and g. — BAGE 22:22
groans g. of love to those of the dying — LOWR 204:6
grooves moves In determinate g. — HARE 152:7
ringing g. of time — TENN 312:15
grosser g. name — SHAK 273:9
Grosvenor Gallery greenery-yallery, G. — GILB 140:27
grotesque g. situation — HAUG 153:7
Groucho of the G. tendency — ANON 11:15
ground as water spilt on the g. — BIBL 35:32

Grammar, the g. of al	LANG 193:2
G. control to Major Tom	BOWI 65:16
g. won to-day	ARNO 15:18
holy g.	BIBL 34:1
in a fair g.	BOOK 61:2
see me cover the g.	GROS 148:3
seven feet of English g.	HARO 152:12

grounds laying out of g. — PEAC 242:13
grove g. of chimneys — MORR 228:12
olive g. of Academe — MILT 222:28
grovelled g. before him — THAC 314:20
groves g. of Academe — HORA 164:4
g. of their academy — BURK 74:8
grow g. up with the country — GREE 146:22
They shall g. not old — BINY 54:4
growed I s'pect I g. — STOW 304:19
grows That which is g. — GALE 135:12
growth children of a larger g. — CHES 89:11
children of a larger g. — DRYD 116:27
root of all genuine g. — SMIL 297:6
grudge ancient g. I bear him — SHAK 282:4
Grundy more of Mrs G. — LOCK 201:9
gruntled far from being g. — WODE 338:1
guard G. us, guide us — EDME 119:23
g. us, guide us — EDME 119:23

guarded well-g. mind	PALI 240:5
guardian G. and my Guide	WILL 336:5
guardians good grey g. of art	WILB 334:19
guards Brigade of G.	MACM 208:11
G. die	CAMB 80:16
Up G. and at them	WELL 331:6
who is to guard the g.	JUVE 179:24

gubu acronym G. — HAUG 153:7
gude g. time coming — SCOT 266:25
guerre ce n'est pas la g. — BOSQ 64:17
guest speed the going g. — POPE 248:23
Speed the parting g. — POPE 248:23
guidance sent down to be a g. — KORA 190:7
guide God to be his g. — BUNY 73:8
Guardian and my G. — WILL 336:5
guides blind g. — BIBL 44:31
guiding g.-star of a whole brave nation — MOTL 229:13
Guildenstern Rosencrantz and G. — SHAK 273:24
guile in whom is no g. — BIBL 47:25
guilt beggar would recognise g. — PARS 241:13
dwell on g. — AUST 19:18
Life without industry is g. — RUSK 262:8
unfortunate circumstance of g. — STEV 303:26
wash her g. away — GOLD 144:4
without its g. — SOME 299:1
guilty crimes of this g. land — BROW 68:14
g. man is acquitted — JUVE 180:5
G. of dust and sin — HERB 157:16
g. thing surprised — WORD 340:12
started like a g. thing — SHAK 270:24
ten g. persons escape — BLAC 55:5
guitar blue g. — STEV 303:6
gulag G. archipelago — SOLZ 298:28
word 'g.' did not appear — WU 341:28
gulf great g. fixed — BIBL 47:4
redwood forest to the G. Stream — GUTH 148:15
gulfs g. will wash us down — TENN 313:32
whelmed in deeper g. — COWP 101:18
gullet g. of New York — MILL 218:15
gum can't fart and chew g. — JOHN 173:7
gun grows out of the barrel of a g. — MAO 211:12
Happiness is a warm g. — LENN 197:8
Maxim G. — BELL 28:18
no g., but I can spit — AUDE 18:15
through the door with a g. — CHAN 87:7
gunfire towards the sound of g. — GRIM 148:1
Gunga Din than I am, G. — KIPL 187:19
gunner Sink me the ship, Master G. — TENN 313:23

gunpowder G., Printing — CARL 82:16
g. ran out — FOOT 130:23
G. Treason and Plot — ANON 9:12
Printing, g. — BACO 22:5
guns G. aren't lawful — PARK 240:18
hundred men with g. — PUZO 252:26
monstrous anger of the g. — OWEN 238:21
rather have butter or g. — GOER 142:14
with g. not with butter — GOEB 142:12
guru G. Granth Sahib — SIKH 295:19
Gutenberg G. made everybody — MCLU 208:6
guts g. of the last priest — DIDE 111:20
lug the g. — SHAK 272:29
Spill your g. at Wimbledon — CONN 99:6
strangled with the g. — MESL 217:12
gutta G. cavat lapidem — OVID 238:13
gutter We are all in the g. — WILD 335:6
guys G. and dolls — RUNY 262:1
Nice g. finish last — DURO 118:16
gyre Did g. and gimble — CARR 84:3
gyves With g. upon his wrist — HOOD 162:2

H

ha H., ha — BIBL 37:14
habit Cocaine h.-forming — BANK 24:23
H. is second nature — AUCT 17:18
H. with him was all — CRAB 102:11
Sow a h. — READ 254:21
habitation h. of dragons — BIBL 40:3
local h. and a name — SHAK 283:22
hack Do not h. me — MONM 225:18
Hackney Marshes You could see to H. — BATE 26:4
Hades dark H.' door — VIRG 324:20
haggard prove her h. — SHAK 284:22
Haggards H. ride no more — STEP 302:15
hags black, and midnight h. — SHAK 281:7
hail beaten dog beneath the h. — POUN 250:12
H., fellow, well met — SWIF 307:6
H. Mary — ANON 12:9
h. the power — PERR 244:4
H., thou that art highly favoured — BIBL 45:32
H. to thee, blithe Spirit — SHEL 293:29
hair All her h. — BROW 71:1
amber-dropping h. — MILT 219:18
bind my h. — HUNT 167:6
bracelet of bright h. — DONN 114:10
colour of his h. — HOUS 164:23
fell her golden h. — TURN 320:20
h. is grey — BYRO 79:13
h. of his head — BIBL 41:10
h. of my flesh stood up — BIBL 37:4
Her h. was long — KEAT 181:19
if a woman have long h. — BIBL 49:29
long essenced h. — MACA 206:3
part my h. behind — ELIO 122:14
pin up my h. with prose — CONG 98:18
raiment of camel's h. — BIBL 42:7
right outa my h. — HAMM 150:18
soft brown h. — CALV 80:13
with a single h. — DRYD 117:13
with a single h. — POPE 249:1
with such h. — BROW 71:11
you have lovely h. — CHEK 88:34
hairless white and h. — HERR 158:5
hairs bring down my grey h. — BIBL 33:35
h. of your head — BIBL 43:26
hairy my brother is a h. man — BIBL 33:28
halcyon h. days — SHAK 275:12
half content with h. knowledge — KEAT 183:6
h.-angel and half-bird — BROW 71:4

h. as old as Time — BURG 73:18
h.-brother of the world — BAIL 23:1
H. dead and half alive — BETJ 31:18
h. is greater — HESI 158:14
h. slave — LINC 199:6
h. that's got my keys — GRAH 145:7
h. was not told me — BIBL 36:3
image of myself and dearer h. — MILT 222:9
Too clever by h. — SALI 263:18
Too clever by h. — SALI 263:23
hall fly swiftly into the h. — BEDE 27:5
halloo H. your name — SHAK 288:10
hallow cannot h. this ground — LINC 199:8
hallowed H. be thy name — BIBL 42:23
halls dwelt in marble h. — BUNN 72:17
h. of Montezuma — ANON 7:3
halt h., and the blind — BIBL 46:27
h. ye between two opinions — BIBL 36:10
Hamlet H. without the Prince — SCOT 266:26
not Prince H. — ELIO 122:12
hammer ring of a h. — WILB 334:17
hammering make such a h. — LICH 198:24
hammers hear the h. ring — KIPL 187:6
worn out many h. — MACL 207:20
hammock Drake he's in his h. — NEWB 232:18
hams h., Bayonne — POPE 246:23
hand bloody and invisible h. — SHAK 280:25
bringing me up by h. — DICK 110:14
by the h. of God — MARA 211:15
by the h. of the Lord — BIBL 34:11
go into his h. — BIBL 36:33
h. delights to trace — WINC 337:11
h. into the Hand of God — HASK 153:4
h. of Jean Jacques Rousseau — HEIN 155:9
h. on the cockatrice' den — BIBL 39:23
h. that lays the golden egg — GOLD 144:8
h. that rocks the cradle — WALL 327:3
h. that signed the paper — THOM 316:5
h. that wrote it — CRAN 102:23
h. to execute — CLAR 93:12
h. to execute — GIBB 139:5
Have still the upper h. — COWA 101:10
Heaving up my either h. — HERR 157:25
His [Ishmael's] h. — BIBL 33:24
If someone claps his h. — HAKU 149:10
into mine h. — BIBL 35:25
invisible h. in politics — FRIE 133:24
kingdom of heaven is at h. — BIBL 42:5
let not thy left h. know — BIBL 42:22
licks the h. just raised — POPE 248:9
like a man's h. — BIBL 36:11
like the dyer's h. — SHAK 290:5
my h. into his side — BIBL 48:20
put his h. to the plough — BIBL 46:13
Put out my h. and touched — MAGE 209:9
right h. forget her cunning — BOOK 63:24
sweeten this little h. — SHAK 281:17
sweet Roman h. — SHAK 288:26
sword sleep in my h. — BLAK 55:27
They h. in hand — MILT 222:25
Thy h., great Anarch — POPE 246:24
Took me by the h. — TURN 320:23
Whatsoever thy h. findeth — BIBL 38:26
Wouldst hold my h. — HART 152:21
handbag LADY BRACKNELL: A h. — WILD 334:25
handbook constable's h. — KING 187:1
handclasp h.'s a little stronger — CHAP 87:13
handcuffs h. on his wrists — HOUS 164:23
Handel tunes of H. — SITW 296:15
handful fear in a h. of dust — ELIO 122:21
h. of meal — BIBL 36:9
handiwork firmament sheweth his h. — BOOK 61:3
handkerchief That h. — SHAK 284:28

handles Everything has two h. — EPIC 124:24
handmaiden low estate of his h. — BIBL 45:33
hands blood on their h. — SPEN 300:5
Father, into thy h. — BIBL 47:14
folding of the h. — BIBL 37:22
h., and handle not — BOOK 63:7
h. are the hands of Esau — BIBL 33:29
h. of men — BIBL 41:23
h. of the living God — BIBL 51:15
h. so deeply inserted — BIER 53:18
Holding h. at midnight — GERS 138:17
horny h. of toil — LOWE 203:17
house not made with h. — BIBL 50:10
house not made with h. — BROW 69:24
Into thy h. — BOOK 61:12
keep my h. from picking — BOOK 60:10
knit h., and beat the ground — MILT 219:11
laid violent h. upon themselves — BOOK 60:22
License my roving h. — DONN 113:18
not into the h. of Spain — TENN 313:23
Pale h. I loved — HOPE 162:19
reached out their h. in longing — VIRG 324:22
shook h. with time — FORD 131:7
spits on its h. — SAND 264:12
union of h. and hearts — TAYL 310:2
washed his h. — BIBL 45:19
With mine own h. — SHAK 285:27
world's great h. — HUNT 167:3
handsaw know a hawk from a h. — SHAK 271:32
hang all h. together — FRAN 133:7
Go h. thyself — SHAK 273:29
h. a man first — MOLI 225:14
H. it all, Robert Browning — POUN 250:7
h. my hat — JERO 172:7
in them which will h. him — RICH 257:2
let him h. there — EHRL 120:9
wretches h. — POPE 249:5
hanged h., drawn, and quartered — PEPY 243:13
h. for stealing horses — HALI 150:4
h. in a fortnight — JOHN 175:22
my poor fool is h. — SHAK 278:14
see him h. — BELL 28:14
hanging H. and marriage — FARQ 126:13
h. Danny Deever — KIPL 187:12
H. is too good for him — BUNY 73:3
h.-look to me — CONG 98:12
h. men an' women — ANON 8:1
Many a good h. — SHAK 288:6
hangman naked to the h.'s noose — HOUS 165:3
hangs thereby h. a tale — SHAK 269:18
What h. people — STEV 303:26
hank bone and a h. of hair — KIPL 188:13
happen can't h. here — LEWI 198:20
h. to your mother — WALK 326:19
happens be there when it h. — ALLE 4:8
Nothing h. — BECK 26:21
Nothing, like something, h. anywhere — LARK 193:13
what h. to her — ELIO 121:6
happier seek No h. state — MILT 222:5
happiest h. and best minds — SHEL 294:5
happily h. ever after — ANON 5:18
happiness enemy to human h. — JOHN 176:10
flaw In h. — KEAT 182:24
greatest h. — HUTC 167:13
H. depends on being free — THUC 317:25
h. he feels — LACL 191:12
H. is an imaginary — SZAS 308:9
H. is a warm gun — LENN 197:8
H. is not an ideal — KANT 180:14
H. lies in conquering — GENG 137:20
h. of the greatest number — BENT 30:3
H. was but the occasional — HARD 151:17
home-born h. — COWP 102:4

lifetime of h. — SHAW 291:7
more for human h. — BRIL 67:4
only one h. in life — SAND 264:6
or justice or human h. — BERL 31:1
pursuit of h. — ANON 10:14
pursuit of h. — JEFF 171:12
result h. — DICK 110:3
suited to human h. — DEFO 107:13
happy all be as h. as kings — STEV 303:28
ask if they were h. — CHAN 87:8
bread-sauce of the h. ending — JAME 170:22
Call no man h. — SOLO 298:26
conspiracy to make you h. — UPDI 321:26
had a h. life — HAZL 154:6
H. birthday to you — HILL 159:4
h. could I be with either — GAY 137:5
h. families resemble — TOLS 318:15
H. field or mossy cavern — KEAT 181:26
h. he who crowns in shades — GOLD 143:8
H. he who like Ulysses — DU B 117:20
H. in this — SHAK 282:17
H. is the man — BOOK 63:19
H. is the man who fears — BIBL 52:32
h. noise to hear — HOUS 165:4
H. Rome, born when I — CICE 93:3
H. the man — DRYD 117:12
H. the people — MONT 226:17
H. those early days — VAUG 322:21
h. while y'er leevin — ANON 6:2
make a man h. — HORA 163:23
make men h. — POPE 248:25
man would be as h. — JOHN 176:2
one who has been h. — BOET 57:6
policeman's lot is not a h. one — GILB 141:6
remember a h. time — DANT 105:20
someone, somewhere, may be h. — MENC 216:13
splendid and a h. land — GOLD 143:13
stayed me in a h. hour — SHAK 284:4
This is the h. warrior — READ 254:19
touch the H. Isles — TENN 313:32
whether you are h. — MILL 218:1
Who is the h. Warrior — WORD 339:17
harbinger Love's h. — MILT 222:24
hard h. day's night — LENN 197:13
h.-faced men — BALD 23:8
h. rain's a gonna fall — DYLA 119:3
Long is the way, And h. — MILT 221:20
made up of h. words — OSBO 237:24
soft can wear away the h. — TALM 309:8
thou art an h. man — BIBL 45:6
harden h. not your hearts — BOOK 62:19
h. Pharaoh's heart — BIBL 34:4
hardly Johnny, I h. knew ye — BALL 23:19
Hardy Kiss me, H. — NELS 232:12
hare h. limped trembling — KEAT 181:3
h. sits snug in leaves — HOFF 160:17
h. sitting up — LAWR 194:11
h. when it is cased — GLAS 142:7
hark H., the dominant's persistence — BROW 71:9
H.! the herald-angels — WESL 331:23
harlot h.'s cry — BLAK 55:15
prerogative of the h. — KIPL 189:2
harlots MOTHER OF H. — BIBL 52:21
Harlow silent, as in H. — ASQU 17:1
harm does h. to my wit — SHAK 288:4
do so much h. — CREI 103:8
do the sick no h. — NIGH 234:12
meaning no h. — GREE 147:2
to prevent h. — MILL 218:3
What h. have I ever done — TAWN 309:17
harmless h. as doves — BIBL 43:25
only h. great thing — DONN 114:1
harmonious h. madness — SHEL 294:1

harmony Discordant h.	HORA 163:25
harness joints of the h.	BIBL 36:18
harp H. not on that string	SHAK 286:8
h. that once through Tara's halls	MOOR 227:15
No h. like my own	CAMP 81:2
wild h. slung behind him	MOOR 227:17
harps touch their h. of gold	SEAR 267:2
harrow toad beneath the h.	KIPL 188:3
Harry God for H.	SHAK 274:34
little touch of H.	SHAK 274:35
thy H.'s company	SHAK 274:1
harsh Not h. nor grating	WORD 340:3
so h. to the clever	WORD 339:16
hart As pants the h.	TATE 309:11
as the h. desireth	BOOK 61:21
footed like a h.	MALO 210:10
h. ungallèd	SHAK 272:16
Harvard glass flowers at H.	MOOR 227:10
Yale College and my H.	MELV 216:10
harvest h. is past	BIBL 40:23
h. of a quiet eye	WORD 340:20
laughs with a h.	JERR 172:9
shine on, h. moon	NORW 235:1
harvests Deep h. bury all	POPE 247:21
haste Make h. slowly	AUGU 19:8
maketh h. to be rich	BIBL 38:8
Men love in h.	BYRO 79:5
repent in h.	CONG 98:15
said in my h.	BOOK 63:9
what h. I can to be gone	CROM 104:3
Ye shall eat it in h.	BIBL 34:7
hasten minutes h. to their end	SHAK 289:30
hat hang my h.	JERO 172:7
looking for a black h.	BOWE 65:14
hatches continually under h.	KEAT 183:8
hatchet cut it with my h.	WASH 328:22
hatching H. vain empires	MILT 221:19
hate creative h.	CATH 85:13
h. all Boets and Bainters	GEOR 137:21
h. a song that has sold	BERL 30:22
h. is conquered by love	PALI 240:4
H. takes a long time	THOM 316:23
h. the man you have hurt	TACI 308:15
how much men h. them	GREE 147:6
If h. killed men	BROW 71:5
I h. and I love	CATU 86:2
I h. war	ROOS 259:17
immortal h.	MILT 221:4
letter of h.	OSBO 237:30
Let them h.	ACCI 1:4
make us h.	SWIF 307:1
never bother with people I h.	HART 152:19
People must learn to h.	MAND 210:20
seen much to h. here	MILL 218:11
sprung from my only h.	SHAK 286:17
them also that h. him	BOOK 62:6
them which h. you	BIBL 46:10
time to h.	BIBL 38:18
We can scarcely h.	HAZL 154:5
you h. something in him	HESS 158:16
hateful What is h. to you	HILL 159:8
hates h. dogs and babies	ROST 261:4
marry a man who h. his mother	BENN 29:26
hateth h. his brother	BIBL 51:35
hath Unto every one that h.	BIBL 45:7
hating h. all other nations	GASK 136:17
hatless lands h. from the air	BETJ 31:20
hatred envy, h., and malice	BOOK 59:4
Great h., little room	YEAT 343:15
H. is a tonic	BALZ 24:22
h. is by far the longest	BYRO 79:5
h. therewith	BIBL 37:34
love to h. turned	CONG 98:14

Regulated h.	HARD 151:13
What we need is h.	GENE 137:18
hats H. off, gentlemen	SCHU 265:19
shocking bad h.	WELL 331:11
Haughey H. buried at midnight	O'BR 235:12
haunts h. of coot and hern	TENN 310:13
have h.-his-carcase, next to the perpetual	DICK 111:9
haves and the h.-nots	CERV 86:14
h. to take you in	FROS 134:7
I h. thee not	SHAK 280:5
To h. and to hold	BOOK 60:18
will not let you h. it	HAZL 154:4
haven h. under the hill	TENN 310:10
Havergal Luke H.	ROBI 258:2
haves h. and the have-nots	CERV 86:14
havoc Cry, 'H.!' and let slip	SHAK 276:11
hawk h. of the tower	SKEL 296:16
his h., his hound	BALL 24:13
know a h. from a handsaw	SHAK 271:32
Hawkshaw H., the detective	TAYL 310:3
hay lie tumbling in the h.	SHAK 289:6
live on h.	HILL 159:2
hazelnut no bigger than a h.	JULI 179:9
he Art thou h.	BIBL 43:29
H. would, wouldn't he	RICE 256:17
While H. is mine, and I am His	HERB 157:21
head dark hole of the h.	HUGH 166:12
God be in my h.	ANON 7:4
Go up, thou bald h.	BIBL 36:21
hairs of your h.	BIBL 43:26
h. beneath the feet	OVID 238:17
h. that once was crowned	KELL 183:25
h. that wears a crown	SHAK 274:20
h. thou dust	SCOT 266:29
h. to contrive	CLAR 93:12
h. to contrive	GIBB 139:5
ideas of its "h."	DISR 112:8
If you can keep your h.	KIPL 187:20
It shall bruise thy h.	BIBL 33:10
Johnny-h.-in-air	PUDN 252:2
My h. is bloody, but unbowed	HENL 156:7
Off with her h.	CARR 83:21
Off with his h.	CIBB 92:19
one small h. could carry	GOLD 143:12
Or in the heart or in the h.	SHAK 282:16
show my h. to the people	DANT 106:2
so old a h.	SHAK 282:19
where to lay his h.	BIBL 43:16
which way the h. lies	RALE 254:8
headache with a dismal h.	GILB 140:5
heading do you know where we're h.	DYLA 119:7
headland Be like a h.	AURE 19:12
heads h. Do grow beneath	SHAK 284:12
hold our h. erect	JERO 172:4
Lift up your h.	BOOK 61:9
headstrong h. as an allegory	SHER 294:15
heal Physician, h. thyself	BIBL 46:9
healed h. of a suffering	PROU 251:19
my soul shall be h.	MISS 224:7
ransomed, h.	LYTE 205:6
healing h. in his wings	BIBL 41:19
h. of the nations	BIBL 52:27
health in sickness and in h.	BOOK 60:18
no h. in us	BOOK 58:6
When you have both, it's h.	DONL 113:16
healthy h. bones of a single Pomeranian	BISM 54:15
hear hath ears to h.	BIBL 45:26
h. a smile	CROS 104:6
H., O Israel	BIBL 34:27
h. our prayers	BOOK 60:12
h. the word of the Lord	BIBL 41:6
h. thy shrill delight	SHEL 293:31

hear (*cont.*)

in such wise h. them	BOOK 59:13
prefer not to h.	AGAR 2:25
heard have ye not h.	BIBL 40:10
I will be h.	GARR 136:11
You ain't h. nuttin' yet	JOLS 177:7
heareth thy servant h.	BIBL 35:14
hearses frequent h.	POPE 247:1
heart Ancient person of my h.	ROCH 258:16
As my poor h. doth think	LYLY 204:25
Batter my h.	DONN 113:21
beak form out my h.	POE 246:14
Beware my foolish h.	WASH 328:25
bicycle-pump the human h.	AMIS 4:21
Bury my h. at Wounded Knee	BENÉ 29:11
But break, my h.	SHAK 271:1
Chuang Tzu's dreaming h.	BASH 26:3
committed adultery in my h.	CART 84:23
deep h.'s core	YEAT 343:7
desires of the h.	AUDE 17:2
ease a h. like a satin gown	PARK 240:19
examine my own h.	DE V 109:5
fed the h. on fantasies	YEAT 343:10
Fourteen h. attacks	JOPL 178:12
from hell's h.	MELV 216:11
given you her h.	VANB 322:10
great have no h.	LA B 191:7
harden Pharaoh's h.	BIBL 34:4
h. and hands and voices	WINK 337:13
h. and stomach of a king	ELIZ 123:6
h. be troubled	BIBL 48:4
heart-break in the h. of things	GIBS 139:16
h. has its reasons	PASC 241:18
h.—how shall I say?	BROW 70:23
h. in the business	WATS 329:1
h. is deceitful	BIBL 40:26
h. is Highland	GALT 135:16
h. is inditing	BOOK 61:22
h. is like a singing bird	ROSS 260:10
h. is on the left	MOLI 225:13
h. leaps up	WORD 340:5
h. likes a little disorder	DE B 107:9
H. of England	DRAY 116:6
h. of furious fancies	ANON 11:4
h. of man	DOST 114:25
H. of oak	GARR 136:7
h. speaks to heart	FRAN 133:1
H. speaks to heart	NEWM 233:9
h. the keener	ANON 13:5
h. to a dog to tear	KIPL 188:4
h. to resolve	GIBB 139:5
h. upon my sleeve	SHAK 284:7
h. would hear her and beat	TENN 312:24
his little h.	JAME 170:24
holiness of the h.'s affections	KEAT 183:4
If thy h. fails thee	ELIZ 123:10
I would eat his h.	SHAK 284:5
language of the h.	POPE 247:12
left my h. in San Francisco	CROS 104:5
let your h. be strong	LAUD 194:6
look in thy h. and write	SIDN 295:8
lying in my h.	MARY 214:15
make a stone of the h.	YEAT 342:21
Make me a clean h.	BOOK 61:28
maketh the h. sick	BIBL 37:29
man after his own h.	BIBL 35:19
Mercy has a human h.	BLAK 56:6
merry h.	BIBL 37:33
most plotting h.	RICH 256:20
My h. aches	KEAT 182:9
My h. is heavy	GOET 142:19
my h. is pure	TENN 313:24
My h.'s in the Highlands	BURN 75:18

no longer tear his h.	SWIF 307:15
no matter from the h.	SHAK 288:1
Open my h.	BROW 70:2
Or in the h. or in the head	SHAK 282:16
O tiger's h.	SHAK 275:19
pondered them in her h.	BIBL 46:6
rag-and-bone shop of the h.	YEAT 342:14
Shakespeare unlocked his h.	BROW 70:12
softer pillow than my h.	BYRO 79:25
So the h. be right	RALE 254:8
squirrel's h. beat	ELIO 121:10
Sweeping up the H.	DICK 111:14
tears out the h. of it	KNOW 189:14
there will your h. be	BIBL 42:25
true love hath my h.	SIDN 295:7
where my h. is turning ever	FOST 132:8
wounding h.	CRAS 102:25
heartbeat h. from the Presidency	STEV 303:11
heartbreak h. in the heart of things	GIBS 139:16
hearth By this still h.	TENN 313:28
cricket on the h.	MILT 219:22
hearthstone squats on the h.	QUIL 253:8
heartily let us h. rejoice	BOOK 62:18
hearts all h. be open	BOOK 59:18
all that human h. endure	GOLD 143:23
harden not your h.	BOOK 62:19
h. and minds	BIBL 50:27
h. beating	BROW 70:20
h. of his countrymen	LEE 196:10
heedless h.	GRAY 146:20
imagination of their h.	BIBL 45:34
Incline our h.	BOOK 59:20
Kind h. are more than coronets	TENN 311:4
Lift up your h.	BOOK 60:1
O you hard h.	SHAK 275:28
Pluck their h. from them	SHAK 275:6
queen in people's h.	DIAN 109:10
Two h. that beat as one	HALM 150:11
union of hands and h.	TAYL 310:2
heat can't stand the h.	TRUM 320:6
furnace that gives no h.	RAYM 254:17
h. of the day	BIBL 44:23
not without dust and h.	MILT 223:15
white h. of revolution	WILS 336:17
white h. of technology	WILS 336:17
heath Upon this blasted h.	SHAK 279:5
heathen exalted among the h.	BOOK 61:26
h. in his blindness	HEBE 155:2
h. in 'is blindness	KIPL 187:13
h. so furiously rage	BOOK 60:26
heather bonnie bloomin' h.	LAUD 194:7
cries 'Nothing but h.'	MACD 207:4
heave H. arf a brick at 'im.	PUNC 252:10
heaven all going the H.	GAIN 135:5
All this, and h. too	HENR 156:23
all we know of h.	DICK 111:16
ascend to h.	FIRM 128:2
Bread of h.	WILL 336:6
by a whirlwind into h.	BIBL 36:19
climb up into the h.	BOOK 63:25
face of h. so fine	SHAK 286:29
fallen from h.	BIBL 39:25
gazing up into h.	BIBL 48:23
Give the jolly h. above	STEV 304:3
God's in his h.	BROW 70:27
gold bar of H.	ROSS 260:16
great wonder in h.	BIBL 52:13
H. and Charing Cross	THOM 317:3
h. and earth shall pass	BIBL 45:2
h. and the earth	BIBL 32:21
h. doing good on earth	TERE 314:13
h. expands	BROW 69:24
H. has no rage	CONG 98:14

H. in a rage	BLAK 55:12	all we need of h.	DICK 111:16
h. in a wild flower	BLAK 55:11	Better to reign in h.	MILT 221:7
H. lies about us	WORD 340:10	descended into h.	BOOK 58:16
H. sends us good meat	GARR 136:10	do science in h.	VAUG 323:5
h.'s vaults should crack	SHAK 278:12	from h.'s heart	MELV 216:11
H. take my soul	SHAK 277:3	gates of h.	BIBL 44:10
H. what I cannot	DICK 111:15	H. has no terror for me	LARK 193:9
H. will protect	SMIT 297:15	H. is a city	SHEL 293:13
h. with their tears	BLAK 56:15	H. is oneself	ELIO 121:17
house as nigh h.	MORE 228:1	H. is other people	SART 264:23
hymns at h.'s gate	SHAK 289:26	H. is to love no more	BERN 31:3
idea of h.	SMIT 298:14	h. of heaven	MILT 221:6
into the kingdom of h.	BIBL 44:13	H. or Connaught	CROM 104:1
kingdom of h.	BIBL 42:14	H. to ships	AESC 2:23
kingdom of h.	BIBL 44:2	if I go down to h.	BOOK 63:25
kingdom of h. is at hand	BIBL 42:5	Into the mouth of H.	TENN 310:17
King of h.	LYTE 205:6	I say the h. with it	WHIT 333:8
lead you to H.'s gate	BLAK 55:19	it is all h.	SHER 294:26
leave to h. the measure	JOHN 174:8	made an excursion to h.	PRIE 251:7
make a h. of hell	MILT 221:6	myself am h.	MILT 221:29
merrily meet in h.	MORE 228:2	never mentions H.	POPE 247:20
more than all in h.	BYRO 78:12	Nor H. a fury	CONG 98:14
near to h. by sea	GILB 139:18	out of h. leads up to light	MILT 221:20
new h. and a new earth	BIBL 52:24	pains of h.	BOOK 63:8
new h., new earth	SHAK 268:12	riches grow in h.	MILT 221:14
nurseries of h.	THOM 317:5	rocks whose entrance leads to h.	MILT 219:15
open face of h.	KEAT 182:25	shout that tore h.'s concave	MILT 221:12
open the Kingdom of H.	BOOK 58:12	start raising h.	LEAS 195:22
pennies from h.	BURK 74:23	tell you to go to h.	STIN 304:10
ring the bells of H.	HODG 160:11	there was a way to H.	BUNY 73:5
silence in h.	BIBL 52:12	they think it is h.	TRUM 320:7
sinned against h.	BIBL 46:33	this is h.	MARL 212:5
starry h. above me	KANT 180:12	though h. should bar the way	NOYE 235:5
summons thee to h.	SHAK 280:6	to heaven or to h.	SHAK 280:6
that serve in h.	MILT 221:7	to the gates of H.	PIUS 245:16
things are the sons of h.	JOHN 173:11	walked eye-deep in h.	POUN 250:9
things in h. and earth	SHAK 271:21	War is h., and all that	HAY 153:16
thirtieth year to h.	THOM 316:6	with h. are we at agreement	BIBL 39:30
top of it reached to h.	BIBL 33:30	working definition of h.	SHAW 291:26
waitest for the spark from h.	ARNO 15:18	would be h. on earth	SHAW 291:7
war in h.	BIBL 52:14	Yours till H. freezes	FISH 128:7
we know the way to h.	ELST 124:4	**helluva** h. town	COMD 97:18
what's a h. for	BROW 69:17	**help** Can't h. lovin' dat man	HAMM 150:16
which art in h.	BIBL 42:23	God h. me	LUTH 204:16
young was very h.	WORD 339:21	h. and support of the woman	EDWA 120:4
heavens behold, I create new h.	BIBL 40:22	h. in time of trouble	ANON 5:12
H., and all the Powers therein	BOOK 58:10	here did England h. me	BROW 70:11
h. declare the glory	BOOK 61:3	look on and h.	LAWR 194:24
h. my wide roof-tree	AYTO 20:14	make him an h. meet	BIBL 33:2
starry h. above	THOM 317:13	no h. but Thee	EDME 119:23
heaventree h. of stars	JOYC 179:4	O! h. me, heaven	FIRB 127:24
heaviness H. may endure	BOOK 61:11	scream for h. in dreams	CANE 81:10
Hebrew in the H. Golgotha	BIBL 48:11	Since there's no h.	DRAY 116:5
Hebrides in dreams behold the H.	GALT 135:16	very present h. in trouble	BOOK 61:25
seas colder than the H.	FLEC 129:21	whence cometh my h.	BOOK 63:12
Hector H. took off his plume	CORN 100:7	Who ran to h. me	TAYL 309:20
Hecuba What's H. to him	SHAK 271:36	with a little h. from my friends	LENN 197:17
hedge divinity doth h. a king	SHAK 273:4	you can't h. it	SMIT 297:17
hedgehog h. knows one big one	ARCH 13:22	**helper** mother's little h.	JAGG 170:2
hedgehogs personality belongs to the h.	BERL 30:23	**helpless** H., naked, piping loud	BLAK 56:10
Thorny h., be not seen	SHAK 283:13	**helps** Nobody ever h. me	TRUT 320:12
throwing h. under me	KHRU 185:20	**hemisphere** portion of this h.	MONR 225:21
hedges into the highways and h.	BIBL 46:28	**hemlock** of h. I had drunk	KEAT 182:9
heedless H. of grammar	BARH 25:3	**hempen** sing in a h. string	FLET 130:6
heel thou shalt bruise his h.	BIBL 33:10	What h. home-spuns	SHAK 283:16
heels champagne or high h.	BENN 29:24	**hen** better take a wet h.	KHRU 185:19
height pleasure lives in h.	TENN 313:17	**hence** H., loathèd Melancholy	MILT 219:25
heir h. of all the ages	TENN 312:14	H., vain deluding joys	MILT 219:20
own h.-apparent garters	SHAK 273:29	**Heraclitus** They told me, H.	CORY 100:14
Helena far is St. H.	KIPL 188:8	**herald** Hark! the h.-angels	WESL 331:23
Helicon watered our houses in H.	CHAP 87:15	**herb** call it h. of grace	SHAK 273:6
hell agreement with h.	GARR 136:12	rue, sour h. of grace	SHAK 285:25
all h. broke loose	MILT 222:7		

herbs bitter h. — BIBL 34:6
  bitter h. — HAGG 148:19
  dinner of h. — BIBL 37:34
Hercules I to H. — SHAK 270:33
  some of H. — ANON 9:22
herd h. wind slowly o'er the lea — GRAY 146:13
here can't happen h. — LEWI 198:20
  H. am I — BIBL 39:15
  H. I am — MACM 208:7
  H.'s a how-de-doo — GILB 140:13
  H.'s tae us — ANON 7:10
  h.'s to you, Mrs Robinson — SIMO 295:25
  If we can't stay h. alive — MONT 226:18
  I have been h. before — ROSS 260:19
  I'm still h. — HOPE 162:18
  Mr Watson, come h. — BELL 28:2
  We're h. — ANON 10:15
hereafter died h. — SHAK 281:24
  h. for ever — BOOK 60:16
  world may talk of h. — COLL 97:2
hereditary h. monarch was insane — BAGE 22:14
  idea of h. legislators — PAIN 239:12
hereditas Damnosa h. — GAIU 135:8
heresies begin as h. — HUXL 168:1
  hateful h. — SPEN 300:22
heresy h. signifies no more — HOBB 159:23
heretics H. the only bitter remedy — ZAMY 344:22
heritage I have a goodly h. — BOOK 61:2
hermitage for an h. — LOVE 203:6
  palace for a h. — SHAK 285:23
hern haunts of coot and h. — TENN 310:13
hero acted like a h. — WALP 327:18
  aspires to be a h. — JOHN 176:3
  conquering h. comes — MORE 228:5
  h. to his valet — CORN 100:11
  Millions a h. — PORT 249:22
  seemed a h. — BYRO 77:24
Herod for an hour of H. — HOPE 162:16
  out-herods H. — SHAK 272:10
heroes Canadians do not like h. — WOOD 339:3
  feats worked by those h. — ANON 13:4
  fit country for h. — LLOY 200:20
  h. of old — BROW 71:2
  of all the worlds brave h. — ANON 9:22
  speed glum h. — SASS 264:26
  Thin red line of h. — KIPL 188:11
heroic H. womanhood — LONG 202:2
heroine take a h. — AUST 20:5
  when a h. goes mad — SHER 294:10
herring plague o' these pickle h. — SHAK 288:7
  shoals of h. — MACC 206:24
Herz Mein H. ist schwer — GOET 142:19
hesitates She floats, she h. — RACI 253:18
Hesperus H. entreats thy light — JONS 177:14
  It was the schooner H. — LONG 202:9
heterodoxy h. is another man's doxy — WARB 328:8
heures h. propices — LAMA 191:23
hewers h. of wood — BIBL 34:32
hewn h. out her seven pillars — BIBL 37:23
hey h. for boot and horse — KING 186:22
hic H. jacet — RALE 254:6
hid cannot be h. — BIBL 42:16
  I h. from Him — THOM 316:26
  Which is, to keep that h. — DONN 114:1
hidden h. persuaders — PACK 239:3
  teems with h. meaning — GILB 141:8
hide he can't h. — LOUI 203:4
  Let me h. myself — TOPL 318:19
  wrapped in a player's h. — GREE 147:4
hides H. from himself his state — JOHN 174:7
hiding bloody good h. — GRAN 145:14
Hieronimo H. is mad again — KYD 191:5
high cannot rate me very h. — LACL 191:11

corn as h. as an elephant's eye — HAMM 150:21
  get h. with a little help — LENN 197:17
  h. road — JOHN 174:23
  slain upon thy h. places — BIBL 35:26
  thing with h.-tech — HOCK 160:10
  This h. man — BROW 70:7
  wickedness in h. places — BIBL 50:23
  ye'll tak' the h. road — ANON 9:9
higher Friend, go up h. — BIBL 46:24
highest h. good — CICE 92:24
  needs must love the h. — TENN 311:6
Highland heart is H. — GALT 135:16
  solitary H. lass! — WORD 341:9
highlands H. and ye Lawlands — BALL 23:17
  My heart's in the H. — BURN 75:18
highness his H.' dog at Kew — POPE 247:4
highway h. for our God — BIBL 40:7
  passes over a h. — STEN 302:13
highways into the h. and hedges — BIBL 46:28
hill city that is set on an h. — BIBL 42:16
  city upon a h. — WINT 337:16
  dancers are all gone under the h. — ELIO 121:24
  haven under the h. — TENN 310:12
  hides the green h. — KEAT 182:7
  hunter home from h. — STEV 304:7
  On a huge h. — DONN 114:2
  On the cold h.'s side — KEAT 181:21
  self-same h. — MILT 220:11
hills and the little h. — BOOK 62:7
  Black H. belong to me — SITT 296:10
  blue remembered h. — HOUS 165:7
  convictions are h. — FITZ 129:6
  h. are alive — HAMM 150:24
  h. like young sheep — BOOK 63:5
  H. of the North — OAKL 235:10
  H. peep o'er hills — POPE 247:30
  I to the h. will lift — SCOT 267:1
  mine eyes unto the h. — BOOK 63:12
  Over the h. — GAY 137:4
  red h. of Georgia — KING 186:11
  to the reverberate h. — SHAK 288:10
him cried, 'That's h.!' — BARH 25:3
himself He h. said — CICE 92:23
hinan Ewig-Weibliche zieht uns h. — GOET 142:21
hindsight H. is always twenty-twenty — WILD 335:24
Hindu neither H. nor Muslim — SIKH 295:21
hinterland She has no h. — HEAL 154:9
hip once upon the h. — SHAK 282:4
  smote them h. and thigh — BIBL 35:8
Hippocrene blushful H. — KEAT 182:11
hippopotamus shoot the H. — BELL 28:7
hire labourer is worthy of his h. — BIBL 46:14
hired They h. the money — COOL 99:22
Hiroshima genius of Einstein leads to H. — PICA 244:20
hiss fright and a h. — DEAN 107:6
hissed h. along the polished ice — WORD 339:23
historians h. left blanks in their writings — POUN 250:8
histories studied H. — PEPY 243:18
history blank in h.-books — MONT 226:17
  Does h. repeat itself — BARN 25:9
  dustbin of h. — TROT 320:3
  dust-heap called 'h.' — BIRR 54:8
  H. came to a . — SELL 267:21
  H. gets thicker — TAYL 309:18
  H. is a gallery of pictures — TOCQ 318:10
  H. is a nightmare — JOYC 179:3
  H. . . . is, indeed, little more — GIBB 139:2
  H. is nothing more — VOLT 326:7
  H. is not what you thought — SELL 267:16
  h. is now and England — ELIO 121:29
  h. is on our side — KHRU 185:18
  H. is past politics — FREE 133:15
  H. is philosophy — DION 112:2

H. littered with the wars	POWE 250:22
H. more or less bunk	FORD 131:6
H., n. An account	BIER 53:20
h. of class struggles	MARX 214:9
H. to the defeated	AUDE 18:21
H. will absolve me	CAST 85:9
learned anything from h.	HEGE 155:4
Living in h.	FITZ 129:11
no h.; only biography	EMER 124:12
Read no h.	DISR 112:20
Thames is liquid h.	BURN 74:28
thousand years of h.	GAIT 135:7
too much h.	KING 186:15
what's her h.	SHAK 288:21
world's h.	SCHI 265:14
writing h. with lightning	WILS 337:3
hit very palpable h.	SHAK 273:17
hitch H. your wagon to a star	EMER 124:15
Hitler H. thought he might	CHAM 86:22
kidding, Mister H.	PERR 244:5
When H. attacked the Jews	NIEM 234:5
hitting without h. below it	ASQU 17:2
hoarder h. of two things	SPAR 299:22
hoarse raven himself is h.	SHAK 279:13
Hobbes in for H.'s voyage	VANB 322:9
hobbit there lived a h.	TOLK 318:14
hobgoblin h. of little minds	EMER 124:13
Hobson H. has supped	MILT 220:30
hock weak h. and seltzer	BETJ 31:15
hodgepodge gallimaufry or h.	SPEN 300:26
hoe tickle her with a h.	JERR 172:9
hog all England under a h.	COLL 97:1
disadvantage of being a h.	MORT 229:5
Not the whole h.	MILL 218:18
hogamus H., higamous	JAME 171:5
hogs Men eat H.	STEV 303:4
hoist H. with his own petar	SHAK 272:28
hold can neither h. him	JEFF 171:16
can't h. a man down	WASH 328:18
gat h. upon me	BOOK 63:8
H., enough	SHAK 281:26
h. fast that which is good	BIBL 51:5
H. the fort	BLIS 56:20
H. the fort	SHER 294:25
To have and to h.	BOOK 60:18
holding h. on comes easily	RILK 257:9
hole dark h. of the head	HUGH 166:12
first h. made through	MOOR 227:8
h. to go out of this world	HOBB 160:6
if you knows of a better h.	BAIR 23:3
In a h. in the ground	TOLK 318:14
maketh a h. in the stone	LATI 194:4
poisoned rat in a h.	SWIF 306:22
holiday Butchered to make a Roman h.	BYRO 78:6
perpetual h.	SHAW 291:26
to take a h.	RUSS 262:19
holier h. than thou	BIBL 40:21
holiest Praise to the H.	NEWM 233:6
holiness beauty of h.	BOOK 62:20
beauty of h.	MONS 225:23
holiness but social h.	WESL 332:4
h. of the heart's affections	KEAT 183:4
hollow hate the dreadful h.	TENN 312:19
We are the h. men	ELIO 122:4
Within the h. crown	SHAK 285:21
Hollywood H. money isn't money	PARK 241:2
Holy and to the H. Ghost	BOOK 58:9
holy coming to that h. room	DONN 113:24
H. deadlock	HERB 157:4
h. ground	BIBL 34:1
H., Holy, Holy	HEBE 155:3
H., holy, holy, Lord	BIBL 52:8
h. simplicity	JERO 172:3

h.-water death	MCGO 207:12
neither h., nor Roman	VOLT 326:6
sabbath day, keep it h.	BIBL 34:15
that which is h.	PLAT 245:24
Holy Ghost be any H.	BIBL 48:36
blasphemy against the h.	BIBL 43:34
gifts of the H.	BUTL 77:2
H. over the bent World	HOPK 162:23
home all the h. I have	AYTO 20:14
by staying at h.	LIN 200:5
can't go h. again	WOLF 338:17
children who leave h.	SLOV 296:21
come h. Bill Bailey	CANN 81:18
comes safe h.	SHAK 275:9
England, h. and beauty	ARNO 16:6
for to carry me h.	ANON 10:4
go h. in the dark	HENR 156:20
H. is the place	FROS 134:7
H. is the sailor	STEV 304:7
h. is the Sule Skerry	BALL 23:18
H. James	HILL 159:7
h. life of our own dear Queen	ANON 7:12
H. of lost causes	ARNO 15:29
h. of the brave	KEY 185:6
h. sweet home	JERO 172:7
H., sweet home	PAYN 242:10
H. they brought her warrior	TENN 313:11
house is not a h.	ADLE 2:20
hunter h. from hill	STEV 304:7
Keep the H.-fires burning	FORD 131:9
man goeth to his long h.	BIBL 38:34
murder into the h.	HITC 159:15
never h. came she	KING 186:20
never is at h.	COWP 101:19
no place like h.	PAYN 242:11
Sweet Stay-at-h.	DAVI 106:20
there's nobody at h.	POPE 247:3
Till the boys come h.	FORD 131:9
unto God all things come h.	KORA 190:23
What's the good of a h.	GROS 148:4
won't go h. till morning	BUCK 72:5
years in a geriatric h.	AMIS 5:1
homeland loved my h.	BELL 29:5
Homer excellent H. nods	HORA 163:18
H. dead	ANON 9:19
H. smote 'is bloomin' lyre	KIPL 188:16
H. sometimes sleeps	BYRO 78:25
more than H. knew	SWIF 307:8
warred for H., being dead	HEYW 158:23
Home Rule morning H. passes	CARS 84:18
homes Stately H. of England	COWA 101:10
stately h. of England	HEMA 155:18
homespuns What hempen h.	SHAK 283:16
homeward Look h. angel	MILT 220:18
homo Ecce h.	BIBL 53:11
et h. factus est	MISS 224:2
honest buy it like an h. man	NORT 234:22
h. broker	BISM 54:17
h. God	INGE 169:2
h. man is laughed at	HALI 150:5
h. man's the noblest work	POPE 248:20
h., sonsie face	BURN 75:28
H. to God	ROBI 258:4
I am not naturally h.	SHAK 289:14
most h. of men	RICH 257:2
poor but she was h.	ANON 9:20
honestly If possible h.	HORA 163:20
honesty H. is praised	JUVE 179:19
honey flowing with milk and h.	BIBL 34:2
hives with h. and wax	SWIF 306:15
H. of roses	HERB 157:14
h. shall he eat	BIBL 39:17
h. still for tea	BROO 67:21

honey (cont.)

H., your silk stocking	SELL 267:17
How a bear likes h.	MILN 219:4
locusts and wild h.	BIBL 42:7
sweeter also than h.	BOOK 61:4
took some h.	LEAR 195:14
With milk and h. blessed	NEAL 232:2
honeycomb honey, and the h.	BOOK 61:4
honeydew he on h. hath fed	COLE 96:7
honeysuckle You are my honey, h.	FITZ 128:12
honi H. soie qui mal y pense	SELL 267:17
H. soit qui mal y pense	ANON 11:12
honking goose h. amongst tuneful swans	VIRG 325:13
honour As he was valiant, I h. him	SHAK 276:13
cannot be maintained with h.	RUSS 263:2
Fear God. H. the King	KITC 189:6
flowery plains of h.	JONS 177:21
fountain of h.	BACO 21:1
greater share of h.	SHAK 275:7
H. all men	BIBL 51:27
h., and keep her	BOOK 60:17
h. and life	FRAN 132:19
H. a physician	BIBL 41:28
h. rooted in dishonour	TENN 311:8
h. sinks where commerce	GOLD 143:21
h. therof	EDWA 120:2
H. thy father and thy mother	BIBL 34:16
h. unto the wife	BIBL 51:28
Keeps h. bright	SHAK 287:31
Leisure with h.	CICE 93:2
louder he talked of his h.	EMER 124:11
Loved I not h. more	LOVE 203:7
peace I hope with h.	DISR 112:14
peace with h.	CHAM 86:20
pluck bright h.	SHAK 273:28
post of h.	ADDI 2:10
prophet is not without h.	BIBL 44:4
roll of h.	CLEV 94:11
safety, h., and welfare	CHAR 87:23
signed with their h.	SPEN 300:10
some share of h.	SHAK 276:31
What is h.	SHAK 274:9
whence h. springs	MARL 212:17
honourable Brutus is an h. man	SHAK 276:16
designs were strictly h.	FIEL 127:15
h. alike in what we give	LINC 199:7
honoured h. me of late	SHAK 279:23
honours good card to play for H.	BENN 29:25
neither h. nor wages	GARI 136:5
hook with an h.	BIBL 37:16
hop H. forty paces	SHAK 268:19
hope Abandon all h.	DANT 105:17
All my h. on God	BRID 66:18
believed in h.	BIBL 49:9
Evelyn H. is dead	BROW 70:4
From h. and fear set free	SWIN 307:24
God is our h.	BOOK 61:25
He that lives upon h.	FRAN 133:6
H. deferred	BIBL 37:29
h. for the best	SMIT 298:8
h. for years to come	WATT 329:13
H. raises no dust	ÉLUA 124:5
H. springs eternal	POPE 248:10
I can give you no h.	EDDI 119:14
in the store we sell h.	REVS 256:3
Land of H. and Glory	BENS 29:27
last best h.	LINC 199:7
look forward to with h.	FROS 134:6
Never to h. again	SHAK 275:24
no h. without fear	SPIN 300:27
not another's h.	WALS 328:1
nursing the unconquerable h.	ARNO 15:19
only h. that keeps up	GAY 137:3

Some blessed H.	HARD 151:23
sure and certain h.	BOOK 60:25
There is no h.	CHES 89:4
triumph of h. over experience	JOHN 175:7
True h. is swift	SHAK 286:9
two thousand years of h.	WEIZ 330:26
Was the h. drunk	SHAK 279:24
Where there is despair, h.	FRAN 133:3
Youth and H.	COLE 96:26
hopeful droopingly, but with a h. heart	LAWR 194:13
hopefully travel h. is a better thing	STEV 303:25
hopefulness Lord of all h.	STRU 305:8
hopeless doctors know a h. case	CUMM 104:18
perennially h.	DICK 109:16
hopes no great h. from Birmingham	AUST 19:17
vanity of human h.	JOHN 173:23
wholly h. to be	BROW 70:1
hops apples, cherries, h.	DICK 111:3
horizon just beyond the h.	KISS 189:5
horizontal h. desire	SHAW 292:5
Life is a h. fall	COCT 95:11
horn blow his wreathèd h.	WORD 341:19
h. of the hunter	CRAW 103:5
one of which is made of h.	VIRG 325:2
sound of the h.	VIGN 324:3
Hornby H. and my Barlow	THOM 316:25
horned h. moon	WORD 339:14
horns h. of Elfland	TENN 313:6
memories are hunting h.	APOL 13:10
horny H.-handed sons of toil	SALI 263:21
h. hands of toil	LOWE 203:17
horribilis annus h.	ELIZ 123:14
horrible h. imaginings	SHAK 279:8
O, horrible! O, h.	SHAK 271:19
horrid she was h.	LONG 202:10
very h. thing	BUTL 77:2
With h. warning	KEAT 181:21
horror h. of sunsets	PROU 251:18
h.! The horror	CONR 99:7
horrors supped full with h.	SHAK 281:23
horse behold a pale h.	BIBL 52:9
Boot, saddle, to h.	BROW 69:23
dearer than his h.	TENN 312:8
feeds the h. enough oats	GALB 135:10
h. designed by a committee	ISSI 169:14
h. he can ride	THOM 317:14
h. of air	ANON 11:4
h. of that colour	SHAK 288:16
h. on the mountain	GARC 136:1
h. was made Consul	RAND 254:12
my kingdom for a h.	SHAK 286:11
owe it to h. and hound	WHYT 334:11
sick h. nosing around	KAVA 180:23
sounds like a saddle h.	ONAS 236:9
strength of an h.	BOOK 63:28
torturer's h. scratches	AUDE 18:9
two things about the h.	ROYD 261:18
where's the bloody h.	CAMP 80:21
young corner of h.	WALP 327:22
horseback ride On h.	COWP 101:22
Horseguards be in the H.	RATT 254:16
horseman H., pass by	YEAT 343:30
sits behind the h.	HORA 164:13
horses breed of their h.	PENN 243:10
Bring on the empty. H.	CURT 105:7
don't spare the h.	HILL 159:7
frighten the h.	CAMP 80:20
generally given to h.	JOHN 173:15
h. of instruction	BLAK 55:25
h. of the night	OVID 238:10
if you cannot ride two h.	MAXT 215:13
swap h. when crossing	LINC 199:10
that h. may not be stolen	HALI 150:4

They shoot h. don't they	MCCO 207:2
watered our h. in Helicon	CHAP 87:15
wild white h. play	ARNO 15:7
hortus H. ubi et tecto vicinus iugis	HORA 164:21
hosanna H. in excelsis	MISS 224:4
hosannas sweet h. ring	NEAL 231:23
hospital first requirement in a H.	NIGH 234:12
not an inn, but an h.	BROW 69:9
host h., of golden daffodils	WORD 340:1
hostages h. to fortune	BACO 21:17
h. to the fates	LUCA 204:9
hostile universe is not h.	HOLM 161:8
hot h. for certainties	MERE 217:6
neither cold nor h.	BIBL 52:6
hound his hawk, his h.	BALL 24:13
loves the h. more	SURT 306:9
owe it to horse and h.	WHYT 334:11
hounds h. and his horn in the morning	GRAV 146:3
h. of spring	SWIN 307:17
hour books of the h.	RUSK 262:12
finest h.	CHUR 91:16
for an h. of Herod	HOPE 162:16
h. is come	SCOT 266:23
h. of death	BOOK 59:7
h. of glorious life	MORD 227:21
I also had my h.	CHES 89:19
Improve each shining h.	WATT 329:5
its h. come round at last	YEAT 343:20
known as the Children's H.	LONG 201:19
know not what h.	BIBL 45:4
man and the h.	YANC 342:9
matched us with His h.	BROO 67:22
mine h. is not yet come	BIBL 47:26
most carefully upon your h.	SHAK 270:21
stayed me in a happy h.	SHAK 284:4
Time and the h.	SHAK 279:9
to serve the h.	TENN 313:1
watch with me one hour	BIBL 45:16
hours h. will take care of themselves	CHES 89:8
leaden-stepping h.	MILT 220:29
see the h. pass	CIOR 93:5
house angel in the h.	PATM 242:2
beat upon that h.	BIBL 43:12
doll in the doll's h.	DICK 111:2
heap of stones is a h.	POIN 246:16
h. as nigh heaven	MORE 228:1
h. divided	LINC 199:6
h. is a machine for living in	LE C 196:6
h. is his castle	COKE 95:17
h. is much more	MORR 228:12
h. is not a home	ADLE 2:20
h. not made with hands	BIBL 50:10
h. not made with hands	BROW 69:24
H. of Peers	GILB 140:4
h. of prayer	BIBL 40:19
h. of prayer	BIBL 44:25
h. where I was born	HOOD 162:5
If a h. be divided	BIBL 45:25
In my Father's h.	BIBL 48:5
in the h. of Rimmon	BIBL 36:25
join house to h.	BIBL 39:13
little plaything-h.	WALP 327:7
Lord build the h.	BOOK 63:18
make a H.	CANN 81:17
mind to sell his h.	SWIF 306:18
Set thine h. in order	BIBL 40:5
so in the way in the h.	GASK 136:15
sparrow hath found her an h.	BOOK 62:10
This H. today is a theatre	BALD 23:12
What! in our h.	SHAK 280:18
housekeeping good h. to the winds	KEYN 185:14
houses friends' h.	JOHN 176:11
h. are all gone under the sea	ELIO 121:24

h. go wheeling back	THOM 317:13
h. in between	BATE 26:4
h. thick and sewers	MILT 222:15
nothing in your h.	MORR 228:19
plague o' both your h.	SHAK 286:26
spaces between the h.	FENT 126:19
very h. seem asleep	WORD 339:19
watered our h. in Helicon	CHAP 87:15
housework no need to do any h.	CRIS 103:12
Houston H., we've had a problem	LOVE 203:8
hover H. through the fog	SHAK 278:26
how Here's a h.-de-doo	GILB 140:13
H. do I love thee	BROW 69:14
H. do they know	PARK 241:1
H. NOT TO DO IT	DICK 110:16
not say why and h.	WILS 337:1
howl H., howl, howl, howl	SHAK 278:12
Howth H. Castle and Environs	JOYC 178:19
huddled h. masses yearning	LAZA 195:2
hues all her lovely h.	DAVI 106:18
Hugo H.—alas	GIDE 139:17
hum busy h. of men	MILT 220:6
human all h. life is there	JAME 170:17
full tide of h. existence	JOHN 175:14
guide of h. life	HUME 166:18
h. condition	MALR 210:13
h. hearts endure	JOHN 174:3
H. kind Cannot bear	ELIO 121:20
H. on my faithless arm	AUDE 18:7
H. speech	FLAU 129:17
h. zoo	MORR 228:13
knowledge of h. nature	AUST 19:19
milk of h. kindness	SHAK 279:12
nothing h. foreign to me	TERE 314:7
Peace, the h. dress	BLAK 56:6
people are only h.	COMP 98:2
robot may not injure a h.	ASIM 16:15
socialism would not lose its h. face	DUBČ 117:18
To err is h.	POPE 248:6
wish I loved the H. Race	RALE 254:10
humane Heaven and earth not h.	LAO 193:4
humanity crooked timber of h.	KANT 180:15
freeze my h.	MACN 208:19
religion of h.	PAIN 239:9
sad music of h.	WORD 340:3
teach governments h.	PAIN 239:11
humble Be it ever so h.	PAYN 242:11
He that is h.	BUNY 73:8
Neither too h.	MALL 210:7
humbleth he that h. himself	BIBL 46:25
humbly walk h. with thy God	BIBL 41:17
humbug 'Bah,' said Scrooge. 'H.!'	DICK 109:19
humiliation Art is born of h.	AUDE 18:23
collapse in deepest h.	EDDI 119:14
valley of H.	BUNY 72:23
humility pride that apes h.	COLE 95:23
small book on H.	LONG 202:11
humour h., sincerity	NEIL 232:6
in this h. won	SHAK 286:2
hump without a positive h.	THAC 314:19
Humpty Dumpty heard H.	JAME 171:2
hundred h. flowers blossom	MAO 211:14
Six h. threescore and six	BIBL 52:16
hunger bodily h. in his eyes	SHAW 291:3
h. and poverty	LARK 193:9
h. to be beautiful	RHYS 256:10
sacred h.	SPEN 300:20
shall never h.	BIBL 47:31
hungry h. for dinner at eight	HART 152:19
h. sheep look up	MILT 220:15
If thine enemy be h.	BIBL 38:3
lean and h. look	SHAK 276:1
Let all who are h.	HAGG 148:18

Huns H. or Wops — MITF 225:2
hunter h. home from hill — STEV 304:7
Man is the h. — TENN 313:10
Nimrod the mighty h. — BIBL 33:23
snare of the h. — BOOK 62:16
Hunter Dunn Miss J. H. — BETJ 32:3
hunting H. is all that's worth — SURT 306:8
preserved as h.-grounds — ELIO 121:8
weary wi' h. — BALL 23:20
huntress Queen and h. — JONS 177:14
hurdles don't every see the h. — MOSE 229:12
hurled Swift to be h. — HOOD 162:1
hurricane h. on the way — FISH 128:3
hurry h., hurry, hurry — MIDD 217:21
old man in a h. — CHUR 91:5
hurt hate the man you have h. — TACI 308:15
h. you to the heart — TWAI 321:6
no one was to be h. — BROO 68:2
power to h. us — BEAU 26:14
wish to h. — BRON 67:7
hurting If the policy isn't h. — MAJO 209:21
husband Chaste to her h. — POPE 247:13
crown to her h. — BIBL 37:26
h. what is left of a lover — ROWL 261:15
in her h.'s heart — SHAK 288:18
left her h. because — MURD 230:4
one h. too many — ANON 6:4
over hir h. as hir love — CHAU 88:21
quarrels with one's h. — BONA 57:18
reproach a h. — LA F 191:16
husbandry h. in heaven — SHAK 280:4
husbands Chumps make the best h. — WODE 337:25
hands of the h. — ADAM 1:9
H. at chirche dore — CHAU 88:11
H., love your wives — BIBL 51:2
in spite of their h. — LEE- 196:16
When h. or when lapdogs — POPE 249:7
hush breathless h. in the Close — NEWB 232:20
H., hush — MORT 229:6
H.! Hush! Whisper who dares — MILN 219:3
hushing H. the latest traffic — BRID 66:19
hut Love in a h. — KEAT 181:23
hyacinths h. and biscuits — SAND 264:11
Hyde Dr Jekyll and Mr H. — STEV 303:18
hyena h. in petticoats — WALP 327:17
hymns h. at heaven's gate — SHAK 289:26
Hyperion H. to a satyr — SHAK 270:31
hyphenated h. Americanism — ROOS 260:4
hypocrisy H. is a tribute — LA R 193:20
H., the only evil — MILT 221:28
organized h. — DISR 112:8
hypocrite H. lecteur,—mon semblable — BAUD 26:6
hypocrites scribes and Pharisees, h. — BIBL 44:30
hypothermia dying of h. — BENN 29:18
hypotheses do not feign h. — NEWT 233:13
hypothesis discard a pet h. — LORE 202:17
slaying of a beautiful h. — HUXL 167:21
hysterics h. of the Celt — TENN 311:32

I

I I am a camera — ISHE 169:13
I am not I — WAUG 329:16
I AM THAT I AM — BIBL 34:3
I am the State — LOUI 202:18
I plus my surroundings — ORTE 236:22
Through which we go Is I — DE L 108:9
ibant I. obscuri sola sub nocte — VIRG 324:21
ice along the polished i. — WORD 339:23
Alps of green i. — PHIL 244:17
caves of i. — COLE 96:5

emperor of i.-cream — STEV 303:3
I. formed — WODE 338:7
i., mast-high — COLE 96:10
Some say in i. — FROS 134:8
iceberg ill-concealed i. — LAWS 195:1
iced three parts i. over — ARNO 16:3
Iceland Natural History of I. — JOHN 175:26
iceman i. cometh — O'NE 236:11
Ichabod named the child I. — BIBL 35:15
icicle Chaste as the i. — SHAK 270:15
icicles When i. hang by the wall — SHAK 278:23
id PUT THE I. BACK IN YID — ROTH 261:6
idea better to entertain an i. — JARR 171:7
does get an i. — MARQ 212:23
i. first occurs — DARW 106:10
i. whose time has come — ANON 10:7
invasion by an i. — HUGO 166:16
landed with an i. — BIRT 54:9
more dangerous than an i. — ALAI 3:8
possess but one i. — JOHN 175:6
teach the young i. — THOM 317:9
wilderness of i. — BUTL 77:13
ideal i. for which I am prepared — MAND 210:19
i. of reason — KANT 180:14
idealism morphine or i. — JUNG 179:15
ideas Colourless green i. — CHOM 90:17
From it our i. are born — GENE 137:18
signs of i. — JOHN 173:11
identical Two things are i. — LEIB 196:22
identify I can i. with her — MADO 209:6
ides Beware the i. of March — SHAK 275:29
idiot i. who praises — GILB 140:9
portrait of a blinking i. — SHAK 282:11
tale Told by an i. — SHAK 281:24
idle be not i. — BURT 76:18
For i. hands to do — WATT 329:6
i. singer of an empty day — MORR 228:16
little profits that an i. king — TENN 313:28
most i. and unprofitable — GIBB 139:6
only i. chatter — GILB 140:23
Tears, i. tears — TENN 313:7
We would all be i. — JOHN 175:18
idol one-eyed yellow i. — HAYE 154:1
idolatry god of our i. — COWP 101:27
idols i. I have loved — FITZ 128:21
if I. it moves, salute i. — ANON 7:14
I. you can keep your head — KIPL 187:20
much virtue in 'i.' — SHAK 270:7
ifs Talk'st thou to me of 'i.' — SHAK 286:6
ignis fatuus Reason, an i. — ROCH 258:12
ignominy i. sleep with thee — SHAK 274:11
ignorance Disease, I., and Idleness — BEVE 32:12
fact of my i. — SOCR 298:21
i. is never better — FERM 127:3
i. it accumulates — ADAM 1:17
i. of nature — HOLB 161:2
I. of the law — SELD 267:11
i. or profaneness — MATH 215:3
no sin but i. — MARL 212:10
pure i. — JOHN 174:21
Where i. is bliss — GRAY 146:19
women in a state of i. — KNOX 189:19
ignorant Asking the i. — ZOBE 345:6
In language, the i. — DUPP 118:13
many i. men are sure — DARR 106:5
ignores most poetry i. most people — MITC 224:15
ill ill-clad, i.-nourished — ROOS 259:18
I. fares the land — GOLD 143:7
i.-favoured thing, sir — SHAK 270:5
I. met by moonlight — SHAK 283:8
I. news hath wings — DRAY 116:4
one-third of a nation i.-housed — ROOS 259:18
she's not really i. — JAGG 170:2

Some think him i.-tempered LEAR 195:13
vain, i.-natured DEFO 107:19
warn you not to fall i. KINN 187:3
illegal i., immoral, or fattening WOOL 339:13
means that it is not i. NIXO 234:16
Nothing is i. if YOUN 344:9
illegitimate i. child of Karl Marx ATTL 17:11
no i. children GLAD 141:17
illiterate I. him, I say SHER 294:11
illness i. identified with evil SONT 299:6
ills i. of democracy SMIT 297:12
i. to come GRAY 146:18
illuminatio *Dominus i. mea* ANON 12:11
Dominus i. mea BIBL 52:29
illumine What in me is dark, I. MILT 221:2
illusion great i. ANGE 5:11
sophistry and i. HUME 166:19
illustration i. of character JAME 170:19
image Best i. of myself MILT 222:9
created him in his own i. DOST 115:1
his i., cut in ebony FULL 134:25
i. of the Creator BONA 57:21
votre i. me suit RACI 253:20
imagination hunting-grounds for the poetic i.
ELIO 121:8
ideal of i. KANT 180:14
i. amend them SHAK 283:23
i. droops her pinion BYRO 78:26
i. of their hearts BIBL 45:34
i. resembled MACA 205:23
i. the rudder KEAT 183:3
save those that have no i. SHAW 291:33
shaping spirit of i. COLE 95:22
takes a lot of i. BAIL 22:25
Television contracts i. WOGA 338:8
truth of i. KEAT 183:4
imagine people i. a vain thing BOOK 60:26
imaginings horrible i. SHAK 279:8
imitate Immature poets i. ELIO 123:1
imitation art of I. LLOY 200:16
child of i. REYN 256:6
i. in lines and colours POUS 250:16
imitatores *O i., servum pecus* HORA 164:2
immanent I. Will HARD 151:21
Immanuel call his name I. BIBL 39:17
immemorial in i. elms TENN 313:19
immense error is i. BOLI 57:14
immoral illegal, i., or fattening WOOL 339:13
moral or an i. book WILD 335:8
immortal I have I. longings SHAK 269:6
i. hand or eye BLAK 56:14
I., invisible SMIT 298:15
i. part of myself SHAK 284:17
immortality belief in i. DOST 114:24
i. through my work ALLE 4:10
just Ourselves— And I. DICK 111:12
lead me to i. UPAN 321:21
Milk's leap toward i. FADI 125:19
impediment cause, or just i. BOOK 60:13
imperative i. is Categorical KANT 180:13
imperial act Of the i. theme SHAK 279:7
our great I. family ELIZ 123:13
imperialisms prey of rival i. KENY 184:20
impertinent ask an i. question BRON 67:6
implacable i. in hate DRYD 116:18
important being less i. MONT 226:10
i. book, the critic assumes WOOL 339:8
trivial and the i. POTT 249:27
importunate no less i. MONT 226:10
impossibility Upon I. MARV 213:14
impossible certain because it is i. TERT 314:16
Dream the i. DARI 106:3
eliminated the i. DOYL 115:18

i. takes a little longer ANON 6:12
i. takes a little longer NANS 231:1
i.? that will be done CALO 80:12
six i. things CARR 84:9
something is i. CLAR 93:18
That not i. she CRAS 103:4
wish it were i. JOHN 176:21
impostors treat those two i. KIPL 187:20
impotent i. people, sick THOM 316:24
imprisoned taken or i. MAGN 209:11
improbability life is statistical i. DAWK 107:2
improbable i. possibilities ARIS 14:16
whatever remains, *however* i. DOYL 115:18
improper noun, proper or i. FULL 134:23
impropriety without i. GILB 140:5
improve I. each shining hour WATT 329:5
improved i. by death SAKI 263:13
improvement schemes of political i. JOHN 175:5
improvisation I. is too good SIMO 296:1
impulse first i. CORN 100:4
impulses no truck with first i. MONT 226:21
impune *Nemo me i. lacessit* ANON 12:14
impunity provokes me with i. ANON 12:14
impure to the Puritan all things are i. LAWR 194:11
in going out, and thy coming i. BOOK 63:14
inability i. to live GONC 144:12
inactivity masterly i. MACK 207:19
inadequate not that we are i. WILL 336:11
incarnadine multitudinous seas i. SHAK 280:12
incest i. and folk-dancing ANON 11:8
inch every i. a king SHAK 278:1
inches die by i. HENR 156:18
thirty i. from my nose AUDE 18:15
incident curious i. of the dog DOYL 115:16
determination of i. JAME 170:19
incisors i. and grinders BAGE 22:22
inclination greatest enemy is i. BAHY 22:24
just as i. leads him JOHN 174:24
incline I. our hearts BOOK 59:20
include i. me out GOLD 144:7
income Annual i. twenty pounds DICK 110:3
Expenditure rises to meet i. PARK 241:6
moderate i. DURH 118:14
income tax I. made more liars ROGE 259:4
incomparable i. Max SHAW 292:2
incompatible Thought i. by men LEWI 198:15
united things long i. TACI 308:13
incompetence rise to his level of i. PETE 244:8
incomprehensible use the i. ZOBE 345:6
inconstant i. toads MONT 226:2
i. woman GAY 137:10
inconvenience Change without i. JOHN 173:10
inconveniences i., and those weighty HOOK 162:9
inconvenient cause may be i. BENN 29:24
incorruptible seagreen I. CARL 82:19
increase Some races i. LUCR 204:14
we desire i. SHAK 289:22
increasing has increased, is i. DUNN 118:12
incurable Life is an i. disease COWL 101:15
indecent sent down for i. behaviour WAUG 329:18
independence i. of judges DENN 108:17
right to i. NAMI 230:21
index i. of a feeling mind CRAB 102:16
indexes memories are card-i. CONN 99:3
India I.'s coral strand HEBE 155:1
I. will awake to life NEHR 232:3
Indian I. Crown ROSS 260:15
I. wilderness MATH 215:2
Like the base I. SHAK 284:4
Lo! the poor I. POPE 248:11
Indians only good I. SHER 294:9
to convert the I. WESL 332:6
indictment i. against an whole people BURK 74:1

indifference i. and a coach and six COLM 97:12
indifferent delayed till I am i. JOHN 174:20
It is simply i. HOLM 161:8
indignation fierce i. SWIF 307:15
i. makes me write verse JUVE 179:20
Savage i. there YEAT 343:25
inditing i. of a good matter BOOK 61:22
individual i. men and women THAT 315:12
individualism system of rugged i. HOOV 162:12
indivisible Peace is i. LITV 200:8
indolent i. expression BELL 28:19
indomitable i. Irishry YEAT 343:29
indulgent makes one very i. STAË 301:9
industry Captains of i. CARL 82:26
i. will improve them REYN 256:5
i. without art RUSK 262:8
national i. of Prussia MIRA 223:23
not his i. only BURK 74:17
spur of i. HUME 166:20
inebriate cheer but not i. BERK 30:14
cheer but not i. COWP 102:3
ineffectual beautiful and i. angel ARNO 16:1
Remote and i. Don BELL 28:17
inefficient efficient and the i. SHAW 290:30
inevitability i. of gradualness WEBB 330:1
inevitable i. the Titanic HAGU 149:4
inexactitude terminological i. CHUR 91:7
inexorable deaf, i. SIDN 295:6
infamy date which will live in i. ROOS 259:21
infancy about us in our i. WORD 340:10
infant i. crying in the night TENN 311:19
i. phenomenon DICK 110:24
infantile second i. ARIS 14:10
infection i. of things gone LOWE 204:3
inferior make you feel i. ROOS 259:12
inferno i. of his passions JUNG 179:13
infini l'i. me tourmente MUSS 230:14
infinite door to i. wisdom BREC 66:8
I. riches MARL 212:11
i. spaces PASC 241:17
I. torments MUSS 230:14
I. wrath MILT 221:29
number of worlds is i. ALEX 3:14
infinitive care what a split i. FOWL 132:11
when I split an i. CHAN 87:6
infirmities i. were not noxious JOHN 174:22
inflation pay to get i. down LAMO 192:15
inflections beauty of i. STEV 303:7
influence i. of the Crown DUNN 118:12
i. to your son ICE 168:15
planetary i. SHAK 277:10
win friends and i. people CARN 83:8
influences bind the sweet i. BIBL 37:13
inform not to i. the reader ACHE 1:7
occasions do i. against me SHAK 272:31
ingratitude so unkind As man's i. SHAK 269:25
inhale didn't i. CLIN 94:15
if he doesn't i. STEV 303:8
inherit i. the earth BIBL 42:14
inheritance Ruinous i. GAIU 135:8
inherited i. it brick AUGU 19:9
inhumanity Man's i. to man BURN 75:16
inimitable i. rose WINC 337:11
iniquity hated i. BOOK 61:23
hated i. GREG 147:8
injuries insult to i. MOOR 227:3
revenge for slight i. MACH 207:15
injury i. is much sooner forgotten CHES 89:6
injustice I. anywhere a threat KING 186:9
i. makes democracy necessary NIEB 234:4
justice or i. JOHN 174:9
No i. is done ULPI 321:19
injustices justify their i. VOLT 326:2

ink all the sea were i. LYLY 204:25
i. in my pen ran cold WALP 327:8
inlaid thick i. with patines SHAK 282:29
inlet At a small i. YOUN 344:17
inn Do you remember an I., Miranda BELL 28:26
gain the timely i. SHAK 280:26
no room for them in the i. BIBL 46:3
not an i., but an hospital BROW 69:9
innavigable nor sea i. THOR 317:23
Innisfree go to I. YEAT 343:6
innocence ceremony of i. is drowned YEAT 343:19
i. is like a dumb leper GREE 147:2
not in i. ARDR 14:3
innocent i. of the blood BIBL 45:19
one i. suffer BLAC 55:5
shall not be i. BIBL 38:8
We are i. ROSE 260:9
innocents i. abroad TWAI 321:7
innovator time is the greatest i. BACO 21:16
innuendoes beauty of i. STEV 303:7
innuendos i. Will serve him no longer PULT 252:6
inoperative all previous statements i. ZIEG 345:4
inquisition Spanish I. MONT 227:1
insane hereditary monarch was i. BAGE 22:14
inscription altar with this i. BIBL 48:34
like a rough i. YEVT 344:6
inscriptions In lapidary i. JOHN 175:17
insculped I. and embossed THOM 317:6
insect 'Tortis' is a i. PUNC 252:13
transformed into a gigantic i. KAFK 180:7
insensibility stark i. JOHN 174:15
inseparable one and i. WEBS 330:6
inside i. the tent pissing out JOHN 173:6
insight i. and the stretch BROW 69:18
insignificance of the utmost i. CURZ 105:9
insolence flown with i. and wine MILT 221:11
i. of wealth JOHN 176:1
supports with i. JOHN 173:16
inspiration Genius is one per cent i. EDIS 119:22
inspissated i. gloom JOHN 175:4
instantaneous i. courage NAPO 231:6
instinct believe upon i. BRAD 65:20
instincts i. and abilities BALZ 24:21
true to your i. LAWR 194:16
institution change an i. TUSA 321:1
i. which does not suppose ROBE 257:18
It's an i. HUGH 166:14
instruct i. them AURE 19:14
instruction better the i. SHAK 282:14
horses of i. BLAK 55:25
I. is the pill RICH 257:1
no i. book came with it FULL 134:24
instrument i. of science JOHN 173:11
i. of Your peace FRAN 133:3
insubstantial this i. pageant SHAK 287:15
insular i. country, subject to fogs DISR 112:22
insularum Paene i. CATU 85:21
insult i. to injuries MOOR 227:3
sooner forgotten than an i. CHES 89:6
threatened her with i. BURK 74:6
insulted never hope to get i. DAVI 106:21
insulting i. Christmas card GROS 148:6
insuppressible i. island KETT 185:5
intact is there, i. TRIM 319:12
integral i. and differential calculus GILB 141:5
integration policy of European i. KOHL 190:2
intellect Our meddling i. WORD 341:13
restless and versatile i. HUXL 168:4
tickle the i. LAMB 192:5
intellectual i. All-in-all WORD 340:19
i., amongst the noblest CALV 80:14
'I.' suggests AUDE 18:10
to the i. world STER 302:23

intellectuals treachery of the i. — BEND 29:9
intelligence arresting human i. — LEAC 195:3
  I. is quickness to apprehend — WHIT 333:14
  people have little i. — LA B 191:7
  started at the i. — SOUT 299:18
intelligent Most i., very elegant — BUCK 72:2
  pleasing one i. man — MAIM 209:19
  so i. — ELIO 122:25
intent first avowed i. — BUNY 73:9
  told with bad i. — BLAK 55:13
intentions i. make blackguards — LACL 191:10
  only had good i. — THAT 315:5
inter children i. their parents — HERO 157:23
interest passion or i. — LOCK 201:6
interested i. in the arts — AYCK 20:9
  i. in things — CURI 105:4
  only i. in art — SHAW 292:4
interesting things and characters i. — SCOT 266:27
interests Our i. are eternal — PALM 240:6
Internet I. is an élite — CHOM 90:18
  thanks to the I. — WILE 335:26
interpose i. my body — STRA 304:23
interpretation lost in i. — FROS 134:16
interstellar vacant i. spaces — ELIO 121:25
interstices i. between the intersections — JOHN 173:14
interviewer i. allows you to say — BENN 29:17
intimacy avoid any i. — KITC 189:6
intimidation without i. — ROBE 257:19
intolerable burden of them is i. — BOOK 59:27
intoxicated God-i. man — NOVA 235:3
intreat I. me not to leave thee — BIBL 35:13
intricated Poor i. soul — DONN 114:22
intruding rash, i. fool — SHAK 272:24
invasion i. by an idea — HUGO 166:16
invent necessary to i. him — VOLT 326:5
  one man can i. — DOYL 115:17
invented England i. the phrase — BAGE 22:12
  Truth exists, lies are i. — BRAQ 66:5
invention brightest heaven of i. — SHAK 274:26
  [bureaucracy's] specific i. — WEBE 330:3
  i. of a barbarous age — MILT 220:31
  i. of a mouse — DISN 112:3
  is a happy i. — ANON 13:3
  Marriage a wonderful i. — CONN 98:24
  Pure i. — BYRO 79:23
  use of a new i. — FRAN 133:11
inventions sought out many i. — BIBL 38:22
  with their own i. — BOOK 62:27
inventor plague the i. — SHAK 279:20
inverse i. proportion to the sum — PARK 241:8
invida fugerit i. Aetas — HORA 164:7
inviolable clutching the i. shade — ARNO 15:19
inviolate secret and i. Rose — YEAT 343:21
invisible all things visible and i. — BOOK 59:22
  bloody and i. hand — SHAK 280:25
  Immortal, i. — SMIT 298:15
  I., except to God — MILT 221:28
  i. hand in politics — FRIE 133:24
  no i. means of support — BUCH 71:25
  representation of i. things — LEON 197:21
inward i. and spiritual grace — BOOK 60:11
ipse I. dixit — CICE 92:23
ira Ça i. — ANON 11:9
  I. furor brevis est — HORA 163:22
  Sine i. et studio — TACI 308:16
irae Dies i. — MISS 224:11
Ireland coming to I. today — GEOR 138:3
  daunce wyt me, in i. — ANON 7:13
  evacuation of I. — GRIF 147:16
  God save I. — SULL 305:17
  great Gaels of I. — CHES 89:18
  how's poor ould I. — ANON 8:1
  I. gives England her soldiers — MERE 216:25

I. hurt you into poetry — AUDE 18:3
I. is a small — KETT 185:5
I. is the old sow — JOYC 178:25
I., long a province — DAVI 106:22
I.'s battle — CONN 99:5
I.'s present story — BYRO 79:2
I. unfree shall never be at peace — PEAR 242:17
I. we dreamed of — DE V 109:6
Out of I. have we come — YEAT 343:15
pacify I. — GLAD 141:18
parties in Northern I. — MITC 224:17
programme for I. — KETT 185:4
Romantic I.'s dead and gone — YEAT 343:23
split I. — BRUG 71:16
what I have got for I. — COLL 97:7
would had been for I. — SARS 264:21
iris livelier i. changes — TENN 312:7
Irish answer to the I. Question — SELL 267:20
  become deeply I. — KETT 185:4
  I'm I. — MOOR 227:11
  I. and Ireland ridiculous — EDGE 119:21
  I. poets, learn your trade — YEAT 343:28
  I. Question — DISR 112:5
  Let the I. vessel lie — AUDE 18:4
  symbol of I. art — JOYC 179:1
  what the I. people wanted — DE V 109:5
Irishmen appeal to all I. — GEOR 138:3
Irishry indomitable I. — YEAT 343:29
iron Any old i. — COLL 97:4
  blood and i. — BISM 54:18
  Even an i. partition — TALM 309:6
  he's got i. teeth — GROM 148:2
  i. curtain — CHUR 91:23
  I. Curtain did not reach — SOLZ 298:29
  i. entered into his soul — BOOK 62:26
  i. gates of life — MARV 213:23
  I. Lady — THAT 315:4
  nobles with links of i. — BOOK 63:29
  Nor i. bars a cage — LOVE 203:6
  Torah, hard like i. — TALM 309:8
irrationally I. held truths — HUXL 168:2
irregulars Baker Street i. — DOYL 115:20
irrevocabile volat i. verbum — HORA 163:26
irritabile genus i. vatum — HORA 164:5
irrt Es i. der Mensch — GOET 142:16
is That which i. grows — GALE 135:12
  Whatever I., is RIGHT — POPE 248:14
Ishmael Call me I. — MELV 216:9
Islam I. has established them — KHOM 185:15
  true religion is I. — KORA 190:11
island insuppressible i. — KETT 185:5
  i. is moored only lightly — BARR 25:18
  i. made mainly of coal — BEVA 32:7
  i.-valley of Avilion — TENN 311:16
  John Bull's other i. — SHAW 290:29
  No man is an I. — DONN 114:18
  snug little I. — DIBD 109:15
  soggy little I. — UPDI 321:25
islands favourite i. — AUDE 17:27
  peninsulas and i. — CATU 85:21
isle Fairest I. — DRYD 117:2
  i. is full of noises — SHAK 287:14
  men, of the Emerald I. — DREN 116:9
  sad, black i. — BAUD 26:8
isles i. of Greece — BYRO 78:23
isolated Continent i. — BROC 67:5
  fine i. verisimilitude — KEAT 183:6
Israel between I. and their Father — TALM 309:6
  Hear, O I. — SIDD 295:4
  I. shall be a proverb — BIBL 36:1
  I. was in Egypt land — ANON 10:20
  mother in I. — BIBL 35:1
  sweet psalmist of I. — BIBL 35:35

Israel (*cont.*)
These be thy gods, O I.   BIBL 34:18
waters of I.   BIBL 36:24
Israelite Behold an I.   BIBL 47:25
isst *Der Mensch ist, was er i.*   FEUE 127:5
ist *Der Mensch i., was er isst*   FEUE 127:5
it It's just I.   KIPL 189:1
Italian to women I.   CHAR 87:27
Italy inside of it, 'I.'   BROW 70:2
I. is a geographical expression   METT 217:14
Paradise of exiles, I.   SHEL 292:26
itch i. of literature   LOVE 203:9
itching have an i. palm   SHAK 276:28
ite *I. missa est*   MISS 224:8
itur *sic i. ad astra*   VIRG 325:4
iudice *se i.*   JUVE 180:5
sub i. lis est   HORA 163:13
ivory as if done in i.   FULL 134:25
cargo of i.   MASE 214:16
gleaming white i.   VIRG 325:2
in his i. tower   SAIN 263:11
i., and apes   BIBL 36:4
i. on which I work   AUST 20:3
out of the i. gate   BROW 69:10

J

Jabberwock Beware the J., my son   CARR 84:3
jack banish plump J.   SHAK 274:1
Damn you, J.   BONE 58:1
news of my boy J.   KIPL 188:2
jackals J. piss at their foot   FLAU 129:20
jackdaw J. sat on the Cardinal's chair   BARH 25:2
jackknife j. has Macheath   BREC 66:11
jacks calls the knaves, J.   DICK 110:13
Jackson J. with his Virginians   BEE 27:7
Jacob as the Angel did with J.   WALT 328:6
J. served seven years   BIBL 33:31
traffic of J.'s ladder   THOM 317:3
voice is J.'s voice   BIBL 33:29
jade Let the galled j. wince   SHAK 272:15
jades pampered j.   MARL 212:19
pampered j. of Asia   SHAK 274:18
jail dey gits you in j.   O'NE 236:10
Go to j.   ANON 7:6
jam j. to-morrow   CARR 84:8
j. we thought was for   BENN 29:15
jamais j. triste archy   MARQ 212:22
James Home J.   HILL 159:7
J. I, James II, and the Old Pretender   GUED 148:9
J. James Morrison Morrison   MILN 219:1
King J. stay behind   WHAR 332:25
Jane J., Jane, tall as a crane   SITW 296:11
you J.   WEIS 330:25
Janvier J. and Février   NICH 233:21
Japan J.'s advantage   HIRO 159:12
jar does so j.   GASK 136:18
jargon from J. born to rescue Law   LLOY 200:15
Jarndyce J. and Jarndyce   DICK 109:16
Wards in J.   DICK 109:18
jaw j.-jaw is always better   CHUR 92:4
jawbone with the j. of an ass   BIBL 35:9
jaws Into the j. of Death   TENN 310:17
j. of power   ADAM 1:21
jazz J. music is to be played   MORT 229:8
jealous am a j. God   BIBL 34:13
As thou Art j., Lord   DONN 113:23
to the j.   SHAK 284:24
jealousy Anger and j.   ELIO 121:11
beware, my lord, of j.   SHAK 284:21
J. a human face   BLAK 56:16

j. is cruel as the grave   BIBL 39:8
J. is feeling alone   BOWE 65:12
To j. nothing is more frighful   SAGA 263:10
Jeanie J. with the light brown hair   FOST 132:7
jeepers J. Creepers   MERC 216:22
Jehovah O thou great J.   WILL 336:6
Jehu J., the son of Nimshi   BIBL 36:28
Jekyll Dr J. and Mr Hyde   STEV 303:18
Jellicoe J. was the only man on either side   CHUR 92:12
jellies With j. soother   KEAT 181:8
jelly Out, vile j.   SHAK 277:29
je-ne-sais-quoi J. young man   GILB 140:26
Jenny J. kissed me   HUNT 167:4
jerks bring me up by j.   DICK 110:14
Jerusalem holy city, new J.   BIBL 52:24
J. the golden   NEAL 232:2
Next year in J.   HAGG 149:1
peace of J.   BOOK 63:15
Till we have built J.   BLAK 55:27
waste places of J.   BIBL 40:15
jessamine j. faint   SHEL 293:23
pale j.   MILT 220:17
Jesse stem of J.   BIBL 39:21
jest fellow of infinite j.   SHAK 273:11
good j. for ever   SHAK 273:30
Life is a j.   GARR 136:9
poison in j.   SHAK 272:14
jests He j. at scars   SHAK 286:18
Jesu J., good above all other   DEAR 107:7
J., lover of my soul   WESL 332:1
J., the very thought   CASW 85:10
Jesus At the name of J.   BIBL 50:24
At the name of J.   NOEL 234:18
come, Lord J.   BIBL 52:28
cross of J.   BARI 25:5
J. Christ   BIBL 51:19
J. Christ, her Lord   STON 304:11
J. Christ his only Son   BOOK 58:16
J. loves you more   SIMO 295:25
J. shall reign   WATT 329:12
j. told him; he wouldn't   CUMM 104:16
J. wants me for a sunbeam   TALB 308:23
J. wept   BIBL 48:1
J.! with all thy faults   BUTL 77:14
O J., I have promised   BODE 57:4
power of J.' Name   PERR 244:4
stand up for J.   DUFF 117:23
sweet the name of J.   NEWT 233:19
this J. will not do   BLAK 55:17
When J. came to Birmingham   STUD 305:9
jeunesse *Si j. savait*   ESTI 125:4
Jew especially a J.   MALA 210:3
for Englishman or J.   BLAK 55:17
Just J.-*ish*   MILL 218:18
saved one J. from Auschwitz   AUDE 18:24
jewel j. in the crown   GRAY 146:9
j. of the just   VAUG 323:3
Wears out a precious j.   SHAK 269:14
jewellery just rattle your j.   LENN 197:9
Jewish founded the J. state   HERZ 158:13
J. man with parents alive   ROTH 261:5
murderers of J. children   WIES 334:14
my J. gabardine   SHAK 282:7
national home for the J. people   BALF 23:14
total solution of J. question   GOER 142:15
Jews born King of the J.   BIBL 42:2
But spurn the J.   BROW 68:19
choose The J.   EWER 125:14
conversion of the J.   MARV 213:20
J. require a sign   BIBL 49:22
J. which believed not   BIBL 48:32
last J. to die   MEIR 216:2
unto the J. a stumbling-block   BIBL 49:23

When Hitler attacked the J.	NIEM 234:5
jingo by j. if we do	HUNT 166:24
jo John Anderson my j.	BURN 75:14
Joan J. as my Lady	HERR 158:4
job do his j. when he doesn't feel	AGAT 3:2
finish the j.	CHUR 91:18
I am as poor as J.	SHAK 274:15
j. working-class parents	ABBO 1:1
neighbour loses his j.	TRUM 320:9
patience of J.	BIBL 51:23
read the book of J.	WOOL 339:10
jog as a man *might j. on with*	DURH 118:14
j. on the foot-path	SHAK 289:8
jogging alternative to j.	FITT 128:10
John christen him J.	KEAT 183:15
D'ye ken J. Peel	GRAV 146:3
J. Anderson my jo	BURN 75:14
J. Bull's other island	SHAW 290:29
Old J. of Gaunt	SHAK 285:6
Johnny J.-head-in-air	PUDN 252:2
J., I hardly knew ye	BALL 23:19
Little J. Head-In-Air	HOFF 160:14
joie *j. venait toujours après la peine*	APOL 13:11
joined God hath j. together	BIBL 44:18
j. together in holy Matrimony	BOOK 60:13
whom God hath j.	BOOK 60:20
joint time is out of j.	SHAK 271:24
joke every j. a custard pie	ORWE 237:20
jokes civil servant doesn't make j.	IONE 169:7
difference of taste in j.	ELIO 121:4
Forgive, O Lord, my little j.	FROS 134:5
jolly J. boating weather	CORY 100:13
Jonathan Saul and J.	BIBL 35:28
jonquil j. o'ercomes the feeble brain	WINC 337:10
Jonson Ben J. his best piece	JONS 178:1
J.'s learnèd sock	MILT 220:7
learn'd J.	DRAY 116:7
Josephine Not tonight, J.	NAPO 231:11
journal page of my J.	BOSW 64:21
page of your J.	HUGH 166:13
journalism J. largely consists	CHES 90:8
journalist thank God! the British j.	WOLF 338:13
journalistic j. activity	TOLS 318:17
journalists j. have constructed	LICH 198:24
journey day's j. take the whole day	ROSS 260:14
Here is my j.'s end	SHAK 285:3
I woll this j. be his	EDWA 120:2
j. towards oblivion	LAWR 194:20
long day's j.	O'NE 236:12
more of a J.	CLAU 93:21
now begin the j.	REAG 255:4
prepare for a j.	MANS 211:8
such a long J.	ELIO 122:7
journeying sat the j. boy	HARD 152:1
journeys J. end in lovers meeting	SHAK 288:12
Jove from J. the lightning	MANI 211:5
joy bed Of crimson j.	BLAK 56:13
binds to himself a j.	BLAK 56:2
Break forth into j.	BIBL 40:15
from too much j.	GRAV 146:5
good tidings of great j.	BIBL 46:4
J. always came after pain	APOL 13:11
j. and glory	ABEL 1:2
j. as it flies	BLAK 56:2
J., beautiful radiance	SCHI 265:11
j. cometh in the morning	BOOK 61:11
j. for ever	KEAT 181:2
J. is ever on the wing	MILT 222:31
J. of heav'n	WESL 332:2
j. of the worm	SHAK 269:5
J. shall be in heaven	BIBL 46:31
J., whose hand	KEAT 182:8
Labour without j. is base	RUSK 262:17
let j. be unconfined	BYRO 77:26
Lord of all J.	STRU 305:8
reap in j.	BOOK 63:17
shock of your j.	HUGH 166:13
Surprised by j.	WORD 341:12
Where there is sadness, j.	FRAN 133:3
joyful be j. in the Lord	BOOK 62:22
joys All my j. to this are folly	BURT 76:9
lasting j. the man attend	WHUR 334:9
vain deluding j.	MILT 219:20
jubilate *J. Deo, omnis terra*	BIBL 52:31
Judah J.'s seer	MANT 211:10
Judaism J. knows nothing of	MEND 216:16
Judas boyhood of J.	Æ 2:22
Damned below J.	COWP 101:20
J. who writes the biography	WILD 335:4
that of J.	STAL 301:14
judge after a time they j. them	WILD 335:13
Before you j. me	JACK 169:19
decided by the J.	JOHN 174:9
J. none blessed	BIBL 41:25
J. not	BIBL 43:2
j. thou my cause	BIBL 40:29
Justly to j.	BROO 67:18
judged if j. by himself	JUVE 180:5
judgement Daniel come to j.	SHAK 282:23
day of j.	BOOK 59:7
fit to sit in j.	WILS 337:4
j. of his peers	MAGN 209:11
j. will probably	MANS 211:9
leaves of the J. Book unfold	TAYL 309:22
not give his j. rashly	ADDI 2:12
owes you his j.	BURK 74:17
people's j.	DRYD 116:21
world's j.	SCHI 265:11
judgements j. of the Lord	BOOK 61:4
judges hundred j. have declared it	QUIL 253:7
independence of j.	DENN 108:17
J. must follow their oaths	ZOBE 345:2
j. of fact	PULT 252:6
j. soon the sentence sign	POPE 249:5
Judy J. O'Grady	KIPL 187:24
jug j., jug, jug	LYLY 204:23
'J. Jug' to dirty ears	ELIO 122:23
Julia in silks my J. goes	HERR 158:10
my J.'s dainty leg	HERR 158:5
my J.'s lips do smile	HERR 158:2
July Born on the fourth of J.	COHA 95:14
on the Fourth of J.	HAMM 150:26
winter—ending in J.	BYRO 79:6
Jumblies where the J. live	LEAR 195:11
jumpers Angels in j.	LEWI 198:21
June J. is bustin' out	HAMM 150:19
meetings made December J.	TENN 311:27
newly sprung in J.	BURN 75:21
When J. is past	CARE 82:7
Jungfrau looking like the J.	CHAN 87:10
jungle city is not a concrete j.	MORR 228:13
J. will think	KIPL 188:19
Law of the J.	KIPL 188:28
juniper under a j.-tree	ELIO 121:16
Juno J.'s never-forgetting anger	VIRG 324:9
Jupiter J. from on high laughs	OVID 238:11
jurisdiction j. in this Realm	BOOK 64:5
jury j.-men may dine	POPE 249:5
Trial by j. itself	DENM 108:16
just actions of the j.	SHIR 294:28
all j. works	BOOK 58:23
faithful and j. to me	SHAK 276:17
God is j.	JEFF 171:18
gods are j.	SHAK 278:10
hath his quarrel j.	SHAK 275:15
jewel of the j.	VAUG 323:3

just (*cont.*)

J. are the ways of God	MILT 223:4
J. as I am	ELLI 123:21
j. cause reaches its flood-tide	CATT 85:17
may not be a j. peace	IZET 169:15
ninety and nine j. persons	BIBL 46:31
on the J. and on the unjust	BIBL 42:20
rain, it raineth on the j.	BOWE 65:15
support to the J. One	ZORO 345:12
Thou art indeed j., Lord	HOPK 163:6
justest wisest and j.	PLAT 246:1
justice call for j.	MORE 227:25
Die he or j. must	MILT 221:26
friendship than of j.	THOM 315:24
in the dirt lay j.	HEAN 154:13
J. denied	MILL 218:9
J. is in one scale	JEFF 171:16
j. is open to all	MATH 215:5
j. makes democracy possible	NIEB 234:4
j. of my quarrel	ANON 7:18
j. or injustice	JOHN 174:9
J. should not only be done	HEWA 158:17
J., though she's painted blind	BUTL 77:9
'J.' was done	HARD 151:18
J. with mercy	MILT 222:11
Let j. be done	FERD 126:21
Let j. be done	WATS 329:2
liberty plucks j.	SHAK 281:27
loved j.	GREG 147:8
moderation in the pursuit of j.	GOLD 144:6
Poetic J.	POPE 246:18
Revenge is a kind of wild j.	BACO 21:23
right or j.	MAGN 209:12
think j. requires	MANS 211:9
Though j. be thy plea	SHAK 282:21
justifiable j. act of war	BELL 28:3
j. to men	MILT 223:4
justified confessions of a j. sinner	HOGG 161:1
justifies end j. the means	BUSE 76:19
justify j. God's ways	HOUS 165:10
j. the ways of God	MILT 221:2
justitia Fiat j.	FERD 126:21
justly do j.	BIBL 41:17
juvenes *Gaudeamus igitur, J. dum sumus*	ANON 12:13

K

K wear the Five Ks	SIKH 295:20
Kaiser put the kibosh on the K.	ELLE 123:18
Kansas corny as K. in August	HAMM 150:26
K. had better stop raising corn	LEAS 195:22
Kate Kiss me K.	SHAK 286:37
Kathleen Mavourneen K.! the grey dawn	CRAW 103:5
keener edged tool that grows k.	IRVI 169:10
with his k. eye	MARV 213:18
keep honour, and k. her	BOOK 60:17
If you can k. your head	KIPL 187:20
k. the bridge with me	MACA 206:8
some day it'll k. you	WEST 332:11
keeper my brother's k.	BIBL 33:14
keeps gave it us for k.	AYRE 20:12
Kelly K. from the Isle of Man	MURP 230:8
ken D'ye k. John Peel	GRAV 146:3
Kennedy you're no Jack K.	BENT 30:10
kennst *K. du das Land*	GOET 142:25
Kensal Green Paradise by way of K.	CHES 89:26
Kent everybody knows K.	DICK 111:3
kept k. the faith	BIBL 51:13
kersey honest k. noes	SHAK 278:21
kettle speech is like a cracked k.	FLAU 129:17
Kew Go down to K.	NOYE 235:4

his Highness' dog at K.	POPE 247:4
key possession of the k.	PAIN 239:7
Turn the k.	KEAT 182:20
With this k. Shakespeare	WORD 341:2
keys half that's got my k.	GRAH 145:7
keystone k. which closeth	STRA 305:3
Khatmandu to the north of K.	HAYE 154:1
kibosh put the k. on the Kaiser	ELLE 123:18
kick get no k. from champagne	PORT 249:17
great k. at misery	LAWR 194:23
k. against the pricks	BIBL 48:27
k. me downstairs	BICK 53:15
k. to come to the top	KEAT 183:9
kicked k. up stairs	HALI 150:7
no body to be k.	THUR 318:2
kid comeback k.	CLIN 94:16
lie down with the k.	BIBL 39:22
kiddies k. have crumpled the serviettes	BETJ 31:21
kidding k., Mister Hitler	PERR 244:5
kids just a couple of k.	HOLI 161:5
kill get out and k. something	LEAC 195:5
in every war they k. you in a new way	ROGE 259:7
k. all the lawyers	SHAK 275:16
k. a mockingbird	LEE 196:9
k. animals and stick in stamps	NICO 234:3
k. a wife with kindness	SHAK 286:38
K. millions of men	ROST 261:3
k. the patient	BACO 21:11
k. us for their sport	SHAK 277:30
Licensed to k.	ANON 8:7
not to k. anything	JAIN 170:6
or I k. you	CHAM 87:2
Otherwise k. me	MACN 208:20
prepared to k. one another	SHAW 291:6
Thou shalt not k.	BIBL 34:16
Thou shalt not k.	CLOU 95:2
we are going to k. it	POWE 250:21
won't k. me	COLL 97:9
killed don't mind your being k.	KITC 189:7
I am the enemy you k.	OWEN 238:26
If hate k. men	BROW 71:5
I'm k., Sire	BROW 70:15
kissed thee ere I k. thee	SHAK 285:5
killer lover and k. are mingled	DOUG 115:6
killeth letter k.	BIBL 50:9
killing K. no murder	SEXB 268:4
k. time Is only the name	SITW 296:14
medal for k. two men	MATL 215:7
talk of k. time	BOUC 65:4
kills grip that k. it	TAGO 308:21
k. the thing he loves	WILD 335:16
pity k.	BALZ 24:22
suicide k. two people	MILL 218:12
Kiltartan My country is K. Cross	YEAT 343:4
kimonos girls in silk k.	YEAT 343:3
kin little more than k.	SHAK 270:27
makes the whole world k.	SHAK 287:32
kind cruel only to be k.	SHAK 272:27
for my own k.	THOM 316:23
had been k.	JOHN 174:20
if ye be k. towards women	KORA 190:16
K. hearts are more than coronets	TENN 312:1
less than k.	SHAK 270:27
People will always be k.	SASS 265:1
Too k., too kind	NIGH 234:13
kindness generates k.	JOHN 174:14
kill a wife with k.	SHAK 286:38
milk of human k.	SHAK 279:12
on the k. of strangers	WILL 336:9
tak a cup o' k. yet	BURN 75:5
king authority forgets a dying k.	TENN 311:13
authority of a K.	STRA 305:3
born K. of the Jews	BIBL 42:2

Cotton is K.	CHRI 90:20	k. against kingdom	BIBL 44:34
cotton is k.	HUGO 166:17	k. by the sea	POE 246:11
cuts off his k.'s head	SHAW 291:22	k. of God is within you	BIBL 47:5
despised and dying k.	SHEL 293:26	k. of heaven	BIBL 42:14
divinity doth hedge a k.	SHAK 273:4	k. of heaven	BIBL 44:2
duty is the k.'s	SHAK 275:3	k. of heaven is at hand	BIBL 42:5
every inch a k.	SHAK 278:1	k. stretch from shore to shore	WATT 329:12
fight for its K. and Country	GRAH 145:5	mind to me a k. is	DYER 118:20
God bless the K.	BYRO 77:21	my k. for a horse	SHAK 286:11
God for K. Charles	BROW 70:19	of such is the k. of God	BIBL 45:30
God save k. Solomon	BIBL 35:36	Thy k. come	BIBL 42:23
God save our gracious k.	ANON 7:5	voice of the k.	SWIF 306:16
God save the k.	BIBL 35:18	**kingdoms** all the k. of the world	BIBL 42:12
God save the k.	SHAK 285:26	goodly states and k.	KEAT 182:18
great and mighty k.	ROCH 258:10	out of three k.	WHAR 333:1
have served the K.	WOLS 338:26	**kingfish** call me the K.	LONG 201:15
He played the K.	FIEL 127:9	**kingly** k. crop	DAVI 106:13
Honour the k.	BIBL 51:27	**kings** all be as happy as k.	STEV 303:28
K. and country need you	ANON 11:7	bind their k. in chains	BOOK 63:29
K. asked the Queen	MILN 219:2	captains and the k.	KIPL 188:5
k. can do no wrong	BLAC 55:4	Conquering k.	CHAN 87:3
K. David and King Solomon	NAYL 231:22	death of k.	SHAK 285:20
K. enjoys his own again	PARK 241:4	dominion of k. changed	PRIC 251:5
K. in Babylon	HENL 156:10	end of k.	DEFO 107:21
k. is but a man	SHAK 275:1	five K. left	FARO 126:9
k. is truly *parens patriae*	JAME 170:10	keep even k. in awe	D'AV 106:11
k. never dies	BLAC 55:2	last of the k. strangled	MESL 217:12
K., observing with judicious	TRAP 319:5	laws or k.	JOHN 174:3
K. of England's eyes	TYND 321:18	laws or k. can cause	GOLD 143:23
K. of glory	BOOK 61:9	lays his icy hand on k.	SHIR 294:27
K. of glory now	NOEL 234:18	meaner creatures k.	SHAK 286:9
K. of heaven	LYTE 205:6	Of cabbages—and k.	CARR 84:6
k. of intimate delights	COWP 102:4	politeness of k.	LOUI 203:2
K. of love	BAKE 23:4	Right Divine of K.	POPE 246:21
k. of shreds and patches	SHAK 272:25	ruin k.	DRYD 116:14
K. of tremendous majesty	MISS 224:12	sport of k.	SOME 299:1
K. over the Water	ANON 8:5	sport of k.	SURT 306:8
K. refused a lesser sacrifice	MARY 214:12	Vain the ambition of k.	WEBS 330:8
k.'s a bawcock	SHAK 274:36	walk with K.	KIPL 187:21
k.'s daughter o' Noroway	BALL 24:8	War is the trade of k.	DRYD 117:1
K.'s daughter	BOOK 61:24	**Kipling** K. and his views	AUDE 18:5
k. sits in Dunfermline	BALL 24:7	Rudyards cease from k.	STEP 302:15
K.'s life moving peacefully	DAWS 107:3	**kiss** Ae fond k.	BURN 75:2
k.'s name	SHAK 286:10	Fain would I k.	HERR 158:5
K. to Oxford sent	BROW 69:11	k. again with tears	TENN 313:3
k. was much moved	BIBL 35:33	k. but in the cup	JONS 178:4
lay on the k.	SHAK 275:4	k. is still a kiss	HUPF 167:8
leave without the k.	ELIZ 123:17	K. me, Hardy	NELS 232:12
man who would be k.	KIPL 188:25	K. me Kate	SHAK 286:37
Moloch, horrid k.	MILT 221:10	k. my ass in Macy's window	JOHN 173:5
My dead k.	JOYC 178:24	k. of the sun for pardon	GURN 148:13
my life to make you K.	CHAR 87:22	k. on the hand	ROBI 257:20
neck of the last k.	DIDE 111:20	let us k. and part	DRAY 116:5
No bishop, no K.	JAME 170:9	O! a k. Long as my exile	SHAK 270:14
no k. can govern	ROCH 258:7	sweetly did me k.	WYAT 342:2
not offended the k.	MORE 228:4	wanting to k. me	MACD 207:7
once and future K.	MALO 210:12	Wouldst k. me pretty	HART 152:21
Ozymandias, k. of kings	SHEL 293:12	**kissed** k. each other	BOOK 62:13
passing brave to be a k.	MARL 212:15	k. his sad Andromache	CORN 100:7
rightwise K.	MALO 210:9	k. thee ere I killed thee	SHAK 285:5
Ruin seize thee, ruthless K.	GRAY 146:11	**kisses** fine romance with no k.	FIEL 127:17
sang a k. out of three kingdoms	WHAR 333:1	Give me a thousand k.	CATU 85:20
smote the k. of Israel	BIBL 36:18	more than k.	DONN 114:16
stomach of a k.	ELIZ 123:6	remembered k.	TENN 313:8
thy k. is a child	BIBL 38:29	**kissing** I wasn't k. her	MARX 214:1
To be a Pirate K.	GILB 141:4	K. don't last	MERE 217:1
What must the k. do	SHAK 285:22	k. had to stop	BROW 71:10
With a k.'s son	SURR 306:6	k. your hand	LOOS 202:15
your K. and your Country	RUBE 261:19	like k. God	BRUC 71:14
zeal I served my k.	SHAK 275:26	wonder who's k. her	ADAM 1:12
kingdom comest into thy k.	BIBL 47:12	**kit** old k.-bag	ANON 10:19
found a k.	MILT 222:27	**kitchen** get out of the k.	TRUM 320:6
into the k. of heaven	BIBL 44:13	send me to eat in the k.	HUGH 166:8

kleine eine k. Pause — FERR 127:4
knave k. is not punished — HALI 150:5
makes an honest man a k. — DEFO 107:15
knaves calls the k., Jacks — DICK 110:13
knee blude to the k. — BALL 24:12
Every k. shall bow — NOEL 234:18
every k. should bow — BIBL 50:24
knees body between your k. — CORY 100:13
creeps rustling to her k. — KEAT 181:5
live on your k. — IBAR 168:7
knell it is a k. — SHAK 280:6
k. of parting day — GRAY 146:13
knew If you looked away, you k. — SERE 267:24
Johnny, I hardly k. ye — BALL 23:19
k. it best — BACO 21:5
world k. him not — BIBL 47:20
knife cannibal uses k. and fork — LEC 196:4
my oyster k. — HURS 167:9
smyler with the k. — CHAU 88:15
War to the k. — PALA 239:19
knight as the armèd k. — ASKE 16:16
Fearless, blameless k. — ANON 11:11
gentle k. was pricking — SPEN 300:13
k. at arms — KEAT 181:17
k. like the young Lochinvar — SCOT 266:17
K. of the Doleful Countenance — CERV 86:13
new-slain k. — BALL 24:13
that was your k. — PEEL 243:2
verray, parfit gentil k. — CHAU 88:6
knighthoods MBEs and your k. — KEAT 181:1
knits Sleep that k. up — SHAK 280:9
knitter beautiful little k. — SITW 296:13
knives night of the long k. — HITL 159:17
knock k., and it shall be opened — BIBL 43:5
K. as you please — POPE 247:3
K. at a star — HERR 158:1
k. at the door — LAMB 192:4
k., breathe, shine — DONN 113:21
stand at the door, and k. — BIBL 52:7
when you k. — COWP 101:19
knocked ruin that Cromwell k. about — BEDF 27:6
we k. the bastard off — HILL 159:6
what they k. down — FENT 126:19
knocking k. at Preferment's door — ARNO 15:15
K. on the moonlit door — DE L 108:7
knocks k. you down with the butt — GOLD 144:5
knot crowned k. of fire — ELIO 121:30
political k. — BIER 53:19
knotted Sat and k. — SEDL 267:4
know all I k. is what I read — ROGE 259:6
all ye need to k. — KEAT 182:5
do not pretend to k. — DARR 106:5
don't k. what I'm doing — BRAU 66:7
hate any one that we k. — HAZL 154:5
He must k. sumpin' — HAMM 150:22
How do they k. — PARK 241:1
I k. nothing — SOCR 298:21
k. better what is good for people — JAY 171:8
k. not what they do — BIBL 47:11
k. that I am God — BOOK 61:26
k. that my redeemer liveth — BIBL 37:9
K. then thyself — POPE 248:15
k. the world — YOUN 344:18
K. what I mean, Harry — MILT 222:5
k. what I think — BRUN 71:21
k. what we are talking about — WALL 327:4
K. you the land — RUSS 262:22
let me k. mine end — GOET 142:25
men naturally desire to k. — BOOK 61:19
no one so k. — AUCT 17:21
Tell me what you k. — ANON 6:9
things they didn't k. — EMER 124:16
— POUN 250:8

those who do not wish to k. — RALE 254:9
thought so once; but now I k. it — GARR 136:9
To k. this only — MILT 222:29
What do I k. — MONT 226:13
what should they k. of England — KIPL 187:14
You k. more than you think — SPOC 300:28
you'll never k. — ARMS 14:26
knowed all that there is to be k. — GRAH 145:12
knoweth k. not God — BIBL 51:33
knowing Bewrapt past k. — HARD 152:1
lust of k. — FLEC 129:23
knowledge After such k., what forgiveness — ELIO 122:2
all k. to be my province — BACO 22:1
All our k. is — POPE 248:21
dotage of k. — JACK 169:17
Friendship from k. — BUSS 76:24
increaseth k. — BIBL 38:15
k. in the making — MILT 223:20
k. is dangerous — HUXL 167:22
k. itself is power — BACO 22:2
k. of a lifetime — WHIS 333:5
k. of good and evil — BIBL 32:25
k. of human nature — AUST 19:19
k. of nature — HOLB 161:2
k. which they cannot lose — OPPE 236:9
Language and k. — SULL 305:14
make k. available — BLAC 54:21
never better than k. — FERM 127:3
no k. but I know it — BEEC 27:10
No man's k. — LOCK 201:4
organized k. — SPEN 299:26
price for k. — TICK 318:4
province of k. to speak — HOLM 161:9
tree of diabolical k. — SHER 294:12
tree of the k. — BIBL 33:1
known Have ye not k. — BIBL 40:10
k. too late — SHAK 286:17
k. unto God — ANON 9:21
till I am k. — JOHN 174:20
knows Every schoolboy k. — MACA 205:17
He k. nothing — SHAW 291:5
if you k. of a better 'ole — BAIR 23:3
k. what he fights for — CROM 103:16
knuckle k.-end of England — SMIT 298:7
koompartoo make a K. — BURN 76:2
Koran K. was sent down — KORA 190:7
Kruger killing K. with your mouth — KIPL 187:5
Kubla In Xanadu did K. Khan — COLE 96:3
Kurtz Mistah K.—he dead — CONR 99:8
Kyrie K. eleison — MISS 223:27

L

label without a rag of a l. — HUXL 167:20
labour all ye that l. — BIBL 43:31
brow of l. — BRYA 71:22
done to the L. Party — TAWN 309:17
l. against our own cure — BROW 69:8
l. and not to ask — IGNA 168:17
l. of love — BIBL 51:4
l. of your life — MONT 226:8
l. we delight in — SHAK 280:15
their l. is but lost — RUSK 262:17
youth of l. — BOOK 63:18
labourer l. is worthy of his hire — GOLD 143:8
labouring sleep of a l. man — BIBL 46:14
women l. of child — BIBL 38:20
labours Children sweeten l. — BACO 21:20
no l. tire — JOHN 174:5
laburnums L., dropping-wells of fire — TENN 311:23

labyrinthical perplexed, l. soul DONN 114:22
labyrinthine down the l. ways THOM 316:26
lace Nottingham l. of the curtains BETJ 31:15
lacessit Nemo me impune l. ANON 12:14
lack can I l. nothing BOOK 61:6
lacked questioning, If I l. any thing HERB 157:16
lacking nothing is l. LEON 197:20
lacrimae Hinc illae l. TERE 314:6
Sunt l. rerum VIRG 324:12
lad l. that is gone STEV 304:2
ladder behold a l. BIBL 33:30
traffic of Jacob's l. THOM 317:3
Wiv a l. BATE 26:4
ladders Holy One makes l. MIDR 217:23
where all the l. start YEAT 342:14
laden heavy l. BIBL 43:31
ladies made the carlines l. JAME 170:12
remember the l. ADAM 1:9
lady called her his l. fair KIPL 188:13
I met a l. KEAT 181:19
Joan as my L. HERR 158:4
l. doth protest too much SHAK 272:13
l. fair BALL 24:13
l. of a 'certain age' BYRO 79:1
l. of Christ's College AUBR 17:14
L. of Shalott TENN 312:4
L. of Spain REAV 255:5
l.'s in the case GAY 137:6
l.'s not for burning FRY 134:18
l.'s not for turning THAT 315:6
l. sweet and kind ANON 10:6
L. with a Lamp LONG 202:2
little l. comes by GAY 137:13
lovely l., garmented SHEL 294:4
My L. Bountiful FARQ 126:10
Our L. of Pain SWIN 307:22
talk like a l. SHAW 291:29
to be called First L. ONAS 236:9
why the l. is a tramp HART 152:19
Lafayette L., nous voilà STAN 301:17
laid where they have l. him BIBL 48:17
lain There hath he l. for ages TENN 311:35
laissez-faire L. ARGE 14:5
laissez-faire L. ANON 11:16
laity conspiracies against the l. SHAW 290:26
lake l. water lapping YEAT 343:7
slips into the l. of the lake TENN 313:16
lama Eli, Eli, l. sabachthani BIBL 45:21
lamb Behold the L. of God BIBL 47:23
he who made the L. BLAK 56:15
holy L. of God BLAK 55:27
l. to the slaughter BIBL 40:18
Little L. who made thee BLAK 56:8
Mary had a little l. HALE 149:17
one little ewe l. BIBL 35:30
white in the blood of the L. BIBL 52:10
wolf shall dwell with the l. BIBL 39:22
lambs gather the l. BIBL 40:9
lame l. dogs over stiles KING 186:18
Science without religion is l. EINS 120:11
laments forest l. CHUR 91:2
lamp Lady with a L. LONG 202:2
l. is shattered SHEL 293:2
Slaves of the L. ARNO 15:3
too strong of the l. STER 302:21
unlit l. BROW 71:8
lampada vitai l. LUCR 204:14
lamp post leaning on a l. GAY 137:13
lamp posts drunken man uses l. LANG 192:25
lamprey surfeit by eating of a l. FABY 125:17
lamps l. are going out all over Europe GREY 147:13
old l. for new ARAB 13:15
Lancaster time-honoured L. SHAK 285:6

land by sea as by l. GILB 139:18
Ceres re-assume the l. POPE 247:21
empire of the l. RICH 257:4
fat of the l. BIBL 33:36
if by l., one REVE 256:2
Ill fares the l. GOLD 143:7
l. flowing with milk BIBL 34:2
l. God gave to Cain CART 85:1
l. of counterpane STEV 303:29
L. of Hope and Glory BENS 29:27
l. of lost content HOUS 165:7
l. of my fathers JAME 170:14
l. of my fathers THOM 316:11
l. of pure delight WATT 329:11
l. of the free KEY 185:6
L. that I love BERL 30:17
l. was ours before FROS 134:9
L. where my fathers died SMIT 297:23
lane to the l. of the dead AUDE 17:25
more precious than l. SADA 263:9
no l. unhabitable THOR 317:23
one if by l. LONG 202:5
piece of l. HORA 164:21
ready by water as by l. ELST 124:4
seen the promised l. KING 186:12
splendid and a happy l. GOLD 143:13
spy out the l. BIBL 34:24
There's the l., or cherry-isle HERR 158:2
This l. is your land GUTH 148:15
travel by l. or by water BOOK 59:8
Woe to the l. SHAK 286:4
landed l. with an idea BIRT 54:9
landing fight on the l. grounds CHUR 91:15
landlord paid to the l. RICA 256:13
lands take us l. away DICK 111:13
landscape gardening is but l.-painting POPE 249:10
l. of the world YOUN 344:17
Who owns this l. MCCA 206:16
lane l. to the land of the dead AUDE 17:25
lang For auld l. syne BURN 75:5
How l., O Lord BULL 72:10
language any l. you choose GILB 140:5
best chosen l. AUST 19:19
clear and beautiful l. EMPS 124:22
cool web of l. GRAV 146:5
divided by a common l. SHAW 292:6
entrance into the l. BACO 21:29
everything else in our l. MACA 205:22
except, of course, l. WILD 334:21
In l., the ignorant DUPP 118:13
In such lovely l. LAWR 194:22
L. grows out of life SULL 305:14
l. in her eye SHAK 287:33
L. is only the instrument JOHN 173:11
L. is the dress JOHN 173:19
l. of the heart POPE 247:12
l. of the unheard KING 186:13
L. tethers us LIVE 200:9
L. was not powerful enough DICK 110:24
laogai in every l. WU 341:28
laughter in a l. GOLD 143:4
Life is a foreign l. MORL 228:8
limits of my l. WITT 337:23
Lovely enchanting l. HERB 157:14
mobilized the English l. MURR 230:12
mystery of l. KELL 183:24
no l. but a cry TENN 311:19
not to be his l. STAË 301:11
obscurity of a learned l. GIBB 139:9
Political l. . . . . is designed ORWE 237:19
rich and delicate l. WAUG 329:23
Sithe off oure l. LYDG 204:21
world understands my l. HAYD 153:18

language (*cont.*)
You taught me l. — SHAK 287:5
languages between and across l. — CRAW 103:6
l. are the pedigree — JOHN 174:11
None of your live l. — DICK 110:10
silent in seven l. — BAGE 22:15
languors lilies and l. — SWIN 307:21
lanterns show two l. — REVE 256:2
laogai want to see l. ended — WU 341:28
lap in the l. of the gods — HOME 161:19
strew the green l. — SHAK 285:29
lapdogs l. breathe their last — POPE 249:7
lapidary In l. inscriptions — JOHN 175:17
lapping lake water l. — YEAT 343:7
lards l. the lean earth — SHAK 273:31
large as l. as life — CARR 84:13
lark bisy l., messager of day — CHAU 88:14
l. ascending — MERE 217:2
l. at break of day — SHAK 289:26
l. at heaven's gate sings — SHAK 270:18
l. becomes a sightless song — TENN 311:33
l. now leaves his wat'ry nest — D'AV 106:12
l.'s on the wing — BROW 70:27
sweet l. sing — FERG 127:1
larks Four L. and a Wren — LEAR 195:8
larkspur l. listens — TENN 312:23
Lars Porsena L. of Clusium — MACA 206:6
lasciate L. OGNI SPERANZA — DANT 105:17
lascivious l. gloating — STOP 304:12
lash rum, sodomy, prayers, and the l. — CHUR 92:3
lass every l. a queen — KING 186:22
It came with a l. — JAME 170:13
lies A l. unparalleled — SHAK 269:9
lover and his l. — SHAK 270:4
lassie I love a l. — LAUD 194:7
love she's but a l. — BURN 75:19
last give unto this l. — BIBL 44:24
l. and best — MILT 222:19
l. article of my creed — GAND 135:18
l. best gift — MILT 222:8
l. breath of Julius Caesar — JEAN 171:9
l. day of an era past — YELT 344:5
l. gasp — BIBL 42:1
l. gentleman in Europe — LEVE 198:5
l. great Englishman — TENN 312:28
l. my time — CARL 82:13
l. person who has sat on him — HAIG 149:6
l. red leaf — TENN 311:17
l. rose of summer — MOOR 227:18
l. shall be first — BIBL 44:22
L.-supper-carved-on-a-peach-stone — LANC 192:20
l. taste of sweets — SHAK 285:11
l. thing I shall do — PALM 240:9
l. time I saw Paris — HAMM 150:20
Look thy l. on all things lovely — DE L 108:6
Nice guys finish l. — DURO 118:16
this day as if thy l. — KEN 184:2
We were the l. romantics — YEAT 342:15
world's l. night — DONN 113:22
latchet shoe's l. — BIBL 47:22
late l. into the night — BYRO 79:16
not too l. to-morrow — ARMS 14:25
offering even that too l. — NEVI 232:16
rather l. for me — LARK 193:10
This is a l. parrot — MONT 226:25
Too l. came I — AUGU 19:2
later l. it would be bitter — KIER 185:21
l. than you think — SERV 267:26
latet L. *anguis in herba* — VIRG 325:9
Latin half Greek, half L. — SCOT 266:2
he speaks L. — SHAK 275:18
L., ne of Greek — SPEN 300:22
No more L. — ANON 9:1

small L. — JONS 178:7
latrine mouth had been used as a l. — AMIS 4:19
latter former and the l. — BOOK 59:11
laudant L. *illa* — MART 213:8
laudate l. *et superexaltate eum* — BIBL 53:6
laudator l. *temporis acti* — HORA 163:17
laugh do we not l. — SHAK 282:13
L., and the world laughs — WILC 334:20
l. at them — AUST 20:1
L. no man to scorn — BIBL 41:24
L. where we must — POPE 248:8
loud l. that spoke — GOLD 143:9
more unbecoming than to l. — CONG 98:9
sillier than a silly l. — CATU 86:1
time to l. — BIBL 38:17
laughable very l. things — JOHN 175:5
laughed honest man is l. at — HALI 150:5
when he l. — AUDE 18:1
laughing l. devil — BYRO 78:11
l. queen — HUNT 167:3
laughs l. to see the green man — HOFF 160:17
l. with a harvest — JERR 172:9
laughter faculty of l. — ADDI 2:14
l. and the love — BELL 29:1
l. for a month — SHAK 273:30
L. hath only a scornful — SIDN 295:15
l. in a language — GOLD 143:4
l. is pleasant — PEAC 242:15
l. of a fool — BIBL 38:21
L. . . . the most civilized music — USTI 322:2
Laugh thy girlish l. — WATS 329:3
nothing more frightful than l. — SAGA 263:10
Our sincerest l. — SHEL 293:32
present l. — SHAK 288:13
launched l. a thousand ships — MARL 212:6
laureate became Poet L. — TENN 314:3
laurel Caesar's l. crown — BLAK 55:14
laurels l. all are cut — ANON 11:18
Once more, O ye l. — MILT 220:9
lauriers l. *sont coupés* — ANON 11:18
lava in its l. I still find — WOOL 339:11
lave Let the l. go by me — STEV 304:3
law according to the l. — BIBL 41:9
army of unalterable l. — MERE 217:5
breaks the l. — PLAT 245:24
built with stones of L. — BLAK 55:24
but by the l. — BIBL 49:14
chief l. — CICE 92:22
Custom, that unwritten l. — D'AV 106:11
end of l. is — LOCK 201:7
fear of the l. — JOYC 178:20
fence around the L. — TALM 309:4
from Jargon born to rescue L. — LLOY 200:15
had people not defied the l. — SCAR 265:9
Ignorance of the l. — SELD 267:11
it is of no force in l. — COKE 95:16
judgement of the l. — JACK 169:20
keep this l. — BOOK 59:20
keystone of the rule of l. — DENN 108:17
l. and the prophets — BIBL 43:7
l. doth give it — SHAK 282:24
l. floats in a sea of ethics — WARR 328:16
l. is a ass — DICK 110:28
L. is a bottomless pit — ARBU 13:21
L. is boldly — BURR 76:3
l. is contrary to liberty — BENT 30:5
l. is established — SIDN 295:6
l. is such an ass — CHAP 87:16
L. is the true embodiment — GILB 140:1
l. is to be to restraint — MILT 223:16
L. of the Jungle — KIPL 188:28
l. of the Yukon — SERV 268:1
L. to our selves — MILT 222:17

l. unto themselves — BIBL 49:6
lesser breeds without the L. — KIPL 188:7
majestic equality of the l. — FRAN 132:18
moral l. within me — KANT 180:12
Necessity has no l. — PUBL 252:1
No brilliance is needed in the l. — MORT 229:3
Nor l., nor duty — YEAT 343:5
not a l. at all — ROBE 257:17
old father antick, the l. — SHAK 273:26
purlieus of the L. — ETHE 125:5
purlieus of the l. — TENN 311:24
this is the royal l. — CORO 100:12
where no l. is — BIBL 49:8
whole of the L. — CROW 104:10
windward of the l. — CHUR 90:24
windy side of the l. — SHAK 288:30
Wrest once the l. — SHAK 282:22
lawful L. as eating — SHAK 289:16
their l. occasions — BOOK 63:32
lawn bird-haunted English l. — ARNO 15:9
Get your tanks off my l. — WILS 336:20
on the l. I lie in bed — AUDE 18:13
laws bad or obnoxious l. — GRAN 145:19
breaking of l. — MORE 227:22
care who should make the l. — FLET 130:5
dole Unequal l. — TENN 313:28
dominion of l. — PRIC 251:5
do with the l. — HORS 164:22
government of l. — ADAM 1:19
Government of l. and not of men — FORD 131:4
If l. are needed — KHOM 185:15
L. are like cobwebs — SWIF 306:17
L. are silent — CICE 92:29
L. grind the poor — GOLD 143:22
L., like houses — BURK 74:15
l. or kings — JOHN 174:3
l. or kings can cause — GOLD 143:23
Nature, and Nature's l. — POPE 247:28
neither l. made — JOHN 172:11
not judges of l. — PULT 252:6
part of the l. of England — HALE 149:15
planted thick with l. — BOLT 57:16
prescribed l. to the learned — DUPP 118:13
scientist's l. — QUIN 253:10
sweeps a room as for Thy l. — HERB 157:13
their l. approve — DRYD 116:29
Written l. — ANAC 5:3
lawyer l. has no business — JOHN 174:9
l. with his briefcase — PUZO 252:26
lawyers crowd of l. — WYCH 342:5
kill all the l. — SHAK 275:16
lay I l. me down to sleep — ANON 9:3
l. down his life — BIBL 48:8
l. mee downe — BALL 24:6
L. on, Macduff — SHAK 281:26
L. your sleeping head — AUDE 18:7
layman neither cleric nor l. — BERN 31:6
lays constructing tribal l. — KIPL 187:22
l. it on with a trowel — CONG 98:10
lazy l. leaden-stepping hours — MILT 220:29
lead blind l. the blind — BIBL 44:7
evening l. — CHUR 92:9
L., kindly Light — NEWM 233:7
L. us, Heavenly Father — EDME 119:23
leaden With l. foot — JAGO 170:5
leader fanatic is a great l. — BROU 68:11
I am their l. — LEDR 196:7
leaf And I were like the l. — SWIN 308:5
last red l. — TENN 311:17
yellow l. — SHAK 281:20
league Half a l. onward — TENN 310:15
lean if a man l. — BIBL 36:33
l. and hungry look — SHAK 276:1

l. as much to the contrary — HALI 149:19
l. on one another — BURK 74:15
leap giant l. for mankind — ARMS 15:1
great l. in the dark — VANB 322:9
l. in the dark — HOBB 160:6
l. into the dark — BROW 68:17
methinks it were an easy l. — SHAK 273:28
leaped have I l. over a wall — BIBL 35:34
leaping l. from place to place — HARD 151:24
too broad for l. — HOUS 165:9
learn craft so long to l. — CHAU 88:24
l., and inwardly digest — BOOK 59:13
much desire to l. — MILT 223:20
People must l. to hate — MAND 210:20
while they teach, men l. — SENE 267:22
learned been l. has been forgotten — SKIN 296:20
l. anything from history — HEGE 155:4
obscurity of a l. language — GIBB 139:9
prescribed laws to the l. — DUPP 118:13
learning attain good l. — ASCH 16:10
cry both arts and l. — QUAR 253:6
deep l. little had he — SPEN 300:22
enough of l. to misquote — BYRO 79:8
l. lightly like a flower — TENN 311:34
l. many things — SOLO 298:25
little l. is a dangerous thing — POPE 247:29
loyal body wanted l. — TRAP 319:5
much l. doth make thee mad — BIBL 49:3
Wear your l. — CHES 89:10
will to l. — ASCH 16:11
written for our l. — BOOK 59:13
learnt forgotten nothing and l. nothing — DUMO 118:4
They have l. nothing — TALL 309:2
lease summer's l. — SHAK 289:23
least faithful in that which is l. — BIBL 47:2
l. of these my brethren — BIBL 45:10
leave for ever taking l. — RILK 257:8
Intreat me not to l. thee — BIBL 35:13
l. the outcome — CORN 100:3
l. without the King — ELIZ 123:17
shall a man l. his father — BIBL 33:5
leaven l. leaveneth the whole lump — BIBL 49:25
leaves burning of the l. — BINY 54:5
l. of the tree — BIBL 52:27
l. to a tree — KEAT 183:7
Thick as autumnal l. — MILT 221:9
leaving L. his country — FITZ 128:13
like the l. it — SHAK 279:10
left better to be l. — CONG 98:17
goats on the l. — BIBL 45:8
l. thy first love — BIBL 52:4
let not thy l. hand know — BIBL 42:22
other l. — BIBL 45:3
something l. to treat — MALL 210:7
leg does not resemble a l. — APOL 13:12
here I leave my second l. — HOOD 162:3
my Julia's dainty l. — HERR 158:5
lege Tolle l. — AUGU 19:1
legend before Your l. ever did — JOHN 172:16
before your l. will — JOHN 172:18
true l. — STAL 301:14
Legion My name is L. — BIBL 45:27
legions give me back my l. — AUGU 19:9
legislation possess divine l. — MEND 216:16
legislator l. of mankind — JOHN 173:24
legislators idea of hereditary l. — PAIN 239:12
unacknowledged l. — SHEL 294:6
legs dog's walking on his hinder l. — JOHN 175:1
Four l. good — ORWE 237:4
vast and trunkless l. — SHEL 293:11
legunt sed ista l. — MART 213:8
Leicestershire finest run in L. — PAGE 239:4

leisure absence of l. to reflect	HAVE 153:8
At l. married	CONG 98:15
detest at l.	BYRO 79:5
fill l. intelligently	RUSS 262:20
L. with honour	CICE 93:2
lemon l.-trees bloom	GOET 142:25
lend l. me your ears	SHAK 276:15
lender borrower, nor a l. be	SHAK 271:8
length drags its dreary l.	DICK 109:16
drags its slow l.	POPE 248:4
lente Festina l.	AUGU 19:8
L. currite noctis equi	OVID 238:10
l., lente, currite	MARL 212:7
Léonie Weep not for little L.	GRAH 145:6
leopard l. change his spots	BIBL 40:25
l. does not change	COMP 98:4
l. shall lie down	BIBL 39:22
leopards three white l. sat	ELIO 121:16
leper innocence is like a dumb l.	GREE 147:2
Lesbia Let us live, my L.	CATU 85:19
Lesley bonnie L.	BURN 75:7
less L. is a bore	VENT 323:9
L. than the dust	HOPE 162:20
little l.	BROW 69:25
more and more about l. and less	BUTL 77:3
small Latin, and l. Greek	JONS 178:7
lesser l. breeds	KIPL 188:7
lessons l. to be drawn	ELIZ 123:15
lest L. we forget	KIPL 188:5
let L. my people go	ANON 10:20
L. my people go	BIBL 34:5
L. us with a gladsome mind	MILT 220:8
Lethe go not to L.	KEAT 182:6
letter by speech than by l.	BACO 21:19
l. killeth	BIBL 50:9
made this [l.] longer	PASC 241:14
scarlet l.	HAWT 153:14
thou unnecessary l.	SHAK 277:13
when he wrote a l.	BACO 21:8
letters can't write l.	BISH 54:11
L. for the rich	AUDE 18:11
l. get in the wrong places	MILN 219:6
l., methinks, should be free	OSBO 237:24
l. mingle souls	DONN 114:16
l. to a non-existent	LEWI 198:13
like women's l.	HAZL 154:2
than a man of l.	STER 302:25
letting l. each other go	RILK 257:9
lettuce eating too much l.	POTT 249:25
levee Drove my Chevy to the l.	MCLE 208:1
level l. of provincial existence	ELIO 121:12
Leviathan draw out l.	BIBL 37:16
L., called a commonwealth	HOBB 159:22
L. Hugest of living creatures	MILT 222:12
there is that L.	BOOK 62:25
lewd certain l. fellows	BIBL 48:32
lex suprema est l.	CICE 92:22
lexicographer L. A writer of dictionaries	JOHN 173:13
wake a l.	JOHN 173:12
lexicons We are walking l.	LIVE 200:10
liar answered 'Little L.'	BELL 28:13
best l.	BUTL 77:10
l. should be outlawed	HALI 150:1
proved l.	HAIL 149:8
liars All men are l.	BOOK 63:9
Income Tax made more L.	ROGE 259:4
liberal either a little L.	GILB 140:2
first L. leader	STEE 302:1
is a l. education	STEE 302:3
l. is a conservative who	WOLF 338:19
liberation l. of the human mind	GOLD 143:5
liberties l. are taken in thy name	GEOR 138:12
L. . . . depend on the silence	HOBB 160:4

liberty ardour for l.	PRIC 251:5
be light! said L.	SHEL 292:24
Brightest in dungeons, L.	BYRO 79:15
certainly destroys l.	JOHN 176:10
chosen music, L.	WORD 341:14
conceived in all l.	LINC 199:8
contend for their l.	HALI 150:3
contrary to l.	BENT 30:5
end to a woman's l.	BURN 74:27
extremism in the defence of l.	GOLD 144:6
given l. to man	CURR 105:5
L. and Union	WEBS 330:6
L. cannot be	SUMN 306:4
L. consists in doing	MILL 218:4
L. is liberty, not	BERL 31:1
L. is precious	LENI 197:7
L. is unfinished business	ANON 8:6
L. means responsibility	SHAW 291:15
L. of the press	JUNI 179:17
L., or give me death	HENR 156:22
l. plucks justice	SHAK 281:27
L.'s in every blow	BURN 75:23
L., when it begins to take root	WASH 328:23
life, and l.	JEFF 171:12
life, l.	ANON 10:14
mansion-house of l.	MILT 223:19
O l.! what crimes	ROLA 259:9
pinch the sea of its l.	COTT 100:15
principate and l.	TACI 308:13
so easy as l.	ASTE 17:4
survival and the success of l.	KENN 184:8
Sweet land of l.	SMIT 297:23
tree of l.	JEFF 171:13
wait for l.	MACA 205:14
what cannot be sold—l.	GRAT 146:1
when they cry l.	MILT 223:8
who ever gives, takes l.	DONN 113:23
Liberty-Hall This is L., gentlemen	GOLD 144:2
libraries circulating l.	RUSK 262:14
l. of the Commons	CHAN 87:11
library Alexandria's l. burned	HUGH 166:11
choice of all my l.	SHAK 287:27
circulating l.	SHER 294:12
In his l.	AUST 19:25
l. in every county town	CARL 83:3
l. is thought in cold storage	SAMU 264:3
My l. Was dukedom	SHAK 287:3
public l.	BENN 29:16
public l.	JOHN 173:23
sit in a l.	FITZ 129:7
licence L. they mean	MILT 223:8
l. to print money	THOM 317:15
universal l. to be good	COLE 95:20
license L. my roving hands	DONN 113:18
licensed based upon l. premises	O'BR 235:14
L. to kill	ANON 8:7
licentious l. passages	GIBB 139:9
Licht Mehr L.	GOET 143:1
lick l. it into form	BURT 76:11
lie can't tell a l.	WASH 328:22
definition of a l.	ANON 5:12
Every word she writes is a l.	MCCA 206:21
fain wald l. down	BALL 23:20
fall victim to a big l.	HITL 159:16
home to a l.	POUN 250:9
L. heavy on him, Earth	EVAN 125:11
l. in the soul	JOWE 178:17
l. will go round the world	SPUR 301:6
no worse l.	JAME 171:3
old L.: Dulce et decorum	OWEN 238:24
possible to l. for the truth	ADLE 2:19
sent to l. abroad	WOTT 341:25
when dead, l. as quietly	EDWA 120:6

Whoever would l. usefully	HERV 158:11	L. is a rainbow which	YEVT 344:7
lied because our fathers l.	KIPL 187:10	L. is a top	GREV 147:12
lies Beats all the l.	BLAK 55:13	L. is Colour and Warmth	GREN 147:10
certain, and the rest is l.	FITZ 128:18	L. is doubt	UNAM 321:20
L. are the mortar	WELL 331:16	L. is just a bowl of cherries	BROW 68:15
l. beneath your spell	HOPE 162:19	L. is just one damned	HUBB 166:3
l., damned lies and statistics	DISR 113:8	L. is mostly froth	GORD 144:16
l. it lives on and propagates	FOSD 132:2	L. is real	LONG 201:25
l. of tongue and pen	CHES 89:21	L. is short, the art long	HIPP 159:11
make l. sound truthful	ORWE 237:19	L. is the desert	YOUN 344:19
produces l. like sand	ANON 12:2	L. is the other way round	LODG 201:11
Truth exists, l. are invented	BRAQ 66:5	l. is the thing	SMIT 297:22
life actor's l. for me	WASH 328:24	l. is washed	BARZ 25:22
all human l. is there	JAME 170:17	l., its enemy	ANOU 13:8
all part of l.'s rich pageant	MARS 213:3	l., liberty	ANON 10:14
as large as l.	CARR 84:13	L., like a dome	SHEL 292:20
believe in l.	DU B 117:21	l. of his beast	BIBL 37:27
Book of L. begins	WILD 335:12	l. of men on earth	BEDE 27:5
careful of the single l.	TENN 311:20	l. of the world	DOST 114:24
changing scenes of l.	TATE 309:12	l. protracted	JOHN 174:7
criticism of l.	ARNO 16:2	L. says: she did this	BARN 25:8
crown of l.	BIBL 52:5	l. sentence goes on	CONL 98:21
day-to-day business l. is	LAFO 191:17	L.'s longing for itself	GIBR 139:15
death after l.	SPEN 300:14	L.'s not just being alive	MART 213:9
death, nor l.	BIBL 49:18	L., the Universe and Everything	ADAM 1:11
Does thy l. destroy	BLAK 56:13	L., to be sure, is nothing much	HOUS 165:1
doors to let out l.	FLET 130:7	L. too short to stuff a mushroom	CONR 99:10
doors to let out l.	MASS 215:1	l. was duty	HOOP 162:10
escape the l-sentence	LAWR 194:25	l. went through with death	FORT 131:20
essence of l.	DAWK 107:2	L. without industry is guilt	RUSK 262:8
everlasting l.	BIBL 47:28	l. without theory	DISR 112:20
everlasting l.	BIBL 47:32	L. would be tolerable	LEWI 198:16
evidence of l. after death	SOPE 299:8	L. would be very pleasant	SURT 306:10
Fill me with l. anew	HATC 153:5	L. would ring the bells	GINS 141:13
findeth his l.	BIBL 43:28	live a l. half dead	MILT 223:3
fountain of the water of l.	BIBL 52:26	Mad from l.'s history	HOOD 162:1
gained in the university of l.	BOTT 65:3	matter of l. and death	SHAN 290:19
gave my l. for freedom	EWER 125:13	measured out my l. with coffee spoons	ELIO 122:10
give for his l.	BIBL 36:38	more a way of l.	ANON 9:2
giveth his l. for the sheep	BIBL 47:38	more of a l.	CLAU 93:21
golden tree of actual l.	GOET 142:18	my l. to make you King	CHAR 87:22
great l. if you don't weaken	BUCH 71:24	my whole l., long or short	ELIZ 123:13
had a happy l.	HAZL 154:6	No, no, no l.	SHAK 278:14
hath a l. to live	RAIN 253:22	not a L. at all	GLAD 142:5
honour and l.	FRAN 132:19	not a new form of l.	DYSO 119:11
hour of glorious l.	MORD 227:21	Nothing in his l.	SHAK 279:10
Human l. is everywhere	JOHN 173:25	not the men in my l. that counts	WEST 332:13
in mourning for my l.	CHEK 88:32	now my l. is done	TICH 318:3
in our l. alone	COLE 95:21	of man's l. a thing apart	BYRO 78:18
In the midst of l.	BOOK 60:24	O for a l. of sensations	KEAT 183:5
I've had a wonderful l.	WITT 337:24	one l. to lose	HALE 149:16
last of l.	BROW 71:3	Our end is L.	MACN 208:21
lay down his friends for his l.	THOR 317:24	path of our l.	DANT 105:16
lay down his l.	BIBL 48:8	priceless gift of l.	ROSE 260:9
lay down my l.	CLOU 94:20	Pride of L.	HARD 151:20
leadeth us unto l.	BIBL 43:9	resurrection, and the l.	BIBL 47:39
Lead me from death to l.	KUMA 191:1	shilling l. will give you	AUDE 18:18
l. a glorious cycle of song	PARK 240:14	single page of our l.	SAND 264:5
l., and liberty	JEFF 171:12	slits the thin-spun l.	MILT 220:14
l. and loves of a she-devil	WELD 331:2	spice of l.	COWP 102:1
l. began by flickering out	GONC 144:11	spirit giveth l.	BIBL 50:9
L. begins at forty	PITK 245:8	Style is l.	FLAU 129:19
l. beyond life	MILT 223:14	That l. so short	CHAU 88:24
L. exists in the universe	JEAN 171:10	There is l., but not for you	MORT 229:4
L. for life	BIBL 34:17	third of my l.	ALLE 4:11
l. had been ruined	BROO 68:3	this long disease, my l.	POPE 247:8
l. hath been one chain	CLAR 93:8	tired of l.	JOHN 175:23
l. in the village	LEE 196:11	torch of l.	LUCR 204:14
l. is 6 to 5 against	RUNY 262:3	Touch my l.	TAGO 308:22
L. is a foreign language	MORL 228:8	tree of l.	BIBL 32:25
L. is a horizontal fall	COCT 95:11	upon the thorns of l.	SHEL 293:8
L. is a jest	GARR 136:9	walk in newness of l.	BIBL 49:11
L. is an incurable disease	COWL 101:15	way, the truth, and the l.	BIBL 48:6

life (cont.)
well-written L.   CARL 82:14
What is this l.   DAVI 106:19
Who saw l. steadily   ARNO 15:24
you lived your l.   JOHN 172:15
life-blood l. of a master spirit   MILT 223:14
lifetime in their l.   BELL 29:4
knowledge of a l.   WHIS 333:5
l. of happiness   SHAW 291:7
lift l. up mine eyes   BOOK 63:12
L. up your heads   BOOK 61:9
L. up your hearts   BOOK 60:1
light armour of l.   BOOK 59:12
armour of l.   BIBL 49:21
bear witness of that L.   BOOK 59:1
children of l.   BIBL 47:19
Creature, which was L.   BIBL 46:36
crying for the l.   BACO 22:3
dark is l. enough   TENN 311:19
dim religious l.   FRY 134:17
excess of l.   MILT 219:24
fierce l. which beats   GRAY 146:21
From darkness lead me to L.   TENN 311:3
garmented in l.   UPAN 321:21
gives a lovely l.   SHEL 294:4
how my l. is spent   MILT 218:8
infinite ocean of l.   MILT 223:9
into the world of l.   FOX 132:14
Jeanie with the l. brown hair   VAUG 323:2
know what l. is   FOST 132:7
Lead, kindly L.   JOHN 175:20
Let there be l.   NEWM 233:7
Let there be l.   BIBL 32:21
Let there be l.   MARR 212:26
Let your l. so shine   SHEL 292:24
l. at the end of the tunnel   BIBL 42:17
l. at the end of the tunnel   DICK 111:19
l. fantastic round   LOWE 204:1
l. fantastic toe   MILT 219:11
l. gleams an instant   MILT 220:2
L. (God's eldest daughter)   BECK 27:1
l. has gone out of our lives   FULL 134:27
l. in the darkness of mere being   NEHR 232:4
l. in the dust   JUNG 179:14
l. is come   SHEL 293:2
l. my fire   BIBL 40:20
l. of common day   MORR 228:20
l. of evening, Lissadell   WORD 340:11
L. of Light   YEAT 343:3
l. of the world   BOOK 59:22
l. shineth in darkness   BIBL 42:16
l. that never was   BIBL 47:17
l. to them that sit in darkness   WORD 339:20
l. within his own clear breast   BIBL 46:1
line of festal l.   MILT 219:12
More l.   ARNO 15:17
once we lose this l.   GOET 143:1
particles of l.   JONS 177:22
perpetual l.   BLAK 56:1
progeny of l.   MISS 224:10
pure and endless l.   MILT 222:11
Put out the l.   VAUG 323:4
seen a great l.   SHAK 285:1
speed far faster than l.   BIBL 39:18
sweetness and l.   BULL 72:9
sweetness and l.   ARNO 15:27
Teach l. to counterfeit a gloom   SWIF 306:15
tried to mend the Electric L.   MILT 219:22
Warmth and l.   BELL 28:21
where sweetness and l. failed   GREN 147:10
while the l. fails   FORS 131:12
with a l. behind her   ELIO 121:29
with Thee l.   GILB 141:10
                                          BONH 58:2

lighten L. our darkness   BOOK 59:1
lighter l. than vanity   BUNY 73:2
lighting l. devils   BINC 54:2
lightness unbearable l. of being   KUND 191:5
lightning from Jove the l.   MANI 211:5
Shakespeare by flashes of l.   COLE 96:23
snatched the l.   TURG 320:18
writing history with l.   WILS 337:3
lights all-the-l.-on man   REED 255:11
l. are dim and low   ORRE 236:21
l. around the door   ROSS 260:19
northern l. astream   SMAR 297:3
Turn up the l.   HENR 156:20
watching the tail l.   CRAN 102:20
ligno *Regnavit a l. Deus*   FORT 132:1
like Do what you l.   RABE 253:13
L. cures like   ANON 12:23
l. it the least   CHES 89:9
l. this sort of thing   LINC 199:13
l. what you get   SHAW 291:20
look upon his l. again   SHAK 271:3
man you don't l.   THOM 316:12
none of his friends l. him   WILD 335:21
wha's l. us   ANON 7:10
will much l.   AUST 20:5
liked l. whate'er She looked on   BROW 70:23
likely Not bloody l.   SHAW 291:31
likerous l. mouth   CHAU 88:19
likes does what he l. to do   GILL 141:11
likewise Go, and do thou l.   BIBL 46:17
liking Being alone and l. it   HASK 153:3
Not l. the person   THOM 316:18
lilac Kew in l.-time   NOYE 235:4
l. and the roses   ARAG 13:19
lilacs breeding l.   ELIO 122:20
l. last in the dooryard   WHIT 334:2
Lilian Airy, fairy L.   TENN 312:6
lilies braids of l. knitting   MILT 219:18
feedeth among the l.   BIBL 39:5
l. and languors   SWIN 307:21
l. in armfuls   VIRG 325:1
l. of the field   BIBL 42:27
L. that fester   SHAK 290:1
peacocks and l.   RUSK 262:16
three l. in her hand   ROSS 260:16
lilting l., before dawn of day   ELLI 123:20
lily Elaine, the l. maid   TENN 311:7
folds the l. all her sweetness up   TENN 313:16
l. of Florence   LONG 201:23
l. of the valleys   BIBL 39:3
l. on thy brow   KEAT 181:18
l.-white boys   ANON 7:17
little l.-handed baronet   TENN 313:20
paint the l.   SHAK 277:2
pure as the l.   LAUD 194:7
with a poppy or a l.   GILB 140:25
limb on every airth a l.   MONT 226:22
limbs deck your lower l. in pants   NASH 231:18
l. of a poet   HORA 164:20
lime l.-tree bower my prison   COLE 96:20
limestone l. quarried near   YEAT 343:30
limited whizzed the L.   CRAN 102:20
limits l. of my language   WITT 337:23
limousine All we want is a l.   MACN 208:16
One perfect l.   PARK 240:17
Limpopo grey-green, greasy, L.   KIPL 188:23
Lincoln I am a Ford, not a L.   FORD 131:3
L. County Road or Armageddon   DYLA 119:7
line active l. on a walk   KLEE 189:9
carved not a l.   WOLF 338:12
cut, the style, the l.   LOES 201:13
horizontal l.   WHEW 333:3
l. is length without breadth   EUCL 125:7

l. upon line BIBL 39:29
lives along the l. POPE 248:13
thin red l. RUSS 263:3
linen fair white l. cloth BOOK 59:17
In blanchèd l. KEAT 181:8
Love is like l. FLET 130:12
very fine l. BRUM 71:18
lines I plant l. WALC 326:17
Just say the l. COWA 101:13
l. and colours POUS 250:16
l. are fallen unto me BOOK 61:2
l. like these CALV 80:13
Prose is when all the l. BENT 30:6
six l. written RICH 257:2
lingering alone sit l. here VAUG 323:2
l., with boiling oil GILB 140:17
lingua Pange, l. FORT 131:19
Pange, l. THOM 315:22
lining There's a silver l. FORD 131:9
lion as a roaring l. BIBL 51:30
bold as a l. BIBL 38:7
buttocked like a l. MALO 210:10
calf and the young l. BIBL 39:22
dead l. BIBL 38:25
l. to frighten the wolves MACH 207:17
nation that had l.'s heart CHUR 92:5
lions L. led by donkeys ANON 8:8
l. roaring BOOK 62:24
my darling from the l. BOOK 61:15
lips ever at his l. KEAT 182:8
l. cannot fail BURG 73:9
l. of dying men ARNO 15:21
l. that touch liquor YOUN 344:20
moisten poor Jim's l. FARM 126:8
my Julia's l. do smile HERR 158:2
My l. are sealed BALD 23:11
Read my l. BUSH 76:22
saw their starved l. KEAT 181:21
lipstick bears a l.'s traces MARV 213:24
liquefaction l. of her clothes HERR 158:10
liquid Cats, no less l. TESS 314:17
Thames is l. history BURN 74:28
liquor lips that touch l. YOUN 344:20
l. is quicker NASH 231:15
lisped I l. in numbers POPE 247:7
list I've got a little l. GILB 140:8
List, list, O, l. SHAK 271:15
listen Darkling I l. KEAT 182:13
L., my children LONG 202:4
l. the more ZENO 345:3
politicians have had to l. FITT 128:11
privilege of wisdom to l. HOLM 161:9
world should l. then SHEL 294:1
listening disease of not l. SHAK 274:14
l., lying in wait THOM 316:16
listeth wind bloweth where it l. BIBL 47:27
lit whole Fleet's l. up WOOD 339:4
literary l. cooks MORE 227:23
l. productions GIBB 139:3
Never l. attempt HUME 166:22
Of all the l. scenes PRES 251:3
parole of l. men JOHN 176:9
unsuccessful l. man BELL 28:19
literature great Cham of l. SMOL 298:16
in l., the oldest BULW 72:16
in the locks of l. TENN 314:5
itch of l. LOVE 203:9
life ruined by l. BROO 68:3
like their l. clear and cold LEWI 198:18
l. can and should do BYAT 77:17
L. cannot be the business SOUT 299:20
l. is my mistress CHEK 89:1
L. is news POUN 250:14

L. mostly about having sex LODG 201:11
L.'s always a good card BENN 29:25
L. the orchestration of platitudes WILD 335:25
province of l. MACA 206:1
rest is l. COLE 96:29
rest is l. VALÉ 322:5
littérature tout le reste est l. VERL 323:11
little cry of the L. Peoples LE G 196:17
Go, l. bok CHAU 88:28
having too l. COMP 98:3
here a l., and there a little BIBL 39:29
hobgoblin of l. minds EMER 124:13
L. boxes on the hillside REYN 256:7
L. drops of water CARN 83:9
L. Englanders ANON 8:9
l. grey cells CHRI 90:19
l. learning is a dangerous thing POPE 247:29
Little man, l. man ELIZ 123:9
L. man, you've had a busy day SIGL 295:18
l. more BROW 69:25
L. one! Oh, little one STEP 302:18
l. people pay taxes HELM 155:16
l. ships of England GUED 148:8
L. subject, little wit CARE 82:9
l. woman who wrote LINC 199:14
Man wants but l. GOLD 143:14
Offering Germany too l. NEVI 232:16
She gives but l. YOUN 344:18
So l. done RHOD 256:9
so l. done TENN 311:22
though she be but l. SHAK 283:18
very l. one MARR 213:1
live cannot l. with you MART 213:10
Can these bones l. BIBL 41:5
Come l. with me DONN 114:5
Come l. with me MARL 212:13
desires to l. long SWIF 307:4
enable its citizens to l. WEIL 330:23
forgets to l. LA B 191:8
he isn't fit to l. KING 186:10
He shall l. by them TALM 309:7
he shall l. in them BIBL 34:21
He shall not l. SHAK 276:27
how long I have to l. BOOK 61:19
in him we l., and move BIBL 48:35
L. a thousand years SHAK 276:9
l. in peace ARIS 14:13
l. in society ARIS 14:18
l. on your knees IBAR 168:7
l. or die wi' Charlie HOGG 160:23
l. their creeds GUES 148:10
l. this long BLAK 55:10
l. well on nothing a year THAC 314:24
l. your life not as simple PAST 241:21
Man is born to l. PAST 241:20
might as well l. PARK 240:18
must l. ARGE 14:6
nations how to l. MILT 223:21
not l. to eat MOLI 225:9
Sacco's name will l. VANZ 322:17
see so much, nor l. so long SHAK 278:16
short time to l. BOOK 60:23
sometimes l. apart SAKI 263:16
taught us how to l. TICK 318:4
Teach me to l. KEN 184:3
To l. with thee RALE 253:24
turn and l. with animals WHIT 333:24
We l. our lives RILK 257:8
wouldn't l. under Niagara CARL 83:5
would you l. for ever FRED 133:14
lived I have l. long enough SHAK 281:20
Never to have l. is best YEAT 342:24
lively l. Oracles of God CORO 100:12

liver l. is on the right — MOLI 225:13
l.-wing of a fowl — TENN 314:3
open and notorious evil l. — BOOK 59:16
lives Clarissa l. — RICH 256:21
He that l. upon hope — FRAN 133:6
he who l. more lives than one — WILD 335:17
light wind l. or dies — KEAT 182:10
l. along the line — POPE 248:13
l. of quiet desperation — THOR 317:19
make our l. sublime — LONG 201:26
ninety l. have been taken — MCGO 207:10
pleasant in their l. — BIBL 35:28
woman who l. for others — LEWI 198:12
liveth know that my redeemer l. — BIBL 37:9
name l. for evermore — ANON 10:5
name l. for evermore — BIBL 41:30
living even for the l. God — BOOK 61:21
fight for the l. — JONE 177:10
go on l. even after death — FRAN 133:4
hands of the l. God — BIBL 51:15
house is a machine for l. in — LE C 196:6
L. and partly living — ELIO 122:15
l. at this hour — WORD 340:4
l. death — MILT 223:3
l. dog — BIBL 38:25
L. in history — FITZ 129:11
l. in Philadelphia — FIEL 127:23
l. sacrifice — BIBL 49:19
L.? The servants will do that — VILL 324:5
l. to some purpose — PAIN 239:17
machine for l. — TOLS 318:16
nets to catch the l. — WEBS 330:8
noble L. — WORD 340:24
no l. of its own — JENN 172:2
Plain l. and high thinking — WORD 340:16
respect to the l. — VOLT 326:10
riotous l. — BIBL 46:32
Summer time an' the l. is easy — HEYW 158:20
too much love of l. — SWIN 307:24
well and l. in Paris — ANON 8:3
Who, l., had no roof — HEYW 158:23
world does not owe us a l. — PHIL 244:14
Livingstone Dr L., I presume — STAN 301:16
llama L. is a sort of fleecy goat — BELL 28:19
Lloyd George L. knew my father — ANON 8:11
lo L.! He comes — WESL 332:3
L.! the poor Indian — POPE 248:11
load l. and bless With fruit — KEAT 182:21
L. every rift — KEAT 183:16
loaf l. with a field in the middle — WILD 335:19
with a l. of bread — FITZ 128:15
loafing cricket as organized l. — TEMP 310:9
local little l. difficulties — MACM 208:9
l., but prized elsewhere — AUDE 18:20
l. habitation and a name — SHAK 283:22
Lochinvar young L. is come — SCOT 266:16
loci Geniumque l. — VIRG 325:3
locks in the l. of literature — TENN 314:5
l. were like the raven — BURN 75:14
never shake Thy gory l. — SHAK 280:29
locust years that the l. hath eaten — BIBL 41:13
locusts l. and wild honey — BIBL 42:7
locuta Roma l. est — AUGU 19:6
lodestar he was the l. — LYDG 204:21
lodge best to l. — SHAK 288:25
lodged L. with me useless — MILT 223:9
log L.-cabin to White House — THAY 315:16
logic l. of our times — DAY- 107:4
Second L. then — ARIS 14:9
logical L. consequences — HUXL 168:3
loin ungirt l. — BROW 71:8
loins girded up his l. — BIBL 36:12
shudder in the l. engenders — YEAT 343:8

thicker than my father's l. — BIBL 36:6
loitering Alone and palely l. — KEAT 181:17
Lolita L., light of my life — NABO 230:17
Lombardy waveless plain of L. — SHEL 293:3
London 1938 in L. — MIDL 217:22
arch of L. Bridge — MACA 205:18
best club in L. — DICK 111:1
city much like L. — SHEL 293:13
gazed at the L. skies — BETJ 31:15
L. is a fine town — COLM 97:13
L. is a modern Babylon — DISR 112:28
L. is to Paddington — CANN 81:14
L. particular . . . A fog — DICK 109:17
L., small and white and clean — MORR 228:18
L., thou art the flower — ANON 8:12
lungs of L. — PITT 245:12
rainy Sunday in L. — DE Q 108:20
tired of L. — JOHN 175:23
lone From the l. shieling — GALT 135:16
l. lorn creetur — DICK 109:22
loneliness l. of the long-distance — SILL 295:22
well of l. — HALL 150:9
lonely All the l. people — LENN 197:11
Only the l. — ORBI 236:19
lonesome on a l. road — COLE 96:17
long foot and a half l. — HORA 163:14
How l. a time — SHAK 285:9
how l. I have to live — BOOK 61:19
if a man have l. hair — BIBL 49:29
In the l. run — KEYN 185:13
it hath very l. arms — HALI 150:2
live this l. — BLAK 55:10
l. and the short and the tall — HUGH 166:7
l. day's task — SHAK 268:25
l.-distance runner — SILL 295:22
l. in city pent — KEAT 182:25
L. is the way — MILT 221:20
l., long trail — KING 186:14
l. time deid — ANON 6:2
l. way to Tipperary — JUDG 179:8
l. week-end — FORS 131:13
Lord, how l. — BIBL 39:16
love me l. — ANON 8:13
man goeth to his l. home — BIBL 38:34
night of the l. knives — HITL 159:17
Nor wants that little l. — GOLD 143:14
story need be l. — THOR 317:17
week is a l. time in politics — WILS 336:18
your way be l. — CAVA 86:5
longa Ars l., vita brevis — HIPP 159:11
longer no l. my own — METH 217:13
longeth l. my soul after thee — BOOK 61:21
longitude l. with no platitude — FRY 134:19
look do we l. for another — BIBL 43:29
I l. at the senators — HALE 149:14
l. after our people — SCOT 266:4
l., and pass on — DANT 105:18
L. back in anger — OSBO 237:27
L. for me by moonlight — NOYE 235:5
l. forward to the trip — STIN 304:10
l. in thy heart and write — SIDN 295:8
l. no way but downwards — BUNY 73:7
l. on and help — LAWR 194:24
L., stranger — AUDE 18:6
l. the East End in the face — ELIZ 123:16
L. thy last on all things lovely — DE L 108:6
l. to his bond — SHAK 282:12
l. to the end — ANON 12:19
l. upon a monkey — CONG 98:20
l. upon his like again — SHAK 271:3
One cannot l. at this — GOYA 145:1
row one way and l. another — BURT 76:12
sit and l. at it for hours — JERO 172:6

'Tis very sweet to l. KEAT 182:25
looked If you l. away, you knew SERE 267:24
more he l. inside MILN 218:23
looketh man l. on the outward BIBL 35:20
looking l. back BIBL 46:13
l. one way, and rowing BUNY 73:4
someone may be l. MENC 216:15
stop other people from l. BLAC 54:21
looking glass cracked l. of a servant JOYC 179:1
looks her l. went everywhere BROW 70:23
l. like a duck REUT 256:1
needs good l. TUCK 320:14
loon cream-faced l. SHAK 281:19
loophole l. through which the pervert BRON 67:7
loose all hell broke l. MILT 222:7
l. the bands of Orion BIBL 37:13
man who should l. me LOWE 203:13
loquitur *Cor ad cor* l. NEWM 233:9
lord And I replied, 'My L.' HERB 157:11
by the hand of the L. BIBL 34:11
come, L. Jesus BIBL 52:28
coming of the L. HOWE 165:15
dwell in the house of the L. BOOK 61:7
earth is the L.'s BIBL 49:28
earth is the L.'s BOOK 61:8
Go, and the L. be with thee BIBL 35:21
great l. BEAU 26:13
Great l. of all things POPE 248:16
L. and Father of mankind WHIT 334:5
L., dismiss us BUCK 72:4
l. gave, and the Lord BIBL 36:37
L., how long BIBL 39:16
L. in His mercy CRAI 102:18
L. is my shepherd BOOK 61:6
L. is One SIDD 295:4
L. looketh on the heart BIBL 35:20
L. make his face shine BIBL 34:23
L., now lettest thou BIBL 46:7
L. of all hopefulness STRU 305:8
L. Of life and death CRAS 103:1
L. of the Dance CART 84:24
l. of the foul and the brute COWP 102:9
L. our God is one Lord BIBL 34:27
L. Randal BALL 23:20
L., remember me BIBL 47:12
L. shall raise me up RALE 254:5
L.'s my shepherd SCOT 266:28
L. Tomnoddy is thirty-four BROU 68:7
L. watch between BIBL 33:32
L., what fools SHAK 283:17
L., ye know, is God KETH 185:3
Name of the L. BOOK 63:11
O L., to what a state TERE 314:12
Praise the L. FORG 131:10
Rejoice in the L. BIBL 50:26
saying 'L. Jones Dead' CHES 90:8
soul doth magnify the L. BIBL 45:33
taken away my L. BIBL 48:17
those who love the L. HUNT 167:1
Up to a point, L. Copper WAUG 329:21
way of the L. BIBL 40:7
what hour your L. doth come BIBL 45:4
when they crucified my L. ANON 10:16
Whom the L. loveth BIBL 51:17
lords I made the carles l. JAME 170:12
L. in ermine ROBI 258:5
l. who lay ye low SHEL 293:25
l. will alway BARC 25:1
wit among L. JOHN 176:13
lose is to l. it ORWE 237:21
l. his own soul BIBL 45:28
l. one parent WILD 334:24
l. the war in an afternoon CHUR 92:12

l. to-morrow ARNO 15:18
nothing much to l. HOUS 165:1
nothing to l. MARX 214:10
shall l. it BIBL 43:28
we don't want to l. you RUBE 261:19
win or l. it all MONT 226:23
losing l. your sight SASS 265:1
loss do our country l. SHAK 275:7
lost All is not l. MILT 221:4
all was l. MILT 222:18
and we are l. PYRR 253:1
Are you l. daddy LARD 193:8
Balls will be l. always BERR 31:11
better to have loved and l. TENN 311:18
country is l. WILL 336:3
every day to be l. JOHN 176:20
found my sheep which was l. BIBL 46:30
France has not l. the war DE G 107:23
Home of l. causes ARNO 15:29
I have l. a day TITU 318:8
land of l. content HOUS 165:7
l. an empire ACHE 1:6
l. chord PROC 251:13
l. generation STEI 302:8
l. the only Playboy SYNG 308:8
l. the world for love DRYD 117:5
never l. till won CRAB 102:15
Next to a battle l. WELL 331:7
Not l. but gone before NORT 234:23
not l. but sent before CYPR 105:11
not that you won or l. RICE 256:14
OK. We l. MAJO 210:2
paradises we have l. PROU 251:20
Though lovers be l. THOM 316:2
was l., and is found BIBL 46:35
what is l. in translation FROS 134:16
who deliberates is l. ADDI 2:8
lot l. is fallen unto me BOOK 61:2
policeman's l. is not a happy one GILB 141:6
Remember L.'s wife BIBL 47:6
Lothario gay L. ROWE 261:14
lots cast l. upon my vesture BOOK 61:5
lottery genetic l. comes up with PIML 245:1
l. is a taxation FIEL 127:13
L., with weekly pay-out ORWE 237:16
Lou lady that's known as L. SERV 268:3
loud upon the l. cymbals BOOK 63:30
louder l. he talked of his honour EMER 124:11
louse l. and a flea JOHN 176:13
l. in the locks of literature TENN 314:5
lout l.'s game WEST 332:17
Louvre You're the L. PORT 249:21
love Absence is to l. BUSS 76:25
Ah! what is l. GREE 147:3
all for l. SPEN 300:16
All that matters is l. and work FREU 133:21
Amazing l. WESL 331:22
and be my l. MARL 212:13
and be thy l. RALE 253:24
be wise, and l. SHAK 287:29
bring those who l. Thee TERE 314:12
but one true l. BALL 24:14
came I to l. thee AUGU 19:2
come unto my l. SPEN 300:12
commonly called l. FIEL 127:14
corner in the thing I l. SHAK 284:23
could l. thee, Dear LOVE 203:7
dark secret l. BLAK 56:13
doesn't l. a wall FROS 134:10
do not l. thee, Dr Fell BROW 68:18
every man's l. affair with America MAIL 209:17
fall in l. today GERS 138:14
fit l. for gods MILT 222:16

love (*cont.*)

For ever wilt thou l.	KEAT 182:1
Friendship is L.	BYRO 79:10
gin l. be bonnie	BALL 24:15
God is l., but	LEE 196:8
God of l.	HERB 157:21
good man's l.	SHAK 270:2
got l. well weighed up	AMIS 4:22
Greater l. hath no man	BIBL 48:8
greater l. hath no man	THOR 317:24
groans of l. to those of the dying	LOWR 204:6
had a l. for Charlotte	THAC 314:27
hate is conquered by l.	PALI 240:4
Hell is l. no more	BERN 31:3
hid in the heart of l.	YEAT 343:14
how can he l. God	BIBL 51:35
How do I l. thee	BROW 69:14
how I l. my country	PITT 245:15
How should I your true l. know	SHAK 272:32
hurt us that we l.	BEAU 26:14
I don't l. you	MART 213:7
I hate and I l.	CATU 86:2
I knew it was l.	BYRO 79:17
I l. a lass	O'KE 235:24
I l. but you alone	BALL 24:3
in l. to practise only this	RILK 257:9
in l. with a cold climate	SOUT 299:19
in the world is l.	BREN 66:13
It's so simple, l.	PRÉV 251:4
King of l.	BAKE 23:4
labour of l.	BIBL 51:4
Land that I l.	BERL 30:17
left thy first l.	BIBL 52:4
let me l.	DONN 114:6
let me sow l.	FRAN 133:3
Let's fall in l.	PORT 249:18
let us l.	CATU 85:19
lightly turns to thoughts of l.	TENN 312:7
live with me, and be my l.	DONN 114:5
lost the world for l.	DRYD 117:5
L., a child	WROT 341:27
L. alters not	SHAK 290:7
L. and a cottage	COLM 97:12
L. and do what you will	AUGU 19:4
l. and fame	KEAT 183:2
l. and murder will out	CONG 98:11
l. a thing that can never go wrong	PARK 240:14
l. bade me welcome	HERB 157:16
l. can find you at every time	CHER 89:3
L. comes from blindness	BUSS 76:24
L. comforteth like sunshine	SHAK 290:14
L. conquers all things	VIRG 325:14
L., curiosity, freckles, and doubt	PARK 240:15
L. divine	WESL 332:2
l. Flames for a year	LAMP 192:19
L. has pitched his mansion	YEAT 342:17
l. her, comfort her	BOOK 60:17
l. her is a liberal education	STEE 302:3
l. her till I die	ANON 10:6
L. in a cold climate	MITF 225:1
l. in a golden bowl	BLAK 55:16
L. in a hut	KEAT 181:23
L. is a boy	BUTL 77:7
L. is a spirit	SHAK 290:13
L. is here to stay	GERS 138:16
L. is just a system	BARN 25:10
L. is like any other luxury	TROL 319:21
L. is like linen	FLET 130:12
L. is not love	SHAK 290:6
l. is of a birth as rare	MARV 213:14
L. is of the valley	TENN 313:18
l. is slight	MARL 212:9
L. is strong as death	BIBL 39:8

L. is the discovery of reality	MURD 230:6
L. is the fart	SUCK 305:12
L. iz like the meazles	BILL 54:1
L. just makes it safer	ICE- 168:16
L. looks not with the eyes	SHAK 283:2
L. means not ever having	SEGA 267:8
L. me little	ANON 8:13
l. of friends	BELL 29:1
l. of money	BIBL 51:11
l. one another or die	AUDE 18:17
L.'s a disease	MACA 205:9
L. set you going	PLAT 245:22
L.'s harbinger	MILT 222:24
l. she's but a lassie	BURN 75:19
l. slights it	BACO 21:10
L.'s like a red, red rose	BURN 75:21
L.'s passives	CRAS 102:25
L.'s pleasure lasts but a moment	FLOR 130:14
l's proper exercise	DAVI 106:15
L.'s the noblest frailty	DRYD 116:30
L.'s tongue is in the eyes	FLET 130:11
l's young dream	MOOR 227:16
l. that asks no question	SPRI 301:3
L. that dare not	DOUG 115:2
l. that moves the sun	DANT 105:22
L. the Beloved Republic	FORS 131:18
l., the beloved Republic	SWIN 307:25
L. the brotherhood	BIBL 51:27
l. thee better after death	BROW 69:15
L., the human form divine	BLAK 56:6
l. the Lord thy God	BIBL 44:29
L. the sinner	AUGU 19:5
L.-thirty, love-forty	BETJ 32:4
L., thou art absolute	CRAS 103:1
l. thy neighbour	BIBL 34:22
l. thy neighbour as thyself	BIBL 44:29
l. to hatred turned	CONG 98:14
L. to the loveless shown	CROS 104:8
l. up groweth	CHAU 88:29
L. was a terrible thing	RHYS 256:11
l. were what the rose is	SWIN 308:5
l . . . whatever that may	CHAR 88:1
L. wol nat been constreyned	CHAU 88:13
l. you just the same	KIER 185:21
L. your enemies	BIBL 46:10
L. you ten years before	MARV 213:20
making l. all year round	BEAU 26:12
Man's l. is of man's life	BYRO 78:18
Men l. in haste	BYRO 79:5
money can't buy me l.	LENN 197:10
music be the food of l.	SHAK 288:2
my l. and I did meet	YEAT 342:18
My l. for Heathcliff	BRON 67:14
My only l.	SHAK 286:17
My song is l. unknown	CROS 104:8
needs must l. the highest	TENN 311:6
never l. a stranger	BENS 30:1
no l. for such	THOM 316:22
not enough to make us l.	SWIF 307:1
O lyric L.	BROW 71:4
Only by l. can men see me	BHAG 32:18
our l. hath no decay	DONN 114:4
over hir housbond as hir l.	CHAU 88:21
passing the l. of women	BIBL 35:29
perfect l. casteth out fear	BIBL 51:34
power and effect of l.	BURT 76:17
programmed to l. completely	BAIN 23:2
putting L. away	DICK 111:14
quick-eyed L., observing	HERB 157:16
search for l.	WALE 326:18
some l. but little policy	SHAK 285:28
sports of l.	JONS 177:23
support of the woman I l.	EDWA 120:4

survive of us is l. — LARK 193:11
them that l. God — BIBL 49:16
there are those who l. it — WEBS 330:4
There is l. of course — ANOU 13:8
They l. indeed — SIDN 295:10
this spring of l. — SHAK 288:34
those who l. the Lord — HUNT 167:1
thought that l. would last — AUDE 18:2
time to l. — BIBL 38:18
tired of L. — BELL 28:16
to l. and be loved — SAND 264:6
to l. and rapture's due — ROCH 258:9
To see her is to l. her — BURN 75:7
true l. hath my heart — SIDN 295:7
true l. is a durable fire — RALE 254:3
true l. is, it showeth — DE P 108:19
vegetable l. should grow — MARV 213:20
very few to l. — WORD 341:3
vividly gifted in l. — DUFF 117:24
waters cannot quench l. — BIBL 39:9
well-nourished l. — COLE 96:29
What is l. — SHAK 288:13
When l. congeals — HART 152:18
who l., time is eternity — VAN 322:15
Whom the gods l. — MENA 216:12
wilder shores of l. — BLAN 56:19
woman wakes to l. — TENN 311:11
world and l. were young — RALE 253:24
'You must sit down,' says L. — HERB 157:17
loved all we l. of him — SHEL 292:16
And the l. one — BROW 70:24
better to have l. and lost — TENN 311:18
feared than l. — MACH 207:16
God so l. the world — BIBL 47:28
idols I have l. — FITZ 128:21
I have l. — SUCK 305:13
I l. a lass — WITH 337:19
l. by the gods — PLAT 245:24
l. Caesar less — SHAK 276:12
l. him so — BROW 70:17
l. him too much — RACI 253:17
l. not at first sight — MARL 212:9
l. the doctrine — DEFO 107:16
l. you, so I drew these tides — LAWR 194:26
never to have been l. — CONG 98:17
she l. much — BIBL 46:12
Solomon l. many strange women — BIBL 36:5
thirst to be l. — RHYS 256:10
till we l. — DONN 114:7
wish I l. the Human Race — RALE 254:10
loveless Love to the l. shown — CROS 104:8
loveliness miracle of l. — GILB 140:16
portion of the l. — SHEL 292:19
woman of shining l. — YEAT 343:22
lovely Look thy last on all things l. — DE L 108:6
l. and pleasant — BIBL 35:28
L. enchanting language — HERB 157:14
l. is the rose — WORD 340:8
l. woman stoops to folly — ELIO 122:28
l. woman stoops to folly — GOLD 144:4
more l. and more temperate — SHAK 289:23
once he made more l. — SHEL 292:19
what a l. war — LITT 200:7
whatsoever things are l. — BIBL 50:28
woods are l. — FROS 134:14
You have l. eyes — CHEK 88:34
lover binds the l. — SANS 264:15
dividing l. and lover — SWIN 307:18
l. and his lass — SHAK 270:4
l. and killer are mingled — DOUG 115:6
l., and the poet — SHAK 283:21
l. of my soul — WESL 332:1
sighed as a l. — GIBB 139:7

some old l.'s ghost — DONN 114:8
what is left of a l. — ROWL 261:15
lovers Journeys end in l. meeting — SHAK 288:12
laughs at l.' perjuries — OVID 238:11
L., to bed — SHAK 283:24
star-crossed l. — SHAK 286:12
These l. fled away — KEAT 181:10
Though l. be lost — THOM 316:2
loves because God l. it — JULI 179:9
die to that which one l. — HARA 151:5
For who l. that — MILT 223:8
kills the thing he l. — WILD 335:16
life and l. of a she-devil — WELD 331:2
l. the fox less — SURT 306:9
our l., must I remember them — APOL 13:11
reigned with your l. — ELIZ 123:8
lovesome garden is a l. thing — BROW 68:16
loveth He that l. not — BIBL 51:33
prayeth well, who l. well — COLE 96:18
whom the Lord l. — BIBL 37:18
Whom the Lord l. — BIBL 51:17
loving Can't help l. dat man — HAMM 150:16
discharge for l. one — MATL 215:7
heart be still as l. — BYRO 79:16
I ain't had no l. — NORW 235:1
most l. mere folly — SHAK 269:26
savage l. has made me — BECK 27:3
low Malice is of a l. stature — HALI 150:2
Sweet and l. — TENN 313:4
That l. man — BROW 70:7
upper station of l. life — DEFO 107:13
Lowells L. talk to the Cabots — BOSS 64:18
lower l. than vermin — BEVA 32:8
While there is a l. class — DEBS 107:10
lowlands Highlands and ye l. — BALL 23:17
lowliness l. become mine inner clothing — LITT 200:6
loyal l. to his own career — DALT 105:13
loyalties tragic conflict of l. — HOWE 165:14
loyalty I want l. — JOHN 173:5
learned body wanted l. — TRAP 319:5
L. the Tory's secret weapon — KILM 186:3
LSD PC is the L. of the '90s — LEAR 195:20
Lucifer falls like L. — SHAK 275:24
L. arose — MERE 217:4
L., son of the morning — BIBL 39:25
luck believes in l. — STEA 301:22
watching his l. — SERV 268:3
Lucy L. ceased to be — WORD 341:5
lug l. the guts — SHAK 272:29
lugete L., O Veneres — CATU 85:18
lugger Once aboard the l. — JOHN 177:5
lukewarm thou art l. — BIBL 52:6
lullaby Once in a l. — HARB 151:9
lumber l. of the schools — SWIF 307:7
luminous beating his l. wings — ARNO 16:1
with a l. nose — LEAR 195:10
lump leaven leaveneth the whole l. — BIBL 49:25
l. bred up in darkness — KYD 191:3
lumps l. in it — STEP 302:17
luna great Lord of L. — MACA 206:10
lunatic l., the lover — SHAK 283:21
lunatics l. have taken charge — ROWL 261:16
lunch cork out of my l. — FIEL 127:20
unable to l. today — PORT 249:19
lungs dangerous to the l. — JAME 170:8
from froth-corrupted l. — OWEN 238:24
l. of London — PITT 245:12
lure l. this tassel-gentle — SHAK 286:22
lurk l. outside — GRAC 145:3
lurks l. a politician — ARIS 14:12
lust generous in mere l. — ROCH 258:11
l. and calls it advertising — LAHR 191:20
l. of knowing — FLEC 129:23

lust (cont.)
to l. after it
lustily sing praises l. unto him   LEWI 198:14
lustre Where is thy l. now   BOOK 61:14
lusts l. of the flesh   SHAK 277:29
   BOOK 60:9
lute Apollo's l.   MILT 219:14
   Orpheus with his l.   SHAK 275:22
   rift within the l.   TENN 311:9
lux l. perpetua   MISS 224:10
luxury height of l.   TENN 314:4
   like any other l.   TROL 319:21
   l., not a necessity   ANTH 13:9
   l., peace   BAUD 26:7
   l. was doing good   GART 136:13
Lycidas L. is dead   MILT 220:10
lying branch of the art of l.   CORN 100:10
   listening, l. in wait   THOM 316:16
   L. lips are abomination   BIBL 37:28
   One of you is l.   PARK 240:20
   smallest amount of l.   BUTL 77:10
Lyonnesse When I set out for L.   HARD 152:4
lyre Make me thy l.   SHEL 293:9
   'Omer smote 'is bloomin' l.   KIPL 188:16

M

M dreaded four M's   STRE 305:6
Mab M., the Mistress-Fairy   JONS 177:15
   Queen M. hath been with   SHAK 286:14
macaroni called it M.   ANON 11:6
Macaulay as Tom M.   MELB 216:5
Macavity M. WASN'T THERE   ELIO 122:17
Macbeth had Lady M.   KNIG 189:13
   M. does murder sleep   SHAK 280:9
   M. shall never vanquished be   SHAK 281:10
   M. shall sleep no more   SHAK 280:10
   night I appeared as M.   HARG 152:9
MacCorley Rody M. goes to die   CARB 82:3
Macduff Lay on, M.   SHAK 281:26
   M. was from his mother's womb   SHAK 281:25
mace fool's bauble, the m.   CROM 103:21
Macheath jack-knife has M.   BREC 66:11
machine body is a m.   TOLS 318:16
   Ghost in the M.   RYLE 263:7
   house is a m. for living in   LE C 196:6
   m. for turning the red wine   DINE 111:27
machines whether m. think   SKIN 296:19
macht Arbeit m. frei   ANON 11:21
mackerel like rotten m.   RAND 254:13
   Not so the m.   FRER 133:18
mackintosh bit of black m.   WELB 331:1
mad All poets are m.   BURT 76:13
   bad and m. it was   BROW 69:28
   called me m.   LEE 196:13
   glad m. brother's name   SWIN 307:19
   Hieronimo is m. again   KYD 191:5
   M. about the boy   COWA 101:6
   m. all my life   JOHN 174:10
   m. and savage master   SOPH 299:11
   M., bad, and dangerous   LAMB 192:1
   M. dogs and Englishmen   COWA 101:7
   m. north-north-west   SHAK 271:32
   men that God made m.   CHES 89:18
   much learning doth make thee m.   BIBL 49:3
   old, m., blind   SHEL 293:26
   O! let me not be m.   SHAK 277:12
   pleasure sure, In being m.   DRYD 116:17
   when a heroine goes m.   SHER 294:10
   Whom the m. would destroy   LEVI 198:8
madam globe-trotting M.   YEAT 343:27
madding Far from the m. crowd's   GRAY 146:17

made All things were m. by him   BIBL 47:16
   Begotten, not m.   BOOK 59:22
   fearfully and wonderfully m.   BOOK 63:26
   Little Lamb who m. thee   BLAK 56:8
Madeira M., m'dear   FLAN 129:14
madeleine little piece of m.   PROU 251:17
mademoiselle M. from Armenteers   ANON 8:14
madhouses M., prisons   CLAR 93:8
madmen M. in authority   KEYN 185:12
   none but m. know   DRYD 117:10
madness despondency and m.   WORD 340:26
   destroyed through m.   GINS 141:14
   harmonious m.   SHEL 294:1
   m. is terrific   WOOL 339:11
   M. need not be all breakdown   LAIN 191:22
   m. of many   POPE 249:8
   moon-struck m.   MILT 222:23
   O! that way m. lies   SHAK 277:21
   Though this be m.   SHAK 271:28
   to m. near allied   DRYD 116:11
   very midsummer m.   SHAK 288:27
magazines graves of little m.   PRES 251:3
Magdalen fourteen months at M. College   GIBB 139:6
magic daylight in upon m.   BAGE 22:20
   If this be m.   SHAK 289:16
   indistinguishable from m.   CLAR 93:19
   m. casements   KEAT 182:14
   m. of your fire   TAGO 308:22
   mistake medicine for m.   SZAS 308:11
   old black m.   MERC 216:24
   rough m. I here abjure   SHAK 287:17
   secret m. of numbers   BROW 69:3
   tightness of the m. circle   MACL 208:3
magistrate m. corruptible   ROBE 257:18
   shocks the m.   RUSS 262:24
magna M. Charta is such a fellow   COKE 95:19
   M. est veritas, et praevalet   BIBL 53:14
magnificat M. anima mea Dominum   BIBL 53:7
magnificent M. desolation   ALDR 3:12
   mild and m. eye   BROW 70:17
magnifique C'est m.   BOSQ 64:17
magnify soul doth m. the Lord   BIBL 45:33
   we m. thee   BOOK 58:13
magpie swollen m. in a fitful sun   POUN 250:12
magpies pair of m. fly   HO 159:21
magus M. Zoroaster, my dead child   SHEL 293:14
maid m. is mine   JOHN 177:5
   m. is not dead   BIBL 43:23
   man with a m.   BIBL 38:10
   She could not live a m.   PEEL 242:23
maiden m. of bashful fifteen   SHER 294:19
maidens laughter of comely m.   DE V 109:6
   What m. loth   KEAT 181:28
maids Old m. biking   ORWE 237:11
   Three little m.   GILB 140:10
maimed M. us at the start   YEAT 343:15
   poor, and the m.   BIBL 46:27
Maine As M. goes   FARL 126:7
maintenance art of motorcycle m.   PIRS 245:6
maior M. erat natu   LUCI 204:11
maistrye constreyned by m.   CHAU 88:13
maîtresses j'aurai des m.   GEOR 137:22
majestic m. equality of the law   FRAN 132:18
   M. though in ruin   MILT 221:18
majesty as his m.   BIBL 41:23
   Her M.'s Opposition   BAGE 22:12
   ride on in m.   MILM 218:22
   Thy M. how bright   FABE 125:16
   touching in its m.   WORD 339:17
major Ground control to M. Tom   BOWI 65:16
   modern M.-General   GILB 141:5
   With M. Major it had been all three   HELL 155:13
majority big enough m.   TWAI 321:3

black m. rule	SMIT 297:19	M., I assure you	MOLI 225:15
gone to join the m.	PETR 244:10	M. is a noble animal	BROW 69:2
m. never has right	IBSE 168:9	M. is a tool-using animal	CARL 83:1
m. . . . one is enough	DISR 112:23	M. is born unto trouble	BIBL 37:5
to the great m.	YOUN 344:19	m. is dead	FROM 134:3
majors live with scarlet M.	SASS 264:26	M. is man's A.B.C.	QUAR 253:5
make does not usually m. anything	PHEL 244:12	m. . . . is *so* in the way	GASK 136:15
Scotsman on the m.	BARR 25:17	M. is something to be surpassed	NIET 234:6
wrote M. IT NEW	POUN 250:6	M. is the hunter	TENN 313:10
maker M. of heaven and earth	BOOK 58:16	M. is the measure	PROT 251:15
M. of heaven and earth	BOOK 59:22	m. made the town	COWP 101:28
watch must have had a m.	PALE 239:20	M. may not marry his Mother	BOOK 64:7
malady m. of not marking	SHAK 274:14	m. of restless intellect	HUXL 168:4
male m. and the female	BIBL 33:19	M. owes his entire existence	HEGE 155:5
M. bonding	TIGE 318:5	M. partly is	BROW 70:1
m., middle class, middle-aged	STRE 305:6	m. proposes	THOM 315:19
more deadly than the m.	KIPL 187:15	M., proud man	SHAK 281:30
malice envy, hatred, and m.	BOOK 59:4	m. recovered of the bite	GOLD 143:16
M. domestic	SHAK 280:24	m.'s a man for a' that	BURN 75:10
M. is of a low stature	HALI 150:2	m. sent from God	BIBL 47:18
m., to breed causes	JONS 177:24	m.'s first disobedience	MILT 220:33
m. toward none	LINC 199:11	M. shall not live	BIBL 42:10
malicious God is subtle but not m.	EINS 120:13	M.'s inhumanity to man	BURN 75:16
malignant part of Randolph that was not m.		M. stole the fruit	HERB 157:20
	WAUG 329:24	M. that is born	BIBL 37:6
Malmesey drowned in a barrel of M.	FABY 125:18	M. that is born of a woman	BOOK 60:23
malt m. does more than Milton	HOUS 165:10	M. wants but little	GOLD 143:14
Malvern on M. hilles	LANG 192:27	m. who has no office	SHAW 290:28
mama M. may have	HOLI 161:3	m. who should loose me	LOWE 203:13
m. of dada	FADI 125:20	m. who would be king	KIPL 188:25
mammon God and m.	BIBL 42:26	M. will err	GOET 142:16
M. led them on	MILT 221:13	m. with a maid	BIBL 38:10
m. of unrighteousness	BIBL 47:1	m. write a better book	EMER 124:18
man against every m.	BIBL 33:24	met a m. who wasn't there	MEAR 215:18
all that may become a m.	SHAK 279:26	more like a m.	LERN 197:25
And was made m.	MISS 224:2	more wonderful than m.	SOPH 299:9
arms and the m.	VIRG 324:9	My m. Friday	DEFO 107:14
Arms, and the m. I sing	DRYD 117:14	new m. may be raised up	BOOK 60:7
arose as one m.	BIBL 35:12	nor no m. ever loved	SHAK 290:7
become the servant of a m.	SHAW 290:27	not m. for the sabbath	BIBL 45:23
Both m. and bird	COLE 96:18	one small step for a m.	ARMS 15:1
by m. shall his blood	BIBL 33:21	only m. is vile	HEBE 155:2
century of the common m.	WALL 327:2	piece of work is a m.	SHAK 271:31
chief end of m.	SHOR 295:3	repelled by m.	INGE 168:20
come, but not the m.	SCOT 266:23	said, ask a m.	THAT 315:3
demolition of a m.	LEVI 198:6	Stand by your m.	WYNE 342:6
every m. against every man	HOBB 160:1	standing by my m.	CLIN 94:13
every m. and nation	LOWE 203:18	study of m. is man	CHAR 88:3
everyone has sat except a m.	CUMM 104:15	Style is the m.	BUFF 72:7
father of the M.	WORD 340:6	that the m. should be alone	BIBL 33:2
first m.	BIBL 50:6	This bold bad m.	SHAK 275:21
fit night out for m. or beast	FIEL 127:21	this M. and this Woman	BOOK 60:14
from pig to m.	ORWE 237:6	This was a m.	SHAK 276:33
God has more right than m.	JOHN 172:11	Thou art the m.	BIBL 35:31
Greater love hath no m.	BIBL 48:8	To the m.-in-the-street	AUDE 18:10
Happy is the m.	BOOK 63:19	What bloody m.	SHAK 278:27
He was a m.	SHAK 271:3	what is m.	LENO 197:18
He was her m.	ANON 7:11	when a m. should marry	BACO 21:18
in m. there is nothing great	HAMI 150:15	When God at first made m.	HERB 157:18
just the m. to do it	BOLT 57:16	when I became a m.	BIBL 49:33
let him pass for a m.	SHAK 282:2	Who's master, who's m.	SWIF 307:6
let no m. put asunder	BOOK 60:20	woman was made for m.	STAN 301:19
make a m. a woman	PEMB 243:6	woman without a m.	STEI 302:12
m. after his own heart	BIBL 35:19	You'll be a M., my son	KIPL 187:21
m. and a brother	WEDG 330:21	**manage** m. without butter	GOEB 142:12
m. and the hour	YANC 342:9	**management** M. that wants to change	TUSA 321:1
m. at the gate of the year	HASK 153:4	**manager** m. who gets the blame	LINE 200:1
m. bites a dog	BOGA 57:8	**managers** m. of affairs of women	KORA 190:13
m. could ease a heart	PARK 240:19	**Manchester** school of M.	DISR 113:7
M. dreams of fame	TENN 311:11	**Mandalay** road to M.	KIPL 187:26
m. for all seasons	WHIT 334:7	**Manderley** dreamt I went to M.	DU M 118:3
m. from animals	OSLE 238:4	**manger** in the rude m. lies	MILT 220:24
m. have the upper hand	BOOK 60:28	laid him in a m.	BIBL 46:3

manger (*cont.*)
m. for his bed — ALEX 3:17
manhood m. an opportunity — KEIL 183:23
M. taken by the Son — NEWM 233:5
manibus *M. date lilia plenis* — VIRG 325:1
manifestoes in the party m. — ROTH 261:7
manifold m. sins and wickedness — BOOK 58:4
manilla misery of m. folders — ROET 258:21
mankind all m. — BALL 24:3
crucify m. — BRYA 71:22
giant leap for m. — ARMS 15:1
legislator of m. — JOHN 173:24
m. and womankind — BAHA 22:23
M. has done more damage — COUS 101:1
M. is on the move — SMUT 298:17
not in Asia, was m. born — ARDR 14:3
proper study of m. — POPE 248:15
proper study of m. is books — HUXL 167:14
manna his tongue Dropped m. — MILT 221:17
manner after the m. of men — BIBL 50:4
all m. of thing — JULI 179:10
to the m. born — SHAK 271:12
manners bring good m. — BURN 76:2
corrupt good m. — BIBL 50:5
gentleness of your m. — CLAI 93:6
good table m. — MIKE 217:25
had very good m. — SELL 267:17
lack of m. — HATH 153:6
m. of a dancing master — JOHN 174:19
m. of a Marquis — GILB 141:7
Oh, the m. — CICE 92:25
polished m. — COWP 102:7
rectify m. — MILT 223:17
Manningtree roasted M. ox — SHAK 273:34
mansion everlasting m. — SHAK 287:25
Love has pitched his m. — YEAT 342:17
m.-house of liberty — MILT 223:19
mansions m. of the dead — CRAB 102:12
many m. — BIBL 48:5
mantle cast his m. upon him — BIBL 36:14
green m. — SHAK 277:25
in russet m. clad — SHAK 270:26
twitched his m. blue — MILT 220:21
manunkind this busy monster, m. — CUMM 104:17
manure liquid m. from the West — SOLZ 298:29
natural m. — JEFF 171:13
manuscript youth's sweet-scented m. — FITZ 129:1
many How m. things — SOCR 298:20
m. are called — BIBL 44:26
m.-headed monster — POPE 248:29
m.-splendoured thing — THOM 317:2
So m. worlds — TENN 311:22
so much owed by so m. to so few — CHUR 91:17
we are m. — BIBL 45:27
map Roll up that m. — PITT 245:14
mapmakers m. should place the Mississippi — BELL 29:3
maps Geography is about M. — BENT 30:7
in Afric-m. — SWIF 307:9
marathon M. looks on the sea — BYRO 78:24
trivial skirmish fought near M. — GRAV 146:6
marble dwelt in m. halls — BUNN 72:17
Glowed on the m. — ELIO 122:22
left it m. — AUGU 19:9
m., nor the gilded monuments — SHAK 289:29
march Beware the ides of M. — SHAK 275:29
boundary of the m. of a nation — PARN 241:10
do not m. on Moscow — MONT 226:19
droghte of M. — CHAU 88:4
in the front of M. — TENN 311:11
m. as an alternative — FITT 128:10
m. my troops towards — GRIM 148:1
m. towards it — CALL 80:9
Men who m. away — HARD 151:25

take The winds of M. — SHAK 289:11
marche *congrès ne m. pas* — LIGN 199:3
marching M. as to war — BARI 25:5
m., charging feet — JAGG 170:4
soul is m. on — ANON 8:4
truth is m. on — HOWE 165:15
mare brought him a Flanders m. — HENR 156:16
lend me your grey m. — BALL 24:16
Margaret M. you mourn for — HOPK 163:5
Merry M. — SKEL 296:16
margerain With m. gentle — SKEL 296:17
margin m. too narrow — FERM 127:2
Maria *Ave M.* — ANON 12:9
Mariana this dejected M. — SHAK 282:1
Marie I am M. of Roumania — PARK 240:14
Maries Queen had four M. — BALL 24:5
marigold m., that goes to bed — SHAK 289:10
marijuana experimented with m. — CLIN 94:15
mariner It is an ancient M. — COLE 96:8
m. with the gentleman — DRAK 116:2
mark man's distinctive m. — BROW 70:1
m., or the name of the beast — BIBL 52:15
m. upon Cain — BIBL 33:15
no drowning m. — SHAK 287:1
read, m., learn — BOOK 59:13
market enterprise of the m. — ANON 6:8
heart in the m.-place — SHAK 284:5
Market Harborough AM IN M. — CHES 90:10
marking malady of not m. — SHAK 274:14
marks m. of the beast — HARD 151:16
marl Over the burning m. — MILT 221:8
marquis manners of a M. — GILB 141:7
married man that's m. — SHAK 268:11
marriage by way of m. — FIEL 127:15
definition of m. — SMIT 298:10
furnish forth the m. tables — SHAK 271:2
get anywhere in a m. — MURD 230:5
Hanging and m. — FARQ 126:9
M. a wonderful invention — CONN 98:24
M. has many pains — JOHN 173:26
M. is popular because — SHAW 291:17
M. is the grave — CAVE 86:8
M. may often be a stormy lake — PEAC 242:14
m. of true minds — SHAK 290:6
M., to women — ANTH 13:9
prevents a bad m. — SHAK 288:6
three of us in this m. — DIAN 109:11
marriages All the unhappy m. — WODE 337:25
have no more m. — SHAK 272:6
There are good m. — LA R 193:19
married At leisure m. — CONG 98:15
delight we m. people have — PEPY 243:15
if ever we had been m. — GAY 137:2
imprudently m. the barber — FOOT 130:23
In m. life three is company — WILD 334:23
let us be m. — LEAR 195:15
like other m. couples — SAKI 263:16
m. beneath me — ASTO 17:6
m. me with a ring — RAIN 253:23
m. to a poem — KEAT 183:13
m.—to be the more together — MACN 208:18
Mocks m. men — SHAK 278:22
Reader, I m. him — BRON 67:9
Trade Unionism of the m. — SHAW 291:14
when they got m. — HOLI 161:5
young man m. — SHAK 268:11
marries signify whom one m. — ROGE 259:3
marry better to m. than to burn — BIBL 49:26
Can't get away to m. you — LEIG 196:23
m. a man who hates his mother — BENN 29:26
M. my body to that dust — KING 186:6
m. one another — BUTL 77:11
m. whom she likes — THAC 314:19

may not m. his Mother	BOOK 64:7	**mater** *Stabat M. dolorosa*	JACO 169:23
men we wanted to m.	STEI 302:11	**materialism** deteriorate into m.	MOLT 225:16
neither m., nor are given	BIBL 44:28	**materials** I use simple m.	LOWR 204:5
persons about to m.	PUNC 252:7	**mathematical** of m. celebrity	DOYL 115:15
when a man should m.	BACO 21:18	**mathematician** appear as a pure m.	JEAN 171:11
while ye may, go m.	HERR 158:9	**mathematics** M. may be defined	RUSS 262:22
marrying m. in haste	THOM 316:18	M., rightly viewed	RUSS 262:23
Mars Men are from M.	GRAY 146:8	no place for ugly m.	HARD 151:14
marshal m.'s baton	LOUI 203:1	**matrimony** as that of m.	TROL 319:17
Martha M. was cumbered	BIBL 46:18	critical period in m.	HERB 76:9
Martin Saint M.'s summer	SHAK 275:12	joined together in holy M.	BOOK 60:13
Martini medium Vodka dry M.	FLEM 130:1	**matter** altering the position of m.	RUSS 262:21
Martinis Those dry M.	ADE 2:18	Does it m.	SASS 265:1
martlet temple-haunting m.	SHAK 279:18	if it is it doesn't m.	GILB 141:9
martyr regarded as a m.	KHOM 185:16	inditing of a good m.	BOOK 61:22
martyrdom m. must run its course	AUDE 18:9	m. out of place	GRAY 146:9
martyred shrouded oft our m. dead	CONN 98:22	More m. with less art	SHAK 271:26
martyrs army of M.	BOOK 58:11	root of the m.	BIBL 37:10
marvel m. at nothing	HORA 163:23	this m. better in France	STER 302:19
marvellous Chatterton, the m. boy	WORD 340:25	'twas no m. what he said	BYRO 79:3
hath done m. things	BOOK 62:21	What is M.	PUNC 252:11
m. demonstration	FERM 127:2	wretched m. and lame metre	MILT 220:31
m. in our eyes	BOOK 63:10	**matters** else you do well m.	ONAS 236:8
Marx illegitimate child of Karl M.	ATTL 17:11	Nobody that m.	MILL 218:6
in M.'s pages	SCHU 265:20	**Matthew** M. Mark, Luke, and John	ANON 8:17
Marxist I am a M.	ANON 11:15	**mature** m. women, *dancing*	FRIE 133:25
Marxiste *Je suis M.*	ANON 11:15	**Maud** into the garden, M.	TENN 312:21
Mary Hail M.	ANON 12:9	**mausoleum** as its m.	AMIS 4:19
M. Ambree	BALL 24:2	**Max** incomparable M.	SHAW 292:2
M. had a little lamb	HALE 149:17	**maxim** M. Gun	BELL 28:18
M. hath chosen	BIBL 46:19	**maxima** *mea m. culpa*	MISS 223:26
M.'s prayers	FABE 125:15	**may** darling buds of M.	SHAK 289:23
Mary Magdalene cometh M. early	BIBL 48:16	fressh as is the month of M.	CHAU 88:7
mask had a m. like Castlereagh	SHEL 293:5	I'm to be Queen o' the M.	TENN 312:25
m. that eats into the face	UPDI 322:1	matter for a M. morning	SHAK 288:29
masochistic m. form of exhibitionism	OLIV 236:6	M. to December	ANDE 5:7
mass M. is ended	MISS 224:8	merry month of M.	BALL 23:16
Paris is well worth a m.	HENR 156:12	on a M. morning	LANG 192:27
two thousand years of m.	HARD 151:19	rose in M.	CHAU 88:23
Massachusetts denied in M.	MILL 218:9	**maypole** M. in the Strand	BRAM 66:1
massacre not as sudden as a m.	TWAI 321:4	**maypoles** I sing of M.	HERR 157:26
masses calling 'em the m.	PRIE 251:6	**MBEs** M. and your knighthoods	KEAT 181:1
huddled m. yearning	LAZA 195:2	**McCarthyism** M. is Americanism with	MCCA 206:18
m. against the classes	GLAD 142:1	**McGregor** Mr M.'s garden	POTT 249:26
m. conveying an emotion	HEPW 156:24	**McNamara** M.'s War	MCNA 208:14
massy huge m. face	MACA 205:13	**me** M. Tarzan	WEIS 330:25
master Caliban, Has a new m.	SHAK 287:11	save thee and m.	OWEN 238:19
Death is a m. from Germany	CELA 86:11	**meadows** M. trim with daisies pied	MILT 220:3
mad and savage m.	SOPH 299:11	**meal** handful of m.	BIBL 36:9
M.-morality	NIET 234:10	**mean** citizen of no m. city	BIBL 48:39
m. of my fate	HENL 156:8	Down these m. streets	CHAN 87:5
m. of the Party	HEAL 154:10	having a m. Court	BAGE 22:18
slew his m.	BIBL 36:30	Know what I m., Harry	BRUN 71:21
This is our m.	BROW 70:6	loves the golden m.	HORA 164:10
which is to be m.	CARR 84:11	nothing common did or m.	MARV 213:18
Who's m., who's man	SWIF 307:6	poem should not m. but be	MACL 208:2
Why eateth your M.	BIBL 43:18	say what you m.	CARR 83:19
masterly m. inactivity	MACK 207:19	They may not m. to	LARK 193:14
masterpiece Nature's great m.	DONN 114:1	whatever that may m.	CHAR 88:1
masters anything but new m.	HALI 150:3	**meaner** m. beauties of the night	WOTT 341:22
never wrong, the Old M.	AUDE 18:8	only m. things	ELIO 121:6
people are the m.	BURK 74:18	**meaning** m. doesn't matter	GILB 140:23
serve two m.	BIBL 42:26	teems with hidden m.	GILB 141:8
We are not the m.	BLAI 55:8	to some faint m. make pretence	DRYD 117:3
We are the m. now	SHAW 292:7	within the m. of the Act	ANON 9:10
mastiff m.? the right hon. Gentleman's poodle		**meanings** two m. packed up	CARR 84:12
	LLOY 200:17	wrestle With words and m.	ELIO 121:23
mastodons like m. bellowing	WODE 338:4	**meanly** all m. wrapped	MILT 220:24
match lighted m.	BROW 70:20	m. lose	LINC 199:7
matched m. us with His hour	BROO 67:22	**means** between ends and scarce m.	ROBB 257:16
matches with that stick of m.	MAND 211:2	by the best m.	HUTC 167:12
matchless m. deed's achieved	SMAR 297:4	die beyond my m.	WILD 335:20
mate great artificer Made my m.	STEV 304:1	end justifies the m.	BUSE 76:19

means (*cont.*)
It m. everything	RUSH 262:5
live within our m.	WARD 328:9
m. of rising	JOHN 175:16
politics by other m.	CLAU 94:1
Whatever 'in love' m.	DUFF 117:24

meant damned dots m.
	CHUR 91:6
knew what it m.	BROW 71:13
knew what it m.	KLOP 189:10
'w-a-t-e-r' m. the wonderful	KELL 183:24
what he m. by that	LOUI 203:3

measure good m., pressed down
	BIBL 46:11
If you cannot m. it	KELV 183:26
leave to heaven the m.	JOHN 174:8
m. of all things	PROT 251:15
m. of movement	AUCT 17:23
m. of the universe	SHEL 293:17
serves to grace my m.	PRIO 251:9

measured dance is a m. pace
	BACO 20:20
m. out my life with coffee spoons	ELIO 122:10

measures M. not men
	CANN 81:15
M. not men	GOLD 143:25
Not men, but m.	BURK 74:14

meat came forth m.
	BIBL 35:7
have m. and cannot eat	BURN 75:15
Heaven sends us good m.	GARR 136:10
taste my m.	HERB 157:17

meats funeral baked m. SHAK 271:2
meazles Love iz like the m. BILL 54:1
méchant *m. animal* MOLI 225:15
medal m. for killing two men MATL 215:7
meddles Minister that m. with art MELB 216:4
Medes M. and Persians BIBL 41:9
medias *in m. res* HORA 163:16
medical in advance of m. thought WODE 338:5
medicinal M. discovery AYRE 20:12
medicine desire to take m. OSLE 238:4
M. is my lawful wife	CHEK 89:1
mistake m. for magic	SZAS 308:11
patent m. advertisement	JERO 172:5
practise m.	MOLI 225:13

medieval lily in your m. hand GILB 140:25
medio *M. tutissimus ibis* OVID 238:14
mediocre middle-aged and m. STRE 305:6
Some men are born m. HELL 155:13
mediocritatem *Auream quisquis m.* HORA 164:10
mediocrity m. thrust upon them HELL 155:13
medium m. because nothing's well done ACE 1:5
m. is the message MCLU 208:5
meek Blessed are the m. BIBL 42:14
meet If I should m. thee BYRO 79:19
make him an help m.	BIBL 33:2
m. and right so to do	BOOK 60:2
m. 'em on your way down	MIZN 225:4
m. thee in that hollow vale	KING 186:6
very m., right	BOOK 60:3
When shall we three m.	SHAK 278:25

meeting Journeys end in lovers m. SHAK 288:12
meetings m. made December June TENN 311:27
melancholy Hence, loathèd M. MILT 219:25
inherited a vile m.	JOHN 174:10
m. fit shall fall	KEAT 182:7
m. god protect thee	SHAK 280:20
m., long	ARNO 15:4
moping m.	MILT 222:23
Naught so sweet as M.	BURT 76:9
soothe her m.	GOLD 144:4

Melchisedech order of M. BOOK 63:3
meliora *Video m.* OVID 238:15
mellow m. fruitfulness KEAT 182:21
melodie Luve's like the m. BURN 75:21
melodies Heard m. are sweet KEAT 181:29
melody M. is the essence MOZA 229:16

pretty girl is like a m. BERL 30:19
smale foweles maken m. CHAU 88:5
melons Stumbling on m. MARV 213:16
Melrose would'st view fair M. SCOT 266:9
melt Let Rome in Tiber m. SHAK 268:13
m. with ruth MILT 220:18
solid flesh would m. SHAK 270:29
melted m. into air SHAK 287:15
melting M.-Pot where all the races ZANG 344:23
member that will accept me as a m. MARX 214:2
members m. one of another BIBL 50:18
membra *Etiam disiecti m. poetae* HORA 164:20
même *plus c'est la m. chose* KARR 180:17
meminisse *Forsan et haec olim m. iuvabit* VIRG 324:10
memoirs M. are true and useful stars PEPY 243:18
write one's m. is to speak ill PÉTA 244:7
memorable that m. scene MARV 213:18
memorandum m. is written ACHE 1:7
memorial have no m. BIBL 41:30
out of the M. DICK 110:4
whole earth as their m. PERI 243:21
memorials there are no m. YEVT 344:6
memories m. are card-indexes CONN 99:3
m. are hunting horns APOL 13:10
memory Fond M. brings the light MOOR 227:20
Footfalls echo in the m.	ELIO 121:19
grand m. for forgetting	STEV 303:16
His m. is going	JOHN 176:12
m. revealed itself	PROU 251:17
Queen Elizabeth of most happy m.	BIBL 32:20
sense them like a m.	MOSE 229:12
Some women'll stay in a man's m.	KIPL 189:1
Thanks for the m.	ROBI 257:21
Vibrates in the m.	SHEL 293:27

men 200,000 m. NAPO 231:8
all m. are created equal	ANON 10:14
all things to all m.	BIBL 49:27
Bring forth m.-children	SHAK 280:2
conditions of m.	BOOK 59:9
finds too late that m. betray	GOLD 144:4
fishers of m.	BIBL 42:13
form Christian m.	ARNO 16:7
hell to m.	AESC 2:23
how much m. hate them	GREE 147:6
I eat m. like air	PLAT 245:21
If m. could get pregnant	KENN 184:5
Measures not m.	CANN 81:15
M. are April when they woo	SHAK 270:3
M. are but children	DRYD 116:27
M. are so honest	LERN 197:25
M. are vile	MONT 226:2
M. eat Hogs	STEV 303:4
m. have got love	AMIS 4:22
M. have had every advantage	AUST 19:23
m. in women do require	BLAK 56:3
m., like satyrs	MARL 212:8
m. may come	TENN 310:14
m. must work	KING 186:21
M., my brothers	TENN 312:9
m. naturally desire to know	AUCT 17:21
M. seldom make passes	PARK 240:16
m.'s lack of manners	HATH 153:6
M.! the only animal to fear	LAWR 194:18
M. were deceivers ever	SHAK 284:1
m. we wanted to marry	STEI 302:11
M. who march away	HARD 151:25
m. who will support me	MELB 216:7
m. with the muck-rakes	ROOS 260:2
Not m., but measures	BURK 74:14
not the m. in my life that counts	WEST 332:13
power over m.	WOLL 338:23
schemes o' mice an' m.	BURN 75:31
two strong m.	KIPL 187:8

wealth accumulates, and m. decay — GOLD 143:7
We are the hollow m. — ELIO 122:4
What m. or gods — KEAT 181:28
mend shine, and seek to m. — DONN 113:21
mene M., TEKEL, UPHARSIN — BIBL 41:8
meningitis M. It was a word — DEAN 107:6
mens M. sana in corpore sano — JUVE 180:4
mental cease from m. fight — BLAK 55:27
mer Poème De la M. — RIMB 257:10
merchant like unto a m. man — BIBL 44:3
m. shall hardly keep himself — BIBL 41:27
merchantman monarchy is a m. — AMES 4:17
mercies For his m. ay endure — MILT 220:8
tender m. of the wicked — BIBL 37:27
Thanks for m. past — BUCK 72:4
merciful God be m. — BIBL 47:8
Name of God, the M. — KORA 190:5
these were m. men — BIBL 41:30
merciless black and m. things — JAME 170:16
mercury pick up m. with a fork — LLOY 201:2
words of M. — SHAK 278:24
mercy belle dame sans m. — KEAT 181:9
crowning m. — CROM 103:19
God's gracious m. — BOOK 60:21
Have m. upon us — BOOK 59:3
Justice with m. — MILT 222:21
love m. — BIBL 41:17
M. and truth — BOOK 62:13
m. embraceth him — BOOK 61:13
m. endureth for ever — BOOK 63:22
M. has a human heart — BLAK 56:6
M. I asked, mercy I found — ANON 6:3
quality of m. — SHAK 282:20
render The deeds of m. — SHAK 282:21
so is his m. — BIBL 41:23
merde M. — CAMB 80:16
merit m. for a bishopric — WEST 332:20
mermaid M. Tavern — KEAT 181:26
mermaids heard the m. singing — ELIO 122:14
hear m. singing — DONN 114:11
merrily m. hent the stile-a — SHAK 289:8
m. meet in heaven — MORE 228:2
Merrily, m. shall I live — SHAK 287:19
merriment m. of parsons — JOHN 176:7
merry all their wars are m. — CHES 89:18
be m. — BIBL 38:24
eat, drink, and be m. — BIBL 46:22
Have they been m. — SHAK 286:36
m. heart — BIBL 37:33
m. heart goes all the day — SHAK 289:8
m. monarch — ROCH 258:15
m. month of May — BALL 23:16
m. someris day — CHAU 88:25
never a m. world — SELD 267:12
merrygoround It's no go the m. — MACN 208:16
mess Another fine m. — LAUR 194:9
In every m. I finds — DIBD 109:14
m. of pottage — BIBL 33:27
message if there is a m. — PAXM 242:8
medium is the m. — MCLU 208:5
messager bisy larke, m. of day — CHAU 88:14
messages m. should be delivered — GOLD 144:10
messenger M. of God — KORA 190:21
messing m. about in boats — GRAH 145:9
met Hail, fellow, well m. — SWIF 307:6
Ill m. by moonlight — SHAK 283:8
m. together — BOOK 62:13
metal with rich m. loaded — SPEN 300:15
metamorphoses month of m. — ARAG 13:19
metaphysical m. brothel for the emotions — KOES 189:21
metaphysics Explaining m. — BYRO 78:15
M. is the finding — BRAD 65:20

meteor cloud-encircled m. — SHEL 293:1
method yet there is m. in't — SHAK 271:28
Methodist morals of a M. — GILB 141:7
methods You know my m. — DOYL 115:19
methought M. I saw — MILT 223:11
métier c'est son m. — HEIN 155:10
metre wretched m. and lame m. — MILT 220:31
metropolis m. of the empire — COBB 95:8
meurt La Garde m. — CAMB 80:16
Mexico M., so far from God — DIAZ 109:12
Mexique beyond the M. Bay — MARV 213:13
mezzo Nel m. del cammin — DANT 105:16
mice as long as it catches m. — DENG 108:14
Like little m. — SUCK 305:11
schemes o' m. an' men — BURN 75:31
Michael M. and his angels — BIBL 52:14
Michelangelo M. left a proof — YEAT 343:27
Mickey Mouse M. could direct — HYTN 168:6
microbes on the antiquity of m. — ANON 5:14
microscopic man a m. eye — POPE 248:12
middle beginning, a m. — ARIS 14:15
Heaven, a m. state — MALL 210:7
m. way is none at all — ADAM 1:20
mine was the m. state — DEFO 107:13
safely by the m. way — OVID 238:14
middle age dead centre of m. — ADAM 1:13
enchantments of the M. — BEER 27:12
last enchantments of the M. — ARNO 15:29
middle class M. was quite prepared — BELL 28:12
Philistines proper, or m. — ARNO 15:28
midnight a-bed after m. — SHAK 288:11
black, and m. hags — SHAK 281:7
came upon a m. clear — SEAR 267:2
cease upon the m. — KEAT 182:13
Cerberus, and blackest M. — MILT 219:25
chimes at m. — SHAK 274:22
Holding hands at m. — GERS 138:17
iron tongue of m. — SHAK 283:24
m. ride of Paul Revere — LONG 202:4
our m. oil — QUAR 253:4
stroke of the m. hour — NEHR 232:3
'Tis the year's m. — DONN 114:9
woes at m. rise — LYLY 204:23
midst In the m. of life — BOOK 60:24
there am I in the m. — BIBL 44:16
midsummer very m. madness — SHAK 288:27
midway M. along the path — DANT 105:16
midwife fairies' m. — SHAK 286:14
midwinter In the bleak m. — ROSS 260:12
mieux m. est l'ennemi du bien — VOLT 326:3
tout est au m. — VOLT 325:20
might as our m. lessens — ANON 13:5
do it with thy m. — BIBL 38:26
Exceeds man's m. — SHAK 287:29
It m. have been — HART 152:22
It m. have been — WHIT 334:6
my name is M.-have-been — ROSS 260:17
Through the dear m. — MILT 220:20
mightier pen m. than the sword — BULW 72:15
mighty all that m. heart — WORD 339:19
how are the m. fallen — BIBL 35:26
How are the m. fallen — BIBL 35:29
Marlowe's m. line — JONS 178:6
M. lak' a rose — STAN 301:20
m. man is he — LONG 202:7
Nimrod the m. hunter — BIBL 33:23
put down the m. — BIBL 45:34
rushing m. wind — BIBL 48:24
thou art m. yet — SHAK 276:30
mild m. and magnificent eye — BROW 70:17
mile compel thee to go a m. — BIBL 42:19
miles m. to go before I sleep — FROS 134:14
milestones m. on the Dover Road — DICK 110:17

militant Christ's Church m. | BOOK 59:24
militarism M. . . . is fetish worship | TAWN 309:14
military entrust to m. men | CLEM 94:7
m. man approaches | SHAW 291:13
order and m. discipline | ANON 6:10
milk Adversity's sweet m. | SHAK 288:30
drunk the m. of Paradise | COLE 96:7
end is moo, the other, m. | NASH 231:13
flowing with m. and honey | BIBL 34:2
Gin was mother's m. | SHAW 291:30
his mother's m. | SHAK 288:8
m. and the yoghurt | TRIL 319:10
m. of human kindness | SHAK 279:12
M.'s leap toward immortality | FADI 125:19
M.-soup men call domestic | PATM 242:3
m. the cow of the world | WILB 334:18
m.-white steed | BALL 24:11
putting m. into babies | CHUR 91:22
take my m. for gall | SHAK 279:15
trout in the m. | THOR 317:16
With m. and honey blessed | NEAL 232:2
mill at the m. with slaves | MILT 222:32
old m. by the stream | ARMS 14:23
mille Da mi basia m. | CATU 85:20
million Fifty m. Frenchmen | ANON 6:22
m. deaths a statistic | STAL 301:15
want to make a m. | ANON 7:15
millionaire And an old-fashioned m. | FISH 128:9
I am a M. | SHAW 291:2
m. who bought it | MCCA 206:16
millions I will be m. | PERÓ 244:2
mills dark Satanic m. | BLAK 55:27
m. of God grind slowly | LONG 202:1
millstone m. were hanged about his neck | BIBL 44:14
millstones Turned to m. | SHEL 293:6
Milton malt does more than M. | HOUS 165:10
M.! thou shouldst be living | WORD 340:4
miminy Francesca di Rimini, m. | GILB 140:26
mimsy m. were the borogoves | CARR 84:3
mince dined on m. | LEAR 195:16
mind absence of m. | SEEL 267:7
damages his m. | ANON 12:4
frailty of the m. | SHAD 268:6
Georgia on my m. | GORR 144:19
give a sex to m. | WOLL 338:22
human m. in ruins | DAVI 106:17
index of a feeling m. | CRAB 102:16
in m., body, or estate | BOOK 59:10
know the m. of God | HAWK 153:13
liberation of the human m. | GOLD 143:5
man's unconquerable m. | WORD 341:16
m. diseased | BYRO 78:4
m. has mountains | HOPK 162:26
M. has no sex | WOLL 338:22
m. is its own place | MILT 221:6
m. is not a bed | AGAT 3:1
m.'s construction | SHAK 279:11
m. serene for contemplation | GAY 137:8
m. to me a kingdom is | DYER 118:20
m. was that of Lord Beaverbrook | ATTL 17:9
m. which cannot bear | MENG 216:17
m. which reveres details | LEWI 198:19
minister to a m. diseased | SHAK 281:21
my m. a gap of danger | HEAN 154:13
my m.'s unsworn | EURI 125:9
no female m. | GILM 141:12
nothing great but m. | HAMI 150:15
not in my perfect m. | SHAK 278:7
out of my m. | BELL 29:2
O! what a noble m. | SHAK 272:7
padlock—on her m. | PRIO 251:8
so-called mortal m. | EDDY 119:16
sound m. | JUVE 180:4

travel broadens the m. | CHES 90:6
Until reeled the m. | GIBB 139:13
What is M. | PUNC 252:11
minds hearts and m. | BIBL 50:27
marriage of true m. | SHAK 290:6
M. are like parachutes | DEWA 109:7
M. innocent and quiet | LOVE 203:6
M. like beds always made up | WILL 336:10
m. of ordinary men | BRON 67:7
spur of all great m. | CHAP 87:17
mine but m. own | SHAK 270:5
lovin' dat man of m. | HAMM 150:16
m. own familiar friend | BOOK 62:2
minefield grief is like a m. | WARN 328:15
miner Dwelt a m. | MONT 226:24
miners like m.' coal dust | BOOT 64:11
mineworkers National Union of M. | MACM 208:11
minion morning's m. | HOPK 163:8
minister cheer the m. | CANN 81:17
God help the M. | MELB 216:4
m. to a mind diseased | SHAK 281:21
M., whoever he at any time | PAIN 239:14
m. who moves about | CHOI 90:16
Yes, M.! No, Minister | CROS 104:7
ministering m. angel | SHAK 273:13
m. angel thou | SCOT 266:19
ministers Angels and m. of grace | SHAK 271:13
group of Cabinet M. | CURZ 105:8
my actions are my m.' | CHAR 87:24
you murdering m. | SHAK 279:15
ministries Times has made many m. | BAGE 22:13
ministry m. of all the talents | ANON 8:16
performs its secret m. | COLE 96:1
mink trick of wearing m. | BALM 24:20
minnows death for the m. | TAWN 309:15
Triton of the m. | SHAK 270:10
minstrel M. Boy to the war | MOOR 227:17
wandering m. I | GILB 140:6
minute sucker born every m. | BARN 25:12
minutes famous for fifteen m. | WARH 328:12
have the seven m. | COLL 97:8
m. hasten to their end | SHAK 289:30
take care of m. | CHES 89:8
Mirabeau Under M. Bridge | APOL 13:11
miracle m. of our age | CARE 82:5
m. of rare device | COLE 96:5
Miranda Do you remember an Inn, M. | BELL 28:26
mirror m. cracked from side to side | TENN 312:5
m. up to nature | SHAK 272:12
novel is like a m. | STEN 302:13
mirth I love such m. | WALT 328:4
mischief execute any m. | CLAR 93:12
In every deed of m. | GIBB 139:5
m., thou art afoot | SHAK 276:25
m. thou hast done | NEWT 233:16
punishment is m. | BENT 30:4
misdoings these our m. | BOOK 59:27
miserable Me m.! which way shall I fly | MILT 221:29
M. comforters | BIBL 37:7
m. sinners | BOOK 59:3
two people m. | BUTL 77:11
miserere m. nobis | MISS 224:6
miseria Nella m. | DANT 105:20
misery full of m. | BOOK 60:23
great kick at m. | LAWR 194:23
guilt and m. | AUST 19:18
mine affliction and my m. | BIBL 40:28
M. acquaints a man | SHAK 287:10
m. is a battle gained | WELL 331:7
m. of manilla folders | ROET 258:21
m. which it is his duty | LOWE 203:12
result m. | DICK 110:3
splendid m. | ROSS 260:15

vale of m.	BOOK 62:11	**mome** m. raths outgrabe	CARR 84:3
when one is in m.	DANT 105:20	**moment** Every m. dies a man	BABB 20:15
misfortune m. of our best friends	LA R 194:2	m. dies a man	TENN 314:2
misfortunes crimes and m.	VOLT 326:7	m. in childhood	GREE 147:1
crimes, follies, and m.	GIBB 139:2	one brief shining m.	LERN 197:24
make m. more bitter	BACO 21:20	**momentary** pleasure is m.	CHES 89:15
m. of others	LA R 193:18	**moments** Wagner has lovely m.	ROSS 260:21
mislead one to m. the public	ASQU 16:20	**monarch** hereditary m. was insane	BAGE 22:14
misleading bound to be m.	WATS 328:26	merry m.	ROCH 258:15
misquote enough of learning to m.	BYRO 79:8	m. of all I survey	COWP 102:9
missa *Ite m. est*	MISS 224:8	**monarchies** elective m.	GIBB 139:1
missed m. the bus	CHAM 86:22	**monarchs** righteous m.	BROO 67:13
never would be m.	GILB 140:8	**monarchy** absolute M.	PAIN 239:7
Woman much m.	HARD 152:2	constitutional m.	BAGE 22:21
mission My m. is to pacify	GLAD 141:18	m. is a merchantman	AMES 4:17
missionaries eaten by m.	SPOO 301:2	M. is only	SHEL 294:7
missionary I would eat a m.	WILB 334:15	universal m. of wit	CARE 82:6
Mississippi place the m.	BELL 29:3	US presidency a Tudor m.	BURG 73:16
misspent thy m. time	KEN 184:2	**money** ain't got a barrel of m.	WOOD 339:5
mist Fuji through m.	BASH 26:1	bank will lend you m.	HOPE 162:17
mistake make a m.	LA G 191:18	draining m. from the pockets	SMIT 297:11
m. in the translation	VANB 322:8	getting m.	JOHN 175:12
m. shall not be repeated	ANON 9:16	haven't got the m.	RUTH 263:5
mistaken possible you may be m.	CROM 103:18	have to borrer the m.	WARD 328:9
mistakes knows some of the worst m.	HEIS 155:11	He had m. as well	THAT 315:5
man who makes no m.	PHEL 244:12	Hollywood m. isn't money	PARK 241:2
mistress In ev'ry port a m.	GAY 137:12	if you can count your m.	GETT 138:18
literature is my m.	CHEK 89:1	licence to print m.	THOM 317:15
m. of herself	POPE 247:15	long enough to get m. from	LEAC 195:3
m. of the Earl of Craven	WILS 337:1	love of m.	BIBL 51:11
m. of the months	SWIN 307:16	man without m.	WYCH 342:5
m. of the Party	HEAL 154:10	m. answereth all things	BIBL 38:30
O m. mine	SHAK 288:12	m. can't buy me love	LENN 197:10
teeming m.	POPE 247:13	M. couldn't buy friends	MILL 218:19
mistresses I shall have m.	GEOR 137:22	M. doesn't talk, it swears	DYLA 119:4
or your Lordship's m.	WILK 336:1	M. gives me pleasure	BELL 28:16
mists Season of m.	KEAT 182:21	m.-grabbing cronies	HAGU 149:5
misty ful m. morwe	CHAU 88:25	m. gushes into politics	WHIT 333:12
misunderstood truth m.	JAME 171:3	M. has no smell	VESP 323:15
mites with m. of stars	MAYA 215:15	M. is like a sixth sense	MAUG 215:9
Mithra M. of wide pastures	ZORO 345:10	M. is like muck	BACO 21:24
Mithridates M., he died old	HOUS 165:11	M. . . . is none of the wheels	HUME 166:21
mix m. them with my brains	OPIE 236:15	m. I spend on advertising	LEVE 198:4
mixture strange m. of blood	CEÈV 103:9	M. is the sinews of love	FARQ 126:11
Moab M. is my wash-pot	BOOK 62:5	m. perish with thee	BIBL 48:25
moan of doves	TENN 313:19	m. the sinews of war	BACO 21:28
moanday m., tearsday, wailsday	JOYC 178:20	M. was exactly like sex	BALD 23:6
moaning no m. of the bar	TENN 310:18	only interested in m.	SHAW 292:4
moated at the m. grange	SHAK 282:1	pleasant it is to have m.	CLOU 94:22
lonely m. grange	TENN 312:18	plenty of m.	ANOU 13:7
mob do what the m. do	DICK 111:5	poor know that it is m.	BREN 66:13
M., Parliament, Rabble	COBB 95:7	rub up against m.	RUNY 262:2
supreme governors, the m.	WALP 327:6	somehow, make m.	HORA 163:20
mocked God is not m.	BIBL 50:15	they have more m.	FITZ 129:4
mocker Wine is a m.	BIBL 37:38	They hired the m.	COOL 99:22
mockingbird kill a m.	LEE 196:9	unlimited m.	CICE 92:28
model I am the very m.	GILB 141:5	use the m. for the poor	PERÓ 244:1
moderate m. income	DURH 118:14	voter who uses his m.	SAMU 264:4
moderation astonished at my own m.	CLIV 94:19	way the m. goes	MAND 210:18
m. in everything	HORA 164:19	When you have m., it's sex	DONL 113:16
m. in the pursuit of justice	GOLD 144:6	wrote, except for m.	JOHN 175:19
m. is a sort of treason	BURK 73:21	You pays your m.	PUNC 252:8
modern m. Babylon	DISR 112:28	**moneybag** Aristocracy of the M.	CARL 82:21
m. Major-General	GILB 141:5	**moneys** m. are for values	BACO 20:19
modest M.? My word, no	REED 255:11	**mongoose** motto of all the m. family	KIPL 188:20
modified M. rapture	GILB 140:11	**mongrels** continent of energetic m.	FISH 128:4
modus *Est m. in rebus*	HORA 164:19	**monk** m. who shook the world	MONT 226:20
mois *m. des floraisons*	ARAG 13:19	**monkey** descent from a m.	WILB 334:16
molecule inhales one m. of it	JEAN 171:9	look upon a m.	CONG 98:20
moll Me and M. Maloney	GRAV 146:2	**monkeys** Cats and m.	JAME 170:17
Moloch great M., national sovereignty	MEYE 217:17	m. banging on typewriters	WILE 335:26
M., horrid king	MILT 221:10	m. strumming on typewriters	EDDI 119:13
mom place called M.'s	ALGR 4:2	**monogamous** Woman m.	JAME 171:5

monogamy M. is the same ANON 6:4
Monroe M. Doctrine MONR 225:21
mouth of Marilyn M. MITT 225:3
monster become a m. NIET 234:9
green-eyed m. SHAK 284:21
many-headed m. POPE 248:29
m., which the Blatant beast SPEN 300:21
m. whom I had created SHEL 292:11
this busy m., manunkind CUMM 104:17
monsters reason produces m. GOYA 145:2
monstrous m. carbuncle CHAR 88:2
M. carbuncles SPEN 300:7
m. regiment of women KNOX 189:15
montes *Parturient m.* HORA 163:15
Montezuma halls of M. ANON 7:3
who imprisoned M. MACA 205:17
month April is the cruellest m. ELIO 122:20
fressh as is the m. of May CHAU 88:7
m. of metamorphoses ARAG 13:19
m. of tension LESS 198:2
months mistress of the m. SWIN 307:16
Montreal O God! O M. BUTL 77:15
monument If you seek a m. ANON 13:1
m. more lasting than bronze HORA 164:16
m. of the insufficiency JOHN 174:2
m. sticks like a fishbone LOWE 203:20
patience on a m. SHAK 288:21
monumentum *Exegi m. aere perennius* HORA 164:16
Si m. requiris, circumspice ANON 13:1
moo One end is m. NASH 231:13
moocow m. coming down along the road JOYC 178:23
moon auld m. in her arm BALL 24:9
beneath a waning m. COLE 96:4
Beneath the visiting m. SHAK 268:28
by the light of the m. LEAR 195:16
danced in the m. CART 84:24
Daughter of the M. LONG 202:3
hornèd M. COLE 96:15
horned m. WORD 339:14
i' the cold o' the m. BROW 69:26
minions of the m. SHAK 273:25
m. belongs to everyone DE S 109:4
m. be still as bright BYRO 79:16
m. by night BOOK 63:13
m. is in the seventh house RADO 253:21
m.'s an arrant thief SHAK 287:24
m. shines bright SHAK 282:26
m. shone bright on Mrs Porter ELIO 122:26
m. under her feet BIBL 52:13
m. walks the night DE L 108:10
mortals call the M. SHEL 292:22
only a paper m. HARB 151:8
sad steps, O M. SIDN 295:9
shine on, harvest m. NORW 235:1
silent as the m. MILT 223:2
voyage to the m. LARD 193:7
when the m. shall rise WOTT 341:22
moonlight How sweet the m. sleeps SHAK 282:28
Ill met by m. SHAK 283:8
visit it by the pale m. SCOT 266:9
Watch for me by m. NOYE 235:5
moonlit Knocking on the m. door DE L 108:7
moons m. shall wax and wane no more WATT 329:12
moonshine find out m. SHAK 283:15
Transcendental m. CARL 82:25
moonstruck m. madness MILT 222:23
moored island is m. only lightly BARR 25:18
moral Debasing the moral m. ELIO 121:7
m. flabbiness JAME 171:4
m. law within me KANT 180:12
m. or an immoral book WILD 335:8
m. principles please MENG 216:18
M. science is better occupied THOM 315:24

nature of m. sciences COND 98:5
O m. Gower CHAU 88:30
point a m. JOHN 174:6
morality Absolute m. SPEN 300:2
fits of m. MACA 205:15
Goodbye, m. HERB 157:2
know about m. CAMU 81:9
may be called M. KANT 180:13
m. for morality's sake COUS 100:19
m. touched by emotion ARNO 16:4
slave-m. NIET 234:10
some people talk of m. EDGE 119:20
morals either m. or principles GLAD 141:22
lack of m. HATH 153:6
m. of a Methodist GILB 141:7
m. of a whore JOHN 174:19
more For, I have m. DONN 113:25
I want some m. DICK 110:26
little m. BROW 69:25
m. and m. about less and less BUTL 77:3
m. equal than others ORWE 237:5
m. Piglet wasn't there MILN 218:23
m. than Homer knew SWIF 307:8
mores *O tempora, O m.* CICE 92:25
mori *pro patria m.* HORA 164:14
moriar *Non omnis m.* HORA 164:17
morituri *Ave Caesar, m. te salutant* ANON 12:8
morn But, look, the m. SHAK 270:26
From m. to noon he fell MILT 221:15
Salute the happy m. BYRO 77:19
morning arrested one fine m. KAFK 180:8
danced in the m. CART 84:24
Early one m. ANON 6:15
evening and the m. BIBL 32:22
glad confident m. BROW 70:18
joy cometh in the m. BOOK 61:11
Lucifer, son of the m. BIBL 39:25
many a glorious m. SHAK 289:28
m. after ADE 2:18
m. cometh BIBL 39:26
m. had been golden CHUR 92:9
M. has broken FARJ 126:5
M. in the bowl of night FITZ 128:14
M. light creaks down again SITW 296:11
m. rose KEAT 182:7
M.'s at seven BROW 70:27
m.'s minion HOPK 163:8
New every m. KEBL 183:19
pay thy m. sacrifice KEN 184:1
shining m. face SHAK 269:21
take you in the m. BALD 23:7
What a glorious m. ADAM 2:2
wings of the m. BOOK 63:25
won't go home till m. BUCK 72:5
Mornington present of M. Crescent HARG 152:9
Morocco we're M. bound BURK 74:24
moron consumer isn't a m. OGIL 235:20
See the happy m. ANON 9:18
morphine m. or idealism JUNG 179:15
Morris M. Minor prototype NUFF 235:6
nine men's m. SHAK 283:9
morrow no thought for the m. BIBL 43:1
mort *La m. ne surprend* LA F 191:15
mortal Her last disorder m. GOLD 143:15
shuffled off this m. coil SHAK 272:1
this m. life BOOK 60:6
mortality m. touches the heart VIRG 324:12
Old m. BROW 68:20
sepulchres of m. CREW 103:10
mortals not for m. ARMS 14:24
not in m. ADDI 2:7
what fools these m. be SHAK 283:17
mortar Lies are the m. WELL 331:16

mortifying m. reflections — CONG 98:20
mortis Timor m. conturbat me — DUNB 118:6
morts Il n'y a pas de m. — MAET 209:7
mortuus Passer m. est — CATU 85:18
Moscow do not march on M. — MONT 226:19
  M.: those syllables — PUSH 252:22
Moses From M. to Moses — ANON 7:2
  Go down, M. — ANON 10:20
Mosque from the Holy M. — KORA 190:18
mosquito just another m. — OKPI 236:3
mossy Happy field or m. cavern — KEAT 181:26
  violet by a m. stone — WORD 341:4
mote m. that is in thy brother's eye — BIBL 43:3
moth Both m. and flame — ROET 258:22
  m. and rust doth corrupt — BIBL 42:24
  m. for the star — SHEL 293:28
mother artist man and the m. woman — SHAW 291:9
  As is the m. — BIBL 40:30
  Behold thy m. — BIBL 48:13
  church for his m. — CYPR 105:10
  France, m. of arts — DU B 117:19
  gave her m. forty whacks — ANON 8:10
  Gentle Child of gentle M. — DEAR 107:7
  happen to your m. — WALK 326:19
  heaviness of his m. — BIBL 37:25
  Honour thy father and thy m. — BIBL 34:16
  I arose a m. — BIBL 35:1
  leave his father and his m. — BIBL 33:5
  marry a man who hates his m. — BENN 29:26
  may not marry his M. — BOOK 64:7
  m. bids me bind — HUNT 167:6
  m. bore me in the southern wild — BLAK 56:9
  m., do not cry — FARM 126:8
  M., give me the sun — IBSE 168:11
  m. laid my baby — ALEX 3:17
  m. of all battles — HUSS 167:11
  m. of all treachery — PAIS 239:18
  M. OF HARLOTS — BIBL 52:21
  m. of Parliaments — BRIG 67:1
  m. of sciences — BACO 22:4
  M. of the Free — BENS 29:27
  m.'s little helper — JAGG 170:2
  My m. groaned — BLAK 56:10
  never called me m. — WOOD 339:2
  their Dacian m. — BYRO 78:6
  to make it well? My M. — TAYL 309:20
  Took great care of his M. — MILN 219:1
mothers Come m. and fathers — DYLA 119:10
  happy m. made — SHAK 286:13
  m.-in-law and Wigan Pier — BRID 66:17
  m. of large families — BELL 28:8
  women become like their m. — WILD 335:1
motion m. of the wheels — HUME 166:21
  perpetual m. — DICK 111:9
  poetry in m. — KAUF 180:20
  poetry of m. — GRAH 145:10
  uniform m. in a right line — NEWT 233:11
motley made myself a m. — SHAK 290:4
  M.'s the only wear — SHAK 269:19
motorcycle art of m. maintenance — PIRS 245:6
mould broke the m. — ARIO 14:7
  frozen in an out-of-date m. — JENK 171:21
mouldering many a m. heap — GRAY 146:14
mount m. up with wings — BIBL 40:11
mountain Climb ev'ry m. — HAMM 150:17
  exceeding high m. — BIBL 42:12
  Flatter the m.-tops — SHAK 289:28
  from yonder m. height — TENN 313:17
  go up to the m. — KING 186:12
  In a m. greenery — HART 152:20
  misty m. tops — SHAK 286:32
  m. and hill — BIBL 40:7
  say unto this m., Remove — BIBL 44:12

mountains beautiful upon the m. — BIBL 40:14
  m. also shall bring peace — BOOK 62:7
  M. are the beginning — RUSK 262:11
  m. by the winter sea — TENN 311:12
  m. look on Marathon — BYRO 78:24
  M. of Mourne — FREN 133:17
  m. skipped like rams — BOOK 63:5
  M. will go into labour — HORA 163:15
  One of the m. — WORD 341:14
  so that I could remove m. — BIBL 49:30
mountebank m. and his zany — WALP 327:14
mourir Partir c'est m. un peu — HARA 151:5
mourn Blessed are they that m. — BIBL 42:14
  countless thousands m. — BURN 75:16
  each will m. her own — INGE 169:1
  Margaret you m. for — HOPK 163:5
  M., you powers of Charm — CATU 85:18
  time to m. — BIBL 38:17
Mourne Mountains of M. — FREN 133:17
mournful m. Ever weeping Paddington — BLAK 55:18
mourning in m. for my life — CHEK 88:32
  M. becomes Electra — O'NE 236:13
  widow bird sat m. — SHEL 292:21
mouse invention of a m. — DISN 112:3
  little m. will be born — HORA 163:15
  Not a m. Shall disturb — SHAK 283:25
  not even a m. — MOOR 227:2
mousetrap make a better m. — EMER 124:18
  The M. — SHAK 272:14
mouth Englishman to open his m. — SHAW 291:28
  m. became the Brahmin — RIG 257:7
  m. had been used as a latrine — AMIS 4:19
  m. of Marilyn Monroe — MITT 225:3
  m. of very babes — BOOK 60:27
  only one m. — ZENO 345:3
  out of the m. of God — BIBL 42:10
  silver foot in his m. — RICH 256:18
  spew thee out of my m. — BIBL 52:6
mouthful gold filling in a m. of decay — OSBO 237:29
mouths m., and speak not — BOOK 63:7
  poet's m. be shut — YEAT 343:13
  pork please our m. — MENG 216:18
  stuffed their m. with gold — BEVA 32:11
moutons Revenons à ces m. — ANON 11:19
movable Paris is a m. feast — HEMI 156:2
move But it does m. — GALI 135:13
  feel the earth m. — HEMI 156:1
  great affair is to m. — STEV 303:19
  in him we live, and m. — BIBL 48:35
  m. the earth — ARCH 14:2
moved king was much m. — BIBL 35:33
  m. about like the wind — GERO 138:13
movement measure of m. — AUCT 17:23
movers m. and shakers — O'SH 238:1
moves If it m., salute it — ANON 7:14
movie could direct a m. — HYTN 168:6
movies M. should have a beginning — GODA 142:10
moving m. accident is not my trade — WORD 339:22
  m. finger writes — FITZ 128:19
  m. in opposite directions — SMIT 298:10
  m. toyshop of the heart — POPE 248:32
Mozart no female M. — PAGL 239:5
  when M. was my age — LEHR 196:20
MP Being an M. — ABBO 1:1
  Being an M. — PARR 241:12
MPs dull M. in close proximity — GILB 140:3
much just so m., no more — BROW 71:12
  not m. for them to be — COMP 98:2
  Sing 'em m. — MELB 216:3
  so m. owed by so many to so few — CHUR 91:17
  so m. to do — RHOD 256:9
  so m. to do — TENN 311:22

muck Money is like m.	BACO 21:24
muckrake m. in his hand	BUNY 73:7
muckrakes men with the m.	ROOS 260:2
mud back in the m.	AUGI 18:25
filled up with m.	SHAK 283:9
M.! Glorious mud	FLAN 129:15
muddle beginning, a m.	LARK 193:17
muddy almost always a m. horsepond	PEAC 242:14
M., ill-seeming	SHAK 286:39
muero *Muero porque no m.*	JOHN 172:13
Muhammad M. is not the father	KORA 190:21
mule m. of politics	DISR 112:19
mules m. of politics	POWE 250:26
Mulligan plump Buck M.	JOYC 178:26
multiply m. my signs and my wonders	BIBL 34:4
multitude m. is in the wrong	DILL 111:24
m. of sins	BIBL 51:29
multitudes I contain m.	WHIT 334:1
mum oafish louts remember M.	BETJ 31:16
They fuck you up, your m. and dad	LARK 193:14
mundane in this m. life	MURA 230:3
mundi *peccata m.*	MISS 224:6
Sic transit gloria m.	ANON 12:22
muove *amor che m. il sole*	DANT 105:22
Eppur si m.	GALI 135:13
murder battle and m.	BOOK 59:6
commit a m.	VAN 322:14
do no m.	BOOK 59:21
I met M. on the way	SHEL 293:5
Killing no m.	SEXB 268:4
love and m. will out	CONG 98:11
m. by the law	YOUN 344:12
m. by the throat	LLOY 201:1
m. cannot be hid long	SHAK 282:9
M. considered	DE Q 108:22
m. into the home	HITC 159:15
M. most foul	SHAK 271:17
m. respectable	ORWE 237:19
M.'s out of tune	SHAK 285:2
m. the thinker	WESK 331:21
m. to dissect	WORD 341:19
M. wol out	CHAU 88:16
One m. made a villain	PORT 249:22
story is about not m.	JAME 171:1
to m., for the truth	ADLE 2:19
Vanity, like m., will out	COWL 101:15
murdered m. reputations	CONG 98:16
Our royal master's m.	SHAK 280:18
their m. man	KEAT 181:14
murderer m. for fancy prose style	NABO 230:18
murderers m. of Jewish children	WIES 334:14
m. take the first step	KARR 180:16
murmur m. of a summer's day	ARNO 15:14
murmuring m. of innumerable bees	TENN 313:19
Murray slain the Earl of M.	BALL 23:17
mus *nascetur ridiculus m.*	HORA 163:15
muscular His Christianity was m.	DISR 112:21
muse M. but served to ease	POPE 247:8
O! for a M. of fire	SHAK 274:26
tenth M.	TROL 319:20
muses charm of all the M.	TENN 313:27
museum m. inside our heads	LIVE 200:10
mushroom Life too short to stuff a m.	CONR 99:10
music alive with the sound of m.	HAMM 150:24
but the m. there	POPE 248:3
chosen m., liberty	WORD 341:14
Classic m. is th'kind	HUBB 166:5
compulsion doth in m. lie	MILT 219:8
dance to the m. of time	POWE 250:18
day the m. died	MCLE 207:21
essence of m.	MOZA 229:16
Fading in m.	SHAK 282:15
finds its food in m.	LILL 199:4

Fled is that m.	KEAT 182:16
frozen m.	SCHE 265:10
how potent cheap m. is	COWA 101:12
How sour sweet m. is	SHAK 285:30
I shall be made thy m.	DONN 113:24
Let's face the m. and dance	BERL 30:18
make the m. mute	TENN 311:9
most civilized m.	USTI 322:2
M. and women	PEPY 243:16
M. begins to atrophy	POUN 250:13
m. be the food of love	SHAK 288:2
M. has charms	CONG 98:13
m. in the air	ELGA 121:3
M. that gentlier on the spirit	TENN 312:17
m. the brandy of the damned	SHAW 291:11
M., when soft voices die	SHEL 293:27
Of m. Dr Johnson used to say	JOHN 177:2
passion cannot M. raise	DRYD 117:9
practising your pastoral m.	VIRG 325:83
sound of soft m.	DISR 113:1
still, sad m.	WORD 340:3
thou hast thy m. too	KEAT 182:22
We are the m. makers	O'SH 238:1
musical m. as is Apollo's lute	MILT 219:14
musician far below the m.	LEON 197:21
Muslim neither Hindu nor M.	SIKH 295:21
Muslims named you M.	KORA 190:20
zealous M. to execute	KHOM 185:16
Muss *M. es sein*	BEET 27:15
must It m. be	BEET 27:15
Must! Is m. a word	ELIZ 123:9
whispers low, *Thou m.*	EMER 124:10
mustard faith as a grain of m. seed	BIBL 44:12
grain of m. seed	BIBL 44:2
mutabile *Varium et m. semper Femina*	VIRG 324:16
mutantur *spatio m.*	LUCR 204:14
mute m. recommendation	PUBL 251:21
mutilate spindle or m.	ANON 6:13
my m.-lorded him	THAC 314:20
myriad There died a m.	POUN 250:10
myrrh frankincense, and m.	BIBL 42:3
myrtles Ye m. brown	MILT 220:9
myself If I am not for m.	HILL 159:9
mysterious moves in a m. way	COWP 101:23
mystery grasped the m. of the atom	BRAD 65:23
heart of my m.	SHAK 272:17
I shew you a m.	BIBL 50:7
M., BABYLON THE GREAT	BIBL 52:21
my tongue, the m. telling	THOM 315:22
penetralium of m.	KEAT 183:6
riddle wrapped in a m.	CHUR 91:13
mystic m., wonderful	TENN 311:4
mystical m. way of Pythagoras	BROW 69:3
myths Science must begin with m.	POPP 249:13
where m. Go when they die	FENT 126:20

N

nagging N. is the repetition	SUMM 306:3
nail blows his n.	SHAK 278:23
I n. my pictures together	SCHW 265:22
nails n. bitten and pared	MACA 205:13
print of the n.	BIBL 48:20
naive n. domestic Burgundy	THUR 317:27
naked Half n., loving	BYRO 78:21
left me n. to mine enemies	SHAK 275:26
n. ape	MORR 228:14
n. into the conference chamber	BEVA 32:9
n. to the hangman's noose	HOUS 165:3
stark n. truth	CLEL 94:6
starving hysterical n.	GINS 141:14

With n. foot WYAT 342:1
name at the n. of Jesus BIBL 50:24
At the n. of Jesus NOEL 234:18
dare not speak its n. DOUG 115:2
fear my n. BIBL 41:19
filches from me my good n. SHAK 284:20
gathered together in my n. BIBL 44:16
ghost of a great n. LUCA 204:7
glory in the n. of Briton GEOR 137:24
Halloo your n. SHAK 288:10
Hallowed be thy n. BIBL 42:23
In the n. of God, go AMER 4:16
In the n. of God, go CROM 103:20
In the N. of the Father MISS 223:25
king's n. SHAK 286:10
left the n. JOHN 174:6
Let me not n. it SHAK 284:33
liberties are taken in thy n. GEOR 138:12
local habitation and a n. SHAK 283:22
mark, or the n. of the beast BIBL 52:15
my n. is Jowett BEEC 27:10
My n. is Legion BIBL 45:27
My n. is Ozymandias SHEL 293:12
n. Achilles assumed BROW 68:21
n. had been Edmund KEAT 183:15
n. liveth for ever SASS 265:4
n. liveth for evermore ANON 10:5
n. liveth for evermore BIBL 41:30
n. of God in vain BIBL 34:14
N. of God, the Merciful KORA 190:5
N. of the Lord BOOK 63:11
n. to all succeeding ages curst DRYD 116:15
n. we give the people FLER 130:4
nothing of a n. BYRO 78:10
one whose n. was writ KEAT 183:17
power of Jesus' N. PERR 244:4
problem that has no n. FRIE 133:23
unto thy N. give the praise BOOK 63:6
What's in a n. SHAK 286:20
Who gave you this N. BOOK 60:8
worshipped with spoken n. ZORO 345:10
worth an age without a n. MORD 227:21
named n. you Muslims KORA 190:20
names Called him soft n. KEAT 182:13
called them by wrong n. BROW 69:22
in love with American n. BENÉ 29:10
N. Most Beautiful KORA 190:24
n. of men TROL 319:19
n. of those who love HUNT 167:1
naming n. of parts REED 255:8
Napoleon N. of crime DOYL 115:15
Napoleons Caesars and N. HUXL 167:16
narcotic n. be alcohol JUNG 179:15
Narragansett Where are the N. TECU 310:6
narrative unconvincing n. GILB 140:18
narrow find the road n. MAIM 209:19
n. is the way BIBL 43:9
nastiest n. thing in the nicest way GOLD 143:2
nasty is a n. creature MOLI 225:15
n., brutish, and short HOBB 160:3
Something n. in the woodshed GIBB 139:12
nation AMERICA thus top n. SELL 267:21
boundary of the march of a n. PARN 241:10
broad mass of a n. HITL 159:16
can deprive a n. NAMI 230:21
create a n. Europe MONN 225:19
every man and n. LOWE 203:18
n. a le gouvernment MAIS 209:20
n. of dancers EQUI 125:1
n. of shop-keepers ADAM 2:3
n. of shopkeepers NAPO 231:10
n. of shopkeepers SMIT 297:9
N. once again DAVI 106:22

n. shall not lift up sword BIBL 39:11
n. shall rise BIBL 44:34
N. shall speak peace REND 255:17
n. talking to itself MILL 218:16
n. that had lion's heart CHUR 92:5
new n. LINC 199:8
No n. is fit WILS 337:4
no rainbow n. MAND 211:3
old and haughty n. MILT 219:10
one-third of a n. ill-housed ROOS 259:18
terrorize a whole n. MURR 230:11
voice of a n. RUSS 263:1
what our N. stands for BETJ 31:22
national n. debt HAMI 150:13
N. Debt is a very Good Thing SELL 267:19
n. flag SUMN 306:5
n. home for the Jewish people BALF 23:14
nationalism n. is a silly cock ALDI 3:11
nationality what n. he would prefer RHOD 256:8
nations belong to other n. GILB 141:3
belong to two different n. FOST 132:4
day of small n. CHAM 86:18
Europe of n. DE G 107:25
father of many n. BIBL 49:9
fierce contending n. ADDI 2:11
great n. acted like gangsters KUBR 190:27
hating all other n. GASK 136:17
healing of the n. BIBL 52:27
n. how to live MILT 223:21
pedigree of n. JOHN 174:11
place among the n. EMME 124:19
rule n. by your government VIRG 324:23
Two n. DISR 112:27
two n. have been at war VOLT 325:21
two n. warring DURH 118:15
native by their n. shore COWP 101:25
in his n. place JOHN 175:8
my n. land SCOT 266:10
n. wood-notes wild MILT 220:7
our ideas about the n. LESS 198:1
with his n. land EDGE 119:21
natural I do it more n. SHAK 288:14
N. rights BENT 30:2
N. Selection DARW 106:7
n., simple, affecting GOLD 143:19
twice as n. CARR 84:13
naturalists n. observe, a flea SWIF 307:11
nature [Death is] n.'s way ANON 6:11
does N. live COLE 95:21
drive out n. HORA 163:24
Eye N.'s walks POPE 248:8
fair defect of n. MILT 222:22
God and n. AUCT 17:20
How N. always does contrive GILB 140:2
ignorance of n. HOLB 161:2
interpreter of n. JOHN 173:24
mirror up to n. SHAK 272:12
My n. is subdued SHAK 290:5
N. abhors a vacuum RABE 253:12
N., and Nature's laws POPE 247:28
n. cannot be fooled FEYN 127:6
N. does nothing uselessly ARIS 14:19
N. from her seat MILT 222:18
N. in awe to him MILT 220:24
N. in you stands SHAK 277:14
N. is not a temple TURG 320:15
n. is the art of God BROW 69:5
n. itselfe cant endure FLEM 130:2
n. made him ARIO 14:7
n. of war HOBB 160:2
N., red in tooth and claw TENN 311:21
N.'s agreeable blunders COWL 101:17
N.'s great masterpiece DONN 114:1

nature (*cont.*)
N. to advantage dressed — POPE 248:1
N. wears one universal grin — FIEL 127:16
next to N. — LAND 192:21
not n. — CONS 99:12
One touch of n. — SHAK 287:32
paint too much direct from n. — GAUG 136:19
priketh hem n. — CHAU 88:5
Secretary of N. — WALT 328:7
simply follow N. — LAO 193:5
state of war by n. — SWIF 307:10
Treat n. in terms — CÉZA 86:16
violates the order of n. — HERO 157:23
whatever N. has in store — FERM 127:3
naught n. for your comfort — CHES 89:17
naughty in a n. world — SHAK 282:30
naval N. tradition — CHUR 92:3
navies nations' airy n. — TENN 312:11
navy Ruler of the Queen's N. — GILB 140:30
upon the n. — CHAR 87:23
nay royal n. of England — BLAC 55:3
your n., nay — BIBL 51:24
Nazareth come out of N. — BIBL 47:24
Neaera tangles of N.'s hair — MILT 220:12
Neanderthal N. skeleton — HAWK 153:11
of N. man — STRA 305:4
near come not n. to me — BIBL 40:21
so n. and yet so far — TENN 311:28
nearer N., my God, to thee — ADAM 2:4
neat N., but not gaudy — WESL 332:10
Still to be n. — JONS 177:16
Nebuchadnezzar N. the king — BIBL 41:7
necessarily ain't n. so — HEYW 158:19
necessary absolutely n. — OCCA 235:19
little visible delight, but n. — BRON 67:14
n. evil — BRAD 65:21
n. not to change — FALK 126:1
n. to salvation — BOOK 64:2
necessity Cruel n. — CROM 103:17
do not see the n. — ARGE 14:6
N. has no law — PUBL 252:1
N. makes an honest man — DEFO 107:15
N. never made — FRAN 133:5
no virtue like n. — SHAK 285:10
neck had but one n. — CALI 80:7
hanged about his n. — BIBL 44:14
Some chicken! Some n. — CHUR 91:19
necklace with our n. — MAND 211:2
necks bowing our n. — JERO 172:4
nectarine n., and curious peach — MARV 213:16
need all ye n. to know — KEAT 182:5
face of total n. — BURR 76:4
not enough for everyone's n. — BUCH 72:1
O reason not the n. — SHAK 277:15
People who n. people — MERR 217:10
thy n. is greater — SIDN 295:16
What can I want or n. — HERB 157:21
Will you still n. me — LENN 197:16
needle eye of a n. — BIBL 44:20
n. and the pen — LEWI 198:15
upon a n.'s point — CUDW 104:11
needs according to his n. — MARX 214:5
negative Europe the unfinished n. — MCCA 206:19
N. Capability — KEAT 183:6
neglect Such sweet n. — JONS 177:17
negotiate n. out of fear — KENN 184:10
not here to n. — TRIM 319:11
negotiating N. with de Valera — LLOY 201:2
Negro places where the average N. — DAVI 106:21
neiges *où sont les n. d'antan* — VILL 324:6
neighbour do not to your n. — HILL 159:8
guts into the n. room — SHAK 272:29
love thy n. — BIBL 34:22

love thy n. as thyself — BIBL 44:29
n.'s house is on fire — BURK 74:5
policy of the good n. — ROOS 259:16
rob a n. — MACA 205:11
thy n.'s house — BIBL 34:16
thy n.'s house — BIBL 38:2
neighbourhood n. of voluntary spies — AUST 19:21
neighbouring cynosure of n. eyes — MILT 220:4
neighbours Good fences make good n. — FROS 134:11
have good n. — ELIZ 123:4
sport for our n. — AUST 20:1
Nell Pretty witty N. — PEPY 243:14
Nellie N. Dean — ARMS 14:23
Nelly Let not poor N. starve — CHAR 87:26
Nelson N. touch — NELS 232:8
Nemo N. *me impune lacessit* — ANON 12:14
nerve after the n. has been extracted — ROWL 261:15
nervous approaching n. breakdown — RUSS 262:19
nervousness only n. or death — LEBO 196:2
nest her soft and chilly n. — KEAT 181:6
leaves his wat'ry n. — D'AV 106:12
n. of singing birds — JOHN 174:16
theek our n. — BALL 24:13
nests Birds in their little n. agree — WATT 329:8
built their n. in my beard — LEAR 195:8
net n. is spread — BIBL 37:17
play tennis with the n. down — FROS 134:15
too old to rush up to the n. — ADAM 1:13
nets n. to catch the living — WEBS 330:8
nettle Out of this n., danger — SHAK 273:32
Tender-handed stroke a n. — HILL 158:24
network N. Anything reticulated — JOHN 173:14
neurosis n. is a secret — TYNA 321:16
N. is a way of avoiding — TILL 318:6
neutral studiously n. — WILS 337:6
neutrality Just for a word 'n.' — BETH 31:14
N. helps the oppressor — WIES 334:13
never come no more, N., never — SHAK 278:14
N. do to-day — PUNC 252:9
N. explain — FISH 128:6
N. explain — HUBB 166:2
n. had it so good — MACM 208:8
n. home came she — KING 186:20
N. in the field of human conflict — CHUR 91:17
N. the time — BROW 70:24
n. to have been loved — CONG 98:17
N. to have lived is best — YEAT 342:24
This will n. do — JEFF 171:19
We n. closed — VAN 322:11
nevermore Quoth the Raven, 'N.' — POE 246:14
new called the N. World — CANN 81:16
Emperor's n. clothes — ANDE 5:5
just a n. activity — DYSO 119:11
make a n. acquaintance — JOHN 176:20
making n. enemies — VOLT 326:15
n. deal for the American people — ROOS 259:15
N. every morning — KEBL 183:19
n. heaven and a new earth — BIBL 52:24
new heavens and a n. earth — BIBL 40:22
n. man may be raised up — BOOK 60:7
N. opinions are always suspected — LOCK 201:3
n. race is sent down — VIRG 325:10
n. wine into old bottles — BIBL 43:21
n. world order — BUSH 76:23
no n. thing under the sun — BIBL 38:14
O brave n. world — SHAK 287:20
old lamps for n. — ARAB 13:15
shock of the n. — DUNL 118:8
something n. out of Africa — PLIN 246:4
songs for ever n. — KEAT 182:2
unto the Lord a n. song — BOOK 61:14
unto the Lord a n. song — BOOK 62:21
wrote MAKE IT N. — POUN 250:6

newborn use of a n. child — FRAN 133:11
newest n. works — BULW 72:16
newness walk in n. of life — BIBL 49:11
news get the n. to you — TWAI 321:6
good n. from a far country — BIBL 38:4
good n. from Ghent to Aix — BROW 70:13
good n. yet to hear — CHES 89:26
how much n. there is — DOUG 115:7
Ill n. hath wings — DRAY 116:4
it is an item of n. — TALL 308:25
love of n. — CRAB 102:14
news that STAYS n. — POUN 250:14
that is n. — BOGA 57:8
What n. on the Rialto — SHAK 282:3
New South Wales govern N. — BELL 28:12
newspaper n. and journalistic activity — TOLS 318:17
N. editors — TROL 319:19
n. is a nation talking — MILL 218:16
newspapers n. I can't stand — STOP 304:15
read the n. — BEVA 32:10
newt Eye of n. — SHAK 281:5
Newton Let N. be — POPE 247:28
N. at Peru — WALP 327:12
New York California to the N. Island — GUTH 148:15
gullet of N. — MILL 218:15
New York, N. — COMD 97:18
three o'clock in N. — MIDL 217:22
next At forty-five, what n. — LOWE 203:22
n. to god america — CUMM 104:14
n. to Nature — LAND 192:21
nexus n. of man to man — CARL 82:12
Niagara wouldn't *live* under N. — CARL 83:5
nice N. guys finish last — DURO 118:16
n. to people on your way up — MIZN 225:4
N. work if you can get it — GERS 138:17
Too n. for a statesman — GOLD 143:18
nicens n. little boy — JOYC 178:23
nicest nastiest thing in the n. way — GOLD 143:2
niche your n. in creation — HALL 150:10
Nicodemus N. saw such light — VAUG 322:19
Nigeria daughter of N. — EMEC 124:7
nigger n. of the world — ONO 236:14
night armies clash by n. — ARNO 16:5
black bat, n., has flown — TENN 312:21
blue of the n. — CROS 104:4
borrower of the n. — SHAK 280:22
by n. in a pillar of fire — BIBL 34:10
carried His servant by n. — KORA 190:18
Chaos and old N. — MILT 221:12
city of dreadful n. — THOM 317:12
dangers of this n. — BOOK 59:1
dark and stormy n. — BULW 72:12
dark n. of the soul — FITZ 129:8
dark n. of the soul — JOHN 172:14
dog in the n.-time — DOYL 115:16
endure for a n. — BOOK 61:11
Farewell n. — BUNY 73:10
fit n. out for man or beast — FIEL 127:21
forests of the n. — BLAK 56:14
gentle into that good n. — THOM 316:3
hard day's n. — LENN 197:13
Harry in the n. — SHAK 274:35
horses of the n. — OVID 238:10
in endless n. — GRAY 146:21
infant crying in the n. — TENN 311:19
journey into n. — O'NE 236:12
know his God by n. — VAUG 322:19
late into the n. — BYRO 79:16
meaner beauties of the n. — WOTT 341:22
moon by n. — BOOK 63:13
moon walks the n. — DE L 108:10
Morning in the bowl of n. — FITZ 128:14
n. and day, brother — BORR 64:16

n. before Christmas — MOOR 227:2
n. Darkens the streets — MILT 221:11
n. has a thousand eyes — BOUR 65:8
N. hath a thousand eyes — LYLY 204:24
n. is far spent — BIBL 49:21
N. Mail crossing the Border — AUDE 18:11
n. Of cloudless climes — BYRO 79:14
n. of doubt — BARI 25:6
n. of the long knives — HITL 159:17
N.'s candles — SHAK 286:32
n.'s starred face — KEAT 183:1
n. that he was betrayed — BOOK 60:5
one other gaudy n. — SHAK 268:22
pass in the n. — LONG 202:6
perpetual n. — JONS 177:22
revelry by n. — BYRO 77:25
Sable-vested N. — MILT 221:24
something of the n. — WIDD 334:12
son of the sable N. — DANI 105:14
Spirit of N. — SHEL 294:2
such a n. as this — SHAK 282:26
tender is the n. — KEAT 182:12
terror by n. — BOOK 62:17
that it may be n. — BOOK 62:24
This ae n. — BALL 24:1
Through the dim n. — SHEL 293:19
tire the n. in thought — QUAR 253:4
under the lonely n. — VIRG 324:21
watch in the n. — BOOK 62:14
Watchman, what of the n. — BIBL 39:26
witching time of n. — SHAK 272:20
world's last n. — DONN 113:22
nightingale describing a n. — ANON 13:2
n., and not the lark — SHAK 286:31
ravished n. — LYLY 204:23
roar you as 'twere any n. — SHAK 283:4
nightingales n. are singing near — ELIO 122:19
nightmare History is a n. — JOYC 179:3
long national n. is over — FORD 131:4
nihil Aut Caesar, aut n. — BORG 64:15
N. est sine ratione — LEIB 196:21
nil N. actum credens — LUCA 204:8
N. admirari — HORA 163:23
N. desperandum — HORA 164:6
N. posse creari — LUCR 204:13
Nile my serpent of old N. — SHAK 268:15
on the banks of the N. — SHER 294:15
waters of the N. — CARR 83:15
nimini-pimini pronouncing to yourself n. — BURG 73:19
Nimrod N. the mighty hunter — BIBL 33:23
nine By the n. gods — MACA 206:6
N. bean rows — YEAT 343:6
n. men's morris — SHAK 283:9
nineteenth n. century — LAUR 194:10
ninety fears to speak of N.-Eight — INGR 169:5
Leave the n. and nine — BIBL 46:29
nurse of n. years — TENN 313:12
Nineveh N. and Tyre — KIPL 188:6
Quinquireme of N. — MASE 214:16
nip n. him in the bud — ROCH 258:8
nipping n. and an eager air — SHAK 271:11
nirvana called N. because — PALI 240:2
nisi N. Dominus — BIBL 53:2
N. Dominus frustra — ANON 12:15
no everlasting N. — CARL 83:2
I am also called N.-more — ROSS 260:17
It's n. go the merrygoround — MACN 208:16
land of the omnipotent N. — BOLD 57:12
man who says n. — CAMU 81:7
N.! No! No — THAT 315:15
There is n. God — BOOK 61:1
Noah N. he often said to his wife — CHES 90:2
nobility N. has obligations — LÉVI 198:9

nobis *Non n., Domine* — BIBL 53:1
noble days of the N. Savage — BIKO 53:22
Do n. things — KING 186:17
echo of a n. mind — LONG 202:12
fredome is a n. thing — BARB 24:26
Man is a n. animal — BROW 69:2
n. and nude and antique — SWIN 307:20
n. grand book — GASK 136:18
n. Living — WORD 340:24
n. savage ran — DRYD 116:28
O! what a n. mind — SHAK 272:7
nobleman Underrated N. — GILB 139:19
nobles n. with links of iron — BOOK 63:29
noblesse *N. oblige* — LÉVI 198:9
noblest n. of mankind — CALV 80:14
n. prospect — JOHN 174:23
n. Roman of them all — SHAK 276:32
n. work of God — POPE 248:20
n. work of man — INGE 169:2
nobly N., nobly Cape Saint Vincent — BROW 70:10
n. save — LINC 199:7
nobody care for n. — BICK 53:16
N. came — GINS 141:13
n. comes — BECK 26:21
n. will come — SAND 264:10
noctis *currite n. equi* — MARL 212:7
currite n. equi — OVID 238:10
nod dwelt in the land of N. — BIBL 33:16
nods excellent Homer n. — HORA 163:18
N., and becks — MILT 220:1
noes honest kersey n. — SHAK 278:21
noire *triste et n.* — BAUD 26:8
noise Go placidly amid the n. — EHRM 120:10
happy n. to hear — HOUS 165:4
loud n. at one end — KNOX 189:18
n. is an effective means — GOEB 142:13
n., my dear — ANON 8:22
n. of battle rolled — TENN 311:12
those who make the n. — BURK 74:9
noises isle is full of n. — SHAK 287:14
Nokomis wigwam of N. — LONG 202:3
noli *N. me tangere* — BIBL 53:13
nominate n. a spade a spade — JONS 177:19
nominative her n. case — O'KE 235:24
nomine *In N. Patris* — MISS 223:25
non avoiding n.-being — TILL 318:6
no fury like a n.-combatant — MONT 226:6
n.-cooperation with evil — GAND 135:19
N.-violence is the first article — GAND 135:18
none answer came there n. — CARR 84:7
answer came there n. — SCOT 266:5
answer made it n. — SHAK 271:4
malice toward n. — LINC 199:11
nonexistent obsolescent and n. — BREN 66:14
nonsense n., and learning — GOLD 143:26
n. upon stilts — BENT 30:2
your damned n. — RICH 257:3
noon amid the blaze of n. — MILT 223:1
returned before n. — SAIN 263:11
noonday destroyeth in the n. — BOOK 62:17
noose naked to the hangman's n. — HOUS 165:3
Norfolk bear him up the N. sky — BETJ 31:19
Very flat, N. — COWA 101:11
normal n. and easy — JAME 170:21
Norman simple faith than N. blood — TENN 312:1
Noroway To N. o'er the faem — BALL 24:8
north He was my N., my South — AUDE 18:2
mad n.-north-west — SHAK 271:32
N.-west passage — STER 302:23
tender is the N. — TENN 313:9
to us the near n. — MENZ 216:19
northern constant as the n. star — SHAK 276:7
n. lights astream — SMAR 297:3

N. reticence, the tight gag — HEAN 154:14
Norval My name is N. — HOME 161:14
nose at the end of his n. — LEAR 195:15
Cleopatra's n. been shorter — PASC 241:16
hateful to the n. — JAME 170:8
insinuated n. — WATS 329:4
large n. is in fact the sign — ROST 260:22
lifts his n. — SWIF 307:5
n. May ravage with impunity — BROW 71:7
n. was as sharp as a pen — SHAK 274:32
plucks justice by the n. — SHAK 281:27
run up your n. dead against — BALD 23:13
thirty inches from my n. — AUDE 18:15
very shiny n. — MARK 212:1
with a luminous n. — LEAR 195:10
noses Athwart men's n. — SHAK 286:14
n. cast is of the roman — FLEM 130:3
n. have they, and smell not — BOOK 63:7
nostalgie *n. de la boue* — AUGI 18:25
noster *Pater n.* — MISS 224:5
not n. I, but the wind — LAWR 194:21
N. so much a programme — ANON 9:2
N. unto us, O Lord — BOOK 63:6
Thou shalt n. kill — BIBL 34:16
note living had no n. — GIBB 139:10
longest suicide n. — KAUF 180:19
n. I wanted — JAME 170:21
only the n. of a bird — SIMP 296:4
When found, make a n. — DICK 110:11
notes n. I handle no better — SCHN 265:16
right n. at the right time — BACH 20:17
thick-warbled n. — MILT 222:28
too many n. — JOSE 178:14
nothing brought n. into this world — BIBL 51:10
Caesar or n. — BORG 64:15
Death is n. to us — EPIC 124:25
don't believe in n. — CHES 90:11
Emperor has n. on — ANDE 5:6
forgotten nothing and learnt n. — DUMO 118:4
good man to do n. — BURK 74:22
Goodness had n. to do with it — WEST 332:14
have not charity, I am n. — BIBL 49:30
I have done n. yet — BRON 67:11
individually can do n. — ALLE 4:7
live well on n. a year — THAC 314:24
marvel at n. — HORA 163:23
N. — LOUI 202:21
N. ain't worth nothin' — KRIS 190:26
n. a-year, paid quarterly — SURT 306:12
N. can be created — LUCR 204:13
n. can be sole or whole — YEAT 342:17
N. happens — AURE 19:13
N. happens — BECK 26:21
N. in excess — ANON 12:3
N. is ever done in this world — SHAW 291:6
N. is here for tears — MILT 223:5
N. is more dangerous — ALAI 3:8
N., like something, happens anywhere — LARK 193:13
n. of a name — BYRO 78:10
n. should be done for the first time — CORN 100:9
N. to do but work — KING 186:5
n. to do with the case — GILB 140:19
n. to look backward to — FROS 134:6
n. to say — CAGE 80:5
n. to say — COLT 97:15
n. to you — BIBL 40:27
N. will come of nothing — SHAK 277:5
power over n. — HERO 157:24
resent having n. — COMP 98:3
say n. — HEAN 154:14
Tar-baby ain't sayin' n. — HARR 152:16
that he n. knows — MILT 222:29
Thinking n. done — LUCA 204:8

Think n. done ROGE 259:1
You ain't heard n. yet JOLS 177:7
nothingness to n. do sink KEAT 183:2
notice escaped our n. CRIC 103:11
n. of my labours JOHN 174:20
notorious open and n. evil liver BOOK 59:16
noun n., proper or improper FULL 134:23
nouns N. of number COBB 95:7
novel end of a n. TROL 319:15
given away by a n. KEAT 183:13
no more n.-writing HARD 152:5
n. is like a mirror STEN 302:13
n. tells a story FORS 131:11
only a n. AUST 19:19
reading a n. ELIO 121:9
subject of a n. MURA 230:3
want to read a n. DISR 113:9
novelists great—the major n. LEAV 195:24
novelty This n. on earth MILT 222:22
November N. at the gate PUSH 252:21
remember the Fifth of N. ANON 9:12
novo N. cedat ritui THOM 315:23
now If it be n. SHAK 273:16
If not n. when HILL 159:9
N. I lay me down to sleep ANON 9:3
Right N. is better BINC 54:3
We are the masters n. SHAW 292:7
nowhere circumference is n. ANON 8:21
Eclipse first, the rest n. O'KE 236:2
nowness n. of everything POTT 249:27
noxious Of all n. animals KILV 186:4
nude keep one from going n. KING 186:5
noble and n. and antique SWIN 307:20
nuisance one n. for another nuisance ELLI 124:2
nuisances small n. of peace-time HAY 153:16
null splendidly n. TENN 312:20
nullius N. in verba ANON 12:16
NUM against the Pope or the N. BALD 23:13
number called the wrong n. THUR 317:28
full of a n. of things STEV 303:28
happiness of the greatest n. BENT 30:3
I am not a n. MCGO 207:11
Nouns of n. COBB 95:7
n. of my days BOOK 61:19
n. of the beast BIBL 52:16
numbered all n. BIBL 43:26
numbers divinity in odd n. SHAK 282:32
greatest n. HUTC 167:13
I lisped in n. POPE 247:7
secret magic of n. BROW 69:3
numbness drowsy n. pains KEAT 182:9
numerus Nos n. sumus HORA 163:21
nun Come, pensive n. MILT 219:21
nunc N. dimittis BIBL 53:8
N. est bibendum HORA 164:9
nunnery Get thee to a n. SHAK 272:4
Nuremberg prosecution at N. JACK 169:20
nurse always keep a-hold of N. BELL 28:11
n. of ninety years TENN 313:12
sucks the n. asleep SHAK 269:8
nursed n. a dear gazelle MOOR 227:19
n. the self-same hill MILT 220:11
nurseries n. of heaven THOM 317:5
nut spicy n.-brown ale MILT 220:5
nuts N. MCAU 206:15
where the n. come from THOM 316:1
nutshell bounded in a n. SHAK 271:30
nymph N., in thy orisons SHAK 272:3

O

O Within this wooden O SHAK 274:27
oafish o. louts remember Mum BETJ 31:16
oafs muddied o. at the goals KIPL 187:23
oak Heart of o. GARR 136:7
O., and Ash, and Thorn KIPL 188:12
o. would sprout in Derry HEAN 154:13
round that o. hangs PUSH 252:23
oaks families last not three o. BROW 69:1
oatcakes o., and sulphur SMIT 298:7
oath cheats with an o. PLUT 246:10
man is not upon o. JOHN 175:17
oaths Judges must follow their o. ZOBE 345:7
oats feeds the horse enough o. GALB 135:10
O. A grain JOHN 173:15
obedience o. to God BRAD 65:24
obedient o. to their laws we lie SIMO 296:2
penitent, and o. heart BOOK 58:4
obey o. them HORS 164:22
obeyed o. as a son GIBB 139:7
right to be o. JOHN 172:11
She who must be o. HAGG 149:3
obituary o. in serial form CRIS 103:13
your own o. BEHA 27:18
object My o. all sublime GILB 140:15
oblation o. of himself BOOK 60:4
oblations alms and o. BOOK 59:25
obligations Nobility has o. LÉVI 198:9
oblige Noblesse o. LÉVI 198:9
obliteration policy is o. BELL 28:3
oblivion from place to place over o. HARD 151:24
journey towards o. LAWR 194:20
mere o. SHAK 269:24
puts alms for o. SHAK 287:30
To cold o. SHEL 292:23
obnoxious I am o. BRAD 65:25
obscenity 'o.' not capable of exact definition
RUSS 262:24
obscure become o. HORA 163:12
obscuri Ibant o. sola sub nocte VIRG 324:21
obscurity man from o. REYN 256:4
o. of a learned language GIBB 139:9
obscurus O. fio HORA 163:12
observation o. is concerned PAST 241:22
o. of facts COND 98:5
o. with extensive view JOHN 174:4
observer keen o. of life AUDE 18:10
obsolescence adolescence and o. LINK 200:3
planned o. STEV 303:2
obsolescent o. and nonexistent BREN 66:14
obstruction consecrated o. BAGE 22:17
Occam O.'s Razor OCCA 235:19
occasion o.'s forelock watchful MILT 222:26
occasions o. do inform against me SHAK 272:31
their lawful o. BOOK 63:32
occupation Othello's o.'s gone SHAK 284:27
occupy o. their business BOOK 63:1
occurred never to have o. BENT 30:8
ocean day-star in the o. bed MILT 220:19
deep and dark blue O. BYRO 78:9
great o. of truth NEWT 233:15
In the o.'s bosom MARV 213:12
mighty o. deep WHIT 333:18
o. of darkness FOX 132:14
o. on a western beach LANG 192:24
O.'s child SHEL 293:4
October O., that ambiguous month LESS 198:2
octopus dear o. SMIT 297:14
odd But not so o. BROW 68:19
divinity in o. numbers SHAK 282:32
God must think it exceedingly o. KNOX 189:17

odd (*cont.*)
How o. Of God — EWER 125:14
odds facing fearful o. — MACA 206:7
oderint O., *dum metuant* — ACCI 1:4
odi O. *et amo* — CATU 86:2
odious O.! in woollen — POPE 247:24
odorous Comparisons are o. — SHAK 284:3
odours haste with o. sweet — MILT 220:23
Odyssey thunder of the O. — LANG 192:24
off I want to be o. it — PAXM 242:8
O. with her head — CARR 83:21
O. with his head — CIBB 92:19
O. with his head — SHAK 286:6
offence detest th'o. — POPE 247:2
o. inspires less horror — GIBB 139:4
only defence is in o. — BALD 23:10
where the o. is — SHAK 273:7
offended him have I o. — SHAK 276:14
not o. the king — MORE 228:4
offender love th'o. — POPE 247:2
offenders society o. — GILB 140:8
offensive extremely o. — SMIT 297:17
offer o. he can't refuse — PUZO 252:25
offering o. too little — CANN 81:11
office for o. boys — SALI 263:22
in o. but not in power — LAMO 192:17
no o. to go to — SHAW 290:28
receives the seals of office — ROSE 260:8
waters of o. — TROL 319:16
officer o. and a gentleman — ANON 5:19
official concept of the o. secret — WEBE 330:3
This high o., all allow — HERB 157:3
oft O. in danger — WHIT 333:9
o. was thought — POPE 248:1
oil o. controlling American soil — DYLA 119:8
o. in a cruse — BIBL 36:9
o. of gladness — BOOK 61:23
O., vinegar, sugar — GOLD 143:17
o. which renders — HUME 166:21
with boiling o. in it — GILB 140:17
with o. anoint — SCOT 266:29
oiled in the o. wards — KEAT 182:20
oily glib and o. art — SHAK 277:7
OK O. We lost — MAJO 210:2
Okie O. means you're scum — STEI 302:10
old Any o. iron — COLL 97:4
As with gladness men of o. — DIX 113:10
balance of the O. — CANN 81:16
better than the Good O. Days — BINC 54:3
boys of the o. Brigade — WEAT 329:25
chilly and grown o. — BROW 71:11
die before I get o. — TOWN 319:1
dressing o. words new — SHAK 289:32
ere thou grow o. — ROCH 258:16
foolish, fond o. man — SHAK 278:7
good o. Cause — MILT 223:22
Growing o. is like — POWE 250:20
Grow o. along with me — BROW 71:3
I grow o. — SOLO 298:25
I grow o. . . . I grow old — ELIO 122:13
instead of the o. ones — PEEL 242:19
make me conservative when o. — FROS 134:12
man who reviews the o. — CONF 98:7
Mithridates, he died o. — HOUS 165:11
name thee O. Glory — DRIV 116:11
no country for o. men — YEAT 343:16
no man would be o. — SWIF 307:4
now am o. — BOOK 61:16
o. Adam in this Child — BOOK 60:7
o. age always fifteen years older — BARU 25:21
O. Age, and Experience — ROCH 258:13
O. age is the most unexpected — TROT 320:1
o. age of cards — POPE 247:14
o. age, the last gap but one — WHIT 333:10
o. black magic — MERC 216:24
o. familiar faces — LAMB 192:7
o. heads on your young shoulders — SPAR 299:23
o. in a second childhood — ARIS 14:10
o. lamps for new — ARAB 13:15
o. Lie: *Dulce et decorum* — OWEN 238:24
o., mad, blind — SHEL 293:26
o. man in a dry month — ELIO 122:1
o. man in a hurry — CHUR 91:5
o. man of Thermopylae — LEAR 195:12
O. man river — HAMM 150:22
o. men from the chimney corner — SIDN 295:13
o. men shall dream dreams — BIBL 41:14
o. order changeth — TENN 311:14
O. soldiers never die — FOLE 130:18
o., unhappy, far-off things — WORD 341:10
O, sir! you are o. — SHAK 277:14
planned by o. men — RICE 256:15
so o. a head — SHAK 282:19
suppose an o. man decayed — JOHN 176:12
Tell me the o., old story — HANK 151:2
They shall grow not o. — BINY 54:4
too o. to rush up to the net — ADAM 1:13
want an o.-fashioned house — FISH 128:9
warn you not to grow o. — KINN 187:3
When I am an o. woman — JOSE 178:16
when 'tis o. — BALL 24:15
When you are very o. — RONS 259:11
you are o. and grey — YEAT 344:1
You are o., Father William — CARR 83:16
You are o., Father William — SOUT 299:16
older Another day o. — TRAV 319:6
As we get o. — REED 255:7
o. than the rocks — PATE 241:24
oldest o. hath borne most — SHAK 278:16
o. rule in the book — CARR 84:1
olet *Pecunia non o.* — VESP 323:15
olive children like the o.-branches — BOOK 63:20
Olympus O. on top of Ossa — VIRG 325:16
Pelion on top of shady O. — HORA 164:15
Omega Alpha and O. — BIBL 52:3
omelette fuss about an o. — VOLT 326:14
omen gods avert this o. — CICE 92:27
omnia *Amor vincit o.* — CHAU 88:9
non o. possumus omnes — LUCI 204:11
Non o. possumus omnes — VIRG 325:12
O. vincit Amor — VIRG 325:14
omnibus man on the Clapham o. — BOWE 65:13
omnipotent land of the o. No — BOLD 57:12
omnis *Non o. moriar* — HORA 164:1
once I was adored o. — SHAK 288:17
oblation of himself o. offered — BOOK 60:4
o. and future king — MALO 210:12
O. in royal David's city — ALEX 3:17
O. more unto the breach — SHAK 274:33
O. to every man — LOWE 203:18
O. upon a time — ANON 9:6
one All for o., one for all — DUMA 118:2
How to be o. up — POTT 250:1
Lord is O. — SIDD 295:4
o. day in thy courts — BOOK 62:12
o.-eyed man is king — ERAS 125:2
o. for my baby — MERC 216:23
o. if by land — LONG 202:5
o. man fewer — METT 217:15
O. man shall have one vote — CART 85:4
oneself Hell is o. — ELIO 121:17
how to be o. — MONT 226:11
only his o. begotten Son — BIBL 47:28
It's the o. thing — SAND 264:13
o. begotten of the Father — BIBL 47:21
O. connect — FORS 131:15

O. the lonely	ORBI 236:19
To the o. begetter	SHAK 289:21
only-begotten o. Son of God	BOOK 59:22
onward O., Christian soldiers	BARI 25:5
O. goes the pilgrim band	BARI 25:6
open function when they are o.	DEWA 109:7
o. and notorious evil liver	BOOK 59:16
O. Sesame	ARAB 13:16
o. the Kingdom of Heaven	BOOK 58:12
opera *Benedicite, omnia o. Domini*	BIBL 53:6
O. is when a guy gets stabbed	GARD 136:3
operas German text of French o.	WHAR 332:23
operatic so romantic, so o.	PROU 251:18
operations o. which we can perform	WHIT 333:15
opiate some dull o.	KEAT 182:9
opiates curing diverse maladies as o.	SYDE 308:6
opinion approve a private o.	HOBB 159:23
form a clear o.	BONH 58:3
Government and public o.	SHAW 291:12
man can brave o.	STAÉ 301:10
of his own o. still	BUTL 77:8
O. in good men	MILT 223:20
Party is organized o.	DISR 112:9
think the last o. right	POPE 248:5
opinions as many o. as people	TERE 314:9
Golden o.	SHAK 279:23
halt ye between two o.	BIBL 36:10
New o. are always suspected	LOCK 201:3
opium o.-dose for keeping beasts	KING 187:1
o. of the people	MARX 214:4
subtle, and mighty o.	DE Q 108:21
with an o. wand	PAIN 239:14
opponents o. eventually die	PLAN 245:18
opportunity maximum of o.	SHAW 291:17
o. for achievement	KEIL 183:23
oppose o. everything	DERB 108:23
opposing by o. end them	SHAK 272:1
opposition duty of an O.	DERB 108:23
effective means of o.	GOEB 142:13
formidable O.	DISR 112:17
Her Majesty's O.	BAGE 22:12
His Majesty's O.	HOBH 160:7
oppressor Neutrality helps the o.	WIES 334:13
optimist o. proclaims that we live	CABE 79:26
oracles lively O. of God	CORO 100:12
oracular use of my o. tongue	SHER 294:14
orange clockwork o.	BURG 73:15
O. card	CHUR 91:3
oration studied as an o.	OSBO 237:24
orator I am no o., as Brutus is	SHAK 276:22
without an o.	SHAK 289:19
orators play the o.	MARL 212:14
oratory first in o.	DEMO 108:12
orbed o. maiden	SHEL 292:22
orchestra golden rules for an o.	BEEC 27:8
orchestration o. of platitudes	WILD 335:25
order all is in o.	MANS 211:8
best words in the best o.	COLE 96:24
decently and in o.	BIBL 49:34
new world o.	BUSH 76:23
not necessarily in that o.	GODA 142:10
old o. changeth	TENN 311:14
o. and beauty	BAUD 26:7
o. of Melchisedech	BOOK 63:3
o. of the acts is planned	PAST 241:21
o. of your going	SHAK 281:1
O. reigns in Warsaw	ANON 11:17
prejudice of good o.	ANON 6:10
restoration of o.	JAME 171:1
Set thine house in o.	BIBL 40:5
They o., said I	STER 302:19
violates the o. of nature	HERO 157:23
ordering o. of the universe	ALFO 3:20

orders Almighty's o. to perform	ADDI 2:6
don't obey no o.	KIPL 187:13
gave them their o.	WELL 331:13
ordinary learn to see the o.	BAIL 22:25
o. mind	WOOL 339:6
see God in the o. things	AWDR 20:8
warn you not to be o.	KINN 187:3
ore Load your subject with o.	KEAT 183:16
organ o.-voice of England	TENN 312:27
organization o. man	WHYT 334:10
o. of forms	CART 85:2
organize Don't waste time mourning—o.	HILL 159:3
organized it's got to be o.	HOCK 160:9
o. hypocrisy	DISR 112:8
Party is o. opinion	DISR 112:9
organizing Only an o. genius	BEVA 32:7
orient corn was o.	TRAH 319:3
original Behold the bright o.	GAY 137:9
gone from o. righteousness	BOOK 64:3
great and o. writer	WORD 341:21
o. is unfaithful	BORG 64:13
saves o. thinking	SAYE 265:7
originality o. of your countenance	CLAI 93:6
originals few o. and many copies	TOCQ 318:10
Orion bands of O.	BIBL 37:13
Orlando Run, run, O.	SHAK 269:27
ornament study's o.	MIDD 217:20
orphan defeat is an o.	CIAN 92:17
Orpheus O. with his lute	SHAK 275:22
orthodoxy O. is my doxy	WARB 328:8
ortolans die eating o.	DISR 113:1
Oscar You will, O.	WHIS 333:6
Ossa pile O. on Pelion	VIRG 325:16
ossibus *ex o. ultor*	VIRG 324:17
ostentation use rather than o.	GIBB 139:3
ostrich wings of an o.	MACA 205:23
Othello O.'s occupation's gone	SHAK 284:27
other I am not as o. men are	BIBL 47:7
o. Eden	SHAK 285:12
o. men's flowers	MONT 226:14
O. voices, other rooms	CAPO 81:21
Were t'o. dear charmer away	GAY 137:5
wonderful for o. people	KERR 184:22
others woman who lives for o.	LEWI 198:12
otherwise gods thought o.	VIRG 324:14
Otis Miss O. regrets	PORT 249:19
ought hadn't o. to be	HART 152:22
o. to have done	BOOK 58:6
our O. Father	BIBL 42:23
out counted them all o.	HANR 151:3
get o. while we're young	SPRI 301:5
include me o.	GOLD 144:7
Mordre wol o.	CHAU 88:16
O.-babying Wordsworth	BULW 72:14
O., damned spot	SHAK 281:14
o.-glittering Keats	BULW 72:14
o.-herods Herod	SHAK 272:10
O. of the deep	BOOK 63:21
preserve thy going o.	BOOK 63:14
outcasts o. always mourn	WILD 335:18
outdated o. methods	WILS 336:17
outdoor system of o. relief	BRIG 66:21
outgrabe mome raths o.	CARR 84:3
outlawed liar should be o.	HALI 150:1
o. or exiled	MAGN 209:11
outlive o. this powerful rhyme	SHAK 289:29
outlives o. this day	SHAK 275:9
outside just going o.	OATE 235:11
o. of the text	DERR 108:4
o. pissing in	JOHN 173:6
outsoared hath o. the shadow	SHEL 292:18
outstretched o. beneath the tree	BLAK 56:12
outvoted they o. me	LEE 196:13

outward American-o.-bound   HOPK 163:9
man looketh on the o.   BIBL 35:20
o. and visible sign   BOOK 60:11
over ain't o. till it's over   BERR 31:9
O. hill, over dale   SHAK 283:6
oversexed, and o. here   TRIN 319:13
O. the hills   GAY 137:4
O. there   COHA 95:13
They think it's all o.   WOLS 339:1
overcome never o. them   JUNG 179:13
overpaid grossly o.   HERB 157:3
O., overfed, oversexed   TRIN 319:13
oversexed o., and over here   TRIN 319:13
owe o. God a death   SHAK 274:23
owed so much o. by so many to so few   CHUR 91:17
owest o. God a death   SHAK 274:8
owl fat greedy o.   RICH 256:19
mousing o.   SHAK 280:21
O. and the Pussy-Cat   LEAR 195:14
o., for all his feathers   KEAT 181:3
o. of Minerva   HEGE 155:6
o. that shrieked   SHAK 280:7
owls companion to o.   BIBL 37:12
court for o.   BIBL 40:3
eagle among blinking o.   SHEL 293:1
Two O. and a Hen   LEAR 195:8
own but mine o.   SHAK 270:5
his o. received him not   BIBL 47:20
marked him for his o.   WALT 328:6
money and a room of her o.   WOOL 339:7
my words are my o.   CHAR 87:24
only to those who o. one   LIEB 199:2
To each his o.   ANON 12:1
ownership common o.   ANON 10:13
ox brother to the o.   MARK 211:19
eateth grass as an o.   BIBL 37:15
eat straw like the o.   BIBL 39:23
not covet his o.   BIBL 34:16
roasted Manningtree o.   SHAK 273:34
stalled o.   BIBL 37:34
oxen breath of the o.   HAGG 149:2
great black o.   YEAT 342:16
Who drives fat o.   JOHN 176:18
Oxenford Clerk there was of O.   CHAU 88:10
Oxford academia in O.   AUNG 19:10
clever men at O.   GRAH 145:12
King to O. sent   BROW 69:11
sends his son to O.   STEA 301:22
To O. sent a troop   TRAP 319:5
To the University of O.   GIBB 139:6
oxlips o. and the nodding violet   SHAK 283:12
oxygen o. of publicity   THAT 315:11
oyster my o. knife   HURS 167:9
world's mine o.   SHAK 282:31
Ozymandias My name is O.   SHEL 293:12

P

pace dance is a measured p.   BACO 20:20
requiescant in p.   MISS 224:13
pacific stared at the P.   KEAT 182:19
pacifist quietly p. peaceful   WALK 326:21
pacify p. Ireland   GLAD 141:18
pack changed the form of the p.   TROT 320:2
p. up your troubles   ANON 10:19
Pay, p., and follow   BURT 76:8
running with the p.   BUTL 77:5
whole p. of you   SHAK 288:32
packhorses P., And hollow pampered jades   SHAK 274:18
Paddington Ever weeping P.   BLAK 55:18

London is to P.   CANN 81:14
paddocks Cold as p.   HERR 157:25
padlock p.—on her mind   PRIO 251:8
paene *P. insularum*   CATU 85:21
pagan P. suckled in a creed outworn   WORD 341:19
page allowed P. 3 to develop   MURD 230:7
foot of the first p.   SAND 264:14
single p. of our life   SAND 264:5
pageant all part of life's rich p.   MARS 213:3
paid we ha' p. in full   KIPL 188:10
well p. that is well satisfied   SHAK 282:25
pain beneath the aromatic p.   WINC 337:10
cost Ceres all that p.   MILT 221:32
Eternal P.   ARNO 15:10
general drama of p.   HARD 151:17
I have no p., dear mother   FARM 126:8
intoxication with p.   BRON 67:7
Joy always came after p.   APOL 13:11
never inflicts p.   NEWM 233:1
no greater p.   DANT 105:20
No p., no palm   PENN 243:9
Our Lady of P.   SWIN 307:22
p. and grief   BOOK 61:18
p. shall not be inflicted   SPEN 300:2
p. to the bear   MACA 205:21
physics p.   SHAK 280:15
pleasure after p.   DRYD 116:24
sure she felt no p.   BROW 71:1
with no p.   KEAT 182:13
With some p. is fraught   SHEL 293:32
pains Marriage has many p.   JOHN 173:26
no gains without p.   STEV 303:9
p. a man when 'tis kept close   SUCK 305:12
p. of hell   BOOK 63:8
paint can't pick it up, p. it   ANON 7:14
flinging a pot of p.   RUSK 262:7
I p. with my prick   RENO 255:18
p. the lily   SHAK 277:2
p. too much direct from nature   GAUG 136:19
price of the p.   VAN 322:16
should not p. the chair   MUNC 230:2
throws aside his p.-pots   HORA 163:14
painted fears a p. devil   SHAK 280:11
p. her face   BIBL 36:29
p. on the wall   BROW 70:22
painter I am a p.   SCHW 265:22
ranks far below the p.   LEON 197:21
scenes made me a p.   CONS 99:11
painting chapel I was p.   MICH 217:18
no matter what you're p.   HOCK 160:9
P. became everything   BROW 68:12
P. is saying 'Ta'   SPEN 300:8
P. is silent poetry   SIMO 296:3
p. not made to decorate   PICA 244:18
poem is like a p.   HORA 163:19
paints God p. the scenery   HART 152:20
pair Sleep on Blest p.   MILT 222:5
Take a p. of sparkling eyes   GILB 139:21
palace p. and a prison on each hand   BYRO 78:2
p. for a hermitage   SHAK 285:23
palaces Dragons in their pleasant p.   BIBL 39:24
pleasures and p.   PAYN 242:11
pale behold a p. horse   BIBL 52:9
p. fire she snatches   SHAK 287:24
P. hands I loved   HOPE 162:19
P. prime-roses   SHAK 289:12
turned p.   SOUT 299:18
whiter shade of p.   REID 255:15
Why so p. and wan   SUCK 305:10
world grew p.   JOHN 174:6
palely Alone and p. loitering   KEAT 181:17
Palestine establishment in P.   BALF 23:14
Palladium P. of all the civil   JUNI 179:17

pallor p. of girls' brows — OWEN 238:23
palls everything p. — ANON 11:20
palm has won it bear the p. — JORT 178:13
  have an itching p. — SHAK 276:28
  No pain, no p. — PENN 243:9
  win the p. — MARV 213:15
palms p. before my feet — CHES 89:19
  p. of her hands — BIBL 36:32
palpable very p. hit — SHAK 273:17
paltry aged man is but a p. thing — YEAT 343:17
pampered p. jades — MARL 212:19
pan great god P. — BROW 69:13
panache My p. — ROST 261:1
pancreas adorable p. — KERR 185:1
pandemonium P., the high capital — MILT 221:16
Pandora open that P.'s Box — BEVI 32:14
panem P. et circenses — JUVE 180:3
pange P., lingua — FORT 131:19
  P., lingua — THOM 315:22
panic p.'s in thy breastie — BURN 75:30
Panjandrum grand P. himself — FOOT 130:23
pansies p., that's for thoughts — SHAK 273:5
pantaloon lean and slippered p. — SHAK 269:23
panteth As the hart p. — BOOK 61:21
panther Black P. Party — NEWT 233:10
panting For ever p. — KEAT 182:3
pants As p. the hart — TATE 309:11
  deck your several limbs in p. — NASH 231:18
papa word P., besides — DICK 110:18
papacy p. is not other — HOBB 160:5
paper All reactionaries are p. tigers — MAO 211:13
  all the earth were p. — LYLY 204:25
  only a p. moon — HARB 151:8
  p. hats and wooden swords — USTI 322:4
  scrap of p. — BETH 31:14
  worth the p. it is written on — GOLD 144:9
papers He's got my p. — PINT 245:3
  what I read in the p. — ROGE 259:6
parachutes Minds are like p. — DEWA 109:7
parade p. of riches — SMIT 297:3
parades produce victory p. — HOBS 160:8
paradise cannot catch the bird of p. — KHRU 185:19
  drunk the milk of P. — COLE 96:7
  keys of P. — DE Q 108:21
  P. by way of Kensal Green — CHES 89:26
  P. of exiles — SHEL 292:26
  paved p. — MITC 224:19
  wilderness is p. enow — FITZ 128:15
  with me in p. — BIBL 47:13
paradises true p. are — PROU 251:20
parallelograms Princess of P. — BYRO 79:21
paranoid Only the p. survive — GROV 148:7
parapets of the ancient p. — RIMB 257:11
pardlike p. Spirit — SHEL 292:17
pardon Alas but cannot p. — AUDE 18:21
  God will p. me — HEIN 155:10
  kiss of the sun for p. — GURN 148:13
  P. me boy — GORD 144:17
pardoned praised than to be p. — JONS 178:11
pardons P. him — AUDE 18:5
parens king is truly p. patriae — JAME 170:10
parent lose one p. — WILD 334:24
  one child makes you a p. — FROS 134:4
parents begin by loving their p. — WILD 335:13
  bondage to p. — WOLL 338:24
  children inter their p. — HERO 157:23
  girl needs good p. — TUCK 320:14
  In mine it was the p. — SLOV 296:21
  Jewish man with p. alive — ROTH 261:5
  only illegitimate p. — GLAD 141:17
  P. love their children — AUCT 17:22
  produce bad p. — MORS 229:2
  sacrifice and p.' tears — MILT 221:10

sharp and severe p. — GREY 147:14
sue its p. — WATS 328:27
parfit verray, p. gentil knyght — CHAU 88:6
paries p. cum proximus ardet — HORA 164:1
Paris after they've seen P. — LEWI 198:17
  Down and out in P. — ORWE 237:9
  go to P. — APPL 13:13
  last time I saw P. — HAMM 150:20
  P. is a movable feast — HEMI 156:2
  P. is well worth a mass — HENR 156:12
  P. was French—and silent — TUCH 320:13
  they go to P. — WILD 335:10
parish all the world as my p. — WESL 332:7
park gentleman's p. — CONS 99:12
  p., a policeman — CHAP 87:12
  Poisoning pigeons in the p. — LEHR 196:19
parking put up a p. lot — MITC 224:19
parks p. are the lungs of London — PITT 245:12
parles their treasonous p. — BROW 70:19
parley-voo Hinky, dinky, p. — ANON 8:14
parliament enables P. to do things — SHAW 291:4
  of [P.] — BOOT 64:11
  [p.] a lot of hard-faced men — BALD 23:8
  p. can do any thing — PEMB 243:6
  P. itself would not exist — SCAR 265:9
  P. of man — TENN 312:12
  P. speaking through reporters — CARL 82:23
parliamentarian safe pleasure for a p. — CRIT 103:14
parliaments mother of P. — BRIG 67:1
parlour walk into my p. — HOWI 165:21
Parnell Poor P. — JOYC 178:24
parole p. of literary men — JOHN 176:9
paroles n'emploient les p. — VOLT 326:2
parrot This is a late p. — MONT 226:25
parson If P. lost his senses — HODG 160:11
  P. left off conjuring — SELD 267:12
  Whig in a p.'s gown — JOHN 174:12
parsons merriment of p. — JOHN 176:7
part chosen that good p. — BIBL 46:19
  death p. thee and me — BIBL 35:13
  if we were ever to p. — KIER 185:21
  let us kiss and p. — DRAY 116:5
  My soul, bear thou thy p. — GURN 148:14
  p. to tear a cat in — SHAK 283:3
  we know in p. — BIBL 49:32
  What isn't p. of ourselves — HESS 158:16
parted Mine never shall be p. — MILT 222:20
partiality neither anger nor p. — TACI 308:16
particles p. of light — BLAK 56:1
particular bright p. star — SHAK 268:9
  Did nothing in p. — GILB 140:4
  London p. . . . . A fog — DICK 109:17
parting P. is all we know — DICK 111:16
  p. is such sweet sorrow — SHAK 286:23
  p. of the ways — BIBL 41:3
  Speed the p. guest — POPE 248:23
partir P. c'est mourir un peu — HARA 151:5
partly Living and p. living — ELIO 122:15
parts dignified p. — BAGE 22:10
  naming of p. — REED 255:8
  P. of it are excellent — PUNC 252:18
parturient P. montes — HORA 163:15
party Collapse of Stout P. — ANON 6:6
  in the p. manifestoes — ROTH 261:7
  master of the P. — HEAL 154:10
  none was for a p. — MACA 206:9
  P. is organized opinion — DISR 112:9
  p. not to be brought down — HAIL 149:8
  p.'s over — COMD 97:19
  P-spirit, which at best is — POPE 249:8
  save the P. we love — GAIT 135:6
  spirit of p. — WASH 328:21
  Stick to your p. — DISR 113:2

party (cont.)
stupidest p.
voted at my p.'s call — MILL 218:2
pasarán No p. — GILB 141:1
pass Do not p. go — IBAR 168:8
let him p. for a man — ANON 7:6
let this cup p. — SHAK 282:2
look, and p. on — BIBL 45:15
my words shall not p. — DANT 105:18
O! let him p. — BIBL 45:2
p., and turn again — SHAK 278:15
p. for forty-three — EMER 124:8
p. in the night — GILB 141:10
p. the ammunition — LONG 202:6
They shall not p. — FORG 131:10
They shall not p. — ANON 11:14
passage North-west p. — IBAR 168:8
p. which is particularly fine — STER 302:23
passed p. by on the other side — JOHN 175:11
passer P. mortuus est — BIBL 46:16
passeront Ils ne p. pas — CATU 85:18
passes Everything p. — ANON 11:14
Men seldom make p. — ANON 11:20
p. the glory of the world — PARK 240:16
passeth p. all understanding — ANON 12:22
passing did but see her p. by — BIBL 50:27
p.-bells for these who die — ANON 10:6
p. brave to be a king — OWEN 238:21
p. the love of women — MARL 212:15
passion all p. spent — BIBL 35:29
Eternal P. — MILT 223:6
in such a p. about — ARNO 15:10
p. cannot Music raise — SHAW 292:8
p. in the human soul — DRYD 117:9
P. makes the world go — LILL 199:4
p. or interest — ICE- 166:16
p. shall have spent — LOCK 201:6
prose and the p. — TENN 312:8
ruling p. conquers — FORS 131:15
Search then the Ruling P. — POPE 247:18
stubborn with his p. — POPE 247:23
vows his p. is infinite — YEAT 342:12
passions diminishes commonplace p. — PARK 240:20
inferno of his p. — LA R 193:21
p. break not through — JUNG 179:13
passives Love's p. — PALI 240:5
Passover come to our P. feast — CRAS 102:25
it is the Lord's p. — HAGG 148:18
passport My p.'s green — BIBL 34:7
past cannot remember the p. — HEAN 154:12
change the p. — SANT 264:17
Ghost of Christmas P. — AGAT 3:3
last day of an era p. — DICK 109:20
looking forward to the p. — YELT 344:5
nothing but the p. — OSBO 237:28
p. as a watch — KEYN 185:10
p., brittle with relics — BOOK 62:14
p. is a foreign country — THOM 316:24
p. never dead — HART 153:1
p. our dancing days — FAUL 126:16
remembrance of things p. — SHAK 286:15
things long p. — SHAK 289:27
Things p. redress — SHAK 285:11
Time present and time p. — SHAK 285:16
under the bloody p. — ELIO 121:18
Utopia is a blessed p. — AHER 3:4
What's p. is prologue — KISS 189:5
pastime take his p. therein — SHAK 287:8
pastoral practising your p. music — BOOK 62:25
pasture feed me in a green p. — VIRG 325:8
pastures fresh woods, and p. new — BOOK 61:6
In p. green — MILT 220:21
pat Now might I do it p. — SCOT 266:28
— SHAK 272:21

patches king of shreds and p. — SHAK 272:25
pate beat your p. — POPE 247:3
pâté de foie gras eating p. — SMIT 298:14
pater P. noster — MISS 224:5
path beaten p. to his door — EMER 124:18
Eightfold P. — PALI 240:3
pathetic P. Fallacy — RUSK 262:9
pathless pleasure in the p. woods — BYRO 78:8
paths all her p. are peace — BIBL 37:19
craggy p. of study — JONS 177:21
p. of glory — GRAY 146:15
patience aptitude for p. — BUFF 72:8
childhood had taught her p. — COLE 96:28
my p. is now at an end — HITL 159:20
p., and shuffle the cards — CERV 86:15
p. of Job — BIBL 51:23
p. on a monument — SHAK 288:21
patient fury of a p. man — DRYD 116:22
kill the p. — BACO 21:11
not so p. — SHAK 274:15
P. continuance — BIBL 49:5
p. etherized upon a table — ELIO 122:9
patients poets are their own p. — THOM 316:21
patines p. of bright gold — SHAK 282:29
patria Died some, pro p. — POUN 250:9
pro p. mori — HORA 164:14
patrician This is the P. — DONN 114:20
patrie enfants de la p. — ROUG 261:8
patries Europe des p. — DE G 107:25
patriot p. of the world — CANN 81:12
Such is the p.'s boast — GOLD 143:20
patriotism knock the p. out of the human race — SHAW 291:25
P. is a lively sense — ALDI 3:11
P. is not enough — CAVE 86:7
P. is the last refuge — JOHN 175:15
That kind of p. — GASK 136:17
patriots blood of p. — JEFF 171:13
True p. we — CART 84:21
patron not a P., my Lord — JOHN 174:20
P. Commonly a wretch — JOHN 173:16
patter rapid, unintelligible p. — GILB 141:9
pattern p. informed by sensibility — READ 254:18
shewed as a p. — SWIF 306:18
patterns weaves algebraic p. — LOVE 203:5
What are p. for — LOWE 203:13
pauper He's only a p. — NOEL 234:19
pause eine kleine P. — FERR 127:4
I p. for a reply — SHAK 276:14
p. in the day's occupations — LONG 201:19
pauses p. between the notes — SCHN 265:16
paved p. paradise — MITC 224:19
streets are p. with gold — COLM 97:13
pavement P. slippery — ROBI 258:5
pavilioned P. in splendour — GRAN 145:15
paw ear on its p. — MAYA 215:15
pax in terra p. — MISS 223:28
P. Vobis — BIBL 53:9
pay Not a penny off the p. — COOK 99:18
p. any price — KENN 184:8
P., pack, and follow — BURT 76:8
p. us, pass us — CHES 89:27
saved the sum of things for p. — HOUS 164:16
We won't p. — FO 130:15
paycock mornin' til night like a p. — O'CA 235:16
paying P. the Dane-geld — KIPL 188:15
price well worth p. — LAMO 192:15
pays You p. your money — PUNC 252:8
PC P. is the LSD of the '90s — LEAR 195:20
pea beautiful p.-green boat — LEAR 195:14
peace all her paths are p. — BIBL 37:19
arch of p. morticed — NICO 234:1
author of p. — BOOK 58:18

call it p.	TACI 308:14
came not to send p.	BIBL 43:27
for ever hold his p.	BOOK 60:16
for p. like retarded pygmies	PEAR 242:18
Give p. a chance	LENN 197:12
good war, or a bad p.	FRAN 133:8
Had Zimri p.	BIBL 36:30
If you want p.	VEGE 323:8
inordinate demand for p.	PEEL 242:20
In p.; goodwill	CHUR 92:11
instrument of Your p.	FRAN 133:3
into the way of p.	BIBL 46:1
in what p. a Christian can die	ADDI 2:16
just and lasting p.	LINC 199:11
Let p. fill our heart	KUMA 191:1
luxury, p.	BAUD 26:7
Make it a *green* p.	DARN 106:4
may not be a just p.	IZET 169:15
mountains also shall bring p.	BOOK 62:7
My p. is gone	GOET 142:19
no p. unto the wicked	BIBL 40:13
no such thing as inner p.	LEBO 196:2
not a p. treaty	FOCH 130:17
on earth p.	BIBL 46:5
Over all the mountain tops is p.	GOET 142:24
p. at the last	NEWM 233:4
p. between equals	WILS 337:7
P. be unto you	BIBL 53:9
p. cannot be maintained	RUSS 263:2
p. for our time	CHAM 86:20
P. hath her victories	MILT 223:13
p. I hope with honour	DISR 112:14
P. I leave with you	BIBL 48:7
p. in our time	BOOK 58:17
p. is a dream	MOLT 225:16
P. is indivisible	LITV 200:8
P. is much more precious	SADA 263:9
'P.! it is I.'	ANAT 5:4
P. its ten thousands	PORT 249:23
p., n. in international affairs	BIER 53:21
P. no longer a dream	CLIN 94:18
p. of God	BIBL 50:27
p. of God	JAME 170:11
p. of Jerusalem	BOOK 63:15
p. of the double-bed	CAMP 80:19
P. on earth	WESL 331:23
P.! Peace! Peace	UPAN 321:22
P., perfect peace	BICK 53:17
P., retrenchment, and reform	BRIG 66:22
P., the human dress	BLAK 56:6
p. there may be in silence	EHRM 120:10
'P. upon earth!' was said	HARD 151:19
p. which the world cannot give	BOOK 58:23
p. with honour	CHAM 86:20
people want p. so much	EISE 120:16
potent advocates of p.	GEOR 138:4
publisheth p.	BIBL 40:14
righteousness and p.	BOOK 62:13
servant depart in p.	BIBL 46:7
So enamoured on p.	CLAR 93:13
speak p. unto nation	REND 255:17
tell me p. has broken out	BREC 66:9
than to make p.	CLEM 94:9
that we may live in p.	ARIS 14:13
time of p.	SHAK 286:1
war and p. in 21st century	KOHL 190:2
peaceably p. if we can	CLAY 94:2
peaceful quietly pacifist p.	WALK 326:21
peacefully p. towards its close	DAWS 107:3
peach dare to eat a p.	ELIO 122:14
Last-supper-carved-on-a-p.-stone	LANC 192:20
nectarine, and curious p.	MARV 213:16
peacock Eyed like a p.	KEAT 181:22

mornin' 'til night like a p.	O'CA 235:16
peacocks apes, and p.	BIBL 36:4
p. and lilies	RUSK 262:16
peak small things from the p.	CHES 90:3
pear *Here we go round the prickly p.*	ELIO 122:5
pearl p. in every cowslip's ear	SHAK 283:7
p. of great price	BIBL 44:3
threw a p. away	SHAK 285:4
pearls He who would search for p.	DRYD 116:26
p. before swine	BIBL 43:4
p. fetch a high price	WHAT 333:2
p. that were his eyes	SHAK 287:7
Pearse Tom P.	BALL 24:16
peasant I am a West Indian p.	MCDO 207:8
rogue and p. slave	SHAK 271:35
peasantry p. its pack animal	TROT 320:2
peasants cricket with their p.	TREV 319:8
pebble smoother p.	NEWT 233:15
peccata p. mundi	MISS 224:6
peccavi P.—I have Sindh	WINK 337:15
p. nimis cogitatione	MISS 223:26
pectora *non mortalia p. cogis*	VIRG 324:15
peculiar Funny-p. or funny ha-ha	HAY 153:17
p. people	BIBL 51:26
pecunia *P. non olet*	VESP 323:15
pedant apothegmatical P.	NASH 231:19
pedantry P. is the dotage	JACK 169:17
pede *nunc p. libero*	HORA 164:9
pedestrians two classes of p.	DEWA 109:8
pedigree languages are the p.	JOHN 174:11
peel orange p. picked out	RALE 254:11
p. me a grape	WEST 332:12
peepers where you get them p.	MERC 216:22
peeping sun Came p. in at morn	HOOD 162:5
peepshow ticket for the p.	MACN 208:16
peer hath not left his p.	MILT 220:10
reluctant p.	BENN 29:14
peerage should study the P.	WILD 335:14
When I want a p.	NORT 234:22
peers House of P.	GILB 140:4
judgement of his p.	MAGN 209:11
Lord in the P.	BROU 68:7
peine *joie venait toujours après la p.*	APOL 13:11
pelican bird is the p.	MERR 217:11
Pelion *P. imposuisse Olympo*	HORA 164:15
pile Ossa on P.	VIRG 325:16
pen Biting my truant p.	SIDN 295:8
mightier than the p.	HOGB 160:21
My tongue is the p.	BOOK 61:22
needle and the p.	LEWI 198:15
nose was as sharp as a p.	SHAK 274:32
p. has been in their hands	AUST 19:23
p. in his hand	JOHN 176:6
p. is worse than the sword	BURT 76:14
p. mightier than the sword	BULW 72:15
scratching of a p.	LOVE 203:9
squat p. rests	HEAN 154:11
pence Take care of the p.	LOWN 204:4
pencils sadness of p.	ROET 258:21
penetralium p. of mystery	KEAT 183:6
peninsulas bright eye of p.	CATU 85:21
pennies p. from heaven	BURK 74:23
penny Not a p. off the pay	COOK 99:18
p. plain and twopence coloured	STEV 303:20
pens Let other p. dwell	AUST 19:18
pension p. list of the republic	CLEV 94:11
pensive Come, p. nun	MILT 219:21
pentagon P., that immense monument	FRAN 133:12
penthouse his p. lid	SHAK 279:1
people All p. that on earth do dwell	KETH 185:2
And the p.	ANON 8:22
as if p. mattered	SCHU 265:18
as many opinions as p.	TERE 314:9

people (*cont.*)
August for the p. — AUDE 17:27
Before we were her p. — FROS 134:9
die for the p. — BIBL 48:2
fiery, impulsive p. — HOUS 165:12
fool all the p. — LINC 199:15
good of the p. — CICE 92:22
indictment against an whole p. — BURK 74:1
I would be of the p. — LA B 191:7
Let my p. go — ANON 10:20
Let my p. go — BIBL 34:5
look after our p. — SCOT 266:4
made for the p. — WEBS 330:5
Most p. ignore most poetry — MITC 224:15
no petty p. — YEAT 344:3
opium of the p. — MARX 214:4
p. are only human — COMP 98:2
p. are the masters — BLAI 55:8
p. are the masters — BURK 74:18
p. arose as one — BIBL 35:12
p. as base as itself — PULI 252:5
p. don't do such things — IBSE 168:12
p. have spoken — FITT 128:11
p. imagine a vain thing — BOOK 60:26
p. is grass — BIBL 40:8
p. made the Constitution — MARS 213:5
P.'s Princess — BLAI 55:9
p.'s voice is odd — POPE 248:26
p. that read — SHEN 294:8
p. that walked in darkness — BIBL 39:18
p. who got there first — USTI 322:3
People who need p. — MERR 217:10
suppose the p. good — ROBE 257:18
thy p. shall be my people — BIBL 35:13
understanded of the p. — BOOK 64:4
voice of the p. — ALCU 3:10
What is the city but the p. — SHAK 270:11
peopled conquered and p. — SEEL 267:7
peoples cry of the Little P. — LE G 196:17
pepper Sergeant P. — TYNA 321:15
percentage reasonable p. — BECK 26:19
perception doors of p. — BLAK 55:26
no p., appellation — Mahâ 209:13
perdition led to p. by a man — WEST 332:19
P. catch my soul — SHAK 284:19
perennial Falsehood has a p. spring — BURK 73:23
perennius *Exegi monumentum aere p.* — HORA 164:16
perestroika restructuring [p.] — GORB 144:15
perfect Be ye therefore p. — BIBL 42:21
end of a p. day — BOND 57:22
ever more p. eyes — TEIL 310:7
If thou wilt be p. — BIBL 44:19
Nothing is p. — STEP 302:17
One p. rose — PARK 240:17
p. woman; nobly planned — WORD 341:7
service is p. freedom — BOOK 58:18
perfection Dead p., no more — TENN 312:20
P. is the child — HALL 150:8
Pictures of p. — AUST 20:4
pursuit of p. — ARNO 15:27
very pink of p. — GOLD 144:1
perfectly P. pure and good — BROW 70:28
small, but p. formed — COOP 99:23
perfide *ah, la p. Angleterre* — BOSS 64:19
perfidious p. Albion — XIMÉ 342:8
p. friends — MEDI 216:1
perform Almighty's orders to p. — ADDI 2:6
p. without thinking — WHIT 333:15
zeal will p. this — BIBL 39:20
performance so many years outlive p. — SHAK 274:19
takes away the p. — SHAK 280:14
performing aroma of p. seals — HART 152:18
perfume curious p. — AUBR 17:17

perfumes No p. — BRUM 71:18
p. of Arabia — SHAK 281:17
perhaps grand P. — BROW 69:20
seek a great p. — RABE 253:15
Perigord truffles, P. — POPE 246:23
peril p. in the fight — CORN 100:2
those in p. on the sea — WHIT 333:18
perils defend us from all p. — BOOK 59:1
perish if I p., I perish — BIBL 36:35
Let the day p. — BIBL 37:2
money p. with thee — BIBL 48:25
people p. — BIBL 38:9
P. the thought — CIBB 92:20
p. with the sword — BIBL 45:18
should not p. — BIBL 47:28
venal city ripe to p. — SALL 264:1
perished p., each alone — COWP 101:18
perjured p. Clarence — SHAK 286:3
perjuries laughs at lovers' p. — OVID 238:11
permitted p. to make all the ballads — FLET 130:5
perpendicular p. expression of horizontal — SHAW 292:5
perpetua *lux p.* — MISS 224:10
perpetual p. light — MISS 224:10
p. motion — DICK 111:9
p. night — JONS 177:22
p. quarrel — BURK 74:2
persecuted I p. the church of God — BIBL 50:1
merely because he is p. — GOUL 144:21
persecutest Saul, why p. thou me — BIBL 48:26
persecution P. is a bad and indirect way — BROW 69:6
Persepolis through P. — MARL 212:15
perseverance P., dear my lord — SHAK 287:31
persevere Give us grace to p. — DEAR 107:7
persevering no dignity in p. in error — PEEL 242:21
Persians Medes and P. — BIBL 41:9
Truth-loving P. — GRAV 146:6
persistence Hark, the dominant's p. — BROW 71:9
person most superior p. — ANON 8:20
p. on business from Porlock — COLE 96:2
p. you and I took me for — CARL 82:11
personality From 35 to 55, good p. — TUCK 320:14
persons no respecter of p. — BIBL 48:30
things, not in p. — CURI 105:4
perspiration ninety-nine per cent p. — EDIS 119:22
perspire Gladstone may p. — CHUR 91:2
persuaders hidden p. — PACK 239:3
persuadest Almost thou p. me — BIBL 49:4
persuading By p. others — JUNI 179:18
persuasion p. only is to work — MILT 223:16
perturbed rest, p. spirit — SHAK 271:23
Peru China to P. — JOHN 174:4
perversions of all the sexual p. — HUXL 167:17
pervert loophole through which the p. — BRON 67:7
pessimist p. fears this is true — CABE 79:26
pestilence p. that walketh in darkness — BOOK 62:17
plague and p. — NASH 231:21
petal dropping a rose p. — MARQ 212:24
Now sleeps the crimson p. — TENN 313:14
petar Hoist with his own p. — SHAK 272:28
Peter Shock-headed P. — HOFF 160:19
Thou art P. — BIBL 44:10
Where P. is — AMBR 4:13
petrifactions p. of a plodding brain — BYRO 79:9
pets hate a word like 'p.' — JENN 172:2
petticoat feet beneath her p. — SUCK 305:11
petticoats hyena in p. — WALP 327:17
petty no p. people — YEAT 344:3
phagocytes Stimulate the p. — SHAW 290:25
phantom p. of delight — WORD 341:6
Pharisees drowns in the P.'s hypocrisy — PAST 241:21
scribes and P., hypocrites — BIBL 44:30
phenomenon infant p. — DICK 110:24

Philadelphia living in P.	FIEL 127:23	**pieces** P. of eight	STEV 303:23
Philip from P. drunk	ANON 5:20	thirty p. of silver	BIBL 45:11
Philistines daughters of the P.	BIBL 35:27	**pierce** his hand, and p. it	BIBL 36:33
P. be upon thee, Samson	BIBL 35:10	**Pierian** P. spring	DRAY 116:7
P. proper	ARNO 15:28	taste not the P. spring	POPE 247:25
philosopher in my time to be a p.	EDWA 120:7	**piety** nor all thy p. nor wit	FITZ 128:19
philosophy divine p.	MILT 219:14	p. more prone	ALEX 3:19
dreamt of in your p.	SHAK 271:21	**piffle** p. before the wind	ASHF 16:14
History is p.	DION 112:2	**pig** from p. to man	ORWE 237:6
mere touch of cold p.	KEAT 181:24	p. got up and slowly walked away	BURT 76:5
p. inclineth man's mind	BACO 21:2	p. in a sausage	TROL 319:22
P. is the replacement	RYLE 263:6	**pigeon** branded, p.-holed	PRES 251:1
p. paints its grey	HEGE 155:6	**pigeons** Poisoning p.	LEHR 196:19
p. quenches them	VOLT 326:4	**pigs** P. treat us as equals	CHUR 92:14
P.! the lumber	SWIF 307:7	whether p. have wings	CARR 84:6
P. will clip	KEAT 181:25	**pike** freedom for the p.	TAWN 309:15
superstition to enslave a p.	INGE 168:19	**Pilate** jesting P.	BACO 21:30
sweet milk, p.	SHAK 286:30	P. saith unto him	BIBL 48:9
Phoebus P., arise	DRUM 116:13	Suffered under Pontius P.	BOOK 58:16
phoenix privilege of P.	GRAC 145:4	water like P.	GREE 146:23
phoenixes envy the pair of p.	HO 159:21	**pile** p. Ossa on Pelion	VIRG 325:16
phone answer the p.	THUR 317:28	P. the bodies high	SAND 264:9
never even made a p. call	CHOM 90:18	**pilfering** quiet, p.	CLAR 93:9
P. for the fish-knives	BETJ 31:21	**pilgrim** Onward goes the p. band	BARI 25:6
photograph p. is a secret	ARBU 13:20	To be a p.	BUNY 73:9
photographer be a good p.	BAIL 22:25	**pilgrimage** I'll take my p.	RALE 254:2
p. is like the cod	SHAW 292:3	succeed me in my p.	BUNY 73:11
photography mission of p.	STEI 302:6	**pilgrimages** longen folk to goon on p.	CHAU 88:5
P. is truth	GODA 142:9	**pilgrims** land of the p.	CUMM 104:14
p. of an event	CART 85:2	Land of the p.' pride	SMIT 297:23
phrase ancient Saxon p.	LONG 201:24	**pill** any p. can be swallowed	TROL 319:16
phrases Taffeta p.	SHAK 278:20	Instruction is the p.	RICH 257:1
physic Take p., pomp	SHAK 277:22	little yellow p.	JAGG 170:2
Throw p. to the dogs	SHAK 281:22	women may take the p.	THOM 316:20
physician died last night of my p.	PRIO 251:10	**pillar** became a p. of salt	BIBL 33:25
Honour a p.	BIBL 41:28	p. of a cloud	BIBL 34:10
need not a p.	BIBL 43:19	seemed A p. of state	MILT 221:18
p. can bury his mistakes	WRIG 341:26	**pillars** hewn out her seven p.	BIBL 37:23
P., heal thyself	BIBL 46:9	p. bare like nude	SPEN 300:11
physicians P. of the Utmost Fame	BELL 28:10	**pillow** like the feather p.	HAIG 149:6
physicists p. have known sin	OPPE 236:17	softer p. than my heart	BYRO 79:25
physics p. or stamp collecting	RUTH 263:4	upon the p.-hill	STEV 303:29
p. pain	SHAK 280:15	**pillows** P. his chin	MILT 220:26
pianist shoot the p.	ANON 9:11	**pilot** daring p. in extremity	DRYD 116:16
pianists no better than many p.	SCHN 265:16	Dropping the p.	TENN 310:10
Picardy Roses are flowering in P.	WEAT 329:26	See my p. face to face	TENN 310:19
Piccadilly Goodbye, P.	JUDG 179:8	**pilots** P. of the purple twilight	TENN 312:10
walk down P.	GILB 140:25	**piminy** Francesca di Rimini, miminy, p.	GILB 140:26
picket p.'s off duty forever	BEER 27:14	**Pimpernel** demmed, elusive P.	ORCZ 236:20
picking keep my hands from p.	BOOK 60:10	**pimples** scratching of p. on the body	WOOL 339:9
pickle weaned on a p.	ANON 10:11	**pin** p. up my hair with prose	CONG 98:18
picklocks p. of biographers	BENÉ 29:12	**pineapple** p. of politeness	SHER 294:13
pickpockets crowd of p.	WYCH 342:5	**pinion** imagination droops her p.	BYRO 78:26
pickpurse no p. of another's wit	SIDN 295:11	**pinions** with p. skim the air	FRER 133:18
picnic Teddy Bears have their P.	BRAT 66:6	**pink** very p. of courtesy	SHAK 286:24
pictura Ut p. poesis	HORA 163:19	very p. of perfection	GOLD 144:1
picture look Not on his p.	JONS 178:3	**pinko** really p.-grey	FORS 131:16
One p. is worth ten thousand	BARN 25:7	**pinstripe** come in a p. suit	FEIN 126:18
speaking p., with this end	SIDN 295:12	**pint** p. of plain	O'BR 235:15
your p. chases me	RACI 253:20	p.—that's very nearly	GALT 135:17
pictured my friends p. within	ELGA 121:2	**pioneers** are simply p.	MURR 230:10
pictures cutting all the p. out	BELL 28:6	P.! O pioneers	WHIT 333:22
furnish the p.	HEAR 154:16	**pious** rarther p.	ASHF 16:13
P. are for entertainment	GOLD 144:10	**pipes** open the p.	BYRD 77:18
p. aren't good enough	CAPA 81:20	What p. and timbrels	KEAT 181:28
p. do not sell	VAN 322:16	**piping** For ever p. songs	KEAT 182:2
P. of perfection	AUST 20:4	Helpless, naked, p. loud	BLAK 56:10
sees more in my p.	TURN 320:21	P. songs of pleasant glee	BLAK 56:4
without p. or conversations	CARR 83:13	weak p. time	SHAK 286:1
picturesque p. and the beautiful	PEAC 242:13	**Pippa** P. passes	BEER 27:11
pie Miss American P.	MCLE 208:1	**pips** until the p. squeak	GEDD 137:14
p. in the sky	HILL 159:2	**pirate** To be a P. King	GILB 141:4
put into a p.	POTT 249:26	**piss** pitcher of warm p.	GARN 136:6

pissing inside the tent p. out — JOHN 173:6
pistol I reach for my p. — JOHS 177:6
  p. in your pocket — WEST 332:16
  pun is a p. — LAMB 192:5
  when his p. misses fire — GOLD 144:5
piston steam and p. stroke — MORR 228:18
pit digged a p. before me — BOOK 62:3
  He that diggeth a p. — BIBL 38:28
  Law is a bottomless p. — ARBU 13:21
  monster of the p. — POPE 248:29
pitch He that toucheth p. — BIBL 41:26
pitcher p. be broken at the fountain — BIBL 38:34
pitchfork drive out nature with a p. — HORA 163:24
  use my wit as a p. — LARK 193:15
pith p. is in the postscript — HAZL 154:2
pitiful God be p. — BROW 69:12
pity by means of p. and fear — ARIS 14:14
  cherish p. — BLAK 56:7
  O source of p. — MISS 224:12
  P. a human face — BLAK 56:6
  p. beyond all telling — YEAT 343:14
  p. kills — BALZ 24:22
  p. never ceases to be shown — DRYD 116:20
  p. this busy monster — CUMM 104:17
  Poetry is in the p. — OWEN 238:20
  she did p. them — SHAK 284:13
  yet the p. of it, Iago — SHAK 284:30
place all other things give p. — GAY 137:6
  and the p. thereof — BOOK 62:23
  genius of the p. — POPE 247:19
  Get p. and wealth — POPE 248:24
  Gratitude of p.-expectants — WALP 327:23
  In p. of strife — CAST 85:8
  keep in the same p. — CARR 84:5
  no p. to go — WHIT 333:17
  p. in the sun — BÜLO 72:11
  p. in the sun — WILH 335:27
  p. within the meaning — ANON 9:10
  p. without power — ROSE 260:7
  prepare a p. for you — BIBL 48:5
  rising to great p. — BACO 21:15
  spirit of the p. — VIRG 325:3
  till there be no p. — BIBL 39:13
  time and the p. — BROW 70:24
  Time, P. — DRYD 117:15
placem ut p. genus irritabile vatum — HORA 164:5
places all p. were alike to him — KIPL 188:21
  P. where they sing — BOOK 58:20
  Proper words in proper p. — SWIF 306:21
  quietest p. — HOUS 165:8
placidly Go p. amid the noise — EHRM 120:10
plagiarism from one author, it's p. — MIZN 225:5
plagiarize P.! Let no one else's work — LEHR 196:18
plague instruments to p. us — SHAK 278:10
  p. and pestilence — NASH 231:21
  p. o' both your houses — SHAK 286:26
  p. the inventor — SHAK 279:20
plagues Great p. remain — BOOK 61:13
plain best p. set — BACO 21:3
  Books will speak p. — BACO 21:7
  darkling p. — ARNO 15:5
  make it p. upon tables — BIBL 41:18
  penny p. and twopence coloured — STEV 303:20
  pint of p. — O'BR 235:15
  p., blunt man — SHAK 276:22
  'p.' cooking cannot be entrusted — MORP 228:11
  P. living and high thinking — WORD 340:16
  pricking on the p. — SPEN 300:13
  truth for p. people — WESL 332:5
plains flowery p. of honour — JONS 177:21
  p. of windy Troy — TENN 313:29
plaisir P. d'amour — FLOR 130:14
plan by his p. of attack — SASS 265:3

planes search me going into p. — KEYE 185:7
planet born under a rhyming p. — SHAK 284:6
  new p. swims into his ken — KEAT 182:19
planetary p. influence — SHAK 277:10
planned order of the acts is p. — PAST 241:21
  p. obsolescence — STEV 303:2
plant I p. lines — WALC 326:17
  p. of rapid growth — WASH 328:23
  Sensitive P. — SHEL 293:22
  time to p. — BIBL 38:16
  What is a weed? A p. — EMER 124:14
Plantagenet where is P. — CREW 103:10
planting p. my cabbages — MONT 226:7
plants forced p. — JOHN 176:5
  He that p. trees — FULL 135:1
plasters p., pills, and ointment — LOCK 201:10
platinum bullets made of p. — BELL 28:7
platitude longitude with no p. — FRY 134:19
  stroke a p. until it purrs — MARQ 212:25
platitudes orchestration of p. — WILD 335:25
Plato attachment à la P. — GILB 140:24
  P. is dear to me — ARIS 14:20
  P.'s retirement — MILT 222:28
  p. told him: he couldn't — CUMM 104:16
plausibly p. maintained — BURR 76:3
play all the p., the insight — BROW 69:18
  children at p. — MONT 226:9
  Did that p. of mine send out — YEAT 343:9
  Games people p. — BERN 31:7
  holdeth children from p. — SIDN 295:13
  I could p. Ercles rarely — SHAK 283:3
  little victims p. — GRAY 146:18
  our p. is played out — THAC 314:26
  p.'s the thing — SHAK 271:37
  p. the game — NEWB 232:20
  p. things as they are — STEV 303:6
  p. with my cat — MONT 226:12
  written a damned p. — REYN 256:4
playboy lost the only P. — SYNG 308:8
played He p. the King — FIEL 127:9
player wrapped in a p.'s hide — GREE 147:4
players men and women merely p. — SHAK 269:20
playing won on the p. fields — WELL 331:12
plays English p. are like — VOLT 326:12
plaything child's a p. — LAMB 192:8
  little p.-house — WALP 327:7
Plaza Toro Duke of P. — GILB 139:19
plea Though justice be thy p. — SHAK 282:21
  without one p. — ELLI 123:21
pleasance Youth is full of p. — SHAK 289:17
pleasant green and p. land — BLAK 55:27
  in p. places — BOOK 61:2
  Life would be very p. — SURT 306:10
  p. it is to have money — CLOU 94:22
  P. to know Mr Lear — LEAR 195:13
pleasantness ways are ways of p. — BIBL 37:19
please do what I p. — FRED 133:13
  p. the touchy breed of poets — HORA 164:5
  To tax and to p. — BURK 73:24
pleased in whom I am well p. — BIBL 42:9
  p. not the million — SHAK 271:33
pleases every prospect p. — HEBE 155:2
pleasing p. one intelligent man — MAIM 209:19
pleasure egg by p. laid — COWP 101:26
  go to my p., business — WYCH 342:3
  harmless p. — JOHN 173:21
  heart with p. fills — WORD 340:2
  I' the east my p. lies — SHAK 268:21
  no p. in the strength — BOOK 63:28
  No p. worth giving up — AMIS 5:1
  pay a debt to p. — ROCH 258:9
  p. after pain — DRYD 116:24

p. afterwards THAC 314:18
P. at the helm GRAY 146:12
p. in the pathless woods BYRO 78:8
p. is momentary CHES 89:15
p. lives in height TENN 313:17
p. me in his top-boots MARL 212:2
P. never is at home KEAT 181:11
p. sure, In being mad DRYD 117:10
p. to the spectators MACA 205:21
read without p. JOHN 177:3
soul of p. BEHN 27:20
stately p.-dome decree COLE 96:3
Youth and P. meet BYRO 77:26
pleasures all the p. prove MARL 212:13
celibacy has no p. JOHN 173:26
English take their p. SULL 306:1
p. and palaces PAYN 242:11
purest of human p. BACO 21:12
some new p. prove DONN 114:5
tear our p. MARV 213:23
two supreme p. ROSE 260:8
plebeian this the P. bran DONN 114:20
plebiscite justice by p. ZOBE 345:7
pledge I will p. with mine JONS 178:4
p. allegiance BELL 28:4
Pleiades influences of P. BIBL 37:13
pleni P. sunt coeli MISS 224:4
plenty but just had p. BURN 75:9
here is God's p. DRYD 117:17
pleuré quelquefois p. MUSS 230:15
pleut il p. sa ville VERL 323:13
plie taking their p. BURG 73:19
plot Gunpowder Treason and P. ANON 9:12
now the p. thickens BUCK 72:3
This blessèd p. SHAK 285:13
plots P., true or false DRYD 116:14
plotting most p. heart RICH 256:20
plough boy that driveth the p. TYND 321:17
p. the fields CAMP 80:18
put his hand to the p. BIBL 46:13
wherefore p. SHEL 293:25
ploughman p. homeward plods GRAY 146:13
wrong even the poorest p. CHAR 87:20
ploughshares swords into p. BIBL 39:11
pluck it out BIBL 44:15
p. till time and times are done YEAT 343:24
plume blast-beruffled p. HARD 151:22
plummet did ever p. sound SHAK 287:18
plums p. and orange peel RALE 254:11
plunder no man stop to p. MACA 206:5
What a place to p. BLÜC 57:1
plures Abiit ad p. PETR 244:10
plus Il n'y a p. de Pyrénées LOUI 202:20
P. ça change KARR 180:17
Plutonian Night's P. shore POE 246:13
poacher p. staggering MCCA 206:16
Pobble P. who has no toes LEAR 195:17
pocket gun in your p. WEST 332:16
in Britain, in your p. WILS 336:19
in each other's p. BIER 53:18
pockets in the p. of the people GLAD 142:6
poem begin a p. MCGO 207:13
being the author of that p. WOLF 338:14
essentially the greatest p. WHIT 334:3
long p. is a test KEAT 183:3
married to a p. KEAT 183:13
p. is like a painting HORA 163:19
p. lovely as a tree KILM 186:1
P. of the Sea RIMB 257:10
p. should not mean but be MACL 208:2
write a p. after Auschwitz ADOR 2:1
poemata Scribimus indocti doctique p. HORA 164:3
poems P. are made by fools like me KILM 186:2

p. should be Clyde-built DUNN 118:10
we all scribble p. HORA 164:3
poesis Ut pictura p. HORA 163:19
poet and the P.'s dream WORD 339:20
dreams of a p. JOHN 173:12
every fool is not a p. POPE 247:5
have a p. able-bodied MACN 208:22
limbs of a p. HORA 164:20
lover, and the p. SHAK 283:21
Not deep the P. sees ARNO 15:12
p. ranks far below the painter LEON 197:21
p.'s eye, in a fine frenzy SHAK 283:22
p.'s hope: to be AUDE 18:20
p.'s mouth be shut YEAT 343:13
p. stubborn with his passion YEAT 342:12
starved p. LOCK 201:10
was a true P. BLAK 55:21
poetae Etiam disiecti membra p. HORA 164:20
poetic constitutes p. faith COLE 96:21
nurse for a p. child SCOT 266:12
P. Justice POPE 246:18
poetry best piece of p. JONS 178:1
campaign in p. CUOM 105:2
cradled into p. by wrong SHEL 292:27
Emptied of its p. AUDE 18:4
If p. comes not KEAT 183:7
Ireland hurt you into p. AUDE 18:3
It is not p. POPE 247:9
most p. ignores most people MITC 224:15
p. begins to atrophy POUN 250:13
p. in motion KAUF 180:20
P. is a subject as precise FLAU 139:8
P. is at bottom ARNO 16:2
p. is eloquent painting SIMO 296:3
P. is in the pity OWEN 238:20
P. is not most important THOM 316:13
P. is the achievement SAND 264:11
P. is the record of the best SHEL 294:5
P. is the spontaneous overflow WORD 341:20
P. is the supreme fiction STEV 303:5
P. is what is lost FROS 134:16
P. is when some of them BENT 30:6
P. must be as well written POUN 250:15
p. of motion GRAH 145:10
p., prophecy, and religion RUSK 262:10
P.'s a mere drug FARQ 126:12
P.'s the feverish fit WINC 337:9
p. = the best words COLE 96:24
polar star of p. KEAT 183:3
quarrel with ourselves, p. YEAT 344:2
saying it and that is p. CAGE 80:5
Sir, what is p. JOHN 175:20
Writing a book of p. MARQ 212:24
poets All p. are mad BURT 76:13
impossible to hold the p. back GIRA 141:16
Irish p., learn your trade YEAT 343:28
mature p. steal ELIO 123:1
No death has hurt p. more HEAN 154:15
p. are their own patients THOM 316:21
P. are the unacknowledged SHEL 294:6
p. bicycle-pump the human heart AMIS 4:21
powerful p. of the century ELIO 123:2
romantic p. LEAP 195:6
Souls of p. dead KEAT 181:26
think all p. were Byronic COPE 99:25
touchy breed of p. HORA 164:5
We p. in our youth WORD 340:26
point from p. to point TENN 312:13
p. a moral JOHN 174:6
still p. of the turning world ELIO 121:21
upon a needle's p. CUDW 104:11
Up to a p., Lord Copper WAUG 329:21

poison coward's weapon, p. — FLET 130:13
food only a cover for p. — BURK 74:12
got as far as p.-gas — HARD 151:19
p. in jest — SHAK 272:14
put p. in your coffee — CHUR 92:15
strongest p. ever known — BLAK 55:14
poisoned p. rat in a hole — SWIF 306:22
poisoning P. pigeons — LEHR 196:19
poisonous for its p. wine — KEAT 182:6
polar p. star of poetry — KEAT 183:3
pole top of the greasy p. — DISR 113:4
polecat semi-house-trained p. — FOOT 130:21
polemic don't watch BBC for p. — SIMP 296:5
police citizen or the p. — AUDE 18:17
p. can beat you — SHAW 291:23
p. were to blame — GRAN 145:14
policeman p. and a pretty girl — CHAP 87:12
p.'s lot — GILB 141:6
terrorist and the p. — CONR 99:9
policy English p. is to float — SALI 263:19
home p.: I wage war — CLEM 94:8
If the p. isn't hurting — MAJO 209:21
My [foreign] p. — BEVI 32:13
national p. — BRIA 66:16
p. of retaliation — PARN 241:9
p. of the good neighbour — ROOS 259:16
some love but little p. — SHAK 285:28
polite no allies to be p. to — GEOR 138:9
p. meaningless words — YEAT 342:19
time to be p. — MONT 226:16
politeness pineapple of p. — SHER 294:13
p. of kings — LOUI 203:2
suave p. — KNOX 189:16
political fear of P. Economy — SELL 267:19
points to a p. career — SHAW 291:5
p. animal — ARIS 14:17
p. Cave of Adullam — BRIG 67:2
P. language . . . is designed — ORWE 237:19
p. lives end in failure — POWE 250:25
p. will — LYNN 205:2
schemes of p. improvement — JOHN 175:5
politician greatest art of a p. — BOLI 57:15
like a scurvy p. — SHAK 278:3
lurks a p. — ARIS 14:12
makes the p. wise — POPE 249:6
P.'s corpse — CUMM 104:15
p. to complain about — BELL 28:14
statesman is a p. — POWE 250:24
when a p. does get an idea — TRUM 320:8
politicians die for p. — MARQ 212:23
Old p. chew — THOM 317:7
p. have had to listen — POPE 247:25
whole race of p. — FITT 128:11
politics continuation of p. — SWIF 306:19
From p., it was an easy step — CLAU 94:1
In p., if you want anything — AUST 19:20
in p. the middle way — THAT 315:3
In p., what begins in fear — ADAM 1:20
invisible hand in p. — COLE 96:25
mule of p. — FRIE 133:24
no true friends in p. — DISR 112:19
P. are now nothing more — CLAR 93:15
p. consists in ignoring facts — JOHN 175:16
P. has got to be fun — ADAM 1:16
P. is not the art — CLAR 93:17
p. is present history — GALB 135:11
P. is the art of preventing — FREE 133:15
P. is the Art of the Possible — VALÉ 322:7
P. is war without bloodshed — BUTL 77:4
p. of the left — MAO 211:11
P. supposed to be — JENK 171:21
week is a long time in p. — REAG 255:1
— WILS 336:18

zeal in p. — JUNI 179:18
politique p. father — JAME 170:10
Polka see me dance the P. — GROS 148:3
pollution engine of p., the dog — SPAR 299:25
p. of democracy — WHIT 333:12
Polly Our P. is a sad slut — GAY 137:1
polygamous Man is p. — JAME 171:5
Pomeranian P. grenadier — BISM 54:15
pomp p. of yesterday — KIPL 188:6
Pride, p., and circumstance — SHAK 284:26
Take physic, p. — SHAK 277:22
Pompey Knew you not P. — SHAK 275:28
pompous p. in the grave — BROW 69:2
pomps p. and vanity — BOOK 60:9
pond Old p., leap-splash — BASH 26:2
pondered p. them in her heart — BIBL 46:6
ponies Five and twenty p. — KIPL 188:9
poodle in a p. parlour — PARR 241:11
right hon. Gentleman's p. — LLOY 200:17
pools p. are filled with water — BOOK 62:11
Where the p. are bright — HOGG 160:22
poop O p.-poop — GRAH 145:11
poor Blessed are the p. — BIBL 42:14
bring in hither the p. — BIBL 46:27
give food to the p. — CAMA 80:15
give to the p. — BIBL 44:19
grind the faces of the p. — BIBL 39:12
help the many who are p. — KENN 184:9
Laws grind the p. — GOLD 143:22
murmuring p. — CRAB 102:13
My countrymen Kiltartan's p. — YEAT 343:4
no disgrace t'be p. — HUBB 166:6
no peasant in my kingdom so p. — HENR 156:11
p. always ye have — BIBL 48:3
p. are Europe's blacks — CHAM 87:1
p. but she was honest — ANON 9:20
p. get children — KAHN 180:11
p. know that it is money — BREN 66:13
P. little rich girl — COWA 101:9
p. man had nothing — BIBL 35:30
p. soul sat sighing — SHAK 284:32
Resolve not to be p. — JOHN 176:10
RICH AND THE P. — DISR 112:27
your tired, your p. — LAZA 195:2
poorer for richer for p. — BOOK 60:18
poorest p. he that is in England — RAIN 253:22
pop P. goes the weasel — MAND 210:18
pope against the P. or the NUM — BALD 23:13
P.! How many divisions — STAL 301:13
P. is quite satisfied — MICH 217:18
to the P. afterwards — NEWM 233:3
poppies In Flanders p. the poppies blow — MCCR 207:3
poppy with a p. or a lily — GILB 140:25
populace clamours of the p. — ADAM 1:18
population p., when unchecked — MALT 210:15
populi Salus p. — CICE 92:22
Vox p. — ALCU 3:10
porcelain dainty rogue in p. — MERE 216:26
porcupines throw p. under you — KHRU 185:20
pork p. please our mouths — MENG 216:18
Porlock on business from P. — COLE 96:2
pornography p. is really about — SONT 299:7
P. the attempt to insult sex — LAWR 194:14
porpentine quills upon the fretful p. — SHAK 271:16
porridge consistency of cold p. — TURI 320:19
port be p. if it could — BENT 30:9
In every p. a wife — DIBD 109:14
In ev'ry p. a mistress — GAY 137:12
little p. Had seldom seen — TENN 310:23
p., for men — JOHN 176:3
porter moon shone bright on Mrs P. — ELIO 122:26
portmanteau like a p. — CARR 84:12
portrait Every time I paint a p. — SARG 264:19

p. of a blinking idiot | SHAK 282:11
p. of the artist | JOYC 178:22
portraits put up and take down p. | LICH 198:24
position altering the p. of matter | RUSS 262:21
only p. for women | CARM 83:6
p. must be held to the last man | HAIG 149:7
p. ridiculous | CHES 89:15
positive ac-cent-tchu-ate the p. | MERC 216:21
power of p. thinking | PEAL 242:16
possessed much p. by death | ELIO 122:30
possessing too dear for my p. | SHAK 289:34
possession in the glad p. | JONS 177:20
possessions All my p. | ELIZ 123:12
behind the great p. | JAME 170:16
possibilities improbable p. | ARIS 14:16
possibility deny the p. of anything | HUXL 168:5
possible art of the p. | BISM 54:13
Art of the P. | BUTL 77:4
art of the p. | GALB 135:11
best of all p. worlds | BRAD 65:21
if a thing is p. | CALO 80:12
p. you may be mistaken | CROM 103:18
something is p. | CLAR 93:18
With God all things are p. | BIBL 44:21
possum said the Honourable P. | BERR 31:13
possumus Non omnia p. omnes | VIRG 325:12
possunt p., quia posse videntur | VIRG 324:18
post driving briskly in a p.-chaise | JOHN 175:21
P. coitum | ANON 12:18
p. of honour | ADDI 2:10
posted p. presence of the watcher | JAME 170:20
poster Kitchener is a great p. | ASQU 16:21
p. a visual telegram | CASS 85:6
posteri Credite p. | HORA 164:12
posterity go down to p. | DISR 112:16
hope of p. | POWE 250:26
P. do something for us | ADDI 2:15
Think of your p. | ADAM 1:22
write for p. | ADE 2:17
posters P. of the sea and land | SHAK 279:2
postman p. always rings twice | CAIN 80:6
postscript but in her p. | STEE 302:2
most material in the p. | BACO 21:8
pith is in the p. | HAZL 154:2
pot chicken in every p. | HOOV 162:13
chicken in his p. | HENR 156:11
death in the p. | BIBL 36:23
flinging a p. of paint | RUSK 262:7
under a p. | BIBL 38:21
who the p. | FITZ 128:20
potato bashful young p. | GILB 140:24
potent how p. cheap music is | COWA 101:12
Potomac All quiet along the P. | BEER 27:14
quiet along the P. | MCCL 206:23
pottage mess of p. | BIBL 33:27
potter Who is the p., pray | FITZ 128:20
poultry lives of the p. | ELIO 121:5
pound p. here in Britain | WILS 336:19
pounds p. will take care | LOWN 204:4
poverty hunger and p. | LARK 193:9
misfortunes of p. | JUVE 179:21
P. is a great enemy | JOHN 176:10
p.'s catching | BEHN 27:21
worst of crimes is p. | SHAW 291:1
powder keep your p. dry | BLAC 55:1
when your p.'s runnin' low | NEWB 232:17
powdered Still to be p. | JONS 177:16
power balance of p. | NICO 234:1
corridors of p. | SNOW 298:18
desires to have—P. | BOUL 65:7
friend in p. | ADAM 1:15
his p. and his love | GRAN 145:15
in office but not in p. | LAMO 192:17

jaws of p. | ADAM 1:21
knowledge itself is p. | BACO 22:2
live without a common p. | HOBB 160:1
only have p. over people | SOLZ 298:27
O wad some P. | BURN 75:29
place without p. | ROSE 260:7
p. can be rightfully exercised | MILL 218:3
p. grows out of the barrel of a gun | MAO 211:12
p. in trust | DRYD 116:19
p. is a trust | DISR 112:29
P. is the great aphrodisiac | KISS 189:3
p. of Jesus' Name | PERR 244:4
p. of suppress | NORT 234:21
p. over men | WOLL 338:23
p. over nothing | HERO 157:24
P. tends to corrupt | ACTO 1:8
p. to tax | MARS 213:4
p. Which erring men call chance | MILT 219:17
P. without responsibility | KIPL 189:2
responsibility without p. | STOP 304:14
Unlimited p. | PITT 245:10
with Eternal God for p. | TENN 313:1
powerful fear is that we are p. | WILL 336:11
P. women only succeed | LEE- 196:16
powers against p. | BIBL 50:23
high contracting p. | BRIA 66:16
principalities, nor p. | BIBL 49:18
principalities, or p. | BIBL 51:1
real separation of p. | DENN 108:17
virtues, p. | MILT 222:11
we lay waste our p. | WORD 341:18
pox or of the p. | WILK 336:1
praevalet Magna est veritas, et p. | BIBL 53:14
praise Apostles: p. thee | BOOK 58:11
as is p. | ASCH 16:11
Damn with faint p. | POPE 247:10
is p. indeed | MORT 229:10
lack tongues to p. | SHAK 290:3
p. at morning | POPE 248:5
p. famous men | BIBL 41:29
P. my soul | LYTE 205:6
P. the green earth | BUNT 72:18
P. the Lord | FORG 131:10
P. the Lord, for he is kind | MILT 220:8
p. those works | MART 213:8
P. to the Holiest | NEWM 233:6
P. to the Lord | WINK 337:14
unto thy Name give the p. | BOOK 63:6
We p. thee, O God | BOOK 58:10
praised God be p. | BROW 69:12
more in him to be p. | JONS 178:11
p., and got rid of | CICE 93:4
p. his fleas | YEAT 343:26
praiser p. of past times | HORA 163:17
praises with faint p. | WYCH 342:4
pray as lief p. with Kit Smart | JOHN 174:22
came to scoff, remained to p. | GOLD 143:11
I p. for the country | HALE 149:14
Often when I p. | LEWI 198:13
P. for the dead | JONE 177:10
p. you, master Lieutenant | MORE 228:3
Watch and p. | BIBL 45:17
Work and p. | HILL 159:2
prayer Conservative Party at p. | ROYD 261:17
Father, hear the p. | WILL 336:13
house of p. | BIBL 40:19
house of p. | BIBL 44:25
lift up the hands in p. | HOPK 163:10
on a wing and a p. | ADAM 2:5
perfect p. | LESS 198:3
p. at sinking of the sun | KORA 190:19
p. reduces itself | TURG 320:17
things are wrought by p. | TENN 311:15

prayer (*cont.*)
wish for p. is a prayer — BERN 31:2
prayers addicted to p. — ASHF 16:13
among my p. — HORA 164:21
Christopher Robin is saying his p. — MILN 219:3
hear our p. — BOOK 60:12
prayeth p. well, who loveth well — COLE 96:18
praying Amelia was p. for George — THAC 314:23
No p. — OTWA 238:9
now he is p. — SHAK 272:21
past p. for — SHAK 273:33
preach p. the gospel — BIBL 45:31
preached p. to death by wild curates — SMIT 298:11
preachers best of all p. — GUES 148:10
preaching woman's p. — JOHN 175:1
precedency point of p. — JOHN 176:13
precedent from p. — LLOY 200:15
is a dangerous p. — CORN 100:9
p. embalms a principle — STOW 304:21
precept more efficacious than p. — JOHN 174:1
p. must be upon precept — BIBL 39:29
precious Deserve the p. bane — MILT 221:14
so p. it must be rationed — LENI 197:7
This p. stone — SHAK 285:12
predicament It is a p. — BENN 29:22
preference special p. for beetles — HALD 149:12
preferment knocking at P.'s door — ARNO 15:15
pregnant If men could get p. — KENN 184:5
prejudice p. runs in favour of two — DICK 110:22
PRIDE AND P.
religious p. — BURN 74:26
prejudices it p. a man so — HUXL 168:4
proprietor's p. — SMIT 298:13
premises based upon licenced p. — SWAF 306:13
prepare not to p. for life — O'BR 235:14
p. a place for you — PAST 241:20
p. to shed them now — BIBL 48:5
P. ye the way — SHAK 276:19
P. ye the way of the Lord — BIBL 40:7
prepared BE P. — BIBL 42:6
favours only the p. — BADE 22:9
world not yet p. — PAST 241:22
prerogative p. of the eunuch — DOYL 115:13
p. of the harlot — STOP 304:14
presbyter New P. is but old *Priest* — KIPL 189:2
presence before his p. with a song — MILT 220:28
posted p. of the watcher — BOOK 62:22
p. on the field — JAME 170:20
present All p. and correct — WELL 331:9
know nothing but the p. — ANON 5:16
no p. in Wales — KEYN 185:10
p. in spirit — THOM 316:24
p. laughter — BIBL 49:24
p., yes, we are in it — SHAK 288:13
Time p. and time past — LOWE 204:3
un-birthday p. — ELIO 121:18
very p. help in trouble — CARR 84:10
What if this p. — BOOK 61:25
presents P., I often say, endear Absents — DONN 113:22
preservation p. of their property — LAMB 192:2
preserve do not p. myself — LOCK 201:8
Dr Strabismus (Whom God P.) — ORTE 236:22
p. and enlarge freedom — MORT 229:7
p. thy going out — LOCK 201:7
preserved need not be p. — BOOK 63:14
Union: it must be p. — OMAR 236:7
presidency cancer close to the P. — JACK 169:16
heart-beat from the P. — DEAN 107:5
US p. a Tudor monarchy — STEV 303:11
vice-p. isn't worth a pitcher — BURG 73:16
president any boy may become P. — GARN 136:6
As P., I have no eyes — STEV 303:10
P. of the Immortals — LINC 199:12
HARD 151:18

P.'s spouse — BUSH 76:20
rather be right than be P. — CLAY 94:3
security around the p. — MAIL 209:18
We are the P.'s men — KISS 189:4
When the P. does it — NIXO 234:16
press be named P.-men — ARNO 15:3
complain about the p. — POWE 250:24
dead-born from the p. — HUME 166:22
demagogic, corrupt p. — PULI 252:5
Freedom of the p. guaranteed — LIEB 199:2
Freedom of the p. in Britain — SWAF 306:13
liberty of the p. — JUNI 179:17
lose your temper with the P. — PANK 240:10
of our idolatry, the p. — COWP 101:27
people from the p. — TWAI 321:8
periodical p. — TROL 319:20
popular p. is drinking — MELL 216:8
power of the p. — NORT 234:21
with you on the free p. — STOP 304:15
pressure Grace under p. — HEMI 156:4
presume Dr Livingstone, I p. — STAN 301:16
presumption amused by its p. — THUR 317:27
prêt toujours p. à partir — LA F 191:15
pretence to some faint meaning make p. — DRYD 117:3
pretended p. friend is worse — GAY 137:7
pretender blessing—the P. — BYRO 77:21
James I, James II, and the Old P. — GUED 148:9
pretending p. to extraordinary revelations — BUTL 77:2
pretio Omnia Romae Cum p. — JUVE 179:22
pretty all my p. chickens — SHAK 281:13
He is a very p. weoman — FLEM 130:3
It is a p. thing — GREE 147:3
lived in a p. how town — CUMM 104:13
policeman and a p. girl — CHAP 87:12
p. girl is like a melody — BERL 30:19
P. witty Nell — PEPY 243:14
prevail truth, and shall p. — BROO 68:6
prevent try to p. it — MILN 219:7
preventing p. people from taking part — VALÉ 322:7
prey destined p. — SHAW 291:10
to hast'ning ills a p. — GOLD 143:7
yet a p. to all — POPE 248:16
Priam P.'s sons of Troy — SURR 306:6
price bought it at any p. — CLAR 93:13
in Rome has its p. — JUVE 179:22
pay any p. — KENN 184:8
pearl of great p. — BIBL 44:3
pearls fetch a high p. — WHAT 333:2
p. is far above rubies — BIBL 38:11
p. of admiralty — KIPL 188:10
p. of a large turbot — RUSK 262:13
p. of everything — WILD 335:7
p. of the paint — VAN 322:16
p. of wisdom — BIBL 37:11
p. well worth paying — LAMO 192:15
those men have their p. — WALP 327:20
What p. glory — ANDE 5:8
prices contrivance to raise p. — SMIT 297:7
prick If you p. us — SHAK 282:13
I paint with my p. — RENO 255:18
pricking By the p. of my thumbs — SHAK 281:6
p. on the plain — SPEN 300:13
prickly *Here we go round the p. pear* — ELIO 122:5
pricks kick against the p. — BIBL 48:27
pride contempt on all my p. — WATT 329:10
look backward to with p. — FROS 134:6
P. AND PREJUDICE — BURN 74:26
p., cruelty, and ambition — RALE 254:6
P. goeth before destruction — BIBL 37:36
P. of Life — HARD 151:20
p. that apes humility — COLE 95:23
save its p. — MEYE 217:17
soldier's p. — BROW 70:15

priest As a p.   COWP 102:8
great being a p.   LINE 199:17
guts of the last p.   DIDE 111:20
New *Presbyter* is but old *P.*   MILT 220:28
p. doth reign   MACA 206:4
P. for ever   BOOK 63:3
rid me of this turbulent p.   HENR 156:14
priesthood royal p.   BIBL 51:26
priests dominion of p.   PRIC 251:5
treen p.   JEWE 172:10
with the guts of p.   MESL 217:12
priggish p. schoolgirl   GRIG 147:18
prime having lost but once your p.   HERR 158:9
My p. of youth   TICH 318:3
One's p. is elusive   SPAR 299:24
Prime Minister buried the Unknown P.   ASQU 16:19
HOW DARE YOU BECOME P.   ASQU 17:3
next P. but three   BELL 28:12
No woman will be P.   THAT 315:2
Prime Ministers P. are wedded   SAKI 263:16
P. dissatisfied   JENK 172:1
wild flowers, and P.   BALD 23:9
primeval forest p.   LONG 201:21
primrose p. path of dalliance   SHAK 271:6
p. that forsaken dies   MILT 220:17
primroses Pale p.   SHAK 289:12
prince bless the P. of Wales   LINL 200:4
danced with the P. of Wales   FARJ 126:6
Good-night, sweet p.   SHAK 273:23
Hamlet without the P.   SCOT 266:26
in a p. the virtue   MASS 214:19
p. must be a fox   MACH 207:17
p. of Aquitaine   NERV 232:14
p. of darkness   SHAK 277:26
p. of glory died   WATT 329:10
P. of Wales not a position   BENN 29:22
safer for a p.   MACH 207:16
send the companion a better p.   SHAK 274:16
princedoms p., virtues   MILT 222:11
princes P. and lords may flourish   GOLD 143:7
trust in p.   BOOK 63:27
princess People's P.   BLAI 55:9
P. leave the Englishwoman   BISM 54:12
P. of Parallelograms   BYRO 79:21
principalities against p.   BIBL 50:23
angels, nor p.   BIBL 49:18
p., or powers   BIBL 51:1
principate p. and liberty   TACI 308:13
principle precedent embalms a p.   STOW 304:21
p. of all social progress   FOUR 132:10
useful thing about a p.   MAUG 215:8
principles Damn your p.   DISR 113:2
denies the first p.   AUCT 17:19
either morals or p.   GLAD 141:22
embrace your Lordship's p.   WILK 336:1
print *devils* must p.   MOOR 227:12
licence to p. money   THOM 317:15
say in p.   ROBI 257:22
printing Gunpowder, P.   CARL 82:16
P., gunpowder   BACO 22:5
regulate p.   MILT 223:17
printless set my p. feet   MILT 219:19
prism prunes and p.   DICK 110:18
prison at home in p.   WAUG 329:19
born in p.   MALC 210:4
Come, let's away to p.   SHAK 278:9
do not a p. make   LOVE 203:6
forever p.-pent   WOLF 338:16
lime-tree bower my p.   COLE 96:20
palace and a p. on each hand   BYRO 78:2
Shades of the p.-house   WORD 340:10
ship but a p.   BURT 76:16
So cruel p.   SURR 306:6

while there is a soul in p.   DEBS 107:10
prisoner object to your being taken p.   KITC 189:7
prisoners all p. and captives   BOOK 59:8
p. call the sky   WILD 335:15
p. of addiction   ILLI 168:18
weapons of all p.   COLE 96:28
prisons P. are built with stones   BLAK 55:24
private fine and p. place   MARV 213:22
Give me a p. station   GAY 137:8
P. faces in public places   AUDE 18:12
p. life is a disgrace   ANON 9:14
P. property is a necessary   TAWN 309:16
p. station   ADDI 2:10
prize lawful p.   GRAY 146:20
prized local, but p. elsewhere   AUDE 18:20
prizes glittering p.   SMIT 297:16
winners of the big p.   ORWE 237:16
probable P. impossibilities   ARIS 14:16
problem Houston, we've had a p.   LOVE 203:8
p.-solving minds   KAUN 180:2
p. that has no name   FRIE 133:23
p. to be overcome   KEIL 183:23
three-pipe p.   DOYL 115:12
you're part of the p.   CLEA 94:5
proceed just works do p.   BOOK 58:23
procession torchlight p.   O'SU 238:6
proclaims apparel oft p. the man   SHAK 271:7
procrastination p. is the art of   MARQ 212:20
P. is the thief   YOUN 344:14
proctors prudes for p.   TENN 313:2
prodigies Africa and her p.   BROW 69:4
production means of p.   ANON 10:13
purpose of p.   SMIT 297:10
productions literary p.   GIBB 139:3
profane p. and old wives' fables   BIBL 51:8
profession most ancient p.   KIPL 188:18
second oldest p.   REAG 255:1
professional p. is a man who can   AGAT 3:2
professions p. are conspiracies   SHAW 290:26
professor called a *p. emeritus*   LEAC 195:4
profit To whose p.   CICE 93:1
what shall it p. a man   BIBL 45:28
profits little p. that an idle king   TENN 313:28
nothing p. more   MILT 222:13
profundis De p. clamavi   BIBL 53:3
programme Not so much a p.   ANON 9:2
programmed p. to love completely   BAIN 23:2
progress Congress makes no p.   LIGN 199:3
no summer p.   ANDR 5:10
principle of all social p.   FOUR 132:10
p. if a cannibal uses   LEC 196:4
P. is a comfortable disease   CUMM 104:17
P., man's distinctive mark   BROW 70:1
Time's thievish p.   SHAK 289:33
What we call 'p.'   ELLI 124:2
prohibition enacting P.   HOOV 162:11
proie *à sa p. attachée*   RACI 253:19
proletariat dictatorship of the p.   MARX 214:7
prologue What's past is p.   SHAK 287:8
prologues happy p.   SHAK 279:7
Promethean true P. fire   SHAK 278:19
promise P., large promise   JOHN 173:18
p. made is a debt unpaid   SERV 267:25
promised O Jesus, I have p.   BODE 57:4
reach the p. land   CALL 80:9
seen the p. land   KING 186:12
promises have p. to keep   FROS 134:14
p. and panaceas   ROTH 261:7
young man of p.   BALF 23:15
promising first call p.   CONN 99:1
promontory See one p.   BURT 76:15
Stretched like a p.   MILT 222:12

promotion p. cometh neither from	BOOK 62:8	**Protestants** in the hands of P.	PUGI 252:4
You'll get no p.	HUGH 166:7	**Proteus** sight of P. rising	WORD 341:19
prone position for women is p.	CARM 83:6	**protoplasmal** p. primordial globule	GILB 140:7
pronounce could not frame to p. it	BIBL 35:6	**protracted** p. woe	JOHN 174:7
pronounced p. the letter R	AUBR 17:15	**proud** all the p. and mighty have	DYER 118:21
proof America is the p.	MCCA 206:19	Death be not p.	DONN 113:19
proofs p. of holy writ	SHAK 284:24	make death p.	SHAK 269:1
propaganda on p.	CORN 100:10	p. in arms	MILT 219:10
proper noun, p. or improper	FULL 134:23	p. me no prouds	SHAK 286:33
p. man	SHAK 283:5	scattered the p.	BIBL 45:34
P. words in proper places	SWIF 306:21	too p. for a wit	GOLD 143:18
properly never did anything p.	LEAR 195:12	too p. to fight	WILS 337:5
property give me a little snug p.	EDGE 119:20	**prove** I could p. everything	PINT 245:3
preservation of their p.	LOCK 201:8	P. all things	BIBL 51:5
Private p. is a necessary	TAWN 309:16	p. our chance	DRAY 116:8
P. has its duties	DRUM 116:12	**proverb** Israel shall be a p.	BIBL 36:1
P. is theft	PROU 251:16	**proverbs** Solomon wrote the P.	NAYL 231:22
p.-owning democracy	SKEL 296:18	**providence** assert eternal p.	MILT 221:2
public p.	JEFF 171:15	P. had sent a few men	RUMB 261:20
Thieves respect p.	CHES 90:4	P. their guide	MILT 222:25
prophecy poetry, p., and religion	RUSK 262:10	way that P. dictates	HITL 159:18
prophesy sons and daughters shall p.	BIBL 41:14	**provident** They are p. instead	BOGA 57:7
prophet arise among you a p.	BIBL 34:28	**province** all knowledge to be my p.	BACO 22:1
p. is not without honour	BIBL 44:4	p. they have desolated	GLAD 141:20
prophetic In her p. fury	SHAK 284:29	**provincial** level of p. existence	ELIO 121:12
O my p. soul	SHAK 271:18	**provocation** as in the p.	BOOK 62:19
p. greeting	SHAK 279:5	**provoke** fathers, p. not	BIBL 50:21
prophets Beware of false p.	BIBL 43:10	**provoker** Drink, sir, is a great p.	SHAK 280:14
ceased to pose as its p.	POPP 249:12	**provokes** No one p. me	ANON 12:14
fellowship of the P.	BOOK 58:11	**proximus** paries cum p. ardet	HORA 164:1
Is Saul also among the p.	BIBL 35:17	**prudes** p. for proctors	TENN 313:2
law and the p.	BIBL 43:7	**prunes** p. and prism	DICK 110:18
proportion strangeness in the p.	BACO 21:4	**pruninghooks** spears into p.	BIBL 39:11
proposes man p.	THOM 315:19	**prurient** p. curiosity	STOP 304:12
proposition accept the p.	AYER 20:10	**Prussia** national industry of P.	MIRA 223:23
meaning of a p.	SCHL 265:15	**psalmist** sweet p. of Israel	BIBL 35:35
proprietor p.'s prejudices	SWAF 306:13	**psalms** David wrote the P.	NAYL 231:22
prose All that is not p.	MOLI 225:10	**psychopath** p. is the furnace	RAYM 254:17
as well written as p.	POUN 250:15	**public** as if I was a p. meeting	VICT 323:20
but p. run mad	POPE 247:9	assumes a p. trust	JEFF 171:15
for p. and verse	CARE 82:5	Desolation in immaculate p. places	ROET 258:21
Good p. like a window-pane	ORWE 237:7	English p. school	WAUG 329:19
govern in p.	CUOM 105:2	hand into the p. purse	PEEL 242:22
in p. or rhyme	MILT 221:1	I and the p. know	AUDE 18:16
nearest p.	DRYD 117:7	one to mislead the p.	ASQU 16:20
pin up my hair with p.	CONG 98:18	precedence over p. relations	FEYN 127:6
p. and the passion	FORS 131:15	Private faces in p. places	AUDE 18:12
P. is when all the lines	BENT 30:6	p. be damned	VAND 322:12
P. = words in their best order	COLE 96:24	tell the p. which way	SULZ 306:2
shut me up in p.	DICK 111:17	**publicans** p. and sinners	BIBL 43:18
speaking p. without knowing it	MOLI 225:11	**publicity** bad p.	BEHA 27:18
Proserpine P. gathering flowers	MILT 221:32	oxygen of p.	THAT 315:11
prospect every p. pleases	HEBE 155:2	**publish** P. and be damned	WELL 331:8
noblest p.	JOHN 174:23	p. it not	BIBL 35:27
prosper I grow, I p.	SHAK 277:9	**publisher** Barabbas was a p.	CAMP 81:4
sinners' ways p.	HOPK 163:6	makes everybody a p.	MCLU 208:6
Treason doth never p.	HARI 152:10	**publishers** numerous p.	ADE 2:17
prosperity man to han ben in p.	CHAU 88:26	p. are not women	ROBI 257:22
prostitute doormat or a p.	WEST 332:18	**publishing** p. faster than think	PAUL 242:7
prostitutes small nations like p.	KUBR 190:27	**pudding** chieftain o' the p.-race	BURN 75:28
protect p. a working-girl	SMIT 297:15	p. in his belly	SHAK 273:34
p. the writer	ACHE 1:7	**puddings** like their English p.	VOLT 326:12
protection calls mutely for p.	GREE 147:2	**puero** p. reverentia	JUVE 180:6
mercy and p.	BOOK 60:21	**pugna** P. magna victi sumus	LIVY 200:13
protest lady doth p. too much	SHAK 272:13	**pull** P. down thy VANITY	POUN 250:12
Protestant Hitler attacked the P. church	NIEM 234:5	**pulls** p. a lady through	MARQ 212:21
I am the P. whore	GWYN 148:16	**pulp** p. my acquaintance	TROL 319:22
P. counterpoint	BEEC 27:9	**pulpit** such a bully p.	ROOS 260:6
p. ethic	WEBE 330:2	white glove p.	REAG 254:22
P. Province of Ulster	CARS 84:18	**pulsanda** P. tellus	HORA 164:9
P. Religion	CARL 82:16	**pulse** My P., like a soft drum	KING 186:7
P. with a horse	BEHA 27:16	**pumpkins** early p. blow	LEAR 195:9
'tis a P. wind	WHAR 332:25	**pun** p. is a pistol	LAMB 192:5

punctuality P. is the politeness LOUI 203:2
Punica *P. fide* SALL 264:2
punish God p. England FUNK 135:3
punishing p. anyone who comes between SMIT 298:10
punishment cruel and unusual p. CONS 99:17
less horror than the p. GIBB 139:4
p. fit the crime GILB 140:15
p. is mischief BENT 30:4
p. is not for revenge FRY 134:20
restraint and p. MILT 223:16
suffer first p. CRAN 102:23
punishments sanguinary p. PAIN 239:11
punt better fun to p. than to be punted SAYE 265:6
pupped down to Brighton and p. SMIT 298:12
puppets shut up the box and the p. THAC 314:26
purchase p. of my wealth JONS 177:20
pure as p. as snow SHAK 272:5
Blessed are the p. in heart KEBL 183:18
my heart is p. TENN 313:24
Perfectly p. and good BROW 70:28
p. as the driven slush BANK 24:24
p. as the lily LAUD 194:7
truth is rarely p. WILD 334:22
Unto the p. BIBL 51:14
whatsoever things are p. BIBL 50:28
purgation p. of such emotions ARIS 14:14
purgatory no other p. but a woman BEAU 26:15
purify p. the dialect of the tribe ELIO 121:27
puritan P. hated bear-baiting MACA 205:21
to the P. all things are impure LAWR 194:11
puritanism P. The haunting fear MENC 216:13
purlieus p. of the Law ETHE 125:5
p. of the law TENN 311:24
purling to p. brooks POPE 247:26
purple colour p. WALK 326:22
deep p. falls PARI 240:13
in p. and gold BYRO 78:13
in the p. of Emperors KIPL 188:26
I shall wear p. JOSE 178:16
never saw a P. Cow BURG 73:17
p. patch or two HORA 163:11
purpose any p. perverts art CONS 99:13
Infirm of p. SHAK 280:11
My p. is, indeed SHAK 288:16
p. of human existence JUNG 179:14
time to every p. BIBL 38:16
working his p. out AING 3:6
purpureus *P. Adsuitur pannus* HORA 163:1
purrs p. like an epigram MARO 212:25
purse consumption of the p. SHAK 274:17
empty p. BRET 66:15
hand into the public p. PEEL 242:22
steals my p. SHAK 284:20
pursued you who are the p. SHAW 291:10
pursueth flee when no man p. BIBL 38:7
pursuing Faint, yet p. BIBL 35:5
pursuit common p. LEAV 195:23
p. of happiness ANON 10:14
p. of happiness JEFF 171:12
p. of perfection ARNO 15:27
p. of the uneatable WILD 335:11
What mad p. KEAT 181:28
pushed was he p. JAME 171:2
pussy Owl and the P.-Cat LEAR 195:14
put P. me to what you will METH 217:13
p. not your trust BOOK 63:27
P. out the light SHAK 285:1
up with which I will not p. CHUR 92:2
pylons P., those pillars bare SPEN 300:11
pyramid bottom of the economic p. ROOS 259:13
pyramids not like children but like p. FLAU 129:20
summit of these p. NAPO 231:2
Pyrenees P. are no more LOUI 202:20

Pythagoras mystical way of P. BROW 69:3

Q

quad No one about in the Q. KNOX 189:17
quadrille q. in a sentry-box JAME 170:15
quadruped hairy q. DARW 106:6
quailing No q., Mrs Gaskell BRON 67:17
quake q. to say they love SIDN 295:10
qualis *Non sum q. eram* HORA 164:18
qualities such q. as would wear well GOLD 144:3
quality q. of mercy SHAK 282:20
quanta *O q. qualia* ABEL 1:2
quantities ghosts of departed q. BERK 30:13
quarks Three q. for Muster Mark JOYC 178:21
quarrel hath his q. just SHAK 275:15
justice of my q. ANON 7:18
perpetual q. BURK 74:2
q. in a far away country CHAM 86:19
q. with ourselves, poetry YEAT 344:2
takes one to make a q. INGE 168:21
quarrels q. with one's husband BONA 57:18
quarry marked down a q. SHAW 291:10
quarterly nothing a-year, paid q. SURT 306:12
quarters awful q. of an hour ROSS 260:21
quarto beautiful q. page SHER 294:17
quean flaunting, extravagant q. SHER 294:19
queen Cinara was my q. HORA 164:18
cold q. of England CHES 89:22
Famine Q. GONN 144:13
home life of our own dear Q. ANON 7:12
I'm to be Q. o' the May TENN 312:25
laughing q. HUNT 167:3
Ocean's child, and then his q. SHEL 293:4
Q. and country THOM 317:7
Q. and huntress JONS 177:14
Q. had four Maries BALL 24:5
q. in people's hearts DIAN 109:10
Q. must sign BAGE 22:19
q. of curds and cream SHAK 289:13
q. of Scots ELIZ 123:3
q. of Sheba BIBL 36:2
Q. rose of the rosebud garden TENN 312:22
Ruler of the Q.'s Navee GILB 140:30
To toast *The Q.* HEAN 154:12
queens Q. have died young NASH 231:20
queer All the world is q. OWEN 238:19
q. sort of thing BARH 25:4
queerer universe q. than we suppose HALD 149:11
quench shall he not q. BIBL 40:12
waters cannot q. love BIBL 39:9
questing passes the q. vole WAUG 329:22
q. beast MALO 210:10
question Answer to the Great Q. ADAM 1:11
ask an impertinent q. BRON 67:6
asked any clear q. CAMU 81:6
not to q. other KIPL 187:7
Others abide our q. ARNO 15:20
q. is CARR 84:11
q. why we died KIPL 187:10
secretly changed the Q. SELL 267:20
such a silly q. STER 302:20
that is the q. SHAK 272:1
what is the q. STEI 302:9
questionings for those obstinate q. WORD 340:12
questions *all* q. were stupid WEIS 330:24
ask q. of those who cannot tell RALE 254:9
puzzling q. BROW 68:21
queue orderly q. of one MIKE 217:26
quick Come! q. as you can DE L 108:3
q., and the dead DEWA 109:8

quick (*cont.*)
q. could never rest · SURR 306:7
q. to blame · AESC 2:24
quickly It were done q. · SHAK 279:19
Quicunque Q. vult · BOOK 59:2
quiet All q. along the Potomac · BEER 27:14
alone with the q. day · JAME 170:24
Anything for a q. life · MIDD 217:19
Easy live and q. die · SCOT 266:20
harvest of a q. eye · WORD 340:20
lives of q. desperation · THOR 317:19
never have a q. world · SHAW 291:25
q. along the Potomac · MCCL 206:23
q. flows the Don · SHOL 294:29
q. on the western front · REMA 255:16
q., pilfering · CLAR 93:9
sleepers in that q. earth · BRON 67:15
quietest q. places · HOUS 165:8
quietly q. pacifist peaceful · WALK 326:21
quietness unravished bride of q. · KEAT 181:27
quietus q. make With a bare bodkin · SHAK 272:2
quills q. upon the fretful porpentine · SHAK 271:16
quince slices of q. · LEAR 195:16
quinquireme Q. of Nineveh · MASE 214:16
quintessence q. of dust · SHAK 271:31
quip q. modest · SHAK 270:6
quires Q. and Places · BOOK 58:20
quis q. *custodiet ipsos Custodes* · JUVE 179:24
quiver hath his q. full · BOOK 63:19
quo Q. *vadis* · BIBL 53:10
quotation always have a q. · SAYE 265:7
q. what a speaker wants · BENN 29:17
quotations I hate q. · EMER 124:16
read books of q. · CHUR 92:10
swathed himself in q. · KIPL 188:26

R

R pronounced the letter R · AUBR 17:15
rabbit r. has a charming face · ANON 9:14
r. in a snare · STEP 302:18
race avails the sceptred r. · LAND 192:22
melted into a new r. · CEEV 103:9
No r. can prosper · WASH 328:17
play the r. card · SHAP 290:2
r. is not to the swift · BIBL 38:27
r. is to the swift · DAVI 106:14
r. that is set before us · BIBL 51:16
run out thy r. · MILT 220:29
unprotected r. · CLAR 93:9
racer melodist to a fine r. · MOZA 229:16
races so-called white r. · FORS 131:16
Some r. increase · LUCR 204:14
Rachel R. weeping · BIBL 42:4
served seven years for R. · BIBL 33:31
rack r. of a too easy chair · POPE 246:22
r. of this tough world · SHAK 278:15
racket all a German r. · RIDL 257:5
rackets r. to these balls · SHAK 274:29
radical never dared be r. when young · FROS 134:12
R. Chic . . . only radical in Style · WOLF 338:21
radio r. expands it · WOGA 338:8
radish r. and an egg · COWP 102:5
rag foul r.-and-bone shop · YEAT 342:14
r. and a bone · KIPL 188:13
Shakespeherian R. · ELIO 122:25
rage die here in a r. · SWIF 306:22
heathen so furiously r. · BOOK 60:26
Heaven has no r. · CONG 98:14
Heaven in a r. · BLAK 55:12
r. against the dying of the light · THOM 316:3

rages weight of r. · SPOO 301:1
ragged pair of r. claws · ELIO 122:11
raging strong drink is r. · BIBL 37:38
ragout fricassee, or a r. · SWIF 306:23
railway by r. timetables · TAYL 309:19
R. termini · FORS 131:14
rain buried in the r. · MILL 218:10
drop of r. maketh a hole · LATI 194:4
gentle r. from heaven · SHAK 282:20
hard r.'s a gonna fall · DYLA 119:3
latter r. · BOOK 59:11
like sunshine after r. · SHAK 290:14
r. in Spain · LERN 197:26
r. is destroying his grain · HERB 157:1
r. it raineth every day · SHAK 288:33
r., it raineth on the just · BOWE 65:15
R.! Rain! Rain · KEAT 183:8
sendeth r. · BIBL 42:20
small drops of r. · BALL 24:14
small r. down can rain · ANON 10:18
waiting for r. · ELIO 122:1
rainbow no r. nation · MAND 211:3
r. coalition · JACK 169:18
r. comes and goes · WORD 340:8
R. gave thee birth · DAVI 106:18
r.'s glory is shed · SHEL 293:2
r. which includes black · YEVT 344:7
Somewhere over the r. · HARB 151:9
when I behold A r. · WORD 340:5
raineth R. drop and staineth slop · POUN 250:5
rains r. pennies from heaven · BURK 74:23
rainy r. Sunday in London · DE Q 108:20
raise Lord shall r. me up · RALE 254:5
raised It is easily r. · FIEL 127:13
r. not a stone · WOLF 338:12
raising stop r. corn · LEAS 195:22
rake r. in reading · MONT 226:3
ram r. caught in a thicket · BIBL 33:26
Rama In R. was there a voice · BIBL 42:4
Ramadan month of R. · KORA 190:7
rampart corse to the r. · WOLF 338:10
rams mountains skipped like r. · BOOK 63:5
Ramsbottom Mr and Mrs R. · EDGA 119:19
ran Who r. to help me · TAYL 309:20
Randal Lord R. · BALL 23:20
random word, at r. spoken · SCOT 266:13
rank r. me with whom you will · METH 217:13
rankers Gentlemen-r. · KIPL 187:17
ranks In the r. of death · MOOR 227:17
r. of Tuscany · MACA 206:13
ransomed R., healed · LYTE 205:6
rap r. at the ballot box · CHIL 90:12
rape procrastinated r. · PRIT 251:12
you r. it · DEGA 107:22
rapid r., unintelligible patter · GILB 141:9
rapist r. bothers to buy a bottle · DWOR 118:18
rapper to your son as a r. · ICE 168:15
rappers first r. of Europe · BJÖR 54:20
rapture first fine careless r. · BROW 70:9
Modified r. · GILB 140:11
rara R. *avis* · JUVE 179:23
rare man of culture r. · GILB 140:22
O r. Ben Jonson · ANON 9:8
was indeed a r. one · WITH 337:19
rarely R., rarely, comest thou · SHEL 293:24
rascals R., would you live · FRED 133:14
rash too r., too unadvised · SHAK 286:21
Rasputin Like—like R. · RHYS 256:11
rat Anyone can r. · CHUR 91:10
Cat, the R., and Lovell · COLL 97:1
creeps like a r. · BOWE 65:11
giant r. of Sumatra · DOYL 115:13
How now! a r. · SHAK 272:23

poisoned r. in a hole — SWIF 306:22
r. without a tail — SHAK 278:28
smell a r. — ROCH 258:8
rate cannot r. me very high — LACL 191:11
rathe r. primrose that forsaken dies — MILT 220:17
ratio geometrical r. — MALT 210:15
rationed so precious it must be r. — LENI 197:7
rats r.' alley — ELIO 122:24
R.! They fought the dogs — BROW 70:26
rattle Pleased with a r. — POPE 248:17
R. his bones — NOEL 234:19
ravage nose May r. with impunity — BROW 71:7
raved as I r. and grew more fierce — HERB 157:11
raven grim and ancient r. — POE 246:13
Poe with this r. — LOWE 203:16
r. himself is hoarse — SHAK 279:13
ravening r. wolves — BIBL 43:10
ravished would have r. her — FIEL 127:12
ravishing dear r. thing — BEHN 27:19
razor hew blocks with a r. — POPE 249:9
mirror and a r. — JOYC 178:26
Occam's R. — OCCA 235:19
reach could not r. it — SAPP 264:18
I r. for my pistol — JOHS 177:6
man's r. should exceed — BROW 69:17
r. the promised land — CALL 80:9
reaction can't get no girl r. — JAGG 170:3
opposed an equal r. — NEWT 233:12
reactionaries All r. are paper tigers — MAO 211:13
read Being r. to by a boy — ELIO 122:1
but r. these — MART 213:8
In science, r. — BULW 72:16
man ought to r. — JOHN 174:24
people that r. — SHEN 294:8
people who can't r. — ZAPP 345:2
r. a book before reviewing it — SMIT 298:13
r. books *through* — JOHN 175:10
r. in the train — WILD 335:3
r., mark, learn — BOOK 59:13
R. my lips — BUSH 76:22
r. strange matters — SHAK 279:16
r. without pleasure — JOHN 177:3
Take up and r. — AUGU 19:1
want to r. a novel — DISR 113:9
What do you r. — SHAK 271:27
what I r. in the papers — ROGE 259:6
who don't r. the books — BYAT 77:17
reader Hypocrite r. — BAUD 26:6
R., I married him — BRON 67:9
readeth he may run that r. it — BIBL 41:18
readiness r. is all — SHAK 273:16
reading get nowadays from r. — GREE 146:25
he was r. — AUGU 18:27
lie in a hot bath r. — THOM 316:13
prefer r. — SMIT 297:22
rake in r. — MONT 226:3
r. is right — JOHN 173:22
R. maketh a full man — BACO 21:27
vile hard r. — SHER 294:22
what is worth r. — TREV 319:9
ready always r. to go — LA F 191:15
conference a r. man — BACO 21:27
of a r. writer — BOOK 61:22
real Life is r. — LONG 201:25
r. Simon Pure — CENT 86:12
speechless r. — BARZ 25:22
realistic make a 'r. decision' — MCCA 206:20
reality bear very much r. — ELIO 121:20
It is a r. — CLIN 94:18
Love is the discovery of r. — MURD 230:6
r. take precedence — FEYN 127:6
really be a R. Useful Engine — AWDR 20:7
what I r. really want — ROWB 261:13

realms r. of gold — KEAT 182:18
whom three r. obey — POPE 249:3
reap r. a character — READ 254:21
r., if we faint not — BIBL 50:16
r. in joy — BOOK 63:17
r. the whirlwind — BIBL 41:12
that shall he also r. — BIBL 50:15
reaping ever r. something new — TENN 312:9
No, r. — BOTT 65:2
r. where thou hast not sown — BIBL 45:6
rear r. the tender thought — THOM 317:9
reason appear the better r. — MILT 221:17
conquers r. still — POPE 247:18
erring R.'s spite — POPE 248:14
ideal of r. — KANT 180:14
if it be against r. — COKE 95:16
most sovereign r. — SHAK 272:8
Nothing without a r. — LEIB 196:21
O r. not the need — SHAK 277:15
R. always means — GASK 136:16
r. and conscience — PRIC 251:5
R., an *ignis fatuus* — ROCH 258:12
r. is our law — MILT 222:17
r. knows nothing of — PASC 241:18
r. produces monsters — GOYA 145:2
R. the natural image — BONA 57:21
r. why I cannot tell — BROW 68:18
right deed for the wrong r. — ELIO 122:9
Their's not to r. why — TENN 310:16
triumph of human r. — HAWK 153:13
reasonable They were r. people — BROO 68:2
reasoning abstract r. — HUME 166:19
cowards in r. — SHAF 268:8
in dirt the r. engine — ROCH 258:13
r., self-sufficing thing — WORD 340:19
reasons finding of bad r. — BRAD 65:20
heart has its r. — PASC 241:18
R. are not like garments — ESSE 125:3
r. will certainly — MANS 211:9
rebel die like a true-blue r. — HILL 159:3
What is a r. — CAMU 81:7
rebellion R. lay in his way — SHAK 274:6
R. to tyrants — BRAD 65:24
rum, Romanism, and r. — BURC 73:13
rebels r. are our countrymen — GRAN 145:18
r. their gifts — TENN 313:26
takes wing beyond r. — HORA 163:26
receive r. but what we give — COLE 95:21
r. one such little child — BIBL 44:14
than to r. — BIBL 48:38
received his own r. him not — BIBL 47:20
receiver have left the r. off the hook — KOES 190:1
recession r. when your neighbour — TRUM 320:9
recipes like r. in a cookbook — STEW 304:8
r. that are always successful — VALÉ 322:5
recirculation commodious vicus of r. — JOYC 178:19
recognize only a trial if I r. it — KAFK 180:9
reconciliation bridge of r. — RUNC 261:21
True r. does not — MAND 211:1
recording R. Angel, as he wrote it down — STER 302:24
rectangular proceedings are quite r. — BYRO 79:21
recte *Si possis r.* — HORA 163:20
rectum one in the r. — OSLE 238:3
recurret *usque r.* — HORA 163:24
red blows so r. The rose — FITZ 128:17
her lips' r. — SHAK 290:9
keep the r. flag flying — CONN 98:23
Luve's like a r., red rose — BURN 75:21
Making the green one r. — SHAK 280:12
my skin is r. — SITT 296:9
people's flag is deepest r. — CONN 98:22
Pluck a r. rose — SHAK 275:14
r. in tooth and claw — TENN 311:21

red (cont.)
r. men scalped each other — MACA 205:11
rise with my r. hair — PLAT 245:21
thin r. line — RUSS 263:3
Thin r. line of 'eroes — KIPL 188:11
wine when it is r. — BIBL 37:40
reddens sweet-apple r. — SAPP 264:18
redeem R. thy mis-spent time — KEN 184:2
redeemed r. Jerusalem — BIBL 40:15
redeemer know that my r. liveth — BIBL 37:9
O thou great R. — WILL 336:6
such a mighty R. — MISS 224:14
To thee, R. — NEAL 231:23
redeeming devastating or r. fires — GONC 144:11
R. the time — BIBL 50:20
redemption r.'s happy dawn — CASW 85:11
redemptorem meruit habere R. — MISS 224:14
redress Things past r. — SHAK 285:16
reds honour the indomitable R. — DUNN 118:10
redwood r. forest to the Gulf Stream — GUTH 148:15
reed bruised r. — BIBL 36:33
bruised r. — BIBL 40:12
he is a thinking r. — PASC 241:19
r. shaken with the wind — BIBL 43:30
reeds in the r. by the river — BROW 69:13
reeking r. into Cadiz Bay — BROW 70:10
reel They r. to and fro — BOOK 63:2
reeled Until r. the mind — GIBB 139:13
referee having two you are a r. — FROS 134:4
references verify your r. — ROUT 261:12
refined Englishwoman is so r. — SMIT 298:4
reform Peace, retrenchment, and r. — BRIG 66:22
r. the criminal — FRY 134:20
reformation plotting some new r. — DRYD 117:6
reformer r. is a guy who rides — MIZN 225:6
reformers r. are bachelors — MOOR 227:5
refreshed r. with wine — BOOK 62:9
refuge easy to take r. in — IBSE 168:13
God is thy r. — BIBL 34:30
Patriotism is the last r. — JOHN 175:15
refusal great r. — DANT 105:19
refuse offer he can't r. — PUZO 252:25
refute I r. it thus — JOHN 175:2
r. a sneer — PALE 240:1
regardless r. of their doom — GRAY 146:18
regiment r. of women — KNOX 189:15
register r. of the crimes, follies — GIBB 139:2
regnavit R. a ligno Deus — FORT 132:1
regnum adveniat r. tuum — MISS 224:5
regrets Miss Otis r. — PORT 249:19
no r. — VAUC 322:18
regrette je ne r. rien — VAUC 322:18
Je r. l'Europe — RIMB 257:11
regular icily r. — TENN 312:20
regulate r. printing — MILT 223:17
regulated R. hatred — HARD 151:13
reign Better to r. in hell — MILT 221:7
Long to r. over us — ANON 7:5
r. of Chaos and old Night — MILT 221:12
reigned if he had not r. — TACI 308:18
r. with your loves — ELIZ 123:8
reindeer Red-Nosed R. — MARK 212:1
rejected despised and r. — BIBL 40:16
rejoice let us heartily r. — BOOK 62:18
Let us then r. — ANON 12:13
Philistines r. — BIBL 35:27
r. at that news — THAT 315:7
R. in the Lord — BIBL 50:26
rejoiced spirit hath r. — BIBL 45:33
relation cold r. — BURK 74:10
nobody like a r. — THAC 314:21
relations not have sexual r. — CLIN 94:17
relationship r. that goes bad — FAIT 125:22

relent make him once r. — BUNY 73:9
relief For this r. much thanks — SHAK 270:22
system of outdoor r. — BRIG 66:21
relieve comfort and r. them — BOOK 59:10
relieved By desperate appliances are r. — SHAK 272:30
religio Tantum r. potuit — LUCR 204:12
religion all of the same r. — DISR 112:24
become a popular r. — INGE 168:19
brothels with bricks of r. — BLAK 55:24
but of one r. — SHAF 268:7
can't talk r. to — SHAW 291:3
concerned with r. — TEMP 310:8
dominion of r. — GOLD 143:5
establishment of r. — CONS 99:15
Every dictator uses r. — BHUT 32:19
just enough r. — SWIF 307:1
men's minds to r. — BACO 21:2
much wrong could r. induce — LUCR 204:12
No compulsion in r. — KORA 190:8
no r. but social — WESL 332:4
only one r. — SHAW 291:27
poetry, prophecy, and r. — RUSK 262:10
politics as well as in r. — JUNI 179:18
r. but a childish toy — MARL 212:10
r. for religion's sake — COUS 100:19
r. has always been to me — POTT 249:28
r. into after-dinner toasts — NEWM 233:3
R. is by no means — CHES 89:5
r. is powerless to bestow — FORB 131:1
R. is the sigh — MARX 214:4
r. is to do good — PAIN 239:16
r. of humanity — PAIN 239:9
R. the frozen thought of men — KRIS 190:25
r. weak — SZAS 308:11
r. without science is blind — EINS 120:11
rum and true r. — BYRO 78:19
some of r. — EDGE 119:20
start your own r. — ANON 7:15
That is my r. — SHAW 291:2
too late to trust the old r. — LOWE 204:2
true meaning of r. — ARNO 16:4
true r. is Islam — KORA 190:11
way to plant r. — BROW 69:6
religions sixty different r. — CARA 82:2
religious dim r. light — MILT 219:24
Old r. factions — BURK 74:20
r. prejudice — HUXL 168:4
relished by which he is to be r. — WORD 341:21
reluctant r. peer — BENN 29:14
rem quocumque modo r. — HORA 163:20
R. tene — CATO 85:16
remain things have been, things r. — CLOU 95:4
remains aught r. to do — ROGE 259:1
remarkable nothing left r. — SHAK 268:28
remarks said our r. before us — DONA 113:15
remedies will not apply new r. — BACO 21:16
remedy bestowed on mankind a r. — SYDE 308:6
dangerous r. — FAWK 126:17
r. is worse than the disease — BACO 21:25
Things without all r. — SHAK 280:23
'Tis a sharp r. — RALE 254:7
remember cannot r. the past — SANT 264:17
Do you r. an Inn, Miranda — BELL 28:26
I r., I remember — HOOD 162:5
Lord, r. me — BIBL 47:12
r. a happy time — DANT 105:20
r. and be sad — ROSS 260:13
r. even these things — VIRG 324:10
r. for ever — WARN 328:14
R. me when I am dead — DOUG 115:5
r. more than seven — BELL 28:5
R. now thy Creator — BIBL 38:33
R. the Alamo — SHER 294:24

r. the Fifth of November — ANON 9:12
R. the sabbath day — BIBL 34:15
r., whan it passed is — CHAU 88:26
We will r. them — BINY 54:4
what you can r. — SELL 267:16
Yes; I r. Adlestrop — THOM 316:14
yet never can, r. — THOM 316:16
You must r. this — HUPF 167:8
remembered blue r. hills — HOUS 165:7
r. around the world — DISN 112:3
r. for a very long time — MCGO 207:10
r. kisses — TENN 313:8
remembering R. without ceasing — BIBL 51:4
remembrance Do this in r. of me — BOOK 60:5
r. of them is grievous — BOOK 59:27
r. of things past — SHAK 289:27
rosemary, that's for r. — SHAK 273:5
Writ in r. more — SHAK 285:11
remind R. me of you — MARV 213:24
remorse R., the fatal egg — COWP 101:26
R.! Those dry Martinis — ADE 2:18
remove bowl of the R. — RICH 256:19
say unto this mountain, R. — BIBL 44:12
render R. unto Caesar — BIBL 44:27
rendezvous r. with Death — SEEG 267:5
renew r. a right spirit — BOOK 61:28
R. your brilliance — GRAC 145:4
renounce I r. war — FOSD 132:2
r. the devil — BOOK 60:9
rent R. is that portion — RICA 256:13
r. we pay for our room — CLAY 94:4
repay I will r. — BIBL 49:20
repeal r. of bad or obnoxious laws — GRAN 145:19
repeat condemned to r. it — SANT 264:17
r. what we all know — BELL 29:3
repeated mistake shall not be r. — ANON 9:16
repelled r. by man — INGE 168:20
repent r. in haste — CONG 98:15
R. ye — BIBL 42:5
repentance sinners to r. — BIBL 43:20
repented strove, and much r. — BYRO 78:17
repenteth sinner that r. — BIBL 46:31
repetition r. of unpalatable truths — SUMM 306:3
reply I pause for a r. — SHAK 276:14
r. churlish — SHAK 270:6
Their's not to make r. — TENN 310:16
report of good r. — BIBL 50:28
reporters speaking through r. — CARL 82:23
reports R. of my death — TWAI 321:13
repose earned a night's r. — LONG 202:8
representation Taxation without r. — OTIS 238:7
representative Your r. owes you — BURK 74:17
repression result of forced r. — MILL 218:5
reproach r. a husband — LA F 191:16
reproche *Chevalier sans peur et sans r.* — ANON 11:11
reproof r. valiant — SHAK 270:6
republic Love the Beloved R. — FORS 131:18
love, the beloved R. — SWIN 307:25
r. is a raft — AMES 4:17
republican on r. principles — SHAW 291:22
understood by r. government — TOCQ 318:11
Republicans We are R. — BURC 73:13
repugnant r. to the Word of God — BOOK 64:4
reputation honour and r. — JONS 177:21
O! I have lost my r. — SHAK 284:17
r. dies — POPE 249:4
Seeking the bubble r. — SHAK 269:22
sold my r. for a song — FITZ 128:21
spotless r. — SHAK 285:7
reputations murdered r. — CONG 98:16
request No flowers, by r. — AING 3:5
requiem R. *aeternam dona eis* — MISS 224:10
requiescant *r. in pace* — MISS 224:13

require thought 'e might r. — KIPL 188:16
required soul shall be r. of thee — BIBL 46:23
re-rat ingenuity to r. — CHUR 91:10
res *in medias r.* — HORA 163:16
rescuers firing on the r. — WOOL 339:12
research Basic r. is what — BRAU 66:7
r. the art of the soluble — MEDA 215:19
steal from many, it's r. — MIZN 225:5
resign Few die and none r. — JEFF 171:14
resignation by r. none — JEFF 171:14
resigned I am not r. — MILL 218:7
resist r. everything except temptation — WILD 335:5
resistance no length of r. — BONA 57:19
resistible r. rise of Arturo Ui — BREC 66:10
resolute bloody, bold, and r. — SHAK 281:8
resolve R. not to be poor — JOHN 176:10
resources born to consume r. — HORA 163:21
respect owed the greatest r. — JUVE 180:6
r. to the living — VOLT 326:10
respectable more r. he is — SHAW 291:8
respecter no r. of persons — BIBL 48:30
respice *r. finem* — ANON 12:19
responsibility Liberty means r. — SHAW 291:15
no sense of r. — KNOX 189:18
Power without r. — KIPL 189:2
r. without power — STOP 304:14
rest choose Their place of r. — MILT 222:25
dove found no r. — BIBL 33:20
far, far better r. — DICK 111:11
flee away, and be at r. — BOOK 62:1
Grant them eternal r. — MISS 224:10
holy r. — NEWM 233:4
I will give you r. — BIBL 43:31
no r. day or night — BIBL 52:18
R. in soft peace — JONS 178:1
r. is literature — COLE 96:29
r. is mere fine writing — VERL 323:11
r. is silence — SHAK 273:22
R., rest, perturbèd spirit — SHAK 271:23
Swift has sailed into his r. — YEAT 343:25
talk about the r. of us — ANON 10:8
weary be at r. — BIBL 37:3
restaurant table at a good r. — LEBO 196:3
resteth Wyatt r. here — SURR 306:7
resting give us a r.-place — WEIZ 330:26
restored r., forgiven — LYTE 205:6
restraint r. with which they write — CAMP 80:21
restructuring r. [*perestroika*] — GORB 144:15
result r. happiness — DICK 110:3
resurrection in the r. — BIBL 44:28
on the Day of R. — KORA 190:12
r., and the life — BIBL 47:39
R. to eternal life — BOOK 60:25
retaliation policy of r. — PARN 241:9
reticence Northern r., the tight gag — HEAN 154:14
R., in three volumes — GLAD 142:5
reticulated *Network.* Anything r. — JOHN 173:14
retort r. courteous — SHAK 270:6
retreating Have you seen yourself r. — NASH 231:18
my right is r. — FOCH 130:16
retrenchment Peace, r., and reform — BRIG 66:22
retrograde be not r. — JONS 177:19
return I shall r. — MACA 205:8
I will r. — PERÓ 244:2
not r. your blow — SHAW 291:21
Should I never r. — MANS 211:8
unto dust shalt thou r. — BIBL 33:13
returning R. were as tedious — SHAK 281:3
reveal r. Himself — MILT 223:18
revealed nothing of r. religion — MEND 216:16
revelation except by r. — KORA 190:22
first hole is a r. — MOOR 227:8

revelations ends with R.   WILD 335:12
  extraordinary r.   BUTL 77:2
  offers stupendous r.   HOFF 160:20
revelry r. by night   BYRO 77:25
revels Our r. now are ended   SHAK 287:15
revenge Punishment is not for r.   FRY 134:20
  r. for slight injuries   MACH 207:15
  r. is a kind of wild justice   BACO 21:23
  r.! Timotheus cries   DRYD 116:25
  R. triumphs over death   BACO 21:10
  spur my dull r.   SHAK 272:31
  study of r.   MILT 221:4
  sweet r. grows harsh   SHAK 285:2
revenged I'll be r.   SHAK 288:32
revenges brings in his r.   SHAK 288:31
revenons R. à ces moutons   ANON 11:19
revenue standing r.   BURK 74:2
reverence In deeper r. praise   WHIT 334:5
review your r. before me   REGE 255:14
reviewing read a book before r. it   SMIT 298:13
revisited r. ideas   OLDF 236:4
revolt It is a big r.   LA R 194:3
revolution crust over a volcano of r.   ELLI 124:3
  it is a big r.   LA R 194:3
  R., like Saturn   VERG 323:10
  r. of rising expectations   CLEV 94:12
revolutionary can't feel r. in a bathroom   LINK 200:2
  forge his r. spirit   GUEV 148:11
revolutions All modern r.   CAMU 81:8
  share in two r.   PAIN 239:17
revolver resembles a r.   FANO 126:2
revolving with the r. year   SHEL 292:15
reward nothing for r.   SPEN 300:16
  not to ask for any r.   IGNA 168:17
rewards r. and Fairies   CORB 100:1
rex r. quondam   MALO 210:12
  R. tremendae maiestatis   MISS 224:12
rhetoric aimless r.   HUXL 168:4
  quarrel with others, r.   YEAT 344:2
rhetorician sophistical r.   DISR 112:15
Rhodesia black majority rule in R.   SMIT 297:19
rhyme could not get a r.   FLEM 130:3
  in prose or r.   MILT 221:1
  outlive this powerful r.   SHAK 289:29
  R. being . . . but the invention   MILT 220:31
  R. still the most effective drum   GIRA 141:16
  r. the rudder is   BUTL 77:6
  still more tired of R.   BELL 28:16
rhyming bondage of r.   MILT 220:32
  born under a r. planet   SHAK 284:6
  Thy drasty r.   CHAU 88:17
rhythm I got r.   GERS 138:15
  sweet, soft, plenty r.   MORT 229:8
Rialto What news on the R.   SHAK 282:3
rib r., which the Lord God   BIBL 33:3
riband Just for a r.   BROW 70:16
ribbon blue r. of the turf   DISR 112:26
  changing a typewriter r.   BENC 29:6
Ribstone Pippin Right as a R.   BELL 28:15
rich fell from the r. man's table   BIBL 47:3
  maketh haste to be r.   BIBL 38:8
  man who dies . . . r.   CARN 83:7
  never be too r. or too thin   WIND 337:12
  not really a r. man   GETT 138:18
  Poor little r. girl   COWA 101:9
  potentiality of growing r.   JOHN 176:8
  R. AND THE POOR   DISR 112:27
  r. are different from you and me   FITZ 129:4
  r. beyond the dreams   MOOR 227:4
  r. get rich   KAHN 180:11
  r. he hath sent empty away   BIBL 45:34
  r. with forty pounds a year   GOLD 143:10
  r. wot gets the gravy   ANON 9:20

save the few who are r.   KENN 184:9
  sincerely want to be r.   CORN 100:6
Richard put down R.   SHAK 273:27
  R.'s himself again   CIBB 92:21
richer for r. for poorer   BOOK 60:18
  R. than all his tribe   SHAK 285:4
riches embarrassment of r.   ALLA 4:6
  Infinite r.   MARL 212:11
  parade of r.   SMIT 297:8
  r. grow in hell   MILT 221:14
  unsearchable r. of Christ   BIBL 50:17
  world's r., which dispersed lie   HERB 157:18
rid decorated, and got r. of   CICE 93:4
riddle r. of the sands   CHIL 90:13
  r. of the world   POPE 248:16
  r. wrapped in a mystery   CHUR 91:13
ride if you cannot r. two horses   MAXT 215:13
  r. in triumph   MARL 212:15
  r. of Paul Revere   LONG 202:4
  R. on! ride on in majesty   MILM 218:22
  She's got a ticket to r.   LENN 197:15
ridentem Dulce r.   HORA 164:8
ridicule r. is the best test   CHES 89:13
  stand the test of r.   SHAF 268:8
ridiculous makes men r.   JUVE 179:21
  no spectacle so r.   MACA 205:15
  position r.   CHES 89:15
  step above the r.   PAIN 239:6
  sublime to the r.   NAPO 231:5
ridiculus nascetur r. mus   HORA 163:15
Ridley good comfort, Master R.   LATI 194:5
rien Ils n'ont r. appris   TALL 309:2
  je ne regrette r.   VAUC 322:18
  R.   LOUI 202:21
rifle r. all the breathing spring   COLL 97:10
rift loaded every r.   SPEN 300:15
  Load every r.   KEAT 183:16
  r. within the lute   TENN 311:9
right All's r. with the world   BROW 70:27
  convinced that they are r.   VAN 322:13
  defend to the death your r.   VOLT 326:13
  everyone is r.   LA C 191:9
  firmness in the r.   LINC 199:11
  grounded on just and r.   MILT 222:13
  if r., to be kept right   SCHU 265:21
  I had rather be r.   CLAY 94:3
  It must be r.   CRAB 102:11
  Jack — I'm all r.   BONE 58:1
  majority never has r.   IBSE 168:9
  my r. is retreating   FOCH 130:16
  never r. to do wrong   SOCR 298:22
  no r. in the circus   MAXT 215:13
  of—them—is—r.   KIPL 189:22
  our country, r. or wrong   DECA 107:11
  renew a r. spirit   BOOK 61:28
  r., and our bounden duty   BOOK 60:3
  R. as a Ribstone Pippin   BELL 28:15
  r. deed for the wrong reason   ELIO 122:16
  R. Divine of Kings   POPE 246:21
  r. little, tight little Island   DIBD 109:15
  r. notes at the right time   BACH 20:17
  r. there is none to dispute   COWP 102:9
  r. thought   PALI 240:3
  r. to be consulted   BAGE 22:21
  r. to be obeyed   JOHN 172:11
  Self-government is our r.   CASE 85:5
  sheep on his r. hand   BIBL 45:8
  to be decorative and to do r.   FIRB 127:24
  To do a great r.   SHAK 282:22
  Whatever is, is R.   POPE 248:14
righteous godly, r., and sober life   BOOK 58:7
  never the r. forsaken   BOOK 61:16
  not come to call the r.   BIBL 43:20

r. are bold	BIBL 38:7	Goodbye yellow brick r.	JOHN 172:19
r. man	BIBL 37:27	high r.	JOHN 174:23
souls of the r.	BIBL 41:21	on a lonesome r.	COLE 96:17
righteousness clouds rain down r.	BIBL 53:5	one more for the r.	MERC 216:23
loved r., and hated iniquity	BOOK 61:23	on to the end of the r.	LAUD 194:6
r. and peace	BOOK 62:13	r. of excess	BLAK 55:22
r. hath not been forgotten	BIBL 41:30	r. to the City of Emeralds	BAUM 26:10
Sun of r.	BIBL 41:19	r. to wealth	TROL 319:17
rights duties as well as its r.	DRUM 116:12	r. up and the road down	HERA 156:27
extension of women's r.	FOUR 132:10	r. wind up-hill	ROSS 260:14
inalienable r.	ROBE 257:17	rolling English r.	CHES 89:24
Natural r.	BENT 30:2	r. through the woods	KIPL 188:14
r. of an Englishman	JUNI 179:17	watched the ads and not the r.	NASH 231:14
Stand up for your r.	MARL 212:3	ye'll tak' the high r.	ANON 9:9
unalienable r.	ANON 10:14	**roads** How many r.	DYLA 119:2
rigs Corn r., an' barley rigs	BURN 75:13	Two r. diverged	FROS 134:13
rime r. was on the spray	HARD 152:4	without fear the lawless r.	MUIR 229:18
Rimmon in the house of R.	BIBL 36:25	**roam** Everywhere I r.	FOST 132:9
ring Like a great r.	VAUG 323:4	**roaming** R. in the gloamin'	LAUD 194:8
now r. the bells	WALP 327:19	where are you r.	SHAK 288:12
One R. to rule them all	TOLK 318:13	**roar** called upon to give the r.	CHUR 92:5
only pretty r. time	SHAK 270:4	die of that r.	ELIO 121:10
r. at the end of his nose	LEAR 195:15	r. you as gently	SHAK 283:4
r. is worn away	OVID 238:13	**roareth** What is this that r. thus	GODL 142:11
r. of bright water	RAIN 253:23	**roaring** r. of the wind	KEAT 183:12
R. out, wild bells	TENN 311:29	**roast** r. their eggs	BACO 21:34
r. the bells of Heaven	HODG 160:11	**rob** r. a lady of her fortune	FIEL 127:15
small circle of a wedding-r.	CIBB 92:18	**robbed** We was r.	JACO 169:21
What shall we do for a r.	LEAR 195:15	**robber** Barabbas was a r.	BIBL 48:10
With this R. I thee wed	BOOK 60:19	r.'s bundle	SHEL 294:7
ringleaders fling the r.	ARNO 16:8	**robbing** r. a bank	BREC 66:12
rings postman always r. twice	CAIN 80:6	**robe** Give me my r.	SHAK 269:6
riot r. is at bottom	KING 186:13	**robes** washed their r.	BIBL 52:10
riotous r. living	BIBL 46:32	**robin** Call for the r.-red-breast	WEBS 330:17
ripe Cherry r.	CAMP 81:5	r. red breast	BLAK 55:12
we r. and ripe	SHAK 269:18	**Robinson** here's to you, Mrs R.	SIMO 295:25
ripeness R. is all	SHAK 278:8	**robot** r. may not injure a human	ASIM 16:15
ripper no female Jack the R.	PAGL 239:5	**robotics** Rules of R.	ASIM 16:15
rise Created half to r.	POPE 248:16	**rock** founded upon a r.	BIBL 43:12
fall to r.	BROW 69:19	from the Tarpeian r.	ARNO 16:8
resistible r. of Arturo Ui	BREC 66:10	I've gotten a r.	BLAM 56:17
r. against nation	BIBL 44:34	knew the perilous r.	SOUT 299:14
r. and fight againe	BALL 24:6	R. journalism is people	ZAPP 345:2
r. at ten thirty	HARG 152:8	R. of Ages	TOPL 318:19
rises sun also r.	HEMI 156:3	Sex and drugs and r. and roll	DURY 118:17
rising means of r.	JOHN 175:16	upon this r.	BIBL 44:10
revolution of r. expectations	CLEV 94:12	**rocked** R. in the cradle of the deep	WILL 336:2
r. to great place	BACO 21:15	r. the system	ROBI 258:6
risk life without r.	LAHR 191:19	**rocket** rose like a r.	PAIN 239:10
risks just one of the r. he takes	STEV 303:10	**Rockies** R. may crumble	GERS 138:16
ritui Novo cedat r.	THOM 315:23	**rocks** eternal r. beneath	BRON 67:14
Ritz open to all—like the R.	MATH 215:5	hand that r. the cradle	WALL 327:3
river Among the r. sallows	KEAT 182:23	older than the r.	PATE 241:24
black flowing r.	HOOD 161:22	**rod** shall come forth a r.	BIBL 39:21
daughter went through the r.	BUNY 73:10	spare the r., and spoil the child	BUTL 77:7
either side the r. lie	TENN 312:2	spareth his r.	BIBL 37:31
Fame is like a r.	BACO 21:21	thy r. and thy staff	BOOK 61:7
in the reeds by the r.	BROW 69:13	**rogue** dainty r. in porcelain	MERE 216:26
Ol' man r.	HAMM 150:22	r. and peasant slave	SHAK 271:35
r. Is a strong brown god	ELIO 121:26	r.'s face	CONG 98:12
r. of crystal light	FIEL 127:8	**roi** que le r.	ANON 11:13
twice into the same r.	HERA 156:25	**Roland** Childe R. to the Dark Tower	BROW 69:27
riverrun r., past Eve and Adam's	JOYC 178:19	Child R. to the dark tower	SHAK 277:28
rivers discourse of r.	WALT 328:5	**roll** drugs and rock and r.	DURY 118:17
I've known r.	HUGH 166:9	r. all our strength	MARV 213:23
R. and mountain-spring	OAKL 235:10	R. on, thou deep	BYRO 78:9
r. of blood	JEFF 171:17	R. up that map	PITT 245:14
r. of Damascus	BIBL 36:24	**rolled** bottoms of my trousers r.	ELIO 122:13
r. run into the sea	BIBL 38:13	**rolling** jus' keeps r. along	HAMM 150:22
rivulet neat r. of text	SHER 294:17	r. English road	CHES 89:24
road And the r. below me	STEV 304:4	**Roman** by a R. Valiantly vanquished	SHAK 268:27
Follow the yellow brick r.	HARB 151:10	deceased R. Empire	HOBB 160:5
Golden R. to Samarkand	FLEC 129:23	high R. fashion	SHAK 269:1

Roman (*cont.*)
I am a R. citizen — CICE 92:26
make a R. holiday — BYRO 78:6
more an antique R. — SHAK 273:20
neither holy, nor R. — VOLT 326:6
noblest R. of them all — SHAK 276:32
noses cast is of the r. — FLEM 130:3
R. and his trouble — HOUS 165:6
R., make your task to rule — VIRG 324:23
R. meal . . . . . . a radish — COWP 102:5
R. people — CALI 80:7
R.-Saxon-Danish-Norman — DEFO 107:20
R.'s life — MACA 206:12
R. thought hath struck him — SHAK 268:14
R. world is falling — JERO 172:4
sweet R. hand — SHAK 288:26
Roman Catholic R. Church — MACA 205:18
romance fine r. with no kisses — FIEL 127:17
symbols of a high r. — KEAT 183:1
Romanism rum, R., and rebellion — BURC 73:13
Romans Friends, R., countrymen — SHAK 276:15
romantic airline ticket to r. places — MARV 213:24
R. Ireland's dead and gone — YEAT 343:23
r. poets — LEAP 195:6
ruin that's r. — GILB 140:21
Wrong but R. — SELL 267:18
romantics We were the last r. — YEAT 342:15
Romanus Civis R. sum — CICE 92:26
Rome Bishop of R. — BOOK 64:5
cruel men of R. — SHAK 275:28
Everything in R. — JUVE 179:22
grandeur that was R. — POE 246:15
happy R., born when I — CICE 93:3
Let R. in Tiber melt — SHAK 268:13
loved R. more — SHAK 276:12
Men, I'm getting out of R. — GARI 136:5
Oh R.! my country — BYRO 78:3
R. has spoken — AUGU 19:6
R. shall stand — BYRO 78:7
second at R. — CAES 80:1
voice of R. — JONS 177:13
When I go to R. — AMBR 4:14
Romeo wherefore art thou R. — SHAK 286:19
romping r. of sturdy children — DE V 109:6
Ronsard R. me célébrait — RONS 259:11
roof cat on a hot tin r. — WILL 336:8
come under my r. — BIBL 43:13
enter under my r. — MISS 224:7
heavens my wide r.-tree — AYTO 20:14
Who, living, had no r. — HEYW 158:23
rooks r. are blown — TENN 311:17
room always r. at the top — WEBS 330:7
Books do furnish a r. — POWE 250:17
boys in the back r. — LOES 201:12
Great hatred, little r. — YEAT 343:15
into the next r. — HOLL 161:7
just entering the r. — BROU 68:11
large upper r. — BIBL 47:9
money and a r. of her own — WOOL 339:7
no r. for them in the inn — BIBL 46:3
riches in a little r. — MARL 212:11
smallest r. of my house — REGE 255:14
smoke-filled r. — SIMP 296:6
struggle for r. — MALT 210:16
rooms boys in the back r. — BEAV 26:16
Other rooms, other r. — CAPO 81:21
root axe to the r. — PAIN 239:11
begins to take r. — WASH 328:23
perced to the r. — CHAU 88:7
r. of all evil — BIBL 51:11
r. of the matter — BIBL 37:10
roots drought is destroying his r. — HERB 157:1
rope fourfold r. of nerves — HEAT 154:18

refuse to set his hand to a r. — DRAK 116:2
rorate R., coeli — BIBL 53:5
rose American beauty r. — ROCK 258:17
beauty's r. — SHAK 289:22
blossom as the r. — BIBL 40:4
blows so'd The r. — FITZ 128:17
English unofficial r. — BROO 67:20
expectancy and r. — SHAK 272:7
fading r. — CARE 82:7
fayr as is the r. — CHAU 88:23
fire and the r. are one — ELIO 121:30
Go, lovely r. — WALL 327:5
Goodbye, England's r. — JOHN 172:17
I know the colour r. — ABSE 1:3
inimitable r. — WINC 337:11
Into the r.-garden — ELIO 121:19
last r. of summer — MOOR 227:18
lovely is the r. — WORD 340:8
love were what the r. is — SWIN 308:5
Luve's like a red, red r. — BURN 75:21
Mighty lak' a r. — STAN 301:20
morning r. — KEAT 182:7
One perfect r. — PARK 240:17
Pluck a red r. — SHAK 275:14
pluck a white r. — SHAK 275:13
Queen r. of the rosebud garden — TENN 312:22
ravage with impunity a r. — BROW 71:7
r. By any other name — SHAK 286:20
r. in dark and evil days — INGR 169:4
R. is a rose — STEI 302:7
r. of Sharon — BIBL 39:3
r.-red city — BURG 73:18
r. should shut — KEAT 181:7
R., thou art sick — BLAK 56:13
R., were you not — PRIO 251:11
r. without the thorn — HERR 158:6
Roves back the r. — DE L 108:4
secret and inviolate R. — YEAT 343:21
sweet lovely r. — SHAK 273:27
vanish with the r. — FITZ 129:1
white r. of Scotland — MACD 207:5
white r. weeps — TENN 312:23
without thorn the r. — MILT 221:31
rosebuds Gather ye r. — HERR 158:8
rosemary r. and rue — SHAK 289:9
r., that's for remembrance — SHAK 273:5
Rosencrantz R. and Guildenstern — SHAK 273:24
roses days of wine and r. — DOWS 115:11
Everything's coming up r. — SOND 299:4
Honey of r. — HERB 157:14
let fall a shower of r. — TERE 314:14
lilac and the r. — ARAG 13:19
R. are flowering in Picardy — WEAT 329:26
roses, r., all the way — BROW 70:25
smells like r. — JOHN 173:5
rosy R.-fingered dawn — HOME 161:21
rot in cold obstruction and to r. — SHAK 281:33
we r. and rot — SHAK 269:18
rotten like r. mackerel — RAND 254:13
shines like r. wood — RALE 254:1
Something is r. — SHAK 271:14
rough R.-hew them how we will — SHAK 273:15
r. magic I here abjure — SHAK 287:17
R. winds do shake — SHAK 289:23
round in that little r. — FORD 131:8
r. as a ball — JULI 179:9
R. both the shires — HOUS 165:4
R. the world — ARNO 15:8
r. unvarnished tale — SHAK 284:11
Roundheads R. (Right but Repulsive) — SELL 267:18
roving go no more a-r. — BYRO 79:16
row r. one way and look another — BURT 76:12
rowed All r. fast — COKE 95:15

rowing looking one way, and r. BUNY 73:4
royal If you have a R. Family PIML 245:1
  needed no r. title SPEN 300:6
  r. banners forward go FORT 131:20
  r. priesthood BIBL 51:26
  'r. road' to geometry EUCL 125:8
  r. road to the unconscious FREU 133:20
  this is the r. Law CORO 100:12
royalist more of a r. ANON 11:13
royaliste plus r. ANON 11:13
royalty r. is to be reverenced BAGE 22:20
  R. the gold filling OSBO 237:29
  when you come to R. DISR 113:3
rub ay, there's the r. SHAK 272:1
  r. up against money RUNY 262:2
rubbish What r. BLÜC 57:1
rubies above r. BIBL 37:11
  price is far above r. BIBL 38:11
rudder rhyme the r. is BUTL 77:6
rude so r. to the good WORD 339:16
Rudolph R., the Red-Nosed MARK 212:1
rue rosemary and r. SHAK 289:9
  set a bank of r. SHAK 285:25
  There's r. for you SHAK 273:6
ruffle r. up your spirits SHAK 276:23
rugged harsh cadence of a r. line DRYD 117:11
  old r. cross BENN 29:19
  r. verse I chose DRYD 117:7
  system of r. individualism HOOV 162:12
rugs like a million bloody r. FITZ 129:9
Ruh Meine R.' ist hin GOET 142:19
  Über allen Gipfeln Ist R.' GOET 142:24
Ruhm Tat ist alles, nichts der R. GOET 142:20
ruin Majestic though in r. MILT 221:18
  Resolved to r. DRYD 116:18
  r. himself in twelve months GEOR 138:5
  R. seize thee GRAY 146:11
  r. that Cromwell knocked about BEDF 27:6
  r. that's romantic GILB 140:21
  r. upon ruin MILT 221:25
ruinous R. inheritance GAIU 135:8
ruins human mind in r. DAVI 106:17
Ruislip Gaily into R. gardens BETJ 32:1
rule Ill can he r. the great SPEN 300:19
  oldest in the book CARR 84:1
  One Ring to r. them all TOLK 318:13
  R. 1, on page 1 MONT 226:19
  R., Britannia THOM 317:8
  r. o'er freemen BROO 67:18
  r. the state DRYD 116:18
ruler r. in Israel BIBL 41:16
  R. of the Queen's Navee GILB 140:30
rulers best r. LAO 193:5
  r., mostly knaves BIER 53:20
  r. of the darkness BIBL 50:23
rules hand that r. the world WALL 327:3
  R. of Robotics ASIM 16:15
ruling r. passion conquers POPE 247:18
  Search then the R. Passion POPE 247:23
rum r. and true religion BYRO 78:19
  r., Romanism, and rebellion BURC 73:13
  r., sodomy, prayers, and the lash CHUR 92:3
rumble r. of a distant drum FITZ 128:16
  R. thy bellyful SHAK 277:19
rumours wars and r. of wars BIBL 44:33
run born to r. SPRI 301:5
  enabled him to r. MACA 205:23
  finest r. in Leicestershire PAGE 239:4
  He can r. LOUI 203:4
  he may r. that readeth it BIBL 41:18
  In the long r. KEYN 185:13
  never did r. smooth SHAK 282:33
  Now Teddy must r. KENN 184:19

  R. and find out KIPL 188:20
  R., run, Orlando SHAK 269:27
  r.-stealers flicker THOM 316:25
  r. with patience BIBL 51:16
  shine, and r. to and fro BIBL 41:22
  we will make him r. MARV 213:23
  What makes Sammy r. SCHU 265:17
runcible ate with a r. spoon LEAR 195:16
  R. Cat with crimson whiskers LEAR 195:18
runnable r. stag DAVI 106:13
runner long-distance r. SILL 295:22
running all the r. you can do CARR 84:5
  r. over BIBL 46:11
  r. with the pack BUTL 77:5
Rupert Prince R. DISR 112:6
  R. of Debate BULW 72:13
  R. of the Rhine MACA 206:3
rural Retirement, r. quiet THOM 317:10
rus R. in urbe MART 213:11
rush fools r. in POPE 248:7
rushes Green grow the r. O ANON 7:17
  Green grow the r., O BURN 75:11
rushing r. mighty wind BIBL 48:24
russet plain r.-coated captain CROM 103:16
  r. yeas SHAK 278:21
Russia forecast the action of R. CHUR 91:13
  power of R. MITC 224:18
  R. an empire or democracy BRZE 71:23
  R. has two generals NICH 233:21
Russian he might have been a R. GILB 141:3
  tumult in the R. heart PUSH 252:22
rust moth and r. doth corrupt BIBL 42:24
  wear out than to r. out CUMB 104:12
Ruth sad heart of R. KEAT 182:14
ruthless Ruin seize thee, r. King! GRAY 146:11
rye catcher in the r. SALI 263:17
  Comin thro' the r. BURN 75:8
  fields of barley and of r. TENN 312:2
  r. reach to the chin PEEL 242:23

S

sabachthani Eli, Eli, lama s. BIBL 45:21
sabbath Remember the s. day BIBL 34:15
  s. was made for man BIBL 45:23
sabbaths endless S. ABEL 1:2
Sabidi Non amo te, S. MART 213:7
sable paint the s. skies DRUM 116:13
  S.-vested Night MILT 221:24
Sabrina S. fair MILT 219:18
Sacco S.'s name will live VANZ 322:17
sack intolerable deal of s. SHAK 274:2
  S. the lot FISH 128:5
sacrament abortion would be a s. KENN 184:5
  great S. revere THOM 315:23
sacred only s. thing FRAN 132:17
sacrifice approaching s. MILM 218:22
  blood Of human s. MILT 221:10
  highest s. is ELEA 121:1
  King refused a lesser s. MARY 214:12
  living s. BIBL 49:19
  Passover s. HAGG 148:19
  pay thy morning s. KEN 184:1
  sufficient s. BOOK 60:4
  Thine ancient S. KIPL 188:5
  Too long a s. YEAT 342:21
sacrificed be s. to expediency MAUG 215:8
sad all their songs are s. CHES 89:18
  How s. and bad BROW 69:28
  of all s. words WHIT 334:6
  remember and be s. ROSS 260:13

sad (*cont.*)
s. bad glad mad | SWIN 307:19
s., black isle | BAUD 26:8
s.-coloured sect | HOOD 162:8
s. steps, O Moon | SIDN 295:9
s. tires in a mile-a | SHAK 289:8
world is s. and dreary | FOST 132:9
sadder s. and a wiser man | COLE 96:19
saddest tell of s. thought | SHEL 293:32
saddle Boot, s., to horse | BROW 69:23
saddled s. and bridled | RUMB 261:20
sadly take their pleasures s. | SULL 306:1
saeclum *Solvet s. in favilla* | MISS 224:11
safe made s. for democracy | WILS 337:8
S. is spelled D-U-L-L | CLAR 93:17
s. lodging | NEWM 233:4
see me s. up | MORE 228:3
safeguard s. of the West | WORD 340:17
safer Love just makes it s. | ICE- 168:16
s. for a prince | MACH 207:16
safety s., honour, and welfare | CHAR 87:23
strike against public s. | COOL 99:20
sagas frosty s. | CRAN 102:19
peoples who memorized s. | BJÖR 54:20
sage *ne surprend point le s.* | LA F 191:15
said fool hath s. in his heart | BOOK 61:1
He himself s. | CICE 92:23
if you want anything s. | THAT 315:3
nobody had s. it before | TWAI 321:9
s. on both sides | ADDI 2:12
s. our remarks before us | DONA 113:15
what the soldier s. | DICK 111:8
sail s. on, O Ship of State | LONG 201:18
sea-mark of my utmost s. | SHAK 285:3
sailed I have s. the seas | YEAT 343:18
Saturday s. from Bremen | HOPK 163:9
sailing S. over a cardboard sea | HARB 151:8
sailor Home is the s. | STEV 304:7
sailors tell thee, s., when away | GAY 137:12
saint call me a s. | CAMA 80:15
my late espousèd s. | MILT 223:11
S. Martin's summer | SHAK 275:12
s. or incarnation of Satan | MADO 209:6
Sloane turned secular s. | BURC 73:14
saints Christ and His s. | ANON 13:6
s. immortal reign | WATT 329:11
saisons *Ô s.* | RIMB 257:12
sake Art for art's s. | CONS 99:13
for his country's s. | FITZ 128:13
loseth his life for my s. | BIBL 43:28
Saki like her, O S. | FITZ 129:2
salad Our Garrick's a s. | GOLD 143:17
s. days | SHAK 268:16
salesman Death of a s. | MILL 218:13
s. is got to dream | MILL 218:14
salley by the s. gardens | YEAT 342:18
sally none like pretty S. | CARE 82:10
saloon in the last chance s. | MELL 216:8
salt became a pillar of s. | BIBL 33:25
grain of s. | PLIN 246:5
how s. is the taste | DANT 105:21
s. of the earth | BIBL 42:15
seasoned with s. | BIBL 51:3
unplumbed, s., estranging sea | ARNO 15:26
verge of the s. flood | SHAK 287:25
Salteena S. was an elderly man | ASHF 16:12
saltness sugar, and s. | GOLD 143:17
salus S. populi | CICE 92:22
salutant *Ave Caesar, morituri te s.* | ANON 12:8
salute If it moves, s. it | ANON 7:14
S. the happy morn | BYRO 77:19
those about to die s. you | ANON 12:8
salva *S. me* | MISS 224:12

salvaged ships have been s. | HALS 150:12
salvation bottle of s. | RALE 254:2
cannot be s. | CYPR 105:12
necessary to s. | BOOK 64:2
no s. outside the church | AUGU 19:3
strength of our s. | BOOK 62:18
Work out your own s. | BIBL 50:25
Samaritan remember the Good S. | THAT 315:5
Samarkand Golden Road to S. | FLEC 129:23
Samarra appointment with him in S. | MAUG 215:10
same all say *the s.* | MELB 216:6
Ever the s. | ANON 12:20
more they are the s. | KARR 180:17
much the s. | ANON 5:17
s. yesterday, and to day | BIBL 51:12
you are the s. | MART 213:10
samite Clothed in white s. | TENN 311:4
Sammy What makes S. run | SCHU 265:17
sancta *s. simplicitas* | JERO 172:3
sanctuary classes which need s. | BALD 23:9
sanctus *S., sanctus, sanctus* | MISS 224:4
sand Little grains of s. | CARN 83:9
on the edge of the s. | LEAR 195:16
world in a grain of s. | BLAK 55:11
sandal s. shoon | SHAK 272:32
sands Across the s. of Dee | KING 186:19
Come unto these yellow s. | SHAK 287:6
Footprints on the s. | LONG 201:26
riddle of the s. | CHIL 90:13
s. upon the Red sea shore | BLAK 56:1
sandwich ask for a watercress s. | WILD 335:19
cheaper than a prawn s. | RATN 254:15
taste again that raw-onion s. | BARN 25:9
sane if he was s. he had to fly | HELL 155:12
San Francisco left my heart in S. | CROS 104:5
sang s. a king out of three kingdoms | WHAR 333:1
Sangreal story of the S. | MALO 210:11
sank s. my boat | KENN 184:16
Sighted sub, s. same | MASO 214:18
sano *Mens sana in corpore s.* | JUVE 180:4
sans S. teeth, sans eyes | SHAK 269:24
Santa Claus there is a S. | CHUR 90:22
sap dried the s. of my veins | YEAT 342:23
sapienti *Dictum s.* | PLAU 246:3
Sappho Where burning S. loved | BYRO 78:23
sardines s. will be thrown | CANT 81:19
sash s. my father wore | ANON 10:2
sashes one of his nice new s. | GRAH 145:8
sat everyone has s. except a man | CUMM 104:15
S. and knotted | SEDL 267:4
s. too long here | CROM 103:20
we s. down and wept | BOOK 63:23
Satan Get thee behind me, S. | BIBL 44:11
high capital of S. | MILT 221:16
Lord said unto S. | BIBL 36:36
saint or incarnation of S. | MADO 209:6
S. cast out Satan | BIBL 45:24
S. finds some mischief still | WATT 329:6
Satanic dark S. mills | BLAK 55:27
satiable full of s. curtiosity | KIPL 188:22
satin ease a heart like a s. gown | PARK 240:19
satire S. is a sort of glass | SWIF 306:14
S. is what closes Saturday | KAUF 180:18
S. or sense | POPE 247:11
satirical sign of a s. wit | AUBR 17:15
satisfaction can't get no s. | JAGG 170:3
satisfied well paid that is well s. | SHAK 282:25
satisfy poorly s. our eyes | WOTT 341:22
satisfying s. a voracious appetite | FIEL 127:14
Saturday closes S. night | KAUF 180:18
Glasgow Empire on a S. night | DODD 113:13
Saturn Revolution, like S. | VERG 323:10
Saturnia *redeunt S. regna* | VIRG 325:10

satyr Hyperion to a s. — SHAK 270:31
satyrs men, like s. — MARL 212:8
sauce only one s. — CARA 82:2
Saul Is S. also among the prophets — BIBL 35:17
S. and Jonathan — BIBL 35:28
S. hath slain his thousands — BIBL 35:23
S., why persecutest thou me — BIBL 48:26
sausage pig in a s. — TROL 319:22
savage days of the Noble S. — BIKO 53:22
laws unto a s. race — TENN 313:28
mad and s. master — SOPH 299:11
noble s. ran — DRYD 116:28
s. loving has made me — BECK 27:3
sooth a s. breast — CONG 98:13
savaged s. by a dead sheep — HEAL 154:8
save destroy the town to s. it — ANON 8:2
God's king Solomon — BIBL 35:36
helped s. the world — KEYN 185:14
himself he cannot s. — BIBL 45:20
s. his soul — BIBL 41:2
s. me — MISS 224:12
Save me, oh, s. me — CANN 81:13
s. those that have no imagination — SHAW 291:33
To s. your world — AUDE 17:29
saved He s. others — BIBL 45:20
only s. the world — CHES 89:20
we are not s. — BIBL 40:23
What must I do to be s. — BIBL 48:31
Whosoever will be s. — BOOK 59:2
saviour S.'s birth is celebrated — SHAK 270:25
s. spring to life — BIBL 53:5
savour keep Seeming and s. — SHAK 289:9
salt have lost his s. — BIBL 42:15
saw I came, I s., I conquered — CAES 80:3
Saxon ancient S. phrase — LONG 201:24
say all s. *the same* — MELB 216:6
anything good to s. — LONG 202:13
don't s. nothin' — HAMM 150:22
Have something to s. — ARNO 16:5
Lat thame s. — ANON 10:9
more to s. when I am dead — ROBI 258:1
nothing to s. — CAGE 80:5
nothing to s. — COLT 97:15
not s. what one thinks — EURI 125:10
not s. why and how — WILS 337:1
S. it ain't so — ANON 9:17
S. little and do much — SHAM 290:18
s. only the word — MISS 224:7
s. something — GOOD 144:14
s. what they please — FRED 133:13
s. what you mean — CARR 83:19
see what I s. — WALL 327:4
someone else has got to s. — GASK 136:16
whatever you s. — HEAN 154:14
saying were s. yesterday — LUIS 204:15
sayings s. are like women's letters — HAZL 154:2
scabbard threw away the s. — CLAR 93:11
scaffold forever on the s. — LOWE 203:19
s. and the doom — AYTO 20:13
scale sufficiently large s. — SPEN 300:4
with her lifted s. — POPE 246:18
scallop s.-shell of quiet — RALE 254:2
scandal s. by a woman of easy virtue — HAIL 149:8
scandalous s. and poor — ROCH 258:15
scapegoat Let him go for a s. — BIBL 34:20
scar wears their going like a s. — DUNN 118:11
scarecrows s. of fools — HUXL 168:3
scarf S. up the tender eye — SHAK 280:25
scarlet Cowards in s. — GRAN 145:21
His sins were s. — BELL 28:24
raise the s. standard — CONN 98:23
s. letter — HAWT 153:14
s. soldiers — AUDE 18:14

sins be as s. — BIBL 39:10
scars He jests at s. — SHAK 286:18
show his s. — SHAK 275:10
scattered enemies be s. — BOOK 62:6
s. the proud — BIBL 45:34
scenery among savage s. — HOFF 160:20
end of all natural s. — RUSK 262:11
God paints the s. — HART 152:20
scenes behind your s. — JOHN 174:17
s. where man hath never — CLAR 93:10
scent sweetest flower for s. — SHEL 293:23
sceptered s. isle — SHAK 285:12
sceptic too much of a s. — HUXL 168:5
sceptred avails the s. race — LAND 192:22
schemes s. of political improvement — JOHN 175:5
s. o' mice an' men — BURN 75:31
schizophrenic you are a s. — SZAS 308:10
Schleswig-Holstein S. question — PALM 240:8
scholar s. all Earth's volumes carry — CHAP 87:18
scholars S. dispute — HORA 163:13
school every s. knows it — TAYL 310:1
goeth to s. — BACO 21:29
learned about in s. — JARR 171:6
s. of Manchester — DISR 113:7
s. of Stratford atte Bowe — CHAU 88:8
schoolboy Every s. knows — MACA 205:17
Not the s. heat — TENN 311:32
tell what every s. knows — SWIF 307:5
whining s., with his satchel — SHAK 269:21
schoolboys s. playing in the stream — PEEL 242:23
schoolchildren What all s. learn — AUDE 18:16
schoolgirl priggish s. — GRIG 147:18
schoolman no s.'s subtle art — POPE 247:12
schoolmaster becoming a s. — WAUG 329:18
s. is abroad — BROU 68:9
so gentle a s. — GREY 147:14
schoolmasters s. puzzle their brain — GOLD 143:26
schoolrooms s. for 'the boy' — COOK 99:19
schools hundred s. of thought contend — MAO 211:14
lumber of the s. — SWIF 307:7
schooner It was the s. Hesperus — LONG 202:9
sciatica S.: he cured it — AUBR 17:16
science aim of s. — BREC 66:8
All s. physics or stamp collecting — RUTH 263:4
applications of s. — PAST 241:23
Dismal S. — CARL 82:24
do s. in hell — VAUG 323:5
essence of s. — BRON 67:6
How s. dwindles — YOUN 344:13
In s., read — BULW 72:16
In s. the credit goes — DARW 106:10
In s., we must be — CURI 105:4
instrument of s. — JOHN 173:11
it is not s. — KELV 183:26
S. is an edged tool — EDDI 119:15
S. is built up of facts — POIN 246:16
S. is organized knowledge — SPEN 299:26
S. is part of culture — GOUL 144:22
s. is satisfying the curiosity — ARTS 16:9
s. is strong — SZAS 308:11
S. moves, but slowly — TENN 312:13
S. must begin with myths — POPP 249:13
s. reassures — BRAQ 66:4
S. the aggregate of all — VALÉ 322:5
S. without religion is lame — EINS 120:11
tragedy of S. — HUXL 167:21
triumph of modern s. — WAUG 329:24
true s. and study — CHAR 88:3
sciences mother of s. — BACO 22:4
scientific new s. truth — PLAN 245:18
on the most s. principles — PEAC 242:12
plunges into s. questions — HUXL 168:4
s. faith's absurd — BROW 70:3

scientist elderly s. states — CLAR 93:18
exercise for a research s. — LORE 202:17
s.'s laws — QUIN 253:10
scissor long, red-legged s.-man — HOFF 160:15
scissors end up using s. — HOCK 160:10
scoff fools, who came to s. — GOLD 143:11
scold what a s. you are — BULL 72:10
scope that man's s. — SHAK 289:25
score time required to s. 500 — COMP 98:1
scorer One Great S. — RICE 256:14
scorn Laugh no man to s. — BIBL 41:24
S. not the Sonnet — WORD 341:2
think foul s. — ELIZ 123:6
scorned fury, like a woman s. — CONG 98:14
scornful only a s. tickling — SIDN 295:15
scorpions chastise you with s. — BIBL 36:7
Scotch as a S. banker — DAVI 106:16
Mary, ma S. Bluebell — LAUD 194:7
scotched s. the snake — SHAK 280:23
Scotchman S. ever sees — JOHN 174:23
Scotland flower of S. — WILL 336:12
in S. supports the people — JOHN 173:15
In S. we live between — CRAW 103:6
our infinite S. — MACD 207:4
S., land of the omnipotent No — BOLD 57:12
Stands S. — SHAK 281:11
white rose of S. — MACD 207:5
Scots S. lords at his feet — BALL 24:10
S., wha hae wi' Wallace bled — BURN 75:22
Scotsman S. on the make — BARR 25:17
Scotty Beam me up, S. — RODD 258:19
scoundrel refuge of a s. — JOHN 175:15
scouts s.' motto — BADE 22:9
scrap s. of paper — BETH 31:14
scratch quick sharp s. — BROW 70:20
scratching s. of a pen — LOVE 203:9
s. of my finger — HUME 166:23
s. of pimples on the body — WOOL 339:9
scream s. in a low voice — BYRO 79:22
screw s. your courage — SHAK 280:1
turn of the s. — JAME 170:23
scribblative babblative and s. — SOUT 299:17
scribble Always s., scribble, scribble — GLOU 142:8
scrawl, and s. — POPE 248:27
scribbling mob of s. women — HAWT 153:15
s. fry — YOUN 344:11
scribendi S. cacoethes — JUVE 180:1
scribes and Pharisees, hypocrites — BIBL 44:30
scribimus S. indocti doctique poemata — HORA 164:3
scrip My s. of joy — RALE 254:2
scripture devil can cite S. — SHAK 282:5
Holy S. containeth — BOOK 64:2
know more of the s. — TYND 321:17
S. moveth us — BOOK 58:4
scriptures all holy S. — BOOK 59:13
Let us look at the s. — SELD 267:10
S. in the hands — PUGI 252:4
scrotumtightening s. sea — JOYC 178:27
scrutamini s. scripturas — SELD 267:10
sculpture like that of s. — RUSS 262:23
S. in stone — MOOR 227:7
scum Okie means you're s. — STEI 302:10
s. of the earth — WELL 331:10
scuttling S. across the floors of silent seas — ELIO 122:11
se s. Iudice — JUVE 180:5
sea all the s. were ink — LYLY 204:25
around the glassy s. — HEBE 155:3
as the waters cover the s. — BIBL 39:23
beneath a rougher s. — COWP 101:18
best thing is—the s. — JERR 172:8
burst Into that silent s. — COLE 96:12
cloud out of the s. — BIBL 36:11
cold grey stones, O S. — TENN 310:11

complaining about the s. — POWE 250:24
dominion of the s. — COVE 101:2
down to the s. again — MASE 214:17
flowing s. — CUNN 105:1
having been at s. — JOHN 175:25
home from s. — STEV 304:7
houses are all gone under the s. — ELIO 121:24
In a solitude of the s. — HARD 151:20
Into a s. of dew — FIEL 127:8
near to heaven by s. — GILB 139:18
one is of the s. — WORD 341:14
Over the s. to Skye — STEV 304:2
over the summer s. — TENN 313:22
pinch the s. of its liberty — COTT 100:15
Poem of the S. — RIMB 257:10
Put out to s. — MACN 208:21
sailed the wintry s. — LONG 202:9
s. gave up the dead — BIBL 52:23
s. is not full — BIBL 38:13
s.-mark of my utmost sail — SHAK 285:3
S. of Faith — ARNO 15:4
S. shall give up her dead — BOOK 64:1
s.! the sea! — XENO 342:7
s. to shining sea — BATE 26:5
s. was made his tomb — BARN 25:11
serpent-haunted s. — FLEC 129:22
set in the silver s. — SHAK 285:12
smiling surface of the s. — PLUT 246:9
snotgreen s. — JOYC 178:27
spread like a green s. — SHEL 293:3
suffer a s.-change — SHAK 287:7
there was no more s. — BIBL 52:24
those in peril on the s. — WHIT 333:18
to the English that of the s. — RICH 257:4
to the s. in ships — BOOK 63:1
two if by s. — LONG 202:5
unplumbed, salt, estranging s. — ARNO 15:26
uttermost parts of the s. — BOOK 63:25
water in the rough rude s. — SHAK 285:17
went to s. — LEAR 195:14
why the s. is boiling hot — CARR 84:6
willing foe and s. room — ANON 11:3
wrinkled s. beneath him — TENN 310:22
seagreen S. Incorruptible — CARL 82:19
seagulls When s. follow a trawler — CANT 81:19
seal opened the seventh s. — BIBL 52:12
S. of the Prophets — KORA 190:21
sealed My lips are s. — BALD 23:11
sealing wax ships—and s. — CARR 84:6
seals receives the s. of office — ROSE 260:8
sear fall'n into the s. — SHAK 281:20
search in s. of an author — PIRA 245:5
travels the world in s. — MOOR 227:6
seas dangers of the s. — PARK 241:3
foam Of perilous s. — KEAT 182:14
Scuttling across the floors of silent s. — ELIO 122:11
s. colder than the Hebrides — FLEC 129:21
such as pass on the s. — BOOK 63:32
seashells She sells s. — SULL 305:16
seashore boy on the s. — NEWT 233:15
season dry brain in a dry s. — ELIO 122:3
In a summer's s. — LANG 192:26
man has every s. — FOND 130:19
S. of mists — KEAT 182:21
s. of snows and sins — SWIN 307:18
there is a s. — BIBL 38:16
word spoken in due s. — BIBL 37:35
seasoned s. with salt — BIBL 51:3
seasons lovers' s. run — DONN 114:12
man for all s. — WHIT 334:7
O s., O castles — RIMB 257:12
s. alter — SHAK 283:10
seaworms Battening upon huge s. — TENN 311:35

second for my s. race — VAUG 322:21
Habit is s. nature — AUCT 17:18
my s. best bed — SHAK 290:16
no s. acts — FITZ 129:10
no s. spring — PHIL 244:16
not a s. on the day — COOK 99:18
s. at Rome — CAES 80:1
s. childhood — ARIS 14:10
s. oldest profession — REAG 255:1
things have s. birth — WORD 340:23
truth 24 times per s. — GODA 142:9
when you come s. — HILL 159:1
secrecy S. the human dress — BLAK 56:16
secret alms may be in s. — BIBL 42:22
concept of the official s. — WEBE 330:3
Et Vigny plus s. — SAIN 263:11
neurosis is a s. — TYNA 321:16
photograph is a s. — ARBU 13:20
s. and inviolate Rose — YEAT 343:21
s., black, and midnight hags — SHAK 281:7
s. magic of numbers — BROW 69:3
s. of the Lord — KEBL 183:18
secretary S. of Nature — WALT 328:7
secrets no s. are hid — BOOK 59:18
s. are edged tools — DRYD 117:8
sect attached to that great s. — SHEL 292:23
sad-coloured s. — HOOD 162:8
sects diversity of s. — SPEN 300:22
security fear, otherwise styled s. — MADA 209:3
s. around the president — MAIL 209:18
s. of Europe — MITC 224:18
sedentary s. humour — MONT 226:3
sedge s. has withered — KEAT 181:17
seduction In s., the rapist — DWOR 118:18
sedulous played the s. ape — STEV 303:17
see In all things Thee to s. — HERB 157:1
into the wilderness to s. — BIBL 43:30
I shall never s. — KILM 186:1
last s. your father — YEAM 342:10
never s. so much — SHAK 278:16
not worth going to s. — JOHN 176:4
rather s. than be one — BURG 73:17
s. and hear nothing — THOM 316:16
s. beyond our bourn — KEAT 182:24
s. me dance the Polka — GROS 148:3
s. me sometime — WEST 332:15
S. one promontory — BURT 76:15
s. oursels as others see us — BURN 75:29
s. the goodness — BOOK 61:10
s. the hours pass — CIOR 93:5
s. the things thou dost not — SHAK 278:3
s. what I eat — CARR 83:19
s. what I say — WALL 327:4
they shall s. our God — KEBL 183:18
To s. her is to love her — BURN 75:7
wait and s. — ASQU 16:18
yet I s. thee still — SHAK 280:5
seed blood of Christians is the s. — TERT 314:15
good s. on the land — CAMP 80:18
seeds into the s. of time — SHAK 279:4
s. fell by the wayside — BIBL 44:1
seeing s. what everybody has seen — SZEN 308:12
seek All I s., the heaven above — STEV 304:4
go s. the asses — BIBL 35:16
If you s. a monument — ANON 13:1
s., and ye shall find — BIBL 43:5
sometime did me s. — WYAT 342:1
strive, to s., to find — TENN 314:1
We s. him here — ORCZ 236:20
seeking s. asses found — MILT 222:27
seeming keep S. and savour — SHAK 289:9
seen anybody here s. Kelly — MURP 230:8
God whom he hath not s. — BIBL 51:35

I have s. war — ROOS 259:17
not s., and yet have believed — BIBL 48:21
should be s. to be done — HEWA 158:17
Too early's unknown — SHAK 286:17
when you've s. one Western — WHIT 333:16
sees s. more in my pictures — TURN 320:21
segregation S. now — WALL 327:1
Seine flows the S. — APOL 13:11
seize s. the day — HORA 164:7
select each one should s. — SHEL 292:23
selection Natural S. — DARW 106:7
self divided s. — LAIN 191:21
to thine own s. be true — SHAK 271:9
self-assertion s. abroad — WAUG 329:20
self-contempt S., well-grounded — LEAV 196:1
self-defence it was in s. — MARL 212:4
self-esteem s., grounded on just — MILT 222:13
self-evident s. beings — NEWM 232:22
truths to be s. — ANON 10:14
self-government S. is our right — CASE 85:5
self-help spirit of s. — SMIL 297:6
self-love s. and social — POPE 248:19
self-made s. man is one who believes — STEA 301:22
self-preservation s. in the other — JEFF 171:16
self-respect starves your s. — PARR 241:12
self-slain As a god s. — SWIN 307:23
self-sufficiency S. at home — WAUG 329:20
self-sufficing reasoning, s. thing — WORD 340:19
selkie s. in the sea — BALL 23:18
sell dreams to s. — BEDD 27:4
I s. here, Sir — BOUL 65:7
mind to s. his house — SWIF 306:18
no man might buy or s. — BIBL 52:15
One does not s. the earth — CRAZ 103:7
s. Jack like soapflakes — KENN 184:17
s., or deny, or delay — MAGN 209:12
s. that thou hast — BIBL 44:19
selling S. off the family silver — MACM 208:12
seltzer weak hock and s. — BETJ 31:15
semblable Hypocrite lecteur,—mon s. — BAUD 26:6
semen no frozen s. ever read a story — WILL 336:7
semi s.-house-trained polecat — FOOT 130:21
semper Quod ubique, quod s. — VINC 324:8
S. aliquid novi — PLIN 246:4
S. eadem — ANON 12:20
Sic s. tyrannis — ANON 12:21
senator S., and a Democrat — JOHN 173:1
senators I look at the s. — HALE 149:14
s. burst with laughter — AUDE 18:1
send S. in the clowns — SOND 299:5
s. me — BIBL 39:15
sennights Weary s. — SHAK 279:1
sensational s. to read in the train — WILD 335:3
sensations easy prey to s. — TREV 319:9
O for a life of s. — KEAT 183:5
sense deviates into s. — DRYD 117:3
light of nature, s. — ROCH 258:12
men of s. never tell — SHAF 268:7
Money is like a sixth s. — MAUG 215:9
Satire or s. — POPE 247:11
Take care of the s. — CARR 83:22
talk s. to the American people — STEV 303:9
want of s. — DILL 111:23
sensibility dissociation of s. — ELIO 123:2
pattern informed by s. — READ 254:18
sensible S. men — DISR 112:24
sensitive S. Plant — SHEL 293:22
sensual s. pleasure without vice — JOHN 177:2
sent man s. from God — BIBL 47:18
sentence life s. goes on — CONL 98:21
No! No! S. first — CARR 84:2
s. is enough — PLAU 246:3
s. is factually significant — AYER 20:10

sentenced s. to death in my absence BEHA 27:17
sentences Backward ran s. GIBB 139:13
sentiments Them's my s. THAC 314:22
sentinels s. to warn MARL 212:18
sentry quadrille in a s.-box JAME 170:15
  stands a wingèd s. VAUG 322:20
separated they cannot be s. SMIT 298:10
separately all hang s. FRAN 133:7
separation prepare for a s. QUIN 253:9
  real s. of powers DENN 108:17
September days hath S. ANON 10:10
  When you reach S. ANDE 5:7
sepulchre taken away from the s. BIBL 48:16
sepulchres s. BIBL 44:32
  s. of mortality CREW 103:10
seraglio s. of eunuchs FOOT 130:20
seraphims Above it stood the s. BIBL 39:14
sere Now my s. fancy BYRO 78:26
serfdom abolish s. ALEX 3:15
sergeant S. Pepper TYNA 321:15
  This fell s., death SHAK 273:19
serial obituary in s. form CRIS 103:13
serious s.-minded activity MONT 226:9
  War is too s. CLEM 94:7
sermon rejected the S. on the Mount BRAD 65:23
sermons S. and soda-water BYRO 78:20
  S. in stones SHAK 269:14
sero S. te amavi AUGU 9:2
serpent be the s. under't SHAK 279:17
  my s. of old Nile SHAK 268:15
  Now the s. was more subtil BIBL 33:6
  s. beguiled me BIBL 33:9
  s.-haunted sea FLEC 129:22
  s. subtlest beast MILT 222:14
  s. upon a rock BIBL 38:10
  sharper than a s.'s tooth SHAK 277:11
serpents wise as s. BIBL 43:25
servant become the s. of a man SHAW 290:27
  carried His s. by night KORA 190:18
  cracked lookingglass of a s. JOYC 179:1
  good and faithful s. BIBL 45:5
  Is thy s. a dog BIBL 36:27
  s. depart in peace BIBL 46:7
  s. of the Living God SMAR 296:22
  s. to the devil SISS 296:8
  s. with this clause HERB 157:13
  thy s. heareth BIBL 35:14
  Your s.'s cut in half GRAH 145:7
servants Between them and s. BARC 25:1
  equality in the s.' hall BARR 25:13
  s. will do that for us VILL 324:5
  wife or your s. to read GRIF 147:17
serve Fleet in which we s. BOOK 63:31
  love to s. my country GIBR 139:14
  s. in the wars BOOK 64:6
  s. the Lord with gladness BOOK 62:22
  s. two masters BIBL 42:26
  s. your captives' need KIPL 188:17
  than s. in heaven MILT 221:7
  They also s. MILT 223:10
served s. her, perhaps mistakenly GLAD 142:3
service devoted to your s. ELIZ 123:13
  done the state some s. SHAK 285:4
  s. is perfect freedom BOOK 58:18
  s.? The rent we pay CLAY 94:4
serviettes kiddies have crumpled the s. BETJ 31:21
serving cumbered about much s. BIBL 46:18
servitude base laws of s. DRYD 116:28
servum O imitatores, s. pecus HORA 164:2
sesame Open S. ARAB 13:16
sesquipedalia s. verba HORA 163:14
sesquippedlan S. verboojuice WELL 331:15
sessions s. of sweet silent thought SHAK 289:27

set S. thine house in order BIBL 40:5
Setebos S., Setebos BROW 69:26
sets sun never s. NORT 234:20
setting against a s. sun SHAK 287:21
settlement through the Act of S. RICE 256:16
seven acts being s. ages SHAK 269:20
  have the s. minutes COLL 97:8
  hewn out her s. pillars BIBL 37:23
  Jacob served s. years BIBL 33:31
  remember more than s. BELL 28:5
  s. feet of English ground HARO 152:12
  S. types of ambiguity EMPS 124:21
  Until seventy times s. BIBL 44:17
  We are s. WORD 341:17
seventh moon is in the s. house RADO 253:21
  opened the s. seal BIBL 52:12
seventy s. years young HOLM 161:12
  Until s. times seven BIBL 44:17
sever kiss, and then we s. BURN 75:2
severity with its usual s. COLE 96:27
sewer s. in a glass-bottomed boat MIZN 225:6
sewers houses thick and s. MILT 222:15
sex attempt to insult s. LAWR 194:14
  call your darling after s. BARN 25:10
  give a s. to mind WOLL 338:22
  have s. with a man WESL 332:9
  isn't s. but death SONT 299:7
  Mind has no s. WOLL 338:22
  Money was exactly like s. BALD 23:6
  mostly about having s. LODG 201:11
  only unnatural s. act KINS 187:4
  practically conceal its s. NASH 231:12
  S. and drugs and rock and roll DURY 118:17
  S. and taxes JONE 177:11
  S. never an obsession BOY 65:18
  soft, unhappy s. BEHN 28:1
  weaker s. ALEX 3:19
  When you have money, it's s. DONL 113:16
sexton s. tolled the bell HOOD 162:4
sexual man's idea of his s. rights STAN 301:19
  not have s. relations CLIN 94:17
  of all the s. perversions HUXL 167:17
  S. intercourse began LARK 193:10
sexuality relinquish their s. WOLF 338:9
shabby tamed and s. tigers HODG 160:11
shade clutching the inviolable s. ARNO 15:19
  gentlemen of the s. SHAK 273:25
  in a green s. MARV 213:17
  sitting in the s. KIPL 187:18
  whiter s. of pale REID 255:15
shades S. of the prison-house WORD 340:10
  till the s. lengthen NEWM 233:4
shadow but the s. of heaven MILT 222:10
  days on the earth are as a s. BIBL 36:34
  Falls the S. ELIO 122:5
  fleeth also as a s. BIBL 37:6
  in the s. of death BIBL 46:1
  little s. that goes STEV 303:30
  little s. that runs CROW 104:9
  little s. that runs HAGG 149:2
  s. of death BIBL 39:18
  s. of death BOOK 62:28
  s. of our night SHEL 292:18
  s. of the Valois CHES 89:22
  s. will be shown NIET 234:8
  valley of the s. of death BOOK 61:7
shadows but s. SHAK 283:23
  half sick of s. TENN 312:4
  less liquid than their s. TESS 314:17
  long s. on county grounds MAJO 209:23
  see only their own s. PLAT 246:2
  s. and twilights Æ 2:22
  s. flee away BIBL 39:5

Types and s. | THOM 315:23
shaft s., at random sent | SCOT 266:13
shag common cormorant (or s.) | ISHE 169:12
shake Earth must s. | HORA 164:9
only S.-scene in a country | GREE 147:4
s. off the dust | BIBL 43:24
shaken S. and not stirred | FLEM 130:1
s. me by the hand | WESL 332:8
shakers movers and s. | O'SH 238:1
Shakespeare less S. he | BROW 70:12
Our sweetest S. | MILT 220:7
reproduce works of S. | WILE 335:26
S. by flashes of lightning | COLE 96:23
S. unlocked his heart | WORD 341:2
She had read S. | WELL 331:14
S.—the nearest thing | OLIV 236:5
When I read S. | LAWR 194:22
Shakespearean That S. rag | BUCK 72:2
Shakespeherian S. Rag | ELIO 122:25
Shalimar loved beside the S. | HOPE 162:19
shallow s. in himself | MILT 222:30
Shalott Lady of S. | TENN 312:4
shalt Thou s. have no other gods | BIBL 34:12
shame mourn with her in s. | EMEC 124:7
s. unto him | BIBL 49:29
terrible s. for me | YOKO 344:8
waste of s. | SHAK 290:8
Shannon green banks of S. | CAMP 81:2
shantih S., shantih | ELIO 122:29
shape s. of things to come | WELL 331:17
shapen s. in wickedness | BOOK 61:27
shaping s. spirit of imagination | COLE 95:22
shark s. has pretty teeth | BREC 66:11
sharks s. circling, and waiting | CLAR 93:15
Sharon rose of S. | BIBL 39:3
sharp 'Tis a s. remedy | RALE 254:7
sharpening s. my oyster knife | HURS 167:9
sharper s. than a serpent's tooth | SHAK 277:11
sharpness s. of death | BOOK 58:12
shaves and takes a train | WHIT 333:7
she chaste, and unexpressive s. | SHAK 269:27
life and loves of a s.-devil | WELD 331:2
S. sells sea-shells | SULL 305:16
S. who must be obeyed | HAGG 149:3
That not impossible s. | CRAS 103:4
shearers sheep before her s. | BIBL 40:18
shears resembles a pair of s. | SMIT 298:10
with th' abhorrèd s. | MILT 220:14
sheaves bring his s. with him | BOOK 63:17
Sheba Another S. queen | WITH 337:19
queen of S. | BIBL 36:2
shed prepare to s. them now | SHAK 276:19
shall his blood be s. | BIBL 33:21
sheep Feed my s. | BIBL 48:22
found my s. which was lost | BIBL 46:30
get back to these s. | ANON 11:19
giveth his life for the s. | BIBL 47:38
hills like young s. | BOOK 63:5
hungry s. look up | MILT 220:15
in s.'s clothing | BIBL 43:10
like lost s. | BOOK 58:5
like s. have gone astray | BIBL 40:17
savaged by a dead s. | HEAL 154:8
s. before her shearers | BIBL 40:18
s. born carnivorous | FAGU 125:21
s. in sheep's clothing | CHUR 92:16
s. on his right hand | BIBL 45:8
s. that have not a shepherd | BIBL 36:16
s., that were wont to be | MORE 227:24
s. to pass resolutions | INGE 168:21
two hundred years like a s. | TIPU 318:7
sheet brought in the white s. | GARC 135:21
England's winding s. | BLAK 55:15

turn over the s. | SAND 264:14
waters were his winding s. | BARN 25:11
wet s. | CUNN 105:1
shelf s. life of the modern | TRIL 319:10
shell prettier s. | NEWT 233:15
thou s. of death | MIDD 217:20
Shelley did you once see S. | BROW 70:21
shells choirs of wailing s. | OWEN 238:22
shelter s. from the stormy blast | WATT 329:13
shelves symmetry of s. | LAMB 192:3
shepherd call you, S. | ARNO 15:13
Dick the s. | SHAK 278:23
God of love my S. is | HERB 157:21
good s. | BIBL 47:38
like a s. | BIBL 40:9
Lord is my s. | BOOK 61:6
Lord's my s. | SCOT 266:28
my s. is | BAKE 23:4
sheep that have not a s. | BIBL 36:16
sweet unto a s. | GREE 147:3
shepherds s. abiding in the field | BIBL 46:3
s. and butchers | VOLT 326:8
s. give a grosser name | SHAK 273:9
s. watched their flocks | TATE 309:13
sheriff I shot the s. | MARL 212:4
Sherman general (yes mam) s. | CUMM 104:16
sherry s. flowing into second-rate whores | PLOM 246:7
shibboleth Say now S. | BIBL 35:6
shield faith shall be my s. | ASKE 16:16
Our S. and Defender | GRAN 145:15
trusty s. | LUTH 204:18
shieling From the lone s. | GALT 135:16
shift let me s. for myself | MORE 228:3
shilling s. life will give you | AUDE 18:18
shine Arise, s. | BIBL 40:20
Boy you can gimme a s. | GORD 144:17
Let your light so s. | BIBL 42:17
Lord make his face s. | BIBL 34:23
s., and run to and fro | BIBL 41:22
s. on, harvest moon | NORW 235:1
shines s. and stinks | RAND 254:13
shining s. from shook foil | HOPK 162:22
s. morning face | SHAK 269:21
S. nowhere but in the dark | VAUG 323:3
woman of s. loveliness | YEAT 343:22
ship all I ask is a tall s. | MASE 214:17
build your s. of death | LAWR 194:20
like a sinking s. | WOOL 339:12
O S. of State | LONG 201:18
s. has weathered every rack | WHIT 333:20
s. in a black storm | WEBS 330:19
S. me somewhere | KIPL 188:1
s. on the sea | GARC 136:1
Sink me the s., Master Gunner | TENN 313:23
What is a s. | BURT 76:16
ships Hell to s. | AESC 2:23
launched a thousand s. | MARL 212:6
little s. of England | GUED 148:8
Of shoes—and s. | CARR 84:6
s. empty of men | NICI 233:22
s. have been salvaged | HALS 150:12
s. sail like swans asleep | FLEC 129:24
S. that pass in the night | LONG 202:6
something wrong with our bloody s. | BEAT 26:11
stately s. go on | TENN 310:12
There go the s. | BOOK 62:25
to the sea in s. | BOOK 63:1
we've got the s. | HUNT 166:24
wooden wall is your s. | THEM 315:17
shire That s. which we may call | DRAY 116:6
shires bugles calling from sad s. | OWEN 238:22
Round both the s. | HOUS 165:4
shirt Song of the S. | HOOD 162:7

shit shock-proof s. detector HEMI 156:5
shiver praised and left to s. JUVE 179:19
  tremble and s. HOOD 161:22
shoal bank and s. of time SHAK 279:19
shoals s. of herring MACC 206:24
shock Future s. TOFF 318:12
  S.-headed Peter HOFF 160:19
  s. of the new DUNL 118:8
  s. of your joy HUGH 166:13
  short, sharp s. GILB 140:12
  we shall s. them SHAK 277:4
shocked s. by this subject BOHR 57:9
shocking looked on as something s. PORT 249:15
shocks s. the magistrate RUSS 262:24
shoe cast out my s. BOOK 62:5
  s.'s latchet BIBL 47:22
shoes in cheap s. AMIE 4:18
  Of s.—and ships CARR 84:6
  Put off thy s. BIBL 34:1
shoeshine riding on a smile and a s. MILL 218:14
shook monk who s. the world MONT 226:20
  more it's s. it shines HAMI 150:14
  s. hands with time FORD 131:7
  Ten days that s. the world REED 255:13
shoot S., if you must WHIT 334:4
  s. me in my absence BEHA 27:17
  s. the Hippopotamus BELL 28:7
  s. the pianist ANON 9:11
  s. the sleepy, green-coat man HOFF 160:18
  They's horses don't they MCCO 207:2
  young idea how to s. THOM 317:9
shoots green s. of recovery LAMO 192:16
  man who s. him gets caught MAIL 209:18
shop back to the s. LOCK 201:10
  foul rag-and-bone s. YEAT 342:14
shopkeepers nation of s. ADAM 2:3
  nation of s. NAPO 231:10
  nation of s. SMIT 297:9
shore for the further s. VIRG 324:22
  s. Of the wide world KEAT 183:2
  sounds by the s. YEAT 343:7
  stretch from s. to shore WATT 329:12
  unknown and silent s. LAMB 192:6
shores wilder s. of love BLAN 56:19
shorn green grass s. BACO 21:13
short Anger is a. madness HORA 163:22
  long and the s. and the tall HUGH 166:7
  nasty, brutish, and s. HOBB 160:3
  s., sharp shock GILB 140:12
  s. time to live BOOK 60:23
  Take s. views SMIT 298:8
  That lyf so s. CHAU 88:24
  while to make it s. THOR 317:17
shorter time to make it s. PASC 241:14
shot be s. at HARD 152:5
  Certain men the English s. YEAT 343:9
  I s. the sheriff MARL 212:4
  s. at for sixpence a-day DIBD 109:13
  s. heard round the world EMER 124:9
  They've s. our fox BIRC 54:7
shots of the best s. VOLT 326:9
shoulder giant's s. to mount on COLE 96:22
  left s.-blade GILB 140:16
shoulders Borne on our s. BROW 70:6
  City of the Big S. SAND 264:7
  from her s. did fall WYAT 342:2
  grow beneath their s. SHAK 284:12
  on the s. of giants NEWT 233:14
  on your young s. SPAR 299:23
  s. held the sky suspended HOUS 164:26
  s. of giants BERN 31:4
shout shouted with a great s. BIBL 34:31
  s. that tore hell's concave MILT 221:12

S. with the largest DICK 111:5
shouting thunder and the s. BIBL 37:14
  tumult and the s. KIPL 188:5
show business like s. business BERL 30:20
  s. any just cause BOOK 60:16
  s. business with blood BRUN 71:20
  s. that you have one CHES 89:10
showers with his s. soote CHAU 88:4
showery S., Flowery, Bowery ELLI 124:1
showeth true love is, it s. DE P 108:19
showing worth s. DANT 106:2
shreds king of s. and patches SHAK 272:25
  thing of s. and patches GILB 140:6
shrewishly speaks very s. SHAK 288:8
shrieks Not louder s. POPE 249:7
shrimp s. learns to whistle KHRU 185:17
shrink all the boards did s. COLE 96:13
shroud April s. KEAT 182:7
  stain the stiff dishonoured s. ELIO 122:19
  striped s. THOM 316:19
shrug with a patient s. SHAK 282:6
shudder s. in the loins engenders YEAT 343:8
shuffle s. the cards CERV 86:15
shuffled s. off this mortal coil SHAK 272:1
shun let me s. that SHAK 277:21
shut Men s. their doors SHAK 287:21
  ought to be s. up JOHN 174:22
  S. up he explained LARD 193:8
shutter before her on a s. THAC 315:1
  click the s. EISE 120:17
shuttered s. mansion FITZ 129:11
si S. possis recte HORA 163:20
Sibyl saw the S. at Cumae ROSS 260:20
Sibyllam Nam S. quidem Cumis PETR 244:11
sick do not make me s. WHIT 333:24
  do the s. no harm NIGH 234:12
  extremely s. PRIO 251:11
  half's. of shadows TENN 312:4
  I am s., I must die NASH 231:20
  Rose, thou art s. BLAK 56:13
  s. and wicked AUST 20:4
  s. for home KEAT 182:14
  they that are s. BIBL 43:19
  when he is s. JOHN 176:11
sickness age, grief, or s. KING 186:6
  falling s. SHAK 276:2
  in s. and in health BOOK 60:18
  s. that destroyeth BOOK 62:17
Sidcup get down to S. PINT 245:3
side my hand into his s. BIBL 48:20
  on every s. BOOK 61:13
  on our s. today MACA 206:5
  on the other s. BUNY 73:12
  on the s. of those ANOU 13:7
  passed by on the other s. BIBL 46:16
  S. by side WOOD 339:5
  Who is on my s. BIBL 36:31
sides said on both s. ADDI 2:12
Siegfried washing on the S. Line KENN 184:6
sieve in a s. I'll thither sail SHAK 278:28
  went to sea in a S. LEAR 195:11
sifted s. a nation STOU 304:18
sigh s. no more, ladies SHAK 284:1
sighed S. and looked THOM 317:11
  s. as a lover GIBB 139:7
  s. his soul SHAK 282:26
sighing poor soul sat s. SHAK 284:32
sighs on the Bridge of S. BYRO 78:2
sight in the s. of God BOOK 60:14
  thousand years in thy s. BOOK 62:14
sights few more impressive s. BARR 25:17
sign if you s. this BRUG 71:16
  In this s. shalt thou conquer CONS 99:14

Jews require a s. BIBL 49:22
outward and visible s. BOOK 60:11
Queen must s. BAGE 22:19
signal do not see the s. NELS 232:7
signed hand that s. the paper THOM 316:5
I s. my death warrant COLL 97:7
What I have s. GRIF 147:15
significance s. of an event CART 85:2
signo In hoc s. vinces CONS 99:14
signs multiply my s. and my wonders BIBL 34:4
no 'white' or 'coloured' s. KENN 184:13
read s. of the times CHOI 90:16
s. and wonders BIBL 47:29
s. of the times BIBL 44:9
words are but the s. JOHN 173:11
silence Deep is the s. DRIN 116:10
easy step to s. AUST 19:20
eternal s. PASC 241:17
foster-child of s. KEAT 181:27
Gospel of S. MORL 228:9
Go to where the s. is GOOD 144:14
I kept s. BOOK 61:18
My gracious s., hail SHAK 270:9
other side of s. ELIO 121:10
rest is s. SHAK 273:22
S. alone is great VIGN 324:4
S. augmenteth grief DYER 118:19
s. in heaven BIBL 52:12
s. of a dream ROSS 260:11
s. of the law HOBB 160:4
S., sing to me HOPK 162:24
With s. and tears BYRO 79:19
silenced because you have s. him MORL 228:10
silent All s., and all damned WORD 340:18
Laws are s. CICE 92:29
mornings are strangely s. CARS 84:20
one must be s. WITT 337:21
Paris was French—and s. TUCH 320:13
s. in seven languages BAGE 22:15
S., upon a peak in Darien KEAT 182:19
strong, s. man MORL 228:9
t is s. ASQU 17:1
unlocked her s. throat GIBB 139:10
silk breed the s. SHAK 284:29
he was shot s. STRA 304:22
make a s. purse MORT 229:5
s. makes the difference FULL 135:2
s. stockings JOHN 174:17
soft as s. remains HILL 158:24
silken s. terms precise SHAK 278:20
silks in s. my Julia goes HERR 158:10
sillier s. than a silly laugh CATU 86:1
silliest s. woman can manage a clever man KIPL 188:27
silly such a s. question STER 302:20
You were s. like us AUDE 18:3
silvae paulum s. super his HORA 164:21
silvas inter s. Academi HORA 164:4
silver all the Georgian s. MACM 208:12
bringing gold, and s. BIBL 36:4
for a handful of s. BROW 70:16
in her s. shoon DE L 108:10
Selling off the family s. MACM 208:12
s. apples of the moon YEAT 343:24
s. cord be loosed BIBL 38:34
s. foot in his mouth RICH 256:18
s. plate on a coffin CURR 105:6
s., snarling trumpets KEAT 181:4
There's a s. lining FORD 131:9
thirty pieces of s. BIBL 45:11
time hath to s. turned PEEL 243:1
Silvia Who is S. SHAK 288:35
similia S. similibus curantur ANON 12:23
Simon real S. Pure CENT 86:12

simple and never s. WILD 334:22
beautiful and s. HENR 156:19
C'est tellement s. PRÉV 251:4
I'm a s. man LOWR 204:5
too clear, too s. STEN 302:14
simplicitas O sancta s. HUSS 167:10
simplicity Cultivate s. LAMB 192:10
elegant s. STOW 304:20
holy s. JERO 172:3
O holy s. HUSS 167:10
s. of the three per cents DISR 112:25
simplify s. me when I'm dead DOUG 115:5
sin And the s. I impute BROW 71:8
beauty is only s. deep SAKI 263:15
brother s. against me BIBL 44:17
dark world of s. BICK 53:17
fall into no s. BOOK 58:19
go, and s. no more BIBL 47:35
hate the s. AUGU 19:5
He that is without s. BIBL 47:34
I had not known s. BIBL 49:14
in s. hath my mother BOOK 61:27
lose the s. POPE 247:2
My s., my soul NABO 230:17
no s. but ignorance MARL 212:10
physicists have known s. OPPE 236:17
Shall we continue in s. BIBL 49:10
single venial s. NEWM 233:2
S. is behovely JULI 179:10
s. not BIBL 50:19
taketh away the s. BIBL 47:23
wages of s. is death BIBL 49:13
we have no s. BIBL 51:32
Which is my s. DONN 113:25
Would you like to s. ANON 11:5
your s. will find you out BIBL 34:26
sincerely s. want to be rich CORN 100:6
Sindh I have S. WINK 337:15
sinews Money is the s. of love FARQ 126:11
money the s. of war BACO 21:28
s. of the soul FULL 134:26
s. of war CICE 92:28
sing come, let us s. BOOK 62:18
I'll s. you twelve O ANON 7:17
I s. of brooks HERR 157:26
I, too, s. America HUGH 166:8
Places where they s. BOOK 58:20
Silence, s. to me HOPK 162:24
S. 'em muck MELB 216:3
s. in a hempen string FLET 130:6
s. in the robber's face JUVE 180:2
s. like birds i' the cage SHAK 278:9
S. me a song STEV 304:2
S., my tongue FORT 131:19
s. the body electric WHIT 333:19
S. unto the Lord BOOK 61:14
s. unto the Lord BOOK 62:21
think that they will s. to me ELIO 122:14
thousand tongues to s. WESL 331:24
Who would not sing for S. MILT 220:10
world in ev'ry corner s. HERB 157:8
singeing s. of the King of Spain's Beard DRAK 116:1
singer s. of an empty day MORR 228:16
singing exercise of s. BYRD 77:18
hear mermaids s. DONN 114:11
like a s. bird ROSS 260:10
nest of s. birds JOHN 174:16
s. of birds BIBL 39:4
s. still dost soar SHEL 293:30
suddenly burst out s. SASS 265:2
waves of thy sweet s. SHEL 293:18
single but a s. thought HALM 150:11
come not s. spies SHAK 273:3

single (cont.)
s. in the field — WORD 341:9
s. man in possession — AUST 19:24
with a s. hair — DRYD 117:13
sings instead of bleeding, he s. — GARD 136:3
why the caged bird s. — DUNB 118:5
sinister strange and s. — JAME 170:21
sink S. me the ship, Master Gunner — TENN 313:23
sinking like a s. ship — WOOL 339:12
sinned More s. against than sinning — SHAK 277:20
s. against heaven — BIBL 46:33
s. exceedingly — MISS 223:26
sinner confessions of a justified s. — HOGG 161:1
Love the s. — AUGU 19:5
s. that repenteth — BIBL 46:31
to me a s. — BIBL 47:8
who is that young s. — HOUS 164:23
sinners favoured s. slain — WESL 332:3
God and s. reconciled — WESL 331:23
miserable — BOOK 59:3
publicans and s. — BIBL 43:18
S.; of whom I am chief — BIBL 51:7
s. to repentance — BIBL 43:20
s.' ways prosper — HOPK 163:6
sinning More sinned against than s. — SHAK 277:20
sins Be all my s. remembered — SHAK 272:3
Her s. are forgiven — BIBL 46:12
His s. were scarlet — BELL 28:24
manifold s. and wickedness — BOOK 58:4
multitude of s. — BIBL 51:29
s. are attempts to fill — WEIL 330:22
s. be as scarlet — BIBL 39:10
s. of the fathers — BOOK 59:19
sint *S. ut sunt* — CLEM 94:10
Sion remembered thee, O S. — BOOK 63:23
sirens Blest pair of S. — MILT 219:9
Sirmio S., bright eye — CATU 85:21
Sisera fought against S. — BIBL 35:2
sister my s., my spouse — BIBL 39:7
s. and my sister's child — COWP 101:22
s. throw up a lot — WALK 326:19
s., thy first-begotten — SWIN 308:3
trying to violate your s. — STRA 304:23
sisterhood S. is powerful — MORG 228:7
sisters And so do his s. — GILB 140:29
harmonious — MILT 219:9
s. under their skins — KIPL 187:24
weird s. — SHAK 279:2
Sistine on the S. Chapel roof — YEAT 343:27
sit So I did s. and eat — HERB 157:17
Teach us to s. still — ELIO 121:15
sits I s. and thinks — PUNC 252:20
sitting stay s. down — CART 85:3
situation s. excellent — FOCH 130:16
six Rode the s. hundred — TENN 310:15
S. hundred threescore and six — BIBL 52:16
sixpence bang—went s. — PUNC 252:12
sixty past S. it's the young — AUDE 18:19
turned s. — ALLE 4:11
When I'm s. four — LENN 197:16
Skiddaw S. saw the fire — MACA 206:2
skies danced the s. — MAGE 209:8
paint the sable s. — DRUM 116:13
thou climb'st the s. — SIDN 295:9
watcher of the s. — KEAT 182:19
skilled S. or unskilled — HORA 164:3
skin beauty being only s.-deep — KERR 185:1
Can the Ethiopian change his s. — BIBL 40:25
castle of my s. — LAMM 192:14
my s. is red — SITT 296:9
s. of my teeth — BIBL 37:8
skull beneath the s. — ELIO 122:30
skins sisters under their s. — KIPL 187:24

skipped mountains s. like rams — BOOK 63:5
skipper s. had taken his little daughter — LONG 202:9
skirmish trivial s. fought near Marathon — GRAV 146:6
skivvies take a dozen s. — MCGR 207:14
skull place of a s. — BIBL 48:11
s., and the feet — BIBL 36:32
s. beneath the skin — ELIO 122:30
sky diamond in the s. — TAYL 309:21
evening is spread out against the s. — ELIO 122:9
pie in the s. — HILL 159:2
prisoners call the s. — WILD 335:15
shoulders held the s. suspended — HOUS 164:26
wide and starry s. — STEV 304:6
Skye Over the sea to S. — BOUL 65:6
Over the sea to S. — STEV 304:2
slag post-industrial s.-heap — DRAB 115:21
slain fifty thousand men s. — WALP 327:21
new-s. knight — BALL 24:13
s. a thousand men — BIBL 35:9
s. his thousands — BIBL 35:23
s. think he is slain — EMER 124:8
slander one to s. you — TWAI 321:6
slang S. is a language — SAND 264:12
slanged sneered and s. — BELL 28:14
slaughter lamb to the s. — BIBL 40:18
slave always the s. of the other — LERM 197:22
Better be a s. — BRON 67:10
female worker slave of that s. — CONN 99:4
freedom to the s. — LINC 199:7
half s. — LINC 199:6
s.-morality — NIET 234:10
s.'s condition — EURI 125:10
you were a Christian s. — HENL 156:10
slavery S. is — SUMN 306:4
S. they can have — BURK 74:3
sold off into s. — TRUT 320:12
state of s. — GILL 141:11
testimony against s. — DOUG 115:8
wise and good in s. — MACA 205:14
slaves Air for S. to breathe — ANON 9:7
at the mill with s. — MILT 222:32
Britons never will be s. — THOM 317:8
Englishmen never will be s. — SHAW 291:12
millions of royal s. — GENE 137:19
S. cannot breathe in England — COWP 101:29
S. of the Lamp — ARNO 15:3
sons of former s. — KING 186:11
slavish O imitators, you s. herd — HORA 164:3
slay s. and slay and slay — MACA 206:5
slayer s. think he slays — EMER 124:8
slew the s. — MACA 206:4
slays If any man thinks he s. — UPAN 321:24
man thinks he s. — BHAG 32:16
slayer think he s. — EMER 124:8
sleekit Wee, s., cow'rin' — BURN 75:30
sleep borders of s. — THOM 316:15
Care-charmer S. — DANI 105:14
Care-charming S. — FLET 130:8
Death and his brother S. — SHEL 293:20
do I wake or s. — KEAT 182:16
grey and full of s. — YEAT 344:1
How s. the brave — COLL 97:11
I lay me down to s. — ANON 9:3
In s. a king — SHAK 289:35
in soot I s. — BLAK 56:5
Let us s. now — OWEN 239:1
little s. — BIBL 37:22
Macbeth does murder s. — SHAK 280:9
Macbeth shall s. no more — SHAK 280:10
Me biful for to s. — LANG 192:27
miles to go before I s. — FROS 134:14
One short s. past — DONN 113:20
Shake off this downy s. — SHAK 280:17

S. after toil SPEN 300:14
s. and a forgetting WORD 340:10
s. is so deep CHAN 87:11
S. no more SHAK 280:9
s. of a labouring man BIBL 38:20
S. on Blest pair MILT 222:5
S. on (my Love!) KING 186:6
S. shall neither night SHAK 279:1
S. to wake BROW 69:19
slept an azure-lidded s. KEAT 181:8
some must s. SHAK 272:16
two gates of S. VIRG 325:2
We shall not all s. BIBL 50:7
sleepers seven s. den DONN 114:7
s. in that quiet earth BRON 67:15
sleepeth not dead, but s. BIBL 43:23
sleeping Lay your s. head AUDE 18:7
s. with an elephant TRUD 320:5
sleepless s. soul that perished WORD 340:25
s. with cold commemorative ROSS 260:18
sleeps Homer sometimes s. BYRO 78:25
it s. obedience PAIN 239:14
Now s. the crimson petal TENN 313:14
while the world s. NEHR 232:3
sleepwalker assurance of a s. HITL 159:18
sleeve heart upon my s. SHAK 284:7
sleeves Americanism with its s. rolled MCCA 206:18
language that rolls up its s. SAND 264:12
slepen s. al the nyght with open ye CHAU 88:5
slept His saints s. ANON 13:6
slew s. his master BIBL 36:30
s. the slayer MACA 206:4
slimy thousand s. things COLE 96:16
slings s. and arrows SHAK 272:1
slippered lean and s. pantaloon SHAK 269:23
slit S. your girl's KING 187:2
slits s. the thin-spun life MILT 220:14
sliver envious s. broke SHAK 273:10
Sloane S. turned secular saint BURC 73:14
slop woman with a s.-pail HOPK 163:10
slopes butler's upper s. WODE 338:7
sloth Shake off dull s. KEN 184:1
slouches S. towards Bethlehem YEAT 343:20
slough friendly bombs, fall on S. BETJ 32:2
s. was Despond BUNY 72:22
slow come he s. SCOT 266:15
comes ever s. DRAY 116:4
telling you to s. down ANON 6:11
Time is too s. VAN 322:15
slowly angel to pass, flying s. FIRB 128:1
Architecture acts the most s. DIMN 111:25
Make haste s. AUGU 19:8
mills of God grind s. LONG 202:1
Run s. OVID 238:10
Science moves, but s. TENN 312:13
twist s. in the wind EHRL 120:9
sluggard foul s.'s comfort CARL 82:13
thou s. BIBL 37:21
slughorn Dauntless the s. BROW 69:27
sluicing browsing and s. WODE 338:6
slumber little s. BIBL 37:22
s. did my spirit steal WORD 341:8
S.'s chain had bound me MOOR 227:20
slumbers Golden s. kiss your eyes DEKK 108:2
slums gay intimacy of the s. WAUG 329:19
slush pure as the driven s. BANK 24:24
small big squadrons against the s. BUSS 77:1
both great and s. COLE 96:18
day of s. nations CHAM 86:18
grind exceeding s. LONG 202:1
s., but perfectly formed COOP 99:23
s. college WEBS 330:4
S. is beautiful SCHU 265:18

s. Latin JONS 178:7
s.-talking world FRY 134:19
still s. voice BIBL 36:13
that cannot reach the s. SPEN 300:19
smaller s. fleas to bite 'em SWIF 307:11
smallest s. amount of lying BUTL 77:10
s. room of my house REGE 255:14
smart girls that are so s. CARE 82:10
smatch some s. of honour SHAK 276:31
smell ancient and fish-like s. SHAK 287:9
I s. the blood SHAK 277:28
Money has no s. VESP 323:15
s. and hideous hum GODL 142:11
s. a rat ROCH 258:8
s. too strong STER 302:21
sweet keen s. ROSS 260:19
smelleth s. the battle afar off BIBL 37:14
smells s. like roses JOHN 173:5
smile Asians could still s. HEAD 154:7
call me that, s. WIST 337:18
has a nice s. GROM 148:2
hear a s. CROS 104:8
my Julia's lips do s. HERR 158:2
riding on a s. and a shoeshine MILL 218:14
s., and be a villain SHAK 271:20
S. at us, pay us CHES 89:27
s. dwells a little longer CHAP 87:13
s. of cosmic Cheshire cat HUXL 167:19
s. of fate DYER 118:21
s., smile, smile ANON 10:19
smiler s. with the knyf CHAU 88:15
smiles daggers in men's s. SHAK 280:20
s. surface of the sea PLUT 246:9
S. through her tears HOME 161:18
smite ready to s. once MILT 220:16
s. all the firstborn BIBL 34:8
s. thee on thy right cheek BIBL 42:18
smith Chuck it, S. CHES 89:16
s., a mighty man is he LONG 202:7
s. of his own fortune CLAU 93:22
smithy village s. stands LONG 202:7
smoke s.-filled room SIMP 296:6
S. gets in your eyes HARB 151:6
s. of their torment BIBL 52:18
Stygian s. JAME 170:8
smoking s. flax BIBL 40:12
smooth I am a s. man BIBL 33:28
never did run s. SHAK 282:33
smote s. the king of Israel BIBL 36:18
s. them hip and thigh BIBL 35:8
snail creeping like s. SHAK 269:21
said a whiting to a s. CARR 83:23
s.'s on the thorn BROW 70:27
snake like a wounded s. POPE 248:4
scotched the s. SHAK 280:23
s. hidden in the grass VIRG 325:9
snakes no s. to be met with JOHN 175:26
S. eat Frogs STEV 303:4
You spotted s. SHAK 283:13
snapper s.-up of unconsidered trifles SHAK 289:7
snare mockery, and a s. DENM 108:16
rabbit in a s. STEP 302:18
s. of the fowler BOOK 63:16
s. of the hunter BOOK 62:16
world's great s. SHAK 268:23
snares s. of death BOOK 63:8
Snark S. was a Boojum CARR 84:16
snatched s. from Jove MANI 211:5
s. the lightning TURG 320:18
sneaky snouty, s. mind NICO 234:2
sneer devil in his s. BYRO 78:11
refute a s. PALE 240:1

sneer (*cont.*)
teach the rest to s. POPE 247:10
with solemn s. BYRO 78:1
sneering I was born s. GILB 140:7
sneezing people s. ROBI 258:5
snip S.! Snap! Snip HOFF 160:16
snipe so wet you could shoot s. off him POWE 250:19
snobbery S. with Violence BENN 29:21
snorted Or s. we DONN 114:7
snotgreen s. sea JOYC 178:27
snouty s., sneaky mind NICO 234:2
snow amid the winter's s. CASW 85:11
congealed s. PARK 241:2
dark over the s. THOM 316:17
few acres of s. VOLT 325:21
I, this incessant s. DE L 108:9
like the s. geese OKPI 236:3
shivering in the s. SOUT 299:21
s. before the summer sun TECU 310:6
s. came flying BRID 66:19
s. of ferne yere CHAU 88:27
S. on snow ROSS 260:12
very s.-broth SHAK 281:28
white as s. BIBL 39:10
snows s. of yesteryear VILL 324:6
snowy S., Flowy, Blowy ELLI 124:1
snug s. little Island DIBD 109:15
so And s. do I HARD 152:3
soap S. and education TWAI 321:4
What! no s. FOOT 130:23
soapflakes sell Jack like s. KENN 184:17
soar creep as well as s. BURK 74:11
not to s. MACA 205:23
soaring s. ever singest SHEL 293:30
sober at least not s. JOHN 174:10
Be s., be vigilant BIBL 51:30
godly, righteous, and s. life BOOK 58:7
s. me up FITZ 129:7
S., steadfast, and demure MILT 219:21
to Philip s. ANON 5:20
social no religion but s. WESL 332:4
self-love and s. POPE 248:19
s. and economic experiment HOOV 162:11
s. contract ROUS 261:10
S. Contract is nothing more WELL 331:16
socialism S. can only arrive VIER 324:2
s. would not lose its human face DUBČ 117:18
socialists We are all s. now HARC 151:11
society action of s. upon itself TOCQ 318:11
affluent s. GALB 135:9
consolidates s. JOHN 174:14
Great S. JOHN 173:3
live in s. ARIS 14:18
moves about in s. CHOI 90:16
no such thing as S. THAT 315:12
One great s. WORD 340:24
S. needs to condemn MAJO 209:22
sock Jonson's learnèd s. MILT 220:7
socks inability to put on your s. GONC 144:12
Socrates contradict S. SOCR 298:23
soda Sermons and s.-water BYRO 78:20
sodomy rum, s., prayers, and the lash CHUR 92:3
sods s. with our bayonets turning WOLF 338:11
soft her s. and chilly nest KEAT 181:6
s. answer BIBL 37:32
s. as the dawn LOVE 203:10
s. as the dawn THUR 318:1
s. can wear away the hard TALM 309:8
s. under-belly of Europe CHUR 91:21
s., unhappy sex BEHN 28:1
s. was the sun LANG 192:26
softly s. and suddenly vanish CARR 84:15
S. come and softly go ORRE 236:21

Tread s. YEAT 343:2
softness s. of my body will be guarded LOWE 203:13
soggy s. little island UPDI 321:25
soil grows in every s. BURK 74:3
powers of the s. RICA 256:13
sojourners s., as were all our fathers BIBL 36:34
sold Never s. the truth TENN 313:1
s. all that he had BIBL 44:3
s. my reputation FITZ 128:21
what cannot be s.—liberty GRAT 146:1
soldier British s. can stand up to SHAW 290:24
chocolate cream s. SHAW 290:22
death, who had the s. singled DOUG 115:6
For a s. I listed DIBD 109:13
having been a s. JOHN 175:25
s. is no more exempt STER 302:25
s. of the Great War ANON 9:21
s.'s life is terrible hard MILN 218:26
s.'s pride BROW 70:15
what the s. said DICK 111:8
soldiers gives England her s. MERE 216:25
Old s. never die FOLE 130:18
Onward, Christian s. BARI 25:5
our s. slighted QUAR 253:3
scarlet s. AUDE 18:14
s., mostly fools BIER 53:20
S., this solitude DE L 108:9
s. under me BIBL 43:14
steel my s.' hearts SHAK 275:6
young Argentinian s. RUNC 261:21
sole *amor che muove il* s. DANT 105:22
s. of her foot BIBL 33:20
solemn Sapping a s. creed BYRO 78:1
solidity appearance of s. to pure wind ORWE 237:19
solitary Be not s. BURT 76:18
ennui of a s. existence BONA 57:18
s. Highland lass! WORD 341:9
Their s. way MILT 222:25
till I am s. JOHN 174:20
solitude feel his s. more keenly VALÉ 322:6
s. of the sea HARD 151:20
s. Through which we go DE L 108:9
solitudinem S. *faciunt pacem* TACI 308:14
Solomon all S.'s wisdom BIBL 36:2
anointed S. BIBL 35:36
greater than S. BIBL 43:35
S. in all his glory BIBL 42:27
S. loved many strange women BIBL 36:5
S. wrote the Proverbs NAYL 231:22
soluble art of the s. MEDA 215:19
solution either part of the s. CLEA 94:5
final s. HEYD 158:18
kind of s. CAVA 86:6
total s. GOER 142:15
some fool s. of the people LINC 199:15
somebody When every one is s. GILB 139:22
someone it was s. else ROGE 259:3
s., somewhere, may be happy MENC 216:13
something s. for Posterity ADDI 2:15
S. must be done EDWA 120:3
s. of the night WIDD 334:12
S. should be done EDWA 120:3
Time for a little s. MILN 219:5
sometime see me s. WEST 332:15
woman is a s. thing HEYW 158:21
sometimes s. always RICH 257:3
somewhat s. against thee BIBL 52:4
somewhere get s. else CARR 84:5
S. over the rainbow HARB 151:9
son bear a s. BIBL 39:17
bear our s. KYD 191:4
be called thy s. BIBL 46:33
brought forth her firstborn s. BIBL 46:3

Fitzdotterel's eldest s.	BROU 68:7
Forgive your s.	JOYC 179:5
hateth his s.	BIBL 37:31
his only begotten S.	BIBL 47:28
if his s. ask bread	BIBL 43:6
leichter of a fair s.	ELIZ 123:3
my s. was dead	BIBL 46:35
O Absalom, my s., my son	BIBL 35:33
S. of man	BIBL 43:16
S. of Saint Louis	FIRM 128:2
This is my beloved S.	BIBL 42:9
This is my s.	TENN 313:30
unto us a s. is given	BIBL 39:19
what's a s.	KYD 191:3
wise s.	BIBL 37:25
With a king's s.	SURR 306:6
Woman, behold thy s.	BIBL 48:13
your s.'s tender years	JUVE 180:6
song ane end of ane old s.	OGIL 235:21
becomes a sightless s.	TENN 311:33
before his presence with a s.	BOOK 62:22
burthen of his s.	BICK 53:16
glorious s. of old	SEAR 267:2
hate a s. that has sold	BERL 30:22
My s. is love unknown	CROS 104:8
On wings of s.	HEIN 155:8
play a s. for me	DYLA 119:6
sold my reputation for a s.	FITZ 128:21
s. charms the sense	MILT 221:21
s. of praise be sung	POTT 249:24
S. of the Shirt	HOOD 162:7
s. that found a path	KEAT 182:14
s. that never ends	GOET 142:17
s. the Syrens sang	BROW 68:21
start a s.	VIRG 325:11
till I end my s.	SPEN 300:24
Time is our tedious s.	MILT 220:27
unto the Lord a new s.	BOOK 61:14
unto the Lord a new s.	BOOK 62:21
what they teach in s.	SHEL 292:27
wine and s.	LUTH 204:19
songs all their s. are sad	CHES 89:18
For ever piping s.	KEAT 182:2
s. of Apollo	SHAK 278:24
s. of pleasant glee	BLAK 56:4
s. of Spring	KEAT 182:22
sweetest s. are those	SHEL 293:32
with a few good s.	FAIT 125:22
sonnet Scorn not the S.	WORD 341:2
sonnets written s. all his life	BYRO 78:22
sons Bears all its s. away	WATT 329:15
cruel s. of Cain	LE G 196:17
God's s. are things	MADD 209:4
s. and daughters of Life	GIBR 139:15
s. and daughters shall prophesy	BIBL 41:14
s. Of Belial, flown with insolence	MILT 221:1
S. of the dark and bloody ground	O'HA 235:23
s. of the morning	HEBE 154:19
soot in s. I sleep	BLAK 56:5
sophistry s. and illusion	HUME 166:19
soporific lettuce is 's.'	POTT 249:25
Sordello but the one 'S.'	POUN 250:7
sorrow any sorrow like unto my s.	BIBL 40:27
beguile thy s.	SHAK 287:27
doubt and s.	BARI 25:6
Give s. words	SHAK 281:12
glut thy s.	KEAT 182:7
increaseth s.	BIBL 38:15
In s. thou shalt bring forth	BIBL 33:11
Labour without s.	RUSK 262:17
Love's s. lasts all through life	FLOR 130:14
more in s. than in anger	SHAK 271:5
S. is tranquillity remembered	PARK 240:22

sphere of our s.	SHEL 293:28
such sweet s.	SHAK 286:23
whipping S. driveth	GREV 147:12
with s. to the grave	BIBL 33:35
sorrows man of s.	BIBL 40:16
When s. come	SHAK 273:3
sorry having to say you're s.	SEGA 267:8
heartily s.	BOOK 59:27
S. for itself	LAWR 194:19
sorts all s. and conditions	BOOK 59:9
sought Being, of all, least s. for	CRAN 102:21
soul bitterness of his s.	BIBL 41:24
captain of my s.	HENL 156:8
casket of my s.	KEAT 182:20
city of the s.	BYRO 78:3
dark night of the s.	FITZ 129:8
dark night of the s.	JOHN 172:14
engineers of the s.	GORK 144:18
every subject's s.	SHAK 275:3
give his own s.	BOLT 57:17
Heaven take my s.	SHAK 277:3
if I have a s.	ANON 9:5
iron entered into his s.	BOOK 62:26
lie in the s.	JOWE 178:17
like s., my soul	SHAK 270:20
longeth my s. after thee	BOOK 61:21
lose his own s.	BIBL 45:28
lover of my s.	WESL 332:1
My s., bear thou thy part	GURN 148:14
my s. is white	BLAK 56:9
My s., like to a ship	WEBS 330:19
My s., there is a country	VAUG 322:20
No coward s. is mine	BRON 67:12
no s. to be damned	THUR 318:2
not engineers of the s.	KENN 184:15
One s. inhabiting two bodies	ARIS 14:21
owe my s. to the company store	TRAV 319:6
Perdition catch my s.	SHAK 284:19
Poor intricated s.	DONN 114:22
pray the Lord my s. to take	ANON 9:3
save his s.	BIBL 41:2
sighed his s.	SHAK 282:26
sinews of the s.	FULL 134:26
s. doth magnify the Lord	BIBL 45:33
s. in bliss	SHAK 278:6
s. is an enchanted boat	SHEL 293:18
s. is Christ's abode	KEBL 183:18
s. is marching on	ANON 8:4
s. of fire	JOHN 174:5
s. of our dear brother	BOOK 60:25
s. of pleasure	BEHN 27:20
S. of the Age	JONS 178:5
s. shall be required of thee	BIBL 46:23
S., thou hast much goods	BIBL 46:22
than that one s.	NEWM 233:2
two to bear my s. away	ANON 8:17
with s. so dead	SCOT 266:10
souls engineers of human s.	STAL 301:12
letters mingle s.	DONN 114:16
open windows into men's s.	ELIZ 123:11
S. of poets dead	KEAT 181:26
s. of the righteous	BIBL 41:21
they have no s.	COKE 95:18
times that try men's s.	PAIN 239:8
Two s.	HALM 150:11
sound alive with the s. of music	HAMM 150:24
in a s. body	JUVE 180:4
s. and fury	SHAK 281:24
s. of surprise	BALL 24:19
what is that s.	AUDE 18:14
soundbite s. all an interviewer	BENN 29:17
sounds better than it s.	NYE 235:8
S. and sweet airs	SHAK 287:14

sounds (*cont.*)
s. will take care CARR 83:22
soup cake of portable s. BOSW 64:21
S. of the evening CARR 83:25
sour How s. sweet music is SHAK 285:30
s. grapes BIBL 41:1
source s. of little visible delight BRON 67:14
south fickle is the S. TENN 313:9
full of the warm S. KEAT 182:11
nor yet from the s. BOOK 62:8
S. is avenged BOOT 64:8
Yes, but not in the S. POTT 250:2
southern bore me in the s. wild BLAK 56:9
S. trees bear strange HOLI 161:4
souvenirs s. sont cors de chasse APOL 13:10
sovereign Here lies our s. lord ROCH 258:10
he will have no s. COKE 95:19
S. has BAGE 22:21
subject and a s. CHAR 87:21
to be a S. ELIZ 123:4
sovereignty s. is an artificial soul HOBB 159:22
sovereynetee Wommen desiren to have s. CHAU 88:21
soviet Communism is S. power LENI 197:4
S. Union has indeed FULB 134:22
sow hath the s. by the right ear HENR 156:15
old s. that eats her farrow JOYC 178:25
s. in tears BOOK 63:17
went forth to s. BIBL 44:1
sower s. went forth BIBL 44:1
soweth whatsoever a man s. BIBL 50:15
sown s. the wind BIBL 41:12
where thou hast not s. BIBL 45:6
space art of how to waste s. JOHN 173:9
S. isn't remote HOYL 166:1
untrespassed sanctity of s. MAGE 209:9
spaces s. between the houses FENT 126:19
vacant interstellar s. ELIO 121:25
spaceship regarding S. Earth FULL 134:24
spade call a s. a spade BURT 76:10
nominate a s. a spade JONS 177:15
Spain Lady of S. REAV 255:5
leave S. JUAN 179:7
not into the hands of S. TENN 313:23
rain in S. LERN 197:26
span Contract into a s. HERB 157:18
Eternity shut in a s. CRAS 103:3
Less than a s. BACO 22:7
Spaniards thrash the S. too DRAK 116:3
spanieled hearts That s. me SHAK 268:24
Spanish To God I speak S. CHAR 87:27
spare Brother can you s. a dime HARB 151:7
do in his s. time GILL 141:11
s. the beechen tree CAMP 81:1
s. your country's flag WHIT 334:4
Woodman, s. that tree MORR 228:15
spared better s. a better man SHAK 274:12
spareth s. his rod BIBL 37:31
spark s.-gap is mightier HOGB 160:21
Vital s. POPE 246:25
waitest for the s. from heaven ARNO 15:18
sparkling s. in the sun CHAN 87:10
sparks as the s. fly upward BIBL 37:5
s. among the stubble BIBL 41:22
sparrow fall of a s. SHAK 273:16
My lady's s. is dead CATU 85:18
s. hath found her an house BOOK 62:10
s. should fly swiftly BEDE 27:5
sparrows five s. sold BIBL 46:21
pass through for the s. GALB 135:10
two s. sold BIBL 43:26
Spartans Go, tell the S. SIMO 296:2
speak Books will s. plain BACO 21:7
dare not s. its name DOUG 115:2

didn't s. up NIEM 234:5
fears to s. of Ninety-Eight INGR 169:5
grief that does not s. SHAK 281:12
let him now s. BOOK 60:16
Let us not s. of them DANT 105:18
neither s. they BOOK 63:7
province of knowledge to s. HOLM 161:9
s. for Britain BOOT 64:10
S. for England AMER 4:15
s. ill of everybody except oneself PÉTA 244:7
S., Lord BIBL 35:14
S. softly ROOS 259:22
S. the speech SHAK 272:9
S. ye comfortably BIBL 40:6
whereof one cannot s. WITT 337:21
speaking s. picture, with this end SIDN 295:12
speaks He s. to Me VICT 323:20
spear Bring me my s. BLAK 55:27
With a burning s. ANON 11:4
spears s. into pruninghooks BIBL 39:11
stars threw down their s. BLAK 56:15
spectacle no s. so ridiculous MACA 205:15
spectre s. of Communism MARX 214:8
speech abridging the freedom of s. CONS 99:15
deal by s. BACO 21:19
freedom of the press's s. TWAI 321:8
function of s. to free BRAN 66:2
our concern was s. ELIO 121:27
Speak the s. SHAK 272:9
s. be alway with grace BIBL 51:3
s. created thought SHEL 293:17
S. happens not to be STAË 301:11
s. is like a cracked kettle FLAU 129:17
s. only to conceal VOLT 326:2
true use of s. GOLD 143:24
verse is a measured s. BACO 20:20
speechless s. real BARZ 25:22
speed S., bonnie boat BOUL 65:6
s. far faster than light BULL 72:9
s. glum heroes SASS 264:26
s. the going guest POPE 248:23
S. the parting guest POPE 248:23
Unsafe at any s. NADE 230:19
spell lies beneath your s. HOPE 162:19
s. it with a "V" DICK 111:7
speller fancy of the s. DICK 111:7
spelling s. is Wobbly MILN 219:6
spend s. more time with my family FOWL 132:12
whatever you have, s. less JOHN 176:10
spending Getting and s. WORD 341:18
S. again SHAK 289:32
spent all passion s. MILT 223:6
speranza LASCIATE OGNI S. DANT 105:17
spew s. thee out of my mouth BIBL 52:6
sphere motion in one s. SHAK 274:10
s., the cone CÉZA 86:16
these walls thy s. DONN 114:13
spice s. of life COWP 102:1
spicy s. nut-brown ale MILT 220:5
spider said a s. to a fly HOWI 165:21
seen the s. SHAK 289:2
s.'s touch, how exquisitely fine POPE 248:13
spiders like s.' webs ANAC 5:3
seen s. fly EDWA 120:5
Weaving s. come not SHAK 283:14
spies come not single s. SHAK 273:3
voluntary s. AUST 19:21
spill let them not s. me MACN 208:20
S. your guts at Wimbledon CONN 99:6
spilt as water s. on the ground BIBL 35:32
spin great world s. for ever TENN 312:15
neither do they s. BIBL 42:27
ye whores, go s. PEMB 243:5

spinach I say it's s. — WHIT 333:8
spindle s. or mutilate — ANON 6:13
spinnage world of gammon and s. — DICK 110:7
spinners long-legged s. — SHAK 283:14
spinning at evening s. — RONS 259:11
spinning-wheel wee bit s. — BLAM 56:17
spires dreaming s. — ARNO 15:22
  three steeple-house s. — FOX 132:15
spirit blithe S. — SHEL 293:29
  Come, Holy S. — LANG 193:3
  commend my s. — BIBL 47:14
  commend my s. — BOOK 61:12
  did my s. steal — WORD 341:8
  forge his s. spirit — GUEV 148:11
  Love is a s. — SHAK 290:13
  never approached my s. — METT 217:16
  no more s. in her — BIBL 36:2
  no s. can walk abroad — SHAK 270:25
  pardlike S. — SHEL 292:17
  poor in s. — BIBL 42:14
  present in s. — BIBL 49:24
  renew a right s. — BOOK 61:28
  shaping s. of imagination — COLE 95:22
  s. giveth life — BIBL 50:9
  s. hath rejoiced — BIBL 45:33
  s. indeed is willing — BIBL 45:17
  S. of Delight — SHEL 293:24
  s. of Elijah — BIBL 36:20
  S. of God — BIBL 32:21
  s. of party — WASH 328:21
  s. of the chainless mind — BYRO 79:15
  s. of the place — VIRG 325:3
  s. passed before my face — BIBL 37:4
  Thy s. walks abroad — SHAK 276:30
spirits insult to the s. — RED 255:6
  ruffle up your s. — SHAK 276:23
  s. from the vasty deep — SHAK 274:3
  S. of well-shot woodcock — BETJ 31:19
  thousands of s. dancing — CUDW 104:11
  two primal S. — ZORO 345:11
spiritu Et cum s. tuo — MISS 223:24
spiritual inward and s. grace — BOOK 60:11
  Millions of s. creatures — MILT 222:4
  not being a s. people — MANC 210:17
spiritualist you are a s. — SZAS 308:10
spiritus Sancte S. — LANG 193:3
spit no gun, but I can s. — AUDE 18:15
  s. upon my Jewish gabardine — SHAK 282:7
splash Old pond, leap-s. — BASH 26:2
splendeat late qui s. — HORA 163:11
splendid by the vision s. — WORD 340:11
  having a s. Court — BAGE 22:18
  s. and a happy land — GOLD 143:13
splendour s. falls on castle walls — TENN 313:5
  s. in the grass — WORD 340:13
  Stung by the s. — BROW 69:29
splendoured many-s. thing — THOM 317:2
splinters teeth like s. — CAUS 86:4
split care what a s. infinitive — FOWL 132:11
  make all s. — SHAK 283:3
  s. Ireland — BRUG 71:16
  when I s. an infinitive — CHAN 87:6
spoiled s. the Egyptians — BIBL 34:9
spoils belong the s. — MARC 211:16
spoken never have s. yet — CHES 89:27
  Rome has s. — AUGU 19:6
spongy Patrol the halls on s. shoes — WILB 334:19
spoon ate with a runcible s. — LEAR 195:16
  trifle with the s. — POPE 247:27
spoons counted our s. — EMER 124:11
  let us count our s. — JOHN 174:25
  world locks up its s. — SHAW 291:13
sport ended his s. with Tess — HARD 151:18

  kill us for their s. — SHAK 277:30
  owe to s. — CAMU 81:9
  s. for our neighbours — AUST 20:1
  s. of kings — SOME 299:1
  s. of kings — SURT 306:8
  s. with Amaryllis — MILT 220:12
sports s. of love — JONS 177:23
sportsman s. is a man who — LEAC 195:5
spot Out, damned s. — SHAK 281:14
  Tip me the black s. — STEV 303:22
  with a s. I damn him — SHAK 276:27
spots leopard change his s. — BIBL 40:25
  s. rather a credit — COMP 98:4
spotted You s. snakes — SHAK 283:13
spouse my sister, my s. — BIBL 39:7
  President's s. — BUSH 76:20
sprang s. to the stirrup — BROW 70:14
spread except it be s. — BACO 21:24
  S. ALARM AND DESPONDENCY — PENI 243:8
  s. my dreams under your feet — YEAT 343:3
spring Alas, that s. should vanish — FITZ 129:1
  bloom in the s. — GILB 140:19
  can S. be far behind — SHEL 293:10
  commonly called the s. — COWP 102:10
  easing the S. — REED 255:9
  Falsehood has a perennial s. — BURK 73:23
  hounds of s. — SWIN 307:17
  In the s. a young man's fancy — TENN 312:7
  in the s. to follow — SWIN 308:2
  new come s. — SHAK 285:29
  no second s. — PHIL 244:16
  No s., nor summer beauty — DONN 113:17
  only the right to s. — FOND 130:19
  Pierian s. — DRAY 116:7
  rifle all the breathing s. — COLL 97:10
  songs of S. — KEAT 182:22
  s. has kept in its folds — ARAG 13:19
  s. now comes unheralded — CARS 84:20
  s. of business — BAGE 22:11
  s. shut up, a fountain sealed — BIBL 39:7
  Sweet lovers love the s. — SHAK 270:4
  Sweet s., full of sweet days — HERB 157:22
  this s. of love — SHAK 288:34
  year's at the s. — BROW 70:27
springe woodcock to mine own s. — SHAK 273:18
springes s. to catch woodcocks — SHAK 271:10
sprite fleeting, wav'ring s. — HADR 148:17
sprites s. and goblins — SHAK 289:1
spur Fame is the s. — MILT 220:13
  I have no s. — SHAK 279:22
  s. of all great minds — CHAP 87:17
spurious s. brat, Tom Jones — RICH 256:22
spurs this day to wynne his s. — EDWA 120:2
  win his s. — EDWA 120:2
spy s. out the land — BIBL 34:24
  s. who came in from the cold — LE C 196:5
squad awkward s. fire over me — BURN 76:1
squadrons big s. against the small — BUSS 77:1
  winged s. of the sky — MILM 218:22
square S. deal afterwards — ROOS 260:1
squat s. like a toad — MILT 222:6
  s. pen rests — HEAN 154:11
squats s. on the hearthstone — QUIL 253:8
squawking seven stars go s. — AUDE 17:24
squeak s. and gibber — SHAK 270:23
  until the pips s. — GEDD 137:14
squeaking s. Cleopatra — SHAK 269:4
stab do I s. at thee — MELV 216:11
  No iron can s. the heart — BABE 20:16
  saw him s. — READ 254:19
stabat S. Mater dolorosa — JACO 169:23
staff cockle hat and s. — SHAK 272:32
  s. of faith to walk upon — RALE 254:2

staff (*cont.*)
thy rod and thy s. — BOOK 61:7
trustest upon the s. — BIBL 36:33
stag runnable s. — DAVI 106:13
S. at Bay — LEVI 198:7
stage All the world's a s. — SHAK 269:20
Don't put your daughter on the s. — COWA 101:8
On the s. — GOLD 143:19
played upon a s. — SHAK 288:28
this great s. of fools — SHAK 278:4
wonder of our s. — JONS 178:5
stages four s. of man — LINK 200:3
stagger s. like a drunken man — BOOK 63:2
stagnant fen Of s. waters — WORD 340:4
stagnation keeps life from s. — BURN 74:25
stained kick a hole in a s. glass window — CHAN 87:4
s. with their own works — BOOK 62:27
stair by a winding s. — BACO 21:15
stairs another man's s. — DANT 105:21
stake s. driven through his heart — O'BR 235:12
stale How weary, s., flat — SHAK 270:30
Stalingrad cultural S. — BALL 24:17
stalking like a s.-horse — SHAK 270:8
s.-horse to error — BOLI 57:13
s. in my chamber — WYAT 342:1
stall Baby in an ox's s. — BETJ 31:17
stamp physics or s. collecting — RUTH 263:4
stamps kill animals and stick in s. — NICO 234:3
stand By uniting we s. — DICK 111:18
can't s. the heat — TRUM 320:6
firm spot on which to s. — ARCH 14:2
Get up, s. up — MARL 212:3
Here's I — LUTH 204:16
I will s. by — GRIF 147:15
no time to s. and stare — DAVI 106:19
s. and look at them — WHIT 333:24
s. at the door, and knock — BIBL 52:7
S. by thyself — BIBL 40:21
S. by your man — WYNE 342:6
s. on either hand — MACA 206:8
s. out of my sun — DIOG 112:1
s. up for bastards — SHAK 277:9
s. up for Jesus — DUFF 117:23
s. up to anything except — SHAW 290:24
who only s. and wait — MILT 223:10
standard raise the scarlet s. — CONN 98:23
standards S. are always out of date — BENN 29:20
standing mantle of the s. pool — SHAK 277:25
ought to die s. — VESP 323:17
s. by my man — CLIN 94:13
stands S. Scotland — SHAK 281:11
S. the Church clock — BROO 67:21
sun now was — JOSE 178:5
star Being a s. has made it possible — DAVI 106:21
bright Occidental s. — BIBL 32:20
bright particular s. — SHAK 268:9
By a high s. our course — MACN 208:21
catch a falling s. — DONN 114:11
constant as the northern s. — SHAK 276:7
evening s. — MILT 222:24
guests s.-scattered — FITZ 129:2
guiding s. — CARS 84:19
guiding s. behold — DIX 113:10
Hitch your wagon to a s. — EMER 124:15
Knock at a s. — HERR 158:1
like a falling s. — MILT 221:15
moth for the s. — SHEL 293:28
O eastern s. — SHAK 269:8
S. captains glow — FLEC 129:21
s.-crossed lovers — SHAK 286:12
S. for every State — WINT 337:17
s.-led wizards — MILT 220:23
s.-spangled banner — KEY 185:6

s. to steer her by — MASE 214:17
Sunset and evening s. — TENN 310:18
There was a s. danced — SHAK 283:27
twinkle, little s. — TAYL 309:21
we have seen his s. — BIBL 42:2
with one bright s. — COLE 96:15
stardust We are s. — MITC 224:20
stare no time to stand and s. — DAVI 106:19
s. of the deer — WILB 334:17
stark Molly S.'s a widow — STAR 301:21
s. insensibility — JOHN 174:15
starless s. and bible-black — THOM 316:9
starlight S. and dewdrop — FOST 132:5
s. lit my lonesomeness — HARD 152:4
starred On a s. night — MERE 217:4
starry beautiful evening, very s. — WORD 339:14
entertain this s. stranger — CRAS 103:2
wide and s. sky — STEV 304:6
stars all Danaë to the s. — TENN 313:15
climb half-way to the s. — CROS 104:5
crown of twelve s. — BIBL 52:13
cut him out in little s. — SHAK 286:29
Far beyond the s. — VAUG 322:20
heaventree of s. — JOYC 179:4
looking at the s. — WILD 335:6
not in our s. — SHAK 275:30
of the months and s. — SWIN 307:16
puts the s. to flight — FITZ 128:14
seven s. go squawking — AUDE 17:24
s. are old — TAYL 309:22
s. came out — TENN 313:22
s. in her hair — ROSS 260:16
s. in their courses — BIBL 35:2
s. keep not their motion — SHAK 274:10
s. rush out — COLE 96:14
S. scribble on our eyes — CRAN 102:19
Stars, s. — SHAK 289:15
s.' tennis-balls — WEBS 330:14
s. threw down their spears — BLAK 56:15
s. through the window pane — KEAT 183:12
struggle to the s. — ANON 12:17
sun and the other s. — DANT 105:22
useful s. — PEPY 243:18
way to the s. — VIRG 325:4
with mites of s. — MAYA 215:15
you chaste s. — SHAK 284:33
starshine s. at night — STEV 303:31
starship voyages of the s. *Enterprise* — RODD 258:18
start end is where we s. from — ELIO 121:28
s. together and finish — BEEC 27:8
started s. like a guilty thing — SHAK 270:24
starter few thought he was a s. — ATTL 17:10
starve Let not poor Nelly s. — CHAR 87:26
let our people s. — NYER 235:9
starved s. poet — LOCK 201:10
starving you have a s. population — DISR 112:5
state all were for the s. — MACA 206:9
bosom of a single s. — DURH 118:15
done the s. some service — SHAK 285:4
first duty of a S. — RUSK 262:18
glories of our blood and s. — SHIR 294:27
Here's a s. of things — GILB 140:14
I am the S. — LOUI 202:18
in a free s. — CAVO 86:9
mine was the middle s. — DEFO 107:13
no such thing as the S. — AUDE 18:17
Only in the s. — HEGE 155:5
O Ship of S. — LONG 201:18
reinforcement of the S. — CAMU 81:8
rule the s. — DRYD 116:13
S. business is a cruel trade — HALI 150:6
S. for every Star — WINT 337:17
s. has no place — TRUD 320:4

S. is not 'abolished' ENGE 124:23
s. to be endured JOHN 173:25
to what a s. dost Thou bring TERE 314:12
While the S. exists LENI 197:2
stately S. Homes of England COWA 101:10
s. homes of England HEMA 155:18
S., plump Buck Mulligan JOYC 178:26
with his s. stride MACA 206:10
statements all previous s. inoperative ZIEG 345:4
states goodly s. and kingdoms KEAT 182:18
statesman set a s. right YEAT 343:13
s. is a politician TRUM 320:8
Too nice for a s. GOLD 143:18
station antique s. BEER 27:12
her s. keeping JACO 169:23
private s. ADDI 2:10
statistic million deaths a s. STAL 301:15
statistical life is s. improbability DAWK 107:2
statistics lies, damned lies and s. DISR 113:8
uses s. as a drunken man LANG 192:25
We are just s. HORA 163:21
stature Malice is of a low s. HALI 150:2
status quo restored the s. SQUI 301:8
statutes keep my s. BIBL 34:21
stay here I s. MACM 208:7
If we can't s. here alive MONT 226:18
love is here to s. GERS 138:16
S. for me there KING 186:6
things to s. as they are LAMP 192:18
steady S., boys, steady GARR 136:7
steal silently s. away LONG 201:20
s. a goose ANON 10:12
s. from many, it's research MIZN 225:5
s. more than a hundred men PUZO 252:26
s. my Basil-pot KEAT 181:15
s. my thunder DENN 108:18
s. the very teeth ARAB 13:18
thieves break through and s. BIBL 42:24
Thou shalt not s. BIBL 34:16
stealing For de little s. O'NE 236:10
hanged for s. horses HALI 150:4
picking and s. BOOK 60:10
s. ducks ARAB 13:17
steals s. my purse SHAK 284:20
stealth Do good by s. POPE 248:30
steam employ s. navigation LARD 193:7
steamers little holiday s. PRIE 251:7
steed his s. was the best SCOT 266:16
milk-white s. BALL 24:11
steel All shod with s. WORD 339:23
clad in complete s. MILT 219:13
Give them the cold s. ARMI 14:22
long divorce of s. SHAK 275:20
more than complete s. ANON 7:18
S.-true and blade-straight STEV 304:1
with a line of s. RUSS 263:3
worthy of their s. SCOT 266:8
steeple North Church s. REVE 256:2
three s.-house spires FOX 132:15
steeples dreary S. of Fermanagh CHUR 91:9
s. far and near HOUS 165:4
steer s. their courses BUTL 77:6
stelle muove il sole e l'altre s. DANT 105:22
stem s. of Jesse BIBL 39:21
step first s. that is difficult DU D 117:22
One more s. along CART 84:25
one small s. for a man ARMS 15:1
stepped in blood S. in SHAK 281:3
stepping s. westward WORD 341:11
steps sad s., O Moon SIDN 295:9
uneasy s. Over the burning marl MILT 221:8
very long flight of s. GUIB 148:12
wandering s. and slow MILT 222:25

stern S. daughter of the voice of God WORD 340:15
sterner made of s. stuff SHAK 276:18
steward commended the unjust s. BIBL 46:36
stick carry a big s. ROOS 259:22
fell like the s. PAIN 239:10
rattling of a s. inside ORWE 237:23
s. and a string SWIF 307:14
sticketh friend that s. closer BIBL 37:37
stiffnecked thou art a s. people BIBL 34:19
still Because they liked me 's.' DICK 111:17
beside the s. waters BOOK 61:6
Be s. then, and know BOOK 61:26
heart is lying s. WORD 339:19
I'm s. here HOPE 162:18
S. glides the Stream WORD 340:27
s. point of the turning world ELIO 121:21
s., sad music WORD 340:3
s. small voice BIBL 36:13
s. they gazed GOLD 143:12
s.-vexed Bermoothes SHAK 287:4
stilly Oft, in the s. night MOOR 227:20
stilts nonsense upon s. BENT 30:2
stimulate S. the phagocytes SHAW 290:25
stimulation unnatural s. MILL 218:5
sting death, where is thy s. BIBL 50:8
s. like a bee ALI 4:5
where is thy s.-a-ling-a-ling ANON 9:4
stings s. you for your pains HILL 158:24
stir S. up, we beseech thee BOOK 59:15
stirbt er s. ab ENGE 124:23
stirred Shaken and not s. FLEM 130:1
something s. SIMP 296:4
stirrup sprang to the s. BROW 70:14
s. and the ground ANON 6:3
stirs Will that s. and urges HARD 151:21
stitch S.! stitch! stitch HOOD 162:7
stock Woman s. is rising CHIL 90:12
stocking glimpse of s. PORT 249:15
silk s.'s hanging down SELL 267:17
stockings thy yellow s. SHAK 288:24
stocks hurt in the s. BOOK 62:26
stoical s. scheme of supplying SWIF 307:3
stolen s. his wits away DE L 108:5
S. waters are sweet BIBL 37:24
stolid S. and stunned MARK 211:19
stomach army marches on its s. NAPO 231:7
for thy s.'s sake BIBL 51:9
no s. to this fight SHAK 275:8
s. of a king ELIZ 123:6
stone At his heels a s. SHAK 273:1
blossoming in s. LONG 201:23
bomb them back into the S. Age LEMA 197:1
flung the s. FITZ 128:14
give him a s. BIBL 43:6
give them the s. MONT 226:5
hollows out a s. OVID 238:13
let him first cast a s. BIBL 47:34
Let him not make me a s. MACN 208:20
like a s. wall BEE 27:7
look honestly like s. MOOR 227:7
make a s. of the heart YEAT 342:21
Raise the s. ANON 9:15
s. taken away BIBL 48:16
S. walls do not a prison make LOVE 203:6
s. which the builders refused BOOK 63:10
sword out of this s. MALO 210:9
This precious s. SHAK 285:12
through a piece of s. MOOR 227:8
Under every s. ARIS 14:12
Virtue is like a rich s. BACO 21:3
stones chose him five smooth s. BIBL 35:22
Sermons in s. SHAK 269:14
s. will teach you BERN 31:5

stony morre s. than a shore — WILL 336:10
stood should of s. in bed — JACO 169:22
stop come to the end: then s. — CARR 83:26
  could not s. for Death — DICK 111:12
  full s. at the right place — BABE 20:16
  kissing had to s. — BROW 71:10
  Might s. a hole — SHAK 273:12
  S. the world — NEWL 232:21
stoppeth s. one of three — COLE 96:8
stops buck s. here — TRUM 320:10
  know my s. — SHAK 272:17
storage thought in cold s. — SAMU 264:3
store in the s. we sell hope — REVS 256:3
storied S. of old — MILT 219:15
stories beset him round With dismal s. — BUNY 73:9
  S. to rede ar delitabill — BARB 24:25
  tell sad s. — SHAK 285:20
storm directs the s. — ADDI 2:6
  fled away into the s. — KEAT 181:10
  ship in a black s. — WEBS 330:19
  S. and stress — KAUF 180:21
Stormont Ulster Parliament at S. — GEOR 138:3
stormy dark and s. night — BULW 72:12
  S. weather — KOEH 189:20
story It's our *own* s. — THUR 318:1
  novel tells a s. — FORS 131:11
  s. and a byword — WINT 337:16
  s. chronicled — MALO 210:11
  s. need be long — THOR 317:17
  s. of our days — RALE 254:5
  tell my s. — SHAK 273:21
stout Collapse of S. Party — ANON 6:6
St Paul's ruins of S. — MACA 205:18
  ruins of S. — WALP 327:12
  S. had slipped down — SMIT 298:12
strabismus Dr S. (Whom God Preserve) — MORT 229:7
straight line which is accurately s. — WHEW 333:3
  no s. thing — KANT 180:15
  nothing ever ran quite s. — GALS 135:14
  street which is called S. — BIBL 48:28
  unflexible as s. — LOCK 201:5
strain s. at a gnat — BIBL 44:31
  s., Time's eunuch — HOPK 163:7
  That s. again — SHAK 288:3
strait S. is the gate — BIBL 43:9
strand Maypole in the S. — BRAM 66:1
  walk down the S. — HARG 152:8
strange s. and sinister — JAME 170:21
  s., and unnatural — SHAK 271:17
  stranger in a s. land — BIBL 33:38
strangeness s. in the proportion — BACO 21:4
stranger entertain this starry s. — CRAS 103:2
  I, a s. and afraid — HOUS 164:25
  Look, s. — AUDE 18:6
  never love a s. — BENS 30:1
  s. and alone — WOLF 338:16
  s., and ye took me in — BIBL 45:9
  s.? 'Eave 'arf a brick — PUNC 252:10
  s. in a strange land — BIBL 33:38
  S. than fiction — BYRO 79:7
  You may see a s. — HAMM 150:23
strangers courteous to s. — BACO 21:14
  entertain s. — BIBL 51:18
  on the kindness of s. — WILL 336:9
  we are s. before thee — BIBL 36:34
strangled And s. her — BROW 71:1
  s. with the guts — MESL 217:12
strangling s. in a string — HOUS 165:3
  S. is a very quiet death — WEBS 330:13
Stratford atte Bowe scole of S. — CHAU 88:8
straw all things as s. dogs — LAO 193:4
strawberries S. swimming in the cream — PEEL 242:23
strawberry of the s. — BUTL 77:16

S. fields forever — LENN 197:14
Strawberry Hill [S.] is — WALP 327:7
strawed where thou hast not s. — BIBL 45:6
stray If with me you'd fondly s. — GAY 137:4
strayed erred, and s. from thy ways — BOOK 58:5
streak thin red s. — RUSS 263:3
stream like an ever-rolling s. — WATT 329:15
  old mill by the s. — ARMS 14:23
  Still glides the S. — WORD 340:27
streamers s. waving in the wind — GAY 137:11
streams hart for cooling s. — TATE 309:11
  s. in the firmament — MARL 212:7
strebt so lang er s. — GOET 142:16
street don't do it in the s. — CAMP 80:20
  s. which is called Straight — BIBL 48:28
  sunny side of the s. — FIEL 127:18
streets children died in the s. — AUDE 18:1
  Down these mean s. — CHAN 87:5
  grass will grow in the s. — HOOV 162:14
  s. are paved with gold — COLM 97:13
  s. FLOODED — BENC 29:8
  s. that no longer exist — FENT 126:19
strength as the s. of ten — TENN 313:24
  from s. to strength — BOOK 62:11
  giant's s. — SHAK 281:29
  His s. the more is — BUNY 73:9
  ordained s. — BOOK 60:27
  our hope and s. — BOOK 61:25
  roll all our s. — MARV 213:23
  s. of an horse — BOOK 63:28
  s. with his arm — BIBL 45:34
  s. without insolence — BYRO 79:20
  tower of s. — SHAK 286:10
strengtheneth Christ which s. me — BIBL 50:29
stress Storm and s. — KAUF 180:21
stretch insight and the s. — BROW 69:18
  S. him out longer — SHAK 278:15
  s. the human frame — SCAR 265:8
stretched things he s. — TWAI 321:2
stricken I was a s. deer — COWP 102:2
  s. deer — SHAK 272:16
stride At one s. comes the dark — COLE 96:14
strife In place of s. — CAST 85:8
  none was worth my s. — LAND 192:21
  step towards an end of s. — GEOR 138:3
  s. is o'er — POTT 249:24
strike in doubt, s. it out — TWAI 321:12
  s. against public safety — COOL 99:20
  S. him — CALI 80:8
  s. it in anger — SHAW 291:18
  s. it out — JOHN 175:11
  yet afraid to s. — POPE 247:10
string end of a golden s. — BLAK 55:19
  one long yellow s. — BROW 71:1
  strangling in a s. — HOUS 165:3
  s. that ties — SHEL 294:7
  s. that ties them — MONT 226:14
  untune that s. — SHAK 287:28
stringent s. execution — GRAN 145:19
strip s. his sleeve — SHAK 275:10
striped s. like a zebra — KEAT 181:22
  s. shroud — THOM 316:19
stripling s. Thames — ARNO 15:16
strive need's not s. — CLOU 95:2
  s., to seek, to find — TENN 314:1
strives err while yet he s. — GOET 142:16
striving s. evermore for these — GREN 147:10
stroke none so fast as s. — COKE 95:15
strong all s. enough — LA R 193:18
  battle to the s. — BIBL 38:27
  battle to the s. — DAVI 106:14
  men be so s. — BOOK 62:15
  nature of s. people — BONH 58:3

only the S. shall thrive — SERV 268:1
out of the s. — BIBL 35:7
s., silent man — MORL 228:9
weak overcomes the s. — LAO 193:6
stronger on the side of the s. — TACI 308:19
stronghold safe s. — LUTH 204:18
strove s., and much repented — BYRO 78:17
s. with none — LAND 192:21
struck I s. the board — HERB 157:9
they s. at my life — FOX 132:15
structure good s. in a winding stair — HERB 157:15
struggle class s. — MARX 214:7
gods themselves s. — SCHI 265:13
s. between the artist man — SHAW 291:9
S. for Existence — DARW 106:8
s. for room — MALT 210:16
s. naught availeth — CLOU 95:4
What s. to escape — KEAT 181:28
struggles history of class s. — MARX 214:9
stubble sparks among the s. — BIBL 41:22
studies Fred's s. — ELIO 121:9
studio Sine ira et s. — TACI 308:16
studiously s. neutral — WILS 337:6
study craggy paths of s. — JONS 177:21
much s. is a weariness — BIBL 38:35
proper s. of mankind — POPE 248:15
proper s. of mankind is books — HUXL 167:14
s. of man is man — CHAR 88:3
s.'s ornament — MIDD 217:20
stuff Life too short to s. a mushroom — CONR 99:10
made of sterner s. — SHAK 276:18
Was there ever such s. — GEOR 137:25
stumbles how the strong man s. — ROOS 260:3
stumbling-block unto the Jews a s. — BIBL 49:23
stung S. by the splendour — BROW 69:29
stupid all questions were s. — WEIS 330:24
stupidest s. party — MILL 218:2
stupidity With s. the gods themselves — SCHI 265:13
stupidvision It is S. — TOYN 319:2
Sturm S. und Drang — KAUF 180:21
Stygian In S. cave forlorn — MILT 219:25
S. smoke — JAME 170:8
style cut, the s., the line — LOES 201:13
definition of a s. — SWIF 306:21
forges one's s. — ZOLA 345:8
has no real s. — PICA 244:19
murderer for fancy prose s. — NABO 230:18
only secret of s. — ARNO 16:5
see a natural s. — PASC 241:15
s. cannot be too clear — STEN 302:14
S. is life — FLAU 129:19
S. is the dress of thought — WESL 332:10
S. is the man — BUFF 72:7
sub Sighted s., sank same — MASO 214:18
subdue chasten and s. — WORD 340:3
s. the arrogant — VIRG 324:23
subdued My nature is s. — SHAK 290:5
subject Every s.'s duty — SHAK 275:3
Grasp the s. — CATO 85:16
Little s., little wit — CARE 82:9
shocked by this s. — BOHR 57:9
s. and a sovereign — CHAR 87:21
s. of a novel — MURA 230:3
s. of conversation — CHES 89:5
what it is to be a s. — ELIZ 123:4
subjects good of s. — DEFO 107:21
sublime egotistical s. — KEAT 183:11
My object all s. — GILB 140:15
step above the s. — PAIN 239:6
s. to the ridiculous — NAPO 231:5
sublimity S. is the echo — LONG 202:12
submerged s. tenth — BOOT 64:9
submit Must he s. — SHAK 285:22

subsistence S. only increases — MALT 210:15
substance wasted his s. — BIBL 46:32
subtle God is s. but not malicious — EINS 120:13
Now the serpent was more s. — BIBL 33:6
subtlest serpent s. beast — MILT 222:14
subtopia it will stick—s. — NAIR 230:20
suburb new s. beyond the runway — BETJ 31:20
suburbs In the south s. — SHAK 288:25
subversive Whatever is funny is s. — ORWE 237:20
subway in a New York s. — STRA 305:4
succeed How to s. in business — MEAD 215:17
not going to s. — MORT 229:4
succeeds Whenever a friend s. — VIDA 324:1
success bitch-goddess s. — JAME 171:4
command s. — ADDI 2:7
first requisite to s. — SPEN 300:1
this ecstasy, is s. — PATE 241:25
successful recipes that are always s. — VALÉ 322:5
S. crimes alone — DRYD 117:4
whether s. or otherwise — ADAM 2:1
successors dissatisfield with s. — JENK 172:1
successus Hos s. alit — VIRG 324:18
such of s. is the kingdom of God — BIBL 45:30
sucker Never give a s. an even break — FIEL 127:19
s. born every minute — BARN 25:12
sucking any s. dove — SHAK 283:4
suckle s. fools — SHAK 284:16
sucklings babes and s. — BOOK 60:27
sucks as a weasel s. eggs — SHAK 269:17
Sudan your 'ome in the S. — KIPL 187:16
sudden s. thought — BROW 69:29
too unadvised, too s. — SHAK 286:21
Sudeten problem of the S. Germans — HITL 159:20
sue Less used to s. — SCOT 266:7
s. its parents — WATS 328:27
Suez East of S. — KIPL 188:1
S. Canal — EDEN 119:18
suffer s. fools gladly — BIBL 50:12
S. the little children — BIBL 45:30
sufferance s. is the badge — SHAK 282:6
suffered S. under Pontius Pilate — BOOK 58:16
suffereth Charity s. long — BIBL 49:31
suffering About s. they were never wrong — AUDE 18:8
healed of a s. — PROU 251:19
put me to s. — METH 217:13
s. from the particular disease — JERO 172:5
sufficiency elegant s. — THOM 317:10
sufficient s. sacrifice — BOOK 60:4
S. unto the day — BIBL 43:1
sugar Oil, vinegar, s. — GOLD 143:17
sweetmeats and s.-plums — TROL 319:15
suicide longest s. note — KAUF 180:19
s. 25 years after his death — BEAV 26:17
s. kills two people — MILL 218:12
sui generis say I am s. — LONG 201:16
suis J'y s. — MACM 208:7
suitable s. case for treatment — MERC 216:20
suitor think you are Ann's s. — SHAW 291:10
sukebind s. hangs heavy — GIBB 139:11
Sule Skerry home it is the S. — BALL 23:18
sulk s. about having no boyfriend — FIEL 127:10
sulphur oat-cakes, and s. — SMIT 298:7
sultry where the climate's s. — BYRO 78:16
sum Cogito, ergo s. — DESC 109:2
With a great s. — BIBL 48:40
Sumatra giant rat of S. — DOYL 115:13
summer ensure s. in England — WALP 327:11
Eternal s. gilds them yet — BYRO 78:23
guest of s. — SHAK 279:18
if it takes all s. — GRAN 145:17
In a s. season — LANG 192:26
last rose of s. — MOOR 227:18
like a s. birdcage — WEBS 330:15

summer (cont.)
Like s. tempest | TENN 313:13
murmur of a s.'s day | ARNO 15:14
No spring, nor s. beauty | DONN 113:17
no s. progress | ANDR 5:10
one long bathing of a s.'s day | WORD 340:22
over the s. sea | TENN 313:22
Saint Martin's s. | SHAK 275:12
see in a s.'s day | SHAK 283:5
s. afternoon | JAME 170:27
S. has set in | COLE 96:27
s. is ended | BIBL 40:23
S. is icumen in | ANON 10:3
s.'s lease | SHAK 289:23
S. time and the livin' is easy | HEYW 158:20
thy eternal s. | SHAK 289:24
to a s.'s day | SHAK 289:23
summertime In s. on Bredon | HOUS 165:4
summons Upon a fearful s. | SHAK 270:24
summum S. bonum | CICE 92:24
sun against a setting s. | SHAK 287:21
all, except their s., is set | BYRO 78:23
At the going down of the s. | BINY 54:4
Born of the s. | SPEN 300:10
candle to the s. | SIDN 295:5
candle to the s. | YOUN 344:13
cannot make our s. Stand | MARV 213:23
especially Sir Brother S. | FRAN 133:2
golden apples of the s. | YEAT 343:24
I am too much i' the s. | SHAK 270:28
Juliet is the s. | SHAK 286:18
love that moves the s. | DANT 105:22
maketh his sun to rise | BIBL 42:20
maturing s. | KEAT 182:21
Mother, give me the s. | IBSE 168:11
no new thing under the s. | BIBL 38:14
nothing like the s. | SHAK 290:9
old fool, unruly s. | DONN 114:12
out in the midday s. | COWA 101:7
place in the s. | BÜLO 72:11
place in the s. | WILH 335:27
places Under the s. | HOUS 165:8
prayer at sinking of the s. | KORA 190:19
reign where'er the s. | WATT 329:12
soft was the s. | LANG 192:26
stand out of my s. | DIOG 112:1
staring at the s. | BELL 28:9
s. also rises | HEMI 156:3
s. does not set | SCHI 265:12
S.-girt city | SHEL 293:4
s. go down upon your wrath | BIBL 50:19
s. grows cold | TAYL 309:22
s. never sets | NORT 234:20
s. now stands | JOSE 178:15
S. of righteousness | BIBL 41:19
s. of York | SHAK 285:32
s. shall not burn thee | BOOK 63:13
S.'s rim dips | COLE 96:14
s. to me is dark | MILT 223:2
tired the s. with talking | CORY 100:14
under the midday s. | MILT 219:12
watched the s. going down | VAN 322:14
when the s. in bed | MILT 220:26
woman clothed with the s. | BIBL 52:13
sunbeam Jesus wants me for a s. | TALB 308:23
sunbeams s. out of cucumbers | SWIF 306:20
Sunday Here of a S. morning | HOUS 165:4
rainy S. in London | DE Q 108:20
She was the S. | CLAR 93:20
working week and S. best | AUDE 18:2
sundial s., and I make a botch | BELL 28:23
sunk s. beneath the wave | COWP 101:25
sunny s. pleasure-dome | COLE 96:5

s. side of the street | FIEL 127:18
sunrise Eternity's s. | BLAK 56:2
suns S., that set | JONS 177:22
sunset make a fine s. | MADA 209:2
S. and evening star | TENN 310:18
s. breezes shiver | NEWB 232:19
s. of my life | REAG 255:4
S. ran | BROW 70:10
sunsets Autumn s. exquisitely dying | HUXL 167:18
horror of s. | PROU 251:18
sunshine like s. after rain | SHAK 290:14
sunt Sint ut s. | CLEM 94:10
sup s. with my Lord Jesus Christ | BRUC 71:15
superfluity barren s. of words | GART 136:14
superfluous in the poorest thing s. | SHAK 277:15
nothing is s. | LEON 197:20
s. in me | ADAM 1:10
superior most s. person | ANON 8:20
S. people never make long visits | MOOR 227:10
superman I teach you the s. | NIET 234:6
It's S. | ANON 6:21
superseded has not been s. | LONG 202:11
superstition s. sets the whole world | VOLT 326:4
s. to enslave a philosophy | INGE 168:19
superstitions end as s. | HUXL 168:1
supped Hobson has s. | MILT 220:30
s. full with horrors | SHAK 281:23
supper Last-s.-carved-on-a-peach-stone | LANC 192:20
S. of the Lord | BOOK 60:11
supplications make our common s. | BOOK 58:22
supplies just bought fresh s. | BREC 66:9
support help and s. of the woman | EDWA 120:4
no invisible means of s. | BUCH 71:25
s. me when I am in the wrong | MELB 216:7
s. us all the day long | NEWM 233:4
supports s. with insolence | JOHN 173:16
suppose universe queerer than we s. | HALD 149:11
suppress power of s. | NORT 234:21
supreme in none s. | ARNO 15:25
surcease catch With his s. success | SHAK 279:19
sure What nobody is s. about | BELL 28:20
surface looks dingy on the s. | PIRS 245:7
surfeit s. by eating of a lamprey | FABY 126:17
surfing We are s. food | MACK 207:18
surge s. and thunder | LANG 192:24
surmise with a wild s. | KEAT 182:19
surprise Live frugally on s. | WALK 326:20
sound of s. | BALL 24:19
wise man by s. | LA F 191:15
surprised guilty thing s. | WORD 340:12
S. by joy | WORD 341:12
S. by unjust force | MILT 219:17
surrender die but do not s. | CAMB 80:16
I s. to you | GERO 138:13
unconditional and immediate s. | GRAN 145:16
we shall never s. | CHUR 91:15
surroundings I plus my s. | ORTE 236:22
sursum S. corda | MISS 224:3
survey monarch of all I s. | COWP 102:9
s. the wondrous cross | WATT 329:10
survival S. of the Fittest | DARW 106:9
s. of the fittest | SPEN 300:3
survive Only the paranoid s. | GROV 148:7
s. of us is love | LARK 193:11
survived I s. | SIEY 295:17
survivors more the s.' affair | MANN 211:7
Susan black-eyed S. came aboard | GAY 137:11
suspected New opinions are always s. | LOCK 201:3
suspension willing s. of disbelief | COLE 96:21
suspicion above s. | CAES 79:29
against despots—s. | DEMO 108:11
swaddling wrapped him in s. clothes | BIBL 46:3
swagman Once a jolly s. | PATE 242:1

swains all our s. commend her — SHAK 288:35
swallow and the s. a nest — BOOK 62:10
 before the s. dares — SHAK 289:11
 O summer s. — SWIN 308:3
 speed of a s. — BETJ 32:4
 s. a camel — BIBL 44:31
 S., my sister — SWIN 308:2
swamps across primeval s. — WODE 338:4
swan like a sleeping s. — SHEL 293:18
 silver s. — GIBB 139:10
 so much as a black s. — JUVE 179:23
 Sweet S. of Avon — JONS 178:9
 this pale s. — SHAK 289:20
Swanee down upon the S. River — FOST 132:8
swanlike He makes a s. end — SHAK 282:15
swans amongst tuneful s. — VIRG 325:13
 Dumb s., not chattering pies — SIDN 295:10
 I saw two s. — SPEN 300:23
 ships sail like s. asleep — FLEC 129:24
 s. of others are geese — WALP 327:15
swap s. horses when crossing — LINC 199:10
swear when very angry, s. — TWAI 321:11
swears Money doesn't talk, it s. — DYLA 119:4
sweat Blood, s., and tear-wrung — BYRO 77:22
 blood, toil, tears and s. — CHUR 91:14
 In the s. of thy face — BIBL 33:12
 spend our midday s. — QUAR 253:4
sweats Falstaff s. to death — SHAK 273:31
sweep Mountains of Mourne s. down — FREN 133:17
 s. the dust — SHAK 283:25
 Your chimneys I s. — BLAK 56:5
sweeping S. up the Heart — DICK 111:14
sweeps s. a room as for Thy laws — HERB 157:13
sweet Home, s. home — PAYN 242:10
 how it was s. — BROW 69:28
 How s. the moonlight sleeps — SHAK 282:28
 kiss me, s. and twenty — SHAK 288:13
 Life is very s. — BORR 64:16
 Pyramus is a s.-faced man — SHAK 283:5
 Stolen waters are s. — BIBL 37:24
 such s. sorrow — SHAK 286:23
 suck on a boiled s. — WESL 332:9
 S. and low — TENN 313:4
 S. are the uses of adversity — SHAK 269:14
 s. o' the year — SHAK 289:5
 s. peas, on tip-toe — KEAT 181:16
 S., soft, plenty rhythm — MORT 229:8
 s. the name of Jesus — NEWT 233:19
 took s. counsel — BOOK 62:2
sweeter s. also than honey — BOOK 61:4
 those unheard Are s. — KEAT 181:29
sweetly Lalage, who laughs so s. — HORA 164:8
sweetmeats s. and sugar-plums — TROL 319:15
sweetness came forth s. — BIBL 35:7
 s. and light — ARNO 15:27
 s. and light — SWIF 306:15
 waste its s. — GRAY 146:16
 where s. and light failed — FORS 131:12
sweets bag of boiled s. — CRIT 103:14
 discandy, melt their s. — SHAK 268:24
 last taste of s. — SHAK 285:11
 s. compacted lie — HERB 157:22
 S. into your list — HUNT 167:4
 s. of place with power — ROSE 260:7
 S. to the sweet — SHAK 273:14
swell s. a progress — ELIO 122:12
 Thou s.! Thou witty — HART 152:21
 What a s. party — PORT 249:20
swelling s. act — SHAK 279:7
swept empty, s., and garnished — BIBL 43:36
swift race is not to the s. — BIBL 38:27
 race is to the s. — DAVI 106:14
swiftness O s. never ceasing — PEEL 243:1

swimming Come softly s. — SPEN 300:23
 S. for his life — GLAD 141:19
 s. in the air — EDWA 120:5
swindles all truly great s. — HENR 156:19
swine pearls before s. — BIBL 43:4
swing ain't got that s. — MILL 218:21
 s. for it — KING 187:2
 S. low, sweet chariot — ANON 10:4
 Swing, s. together — CORY 100:13
swoop At one fell s. — SHAK 281:13
sword brave man with a s. — WILD 335:16
 but a s. — BIBL 43:27
 first drew the s. — CLAR 93:11
 His father's s. he has — MOOR 227:17
 I gave them a s. — NIXO 234:15
 My s., I give — BUNY 73:11
 nation shall not lift up s. — BIBL 39:11
 pen is worse than the s. — BURT 76:14
 pen mightier than the s. — BULW 72:15
 perish with the s. — BIBL 45:18
 s. out of this stone — MALO 210:9
 s. sleep in my hand — BLAK 55:27
 wield the s. of France — DE G 107:24
swords books are either dreams or s. — LOWE 203:14
 Keep up your bright s. — SHAK 284:10
 s. In our own proper entrails — SHAK 276:30
 s. into plowshares — BIBL 39:11
 s. shall play the orators — MARL 212:14
 ten thousand s. leapt — BURK 74:6
swore My tongue s. — EURI 125:9
syllables S. govern the world — SELD 267:13
syllogism conclusion of your s. — O'BR 235:14
symbols s. of a high romance — KEAT 181:5
symmetry fearful s. — BLAK 56:14
sympathy messages of s. — AYCK 20:9
 Tea and s. — ANDE 5:9
symphony s. like the world — MAHL 209:16
symptoms hundred good s. — POPE 249:11
syne For auld lang s. — BURN 75:5
Syrens song the S. sang — BROW 68:21
system rocked the s. — ROBI 258:6
 s. of outdoor relief — BRIG 66:21

T

T t is silent — ASQU 17:1
ta saying 'T.' to God — SPEN 300:8
table fall from their masters' t. — BIBL 44:8
 fell from the rich man's t. — BIBL 47:3
 patient etherized upon a t. — ELIO 122:9
 prepare a t. before me — BOOK 61:7
 round about thy t. — BOOK 63:20
 T., at the Communion-time — BOOK 59:17
tableau t. of crimes — VOLT 326:7
tables make it plain upon t. — BIBL 41:18
tablet keep taking The T. — THOM 316:20
taboo t.'d by anxiety — GILB 140:5
taffeta doublet of changeable t. — SHAK 288:20
 T. phrases — SHAK 278:20
tail Improve his shining t. — CARR 83:15
 O! thereby hangs a t. — SHAK 284:18
 sensations of its "t." — DISR 112:8
 t. that wagged — WATS 329:4
tainted t. wether of the flock — SHAK 282:18
take big enough to t. away everything — FORD 131:2
 T. a pair of sparkling eyes — GILB 139:21
 T., eat — BIBL 45:13
 T., eat, this is my Body — BOOK 60:5
 T. up the White Man's Burden — KIPL 188:17
 t. you in the morning — BALD 23:7

taken Lord hath t. away — BIBL 36:37
One shall be t. — BIBL 45:3
shall be t. away — BIBL 45:7
t. away my Lord — BIBL 48:17
takes if it t. all summer — GRAN 145:17
t. just like a woman — DYLA 119:5
taketh t. away the sin — BIBL 47:23
tale adorn a t. — JOHN 174:6
I could a t. unfold — SHAK 271:16
mere t. of a tub — WEBS 330:16
most tremendous t. of all — BETJ 31:17
round unvarnished t. — SHAK 284:11
t. Told by an idiot — SHAK 281:24
t. which holdeth children — SIDN 295:13
Trust the t. — LAWR 194:15
talent sister of t. — CHEK 89:2
T. develops in quiet places — GOET 142:22
T. does what it can — MERE 217:8
t. of a liar — BYRO 79:23
t. to amuse — COWA 101:5
t. which is death to hide — MILT 223:9
tomb of a mediocre t. — SMIT 297:21
talents career open to the t. — NAPO 231:9
If you have great t. — REYN 256:5
ministry of all the t. — ANON 8:16
talk gotta use words when I t. to you — ELIO 122:18
If you t. to God — SZAS 308:10
Money doesn't t., it swears — DYLA 119:4
Most English t. — JAME 170:15
people who can't t. — ZAPP 345:2
t. about the rest of us — ANON 10:8
t. like a lady — SHAW 291:29
t. of many things — CARR 84:6
t. on for ever — HAZL 154:3
t. the less — ZENO 345:3
we had a good t. — BOSW 65:1
world may t. of hereafter — COLL 97:2
talked least t. about by men — PERI 243:22
t. like poor Poll — GARR 138:8
talking know what we are t. about — RUSS 262:22
nation t. to itself — MILL 218:16
stop people t. — ATTL 17:12
tired the sun with t. — CORY 100:14
tall all I ask is a t. ship — MASE 214:17
divinely t. — TENN 310:21
for this the clay grew t. — OWEN 238:25
long and the short and the t. — HUGH 166:7
t. as a crane — SITW 296:11
taller t. than other men — HARO 152:12
tambourine Mr T. Man — DYLA 119:6
tame tongue can no man t. — BIBL 51:22
Tandy met wid Nappy T. — ANON 8:1
tangere Noli me t. — BIBL 53:13
tangled t. web we weave — SCOT 266:18
tangles t. of Neaera's hair — MILT 220:12
tango Takes two to t. — HOFF 160:12
tanks Get your t. off my lawn — WILS 336:20
tantum T. ergo sacramentum — THOM 315:23
T. religio potuit — LUCR 204:12
tapestry Turkey t. — HOWE 165:16
tar T.-baby ain't sayin' nuthin' — HARR 152:16
T. water — BERK 30:14
Tara through T.'s halls — MOOR 227:15
tarnished neither t. nor afraid — CHAN 87:5
Tarquin great house of T. — MACA 206:6
tarried too long we have t. — LEAR 195:15
tarry Why t. the wheels — BIBL 35:4
You may for ever t. — HERR 158:9
Tarzan Me T. — WEIS 330:25
task long day's t. — SHAK 268:25
what he reads as a t. — JOHN 174:24
tasks have been my t. — KOLL 190:3
tassel lure this t.-gentle — SHAK 286:22

tassie fill it in a silver t. — BURN 75:17
taste arbiter of t. — TACI 308:17
bouquet is better than the t. — POTT 250:3
create the t. — WORD 341:21
difference of t. in jokes — ELIO 121:4
ghastly good t. — BETJ 32:5
last t. of sweets — SHAK 285:11
nobody has any t. for them — VOLT 326:12
No! let me t. — BROW 71:2
T. is the feminine — FITZ 129:3
t. my meat — HERB 157:17
undoubtedly wanted t. — WALP 327:9
tasted books are to be t. — BACO 21:26
tasting T. of Flora — KEAT 182:10
Tat T. ist alles, nichts der Ruhm — GOET 142:20
taught Cristes loore He t. — CHAU 88:12
what we have t. her — GAY 137:1
You t. me language — SHAK 287:5
tax power to t. — MARS 213:4
soon be able to t. it — FARA 126:4
To t. and to please — BURK 73:24
taxation lottery is a t. — FIEL 127:13
T. without representation — OTIS 238:7
taxed world should be t. — BIBL 46:2
taxes as true . . . as t. — DICK 110:6
death and t. — DEFO 107:12
death and t. — FRAN 133:9
Death and t. and childbirth — MITC 224:21
little people pay t. — HELM 155:16
no new t. — BUSH 76:22
Sex and t. — JONE 177:11
taxing t. machine — LOWE 203:12
Tay Bridge of the Silv'ry T. — MCGO 207:10
tayl likerous t. — CHAU 88:19
tea and sometimes t. — POPE 249:3
honey still for t. — BROO 67:21
if this is t. — PUNC 252:19
some sipping t. — WORD 340:18
T., although an Oriental — CHES 90:1
T. and sympathy — ANDE 5:9
t. for two — CAES 79:27
t.'s out of the way — REED 255:10
teach change the people who t. — BYAT 77:17
Even while they t. — SENE 267:22
qualified to t. others — CONF 98:7
t. him rather to think — SHEL 292:12
T. me, my God and King — HERB 157:12
T. me to live — KEN 184:3
t. the torches — SHAK 286:16
t. the young idea — THOM 317:9
T. us to care — ELIO 121:15
t. young babes — SHAK 284:31
to t. and delight — SIDN 295:12
teacher for the t.'s sake — DEFO 107:16
teaches experience t. — TACI 308:20
He who cannot, t. — SHAW 291:16
teaching t. nations how to live — MILT 223:21
teacup crack in the t. opens — AUDE 17:25
tear dropped a t. upon the word — STER 302:24
T. him for his bad verses — SHAK 276:26
Wipe the t., baby dear — WEST 332:21
tears big t., for he wept — SHEL 293:6
bitter t. to shed — CORY 100:14
blood, toil, t. and sweat — CHUR 91:14
came her t. — TENN 313:13
crocodiles, that shed t. — BACO 21:35
Drop, drop, slow t. — FLET 130:10
enough of blood and t. — RABI 253:16
God will wipe away t. — BIBL 39:28
Hence those t. — TERE 314:6
If you have t. — SHAK 276:19
Nothing is here for t. — MILT 223:5
Smiling through her t. — HOME 161:18

sow in t.	BOOK 63:17
t. I cannot hide	HARB 151:6
T., idle tears	TENN 313:7
t. out the heart of it	KNOW 189:14
t. shed for things	VIRG 324:12
too deep for t.	WORD 340:14
wipe away all t.	BIBL 52:11
wipe away all t.	BIBL 52:25
With mine own t.	SHAK 285:27
With silence and t.	BYRO 79:19
tearsday moanday, t., wailsday	JOYC 178:20
teases Because he knows it t.	CARR 83:17
tea tray t. in the sky	CARR 83:20
technology advanced t. is	CLAR 93:19
T. . . . the knack of so arranging	FRIS 134:1
white heat of t.	WILS 336:17
tecum *Nec t. possum vivere*	MART 213:10
Ted isn't it, T.	LINE 199:17
teddy Now T. must run	KENN 184:19
T. Bears have their Picnic	BRAT 66:6
teems t. with hidden meaning	GILB 141:8
teeth dig our graves with our t.	SMIL 297:5
gnashing of t.	BIBL 43:15
he's got iron t.	GROM 148:2
old bitch gone in the t.	POUN 250:10
shark has pretty t.	BREC 66:11
skin of my t.	BIBL 37:8
steal the very t.	ARAB 13:18
t. are set on edge	BIBL 41:1
t. like splinters	CAUS 86:4
untying with the t.	BIER 53:19
teetotaller only a beer t.	SHAW 290:23
tekel MENE, T., UPHARSIN	BIBL 41:8
telegram visual t.	CASS 85:6
Telemachus mine own T.	TENN 313:30
telephones Tudor monarchy with t.	BURG 73:16
television daytime t.	TOYN 319:2
It's t., you see	HOWE 165:19
T. contracts imagination	WOGA 338:8
T. has brought back murder	HITC 159:15
T. has made dictatorship	PERE 243:20
T.? word is half Greek	SCOT 266:2
tell Don't ask, don't t.	NUNN 235:7
Go, t. the Spartans	SIMO 296:2
men of sense never t.	SHAF 268:7
t. her she mustn't	PUNC 252:14
T. it not in Gath	BIBL 35:27
T. me the old, old story	HANK 151:2
T. them I came	DE L 108:8
t. them of us and say	EDMO 120:1
telling pity beyond all t.	YEAT 343:14
Téméraire Fighting T.	NEWB 232:19
temper Keep me in t.	SHAK 277:12
lose your t. with the Press	PANK 240:10
t. Justice with mercy	MILT 222:21
temperate more lovely and more t.	SHAK 289:23
tempest Like summer's t.	TENN 313:13
temples out of which they build t.	KRIS 190:25
t. of his gods	MACA 206:7
tempora *O t., O mores*	CICE 92:25
temps *O t.! suspend ton vol*	LAMA 191:23
tempt T. not a desperate man	SHAK 286:35
t. the Lord thy God	BIBL 42:11
temptation enter not into t.	BIBL 45:17
everything except t.	WILD 335:5
last t. is the greatest treason	ELIO 122:16
maximum of t.	SHAW 291:17
resisting t.	KNOX 189:19
t. in the wilderness	BOOK 62:19
under t. to it	LOCK 201:6
tempus *fugit inreparabile t.*	VIRG 325:19
T. *edax rerum*	OVID 238:16
ten as the strength of t.	TENN 313:24

T.-sixty-six and all that	SELL 267:15
tenants T. of the house	ELIO 122:3
tendebantque *T. manus*	VIRG 324:22
tender dark and true and t.	TENN 313:9
I'll be irreproachably t.	MAYA 215:14
t. is the night	KEAT 182:12
t. mercies of the wicked	BIBL 37:27
tends t. and spares us	LYTE 205:7
ténébreux *Je suis le t.*	NERV 232:14
tennis play t. with the net down	FROS 134:15
stars' t.-balls	WEBS 330:14
tent inside the t. pissing out	JOHN 173:6
little t. of blue	WILD 335:15
tenth submerged t.	BOOT 64:9
t. Muse	TROL 319:20
tents Israel's t. do shine	BLAK 56:1
t. have been struck	SMUT 298:17
t. of ungodliness	BOOK 62:12
their tents	LONG 201:20
To your t., O Israel	BIBL 36:8
termagant o'erdoing T.	SHAK 272:10
terminological t. inexactitude	CHUR 91:7
terra *in t. pax*	MISS 223:28
terrible t. as hell	MILT 221:22
t. beauty is born	YEAT 342:20
territorial last t. claim	HITL 159:19
terror another t. to death	LYND 205:1
From all that t. teaches	CHES 89:21
new t. to death	WETH 332:22
T. arises from a sense	KING 186:16
t. by night	BOOK 62:17
T. the human form divine	BLAK 56:16
terrorist t. and the hijacker	THAT 315:11
t. and the policeman	CONR 99:9
terrorize t. a whole nation	MURR 230:11
terrors little t.	GAVA 136:21
t. of the earth	SHAK 277:16
Tess ended his sport with T.	HARD 151:10
test Beauty is the first t.	HARD 151:14
cricket t.	TEBB 310:5
No t. tube can breed love	WILL 336:7
testicles requires t.	VOLT 326:11
testimony t. against slavery	DOUG 115:8
text great t. in Galatians	BROW 71:6
neat rivulet of t.	SHER 294:17
outside of the t.	DERR 108:24
Thames clear T. bordered	MORR 228:18
not of Gennesareth, but T.	THOM 317:4
stripling T.	ARNO 15:16
Sweet T., run softly	SPEN 300:24
T. is liquid history	BURN 74:28
thank God, I t. thee	BIBL 47:7
Now t. we all our God	WINK 337:13
T. heaven, fasting	SHAK 270:2
T. me no thankings	SHAK 286:33
thankit let the Lord be t.	BURN 75:15
thankless have a t. child	SHAK 277:11
thanks give t. unto thee	BOOK 60:3
give t. unto thee	BOOK 63:26
give t. unto the Lord	BOOK 63:22
T. for mercies past	BUCK 72:4
T. for the memory	ROBI 257:21
when he had given t.	BOOK 60:5
that man's a man for a' t.	BURN 75:10
thatch round the t.-eaves run	KEAT 182:21
thcream I'll t. and thcream	CROM 103:15
theatre I like the t.	HART 152:19
shouting fire in a t.	HOLM 161:13
t. of the world	MARY 214:13
This House today is a t.	BALD 23:12
thee save t. and me	OWEN 238:19
theft clever t. was praiseworthy	SPEN 300:4
Property is t.	PROU 251:16

them Lat t. say	ANON 10:9	t. like other people	SHEL 292:12
themselves laid violent hands upon t.	BOOK 60:22	T. of your forefathers	ADAM 1:22
law unto t.	BIBL 49:6	we've got to t.	RUTH 263:5
theories T. pass	ROST 261:2	What the Bandar-log t.	KIPL 188:19
theory All t., dear friend, is grey	GOET 142:18	whether machines t.	SKIN 296:19
life without t.	DISR 112:20	You know more than you t.	SPOC 300:28
sometimes t.	MACA 206:1	**thinker** murder the t.	WESK 331:21
t. against the second law	EDDI 119:14	**thinking** All t. for themselves	GILB 140:3
there Because it's t.	MALL 210:8	he is a t. reed	PASC 241:19
be t. when it happens	ALLE 4:8	Plain living and high t.	WORD 340:16
I am not t.	ANON 6:14	power of positive t.	PEAL 242:16
MACAVITY WASN'T T. T.	ELIO 122:17	saves original t.	SAYE 265:7
met a man who wasn't t.	MEAR 215:18	t. makes it so	SHAK 271:29
Over t.	COHA 95:13	t. man's crumpet	MUIR 229:19
T. but for the grace of God	BRAD 65:19	t. what nobody has thought	SZEN 308:12
thou art t.	BOOK 63:25	**thinks** If any man t. he slays	UPAN 321:24
Were you t.	ANON 10:16	I sits and t.	PUNC 252:20
thereby O! t. hangs a tail	SHAK 284:18	man t. he slays	BHAG 32:16
thereof and the place t.	BOOK 62:23	not say what one t.	EURI 125:10
thermodynamics second law of t.	EDDI 119:14	t. he knows everything	SHAW 291:5
Thermopylae old man of T.	LEAR 195:12	what she t.	ROBI 257:22
they t. are not they	WAUG 329:16	**third** t. of my life	ALLE 4:11
thick thcream till I'm t.	CROM 103:15	**thirst** I t.	BIBL 48:14
thickens now the plot t.	BUCK 72:3	shall never t.	BIBL 47:31
thicker History gets t.	TAYL 309:18	soul is a t. for God	BOOK 61:21
little finger shall be t.	BIBL 36:6	**thirsty** cold waters to a t. soul	BIBL 38:4
thicket ram caught in a t.	BIBL 33:26	Drinking when we are not t.	BEAU 26:12
thief I come as a t.	BIBL 52:19	**thirteen** clocks were striking t.	ORWE 237:13
subtle t. of youth	MILT 223:7	**thirtieth** t. year to heaven	THOM 316:6
t. of time	YOUN 344:14	**thirty** At t. a man suspects	YOUN 344:15
thieves den of t.	BIBL 44:25	I am past t.	ARNO 16:3
fell among t.	BIBL 46:15	I shall soon be t.	BRON 67:11
One of the t.	BECK 26:19	T. days hath	ANON 10:10
t. break through and steal	BIBL 42:24	t. pieces of silver	BIBL 45:11
T. respect property	CHES 90:4	**this** T. was a man	SHAK 276:33
thievish Time's t. progress	SHAK 289:33	**Thomas** ta'en true T.	BALL 24:11
thigh smote them hip and t.	BIBL 35:8	**thorn** Oak, and Ash, and T.	KIPL 188:12
thighs his t. the People	RIG 257:7	rose without the t.	HERR 158:6
thin become unnaturally t.	WOLF 338:9	snail's on the t.	BROW 70:27
never be too rich or too t.	WIND 337:12	t. in the flesh	BIBL 50:13
pale and t. ones	PLUT 248:8	without t. the rose	MILT 221:31
t. man inside every fat man	ORWE 237:8	**thorns** crackling of t.	BIBL 38:21
t. one wildly signalling	CONN 99:2	crown of t.	BRYA 71:22
t. red line	RUSS 263:3	t. shall come up	BIBL 40:3
T. red line of 'eroes	KIPL 188:11	upon the t. of life	SHEL 293:8
thine Not my will, but t., be done	BIBL 47:10	**thou** t. art not he or she	WAUG 329:16
thing ill-favoured t., sir	SHAK 270:5	T. art the man	BIBL 35:31
one damned t. after another	HUBB 166:3	t. shalt have no other gods	BIBL 34:12
play's the t.	SHAK 271:37	T. swell! Thou witty	HART 152:21
sort of t. they like	LINC 199:13	**thought** beautiful clean t.	LAWR 194:17
t. of beauty	KEAT 181:2	dress of t.	JOHN 173:19
things all t. through Christ	BIBL 50:29	dress of t.	POPE 248:2
all t. to all men	BIBL 49:27	father, Harry, to that t.	SHAK 274:24
God's sons are t.	MADD 209:4	forced into a state of t.	GALS 135:15
infection of t. gone	LOWE 204:3	life-blood of t.	FLAU 129:19
people don't do such t.	IBSE 168:12	no t. for the morrow	BIBL 43:1
quick bright t.	SHAK 283:1	oft was t.	POPE 248:1
tears shed for t.	VIRG 324:12	Perish the t.	CIBB 92:20
T. ain't what they used to be	PERS 244:6	rear the tender t.	THOM 317:9
t. are the sons of heaven	JOHN 173:11	Religion the frozen t. of men	KRIS 190:25
t. are wrought by prayer	TENN 311:15	right t.	PALI 240:3
T. fall apart	YEAT 343:19	Roman t. hath struck him	SHAK 268:14
t. they didn't know	POUN 250:8	single grateful t.	LESS 198:3
think comedy to those that t.	WALP 327:13	speech created t.	SHEL 293:17
don't t. I'll fall in love	GERS 138:14	sudden t.	BROW 69:29
don't t. much of it	STRA 305:2	sweet silent t.	SHAK 289:27
Haply I t. on thee	SHAK 289:26	t. in cold storage	SAMU 264:3
I t., therefore I am	DESC 109:2	T. shall be the harder	ANON 13:5
know what I t.	WALL 327:4	t. so once; but now I know it	GARR 136:9
more clearly than you t.	BOHR 57:10	t., word, and deed	MISS 223:26
not so t. as you drunk	SQUI 301:7	To a green t.	MARV 213:17
people that t.	SHEN 294:8	very t. of Thee	CASW 85:10
publishing faster than t.	PAUL 242:7	while, celestial t.	VAUG 322:21

thoughts conceal their t. — VOLT 326:2
have bloody t. — SHAK 287:16
pansies, that's for t. — SHAK 273:5
rather than of t. — KEAT 183:5
T. that do often lie — WORD 340:14
Words without t. — SHAK 272:22
thousand better than a t. — BOOK 62:12
blotted a t. — JONS 178:11
Death has a t. doors — MASS 215:1
Empire lasts for a t. years — CHUR 91:16
first t. days — KENN 184:11
Give me a t. kisses — CATU 85:20
had five t. a year — THAC 314:25
night has a t. eyes — BOUR 65:8
Night hath a t. eyes — LYLY 204:24
not in a t. years — SMIT 297:19
possessing ten t. eyes — ZORO 345:10
t. ages in Thy sight — WATT 329:14
t. doors open on to it — SENE 267:23
t. thousand slimy things — COLE 96:16
t. tongues to sing — WESL 331:24
t. years in thy sight — BOOK 62:14
t. years of history — GAIT 135:7
thrall Thee hath in t. — KEAT 181:20
thread tied, With a silken t. — KEAT 181:12
threatened t., a lion — CHAP 87:14
three divided into t. parts — CAES 79:28
give him t. sides — MONT 226:15
tell you t. times — CARR 84:14
Though he was only t. — MILN 219:1
t. events in his life — LA B 191:8
T. hours a day — TROL 319:14
t. is company — WILD 334:23
t. little maids — GILB 140:10
t. merry boys are we — FLET 130:6
t. o'clock in the morning — FITZ 129:8
t.-o-clock in the morning — THOR 317:20
t. of us in this marriage — DIAN 109:11
t.-pipe problem — DOYL 115:12
T. whole days together — SUCK 305:13
When shall we t. meet — SHAK 278:25
where two or t. — BIBL 44:16
threefold t. cord — BIBL 38:19
threescore t. years and ten — BOOK 62:15
thrice deny me t. — BIBL 45:14
T. is he armed — SHAK 275:15
thrift Thrift, t., Horatio — SHAK 271:2
thrills t. the ear — AUDE 18:14
throat her little t. around — BROW 71:1
if your t. 'tis hard to slit — KING 187:2
in the city's t. — LOWE 203:20
murder by the t. — LLOY 201:1
So he has cut his t. — BYRO 79:11
unlocked her silent t. — GIBB 139:10
throne beats upon a t. — TENN 311:3
Bust outlasts the t. — DOBS 113:11
I saw a great white t. — BIBL 52:22
like a burnished t. — ELIO 122:22
like a burnished t. — SHAK 268:17
Lord sitting upon a t. — BIBL 39:14
t. of bayonets — INGE 168:22
t. of bayonets — YELT 344:4
t. was like the fiery flame — BIBL 41:10
up to the T. — KIPL 187:25
vacancy of the t. — GIBB 139:1
thrones T., dominations — MILT 222:11
t., or dominions — BIBL 51:1
through one who has gone it — VIRG 325:7
read books t. — JOHN 175:10
t. you but not from you — GIBR 139:15
throw sister t. up a lot — WALK 326:19
thrown All this t. away — MARY 214:11
t. out, as good for nothing — JOHN 174:13

thrush aged t. — HARD 151:22
That's the wise t. — BROW 70:9
Thule Ultima T. — VIRG 325:15
thumb t. each other's books — RUSK 262:14
thumbs both his t. are off — HOFF 160:16
By the pricking of my t. — SHAK 281:6
thunder dawn comes up like t. — KIPL 187:26
Glorious the t.'s roar — SMAR 297:3
steal my t. — DENN 108:18
surge and t. — LANG 192:24
T. is the voice of God — MATH 215:4
t. of the captains — BIBL 37:14
voice like t. — DAVI 106:23
thunderbolt like a t. he falls — TENN 310:22
thus T. have I had thee — SHAK 289:35
thusness reason of this t. — WARD 328:10
thyme whereon the wild t. blows — SHAK 283:12
thyself beside t. — BIBL 49:3
Tiber River T. foaming — POWE 250:23
T.! father Tiber — MACA 206:12
T. foaming with much blood — VIRG 324:19
Tiberius Coin, T. — DOBS 113:11
Had T. been a cat — ARNO 15:11
ticket She's got a t. to ride — LENN 197:15
take a t. at Victoria — BEVI 32:13
t. for the peepshow — MACN 208:16
tickle if you t. us — SHAK 282:13
t. her with a hoe — JERR 172:9
tickled t. with a straw — POPE 248:17
tickling only a scornful t. — SIDN 295:15
tide full t. of human existence — JOHN 175:14
Not this t. — KIPL 188:2
tether time or t. — BURN 75:24
t. in the affairs — SHAK 276:29
tides drew these t. of men — LAWR 194:26
tidings bringeth good t. — BIBL 40:14
good t. of great joy — BIBL 46:4
ties string that t. them — MONT 226:14
tiger atom bomb is a paper t. — MAO 211:13
On a t. skin — ANON 11:5
one poor t. — PUNC 252:15
O t.'s heart — SHAK 275:19
t.'s heart wrapped — GREE 147:4
T., Tyger — BLAK 56:14
T. well repay — BELL 28:8
two days like a t. — TIPU 318:7
tigers tamed and shabby t. — HODG 160:11
t. of wrath — BLAK 55:25
t. which they dare not dismount — CHUR 91:12
tight t. gag of place — HEAN 154:14
tights played it in t. — BEER 27:13
timber crooked t. of humanity — KANT 180:15
Timbuctoo plains of T. — WILB 334:15
time abysm of t. — SHAK 287:2
As t. goes by — HUPF 167:8
bid t. return — SHAK 285:18
born out of due t. — BIBL 50:1
but for all t. — JONS 178:8
child of T. — HALL 150:8
chronicle of wasted t. — SHAK 290:2
Cormorant devouring T. — SHAK 278:17
dance to the music of t. — POWE 250:18
devote more t. — FOWL 132:12
Even such is T. — RALE 254:5
Fleet the t. carelessly — SHAK 269:12
Fly envious T. — MILT 220:29
for a moment of t. — ELIZ 123:12
good t. was had by all — SMIT 298:2
half as old as T. — BURG 73:18
idea whose t. has come — ANON 10:7
I forget all t. — MILT 222:3
into the seeds of t. — SHAK 279:4
I T.! arrest your flight — LAMA 191:23

time (*cont.*)

last my t.	CARL 82:13
leave exactly on t.	MUSS 230:16
loved the t. too well	CLAR 93:7
may be some t.	OATE 235:11
now doth t. waste me	SHAK 285:31
old common arbitrator, T.	SHAK 287:34
Once upon a t.	ANON 9:6
on the sands of t.	LONG 201:26
O t. too swift	PEEL 243:1
peace for our t.	CHAM 86:20
peace in our t.	BOOK 58:17
Redeeming the t.	BIBL 50:20
ringing grooves of t.	TENN 312:15
shook hands with t.	FORD 131:7
spend more t. with family	THAT 315:14
strain, T.'s eunuch	HOPK 163:7
talk of killing t.	BOUC 65:4
tether t. or tide	BURN 75:24
thief of t.	YOUN 344:14
T. and the hour	SHAK 279:9
t. and the place	BROW 70:24
t. and times are done	YEAT 343:24
t. creeps along	JAGO 170:5
T. for a little something	MILN 219:5
t. has come	CARR 84:6
T. has shaken me	WESL 332:8
T. hath, my lord, a wallet	SHAK 287:30
t. is fleeing	HORA 164:7
t. is flying	VIRG 325:19
t. is money	HUGO 166:17
T. is our tedious song	MILT 220:27
t. is out of joint	SHAK 271:24
t. is running out	KOES 190:1
t. is the greatest innovator	BACO 21:16
T. is the measure	AUCT 17:23
T. is too slow	VAN 322:15
T., like an ever-rolling stream	WATT 329:15
t. of asking	BOOK 60:13
T., Place	DRYD 117:15
T. present and time past	ELIO 121:18
t. remembered	SWIN 307:18
t.'s arrow	EDDI 119:12
T.'s devouring hand	BRAM 66:1
T. spent on any item	PARK 241:8
T. stays, *we go*	DOBS 113:12
T.'s thievish progress	SHAK 289:33
T.'s wingèd chariot	MARV 213:21
T., the avenger	BYRO 78:5
T. the devourer	OVID 238:16
T. the subtle thief	MILT 223:7
t. to every purpose	BIBL 38:16
t. to win this game	DRAK 116:3
T. which destroys all things	BHAG 32:17
T. will run back	MILT 220:25
T., you thief	HUNT 167:4
to fill the t. available	PARK 241:7
trencher-friends, t.'s flies	SHAK 287:22
unconscionable t. dying	CHAR 87:25
use your t.	HERR 158:9
very good t. it was	JOYC 178:23
ways By which T. kills us	SITW 296:14
When t. is broke	SHAK 285:30
whips and scorns of t.	SHAK 272:2
whirligig of t.	SHAK 288:31
womb of t.	HEIN 155:9
world enough, and t.	MARV 213:19
timely t. compliance	FIEL 127:12
timeo t. *Danaos et dona ferentes*	VIRG 324:13
times It was the best of t.	DICK 111:10
Oh, the t.	CICE 92:25
one year's experience 30 t.	CARR 83:12
possibility of good t.	BRAN 66:3

praiser of past t.	HORA 163:17
signs of the t.	BIBL 44:9
T. has made many ministries	BAGE 22:13
t. that try men's souls	PAIN 239:8
t. they are a-changin'	DYLA 119:9
t. will not mend	PARK 241:4
timetables by railway t.	TAYL 309:19
timor T. *mortis conturbat me*	DUNB 118:6
Timothy T. Winters comes to school	CAUS 86:4
tin cat on a hot t. roof	WILL 336:8
tincture Actions receive their t.	DEFO 107:17
t. in the blood	DEFO 107:18
tintinnabulation To the t.	POE 246:12
tiny Your t. hand is frozen	GIAC 138:19
tip Within the nether t.	COLE 96:15
Tipperary long way to T.	JUDG 179:8
tiptoe Dance t., bull	BUNT 72:19
jocund day Stands t.	SHAK 286:32
sweet peas, on t.	KEAT 181:16
tired Give me your t., your poor	LAZA 195:2
t. her head	BIBL 36:29
t. of London	JOHN 175:23
t. of Love	BELL 28:16
t. the sun with talking	CORY 100:14
Tiresias T., old man with wrinkled dugs	ELIO 122:27
titanic furniture on the deck of the T.	MORT 229:9
inevitable the T.	HAGU 149:4
title needed no royal t.	SPEN 300:6
titles their t. take	CHAN 87:3
T. are shadows	DEFO 107:21
titwillow Willow, t.	GILB 140:20
Tityre T., *tu patulae recubans*	VIRG 325:8
toad Give me your arm, old t.	LARK 193:16
let the t. work	LARK 193:15
like the t., ugly	SHAK 269:14
rather be a t.	SHAK 284:23
squat like a t.	MILT 222:6
t. beneath the harrow	KIPL 188:3
toads imaginary gardens with real t.	MOOR 227:9
inconstant t.	MONT 226:2
toast My t. would be	ADAM 2:1
never had a piece of t.	PAYN 242:9
toasted cheese—t., mostly	STEV 303:24
tobacco leave off t.	LAMB 192:11
that tawney weed t.	JONS 177:12
tocsin t. of the soul	BYRO 78:27
today I have lived it	DRYD 117:12
let us do something t.	COLL 97:2
never jam t.	CARR 84:8
standing here t.	JOHN 173:2
t. I am fifty-five	REED 255:7
T. if ye will hear	BOOK 62:19
T. is the last day	YELT 344:5
T. shalt thou be with me	BIBL 47:13
T. we have naming of parts	REED 255:8
we gave our t.	EDMO 120:1
toe light fantastic t.	MILT 220:2
toes Pobble who has no t.	LEAR 195:17
toff Saunter along like a t.	HARG 152:8
together lived comfortably so long t.	GAY 137:2
toil bleared, smeared with t.	HOPK 162:22
blood, t., tears and sweat	CHUR 91:14
day in t.	QUAR 253:4
Double, double t. and trouble	SHAK 281:4
Horny-handed sons of t.	SALI 263:21
horny hands of t.	LOWE 203:17
strong t. of grace	SHAK 269:10
they t. not	BIBL 42:27
token t. of a covenant	BIBL 33:22
tokens Words are the t.	BACO 20:19
told half was not t. me	BIBL 36:3
I t. you so	WELL 331:19
plato t. him: he couldn't	CUMM 104:16

t. my wrath — BLAK 56:11
t. you from the beginning — BIBL 40:10
tolerable Life would be t. — LEWI 198:16
tolerated women not merely t. — AUNG 19:11
toll T. for the brave — COWP 101:25
t. me back from thee — KEAT 182:15
tolle T. *lege* — AUGU 19:1
tollis t. *peccata mundi* — MISS 224:6
tolls for whom the bell t. — DONN 114:19
Tom Ground control to Major T. — BOWI 65:16
Poor T.'s a-cold — SHAK 277:27
spurious brat, T. Jones — RICH 256:22
T. Pearse — BALL 24:16
Uncle T. Cobbleigh — BALL 24:16
tomb empty in thy t. — KING 186:6
fair Fidele's grassy t. — COLL 97:10
t. of a mediocre talent — SMIT 297:21
t. of wit — CAVE 86:8
Tommy T. this, an' Tommy that — KIPL 188:11
tomorrow For your t. we gave — EDMO 120:1
jam t. — CARR 84:8
put off till t. — PUNC 252:9
This, no t. hath — DONN 114:4
T., and to-morrow — SHAK 281:24
T. do thy worst — DRYD 117:12
t. is another day — MITC 224:23
t. to be brave — ARMS 14:25
t. we shall die — BIBL 39:27
we thought was for t. — BENN 29:15
tomtit little t. Sang — GILB 140:20
tone t. of the company — CHES 89:7
tongs t. and the bones — SHAK 283:20
tongue his t. Dropped manna — MILT 221:17
hold your t. — DONN 114:6
I held my t. — BOOK 61:18
I must hold my t. — SHAK 271:1
iron t. of midnight — SHAK 283:24
lies of t. and pen — CHES 89:21
Love's t. is in the eyes — FLET 130:11
my t. could utter — TENN 310:11
My t. is the pen — BOOK 61:22
My t. swore — EURI 125:9
my t. the mystery telling — THOM 315:22
nor t. to speak — LENT 197:19
sharp t. — IRVI 169:10
Sing, my t. — FORT 131:19
tip of the t. taking — NABO 230:17
t. can no man tame — BIBL 51:22
t. In every wound — SHAK 276:23
t. not understood — BOOK 64:4
t. That Shakespeare spake — WORD 339:25
t. to persuade — CLAR 93:12
use of my oracular t. — SHER 294:14
voice and t. — AUGU 18:27
yield to the t. — BIER 53:19
tongues lack t. to praise — SHAK 290:3
thousand t. to sing — WESL 331:24
time in the t. — SHAK 288:5
t. like as of fire — BIBL 48:24
t. of men and of angels — BIBL 49:30
tonic Hatred is a t. — BALZ 24:22
tonight Not t., Josephine — NAPO 231:11
tons Sixteen t. — TRAV 319:6
too T. kind, too kind — NIGH 234:13
we are t. menny — HARD 151:15
took 'E went an' t. — KIPL 188:16
tool edged t. that grows keener — IRVI 169:10
Man is a t.-making animal — FRAN 133:10
Man is a t.-using animal — CARL 83:1
Science is an edged t. — EDDI 119:15
tools Give us the t. — CHUR 91:18
secrets are edged t. — DRYD 117:8
t. to him that can handle them — CARL 82:15

Toome On the Bridge of T. — CARB 82:3
tooth hadde alwey a coltes t. — CHAU 88:20
red in t. and claw — TENN 311:21
sharper than a serpent's t. — SHAK 277:11
t. for tooth — BIBL 34:17
where each t.-point goes — KIPL 188:3
toothache Venerable Mother T. — HEAT 154:18
toothpaste t. is out of the tube — HALD 149:13
top always room at the t. — WEBS 330:7
I shall die at the t. — SWIF 307:13
Life is a t. — GREV 147:12
t. of it reached to heaven — BIBL 33:30
t. thing in the world — KEAT 183:14
You're the t. — PORT 249:21
Torah found in the T. — ELEA 121:1
T., hard like iron — TALM 309:8
Turn it [T.] — TALM 309:5
torch t. of life — LUCR 204:14
Truth, like a t. — HAMI 150:14
torches teach the t. — SHAK 286:16
torchlight t. procession — O'SU 238:6
Tories T. born wicked — ANON 8:15
T. own no argument — BROW 69:11
torment most hateful t. for men — HERO 157:24
smoke of their t. — BIBL 52:18
torments many t. lie — CIBB 92:18
tornado set off a t. in Texas — LORE 202:16
torpedoes Damn the t. — FARR 126:15
tortoise 'T.' is a insect — PUNC 252:13
torturer t.'s horse scratches — AUDE 18:9
Tory deep burning hatred for the T. Party — BEVA 32:8
Loyalty the T.'s secret weapon — KILM 186:3
T. Corps d'Armée — GLAD 141:21
T. men and Whig measures — DISR 112:18
tossed you t. and gored — BOSW 65:1
total t. solution — GOER 142:15
totter t. into vogue — WALP 327:10
totters Who t. forth — SHEL 294:3
touch little t. of Harry — SHAK 274:35
Nelson — NELS 232:8
nothing, Can t. him further — SHAK 280:24
One t. of nature — SHAK 287:32
puts it not unto the t. — MONT 226:23
T. me not — BIBL 48:19
T. not the cat — SCOT 266:21
t. of earthly years — WORD 341:8
touches Who t. this touches a man — WHIT 333:23
toucheth He that t. pitch — BIBL 41:26
tough t. get going — KENN 184:18
T. on crime — BLAI 55:6
toughness T. doesn't have to come — FEIN 126:18
tourist loathsome is the British t. — KILV 186:4
t. of wars — GELL 137:16
whisper to the t. — BEER 27:12
tourmente *l'infini me t.* — MUSS 230:14
tout T. *passe* — ANON 11:20
toves slithy t. — CARR 84:3
tower Child Roland to the dark t. — SHAK 277:28
Giotto's t. — LONG 201:23
prisoner in the T. — FABY 125:18
to the Dark T. came — BROW 69:27
t. of strength — SHAK 286:10
watchman on the lonely t. — SCOT 266:14
with the blasted t. — NERV 232:14
towered t. cities please us — MILT 220:6
towers branchy between t. — HOPK 162:21
Whispering from her t. — ARNO 15:29
towery T. city — HOPK 162:21
town Country in the t. — MART 213:11
destroy the t. to save it — ANON 8:2
little t. of Bethlehem — BROO 68:5
lived in a pretty how t. — CUMM 104:13
man made the t. — COWP 101:28

town (*cont.*)
never go down to the end of the t. — MILN 219:1
spreading of the hideous t. — MORR 228:18
towns Seven wealthy t. — ANON 9:19
toys brooches and t. — STEV 303:31
Deceive boys with t. — LYSA 205:3
toyshop moving t. of the heart — POPE 248:32
traces on winter's t. — SWIN 307:17
track flying on our t. — THOM 317:13
T. twenty nine — GORD 144:17
tracks hungry on the t. — CRAN 102:20
trade all is seared with t. — HOPK 162:22
autocrat: that's my t. — CATH 85:14
from the vulgar t. — MARL 212:11
great t. — BURK 73:22
Irish poets, learn you t. — YEAT 343:28
It is his t. — HEIN 155:10
People of the same t. — SMIT 297:7
There isn't any T. — HERB 157:3
War is the t. of kings — DRYD 117:1
wheels of t. — HUME 166:21
trade unionism t. of the married — SHAW 291:14
trading t. on the blood — LEE 196:15
tradition t. is a fence — TALM 309:4
T. means giving votes to — CHES 90:5
traduced t. Joseph K. — KAFK 180:8
traffic Hushing the latest t. — BRID 66:19
means of t. — MARL 212:11
t. of Jacob's ladder — THOM 317:3
trafficking permitted t. — KORA 190:9
tragedy composition of a t. — VOLT 326:11
Fate wrote her a t. — BEER 27:13
first time as t. — BARN 25:9
first time as t. — MARX 214:6
go, litel myn t. — CHAU 88:28
That is their t. — WILD 335:1
t. is thus a representation — ARIS 14:14
t. of Science — HUXL 167:21
t. of the classical languages — MADA 209:1
T. ought to be a great kick — LAWR 194:23
t. to those that feel — WALP 327:13
weak, washy way of true t. — KAVA 180:23
what t. means — STOP 304:17
tragic I acted so t. — HARG 152:9
trahison t. *des clercs* — BEND 29:9
trail long, long t. — KING 186:14
t. has its own stern code — SERV 267:25
train biggest electric t. set — WELL 331:4
express-t. drew up there — THOM 316:14
headlight of an oncoming t. — DICK 111:19
light of the oncoming t. — LOWE 204:1
like a runaway t. — CONL 98:21
read in the t. — WILD 335:3
Runs the red electric t. — BETJ 32:1
rush in the t. — THOM 317:13
shaves and takes a t. — WHIT 333:7
t. is arriving on time — MUSS 230:16
T. up a child — BIBL 37:39
waited for the t. — TENN 311:2
traitor hate the t. — DANI 105:15
traitors form of our t. — WEST 332:17
hate t. and the treason love — DRYD 116:29
tram not even a bus, I'm a t. — HARE 152:7
tramp why the lady is a t. — HART 152:19
tranquil Farewell the t. mind — SHAK 284:25
tranquillity feeling of inward t. — FORB 131:1
recollected in t. — WORD 341:20
t. remembered in emotion — PARK 240:22
tranquillized t. *Fifties* — LOWE 203:21
transcendental of a t. kind — GILB 140:23
T. moonshine — CARL 82:25
transgression there is no t. — BIBL 49:8
transgressions wounded for our t. — BIBL 40:17

transgressors way of t. — BIBL 37:30
transient t. is the smile — DYER 118:21
transit *O quam cito t. gloria mundi* — THOM 315:18
Sic t. gloria mundi — ANON 12:22
translated t. into Italian — WHAR 332:23
translation mistake in the t. — VANB 322:8
unfaithful to the t. — BORG 64:13
what is lost in t. — FROS 134:16
translations hold t. not unlike — HOWE 165:16
trapeze on the flying t. — LEYB 198:22
traps recognize the t. — MACH 207:17
trash steals t. — SHAK 284:20
travel *real* way to t. — GRAH 145:10
t. broadens the mind; but — CHES 90:6
t. by land or by water — BOOK 59:8
t. for travel's sake — STEV 303:19
t. hopefully is a better thing — STEV 303:25
t. in the direction of our fear — BERR 31:12
T., in the younger sort — BACO 21:29
T. light — JUVE 180:2
two classes of t. — BENC 29:7
travelled took the one less t. — FROS 134:13
t. a good deal in Concord — THOR 317:18
traveller said the T. — DE L 108:7
spurs the lated t. — SHAK 280:26
t. from an antique land — SHEL 293:11
travels t. the fastest — KIPL 187:25
t. the world in search — MOOR 227:6
trawler When seagulls follow a t. — CANT 81:19
treachery mother of all t. — PAIS 239:18
t. of the intellectuals — BEND 29:9
tread Doth close behind him t. — COLE 96:17
so airy a tread — TENN 312:24
T. softly — YEAT 343:2
treason [corporations] cannot commit t. — COKE 95:18
Gunpowder T. and Plot — ANON 9:12
hate traitors and the t. love — DRYD 116:29
In trust I have found t. — ELIZ 123:5
last temptation is the greatest t. — ELIO 122:16
love the t. — DANI 105:15
moderation is a sort of t. — BURK 73:21
none dare call it t. — HARI 152:10
t. a matter — TALL 309:3
T. has done his worst — SHAK 280:24
t. is not owned — DRYD 117:4
t., make the most of it — HENR 156:21
t. of all clerks — AUDE 17:26
treasonous their t. parles — BROW 70:9
treasure liking his t. — THOM 316:18
purest t. mortal times afford — SHAK 285:7
t. in heaven — BIBL 44:19
Where your t. is — BIBL 42:25
treasures t. upon earth — BIBL 42:24
treasury If the T. were to fill old bottles — KEYN 185:11
T. is the spring — BAGE 22:11
treatise T. of Human Nature — HUME 166:22
treatment suitable case for t. — MERC 216:20
treaty not a peace t. — FOCH 130:17
tree apple on the t. — DICK 111:15
billboard lovely as a t. — NASH 231:17
finds that this t. — KNOX 189:2
golden t. of actual life — GOET 142:18
happy, happy t. — KEAT 181:13
I must climb the t. — HERB 157:20
leaves of the t. — BIBL 52:27
Of that forbidden t. — MILT 220:33
only God can make a t. — KILM 186:2
outstretched beneath the t. — BLAK 56:12
poem lovely as a t. — KILM 186:1
shall be like that t. — SWIF 307:13
she gave me of the t. — BIBL 33:8
spare the beechen t. — CAMP 81:1
Till the t. die — SHAK 270:20

to my mind than a t.   MORR 228:12
t. of knowledge   BIBL 32:25
t. of liberty   JEFF 171:13
t. of life   BIBL 32:25
t. of the knowledge   BIBL 33:1
Under the greenwood t.   SHAK 269:16
where the t. falleth   BIBL 38:32
Woodman, spare that t.   MORR 228:15
treefull t. of angels   BENÉ 29:13
treen t. priests   JEWE 172:10
trees all the t. are green   KING 186:22
apple t. will never get across   FROS 134:11
die when the t. were green   CLAR 93:7
He that plants t.   FULL 135:1
Loveliest of t.   HOUS 165:2
tall ancestral t.   HEMA 155:18
T. and stones will teach   BERN 31:5
t., And the mountain-tops   SHAK 275:22
t. bear strange fruit   HOLI 161:4
t. that grow so fair   KIPL 188:12
while some t. stand   BROW 69:1
Trelawny And shall T. die   HAWK 153:10
tremble t. for my country   JEFF 171:11
trembles t. as I do   WELL 331:5
trembling fear and t.   BIBL 50:25
T., hoping   POPE 246:25
T. in her soft   KEAT 181:6
trencher t.-friends, time's flies   SHAK 287:22
trencherman very valiant t.   SHAK 283:26
trespasses forgive us our t.   BOOK 58:8
tresses Fair t. man's imperial race   POPE 249:1
trial only a t. if I recognize it   KAFK 180:9
T. by jury itself   DENM 108:16
t. is by what is contrary   MILT 223:15
triangle eternal t.   ANON 6:16
triangles t. were to make a God   MONT 226:15
tribal constructing t. lays   KIPL 187:22
tribalism pure t.   FITT 128:10
tribe purify the dialect of the t.   ELIO 121:27
tribute Hypocrisy is a t.   LA R 193:20
trick conjuring t. with bones   JENK 171:20
win the t.   HOYL 165:22
trickle T.-down theory   GALB 135:10
tried Christian ideal has not been t.   CHES 90:7
she for a little t.   WOTT 341:23
trifle t. with the spoon   POPE 247:27
trifles T. light as air   SHAK 284:24
unconsidered t.   SHAK 289:7
trimmer innocent word T.   HALI 149:19
trip don't t. over the furniture   COWA 101:13
forward to the t.   STIN 304:10
t. it as ye go   MILT 220:2
triple t. cord   BURK 73:20
trippingly t. on the tongue   SHAK 272:9
tripwire touch the t.   WARN 328:15
triste jamais t. archy   MARQ 212:22
t. et noire   BAUD 26:8
tristesse Adieu t.   ÉLUA 124:6
Triton T. blow his wreathèd horn   WORD 341:19
T. of the minnows   SHAK 270:10
triumph for evil to t.   BURK 74:22
glory in the t.   CORN 100:2
t. and disaster   KIPL 187:20
T. in God above   GURN 148:14
t. of hope over experience   JOHN 175:7
t. of modern science   WAUG 329:24
Victor's t. won   POTT 249:24
trivial such t. people   LAWR 194:22
t. and the important   POTT 249:27
t. and vulgar way   BROW 69:7
t. round, the common task   KEBL 183:20
Trojan what T. 'orses will jump out   BEVI 32:14
troops t. towards the sound   GRIM 148:1

trophies her weedy t.   SHAK 273:10
trotting T. to the fair   GRAV 146:2
trouble capacity of taking t.   CARL 82:17
Double, double toil and t.   SHAK 281:4
full of t.   BIBL 37:6
help in time of t.   ANON 5:12
In t. and in joy   TATE 309:12
Man is born unto t.   BIBL 37:5
Roman and his t.   HOUS 165:6
There may be t. ahead   BERL 30:18
there's t. brewing   KNIG 189:11
took the t. to be born   BEAU 26:13
When in t., delegate   BORE 64:12
wood's in t.   HOUS 165:5
troubled bridge over t. water   SIMO 295:24
heart be t.   BIBL 48:4
I am t.   MOOR 227:11
troubles against a sea of t.   SHAK 272:1
From t. of the world   HARV 153:2
pack up your t.   ANON 10:19
troubling wicked cease from t.   BIBL 37:3
trousers bottoms of my t. rolled   ELIO 122:13
cloud in t.   MAYA 215:14
have your best t. on   IBSE 168:10
trout t. in the milk   THOR 317:16
Where the gray t. lies   HOGG 160:22
trovato è molto ben t.   ANON 13:3
trowel lay it on with a t.   DISR 113:3
lays it on with a t.   CONG 98:10
Troy another T. for her to burn   YEAT 343:12
from the shores of T.   VIRG 324:9
plains of windy T.   TENN 313:29
Priam's sons of T.   SURR 306:6
sacked T.'s sacred city   HOME 161:20
Where's T.   BRAM 66:1
trucks learn about t.   AWDR 20:7
true always t. to you, darlin'   PORT 249:14
And is it t.   BETJ 31:17
as t. . . . as taxes   DICK 110:6
can the devil speak t.   SHAK 279:6
course of t. love   SHAK 282:33
dark and t. and tender   TENN 313:9
If it is not t.   ANON 13:3
not necessarily t.   WILD 335:9
Ring in the t.   TENN 311:30
said t. things   BROW 69:22
ta'en t. Thomas   BALL 24:11
three times is t.   CARR 84:14
too wonderful to be t.   FARA 126:3
to thine own self be t.   SHAK 271:9
t. legend   STAL 301:14
t. love hath my heart   SIDN 295:7
t. to thyself   BACO 21:33
Whatsoever things are t.   BIBL 50:28
what we are saying is t.   RUSS 262:22
You are not t.   WILB 334:18
truffles t., Perigord   POPE 246:23
trumpet sound of the t.   BIBL 34:31
trumpets saith among the t.   BIBL 37:14
silver, snarling t.   KEAT 181:4
to the sound of t.   SMIT 298:14
t. sounded for him   BUNY 73:12
trunkless vast and t. legs   SHEL 293:11
trust assumes a public t.   JEFF 171:15
In t. I have found treason   ELIZ 123:5
Never t. the artist   LAWR 194:13
no t. in the future   HORA 164:7
power in t.   DRYD 116:19
power is a t.   DISR 112:29
put your t. in God   BLAC 55:1
t. in God   SMIT 298:8
t. in princes   BOOK 63:27

trust (*cont.*)
t. me not at all — TENN 311:10
T. one who has gone through it — VIRG 325:7
trusted friend, whom I t. — BOOK 61:20
in thee have I t. — BOOK 58:14
trustest t. upon the staff — BIBL 36:33
trusting no t. appearances — SHER 294:21
trustworthiness Carthaginian t. — SALL 264:2
truth Beauty is t. — KEAT 182:5
Believing T. — BELL 28:9
best test of t. — CHES 89:13
cinema is t. 24 times per second — GODA 142:9
dearer still is t. — ARIS 14:20
diminution of the love of t. — JOHN 173:17
economical with the t. — ARMS 15:2
economy of t. — BURK 74:16
fight for freedom and t. — IBSE 168:10
forsake this t. — ROSE 260:9
From delusion lead me to T. — UPAN 321:21
Great is T. — BIBL 41:20
great is t. — BROO 68:6
great ocean of t. — NEWT 233:15
Is there in t. no beauty — HERB 157:15
just tell the t. — TRUM 320:7
keep t. safe in its hand — TAGO 308:21
mainly he told the t. — TWAI 321:2
Mercy and t. — BOOK 62:13
Never sold the t. — TENN 313:1
new scientific t. — PLAN 245:18
not only t. — RUSS 262:23
plain t. for plain people — WESL 332:5
positive in error as in t. — LOCK 201:5
seek for t. — ADLE 2:19
spirit of t. — HORA 164:4
stark naked t. — BOOK 59:26
test of t. — CLEL 94:6
T. exists, lies are invented — CRAB 102:11
T. forever on the scaffold — BRAQ 66:5
T. from his lips prevailed — LOWE 203:19
t. is always strange — GOLD 143:11
t. is not in us — BYRO 79:7
t. is pulling its boots on — BIBL 51:32
t. is rarely pure — SPUR 301:6
t. is the first — WILD 334:22
T. is the most valuable thing — ANON 11:2
t., justice and the American way — TWAI 321:5
T. lies within a little — ANON 6:21
T., like a torch — BOLI 57:14
T.-loving Persians — HAMI 150:14
t. makes men free — GRAV 146:6
t. misunderstood — AGAR 2:25
t. of imagination — JAME 171:3
t. serve as a stalking-horse — KEAT 183:4
t. shall make you free — BOLI 57:13
T. sits upon the lips — BIBL 47:36
T. stands — ARNO 15:21
t. that's told with bad intent — DONN 114:2
t. universally acknowledged — BLAK 55:13
t. which you cannot contradict — AUST 19:24
T. will come to light — SOCR 298:23
way, the t., and the life — SHAK 282:9
wedded to the t. — BIBL 48:6
we owe only t. — SAKI 263:16
What is t. — VOLT 326:10
What is t. — BACO 21:30
truths all t. are half-truths — BIBL 48:9
fate of new t. — WHIT 333:13
Irrationally held t. — HUXL 168:1
repetition of unpalatable t. — HUXL 168:2
t. begin as blasphemies — SUMM 306:3
t. he can impart — SHAW 290:21
t. to be self-evident — WORD 340:20
— ANON 10:14

We hold these t. — JEFF 171:12
try t. him afterwards — MOLI 225:14
trying I am t. to be — SMIT 297:17
just goes on t. — PICA 244:19
succeed in business without really t. — MEAD 215:17
tu *Et t., Brute?* — SHAK 276:8
tua *Nam t. res agitur* — HORA 164:1
tub mere tale of a t. — WEBS 330:16
tube toothpaste is out of the t. — HALD 149:13
tuberose sweet t. — SHEL 293:23
Tudor US presidency a T. monarchy — BURG 73:16
tue *je te t.* — CHAM 87:2
tug then was the t. of war — LEE 196:12
tumour ripens in a t. — ABSE 1:3
tumult t. and the shouting — KIPL 188:5
tune I t. the instrument — DONN 113:24
keep thinkin'll turn into a t. — HUBB 166:5
out of t. and harsh — SHAK 272:8
sweetly play'd in t. — BURN 75:21
turn on, t. in and drop out — LEAR 195:19
tunes have all the good t. — HILL 159:5
t. of Handel — SITW 296:15
tunnel back down the time t. — KEAT 181:1
light at the end of the t. — DICK 111:19
light at the end of the t. — LOWE 204:1
turbot price of a large t. — RUSK 262:13
T., Sir — WELB 331:1
turbulent rid me of this t. priest — HENR 156:14
turd nat worth a t. — CHAU 88:17
turf blue ribbon of the t. — DISR 112:26
grass-green t. — SHAK 273:1
Where heaves the t. — GRAY 146:14
Turk French, or T. — GILB 141:3
turkey T. is a dying man — NICH 233:20
Turkish English, not the T. court — SHAK 274:25
Turks Let the T. now carry — GLAD 141:20
turn Because I do not hope to t. — ELIO 121:14
pass, and t. again — EMER 124:8
t. of the screw — JAME 170:23
t. on, tune in and drop out — LEAR 195:19
t. over the sheet — SAND 264:14
t. to him the other — BIBL 42:18
T. up the lights — HENR 156:20
turned having once t. round — COLE 96:17
in case anything t. up — DICK 110:2
t. every one to his own way — BIBL 40:17
turning lady's not for t. — THAT 315:6
still point of the t. world — ELIO 121:21
Turpe *squid T. paras* — JUVE 180:6
turtle t. lives 'twixt plated decks — NASH 231:12
voice of the t. — BIBL 39:4
Tuscany ranks of T. — MACA 206:13
TV blight has hit the T. industry — STRE 305:6
T.—a clever contraction — ACE 1:5
twain go with him t. — BIBL 42:19
with t. he covered — BIBL 39:14
twang melodious t. — AUBR 17:17
Tweedledum 'Twixt T. and Tweedledee — BYRO 77:20
twelve ruin himself in t. months — GEOR 138:5
t. good men into a box — BROU 68:8
t. honest men have decided — PULT 252:6
twentieth fill the twentieth t. — LAUR 194:10
twenty At T. I tried to vex — AUDE 18:19
twenty-twenty Hindsight is always t. — WILD 335:24
twice He gives t. — PUBL 251:22
must be t. as well as men — WHIT 334:8
postman always rings t. — CAIN 80:6
t. as natural — CARR 84:13
t. into the same river — HERA 156:25
twilight in the t. wait — ROBI 258:2
twilights shadows and t. — Æ 2:22
twinkle Twinkle, t., little bat — CARR 83:20
T., twinkle, little star — TAYL 309:21

twinkling in the t. of an eye — BIBL 50:7
twins to have been born t. — MADA 209:1
twist t. slowly in the wind — EHRL 120:9
twitched t. his mantle blue — MILT 220:21
two say that t. plus two make four — ORWE 237:15
Takes t. to tango — HOFF 160:12
tea for t. — CAES 79:27
There went in t. and two — BIBL 33:19
twice t. be not four — TURG 320:17
T. and two only — NEWM 232:22
t. and two would continue to make — WHIS 333:4
t. cultures — SNOW 298:19
t. ears of corn — SWIF 306:19
t.-handed engine — MILT 220:16
t. hundred thousand men — NAPO 231:8
T. nations — DISR 112:27
t. o'clock in the morning — NAPO 231:6
t. or three are gathered — BOOK 58:22
t. people miserable — BUTL 77:11
t. primal Spirits — ZORO 345:11
t. things about the horse — ROYD 261:18
t. things that will be believed — TARK 309:10
where t. or three — BIBL 44:16
twopence penny plain and t. coloured — STEV 303:20
Tyburn damned T.-face — CONG 98:12
tyger T., Tyger — BLAK 56:14
tygers t. of wrath — BLAK 55:25
type careful of the t. — TENN 311:20
types Seven t. of ambiguity — EMPS 124:21
T. and shadows — THOM 315:23
typewriter changing a t. ribbon — BENC 29:6
typewriters banging on million t. — WILE 335:26
monkeys strumming on t. — EDDI 119:13
tyrannis Sic semper t. — ANON 12:21
Sic semper t. — BOOT 64:8
tyrannous t. To use it like a giant — SHAK 281:29
tyranny T. is always better organized — PÉGU 243:3
without representation is t. — OTIS 238:7
tyrants all men would be t. — DEFO 107:18
men would be t. — ADAM 1:9
patriots and t. — JEFF 171:13
Rebellion to t. — BRAD 65:24
sceptre from t. — TURG 320:18
Tyre men still call T. — FLEC 129:24
Nineveh and T. — KIPL 188:6
tyres concrete and t. — LARK 193:12
Tyrian budded T. — KEAT 182:17

U

ubi U. Petrus, íbi ergo ecclesia — AMBR 4:13
ubique Quod u., quod semper — VINC 324:8
ubiquities blazing u. — EMER 124:17
ugly no place for u. mathematics — HARD 151:14
Ulster Protestant Province of U. — CARS 84:18
to which U. will not go — BONA 57:19
U. will fight — CHUR 91:4
ulterioris ripae u. amore — VIRG 324:22
ultima U. Thule — VIRG 325:15
Ulysses Happy he who like U. — DU B 117:20
umble so very 'u. — DICK 110:5
umbrage garden's u. mild — SMAR 297:2
umbrella steals the just's u. — BOWE 65:15
umpire Chaos u. sits — MILT 221:23
unacceptable u. face of capitalism — HEAT 154:17
unacknowledged u. legislators — SHEL 294:6
unarm U., Eros — SHAK 268:25
unattempted u. yet in prose or rhyme — MILT 221:1
unaware And I was u. — HARD 151:23
unbearable in victory u. — CHUR 92:7
u. lightness of being — KUND 191:2

unbeatable In defeat u. — CHUR 92:7
unbecoming u. the character — ANON 5:19
unbelief help thou mine u. — BIBL 45:29
unbirthday u. present — CARR 84:10
unbowed bloody, but u. — HENL 156:7
unbroken part of u. stream — HAWK 153:11
unburied bodies of u. men — WEBS 330:17
uncharitableness from all u. — BOOK 59:4
uncle My u. — SHAK 271:18
u. me no uncle — SHAK 285:14
U. Tom Cobbleigh — BALL 24:16
unclubbable very u. man — JOHN 175:3
unco Address to the u. guid — BURN 75:1
unconditional u. and immediate surrender — GRAN 145:16
unconquerable man's u. mind — WORD 341:16
nursing the u. hope — ARNO 15:19
u. will — MILT 221:4
unconscionable u. time dying — CHAR 87:25
unconscious knowledge of the u. — FREU 133:20
royal road to the u. — FREU 133:20
unconsidered u. trifles — SHAK 289:7
unconvincing bald and u. — GILB 140:18
uncouth U. unkist — SPEN 300:25
uncreating U. word — POPE 246:24
undefiled well of English u. — SPEN 300:18
underbelly soft u. of Europe — CHUR 91:21
u. of the Axis — CHUR 91:21
underground Johnny u. — PUDN 252:2
undergrowth u. is part of the language — EMPS 124:22
underlings ourselves, that we are u. — SHAK 275:30
underneath U. the Arches — FLAN 129:13
understand criticize What you can't u. — DYLA 119:10
doesn't u. the situation — MURR 230:13
failed to u. — BOHR 57:9
Grown-ups never u. anything — SAIN 263:12
I do not u. — FEYN 127:7
u. a little less — MAJO 209:22
u. nothing — CORN 100:5
u. the country — LESS 198:1
understanded tongue not u. — BOOK 64:4
understanding pass all u. — JAME 170:11
passeth all u. — BIBL 50:27
To be totally u. — STAË 301:9
with all thy getting get u. — BIBL 37:20
understands world u. my language — HAYD 153:18
understatement that was an u. — MITC 224:16
undertaking no such u. has been received — CHAM 86:21
undeservedly books u. forgotten — AUDE 18:22
undone John Donne, Anne Donne, U. — DONN 114:23
We have left u. — BOOK 58:6
What's done cannot be u. — SHAK 281:18
undulating u. throat — BELL 28:19
uneasy U. lies the head — SHAK 274:20
uneatable pursuit of the u. — WILD 335:11
uneducated government by the u. — CHES 90:9
u. man to read books — CHUR 92:10
unemployed u. youth — BAGE 22:16
unemployment leave it to u. — KEYN 185:11
rising u. — LAMO 192:15
unequal equal division of u. earnings — ELLI 123:23
unespied In the ocean's bosom u. — MARV 213:12
unexpected Old age is the most u. — TROT 320:1
unexpectedness I call u. — PEAC 242:13
unexplained you're u. as yet — HALL 150:10
unfaithful faith u. — TENN 311:8
original is u. — BORG 64:13
unfathomable u. deep forest — THOM 316:15
unfinished Liberty is u. business — ANON 8:6
unforgiveness alp of u. — PLOM 246:6
unforgiving u. eye — SHER 294:20
unfortunate u. man — BOET 57:6
ungodliness tents of u. — BOOK 62:12

ungodly plagues remain for the u. BOOK 61:13
u. in great power BOOK 61:17
unhabitable no land u. THOR 317:23
unhappily bad end u. STOP 304:17
unhappiness putting-off of u. GREE 146:24
vocation of u. SIME 295:23
unhappy each u. family TOLS 318:15
I'm u. CHEK 88:32
soft, u. sex BEHN 28:1
u., far-off things WORD 341:10
unheard language of the u. KING 186:13
those u. Are sweeter KEAT 181:29
unholy sights u. MILT 219:25
unhonoured Unwept, u. SCOT 266:11
uninspiring may be u. GEOR 138:6
unintelligible rapid, u. patter GILB 141:9
union Act of U. is there TRIM 319:12
determined to preserve this U. HOUS 165:12
devotion to the u. CARS 84:19
Liberty *and* U. WEBS 330:6
O U., strong and great LONG 201:18
Our Federal U. JACK 169:16
u. of hands and hearts TAYL 310:2
unions when Hitler attacked the u. NIEM 234:5
unite Workers of the world, u. MARX 214:10
United States close to the U. DIAZ 109:12
U. themselves WHIT 334:3
unities Three U. DRYD 117:15
uniting By u. we stand DICK 111:18
unity truth, u., and concord BOOK 59:26
universal one u. grin FIEL 127:16
Relaxed into a u. grin COWP 102:6
u. monarchy of wit CARE 82:6
universe Architect of the U. JEAN 171:11
hell of a good u. next door CUMM 104:18
Life, the U. and Everything ADAM 1:11
measure of the u. SHEL 293:17
ordering of the u. ALFO 3:20
Put back Thy u. JONE 177:8
u. go to all the bother HAWK 153:12
u. is not hostile HOLM 161:8
u. queerer than we suppose HALD 149:11
u.'s existence made known PENR 243:11
u. sleeps MAYA 215:15
we and the u. exist HAWK 153:13
university gained in the u. of life BOTT 65:3
God-sustaining U. GLAD 142:3
U. of these days CARL 82:22
unjust commended the u. steward BIBL 46:36
on the just and on the u. BIBL 42:20
u. steals BOWE 65:15
unjustly teach to talk u. ARIS 14:9
unkindest most u. cut of all SHAK 276:20
unkist Uncouth u. SPEN 300:25
unknowable decide on the u. ZOBE 345:6
unknowing cloud of u. ANON 6:5
unknown buried the U. Prime Minister ASQU 16:19
gates to the glorious and u. FORS 131:14
My song is love is u. CROS 104:8
She lived u. WORD 341:5
to the u. god BIBL 48:34
u. and silent shore LAMB 192:6
u. regions preserved ELIO 121:8
Woman is the great u. HARD 151:12
unleavened u. bread BIBL 34:6
u. bread HAGG 148:19
unleaving Goldengrove u. HOPK 163:3
unlessoned u. girl SHAK 282:17
unloose not worthy to u. BIBL 47:22
unluckily good u. STOP 304:17
unmaking things are in the u. KING 186:16
unmarried prime-roses, That die u. SHAK 289:12
unnatural only u. sex act KINS 187:4

unnecessary thou u. letter SHAK 277:13
unofficial English u. rose BROO 67:20
unpalatable disastrous and the u. GALB 135:11
unparalleled lies A lass u. SHAK 269:9
unplumbed u., salt, estranging sea ARNO 15:26
unpolitical no such thing as an u. man MALA 210:3
unprincipled sold by the u. CAPP 82:1
unprofitable flat, and u. SHAK 270:30
most idle and u. GIBB 139:6
unprofitably U. travelling WORD 340:21
unprotected u. race CLAR 93:9
unrest u. which men miscall delight SHEL 292:18
unrighteousness mammon of u. BIBL 47:1
unruly old fool, u. sun DONN 114:12
u. evil BIBL 51:22
unsafe U. at any speed NADE 230:19
unsayable say the u. RUSH 262:4
unscathed u. tourist of wars GELL 137:16
unsearchable u. riches of Christ BIBL 50:17
unseen born to blush u. GRAY 146:16
Thou art u. SHEL 293:31
walk the earth U. MILT 222:4
unsex U. me here SHAK 279:14
unsoiled delicately and u. CHUR 92:8
unspeakable speak the u. RUSH 262:4
u. in full pursuit WILD 335:11
unstable U. as water BIBL 33:37
unsung unhonoured, and u. SCOT 266:11
untalented product of the u. CAPP 82:1
untender So young, and so u. SHAK 277:8
untimely U. ripped SHAK 281:25
unto give u. this last BIBL 44:24
u. us a child is born BIBL 39:19
untried difficult; and left u. CHES 90:7
untrodden among the u. ways WORD 341:3
through an u. forest MURR 230:10
untrue man who's u. to his wife AUDE 18:10
unusual cruel and u. punishment CONS 99:17
unutterable looked u. things THOM 317:11
unvarnished round u. tale SHAK 284:11
unwanted feeling of being u. TERE 314:11
unwept U., unhonoured SCOT 266:11
unwholesome not u. AUST 19:16
unwilling committee is a group of the u. ANON 6:7
unwritten Custom, that u. law D'AV 106:11
up be u. betimes SHAK 288:11
nice to people on your way u. MIZN 225:4
u. go we QUAR 253:6
U. Guards and at them WELL 331:6
u.-hill all the way ROSS 260:14
U., Lord BOOK 60:28
U. to a point, Lord Copper WAUG 329:21
U. with your damned nonsense RICH 257:3
upharsin MENE, TEKEL, U. BIBL 41:8
upper butler's u. slopes WODE 338:7
large u. room BIBL 47:9
Like many of the U. Class BELL 28:22
man have the u. hand BOOK 60:28
prove the u. classes COWA 101:10
u. station of low life DEFO 107:13
upright God hath made man u. BIBL 38:22
stand u. in the winds BOLT 57:16
uprising Our wakening and u. KEBL 183:19
upside world u. down BIBL 48:33
upstairs kicked u. HALI 150:7
upstanding clean u. chap like you KING 187:2
upward Eternal Woman draws us u. GOET 142:21
upwards car could go straight u. HOYL 166:1
urbe Rus in u. MART 213:11
urge u. for destruction BAKU 23:5
urges Will that stirs and u. HARD 151:21
Uricon ashes under U. HOUS 165:6
urine red wine of Shiraz into u. DINE 111:27

urn Pit's long-broken u. — WILD 335:18
urns u. and sepulchres — CREW 103:10
us Not unto u., O Lord — BOOK 63:6
USA Born in the U. — SPRI 301:4
use such as cannot u. them — JONS 177:18
  true u. of speech — GOLD 143:24
  u. alone that sanctifies — POPE 247:22
  U. every man after his desert — SHAK 271:34
  u. of a new-born child — FRAN 133:11
  u. rather than ostentation — GIBB 139:3
  worn away by u. — OVID 238:13
used Things ain't what they u. to be — PERS 244:6
useful be a Really U. Engine — AWDR 20:7
  know to be u. — MORR 228:19
  way to what is u. — COUS 100:19
useless are the most u. — RUSK 262:16
  Lodged with me u. — MILT 223:9
usquebae Wi' u., we'll face — BURN 75:25
usual Business carried on as u. — CHUR 91:8
usury forbidden u. — KORA 190:9
Utopia U. is a blessed past — KISS 189:5
Utrecht (Whom God Preserve) of U. — MORT 229:7
utterly should u. have fainted — BOOK 61:10
uttermost u. parts of the sea — BOOK 63:25
U-turn media catchphrase, the U. — THAT 315:6

V

V with a ''V'' or a ''W'' — DICK 111:7
vacancies v. to be obtained — JEFF 171:14
vacant spoke the v. mind — GOLD 143:9
  v. interstellar spaces — ELIO 121:25
vacations No extras, no v. — DICK 110:21
vacuum Nature abhors a v. — RABE 253:12
vadis Quo v. — BIBL 53:10
vae V. victis — LIVY 200:12
vain name of God in v. — BIBL 34:14
  people imagine a v. thing — BOOK 60:26
  v., ill-natured — DEFO 107:19
  V. the ambition of kings — WEBS 330:8
vainly v. men themselves amaze — MARV 213:15
vale ave atque v. — CATU 86:3
  in that hollow v. — KING 186:6
  v. of misery — BOOK 62:11
valere sed v. vita est — MART 213:9
valet hero to his v. — CORN 100:11
  to his very v. seemed — BYRO 77:24
valiant As he was v., I honour him — SHAK 276:13
  Ring in the v. man — TENN 311:31
  v. never taste of death — SHAK 276:6
valley great things from the v. — CHES 90:3
  How green was my v. — LLEW 200:14
  in the v. of Death — TENN 310:15
  Love is of the v. — TENN 313:18
  V. and lowland, sing — OAKL 235:10
  v. full of bones — BIBL 41:4
  v. of Humiliation — BUNY 72:23
  v. of the shadow of death — BOOK 61:7
  v. shall be exalted — BIBL 40:7
valleys down the v. wild — BLAK 56:4
  lily of the v. — BIBL 39:3
  v., groves, hills — MARL 212:13
Vallombrosa V., where the Etrurian shades — MILT 221:9
Valois shadow of the V. — CHES 89:22
valour true v. see — BUNY 73:9
valuable Truth is the most v. thing — TWAI 321:5
value little v. of fortune — STEE 302:4
  v. of nothing — WILD 335:7
values moneys are for v. — BACO 20:19
  Victorian v. — THAT 315:8
van Follow the v. — COLL 97:5

Vandyke V. is of the company — GAIN 135:5
vanish softly and suddenly v. — CARR 84:15
  v. with the rose — FITZ 129:1
vanished This time it v. — CARR 83:18
  this v. being — HAWK 153:11
  v. before the white man — TECU 310:6
vanishings Fallings from us, v. — WORD 340:12
vanitas V. vanitatum — BIBL 53:4
vanities bonfire of the v. — WOLF 338:18
vanity all is v. — BIBL 38:12
  feeds your v. — PARR 241:12
  name of V.-Fair — BUNY 73:2
  pomps and v. — BOOK 60:9
  Pull down thy v. — POUN 250:12
  V., like murder, will out — COWL 101:16
  v. of human hopes — JOHN 173:23
  V. of vanities — BIBL 38:12
vanquished Valiantly v. — SHAK 268:27
vapour I absorb the v. — GLAD 142:4
variety stale Her infinite v. — SHAK 268:20
  V. is the soul — BEHN 27:20
  V.'s the very spice — COWP 102:1
varium V. et mutabile semper Femina — VIRG 324:16
Varus V., give me back my legions — AUGU 19:7
vase not a v. to be filled — RABE 253:14
  Sèvres v. in the hands — WAUG 329:23
vats boilers and v. — JOHN 176:8
vatum genus irritabile v. — HORA 164:5
vaulting V. ambition — SHAK 279:22
veal Bellamy's v. pies — PITT 245:15
vécu J'ai v. — SIEY 295:17
Vega V. conspicuous overhead — AUDE 18:13
vegetable v., animal, and mineral — GILB 141:5
  v. love should grow — MARV 213:20
veil from behind a v. — KORA 190:22
  wrapped in a gauzy veil — SHEL 294:3
vein not in the giving v. — SHAK 286:7
venal v. city ripe to perish — SALL 264:1
venerable what v. creatures — TRAH 319:4
Veneres V. Cupidinesque — CATU 85:18
vengeance stay the hands of v. — JACK 169:20
  sudden v. waits — POPE 247:1
  V. is mine — BIBL 49:20
veni V., Sancte Spiritus — LANG 193:3
  V., vidi, vici — CAES 80:3
Venice stood in V. — BYRO 78:2
venit Benedictus qui v. — MISS 224:4
venite v., adoremus Dominum — ANON 12:6
venture drew a bow at a v. — BIBL 36:18
Venus V. here will choose her dwelling — DRYD 117:2
  V. tout entière — RACI 253:19
  women are from V. — GRAY 146:8
vera v. incessu patuit dea — VIRG 324:11
verb V. is God — HUGO 166:15
  v. not a noun — FULL 134:23
  word is the V. — HUGO 166:15
verba Nullius in v. — ANON 12:16
  v. sequentur — CATO 85:16
verbal v. contract isn't worth — GOLD 144:9
verbo sed tantum dic v. — MISS 224:7
verboojuice Sesquippledan v. — WELL 331:15
verbosa v. rusticitas — JERO 172:3
verbosity crude v. — JERO 172:3
  exuberance of his own v. — DISR 112:15
verbrennt wo man Bücher V. — HEIN 155:7
verbum V. caro factum est — MISS 224:9
  V. sapienti — PLAU 246:3
  volat irrevocabile v. — HORA 163:26
verdict v. afterwards — CARR 84:2
verge get to the v. — DULL 117:25
verifiability criterion of v. — AYER 20:10
verification method of its v. — SCHL 265:15
verify v. your references — ROUT 261:12

verily v., I say unto you — BIBL 47:32
verisimilitude artistic v. — GILB 140:18
fine isolated v. — KEAT 183:6
veritas *magis amica v.* — ARIS 14:20
Magna est v., et praevalet — BIBL 53:14
vermilion V.-spotted, golden — KEAT 181:22
vermin lower than v. — BEVA 32:8
Vermont so goes V. — FARL 126:7
vero *Se non è v.* — ANON 13:3
verse all that is not v. — MOLI 225:10
as soon write free v. — FROS 134:15
died to make v. free — PRES 251:3
Doctors in v. — THOM 316:21
for prose and v. — CARE 82:5
indignation makes me write v. — JUVE 179:20
No subject for immortal v. — DAY- 107:4
rugged v. I chose — DRYD 117:7
v. is a measured speech — BACO 20:20
v. the subject fit — CARE 82:9
Voice, and V. — MILT 219:9
with those in v. — CONG 98:18
write it out in a v. — YEAT 342:22
verses Tear him for his bad v. — SHAK 276:26
versions hundred v. of it — SHAW 291:27
verum *Ave v. corpus* — ANON 12:10
quaerere v. — HORA 164:4
very V. God of very God — BOOK 59:22
vespers friars were singing v. — GIBB 139:8
vessel gilded v. goes — GRAY 146:12
unto the weaker v. — BIBL 51:28
vesture cast lots upon my v. — BOOK 61:5
Mine outward v. be — LITT 200:6
Vexilla *Vexilla regis prodeunt* — FORT 131:20
vibrates V. in the memory — SHEL 293:27
vibration brave v. each way free — HERR 158:10
vice Art is v. — DEGA 107:22
defence of liberty is no v. — GOLD 144:6
end in sight was a v. — BROW 71:8
in a private man a v. — MASS 214:19
raptures and roses of v. — SWIN 307:21
render v. serviceable — BOLI 57:15
sensual pleasure without v. — JOHN 177:2
v. pays to virtue — LA R 193:20
virtue and v. — JOHN 174:25
vices our pleasant v. — SHAK 278:10
redeemed his v. — JONS 178:11
vicious didn't know what v. was — AUNG 19:10
vicisti V., *Galilae* — JULI 179:11
victi *Pugna magna v. sumus* — LIVY 200:13
victim felt like a v. — WALP 327:18
oppressor, never the v. — WIES 334:13
v. must be found — GILB 140:8
victims blame to its 'v.' — SONT 299:6
gave its v. time to die — GUIB 148:12
little v. play — GRAY 146:18
v. who respect their executioners — SART 264:25
victis *Vae v.* — LIVY 200:12
victor to the v. belong — MARC 211:16
Victoria take a ticket at V. — BEVI 32:13
Victorian V. values — THAT 315:8
victories Peace hath her v. — MILT 223:13
victory grave, where is thy v. — BIBL 50:8
In v.; magnanimity — CHUR 92:11
in v. unbearable — CHUR 92:7
not the v. but the contest — COUB 100:16
One more such v. — PYRR 253:1
peace without v. — WILS 337:7
produce v. parades — HOBS 160:8
swallow up death in v. — BIBL 39:28
'twas a famous v. — SOUT 299:13
v. by a woman — WEST 332:19
V. has a hundred fathers — CIAN 92:17
wallow in our v. — PRES 251:2

vidders Be wery careful o' v. — DICK 111:6
vidi *Veni, v., vici* — CAES 80:3
vie *v. humaine commence* — SART 264:24
vieillesse *si v. pouvait* — ESTI 125:4
Vietnam V. as a war — PILG 244:21
view lends enchantment to the v. — CAMP 81:3
motley to the v. — SHAK 290:4
views Kipling and his v. — AUDE 18:5
vigilance eternal v. — CURR 105:5
vigilant Be sober, be v. — BIBL 51:30
vile only man is v. — HEBE 155:2
V., but viler George the Second — LAND 192:23
village first in a v. — CAES 80:1
image of a global v. — MCLU 208:4
in a country v. — AUST 20:2
life in the v. — LEE 196:11
Sweet Auburn, loveliest v. — GOLD 143:6
villages pleasant v. and farms — MILT 222:15
villain One murder made a v. — PORT 249:22
smiling, damnèd v. — SHAK 282:14
villainy v. you teach me — SHAK 282:14
vinces *In hoc signo v.* — CONS 99:14
vincit *Omnia v. Amor* — VIRG 325:14
vindicate v. the ways of God — POPE 248:8
vine as the fruitful v. — BOOK 63:20
clusters of the v. — MARV 213:16
vinegar Oil, v., sugar — GOLD 143:17
vines advise his client to plant v. — WRIG 341:26
bless With fruit the v. — KEAT 182:21
vintage O, for a draught of v. — KEAT 182:10
trampling out the v. — HOWE 165:15
violations no end to the v. — BOWE 65:10
violence Snobbery with V. — BENN 29:21
v. is necessary — BROW 68:13
violent All v. feelings — RUSK 262:9
laid v. hands upon themselves — BOOK 60:22
violently v. if they must — QUIN 253:9
violet v. by a mossy stone — WORD 341:4
v. smells to him — SHAK 275:1
violets I would give you some v. — SHAK 273:6
Who are the v. now — SHAK 285:29
vipers O generation of v. — BIBL 42:8
vir *Beatus v. qui timet Dominum* — BIBL 52:32
Virgil V. at Mexico — WALP 327:12
virgin v. goddess returns — VIRG 325:10
V. is the possibility — BRAN 66:3
v. shall conceive — BIBL 39:17
virginity for my v. — PRIO 251:11
virtue Assume a v. — SHAK 272:26
Few men have v. to withstand — WASH 328:19
governs his state by v. — CONF 98:6
in a prince the v. — MASS 214:19
lilies and languors of v. — SWIN 307:21
no v. like necessity — SHAK 285:10
O infinite v. — SHAK 268:23
'tis some v. — CONG 98:20
to the cause of v. — BOLI 57:15
vice pays to v. — LA R 193:20
v. and vice — JOHN 174:25
V. is like a rich stone — BACO 21:3
V. is the fount — MARL 212:17
V. may be assailed — MILT 219:17
What is v. — SHAW 291:14
without v. — ROBE 257:19
woman of easy v. — HAIL 149:8
virtues all the v. of Man — BYRO 79:20
makes some v. impracticable — JOHN 176:10
plant whose v. — EMER 124:14
vices with his v. — JONS 178:11
v. made or crimes — DEFO 107:17
v. very kind — PRIO 251:8
v. Will plead — SHAK 279:21
virtuous because thou art v. — SHAK 288:15

v. woman	BIBL 38:11
v. woman is a crown	BIBL 37:26
visible all things v. and invisible	BOOK 59:22
darkness v.	MILT 221:3
it makes v.	KLEE 189:8
outward and v. sign	BOOK 60:11
representation of v. things	LEON 197:21
vision Bright the v.	MANT 211:10
by the v. splendid	WORD 340:11
single central v.	BERL 30:23
v. thing	BUSH 76:21
Was it a v.	KEAT 182:16
Where there is no v.	BIBL 38:9
Write the v.	BIBL 41:18
visionary Whither is fled the v. gleam	WORD 340:9
visions shades send deceptive v.	VIRG 325:2
young men shall see v.	BIBL 41:14
visitation time of their v.	BIBL 41:22
visiting v. the iniquity	BIBL 34:13
visits Superior people never make long v.	MOOR 227:10
visual v. telegram	CASS 85:6
vita *Ars longa, v. brevis*	HIPP 159:11
cammin di nostra v.	DANT 105:16
vitai *v. lampada*	LUCR 204:14
vital V. spark	POPE 246:25
v. spirit	BERG 30:12
vivamus *V., mea Lesbia*	CATU 85:19
vivere *Nec tuam possum v.*	MART 213:10
vivid left the v. air signed	SPEN 300:10
vixen v. when she went to school	SHAK 283:18
vobis *Pax V.*	BIBL 53:9
vobiscum *Dominus v.*	MISS 223:24
vocation v. of unhappiness	SIME 295:23
vodka medium V. dry Martini	FLEM 130:1
vogue totter into v.	WALP 327:10
voice daughter of the v. of God	WORD 340:15
Her v. was ever soft	SHAK 278:13
I have lost my v.	WEBS 330:20
Lord, hear my v.	BOOK 63:21
people's v. is odd	POPE 248:26
scream in a low v.	BYRO 79:22
still small v.	BIBL 36:13
supplicating v.	JOHN 174:8
Thunder is the v. of God	MATH 215:4
v. and nothing more	ANON 13:2
V., and Verse	MILT 219:9
v. is Jacob's voice	BIBL 33:29
v. of a nation	RUSS 263:1
v. of Doris Day	FISH 128:8
v. of one crying	BIBL 42:6
v. of Rome	JONS 177:13
v. of the charmer	BOOK 62:4
v. of the kingdom	SWIF 306:16
v. of the Lord God	BIBL 33:7
v. of the people	ALCU 3:10
v. of the turtle	BIBL 39:4
v. that breathed o'er Eden	KEBL 183:21
v. was that of Mr Churchill	ATTL 17:9
voices Ancestral v. prophesying war	COLE 96:6
Other v., other rooms	CAPO 81:21
Two V. are there	WORD 341:14
when soft v. die	SHEL 293:27
voids attempts to fill v.	WEIL 330:22
vol *suspend ton v.*	LAMA 191:23
volat *v. irrevocabile verbum*	HORA 163:26
volcano crust over a v. of revolution	ELLI 124:3
volcanoes range of exhausted v.	DISR 112:11
v. burnt out	BURK 74:20
vole passes the questing v.	WAUG 329:22
volenti *V. non fit iniuria*	ULPI 321:19
volley v. we have just heard	COLL 97:6
Voltaire V. in the Bastille	DE G 107:26
volume take in our hand any v.	HUME 166:19

volumes all Earth's v.	CHAP 87:18
creators of odd v.	LAMB 192:3
thirty fine v.	MORL 228:9
voluntary Composing's not v.	BIRT 54:9
v. spies	AUST 19:21
voluntas *fiat v.*	MISS 224:5
vomit dog is turned to his own v.	BIBL 51:31
dog returneth to his v.	BIBL 38:6
vote always v. *against*	FIEL 127:22
One man shall have one v.	CART 85:4
v. against somebody	ADAM 1:14
voted v. at my party's call	GILB 141:1
v. cent per cent	BYRO 77:22
votes v. to get the things done	SAMU 264:4
voting If v. changed anything	LIVI 200:11
not the v. that's democracy	STOP 304:13
vow v. to thee, my country	SPRI 301:3
vowels U green, O blue: v.	RIMB 257:13
vows cancel all our v.	DRAY 116:5
vox *V. et praeterea nihil*	ANON 13:2
V. populi	ALCU 3:10
voyage in for Hobbes's v.	VANB 322:9
make the v. over	VIRG 324:22
take my last v.	HOBB 160:6
v. to the moon	LARD 193:7
voyages v. of the starship *Enterprise*	RODD 258:18
vulgar trivial and v. way	BROW 69:7
upon the v. with fine sense	POPE 249:9
v. expression	CONG 98:9
vulgarity human v.	AMIS 5:2

W

W with a ''V'' or a ''W''	DICK 111:7
wabe gimble in the w.	CARR 84:3
wade should I w. no more	SHAK 281:3
waded w. thro' red blude	BALL 24:12
wage home policy: I w. war	CLEM 94:8
wages neither honours nor w.	GARI 136:5
paid in full your w.	KORA 190:12
w. of sin is death	BIBL 49:13
wagged tail that w.	WATS 329:4
Wagner W. has lovely moments	ROSS 260:21
W.'s music	NYE 235:8
wagon Hitch your w. to a star	EMER 124:15
wail nothing to w.	MILT 223:5
wailing w. for her demon-lover	COLE 96:4
wains hangs heavy from the w.	GIBB 139:11
wait too slow for those who w.	VAN 322:15
w. and see	ASQU 16:18
w. for ever	MACA 205:14
w. for what will come	ROBI 258:2
we won't w.	ANON 10:17
who only stand and w.	MILT 223:10
waiting w. for Godot	BECK 26:20
W. for the end	EMPS 124:20
w. seven hundred years	COLL 97:8
wake do I w. or sleep	KEAT 182:16
W. up, England	GEOR 138:3
we w. eternally	DONN 113:20
wakening Our w. and uprising	KEBL 183:19
wakes Hock-carts, wassails, w.	HERR 157:26
Wordsworth sometimes w.	BYRO 78:25
waking w., no such matter	SHAK 289:35
Wales bless the Prince of W.	LINL 200:4
no present in W.	THOM 316:24
still parts of W.	THOM 316:19
whole world . . . But for W.	BOLT 57:17
walk closer w. with God	COWP 101:24
machine that would w.	APOL 13:12
never w. alone	HAMM 151:1

walk (*cont.*)
no easy w.-over to freedom — NEHR 232:5
not easy to w. on ways — JAIN 170:7
take up thy bed, and w. — BIBL 47:30
taking a w. that day — BRON 67:8
upon which the people w. — CRAZ 103:7
w. a little faster — CARR 83:23
W. cheerfully over the world — FOX 132:16
w. circumspectly — BIBL 50:20
w. humbly with thy God — BIBL 41:17
w. in fear and dread — COLE 96:17
w. in newness of life — BIBL 49:11
w. o'er the western wave — SHEL 294:2
w. on the wild side — ALGR 4:1
W. upon England's mountains green — BLAK 55:27
w. within the purlieus — ETHE 125:5
w. ye — BIBL 40:2
Where'er you w. — POPE 248:31
Yea, though I w. — BOOK 61:7
walked He w. by himself — KIPL 188:21
slowly w. away — BURT 76:5
w. through the wilderness — BUNY 72:21
walking empire w. very slowly — FITZ 129:9
Lord God w. in the garden — BIBL 33:7
w. up and down — BIBL 36:36
walks She w. in beauty — BYRO 79:14
wall close the w. up — SHAK 274:33
doesn't love a w. — FROS 134:10
have I leaped over a w. — BIBL 35:34
like a stone w. — BEE 27:7
w. fell down flat — BIBL 34:31
w. next door catches fire — HORA 164:1
Watch the w., my darling — KIPL 188:9
With our backs to the w. — HAIG 149:7
Without a city w. — ALEX 3:18
wooden w. is your ships — THEM 315:17
Wallace hae wi' W. bled — BURN 75:22
wallet Time hath, my lord, a w. — SHAK 287:30
wallow w. in our victory — PRES 251:2
walls angels on the w. — MARL 212:18
not in w. — NICI 233:22
Stone w. do not a prison make — LOVE 203:6
these w. thy sphere — DONN 114:13
w. of stone or brass — COTT 100:15
wooden w. are the best — COVE 101:2
waltzing You'll come a-w., Matilda — PATE 242:1
wan Why so pale and w. — SUCK 305:10
wandered w. far and wide — HOME 161:20
w. lonely as a cloud — WORD 340:1
wanderer do not we, W., await it too — ARNO 15:18
wandering but a w. voice — WORD 341:15
w. minstrel I — GILB 140:6
Werchynge and w. — LANG 193:1
want don't w. him — MILN 218:24
in w. of a wife — AUST 19:24
I shall not w. — BOOK 61:6
I w. some more — DICK 110:26
probably won't w. — HOPE 162:15
that people know what they w. — MENC 216:14
third is freedom from w. — ROOS 259:20
w. it the most — CHES 89:9
w. of decency — DILL 111:23
W. one only of five giants — BEVE 32:12
we w. it now — MORR 228:21
What can I w. or need — HERB 157:7
what I really really w. — ROWB 261:13
wanting found w. — BIBL 41:8
wanton wightly w. — SHAK 278:18
wantonly unadvisedly, lightly, or w. — BOOK 60:15
wantonness in clothes a w. — HERR 158:3
wants Man w. but little — GOLD 143:14
wanwood worlds of w. leafmeal — HOPK 163:4
war After each w. — ATKI 17:7

Ancestral voices prophesying w. — COLE 96:6
another w. in Europe — BISM 54:19
at w. with Germany — CHAM 86:21
better than to w.-war — CHUR 92:4
bungled, unwise w. — PLOM 246:6
but it is not w. — BOSQ 64:17
calamities of w. — JOHN 173:17
clamour for w. — PEEL 242:20
cold w. — BARU 25:20
cold w. warrior — THAT 315:4
condition which is called w. — HOBB 160:1
cruellest and most terrible w. — LLOY 200:19
desolation of w. — GEOR 138:4
done very well out of the w. — BALD 23:8
easier to make w. — CLEM 94:9
enable it to make w. — WEIL 330:23
endless w. still breed — MILT 220:22
except the British W. Office — SHAW 290:24
First World W. had begun — TAYL 309:19
France has not lost the w. — DE G 107:23
furnish the w. — HEAR 154:16
home policy: I wage w. — CLEM 94:8
I am for w. — RED 255:6
if someone gave a w. — GINS 141:13
I hate w. — ROOS 259:17
I have seen w. — ROOS 259:17
Image of w. — SOME 299:1
in every w. they kill you in a new way — ROGE 259:7
In w.; resolution — CHUR 92:11
I renounce w. — FOSD 132:2
justifiable act of w. — BELL 28:3
let slip the dogs of w. — SHAK 276:11
looks on w. as all glory — SHER 294:26
lose the w. in an afternoon — CHUR 92:12
made this great w. — LINC 199:14
make w. that we may live — ARIS 14:13
McNamara's W. — MCNA 208:14
money the sinews of w. — BACO 21:28
nature of w. — HOBB 160:2
neither shall they learn w. — BIBL 39:11
never was a good w. — FRAN 133:8
no declaration of w. — EDEN 119:17
no discharge in that w. — BIBL 38:23
page 1 of the book of w. — MONT 226:19
pattern called a w. — LOWE 203:13
prepare for w. — VEGE 323:8
provoke a new civil w. — JUAN 179:7
recourse to w. — BRIA 66:16
silent in time of w. — CICE 92:29
sinews of w. — CICE 92:28
soon as w. is declared — GIRA 141:16
state of w. by nature — SWIF 307:10
subject is W. — OWEN 238:20
tell us all about the w. — SOUT 299:12
they'll give a w. — SAND 264:10
this is w. — ADAM 1:10
time of w. — BIBL 38:18
to the w. is gone — MOOR 227:17
two nations have been at w. — VOLT 325:21
Vietnam as a w. — PILG 244:21
w. and peace in 21st century — KOHL 190:2
w. has used up words — JAME 170:25
W. hath no fury — MONT 226:6
w. in heaven — BIBL 52:14
w. is a necessary part — MOLT 225:16
W. is continuation of politics — CLAU 94:1
W. is hell, and all that — HAY 153:16
w. is over — GRAN 145:18
w. is politics with bloodshed — MAO 211:11
w. is so terrible — LEE 196:14
W. is the national industry — MIRA 223:23
W. is the trade of kings — DRYD 117:1
W. is too serious — CLEM 94:7

W. its thousands slays	PORT 249:23
w. situation	HIRO 159:12
w. that will end war	WELL 331:18
W. to the knife	PALA 239:19
w. which existed in order to	HOBS 160:8
way of ending a w.	ORWE 237:21
we prepare for w.	PEAR 242:18
what a lovely w.	LITT 200:7
When w. enters a country	ANON 12:2
When w. is declared	ANON 11:2
win an atomic w.	BRAD 65:22
without having won the w.	YOKO 344:8
wardrobe open your w.	WELD 331:3
wards W. in Jarndyce	DICK 109:18
warfare Armed w. must be preceded	ZINO 345:5
w. is accomplished	BIBL 40:6
warlord concubine of a w.	JUNG 179:16
warm For ever w.	KEAT 182:3
O! she's w.	SHAK 289:16
too w. work, Hardy	NELS 232:10
warmth W. and Light	GREN 147:10
warn right to w.	BAGE 22:21
w., to comfort, and command	WORD 341:7
w. you not to be ordinary	KINN 187:3
warning With horrid w.	KEAT 181:21
warrant not a sufficient w.	MILL 218:3
warring two nations w.	DURH 118:15
warrior cold war w.	THAT 315:4
Home they brought her w.	TENN 313:11
This is the happy w.	READ 254:19
Who is the happy W.	WORD 339:17
wars all their w. are merry	CHES 89:18
came to an end all w.	LLOY 200:19
History littered with the w.	POWE 250:22
not armaments that cause w.	MADA 209:3
serve in the w.	BOOK 64:6
tourist of w.	GELL 137:16
w. and rumours of wars	BIBL 44:33
w., horrible wars	VIRG 324:19
w. planned by old men	RICE 256:15
Warsaw Order reigns in W.	ANON 11:17
warts w. and all	CROM 104:2
wash Moab is my w.-pot	BOOK 62:5
w. that man right outa	HAMM 150:18
washed w. his hands	BIBL 45:19
w. in the blood of the Lamb	LIND 199:16
washing country w.	BRUM 71:18
w. on the Siegfried Line	KENN 184:6
Washington come to W. to be loved	GRAM 145:13
Government at W. lives	GARF 136:4
wasp everything about the w.	THOM 316:8
wasps w. and hornets break through	SWIF 306:17
wassails Hock-carts, w., wakes	HERR 157:26
waste art of how to w. space	JOHN 173:9
file your w. basket-paper	BENN 29:16
now doth time w. me	SHAK 285:31
w. howling wilderness	BIBL 34:29
w. of shame	SHAK 290:8
w. places of Jerusalem	BIBL 40:15
we lay w. our powers	WORD 341:18
wasted spend on advertising is w.	LEVE 198:4
w. his substance	BIBL 46:32
watch could ye not watch with me	BIBL 45:16
done much better by a w.	BELL 28:23
keeping w. over their flock	BIBL 46:3
learning, like your w.	CHES 89:10
like a fat gold w.	PLAT 245:22
some must w.	SHAK 272:16
W. and pray	BIBL 45:17
W. and pray	ELLI 123:22
w. a sailing cloud	LIN 200:5
w. between me and thee	BIBL 33:32
w. in the night	BOOK 62:14

w. must have had a maker	PALE 239:20
W. therefore	BIBL 45:4
watcher posted presence of the w.	JAME 170:20
w. of the skies	KEAT 182:19
watchful occasion's forelock w.	MILT 222:26
watching BIG BROTHER IS W. YOU	ORWE 237:14
watchmaker blind w.	DAWK 107:1
watchman w. on the lonely tower	SCOT 266:14
W., what of the night	BIBL 39:26
water as w. spilt on the ground	BIBL 35:32
bridge over troubled w.	SIMO 295:24
conscious w. saw its God	CRAS 102:24
desireth the w.-brooks	BOOK 61:21
drawers of w.	BIBL 34:32
fountain of the w. of life	BIBL 52:26
if I were under w.	KEAT 183:9
King over the W.	ANON 8:5
Little drops of w.	CARN 83:9
little w. clears us	SHAK 280:13
name was writ in w.	KEAT 183:17
ready by w. as by land	ELST 124:4
ring of bright w.	RAIN 253:23
spring of ever-flowing w.	HORA 164:21
Tar w.	BERK 30:14
travel by land or by w.	BOOK 59:8
Unstable as w.	BIBL 33:37
virtues We write in w.	SHAK 275:27
walking on the w.	THOM 317:4
w. and a crust	KEAT 181:23
w. hollows out	OVID 238:13
w. in the rough rude sea	SHAK 285:17
W. is best	PIND 245:2
w. like Pilate	GREE 146:23
'w.' meant the wonderful	KELL 183:24
w. of affliction	BIBL 36:17
W., water, everywhere	COLE 96:13
weaker than w.	LAO 193:6
We'll o'er the w.	HOGG 160:23
where the w. goes	CHES 90:2
watercress ask for a w. sandwich	WILD 335:19
watered w. heaven with their tears	BLAK 56:15
w. our houses in Helicon	CHAP 87:15
Waterloo Austerlitz and W.	SAND 264:9
battle of W.	WELL 331:12
battle of W. won	ORWE 237:12
world-earthquake, W.	TENN 312:29
waterman great-grandfather was but a w.	BUNY 73:4
watermen w., that row one way	BURT 76:12
waters as the w. cover the sea	BIBL 39:23
beside the still w.	BOOK 61:6
By the w. of Babylon	BOOK 63:23
Cast thy bread upon the w.	BIBL 38:31
cold w. to a thirsty soul	BIBL 38:4
face of the w.	BIBL 32:21
in great w.	BOOK 63:1
quiet w. by	SCOT 266:28
seething of the w.	AURE 19:12
Stolen w. are sweet	BIBL 37:24
w. cannot quench love	BIBL 39:9
w. of affliction	BIBL 40:1
w. of comfort	BOOK 61:6
w. of Israel	BIBL 36:24
w. of office	TROL 319:16
w. were his winding sheet	BARN 25:11
Watson Elementary, my dear W.	DOYL 115:14
Mr W., come here	BELL 28:2
wave age is rocking the w.	MAND 211:4
bind the restless w.	WHIT 333:18
cool, translucent w.	MILT 219:18
lift me as a w.	SHEL 293:8
upon an orient w.	MILT 220:26
waveless w. plain of Lombardy	SHEL 293:3

waves Him that walked the w.   MILT 220:20
 Like as the w.   SHAK 289:30
 on which the w. break   AURE 19:12
 w. were always saying   DICK 110:12
 wild w. saying   CARP 83:11
waving not w. but drowning   SMIT 298:3
wax hives with honey and w.   SWIF 306:15
way broad is the w.   BIBL 43:8
 by w. of Beachy Head   CHES 89:25
 every one to his own w.   BIBL 40:17
 going the w. of all the earth   BIBL 34:33
 long w. to Tipperary   JUDG 179:8
 more a w. of life   ANON 9:2
 Prepare ye the w. of the Lord   BIBL 42:6
 there was a w. to Hell   BUNY 73:5
 This is the w.   BIBL 40:2
 W. down upon the Swanee   FOST 132:8
 w. of a man with a maid   BIBL 38:10
 W. of our Master   CONF 98:8
 w. of the Lord   BIBL 40:7
 w. of transgressors   BIBL 37:30
 w., the truth, and the life   BIBL 48:6
 w. to the stars   VIRG 325:4
 your w. be long   CAVA 86:5
ways in whose heart are thy w.   BOOK 62:11
 justify the w. of God   MILT 221:2
 Let me count the w.   BROW 69:14
 parting of the w.   BIBL 41:3
 vindicate the w. of God   POPE 248:8
 w. are ways of pleasantness   BIBL 37:19
 w. be unconfined   PRIO 251:8
wayside seeds fell by the w.   BIBL 44:1
we W. are seven   WORD 341:17
 W.'re here   ANON 10:15
weak flesh is w.   BIBL 45:17
 found him w. in chemistry   WELL 331:14
 w. always have to decide   BONH 58:3
 w. overcomes the strong   LAO 193:6
 w. piping time   SHAK 286:1
weaken great life if you don't w.   BUCH 71:24
weaker to the w. side inclined   BUTL 77:9
 unto the w. vessel   BIBL 51:28
 w. sex   ALEX 3:19
weakness makes our w. weaker   BALZ 24:22
wealth get w. and place   POPE 248:24
 insolence of w.   JOHN 176:1
 purchase of my w.   JONS 177:20
 road to w.   TROL 319:17
 w. accumulates, and men decay   GOLD 143:7
 w. is a sacred thing   FRAN 132:17
wealthy business of the w. man   BELL 28:21
weaned w. on a pickle   ANON 10:11
weapon art is not a w.   KENN 184:15
 Loyalty the Tory's secret w.   KILM 186:3
 offensive and dangerous w.   PICA 244:18
 shield and w.   LUTH 204:18
weapons wear w.   BOOK 64:6
wear better to w. out   CUMB 104:12
 qualities as would w. well   GOLD 144:3
 w. of winning   BELL 29:1
 what you are going to w.   WELD 331:3
weariness for w. of-walked   LANG 192:27
 much study is a w.   BIBL 38:35
 w. May toss him to My breast   HERB 157:19
wearing w. o' the Green   ANON 8:1
weary How w., stale, flat   SHAK 270:30
 not be w. in well doing   BIBL 50:16
 run, and not be w.   BIBL 40:11
 w. be at rest   BIBL 37:3
 w. warl goes round   BLAM 56:17
weasel as a w. sucks eggs   SHAK 269:17
 Pop goes the w.   MAND 210:18
 w. under the cocktail cabinet   PINT 245:4

 w. word   ROOS 260:5
weather Jolly boating w.   CORY 100:13
 Stormy w.   KOEH 189:20
 w. the cuckoo likes   HARD 152:3
 winter and rough w.   SHAK 269:16
 you won't hold up the w.   MACN 208:17
weave tangled web we w.   SCOT 266:18
weaving my own hand's w.   KEAT 181:12
web cool w. of language   GRAV 146:5
 She left the w.   TENN 312:5
 tangled w. we weave   SCOT 266:18
webs like spiders' w.   ANAC 5:3
Webster Like W.'s Dictionary   BURK 74:24
wed With this Ring I thee w.   BOOK 60:19
wedded I have w. fyve   CHAU 88:18
 w. to the truth   SAKI 263:16
wedding as she did her w. gown   GOLD 144:3
 earliest w.-day   KEBL 183:21
 small circle of a w.-ring   CIBB 92:18
wedlock w.'s the devil   BYRO 79:18
wee W., sleekit, cow'rin'   BURN 75:30
 w. wifie waitin'   MORR 228:22
weed w. that grows   BURK 74:3
 What is a w.? A plant   EMER 124:14
weeds coronet w.   SHAK 273:10
 smell far worse than w.   SHAK 290:1
week die in my w.   JOPL 178:12
 Sunday In every w.   CLAR 93:20
 w. a long time in politics   WILS 336:18
weekend long w.   FORS 131:13
weep I w. for Adonais   SHEL 292:14
 That he should w. for her   SHAK 271:36
 time to w.   BIBL 38:17
 W., and you weep alone   WILC 334:20
 W. not for little Léonie   GRAH 145:6
 w. or she will die   TENN 313:11
 women must w.   KING 186:21
weepest Woman, why w. thou   BIBL 48:18
weeping w. and gnashing   BIBL 43:15
 w. for her children   BIBL 42:4
Weib W. und Gesang   LUTH 204:19
weigh w. it down on one side   HALI 149:19
weighed w. in the balances   BIBL 41:8
weight w. of rages   SPOO 301:1
Wein W., Weib und Gesang   LUTH 204:19
weird w. sisters   SHAK 279:2
welcome Advice is seldom w.   CHES 89:9
 Love bade me w.   HERB 157:16
 W., all wonders   CRAS 103:3
 W. the coming   POPE 248:23
 W. the sixte   CHAU 88:18
 W. to your gory bed   BURN 75:22
welfare w. of this realm   CHAR 87:23
welkin all the w. rings   WESL 331:23
well alive and w.   ANON 8:3
 all shall be w.   ELIO 121:30
 all shall be w.   JULI 179:10
 being w.   MART 213:9
 deep as a w.   SHAK 286:25
 foolish thing w. done   JOHN 175:9
 Is it w. with the child   BIBL 36:22
 It is not done w.   JOHN 175:1
 Like a w.-conducted person   THAC 315:1
 not wisely but too w.   SHAK 285:4
 rare as a w.-spent one   CARL 82:14
 sense of being w.-dressed   FORB 131:1
 spent one whole day w.   THOM 315:20
 use it for a w.   BOOK 62:11
 W. done   BIBL 45:5
 w. of English undefiled   SPEN 300:18
 w. of loneliness   HALL 150:9
 w.-tuned cymbals   BOOK 63:30
 w.-written Life   CARL 82:14

Wellesley fat with W.'s glory — BYRO 79:2
Welsh devil understands W. — SHAK 274:4
wen great w. of all — COBB 95:8
Wenceslas Good King W. — NEAL 232:1
wench w. is dead — MARL 212:12
Wenlock On W. Edge — HOUS 165:5
wept Jesus w. — BIBL 48:1
  sometimes w. — MUSS 230:15
  we sat down and w. — BOOK 63:23
Werther W. had a love for Charlotte — THAC 314:27
west Cincinnatus of the W. — BYRO 79:12
  come out of the w. — SCOT 266:16
  Go W., young man — GREE 146:22
  liquid manure from the W. — SOLZ 298:29
  nor from the w. — BOOK 62:8
  O wild W. Wind — SHEL 293:7
  safeguard of the W. — WORD 340:17
  W. is West — KIPL 187:8
  W. of these out to seas — FLEC 129:21
  W.'s awake — DAVI 106:23
  where the W. begins — CHAP 87:13
western delivered by W. Union — GOLD 144:10
  Go to the w. gate — ROBI 258:2
  o'er the w. wave — SHEL 294:2
  Playboy of the W. World — SYNG 308:8
  quiet on the w. front — REMA 255:16
  When you've seen one W. — WHIT 333:16
  Wind of the w. sea — TENN 313:4
Westerners W. have aggressive — KAUN 180:22
West Indian I am a W. peasant — MCDO 207:8
westward stepping w. — WORD 341:11
  w., look, the land — CLOU 95:5
  W. the course of empire — BERK 30:15
wet so w. you could shoot snipe off him — POWE 250:19
  w. and wildness — HOPK 162:25
  w. sheet — CUNN 105:1
wether tainted w. of the flock — SHAK 282:18
whacks gave her mother forty w. — ANON 8:10
whale unconquering w. — MELV 216:11
  Very like a w. — SHAK 272:18
whales great w. come sailing by — ARNO 15:8
whaleship w. was my Yale College — MELV 216:10
what for my own self w. am I — HILL 159:9
  W. is to be done — LENI 197:3
  why, or which, or w. — LEAR 195:7
wheat orient and immortal w. — TRAH 319:3
  w. from the chaff — HUBB 166:4
wheel beneath thy Chariot w. — HOPE 162:20
  butterfly upon a w. — POPE 247:11
  created the w. — APOL 13:12
wheels w. of trade — HUME 166:21
  Why tarry the w. — BIBL 35:4
when If not now w. — HILL 159:9
  w. a man should marry — BACO 21:18
  w. did you last see — YEAM 342:10
  W. you call me that — WIST 337:18
whence W. comest thou — BIBL 36:26
  w. cometh my help — BOOK 63:12
  w. did he whence — LENO 197:18
  w. it cometh — BIBL 47:27
where fixed the w. and when — HAWK 153:10
  I knew not w. — LONG 201:17
  W. are you going — BIBL 53:10
  W. did you come from — MACD 207:6
  w. do they all come from — LENN 197:11
  w. is Plantagenet — CREW 103:10
  w. OUGHT I TO BE — CHES 90:10
wherefore w. art thou Romeo — SHAK 286:19
  W. does he why — LENO 197:18
whereof w. one cannot speak — WITT 337:21
whetstone no such w. — ASCH 16:11
whiff w. of grapeshot — CARL 82:18
Whig ascendancy of the W. party — MACA 205:16

Tory men and W. measures — DISR 112:18
W. in any dress — JOHN 174:12
Whigs caught the W. bathing — DISR 112:7
  W. admit no force — BROW 69:11
whimper Not with a bang but a w. — ELIO 122:6
whip Do not forget the w. — NIET 234:7
  W.'s duty — CANN 81:17
whipped w. the offending Adam — SHAK 274:28
whipping w. Sorrow driveth — GREV 147:12
  who should 'scape w. — SHAK 271:34
whips chastised you with w. — BIBL 36:7
  w. and scorns of time — SHAK 272:2
whirligig w. of time — SHAK 288:31
whirling by the w. rim — BLAM 56:17
whirlwind Elijah went up by a w. — BIBL 36:19
  reap the w. — BIBL 41:12
  Rides in the w. — ADDI 2:6
  w. hath blown — DONN 114:20
whiskers Cat with crimson w. — LEAR 195:18
whisky good old boys drinkin' w. — MCLE 208:1
whisper w. of a faction — RUSS 263:1
  w. to the tourist — BEER 27:12
  W. who dares — MILN 219:3
whispering just w. in her mouth — MARX 214:1
whistle I'd w. her off — SHAK 284:22
  shrimp learns to w. — KHRU 185:17
  W. and she'll come — FLET 130:9
  w., an' I'll come — BURN 75:20
white always goes into w. satin — SHER 294:10
  fat w. woman — CORN 100:8
  garment was w. as snow — BIBL 41:10
  no 'w.' or 'coloured' signs — KENN 184:13
  pluck a w. rose — SHAK 275:13
  see the w. of their eyes — PUTN 252:24
  so-called w. races — FORS 131:16
  tupping your w. ewe — SHAK 284:8
  want to be the w. man's brother — KING 186:8
  w. and hairless — HERR 158:5
  w. and sparkling — CHAN 87:10
  W. as an angel — BLAK 56:9
  w. as snow — BIBL 39:10
  w., celestial thought — VAUG 322:21
  w. Christmas — BERL 30:21
  w. cliffs of Dover — BURT 76:7
  w. heat of technology — WILS 336:17
  W. In a single night — BYRO 79:13
  w. in the blood of the Lamb — BIBL 52:10
  W. Man's Burden — KIPL 188:17
  w. owl in the belfry — TENN 313:25
  wild w. horses play — ARNO 15:7
whited w. sepulchres — BIBL 44:32
Whitehall gentleman in W. — JAY 171:8
White House Log-cabin to W. — THAY 315:16
  no whitewash at the W. — NIXO 234:14
whiter w. shade of pale — REID 255:15
whitewash no w. at the White House — NIXO 234:14
whither W. is he withering — LENO 197:18
  w. it goeth — BIBL 47:27
whiting said a w. to a snail — CARR 83:23
who W. am I going to be today — WELD 331:3
  W. dares wins — ANON 11:1
  W. is on my side — BIBL 36:31
  W., or why, or which — LEAR 195:7
  W.? Whom — LENI 197:5
whole faith hath made thee w. — BIBL 43:22
  greater than the w. — HESI 158:14
  They that be w. — BIBL 43:19
whom Who? W. — LENI 197:5
whooping out of all w. — SHAK 269:28
whore I am the Protestant w. — GWYN 148:16
  I' the posture of a w. — SHAK 269:4
  morals of a w. — JOHN 174:19
  w. and the gambler — BLAK 55:15

whores second-rate w.	PLOM 246:7
to work, ye w.	PEMB 243:5
whoring went a w.	BOOK 62:27
whosoever W. will be saved	BOOK 59:2
why about the wasp, except w.	THOM 316:8
can't tell you w.	MART 213:7
W. not? Why not? Yeah	LEAR 195:21
Would this man ask w.	AUDE 17:29
wicked August is a w. month	O'BR 235:13
desperately w.	BIBL 40:26
no peace unto the w.	BIBL 40:13
sick and w.	AUST 20:4
Something w. this way comes	SHAK 281:6
tender mercies of the w.	BIBL 37:27
Tories born w.	ANON 8:15
w. cease from troubling	BIBL 37:3
w. flee	BIBL 38:7
wickedness manifold sins and w.	BOOK 58:4
shapen in w.	BOOK 61:27
turneth away from his w.	BIBL 41:2
w. in high places	BIBL 50:23
wicket flannelled fools at the w.	KIPL 187:23
Widdicombe Fair want for to go to W.	BALL 24:16
wide Poet sees, but w.	ARNO 15:12
w. as a church door	SHAK 286:25
W. is the gate	BIBL 43:8
wider w. still and wider	BENS 29:27
widow French w. in every bedroom	HOFF 160:20
Molly Stark's a w.	STAR 301:21
retired w.	BAGE 22:16
w. bird sat mourning	SHEL 292:21
w. of fifty	SHER 294:19
widowhood comfortable estate of w.	GAY 137:3
wife Caesar's w.	CAES 79:29
cleave unto his w.	BIBL 33:5
covet thy neighbour's w.	BIBL 34:16
dwindle into a w.	CONG 98:19
his [Lot's] w. looked back	BIBL 33:25
honour unto the w.	BIBL 51:28
If I were your w.	CHUR 92:15
I have a w.	LUCA 204:9
I have married a w.	BIBL 46:26
in want of a w.	AUST 19:24
keeps up a w.'s spirits	GAY 137:3
kill a w. with kindness	SHAK 286:38
look out for a w.	SURT 306:11
man who's untrue to his w.	AUDE 18:10
Medicine is my lawful w.	CHEK 89:1
my sonne's w., Elizabeth	INGE 169:1
My w. won't let me	LEIG 196:23
Petrarch's w.	BYRO 78:22
Remember Lot's w.	BIBL 47:6
riding to and from his w.	WHIT 333:7
she is your w.	OGIL 235:20
some friend, not w.	POPE 247:8
Thane of Fife had a w.	SHAK 281:16
w. and children	BACO 21:17
w. or your servants to read	GRIF 147:17
w. shall be as the fruitful vine	BOOK 63:20
w. talks Greek	JOHN 177:1
wind is my w.	KEAT 183:12
your w. and your dog	HILL 159:1
wig w. with the scorched foretop	MACA 205:13
Wigan mothers-in-law and W. Pier	BRID 66:17
wigwam w. of Nokomis	LONG 202:3
wild call of the w.	LOND 201:14
grew more fierce and w.	HERB 157:11
never saw a w. thing	LAWR 194:19
O Caledonia! stern and w.	SCOT 268:12
three w. lads were we	SCOT 266:22
walk on the w. side	ALGR 4:1
wilder w. shores of love	BLAN 56:19
wilderness crieth in the w.	BIBL 40:7
crying in the w.	BIBL 42:6
grain into the w.	STOU 304:18
in the w.	BIBL 46:29
into the w.	BIBL 34:20
into the w. to see	BIBL 43:30
singing in the w.	FITZ 128:15
temptation in the w.	BOOK 62:19
They make a w.	TACI 308:14
To the w. I wander	ANON 11:4
weeds and the w.	HOPK 162:25
w. of idea	BUTL 77:13
w. of this world	BUNY 72:21
Women have no w.	BOGA 57:7
will complies against his w.	BUTL 77:8
Immanent W.	HARD 151:21
Not my w., but thine, be done	BIBL 47:10
political w.	LYNN 205:2
Thy w. be done	BIBL 42:23
W. in over-plus	SHAK 290:10
W. you, won't you	CARR 83:24
wrote my w. across the sky	LAWR 194:26
You w., Oscar	WHIS 333:6
willed only a w. gentleness	THOM 316:22
William You are old, Father W.	CARR 83:16
willing Barkis is w.	DICK 110:1
spirit indeed is w.	BIBL 45:17
w. suspension of disbelief	COLE 96:21
willow green w. is my garland	HEYW 158:22
Make me a w. cabin	SHAK 288:9
Sing all a green w.	SHAK 284:32
Stood Dido with a w.	SHAK 282:27
w. grows aslant a brook	SHAK 273:8
W., titwillow	GILB 140:20
willows w., old rotten planks	CONS 99:11
W. whiten, aspens quiver	TENN 312:3
wills talk of w.	SHAK 285:19
wilt Do what thou w.	CROW 104:10
Wimbledon Spill your guts at W.	CONN 99:6
win w. an atomic war	BRAD 65:22
w. his spurs	EDWA 120:2
W. just one for the Gipper	GIPP 141:15
w. or lose it all	MONT 226:23
wind answer is blowin' in the w.	DYLA 119:2
appearance of solidity to pure w.	ORWE 237:19
bleak w. of March	HOOD 161:22
Blow, blow, thou winter w.	SHAK 269:25
candle in the w.	JOHN 172:15
east w. made flesh	APPL 13:14
flare up in a w.	FRAN 132:20
Frosty w. made moan	ROSS 260:12
gone with the w.	DOWS 115:10
His hammer of w.	THOM 317:6
how the w. doth ramm	POUN 250:5
impatient as the w.	WORD 341:12
let her down the w.	SHAK 284:22
light w. lives or dies	KEAT 182:23
Lord was not in the w.	BIBL 36:13
moved about like the w.	GERO 138:13
not I, but the w.	LAWR 194:21
Not with this w. blowing	KIPL 188:2
O wild West W.	SHEL 293:7
piffle before the w.	ASHF 16:14
reed shaken with the w.	BIBL 43:30
rushing mighty w.	BIBL 48:24
sown the w.	BIBL 41:12
stood the w. for France	DRAY 116:8
'tis a Protestant w.	WHAR 332:25
twist slowly in the w.	EHRL 120:9
Unhelped by any w.	COLE 96:1
Western w.	ANON 10:18
w. and the rain	SHAK 288:33
w. bloweth where it listeth	BIBL 47:27
w. blow the earth	SHAK 277:17

w. doth blow	BALL 24:14	w. of the morning	BOOK 63:25
w. extinguishes candles	LA R 193:21	with ah! bright w.	HOPK 162:23
w. goeth over it	BOOK 62:23	**winning** glory of the w.	MERE 217:3
w. in that corner	SHAK 284:2	wear of w.	BELL 29:1
w. is to fire	BUSS 76:25	W. is everything	HILL 159:1
w. it into a ball	BLAK 55:19	w. isn't anything	SAND 264:13
w. of change is blowing	MACM 208:10	**wins** Who dares w.	ANON 11:1
W. of the western sea	TENN 313:4	**winter** all the w. long	SHAK 289:9
Woord is but w.	LYDG 204:22	amid the w.'s snow	CASW 85:11
winder w., a casement	DICK 110:23	by the w. sea	TENN 311:12
winding by a w. stair	BACO 21:15	English w.	BYRO 79:6
England's w. sheet	BLAK 55:15	If W. comes	SHEL 293:10
good structure in a w. stair	HERB 157:15	in the Middle of W.	ADDI 2:13
waters were his w. sheet	BARN 25:11	It was the w. wild	MILT 220:24
window appears at a w.	BEER 27:11	on w.'s traces	SWIN 307:17
argument of the broken w.	PANK 240:12	Our severest w.	COWP 102:10
doggie in the w.	MERR 217:9	sad tale's best for w.	SHAK 289:1
Good prose like a w.-pane	ORWE 237:7	very dead of w.	ELIO 122:7
has not one w.	JAME 170:20	w. and rough weather	SHAK 269:16
kick a hole in a stained glass w.	CHAN 87:4	W. is come and gone	SHEL 292:15
kiss my ass in Macy's w.	JOHN 173:5	W. is icummen in	POUN 250:5
little w. where the sun	HOOD 162:5	w. of discontent	CALL 80:10
looked out at a w.	BIBL 36:29	w. of our discontent	SHAK 285:32
windows breaking of w.	MORE 227:22	w., plague and pestilence	NASH 231:21
open the w. of the Church	JOHN 172:12	w.'s rains and ruins	SWIN 307:18
open w. into men's souls	ELIZ 123:11	**wipe** w. away all tears	BIBL 52:11
storied w.	MILT 219:24	w. away all tears	BIBL 52:25
thus, Through w.	DONN 114:12	**wire** Along the electric w.	ANON 5:17
winds Blow, w., and crack	SHAK 277:18	**wisdom** all Solomon's w.	BIBL 36:2
take The w. of March	SHAK 289:11	beginning of w.	BOOK 63:4
w. that would blow	BOLT 57:16	door to infinite w.	BREC 66:8
windward w. of the law	CHUR 90:24	Greeks seek after w.	BIBL 49:22
windy w. side of the law	SHAK 288:30	how little w.	OXEN 239:2
wine days of w. and roses	DOWS 115:11	price of w.	BIBL 37:11
do crush their w.	MARV 213:16	privilege of w. to listen	HOLM 161:9
doesn't get into the w.	CHES 90:2	quintessence of w.	JAIN 170:6
Drinking the blude-red w.	BALL 24:7	to the palace of w.	BLAK 55:22
flask of w.	FITZ 128:15	w. be put in a silver rod	BLAK 55:16
flown with insolence and w.	MILT 221:11	W. denotes the pursuing	HUTC 167:12
have w. and women	BYRO 78:20	W. hath builded her house	BIBL 37:23
I'll not look for w.	JONS 178:4	W. is the principal thing	BIBL 37:20
Look not thou upon the w.	BIBL 37:40	w. of the crocodiles	BACO 21:35
new w. into old bottles	BIBL 43:21	**wise** beacons of w. men	HUXL 168:3
pint o' w.	BURN 75:17	be w., and love	SHAK 287:29
red sweet w. of youth	BROO 67:19	Be w. with speed	YOUN 344:10
red w. of Shiraz into urine	DINE 111:27	consider her ways, and be w.	BIBL 37:21
refreshed with w.	BOOK 62:9	enough for the w.	PLAU 246:3
take a glass of w.	SHER 294:23	more w. when he had	JOHN 176:6
w. for thy stomach's sake	BIBL 51:9	Nor ever did a w. one	ROCH 258:10
W. is a mocker	BIBL 37:38	So w. so young	SHAK 286:5
W. maketh merry	BIBL 38:30	'Tis folly to be w.	GRAY 146:19
W., not water	SANS 264:15	w. as serpents	BIBL 43:25
woman, w. and song	LUTH 204:19	w. father that knows	SHAK 282:8
wing joy is ever on the w.	MILT 222:31	w. in his own conceit	BIBL 38:5
knowst'ou w. from tail	POUN 250:12	w. men from the east	BIBL 42:2
on a w. and a pray'r	ADAM 2:5	w. son	BIBL 37:25
winged Time's w. chariot	MARV 213:21	**wisecracking** w. is simply callisthenics	PARK 240:24
w. life destroy	BLAK 56:2	**wisely** not w. but too well	SHAK 285:4
w. squadrons of the sky	MILM 218:22	**wiser** in their generation w.	BIBL 46:36
W. words	HOME 161:17	sadder and a w. man	COLE 96:19
wings beating his luminous w.	ARNO 16:1	**wisest** first and w. of them	MILT 222:29
beating of his w.	BRIG 66:20	w. and justest	PLAT 246:1
Beteth his w.	CHAU 88:13	w. fool in Christendom	HENR 156:13
clip an Angel's w.	KEAT 181:25	w. man can answer	COLT 97:16
Grief has no w.	QUIL 253:8	**wish** Whoever hath her w.	SHAK 290:10
healing in his w.	BIBL 41:19	w. for prayer is a prayer	BERN 31:2
Ill news hath w.	DRAY 116:4	w. I loved the Human Race	RALE 254:10
Love without his w.	BYRO 79:10	w. was father, Harry	SHAK 274:24
mount up with w.	BIBL 40:11	**wit** Brevity is the soul of w.	SHAK 271:25
on laughter-silvered w.	MAGE 209:8	fancy w. will come	POPE 247:3
On w. of song	HEIN 155:8	His w. invites you	COWP 101:19
spread his w. on the blast	BYRO 78:14	no pick-purse of another's w.	SIDN 295:11
w. like a dove	BOOK 62:1	nor all thy piety nor w.	FITZ 128:19

wit (cont.)

o'erflowing of unbounded w.	WINC 337:9
sharpen a good w.	ASCH 16:11
Staircase w.	DIDE 111:21
tomb of w.	CAVE 86:8
too proud for a w.	GOLD 143:18
True w. is Nature	POPE 248:1
universal monarchy of w.	CARE 82:6
use my w. as a pitchfork	LARK 193:15
w. among Lords	JOHN 174:18
w. and humour	AUST 19:19
W. has truth in it	PARK 240:24
w.'s the noblest frailty	SHAD 268:6
W. will shine	DRYD 117:11
w. with dunces	POPE 246:20
witch Aroint thee, w.	SHAK 278:28
witchcraft w., there has been	WALP 327:16
witches Men feared w.	BRAN 66:2
witching w. time of night	SHAK 272:20
with He that is not w. me	BIBL 43:33
I am w. you alway	BIBL 45:22
withdrawing long, w. roar	ARNO 15:4
wither Age cannot w. her	SHAK 268:20
withered are w. away	COCK 95:9
O! w. is the garland	SHAK 268:28
withereth grass w.	BIBL 51:25
rose Fast w. too	KEAT 181:18
withers it w. away	ENGE 124:23
our w. are unwrung	SHAK 272:15
within kingdom of God is w. you	BIBL 47:5
without forasmuch as w. thee	BOOK 59:14
I can do w.	SOCR 298:20
with you—or w. you	MART 213:10
witness bear false w.	BIBL 34:16
bear w. of that Light	BIBL 47:19
witnesses cloud of w.	BIBL 51:16
w. against mankind	KORA 190:20
w. to the desolation of war	GEOR 138:4
wits Great w.	DRYD 116:17
stolen his w. away	DE L 108:5
warming his five w.	TENN 313:25
witty dull men w.	BACO 22:6
of the w. devil	GRAV 146:4
Thou swell! Thou w.	HART 152:21
w. in myself	SHAK 274:13
wives Husbands, love your w.	BIBL 51:2
profane and old w.' fables	BIBL 51:8
wizards star-led w.	MILT 220:23
wobbly spelling is W.	MILN 219:6
woe discover sights of w.	MILT 221:3
gave signs of w.	MILT 222:18
oft in w.	WHIT 333:9
protracted w.	JOHN 174:7
W. to thee, O land	BIBL 38:29
W. to the land	SHAK 286:4
w. unto them	BIBL 39:13
woes Of w. unnumbered	POPE 248:22
wolf like the w. on the fold	BYRO 78:13
w. by the ears	JEFF 171:16
w. of a different opinion	INGE 168:21
w. shall dwell with the lamb	BIBL 39:22
W. that shall keep it	KIPL 188:28
wolfsbane twist W., tight-rooted	KEAT 182:6
wolves frighten the w.	MACH 207:17
ravening w.	BIBL 43:10
woman aren't I a w.	TRUT 320:12
artist man and the mother w.	SHAW 291:9
body of a weak and feeble w.	ELIZ 123:6
born of a w.	BIBL 37:6
business of a w.'s life	SOUT 299:20
But what is w.	COWL 101:17
changeable always is w.	VIRG 324:16
Come to my w.'s breasts	SHAK 279:15

could be a good w.	THAC 314:25
dead w. bites not	GRAY 146:10
done, ask a w.	THAT 315:3
end to a w.'s liberty	BURN 74:27
Eternal W. draws us upward	GOET 142:21
Every w. adores a Fascist	PLAT 245:19
excellent thing in w.	SHAK 278:13
fat white w.	CORN 100:8
Frailty, thy name is w.	SHAK 270:32
fury, like a w. scorned	CONG 98:14
greatest glory of a w.	PERI 243:22
if a w. have long hair	BIBL 49:29
in a w.'s hide	SHAK 275:19
inconstant w.	GAY 137:10
just like a w.	DYLA 119:5
Let us look for the w.	DUMA 118:1
little w. who wrote	LINC 199:14
lovely w. stoops to folly	GOLD 144:4
made he a w.	BIBL 33:3
make a man a w.	PEMB 243:6
Man that is born of a w.	BOOK 60:23
no, nor w. neither	SHAK 271:31
no other purgatory but a w.	BEAU 26:15
No w. will be Prime Minister	THAT 315:2
One is not born a w.	DE B 107:8
perfect w.; nobly planned	WORD 341:7
post-chaise with a pretty w.	JOHN 175:21
she's a w.	RACI 253:18
sweeter w. ne'er drew breath	INGE 169:1
takes a very clever w.	KIPL 188:27
this Man and this W.	BOOK 60:14
trapped in a w.'s body	BOY 65:17
victory by a w.	WEST 332:19
virtuous w.	BIBL 38:11
virtuous w. is a crown	BIBL 37:26
where w. never smiled	CLAR 93:10
Why can't a w. be	LERN 197:25
W., behold thy son	BIBL 48:13
w. can hardly ever choose	ELIO 121:6
w. clothed with the sun	BIBL 52:13
w. has given you her heart	VANB 322:10
W.! in our hours of ease	SCOT 266:19
w. in this humour	SHAK 286:2
w. is a sometime thing	HEYW 158:21
w. is his game	TENN 313:10
W. is the great unknown	HARD 151:12
w. moved	SHAK 286:39
W. much missed	HARD 152:2
w. must have money	WOOL 339:7
w. must submit to it	STAË 301:10
w. of shining loveliness	YEAT 343:22
w. only the right to spring	FOND 130:19
W.'s degradation	STAN 301:19
w. seldom writes her mind	STEE 302:2
w.'s preaching	JOHN 175:1
W. stock is rising	CHIL 90:12
w.'s whole existence	BYRO 78:18
w. take An elder	SHAK 288:18
w. taken in adultery	BIBL 47:33
W. the nigger of the world	ONO 236:14
w. wakes to love	TENN 311:11
w. was full of good works	BIBL 48:29
W., what have I to do	BIBL 47:26
w. who deliberates	ADDI 2:8
w. who did not care	KIPL 188:13
w. who lives for others	LEWI 198:12
w. whom thou gavest	BIBL 33:8
W., why weepest thou	BIBL 48:18
w., wine and song	LUTH 204:19
w. with a slop-pail	HOPK 163:10
w. with fair opportunities	THAC 314:19
w. without a man	STEI 302:12
womanhood Heroic w.	LONG 202:2

womankind mankind and w. BAHA 22:23
packs off its w. SHAW 291:13
womb from his mother's w. SHAK 281:25
w. of time HEIN 155:9
women blessed art thou among w. BIBL 45:32
claim our right as w. PANK 240:11
comfortable w. STRI 305:7
dream of fair w. TENN 310:20
extension of w.'s rights FOUR 132:10
feelings of w. in a drawing-room WOOL 339:8
going to w. NIET 234:7
Good w. always think BROO 68:1
have wine and w. BYRO 78:20
hops, and w. DICK 111:3
if ye be kind towards w. KORA 190:16
like w.'s letters HAZL 154:2
managers of affairs of w. KORA 190:13
mature w., *dancing* FRIE 133:25
mob of scribbling w. HAWT 153:15
Music and w. PEPY 243:16
now called the nature of w. MILL 218:5
passing the love of w. BIBL 35:29
position for w. is prone CARM 83:6
Powerful w. only succeed LEE- 196:16
publishers are not w. ROBI 257:22
regiment of w. KNOX 189:15
Solomon loved many strange w. BIBL 36:5
Some w.'ll stay in a man's memory KIPL 189:1
to w. as to men ANTH 13:9
to w. Italian CHAR 87:27
Whatever w. do WHIT 334:8
w. are from Venus GRAY 146:8
W. are only children CHES 89:11
W. are programmed to love BAIN 23:2
w. become like their mothers WILD 335:1
w. become unnaturally thin WOLF 338:9
W. can't forgive failure CHEK 88:33
W. desiren to have sovereynetee CHAU 88:21
W. don't seem to think AMIS 4:22
W. have no wilderness BOGA 57:7
W. have very little idea GREE 147:6
w. in a state of ignorance KNOX 189:19
w. in furious secret rebellion SHAW 290:27
w. in men require BLAK 56:3
w. labouring of child BOOK 59:8
w. must weep KING 186:21
w. need to be helped TRUT 320:12
w. not merely tolerated AUNG 19:11
won ground w. to-day ARNO 15:18
has w. it bear the palm JORT 178:13
in this humour w. SHAK 286:2
I w. the count SOMO 299:2
never lost till w. CRAB 102:15
not that you w. or lost RICE 256:14
not to have w. COUB 100:16
woman, therefore may be w. SHAK 287:26
wonder boneless w. CHUR 91:11
great w. in heaven BIBL 52:13
I w. any man alive GAY 137:1
I w. by my troth DONN 114:7
moon-washed apples of w. DRIN 116:10
One can only w. BENT 30:8
still the w. grew GOLD 143:12
w. of our age DYER 118:19
w. of our stage JONS 178:5
w. who's kissing her ADAM 1:12
wonderful God, how w. Thou art FABE 125:16
I've had a w. life WITT 337:24
many w. things SOPH 299:9
most w. wonderful SHAK 269:28
too w. to be true FARA 126:3
Yes, w. things CART 84:22
wonderfully fearfully and w. made BOOK 63:26

wonders His w. to perform COWP 101:23
multiply my signs and my w. BIBL 34:4
signs and w. BIBL 47:29
Welcome, all w. CRAS 103:3
w. in the deep BOOK 63:1
w. we seek without us BROW 69:4
wondrous survey the w. cross WATT 329:10
won't administrative w. LYNN 205:2
wood behind the little w. TENN 312:19
Bows down to w. and stone HEBE 155:2
bows down to w. and stone KIPL 187:13
cleave the w. ANON 9:15
hewers of w. BIBL 34:32
native w.-notes wild MILT 220:7
w.'s in trouble HOUS 165:5
woodcock Spirits of well-shot w. BETJ 31:19
w. to mine own springe SHAK 273:18
woodcocks springes to catch w. SHAK 271:10
wooden Sailed off in a w. shoe FIEL 127:8
Within this w. O SHAK 274:27
w. wall is your ships THEM 315:17
w. walls are the best COVE 101:2
woodland bit of w. HORA 164:21
woodman W., spare that tree MORR 228:15
w., spare the beechen tree CAMP 81:1
woods Enter these enchanted w. MERE 217:7
fresh w., and pastures new MILT 220:21
go down in the w. today BRAT 66:6
once a road through the w. KIPL 188:14
pleasure in the pathless w. BYRO 78:8
We'll to the w. no more ANON 11:18
w. against the world BLUN 57:3
w. are lovely FROS 134:14
woodshed Something nasty in the w. GIBB 139:12
wooed woman, therefore may be w. SHAK 287:26
wooing my w. mind SHAK 278:21
wool like the pure w. BIBL 41:10
Woolf afraid of Virginia W. ALBE 3:9
woollen Odious! in w. POPE 247:24
Wops Huns or W. MITF 225:2
word action to the w. SHAK 272:11
Every w. she writes is a lie MCCA 206:21
every w. that proceedeth BIBL 42:10
flowering in a lonely w. TENN 313:27
Greeks had a w. AKIN 3:7
honour? A w. SHAK 274:9
I kept my w. DE L 108:8
In the beginning was the W. BIBL 47:15
lies in one little w. SHAK 285:9
packed up into one w. CARR 84:12
weasel w. ROOS 260:5
whose eternal W. MARR 212:26
w., at random spoken SCOT 266:13
w. fitly spoken BIBL 38:1
W. is but wynd LYDG 204:22
w. is enough PLAU 246:3
w. is the Verb HUGO 166:15
w. spoken in due season BIBL 37:35
w. takes wing HORA 163:26
W. was made flesh BIBL 47:21
w. was made flesh MISS 224:9
words barren superfluity of w. GART 136:14
comfortable w. BOOK 59:28
dressing w. new SHAK 289:32
fear those big w. JOYC 179:2
few w. of my own EDWA 120:4
Give sorrow w. SHAK 281:12
gotta use w. when I talk to you ELIO 122:18
He w. me, girls SHAK 269:2
In all his w. most wonderful NEWM 233:6
may w. matter to you SMIT 297:18
my w. are my own CHAR 87:24
my w. shall not pass BIBL 45:2

words (*cont.*)
not even with w.	BROO 68:2
of all sad w.	WHIT 334:6
poetry = the *best* w.	COLE 96:24
polite meaningless w.	YEAT 342:19
Proper w. in proper places	SWIF 306:21
wall of w.	BUTL 77:13
war has used up w.	JAME 170:25
Winged w.	HOME 161:17
w. a foot and a half long	HORA 163:14
w. are but the signs	JOHN 173:11
W. are men's daughters	MADD 209:4
w. are the daughters	JOHN 173:11
W. are the tokens	BACO 20:19
w. fail us	AUST 20:6
words, mere w.	SHAK 288:1
w. of Mercury	SHAK 278:24
w. of tongue and pen	HART 152:22
w. will follow	CATO 85:16
W. without thoughts	SHAK 272:22
W., words, words	SHAK 271:27
worth ten thousand w.	BARN 25:7
wrestle With w. and meanings	ELIO 121:23
yea, even from good w.	BOOK 61:18
you can drug, with w.	LOWE 203:14
Wordsworthian W. or egotistical	KEAT 183:11
work All that matters is love and w.	FREU 133:21
Do the w. that's nearest	KING 186:18
goes to w.	SAND 264:12
If any would not w.	BIBL 51:6
I like w.: it fascinates me	JERO 172:6
immortality through my w.	ALLE 4:10
in that w. does what he wants	COLL 97:3
let the toad w.	LARK 193:15
looked for w.	TEBB 310:4
men must w.	KING 186:21
Nice w. if you can get it	GERS 138:17
Nothing to do but w.	KING 186:5
piece of w. is a man	SHAK 271:31
to w., ye whores	PEMB 243:5
We w. in the dark	JAME 170:18
W. and pray	HILL 159:2
W. expands	PARK 241:7
W. is of two kinds	RUSS 262:21
w. is terribly important	RUSS 262:19
W. liberates	ANON 11:21
w. like a fiend	THOM 316:10
W. out your own salvation	BIBL 50:25
w. together for good	BIBL 49:16
worked w. with my blood	KOLL 190:4
worker w. slave of capitalist society	CONN 99:4
workers men the w.	TENN 312:9
secure for the w.	ANON 10:13
W. all demand	SERV 268:2
W. of the world	MARX 214:10
workhouse Christmas Day in the W.	SIMS 296:7
working in his w. time	GILL 141:11
it isn't w.	MAJO 209:21
killin' meself w.	O'CA 235:16
kind of like w.	BISH 54:11
protect a w.-girl	SMIT 297:15
this w.-day world	SHAK 269:13
W. and wandrynge	LANG 193:1
w. like a dog	LENN 197:13
working class job w. parents want	ABBO 1:1
working classes worst fault of w.	MORT 229:4
works all ye W. of the Lord	BOOK 58:15
cast off the w. of darkness	BIBL 49:21
devil and all his w.	BOOK 60:9
Faith without w.	BIBL 51:21
Look on my w.	SHEL 293:12
move immediately upon your w.	GRAN 145:16
seen the future and it w.	STEF 302:5

stained with their own w.	BOOK 62:27
w. of darkness	BOOK 59:12
your good w.	BIBL 42:17
workshop nation may be its w.	CHAM 86:17
not a temple but a w.	TURG 320:15
w. of the world	DISR 112:4
world All's right with the w.	BROW 70:27
all the kingdoms of the w.	BIBL 42:12
All the w. is sad	FOST 132:9
all the w. is young	KING 186:22
All the w.'s a stage	SHAK 269:20
all the w. was gay	POPE 249:2
along the W. I go	CART 84:25
bestride the narrow w.	SHAK 275:30
brought nothing into this w.	BIBL 51:10
citizen of the w.	BOSW 64:20
country is the w.	PAIN 239:16
create the wondrous w.	YOUN 344:17
dark w. of sin	BICK 53:17
deceits of the w.	BOOK 59:5
destruction of the whole w.	HUME 166:23
foppery of the w.	SHAK 277:10
gain the whole w.	BIBL 45:28
glory of the w.	ANON 12:22
glory of this w. passes	THOM 315:18
God so loved the w.	BIBL 47:28
go out of this w.	HOBB 160:6
governs the whole w.	OXEN 239:2
great w. spin for ever	TENN 312:15
half-brother of the w.	BAIL 23:1
Hog Butcher for the W.	SAND 264:7
in 1915 the old w. ended	LAWR 194:12
in a naughty w.	SHAK 282:30
In a w. I never made	HOUS 164:25
know the w.	YOUN 344:18
light of the w.	BIBL 42:16
limits of my w.	WITT 337:23
Little Friend of all the W.	KIPL 188:24
lost the w. for love	DRYD 117:5
makes the whole w. kin	SHAK 287:32
monk who shook the w.	MONT 226:20
new w. order	BUSH 76:23
not as the w. giveth, give I	BIBL 48:7
O brave new w.	SHAK 287:20
observe a w. of variety	FORD 131:8
only saved the w.	CHES 89:20
peace which the w. cannot give	BOOK 58:23
rack of this tough w.	SHAK 278:15
Round the w.	ARNO 15:8
small-talking w.	FRY 134:19
still point of the turning w.	ELIO 121:21
Stop the w.	NEWL 232:21
Syllables govern the w.	SELD 267:13
symphony like the w.	MAHL 209:16
Ten days that shook the w.	REED 255:13
Than this w. dreams of	TENN 311:15
There is a w. elsewhere	SHAK 270:12
this dark w. and wide	MILT 223:9
though the w. perish	FERD 126:21
three corners of the w.	SHAK 277:4
unto the end of the w.	BIBL 45:22
way the w. ends	ELIO 122:6
We want the w.	MORR 228:21
What is the w.	DE L 108:9
What would the w. be	HOPK 162:25
wilderness of this w.	BUNY 72:21
woods against the w.	BLUN 57:3
workshop of the w.	DISR 112:4
w. and love were young	RALE 253:24
w. empty of people	LAWR 194:17
w. enough, and time	MARV 213:19
w. grew pale	JOHN 174:6
w. in a grain of sand	BLAK 55:11

w. is a comedy WALP 327:13
w. is charged HOPK 162:22
w. is everything that is the case WITT 337:22
w. is given over LE G 196:17
w. is so full STEV 303:28
w. is too much with us WORD 341:18
w. knew him not BIBL 47:20
w. must be made safe WILS 337:8
w.'s a bubble BACO 22:7
w.'s great age begins anew SHEL 292:25
w.'s history SCHI 265:14
w. should be taxed BIBL 46:2
w.'s in a state o' chassis O'CA 235:18
w.'s last night DONN 113:22
w.'s mine oyster SHAK 282:31
w.'s worst wound SASS 265:4
w. upside down BIBL 48:33
w. was all before them MILT 222:25
w. will end in fire FROS 134:8
w. without end BOOK 58:9
youth of the w. BACO 20:21
worlds best of all possible w. CABE 79:26
best of all possible w. VOLT 325:20
destroyer of w. OPPE 236:16
number of w. is infinite ALEX 3:14
what w. away BROW 69:25
w. of wanwood leafmeal HOPK 163:4
worm invisible w. BLAK 56:13
joy of the w. SHAK 269:5
sets foot upon a w. COWP 102:7
w. i' the bud SHAK 288:21
worms w. destroy this body BIBL 37:9
w. were hallowed SHAK 284:29
wormwood w. and the gall BIBL 40:28
worrying What's the use of w. ANON 10:19
worse Defend the bad against the w. DAY- 107:4
follow the w. OVID 238:15
for better for w. BOOK 60:18
For fear of finding something w. BELL 28:11
from w. to better HOOK 162:9
from w. to better JOHN 173:10
make the w. appear MILT 221:17
mean the W. one ARIS 14:9
w. than a crime BOUL 65:5
worst are no w. SHAK 283:23
worship earth doth w. thee BOOK 58:10
O w. the King GRAN 145:15
O w. the Lord BOOK 62:20
second is freedom to w. ROOS 259:20
we w. thy Name BOOK 58:13
who w. the beast BIBL 52:18
with my body I thee w. BOOK 60:19
w. the Lord MONS 225:23
worst good in the w. of us ANON 10:8
it was the w. of times DICK 111:10
To-morrow do thy w. DRYD 117:12
world's w. wound SASS 265:4
w. form of Government CHUR 92:1
w. is yet to come JOHN 173:8
w. time of the year ELIO 122:7
worth confident of their own w. AUNG 19:11
not w. going to see JOHN 176:4
Worthington daughter on the stage, Mrs W.
COWA 101:8
worthy am no more w. BIBL 46:33
I am not w. MISS 224:7
labourer is w. of his hire BIBL 46:14
Lord I am not w. BIBL 43:13
not w. to unloose BIBL 47:22
w. of their steel SCOT 266:8
wotthehell w. archy MARQ 212:22
would evil which I w. not BIBL 49:15
He w., wouldn't he RICE 256:17

wound Earth felt the w. MILT 222:18
Willing to w. POPE 247:10
world's worst w. SASS 265:4
w. had been for Ireland SARS 264:21
w., not the bandage POTT 249:28
wounded like a w. snake POPE 248:4
w. for our transgressions BIBL 40:17
You're w. BROW 70:15
Wounded Knee Bury my heart at W. BENÉ 29:11
wounding w. heart CRAS 102:25
wounds bind up the nation's w. LINC 199:11
not to heed the w. IGNA 168:17
wrapped all meanly w. MILT 220:24
wrath day of w. MISS 224:11
flee from the w. to come BIBL 42:8
provoke not your children to w. BIBL 50:21
sun go down upon your w. BIBL 50:19
turneth away w. BIBL 37:32
tygers of w. BLAK 55:25
w. did end BLAK 56:11
wreathed becks, and w. smiles MILT 220:1
Wrekin W. heaves HOUS 165:5
wren Four Larks and a W. LEAR 195:8
w. goes to't SHAK 278:2
wrest W. once the law SHAK 282:22
wrestle w. not against flesh BIBL 50:23
w. With words and meanings ELIO 121:23
wrestled w. for perhaps too long HOWE 165:14
w. with him WALT 328:6
wretched w. men are cradled SHEL 292:27
wring soon w. their hands WALP 327:19
wrinkled w. sea beneath him TENN 310:22
wrinklies not because ageing w. STRA 305:5
wrist With gyves upon his w. HOOD 162:2
writ I never w. SHAK 290:7
name was w. in water KEAT 183:17
write angel should w. MOOR 227:12
I w. one DISR 113:9
I w. them PUNC 252:16
look in thy heart and w. SIDN 295:8
love to w. them BISH 54:11
man ought to w. TROL 319:14
not enough for me to w. LYLY 204:25
people that w. SHEN 294:8
people who can't w. ZAPP 345:2
restraint with which they w. CAMP 80:21
things I w. about WOOL 339:11
those who cannot w. POPE 248:27
w. about it AMIS 4:22
w. all the books EDDI 119:13
w. every other day DOUG 115:7
w. for Antiquity LAMB 192:13
w. for posterity ADE 2:17
W. me as one HUNT 167:2
w. with ease SHER 294:22
writer best fame is a w.'s fame LEBO 196:3
great and original w. WORD 341:21
I'm a w. WALC 326:17
loose, plain, rude w. BURT 76:10
modern hardback w. TRIL 319:10
more interested in the w. AMIS 5:2
of a ready w. BOOK 61:22
things a w. is for RUSH 262:4
This is the w.'s radar HEMI 156:5
writers W., like teeth BAGE 22:22
writes seldom w. mind STEE 302:2
writing Fine w. KEAT 183:14
get it in w. LEE 196:8
If w. did not exist SEI 267:9
incurable disease of w. JUVE 180:1
obstacle to professional w. BENC 29:6
thought *nothing* of her w. SITW 296:13

writing (*cont.*)
w. an exact man — BACO 21:27
W. is not a profession — SIME 295:23
written *as well w. as prose* — POUN 250:15
being w. about — BELL 29:4
I have w. — BIBL 48:12
well w., or badly written — WILD 335:8
w. such volumes of stuff — LEAR 195:13
w. without effort — JOHN 177:3
wrong absent are always in the w. — DEST 109:3
Addison approved, Cannot be w. — BUDG 72:6
always in the w. — DILL 111:24
called them by w. names — BROW 69:22
called the w. number — THUR 317:28
customer is never w. — RITZ 257:14
do a little w. — SHAK 282:22
Eating people is w. — FLAN 129:16
feel that something has gone w. — POTT 250:1
Fifty million Frenchmen can't be w. — ANON 6:22
he done her w. — ANON 7:11
if w., to be set right — SCHU 265:21
I was w. — AUDE 18:2
keep himself from doing w. — BIBL 41:27
king can do no w. — BLAC 55:4
mind being w. — AYER 20:11
much w. could religion induce — LUCR 204:12
never w., the Old Masters — AUDE 18:8
our country, right or w. — DECA 107:11
ran w. through all the land — MUIR 229:18
requite w. with wrong — SOCR 298:22
right deed for the w. reason — ELIO 122:16
something w. with our bloody ships — BEAT 26:11
that is a w. one — JOHN 175:6
thought it w. to fight — BELL 28:25
thou hast seen my w. — BIBL 40:29
very probably w. — CLAR 93:18
We were w. — MCNA 208:15
When everyone is w. — LA C 191:9
when I am in the w. — MELB 216:7
W. but Wromantic — SELL 267:18
w. even the poorest ploughman — CHAR 87:20
W. forever on the throne — LOWE 203:19
w. side of a tapestry — HOWE 165:16
wrongs makes the people's w. his own — DRYD 116:20
wrote w., except for money — JOHN 175:19
w. like an angel — GARR 136:8
wrought What hath God w. — BIBL 34:25
What hath God w. — MORS 229:1
Wyatt W. resteth here — SURR 306:7
Wynken W., Blynken, and Nod — FIEL 127:8

X

X Generation X — COUP 100:18
Xanadu In X. did Kubla Khan — COLE 96:3
xerox X. makes everybody — MCLU 208:6

Y

Yale whaleship was my Y. College — MELV 216:10
Yankee Y. Doodle — ANON 11:6
Y. Doodle Dandy — COHA 95:14
Yanks Y. are coming — COHA 95:13
yawning Y. at a ball — LERM 197:23
yea Let your y. be yea — BIBL 51:24
year man at the gate of the y. — HASK 153:4
Next y. in Jerusalem — HAGG 149:1
one y.'s experience 30 times — CARR 83:12
snow of ferne y. — CHAU 88:27
thirtieth y. to heaven — THOM 316:6

this time next y. — REED 255:7
'Tis the y.'s midnight — DONN 114:9
y. is dying — TENN 311:30
y.'s at the spring — BROW 70:27
years Forty y. on — BOWE 65:9
Jacob served seven y. — BIBL 33:31
more than a hundred y. — FROS 134:9
thousand y. in thy sight — BOOK 62:14
threescore y. and ten — BOOK 62:15
touch of earthly y. — WORD 341:8
two hundred y. like a sheep — TIPU 318:7
two thousand y. of hope — WEIZ 330:26
y. are slipping by — HORA 164:11
y. like great black oxen — YEAT 342:16
y. of desolation — JEFF 171:17
y. that the locust hath eaten — BIBL 41:13
yeas russet y. — SHAK 278:21
yellow Come unto these y. sands — SHAK 287:6
falls into the y. Leaf — BYRO 78:26
Follow the y. brick road — HARB 151:10
Goodbye y. brick road — JOHN 172:19
one long y. string — BROW 71:1
paved with y. brick — BAUM 26:10
thy y. stockings — SHAK 288:24
Y., and black, and pale — SHEL 293:7
Y. God forever gazes — HAYE 154:1
y. leaf — SHAK 281:20
yes getting the answer y. — CAMU 81:6
Y., but not in the South — POTT 250:2
Y., Minister! No, Minister — CROS 104:7
Y., Virginia — CHUR 90:22
yesterday but as y. — BOOK 62:14
give me y. — JONE 177:8
keeping up with y. — MARQ 212:20
O! call back y. — SHAK 285:18
same y., and to day — BIBL 51:19
were saying y. — LUIS 204:15
yesterdays all our y. — SHAK 281:24
yesteryear snows of y. — VILL 324:6
yet but not y. — AUGU 18:26
yid PUT THE ID BACK IN Y. — ROTH 261:6
yield and not to y. — TENN 314:1
yoke my y. is easy — BIBL 43:32
Yonghy-Bonghy-Bó Lived the Y. — LEAR 195:9
Yorick Alas, poor Y. — SHAK 273:11
you cannot live with y. — MART 213:10
Y.'ll never walk — HAMM 151:1
Y. too, Brutus — CAES 80:4
young artist as a y. man — JOYC 178:22
Being y. is overestimated — QUAN 253:2
censor of the y. — HORA 163:17
crime of being a y. man — PITT 245:9
dies y. — MENA 216:12
for ever y. — KEAT 182:3
get out while we're y. — SPRI 301:5
I have been y. — BOOK 61:16
I'll die y. — BRUC 71:14
love's y. dream — MOOR 227:16
on your y. shoulders — SPAR 299:23
O y., fresshe folkes — CHAU 88:29
seventy years y. — HOLM 161:12
So wise so y. — SHAK 286:5
so y. a body — SHAK 282:19
So y., and so untender — SHAK 277:6
what the world would call y. men — PEEL 242:19
While we are y. — ANON 12:13
Y. and foolish — YEAT 342:18
Y. blood must have its course — KING 186:22
y., gifted and black — HANS 151:4
Y., gifted and black — IRVI 169:9
y. man married — SHAK 268:11
y. men shall see visions — BIBL 41:14
y. men think it is — HOUS 165:1

y. was very heaven WORD 339:21
y. whom I hope to bother AUDE 18:19
younger Y. than she SHAK 286:13
yours Y. till Hell freezes FISH 128:7
youth April of your y. HERB 157:7
Crabbed age and y. SHAK 289:17
days of thy y. BIBL 38:33
flattering y. defy ROCH 258:16
flower of their y. VIRG 325:11
If y. knew ESTI 125:4
My prime of y. TICH 318:3
red sweet wine of y. BROO 67:19
sign of an ill-spent y. ROUP 261:9
subtle thief of y. MILT 223:7
unemployed y. BAGE 22:16
Y. and Hope COLE 96:26
Y. and Pleasure meet BYRO 77:26
y., I do adore thee SHAK 289:18
y. of England SHAK 274:30
y. of frolics POPE 247:14
y. of labour GOLD 143:8
y. of the world BACO 20:21
Y. on the prow GRAY 146:12
y. replies, *I can* EMER 124:10
Y.'s a stuff SHAK 288:13
y.'s sweet-scented manuscript FITZ 129:1

y. to the gallows PAIN 239:15
Y., what man's age is like DENH 108:15
Y., which is forgiven SHAW 291:19
yuppie y. version of bulimia EHRE 120:8

Z

Zadok Z. the priest BIBL 35:36
Zaire Z. is the trigger FANO 126:2
zany mountebank and his z. WALP 327:14
Zanzibar count the cats in Z. THOR 317:21
Zauber *Deine Z. binden wieder* SCHI 265:11
zeal all z., Mr Easy MARR 213:2
holy mistaken z. JUNI 179:18
not the slightest z. TALL 309:1
tempering bigot z. KNOX 189:16
z. of the Lord BIBL 39:20
zealous z. citizen BURK 74:10
zed Thou whoreson z. SHAK 277:13
Zen Z. and the art PIRS 245:6
zenith from the z. like a falling star MILT 221:15
Zion Z., city of our God NEWT 233:18
Zitronen *Land, wo die Z. blühn* GOET 142:25
zoo human z. MORR 228:13

Sayings and Slogans

Advertising slogans

1 Access—your flexible friend.
Access credit card, 1981 onwards

2 An ace caff with quite a nice museum attached.
the Victoria and Albert Museum, February 1989

3 All human life is there.
the *News of the World*; used by Maurice Smelt in the late 1950s

4 All the news that's fit to print.
motto of the *New York Times*, from 1896; coined by its proprietor Adolph S. Ochs

5 American Express? . . . That'll do nicely, sir.
American Express credit card, 1970s

6 And all because the lady loves Milk Tray.
Cadbury's Milk Tray chocolates, 1968 onwards

7 Australians wouldn't give a XXXX for anything else.
Castlemaine lager, 1986 onwards

8 Beanz meanz Heinz.
Heinz baked beans, *c.*1967; coined by Maurice Drake

9 Bovril . . . Prevents that sinking feeling.
Bovril, 1920; coined by H. H. Harris

10 . . . But I know a man who can.
Automobile Association, 1980s

11 Can you tell Stork from butter?
Stork margarine, from *c.*1956

12 Cool as a mountain stream.
Consulate menthol cigarettes, early 1960s onwards

13 A diamond is forever.
De Beers Consolidated Mines, 1940s onwards

14 Does she . . . or doesn't she?
Clairol hair colouring, 1950s

15 Don't be vague, ask for Haig.
Haig whisky, *c.*1936

16 Don't forget the fruit gums, Mum.
Rowntree's Fruit gums, 1958–61

17 Drinka Pinta Milka Day.
National Dairy Council, 1958; coined by Bertrand Whitehead

18 Even your closest friends won't tell you.
Listerine mouthwash, US, 1923

19 Every picture tells a story.
advertisement for Doan's Backache Kidney Pills (early 1900s)

20 Full of Eastern promise.
Fry's Turkish Delight, 1950s onwards

21 Go to work on an egg.
British Egg Marketing Board, from 1957; perhaps written by Fay Weldon or Mary Gowing

22 Guinness is good for you.
reply universally given to researchers asking people why they drank Guinness
adopted by Oswald Greene, *c.*1929

23 Happiness is a cigar called Hamlet.
Hamlet cigars, UK

24 Have a break, have a Kit-Kat.
Rowntree's Kit-Kat, from *c.*1955

25 Heineken refreshes the parts other beers cannot reach.
Heineken lager, 1975 onwards

26 High o'er the fence leaps Sunny Jim 'Force' is the food that raises him.
breakfast cereal (1903)

27 Horlicks guards against night starvation.
Horlicks malted milk drink, 1930s

28 If you want to get ahead, get a hat.
the Hat Council, 1965

29 I'm only here for the beer.
Double Diamond beer, 1971 onwards

30 It beats as it sweeps as it cleans.
Hoover vacuum cleaners, 1919

31 It could be you.
British national lottery, from 1994

32 It's finger lickin' good.
Kentucky fried chicken, from 1958

33 It's good to talk.
British Telecom, from 1994

34 It's tingling fresh. It's fresh as ice.
Gibbs toothpaste; the first advertising slogan heard on British television, 22 September 1955

35 I was a seven-stone weakling.
Charles Atlas body-building, originally in US

36 Just when you thought it was safe to go back in the water.
Jaws 2 (1978 film) advertising copy

37 Keep that schoolgirl complexion.
Palmolive soap, from 1917

38 Kills all known germs.
Domestos bleach, 1959

39 Let the train take the strain.
British Rail, 1970 onwards

40 Let your fingers do the walking.
Bell system Telephone Directory Yellow Pages, 1960s

41 The man you love to hate.
billing for Erich von Stroheim in the film *The Heart of Humanity* (1918)

42 A Mars a day helps you work, rest and play.
Mars bar, *c.*1960 onwards

43 Maybe, just maybe.
British national lottery, from 1998

44 The mint with the hole.
Life-Savers, US, 1920; and for Rowntree's Polo mints, UK from 1947

45 My Goodness, My Guinness.
Guinness stout, 1935

46 Never knowingly undersold.
motto of the John Lewis Partnership, from *c.*1920

1 Nice one, Cyril.
taken up by supporters of Cyril Knowles, Tottenham Hotspur footballer; the Spurs team later made a record featuring the line
Wonderloaf, 1972

2 No manager ever got fired for buying IBM.
IBM

3 Oxo gives a meal man-appeal.
Oxo beef extract, c.1960

4 Persil washes whiter—and it shows.
Persil washing powder, 1970s

5 Put a tiger in your tank.
Esso petrol, 1964

6 Say it with flowers.
Society of American Florists, 1917, coined by Patrick O'Keefe

7 Sch . . . you know who.
Schweppes mineral drinks, 1960s

8 Someone, somewhere, wants a letter from you.
British Post Office, 1960s

9 Stop me and buy one.
Wall's ice cream, from spring 1922; coined by Cecil Rodd

10 Tell Sid.
privatization of British Gas, 1986

11 They come as a boon and a blessing to men, The Pickwick, the Owl, and the Waverley pen.
advertisement by MacNiven and H. Cameron Ltd., current by 1879

12 Things go better with Coke.
Coca-Cola, 1963

13 Top people take *The Times*.
The Times newspaper, from January 1959

14 *Vorsprung durch Technik.*
Progress through technology.
Audi motors (advertising slogan, from 1986)

15 We are the Ovaltineys,
Little [*or* Happy] girls and boys.
'We are the Ovaltineys' (song from c.1935); Ovaltine drink

16 We're number two. We try harder.
Avis car rentals

17 We won't make a drama out of a crisis.
Commercial Union insurance

18 Where's the beef?
Wendy's Hamburgers, from January 1984

19 Worth a guinea a box.
Beecham's pills, from c.1859, from the chance remark of a lady purchaser

20 You're never alone with a Strand.
Strand cigarettes, 1960

Catchphrases

21 CECIL: After you, Claude.
CLAUDE: No, after you, Cecil.
ITMA (BBC radio programme, 1939–49), written by Ted Kavanagh

22 And now for something completely different.
Monty Python's Flying Circus (BBC TV programme, 1969–74)

23 Anyone for tennis?
said to be typical of drawing-room comedies; perhaps from George Bernard Shaw 'Anybody on for a game of tennis?' *Misalliance* (1914)

24 Are you sitting comfortably? Then I'll begin.
Listen with Mother (BBC radio programme for children, 1950–82)

25 Can I do you now, sir?
spoken by 'Mrs Mopp'
ITMA (BBC radio programme, 1939–49), written by Ted Kavanagh

26 Can you hear me, mother?
used by Sandy Powell

27 The day war broke out.
customary preamble to radio monologues in the role of a Home Guard
used by Robb Wilton from c.1940

28 Didn't she [*or* he *or* they] do well?
used by Bruce Forsyth in 'The Generation Game' on BBC Television, 1973 onwards

29 Don't forget the diver.
ITMA (BBC radio programme, 1939–49), written by Ted Kavanagh

30 Eat my shorts!
The Simpsons (American TV series, 1990–), created by Matt Groening

31 Ee, it was agony, Ivy.
Ray's a Laugh (BBC radio programme, 1949–61), written by Ted Ray

32 Evening, all.
opening words spoken by Jack Warner as Sergeant Dixon in *Dixon of Dock Green* (BBC television series, 1956–76), written by Ted Willis

33 Everybody wants to get inta the act!
used by Jimmy Durante

34 An everyday story of country folk.
introduction to *The Archers* (BBC radio serial, 1950 onwards), written by Geoffrey Webb and Edward J. Mason

35 Give him the money, Barney.
Have a Go! (BBC radio quiz programme, 1946–67), used by Wilfred Pickles

36 A good idea—son.
Educating Archie, 1950–3 BBC radio comedy series, written by Eric Sykes and Max Bygraves

37 Good morning, sir—was there something?
used by Sam Costa in radio comedy series *Much-Binding-in-the-Marsh*, written by Richard Murdoch and Kenneth Horne, started 2 January 1947

38 Goodnight, children . . . everywhere.
closing words normally spoken by 'Uncle Mac' in the 1930s and 1940s
on *Children's Hour* (BBC Radio programme); written by Derek McCulloch

1 Have you read any good books lately?

used by Richard Murdoch in radio comedy series *Much-Binding-in-the-Marsh*, written by Richard Murdoch and Kenneth Horne, started 2 January 1947

2 Hello, good evening, and welcome.

used by David Frost in 'The Frost Programme' on BBC Television, 1966 onwards

3 Here come de judge.

from the song-title 'Here comes the judge' (1968); written by Dewey 'Pigmeat' Markham, Dick Alen, Bob Astor, and Sarah Harvey

4 Here's one I made earlier.

culmination to directions for making a model out of empty yoghurt pots, coat-hangers, and similar domestic items

children's BBC television programme *Blue Peter*, 1963 onwards

5 I didn't get where I am today without . . . .

used by the manager C. J. in BBC television series *The Fall and Rise of Reginald Perrin* (1976–80); based on David Nobbs *The Death of Reginald Perrin* (1975)

6 I don't like this game, let's play another game—let's play doctor and nurses.

phrase first used by Bluebottle in 'The Phantom Head-Shaver' in *The Goon Show* (BBC radio series) 15 October 1954, written by Spike Milligan; the catchphrase was often 'I do not like this game'

7 I don't mind if I do.

spoken by 'Colonel Chinstrap'

ITMA (BBC radio programme, 1939–49), written by Ted Kavanagh

8 I go—I come back.

spoken by 'Ali Oop'

ITMA (BBC radio programme, 1939–49), written by Ted Kavanagh

9 I have a cunning plan.

Baldrick's habitual overoptimistic promise in *Blackadder II* (1987 television series), written by Richard Curtis and Ben Elton

10 I'm Bart Simpson: who the hell are you?

The Simpsons (American TV series, 1990–), created by Matt Groening

11 I'm in charge.

used by Bruce Forsyth in 'Sunday Night at the London Palladium' on ITV, 1958 onwards

12 I'm worried about Jim.

frequent line in *Mrs Dale's Diary*, BBC radio series 1948–69

13 It all depends what you mean by . . .

habitually used by C. E. M. Joad when replying to questions on 'The Brains Trust' (formerly 'Any Questions'), BBC radio (1941–8)

14 It's being so cheerful as keeps me going.

spoken by 'Mona Lott'

ITMA (BBC radio programme, 1939–49), written by Ted Kavanagh

15 I've arrived and to prove it I'm here!

Educating Archie, 1950–3 BBC radio comedy series, written by Eric Sykes and Max Bygraves

16 I've started so I'll finish.

said when a contestant's time runs out while a question is being put

Magnus Magnusson on *Mastermind*, BBC television (1972–97)

17 Just like that!

used by Tommy Cooper

18 Keep on truckin'.

used by Robert Crumb in cartoons from *c.*1972

19 Left hand down a bit!

The Navy Lark (BBC radio series, 1959–77), written by Laurie Wyman

20 Let's be careful out there.

Hill Street Blues (television series, 1981 onwards), written by Steven Bochco and Michael Kozoll

21 Meredith, we're in!

originating in a stage sketch by Fred Kitchen, *The Bailiff* (1907); J. P. Gallagher *Fred Karno* (1971) ch. 9

22 Mind my bike!

used by Jack Warner in the BBC radio series *Garrison Theatre*, 1939 onwards

23 Nice to see you—to see you, nice.

used by Bruce Forsyth in 'The Generation Game' on BBC Television, 1973 onwards

24 Oh, calamity!

used by Robertson Hare

25 Ohhh, I don't *believe* it!

Victor Meldrew in *One Foot in the Grave* (BBC television series, 1989–2000), written by David Renwick

26 Once again we stop the mighty roar of London's traffic.

In Town Tonight (BBC radio series, 1933–60) preamble

27 Pass the sick bag, Alice.

used by John Junor; in *Sunday Express* and elsewhere, from 1980 or earlier

28 Seriously, though, he's doing a grand job!

popularized by David Frost in 'That Was The Week That Was', on BBC Television, 1962-3; originally deriving from a sketch written for Roy Kinnear

29 Shome mishtake, shurely?

in *Private Eye* magazine, 1980s

30 So farewell then . . .

frequent opening of poems by 'E. J. Thribb' in Private Eye *magazine, usually as an obituary* 1970s onwards

31 Take me to your leader.

from science-fiction stories

32 The truth is out there.

The X Files (American television series, 1993–), created by Chris Carter

33 Very interesting . . . but stupid.

Rowan and Martin's Laugh-In (American television series, 1967–73), written by Dan Rowan and Dick Martin

34 The weekend starts here.

Ready, Steady, Go, British television series, *c.*1963

1 We have ways of making you talk.

perhaps originating in the line 'We have ways of making men talk' in *Lives of a Bengal Lancer* (1935 film), written by Waldemar Young et al.

2 What's up, Doc?

Bugs Bunny cartoons, written by Tex Avery from *c.*1940

3 Who loves ya, baby?

used by Telly Savalas in American TV series *Kojak* (1973-8)

4 You bet your sweet bippy.

Rowan and Martin's Laugh-In (American television series, 1967-73), written by Dan Rowan and Dick Martin

5 You might very well think that. I couldn't possibly comment.

the Chief Whip's habitual response to questioning House of Cards (televised 1990); written by Michael Dobbs

6 You're going to like this . . . not a lot . . . but you'll like it!

used by Paul Daniels in his conjuring act, especially on television from 1981 onwards

7 You rotten swines. I told you I'd be deaded.

phrase first used by Bluebottle in 'Hastings Flyer' in *The Goon Show* (BBC radio series) 3 January 1956, written by Spike Milligan

8 Your starter for ten.

phrase often used by Bamber Gascoigne in *University Challenge* (ITV quiz series, 1962-87)

9 You silly twisted boy.

phrase first used in 'The Dreaded Batter Pudding Hurler' in *The Goon Show* (BBC radio series) 12 October 1954, written by Spike Milligan

Film lines

10 Anyway, Ma, I made it . . . Top of the world!

White Heat (1949 film) written by Ivan Goff and Ben Roberts; last lines—spoken by James Cagney

11 Cancel the kitchen scraps for lepers and orphans. No more merciful beheadings. And call off Christmas!

Robin Hood, Prince of Thieves (1991 film), written by Pen Densham and John Watson; spoken by Alan Rickman

12 Don't let's ask for the moon! We have the stars!

Now, Voyager (1942 film), from the novel (1941) by Olive Higgins Prouty; spoken by Bette Davis

13 Either he's dead, or my watch has stopped.

A Day at the Races (1937 film) written by Robert Pirosh, George Seaton, and George Oppenheimer; spoken by Groucho Marx

14 E.T. phone home.

E.T. (1982 film) written by Melissa Mathison

15 Fasten your seat-belts, it's going to be a bumpy night.

All About Eve (1950 film) written by Joseph L. Mankiewicz; spoken by Bette Davis

16 Frankly, my dear, I don't give a damn!

Gone with the Wind (1939 film) written by Sidney Howard; spoken by Clark Gable

17 Go ahead, make my day.

Sudden Impact (1983 film) written by Joseph C. Stinson; spoken by Clint Eastwood

18 Greed—for lack of a better word—is good. Greed is right. Greed works.

Wall Street (1987 film) written by Stanley Weiser and Oliver Stone

19 Here's looking at you, kid.

Casablanca (1942 film) written by Julius J. Epstein, Philip G. Epstein, and Howard Koch; spoken by Humphrey Bogart to Ingrid Bergman

20 I could have had class. I could have been a contender.

On the Waterfront (1954 film) written by Budd Schulberg; spoken by Marlon Brando

21 If she can stand it, I can. Play it!

usually quoted as 'Play it again, Sam'
Casablanca (1942 film) written by Julius J. Epstein, Philip G. Epstein, and Howard Koch; spoken by Humphrey Bogart

22 If you can't leave in a taxi you can leave in a huff. If that's too soon, you can leave in a minute and a huff.

Duck Soup (1933 film) written by Bert Kalmar, Harry Ruby, Arthur Sheekman, and Nat Perrin; spoken by Groucho Marx

23 I'll have what she's having.

woman to waiter, seeing Sally acting an orgasm
When Harry Met Sally (1989 film) written by Nora Ephron

24 I love the smell of napalm in the morning. It smells like victory.

Apocalypse Now (1979 film) written by John Milius and Francis Ford Coppola; spoken by Robert Duvall

25 In Italy for thirty years under the Borgias they had warfare, terror, murder, bloodshed—they produced Michelangelo, Leonardo da Vinci and the Renaissance. In Switzerland they had brotherly love, five hundred years of democracy and peace and what did that produce . . . ? The cuckoo clock.

The Third Man (1949 film); words added by Orson Welles to Graham Greene's screenplay

26 It's a funny old world—a man's lucky if he gets out of it alive.

You're Telling Me (1934 film), written by Walter de Leon and Paul M. Jones; spoken by W. C. Fields

27 DRIFTWOOD (Groucho Marx): It's all right. That's—that's in every contract. That's—that's what they call a sanity clause.
FIORELLO (Chico Marx): You can't fool me. There ain't no Sanity Claus.

Night at the Opera (1935 film) written by George S. Kaufman and Morrie Ryskind

1 Let's get out of these wet clothes and into a dry Martini.

> line coined in the 1920s by Robert Benchley's press agent and adopted by Mae West in *Every Day's a Holiday* (1937 film)

2 Madness! Madness!

> *The Bridge on the River Kwai* (1957 film of the novel by Pierre Boulle) written by Carl Foreman, closing line

3 Major Strasser has been shot. Round up the usual suspects.

> *Casablanca* (1942 film) written by Julius J. Epstein, Philip G. Epstein, and Howard Koch; spoken by Claude Rains

4 The man you love to hate.

> anonymous billing for Erich von Stroheim in the film *The Heart of Humanity* (1918)

5 Man your ships, and may the force be with you.

> *Star Wars* (1977 film) written by George Lucas

6 Marriage isn't a word . . . it's a *sentence*!

> *The Crowd* (1928 film) written by King Vidor

7 Maybe just whistle. You know how to whistle, don't you, Steve? You just put your lips together and blow.

> *To Have and Have Not* (1944 film) written by Jules Furthman and William Faulkner; spoken by Lauren Bacall

8 Mr Kane was a man who got everything he wanted, and then lost it. Maybe Rosebud was something he couldn't get or something he lost. Anyway, it wouldn't have explained anything. I don't think any word can explain a man's life. No, I guess Rosebud is just a piece in a jigsaw puzzle, a missing piece.

> *Citizen Kane* (1941 film) written by Herman J. Mankiewicz and Orson Welles

9 My momma always said life was like a box of chocolates . . . you never know what you're gonna get.

> *Forrest Gump* (1994 film), written by Eric Ross, based on the novel (1986) by Winston Groom; spoken by Tom Hanks

10 Nature, Mr Allnutt, is what we are put into this world to rise above.

> *The African Queen* (1951 film) written by James Agee; spoken by Katharine Hepburn; not in the novel by C. S. Forester

11 Of all the gin joints in all the towns in all the world, she walks into mine.

> *Casablanca* (1942 film) written by Julius J. Epstein, Philip G. Epstein, and Howard Koch; spoken by Humphrey Bogart

12 Oh no, it wasn't the aeroplanes. It was Beauty killed the Beast.

> *King Kong* (1933 film) written by James Creelman and Ruth Rose, final words

13 The pellet with the poison's in the vessel with the pestle. The chalice from the palace has the brew that is true.

> *The Court Jester* (1955 film) written by Norman Panama and Melvin Frank; spoken by Danny Kaye

14 Remember, you're fighting for this woman's honour . . . which is probably more than she ever did.

> *Duck Soup* (1933 film) written by Bert Kalmar, Harry Ruby, Arthur Sheekman, and Nat Perrin; spoken by Groucho Marx

15 The son of a bitch stole my watch!

> *The Front Page* (1931 film), from the play (1928) by Charles MacArthur and Ben Hecht

16 GERRY: We can't get married at all . . . I'm a man.
OSGOOD: Well, nobody's perfect.

> *Some Like It Hot* (1959 film) written by Billy Wilder and I. A. L. Diamond; closing words spoken by Jack Lemmon and Joe E. Brown

17 What a dump!

> *Beyond the Forest* (1949 film) written by Lenore Coffee; line spoken by Bette Davis, entering a room

18 Why, a four-year-old child could understand this report. Run out and find me a four-year-old child. I can't make head or tail of it.

> *Duck Soup* (1933 film) written by Bert Kalmar, Harry Ruby, Arthur Sheekman, and Nat Perrin; spoken by Groucho Marx

19 NINOTCHKA: Why should you carry other people's bags?
PORTER: Well, that's my business, Madame.
NINOTCHKA: That's no business. That's social injustice.
PORTER: That depends on the tip.

> *Ninotchka* (1939 film) written by Charles Brackett, Billy Wilder, and Walter Reisch

20 You're going out a youngster but you've *got* to come back a star.

> *42nd Street* (1933 film) written by James Seymour and Rian James

21 You're here to stay until the rustle in your dying throat relieves you!

> *Beau Hunks* (1931 film; re-named *Beau Chumps* for British audiences) written by H. M. Walker; addressed to Laurel and Hardy

22 JOE GILLIS: You used to be in pictures. You used to be big.
NORMA DESMOND: I am big. It's the pictures that got small.

> *Sunset Boulevard* (1950 film) written by Charles Brackett, Billy Wilder, and D. M. Marshman Jr

Modern sayings and slogans

23 Been there, done that, got the T-shirt.

> 'been there, done that' recorded from 1980s, expanded form from 1990s

24 Burn your bra.

> feminist slogan, 1970s

1 Close your eyes and think of England.
said to derive from a 1912 entry in the journal of Lady Hillingdon but the journal has never been traced

2 Crime doesn't pay.
a slogan of the FBI and the cartoon detective Dick Tracy

3 Daddy, what did you do in the Great War?
daughter to father in First World War recruiting poster

4 [Death is] nature's way of telling you to slow down.
life insurance proverb; in *Newsweek* 25 April 1960

5 A dog is for life, not just for Christmas.
slogan of the National Canine Defence League

6 Do not fold, spindle or mutilate.
instruction on punched cards (1950s, and in differing forms from the 1930s)

7 Don't get mad, get even.
late twentieth century saying

8 The family that prays together stays together.
motto devised by Al Scalpone for the Roman Catholic Family Rosary Crusade, 1947

9 Garbage in, garbage out.
in computing, incorrect or faulty input will always cause poor output; origin of the acronym GIGO

10 Give me a child for the first seven years, and you may do what you like with him afterwards.
attributed as a Jesuit maxim, in *Lean's Collectanea* vol. 3 (1903)

11 If anything can go wrong, it will.
commonly known as Murphy's Law
mid twentieth century saying; said to have been invented by George Nichols in 1949, based on a remark by his colleague Captain E. Murphy

12 If it ain't broke, don't fix it.
Bert Lance in *Nation's Business* May 1977

13 If you can't beat them, join them.
beat *is usually replaced by* lick *in the US*
mid twentieth century saying

14 If you pay peanuts, you get monkeys.
mid twentieth century saying

15 If you're not part of the solution, you're part of the problem.
late twentieth century saying

16 I married my husband for life, not for lunch.
origin unknown

17 I'm backing Britain.
slogan coined by workers at the Colt factory, Surbiton, Surrey in 1968, and subsequently used in a national campaign

18 It takes 40 dumb animals to make a fur coat, but only one to wear it.
slogan of an anti-fur campaign poster, 1980s

19 Let's run it up the flagpole and see if anyone salutes it.
recorded as an established advertising expression in the 1960s

20 Life is a sexually transmitted disease.
graffito found on the London Underground, in D. J. Enright (ed.) *The Faber Book of Fevers and Frets* (1989)

21 Make love not war.
student slogan, 1960s

22 *Nil carborundum illegitimi.*
Don't let the bastards grind you down.
cod Latin saying in circulation during the Second World War, though possibly of earlier origin

23 Nostalgia isn't what it used to be.
graffito; taken as title of book by Simone Signoret, 1978

24 The opera ain't over 'til the fat lady sings.
Dan Cook, in *Washington Post* 3 June 1978

25 Pile it high, sell it cheap.
slogan coined by John Cohen, founder of Tesco

26 There's no such thing as a free lunch.
colloquial axiom in US economics from the 1960s, much associated with Milton Friedman; recorded in form 'there ain't no such thing as a free lunch' from 1938, which gave rise to the acronym TANSTAAFL

27 Think globally, act locally.
Friends of the Earth slogan, *c.*1985

28 To err is human but to really foul things up requires a computer.
Farmers' Almanac for 1978 'Capsules of Wisdom'

29 What goes around comes around.
late twentieth century saying

30 What you see is what you get.
a computing expression, from which the acronym wysiwyg *derives*
late twentieth century saying

Newspaper headlines and leaders

31 Believe it or not.
title of syndicated newspaper feature (from 1918), written by Robert L. Ripley (1893–1949)

32 Crisis? What crisis?
summarizing James Callaghan's response in an interview at London airport, 'I don't think other people in the world would share the view there is mounting chaos'
headline in *Sun*, 11 January 1979

33 Dewey defeats Truman.
anticipating the result of the Presidential election, which Harry Truman won against expectation
in *Chicago Tribune* 3 November 1948

34 Egghead weds hourglass.
on the marriage of Arthur Miller and Marilyn Monroe
headline in *Variety* 1956; attributed

35 Freddie Starr ate my hamster.
headline in *Sun* 13 March 1986

36 GOTCHA!
on the sinking of the General Belgrano
headline in *Sun* 4 May 1982

37 Go West, young man, go West!
editorial in *Terre Haute* [Indiana] *Express* (1851), by John L. B. Soule

1 Is THIS the most dangerous man in Britain?
*headline beside a picture of Tony Blair, attacking
his perceived sympathy for the euro*
   in *The Sun* 25 June 1998

2 It *is* a moral issue.
leader following the resignation of Profumo
   in *The Times* 11 June 1963

3 It's that man again . . . ! At the head of a
cavalcade of seven black motor cars Hitler
swept out of his Berlin Chancellery last
night on a mystery journey.
   headline in *Daily Express* 2 May 1939; the
   acronym ITMA became the title of a BBC radio
   show, from September 1939

4 It's The Sun wot won it.
following the 1992 general election
   headline in *Sun* 11 April 1992

5 King's Moll Reno'd in Wolsey's home town.
*US newspaper headline on the divorce proceedings
of Wallis Simpson (later Duchess of Windsor) in
Ipswich*
   Frances Donaldson *Edward VIII* (1974) ch. 7

6 Splendid isolation.
   headline in *The Times* 22 January 1896, referring
   to

   In these somewhat troublesome days
      when the great Mother Empire stands
      splendidly isolated in Europe.
   speech by George Foster, 16 January 1896, in
   *Official Report of the Debates of the House of
   Commons of the Dominion of Canada* (1896) vol. 41

7 Sticks nix hick pix.
*front-page headline on the lack of enthusiasm for
farm dramas among rural populations*
   in *Variety* 17 July 1935

8 Unless the people—the people
everywhere—come forward and petition,
ay, thunder for reform.
*leader on the Reform Bill, possibly written by
Edward Sterling, resulting in the nickname 'The
Thunderer'*
   in *The Times* 29 January 1831; the phrase 'we
   thundered out' had been used earlier, 11
   February 1829

9 Wall St. lays an egg.
   crash headline, *Variety* 30 October 1929

10 We shall not pretend that there is nothing
in his long career which those who respect
and admire him would wish otherwise.
on Edward VII's accession to the throne
   in *The Times* 23 January 1901, leading article

11 Who breaks a butterfly on a wheel?
*defending Mick Jagger after his arrest for
cannabis possession*
   leader in *The Times* 1 June 1967, written by
   William Rees-Mogg, and quoting Alexander
   Pope's 'Who breaks a butterfly upon a wheel?'

12 Whose finger do you want on the trigger?
referring to the atom bomb
   headline in *Daily Mirror* 21 September 1951

13 Winter of discontent.
   headline in *Sun* 30 April 1979

Official advice

14 Careless talk costs lives.
   Second World War security slogan (popularly
   inverted as 'careless lives cost talk')

15 Clunk, click, every trip.
   road safety campaign promoting the use of
   seat-belts, 1971

16 Coughs and sneezes spread diseases. Trap
the germs in your handkerchief.
   Second World War health slogan (1942)

17 Dig for Victory.
   Second World War slogan; see below:

   Let 'Dig for Victory' be the motto of every
      one with a garden and of every able-
      bodied man and woman capable of
      digging an allotment in their spare
      time.
   Reginald Dorman-Smith radio broadcast, 3
   October 1939, in *The Times* 4 October 1939

18 Don't ask a man to drink and drive.
   UK road safety slogan, from 1964

19 Don't die of ignorance.
   Aids publicity campaign, 1987

20 Is your journey *really* necessary?
   slogan coined to discourage Civil Servants from
   going home for Christmas, 1939

21 Keep Britain tidy.
   issued by the Central Office of Information,
   1950s

22 Make do and mend.
   wartime slogan, 1940s

23 Slip, slop, slap.
*sun protection slogan, meaning slip on a T-shirt,
slop on some suncream, slap on a hat*
   Australian health education programme, 1980s

24 Smoking can seriously damage your health.
*government health warning now required by
British law to be printed on cigarette packets*
   from early 1970s, in form 'Smoking can
   damage your health'

25 Stop-look-and-listen.
   road safety slogan, current in the US from 1912

26 *Taisez-vous! Méfiez-vous! Les oreilles ennemies
vous écoutent.*
   Keep your mouth shut! Be on your guard!
   Enemy ears are listening to you.
   official notice in France, 1915

27 Tradition dictates that we have a lawn—but
do we really need one? Why not increase
the size of your borders or replace lawned
areas with paving stones or gravel?
   Severn Trent Water 'The Gardener's Water
   Code' (1996)

Political slogans

28 All power to the Soviets.
   workers in Petrograd, 1917

1 All the way with LBJ.
US Democratic Party campaign slogan, 1960

2 As Maine goes, so goes the nation.
American political saying, *c.*1840

3 Ban the bomb.
US anti-nuclear slogan, adopted by the Campaign for Nuclear Disarmament, 1953 onwards

4 A bayonet is a weapon with a worker at each end.
British pacifist slogan (1940)

5 Better red than dead.
slogan of nuclear disarmament campaigners, late 1950s

6 A bigger bang for a buck.
Charles E. Wilson's defence policy, in *Newsweek* 22 March 1954

7 Black is beautiful.
slogan of American civil rights campaigners, mid-1960s

8 Burn, baby, burn.
Black extremist slogan in use during the Los Angeles riots, August 1965

9 Can't pay, won't pay.
anti-Poll Tax slogan, *c.*1990

10 *Ein Reich, ein Volk, ein Führer.*
One realm, one people, one leader.
Nazi Party slogan, early 1930s

11 Fair shares for all, is Labour's call.
slogan for the North Battersea by-election, 1946, coined by Douglas Jay
Douglas Jay *Change and Fortune* (1980) ch. 7

12 Fifty-four forty, or fight!
slogan of expansionist Democrats in the US presidential campaign of 1844, in which the Oregon boundary definition was an issue (in 1846 the new Democratic president, James K. Polk, compromised on the 49th parallel with Great Britain)

13 Hey, hey, LBJ, how many kids did you kill today?
anti-Vietnam marching slogan, 1960s

14 I like Ike.
used when General Eisenhower was first seen as a potential presidential nominee
US button badge, 1947; coined by Henry D. Spalding

15 It'll play in Peoria.
catchphrase of the Nixon administration (early 1970s) meaning 'it will be acceptable to middle America', but originating in a standard music hall joke of the 1930s

16 It's morning again in America.
slogan for Ronald Reagan's election campaign, 1984; coined by Hal Riney in *Newsweek* 6 August 1984

17 It's the economy, stupid.
on a sign put up at the 1992 Clinton presidential campaign headquarters by campaign manager James Carville

18 *Kraft durch Freude.*
Strength through joy.
German Labour Front slogan, from 1933; coined by Robert Ley

19 Labour isn't working.
on poster showing a long queue outside an unemployment office
Conservative Party slogan 1978–9

20 Labour's double whammy.
Conservative Party election slogan 1992

21 *Liberté! Égalité! Fraternité!*
Freedom! Equality! Brotherhood!
motto of the French Revolution, but of earlier origin
the Club des Cordeliers passed a motion, 30 June 1793, 'that owners should be urged to paint on the front of their houses, in large letters, the words: Unity, indivisibility of the Republic, Liberty, Equality, Fraternity or death'; in *Journal de Paris* no. 182 (from 1795 the words 'or death' were dropped)

22 Life's better with the Conservatives. Don't let Labour ruin it.
Conservative Party election slogan, 1959

23 New Labour, new danger.
Conservative slogan, 1996

24 No surrender!
the defenders of the besieged city of Derry to the Jacobite army of James II, April 1689, adopted as a slogan of Protestant Ulster
Jonathan Bardon *A History of Ulster* (1992)

25 Power to the people.
slogan of the Black Panther movement, from *c.*1968 onwards

26 Thirteen years of Tory misrule.
unofficial Labour party election slogan, also in the form 'Thirteen wasted years', 1964

27 Three acres and a cow.
regarded as the requirement for self-sufficiency; associated with the radical politician Jesse Collings and his land reform campaign begun in 1885
Jesse Collings in the House of Commons, 26 January 1886, although used earlier by Joseph Chamberlain in a speech at Evesham (in *The Times* 17 November 1885), by which time it was already proverbial

28 Tippecanoe and Tyler, too.
presidential campaign song for William Henry Harrison, 1840
attributed to A. C. Ross (fl. 1840)

29 Votes for women.
adopted when it proved impossible to use a banner with the longer slogan 'Will the Liberal Party Give Votes for Women?' made by Emmeline Pankhurst, Christabel Pankhurst, and Annie Kenney
slogan of the women's suffrage movement, from 13 October 1905; Emmeline Pankhurst *My Own Story* (1914)

30 War will cease when men refuse to fight.
pacifist slogan, from *c.*1936 (often quoted as, 'Wars will cease . . .')

1 We shall not be moved.

title of labour and civil rights song (1931) adapted from an earlier gospel hymn

2 We shall overcome.

title of song, originating from before the American Civil War, adapted as a Baptist hymn ('I'll Overcome Some Day', 1901) by C. Albert Tindley; revived in 1946 as a protest song by black tobacco workers, and in 1963 during the black Civil Rights Campaign

3 Would you buy a used car from this man?

campaign slogan directed against Richard Nixon, 1968

4 Yes it hurt, yes it worked.

Conservative Party slogan, 1996

5 Yesterday's men (they failed before!).

Labour Party slogan, referring to the Conservatives, 1970; coined by David Kingsley, Dennis Lyons, and Peter Lovell-Davis